A Short History of Western Civilization

A SHORT HISTORY OF
Western Civilization

John B. Harrison and Richard E. Sullivan

MICHIGAN STATE UNIVERSITY

Third Edition

Alfred·A·Knopf New York

THIS IS A BORZOI BOOK PUBLISHED BY ALFRED A. KNOPF, INC.

First Edition published 1960, reprinted six times;
Second Edition published 1966, reprinted seven times

ISBN: 0–394–30245–1

Library of Congress Catalog Card Number: 72–129822

Manufactured in the United States

Third Edition
98765432

to Mary and Vivian

BIBLIOGRAPHICAL NOTE In compiling the bibliographies the authors have made no attempt to supply an exhaustive list of the latest titles. Books have been selected chiefly for their readability. Brief descriptions have been supplied for each title to guide the reader. Note that many older classic works, although cited here with the original publishing data, have been reprinted in recent years. A special effort was made to utilize to the fullest the numerous inexpensive books now available. All books published in paperback or inexpensive hardback editions have been designated by a double asterisk (**). The series in which each volume has been published (Meridian, Penguin, etc.) has also been noted.

PREFACE

In preparing a third edition of this book ten years after its initial publication, the basic concepts that originally inspired its purpose, organization, and approach still hold. The book is designed primarily as a college or university textbook for a survey course in the history of Western civilization or for a humanities course. Over the past decade we have become particularly concerned about the needs of instructors and students in junior and community colleges and have given considerable attention to those needs in shaping our revisions. We still hope, however, that the serious, general reader will find the book profitable and interesting.

Next to accuracy, the qualities we have concentrated on most are clarity, brevity, and specificity. During our many years of college teaching and on the basis of numerous conversations with college students and fellow teachers, we have discovered that there is no substitute for clarity in a textbook. Any serious account of the story of Western civilization is involved and complicated at best; and since most of the students in such a survey course are not history majors, they need all the help they can get in making this long and complex story manageable and clear. We have, therefore, steadfastly refrained from turning the clever or sophisticated phrase or displaying any specialized erudition that we may have acquired in order that the narrative and analysis be as direct as possible. We have concerned ourselves especially with the organization of material, hoping to provide interrelated units each having an inner logic that will facilitate comprehension. In large part the revisions for this third edition have been aimed at achieving greater clarity of expression and organization. Innumerable paragraphs, sections, chapters, and even entire parts have been completely rewritten in order to achieve a smoother narrative, a clearer analysis, and a more logical organization.

Of all our objectives none has been more difficult to achieve than brevity. It would have been twice as easy to write a history twice as long. But our experiences in teaching courses in the history of Western civilization indicate that many textbooks are much too long, presenting more material than can be covered in one academic year and leaving little or no room either for the instructor's personal contribution or for additional readings on the part of the student. In making revisions for the third edition, we have expanded the text somewhat, chiefly in the interest of greater clarity and in order to include materials that experience and advice have shown were treated too briefly in earlier editions. However, we have not enlarged the book to the extent that we have compromised our conviction that a textbook should not be so massive as to dominate completely a course.

Still a third quality we have attempted to give this book is specificity. We believe that it is futile to generalize and philosophize about the past until the student is aware of the basic facts. We also believe that an instructor should have maximum freedom to provide the generalizing, interpretative dimensions of a course without hindrance from the textbook. We are, of course, well aware that writers are always present in their books. To be specific and yet brief requires careful selection of facts, an act which in itself reflects the authors' basic interpretation. Patterns of organization likewise represent the authors' concepts of historical development. Still, we have tried to build our story on specifics. In many cases our revisions for this edition have involved adding such details.

In planning the text originally and in revising it, we have tried to take into account the practical realities of the academic year. In most American colleges and universities there are approximately ninety class meetings during the year, the typical class meeting three times a week. We have broken our story into sixty chapters, each designed as a single day's reading assignment. In this way two of the three weekly meetings may be devoted to textbook material and the third to additional readings, discussions, and quizzes. We have limited our chapters to ten to twelve pages since we believe that this amount of compactly written textbook material is all that the average student is likely to absorb in one day's assignment. We have also kept our bibliographies brief, listing only those readings that will be useful to freshmen, sophomores, and the general reader. We also hope that the completely revised instructor's manual and the student workbook will serve as useful adjuncts to the textbook.

We are quite aware—more so than ever as a consequence of developments since the original publication of our book—of the importance of other civilizations in world history, and we have sought to indicate their basic characteristics as well as to suggest their interactions with the West. However, our conviction of the importance of a grasp of the history of Western civilization in developing perceptive minds aware of the realities of today's world persuades us to continue to place prime emphasis on the Western world. Considerations of space simply have not permitted anything approaching equal treatment to all major civilizations.

This edition has incorporated some basic changes that we hope will improve the book. Every effort has been made to incorporate the fruits of recent historical scholarship into our story. This has necessitated innumerable revisions throughout the book. In many cases, it has demanded revision of an entire section of a chapter. One entire part of the book, the High Middle Ages, has been completely restructured. Extensive changes have been made in the final chapters in an effort to keep up with the changing times. A complete new set of maps has been prepared. Most of the illustrations have been changed, and the illustrative material has been more widely distributed through the text. The suggested reading lists have been completely revised to reflect the vast outpouring of historical literature over the last decade, especially in paperback editions. The format of the bibliographies has been changed from a simple listing of books to a topical organization in the hope that the students' choices of material can be facilitated. Greater emphasis has been given to citing source materials in the suggested reading lists. Special attention has been given to the introductions to the twelve parts of the book, and retrospective essays have been added at the end of each section. It is hoped that these previews and retrospects will focus attention on the larger historical issues raised in each part and prompt significant questions in the students' minds that will encourage more profound study of the past. Six special interpretative essays have been added at various places with a view toward illustrating the complexity of historical problems and sensitizing students to the myriad approaches historians take to the past. This new feature of the book is intended to provoke students to explore new dimensions of the study of the past.

Finally, we wish to acknowledge the help we have received; our debt has greatly increased in preparing this new edition. Since no two historians can write a history of Western civilization based on perfect familiarity with all the sources, we owe an immense obligation to specialized researchers who have explored the myriad aspects of the past. The outcroppings of the labors of this splendid fraternity are everywhere evident in the book. Many fellow teachers who have used previous editions of this book have been most generous in suggesting ways to improve it; their suggestions have been invaluable in developing our plans for this third edition. Our colleagues from many departments at Michigan State University have been ever willing to help us clarify our thinking, especially in matters relating to art, philosophy, and literature. We owe a special debt in this respect to our colleagues in the Department of History and the Department of Humanities. We continue to be impressed with the acuity and the incisiveness of our students in evaluating our labors; many of their suggestions and questions have shaped this edition and we gratefully acknowledge their help.

J. B. H.
R. E. S.

East Lansing, Michigan
October 1970

CONTENTS

Part Six ❧ The Late Middle Ages: 1300–1500

Part Seven ❧ The Beginning of Modern Times— Fifteenth and Sixteenth Centuries

Part Eight ❧ The Age of Royal Absolutism— Seventeenth and Eighteenth Centuries

Part Nine ⚹ The Era of the French Revolution, 1776–1830

Part Ten ⚹ The Industrial Revolution—First Phase: The Dominance of the Middle Class, 1830–1871

Part Eleven ⚹ The Industrial Revolution—Second Phase: The Emergence of the Masses, 1871–1914

Part Twelve ❧ The Era of the Two World Wars, 1914–1970

Where Historians Disagree

MAPS

A Short History of Western Civilization

Part One

The Ancient Near East

4000–300 B.C.

The purpose of this work is to describe the evolution of Western civilization and to make its major characteristics intelligible by describing the numerous ingredients which combined in a chronological sequence to constitute its basic features. Our story will take us back to a remote age and will necessitate a discussion of earlier civilizations which contributed vital elements to Western civilization. This undertaking obviously demands that we first clarify the important concept embraced by the word "civilization." By "civilization" we mean that total pattern of institutions and ideas by which a large group of people conducts a collective life over an extended period of time. Civilizations are characterized primarily by large-scale political organization, complex social groupings, economic systems featuring highly specialized divisions of labor, and cultures marked by the expression of conscious thought patterns in writing and in a variety of art forms. The crucial factor that distinguishes a civilized society from one that has not achieved civilization is the existence of urban life.

Our account of the history of Western civilization will therefore begin with a study of the civilizations that emerged in the great river valleys of the Near East about 6,000 years ago. But first a few introductory remarks must be made about the long era of human history that preceded the birth of the higher civilizations of the Near East.

The origin of man is still shrouded in mystery. The story must be deduced from a pathetically meager collection of skeletons found quite by accident at various places on earth. Some of these remains, bearing a remarkable resemblance to modern man, date back over a million years. Enough such remains have been found in Africa to suggest that that continent was the cradle of the human species. Skeletons from more recent dates show that man was the product of a long process of biological evolution, and that it was probably not until about 30,000 years ago that the human species assumed its present physical form. However, even the earliest manlike creatures possessed a superior combination of physical qualities that distinguished them from the other animals and permitted them to survive and to flourish. Among their assets were an upright posture, better eyesight, a digestive system capable of utilizing nearly any kind of food, a voice mechanism capable of producing a wide variety of sounds, and a complex brain allowing them to remember and to coordinate their bodies better than other creatures.

Even the most primitive manlike creatures of 500,000 or 600,000 years ago were beginning to develop patterns of living. These early societies,

3

traces of which are scattered all over the earth, were all essentially the same and have been given the common name paleolithic, which means Old Stone Age. The distinctive feature of paleolithic society was the fact that man lived as a hunter and food gatherer; the greatest accomplishment of the paleolithic era was man's acquisition of the knowledge and skills to create weapons from stone and wood that made him an effective killer. We know that primitive hunters lived in small groups, their whole existence involved in pursuing the animals that sustained them, but we know very little about paleolithic man's intellectual life. There are scanty bits of evidence to suggest that he had developed religious concepts centering around the belief that spirits existed in all things and that survival depended on getting along with these spirits. In all probability these concepts represent the first attempt at organizing the knowledge man had acquired about the world around him. Evidence in the form of paintings, such as those in the Altamira caves in Spain, indicates that primitive man had an urge to express his inner feelings—to interpret the world as he saw it by visual means. The beauty of these paintings suggests that there was something more noble about paleolithic man than any description of his mode of living would lead us to believe.

If we date the dawn of human history from the time when tools began to be made by hunting societies, then the paleolithic era stretches over nine-tenths of all human history. Not until about 10,000 B.C. did the hunting life begin to disappear in a few parts of the world; and some remnants of it persist even today in Australia, the Pacific islands, and Alaska. The revolutionary changes that brought hunting societies to an end were the development of agriculture and the domestication of animals. These two developments ushered in the neolithic, or New Stone Age, pattern of life. How, when, and where this change first occurred is hotly disputed. The best evidence suggests that agricultural activity first appeared in Southwest Asia about 10,000 or 11,000 years ago. This area was especially favored by climatic changes occurring at this time: The retreat of the ice caps at the end of the last ice age had turned much of Europe and parts of Asia into a heavily forested area and had created conditions that began to produce the deserts of North Africa and Arabia. Both areas, formerly the strongholds of hunting societies, grew inhospitable. In the zone between, the cyclonic storms sweeping around the world from west to east brought regular rainfall and a mild climate, both conducive to grass and grain growing. It was here that man the hunter adapted himself to changing conditions and became man the farmer. During the next few thousand years, this mode of life appeared over most of the earth, probably "invented" several times by enterprising groups faced with difficulties in sustaining a food-gathering economy.

The domestication of plants and animals revolutionized man's living habits. He ceased wandering and settled permanently in villages. He produced new tools and techniques such as houses, hoes, sickles, pottery, and weaving to meet his new needs. With a little foresight he could accumulate enough wealth for better dwellings, clothing, and luxuries. Systematic farming yielded sufficient surplus to permit the specialization of labor, with a resultant increase in skill and efficiency and the broadening of the economic base of society. Neolithic man met the new social problems of the village community by creating tribal governments with authority vested in the hands of one or a few men who directed the activities of the whole community. The family developed into an institution capable of disciplining and directing the activities of all its members. Neolithic man also had to expand his mind to cope with the demands of his new situation. His religion, which increasingly centered around worship of the forces of nature that made a lifeless seed spring from the earth and that added new animals to his precious flocks, challenged him with ideas that were not quite as tangible as the animal spirits with which paleolithic man had grappled daily. Neolithic man's answer to this challenge was to place more trust in

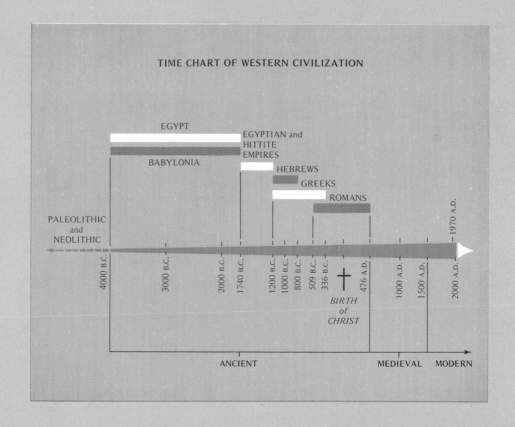

religious experts—his priests—and to dedicate more energy and wealth to the worship of the great spirits that nourished his crops and protected his village.

Neolithic society marked a great advance in human life, but not its ultimate fulfillment. The small isolated village, the limited technology, the routine imposed by nature, the narrowly conceived social system, and the restricted intellectual horizons characteristic of neolithic society combined to inhibit further advances. Men had to discover a new ambience in order to improve their condition. Such a leap forward occurred during the fourth and third millenniums before Christ at a very few spots on the globe. In the great river valley systems of the Near East, China, and India, there existed a physical environment offering opportunity for a more bounteous return from human effort—if men could organize their activities to capitalize on this potential. The response was the development of urban societies embracing much larger groupings of people than had the older neolithic agricultural villages. The urbanization of life in the Near and Far Eastern river valleys constitutes the crucial event inaugurating the history of civilization in the proper sense of the term.

Before becoming engaged in the tumultuous, complicated, fascinating story of the emergence and maturing of civilized human existence, it would be well to pause for a moment to recognize the debt the human species owes to those primitive, savage hunters and simple farmers of old. A solid foundation had been created for civilized life. Because of them it was already decided that city life with all its splendors would be supported by an agricultural economy. They had realized that man was a social being who must concern himself with the bonds attaching him to other men. They had perfected numerous techniques for human control over the natural world. They had sensed the existence of supernatural powers that affected human affairs and had evolved methods of placating these forces. All this accumulation of economic, social and political techniques, technical skills, and religious practices served as the basis upon which life in the emergent cities was constructed. Without them, civilization would have been impossible. Put another way, the leap forward to higher civilization in a few places on the earth did not involve a rent in the fabric of time; rather it marked an extension and elaboration of what had gone before.

In this section attention will be devoted to the civilizations that developed in the Tigris-Euphrates Valley of Mesopotamia and in the Nile Valley of Egypt. By this selection there is no intention of slighting comparable and equally significant advances in China and India. Mesopotamia and Egypt require our full attention because their achievements are vital to the central theme of this book: the history of Western civilization. The first task is to characterize the nature of the civilizations of Mesopotamia and Egypt. Beyond this, the extension of these civilizations into a large area of

Northeast Africa and Southwest Asia must be considered, for numerous other peoples absorbed ideas and institutions from them.   Equally significant, many made unique contributions of their own to the expanding stream of civilized life.   Until at least 500 B.C., the Near East led the civilized world. Its teeming population created a priceless heritage in every realm of human endcavor that was later exploited by other peoples participating in the shaping of Western civilization.

Chapter 1 ❧ Mesopotamian Civilization,

4000–1750 B.C.

It is now generally agreed that the transition from neolithic village society to urban civilization occurred first in the Tigris-Euphrates Valley. The causes of the transition from one level of life to a superior one is still an issue for considerable debate among historians, anthropologists, and archeologists. Some favor an evolutionary approach and stress the natural growth of complex city life out of the simpler village existence. Others speak of a more dramatic leap forward and often cite the development of the use of metals as the decisive factor demanding larger, better-organized communities. Still others argue that an environmental change gripping the entire Near East forced radical changes of life style on peoples long accustomed to the village society of the neolithic period. And not a few authorities emphasize the intrusion of new peoples into the area as a vital factor causing change. There is evidence to give credence to all these views. The strongest evidence, however, seems to point toward a rather sudden transformation of life in the Tigris-Euphrates Valley about 4000 B.C. The change that occurred then set a basic pattern of culture that developed in an unbroken sequence down to about 1750 B.C.

1. THE ENVIRONMENT

The great leap forward that occurred about 4000 B.C. is somehow associated with a new relationship between men and their environment. Mesopotamian [1] civilization came into being as a result of the ability of organized communities to construct an irrigation system which allowed them to capitalize on the agricultural potential of "the land between the rivers." The Tigris and the Euphrates rivers have their sources in the Armenian highlands, from which they flow southward in roughly parallel paths to the Persian Gulf. The land between them is called Mesopotamia, a word of Greek origin meaning "the land between the rivers." In their upper reaches, the rivers

---

[1] The term "Mesopotamian" will be used to refer to the whole cultural tradition that extends from about 4000 B.C. to 1750 B.C. As a label, it is not entirely accurate from any point of view: It does not adequately embrace the total geographical area that will be dealt with; it has no relevance to some of the many peoples that will be involved in the long period being considered; it provides no meaningful clue to the pattern of culture that will be examined. Yet it has become a traditional term, and for this reason suffices better than any other single descriptive term that might be employed.

This statue of Akkadian origin probably represents Sargon I, the creator of the first large-scale empire in Mesopotamia. *Photo: Hirmer Verlag*

BLACK SEA

CASPIAN SEA

Amu Darya (Oxus) R.

Syr Darya R.

MEDITERRANEAN SEA

Tigris R.

Euphrates R.

PERSIAN GULF

Nile R.

RED SEA

ARABIAN SEA

Indus R.

Favorable Zones for Earliest Agriculture
Alluvial Plains of Later Agriculture
● Some Early Agricultural Sites

0   200   400   600   800 mi.

Earliest Civilizations

traverse a semi-arid plateau that is a severe challenge to herders and farmers. Roughly 300 miles north of their mouths, the rivers enter a broad, flat alluvial plain that varies from 20 to 50 miles in width. This area, although relatively small, is immensely rich as a result of the silt constantly deposited by the flood waters of the rivers. However, the richness of the soil of Mesopotamia meant little without an irrigation system, for the hot climate and lack of rainfall made dry-land agriculture nearly impossible.

Tapping the waters of the rivers for irrigation confronted primitive farmers with major problems. The Tigris was of little use, for it ran in a deeply cut bed from which it was nearly impossible to draw water. The Eu-

phrates was different. As it flowed slowly across Mesopotamia, it deposited heavy layers of silt in its bed and along its banks. This process lifted the river above the plain, making it only necessary to cut canals in the banks to get water to the adjacent fields and to extend these canals inland across the flat plain in order to carry water to a large area. But such a system entailed an immense amount of planning and labor in order to retain the river within its banks, keep the canals free from silt, and control the amount of water flowing to the surrounding fields. Any disruption of the dikes would flood the low-lying fields and destroy the crops. The danger of uncontrolled waters was especially great at flood season, which usually occurred between April and June, for the rise of the river, dependent upon the thaw of snow in the Caucasus Mountains, was unpredictable. Since the season of the flood coincided with the chief growing season, failure to control the river spelled disaster to crops and settlements alike. Mesopotamian literature is filled with fearful allusions to devastating floods, and archeological finds confirm that those fears often became reality. Hardly less destructive was the lack of water, for the amount in the rivers apparently varied greatly from season to season. If the supply was short, then the burning sun ruined the crops and brought great suffering. But if the river could be kept within its banks at this critical season and if an orderly system of dikes and canals could be maintained, then water could be drawn off throughout the long growing season to nourish a wide variety of crops and to assure an abundant yield far in excess of the yields of dry-land farming. At the same time, the muddy waters of the Euphrates eternally renewed the fertility of the soil by depositing silt on the fields it watered.

No natural barriers protected Mesopotamia; the peoples who first learned to exploit the waters of the rivers and the rich soil of the valley were exposed to constant attacks. To the east the Zagros Mountains sustained tough herdsmen who were quick to raid the valley. On the west the Arabian Desert supported equally formidable nomads. Hardy farmers inhabited the plateaus along the upper reaches of the rivers. All could and did move into the valley with ease. Their constant assaults had a significant effect on Mesopotamian society, but they also made possible the spread of Mesopotamian influence outward into these more primitive areas.

There is danger in ascribing too much influence to environmental factors in determining the character of a people's history and culture; yet it is difficult to escape the conclusion that physical conditions in the Tigris-Euphrates Valley generated a deep sense of insecurity among its inhabitants. The everlasting threat of flood, drought, famine, and invasion bred an attitude of helplessness, uncertainty, and fatalism that is reflected in Mesopotamian literature and art. But the same conditions can and perhaps did have the reverse effect. Insecurity can breed action, effort, and creative thought in an attempt to overcome adversity. Perhaps this is the reason for the intensity with which life was lived in Mesopotamia and the richly varied response to human existence these people managed to develop.

2. MESOPOTAMIAN POLITICAL HISTORY

The development of higher civilization in the Tigris-Euphrates Valley began about 4000 B.C. with the conquest of the ancient inhabitants of the southern part of the area by a new people. The newcomers were the Sumerians, an agricultural people whose origins have not been established but who appear to have come from the east, perhaps forced to move by the progressive drying up of the entire Near East. The first settlers almost immediately began to irrigate the lands adjacent to the river. This initial effort required relatively simple irrigation techniques, but success apparently attracted more settlers, so that the network of canals had to be pushed back from the river. The growing complexities of the irrigation system and the increasing population placed a premium on management and organization skills. These pressures led to the formation of the more structured and sophisticated city, in which authority to govern both inhabitants and the agricultural operation was vested in a single person or group responsible for the safety and stability of the whole community. Thus, the first political manifestation of advancing civilization in the land of Sumer (as southern Mesopotamia was called) was the appearance of several city-states consisting of an urban center and the surrounding farmlands. By 3000 B.C. many such communities existed, each controlling a definite area of land, each containing a large population, and each jealous of its independence. During this same period Semitic peoples moved from the Arabian Desert into an area of southern Mesopotamia called Akkad, lying immediately north of Sumer. Imitating the more advanced Sumerians, the Semites too developed thriving city-states, some of which matched those of the Sumerians in splendor and wealth.

The governance of the typical Sumerian city-state was grounded in religious faith. The Sumerians believed that each city-state was originally created by a god who had rolled back the primeval flood, made the earth to appear, and fashioned the city and its inhabitants out of the mud. The city therefore belonged to the god, and its citizens were his slaves, charged with serving him in every way required to keep his establishment going. As the city-states first took form, it appears that each was governed by a group of elders who consulted with an assembly of freemen in making the decisions by which the will of the gods was carried out. The system, which has been characterized as a "primitive democracy," did not last long. By a process that is not at all clear but probably caused by the need for efficiency in controlling the water supply and in protecting the lands of the gods from outsiders, power was more and more concentrated in the hands of a single leader. The system grew into an authoritarian, theocratic kingship in which the ruler's power was based on his role as the agent of the patron god, the true ruler of the community. The priest-king, called *ensi* or *lugal*, centered his activities in the temple and surrounded himself with priest-assistants. From the temple flowed orders directing the numerous communal activities required to farm the lands of the gods. Back to the temple came a huge income gathered from the lands reserved for the support of the god, his house (the temple), and his agents (the priest-king and his aides). Added to this income were the sacrificial offerings made to please the god and to win his favor.

The temple complex became the nerve center of the entire community. Specialists whose skills were needed to conduct the numerous rituals in honor of the god congregated there. Gathered there too were the ever-increasing hordes of overseers, tax collectors, surveyors, engineers, recordkeepers (scribes), and planners who enacted the directives of the priest-king. Its many activities nourished the arts, architecture, writing, learning, skilled crafts, and trade—all of which combined to elevate life in the city far above the level in neolithic villages. The civilizing aspects of city life were made possible primarily through the ability and willingness of the priestly community to divert surplus wealth from the city-state economy into such undertakings. Thus the welfare of the entire city-state community depended upon the skill and intelligence of the priest-king and his agents.

There is evidence in the histories of several of the Sumerian city-states that somewhere in the evolution of their government, the *ensi* or *lugal* began to divorce his activities from the temple community to assume a more secular role. His palace, rather than the temple, became the center of civic life. The king did not surrender his role as representative of the patron god; his power was still theocratically based. But he exercised that power more independently by creating a nonpriestly circle of agents to assist him and drawing many civic functions away from the temple to the palace. The priests were increasingly reduced to strictly cult functions. Their role remained important, but it no longer permitted them to monopolize the direction of society in the way they had in the early city-state. In this transformation, badly understood because of the lack of evidence, lies the roots of a type of government which has been called Oriental despotism. It was destined to play a major role in the history of the Near East and was to exercise a great fascination over men who lusted after power and glory in many other parts of the world.

The changing character of Sumerian city-state government was probably related to new political problems in Mesopotamia after 3000 B.C. By that time the individual city-states were solidly established and had mastered the basic issues involved in maintaining internal order. Still, Mesopotamia was plagued by a lack of political stability. In part, the instability resulted from the incessant attacks of less-civilized outsiders, attacks made easy by the absence of any natural barriers. The richer the city-states of the valley grew, the more attracted were the outsiders. Even more disruptive was the violent rivalry among the city-states for land and power. The very nature of the god-centered city-states bred fierce local patriotism and provided little inspiration for a broader political vision. The more successful each city-state was in ordering its internal structure, the more capable it was of harassing its neighbors. The political history of Mesopotamia during much of the third millennium B.C. centered around the search for a solution to the problems of barbarian attacks and incessant intercity warfare. The solution was eventually found in the formation of empires ruled by kings who developed new political techniques for keeping peace and order among smaller political entities, for knitting together the activities of diverse peoples, and for imposing common patterns of life on extensive geographical areas. It was in the course of this search that Oriental despotism, grounded in earlier Sumerian political experience, took on mature form.

The first attempts at shaping a new political order were made by Sumerian cities. At various times between 3000 and 2400 B.C., strong military leaders from Ur, Erech, Lagash, and Umma succeeded in establishing temporary mastery over other cities, but these "empires" were short-lived. The Sumerians seemed to lack the ability to develop political institutions and techniques that could overcome the localism of the old city-states. Ultimately the Semites proved more talented in uniting Mesopotamia.

The first great Semitic empire builder emerged about 2400 B.C. from the city of Akkad in the northern region of the river valley area. His name was Sargon I. Ancient legend cast him in the role of a man of humble origin, set adrift in a basket in the bulrushes by an errant mother when he was an infant, rescued and raised by a peasant who made him a gardener, a calling he followed until the gods raised him to royal greatness. More reliable records indicate that Sargon was a servant in the royal household of a small Semitic kingdom and that he rose to power by usurping the office of king. Whatever the case, Sargon proved to be an effective war leader, utilizing his Semitic troops with great skill to subdue the powerful and more-advanced city-states of the land of Sumer to the south of Akkad. He also led his armies into the Zagros Mountains to the east and to the shores of the Mediterranean in the west, thereby curbing the barbarian assaults on the rich valley region and spreading its culture among more backward peoples. Sargon's empire was sustained until about 2200 B.C. by his descendants. Little is known of how it was governed; it appears that military power was a fundamental factor in holding it together and that Sargon's palace at Akkad was an important administrative center from which efforts were made to impose peace on an extensive area. The excessive size of the Akkadian Empire made it vulnerable to outside attacks and internal resistance from the Sumerian city-states. The main benficiaries of its collapse were these cities, which once more entered an era of independence and glory. Again cities like Ur tried to impose their authority on all Mesopotamia, but with no lasting success.

By 2000 B.C. the renaissance of the old Sumerian city-states was apparently ending. Ascendant now was a new group of Semitic people, the Amorites, who had only recently installed themselves in the river valley after migrating from the Arabian Desert. Early in the second millennium B.C., several Amorite chieftains created petty kingdoms at the expense of the Sumerian city-states. Out of this setting emerged the greatest of the Amorite leaders, Hammurabi, ruler of the city-state of Babylon. His reign, extending from about

Early Mesopotamia

expanse of territory. The Amorite rulers absorbed and spread the high culture of the conquered Sumerians. Under Amorite rule, Mesopotamian civilization reached its apogee.

In spite of the brilliance of Hammurabi and his successors, the Amorite Empire soon suffered from outside assaults. Shortly after 1750 B.C. foreign peoples like the Hittites and the Kassites began to push in from the north. These new peoples moved as part of an extensive disturbance that upset the political order throughout the Near East. Eventually the Kassites seized control of the Tigris-Euphrates Valley. The old Sumerian cities did not have the strength to rise against them; Amorite rule had apparently succeeded in crushing local patriotism. Never again would the people of the valley itself create a strong political power, although the area and its populace were destined to serve as a base upon which future conquerors would build great empires.

The empire builders who dominated the Tigris-Euphrates Valley after 2400 B.C. instituted several new ideas and practices in government that proved to be some of the greatest of all Babylonian contributions to civilization. The great political challenge facing a "king of kings," as Hammurabi called himself, was to overcome the differences that divided the peoples over whom he ruled. He was especially successful in resolving this problem.

One of Hammurabi's achievements was to complete the destruction of the monopoly of power previously held by the priests. He created a new concept in which the king himself was judge, lawgiver, and general in his own right. This powerful figure at the head of the state served as a symbolic center around which his subjects could rally, thus undercutting the utter dependence upon priests who ruled over small areas that a god was believed to have made sacred.

Hammurabi also developed institutions that made it possible for him to exercise the powers he claimed. He was always backed by a well-organized army ready to curb those

1792 to 1750 B.C., was distinguished by military exploits. He repeated the conquests of Sargon I, creating an empire that had its heart in the Tigris-Euphrates Valley and extended from the Mediterranean to the Zagros. By his own description, he was "King of the Four Quarters of the World." Babylon became a great city, the seat of a government that maintained peace and unity over a broad who threatened the peace in his empire. He established at his capital in Babylon a centralized bureaucracy where men of his choice headed specialized departments of finance, public works, justice, and defense. He subdivided his empire into local units and sent out more royal servants to collect taxes, raise troops, suppress uprisings, and judge disputes. He emerges as a tireless administrator, paying careful attention to every detail in his extensive realm. It was not far from the mark when he was called "the efficient king" in his law code. Hammurabi employed religion as a unifying force, promoting the worship of Marduk, once a deity whose worship was confined to the city of Babylon, throughout his empire. Marduk was presented as a god who had conquered the other gods in heaven and therefore had a right to rule their lands on earth. Never, however, was Hammurabi's power dependent solely on religion.

Probably the most significant of all Hammurabi's measures was his famous law code. It is no longer possible to hail Hammurabi as history's first lawgiver, for it is now evident that earlier Sumerian rulers had drawn up law codes and that Hammurabi's code was a synthesis of the previous legal systems. But by the very act of synthesis, he took an important step toward wiping out the diversities that governed the everyday affairs of his subjects by providing them with a common set of rules for property, wages, marriage and family affairs, crime, commercial exchange, inheritance. Here was a practical, utilitarian device for unifying his subjects. There are no startling new legal principles or political concepts to reshape society; rather, the great king reveals in the code a passion for peace and justice, a desire "to destroy the wicked and the evil, so that the strong may not op-

press the weak." The law, clearly defined and honestly administered, was an instrument for achieving ends so vital to the survival of the Amorite empire. In reading the code, one senses the king's full appreciation of the fact that a sound legal system based on widely accepted rules was a prime tool for instituting and maintaining a civilized society. A modern reader is sometimes taken aback by the brutal punishments prescribed: death to a builder who constructs a house so poorly that it falls down and kills its owner; loss of a hand for the surgeon whose patient dies or of the fingers for a son who strikes his father; loss of an eye for anyone who puts out the eye of another. But the code is better characterized by its realistic, commonsense, humane approach to life's basic problems: protection for women, children, and slaves; fairness in commercial exchange; protection for the property of soldiers on duty; regularized procedures for adjudicating disputes; debt relief for vic-

Hammurabi's code. The relief, which shows Hammurabi receiving his code of laws from a god, is carved at the top of a cylinder on which the laws are inscribed in cuneiform symbols. *Photo: Giraudon*

tims of flood and drought. On the whole, the code probably represented an enlightened concept of justice that drew people to accept Hammurabi's rule and to join the larger community of his empire.

3. THE MESOPOTAMIAN SOCIAL AND ECONOMIC SYSTEM

The material base for Mesopotamian society rested on agriculture. That base was sound, for the fertile soil of the valley and the irrigation system combined to permit a rich return in agricultural produce. A wide variety of crops were cultivated, with barley, sesame (for oil), and date palms being the staples. Because no great technical advance, aside from the irrigation system, was required to farm the rich land of Mesopotamia, agricultural techniques advanced little beyond neolithic levels. The spade, the crude wooden plow, the clay sickle, and the flail were the prime tools. Much of the labor was provided by human beings, although oxen and asses were used as sources of power. Despite this primitive technology, yields seem to have been high; some authorities argue that grain yields were as great as those in modern America. The raising of pigs and sheep in large numbers was also of prime importance. The horse was known in ancient Mesopotamia, but seems not to have played any significant role in economic life.

The prime agricultural unit was the large farm. It was tilled by gangs of laborers, some semifree peasants and others slaves, who went forth daily from the villages and cities to plow, sow, reap, and thresh, all under the careful supervision of the landlord or his agents. This labor force also spent large amounts of time repairing the dikes and canals, clearing away the troublesome rushes, and dredging out the silt that constantly threatened the irrigation system. Agricultural laborers were given their pay in produce. Perhaps many of them had a small garden around their huts where they could raise a few vegetables and keep a pig or sheep to help sustain their families. There were also some small independent farmers who cultivated their acreage with the aid of their families and a slave or two. On the whole, however, land ownership tended to be confined to a small group of nobles. In the early Sumerian period the temple priests nearly monopolized control of the land. By Hammurabi's time, large numbers of nonpriestly citizens, chiefly soldiers and royal agents, had gained possession of a considerable part of the land, usually by grant from the king. Although the myth that all land belonged to the patron god of the city-state or empire was sustained, there was active exchange in land and considerable freedom on the part of those who controlled it to exploit it as they saw fit.

Mesopotamian economy was enriched and variegated by a flourishing trade and industry. Many cities maintained well-developed industries devoted to making textiles, pottery, jewelry, metal goods, and especially clay bricks for building. The temples played an important role in promoting industry. The priests used the vast religious offerings as capital to hire labor and procure raw material for industrial production. However, the priests did not have a monopoly on manufacturing; great rulers also sponsored industry. By Hammurabi's time there even existed craftsmen who were able to engage in industrial production on their own.

Lack of many raw materials, especially stone and metals, made trade an absolute necessity in Mesopotamia. Every city maintained a class of people who spent their lives in trading ventures, either with neighboring cities or in the uncivilized areas surrounding the river valley. The code of Hammurabi makes it clear that highly developed business methods had evolved to aid in trading. The commercial class employed complicated contracts, standard weights and measures, credit buying, lending for interest, deeds, promissory notes, and many of the devices that are used today to carry on trade. Traders gave every indication of a truly capitalistic spirit, seeking to increase their wealth by wise investment and to exploit any trading situation for as great a profit as possible.

Mesopotamian society was dominated by a small aristocracy of priests and nobles. As we have seen, the priests were especially powerful in early Sumerian cities, but the lay aristocracy had become more prominent by the time of Hammurabi. Regardless of who constituted this class, however, it was this aristocracy that benefited most from Mesopotamia's wealth and that created a glittering life for itself in every city in Mesopotamia. By twentieth-century standards much of this wealth was ill-gotten. Nonetheless, the aristocracy performed an important function in society by directing the efforts of hundreds of thousands of individuals, each of whom possessed a different talent, toward a common end. Without such a guiding force, the high degree of cooperation needed to control the rivers would have been impossible. In a very real sense, the aristocrats earned their rewards. Perhaps their wealth was not too deeply resented by the rest of society; at least we hear nothing of attempts to overthrow them. It seems likely that many Mesopotamian nobles possessed a highly developed sense of obligation toward the rest of society. At any rate, the principle embodied in Hammurabi's code, according to which nobles should be punished more severely for certain crimes than other members of society, is presumed to reflect the conviction that nobles were expected to conduct themselves better than those with inferior status.

Even though Mesopotamian society was dominated by a small aristocracy, care was taken to define and protect the status of other classes. Hammurabi's code was careful to state the rights and duties of slaves, peasants, merchants, and artisans. The Mesopotamians were class-conscious indeed, but it was understood that each social class had a role in society, a role that all other classes must respect.

4. MESOPOTAMIAN RELIGION

Mesopotamian civilization is comprehensible only in terms of Mesopotamian religion, for religious beliefs and practices permeated every facet of life and gave meaning to every human undertaking. But our knowledge is scanty, and there is no evidence like that available from the writings of theologians of the great modern religions. The origins of Mesopotamian religious beliefs and practices lie in the remote and inaccessible past. When records began to be kept in Mesopotamia, most religious ideas were already formed and stable. And the Mesopotamians were little concerned with describing in a logical fashion the evolution or content of their religious concepts. From the evidence we do have, however, we can draw some conclusions.

We know, for example, that Mesopotamian religion was polytheistic. Perhaps the most basic conviction of all Mesopotamians was the belief that everything in existence was in essence a spirit and that every phenomenon was caused by the spirits living in all things. As a consequence, men were confronted with a bewildering array of spirits. Then men realized that some of these spirits were more powerful than others and thus worthy of greater attention. This heightened sense of awe was felt especially toward the spirits who controlled the forces of nature. Among the Sumerians this worship of the forces of nature fixed on Anu, the sky god, Enlil, god of the air, and Enki (called Ea by Semitic peoples), god of the earth and waters. This triad was worshiped almost universally throughout the river valley by Sumerians and Semites alike. Hardly less important were the astral gods: Nanna (Sin in Semitic), the moon god, and Utu (Shamash to the Semites), the sun god. Often these powerful nature gods were closely associated with a particular city, being accepted as the original founder and present owner of the city and its inhabitants. One deity whose worship had also always been nearly universal in the Tigris-Euphrates Valley was the goddess of fertility, whose munificent power renewed all nature every spring. This great "mother," called Inanna by the Sumerians and Ishtar by the Semites, had a special appeal to the ordinary person living close to the soil, to whom the annual miracle of renewal was most obvious. These gods were all represented as human beings possessing terrible powers and capable of doing great damage to anyone who displeased them. But they were not alone in the universe. Each family and each individual worshiped lesser gods who controlled the multitude of activities that surrounded human existence. Each Mesopotamian likewise believed that the world was filled with demons capable of bringing no end of discomfort and small misfortune to men.

During the long period of Mesopotamian history we are here considering, there was a tendency to clarify the nature and power of these deities, to spell out their relationship to one another, and to define their connections with the human community. One suspects that more energy was expended on this quest than on any other intellectual activity. And, in the final analysis, their success in this intellectual adventure may have constituted one of the main accomplishments of the ancient Mesopotamians, for it was probably crucial that man comprehend his relationship with the gods with precision and a degree of certainty before he could turn his creative talents to other ends. The fruit of this immense effort to know the divine better was a rich and intriguing body of mythology. In part this mythology was directed toward describing the activities of the divine figures—their habits, their quarrels, their love lives, their likes and dislikes, their family ties, their pleasures, etc. Mesopotamians ascribed to their gods a style of life similar to their own: Divine society reflected human society (the Mesopotamian "theologians" would have put it the other way around). The mythologizing effort also tried to spell out the hierarchical relationship among the gods, a problem made more pressing by the incessant political fluctuations in Mesopotamia. Since the Mesopotamians believed that each city-state was the property of a god, some explanation had to be given when one city-state conquered another. Usually the wars between city-states resulted in myths about similar wars between the gods with one conquering the other. Once they realized the impossibility of further resistance, the people of the conquered city usually accepted the conquering god as their chief deity, their old god being reduced to subordinate rank. At one time or another most of the great gods mentioned above were accepted by large numbers of people as a result of conquest. This development culminated in the time of Hammurabi, when the god of the victorious city of Babylon, Marduk, was universally worshiped in Hammurabi's empire.

Mythology also grew from an urge to understand how there came to be order in the universe and what that order consisted of. The result was a series of elaborate creation myths explaining how a particular god, such as Marduk, took things into his hands to subdue the primeval chaos, to fashion the families of gods, to create and position the heavens, the stars, the seas, and the land, and to fill the universe with living things. Accompanying these creation stories were descriptions of the laws ordained by the gods to sustain the harmonious order established at the time of creation. The mythologists also fashioned explanations of how things change; for example, by the age of Hammurabi there existed a rich mythology explaining how the goddess Ishtar and her lover, Tammuz, managed to assure the renewal of life each spring. As a body, this primitive "theology" is an impressive venture into answering the questions that face man. It became an infinitely rich storehouse from which later peoples drew their religious ideas. One suspects that the ordinary peasant or craftsman in ancient Mesopotamia knew little about these exalted myths; he was content to fix his religious interests on performing the time-sanctioned rites aimed at pleasing the gods and warding

Figures from a Sumerian temple at Tell Asmar, Iraq, ca. 2600 B.C. The postures and facial expressions indicate the awe and fear with which the Mesopotamians approached their gods. *Photo: Courtesy of the Oriental Institute, The University of Chicago*

off the demons, especially those close at hand on his farm and in his house. Nonetheless, the mythologizing effort went far to fix and order religious life and to assure thinking men that there was some pattern in the universe.

Where did men fit into this religious scene? A man was viewed as a slave of the gods, created by them to carry out their will without question. Because they were vengeful, angry gods, they were apt at any moment and for any reason to heap disaster on their slaves. Men therefore bore a terrible burden in trying to keep their unpredictable masters

happy. The care and feeding of the gods was crucial in this respect. Magnificent temples were built as dwellings for the great deities, and every care was lavished on decoration and furnishings so that their inhabitants would be comfortable. Sumptuous banquets were prepared each day and served with great pomp. Troops of priests and priestesses, organized by specialties, stood constantly ready to feed, bathe, perfume, fan, sing for, and make love to the gods—or to those whom the gods designated as their surrogates. Whole city-states labored to provide the building materials, the metals, the bread, the beer, the fruit, etc., needed to make life comfortable for the gods. On special occasions, great festivals, like the spring New Year celebration, were organized in honor of the gods. A major part of the wealth and creative talent of the whole community was poured into this effort to make the gods pleased with their earthly slaves. Aside from the great temples, there were countless smaller temples and shrines in houses, on the farms, and in the streets where people made their offerings to placate the spirits who controlled all things. No project, great or small, was ever undertaken without a ritual performance, first to ask the gods to look with favor on the venture before it was initiated and later to thank them for its success. For all this elaborate effort, the Mesopotamians, both as communities and as individuals, were never sure of reward. Their gods were not that predictable and not that favorably disposed toward mankind. So a Mesopotamian's view of life was pessimistic; with no certainty of success or even safety, he lived life as a ritual aimed at pleasing the gods, for this was how things had to be.

As one might expect, the Mesopotamians were especially anxious to find out in advance what the gods might be planning. They developed a whole battery of prediction techniques. Dreams were carefully interpreted in the hope that the gods would reveal themselves to sleepers. The entrails of animals, especially the liver, were studied to find signs of the future. Also, the movement of the stars was carefully observed, and the astrologer was a powerful figure in Mesopotamian society. By adding these many facts together, it is perhaps safe to say that the Mesopotamians explored nearly every mode of external worship conceivable, creating a set of ritual practices that long remained a model for imitation by later peoples.

Mesopotamian religion quite clearly emphasized the outward aspects of religious life, for the Mesopotamians had no god who placed heavy ethical demands on his believers. They hoped that, if they dutifully performed the prescribed rites of worship and made liberal sacrifices, the gods would be happy and would reciprocate with bountiful material rewards. Seldom did the Mesopotamians give much thought to the problem of moral standards as a facet of religious life. Perhaps this lack of concern with morality and ethics was connected with the absence of any deep feeling about immortality among the Mesopotamians. They believed that there was an afterlife, but it was hardly worth working for. The dead passed on to a "land of no return" somewhere underground, "where dust is their feed, clay their sustenance; where they see no light and dwell in darkness." Very little attention was paid to expensive burial or to the care for the dead. Mesopotamian religion was concerned chiefly with sustaining earthly life.

5. MESOPOTAMIAN LITERATURE, ART, AND SCIENCE

The achievements of the Mesopotamians in the arts, literature, and science have always seemed less significant than those of the Egyptians, probably because Egyptian cultural monuments have survived so much better. But what has remained of their culture suggests a great deal of creative power and notable advance over peoples who lived in the area prior to them. By and large, the Sumerians were the original artistic creators in Mesopotamia. The Semites sometimes modified and developed Sumerian cultural accomplishments, but more often they merely imitated them. Culturally, the two peoples merged completely, so that a common pattern of culture rooted in ancient Sumeria embraced the entire area of Mesopotamia.

The Sumerians developed a writing system during the fourth millennium B.C. Their original method of writing employed pictographs, but gradually a system of symbols representing sounds was developed. Eventually, several hundred such symbols were accepted, permitting writers to combine signs to express almost any idea. After the time of Sargon I, the Sumerian written language began to be replaced by the Semitic written language, called Akkadian. However, learned men continued to study Sumerian, much as later scholars preserved classical Greek and Latin, so that a considerable body of Sumerian literature has survived. Both Sumerians and Semites wrote on clay tablets, pressing the symbols into soft clay with a wedge-shaped reed stylus and then baking the tablets. This writing style has been called *cuneiform*, a term derived from the Latin word meaning "wedge."

Writing in the early Sumerian cities probably developed for recordkeeping purposes. Once a usable system was perfected, it was employed to preserve an extensive body of literature which can be classified into a few major genres. The most impressive writings were the magnificent religious epics, of which the *Creation Epic* and the *Epic of Gilgamesh* are the best examples. The *Creation Epic* consists of a series of stirring episodes describing how Marduk won supremacy over the spirit world and created the earth and man. The *Epic of Gilgamesh* recounts the doings of a legendary hero named Gilgamesh, ruler of the city of Erech. The story, which centers on the theme of a fruitless search for immortality, leads Gilgamesh through numerous encounters with angry gods and with the forces they create to destroy him. Woven into these adventures are such themes as war, love, death, and natural catastrophes. The Mesopotamians also wrote impressive hymns addressed to the gods, but containing countless references to worldly affairs. Several pieces of "wisdom" literature, embodying advice on how to get along in this world, have survived. There were attempts at historical writing in the form of chronicles in which the deeds of famous rulers were recounted. The Mesopotamians were prolific letter writers, especially toward the end of the period. Unquestionably these literary works were read by a small circle, since literacy was not general. Nonetheless, Mesopotamian literature clearly

indicates a lively cultural atmosphere. In reading this literature one is often struck by the similarities it bears in theme, style, and form to segments of the Old Testament, written down more than a thousand years later. This likeness suggests that the Mesopotamian literary tradition helped to shape the minds and the esthetic tastes of many later generations who knew little of the history of the men who lived in "the land between the rivers."

From the beginning of their civilization, the Mesopotamians were skilled and creative artists. Their art did not survive well, owing to the lack of stone and the consequent employment of more perishable materials. Their major architectural works were temples. From earliest times, every Sumerian city had a large and elaborate temple to the patron deity at its center. Near it was often a temple tower, called a *ziggurat*. The ziggurats were built of clay bricks, and for this reason have not survived very well. They were constructed by setting a series of terraces one on top of another, each succeeding layer being smaller than the one below it. Thus the towers rose by a series of grand steps toward an apex. A sanctuary, remote from the world, was placed atop the final terrace. The purpose of these towers is not clear. Perhaps they were tombs of some kind, or man-made replicas of the mountains where the dwellers of the river valleys used to worship before they came to the lowlands, or attempts to build a bridge to heaven so that man could approach closer to the gods. Around the main temple there usually developed an extensive complex of offices, dwellings, lesser shrines, storehouses, workshops, and market stalls, all comprising a sacred precinct for conducting the activities associated with serving the gods. Often the temple establishment reached immense size.

Magnificent brick palaces were also built for the kings, especially after the royal establishment began to be separate from the temple. The palace at Mari, an important city at the time when the Amorite Empire was at its peak, covered 6 acres and contained more than two hundred and fifty rooms. Mesopotamian architects knew how to use the column, the dome, the arch, and the vault, but given the limitations of the building materials they had at their disposal, they were unable to apply these techniques very extensively, especially in the monumental architecture of the temples and the palaces. On the whole, Mesopotamian architecture was conservative, following set styles over long centuries.

A considerable amount of sculpture has survived, although this art too was restricted by the shortage of good stone in Mesopotamia. Most of the three-dimensional statues are portrayals of gods and kings. Sculptors took some pains to give a distinctive character to a face, but concerned themselves little with a realistic rendering of the body. The statues are solid, stiff, motionless. A glance at an illustration of Mesopotamian work will indicate that the sculptor was governed by ideal geometrical forms—cylinders and cones—in conceiving his work. More realistic and animated scenes were created by sculptors working in low relief. These *steles*, often devoted to the depiction of historic events or to divine exploits, accentuated action. The most exquisite carving was done by the seal makers, who wrought minaturized scenes on stone that could be used to press an identifying mark into clay. Their portrayals of animals are especially excellent. The same skill is also illustrated in the jewelry, metalwork, and decorated pottery that were created in great abundance. All this work reflects not only a great deal of technical skill, but also a strong sense of beauty.

The Mesopotamians produced a body of knowledge that can be called science. They devised a system of time reckoning in which the length of the year was based on the sun's movement and that of the months on the moon's cycles. They also used a seven-day week. Their system required constant juggling, since the cycles of the sun and moon did not coincide. Extra days were added periodically to keep the two systems together. They also developed a standard of weights and measures, used almost universally by the end of Hammurabi's dynasty. Their number system was based on both a decimal system and units of sixty, a system we still use, for instance, in our divisions of the hour. They were able to add, subtract, multiply, and divide. Also they were able to perform simple geometrical operations, such as finding the area of a plane surface or the volume of a cylinder. Most of their mathematics was practical, intended only to serve the needs of surveyors, architects, and engineers. Mesopotamian medicine mixed intelligent observations about the causes and cures of disease with a tremendous amount of superstition. There existed a rather extensive knowledge of geography, as a result of their wide travels. Since the stars played such a large part in their religious beliefs, they accumulated a large body of accurate information about the movements of the stars, thus laying the basis for astronomy. Their attitude toward this information was typical: Their knowledge of the stars did not lead them to consider the nature of the heavenly bodies; astronomy merely served as a means of foretelling the future. And so it was with all Mesopotamian scientific knowledge. They had no interest in discovering knowledge of the natural world for its own sake. What they knew was retained only because it served a practical purpose. Theoretical science and the inquiring spirit made little progress of any kind.

Taken together, the achievements of the Mesopotamians in literature, the arts, and science suggest a few general characteristics of the outlook that predominated in this ancient culture. Certainly religion was the integrating force in intellectual life. It supplied the basic assumptions that governed all thought and expression and provided the great overarching truths about existence that gave meaning to every intellectual activity. Because the prime focus of religion was the sustaining of earthly life in good order in the face of powerful, capricious divine forces, the Mesopotamian thinkers and artists were basically practical men. They expended their talents toward ends that would keep the gods happy and protect the existing order. There was little room for free expression, experimentation, individual fancy, and speculation. The artist-thinker was conservative, given to saying and doing over and over what had already been proved effective. There is a notable absence of evolution and change in literary and artistic styles and themes across the two thousand years we have reviewed. He was also basically gloomy and pessimistic, seldom hopeful that the burdens imposed on the slaves of the gods would become lighter in an unstable and uncertain cosmic system. Finally, he was anxious, his mind alert for signs that man's efforts were attuned to the forces that governed existence. Perhaps it was this anxiety that supplied a quality of adaptability and pliability that made Mesopotamian civilization tough and durable.

When the semibarbarous Kassites began to occupy the lower Tigris-Euphrates Valley about 1700 B.C., the first phase of Mesopotamian civilization had ended. For 2,000 years the Sumerians and their Semitic imitators had struggled successfully to create an orderly society and a highly developed culture. After 1700 B.C., Mesopotamian civilization began to exert a powerful influence over a much wider area. Hardly a single people was to emerge in the later history of the Near East who did not borrow heavily from Mesopotamia. Mesopotamian influences lived on long after the men from the "land between the rivers" ceased to be politically strong in the Near East.

Suggested Reading*

Overview. The student whose curiosity is piqued by the rather straightforward account of ancient Near Eastern history set forth in Part I (Chapters 1–4) might like to read one or two broad-sweeping, strongly interpretative works. **V. Gordon Childe, *Man Makes Himself* (4th ed., Mentor) is one such book; it emphasizes especially economic and technological development in prehistoric and ancient Near Eastern life. Strongly cultural in orientation and deeply sympathetic is Will Durant, *Our Oriental Heritage . . . (The Story of Civilization*, Vol. I, 1935), the first of a multivolume world history. **Sabatino Moscati, *The Face of the Ancient Orient* (Anchor) spans the ancient Near East with a deft touch, focusing primarily on intellectual history; the book contains ample quotations from ancient literature to illustrate major points. **William H. McNeill, *The Rise of the West: A History of the Human Community* (Mentor), chaps. 1–4, stresses technological advance and cultural diffusion as dynamic factors in Near Eastern development. The first volume of a projected multivolume *History of Mankind* being prepared by UNESCO has been written by Jacquetta Hawkes and Sir Leonard Woolley under the title *Prehistory and the Beginnings of Civilization* (1963). This recent and massive study is thorough, and its organization helps in comparing the many facets of civilization developed in various areas of the Near East. A splendid selection of literature representing all the peoples in the ancient Near East is provided by James B. Pritchard, ed., *Ancient Near Eastern Texts Relating to the Old Testament* (2nd ed., 1955). For a general view of artistic accomplishments, one might turn to **James B. Pritchard, *The Ancient Near East:*

---

* Works available in paperback editions are marked with a double asterisk.

An Anthology of Texts and Pictures (Princeton) or to **Henri Frankfort, *The Art and Architecture of the Ancient Orient* (Penguin).

Always interesting is the way in which historians discover information about the ancient world. Two fascinating books by C. W. Ceram, *Gods, Graves, and Scholars: The Story of Archaeology* (2nd ed., 1967) and *The March of Archaeology* (1958), and another by **Sir Leonard Woolley, *Digging Up the Past* (Penguin), will provide an excellent introduction to archeology. **Ignace J. Gelb, *A Study of Writing* (rev. ed., Phoenix) will help to clear up the difficult problems surrounding the origin and development of writing.

Paleolithic and Neolithic Cultures. Because interpretations of prehistory are diverse and constantly changing, it is difficult to provide in a brief list very sure guidance to a reader wishing to explore this subject more deeply. **William White Howells, *Back of History: The Story of Our Own Origins* (rev. ed., Anchor), is a lively, witty, and reliable book strongly anthropological in orientation. **Robert J. Braidwood, *Prehistoric Men* (7th ed., Scott Foresman), is a masterful study, although some of its conclusions are controversial. Two more difficult but provocative treatments are **Ralph Linton, *The Tree of Culture* (Vintage); and Carleton S. Coon, *The Story of Man: From the First Human to Primitive Culture and Beyond* (2nd rev. ed., 1962). Ashley Montagu, *Man: His First Two Million Years* (1969), is provocative on the controversial subject of the physical development of man. The difficult problem of primitive religion is dealt with by **Robert H. Lowie, *Primitive Religion* (Grosset and Dunlap Universal Library); ** E. O. James, *Prehistoric Religion: A Study in Prehistoric Archaeology* (University Paperbacks); and Johannes Maringer, *The Gods of Prehistoric Man,* ed. and trans. Mary Ilford (1960).

Mesopotamia. The problem of the transition from neolithic society to higher civilization in the ancient Near East has been a much-disputed issued. The issues at stake and various interpretations are well presented in three books, each quite different in its conclusions: **V. Gordon Childe, *New Light on the Most Ancient Near East* (4th ed., Norton); **Henri Frankfort, *The Birth of Civilization in the Near East* (Anchor); and Robert J. Braidwood, *The Near East and the Foundations for Civilization* (1952).

The most complete and balanced survey of Mesopotamian civilization is **H. W. F. Saggs, *The Greatness That Was Babylon: A Sketch of the Ancient Civilization of the Tigris-Euphrates Valley* (Mentor); the book opens with a good survey of political history and then turns to a topical approach to social and cultural history. Two other surveys are also adequate: **Georges Roux, *Ancient Iraq* (Penguin); and **A. Leo Oppenheim, *Ancient Mesopotamia: Portrait of a Dead Civilization* (Phoenix). Roux's book provides a better chronological account, while Oppenheim's provides an excellent characterization of Mesopotamian culture from a topical approach. S. N. Kramer, *The Sumerians: Their History, Culture and Character* (1963) is thorough and up-to-date on Sumerian history. The same author's **History Begins at Sumer* (Anchor) describes the "firsts" achieved by the Sumerians. Leonard Cottrell, *The Land of Shinar* (1965) is a well-written, brief survey of Sumerian history. The nature of Mesopotamian political institutions is brilliantly treated in H. Frankfort, *Kingship and the Gods: A Study of Ancient Near Eastern Religion as the Integration of Society and Nature* (1948). **Cyrus N. Gordon, *Hammurabi's Code: Quaint or Forward Looking?* (Holt, Rinehart, and Winston) is a good introduction to the Mesopotamian legal system.

A reader interested in economic and social conditions and everyday life will find abundant materials in **Georges Contenau, *Everyday Life in Babylon and Assyria* (Norton); and H. W. F. Saggs, *Everyday Life in Babylonia & Assyria* (1965). Also of interest is W. F. Leemans, *The Old-Babylonian Merchant: His Business and His Social Position* (1950).

Aside from the general books already cited, all of which treat religion, art, literature, and science, the following are more specialized works of considerable importance. The fullest treatment of Mesopotamian religion is S. H. Hooke, *Babylonian and Assyrian Religion*

(1963). **S. N. Kramer, *Sumerian Mythology: A Study of Spiritual and Literary Achievement in the Third Millennium B.C.* (rev. ed., Harper Torchbook), brings to bear the author's vast knowledge of Mesopotamian literature and history to produce a rich treatment of religious ideas. A good short essay on Mesopotamian religion by Georges Contenau can be found in **Etienne Drioton, Georges Contenau, and Jacques Duchesne-Guillemin, *Religions of the Ancient East*, trans. M. B. Loraine (Hawthorn). **H. Frankfort *et al.*, *Before Philosophy: The Intellectual Adventure of Ancient Man* (Penguin), presents a splendid synthesis of the mentality of the ancient Mesopotamians by T. Jacobsen. **Otto Neugebauer, *The Exact Sciences in Antiquity* (2nd ed., Dover); and René Taton, *Ancient and Medieval Science From Prehistory to A.D. 1450*, trans. A. J. Pomerans (*A General History of the Sciences*, Vol. I; 1963), chap. 2, will provide good summaries of the scientific achievements of the ancient Mesopotamians. A convenient translation of the Gilgamesh epic is provided by **Nancy Sandars, *The Epic of Gilgamesh: Prose Version* (Penguin).

Chapter 2 ⚜ Ancient Egypt, 4000–1750 B.C.,

and Minoan Civilization

Not long after higher civilization had begun to take shape in Mesopotamia, a similar leap forward occurred in Egypt. Somewhat later still, a comparable advance occurred on the island of Crete. There is some evidence that influences from Mesopotamia played a role in shaping these new civilizations, but in the main, developments in each area, especially Egypt, were indigenous and thus assumed unique forms.

1. THE NILE VALLEY

The Greek historian Herodotus uttered a fundamental truth that still must be the starting point for the history of ancient Egypt: Egypt is the gift of the Nile. Rising in the mountains of equatorial Africa, the river ultimately forms a narrow, cliff-lined trough, seldom more than 10 miles wide, cutting through several hundred miles of bleak desert almost devoid of rainfall. As it nears the Mediterranean, the Nile fans out into a series of channels, forming a triangle of land about 120 miles on each side known as the Delta. Although the river links the land along its course to create a geographical entity, the Delta region differs from the narrow valley to the south. It is less dominated by the desert, less demanding, more open to the outside world, more comfortable. Geography created "two lands" in Egypt, and they always re-

mained visible in Egypt's historic development.

The Egyptians themselves described the valley as the "black land," which they contrasted with the terrible "red land" of the desert. The "black land" was deposited by the benevolent river over the ages. With amazing regularity, each summer the Nile begins to rise, and finally overflows its low banks and covers the flat land on either side of the channel with flood waters. At that point, the harvest would be finished, so the waters could be allowed to spread freely over the land, soaking the parched soil and spreading a new layer of silt to restore the fertility of the fields. When the flood waters receded and the river returned to its normal channel, crops could be planted in the rich, muddy soil. They matured quickly in the hot climate, usually returning high yields because of the fertility of the soil. If the crops needed additional moisture or if a second crop was planted in the same season, it was possible to draw water from the main channel of the river or from reservoirs. But the successful utilization of the waters required careful planning and hard labor; the Nile's gifts were not free. Men had to struggle to keep down the vegetation in the swamps produced by the floods and to push water out from the mainstream to drive back the ever-intrusive "red earth" of the desert. And the river could be capricious, rising too high so that men's handiwork was swept away, or not high enough so that the valley was inadequately watered and famine resulted. On the whole, however, the exploitation of the Nile was less burdensome than the control of the Tigris-Euphrates rivers, which were less predictable in their flooding and which formed a much wider valley to try to irrigate. The Nile inspired trust, confidence, and optimism in those who lived along its course. Well might the Egyptians sing: "Hail to Thee, O Nile, that gushest forth from the earth and comest to nourish Egypt!"

The Nile Valley differed from the Tigris-Euphrates Valley in another significant way: It was shielded from invaders by forbidding natural barriers. The deserts on the east and west, the rapids (cataracts) that block river traffic about 700 miles south of its mouth, and the Mediterranean Sea isolate the valley. The only readily accessible entry into Egypt is a narrow, easily defensible passage connecting the delta region in the north to Asia. This isolation gave Egypt stability, but deprived her of the stimulus of contact with foreigners and limited her ability to influence outsiders.

2. EGYPTIAN POLITICAL HISTORY, 4000–1750 B.C.

From the evidence available to us, it appears that the Nile Valley began to be occupied as early as 5000 B.C. by peoples who had already mastered agricultural life. Perhaps they were North Africans who were being forced to seek new homes by the emerging desert in that area. They may also have been from the south or from western Asia, for the Egyptians were surely a mixed people. The earliest settlers established small agricultural villages typical of neolithic peoples. The villages were built a distance from the river—away from the floods, away from the swamps and from the beasts and insects that infested them. Then began a long struggle to tame the land, a struggle that we must presume placed de-

mands on men that caused them to develop their skills and intelligence. By about 4000 B.C., village settlements had spread throughout the valley, and there was an irrigation system that permitted the inhabitants to begin to gather the gifts of the Nile. There seems to have been no great economic pressure to cause the villages to unite in larger communities, for nothing comparable to the Mesopotamian city-states evolved in early Egypt. However, over the centuries there was a tendency for several contiguous villages to coalesce into petty kingdoms. The survival into later history of many totem symbols and totemic religious ideas from this age suggests that blood ties and shared religious beliefs were factors in drawing the villages together. It is not impossible that the small kingdoms were the handiwork of aggressive, capable landlords who forced their authority on weaker neighboring villages. As larger units were formed, it very likely became obvious that greater cooperation brought greater benefits from the land and the river. However, the primitive villages never disappeared in Egypt; for long ages and under many forms of government, they endured as the basic units of society.

The era of the formation of small kingdoms, called the Predynastic Age, was ended suddenly about 3100 B.C., when all Egypt was unified under a single ruler, the *pharaoh*. Egyptian traditon ascribed this amazing feat to Menes, who founded the first dynasty of pharaohs and whose reign ushered in an era in Egyptian history called the Old Kingdom. Certainly the process of unification had begun before Menes' time, for he was already ruler of a large kingdom in Upper Egypt when he subdued a second well-organized kingdom in Lower Egypt. It required some time after Menes overran Lower Egypt before the unification process was complete. Still, a single Egypt was shaped with impressive speed. Menes preceded Sargon I by nearly seven centuries, and when Hammurabi built his rather temporary Amorite Empire, Egypt had en-

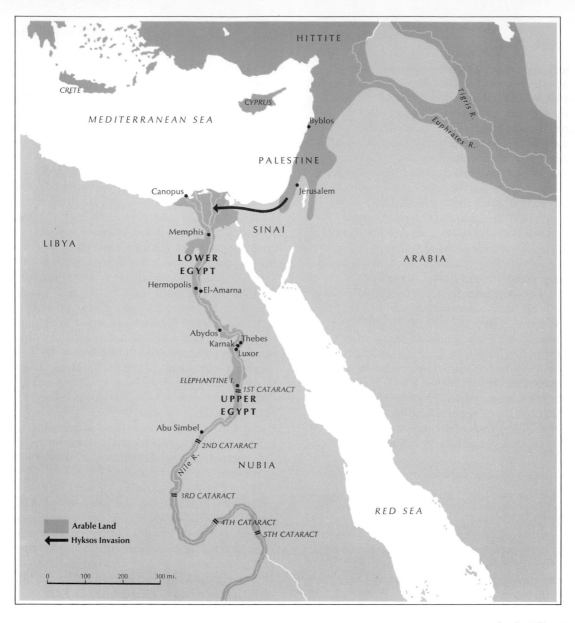

HITTITE

CRETE

CYPRUS

MEDITERRANEAN SEA

Tigris R.

Euphrates R.

Byblos

PALESTINE

Canopus

Jerusalem

SINAI

Memphis

LOWER
EGYPT

LIBYA

ARABIA

Hermopolis   El-Amarna

Abydos
Karnak   Thebes
Luxor

ELEPHANTINE I.
1ST CATARACT

UPPER
EGYPT

Abu Simbel

2ND CATARACT

Nile R.

NUBIA

3RD CATARACT

RED SEA

4TH CATARACT

5TH CATARACT

Arable Land

Hyksos Invasion

0   100   200   300 mi.

Ancient Egypt

joyed about thirteen centuries of almost unin-
terrupted unity.

In part, Egypt's unification was made easy
by the natural unity imposed on the valley by
the Nile, which forms an easily traveled road
from one end of Egypt to the other, drawing
all life to itself. More important was the
absence of strong centers of local patriotism

of the nature of the religiously oriented city-
states in Mesopotamia. The simple agricultural villages lining the Nile offered no real
opposition to a resourceful, determined uni-
fier; probably such a step meant very little in
terms of their basic way of life.

During the era of the Old Kingdom
(3100–2200 B.C.), Egypt was ruled by an or-

derly succession of pharaohs, six dynasties in all. The rulers of the first two dynasties seem to have been absorbed chiefly with the problems of completing Egypt's unification: suppressing rebellion, persuading the people of Lower Egypt to accept a "foreign" ruler from Upper Egypt, working out the details of an effective administration. Success in this venture set the stage for the glorious third and fourth dynasties, the golden age of the Old Kingdom. The pharaohs of these dynasties were truly uncontested masters of the whole valley. Their rule, exercised from their capital at Memphis, situated on the Nile near where the river fans out to form the Delta, brought to the land and its people peace, good order, and great prosperity. And their influence was felt outside the valley: in the Sinai peninsula, in Syria where they maintained a trading outpost at Byblos, and in the south toward Nubia. The splendid pyramids built at Gizeh by the powerful pharaohs of the Fourth Dynasty, Menkaure, Kephren, and Khufu (Cheops), reflect not only the immense wealth and power of their builders, but also the complex and unique cultural pattern that had emerged in Egypt following unification. In a favorable environment, religion, art, architecture, literature, and technology had all made a great leap forward.

By the time of the Third Dynasty, the Egyptian government had assumed the form it was to have for many centuries. The central feature of that government was the absolute power of the pharaoh. Indeed, he was universally accepted as a god; he was supposed to have been sired by the sun god Re, born in a way different from humans, and destined to eternal life with the other gods. How this concept of a god-king came to be formulated and accepted is unknown, but it was the keystone of the entire political order and gave Egypt a political system unique in all history. As god, the pharaoh owned Egypt and its populace. Every person was his servant. His mere word was law. A highly elaborate ritual surrounded his entire existence, and no one dared challenge his authority. He could not

even marry an ordinary mortal, but only his divine sister. Despite their lofty and remote status, most of the pharaohs of the first four dynasties were active statesmen. They were carefully educated for their office, took an active part in administering the state, and emerge as nearly human. They traveled extensively, were informed about the condition of the irrigation system, directed building programs, took special care to render justice to all their subjects, and sponsored trading projects to acquire needed materials from abroad.

The records of the third and fourth dynasties reveal that there had evolved a complex and efficient set of institutions through which the pharaoh exercised his vast powers. At his royal palace in Memphis, the pharaoh gathered a group of trusted friends and delegated to them certain jobs to be carried out under his supervision. Among the high officials prominent in the records of the Old Kingdom were a vizier, a treasurer, a chief of irrigation, a chief justice, recordkeepers, and high priests. Most important was the vizier, who served as chief assistant to the pharaoh. Each of these major officials was assisted by numerous lesser state servants. But the government was not confined to the capital; the pharaoh's officials were spread throughout the country and governed specific local areas in his name. Egypt was divided into forty-two governmental units, called *nomes*, each controlled by royal officials. Every nome was divided into villages, where the mass of the people lived and where officials appeared from time to time to enforce the pharaoh's orders and to collect taxes.

During the fifth and sixth dynasties, this magnificent system began to falter, and Egypt drifted imperceptibly toward disorder. The pyramids built during this time were smaller, their size suggesting a decline in royal wealth and power. There is evidence of the great independence of royal administrators and provincial governors. Complaints about disorder, injustice, and oppression appear in the records. The priests of the national god Re began to challenge the pharaoh's monopoly of the power to intercede with the gods on behalf of the people. The pharaoh's influence outside Egypt disappeared. The causes of the evident decline of a once-successful order are hard to discern. There is no record of any sudden, overpowering internal or external development. Perhaps the pharaohs grew lax in ruling Egypt and tended to place too much trust in their officials. The administrative machine appears to have become so large and complex as to be beyond the control of a single ruler. The opportunity for bureaucratic empire builders to shape their own little circles of power appears not to have been missed; some literary remains suggest that these officials were an aggressive, materialistic group who used the bounty heaped on them by the pharaohs as a means of usurping royal authority. There is some indication that the pharaohs impoverished themselves by overgenerous grants to the nobles and especially to the priests. And the rulers may have discredited themselves by imposing too great a burden on their subjects for such costly, nonproductive projects as the great pyramids. Whatever the reason, Egypt drifted toward chaos.

By the end of the Sixth Dynasty, Egypt entered a period of anarchy sometimes called the Feudal Age (2200–2050 B.C.), but more accurately named the First Intermediate Period. Power rested in the hands of innumerable local princes who made their old offices and grants of land hereditary and did as they pleased. There continued to be pharaohs who together make up the seventh through the tenth dynasties, but they were shadowy, ineffective figures. Political disunity brought with it internal wars, lawlessness, injustice, and economic depression. Sensitive men reacted with shock and moral outrage in the face of these developments. One writer complained of nobles slaving in the workhouses while "he who never slept on a plank now owned a bed," of the robber now possessing riches, of the land deprived of kingship by irresponsible men, of the desert spreading through the land. The end of political unity brought bitter fruit to most Egyptians, even while the strong and the grasping flourished.

Then, about 2050 B.C., the princes of Thebes, previously an insignificant city far to the south in the valley, undertook the task of reunificaiton, perhaps in the name of the god Amon, heretofore only a minor deity. After a fierce struggle, these princes (designated as the Eleventh Dynasty) finally reunited the land and established what is known as the Middle Kingdom (2050–1750 B.C.). It reached its peak during the Twelfth Dynasty. Some of the pharaohs of this dynasty, especially Amenemhet I and Senusret III, remind one of the great pharaohs of the Fourth Dynasty. The rulers of the Middle Kingdom were aware of their role as restorers: they revived many of the political institutions characteristic of the Old Kingdom—the divine power of the pharaoh, the centralized bureaucracy, the provincial administration. They labored to restore the economy, to reclaim land from the desert, and to maintain order. Once again Egypt's influence was felt in Syria, the Sinai region, and Nubia—perhaps more strongly than during the Old Kingdom.

All, however, could not be restored as it had been before. The divine character of the pharaoh was no longer so predominant. One authority has suggested that the pharaohs of the Middle Kingdom might better be called "good shepherds" than gods. The word *ma'at* (*justice*) provides a key to the spirit animating the government during the Twelfth Dynasty. The pharaohs were especially concerned with providing *ma'at* for the lower classes, defining their place in society, ensuring their rights and welfare, and protecting them from greedy and oppressive officials. It appears that the grim experience of the First Intermediate Period had heightened the moral sensitivity of the Egyptians and generated a sense of individual rights, which the rulers of the eleventh and twelfth dynasties sought to put into practice. The strongest pharaohs of the Twelfth Dynasty did modify the shape of the government to some extent by decreasing the power of the old nobility and giving greater authority to a class of professional civil servants, called *scribes*, to carry out the multitude of functions associated with directing a centralized state.

After nearly three hundred years of orderly government and prosperity, the Middle Kingdom also began to decline. Its end was hastened by the emergence of a threat for which the Egyptians were not prepared. About 1750 B.C. a warlike, barbarian horde called the Hyksos swept out of Asia and seized control of the Nile Valley. Lawlessness and violence replaced orderly government. This interlude is usually called the Second Intermediate Period (1750–1550 B.C.). Eventually Egypt recovered from this catastrophe, but that story represents a completely new chapter in the history of the Near East and must be reserved for later.

3. EGYPTIAN ECONOMIC AND SOCIAL LIFE

Organized under a strong government, Egyptian society produced tremendous wealth. The chief source of that wealth was agriculture. Huge yields of wheat, barley, flax, vegetables, and fruit were gathered each harvest. Two or even three crops a year were possible on Egypt's rich soil. Herds of cattle, sheep, pigs, and goats pastured in the valley. The bulk of the Egyptian population devoted itself to farming. The peasants, crowded together in small villages, supplied the farm labor. Their mud huts, their scanty clothing, their monotonous diet of bread, beer, fish, and dried fruit, and their simple furniture certainly do not suggest a high standard of living. Life from one generation to the next consisted of constant labor to keep the irrigation system under control and to cultivate the crops.

Most of the labor was performed by hand and was extremely routinized as a result of the demands imposed by the river. Added to the regular work in the fields was the constant demand for extra labor on the immense building programs undertaken by the phar-

aohs and the priests. The peasant was never permitted to keep much of the product of his labor. After the owners of the land, the state, and the priests claimed their shares, he had only a bare subsistence. In spite of his hard lot and his lack of freedom, the Egyptian peasant appears in literature and art as a happy, contented, healthy man, quite pleased to live in the favored land of the Nile under the good rule of the god-kings. Famine and disorder brought him misery, but these were temporary conditions, made up for by the numerous gifts of the Nile.

Although Egyptian civilization rested chiefly on agriculture, a considerable number of artisans and merchants produced wealth by their handicraft work and their trading ventures. This group produced primarily luxury goods to satisfy the needs of the pharaoh, his court, and the nobility. Most of the artisans and merchants worked directly for the pharaoh, for the rich nobles attached to his court, or for the powerful provincial nobility. Every great household and temple had its own shops where artisans made a variety of items and from which merchants went forth to exchange goods and procure raw materials. In some cases, production was organized on a large scale, for example, stone quarrying, copper mining, and brick making. The social status of the craftsman and merchant was usually much like that of the peasant. They were bound to an overlord, granted little freedom of action, and rewarded for their efforts with little more than subsistence. Egypt never developed urban communities comparable to those of Mesopotamia, where merchants and artisans constituted a class with considerable economic freedom to venture into enterprises of their own.

Egyptian economy and society were dominated by a relatively small aristocracy. At the peak of society stood the pharaoh, whose power permitted him to indulge his every whim. All elements of society and the total wealth of the state were at his command. The rest of the aristocracy consisted of those to whom the pharaoh chose to give high status and to reward with wealth. The priestly class enjoyed an especially high rank. The nonpriestly aristocrats, who served the pharaoh as government officials, played a leading role in organizing the labor of peasants and artisans and enjoyed large incomes derived from land. This wealth was used to provide every comfort—fine homes, costly food and clothing, expensive furniture, and a variety of other luxuries.

In both Egypt and Mesopotamia, economic and social order was marked by certain significant departures from that of neolithic societies. Wealth was produced by extensive division of labor and specialization. Different groups plowed and reaped, built things with their hands, traded, ruled, and prayed, to mention only the broadest divisions. The combination of all these specialties, each as necessary as any other, permitted millions of people to exploit successfully a small but rich geographical area. The efforts of these many "specialists" were rigidly directed from the top down, creating a regimented society. Thus, Egyptian and Mesopotamian civilizations were built upon the leadership of a few people whose intelligence, vigor, and foresight supplied the needed guidance for the labors of the rest of the society. Aristocratic leadership was to remain a keynote of civilized people for long ages after Egypt and Mesopotamia had declined.

4. RELIGION

Like ancient Mesopotamian civilization, every aspect of Egyptian society was given its essential meaning by religious belief and practice. In fact, the modern student of history is forced to agree with Herodotus' conclusion that the Egyptians were the most religious of all peoples. Never has there been a society with more gods, more priests, more temples, or more modes of worship. The problem of the modern historian is to make sense out of Egyptian religious belief and practice, something the Egyptians themselves seldom both-

ered to do. Unfortunately, the gathering of more information about Egyptian religion has not simplified things, for our increasing knowledge has revealed baffling complexity, persistent confusion, and glaring contradictions.

One basic characteristic does emerge clearly: The Egyptians believed that everything that happened was caused by divine forces. Their religion was thus highly polytheistic, the gods worshiped at various times numbering in the thousands. The origins of most of the gods go far back into history. When reliable historical records finally appear, a great host of deities were already familiar to the Egyptians. Because few gods ever disappeared in Egypt, the problem of describing them does not become simpler with passing centuries. Egyptian gods were conceived in a variety of forms—as animals, as humans, as birds, as plants, as inanimate objects, as abstractions, and as mixtures of any two or three of these forms. Most of the gods had some particular place in Egypt or in the skies above it that was their own sacred spot, but all of them roamed about freely and were likely to be present wherever and whenever humans were at work or play. There is some evidence to suggest that Egyptian concepts of the divine forces tended to evolve from a more primitive animal worship toward gods with human forms and cosmic powers, and even toward abstract, disembodied gods (such as *ma'at*). But this trend should not be overemphasized, for seldom were even the most primitive deities abandoned. There is infinite confusion in Egyptian concepts of the functions of the gods, so that any effort to set forth a clear definition of the powers and duties of each god (such as is possible, for instance, in Greek religion) is completely frustrating. For example, the Egyptians had several versions of creation, all accepted as equally valid, even by a single individual. On the whole, it does seem that the Egyptians conceived of their gods as basically benevolent and kindly. In contrast to the Mesopotamians, they did not live in constant fear, but rather viewed the gods and their activities with optimism and hope.

There was, however, an effort to create order among this horde of gods, and especially to decide which were most important. An elaborate body of mythology developed during the centuries prior to the end of the Middle Kingdom, primarily the work of the temple priests. Certain gods emerged as the chief ones in the minds of the Egyptians. During the Predynastic and Old Kingdom periods, there was a tendency for the gods of those who were victorious in war to become supreme. For instance, when Menes unified all Egypt, the falcon god Horus, formerly the god of Upper Egypt, became the supreme god of all Egypt. Myths then developed telling how Horus came to be chief of the gods and made the other gods his servants. Even as late as the Middle Kingdom, a relatively unknown god like Amon could become a powerful force as a result of the political success of the princes of Thebes. However, political changes were not always the cause of the ascendancy of a god. By the end of the Old Kingdom, the sun god Re was accepted as a god demanding reverence from all Egyptians and as the supreme figure in the heavens. The growing popularity of sun-god worship was undoubtedly due to the importance of the sun in the life of every Egyptian. The effort to understand how things came to be could exalt a particular god as the prime creator; such was the case with Ptah, who was brought to prominence by the priests at Memphis as the original creator of an ordered universe and all things in it (including other gods). Especially significant was the emergence of the god Osiris, who was believed to possess the power of granting men a happy life after death. By the end of the Middle Kingdom, this theologizing process had created some order in religious thought and practice. A few gods, especially Re and Osiris, were recognized as most powerful. Most of the other gods had been subordinated to these major

ones, although few had been eliminated. The widespread acceptance of a few great gods who watched over the fate of all Egyptians provided a powerful unifying force in Egyptian society, although Egypt never achieved complete religious unity, for local cults persisted.

Since everything from the Nile floods to the smallest household incident was a consequence of the will of some god, Egyptian religion placed heavy emphasis on man's need to do things that would please the gods. Man's religious obligations became fixed early in Egyptian history and changed little over the centuries. It may be that it was cult and not belief that provided Egyptian religion with unity and organic wholeness. The burden of pleasing the gods fell on all men alike. To the pharaoh belonged the prime responsibility of the care of the great deities, and no little part of the activities of the god-king was devoted to ministering to the needs of other gods. All the rest of society joined the pharaoh in this holy work.

For example, the gods required living quarters. Therefore, the Egyptians built temples and shrines, ranging all the way from the great temples built by the pharaohs in honor of the chief gods to tiny chapels in villages and homes. The gods enjoyed finery, and the Egyptians lovingly decorated the temples with their best artistic efforts. The gods required food and physical care. In every great temple and simple shrine, priests daily enacted an elaborate ritual to ensure that these needs were met. The daily routine of caring for the gods was carried out privately in the inner sanctuaries of the temples; but on occasion great festivals were organized. The statue of the god being honored was brought forth from the temple with great pomp, and crowds came from all over Egypt to pay their respects and make their sacrifices.

Prayers and songs were a regular part of religious worship and were composed in great numbers to fit any request men had to make of the gods. A rich array of magical practices existed to assist in winning the favor of the gods and avoiding the consequences of divine annoyance. In contrast with the Mesopotamians, the Egyptians did not devote much effort to ascertaining the future. They seemed confident that the gods would smile on them and therefore felt no pressing need to know divine intentions. The necessity of addressing, caring for, and pleasing the gods was so great that Egypt maintained a vast number of priests who specialized in this job. Probably most Egyptians felt that their efforts to please the gods were fully repaid. The abundant harvests, the peaceful condition of the kingdom, and the security with which a man could live his life made it seem that the gods were satisfied with the attentions they received.

Besides earthly benefits, the gods held another precious gift for deserving Egyptians—a happy life after death. Concern with immortality was a unique aspect of Egyptian religion and was the source of some of its most dynamic features. The quest for immortality was grounded in the Egyptians' basic view of human nature. From early times, they had believed that every man had a *ka,* which was a double for his body and which lived on after death in some kind of close association with the divine spirits. It was necessary that the *ka* have all it needed to keep it happy after death. In early Egyptian history, that end was met in a rather crude and materialistic fashion. The body was preserved by mummification so that the spirit could return to it. A tomb that would last forever was built to shelter the spirit. Elaborate arrangments were made to ensure that the spirit would have food, drink, luxuries, companions—everything it had enjoyed in life—to make immortal life tolerable. Proper provisions for life after death were expensive; in fact, perhaps only the pharaoh could afford all that was needed. But at least he was willing to help some people live eternally so that they could continue to be his companions and servants. He therefore built tombs for his wives, his children, his officials, and his friends in close proximity to his own great tomb. By

the end of the Old Kingdom, many nobles were constructing their own tombs. The fate of the common man in this early period is not clear, but one must presume that some kind of afterlife was his lot too, even if he could not make the proper preparations.

Gradually the expectation of gaining immortality was democratized and universalized until the gates of heaven were open to all Egyptians. The crucial period of this radical transformation of Egyptian religious belief came in the troubled times of the First Intermediate Period and was probably part of the moral outrage generated against the materialism and greed of the ruling class of the Old Kingdom. The new concept of immortality found its focus in the worship of Osiris, which by the period of the Middle Kingdom had advanced to a central place in religious life. The essence of the new set of beliefs was embodied in a touching myth. Osiris, a good god associated with life forces and the Nile, was murdered by his wicked brother, Seth, who dismembered the god's body and scattered the parts over the face of the earth. Osiris's wife, Isis, patiently gathered the members of her beloved's body. When her task was finished, Osiris returned to life. Thereafter, he had the power to raise everyone from death to life, no matter what a man's social status was. When any Egyptian died, he appeared before Osiris and a panel of judges in the other world. He was required to make a confession in which he testified that his life had been faultless. Osiris placed the dead man's heart on the pan of a balance. On the other pan was a feather. If the heart was weighted with evil, the dead man was not fit for eternal happiness and was tossed to a ferocious beast. If his heart was buoyant with goodness, he was allowed to live forever in a heavenly place very much like the earthly Nile Valley.

The radically new element in this concept of immortal life is the idea of the moral worth attached to each man. Osiris was concerned with goodness in evaluating a man's eligibility for eternal life and not with his wealth and

This Egyptian funerary papyrus from the tomb of a princess shows some of the steps in the transition to the life after death. In the center, the gods weigh the princess' heart in a balance against the figure of the Goddess of Truth. Ca. 1000 B.C. *Photo: The Metropolitan Museum of Art*

social position. In articulating a moral basis for human life, the Egyptians were far in advance of other ancient peoples. The followers of Osiris were compelled to pay heed to the practice of virtue if they expected to be rewarded when they stepped before him to be weighed in the balance. This is not to imply that all of Egyptian life was transformed by this birth of conscience and moral sense. The Egyptians continued to provide for the material welfare of the dead person, although from the Middle Kingdom onward the emphasis was less on the size and luxury of the tomb and more on its decoration—a record in pictures and writing to convince Osiris that the occupant had indeed lived a "good" life. As Osiris worship matured, men busied themselves compiling set lists of virtues that

needed to be observed and devising clever formulas that might conceal their moral faults. Still, Osiris worship heightened moral awareness in a way that would have been unknown in Mesopotamia, and it provided a meaningful place in the cosmic order for all men.

5. EGYPTIAN CULTURAL LIFE

Perhaps the chief glory of Egypt's history down to 1750 B.C. was her intellectual and artistic achievement. This cultural effort is striking for its unity, coherence, and confidence, an effect that stems from the fact that Egyptian culture was basically a product of a single center—the pharaoh's court. A single inspiration, a single set of motifs, a single style, all dictated by court ideals, presided over all intellectual and artistic endeavor. Once that style had been established, there was little questioning or experimenting. Instead, over many centuries thinkers and artists clung to established ideas and styles with complete confidence in their importance and their suitability.

One of Egypt's achievements was her system of hieroglyphic writing, which began to develop about the time of the Old Kingdom (about 3200 B.C.). Egyptian writing began as picture writing, an object being represented by a picture of it. Gradually, various pictures began to be accepted as representations of sound values. By putting several of these symbols together, words could be formed. The Egyptians never developed a

complete alphabet, since symbols representing sounds existed only for consonants. Writing probably developed as a practical tool, useful in government. Once it was perfected, however, it allowed the Egyptians to set down their ideas in a clear and artistic fashion.

Because much of Egyptian literature has survived from religious records, we get the impression that religion supplied the chief inspiration for writing—hardly surprising in a civilization so thoroughly permeated by religious belief. The pyramids were prime repositories for much of Egyptian religious literature. On their walls were carved hymns, prayers, magical incantations, moral exhortations, and bits of mythology, all intended to influence the gods in some way. Although this kind of literature often reflects deep feelings and sophisticated intellectual concepts, on the whole it is traditionalist, bound in form and content by ancient and sacred conventions. Somewhat fresher and more revealing of the character of society were the pyramid texts recounting the splendid deeds of the pharaohs who built the tombs. In a sense, this kind of writing represents an early attempt at history, except that its purpose was religious rather than worldly, so it too became formalized and conventional.

Not all Egyptian literature was intended to serve religious ends. Several kinds of writings of a secular nature have survived either in the form of stone carvings or as texts written on papyrus. Religious themes are never absent from these writings, but their focus is quite different. There are some letters, legal accounts, and business records. The Egyptians appear to have been fond of collections of moral maxims and wise sayings,

This statue of Menkure, a pharaoh of the Fourth Dynasty, and his queen shows the majesty and power that surrounded the Egyptian god-kings. Sculptors used this style—rigid posture, stylized clothing—throughout the history of ancient Egypt. *Photo: Museum of Fine Arts, Boston*

often set down in the form of instruction from a father to his son or a teacher to his pupil. Lyric poetry, often expressing deep feeling about love, nature, and human misfortune, was written. And laments expressing disgust with the world circulated in difficult times. Perhaps most appealing to modern readers are the marvelous tales of fancy and romance recounting the adventures of travelers, shipwrecked sailors, and soldiers.

What has survived of Egyptian literature— and it certainly comprises only a small fraction of a larger production—shows considerable technical skill and a feel for humanity. The mood is often gay, confident, and care-free, although occasionally a writer could work himself into a state of black despair, especially over the talent of men for sin and greed. On the whole, Egyptian literature is not especially profound. It lacks the gloomy spirit of Mesopotamian writing. The Egyptians were more versatile, devising types of literature that never appeared in Mesopotamia —lyric poetry, romances, and tales of fancy. They did not, however, produce anything like the Gilgamesh epic, perhaps because the very concept of a heroic figure seeking to master mysterious cosmic forces and assure immortality for himself was foreign to Egyptian thought. The Egyptian writer sketches a happier, safer, more predictable world.

It is through the visual arts that the character and quality of Egyptian life is most clearly preserved. Who can spend a little time viewing the Egyptian collections in the Louvre or the British Museum without a sense of the marvelous creative power and the amazing technical skill of the self-effacing, anonymous Egyptian artist? And who can avoid a conviction that these artists have conveyed plainly and powerfully what they believed and thought and felt? Egyptian art reveals what may have been the significant character of Egyptian civilization: the ability to work for long ages with set forms and subjects and maintain freshness and vitality. This indeed may have been the spark that sustained eternal Egypt.

Architecture was the queen of all the arts in Egypt, most of the other forms serving to adorn architectural monuments. The Egyptian architects worked in many materials, including mud, reeds, brick, and wood; but the most monumental work was done in stone. The first flowering of stonework occurred in the early years of the Old Kingdom and was devoted chiefly to tomb building, which reached its apogee in the construction of the pyramids. The pyramid of Khufu (built about 2600 B.C.) stands as one of the great construction feats of all time. This structure measured 755 feet on each side at the base, which was intended to be square. It fell short of a geometrically perfect square by about 8 inches of difference between the north and south sides, and by less than ½ inch of difference between the east and west sides. The pyramid once was 480 feet high and contains over two million blocks of stone weighing on an average 2½ tons each. Some of the stones used to roof the internal chambers weigh as much as 30 tons. The outside of the pyramid was covered with polished stone. Most of the stone was precut, probably with copper saws and wedges, in quarries many miles away and floated down the Nile to the pyramid site, a procedure that must have entailed tremendous planning. The huge blocks were probably elevated into position up dirt ramps built alongside the pyramid. The labor was performed by hand with almost no mechanical aid. The masons who fitted the stones together did a remarkably accurate job: The internal passages and rooms that honeycomb the pyramid were skillfully vaulted, again demonstrating the technical progress of Egyptian builders. Pyramid building continued for many centuries, but later architects never equaled those of the Old Kingdom. In later years, shifting concepts of immortality militated against such massive, complex undertakings as the pyramids at Gizeh.

Although the surviving evidence is not as impressive as the pyramids, it seems quite certain that architects had arrived at the basic forms for temple and palace building by the end of the Old Kingdom; by the Middle Kingdom they were constructing impressive structures. The basic temple style was the hypostyle hall—a building consisting of a roof placed on columns. The typical temple was a high-ceilinged central hall flanked by side halls covered by a roof placed on columns shorter than those of the central hall. The builders achieved splendid artistic effects by modeling their columns after plants—the palm tree, the lotus plant, the papyrus plant, the reed. Within the temple, numerous chambers were grouped to serve the sanctuary which was the living place of the god. Before the temple was an open court surrounded by a columned portico. In the center of the court often stood an obelisk in honor of the sun god. (Many of these obelisks have found their way to the cities of Western Europe, the spoils of the nineteenth-century expansion into Africa.) A massive gateway, offering vast expanses of stone for the sculptor, gave access to the courtyard. The palaces of the pharaohs were undoubtedly as splendid as the temples and probably utilized the same basic architectural forms.

Egyptian sculptors matched the architects in skill. At a very early date sculptural styles became fixed and were followed with little change for most of Egyptian history. Sculpture was the handmaiden of religion. The chief subjects of three-dimensional sculpture were the gods, the pharaohs, their families, and their companions, the statues being intended for tombs and temples. The representation of human forms is usually massive, stiff, and unemotional. The portrayal of the body followed strict proportions, so that whatever the size of the figure, there was a fixed relation between the width of the shoulders, the size of the waist, the length of the legs, and so forth. The members of the body were highly formalized and often almost grotesquely unnatural. But the face was another matter. Here the sculptor tried to portray feeling and purpose: the power of a god, the majesty of a pharaoh, the devotion of a royal servant. He was concerned not with realistic portrayal of a particular individual, but with a semblance of the perfection that individual embodied. Thus the face of the typical statue gazes straight out at the viewer as an embodiment of an ideal; captured in stone for eternity is god and man combined to constitute perfect existence. Although the sculptor worked within highly conventionalized canons, each face is different—a reflection again of the dynamic quality of the Egyptian achievement in art.

Egyptian sculptors were also skilled at relief work. Inside the tombs and on the pillars and walls of temples they carved endless series of scenes from Egyptian daily life that tell us more about the way Egyptians lived and worked than does all Egyptian writing. Again, the sculptor seldom tried to be realistic. He let the space he had determine the size and shape of his figures; and he often used conventional designs to represent objects. The human shapes were distorted, the feet and faces usually being shown in profile while the main trunk of the body faces the viewer. Many of the reliefs were painted to heighten the effect. Painting, most of which survives in tombs, bears a striking similarity to relief work in terms of subject matter and form. The artist sketched an outline of the scene to be pictured, often in red, and then colored it in with strong colors of one tone. The effect is stiffness and formality, but every scene has a certain majesty and stability that leaves a vivid impression.

Viewed as a whole, Egyptian art suggests certain generalizations about Egyptian thought. It shows how completely thought was dominated by religion. The Egyptian artist almost always created for eternity—his emphasis was on massiveness, solid construction, and stability. He thereby displayed great confidence in his work and in the civilization he was representing. The unchanging artistic canons of Egypt might be interpreted as evidence of the artist's sense of the permanence of his society, as well as his satisfaction with the existing order. Egyptian art demonstrates pride in Egypt. The emphasis on size in building and sculpture was in part motivated by the desire to show what tremendous things men could do. Their art as a whole portrays a stable, unemotional, proud people, impressed by what they had achieved and eager to maintain it.

The Egyptians made remarkable advances in technology and practical science. They compiled a substantial body of knowledge about the movement of the stars. They devised at an early date an accurate system of reckoning time based on the annual appearance of the star Sirius. Their calendar consisted of twelve months of thirty days each plus five days added at the end of the year. They perfected a system of numbers by which they could perform the basic mathematical operations, although they did not use zero and had great difficulty working with fractions. All their mathematical operations were basically a function of addition and subtraction. Although mathematics was not highly advanced, they did develop a simple form of geometry for the computation of the areas of triangles, rectangles, and hexagons, and the volumes of pyramids and cylinders. The inquiry of Egyptian scientists was not restricted to fields involving the use of mathematics, however. They also accumulated considerable knowledge about metals and their properties. Certainly the Egyptians knew a tremendous amount about plant and animal life. In medicine they developed surgical techniques and learned to use a wide range of drugs. Their knowledge of human anatomy was extensive, undoubtedly because of observations resulting from the mummification process, which required opening the body and removing the internal organs. Egyptian medical knowledge was far in advance of that of other Near Eastern peoples of the age.

However, in spite of all this body of knowledge, pure science held little interest for the Egyptians. They seldom sought new scientific knowledge after the fashion of modern scientists. Most of their scientific knowledge was the result of practical experience and was gained by pragmatic methods. Once they had found a workable solution for a problem of engineering or medicine or metallurgy, they sought no further information. Like the Mesopotamians, they felt no need to search for explanations of nature and of the universe. Religion supplied them with a complete, integrated explanation of the workings of the world about them. Their thinking was mythological, and they found no reason for questioning what religion revealed. In spite of this lack of interest in pure science, credit must be given the Egyptians for accumulating considerable information that not only solved their own problems adequately, but also served people of later civilizations as a solid base from which to proceed toward more fully developed scientific knowledge.

Egypt's history was not yet finished when the Hyksos invaded the Nile Valley about 1750 B.C. But her long isolation had ended; her future role was to be played in a much larger frame of reference than the Nile Valley. (We shall return to a study of this expanded role in a later chapter.) However, the achievements we have just described were to remain the fundamental bases of Egyptian society. The Egyptians had made their creative contributions to the world by the end of the Middle Kingdom; thereafter, their role would be that of a model for other peoples.

6. MINOAN CIVILIZATION

While complex and sophisticated civilizations were being shaped in the great river valleys of the Near East, another center of civilization developed on the island of Crete. Although Greek mythology transmitted a vague memory of this civilization, its fundamental character was unknown until the archeological discoveries of fifty years ago. The emergence of Crete as the focus of a highly developed civilization came considerably later than did the development of Mesopotamia and Egypt. In fact, civilization in Crete owed much to the older Near Eastern centers and did not represent an independent creation. Yet that island civilization is distinctive enough to warrant treatment in conjunction with the older and more powerful societies of the river valleys. Even more important is the fact that the early civilization of Crete provided a link between the civilizations of the Near East and the world toward the west, where new peoples were soon to add fresh elements to civilized life.

The island of Crete offered an entirely new setting for the emergence of higher civilization: Here was no flooding river to water and regenerate the soil, no all-prevailing cycle of nature tying men to an eternal routine. Instead, the inhabitants had to rely on rainfall to nourish crops in the moderately rich soil of small plains interspersed among the mountains that dominate the island. The insular setting, however, gave the Cretans a basic security—and they had the sea. Its mastery provided access to a wider world from which they could buy or borrow what they wanted without danger of being engulfed by greater political powers. The people of Crete advanced to higher civilization as a consequence of their ability to turn the sea to their advantage.

The roots of the higher civilization that developed in Crete lie in the third millennium B.C., when a flourishing neolithic culture developed on the island. This culture was, however, in no way particularly unique to Crete. It was shared by a wide circle of peoples living in Greece, the Aegean islands, and Asia Minor. Probably it had been imported to Crete about 3000 B.C. by invaders from Asia Minor, making the island at the beginning of its history a modest outpost of a vast neolithic village culture complex that had its base in Asia Minor. For most of the millennium between 3000 and 2000 B.C., neolithic culture prevailed in Crete. Life centered in agricultural villages, and society had a clan structure. There was change, however, generated in part by the creative talents of the Cretans themselves and in part by the newcomers from the north who invaded the island from time to time. Technical skills advanced stead-

ily, but the introduction of bronze was of special importance. More complex social organisms developed, the landowners apparently taking the lead in forming larger groupings of people. Cretans learned to sail the seas, and came in contact with new sources of wealth and with the more advanced civilizations in Asia and Egypt. It was their expanding contact with the external world and the resulting influx of techniques, wealth, and ideas that permitted the Cretans to outstrip the peoples of Greece, the Aegean islands, and Asia Minor with whom they had once shared a relatively simple neolithic culture.

About 2000 B.C. there occurred on Crete a sudden advance which marked the beginnings of a mature civilization. That civilization has been named *Minoan* by modern historians after a legendary Cretan king whom the Greeks called Minos. The new age was heralded by the appearance in several cities, especially Knossos, Phaistos, and Mallia, of great palaces. Not only do these palaces bespeak great wealth and technical ability, but they also give evidence of consolidation of society under the direction of kings who had perfected techniques for administering larger areas and greater numbers of people. These kingdoms coexisted on a small island, apparently without any serious conflicts. Their energies were devoted in large part to overseas trading ventures—to Egypt, to Syria, to Asia Minor, to the Aegean islands, to the Greek mainland, and even to the western Mediterranean—and the manufacturing pursuits which supplied this trade. The Minoan thrust was particularly strong toward the Greek peninsula, where the still-backward populace was strongly and decisively influenced by the island civilization. The intrusion of the Minoans into the Greek world marked a significant period in Greek history to which we will return in a later chapter. With the passing of time, Knossos seems to have outstripped the other cities of Crete and to have established dominance over them in a peaceful process of change. Knossos reached the peak of her power between 1600 and 1400 B.C., when she

A view of the ruins of the palace of Knossos on Crete that gives an indication of the splendor of this island civilization during its golden age. *Photo: Hirmer Verlag*

dominated Crete and exercised an influence over a wide circle of the eastern Mediterranean. Then, quite suddenly, about 1400 B.C. the great city was destroyed, and Minoan influence rapidly waned. What brought on this disaster is disputed, but the best explanation seems to be that Crete was invaded by a people from Greece called the Mycenaeans, who had learned most of what they knew about civilized life from the Minoans. The Minoans apparently were not prepared to cope with aggressive, warrior peoples; their talents for centuries had been devoted to peace, trade, and the quest for a comfortable, carefree life.

The nature of Minoan civilization must be derived chiefly from archeological remains. The Minoans developed a system of writing called Linear A, which, although deciphered, reveals little about Minoan culture. Its origins are uncertain, but evidence suggests a kinship with Akkadian. There are some written records in a language called Linear B, deciphered only recently, from the last years of Minoan history, but this language seems to have been an ancestor of Greek brought to Crete by the Mycenaean intruders and does not reflect much of Minoan civilization.

From the evidence we have, we know that a well-developed system of monarchy had developed based upon orderly recordkeeping and bureaucratic administration. Royal power appears to have depended on religious sanction and on the wealth the kings derived from overseas trade, rather than on military strength. A rich, powerful nobility grouped itself around the kings and helped to sustain the royal authority. A productive agricultural system sustained society, but trade and industry contributed a considerable portion of its wealth. Innumerable skilled artisans plied their talents in the workshops of the palaces and the cities of Crete to make products that not only enriched life in Crete, but were also in demand across the seas. Especially skilled were the potters and the metalworkers. Merchants carried these goods abroad in fleets owned by the kings and brought back a variety of raw materials and manufactured goods. Little is known about the condition of the lower classes, but the nobility enjoyed a luxurious life in the fine houses in the cities. The Minoans worshiped a variety of gods representing the forces of nature. The chief deity was the goddess of fertility, whose lifegiving powers were evoked by prayer, ceremony, and sacrifice. Religion played an important but not dominant part in Minoan civilization. No great temples were built, nor was a numerous, powerful priesthood maintained; worship was carried out on hillsides and in groves with considerable popular participation. There was a belief in an afterlife and some attention was given to the care of the dead, but never on the scale that occurred in Egypt.

The genius of the Minoans was in the arts, which also convey best the character of their civilization. Their considerable architectural skills were lavished on palaces and private dwellings rather than temples and tombs. The immense palace at Knossos was a marvel of technical ability and the use of a mixture of architectural forms to create a vast structure that was delicately beautiful, luxuriously comfortable, and utilitarian as well. Palaces and houses were decorated with paintings and carvings that emphasized nature and humanity. Often the artist sought to capture the action of living things in his work, so that Minoan art is mobile, free of stylization, intense, energy-filled. Minoan decorated pottery reflects a fine sense of form and great ingenuity in decoration. The Minoans had a real love for color that adds an element of brilliance to their art. In its general character, Minoan art reflects a civilization that was gay, worldly, lacking in fear, eager for change, pleasure-loving, and amazingly free. Its spirit contrasts sharply with that underlying Mesopotamian and Egyptian civilization, although the Minoans borrowed considerably from both. It points not east, but west toward a world yet to come—to Greece and Europe.

Suggested Reading

Egypt. There are several good narrative histories of Egypt built around political development. Especially to be recommended is an old work (1905), **James Henry Breasted, *A History of Egypt* (Bantam), but one given great distinction by the author's vast knowledge of and enthusiasm for the subject. Other excellent works, all more up to date, are **C. Aldred, *The Egyptians* (Praeger); **C. Aldred, *Egypt to the End of the Old Kingdom* (McGraw-Hill); **Alan H. Gardiner, *Egypt of the Pharaohs* (Galaxy); and William A. Ward, *The Spirit of Ancient Egypt* (1965). Ward's book is especially straightforward and clear in its presentation. All these works contain considerable material on economic and social history, religion, art, literature, and science. The problem of the transition from neolithic culture to higher civilization in the Nile Valley is treated by V. Gordon Childe, Henri Frankfort, and Robert Braidwood in the books cited in the Suggested Reading list in Chapter 1. More specialized treatments of particular periods within the long span of time covered in this chapter are Elise J. Baumgärtel, *The Cultures of Prehistoric Egypt* (1947); **Walter B. Emery, *Archaic Egypt* (Penguin); and Herbert E. Winlock, *The Rise and Fall of the Middle Kingdom in Thebes* (1947). One of the most important books of recent years on ancient Egypt is **John A. Wilson, *The Culture of Ancient Egypt* (Phoenix; originally published as *The Burden of Egypt*, 1951). The analysis of the interactions between political and religious life goes far to make Egyptian history meaningful. H. Frankfort, *Kingship and the Gods* . . . (1948) has a provocative chapter on the nature and role of the pharaoh in Egyptian society.

An excellent synthesis of Egyptian civilization, treating various aspects of society topically, is **Pierre Montet, *Eternal Egypt*, trans. Doreen Weightmann (Mentor). **Jon Manchip White, *Everyday Life in Ancient Egypt* (Capricorn), and **Leonard Cottrell, *Life Under the Pharaohs* (Tempo), provide fascinating material concerning everyday life. An excellent chapter by John A. Wilson in **H. Frankfort *et al.*, *Before Philosophy* . . . (Penguin), summarizes the Egyptian attitude toward life very well. Egyptian religion receives excellent and thorough treatment in **H. Frankfort, *Ancient Egyptian Religion: An Interpretation* (Harper Torchbook), and Jaroslav Černý, *Ancient Egyptian Religion* (1952). An excellent shorter summary has been written by Etienne Drioton in Etienne Drioton, Georges Contenau, and Jacques Duchesne-Guillemin, *Religions of the Ancient East*, trans. M. B. Loraine (1959). Excellent for its clarity and its grasp of technical problems is **I. E. S. Edwards, *The Pyramids of Egypt* (2nd ed., Penguin). A splendid introduction to Egyptian art in its entirety can be gained from K. Lange and M. Hirmer, *Egypt: Architecture, Sculpture, Painting in Three Thousand Years*, trans. R. H. Boothroyd (4th ed., 1968); the illustrations are remarkable. A somewhat less impressive but still good treatment of Egyptian art can be found in **William S. Smith, *The Art and Architecture of Ancient Egypt* (Penguin). An excellent treatment of painting is provided by A. Mekhitarian, *Egyptian Painting*, trans. Stuart Gilbert (1954). A good summary of Egyptian science can be found in **Otto Neugebauer, *The Exact Sciences in Antiquity* (2nd ed., Dover); also useful is René Taton, *Ancient and Medieval Science From Prehistory to A.D. 1450*, trans. A. J. Pomerans (*A General History of the Sciences*, Vol. I, 1963). Well-selected samples of Egyptian literature can be found in Josephine Mayer and Tom Prideaux, *Never to Die: The Egyptians in Their Own Words* (1938), or in Joseph Kaster, ed. and trans., *Wings of the Falcon: Life and Thought in Ancient Egypt* (1968).

Minoan Civilization. The best available synthesis of Minoan history and culture is **R. J. Hutchinson, *Prehistoric Crete* (Penguin); it traces developments chronologically and surveys various aspects of Minoan society topically. **J. D. S. Pendlebury, *The Archaeology of Crete: An Introduction* (Norton), presents a thorough description of Minoan culture on the basis of archeological evidence, but his work is rather formidable to read. Leonard R. Palmer, *Mycenaeans and Minoans: Aegean Prehistory in the Light of the Linear B Tablets* (2nd rev. ed., 1965), develops fresh interpretations of the cultural interchanges working in the Aegean world at the dawn of Greek history on the basis of new literary sources made available by the decipherment of one of the written languages found in Crete. The story of the decipherment of that language is told by **John Chadwick, *The Decipherment of Linear B* (Vintage); the author worked with Michael Ventris to accomplish this important feat. M. P. Nilsson, *Minoan-Mycenaean Religion and Its Survival in Greek Religion* (2nd ed., 1950), provides a clear picture of the main features of Minoan religion.

Chapter 3 ❧ The Diffusion of Near Eastern Civilization

By the beginning of the second millennium B.C., the institutions, techniques, and ideas that had been born in the great river valleys during the preceding two thousand years had begun to spread outward among the peoples living beyond the narrow confines of the valleys. Traders, soldiers, travelers, and diplomats were the prime carriers. This process of diffusion was the characteristic feature of the entire second millennium and the early centuries of the first millennium B.C. It was a process hastened by invasions of new peoples into the Near East. These barbarian intruders upset the existing political system, elevated new leaders to supremacy, and brought significant changes to basic patterns of life. They were, in the words of one authority, catalysts. Their presence, however, did not result in a violent rupture with the past; rather, the catalysts were borrowers from the river valley civilizations, learners of better ways of living. Their intrusion into the established order hastened the process of diffusion and promoted an inexorable trend toward the cultural unification of the entire Near East.

The invaders came in two great waves. The first were Indo-Europeans, who appeared about 1800 B.C. and caused a readjustment of the power structure in the Near East that lasted until about 1200. Then new invasions, involving both Indo-Europeans and Semites, brought about a realignment of power that persisted until about 800 B.C. Underlying the many changes in the political order was a unifying factor of prime historical importance: the civilizing influences spreading outward from the great river valleys to engulf the invaders.

1. THE INDO–EUROPEAN INVASIONS OF THE NEAR EAST

The Indo-Europeans whose invasions opened the era were a people heretofore unknown in the Near East. Although some have argued that the Indo-Europeans were large, fair-skinned, blond men who contrasted sharply with the smaller, darker peoples of ancient Mesopotamia and Egypt, it is by no means certain that they represented a new physical type in the Near East. The only sure significance that can be attached to the term "Indo-European" is linguistic: The newcomers brought with them a new language from

The massive temple at Luxor was built to honor the supreme god Amon, whom the reigning pharaoh traditionally claimed as his father. A series of courts and halls filled with massive columns that supported the roof led to an inner sanctuary from which ordinary worshippers were excluded. Ca. 1400 B.C. *Photo: John Bryson–Rapho Guillumette* which later evolved Sanskrit, Greek, Latin, and most of the modern European languages, including English. In recent times, misled men beginning with unfounded assumptions about the physical characteristics of the ancient Indo-Europeans and infected with racist theories, nationalistic sentiments, and an inflated sense of Western European cultural superiority have exalted these Indo-Europeans —sometimes called Aryans—far beyond their importance as the instigators of all that has been creative in world history. Such nonsense has even been turned into vicious, hate-filled political ideology. An understanding of the initial role of the Indo-Europeans in the ancient Near East will help to restore our perspective.

The Indo-European invasions of the Near East originated from the Eurasian steppe lands north of the great mountain chain that stretches east and west across Europe and Asia to divide each into two parts. Here the Indo-Europeans had practiced a primitive herding economy and lived under a strong clan system as early as 3000 B.C. During the next thousand years they slowly adopted a settled agricultural life, but they were still barbarians by Near Eastern standards when they began to move southward about 2000 B.C. They crossed the mountain barrier between Europe and the Near East by several routes—across the straits connecting the Black Sea and the Aegean Sea into Asia Minor; across the Caucasian Mountains into the area stretching across the upper reaches of the Tigris and Euphrates; across the mountains east of the Caspian Sea into the vast Iranian plateau. The impact of this vast movement was felt in Greece, Italy, Central Europe, and India. Probably because of their superior military strength, based on horse-drawn chariots and a skilled warrior class, the Indo-Europeans were able to establish political dominance over extensive areas of the Near East.

As the invaders moved south, they subdued the natives and formed new political groupings. At first, these groupings consisted of numerous small principalities led by successful Indo-European warlords. Gradually, these principalities coalesced into large kingdoms whose rulers were strongly influenced by the model of river valley monarchies, especially the Amorite Empire of Hammurabi. One powerful group, the Hittites, occupied eastern Asia Minor and began to thrust east and south. Farther to the east, the Mitanni emerged as the dominant force in the upper Tigris-Euphrates area. A group called the Kassites was formed in the mountainous area east of the Tigris River and soon attacked Mesopotamia. Still other Indo-Europeans sifted into the Syria-Palestine area, uniting with Semitic marauders from the Arabian Desert to form the Hyksos, who invaded Egypt and destroyed the Middle Kingdom. All these newcomers quickly adopted the techniques, culture, and religious concepts of their conquered subjects, thus divesting themselves of their barbarism. They retained their older militancy, however, and their presence led to strife and incessant flux throughout the Near East.

2. THE EGYPTIAN EMPIRE, 1600–1200 B.C.

The assault of the barbarian-led hordes on Mesopotamia provoked little resistance. After Hammurabi's death (1750 B.C.), his empire began to weaken internally, and his successors were ineffective in checking its decline and holding back the invaders. The Hittites struck powerful blows from the northwest and finally succeeded in destroying the capital city of Babylon in 1590 B.C. In the meantime, Kassite forces from east of the Zagros Mountains joined in the assault on the faltering Amorite Empire. They were the ultimate conquerors of the land, the Hittites turning their energies elsewhere. Kassite domination lasted over four centuries. Little is known of the regime, except that it was neither strong nor effective. Whatever distinct characteristics the Kassites may have had when they invaded the Tigris-Euphrates Valley soon disappeared as they wholeheartedly adopted

Mesopotamian civilization. Under Kassite rule, the political influence of Mesopotamia was greatly reduced. The Kassite sphere was confined largely to southern Mesopotamia, for in the north, the Assyrians, who were to play a major role in the future of the Near East, had begun to emerge as a power.

Proud Egypt suffered her humiliation with less complacency than did the Mesopotamians, who were more accustomed to foreign intrusion. Egypt's ordeal lasted about two centuries, an interlude called the Second Intermediate Period (ca. 1750–1580 B.C.). It is difficult to ascertain exactly what happened during this period: Probably the Middle Kingdom was already in decline when the Hyksos invaders began to attack from their base in Palestine; local Egyptian princes may again have begun to assert their independence, making effective defense difficult. The Hyksos never succeeded in taking control of all Egypt. Their center of power was in the Delta, but much of Upper Egypt escaped their control. They appear to have assimilated considerable amounts of Egyptian culture and may even have tried to keep the old order intact. On the whole, however, the period of their rule (embracing the fourteenth, fifteenth, and sixteenth dynasties) was a difficult one in Egypt. The "shepherd kings," as the Egyptians contemptuously called the Hyksos, were basically pillagers, enjoying temporary military superiority because they possessed the horse and chariot as implements of war and because they had attacked Egypt at a moment of weakness.

The chief result of Hyksos rule was the generation of a revulsion against foreigners. Eventually this spirit generated the open revolt led by the Theban princes who established the Seventeenth Dynasty. Revolt turned quickly to a war of liberation and then to a crusade to smash the oppressors at the source of their power in Palestine. It was Ahmose I (ca. 1580–1546), the founder of the Eighteenth Dynasty, who crowned this patriotic resurgence with a crushing defeat of the Hyksos in Palestine. His reign opened a third period of glory in Egyptian history—the period of the Egyptian Empire or the New Kingdom, extending from 1580 to 1200 B.C.

During the first century of the Eighteenth Dynasty, a succession of able pharaohs devoted their energies to the restoration of internal order, to "cleansing" the land of the taint of foreign domination. Their avowed aim was the restoration of the ancient system that had existed before Egypt's humiliation, and they succeeded remarkably well. The administrative machine, the agricultural regime, the tax system, the foreign trade connections, the religious order, and artistic and intellectual life all revived in patterns closely parallel to those of the Old and Middle Kingdoms. Especially notable was the religious fervor of the age, which manifested itself in the worship of the god Amon, whose priests became ever more powerful as props of the pharaohs and guardians of Egypt's destiny.

Amid the restoration, there was a new factor at work, tugging the Egyptians out of their old comfortable isolation and challenging their long-standing sense of superiority: a haunting fear of new invasions. The first pharaohs of the Eighteenth Dynasty responded to this sense of insecurity by conducting raids to the south and into Syria-Palestine. Not only did these raids allay fear and restore confidence, but they also demonstrated that the exploitation of foreigners could be profitable. Fear, pride, greed, and internal strength slowly combined to breed imperialism. Conservative elements, content to return to the old Egypt, resisted this tide, but failed to stem it. With the accession of Thutmose III (1484–1447 B.C.), Egypt cast her lot for imperialism.

Thutmose III, called "the Napoleon of Egypt," launched the policy of conquest and occupation of foreign lands. He led a series of brilliantly executed campaigns into Syria-Palestine, Nubia, and Libya that succeeded in crushing all resistance to Egyptian domination. The Egyptians had learned the use of the horse and chariot from the Hyksos, so that their armies proved more than equal to the foreign forces they met. Thutmose's diplomats made Egypt's might felt beyond the area of actual conquest, forcing powers such as the Hittites, Mitanni, Kassites, and Assyrians to seek to remain on friendly terms with her. He marshaled Egypt's internal resources, both material and human, to support the enlarged army, and he established an administration to ensure Egyptian domination over conquered lands. Because heavy tribute was exacted from the conquered peoples, the costs of conquest were met and a substantial surplus remained to enrich Egyptian society. For a century Thutmose's successors pursued his policy and kept Egypt the dominant power in the Near East.

Successful imperialism brought to Egypt a new period of magnificence. Her government reached peak efficiency in exercising absolute control over the population. Agriculture and trade, coupled with the tribute extracted from foreign subjects, produced unprecedented prosperity. Artistic and intellectual life blossomed again, inspired by pride in Egypt's power and supported by her great wealth. The greatest landmarks of Egyptian artistic vigor were the magnificent temples built at Luxor and Karnak in honor of Amon-Re, the chief god in Egypt at this time. Like the pyramids built a thousand years earlier, these giant pillared structures, brilliantly decorated with carvings and paint, illustrate the Egyptian genius for building structures that seem destined to last forever. The artistic outburst of the New Kingdom was not marked by originality or creativity. Artists looked back to earlier times for models, thereby maintaining the static quality in Egyptian art discussed earlier.

Nevertheless, the cultural activity of the New Kingdom kept alive and vital an ancient and rich cultural tradition. And the influences of that culture were felt in a positive way throughout the eastern Mediterranean world. In Nubia huge temples were built in the Egyptian architectural style in honor of Egyptian gods; on their walls were written prayers and hymns in the Egyptian language.

In Syria and Palestine artisans began to imitate Egyptian styles and techniques in the manufacturing of pottery, metalwork, and jewelry. The petty princes of this area, many of whom were educated at the Egyptian royal court, aped the royal style of the pharaohs, as is evident in the considerable body of diplomatic correspondence that has survived from the period (the Amarna letters, discovered in 1887 in the ruins of the city of Amarna). Egyptian manufactured products were exported in quantity to Mesopotamia, the Hittite kingdom, and Crete. Here was cultural diffusion at work.

The Egypt of the New Kingdom, though, was not quite the Egypt of old. Successful imperialism presented serious problems that the Egyptians were ill equipped to handle. One was that of dealing with conquered peoples. Egypt adopted a system of permitting conquered subjects to keep their own rulers, who were compelled to sign treaties with Egypt pledging friendship and loyalty, to pay tribute, and to furnish hostages as security. Egypt sought to hold this intricate alliance system together by establishing garrisons abroad, by organizing periodic displays of military might, and by sending diplomats abroad to monitor semi-independent powers. As long as the armies and diplomats were vigilant, the system worked, but each independent prince always remained a potential source of rebellion.

A second problem facing Egypt was the fear and hostility her expansion aroused among peoples beyond her borders. The Egyptians discovered that expansion did not necessarily safeguard a nation from external attack, but instead increased the possibility of such attacks. Holding her empire thus imposed on Egypt the burden of waging foreign wars against a formidable array of enemies.

Ultimately, the Hittites proved to be Egypt's most dangerous foe. Of all the "new" peoples that had emerged from the Indo-European invasions, the Hittites achieved the greatest power and prominence. Their history began in eastern Asia Minor about 1800 B.C., when

The Ancient Near East ca. 1450 B.C.

Indo-European warlords imposed their rule on the natives of the area and formed a series of small kingdoms. By about 1600 B.C., several of these principalities had been drawn together into a large kingdom with its capital at Hattusas (modern Boghazköy in Turkey). The rulers of this consolidated state played an aggressive role in the Near East, as indicated by their attacks on the declining Amorite Empire. The development of the unified Hittite kingdom was accompanied by the growth of an advanced culture which has been brought to light by modern excavations at Boghazköy and by the decipherment of Hittite writing. Hittite political institutions, religion, literature, architecture, and art were strongly influenced by Mesopotamian models, so that in one sense the Hittite kingdom was a cultural outpost of the Tigris-Euphrates Valley. But there is also a distinctiveness about Hittite culture, for it reflects an amalgam of native elements to which the borrowings were added.

Hittite power, spread over a large area in Asia Minor and reaching out east and south, reached is peak about 1400 B.C. The Hittites drew the Mitanni into their orbit and began to attack the northern fringes of the Egyptian Empire. They successfully encouraged rebellion among the princes ruling the numerous petty states within Egypt's sphere of influence in Syria-Palestine. Such interference of course added greatly to Egypt's difficulties in maintaining her empire.

A third and serious problem was the erosion of the social and spiritual bases of society within Egypt. The demands of war resulted in an increasing regimentation of the lower classes by the government. Occupied with military and diplomatic issues and with pleasures, the pharaohs themselves lost contact with their subjects. Their officials, often newcomers into the world of power and greatly enriched by the spoils of imperialism, constituted a heartless, oppressive ruling class which weighed heavily on the populace. Especially powerful were the priests of Amon-Re; they amassed immense wealth and even challenged the divine authority of the pharaoh for the right to approach the gods. New ideas and new styles of life, often brought in by foreigners, entered the land to compete with the old and to cause doubts about the validity of ancient ways. Excessive wealth tended to vulgarize life and erode long-established social values. As the mass of the populace found itself regimented and exploited by a bureaucratic and priestly caste, it tended to become alienated and preoccupied with the problems of immortality and Osiris worship. The search for eternity lost much of the moral earnestness of earlier times. Men increasingly sought subterfuges whereby Osiris could be inveigled into granting eternal

life. All these trends, perhaps inevitable results of Egypt's thrust out of her small river-valley world, bred tensions and doubts in a society long accustomed to the confident acceptance of an established set of values. The critical question was whether the populace could adjust to these new forces and modify belief and behavior to fit the new situation.

The troubled society of the New Kingdom was finally brought face to face with its problems by an intriguing individual elevated to the throne in about 1375 as Amenhotep IV. This occupant of the office that was the most sacred symbol of the old order turned out to be a revolutionary. His answer to Egypt's problems lay in a new religion: He proclaimed that his subjects must worship a new god, Aton, the sun god. According to the new theology, which the pharaoh personally helped to develop, Aton was the sole god, master of the whole universe and the cause of all things. Symbolizing his break with the old order, Amenhotep IV changed his name to Akhenaton. He abandoned the old capital at Thebes, which was also the center of the powerful Amon-Re cult, and built a new city called Akhetaton. He declared war on the old gods, ordered his subjects to stop worshiping them, destroyed their temples, and demoted their priests. At his new sacred city the cult of Aton was developed. Symbolized by the sun disc, Aton was conceived in more abstract and spiritual terms than the old gods. New rituals, revealing a fresh poetic inspiration, were devised in honor of Aton, and a naturalistic art style, breaking sharply with tradition, was developed to portray his divine powers. Akhenaton personally involved himself in the new cult and the new art; he, his beautiful queen Nefertiti, and his five daughters were the very center of a pulsating movement that turned away from imperialism, bureaucracy, and staid modes of thought and art.

Akhenaton's reforms provoked a storm of protest in Egypt and gripped the population in a struggle that consumed everyone's energies. The opposition to Akhenaton was led by the priests of Amon-Re, the god who had

Akhenaton the Enigma

Every student of history must learn to recognize generalizations about the past and to view them with a healthy skepticism. One such generalization appears in the section of this text on Akhenaton, where it is argued that he was an innovator seeking to move a tradition-bound, proud, self-centered society wallowing in wealth and power into a new world, larger and more complex than the accustomed one. But was this enigmatic figure a leader of this order? A quick glance at the surviving portraits of him may even raise some doubts: his long-faced, pot-bellied, thick-legged figure does not bespeak vigorous, forward-looking leadership. Indeed, not all who have studied his career accept him as he is presented in this book.

Akhenaton's contemporaries were extremely harsh on him. To most of them, he was a heretic who denied the ancient gods in his pursuit of a false deity. His defection bred internal strife and external disaster, as one would expect. The other gods, especially the almighty Amon-Re whose worship had become dominant in Egypt in the two centuries prior to Akhenaton's reign, would surely display their anger. Even before the end of his reign, Akhenaton's mother, Tiy, took the lead in halting his religious reforms and restoring the old order. The pharaoh spent his last years in isolation at his holy city of Akhetaton, while a co-ruler was installed at Thebes to represent the real authority in Egypt. After his death the very name of the "criminal Akhenaton" was dropped from the list of pharaohs and all traces of his religious ideas were erased from the books and chiseled from the stones (with the exception of some tombs at Akhetaton). Not until these tombs were unearthed in the nineteenth century was the existence of Amenhotep IV, renamed Akhenaton, even known to historians.

The initial reaction to the discovery of Akhenaton's existence and his religious ideas was to exalt his role in history. The American Egyptologist James Henry Breasted gave wide popularity to this view. He saw the pharaoh as a sensitive, intelligent man of great individual talent with a new religious vision for which he became a prophet. Steeped in the trends of religious development working in imperial Egypt and offended by the pedestrian, routine religious concepts and practices represented by the traditional priesthood, his seminal thought drew him to monotheism. The unlimited power that was his as pharaoh prompted him to impose this exalted religion on his subjects. The formulation of the new faith was his personal achievement, a witness to his intelligence and depth of feeling. Here then was the first monotheist. Breasted's Akhenaton soon prompted others to see the first monotheist as the teacher of Moses, whose career in Egypt came about a century after his reign. In *Moses and Monotheism*, Sigmund Freud argued that Akhenaton was really the progenitor of Hebrew monotheism.

Not all scholars are persuaded that the evidence points where Breasted and Freud thought. Some have found evidence that Akhenaton was an irresponsible, bigoted religious zealot who insisted on imposing his religious "fads" on a populace that had no desire for innovation and when this did not work withdrew to his own little paradise where he could work his will on his docile retainers, leaving the empire to drift toward ruin. Others see him as demented; perhaps he was a victim of a physical disease, since recent studies of his mummified body suggest he suffered a pituitary disorder that led to physical and mental deterioration. The most careful studies of Akhenaton's religious ideas strongly suggest that he was not a monotheist, but rather the propounder of a faith which proclaimed a new god for the pharaoh to worship while insisting that everyone else worship the pharaoh. This may have been a political ploy: the restoration of the pharaoh's absolute power, the focusing of attention on royal splendor as a key to control over the empire, the curbing of the power of the rich priests. These basically conservative goals would make the pharaoh not even a heretic, much less a religious revolutionary.

Like all significant men in history, Akhenaton will undoubtedly continue to provoke differing viewpoints. Each one must draw his own conclusions on the basis of all information he can gather about one of the first "individuals" to emerge in human history.

leaped to prominence in Egypt during the period of successful expansion. The priests found adequate support elsewhere in society. Akhenaton's reforms were bound to disturb his subjects because religion lay at the very foundation of Egyptian civilization. Although no one can now be sure of his motives it seems that his program offered Egyptian civilization a supreme challenge. Would it continue to progress or would it remain conservative and backward-looking? Akhenaton was trying to hasten his people along a path leading to the worship of one almighty god who demanded moral goodness of his worshipers. This was Akhenaton's substitute for a religious system based on adherence to a welter of gods who asked material offerings. He was seeking to reduce the power of the priests who had been using religion as a means of gaining power and prestige at the expense of the pharaoh. He was trying to guide Egypt's intellectuals and artists into new channels, to divert them from their increasing tendency to worship the past. In short, he was trying to find in a new religion a means of rousing Egyptians to take the lead in exploiting the new currents that were running strong in Near Eastern society in this era of mixing and mingling of cultures. His efforts were fruitless. By the time of his death, his foes had already forced him to abandon his reforms. His successor, Tutankhamon, sealed the victory of reaction by a vigorous restoration of the pre-Akhenaton order in religion, art, and politics.

These internal disturbances proved fatal to the Egyptian Empire. Even before Akhenaton's reforms, Egypt's grip on Syria-Palestine was loosening. His neglect of military affairs encouraged rebellion. Unfortunately for the Egyptians, Hittite power was at its peak at this critical moment. Under the able king Suppilulimas (1375–1335 B.C.), whose reign coincided with that of Akhenaton, they applied great pressure on Egypt's holdings in Syria by direct attack and by encouraging rebellion among Egypt's restless subjects. By the end of the Eighteenth Dynasty, Egypt's power in Asia had been greatly reduced.

The pharaoh Akhenaton, whose attempt to reform Egyptian religion, although unsuccessful, led also to a short-lived artistic revolution that produced works characterized by a realism and freedom of expression that stand in sharp contrast to the traditional style. *Photo: Hirmer Verlag*

The early rulers of the Nineteenth Dynasty (ca. 1320–1200 B.C.), especially Seti I and Rameses II, acted with some success to halt the disintegration of the empire, but at a heavy price. Incessant warfare between Egypt and the Hittites sapped both powers. Although they made peace about 1271 B.C., their days of greatness had ended. The Hittite kingdom was completely destroyed about

1200 by a new wave of invaders surging through the Near East. Egypt's fate was not quite so drastic. She too came under attack from Nubians, Libyans, and the "People of the Sea," seafaring marauders from the Aegean area. These attacks forced her back into her old boundaries and from time to time put foreigners on her throne. Egypt stagnated, imitating and worshiping her past greatness without any marked creative innovations. After 1200 B.C. she never again stood out as a leader, although her achievements left a permanent mark on history.

3. THE ERA OF SMALL NATIONS, 1200–800 B.C.: PHOENICIANS AND ARAMEANS

The collapse of the Hittite and Egyptian empires around 1200 B.C., coupled with the destruction of Minoan power slightly earlier, resulted in a new alignment of political forces in the Near East. The confusion was compounded by the new invasions whose impact on the Hittites and the Egyptians has already been noted. New waves of Indo-Europeans poured into Asia Minor and the Aegean area and spilled over the waterways of the eastern Mediterranean to attack established powers. These newcomers were especially formidable because they possessed iron weapons. Semitic nomads poured out of the Arabian Desert to fill the vacuum created by the collapse of the empires. Several small groups previously under Egyptian or Hittite rule seized the opportunity to establish political independence. For the next four centuries, the Near East was a patchwork of small nations.

The changed political order emerging between 1200 and 800 B.C. did not, however, constitute a break in the broad pattern of historical development. The diffusion of culture remained the basic characteristic of the era. As the small nations struggled to establish and maintain themselves, they borrowed heavily from the cultures of the Mesopotamians and the Egyptians in order to provide a basis for their new life. Their efforts resulted in a continued spread over most of the Near East of ideas and institutions that had originated in the great river valleys. A few of the smaller groups did more than borrow; as a result of their unique experiences, they were able to add new elements to the existing cultural life, thereby enriching the Near Eastern tradition as well as spreading it.

Two small nations stand out especially as borrowers and disseminators of the older civilizations—the Phoenicians and the Arameans. Both these groups were Semitic in origin, migrating from the Arabian Desert into modern Syria prior to 2000 B.C. The Phoenicians settled in the narrow band of territory lying between the Mediterranean Sea and the mountains of Lebanon. The Arameans were located east of these mountains between the northern end of the Arabian Desert and the Euphrates River. Both groups were repeatedly conquered by the Mesopotamians, Egyptians, and Hittites, and were strongly influenced by all their conquerors. Consequently, by 1200 B.C., they were already highly civilized peoples, and when Egypt and the Hittites declined in power, both groups were able to establish their political independence. Ultimately, a number of independent city-states emerged in Phoenicia, the chief of which were Tyre and Sidon. The Arameans organized themselves into a number of small kingdoms, centering around cities like Damascus, Kadesh, and Palmyra. For about four centuries these principalities were among the chief states in the Near East. Their independence was finally crushed, however, by the rising power of the Assyrians in the eighth century B.C.

Phoenician ships such as the one shown in this relief carried goods around the entire Mediterranean Basin in the years between 1200 and 800 B.C. *Photo: Cliché des Musées Nationaux, Versailles*

The Phoenicians and the Arameans were especially active as spreaders of Near Eastern civilization. Both groups derived most of their wealth from trading ventures. The Phoenicians took to the seas, and established a virtual monopoly on trade in the Mediterranean. Phoenician merchants carried manufactured goods from the whole Near East to the backward peoples of Greece, Italy, North Africa, Spain, and southern France, and brought the raw materials of these areas back to the Near East. From these merchants many barbarian peoples got their first taste of higher civilization. The Phoenicians, not content to trade, also established colonies abroad. The chief Phoenician colony was the North African city of Carthage, which became one of the leading centers of civilization in the western Mediterranean after 800 B.C. The Arameans were land traders; they exploited the trade routes that linked Egypt, Mesopotamia, Asia Minor, and points beyond. Both Phoenicians and Arameans reaped a rich reward from their trading ventures which was, in part, devoted to patronizing the arts and learning. Their cities were active cultural centers. Neither people was particularly creative, for they used Egyptian and especially

Mesopotamian models in their art, literature, and religion. The Phoenicians, however, did perfect an alphabet that later served as a model for the written languages of the Mediterranean world.

4. THE ERA OF SMALL NATIONS, 1200– 800 B.C.: THE HEBREWS

The most significant of the small nations for the history of Western civilization was that of the Hebrews. To do them justice in a brief account is virtually impossible, for few people in history have evoked greater interest or more intensive study. We can only hope to place the ancient Hebrews in a larger historical context and try to suggest their unique role in that setting. The Hebrews left one literary record that has been invaluable to the historians of later ages: the Old Testament. Although it is primarily a religious document, the basic Hebrew belief that their God worked out destiny in time makes it historical as well. The history recounted in the Old Testament raises innumerable problems, but it does provide a narrative account far superior to the literature of any other people in the ancient Near East. On the whole, the story it tells has been corroborated by other literary sources and by archeology, and it can be read as a serious introduction to Hebrew history.

The Hebrews originated as Semitic nomads living in the Arabian Desert. About 1800 B.C., roughly at the time of Hammurabi, some tribes led by the patriarch Abraham began a search for a new home. Failing to establish themselves in the Euphrates Valley, the wanderers moved toward Syria-Palestine. In no sense did these migrants constitute a single people; rather, they were divided into numerous tribes, each of which retained a spirit of independence as it struggled for a new home.

In Palestine the newcomers encountered the well-established and highly civilized Canaanites, whose culture was heavily affected by Egyptian and Mesopotamian influences. While some Hebrews quickly adopted Canaan-ite civilization, others, forced to settle in semi-arid parts of Palestine, retained their ancient desert way of life. Grouped into small tribes under patriarchal leaders, such as Isaac and Jacob, and often seminomadic, they sustained a fierce sense of independence and an egalitarian social order. These deeply engrained ways were to influence their future history as a people and as a nation.

Some Hebrews made their way into Egypt to escape famines in Palestine, as part of the Hyksos invasions, or as Egyptian prisoners. In Egypt the Hebrews were assigned lands in the Delta region (the Biblical land of Goshen). Although they preserved many of their ancient ways, they were influenced by Egyptian civilization. Some, like Joseph, even enjoyed great favor in the pharaoh's court. Eventually, however, life in Egypt became intolerable, probably because the Hebrews became victims of the increasing oppression of the pharaohs of the late eighteenth and nineteenth dynasties, who were fighting costly wars to save Egypt's empire. This oppression set the stage for a major turning point in Hebrew history—the Exodus from Egypt, which occurred shortly before 1200 B.C.

The familiar story of the Exodus and of Moses' inspired leadership of those Hebrews who fled Egypt does not need telling here. During forty trying years spent wandering about the Sinai Peninsula, a dramatic transformation occurred among Moses' followers. They underwent a religious experience that laid the basis for a Hebrew nation. The origins and development of Hebrew religious concepts up to the Exodus are extremely obscure and open to debate. The Old Testament probably distorts this development by projecting backward into this early period ideas that developed much later. It cannot be said for sure that the Hebrews had a common religion during the age of the patriarchs; rather, each tribe probably had its own gods. Some of the newcomers into Palestine accepted Canaanite religious practices and abandoned their old desert religion. But at least some of the tribes gave particular allegiance to the god Yahweh. Yahweh was a powerful and somewhat terrible nature god, capable of caring for the material needs of followers who courted his favor with sacrificial offerings and prayers. The tribes which worshiped Yahweh appear from an early date to have given him their sole allegiance, although they did admit that other gods existed. Therefore, prior to 1200 B.C. some of the Hebrews appear to have developed *monolatry*, that is, belief in one god for a particular community while recognizing other gods proper to other groups. If this is the case, the Hebrews were already unique, for no other Near Eastern people—with the exception of the ill-fated circle around Akhenaton—had ever propounded such a belief. Still, monolatry was open to challenge; even during the Exodus, the followers of Moses asked Aaron "to make them a god to go at the head of us," and Aaron responded with the golden calf before which the people worshiped (Exodus, 32, 1–6).

During their stay in the desert, however, the followers of Moses pledged themselves to the worship of Yahweh and accepted certain ideas about that god and their relationship to him. These unique formulations became the basis for all later religious development among the Hebrews. Prompted by the inspired leadership of Moses, the Hebrews of the Exodus entered into a covenant, or contract, with Yahweh: They pledged themselves to worship only Yahweh. In return, their god promised that he would care for them under any circumstances, just as he had done during the escape from Egypt. The Hebrews also accepted from Yahweh a set of laws that were to govern the manner in which each follower conducted himself toward Yahweh and toward his fellow men. Yahweh's wrath would fall on those who violated these commands. By the acceptance of these ideas, Moses' "mixed multitude" became a "nation," the Israelites, bound together by the exclusive worship of one god. The gradual refinement of these concepts and their adjustment to new historical situations led ultimately to the great contribution of the Hebrews to the history of the world—the religion of Judaism.

The first task to which the newly formed Hebrew nation turned was to renew the search for the Promised Land. Armed with the Ark of the Covenant, a wooden chest containing Yahweh's commands, which they carried with them as a mark of their allegiance to him, this impoverished band set themselves against the Canaanites and the other Hebrew tribes in Palestine. Shortly after 1200 B.C., they crossed the Jordan to strike at the Canaanite city of Jericho. For the next hundred and fifty years, the Hebrews devoted their energies to establishing their dominion over Palestine. Usually they were successful, although their own disunity made the task difficult. They were still organized into tribes, each of which fiercely guarded its independence; only in periods of great crisis were they able to overcome tribal jealousies for a united effort. As their control over Palestine widened, the Hebrews enjoyed increasing prosperity. The primitive culture of desert dwellers was greatly modified by the higher culture of settled farmers, which the Hebrews borrowed from the conquered Canaanites.

The worship of Yahweh gained new adherents during the period of conquest, probably because Yahweh seemed to be fulfilling his promise to watch over the interests of those who worshipped him. The Hebrew system of law, still closely allied to the worship of Yahweh, continued to expand and to serve as a common tie among many Hebrew tribes. Another common tie developing in this era was a shared set of religious practices directed by an emerging priesthood and centering around the Ark of the Covenant, which appears to have been located at the town of Shiloh. However, Yahweh worship was still not accepted by all the Hebrews. During the period of conquest, there was a series of leaders who tried to rally backsliding Hebrews to return to the worship of Yahweh. These leaders, called "judges" in the Old Testament and represented by figures like Gideon, Samson, and Samuel, sought to convince the Hebrews that their many military setbacks were punishment for their failure to serve Yahweh and for their tendency to fall under the spell of the Canaanite gods, the Baals.

Although they succeeded in overpowering the Canaanites, the Hebrews eventually met a foe they could not handle so easily. Shortly after 1100 B.C., they began to clash with the Philistines, a people probably from Asia Minor who had recently settled along the Mediterranean shore of southern Palestine after having been rebuffed in an attempt to seize Egypt. By 1050 B.C., most of the Hebrews had been conquered by the Philistines. This disaster eventually proved a blessing for the Hebrews because it forced them into a political union. As a step toward ending Philistine overlordship, several Hebrew tribes agreed to accept a single king. The person they selected for that honor was called Saul.

The reigns of Saul and his successors, David and Solomon, covering the years about 1020 to 930 B.C., mark the high point of Hebrew political history. These kings smashed the Philistine power and subdued many other enemies around Syria-Palestine, making the Hebrew nation the leading power in that area. A centralized government was established at Jerusalem, which gave the king the means to exercise control over all the Hebrews. Active diplomatic relations were established between the kings of the Hebrews and the rulers of most other nations of the Near East. The success of Hebrew traders brought prosperity to the new kingdom. The royal court at Jerusalem patronized the arts and letters. There was occasional dissidence, often in protest against personal conduct of the kings. Saul's jealousy of the youthful David, David's passion for other men's wives, and Solomon's heavy expenditures to satisfy his own tastes outraged the feelings of some Hebrews. For a time, however, the kings were able to curb the dissatisfied elements and to maintain a unified kingdom enjoying power and prestige.

The reigns of Saul, David, and Solomon represented a significant chapter in the history of the Jewish religion. These kings were all active champions of Yahweh, claiming that they were his agents and that they had been anointed to lead the Hebrews to the victory promised in the Covenant. Nearly all the Hebrews now accepted the worship of Yahweh.

David moved the Ark of the Covenant to Jerusalem after he captured that city and made it the seat of his power. Solomon completed the process of making it the religious center of the nation by building a splendid temple, one of the most enduring of all religious centers in the world. The ritual practices devoted to Yahweh took on elaborate form under the guidance of an expanded priesthood richly supported by the kings. A body of religious writings, much of it later to be incorporated in the final form of the Old Testament, was set down at this time. Yahweh worship was becoming a full-fledged religious system, fitted for a prosperous, powerful, civilized people.

Even while Solomon reigned in all his glory, however, deep-seated economic, political, and religious dissension threatened the Hebrew nation. Many Hebrews, remembering their tribal freedom, hated the autocratic methods used by the kings to hold the kingdom together. The old social equality characteristic of tribal life began to be undermined as the Hebrews became more civilized, and a definite aristocracy emerged and sought to subdue the masses. This social and economic inequality was anathema to many Hebrews. As for their religion, despite the fact that Yahweh was championed by their kings, many Hebrews were dissatisfied. They resented the non-Hebrew ideas and practices that had slipped into the rituals at the great temple in Jerusalem. Furthermore, they deplored Solomon's tolerance of the religions of his many non-Jewish wives, for such forbearance of the alien appeared to be a compromise with Yahweh worship. Immediately after Solomon's death, this discontent ended the short-lived unity of the nation. The northern part of the kingdom refused to recognize his son as king and formed a new kingdom called Israel, with its center at Samaria. The southern Hebrews formed a kingdom called Judah, under kings descended from David.

The kingdoms of Israel and Judah proceeded steadily toward destruction, both becoming the victims of internal disturbances and of misrule which sapped their will to resist foreign attack. In 722 B.C. Israel was destroyed by the Assyrians. Her people were carried off into captivity to become the Ten Lost Tribes. Judah survived until 586 B.C., when the Chaldeans (see p. 69) captured Jerusalem and carried off large numbers of Jews into captivity in Babylonia. Thus ended the independent political history of the Hebrews. The Persians did free some of the captives in 538 B.C., allowing them to return to Jerusalem and to reestablish the Hebrew religion, but this did not mean political independence; it simply meant that Hebrew priests were given permission by the Persians to exercise a great deal of influence in Palestine, but always under Persian supervision.

As Hebrew political glory faded in the centuries after 900 B.C., Hebrew religious life took on new depth. During the period of the divided kingdoms and foreign conquests, religion became the sole force that sustained a sense of nationhood and uniqueness among the harassed Hebrews. In part, the priests were responsible for strengthening the religious bond, for they set forth the cult practices and ritual observances that marked one as being a true worshiper of Yahweh. In the process they fashioned a sober, austere religion that cut away much of the magic and superstition surrounding other Near Eastern religions.

Much more significant were the searching examination and the fresh reformulation of the basic concepts of Hebrew religion by a series of powerful religious leaders known as the prophets. Several of the Hebrew prophets deserve individual attention because they rank among the world's greatest spiritual spokesmen: Elijah (ninth century), Amos and Isaiah (eighth century), Jeremiah (seventh–sixth century), Ezekiel and the anonymous second Isaiah (sixth century), and Haggai (late sixth century). As a group, they represent a unique type of religious leader in the ancient Near East. They spoke forth not as members of a priestly caste or as mouthpieces for mighty kings, but as individuals, often of humble origins, who raised their voices as a result of personal conviction and spiritual insight.

With no fear of consequences, they thundered against the rich and the powerful as well as the weak and the insignificant. They all proclaimed a common message built around the idea that the Hebrews were abandoning their covenant with Yahweh and would be punished for their sins. Their prophecies were firmly rooted in Hebrew tradition, but they spoke with such passion and such depth of spiritual understanding that collectively they formulated in nearly final form a set of religious ideas which became the essence of Judaism. Their reformulation of Judaism, put into writing in the prophetic books of the Old Testament, constituted a radical departure from conventional religious thought in the Near East and established a base for much of the religious development of the future. At the risk of oversimplification, the following can be singled out as the fundamental ideas they developed.

First of all, the prophets proclaimed a true monotheism. They made Yahweh the only god and denied that any other gods existed. Before the time of the prophets, the Hebrews had believed that Yahweh was the only god they should worship, but they had never denied the existence of other gods. The prophets repudiated this idea by claiming that only Yahweh existed and that those who did not worship him were idolators.

Second, the prophets proclaimed a whole new concept of the nature of Yahweh. He was a god outside nature, not existing in any natural object; he was a god of justice, acting according to a definite law instead of his own fancy; he was omnipotent, controlling the whole universe and causing everything in the past, present, and future to happen; he was a god with a plan for the world; his will would be worked out in the history of the world. He was a god of righteousness, pleased by those who did good, vengeful toward those who did evil. This was truly the most exalted concept of deity yet expressed in the Near East.

Third, the prophets defined a new basis for human conduct. Just as Yahweh treated men with righteousness and justice, so also must each individual treat his fellow-men according to those same principles. Yahweh had handed down to man a code of law (called the Torah) that must serve as the basis for earthly society. Transgression of the law would invite the wrath of Yahweh and bring down his punishment on the offender. Decent treatment of other men became a major obligation of each Hebrew. Goodness would not be reckoned by Yahweh in terms of wealth or the size of the offering made to him; instead a man would be judged in terms of his treatment of others. The religion of the prophets emphasized ethical concepts far above ritual practices.

Finally, the prophets proclaimed that the Hebrews were the people chosen to carry out Yahweh's will on earth. No matter what disasters had befallen them at the moment, they would eventually emerge victorious over the other peoples of the earth, and through them the one god would eventually be worshiped by all. Yahweh would aid in this venture, since it was his plan for the world, and eventually he would send a Messiah to lead the Hebrews to victory. While awaiting that final victory, the Hebrews must retain their ties with one another. If they could not all live in an inde-

pendent kingdom, they could retain their common religious beliefs as a binding tie. The Hebrew "nation" would live on as a religious community, awaiting its victory over the non-Hebrews.

By the fourth century B.C., when the ancient Near East was conquered by Alexander the Great and its civilization submitted to heavy Greek influences, the Hebrews had made no progress toward winning the world to worship of their god. Near Eastern peoples were too accustomed to the worship of a multitude of nature gods, to their elaborate mythology, and to the ingrained habit of winning the favor of these gods by elaborate sacrifices to listen to Hebrew concepts of a single almighty god living outside nature and expecting men to live by a law requiring high moral standards. But although few men then paid attention to these ideas, they had tremendous impact on later civilizations. They served as the base upon which Christianity and Islam would be built. Despite modest worldly success in the total setting of ancient Near Eastern history, the Hebrews had written one of the great chapters in man's spiritual and moral history.

Suggested Reading

Indo-European and Semitic Invaders. The knotty problem of the Indo-European and Semitic invaders, their origins, and their role is complicated by a lack of information and by an overlay of assumptions about racial origins. Two objective works by renowned experts will be helpful in clearing away some of the clouds: V. Gordon Childe, *The Aryans: A Study of Indo-European Origins* (1926); and **Sabatino Moscati, *Ancient Semitic Civilizations* (Capricorn).

The Egyptian Empire. Most of the works cited in the Suggested Reading for Chapter 2 treat the history of the Egyptian Empire. Especially helpful for political history are the volumes by Breasted, Ward, Aldred, Gardiner,

and Wilson. A detailed study of the history of the Egyptian Empire is provided by **George Steindorff and Karl C. Seele, *When Egypt Ruled the East* (2nd ed., Phoenix). To the works already cited on Egyptian religion should be added **James Henry Breasted, *The Dawn of Conscience* (Scribner Library), in which is developed the author's famous argument that Akhenaton was the first monotheist. Pierre Montet, *Everyday Life in Egypt in the Days of Ramesses the Great* (1958) presents a brilliant picture of Egyptian society in the Nineteenth Dynasty, when the empire was in decline.

Hittites. The best general survey of Hittite history and culture is **O. R. Gurney, *The*

Hittites (2nd ed., Penguin). C. W. Ceram, *The Secret of the Hittites: The Discovery of the Ancient Empire* (1956) provides a well-balanced picture of the nature of Hittite civilization and tells a fascinating story of how it was found by archeologists. Ekrem Akurgal, *Art of the Hittites*, trans. Constance McNab (1962) is thorough and up to date on the subject.

Phoenicians and Arameans. A. T. Olmstead, *History of Palestine and Syria to the Macedonian Conquest* (1939) attempts to provide a general history of the area and its people; the work, however, is old and out of date in many respects. The best work on the Phoenicians is a splendid recent study by Sabatino Moscati, *The World of the Phoenicians*, trans. Alistair Hamilton (1968). Also excellent on the same subject is **Donald Harden, *The Phoenicians* (Praeger).

The Hebrews. There is such a vast literature on the Hebrews that any selection must be arbitrary and subjective; and if the list is short, it may be distorted. Perhaps the best way to begin to study the history of the early Hebrews is to read the Old Testament. Two recent good translations are J. M. P. Smith and E. J. Goodspeed, eds., *The Complete Bible; An American Translation* (1939); and Alexander Jones, ed., *The Jerusalem Bible* (1966), an English version of a translation prepared in French by the Dominican Biblical School of Jerusalem. A student reading the Old Testament in order to learn something of the history of Hebrews will find a good commentary helpful; two convenient ones are *The Abingdon Bible Commentary* (1929) and *A Catholic Commentary on Holy Scripture* (1953). Also useful in interpreting the Old Testament as a historical source are **Stanley Cook, *Introduction to the Bible* (Penguin); and Harry M. Buck, *People of the Lord: The History, Scriptures, and Faith of Ancient Israel* (1966).

There are several excellent brief surveys of Hebrew history during the period covered in this chapter; most of these give considerable attention to religious development. Especially concise, but sound, is **Harry Orlinsky, *Ancient Israel* (2nd ed., Cornell). More challenging and exciting is **William F. Albright,

The Biblical Period From Abraham to Ezra (Harper Torchbook) by a famous archeologist who does an excellent job of reconciling archeology and the Old Testament version of history. That theme is pursued more deeply in the same author's **The Archaeology of Palestine* (Penguin) and **From Stone Age to Christianity: Monotheism and the Historical Process* (Anchor). Another brief survey, somewhat mistitled, is **Cyrus H. Gordon, *The Ancient Near East* (3rd ed. rev., Norton), which seeks to relate Hebrew history to the larger setting in the Near East. The story of the early Hebrews is also excitingly told by the noted French Catholic scholar **Henri Daniel-Rops, *Israel and the Ancient World: A History of the Israelites From the Time of Abraham to the Birth of Christ* (Image). Some of his interpretations, however, are open to challenge. A reader seeking detailed information on Hebrew history might turn to longer histories by T. H. Robinson and W. O. E. Oesterley, *A History of Israel*, Vol. I (2nd ed., 1937); and Salo Wittmayer Baron, *A Social and Religious History of the Jews* (2nd ed. rev., 12 vols., 1952–67), Vol. I, *Ancient Times: To the Beginning of the Christian Era*. **Roland de Vaux, *Ancient Israel: Its Life and Institutions* (2 vols., McGraw-Hill), provides an excellent picture of Hebrew society in Old Testament times.

The student interested in Hebrew religious ideas might turn to one of the following studies: W. O. E. Oesterley and T. H. Robinson, *Hebrew Religion: Its Origins and Development* (2nd ed., 1937); H. H. Rowley, *The Faith of Israel: Aspects of Old Testament Thought* (1956); Th. C. Vriezen, *The Religion of Ancient Israel* (1967); and Helmer Ringgren, *Israelite Religion*, trans. D. E. Green (1966). The difficult problem of early Hebrew religion is well treated by **T. J. Meek, *Hebrew Origins* (Harper Torchbook); and H. H. Rowley, *From Joseph to Joshua: Biblical Traditions in the Light of Archaeology* (1950). For the role of the prophets, see J. Lindblom, *Prophecy in Ancient Israel* (1962). H. H. Rowley, *Worship in Ancient Israel: Its Form and Meaning* (1967) treats an aspect of ancient Hebrew history and religion sometimes overlooked. A difficult but profound treatment of Judaism in the perspective of world culture is Eric Voegelin, *Order and History* (3 vols., 1956–57), Vol. I, *Israel and Revelation*.

Chapter 4 ❧ The Great Empires: Assyria and Persia,

800–300 B.C.

During the ninth century B.C., the rising might of Assyria heralded a new era in Near Eastern history. During the previous millennium the ground had been prepared for a cosmopolitan civilization and a universal political order. The diffusion of the river-valley cultures into a broader society had provided large numbers of men with common techniques and ideas. The formation of new political entities, even though many of them were small, had established local stability and order and had created political building blocks out of which great empires could be shaped. Expanding trade had knit distant communities together with common economic interests. These developments invited attempts at political consolidation, and adventuresome men were at hand to respond to the opportunity. The new "empire builders" revived an earlier tradition of political unification. However, their vision was wider and their efforts resulted in vaster empires. Near Eastern civilization achieved its final maturity.

1. THE ASSYRIAN EMPIRE

The Assyrians were a people of Semitic origin who migrated out of the Arabian Desert as early as 3000 B.C. and settled on either side of the upper Tigris Valley. They eventually spread out toward the Zagros Mountains and into the plateau area between the Tigris and Euphrates rivers. This was a highland area, suited for farming and herding, but incapable of producing such great wealth as the rich valley to the south.

For centuries after 3000 B.C., the main lines of Assyrian history are extremely vague. Perhaps the chief development during this period was the powerful influence exercised by Mesopotamian civilization over the Assyrians, who never demonstrated any ability to create a pattern of life of their own. Mesopotamian art styles, writing techniques, religious ideas, and political and economic institutions were copied to such an extent that Assyria was Mesopotamia's most direct cultural offspring. In fact, so intimate were these cultural ties that many historians treat the two areas as having one history. There were even times, such as under Sargon I and Hammurabi, when the Assyrians were politically incorporated into empires based in the lower Tigris-Euphrates Valley. However, Assyria never lost her identity completely, and when the Amorite Empire began to decline after 1750

The skill of Assyrian artists in portraying the details of everyday life is well illustrated in these reliefs, the originals of which are now in the British Museum. Here the king is shown at war: attacking a city and receiving prisoners. *Photo: The Trustees of the British Museum*

This stele, representing one of Assyria's great conquerors, Esarhaddon (680–669 B.C.), reflects the overpowering might of the Assyrian warrior-kings.
Photo: Staatliche Museen, Berlin

B.C., Assyria continued as an independent nation.

The era from 1750 to 1000 B.C. was the testing period for Assyria. In an age of general confusion, she was subjected to great pressure from beyond her borders, her location making her a constant target for the invading Indo-European hordes sweeping into the Near East. Kassites, Hittites, and Mitanni all assaulted Assyria at one time or another, and new hordes of Semites from the Arabian Desert likewise attacked. The hardy farmers of Assyria met this challenge by subordinating all other interests to a defense of their homeland, and they developed one of the best military forces in the Near East, especially after they adopted the new iron weapons introduced in the late second millennium. These trying centuries, during which the Assyrians strained their meager resources to defend their barren land, were significant for the future. The incessant struggle for survival produced a prime motive for later expansion: fear for the safety of the ancestral homeland which encouraged preventive wars against potential enemies.

As early as 1200 B.C., the Assyrians had demonstrated their military capability by successfully raiding a wide area stretching to the west of the homeland. Perhaps their military dominance might have extended farther at this moment, since this was the time of the collapse of the Hittite and Egyptian empires and the beginning of the era of small nations, but new invasions from the north threatened the Assyrian homeland and tied their forces down in defense.

In the ninth century B.C., the Assyrians returned to a more aggressive posture. The pressure from the north had abated. The small, weak nations which predominated in this period invited attack. A series of capable leaders emerged who harnessed the warlike sentiments of the tough Assyrian farmer-soldiers to launch a wide-sweeping series of raids on surrounding nations. The Hebrews, the Phoenicians, the Arameans, the Mesopotamians, the mountaineers to the north and east of Assyria, and the nomads of the northern part of the Arabian Desert all felt the lash of Assyrian might. No one was capable of standing up against the Assyrian armies, well-armed with iron weapons, excellent siege engines, and strong cavalry units. The Assyrians increased the effectiveness of their military machine by pursuing a deliberate policy of terrorism, using slaughter and torture as a means of frightening their intended victims into submission. The annals recording their exploits are filled with some of the most incredible examples of brutality and inhumanity ever perpetrated by man in his long career of mistreating his fellow-men. Victorious Assyrian kings proclaim their feats as a matter of course in terms such as these: flaying conquered chiefs to death, covering the walls of conquered cities with the skins of the captured populace, impaling victims on sharpened poles, cutting off the ears, noses, fingers, and legs of prisoners, making a pillar of human heads, spanning a river with corpses so as to make a bridge, smashing kingdoms as pots, turning cities into pastures. So awesome did the Assyrian reputation become that many peoples refused to resist, preferring to "embrace the feet" of the conquerors and to pay any price for survival.

These ninth-century forays were primarily tribute-collecting raids, not empire-building expeditions. They demonstrated a second powerful motive generating Assyrian expansion: the desire for a larger sweep of land from which to exact tribute as a way of enriching life in a hard, poor land. The Assyrians were still predators, little concerned with the fate of their victims as long as they turned over their wealth. There thus began a vast flow of wealth from all over the Near East to the tiny kingdom astride the Tigris, and the fortunate recipients began to display this wealth by adopting a grandiose style of life. Perhaps the Assyrians would have remained mere predators if the methods employed by her ninth-century rulers had been permanently successful. This was not the case. Rebellion and refusal to pay tribute occurred as soon as the Assyrian armies departed from any pillaged territory, requiring repeated expeditions to restore respect for Assyrian might and to ensure the flow of tribute. Constant raiding strained Assyrian manpower resources, never over-abundant. The system seems to have caused internal tension in Assyria by setting off struggles for the division of the booty and by breeding resentment

against the ruler for his decisions in splitting up the wealth produced by the new national industry. Assyria was not yet quite prepared for her new role. This internal disarray was so serious that during much of the early eighth century the raiding nearly stopped.

Shortly after 750 B.C., a ruler who was the real founder of the Assyrian Empire appeared. He was Tiglath-Pileser III (745–727 B.C.), and his policy was twofold: Internally, he imposed a new order by strengthening the hand of the king against the great nobles who had been troublesome earlier. Externally, he initiated a policy of establishing permanent, organized, systematic control over conquered subjects as a substitute for the incessant raiding expeditions. A succession of able kings continued his policy: Sargon II (722–705 B.C.), Sennacherib (705–681 B.C.), Esarhaddon (681–669 B.C.), and Ashurbanipal III (669–631 B.C.). These five rulers, several of whose arrogant, cruel visages still stare out on the world in the remarkable stone reliefs wrought by Assyrian artists and all of whom left behind boastful accounts of their exploits, built the first genuinely ecumenical empire in the Near East.

Tiglath-Pileser III and Sargon II shaped the heartland of the empire. They led the Assyrian armies on a series of expeditions that destroyed the bulk of the political powers from southern Mesopotamia around the great sweep of the Tigris-Euphrates Valley into Syria and Palestine. Only the tiny kingdom of Judah escaped, but at a terrible price in tribute. The ruling dynasties of these states were destroyed, and large numbers of the upper classes were deported far from their native homes, probably to suffer the fate of the ten tribes of the kingdom of Israel. These measures destroyed the political leadership of conquered territories and thus reduced the chance of revolt. Assyrian governors were sent to rule the conquered lands and ensure the delivery of tribute. The central administration in Assyria was enlarged to supervise the conduct of imperial affairs, and effective means of communication were devised to keep the royal court informed of affairs in the empire. The army stood ready to crush all signs of resistance. It continued its brutal habits in dealing with those slow to accept the Assyrian yoke and to render tribute to the conquerors. Once this base of power was established in the Fertile Crescent, Sennacherib, Esarhaddon, and Ashurbanipal devoted their energies to dealing with outsiders who insisted on interfering with Assyrian rule over her subjects. Egypt was attacked and forced to accept Assyrian overlordship. The last remnants of local independence in southern Mesopotamia were crushed. Assyrian influences were extended into Asia Minor. Semibarbaric peoples in northern Arabia, in the Zagros Mountains, and in the highlands to the north of Assyria were beaten into submission. By 650 B.C. the whole civilized Near East accepted for the first time a single master, the great king of Assyria, "ruler of the four rims of the world," whose unbeatable armies had left no one a choice.

The Assyrian state, however, was not so strong as its size indicated. Assyrian terrorism had aroused a fierce, irreconcilable hatred among subject peoples, nowhere better reflected than in the writings of the later prophets in the Old Testament. Constant warfare caused a fatal depletion of Assyrian manpower and a consequent crippling of the Assyrian armies. Eventually they had to rely on levies from conquered subjects to replace Assyrian soldiers; the non-Assyrians were much less efficient. Some of the later Assyrian rulers were more inclined to enjoy the fruits of victory than to exercise the active leadership needed to hold their empire together. Worst of all, Assyria encountered the plague of all empire builders—enemies beyond the frontier, aroused by the threat of absorption. Assyria's enemies included the Medes, living east of the Zagros Mountains, Semitic tribes pushing into the lower Tigris-Euphrates Valley, and barbarians pouring into the territory north of Assyria.

Assyria itself began to suffer damage during the time of Ashurbanipal which mounted in fury after his death in 631 B.C. The Egyptians successfully revolted and caused discontent among the Assyrian subjects in Syria and Palestine. A Semitic group, the Chaldeans, raised the standard of revolt in southern Mesopotamia. Assyria committed most of her strength to checking this particular liberation movement, weakening herself beyond repair as a result. Then the Medes, who had learned a great deal by imitating Assyrian military techniques, struck out of the east. In 612 B.C. the forces of the Medes and the Chaldeans destroyed the Assyrian capital at Nineveh. Assyrian power vanished immediately, leaving her empire at the mercy of her many foes.

No one in the Near East lamented the passing of Assyria. The Hebrew prophet Nahum spoke for all the world: "All who hear the news of you clap their hands at your downfall. For who has not felt your unrelenting cruelty?" (Nahum, 3, 19). It was indeed a joyful day when men could join another prophet, Zephaniah, in saying of Nineveh: "All those who pass by her whistle and shake their fists." (Zeph., 2, 15). However, Assyria's bad reputation should not conceal her contributions to history. She broke new ground in trying to solve the complicated problem of creating a single state composed of many different peoples. Her attempt to create a centralized monarchy centering around a single ruler as the common factor in the lives of different peoples was destined to be imitated by others. Assyria had wiped out many artificial political boundaries that kept small groups at sword's point. She had at least briefly imposed a beneficial peace on the Near East, protecting it for nearly three centuries against barbarians who might have destroyed its civilization had they succeeded in seizing control.

Economically, the Assyrian regime had significant results. The Assyrians themselves added very little to Near Eastern economy, remaining simple farmers and warriors. Their own prosperity depended largely on plunder. However, the Assyrians encouraged their subjects to trade and assisted them by

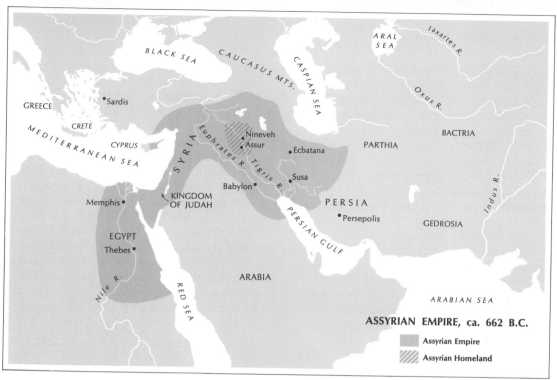

ASSYRIAN EMPIRE, ca. 662 B.C.

▨ Assyrian Empire

▨ Assyrian Homeland

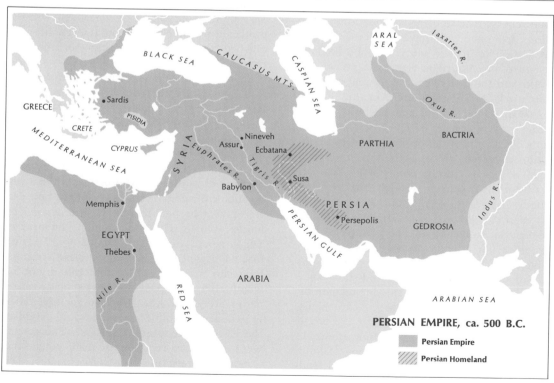

PERSIAN EMPIRE, ca. 500 B.C.

▨ Persian Empire

▨ Persian Homeland

The Assyrian and Persian Empires

breaking down barriers against the movement of goods. People like the Arameans, the Phoenicians, and the residents of the cities of lower Mesopotamia seized this opportunity: through their efforts, goods flowed freely across the Near East, and technical skills associated with the production of goods for trade spread widely among peoples still technologically backward.

In cultural activities, the Assyrians also made a notable contribution. Their efforts were not creative, but their imitations resulted in the continuation of cultural activity. This can be seen best in the fields of architecture and sculpture. Assyrian kings were avid builders, constructing the great cities of Nineveh, Sargonsburg, and Ashur as monuments of their power and glory. In these cities earlier Mesopotamian architectural styles were followed closely and thus kept alive. The temples and palaces were decorated with massive sculptured pieces and with excellent stone reliefs. The vigorous application of traditions from the past gave the Near East a new period of artistic glory. In the field of literature, the Assyrians devoted a great deal of effort to the task of collecting and copying older works in Sumerian and Akkadian. One of Assyria's kings, Ashurbanipal, built a huge library at Nineveh as a repository for thousands of cuneiform tablets copied from Mesopotamian sources. Most of the present knowledge of early Sumerian and Akkadian literature was gained through the copying done by Assyrians. Aside from administrative and economic records, most of the writing in the Assyrian language was merely a re-rendering of earlier literary works, especially the religious epics and creation stories so dear to the Sumerians. The Assyrians did show some originality in compiling annals recounting their innumerable military campaigns, thereby making a contribution to the art of historical writing. Of special importance to the future was their patient copying of large amounts of scientific materials derived from earlier Mesopotamian sources.

Assyrian religion was likewise strongly colored by borrowings from earlier Mesopotamia. The great state god of Assyria, Assur, was very similar to the Amorite Marduk. Assyrian rituals, prayers, and priesthoods are almost indistinguishable from those of the earlier Mesopotamians. Despite the derived character of their religion, there is considerable evidence that the Assyrians were deeply religious and that their society was animated by strong religious forces. Perhaps even their imperialism was motivated by a genuine desire to assert Assur's dominion over the gods of other peoples. In all these ways the Assyrians kept alive some of the most precious cultural traditions in the Near East, and their conquests helped to spread those traditions throughout a vast region.

2. SUCCESSORS OF ASSYRIA, 612–550 B.C.

Assyria's sudden collapse opened a brief but spirited era of competition for the spoils of her empire, and this struggle ended when it produced another empire builder, Persia, who crushed the other contenders for Assyrian power.

Egypt was one power that seemed destined to benefit by the fall of Assyria. Foreign rule had again had the effect of uniting her under a single pharaoh, Psammetichus (also known as Psamtik; reigned 663–609 B.C.), who founded the Twenty-sixth dynasty. Egypt was briefly characterized by internal order, prosperity, and international prestige, but she was incapable of meeting the needs of the new era. Her pharaohs had to rely on foreign mercenaries (chiefly Greeks) to man the armies. These troops, thoroughly hated by the antiforeign Egyptians, caused internal trouble. Egyptian artists and writers, too intent on worshiping the past to detect and reflect newer trends in Near Eastern society, failed to produce anything new that would establish the Egyptian reputation abroad. The priests were even more reactionary, using religion as a means of resisting necessary changes. Old age had gripped Egypt, making her incapable of facing new problems. She failed to capitalize on Assyria's destruction and was unable to check the rise of Persia. She fell to Persian armies with almost no struggle in 525 B.C.

In Asia Minor, the small kingdom of Lydia, which first emerged after the fall of the Hittites, was the chief beneficiary of Assyria's fall, and she quickly established control over nearly all of Asia Minor. The rapid rise of Lydia was especially significant in Greek history, since Lydia lay as a link between the Near East and Greece. During the reign of Croesus (560–546 B.C.), the greatest Lydian king, many Greeks living in Asia Minor were ruled by the Lydians. However, Lydian power was shaky, succumbing in 546 B.C. to one blow by Persia.

Still another contender for the Assyrian power was Media. The Medes, living east of the Zagros Mountains, had long been restless dependents of Assyria. When Assyria began to weaken, the Medes furnished most of the armed might to destroy her. Once Assyria was defeated, the Medes seized control of a large part of the northern areas of the empire and built up a vast state in the Iranian plateau area. However, the state was poorly organized. One of the Median vassal princes, Cyrus of Persia, succeeded in deposing the Median king and laying successful claim to old Median territory.

The most spectacular of all the successor states of Assyria was the Chaldean Empire. The Chaldeans were a Semitic people who had entered lower Mesopotamia while it was under Assyrian rule. When Assyria began to decline, the Chaldean princes led a revolt, representing themselves as champions of ancient Mesopotamian civilization. Once Assyria was destroyed, the Chaldean princes seized some of the most valuable parts of the conquered territory. Under the one great Chaldean ruler, Nebuchadnezzar II (reigned 605–562 B.C.), all of Syria-Palestine was joined with the Tigris-Euphrates Valley in a single empire. Among the victims of Nebuchadnezzar's conquests was the Hebrew kingdom of Judah, which had managed to keep its independence in the great days of Assyria by paying tribute. Jerusalem was destroyed in 586 B.C., and many of its citizens were carried off to Babylon as captives.

Nebuchadnezzar not only prided himself as a conqueror, but also as a champion of culture. In fact, the Chaldean interlude in Mesopotamian history was marked by a cultural renaissance strongly oriented toward the ancient past. Symbolic of this spirit is the story that one of the Chaldean kings had the ruins of ancient Sumerian cities excavated in a search for models for the rebuilding of temples. The prime jewel of this revival was the rebuilding of Babylon by Nebuchadnezzar as his capital. Its massive walls, its beautiful temples and palaces, its fabulous hanging gardens, and its impressive sculpture and painting made it one of the most splendid cities of the ancient world. Even the redoubtable Hebrew prophet Jeremiah, amid his lamentations over the calamities that had befallen his people at the hands of Nebuchadnezzar, had to admit that "Babylon was a golden cup in the hands of Yahweh, she made the whole world drunk" (Jer., 51, 7). The religious revival of the period was especially intense and brought all the ancient Mesopotamian gods, but above all Marduk, again to the center of the stage.

Nonetheless, Nebuchadnezzar's empire was not strong. It was guilty of worshiping the past, and its military resources were limited. Nebuchadnezzar's heirs were weak and little interested in political problems, and when the Persians captured Babylon in 539 B.C., the Chaldean state collapsed immediately.

3. THE PERSIAN EMPIRE, 550–328 B.C.

The final victory in the competition to succeed Assyria fell to a people who hardly seemed in the running—the Persians. The Persians were of Indo-European origin, their ancestors having migrated to the Near East about 2000 B.C. from north of the Black Sea as a part of the wave of Indo-Europeans that descended on the ancient Near East at the beginning of the second millennium. The original Persians settled in the barren plateau of Iran, becoming simple farmers and herders. For many centuries they maintained their own political independence. During these long years, civilizing influences penetrated Persian society, especially from Assyria, so that the Persians began to be drawn into the orbit of the cosmopolitan civilization emerging in the Near East. However, they did retain significant aspects of their old Indo-European pattern of life, especially in religion and language. These ties with their ancient past made the Persians the most distinctively Indo-European of all the peoples who intruded themselves into the ancient Near East prior to the coming of the Greeks. In the seventh century they were forced to accept the overlordship of the Medes, who were closely akin to them in language and culture. In 550 B.C. the Persians suddenly reversed this situation. Their king, Cyrus, overthrew the Median king and began to call himself "king of the Medes and the Persians." This event launched the Persians on their spectaular career as masters of the Near East.

Cyrus' accession to power resulted immediately in a rapid extension of Persia's boundaries. Cyrus (550–529 B.C.) and his successors, Cambyscs (529–522 B.C.) and Darius (521–486 B.C.), destroyed all other powers in the Near East. Cyrus was the most successful conqueror. His first victory was over Lydia, the key to control of all Asia Minor. He then conquered the Chaldean Empire, which made him master of the Tigris-Euphrates Valley and of Syria and Palestine. During his last years he subdued various nations in eastern Iran, pushing Persian power to the borders of India. Cambyses conquered Egypt. Darius pushed Persian power into Europe by conquering a territory west of the Black Sea. However, his expansion into Europe was checked by the Greeks in 490 B.C. in a war we shall describe later. When Darius died in 486 B.C., the Persian Empire stretched from the Aegean and Mediterranean seas to India and from the mountains bounding the Near East on the north to far south in the Nile Valley.

It was one of the largest empires ever created.

The first rulers were intelligent statesmen as well as conquerors. Their statesmanship laid the basis for sound government of their huge empire. Cyrus established a good reputation for Persian rule by practicing a policy of tolerance toward defeated people. He avoided slaughtering captured kings, preferring to proclaim himself the legitimate successor of the conquered local dynasty. Especially meaningful was the respect he showed for the religious systems of his conquered subjects, making their gods his own and contributing to their worship with his resources. It was even said that the god Marduk sought him out to rule the Chaldeans because that god was angry at the misdeeds of the Chaldean rulers. He earned himself a hero's role by allowing the Hebrew exiles to return to Jerusalem to rebuild the temple of Yahweh. These actions convinced most peoples in the Near East that the Persians did not intend to continue the terrorism and brutality of the Assyrians.

Darius was the most constructive of the Achaemenid dynasty, as this line of rulers was called. Borrowing from old ideas and practices in government and adapting them to the new situation, he laid the basis for one of the great political systems of all history. He established himself as absolute ruler, taking the title "king of kings." In this capacity he claimed full authority to make laws, to judge, and to command the services of his subjects. At his court in the capital cities of Ecbatana, Susa, and Persepolis, he created a magnificent court etiquette intended to impress upon everyone that he was lord of the earth. He surrounded his position with powerful religious sanctions, claiming that he was the representative of the great Persian god, Ahura-Mazda, divinely selected to rule all men. Darius gathered around him numerous officials and servants, assigning to each a specific task. These servants, usually of Median or Persian origin, became a kind of aristocracy fanatically devoted to the maintenance of Persian power.

Darius' greatest political innovation lay in the techniques he devised for ruling widely scattered possessions inhabited by many different peoples. He divided his empire into twenty large districts, called *satrapies*. Over each he appointed a governor, usually a Persian and often a member of the royal family, who was given power sufficient to make him a king in his own right. The governors, called *satraps*, were removable at the will of the great king and were held strictly accountable for the administration of their districts. Darius and his successors made it their main business to supervise carefully the conduct of the satraps. An excellent road system was developed binding the satrapies to the capital, and a constant stream of correspondence flowed to and from the royal court, carried by a royal postal system. Periodically Darius sent out inspectors to investigate the administration and report to the king. Spies in the pay of the king swarmed through the empire to keep him informed. Contingents of the royal army under trusted commanders were garrisoned in strategic spots, ready to strike down a rebellious governor. Careful records of taxation were kept at the capital as a means of accounting for each governor's administration. By these methods Darius managed to create twenty semi-independent governments and still keep an eye on each in a fashion that coordinated and unified policy over the whole empire.

In the final analysis, the armed forces of Darius were the key to his power. The Persian army was built around a corps of professional soldiers recruited from the Persians and the Medes. These elite soldiers, sometimes called the Immortals, were given special treatment and were usually fanatically devoted to the king. The army was rounded out by contingents supplied by the conquered peoples as part of their obligations to their king. The quality of these levies left much to be desired; often they deserted at the height of a battle. But they could be recruited in such vast numbers that they made the Persian armies awe-inspiring. The Persians also com-

manded excellent naval forces, composed largely of hired Phoenician, Egyptian, and Greek ships and crews. In view of this armed might, very few peoples were willing to challenge the Persian king. In a real sense, peace reigned within his boundaries.

Darius' imperial system endured about 150 years. The history of Persia after his death contains very few events worthy of our attention. There were wars with outsiders. Because the Persians seldom won these wars, their empire did not increase; on the other hand, they did not lose much territory. Rebellions occurred within the empire, only to be smashed eventually by the superior power of the king. Perhaps the most significant aspect of this period was the slow erosion of the royal power. The Persian royal family declined in vigor and political intelligence. This was a fatal blow because the empire depended so greatly on the ability of one man. The court became corrupt, torn by conspiracy and intrigue among the friends and officials of the king. Several later Persian kings spent more time trying to survive the plots of their many wives and children and their ambitious servants than administering their empire. The satraps could not resist the temptation to overthrow the king. Often they raised a rebellion by putting themselves forward as champions of subject peoples within the empire or by promising great rewards to anyone who would follow them against the king.[1] The only protection against these rebellions was rigid control over the satraps, which the Persian kings were unable to maintain. With the passage of time the Persian army declined in power, still another fatal weakness. By the middle of the fourth century B.C., all that was needed to destroy Persian power was a strong attack from the outside. This attack was soon forthcoming, led by a Macedonian king, Alexander the Great, who was driven in part

---

[1] A good example of this is recounted in the Greek historian Xenophon's *Anabasis*, where the harrowing adventures of ten thousand Greeks who joined a Persian satrap to march from Asia Minor to Ecbatana are described.

by an urge to destroy the Persian menace that had haunted the Greeks since the reign of Darius the Great. Alexander's military genius, coupled with the Persian debility, allowed him to take possession of the whole Persian Empire before his untimely death in 323 B.C.

The Persians, emerging suddenly to mastery of the Near East and confronted constantly with the problem of holding their empire together, devoted most of their talents to administrative and military affairs. As a consequence, their contributions to cultural development in the Near East were not spectacular. In general, they played a role similar to that of the Assyrians, borrowing from the cultural treasure that already existed. They utilized already-existent written languages, especially Aramean, for administrative purposes. The Persian kings were lavish in their patronage of the arts, the results showing chiefly in the royal palaces built at Susa, Persepolis, and Ecbatana. They continued the Assyrian practice of commissioning artists to render in stone pictorial records of their military exploits. The Persians welcomed in their cities men who were schooled in the literary and scientific traditions of the past, and thereby helped to keep alive ancient traditions.

One of the most admirable characteristics of Persian rule was the tolerant attitude held by the Persians toward the many different cultural elements in their empire. They avoided any attempts to smother local differences, and even lent their aid to the support of local institutions as long as their subjects refrained from political revolt. Under Persian rule the Near East remained culturally alive. This fact is of inestimable importance in the history of Western civilization, because it was from the Persians that the Greeks derived and transmitted westward a knowledge of many ancient Near Eastern ideas and institutions.

In spite of their lack of brilliance in cultural affairs, the Persians did make one outstanding contribution to Near Eastern history. They created a new religion, Zoroastrianism, and aided in the spread of some of its ideas. The origins of Zoroastrianism are difficult to discern, since the religion developed over a long period of time. Its beginnings seem certainly to have rested on the original beliefs held by the Persians before they became the rulers of the Near East. Early Persian religion centered around the worship of several gods who represented forces of nature, including especially a god of the sky and a god of fire. Along with the chief gods, the ancient Persians believed in innumerable lesser spirits who were capable of doing both good and evil. A complicated ritual, including sacrifices, magic, and prayer, had developed as a means of winning the favor of the gods and the spirits. A group of priests called the Magi played a prominent role in the early religious life of the Persians.

Out of this setting came one of history's great religious reformers, Zoroaster (Zarathustra in the Persian language), a worthy member of that potent breed of men who by the vigor and freshness of their insights into man's spiritual nature have left an imprint on other men's minds more indelible than many who have wielded more power. Legend has

so clouded Zoroaster's career that it is virtually impossible to speak with certainty of his activities and teachings. It seems likely that he lived in the seventh or sixth century before Christ, prior to the emergence of the Persians as masters of the Near East. According to tradition, he spent the early part of his life in contemplation in the desert, finally receiving a revelation of the true way from Ahura, the god of the sky who had long been among the chief deities worshiped by the Persians. Fortified by his new vision of the truth, Zoroaster returned to the world as a preacher urging all to become converts to his beliefs. At first he enjoyed little success and even suffered persecution, but eventually he began to win adherents, among whom were some princes, perhaps even the father of Darius the Great. This success implanted his religion in Persian society just prior to the emergence of Persia as a world power and launched the new faith on its long career as a major force among the world's religions.

Zoroaster's exact teachings have become as blurred by the passing centuries as are the details of his life. The essence of his religion is contained in a sacred book called the Avesta. It was compiled over many centuries: Only very small parts of it can be identified as Zoroaster's own teachings; the bulk of it represents interpretations and refinements of the original core of doctrines he proclaimed. It seems certain that Zoroaster cast his new message in terms of a protest against existing religious beliefs among the Persians. He was a purifier of the old system, which meant that the new religion was rooted in the old. The central tenet of the new faith was a repudiation of the old polytheistic system and the superstitions surrounding it. Zoroaster preached monotheism, insisting that Ahura was the only god. Ahura was characterized as

The ruins of Persepolis, once the governmental seat of some of the most powerful rulers of the ancient world, the Persian kings. The magnificent stairway led to a great royal audience hall. *Photo: Josephine Powell* the sublime, all-powerful, all-pervading lord of creation whose wisdom was so all-embracing that he was named Ahura-Mazda (Lord of Wisdom). In his monotheism Zoroaster resembles some of the Hebrew prophets whose concepts of the divine nature were taking final shape at about the same time. The good and benevolent spirit of Ahura-Mazda presides over human destiny, emanating such qualities as justice, pure thought, integrity, devotion, good intentions, and immortality; these qualities are but other names for Ahura-Mazda, who embraces all good and all light. But—and this became a key idea in Zoroastrianism—the good spirit of Ahura-Mazda does not prevail unchallenged. Opposed is the diabolical spirit of evil, called Ahriman, struggling to blot out justice, light, wisdom, and good. The warfare between good and evil, going on since the beginning of the world, constitutes the essence of existence. Eventually, in a final day of judgment, Ahura-Mazda will prevail, but in the meantime, the conflict will continue to rage. It extends into the very souls of men, demanding that each individual choose whether to join the good or the evil. On the final day of reckoning, those who had chosen good would be rewarded with perfection and eternal happiness, while those who had elected the way of Ahriman would be damned to eternal misery. This concept of dualism became one of the most fertile grounds for discussion in Zoroastrianism and produced a rich vein of spiritual speculation in later centuries.

By postulating the goodness of Ahura-Mazda and the evil of Ahriman as fundamental to the cosmos, Zoroaster made man's basic obligation clear. Only good conduct could win favor in the eyes of Ahura-Mazda. The worship of the old gods, magic, and sacrifices were irrelevant to the basic issue and constituted surrender to evil because they diverted attention from the fundamental problem of doing good in a positive way. Zoroaster spelled out a vigorous moral code for his followers, derived in its particulars from the qualities of goodness surrounding Ahura-Mazda. Men must tell the truth, keep their vows, think pure thoughts, obey their rulers, help their fellow-men, and perform their daily duties as well as possible. Zoroaster likewise set forth a clear concept of sin, again spelled out in specific terms. Man's choice was between these two paths. The choice was an individual one, and the proof of right choice was revealed only in individual conduct. For it was in the souls of individual men that the decisive battle was fought. Thus there was no need for priests, elaborate rituals, or magical practices. Certainly none of the religions in the world that the Persians were soon to rule, with the exception of Judaism, placed such emphasis on ethical issues—and not even Judaism placed the ethical burden so squarely on each individual man. Zoroaster did not associate goodness and righteousness with a particular chosen people; his message was aimed at all mankind.

Although the record is again vague, it appears that Zoroaster's religion took hold among the Persians and the Medes after the prophet's death and that it became in some fashion the official religion of the rulers of the Achaemenid dynasty at least from the time of Darius the Great onward. But it appears equally clear that the Zoroastrianism of the Persian Empire was not the religion proclaimed by Zoroaster. The Avesta shows that at an early date profound changes occurred in the religion. Some historians have argued that these changes represent a debasement of the prophet's message; almost all agree that the change was brought about by the intrusion of many of the elements of pre-Zoroastrian Persian religion into the framework of thought shaped by the great teacher. Perhaps the architects of the transformation were the Magi, the old priesthood Zoroaster had condemned who now returned as converts to bend the message of the purifier. Ritual practices aimed at pleasing Ahura-Mazda and warding off Ahriman's evil influences grew increasingly prominent. This development tended to blur the ethical principles so central to Zoroaster's original teachings.

Polytheism crept back into religious life.

Ahriman was elevated to the status of a god, standing equal to Ahura-Mazda in the cosmic order. Many of the old gods appeared again as allies of either Ahura-Mazda or Ahriman. Hosts of angels and devils joined the eternal war between good and evil; the urge to placate these spirits provided fertile ground for superstition and magic and diverted attention from doing good. The whole concept of the struggle between good and evil tended to encourage the association of good with purely spiritual things and evil with material things. This version of dualism had the effect of belittling the practice of virtue in everyday life in the world and of emphasizing flight from the world to a secluded life. These new currents working in Zoroastrianism dulled the sharp edge of monotheism and ethical purity and drew the religion back toward the accustomed patterns of ancient Near Eastern religions. Perhaps this was the only way the exalted concepts of Zoroaster could be made appealing and understandable to ordinary mortals, who have always found it difficult to rise to the level of great prophets.

The conquest of the Persian Empire by Alexander the Great represented a setback for Zoroastrianism. Although the Achaemenid dynasty had never been fanatical in its support of Zoroastrianism, still it was the official religion and it suffered from that association when the dynasty collapsed. The general policy of tolerance in the empire had meant that other faiths in the ancient Near East had maintained their hold, and thus Zoroastrianism did not have a very large base in the Persian Empire. In spite of this defeat—and others in the future—Zoroastrianism survives today; its modern adherents, called Parsees, are centered chiefly in Iran and India. During the twenty-five centuries of its existence it has not only satisfied its adherents, but it has powerfully affected other religions, including Judaism, Christianity, and Islam.

The ignominious end of the Persian Empire must not detract from its historical importance. The enlightened and tolerant rule of the Achaemenids had finally built a universal empire in the ancient Near East, one that brought all kinds of people at many levels of civilization into a viable community. The benevolent, cosmopolitan spirit of the Persians permitted the local, native elements of this world to persist while encouraging and providing instruments through which all could mix and fertilize each other. The resulting amalgam was a fitting climax to a long chapter in history.

Suggested Reading

Assyrians. Since Assyrian history is often considered an extension of the history of the lower Tigris-Euphrates Valley, several of the books cited in the Suggested Reading list for Chapter 1 contain relevant material. Especially useful are the books by Roux, Oppenheim, Contenau, Saggs, and Hooke. The best work devoted exclusively to Assyrian history is A. T. Olmstead, *History of Assyria* (1923); it needs updating, however, in the light of recent archeological discoveries and new interpretations of old materials. The confusing history of early Assyria is adequately told by Sidney Smith, *Early History of Assyria to 1000 B.C.* (1928). André Parrot, *Arts of Assyria* (1961), provides an excellent guide to all aspects of art history.

Persians. The most detailed and best survey of Persian history and civilization is supplied by **A. T. Olmstead, *History of the Persian Empire* (Phoenix). More recent and extremely good is the material provided in the first part of **R. N. Frye, *Heritage of Persia* (Mentor); the work is especially strong on intellectual developments. An excellent study of Zoroaster's teachings and the development of his religion is R. C. Zaehner, *Dawn and Twilight of Zoroastrianism* (1961). A detailed study of the same problem is Ernst Herzfeld, *Zoroaster and His World* (2 vols., 1947). R. C. Zaehner in *The Teachings of the Magi* (1956) traces the evolution of Zoroastrianism after its founder's death.

RETROSPECT When in 330 B.C. Alexander the Great stood in triumph over the body of Darius III, a great chapter in the history of the world had ended. The Persians ruled a world that was old and tired, while their youthful conquerer was a fitting symbol of a new world, a world filled with vitality, emerging on the western periphery of the Near East. Before shifting our focus to that new setting, at least an epitaph on the civilizations of the ancient Near East is in order.

For the purposes of this epitaph, let us view the Persians as the last scions of a great family whose origins are rooted in simple neolithic villages and whose members include all the peoples whose history has been reviewed in the preceding pages. The first thing that strikes one is that this family had in the course of five or six millennia put together a great and varied patrimony for the future. The family fortune had grown especially rich after about 4000 B.C., when men had learned to exploit the river valleys and had adjusted their whole life style to that environment. Their treasure included impressive techniques for controlling large groups of people: absolute monarchy, complex tax systems, effective military establishments, organized bureaucracies, recordkeeping systems, legal codes—all representing great advances in government. These same peoples had devised effective systems for wresting sustenance from nature: organized agriculture, skilled technology, trade, transportation. They had developed complex social systems by which large numbers of individuals could relate to other individuals in an orderly and productive fashion. They had learned to enrich their lives through a magnificent art. They had devised writing systems and put into a permanent record descriptions of their daily activities, their thoughts, and their knowledge about themselves, animals, plants, the stars, and all other matter of things. It is indeed an insensitive man who can view this patrimony in all its shapes and forms without being convinced that the peoples of the ancient Near East were amazing creators, a testimony to the ability of the human species to turn the world to its own support and pleasure. Out of this ancient world had come achievements in government, economics, social organization, art, literature, and science from which all men of future ages could draw. And men of succeeding ages did draw on this treasury, and thus did not have to do over again what men in the Near East did so well the first time. In one sense, world history is a story of the diffusion of ancient Near Eastern achievements across much of the face of the earth.

But the Near Eastern patrimony was more than a jumble of things to be borrowed from piecemeal and looked back upon in wonder. The peoples of that area had interrelated the elements of their lives in a pattern that gave meaning to their actions. In a higher sense, the most impressive part of the Near Eastern patrimony was its intellectual component. Men in the ancient Near East had learned how to reflect on the human endeavor and the setting in which it took place. Their reflections resulted in an understanding of the human condition and a sense of its destiny. In the ancient Near East the integrative, unifying, sense-giving aspect of civilized life was supplied by religion. Religion penetrated every facet of life, providing reasons why things happened and justifications for all that was done. All the Near Eastern religions (except Judaism and Zoroastrianism) posited a universe totally occupied and completely directed by powerful cosmic spirits to whose demands men had to adjust in every facet of their existence. Men—even the most powerful—were slaves in this cosmic system, bound forever to repeat in their government, labor, prayer, sacrifice, art, writing, and thinking those kinds of actions and thoughts demanded to sustain harmony in the cosmos. If they acted the part of good slaves, then life went on; the proof that obedience to the established order paid off was the wealth and splendor achieved by the Mesopotamians, the Egyptians, the Persians, and all the rest. The confidence and sense of sureness this approach to existence generated was the vital spark pushing the people of the ancient Near East on to their accomplishments.

Viewed from such a perspective, the achievements of that world were magnificent. Why then did the society grow old and lifeless? Men have for centuries wrestled with the causes of the decline and fall of civilizations. Most great theories on the theme have been discarded soon after their initial expression in favor of newer theories. Here we cannot expect to do more than point to certain limitations on the pattern of civilized life that developed in the ancient Near East by way of suggesting some factors in its decline. The environment imposed a set of limitations, for aside from the river valleys the Near East had limited potential in terms of material resources. Technology imposed another limitation. We must not let the spectacular advances of the last century or two blur a basic fact: Technological advance through most of history has been slow and painful, limiting man's ability to expand his control over nature. The ancient Near East suffered too from the overpowering influence of the river valley peoples. What succeeded so spectacularly in early Mesopotamia and early Egypt became the model of civilized life for every people in the Near East. Although they benefited from imitation, those living beyond the valley flood plains became prisoners of modes of life that were only creative in a small geographical setting. This problem became especially serious when the direction of Near Eastern civilization passed from the people of the valleys to the people from the outside—the Hittites, the small Semitic kingdoms, the Assyrians, the Persians. Slavish imitation of the river valley pattern of civilization brought people to a certain point—and then stopped them from further advance. Still another limitation on the ancient Near Eastern world was its waste of human resources. It was a world directed by small elites who achieved wonders but who ultimately failed to call forth fresh creative talent. The social structure was too inflexible, too closed, to permit genius to break through from unexpected sources.

However, the greatest limitation on ancient Near Eastern civilization and the ultimate cause of its stagnation was in the minds of men. The world view encased in the great religious systems made it extremely difficult for men to use to full capacity their greatest asset: the power to reason. Instead of freeing men to reflect on the nature and potential of themselves and the things around them, the ancient Near Eastern world view required that men pour their intellectual energies into acts of conformity to the directive forces of the cosmos. Because rationality was smothered, men failed to discover themselves. They were reaching in this direction, as the Hebrew prophets and Zoroaster testify, but they never broke through the formidable barriers imposed by the assumptions upon which their civilization was based. Only someone outside their world still had the freedom to discover what man really was. When that discovery was made, the Near Eastern peoples had to surrender the leadership of civilization to others.

Here then is the epitaph of the ancient Near East: It was a world which knew men not well enough.

Part Two

Greco–Roman Civilization

1200 B.C.–A.D. 200

While the civilizations of the Near East were reaching maturity under the political sway of the Assyrians and the Persians, a new civilization was emerging in the lands around the Aegean Sea, especially in the Greek peninsula. The new civilization began to emerge about 1200 B.C. and reached its most creative phase in the fifth century B.C., when the city-states of Greece produced literary, artistic, philosophical, and scientific works that departed radically from those of the Near East. The great intellectual and artistic outburst of fifth-century Greece was nourished in a political and social order that was likewise revolutionary.

From its Aegean center the new civilization exerted a powerful influence over non-Greek peoples. The Greeks themselves propagated their style of life through trading and colonizing ventures that ringed the Mediterranean with Greek city-states. More significant was the role played by non-Greeks as missionaries of Greek civilization. In the latter part of the fourth century, the Macedonians under the meteoric Alexander the Great joined with the Greeks to burst out of the Aegean basin and overrun the old centers of civilization in the Near East. All across this vast area Greek ideas and institutions made a profound impression, and in the territory bordering on the eastern rim of the Mediterranean, the Greek way of life became supreme. In the third century B.C. the Romans, just emerging as a world power, became enamored of Greek civilization and turned their energies to absorbing and spreading it. The Romans eventually conquered Greece and the Greek Near East, but were themselves mastered by Greek ideas and culture. The empire which they forged became the setting for a further extension of the Greek pattern of life so that much of Western Europe and North Africa fell under Greek influence. Roman political genius combined with Greek cultural patterns to forge a vast community of men living around the Mediterranean and a civilization that ranks as a great achievement in human history.

In tracing the complex evolution of Greco-Roman civilization through fourteen or fifteen centuries, one should try to identify in an orderly way the main stages of development and the actors responsible for each new stage. One should try to comprehend the essential ingredients of Greco-Roman civilization, many of which became a permanent part of the total human accomplishment. But perhaps most important, one should grasp the extent to which the Greco-Roman world discovered and unleashed a new range of human talents and turned them to creative ends. To many historians, the key to this chapter of human history was the discovery and development of the idea expressed by the Greek dramatist Sophocles in his *Antigone:* "Many are the wonders of the world, and none so wonderful as Man."

Chapter 5 ❧ The Origins and Development of the

Greek City–State Polity

Greco-Roman civilization was born in a group of small, independent communities around the Aegean Sea. No one can understand that civilization until he understands the unique nature of these communities, which spurred their inhabitants to creative activities radically different from any that had preceded them. However, no city-state sprang full-grown from a void: Each was a product of long experimentation and sometimes painful growth. This chapter will trace that evolution and seek to reveal the nature of these communities by showing how they came into existence. After a look at the general pattern of development, a closer study will be made of Athens and Sparta as examples of city-state society.

1. THE ENVIRONMENT

Greco-Roman civilization had its origins in the setting provided by the Aegean Sea—the lands which surround it on the west, north, and east, and the innumerable islands which dot its surface, all blending together to form a geographical unit. The sea and the land merge intimately, so that no inhabitant of the Aegean is far from the sea, and none using the sea is ever far from land. The whole area is blessed with a beneficent climate, marked by mild winters and long, dry summers, which permits men to sail the Aegean in relative safety and to live on the land without expend-

ing great amounts of energy to clothe and house themselves. But it is not a region of overabundant resources. The topography, especially of Greece proper, is dominated by mountains, valleys, bays, and peninsulas which cut the land into many small pockets of tillable soil and create barriers against political unification. Only a small portion of the land surface, perhaps no more than 20 percent, can be put to the plough; the rest consists of hillsides and mountaintops fit only to feed a few animals. The soil is poor and subject to destructive erosion. It is not particularly suited to the cereal crops so vital to human well-being; the vine and the olive tree fare better. As the Greek historian Herodotus said, "Greece has always poverty as her companion."

This restrictive environment might have doomed its inhabitants to a modest historical role. There was, however, an avenue of escape: the sea. The Aegean Sea blends into the land in a fashion which provides excellent harbors. It is tideless, usually relatively calm, and has good sailing winds. It thus became a roadway for the Greeks out into a larger world from which they could derive wealth and fresh ideas. The topography of the Aegean basin is such that it opens avenues especially to the east and the north. This was an important factor at the time when the Greeks began to emerge as a significant group in history, because it drew them toward the higher civilizations of the Near East and subjected them to the influences of the Indo-European barbarians moving from the north toward the Mediterranean world during the second millennium B.C.

2. PRE-GREEK ORIGINS: THE MYCENAEAN AGE, 2000–1200 B.C.

Greek history in a strict sense did not begin until about 1200 B.C., roughly the time of the era of small nations in the Near East. However, certain events before that time set the stage for the emergence of the Greeks. Although the Aegean world was inhabited at a very early date by peoples with a paleolithic culture, the first significant advance toward civilization occurred during the fourth millennium B.C., when neolithic culture spread over the area from the east, perhaps brought by a migration of peoples. During the ensuing centuries, agricultural villages developed everywhere and a typical neolithic pattern emerged. The archeological record suggests some technical progress and increased population during this period, but on the whole the simple farming communities demonstrated no great innovative talents. The age is important chiefly because the basic population and the fundamental techniques of agricultural life were established as a foundation for later development.

About 2000 B.C. this primitive order was profoundly disturbed by the intrusion of Indo-Europeans from the north. The newcomers imposed their political system on the native population, and their language ultimately became predominant. However, the conquerors adopted from the natives the basic features of agricultural life, so that no radical changes occurred. For the next four or five centuries the history of the Aegean world centered around the activities of numerous agri-

cultural principalities dominated by aggressive warlords and their warrior retainers who demonstrated little talent for advancing their level of civilization.

But about 1500 B.C., there was a change. A series of great fortress-palaces was built in many places in southern and central Greece. The chief one was at Mycenae, and so historians speak of the emergence of Mycenaean culture. The driving force behind this development seems to have been the kings of the small principalities established by the earlier Indo-European invaders. They had increased their power and wealth to the point where they could afford great building projects. The key to their success appears to have been what they learned from their growing contacts with higher civilizations to the south and east. They reached beyond the Aegean world

This fine ivory carving, here greatly enlarged, shows a fiercely-visaged, helmeted Mycenaean warrior. *Photo: Hirmer Verlag*

as booty-seeking pirates and as traders and met the civilized societies of the Near East and Crete. From Crete, where Minoan civilization was reaching its apogee, came the model for a refined style of life. A great influx of Minoan technical skills, art forms, religious ideas, and political techniques swept across Greece, all reflected primarily in the elegant palaces built by the powerful kings for their pleasure and comfort and in the great tombs they constructed to hold their dead bodies. The kings commanded a centralized bureaucracy capable of imposing strong control over the populations of the kingdoms. A written language, which modern scholars call Linear B, had been perfected, chiefly as a device for recording the kings' dealings with their subjects. The decipherment of that language a few years ago furnishes proof that the Mycenaean world spoke Greek and that its people must therefore be counted as Greeks. Mycenaean culture reached its apogee about 1300 B.C. Although it had unique qualities, it was basically derivative. Under its influence the Aegean world appeared to be moving toward a pattern of civilization similar to that characteristic of the ancient Near East. The process of diffusion described earlier as the main feature of Near Eastern history in the second millennium B.C. seemed about to link the Aegean world to the Near Eastern one. Had this happened, the later history of Greece and the West would have been drastically altered.

Mycenaean culture, however, largely a superstructure imposed by kings and heavily dependent on tenuous ties with Crete and the Near East, lacked the vigor to advance on its own. The collapse of Minoan civilization about 1400 B.C., perhaps caused by Mycenaean raids, cut off a vital source of inspiration. The disruptive movements of peoples that afflicted the Hittite and Egyptian empires about 1200 B.C. blocked access to the Near East. The Mycenaean kings reacted to their shrinking world by turning their aggressiveness to attacks on closer neighbors, such as

Troy, and on each other. The decline of Mycenaean culture was climaxed shortly after 1200, when a new horde of Indo-Europeans called the Dorians swept through the Aegean world and laid waste the rich fortress-cities. Although these raids destroyed most of Mycenaean culture, it remained an impressive model of civilized life for the mainland Greeks, who had now to reconstruct their society without strong influences from the outside world.

3. THE FOUNDATIONS OF GREEK SOCIETY: THE DARK AGE, 1200–800 B.C.

From one perspective, the Dorian invasions were catastrophic, sweeping away most of the Mycenaean establishment—the kingdoms, their cities, trade, technical skills, art, and writing. The "dark age" that gripped the Aegean world lasted for four centuries. However, for all its retrogressive character, this age had another side. Cut off from external cultural influences, the invaders and their conquered subjects forged a new pattern of life. To some extent, this new culture was derived from the wreckage of Mycenae, but it was basically a Greek creation, and it was the foundation for later Greece in all its glory. Our information about the dark age comes chiefly from archeology, but at the very end of the period two literary masterpieces, the *Iliad* and the *Odyssey* of Homer, were set down as mirrors of the age and as witnesses to its vitality.

The Dorian invasions caused an extensive movement of peoples in the early part of the period, and Greeks spread to the Aegean islands and the Ionian coast of Asia Minor. Mycenaean culture had never embraced so extensive an area, so that the geographical base for Greek development was larger than before. A common language (with several dialects) spread over this territory, and from it emerged the highly developed written language of the Homeric epics. A common pattern of religion, clearly delineated in the *Iliad*

Early and Classical Greece

and the *Odyssey*, was a major accomplishment. A set of political, economic, and social institutions was shaped to provide order and security to life. The basic political unit was the small kingdom based on agricultural pursuits. Each kingdom was ruled by a chieftain who led his people in war, judged their disputes, and represented them before the gods. In marked contrast with the Mycenaean kings and with monarchies in other ancient societies, the kings of the Greek world had limited powers. A potent nobility played a crucial role in limiting royal power. The authority of the nobles was rooted in the powerful clan structure that grouped people into extended family groups which shared property and religion. As heads of these clans, the noble elders in each petty kingdom met regularly as a council to advise the king on matters of common interest. The peasants and artisans possessed an honorable status in each community by virtue of their membership in the clan structure. They even participated to some degree in political life through an assembly in which they could shout their approval or disapproval of the decisions of kings and elders.

Working within these tiny communities were subtle forces creating bonds attaching the individual to the community. By 800 B.C. kinship ties still provided the chief cohesive force in society. But already the members of the kingdoms were being drawn into another entity that transcended the clan. The communal bonds found their focus in the physical center of each kingdom; and all were so small that every citizen had access to that center. There the king's residence was a fortress where all could gather in times of danger. There temples were built in honor of the gods shared by the members of the kingdom. The same center served as a meeting place for the clan leaders when they gathered from their rural estates to advise the king. A market developed around the king's fortress. Little

Top: Sparta and the Peloponnesus
Bottom: The Dorian Invasion

by little this "city," called the *polis* by the Greeks, became the center of communal life. Those whose lives became increasingly identified with the *polis* became its "citizens"; *citizenship* constituted that total set of conditions which gave a man membership in a *polis*. Participation in military, religious, political, and economic activities centered at a single spot slowly ingrained in men's minds a sense of belonging to a larger group than their kin group, of pride in the group's accomplishments, of a share in its trials and triumphs. This combination of physical and psychological involvement in the *polis*, the city-state, provided the dynamic element in the Greek world. Its deepening in all men in each *polis* and its evocation from them of individual effort on behalf of the community supply the basic key to Greek development.

Perhaps the Dark Age produced another development as unique and important as the institutional patterns just noted, a development that ultimately allowed those who were slowly becoming physically and psychologically attached to the *polis* to do something creative for it. On the basis of Homer's epics and the artistic abilities represented in the pottery fashioned during the later stages of the age, one might venture that the Greeks had assumed a new mental posture. In simplest terms, these sources portray a view of the world that placed a high value on human capability and that took joy in human activity. Moreover, there shows through in verse and pottery decoration a sense of harmony, proportion, balance, and order, each the product of the exercise of one of man's special powers, his reason. Dare we suggest that, amid the darkness at the beginnings of Greek history, humanism and rationalism were somehow born, opening wide vistas to men increasingly inclined to serve the *polis?*

4. GROWTH AND DEVELOPMENT: THE ARCHAIC AGE, 800–500 B.C.

By 800 B.C. the foundation was laid for a new civilization; in the succeeding three centuries,

the edifice was completed. These were centuries of rapid change, for institutions and ideas became ever-more complex and sophisticated. The cultural, intellectual, and religious aspects of change will be treated later. Here the focus of attention will be on the development of the *polis*, on the economic and social forces that helped shape it, and on the strengthening of the bonds that attached men to it as citizens. However, it is well to keep in mind that changing mental attitudes played a crucial role in this development.

The first manifestation of change affecting the *polis* came during the eighth century, with the disappearance of kingship in all but a few communities. Monarchical government in city after city was replaced by a form of government in which decisive authority rested in a council of nobles. The execution of the decisions of the councils was entrusted to elective officials. The causes of this change, running quite contrary to historical development elsewhere in the ancient world, are obscure. Perhaps royal authority as reflected in the Homeric epics had become too tradition-bound to respond to new problems. Some historians argue that a military revolution replacing chariot warfare with the *phalanx*, a massed formation of heavily armored infantrymen, was responsible. The new military system called less for individual leadership than for purposeful action by considerable numbers of men who could afford the necessary armament. Here the landowning aristocrats were crucial, and they expressed their new role by assuming greater political power. One suspects that the growing political consciousness of the aristocrats, based on their long experience in advising the kings, was the prime factor in abolishing monarchy. Whatever the causes, the consequences were great in broadening the political base of the *polis*. Greater numbers of independent men became involved in the crucial decisions of political life in a context which placed emphasis on deliberation and rational resolution of differences.

Aristocratic domination of most *poleis* persisted at least into the sixth century B.C. During the Archaic period, there were few radical changes in the structure of government in the typical *polis*. However, under aristocratic rule, the hold of the *polis* on the inhabitants of each community continued to expand. Although they were often greedy and jealous of their power, the aristocrats themselves formulated during these centuries an ethos that emphasized justice, courage, loyalty, respect for the gods, and responsibility toward others. These were all basically civic concepts. The aristocrats began to lend their wealth and talents to the propagation of these ideas in art, literature, and education, so that other elements of society caught a sense of the larger community. Most important of all, the aristocratic masters of most city-states were ultimately willing to take political action to resolve basic problems affecting the whole population. In general, these solutions worked to strengthen the bonds linking men to the *polis*.

There were indeed serious problems in most *poleis*, arising chiefly from an economic crisis. As reflected so clearly in the lamentations of an eighth-century poet, Hesiod, much of the Greek world began to feel the pinch of severe poverty early in the Archaic Age. The causes of this situation were deep-seated and many: the basic poverty of the Greek soil, increasing population, aristocratic exploitation, and a newborn urge for economic gain driving men to compete for limited resources. In many city-states the aristocratically dominated agricultural system was gradually changing so that previously free small farmers were being reduced to dependency and slavery. Because it threatened to rupture the bonds attaching the common people to the larger community by making them helplessly dependent on aristocratic landowners for their livelihood, this trend could have spelled disaster for the still-immature *poleis*.

The danger was averted in part by overseas colonization. Bold leaders, often of aristocratic origin, and willing followers took to the seas in search of new land where they could assure their livelihood. Often these colonizing ventures were civic undertakings, sponsored and organized by the aristocratic governors of the mother city. Between 800 and 500 B.C. this burst of activity dotted the northern Aegean, Black, and Mediterranean shores with a large number of new Greek cities. These communities were not colonies in the conventional sense; they were independent *poleis* with their own governments, citizens, laws, religion, and patriotism.

More significant in resolving the economic pressures besetting the Aegean world was a great expansion of trade and industry. The colonizing undertakings played a part in this expansion. Although overseas settlement was initially inspired by a search for farmland, many Greeks began to exploit opportunities for trade between overseas Greek cities and the homeland. From this kind of trading activity it was but a short step to involvement in the larger trading world already mapped out in the Near East, especially by the Phoenicians. The Greeks proved energetic and enterprising, and by 500 B.C. they had become the leading traders in the Mediterranean world. Trade nourished a need for manufactured goods. Greek artisans, not averse to borrowing techniques and ideas from the Near East, responded to this demand with numerous superior products, particularly excellent pottery. Even the old agricultural system was altered by expanding trade opportunities. Enterprising farmers abandoned the raising of grain in favor of grapes, olives, and livestock, all of which found profitable markets overseas and in the cities where merchants and artisans were collecting in increasing numbers. For merchants, artisans, and commercial farmers alike, the center of economic life shifted to the marketplace in the city, creating new ties between citizen and *polis*.

The social structure changed under the impact of economic change. Some aristocrats became involved in trade and industry, either as entrepreneurs or as supporters of growth through political action. This development weakened the solidarity of the aristocratic class and bred disagreement among its members. Men from the lower ranks of society succeeded in amassing wealth through trade and industry and became rivals of the land-owning aristocracy for power and prestige. Small farmers, unable to engage in capitalistic farming and unwilling to become dependents of great landowners, left the countryside to move to the cities. This change dissolved ancient family ties, weakened the control of the clan leaders over the populace, and thrust upon public authorities the burden of controlling socially displaced groups.

These mounting tensions evoked from the aristocratic governments of most of the *poleis* deliberate political actions which had the overall effect of expanding the importance of public life and of strengthening the ties binding men to the *polis* as the center of their existence. Each city-state sought its own answers and each ended with a set of unique political and social institutions. However, a broad pattern was discernible throughout the Greek world.

In general, aristocratic regimes tried to relieve mounting tensions by means which did not require surrender of their monopoly on political power. They were "reformers" seeking to ensure justice, greater opportunity, and security to the populace of the *polis* without turning over to the citizens decisive political power. They enacted legal codes which defined rights and obligations more clearly and devised techniques to limit the arbitrary exercise of power. They encouraged overseas colonization and the expansion of trade. They granted relief to debtors and protection to small landowners. These efforts combined to make the *polis* more vital in the life and well-being of every citizen. Aristocratic concern for the lower classes and willingness to advance their cause by deliberate action was a unique feature of Greek political life, contrasting sharply with the viewpoint of the Egyptian and Mesopotamian ruling classes. The Greek aristocrats were undoubtedly motivated in part by economic self-interest and an

urge to retain power, but their effort to improve the city-state was perhaps inspired by another force. It was a manifestation of patriotism, born out of a realization in the minds of aristocrats that steps must be taken to retain the allegiance and services of valuable artisans, sailors, shopkeepers, and farmers who each in his own way made a contribution to the welfare of the *polis*.

As important as they were in strengthening the *polis*, aristocratic "reforms" were not usually sufficient to maintain stability. The growing attachment of men of all levels to the *polis* generated demands for greater political participation that the aristocrats were unwilling to grant. Usually force was required to unseat the nobles and set the stage for refashioning the basic political institutions of the *polis*. This revolt against the nobles was spearheaded in many city-states by individual leaders, called *tyrants* by the Greeks. Tyrants were often men of noble origin and great wealth, acquired in many cases by trading ventures. Usually, however, they had no definite political program. They were zealous for personal power and pursued policies that would ensure they held it. Once established in control of a *polis*, the typical tyrant struck at the wealthy nobles who were the greatest threat to his power. Nobles were taxed severely, sometimes deprived of their lands, and often driven into exile; most important of all, they were deprived of control of political life. Tyrants usually sought to please the poorer elements in society by creating economic opportunities for them. Huge sums of money were spent on beautifying the cities, increasing the people's pride in the *polis* and providing jobs as laborers and artisans. The tyrants exerted every effort to increase trade and industry. Although their political methods were brutal and oppressive, they did help to undermine the bases of the aristocratic power monopoly and increase the economic stake of the common citizen in the *polis*.

The period of tyranny was brief in most cities, chiefly because tyrants had seized power illegally and were incapable of carrying out the changes in political institutions that would prolong and legitimize their rule. The aristocrats who had been their chief victims took the lead in ousting them—but these victorious aristocrats were seldom able to restore their old monopoly. In some city-states, the nobles retained the actual direction of political life but were compelled to conduct public affairs so as to meet the needs of the total citizen body. In progressive city-states, the end of tyranny was accompanied by radical changes in the political system of the *polis* that allowed the total citizen body to take control of civic affairs and to decide for themselves what was in their best interest. With all citizens entitled to participate in government, the last knot binding them to the *polis* was tied. Their whole existence was now completely enmeshed in civic life.

5. ATHENS

This history of Athens provides a case study illustrating the process by which a collection of people grew into a democratic *polis*. At an early date, the region called Attica was inhabited by Indo-Europeans who settled in small agricultural villages in which clan leaders exercised a powerful influence. Eventually these Attic villages coalesced into a single unit centering around Athens with a king as the head of this enlarged community. In the process, Athens became the focus for governmental, economic, religious, and military affairs for all Attica, and thus the embryo of a *polis* which henceforth bore the name of the city at its center. The kings of ancient Athens were assisted by an aristocratic council of clan heads called the Areopagus. Some form of popular assembly where all citizens gathered together to consider public problems also existed, but its role was limited. For political and military purposes, the clans were grouped into four tribes, each of which was divided into three brotherhoods (*phratries*). Citizenship was established by admission to a brotherhood; and since strong kinship ties were the basis for society, citizenship was

therefore hereditary, dependent on clan membership.

About 750 B.C. monarchy began to be replaced by an aristocratic government. Elective officials, called *archons* (for civil affairs) and *polemarchs* (for military leadership), took over the functions of the king. These officials were elected annually by the assembly of all citizens. Only the wealthy of noble birth were eligible for elective office. The directive power in the *polis* rested in the Areopagus, composed of ex-archons who passed from elective office to a life term on the council. The Areopagus supervised the conduct of the *archons*, deliberated on policy decisions, formulated proposals to be submitted to the assembly, and served as the final court of appeal.

The aristocratic political system formed in the eighth century persisted with minor changes for more than two centuries. The nobles who directed civic affairs within this framework provided sound leadership which permitted Athens to grow in wealth and prestige. However, across these centuries there was mounting internal tension. In large part it arose from economic pressures, especially the tendency of the noble landowners to exploit and enslave the less fortunate farmers. And the increasing involvement of Athens in trade and industry caused shifts in the distribution of wealth and the development of new social groups not easily incorporated into a clan structure rooted in landowning. Within the governing aristocratic circle there developed factions whose rivalries sharpened tensions in the city. Ultimately, the aristocracy responded to these pressures by seeking to adjust the political system. Perhaps they were frightened into becoming reformers by the danger of a revolt. As early as 632 B.C., a noble tried unsuccessfully to establish a tyranny in Athens. However, the leaders of the reforming efforts strike one as men genuinely interested in ensuring justice to all citizens and in creating new opportunities for bettering the condition of the citizens—all to the end of making Athens greater.

The first notable reformer was Draco, archon in 621 B.C. Somewhat mistakenly enshrined in history as the giver of a harsh code of laws, Draco was in fact a reformer concerned with the administration of justice. His enactments sought to limit the power of aristocratic judges to oppress the citizenry through the courts and to increase the authority of public courts at the expense of the heretofore-powerful clan-dominated courts.

A more significant reformer was Solon, archon in 594 B.C. Although an aristocrat by birth, Solon was a man of broad vision, perhaps the result of his experience as a trader and perhaps also the result of his intellectual interests, reflected in the surviving fragments of his poetry. His reforms seem to have emerged from a conviction that Athens was endangered by aristocratic exploitation of the poor and by the lack of opportunity for many citizens to improve their economic and social lot. His legislation sought to protect the interests of the lower classes and to give them power to curb illegal activities on the part of the ruling aristocracy.

In his effort to aid the lower classes, Solon reformed the debt laws to end the vicious practice of enslavement for debt. Many who had been enslaved were freed, and some who had fled Athens because of debt were repatriated. He carried through legislation to reduce the power of the clan over the individual and substituted in these matters the public authority as the vessel of power to which the individual could turn. He initiated measures to promote trade and industry, including the adoption of a new coinage system and the recruitment of artisans from abroad. These moves set the stage for future economic growth and gave victims of debt and poverty new opportunities.

To provide checks on aristocratic abuse of power, Solon made changes in the structure of government. Previously, citizens had been classified on the basis of land ownership into two groups—cavalrymen and infantrymen—for military and political purposes. Since landowning was a family function, this system

meant that one had to be wealthy and of good birth to hold office and enter the Areopagus. Solon changed the basis for classification to income from land or other sources. Four groups were now established according to income computed in agricultural terms—500-bushel men, 300-bushel men (the old cavalrymen), 200-bushel men (infantrymen), and laborers (*thetes*). The highest offices of the city-state were opened to the first two classes and minor offices to the third; *thetes* were ineligible for office. The significant aspect of this reform was the opening of offices to men who had achieved wealth but were not of high birth. To stand alongside the powerful Areopagus, composed of ex-archons serving for life, Solon established a new body, called the Council of Four Hundred, made up of one hundred members selected from each of the four tribes. Its main function was to prepare matters for the assembly and provide recommendations on what action that body should take. Probably Solon intended this body as a curb on the assembly, which had great potential power; however, the Council of Four Hundred did bring new people into public service. To curb judicial abuse, Solon created a new court, called the *Heliaea*, composed theoretically of all citizens (including *thetes*) sitting in the assembly, but constituted in practice of a large panel selected from the total citizen body by lot. It was a court of appeal in which citizens had the power to correct abuses perpetrated in the regular courts. Solon's whole system of government was designed to prevent abuse of power while still leaving the operation of the *polis* in aristocratic hands. His reforms broadened the political base of the state somewhat, but they were not democratic. His main importance for later history lay in giving the public authority a vastly wider role in safeguarding the interests of citizens; to a much greater degree, the government was every citizen's government.

Solon's reforms were not sufficient to satisfy the Athenians. Strong factionalism, with noble families in the forefront, marked political life during the first half of the sixth century. In broad terms, the basic issue at stake was whether Athens would revert to an oligarchy—rule by a few—or move toward more popular government. The struggle opened the way for tyranny. Athens' first tyrant was a nobleman, Pisistratus, who finally established control in 546 B.C. after some earlier abortive attempts. He held power until his death in 527, and his sons continued the regime until 510. Pisistratus came to power by force, using foreign mercenaries paid out of his own wealth and the contributions of foreigners hostile toward Athens. His main political support in Athens came from the poorer farmers occupying the less productive hill country of the city-state. His chief opponents were the richest aristocrats from the oldest families, many of whom were driven into exile. Pisistratus and his sons made no changes in the constitutional structure of Athens, but they did direct the overall policy of the government toward safeguarding and promoting the interests of the poor in the *polis*. They promoted a foreign policy that greatly expanded Athenian commercial and industrial interests to the advantage of the merchants and artisans. They patronized public works and the arts with vigor, thereby providing jobs for many and making Athens prominent as a cultural center. Their strict monopoly on all political power imposed order on the city and gave the citizenry considerable security. The general effect of tyranny on Athens was to weaken the power of the aristocracy, to erode family ties, to enrich the city through commerce and industry, to provide new opportunities for those previously poor and weak, and to increase the prestige of the city in the larger Greek world. These trends made the *polis* more and more important to a growing range of citizens.

Tyranny was overthrown in Athens chiefly through the efforts of the aristocrats whose power had been curbed for thirty-five years; their cause was abetted by foreign help. But they had no chance to restore their old monopoly. Another reformer, Cleisthenes (archon in

508 B.C.), took the initiative in establishing a democratic regime in which power rested with the total citizen body acting through agencies to be described later. A member of one of the greatest families victimized by the tyrants, Cleisthenes seems to have been moved to his reforms by confidence in the Athenian citizenry and a realization that oligarchic rule would continue to breed factionalism and tyranny.

Cleisthenes' most important reform consisted in restructuring the base upon which political life was built. From the ancient past Athenian citizenship had been based on membership in one of the twelve brotherhoods (*phratries*) which were combined to create four tribes. These brotherhoods and tribes were ultimately controlled by the powerful clans which interposed a barrier between the citizen and the state. Cleisthenes abolished the political functions of the brotherhoods and the tribes, although leaving them their ancient religious and social functions. To replace the old system, he divided the whole city-state into territorial units called *demes*. All freemen living in a *deme* were registered as citizens, family connections making no difference. The *demes* were combined into ten new tribes. In forming the tribes, Cleisthenes divided the city-state into three regions—the hill country where poor farmers predominated, the plain which was the stronghold of the great noble families, and the coast where artisans and merchants of the city proper prevailed. Each tribe was composed of *demes* drawn from each of these districts; as a result, each of the basic units of political life contained a cross-section of the population. Each *deme* and tribe was a political unit in its own right with officials, courts, taxes, military forces, and so forth, allowing a wide range of opportunity for direct political participation by citizens at the local level.

Cleisthenes then rearranged the main organs of government to fit the new tribal organization. The Council of Four Hundred was replaced by a Council of Five Hundred, fifty citizens of each tribe being selected by lot from an elected panel to serve annual terms in this body. No one could sit on this council more than twice in a lifetime, which meant that over the years a large number of citizens would have the chance to serve in the body which played a major role in guiding the *polis*. The Council of Five Hundred, however, did not have the final authority. Ultimate power rested with an assembly made up of all male citizens over eighteen years of age voting by tribe. This body, called the *ecclesia*, met at least once a month and decided upon matters prepared for its deliberation by the Council of Five Hundred. Thus the citizen body, consisting perhaps of 30,000 or 40,000 males, had the final power in the state. The citizens were further involved in governing the city through the *Heliaea*, which remained as Solon had constituted it. Finally, Cleisthenes ensured popular control over the *polis* by introducing the practice of *ostracism*, through which a majority of citizens in the *ecclesia* could vote an individual dangerous to the state and exile him for ten years. Cleisthenes did not disturb the Areopagus. It continued to retain important powers, but it now lacked the authority to guide crucial decisions in the *polis*. The elected archons remained the executive officers of the city-state. They were still elected by the *ecclesia* and were usually men from aristocratic backgrounds. But now they had to win the support of the total body of citizens, each of whom was politically equal to everyone else. Cleisthenes' real achievement was to provide political equality for the citizens and to devise a way whereby a majority of them could decide all matters. This was democracy.

Cleisthenes' system of government was not much changed in later years. It did require some time to accustom the citizens to using their power to stop aristocratic conservatives and aspiring tyrants from trying to overthrow the democratic constitution; not until the middle of the fifth century B.C. did Athenian democracy reach its full bloom. The guiding spirit of this later era was Pericles, the chief political figure in Athens from 461 to 429 B.C.

Pericles was not primarily a constitution maker, although he did enact legislation which stripped the Areopagus of its last remnants of power. More important, he introduced payment for service in the Council of Five Hundred, the Heliaea, and the elective magistracies. This step gave the poor a chance to engage in political life without sacrificing their livelihood. Pericles' real importance lay in the encouragement he gave to citizens to participate in political life. Although aristocratic by birth and the companion of the leading intellectuals and artists of his day, he felt no fear in entrusting the political destiny of Athens to the common citizens. He encouraged them to discuss issues and to make decisions. His own exemplary conduct as a leader convinced nearly all citizens that public life was a dignified, responsible, and rewarding activity.

In discussing the nature of fifth-century Athenian democracy, one important reservation must be made. Participation in political life was confined to those who were citizens. The right to be a citizen was severely limited in Periclean Athens. Only those whose ancestors had been citizens could qualify for that precious right. Large numbers of foreigners (called *metics*) and slaves, who were not citizens, took no part in the political life of the community. Since metics and slaves outnumbered those who were citizens, a minority of the population actually governed the city.

6. SPARTA

Other cities followed a pattern of development similar to that of Athens, ending with a system that encouraged participation in civic affairs by all citizens. However, still other cities evolved toward different ends, as the history of Sparta illustrates.

Sparta was founded by Indo-European invaders who overran Peloponnesus shortly before 1000 B.C. The invaders first settled in many small villages, which eventually joined into a single city-state. By the seventh century B.C., Sparta was well along toward this unification. Up to that time, her development had been similar to that of Athens and most other Greek cities. In time she too began to feel the sharp edge of poverty, and at this point the Spartans made the decision that determined their future as a city-state. Instead of seeking new wealth through trade and industry, Sparta turned to the conquest of neighboring cities, enslaving her victims and forcing them to labor for her benefit. This policy posed a serious problem. Could Sparta keep her "slaves" under control? The Spartan answer was affirmative: Sparta could continue to live at the expense of her subjects if the Spartan citizens were made into a permanent army to stand guard over those subjects.

The reorganization of Spartan society on a military basis was attributed to a great lawgiver, Lycurgus. The new constitution was probably evolved over several decades in the late seventh and early sixth centuries B.C. Its most fundamental feature was the division of the population into three classes, each with rigidly defined responsibilities. First were the *Spartans*, consisting of about 5 percent of the population. This class served as professional soldiers, each member dedicating his life to ruling the rest of the population. No Spartan was allowed any other occupation. Next were the *perioeci*, a class charged with conducting whatever trading and manufacturing were necessary. Finally there were the *helots*, state slaves who served as laborers on the land or as personal servants. Membership in each class was hereditary, and there was little movement from one class to another.

The Lycurgan reforms prescribed a regimen to be followed by each Spartan to prepare him for his life's service as a soldier. At birth each child of a Spartan citizen was inspected by state officials for physical fitness. If the child was defective, the state ordered death by exposure. If allowed to live, the child was given over to his mother until he reached the age of seven. Then the males were sent to live in barracks, where military training continued until the age of twenty. The training was extremely severe, with an emphasis on physical toughness, bravery, obedience, and other soldierly virtues. The program allowed almost no intellectual pursuits in order that the Spartans would never be "softened" by excessive devotion to the arts, literature, or philosophy. Spartan girls were likewise rigor-

A Spartan warrior, famous among all the Greeks for his strength, courage, and loyalty. This small bronze statue, only about 6 inches high, dates from the late sixth century B.C. *Photo: Courtesy Wadsworth Atheneum, Hartford*

ously trained to become the mothers and wives of future soldiers.

When he was twenty, the Spartan youth became a regular soldier. He and a group of others—usually fifteen—formed a mess group, eating, living, and fighting together as a unit. Each soldier contributed to the support of the mess, deriving his income from a piece of land that the state assigned to him along with enough helots to farm it. A man could marry after he was twenty, although he was not permitted to live with his wife until he was thirty. After he was thirty, the citizen was permitted to take part in political life and maintain his own home. He was probably so accustomed to barrack life by this time that he continued to find the focus of his life there, leaving his wife to rear his children and to supervise his helots. At sixty a Spartan could retire from military service.

The helots and perioeci escaped this regime, but they too were carefully disciplined. Every year the state formally declared war on the helots so that any troublemaker could be killed on the spot. The perioeci had greater freedom, even being allowed to govern themselves in some cases, but they were rigidly excluded from decisions affecting the policy of Sparta and therefore never had a chance to push their commercial interests abroad in a way that would have allowed them to command a leading position in Spartan society.

Finally, the Lycurgan reforms provided a government for Sparta. Sparta always remained a monarchy, with two kings as the formal heads of the state. Actually the power of the kings was very slight; the real power was held by the *gerousia*, a council of elders, consisting of the two kings and twenty-eight other men over sixty years old elected to serve for life. This body formulated all legislation, judged the most important cases, and acted as an advisory body to the administration of the state. Decisions of the *gerousia* had to be presented to an assembly made up of all male Spartans over thirty. Theoretically the assembly had the power to repudiate any policy, but one can well imagine

that this assembly of citizen soldiers, peopled by men taught from childhood to obey orders and to let their superiors do the thinking, was seldom able to render an independent decision. The actual execution of laws was entrusted to a board of five *ephors* elected annually by the assembly. This small group conducted foreign affairs, supervised military training, policed the helots, and handled all matters of military preparation. Throughout most of Spartan history the ephors exercised virtually dictatorial powers, especially if, as was usually the case, they agreed with the thirty members of the council of elders. Sparta was thus ruled by an oligarchy of military commanders.

Once the Lycurgan constitution was finished, it proved effective. The iron discipline of the citizen body resulted in Sparta's possessing the best army in Greece, and by 500 B.C. she had forced most of the city-states in the Peloponnesus to join the Peloponnesian League. The member cities were allowed to keep their independence but were forced to follow Spartan leadership in foreign affairs, thereby ensuring Spartan predominance in the Peloponnesus and enhancing her power in all of Greece. The Spartan system also held the helots in check, for this class constantly threated to revolt but never succeeded.

7. THE CHARACTER OF THE POLIS

To ensure complete understanding of the Greek *polis*, one should look at the institutions of the two or three hundred other city-states that had been shaped by the fifth century, each of which conceived its institutions as excellent and as typically "Greek" as those of Athens and Sparta. Such a wide-ranging study would certainly highlight the infinite variety in the structure of the Greek *poleis*. In fact, discussions of the Greek polity often overemphasize differences, such as those so obvious in the cases of democratic Athens and oligarchic Sparta. The Greeks themselves spent much intellectual energy—and sometimes blood—debating the merits of various political systems. But more significant in the grand historical picture are the features common to all city-states which constitute the essence of the *polis* as an institution.

The city-states were all small, intimate organisms, embracing a territory seldom as large as an American county and a populace often less than that of a modern university. In each *polis* life focused on a spot—a town—familiar to all, where were concentrated political, religious, economic, and cultural activities bearing directly on the lives of all. Each made citizenship a distinctive and precious condition of life. In some fashion or other, citizenship involved direct and active participation in civic life. This direct, physical involvement was at once the highest honor and the gravest responsibility of the citizen. What the Greek historian Thucydides credited Pericles with saying of Athens can serve as a fundamental characterization of all *poleis:*

"We alone regard a man who takes no interest in public affairs, not as harmless, but as a useless character." The giving of one's talents in whatever form to the service of the *polis* was what made one a complete man. Whatever its constitutional form might be, the *polis* drew the individual out of himself, his clan, his calling, his class to make him a participant in a community enterprise. It made him, as Aristotle put it, a political animal. Active involvement nourished a psychological state in the political animal, breeding patriotism—fierce pride in and love for his *polis.* Every *polis* was then a pressure chamber compelling men to discover and exercise their talents in the interests of something larger, more enduring, and more splendid than themselves. As such, the *polis* nourished an intensity of life seldom witnessed in history and brought forth achievements which sometimes seem almost superhuman.

Suggested Reading

General Surveys of Greek History. Three excellent short histories of the Greek world touching on all aspects of Greek civilization are **C. E. Robinson, *Hellas: A Short History of Ancient Greece* (Beacon); **M. Rostovtzeff, *Greece* (Galaxy); and **A. R. Burn, *Pelican History of Greece* (Pelican). These rather straightforward accounts can be supplemented with great profit by two other stimulating works strongly marked by the personal interpretations of their authors: **H. D. F. Kitto, *The Greeks* (Pelican); and **M. I. Finley, *The Ancient Greeks* (Compass). The best detailed history of the Greeks is N. G. L. Hammond, *A History of Greece to 322 B.C.* (1959). Also thorough and excellent is an older work by J. B. Bury, *A History of Greece to the Death of Alexander* (3rd ed., 1959), recently brought up to date by R. Meiggs. A stimulating interpretation of the general sweep

of Greek history is also provided by Finley Hooper, *Greek Realities* (1967).

Mycenaean, Homeric, and Archaic Ages in Greek History. One of the outstanding accomplishments of scholarship in this century has been the reconstruction of the early history of the Greek world down to the end of the Archaic Age. A splendid synthesis of this scholarship is provided by C. G. Starr, *The Origins of Greek Civilization* (1961); this work is especially effective in utilizing archeology to reconstruct history. The complex problems of the Mycenaean period and its civilization are clearly presented in **A. E. Samuel, *The Mycenaeans in History* (Spectrum). More detailed and specialized is L. R. Palmer, *Mycenaeans and Minoans* (1965), which makes excellent use of the recently deciphered Linear B script in reconstructing Mycenaean and Minoan history. A work written with grace is Emily Vermeule, *Greece in the Bronze Age* (1964); this work does an excellent job of treating all aspects of early Greek culture. Also useful on Mycenaean culture is **T. B. L. Webster, *From Mycenae to Homer* (Norton). The Homeric world comes alive in G. S. Kirk, *The Songs of Homer* (1962); and T. D. Seymour, *Life in the Homeric Age* (1963). Enlightening in terms of weighing the Homeric epics as historical sources is **Denys Page, *History and the Homeric Iliad* (University of California).

The Polis and Its Evolution. The nature of the *polis* and the history of its evolution has long intrigued historians; thus there is an immense literature on the subject. A classic treatment that will serve as a good starting point for additional study is **Alfred E. Zimmern, *The Greek Commonwealth: Politics and Economics in Fifth-century Athens* (Galaxy). Another older work especially useful for its description of political institutions is Gustave Glotz, *The Greek City and Its Institutions*, trans. N. Mallinson (1929). More recent is **Kathleen Freeman, *Greek City-States* (Norton), especially good for the treatment it gives to cities other than Athens and Sparta. A stimulating treatment of the *polis* from a sociological standpoint is **Victor Ehrenberg, *The Greek State* (Norton). A brilliant recent work on the development of the Athenian polity is **W. G. Forrest, *The Emergence of Greek Democracy, 800–400 B.C.* (McGraw-Hill). Also useful is C. Hignett, *History of the Athenian Constitution to the End of the Fifth Century* (1952). Another excellent description of the Athenian city-state polity with emphasis on its democratic features is A. H. M. Jones, *Athenian Democracy* (1957). A good study of Sparta is **H. Michell, *Sparta* (Cambridge); also excellent is **W. G. Forrest, *History of Sparta, 950–*

192 B.C. (Norton). The vital role of tyranny in Greek history is described by **A. Andrewes, *Greek Tyrants* (Harper Torchbook).

Economic and Social History. An excellent description of Greek economic life is provided by Hendrik Bolkestein, *Economic Life in Greece's Golden Age* (rev. ed., 1958). Although broader in scope than the Greek world, still extremely valuable is F. W. Heichelheim, *An Ancient Economic History from the Paleolithic Age to the Migration of the Germanic, Slavic, and Arabic Nations* (3 vols., 1958–70). Older but still useful is **Gustave Glotz, *Ancient Greece at Work*, trans. M. R. Dobie (Norton). Social history is well treated by J. P. Mahaffy, *Social Life in Greece From Homer to Menander* (7th ed., 1925); and C. B. Gulick, *The Life of the Ancient Greeks* (1902).

Sources. Essential for an understanding of the origins of the Greek world are **Homer, *Iliad* and *Odyssey* (many editions; an excellent one is the translation by E. V. Rieu [Penguin]). An excellent picture of the stresses and strains in the economic and social life of the sixth-century Greek world is provided by Hesiod, *Works and Days* (many editions; a good translation is by H. G. Evelyn-White in the Loeb Classical Library). The Greeks were deeply interested in their own political institutions. Two works on this theme worth studying are **Aristotle, *On the Constitution of Athens*, trans. K. von Fritz and E. Kapp (Hafner); and Xenophon, "Constitution of the Lacedemonians," in *Scripta Minora*, trans. E. E. Marchant (1925). Plutarch, *Lives* (many editions; a good one is the Modern Library edition) presents short biographical sketches of Lycurgus, Solon, Themistocles, and Pericles which provide insight into the political life of the Greek cities.

Chapter 6 ⚜ The Failure of the Greek City–State Polity

In its full bloom in the fifth century B.C., the *polis* was a marvelous institution for spurring its citizens to expend their talents for the good of the commonwealth. But by 500 B.C., another facet of Greek society took the center of the stage. Even while the city-states, and especially Athens, were pouring forth the many-sided creative effort that marked the golden age of Greek culture, the problem of the relationships among them became more critical and difficult. Small, numerous, crowded together on a poor land, the city-states inevitably became rivals of one another. These rivalries were intensified by the fervent patriotism bred in each *polis*, a state of mind that made men Athenians or Spartans or Thebans or whatever before they were Greeks. A central issue of Greek history in the fifth and fourth centuries B.C. was the extent to which this rivalry could be controlled and constructive. Early in the period the *poleis*, under the threat of a formidable foreign enemy, seemed capable of overcoming petty jealousies and hatreds and joining in common enterprises benefiting all. Eventually, however, they surrendered to their parochialism, and destroyed themselves in what seem in retrospect to have been senseless internecine struggles. Here was one of those countless ironies that confront the student of history: the very institution that made the Greeks magnificently great turned out to be their nemesis.

1. THE PERSIAN WARS, 490–479 B.C.

Throughout the early period of Greek history, there had been wars among the city-states, but prior to 500 B.C., these struggles had been minor. The Greeks poured their energies into the internal development of each *polis*, colonization, and commercial growth. In fact, strong pan-Hellenic forces were operating to unite them. Most Greeks worshiped the same gods and gathered together regularly to pay honor to these deities. They held such all-Greek festivities as the Olympic Games. Moreover, most Greeks had a common language which became the vehicle for a literary tradition shared by all the city-states; the widespread popularity of the Homeric epics supplies an example. Common styles and techniques in art were widely shared. Some progress had even been made toward establishing political unions, such as the already-noted Peloponnesian League.

The practical need for strong pan-Hellenism was dramatically posed at the beginning of the fifth century by the emergence of the Persian Empire, which threatened to engulf all the Greek city-states. For nearly two centuries prior to 500, the Greeks had been increasing their commercial and cultural contacts with the Near East and had benefited greatly from this highly civilized world. Some of the Greek cities on the Ionian coast had even been drawn politically into the Lydian Empire while it was the dominant force in Asia Minor. But the sudden emergence of Persia after 550 B.C. created an entirely new situation in terms of the relationships between the Greek world and the Near East. The conquering exploits of Cyrus and Cambyses destroyed the chief political powers in the area and welded together a political empire greater than any that had existed before. Their expansion westward carried Persian rule to the shores of the Aegean Sea in Asia Minor. Several Greek city-states in this area were forced to accept Persian overlordship. Persian rule, especially as established by Darius (521–486 B.C.), was not unduly harsh, but it seemed burdensome to the Greek city-states, so long accustomed to independence or to the easy overlordship of Lydia. They resented the heavy tribute demanded by Darius and especially chafed at Persian intervention in city-state politics. The city-states in European Greece sympathized with their captive fellow Greeks, and viewed the Persians as a threat to the independence of all Greek cities. They became particularly alarmed when Darius invaded Europe in 512 and established his rule in an area lying north of the Aegean called Thrace. This expansion convinced many Greeks that Persia was intent upon conquering the whole civilized world.

Hostility between Greeks and Persians grew rapidly after 499, when the Greek cities in Asia Minor revolted against the Persians. The rebels called on the European Greeks for aid and received it from Athens and Eretria. Darius crushed the rebellion, however, and determined to punish those who came from Greece to make trouble in his empire.

Developments in certain Greek city-states in the ten years following 500 had helped to increase ill feeling between Greeks and Persians. One of the Spartan kings of the period, Cleomenes, was seeking to foster greater Greek unity under Spartan leadership. He was strongly anti-Persian and felt that the Persian threat, properly exploited, could help unite the Greeks. In Athens a sharp political struggle was in progress, centered in a broad way on the survival of the new democratic institutions begun by Cleisthenes, but involving more directly competition for personal power among ambitious aristocratic leaders. The supporters of the democratic program, now led by Themistocles, were openly anti-Persian, perhaps confident that an encounter with the Persians would demonstrate the vitality of the new form of government. The commercial interests, having sensed the city-state's potential as a result of the policy of Pisistratus and his sons and having grown steadily more important and aggressive in Athenian society, were interested in extending

A very early example of Aegean art, a marble sculpture showing a seated figure playing a harp. Found at Amorgos in the Cycladic islands, this piece displays a discipline and refinement remarkable when we consider the time it was probably made, the second millennium B.C. *Photo: Louis Frédéric–Rapho Guillumette*

The Persian Wars

her influence into the rich trading areas of the northern Aegean and Black seas now dominated by the Persians. Conservatives struggled to curb democratic advances and were not averse to exploiting outside intervention to gain their end. The supporters of the family of Pisistratus hoped for a successful Persian attack which would restore Pisistratus' son, Hippias, as tyrant. Hippias had fled to Asia when he was ousted in 510 B.C. and was still present at Darius' court. The open neutrality of many Greek city-states encouraged the Persians to believe that an attack on Greece might be successful.

Amid these worsening relationships, Darius finally decided to move. In 490 B.C. he sent a fleet bearing a moderate-sized army across the Aegean from Asia Minor, ostensibly to punish Athens and Eretria for intervention in the rebellion of the Ionian city-states, but perhaps to begin the task of conquering the Greeks completely. After destroying Eretria, the Persian army landed in eastern Attica near Marathon, probably expecting that pro-Persian elements in Athens would launch an internal revolt to open the way to the city. The Athenians sought aid from other city-states, but with little success; especially serious was the Spartan inability to deliver promised aid because of her involvement in a religious festival. Although outnumbered, the Athenians decided on an attack. Under the brilliant leadership of Miltiades, they mauled the Persian army at Marathon and forced it back to its ships. The Persians then sailed around to Athens, but by the time they arrived Miltiades had marched his army back from Marathon and was ready to defend the city. The Persians sailed back to Asia Minor. Greece had been saved, and Athens was the savior.

The Persians, preoccupied by revolts within the empire and by political disturbances accompanying the accession of a new ruler, Xerxes I, were unable to resume the war for ten years. The Greek city-states meanwhile felt that the attack would be renewed and made better preparations than they had before Marathon. Athens went through an ex-

tended internal crisis during these years, but finally out of the struggle came a leader whose talent suited the approaching ordeal. He was Themistocles, a staunch supporter of democracy and an astute politician. His greatest achievement at this critical moment was persuading the Athenians to devote a major part of their energy and wealth to building a fleet, an accomplishment made easier by the discovery of rich silver mines in Attica. Several city-states responded to Sparta's suggestion and formed a league in 481 B.C. They agreed to pool their armies and navies in a joint force commanded by Spartan leaders. Ultimately, thirty-one city-states joined this "Greek league"; it was one of the most impressive common undertakings ever agreed to by the individualistic cities. Despite this show of unity, many cities, especially in northern Greece, preferred to remain neutral or to surrender to the Persians.

Early in 480, Xerxes began to move his huge army. It passed across the Hellespont and moved slowly overland around the northern end of the Aegean and into northern Greece. The army depended for supplies on the support of a large fleet, a situation which made sea power the key to the impending encounter. The Greek league decided to make its stand at Thermopylae, where a narrow pass would allow the smaller Greek army to check the massive Persian forces and where the narrow sea lanes between the mainland and the island of Euboea could be advantageously blocked by the Greek fleet. It seemed that the plan might succeed. The Greek fleet fought the Persians, weakened by severe losses suffered in storms, to a standstill, and the Greek army threw back attack after attack in the narrow pass at Thermopylae. But a local traitor showed the Persians a trail around the pass. When the Greek commander, King Leonidas of Sparta, discovered what had happened, he sent the bulk of the Greek army south while he and three hundred Spartans fought to the death to delay the Persians. Once past Thermopylae, the Persians flooded into central Greece. Athens was captured and burned, although her citizens fled to safety.

At this point, Themistocles again exercised a deciding influence. There was strong pressure in the council of the Greek league to withdraw the armies to the Peloponnesus and the fleet to the Gulf of Corinth. Seeing clearly that the issue would be decided by sea power, Themistocles combined persuasion and threats of Athenian withdrawal to convince the league to face the Persians in the waters off Attica. In late September, 480 B.C., Themistocles maneuvered the Persians into an engagement in the narrow strait between Attica and the island of Salamis. Caught in a situation where they could not use their full strength effectively, the Persians suffered a shattering defeat. Xerxes, watching what he surely expected to be the destruction of the Greeks from a high promontory on the Attic shore, saw his campaign come to a disastrous end. Since the winter season was close at hand, he ordered his fleet back to Asia Minor and the withdrawal of his armies from central Greece, for they could not survive without sea support.

His armies spent the winter of 480–479 in northern Greece and undertook a new campaign in the spring of 479. This time a sizable Greek army moved out to meet the Persians and defeated them at Plataea. In the meantime the Greeks sailed boldly across the Aegean and destroyed what was left of the Persian fleet at Mycale. This was a signal for the Greek cities in Asia Minor to revolt once again. Xerxes could do nothing but recall his armies from Europe; the Greek fleet could now cut the path of escape in the straits. The jubilant Greeks had demonstrated their vitality against even so great a foe as Persia: By acting together, they had saved themselves.

2. CONFEDERACY OF DELOS

The Greek victories in 480–479 had been magnificent, but the Persians were still a threat; the source of their potential might had hardly been touched. This realization kept alive the spirit of unity among the Greeks, although leadership passed into new hands. The Spartans, who had directed the Greek league in the critical days of 480 and 479, grew increasingly unwilling to commit their limited strength to projects far removed from the Peloponnesus. They had lost heavily in manpower, and there was always the danger of helot uprisings. Athens, buoyed by her sense of accomplishment over the past decade and by the success of her democratic constitution, took the lead in summoning a meeting of Greek cities on the island of Delos in 478. It was quickly agreed to form the Confederacy of Delos, a voluntary league which was to last until the pieces of iron thrown ceremoniously into the sea on the occasion rose to the surface. The purpose of the confederacy was the continuation of the war against Persia. The league was so constituted that policy decisions were to be made by all the cities meeting annually in an assembly, with Athens executing the decisions. The members pledged to contribute ships and money according to their abilities. The treasury was to be kept at the shrine on the island of Delos. And the cherished independence of each *polis* was protected; no city-state was required to surrender its sovereignty.

The confederacy immediately swung into action. The Athenian statesman Aristides was entrusted with the assessment of dues on each city-state and did so with such fairness that he was called "the Just." Another Athenian, Cimon, was placed in command of the confederacy's forces, and enjoyed immediate success against the Persians. Within about ten years, all the Greek city-states in Asia Minor had been freed from Persian rule, while the Aegean and the straits area were cleared of Persian naval power. Athens was obviously the most powerful city in the league, but she conducted herself with marked restraint in her relationships with her fellow city-states. Cimon's policy was conciliatory even toward nonmembers such as Sparta, although some elements within Athens resented his compromising attitude. Seldom before or after did the Greek world present a more united front than during the first years after the victory over the Persians.

3. THE ATHENIAN EMPIRE

This happy condition did not last long—and Athens was responsible for altering the situation. As the danger from Persia receded, some members of the confederacy desired to withdraw. Athens was unwilling to allow this to happen. Her leaders and many of her citizens saw that Athenian sea power, developed to check the Persians, could be turned to commercial advantage. Instead of conducting herself as one among equals, Athens slowly began to convert the league into an empire under her control and to use its resources for her own ends. She refused to allow members to withdraw, used territories won by league forces to establish her own colonies, and forced cities not yet in the league to join. Members that insisted on withdrawing were subdued by force. The populace in democratic Athens demanded that Athenian interests be put first, and the people had their way.

Athenian imperialism reached its full tide with the emergence of Pericles as the leader of the city in 461 B.C. Pericles came to power in the wake of the downfall of Cimon, who had tried to restrain Athenian imperialism to a degree. Cimon appears to have been especially concerned lest Athens become involved in hostilities with Sparta, an eventuality that might overstrain her resources. In pursuit of this conciliatory policy, in 462 he persuaded the Athenians to send aid to Sparta, which had suffered a destructive earthquake followed by a helot uprising. When the Spartans rebuffed Athenian aid, the angry populace exiled Cimon in favor of the anti-Spartan democratic party led by Pericles.

Since Pericles was a convinced democrat, he pursued a policy he knew was popular; he was also an Athenian patriot who thought that Athenian prosperity and power were all-important. Once in power, he launched a two-pronged drive to spread Athenian influence. In Greece he used every method availa-

ble to force more cities into the confederacy under Athenian control. He supported revolts against nondemocratic governments, tried to entice the members of the Peloponnesian League to abandon Sparta, and used Athenian sea power to bottle up such trading powers as Corinth. Meanwhile, he renewed the assault on Persia, carrying the struggle into the eastern Mediterranean. In both offensives, Pericles enjoyed some success. But about 450 B.C. it became obvious that Athens was overextending her power, and in spite of popular opposition, Pericles arranged peace treaties with both Persia and Sparta. In a treaty of 448 B.C. Persia and Athens agreed to respect each other's spheres of influence. Persia promised to refrain from attacks on the Greeks in Asia Minor, leaving them open to Athenian control, while Athens promised to stop attacking Persian territory. In a treaty of 445 B.C., called the Thirty Years' Truce, Sparta and Athens reached a similar agreement. Sparta promised to refrain from interfering in the affairs of the Confederacy of Delos, while Athens agreed to halt her aggressive policy among Greek cities still free and especially among those in the Peloponnesian League.

These treaties left Athens with a considerable empire, consisting of about three hundred city-states in the Confederacy of Delos. She continued to collect tribute annually, although the Persian danger had vanished. The money was now used in Athens for whatever the Athenians chose, including such things as beautifying the city and paying the common people salaries for serving in the government. Athens forced many of the league members to institute democratic governments in the hope that such governments would be more manageable. She forced subject cities to use her money and her weights and measures. By any standard of judgment, she treated these formerly independent cities as her subjects. And she did this for her own profit.

The profit was indeed great and extremely beneficial to Athens. At the height of the Periclean Age, Athens had grown to a city-state with perhaps 400,000 people, about 160,000 of whom were citizens, and the rest alien artisans (*metics*) and slaves. The tribute money flowing into the city and the wealth from commerce made her richer than all others. A considerable part of this wealth went toward the support of the citizens, who devoted a great part of their time and energies to the public affairs associated with citizenship. Noncitizens, especially slaves, bore the brunt of the labor needed to sustain the complex life of the city-state. Large numbers of citizens drew their main support from payment for service in the Council of Five Hundred, the *ecclesia*, the *Heliaea*, the innumerable administrative offices, and the army and navy; such service was their life. Their experience increased their ability to conduct a democratic state effectively and profitably. The wealth from tribute and trade contributed a considerable share of the expenses of beautifying the city and supporting the artists and writers who made it the "school of Hellas." The master hand of Pericles guided this great city-state with sureness, purpose, and total trust in the citizens, and to his guidance the citizens responded with good judgment and restraint. But fifth-century Athens would not have been the jewel of Hellas had it not been for the price she exacted from her "allies."

The subject city-states, of course, benefited from Athenian domination. They shared the fruits of increased commerce and the security that came from the peace imposed by the Athenians. Still, their hatred for Athens grew steadily. Its source was political. Athens had usurped their one valuable privilege, political independence. She had become a tyrant, endangering liberty everywhere. Not many years before, Athens had inspired the Greek world to a heroic struggle against the Persians to save the independence of the Greek city-state. Now she was acting like the Persians. Even some of the Athenians felt the moral aversion that came with destroying the liberty of any *polis*, and raised their voices in protest. But the mass of the people, aware that the economic welfare of Athens was related to imperial power, overrode these voices.

Athens made no attempt to compensate her subjects for limitations on their freedom. They were not permitted to become citizens of Athens, and they were allowed no representation in the Athenian government. Since the Athenian constitution was based on the principle of direct participation by the citizens, the principle of representation was foreign to any Athenian and to most Greeks. Gradually, anti-Athenian feeling spread throughout the Greek world. These city-states now began to look toward Sparta as a champion of freedom. This was a rather strange development, considering Sparta's own record of domination over the cities of Peloponnesus. The anti-Athenian sentiment heralded a serious war in which Greek assaulted Greek, unmindful of the many things the city-states had in common.

4. THE PELOPONNESIAN WAR, 431–404 B.C.

The uneasy peace in the Greek world was finally shattered in 431 B.C. by the outbreak of the Peloponnesian War, which was born out of the increasing hostility against Athens. The immediate cause of the war was the success of a few cities, and especially Corinth, in convincing Sparta that Athens was violating the Thirty Years' Truce of 445 B.C., thereby threatening the independence of all Greek cities. Athens, still led by Pericles, was not unwilling to join the issue, probably feeling that a showdown was inevitable. She had a large fleet and huge financial resources to pit against the superior land forces of Sparta and her allies. Pericles was confident that the Spartans were incapable of mounting a campaign that would strike at the real sources of Athenian power—her maritime empire.

The first ten years of the war were indecisive. Athens began by pursuing a strategy of refusing to fight on land. She withdrew her troops and her population within the city walls, against which the Spartan armies were powerless. In the meantime, the Athenian

Greece 431 B.C.

fleet harassed the shores of Peloponnesus, seeking to cause enough damage to make Sparta and her allies war-weary. This strategy worked for a time, but a few years after the war opened, conditions began to change. The Athenian population, cooped up in the city, suffered terribly from a serious plague. Pericles himself was a victim in 429 B.C. The populace began to demand a bolder military policy and insisted that the Athenians attack the Spartan armies. A new leader, Cleon, answered this demand by leading the Athenian armies abroad. Sparta produced a general named Brasidas, who convinced the conservative Spartans that they must strike at the Athenian empire if they expected to defeat the city. Brasidas was allowed to take an army into the territory around the northern Aegean to help those cities willing to revolt against Athens. Cleon's aggressiveness was not especially successful. Athens did not possess the strength to defeat Spartan armies, and suffered severe and costly defeats, while the expense of the war was a heavy burden for the Athenians. Brasidas, on the other hand, enjoyed considerable success, although Spartans disliked sending their troops so far from home. In 422, however, both Brasidas and Cleon were killed in battle. This gave the Athenian peace party and the Spartan conservatives a chance to put an end to the war. In 421 B.C. a Fifty-year Truce was agreed upon between Athens and Sparta: Both contestants agreed to return to the situation that existed before the war. Great joy greeted the peace, although it was obvious to some that nothing had really been settled. Athens still had her empire and would obviously resume her former aggressiveness.

The truce lasted only until 415. Again, Athens was responsible for ending the truce. The populace, led by the brilliant but overly ambitious Alcibiades, resumed an aggressive policy toward other cities that aroused old fears among the Greeks. Athenian ambitions culminated in an ill-conceived expedition against the great Greek city of Syracuse in Sicily, where the Athenians suffered a disastrous defeat after a two-year campaign (415–413 B.C.). Even worse, her attack on Syracuse provoked Sparta and her allies to renew the war against an Athens seriously weakened by the Sicilian venture.

After 413 the fortunes of Athens declined steadily. The main theater of war shifted to the Aegean Sea, where the Spartans, brilliantly led by Lysander, proceeded to destroy Athenian sea power while encouraging the cities of the Confederacy of Delos to revolt. At the same time, Sparta allied herself with the Persian king, who supplied money and ships in return for Spartan permission to reestablish Persian control over the Greek cities in Asia Minor. Athens occasionally won an isolated victory, but the net of Spartan-Persian power continued to close around her. Finally in 404 B.C. she surrendered. The victors forced her to tear down her walls, to destroy all but twelve of her ships, and to submit to a government of oligarchs who were guarded by a Spartan army stationed in the city. Although these Thirty Tyrants, as the Athenians called them, were ousted in 403 and democratic government restored, Athens never recovered her former power. The mighty city-state that had united and led the Greeks against the Persians was humbled, the victim of her own attempt to reduce the other city-states to a subordinate position.

5. THE DECLINE OF THE CITY–STATES, 404–336 B.C.

The defeat of Athens in no way solved the problem of intercity rivalry. The Peloponnesian War, which left a legacy of deep hatred, had caused other problems as well. Trade, the source of much wealth, had been badly disturbed, and numerous areas of Greece had been laid waste. Moreover, in many cities the declining economic situation bred serious class struggles. Often the lower classes were prevented from stating their case because democracy had suffered a heavy blow with the defeat of its champion, Athens. Many Greeks, especially intellectual leaders, were pessimistic and sought escape from their civic responsibilities in individual pursuits, thereby depriving the city-states of the leadership they had enjoyed in earlier centuries.

The majority of the Greeks failed to realize what was happening. They persisted in engaging one another in fruitless struggles that merely compounded the problems. At the end of the Peloponnesian War, Sparta was the greatest power in Greece. Her conduct now was even more dishonorable than had been that of Athens. She pursued a reactionary policy of imposing oligarchic government on any Greek city-state she could bully into submission. When the Greek world protested her narrow and often brutal policy, she turned to Persia for help. The Persians were only too glad to assist her and thereby gain the mastery over Greece their armies had not been able to win a century earlier. Sparta's collaboration with Persia only increased the hatred of the other Greeks for the Spartans.

The resentment against Sparta led to a new series of wars. Thebes now became the champion of city-state independence. Under her only great statesman, Epaminondas, Thebes smashed the declining power of Sparta in a single battle in 371 B.C. Sparta, her proud citizen-soldiers having been reduced to a handful and her prestige gone, became a second-rate power. Thebes, however, was ill-suited to assume leadership in the Greek world. She established a new league under her control, but was never able to extend it to all Greece. She too succumbed to the lure of Persian money in the attempt to ensure her own supremacy, but even Persian assistance was insufficient. A new coalition of cities, led once again by Athens, inflicted a fatal defeat on Thebes in 362, ending her dominance.

After the fall of Thebes in 362, the incessant warfare went on. There is no need to follow these struggles in detail. None of the city-states was able to establish the predominant position that might have meant peace. Instead, struggles prompted by the smallest issues continued to waste human and material resources. The material wealth of the Greek world was still very considerable; Greece in the fourth century was perhaps richer than ever before, if the evidence of the numerous building programs and the private fortunes amassed is a yardstick. War pitting Greek against Greek ate up these resources and put the citizens of all the city-states under constant strain. Civic life was being sapped. The engulfing weakness and discouragement was especially dangerous at this moment, for on the northern fringe of the Greek world a powerful giant, the semibarbarous Macedonian kingdom, was casting greedy eyes on the seething turmoil to the south. And in the west in Italy and Sicily, where the Greeks had sired splendid and rich cities, Carthage and Rome were stirring.

Before dealing with the advance of Macedon into Greece and its tragic consequences, we must note that some Greeks became aware of the dangers involved in the intercity warfare and intrigue. They raised eloquent appeals for some kind of union that would stop warfare and protect Greece from foreigners. Some of them, like the Athenian orator and statesman Demosthenes, argued that Athens should take the lead in forming a confederation, but his appeal was not effective in view of Athens' past role as a head of a confederacy. Others turned northward and began to urge the Macedonian king to serve as the head of a Greek confederation. But this idea was also coldly received, since to invite a foreigner into Greece was looked upon as treason. In general, the movement for pan-Hellenism was a lost cause. The Greek city-states were too accustomed to total independence to surrender their sovereignty to a super-organization dedicated to peace and common action. Such great philosophers as Plato and Aristotle, who lived during the fourth century, vigorously maintained that only the traditional small city-state was fit for the Greeks. With this attitude, the Greeks did nothing to put a stop to their quarrels.

6. MACEDONIAN CONQUEST OF GREECE

The Greek city-states, incapable of checking their own struggles, grew increasingly ripe for conquest by some outside power. That conqueror rather unexpectedly turned out to be Macedon. Macedon had not had a particularly brilliant history before the fourth century. The land was poor and inhabited by unruly peoples who resisted organization. Moreover, the Macedonians were far inferior to the Greeks culturally. What little advance they had made was a result of borrowing from the Greeks. Certainly such a backward state was not viewed with any great alarm by most Greeks.

The situation in Macedon changed rapidly as a result of the leadership of Philip II, king from 359–336 B.C. Philip was a masterful political leader, skilled both as a diplomat and as a general, with a clear understanding of the problems besetting the Greek world and a grasp of the potential strength of his own restless subjects. Equally significant was the fact that he genuinely admired Greek culture and wished to preserve it. Once he became king, he turned his energies toward organizing his own kingdom. His first concern was the Macedonian army. Within a short time he welded his wild subjects into a disciplined, loyal, and well-trained army, and he spared no effort to secure an income sufficient to maintain it. The victories won by this force strengthened the loyalty of the whole Macedonian population toward the king.

Philip's own love of all things Greek, along with his personal ambition, soon drew him into Greek affairs. Finding the Greeks engaged in almost constant warfare, Philip used this situation as a means of thrusting himself into Greek political life. His money and his army made him a valuable ally for any Greek city engaged in a war with its neighbors. He was not above intriguing to incite wars in Greece so that his services would be called upon. Wherever he became involved, Philip ended with the upper hand, having isolated individual cities and then forced them into dependence on him. Gradually the confusion in the Greek world began to clear as the Greeks realized the strength of Macedon and as Philip's growing mastery made itself felt. Athens emerged as the champion of the Greeks against Macedon and tried desperately to rally the rest of the Greeks to that cause.

The struggle was one-sided from the beginning. Athens was actually ill-fitted for the heavy burden of leadership of the Greeks. Internal politics crippled her diplomatic efforts, and the Athenian population, constantly encouraged by demagogues, was usually more intent on immediate economic and social gains than on a struggle against a distant foreign power. The chief leader of the party that realized the danger of Macedon was Demosthenes, whose eloquent pleas to the Athenian population to wake up to the threat from the north can still be read in his *Philippics*. On occasion Demosthenes did succeed in persuading the Athenians to send aid to Greek cities besieged by Philip, but usually the aid was too late, and always too little.

Demosthenes' efforts to form a Greek union fared little better. Slowly Philip advanced, finally forcing the Athenian alliance to commit itself to battle at Chaeronea in 338 B.C. In a single engagement the last strength of the Greeks was destroyed by Philip's well-trained army. Greece lay at his feet to be dealt with as he chose.

Philip II, probably inspired by his deep respect for Greek civilization, treated his victims with extreme mildness. He did, however, end the old order in Greece. One of his first moves was to call a meeting of all Greek city-states in 338 B.C. and form them into a Hellenic league, formally called the League of Corinth. Only Sparta refused to comply, but she had sunk to such insignificance that no one noticed. Members of this league were theoretically entitled to complete independence, but in fact crucial restrictions were placed upon that freedom. No city was allowed to change its existing form of government, and without freedom to change its government a city-state certainly was no longer the city-state of old. The league held regular meetings at which each city had representatives to debate and decide league policy. Finally, a common army and navy were created, with each state contributing according to its ability. Although Macedon was not a member of the league, Philip required that the league sign a treaty of alliance with Macedon, thereby giving the Macedonian king an important voice in its decisions.

Philip dictated the first undertaking of the League of Corinth: a war on the Persian Empire, a goal most Greeks could approve. But he did not live to lead the union of Greeks and Macedonians in an Asian campaign. One of his own nobles assassinated him in 336 B.C., perhaps at the behest of his wife, who did not fully approve of Philip's lack of respect for the institution of marriage.

Philip II was certainly one of the most far-seeing statesmen of the fourth century. He was aware of the folly of the rivalry that had kept the Greek cities in a state of warfare for nearly a century. To end this, he used the superior strength of Macedon to force the Greeks into a union sufficiently strong to check the strife among the cities. By penalizing revolutionaries, he tried to discourage the endless internal struggles that plagued each city. Finally, he sought to divert the martial characteristics of the Greeks into a war against Persia. These policies mark a turning point in Greek history. Philip II has seldom been given full credit, for his son, Alexander, put into practice the policies Philip had conceived.

7. THE SIGNIFICANCE OF THE CITY–STATE

The fateful course toward self-destruction followed by the Greek city-states during the fifth and fourth centuries B.C. is hardly inspiring. It may seem that the history of this period involves a contradiction. Much has been made of the unique vitality and strength of the *polis*—but in view of its precipitous decline, could it have been so great an institution? There can be no doubt that the *polis* as an institution generated self-destructive warfare. It obviously limited the political capabilities of the Greeks in terms of regulating relationships among independent, proud, self-contained political units. But perhaps we should recall that man has always had grave difficulty restraining himself from warfare and from the destruction of his best handiwork. The generalization that intercity warfare was the nemesis of the Greek *polis* may be too obvious and too easy.

The study of Greek history in the fifth and fourth centuries B.C. leads one to suspect that the fatal flaw in the *polis* lay in the superhuman demands it made upon the frail creature that man is. The *polis* demanded of its citizens a willingness to recognize the problems

of others, to judge these problems rationally, to weigh them against self-interest, and to sacrifice self-interest in the name of a higher good which the same men had to define. Perhaps for brief periods men are capable of such conduct, but in the long run they cannot sustain it. The history of political life within many *poleis* in the fifth and fourth centuries strongly suggests that the root of the failure lay at this point. Individuals and classes could not sustain the rational, detached posture—what the Greeks themselves defined as the aristocratic view—demanded to keep the *polis* alive. They descended in human fashion to self-seeking and self-interest, and to irrational warfare. It was a failure of men, not institutions, that doomed the *polis*. The city-state suffered from what was perhaps the nemesis of the whole of Greek civilization—

An example of one of the finest of Greek art forms, the painted vase. Here Odysseus is presenting Achilles' armor to his son. *Photo: Kunsthistorischen Museum, Vienna*

too high an estimate of the capabilities of men. Eventually men were forced to accept the dictates of one man because they could not forever meet the political demands placed upon them by Periclean Athens or Lycurgan Sparta. Aristotle may have been wrong when he posited that man was a political animal; probably man is capable of being truly political only for limited periods and within special situations.

Whatever its flaws, the Greek *polis* was amazing, at least for a brief period. For the first time in history, large numbers of men were virtually compelled to rise above themselves to search out and put to work whatever talents they might have. The age-old system of masses of men bent before the will of a few masters was challenged and found wanting. In the typical Greek *polis*, it was demonstrated that even the most common man could do remarkable things if he had the freedom to do so.

Suggested Reading

Fifth- and Fourth-century Greek History. The general works suggested in Chapter 5 all treat this period thoroughly. An excellent detailed work devoted especially to this period is M. L. W. Laistner, *A History of the Greek World from 479 to 323 B.C.* (3rd ed., 1957). An interesting study of the Persian Wars is **A. R. Burn, *Persia and the Greeks* (Minerva). **A. R. Burn, *Pericles and Athens* (Collier), will help to evaluate the policy of Athens in the heyday of her empire.

Sources. Two great works were written by Greek historians of the period covered in this chapter; every student should read them not only for the light they throw on the history of this era, but as great pieces of literature. **Herodotus, *The Persian Wars* (many editions; an excellent one is the translation of Aubrey de Selincourt [Penguin], which pro-

vides a stirring account of the great struggle with the Persians and an insight into how the Greeks reacted to and looked at this epic encounter). **Thucydides, *The Peloponnesian War* (many editions; a good translation is provided by Rex Warner [Penguin], who describes the bitter struggle between the Athenian and Spartan alliances and provides significant reflections on the destructive impact of this war on the Greek world). Plutarch, *Lives* (many editions; a convenient one is the Modern Library edition), supplies short biographies of Themistocles, Aristides, Cimon, Pericles, Alcibiades, Lysander, and Demosthenes which will help in understanding the major developments of this period. A good insight into the tensions of fourth-century Greece is provided by the speeches of Demosthenes; a good edition is Demosthenes, *Public Orations*, trans. A. W. Packard-Cambridge (2 vols., 1912).

Chapter 7 🙰 Greek Culture

Our examination of the Greek *polis* as a political, social, and economic institution revealed it as an instrument capable of evoking from its citizen members intense activity, activity generally creative and beneficial, but sometimes destructive. We must now approach the *polis* from another, more difficult perspective. It provided the setting for one of the most creative cultural outbursts in all history. Living within its confines and interacting with others according to its rules, men were stimulated to modes of thought and expression that still seem amazing for their variety, their quality, and their durability. We must try in this chapter to grasp a sense of the "miracle" of Greek thought and expression as it revealed itself in literature, art, philosophy, and science. It was in this realm that the *polis* produced something shared by all Greeks, something "Hellenic," as they would have said, to balance the divisiveness bred in political life.

In stating his intention to portray the essential features of Greek culture, the historian must enter a warning that arises both from practicality and from humility. In a practical sense it is almost impossible to be comprehensive; it would take several volumes to describe the Greek cultural experience in detail and to explore all its nuances—and a brief summary is bound to be superficial. An attempt to summarize Greek culture is also a humbling experience. In struggling with the problem, the historian finds himself driven back to restudy Greek literature, art, philosophy, and science, and from that experience he learns something new about himself and his intellectual limitations. Greek culture still has a way of being educative, a way of involving the historian. He tends to interpret it from a personal point of view and to present it in terms of the way it affects him. His description tends to be subjective because the subject itself has a vitality that captures the mind and the emotions.

1. AN OVERVIEW

The Greek cultural achievement can be presented in two ways: chronologically, by recounting the stages in which Greek thought and expression evolved from relative simplicity to great complexity; or topically, by describing the essential features of the various modes by which the Greeks expressed what they believed, thought, and felt. The first approach has the advantage of revealing this cultural tradition in all its aspects gathering

The Acropolis, dominated by the symmetry and grace of the Parthenon, is shown in this view in its setting above the city of Athens, but enclosed by the hills beyond. In ancient Athens, the Acropolis was approached by a great stairway which marked the transition from the outer world of the city to the sacred precincts of the gods. *Photo: Alison Frantz* strength step by step and of allowing us to appreciate better the relationship between intellectual and artistic growth and political, economic, and social forces. In this chapter, however, the topical approach will be taken, chiefly because it permits us to identify more easily and clearly the basic features that underlie the Greek cultural achievement in its most mature stage. Before turning to a topical analysis, it might be useful to begin with a very brief overview summarizing the main stages in the development of Greek culture.

The roots of Greek culture lie far back in the history of the Aegean world, the seeds being planted by Paleolithic men, early Indo-European invaders, Minoan influences, and Mycenaean achievements. During the long Dark Age (1200–800 B.C.), that inheritance was shaped within the isolated Aegean world to produce the first uniquely Hellenic culture. The first fruits of this new culture emerged in the eighth century in highly original pottery decoration and in the Homeric epics, both reflections of a well-articulated set of religious ideas. From the eighth through the sixth centuries B.C., the new culture developed rapidly, its unique characteristics being nourished by the changes in society which marked the development of the *polis,* overseas colonization, and commercial expansion. In this period, often called the Archaic Age, new poetic forms, large-scale architecture, and three-dimensional sculpture were developed. By the end of the period, the first signs of rational philosophical inquiry and mature prose literature had appeared. Hellenic culture during the Archaic Age had a strong civic, religious, and aristocratic flavor.

During a relatively short period in the fifth century B.C. extending from the Persian Wars to the Peloponnesian War, Greek culture reached its golden age, with Athens as the chief center. During this period the artistic forms and the ideas that had been shaped in the Archaic Age were honed to perfection by a remarkable group of artists, writers, and thinkers who reflected a strong civic and religious sense but who were powerfully animated by a rational impulse. This was the age of tragic and comic drama, the poetry of Pindar, Herodotus the historian, the architectural and scuptural masterpieces of the Acropolis in Athens, the science of Hippocrates, and the philosophical inquiry of a succession of brilliant thinkers. However, the bright-burning flame of this golden age was relatively short-lived. By the end of the fifth century, the period of the Peloponnesian War, signs of transformation and decline appeared in the form of a sharpened critical spirit and a disillusionment with the values of the golden age. The Sophists and their relativistic concepts, Socrates and his questioning, the dramatist Euripides and his critical attitudes, the historian Thucydides and his disillusionment set the tone of this age. By the fourth century B.C., classical Greek culture had clearly passed its peak. The literature and the art of the era between the end of the Peloponnesian War and Alexander the Great were undistinguished. Only in philosophy, dominated by Plato and Aristotle, was there still vitality. The ground was being prepared for a new phase of culture which is called Hellenistic, one that was derived from the Hellenic experience but was more cosmopolitan, individualistic, and personal.

2. GREEK RELIGION

A description of the Greek cultural achievement must begin with Greek religion. This may strike a modern reader as an unusual point of departure, since we are not accustomed to think of a close kinship between what appear to be the main features of Greek culture and the religious spirit. The Greeks were, however, a deeply religious people, perhaps no less so than other peoples of the ancient world. Their lives, including their thought and expression, were permeated with religious forces, and their main cultural achievements were deeply rooted in religious belief. The most fascinating aspect of Greek culture—and one very difficult to explain—

was the way in which religion provided a spur to cultural innovation, a seedbed for new and fresh cultural growth.

The origins of Greek religion are buried in the earliest stages of Greek history. By the time the historian can begin to find clear evidence for religious belief—toward the end of the Dark Age—religious concepts are well developed in an elaborate mythology, and religious practices are set in a complex ritual pattern. A study of these myths and rituals makes it clear that in its origins Greek religion was a baffling amalgam of concepts and practices derived from Neolithic, Indo-European, Minoan, and Near Eastern sources. It is equally obvious that the early Greeks had put their own stamp on every facet of their borrowings to create a unique body of religious beliefs and practices that never can be understood merely by tracing them back to their origins. But although it is not easy to describe Greek religion as it had developed by 800 B.C., some features do stand out as essential and remain central throughout the classical period under review.

The Greeks, first of all, accepted the existence of a large number of gods; their religion was completely polytheistic. This multitude of spirits circulated freely throughout the world and controlled all things. At an early date, at least before the Homeric Age, the Greeks conceived of most of their gods as having human forms and as conducting themselves in much the same way as earthly men, except that the gods were immortal and infinitely more powerful. This *anthropomorphism*, that is, the endowment of the gods with human characteristics, was highly significant in shaping Greek religion and thought, for it made human access to the gods easier.

As is clearly evident in the Homeric epics, the Greeks had also formulated an elaborate mythology explaining the characters, activities, and functions of their gods. The major deities constituted a tumultuous family living on Mount Olympus under the authority of Zeus, whose position resembled that of an earthly father of a noble household. The activities of this pantheon—their feats, their intrigues against each other, their love lives, their quarrels, their good and evil deeds toward men, their special likes and dislikes—were perfectly familiar to most Greeks. Most of the Olympian gods were worshiped by all Greeks, so that religion constituted a common element in Greek life. Many of the great gods had assumed a specific role: Zeus was the father and ruler of the gods and the world; Hera, his wife, was the protector of marriage and the family; Athena was the goddess of wisdom; Apollo was the bringer of light and the patron of the arts; Hermes was the messenger of the gods and the patron of commerce and the crafts; Dionysus was the god of wine and the regenerative forces of nature; and so forth. Several of the Olympian gods had among their functions the special protection of particular city-states, so that the worship of the Olympian pantheon provided the basis for civic religion and constituted one of the most powerful forces linking men to the *polis*. The great deities honored in mythology were not the only divine forces in the Greek religious system. At a lower, more popular level were the innumerable lesser spirits—nymphs, satyrs, muses, demons, spirits of heroes and departed ancestors—who played a part in every aspect of human behavior and who had to be kept in mind on every occasion and in every undertaking.

The Greeks generally accepted the basic proposition that the gods controlled all human affairs and therefore believed that men must attune their activities to the will of the gods. All good things came from the gods, including life itself, civic well-being, food, comfort, success, honor, and prosperity. Likewise, life's misfortunes at every level were the products of divine disfavor. Basically, the Greeks viewed their gods as capricious and amoral with respect to men, so that there was never assurance that divine action on the human scene would be beneficial. In some respects, the gods' ways toward men were almost repulsive in their crudity and baseness, for example, Zeus' insatiable lust for earthly maidens. In the later stages of Greek history considerable intellectual energy was spent trying to discover moral principles governing divine action and some higher principle of cosmic order transcending the pattern of behavior attributed to the gods in mythology. This struggle to "tame" the gods did not bear a rich harvest; about all it achieved was to posit the rather unappealing idea that over gods and men ruled some inexplicable force of fate or necessity that guided all things. In general, the Greeks persisted in their conviction that powerful, unpredictable divine forces capable of all the good and evil conceivable ruled their destinies. But this was never a fearful proposition for them. Despite their power and whimsy, the gods were basically benevolent, approachable, concerned with human well-being—in short, good. They were too much endowed with life, too human to inflict a burden of terror and helplessness on men. If a man adjusted to their nature and demands, if he did not usurp their powers, he could expect their support in endowing his life with what was good. They did not ask of him a puritanical moral life as a prize for their favors. They demanded only that he be a man. As the Greek philosopher Heraclitus put it, man was like an ape compared to the gods, but he was like a god compared to the apes.

In this kind of relationship, it was especially important that men keep in contact with the gods. This demand gave birth to elaborate ritual as a major feature of Greek religion. Sacrifice and prayer played a part in Greek life at every level: Each home and each clan had its shrines and its rituals. More impressive were the splendid civic cults, for which great temples were built and which called the entire citizenry to pay tribute to the gods. On occasion, the entire Greek world joined in honoring the Olympian pantheon; the Olympic Games in honor of Zeus, first held in 776 B.C. and every four years thereafter, represent such a pan-Hellenic ceremony. Greek ritual life was remarkably open and free. Large numbers of people from all walks

of life participated, as is so dramatically evident in the Parthenon sculpture frieze illustrating the annual procession connected with the civic feast in honor of Athena. Almost every kind of human activity was accepted as worthy of offering to the gods—athletic contests, poetry reading, song, dance, drama, prayer, gift-bearing. The whole spirit of Greek ritual life was characterized by an easy, comfortable relationship between gods and men. There were no elaborate priesthoods in Greece; fathers conducted rituals in the household and elected officials served as priests in the civic ceremonies. After the Greeks offered their gifts of meat and wine, they immediately ate and drank the offerings, leaving only scraps for the gods. In their prayers, they addressed the gods boldly and confidently. A major feature of ritual life among the Greeks was the attempt to get the gods to reveal their intentions. Although the gods often spoke directly to men or let their intentions be revealed in the actions of animals or in dreams, the search for foreknowledge was institutionalized in the *oracles*, where the gods spoke through special people. The most famous of these was at Delphi, where all Greeks went to discover everything from personal destinies to great political issues.

There is evidence that this easy, comfortable, materialistic, nonethical interaction of gods and men characteristic of clan, civic, and pan-Hellenic religion was never completely satisfactory to all. From a rather early date in Greek religious history there developed more emotional, personal religious movements that can be called *mystery* religions. They derived primarily from the ancient worship of the regenerative forces in nature—a baffling mystery to men. The mystery cults centered on belief in a god or goddess who died and then arose to become a savior for those initiated into the cult. The god Dionysus was the center of such a cult throughout much of Greece. An elaborate myth told of his death and rising, associating his fate with that of vegetation. His worship involved his

A detail from a frieze depicting a great procession in honor of Athena which ran completely around the inside of the Parthenon. The Greeks had an attitude to their gods far different from that of the Near Eastern peoples—see the photograph of the Mesopotamian worshipers in Chapter 1. *Photo: Alinari–Art Reference Bureau*

devotees in a highly emotional initiation ritual and in ecstatic rites such as wild dancing and the eating of raw flesh. Another mystery cult grew up in connection with the fertility goddess Demeter and her daughter Persephone; this cult was celebrated annually at Eleusis near Athens with great secrecy and much mystery. While violent and emotional in their origins, the mystery cults tended to grow more subdued, as is illustrated by a poorly understood movement called Orphism, which modified Dionysus worship by emphasizing the need for ethical conduct as a way of pleasing the powerful god. The mystery cults were highly significant in stimulating emotion in Greek life and in focusing attention on the individual. They left an important mark on Christianity at a later date.

Greek religion has an intrinsic importance in itself in terms of the satisfying answers it provided for men seeking to make sense out of their lives, trying to gain insight into the inexplicable that always surrounds life, and attempting to discover modes of living with one another. In the context of this chapter, however, Greek religion has another dimension. In a way that escapes exact definition, it provided the framework and the stimulus for cultural growth. It supplied the Greeks with a profound sense of some higher force guarding their individual and collective destinies and drove them to try to discover and define that force. It postulated a kindly, humane direction of the cosmic order which inspired them to approach the unknown without fear. It cast man in a role that bred confidence and hope that he could become godlike. It invited him to think, to speak, to sing, to dance, to carve as ways of approaching the gods who were always fundamentally pleased with what man did. Thus out of religion grew literature, art, philosophy, and science, each in its own way a form of religious expression, even when the writer or artist or thinker transcended the specific religious belief or ritual that inspired his work. It is symbolic that the Greeks conceived the forces which produced the arts and thought as goddesses, the Muses.

3. LITERATURE

Greek literature is a magnificent artistic creation emerging from a substratum of religious concepts and themes. Most of it is incomprehensible without a familiarity with Greek mythology, for literary artists played upon this material to give it new vitality and meaning in terms of the human situation. In the process they produced masterpieces that still appeal to readers for their imagination, beauty, and insight.

Greek literature was born in glory with the two epic poems of Homer, the *Iliad* and the *Odyssey*. Although the matter is much disputed, these masterpieces were probably set down in the eighth century B.C. Behind them lay a long tradition of oral poetry sung by professional bards in aristocratic courts to tell the deeds of heroic figures who lived in the early Dark Age and the legends pertaining to the gods. A single poetic genius, Homer, who according to tradition lived in Ionia, drew these oral threads together into unified compositions characterized by great artistry and dramatic force. The *Iliad* is a story of the deeds of great warriors who went to Troy to avenge the theft of a Greek woman, Helen, by Paris, the prince of Troy. Its plot centers around the way in which the inflated pride of Achilles, angry at his leader, Agamemnon, for depriving him of his just share of the prizes of war, brought tragedy to the Greeks before he came to his senses and assumed his place as the greatest Greek warrior. The unfolding of this theme provides a framework for stirring action on the field of battle, for the intervention of the gods in human affairs, and for some memorable confrontations between strong individual characters. The *Odyssey* is an adventure story recounting the experiences of one of the heroes of the Trojan War, Ulysses, who takes ten years to return to his home and family. Not a little of the appeal of these epics lies in the gripping story they tell; Homer is a master of narrative poetry. But the poems have other dimensions. They create a heroic picture of men endowed with

courage, nobility, and a deep love for life; the main characters are proper subjects for great poetry by virtue of their own power and talent. While portraying men in such heroic proportions, Homer wrestles with the thought-provoking problem of the relationship of these demigods to the real gods. His probing infuses the poems with a tragic sense of the degree to which human greatness can be faulted when it runs counter to the will of the gods. His poems become a mirror of the Greek concept of the divine and a majestic portrayal of the working of the entire cosmic order. These powerful themes are developed in a language that is masterful and in a verse form that reveals a mature esthetic sense. Homer's epics enshrined a view of gods and men that provided Greeks of all ages with an ideal of heroic greatness.

The epic style of Homer was imitated long after his death, but for all its richness, this one literary form could not contain the Greek literary genius. The impact of changing political and social conditions in the seventh and sixth centuries B.C. brought forth new issues for artistic talent, and the general tenor of life encouraged the artist to respond. In about 700 B.C., the poet Hesiod wrote his *Works and Days,* a bitter reflection on the poverty of small landowners and the injustice of the rich and powerful. It is filled with a search for some deeper understanding of divine justice as an antidote to human misery. Hesiod's work pointed the way to an outburst of lyric poetry in which several poets developed new verse forms to express their personal reactions to man, nature, political developments, the gods, love, and a wide variety of other subjects. Although their view of life was deeply aristocratic and the themes they treated were often so personal as to escape our understanding, several of these poets produced verse that can still command our attention. Among the best were Archilochus of Paros, Alcaeus of Mytilene, and above all the poetess Sappho of Lesbos. Aside from the new literary froms they developed, including the elegy and the choral ode, these lyricists made literature a vehicle for the forceful expression of deep thought and a personal reaction to life. Their work touched an ever-wider circle of people, because much of it was written as part of religious ritual. The nobility, seriousness, and forcefulness of Greek lyric poetry was perhaps best exemplified by Pindar of Thebes (ca. 518–441 B.C.), most of whose lyrics took the form of choral songs to honor victorious athletes at great religious festivals. Into these odes he poured a vision of human greatness that harks back to Homer and a sense of the divine power that ensures good order in the universe. His poems set forth the classic view of aristocratic (in the Greek sense of "the best") man in terms seldom equaled in poetry. His artistry is so powerful that he convinces one of what many Greeks believed—that great poetry can inspire ordinary men to rise above their own limits to the greatness of the athletes who struggled for personal and civic glory and for the honor of the gods.

The burgeoning poetic talent reflected in epic and lyric poetry reached full fruition in the fifth century with the development of tragic drama. Perhaps the greatest literary achievement of the Greeks, the tragic drama not only absorbed and refined previous literary styles and forms, but also took up the great themes of earlier literature and explored them with deep insight and great wisdom. The drama was essentially a public achievement; it was written and produced for large audiences in the *polis*, and paid for by the state from public funds. In this respect, it is a product of the democracy of the fifth century. Its profundity and its artistry suggest an articulate, sensitive, thoughtful populace that speaks well for the power of democracy.

Tragedy originated in religious ceremony and never lost touch with its seedbed. It began in the dramatic choruses and hymns developed to pay honor to the gods and to reflect on the meaning of divine power and its relation to men. By the sixth century B.C., the dramatic element in these ritual acts grew increasingly important, providing opportuni-

ties for poets to attempt to portray the actions of the gods and the heroes enshrined in Greek mythology and to comment on the meaning of these actions through choral interludes interspersed with the dramatic action. The Greek tragedians all built their plots around mythological stories with which their audience was familiar; their art consisted in their ability to endow these old tales with new meaning through the power of word and action.

This developing dramatic art suddenly burst forth in full maturity during the fifth century in the work of three of the world's greatest masters. The first was Aeschylus (525–456 B.C.), a writer of deep religious convictions and strong aristocratic sentiments. He wrote about ninety plays, only seven of which survive. His tragedies spell out with great power and force the consequences that follow human transgressions of the dictates of the divine powers. His most impressive surviving work is a cycle of three plays called the *Oresteia* that traces the tragic fate of the family of Agamemnon resulting from their crime of spilling the blood of their own kinsmen. Out of the portrayal of the punishment meted out to this ill-fated family emerges an almost overpowering awe for divine power and a profound feeling for the suffering that men bring on themselves for defying the gods. Yet Aeschylus had a genius for making his suffering characters noble and admirable, capable of bearing their burden of punishment with dignity and even understanding. Sophocles (495–406 B.C.) was less aristocratic. During his long life, centered chiefly in the period of Athens' greatest power, he produced a large number of plays, all but seven now lost. His dramas remained closely bound to the traditional themes provided by myth and religion, but his interest is more humane, more intent on searching out the psychological effects of suffering on men who ran afoul of the gods. He succeeded in portraying suffering as an experience that uplifted and purified man. In his *Antigone*, for instance, the heroine is ennobled and made more human by the tragic experience of being torn between duty to the gods and to the state, both of which represent good causes. Many would argue that Sophocles' *King Oedipus* is the greatest tragedy ever written. Essentially it is a drama that reveals the measure of man by showing his response when he is trapped by fate into committing an act for which the gods must destroy him. Much more than Aeschylus, Sophocles celebrates the greatness of man.

Euripides (480–406 B.C.) was a dramatist profoundly touched by the growing disillusionment, skepticism, and pessimism of the later fifth century—the generation of the Peloponnesian War. He utilized tragedy as a vehicle for posing profound questions. For example, he presents the gods in a fashion that makes his audience wonder how great their benefactions were for humanity. He probes the weaknesses of men with terrible force, again arousing the suspicion that human powers are limited. His plays, especially *Medea*, represent a search for some understanding of the full nature of man, especially his dark and frightening emotional qualities. Again and again he casts doubt on conventional moral values and accepted religious beliefs. But from this incessant probing emerges a picture of man that is fuller and more subtle—if not nobler—than the portraits of Aeschylus or Sophocles. Seldom have three men living within a single century and employing material already familiar to their audience been able to portray human nature more clearly and probe its multiple facets more profoundly. Their success lay in a rare combination of poetic genius and intellectual power—perhaps the ultimate keys to all literary genius. But they must have written in turn for a great and understanding audience.

While the tragic drama was developing, the Greeks also perfected comic drama to a level where it was as effective in its own way as were the great tragedies. Comedy, like tragedy, began as a part of public religious ceremonies, especially the worship of Dionysus. Its origins were rooted in ribald comic songs evoked by the joy and good humor that apparently surrounded religious feasts. By the fifth century, comedy became independent of religious ceremony and was performed as a distinctive art for the purpose of educating audiences about current affairs by making them laugh. The greatest artist employing this form was Aristophanes (ca. 445–385 B.C.), a conservative Athenian who despised nearly all the developments of the society in which he lived. His comedies held up for the scorn of his audiences politicians, artists, democratic institutions, and Athenian social mores. Typical is his play *Lysistrata*, based on the efforts of Athenian women to deny their husbands any pleasures with them until the men gave up warfare. Much of the comedy of Aristophanes is so close to contemporary Athens that its real force escapes a modern audience, but enough comes through to suggest its devastating effect in the hands of a great artist.

Prose literature in Greece was long overshadowed by the immense talent of the poets. Its first use came in the sixth century in the works of early philosophical and scientific writers and it was thus closely associated with emerging rationalism in Greek life. The best Greek prose writing in the fifth century was devoted to historical literature. Two outstanding historians, Herodotus and Thucydides, not only produced great literature, but also introduced scientific history to the world. Herodotus (ca. 484–425 B.C.) wrote a history of the war between the Greeks and Persia. To make his account as accurate as possible, he traveled extensively and searched through written records for evidence concerning the causes and the events of the Persian wars. His researches produced an immense collection of fact and fiction pertaining to both Persians and Greeks. Herodotus usually tried to sift his material to arrive at the truth; however, he was too good a storyteller to leave out colorful material whether true or not. His finished work was therefore spiced with hundreds of anecdotes and stories, many quite fantastic, intended to illustrate the qualities of the two peoples involved in the war. But he did try to discover the truth about the past, and he insisted that this was the historian's job.

Thucydides' (ca. 470–400 B.C.) masterpiece was a *History of the Peloponnesian War*. He was an Athenian who served as a naval commander in this war but suffered exile as a result of losing a battle. While in exile he wrote his history, in which there is no evidence of personal rancor stemming from his harsh treatment by his fellow citizens. With great industry and complete objectivity, he searched out and reported the details of the military campaigns and the political maneuvers associated with the war. Thucydides was convinced that this was the greatest war in Greek history, and his work is marked by deep seriousness. He tries to let the events of the war illustrate the folly, the nobility, the chicanery, and the bravery of which men under stress are capable. His presentation leads one to the inevitable conclusion that the Athenians lost because of their own mistakes, their pride, their bad judgment. By successfully illustrating what war in any age can do to men and to political institutions, Thucydides did what every modern historian yearns to do: To make the truth about the past enrich our understanding of men.

4. ART

Greek art reflects a spirit akin to that embodied in literature. As one Greek put it: "Painting is silent poetry; poetry is painting that speaks." Art drew its basic themes from the same sources—religion and mythology. Artists labored toward the same ends—to discover man and place him meaningfully in the larger cosmos. Artists found their audiences where writers did: in the citizenry of the *polis*. Artists poured into their work the same talents as did writers: great technical skill and serious intellectual effort. Certainly nature provided them with some of the finest materials in the world, especially marble, and with dramatic sites upon which to place their

buildings, such as the Athenian Acropolis, but it was their genius that produced the magnificent works which so clearly reveal the Greek spirit.

The art of the golden age was the product of a long evolution. During the Mycenaean era, a flourishing art, strongly influenced by Minoan models, had developed on mainland Greece. With the onset of the Dark Age, Mycenaean art styles and technical skills were largely lost, although remnants survived to provide a starting point for a uniquely Greek art. The first signs of this new art appeared near the end of the Dark Age in the form of finely executed pottery decorated with geometric patterns. By the eighth century B.C., potters began to decorate their elegantly shaped vases with human forms, and throughout the Archaic period they continued to perfect the art of pottery painting. Their work established the basic themes for painters and set conventions for representing human beings and animals in action. During the Archaic period, architects developed a basic style for temples and other public buildings: a rectangular form with surrounding columns and low pitched roofs; toward the end of the period, most of these structures were being built of stone. At the same time, sculptors were perfecting a unique style which focused on portraying the human form, especially the nude male and the draped female figure. Architects, sculptors, and painters received increasing support from the city-states, whose leaders and citizens were deeply interested in beautifying the cities and in elaborating civic religious ceremonies. Consequently, Greek art became predominantly a public art, dedicated to the glory of the *polis* and the worship of the gods who protected it.

By the beginning of the fifth century, the long apprenticeship was over. Although there was significant activity in many cities, Athens became the focal point for artistic excellence in the fifth and fourth centuries. Her monuments offer the best examples of Greek art. Unquestionably the crowning glory of Athens was the Acropolis, a hill within the city upon

The Theseum, one of the best-preserved temples in the Greek world, is a good example of the Doric style of architecture and of the basic plan for temples, which changed very little throughout Greek history. *Photo: Hirmer Verlag*

which were built three major temples, the Parthenon, the Erectheum, and the temple to Victorious Athena. A splendid gate and stairway, called the Propylaea, gave access to the Acropolis.

The Parthenon, portions of which still stand, was the noblest of the temples. Built in honor of Athena, this structure embodies all the Greek architectural ideas. It is of moderate size, measuring 228 by 101 feet. Its rectangular shape and accentuated horizontal lines give it the appearance of dignity and simplicity. The inner chamber is surrounded by simple, unadorned columns (called Doric columns), seventeen on each side and eight on each end, which support the roof. The number and size of the columns give the impression of perfect unity. A series of dignified statues and stone reliefs added a

harmonious decorative touch. Many devices were employed by the architects to achieve harmony, balance, and unity. The columns all lean inward slightly and are thickened in the middle to offset the optical illusion that makes a straight column seem to tip outward when viewed from below. The middle of every long horizontal line in or around the temple is slightly higher than the ends to avoid the impression of sagging.

The other Acropolis temples and the Propylaea, all built after the Parthenon, incorporate the same features—horizontal lines, carefully calculated proportions, and technical perfection. The only basic departure was the tendency to make the columns slightly more slender and ornate (in the Ionic style), adding an element of grace lacking in the rather severe Parthenon. Similar temples were built in other cities, although none quite equals the Acropolis group for total effect. The many public buildings constructed in Athens and other cities incorporated the principles employed in temple construction, adding to the simple beauty of the city. Because most such buildings have disappeared, however, we can only guess at their appearances.

Greek sculpture was primarily dedicated to the adornment of temples. The most representative sculptors are Phidias (ca. 500–432 B.C.), Polyclitus (ca. 452–412 B.C.), and Praxiteles (ca. 400–320 B.C.). Phidias designed the sculpture adorning the Parthenon and executed some of the individual pieces. All the surviving Parthenon sculpture is relief work, so it is difficult to tell whether any particular piece is the work of Phidias or of someone working under his direction. Phidias' monumental statues in the round have all been lost. Polyclitus, seeking to create the perfect human form, devoted his talents chiefly to shaping bronze statues of young men. Praxiteles created splendid versions of the gods in human form. The work of all these sculptors concentrated on the human body and was remarkably lifelike. However, none was content to copy nature; all idealized humanity. They created perfect bodies: Their figures are dignified, quiet, and beautifully proportioned. However, some artists did portray violent action. For instance, the fifth-century sculptor Myron, in his statue of the discus thrower, manages to catch the body at a moment of tension just before the cast. When looking at any of the statues of Greek sculptors, the viewer feels that he finally sees man as he should be, although he is aware that he has never seen such perfect men.

Little has survived of Greek painting, except for pottery decoration, which had perhaps passed its peak by the fifth century. However, it remained a significant art during the golden age. The vases are lovely witnesses to the sense of proportion and symmetry characteristic of all Greek art. The decorators adorned them with human and animal forms engaged in an unending variety of activities—walking, standing, leaping, fighting, dancing, riding, eating, praying. Often the scenes represent a mythological story. These vase paintings reflect a fine sense of balance, a flair for portraying action, and a feeling for the joy of human existence. Much more so than sculpture, the vase paintings put us in touch with daily life and permit us to suspect that the Greeks were somewhat less godlike than the sculptured figures indicate. There is evidence from literary sources that artists rendered large-scale paintings to decorate temples and public buildings. For example, the painter Polygnotus decorated a colonnade in the Athenian *agora* with scenes from the Trojan Wars. We may suspect that Greek painting reflected the same idealizing traits seen in sculpture and drew heavily on mythology for its themes. However, painters may have endowed their works with realism; it is said that one painter so realistically portrayed grapes that birds flew down and pecked at them.

5. PHILOSOPHY

The Greeks leaped furthest beyond the achievements of earlier cultures in the realm of philosophical and scientific speculation. They left a heritage that has shaped thinking in the West up to the present. Until the sixth century B.C., most Greeks were content to accept the explanations of mythology for the nature of the universe and man's place in it; Homer and Hesiod provided the basic ingredients of their world view. Then during that century, just when the *polis* was reaching maturity, thinkers began to move beyond these limits, initiating one of the great intellectual revolutions in the history of the world. In part the new movement represented a reaction against the naive and contradictory concepts provided by mythology. Fundamentally, however, the new modes of thought were byproducts of a growing faith in man's capabilities and of the freedom nourished in the atmosphere of the *polis*. In the wake of initial probings into a new understanding of the universe came a breathtaking series of responses to the fundamental questions facing mankind. So bold and so cogent was this activity of the mind that the fifth and fourth centuries B.C. are still regarded as the most productive centuries in the entire history of philosophy and thought.

The prime concern of speculative thinkers during the sixth and fifth centuries centered around the discovery of the fundamental force lying behind and giving unity to the universe. Rejecting traditional religious answers to this question, a series of philosophers tried to give rational answers. One school of thinkers based its answer on a materialistic approach and concluded that such obvious elements as fire, water, and air were the basic substances out of which all other things came. This materialistic tradition continued to be refined until in the early fourth century the philosopher Democritus expounded an atomic theory, according to which the universe is composed of tiny atoms floating at random in space. By mere chance these atoms compose themselves into beings and objects and by the same chance decompose into floating particles again. Another school of philosophers rejected materialism and sought the key to the universe in some nonmaterial force. Perhaps the source of this approach to philosophy was the sixth-century thinker Pythagoras, whose career combined deep scientific interest with a strong religious bent. He argued that the key to the universe lay in a numerical relationship among its many parts. Equally influential in shaping this school of thought was Heraclitus (flourished ca. 500 B.C.), who insisted that change was essence of the physical, material world and therefore that no physical explanation of the universe could have meaning. This whole school of thinkers ultimately concluded that a nonmaterial, changeless being, endowed with perfect intelligence, supplied the creative force of order in the universe.

Only toward the end of the fifth century did the search for a rational explanation of the basic nature of the cosmos lose its attraction for Greek thinkers. Those who had engaged in that search had made a notable contribution to the intellectual development of mankind. They had boldly assumed that the human mind possessed the power to understand the deep mysteries of the universe; they were no longer content to await revelation from the gods or to live in fearful ignorance. They had discovered man's rational power and had turned it toward the resolution of the most profound of all problems. Their feat gave birth to philosophy, the "love of wisdom" which has possessed Western man ever since.

About the middle of the fifth century philosophical inquiry shifted from speculation about the fundamental nature of the universe to an examination of man's nature and his place in that universe. The Sophists, although they were primarily teachers whose interest in philosophy was a byproduct of their ideas on education, led the way into this fresh realm of thought. Protagoras (485–410 B.C.), a famous teacher in Periclean Athens, was chiefly responsible for articulating the basic precepts of the Sophists. He rejected speculative philosophy on the grounds that it could not discover objective truth; for this he had good evidence in the many contradictory schemes put forth by the speculative thinkers. Protagoras even denied that objective, absolute truth existed. To him, man was the measure of all things. Human reason, he said, should be dedicated to a search for the kind of knowledge that would be useful to man in his quest for a comfortable, safe, happy life. He therefore spent his time instructing Athenians in those things that would fit them for citizenship in a democratic society—public speaking, politics, grammar, and the art of being respectable. Greece soon swarmed with his disciples. They delivered withering attacks on all things that were accepted as the truth, preaching that truth was relative and encouraging their audiences to live by any rules of conduct that proved beneficial and workable. The Sophists as a group were condemned, with partial justice, as skeptics, troublemakers, and destroyers of morality. However, they made the Greeks more aware of human problems than had earlier thinkers who were constantly preoccupied with a search for the deepest secrets of the universe. They prepared the way for the greatest Greek philosophers, Socrates, Plato, and Aristotle, whose thought reflected the new humanism without abandoning the search for ultimate truth.

Probably no one was better known in Athens just before 400 B.C. than a homely, dumpy little stonecutter named Socrates (ca. 469–399 B.C.). Socrates left no writings. He set forth his ideas orally; the Athenian *agora*, where the citizens congregated, provided him an ideal setting. Here he locked horns intellectually with anyone interested; the Roman statesman Cicero said with considerable truth that Socrates was the first to bring philosophy down from heaven and to establish it in the cities. But Socrates was more than a street-corner debater. His pupils, especially Plato, recorded enough of his ideas to permit us to grasp the basic thrust of his thought. He believed that objective truth did exist and that man was prevented from discovering it by his own ignorance. Socrates made it his business to purge men's minds of that ignorance. The Socratic method consisted of asking questions until the error of those who claimed to know something was exposed. So skilled and brilliant was Socrates in laying bare the false beliefs and ignorance of his protagonists that he attracted an eager following of youths, including the scions of several of Athens' noblest families. And he earned the anger and distrust of many of the elders of his society. But Socrates was never content with negative, destructive rationalism.

Once having cleared the mind of its errors, he believed that further questioning would reveal the truth. He insisted that precise definition and exact logic were necessary if the mind was to be led from ignorance to enlightenment. Behind all Socrates' questions lay a firm conviction: knowledge alone will serve as a guide to a good life. His annoying questions finally got him into trouble with the state. In 399 B.C., amid the bitterness surrounding Athenian defeat in the Peloponnesian War, he was accused of corrupting the youth of Athens and sentenced to death. Although given a chance to escape, he chose to abide by the state's decision and drank the hemlock, still

Hermes with the Infant Dionysus. Most likely the work of the famed sculptor Praxiteles, this statue is an excellent example of Greek artistic canons; the gods are taken as subject matter and portrayed in an idealized human form that emphasizes physical perfection rather than spiritual qualities. *Photo: Hirmer Verlag*

convinced that the highest virtue consisted of pursuing knowledge, no matter what the consequences.

Plato (427–347 B.C.) carried on the work of Socrates, his master. He was an Athenian whose career spanned an era filled with defeats for Athens and constant civil strife, all of which discouraged him. Most of his life was spent as a teacher in a school called the Academy, which he founded. His voluminous works, elegantly written in dialogue form, offer a complete although sometimes confusing record of his thought. The dialogues reveal an evolution in Plato's intellectual position and demonstrate that his was an active, searching intelligence. There does emerge a basic philosophical position that has exerted an immense influence over all subsequent thought. Plato was a philosophical idealist, his work bringing to a conclusion the nonmaterialistic philosophical movement that had begun with Pythagoras. He argued that the fundamental realities in the universe are *ideas* or abstract forms, the chief of which is good. The so-called realities that man perceives with his senses in the world about him are but imperfect reflections of the perfect universal forms. The justice practiced in Athens was only a shadowy reflection of perfect transcendental justice; the good that an individual did in his daily life was a feeble enactment of perfect good; the man that Plato was was but a pale image of a higher reality, humanity. Life's fundamental task was to comprehend and understand that transcendent reality, those ideas that constituted the ultimate substance of the universe. The intellect, by reflecting on the imperfect earthly embodiments of ideas, opened the path to contemplation of the ultimate, unchanging realities of the universe.

Much of Plato's writing, and presumably his teaching in the Academy, centers on a search for perfect understanding of universal ideas and an effort to make that wisdom and insight applicable to the problems of human existence. His best-known dialogue, *The Republic*, illustrates his idealism, his method, and his earnest concern for the human condition. This work is devoted to the problem of the state and its governance. Plato assumes that the purpose of the state is to achieve justice, the ideal state being an earthly embodiment of the perfect idea of justice. He then seeks to define justice and concludes that justice consists in each man's doing that for which he is best fitted. The ideal state is one in which every man holds that station and does that job for which he is qualified. Such a state, Plato argues, must be ruled by a philosopher-king who will be wise enough to know and recognize the talents of his subjects and put these talents to work. The philosopher-king must train the lower classes to do their jobs and must keep them from learning those things that will distract them from their responsibilities. A completely socialistic economy controlled by the wise king must be instituted so that each will be rewarded according to his merits and so that competition and greed can be eliminated from society. In short, the perfect society is a dictatorial state run by wise men who know each citizen's talents and have the power to put those talents to work. Only in this way will justice be attained and the human condition drawn into concord with perfect justice. In his other dialogues Plato conducts a comparable search for an understanding of the nature of love, friendship, courage, the soul—in fact, virtually the whole range of those elements that constitute the ultimate reality, perfect good.

Aristotle (384–322 B.C.) was Plato's most brilliant and productive pupil. A Macedonian by birth, he came to Athens as a youth to study at the Academy. Here he was steeped in the tenets of Platonic idealism. After Plato's death, Aristotle spent some time as tutor to young Alexander the Great. He then returned to Athens and founded his own school, the Lyceum. His followers were called the Peripatetics because Aristotle often walked about while lecturing (from the Greek *peripatetikos*, meaning "to walk about").

During his career, Aristotle produced a massive body of philosophical work ranging

The Irrational in Greek Culture

Every historian who tries to reconstruct the grand sweep of history in an account of reasonably modest proportions quickly becomes aware of a disturbing consequence of his effort. He finds himself distorting the past by concentrating on what is dominant in any era at the expense of many facets of a society that in his judgment are less momentous. This process of selection, performed for the laudable purpose of educating his readers on those matters that are central to the story of mankind, results in the suppression of matters that were of immense significance to those who lived in the past. Although this kind of distortion is necessary in order to make the immensity of the past manageable and comprehensible, the historian—at least on occasion—owes it to his readers to suggest the limitations of his version of the past by calling attention to his omission of a crucial aspect of a past society.

Our treatment of Greek cultural history provides an example of what we might call the distortion of selection: We have repeatedly and emphatically stressed that the central and crucial theme of Greek thought and expression was rationalism. We have argued that not only did the leading intellectual and artistic spokesmen of Greek culture avow a faith that man's greatest and most distinctive power was his reason, but also that the most active and enduring spokesmen of the Greek world sought to see everything rationally—the natural world, human nature, society, morality, law, religion. Ours is, of course, no new insight and no fresh interpretation. Across long ages, as we shall see in later parts of this book, Greek rationalism was a wonder of the world, passionately admired by those who aspired to be civilized. Near Eastern potentates, Roman aristocrats, medieval churchmen, Renaissance artists, early modern scientists, American revolutionaries, and modern intellectuals have all paid obeisance to the Greek "mind," that is, to the Greek confidence that man was preeminently a thinking creature capable of utilizing his rational faculties to make the world into what he "thought" it should be.

But was what later admirers and interpreters—all in one way or another historians—so much admired and so often talked about the whole story? Did all Greeks perceive all things from a rational perspective? Was even the most sophisticated and intellectually enlightened Greek poet, dramatist, philosopher, scientist, artist, or statesman completely convinced that man was primarily a rational being? Is it possible that the legions of students of the Greek "mind" have been blinded to significant dimensions of the Greek cultural experience as a consequence of their eagerness to permit the Greeks to exemplify that most desirable and admirable of all human traits—reasonableness?

The answers to these questions are buried in an extensive scholarly literature, hardly known except to a few specialists, and certainly not much used by those who have provided the general reader with the standard interpretations of the Greek cultural experience. In the main, this scholarship has been concerned with Greek religion and its relationship to literature, art, philosophy, and science. These important investigations of the Greek religious experience have been broadened and deepened over the last century by valuable insights and techniques supplied to the historian by social scientists interested in the nature of religious experience among men in all ages and every kind of society. Especially illuminating has been the work of anthropologists investigating religious life among primitive societies still in existence and of psychologists seeking to comprehend the nonrational aspects of human behavior. The whole thrust of this approach to the na-

ture of Greek culture has been to cast doubt on the conventional generalization that rationalism is the key to that culture.

Perhaps few who are interested in the fundamental nature of Greek culture will ever find time or energy to pursue the massive and somewhat abstruse literature devoted to Greek religion and its relationship to Greek thought and expression. But such a monumental effort is not necessary: one of the most perceptive and learned of contemporary scholars has brilliantly posed the basic issue and suggested a viable response. He is the Oxford scholar E. R. Dodds, widely known for his profound studies of both classical and early Christian thought and especially their interrelationships. In 1949 Professor Dodds delivered a series of lectures at the University of California, Berkeley; they were published two years later under the title *The Greeks and the Irrational*. Dodds' argument, solidly grounded on vast learning and deep insight into the nature of religion, breeds doubt about the facile generalization that the key to Greek culture is rationalism.

Dodds begins by asserting a fundamental postulate established by modern anthropologists and psychologists: that in the mental behavior of all people in all ages there is a powerful element of the primitive mentality, a mentality that often manifests itself in religion. Without belaboring this point, he argues that, in the main, interpreters of the Greek intellectual experience have failed (or refused?) to take this fact into account. Quite rightly he asks: "Why should we attribute to the ancient Greeks an immunity from 'primitive' modes of thought which we do not find in any society open to our direct observation?" He thinks the attribution is erroneous, and sets out to demonstrate that the Greeks were not "quite so blind to the importance of nonrational factors in man's experience and behavior as is commonly assumed." As he proceeds, he makes it clear that many scholars who have discussed the Greek cultural experience have operated from a narrow, rationalistic concept of religion and have presumed that the major spokesmen for Greek society were "enlightened" about religion in the same way that Western intellectuals since the eighteenth century have been enlightened.

We cannot reconstruct Dodds' argument here in detail. He does succeed, however, in a most persuasive way in demonstrating that Greek literary and philosophical spokesmen were always aware that human conduct was governed by irrational factors and that these men expressed their awareness in religious terms. For example, Dodds finds in the Homeric epics, usually interpreted as reflecting no deep religious concepts, significant evidence that Homer explained irrational conduct among his heroes as a case of "psychic intervention," in which an outside divine agency put something into a man that changed his thinking and behavior. He discerns in the thought and expression of the Archaic Age the emergence of a sense of despair and insecurity stemming from a conviction that the divine forces were hostile toward man. This religious strain bred a sense of guilt, often associated with the idea of pollution. He examines Greek concepts of madness, discovering that there was a strong conviction that the various forms of madness seen among men represented a state of blessedness because the condition indicated the infusion of the divine into man. Especially persuasive is Dodds' demonstration of the presence of shamanistic concepts in Greek thought, concepts that attributed occult powers to "possessed" men, that heightened awareness of the soul in men, and that nourished a puritanical revulsion from the sensual world. Dodds finds evidence to suggest that the "enlightened" views of the great cultural heroes of the fifth century were looked upon with suspicion by many intellectuals, who felt that the rationalist concepts being promulgated did not encompass man's whole existence, and by the great mass of the Greeks, who reacted violently by persecuting the intellectuals. Extending his view beyond the golden age through Plato to the Hellenistic era, Dodds concludes that rationalism never provided an adequate view of man, that something irrational had to be added to human nature in order to explain man's behavior, and that the irrational grew increasingly important in accounting for man's actions.

The implications of Dodds' powerful synthesis are fairly clear. He forces us to realize that the most profound Greek cultural spokesmen recognized in human beings all kinds of irrational behavior patterns and mental reactions. These thinkers and artists explained the presence of the irrational in religious terms that bear a striking resemblance to religious concepts universally present in human societies. Only a rare few Greek thinkers affirmed that man was a rational creature; their affirmation of this concept engendered far more opposition than acceptance, and in the long run their belief in rational man was buried under a belief in man the irrational creature. When one adds to

this conclusion about the awareness of the irrational in the most advanced Greek thinkers the obvious fact that the great mass of Greeks always accepted a religious interpretation of man that made his existence dependent on divine forces, the generalization about rationalism as a key to Greek culture becomes exceedingly suspect.

It thus turns out that what the historian who stresses rationalism as a major feature of Greek culture is doing is distorting Greek history in an important way. He is overlooking a dimension of Greek culture that was of immense importance to the Greeks. This sounds dishonest. Yet in fitting the Greeks into the grand sweep of history, their rationalism is of greater significance than their irrationalism. Their consciousness of man's rational powers marked a fresh insight into human nature, while their awareness of the irrational aspects of human behavior simply provided the common bond with most other societies in history which have tried to cope with the immense and terrifying problems of living in a cosmic order that usually seems hostile to man—unless he assumes that in the cosmos there are beneficent agents who take special care of him.

across the whole spectrum of human knowledge. Perhaps typical of teachers in all ages, he had a passion for systematizing and organizing knowledge, so that his works constitute a kind of encyclopedia of the total learning of the ancient world. Imbedded in his massive scholarship, however, is a basic philosophical position. Aristotle was certainly influenced by Platonic idealism, but his approach is basically different from that of Plato. Perhaps it is best set forth in his *Metaphysics*. Here he argues that reality consists of a combination in individual objects of matter and form (or idea). It is the form that makes the object what it is, but the form or idea has no reality except when it stands in combination with matter. Every object that exists has some purpose in a larger universal order, and its perfection consists in serving that purpose. Behind the wilderness of individual objects lies an ultimate "cause," a higher force that animates everything. The philosopher can understand this ultimate truth only by studying the individual objects of the world to see what the nature of each is and to discover what place it has in the grand design of the universe. The philosopher's path is from the study of nature toward the formulation of concepts about the entire universe.

In most of his works, many of which deal with scientific subjects, Aristotle pursued the course laid down in the *Metaphysics*. He tried to accumulate all the detailed knowledge he could about the natural world and to classify it into a system that would explain how the total natural world operates. In his chief work on political theory, *Politics,* he supplies an illustration of his method. On the basis of a study of the history and organization of more than 150 Greek city-states, he generalized about the nature and function of the state, and concluded that the state is a natural grouping of men for the purpose of promoting virtue. Man is a political animal and cannot fulfill his true nature unless he is a member of a state. In his *Ethics,* Aristotle asked how man should conduct his individual life, and concluded that happiness is the proper goal of every human action. He argued that man is happy and therefore good if he controls his passions by use of his reason and if he seeks a mean between extremes. Although Aristotle's principal method is inductive, proceeding from detailed observations of particulars to general conclusions and although he was the most influential exponent of that method among the Greeks, he is also the founder of formal logic. The last great thinker of Greece, Aristotle was perhaps the most mature and comprehensive.

6. SCIENCE

Aristotle's scientific works were the culmination of a sustained and highly significant interest in science reaching back at least two centuries before him. Because Greek thinkers made no clear-cut distinction between science and philosophy, it is difficult to treat science as a thing apart. Nearly all thinkers derived their conclusions from observations of nature. From the sixth century on, the Greeks steadily accumulated new knowledge about the natural world. Much of this knowledge derived from observations they themselves made; other knowledge came from ancient Mesopotamia and Egypt, from whom they borrowed extensively.

Typical of a Greek interested in observation was Hippocrates (460–377 B.C.), a leading physician to whom is attributed the famous oath defining the responsibilities of a physician which we still know today. He insisted that nothing could be known about sickness except through observation of sick people and through a search for the natural causes of the illness. He repudiated the traditional belief that sickness was due to evil spirits, and taught that it was a result of natural causes. Hippocrates had numerous followers who took the same approach and accumulated an extensive body of knowledge about the human body and its workings.

Other Greeks devoted their energies to compiling information relating to astronomy, physics, geography, botany, and zoology.

Their collective efforts allow us to credit the Greeks with the discovery of the scientific method, which relies on observation as the source of knowledge about nature. But because they lacked instruments for precise observation and measurement, there were limits beyond which Greek scientists were unable to go. And they often made glaring errors in interpreting their observations. Moreover, few were interested in using their knowledge for practical purposes. Scientific knowledge was used chiefly by philosophers who sought to illustrate the operation of the universe by observing how it worked. Aristotle represents the typical point of view: his wide knowledge of nature was useful to him only as it illuminated philosophical speculation, never as it applied to improving the physical and material lot of human society.

7. THE GREEK MIND

Any review of the brilliant work of the Greeks in literature, art, philosophy, and science raises one final question: Did all the leaders of Greek cultural life, whatever their specific interests, share any common ideas and viewpoints that, taken together, might characterize the Greek approach to life? The following basic concepts are offered in answer to that question, although generalization is always dangerous when so many men of such varied talents are in question.

Greek thought was intensely *humanistic;* it placed man on a pedestal for admiration and idealization. Most Greeks believed that the world had been created for man's happiness. They therefore were certain that man was *in harmony with nature* and had no need to struggle against it, try to escape it, or shrink from it in fear. The Greeks were *rationalistic;* they placed a powerful trust in man's ability to understand nature's mysteries through his own intelligence and to act on the basis of his sound judgment to solve any problems that might beset him. The Greeks insisted upon *restraint* and *balance;* nothing was worse than excess in any shape or form. The keenest Greek intellects were inquisitive and searching, never content to accept the obvious or the traditional at face value. This *spirit of inquiry* constantly pushed them into new fields in every aspect of life, and added an element of *boldness* to the Greek way of life. Most Greek intellectual leaders were intensely interested in *society as a whole,* especially in the society of a city-state community, and were ready to offer their talents to the community instead of pursuing individual and introspective ends. Finally, the Greek mind sought *order* and *symmetry* in all things, being unwilling to tolerate disorder in thought or art.

No one would insist that the ideals expressed by a few intellectual giants and artistic geniuses were attained by all Greeks. Greek history is full of cases in which these ideals were violated or denied. Probably most Greeks, engaged in the routine of daily life, seldom paused to think about what their civilization really meant to them, just as most modern men seldom dwell on this question. But even if the Greeks as a whole did not attain or even understand fully what their intellectual leaders set up as ideals for the good life, at least those ideals were clearly expressed and presented to them in poetry, drama, history, sculpture, architecture, and philosophy. Thus values ingrained in the great artistic and philosophical works of the Greeks became a model of civilized life for numerous peoples who rose to prominence in the Mediterranean area after Greece was no longer a leading power.

Suggested Reading

General Cultural Histories. A brilliant introduction to the Greek cultural contribution is **Edith Hamilton, *The Greek Way* (Norton); although it is true that the Greeks are over-idealized, Miss Hamilton presents them with an enthusiasm that is infectious. Almost as stimulating and somewhat more profound is **C. M. Bowra, *The Greek Experience* (Mentor). For a student interested in greater detail, a work by Herbert Newell Couch, *Classical Civilization: Greece* (2nd ed., 1951), will prove invaluable. This work has the great advantage of presenting cultural history in its proper chronological setting so that the reader can sense the evolutionary processes that produced enduring masterpieces. André Bonnard, *Greek Civilization* (3 vols., 1957–62), provides a provocative evaluation of Greek culture and its meaning; many of his conclusions are debatable, but he never fails to stimulate thought. A memorable intellectual experience awaits the student who will devote his time and energy to one of the great scholarly works of recent times, Werner Jaeger, *Paideia: Ideals of Greek Culture* (3 vols., 2nd ed., 1943–45); it provides a penetrating analysis of the uniqueness of Greek thought and expression, stressing especially the aristocratic temper of Greek culture. Also useful, particularly for its abundance of illustrations, is François Chamoux, *The Civilization of Greece*, trans. W. S. Maguinness (1965).

Religion. The best brief introduction to Greek religion is H. J. Rose, *Ancient Greek Religion* (1946). ** W. K. C. Guthrie, *Greeks and Their Gods* (Beacon) also presents a clear statement of the substance of Greek religious belief and practice. **Gilbert Murray, *Five Stages of Greek Religion* (Anchor) supplies a description of Greek religion that emphasizes its development and the forces causing changes. Also excellent in this sense is **M. P. Nilsson, *History of Greek Religion* (2nd ed., Norton). A. J. Festugière, *Personal Religion Among the Greeks* (1960) touches on aspects of Greek religious belief that are sometimes overlooked. A brilliant study of the penetration of religious concepts into all as-

pects of Greek thought is provided by **E. R. Dodds, *The Greeks and the Irrational* (2nd ed., University of California). **Robert Graves, *The Greek Myths* (2 vols., Penguin), brilliantly condenses the essence of Greek mythology. (Since no student of Greek literature or art can proceed far without a knowledge of mythology, it is imperative that he read a book like this.)

Literature. A good introduction to Greek literature is **M. Hadas, *A History of Greek Literature* (Columbia), a work outstanding for its succinct summaries of the accomplishments of individual authors. Also useful as introductions are **H. J. Rose, *Handbook of Greek Literature* (Dutton); and **C. M. Bowra, *Ancient Greek Literature* (Galaxy). **H. D. F. Kitto, *Greek Tragedy* (Anchor) will help in attaining an appreciation of the greatest literary accomplishment of the Greeks. For an excellent study of Greek historians, see **J. B. Bury, *Ancient Greek Historians* (Dover).

Art. An excellent survey of Greek art is **J. Boardman, *Greek Art* (Praeger). More specialized studies are provided by Rhys Carpenter, *Greek Sculpture* (1960); **J. Barron, *Greek Sculpture* (Dutton); **A. W. Lawrence, *Greek Architecture* (Penguin); M. C. Robertson, *Greek Painting* (1959); **P. Devambez, *Greek Painting* (Compass); and **H. Neumayer, *Greek Vase-Painting* (Crown). All these works are well illustrated. Many readers will be fascinated with **R. E. Wycherly, *How the Greeks Built Cities* (2nd ed., Anchor). Extremely provocative in terms of esthetic problems is **Charles Seltman, *Approach to Greek Art* (Dutton).

Philosophy and Science. There is a massive body of literature on Greek philosophy. A brief, well-written treatment is **Rex Warner, *Greek Philosophers* (Mentor). Equally valuable as an introduction is **W. K. C. Guthrie, *Greek Philosophers: From Thales to Aristotle* (Harper Torchbook). An older but still valuable summary is **Eduard Zeller, *Outlines of the History of Greek Philosophy* (Meridian).

**F. Copleston, *History of Philosophy*, Vol. I: *Greece and Rome* (Image), is sound and thorough. Still another excellent general treatment is M. M. Warbeke, *The Searching Mind of Greece* (1930). Three books by **A. E. Taylor, *Plato* (Meridian); *Socrates* (Anchor); and *Aristotle* (Dover), provide sound, readable guides to the basic thought of the three great figures in Greek philosophy. A stimulating description of Greek scientific achievements is **Benjamin Farrington, *Greek Science* (2 vols., Penguin). Also excellent and recent are **Marshall Clagett, *Greek Science in Antiquity* (Collier); **O. Neugebauer, *The Exact Sciences in Antiquity* (2nd ed., Dover); and A. Reymond, *History of Science in Greco-Roman Antiquity*, trans. R. Ghuery de Bray (1963). More detailed is the monumental work of **George Sarton, *A History of Science: Ancient Science Through the Golden Age of Greece* (Wiley).

Sources. The most fruitful way to get at the spirit of Greek culture is to read the literature itself. A convenient way to sample that literature is to turn to anthologies. Among those that are well done and easily accessible are **W. H. Auden, ed., *The Portable Greek Reader* (Viking); G. Howe and G. A. Harrer, eds., *Greek Literature in Translation* (1948); C. T. Murphy, K. Guinagh, and W. J. Oates, eds., *Greek and Roman Classics in Translation* (1947); and **M. I. Finley, ed., *Portable Greek Historians* (Viking). A sampling from these anthologies might persuade a reader to undertake reading some authors in their entirety. The following works are recommended as a starting point:

Basic, of course, is **Homer, *Iliad*, trans. E. V. Rieu (Penguin); and *Odyssey*, trans. E. V. Rieu (Penguin). The works of Aeschylus, Sophocles, Euripides, and Aristophanes are available in many paperback editions. An inexpensive collection of representative works is **L. R. Lind, ed., *Ten Greek Plays in Contemporary Translations* (Riverside Editions). A fuller collection is **Greek Tragedies*, trans. R. Lattimore *et al.* (3 vols., Phoenix). The works of Herodotus and Thucydides are essential reading; the editions cited in Chapter 6 are excellent. The works of Plato and Aristotle are also available in many editions. A good place to start is with selected writings. **Scott Buchanan, ed., *The Portable Plato* (Viking) represents Plato well; it includes his dialogues *Protagoras, Phaedo, Symposium,* and *The Republic*. A good introduction to Aristotle's writings is provided by Richard McKeon, ed., *The Basic Works of Aristotle* (1941); especially recommended are *Politics, Nicomachean Ethics, Metaphysics,* and *Poetics*.

Chapter 8 ❧ Greek Imperialism: The Hellenistic World, 336–31 B.C.

The victorious march of the Macedonians into Greece wrote a tragic note to a brilliant chapter in history; to many Greeks, the coming of the barbarians spelled doom. But as is so often the case when men judge their own age, they were wrong. The Macedonian conquest set the stage for a new chapter in Greek history; it liberated the Greeks from what was becoming a restrictive milieu to work their talents in a new setting. The Greeks were about to discover what one of their own philosophers, Democritus, had realized when he argued that the native land of great souls is the whole earth. Under Macedonian leadership, they exploded out of the Aegean to establish their mastery over a wide circle in Asia and Africa. Their genius and their traditions began to mix with Near Eastern civilizations to produce a new culture which historians have called "Hellenistic" ("like Hellenic" the term often used to designate the civilization of the Greek classical age).

1. ALEXANDER THE GREAT

The military and political genius of Alexander the Great was chiefly responsible for launching the Greeks on this new phase of their history. Endowed with numerous qualities of greatness—intelligence, ambition, industry, imagination, physical attractiveness, boldness, an iron will—Alexander has never ceased to fascinate students of history. Although a Macedonian by birth, he was a Greek in spirit. His education under Aristotle had instilled in him a thorough knowledge and a fanatical admiration of Greek civilization. His conviction that the Greek way represented the ultimate in human excellence, abetted by strong personal ambition, served as the driving force of his fabulous career.

Alexander was twenty when his father was murdered in 336 B.C. Philip had charted the immediate future for his son. Besides being king of Macedon, Alexander was master of the Greek city-states in his role as head of the League of Corinth. Philip had made preparations for a war against Greece's ancient foe, Persia, perhaps hoping to win the approval of all Greeks by rallying them in a crusade. It was this war that absorbed Alexander's interests. He delayed launching it only long enough to cow potential barbarian invaders threatening Macedonia from the north and to reassert his authority in the Greek peninsula by smashing a Macedonian rebellion led by Thebes and Athens.

In 334 B.C. he led his Macedonian-Greek army into Asia Minor in order to attack Persia. Although Persia possessed a huge empire, a rich treasury, and a large army and navy, Alexander was victorious from the beginning. He seems to have conceived a broad strategy for destroying Persia and to have persisted in carrying it out. Perhaps mindful of the role naval power had played in the long struggle between Greeks and Persians, his first campaigns were aimed at winning control of Persia's Mediterranean territories. The Persians tried to stop him in Asia Minor, but he defeated their army at Granicus in 334 B.C. and occupied the key coastal cities. In 333 he again crushed the Persians at the battle of Issus in Syria and proceeded to take over Syria, Palestine, and Egypt, thereby wiping out Persian naval power. Then he marched on the center of Persian power in Mesopotamia and in the spring of 331 destroyed the last major military strength of the Persians at the battle of Arbela. Following this victory, he occupied the chief Persian cities and hunted down the fugitive King Darius III, who was finally murdered in 330 by his own officials as Alexander closed in on him. In four years, Alexander had accomplished his goal—the destruction of the greatest foe of the Greeks. His spectacular success had been compounded of many factors, including the quality of his disciplined Macedonian cavalry and infantry, his own brilliant tactical and strategic talents, his amazing ability to inspire trust in his men, and the weakness of the Persian armies and leadership.

His restless genius would permit no pause.

The end of Persian power, symbolized by the death of Darius III, did not satisfy his ambition. Again he drove eastward. Battling vast distances, native resistance, and defection in his own ranks, he pushed across Persia and the Hindu Kush Mountains into Bactria and eventually India, claiming all this territory as his and leaving behind newly founded cities as centers of Greek power. Beyond the Indus Valley his troops refused to go. Alexander therefore turned back westward through southern Persia and into Mesopotamia, where he fell ill and died in June 323 at the age of thirty-three. Tradition has it that he was planning new conquests, including Arabia, Carthage, and Central Asia beyond the Caspian.

A career so short and so completely occupied with military campaigns left Alexander little time to face the problems of ruling his vast conquests. Probably he had no definite plans when he launched his campaign, and formed his policies as circumstances arose. But before he died he had established certain broad principles of policy that guided his successors. As his career progressed, Alexander had conducted himself more and more like a divine autocrat and had departed radically from the Greek ideal of a citizen-ruled state. Seeing that Greeks alone could not rule his vast empire, Alexander began to employ the talents of the conquered peoples. Persians were employed in some army and administrative posts. The fact that Alexander himself and many of his soldiers had married native women might suggest that Alexander hoped for a merger of the many national groups under his rule, but this point must not be pushed too far. From the beginning of his career Alexander had insisted that the Greeks

The use of portraits of rulers on coins began with the successors of Alexander the Great, whose idealized image appears on this silver coin issued by a Thracian king around 300 B.C. *Photo: Museum of Fine Arts, Boston*

Alexander's Empire 336–323 B.C.

would remain politically, economically, and culturally supreme within his empire. High positions in the army and the civil administration were reserved for Greeks; non-Greeks would remain useful subordinates. In Alexander's eyes Greek dominance of the Near East was a goal much more worth attaining than that of amalgamating the East and West racially, culturally, or politically.

Alexander's death left most of his policies far from fulfilled, and it has often been said that his death was timely for the benefit of his fame, since his reputation might have suffered had he lived to face the task of holding his empire together. The Greek masters sat uneasily atop their vast domain. Greek culture was not firmly planted in the conquered territory, although many Greeks had migrated to the new cities built by Alexander and had become missionaries of the Greek way of life. Furthermore, Alexander left no heir capable of capitalizing on the magic of his name. Aside from his conquests his positive achieve-

ments were few; yet no historian would deny his great importance. His influence lay chiefly in what later generations thought he was trying to do. He established for Greek society the ideal that a statesman of ability could create a government capable of bringing peace, harmony, and prosperity to all men living within a vast empire. He also convinced his successors that a great ruler could uplift his subjects by Hellenizing them. The struggle to attain these goals motivated much of the activity of Mediterranean men for centuries after Alexander's death.

2. HELLENISTIC POLITICAL LIFE, 323–31 B.C.

The task of making sense of the political history of Alexander's empire after his death is so formidable that the historian is tempted to dismiss the whole matter rather than confuse his readers. Such a choice is, however, impossible, for during the last three centuries before the Christian era a large and vital portion of the world's civilized populace was involved in that political order. The difficulty surrounding Hellenistic political history stems from the fact that more than one approach is possible and instructive, but that no one approach succeeds in portraying the whole story.

We can recount Hellenistic political history from the point of view of Alexander's dream of political unity, peace, and harmony. Alexander's successors tried to follow this program, especially in the early years after his death; throughout the Hellenistic period men dreamed of reconstructing the ecumenical empire. From this perspective, Hellenistic political history is a story of failure. Hardly was the great conqueror dead when the struggle began to divide his empire. Out of that struggle emerged a hodgepodge of political entities of various sizes, strengths, and forms of government. Relationships among these "successor states" were constantly embattled, so that war rather than peace was the normal condition. The strife had the overall effect of weakening them and creating opportunities for outside powers. Ultimately, Rome was the chief beneficiary, incorporating into her empire the best parts of Alexander's empire— Macedonia, the Aegean area, Asia Minor, Syria, Palestine, and Egypt.

Again, we might approach Hellenistic history by seeking to discover the fate of Alexander's program of establishing a small minority of Greeks and Macedonians as political masters of the vast territory which a Persian minority had previously ruled. Again there was partial failure. Large segments of Alexander's conquests escaped Greek control. During the third century B.C. the territory lying east of the Tigris-Euphrates Valley was taken over by non-Greeks, and kingdoms of considerable importance to the future, including Bactria and Parthia, were established. Along the southern coast of the Black Sea small but virile kingdoms—Pontus, Bithynia, Cappadocia—were established by local rulers. Despite these losses, the conquering masters did retain power in a large part of the Near

East, especially in Egypt, Syria, Palestine, and the southern shore of Asia Minor. And their power was solidly established; they met little resistance from the native populations. It is true that the ruling elite did to some degree adapt their ways to the political traditions of their subjects, particularly in Egypt. Still, the ability of a relatively few outsiders, nourished in the unique environment of the Greek *polis*, to establish and hold political power over extensive areas where lived highly civilized peoples with ancient political traditions of their own is a great achievement.

Still another approach to Hellenistic history —and the one usually taken—is to concentrate on the most prominent states that developed in the period. Immediately after Alexander's sudden death, a council of his generals decided to maintain a united empire under a single monarch. They elected Alexander's incompetent half-brother as king, with the understanding that should the child which Alexander's widow, Roxanne, was carrying be male, he would share the throne—which is what happened. Despite their royal blood, this pair could provide no direction for the shaky empire, and the generals were soon engaged in a struggle for control. Although the competitors probably did not consciously plan a division of the empire, their struggles demonstrated that no one of them could win a decisive victory that would ensure him control over the entire empire. The next recourse for each was to take what he could get and create a new state for himself and his progeny. The process of partition was not very rational and the exact boundaries of the emerging states were confused, but by about 275 B.C. there were three major kingdoms. In Egypt Ptolemy had established himself as successor to the ancient pharaohs and had laid claim to territories in Palestine and Syria. Another general, Antigonus, claimed the old kingdom of Macedon plus control over the Greek city-states still theoretically bound to Macedon in the league established by Philip in 33 B.C. Seleucus staked out a third kingdom embracing all the lands from Asia Minor to

India; this conglomeration was most nearly similar to Alexander's empire.

Only the briefest summary of the complex histories of these kingdoms can be undertaken here. Macedonian political history centered around the efforts of a succession of kings to maintain control over the Greek city-states and to hold back barbarians constantly pressing on the northern frontiers of the kingdom. These burdens were great for the monarchs, since Macedon was a poor land whose manpower had been badly depleted by the eastern conquests. The Greeks were especially stubborn in resisting Macedonian control, so that the kings were involved in an incessant round of wars and diplomatic maneuvers. In general, they did exert considerable influence over the Greeks, but eventually their involvement brought on their downfall. Shortly before 200 B.C. some of the Greek city-states appealed to Rome for help against Macedon. In the ensuing wars, Roman armies overran and annexed both Macedon and Greece.

The Ptolemaic kingdom was the most stable of the Hellenistic states. The ruling dynasty inherited a homogeneous population and a rich land. They established an autocratic regime such as the Egyptians had long known and exploited the agricultural and commercial potential of Egypt with intelligence and skill. Internal stability and wealth permitted the Ptolemies to play an active role in foreign affairs; they concentrated chiefly on extending their sway in Syria, which involved them in almost constant struggle with the Seleucid kingdom. Not until the second century B.C. did Ptolemaic power begin to decline. In the face of growing internal unrest, the rulers turned to Rome for support. Eventually (in 31 B.C.), Rome annexed Ptolemaic Egypt to her empire.

The history of the Seleucid kingdom is most difficult to tell. Its huge size and mixed populace provided little basis for unity or stability. The burden of its rulers was to supply a common bond, but although some of them were men of ability, the task was too great.

Rather quickly they lost the territories they claimed east of Mesopotamia. Their hold on Asia Minor was always tenuous and ultimately was compromised by the emergence of petty kingdoms in the northern and western portions, of which Pergamum was the most significant. Most of the royal energy was devoted to creating a viable state embracing Syria and Mesopotamia. The Ptolemies constantly challenged the Seleucids for control of Syria. The kings also had to contend with native uprisings, for example, the Maccabean revolt among the Jews. Ultimately the Seleucid kingdom was squeezed to death by Parthian pressure from the east and Roman pressure from the west. The last Seleucid king was overthrown in 64 B.C. by the Romans, called into Asia Minor by the petty kingdoms bent on protecting their independence against Seleucid claims.

Numerous smaller states shared the political scene with these three large kingdoms during the Hellenistic period. Chief among them were several Greek city-states which continued their independent existences and had their own histories. Their internal affairs remained a vital concern, as did their efforts to hold off Macedonian power and their rivalries with other city-states. A noteworthy development in Greek history in this period was the establishment of effective leagues as a means of holding off Macedonian might. The two chief ones were the Aetolian League in central Greece and the Achaean League in the Peloponnesus, both of which demonstrated willingness on the part of some Greeks to compromise total autonomy in the interests of common effort. Among the small states of the era, the most successful were the kingdom of Pergamum in western Asia Minor and the Republic of Rhodes, both of which fared well by capitalizing on the commercial activity of the Hellenistic Age.

The mere listing of the chief states suggests another approach to Hellenistic political history. The existence of so many states growing out of a unified empire created an especially acute problem for interstate relations.

As a consequence, during the Hellenistic Age rulers engaged in a kind of intensive and sophisticated activity in the realm of international relations new to men. Great and small states developed to a high degree a battery of techniques designed to gain advantage over other states: military force, diplomacy, psychological warfare, internal subversion, economic penetration. In a general way, the Hellenistic world moved toward a balance of power structure which safeguarded the status quo rather effectively until a major outside power such as Rome moved onto the scene. For all its unsavory aspects, the history of international relations in the Hellenistic Age constituted a highly significant chapter in the long and difficult story of man's effort to find ways of regulating affairs among competing states. Even the city-states of classical Greece could have learned much from the experience of that period. The Romans did learn, and put what they had learned to excellent use in building and ruling their empire.

Finally, the political history of the Hellenistic Age can be approached from an institutional point of view, for it was perhaps in this realm that Hellenistic political development was most fruitful. Although there were many states in the Hellenistic world and although each had its unique institutions, there were certain common patterns of political life.

The very idea of empire itself was important, especially as so dramatically given embodiment by Alexander. The Near Eastern world was, of course, familiar with this political concept as a result of the efforts of the Amorites, the Egyptians, the Hittites, the Assyrians, and the Persians. But it was new to the Greeks, given their enchantment with the microcosmic world of the *polis*. The experiences of the Hellenistic Age put into the Greek vocabulary and mentality the vision of a great world state where men of many kinds shared a common citizenship and a common destiny. Nowhere was this ideal given more eloquent expression than in the political ideology of the Stoics, who were among the chief philosophical products of the age. And the concept of

empire shaped by Greeks in the Hellenistic Age had a powerful impact on Rome.

The chief development in political institutions during the Hellenistic period, however, was the Greek acceptance of the concept of monarchical government. The Greeks had been schooled to think that a *polis* governed by the collective will of equal citizens (or at least the best of them) was the only civilized form of government. In the fourth century, as is obvious in Plato's *Republic*, that idea began to be questioned in favor of a form of government in which only a hero, a philosopher-king, a superman could provide good government. The success of monarchs like Philip and Alexander served as practical demonstrations of the validity of this idea. During the Hellenistic period, monarchy became the standard form of government among the Greek rulers of the Near East. In most Hellenistic kingdoms the king's power was personal: it derived from his feats at arms, his intelligence, his will, and his favor wth the gods. By virtue of his abilities, he could bestow blessings on his subjects. No constitution limited his power. No entrenched nobility acted to check him. No law other than what he decreed set limits to his authority. Only his ability defined the range of his power. Obviously, this kind of monarchy was shaped by the traditions of the ancient Near East, but it reflected a quality of its own, especially to the extent that it was personal and derived from human ability. In this sense, it bore the stamp of ancient Greece.

To exercise his vast powers efficiently, each Hellenistic king developed a well-organized central government, featuring a strong army, an elaborate bureaucracy, and a carefully structured tax system. The chief offices in the armies and bureaucracies were manned by Greeks, many of them recruited from the old Greek world in the Aegean. Some Orientals held lesser positions, but in the main the Greeks maintained a monopoly on political office and the exercise of power. Elitism supplied a powerful bond of loyalty to the monarch. The old structures of local government were left largely intact, except that again Greeks manned the key posts. One major development was the spread of Greek city-state institutions into the cities of the Near East. Wherever there were Greeks, assemblies, councils, popular courts, and elected officials were instituted in such a way as to give the Greek communities considerable local autonomy. However, while the political institutions nourished in the *polis* penetrated the Near East, the Greek masters were learning from their subjects. In establishing their centralized, autocratic, bureaucratic kingdoms, the Greeks borrowed from their predecessors, especially the Persians and the Egyptians.

While centralized, absolutist monarchy gained the upper hand in the Hellenistic world, the older city-state polity persisted with considerable vitality in Greece and western Asia Minor. Many *poleis* remained completely autonomous during much of the Hellenistic Age. The accustomed forms of city-state government continued—democracies, oligarchies, tyrannies. Assemblies, elected officials, councils, popular courts, and citizen armies still operated to make and carry out a wide range of decisions. The city-state world even demonstrated the power to innovate, as illustrated by the Aetolian and Achaean leagues, both of which were better organized and more effective than earlier Greek confederations. But if the *polis* lived on, it was overshadowed in every way by monarchy. In war, in beautification of cities, in patronage of the arts, in wealth, in security, Athens and Sparta could not match the Seleucid or the Ptolemaic kingdoms.

And for all its confusion, the Hellenistic period was of great importance politically. The Greeks demonstrated an ability to turn their considerable political talents to the creation of units larger than the *polis*. They put their own stamp on monarchy, yet were willing to utilize the political experience of peoples they conquered to refine and to make more effective the art of government. They experimented in the area of establishing local autonomy within a larger framework and in the area of international relations. The whole complex of Hellenistic government prepared the ground for the Romans, who did so much to perpetuate the Greek political experience and to make many of its features applicable to a world far larger than the Aegean basin.

3. HELLENISTIC PROSPERITY

Greek rule in the Hellenistic world resulted in vigorous economic growth, so that one of the highlights of the period was an amazing prosperity. Alexander's conquest might well be compared to Columbus' discovery in the sense that it opened up for Greek exploitation a vast territory endowed with great riches, just as Columbus' discovery supplied Europeans with new wealth and new lands to exploit. The Greeks migrated from their native cities in large numbers and applied themselves with vigor to the exploitation of these new lands. As they broke away from their native *poleis*, they discarded the old attitudes that had placed a higher value on political and cultural life than on economic enterprise. Many of them now became skilled entrepreneurs willing to seek out and exploit the opportunities presented by the larger setting. All over the Near East they found a native population accustomed to economic domination by a narrow ruling group and were therefore able to seize economic control without too much resistance. In many areas of the Hellenistic world well-organized agriculture, skilled industry, and well-developed trading systems already existed, again supplying openings for Greek enterprise. The energetic Greeks missed few of these opportunities. Agriculture, industry, and commerce all expanded under their management.

Agriculture continued to be the basic source of wealth. The new Greek masters did not fundamentally change the well-established and productive farming systems prevailing in the Near East. They did, however, promote greater efficiency and productivity. Greek entrepreneurs, including the kings, sponsored land clearance, directed new irrigation projects, encouraged crop rotation and fertilization, introduced new crops and better breeds of livestock, and organized production more effectively. One senses here an application of the rational spirit of the Greeks at a very mundane level.

The chief advance was in trade and industry. The Greeks displayed tremendous energy in exploiting the markets and the products put at their disposal when they conquered the Near East. Extensive capital came into their hands as a result of their seizure of the treasury of the Persian king and of the wealth controlled by the rich all over the Near East. The Greeks put this capital to work in large-scale trading and industrial ventures. Their activities were centered chiefly in the great seaboard cities of the eastern Mediterranean, but they extended outward to the entire Mediterranean world. The shift of the centers of production and exchange eastward was a grave blow to the prosperity of the old Greek economic centers (especially Athens), but the total effect was to greatly enrich the Greeks in general. The Hellenistic kings led in this activity by creating state monopolies for the exchange and production of many items. They also helped trade by clearing the seas of pirates, keeping roads safe, building canals and harbors, improving marketing facilities in their cities, establishing sound money systems, and abolishing artificial political barriers to trade. But private entrepreneurs were by no means absent; every important city was full of enterprising manufacturers, active traders, and skilled artisans. The horizons of commerce were considerably extended by active geographical exploration which expanded Greek contacts eastward to India and out of the western end of the Mediterranean to the coasts of Africa, Western Europe, and Britain.

Hellenistic prosperity, however, benefited only a few—princes, civil servants, landowners, great merchants, and priests. The mass of the population on the farms and in the cities still labored for small gain. The Greeks who spread over the Near East were usually predominant in the favored upper classes, the natives generally economically oppressed. As the Hellenistic era progressed, this gap between rich and poor caused increasing social conflict. Moreover, the prosperity was not evenly distributed geographically. The great centers of wealth were in a belt stretching from Asia Minor to Egypt. Here were the great cities, like Alexandria and Antioch, the best farms, the chief trade routes, the most skilled workers, and the most capital. Greece itself suffered a constant impoverishment during the Hellenistic Age as economic leadership moved eastward and southward. This situation bred deep hostility and boded ill for the long-run stability of Hellenistic society.

The increasing maldistribution of wealth marking the later stages of Hellenistic history constituted a serious failure on the part of the Greek masters. In many of the ancient Greek city-states, intelligent leadership, often supplied by aristocrats, had directed economic and social development toward the improvement of the lot of the poor and the deprived, a policy that had strengthened the whole fabric of society. The experience might have suggested a similar policy to the Greek rulers and entrepreneurs of the Hellenistic Age, which if followed, might have strengthened their rule. But the Greeks now chose to be exploiters. Perhaps this new posture was a natural product of their position as rulers over subjects rather than sharers of power with fellow citizens. Perhaps too it was the inevitable consequence of their migration from the ancient *poleis,* a process that transformed them from aristocratic political animals into entrepreneurial economic animals.

4. LITERATURE AND ART

The three centuries following Alexander's conquests mark an important era in cultural history. The Greeks were convinced they had conquered "barbarians." No matter how deeply they became involved with Asians, they retained their feeling of superiority and sought to impress their ideas on their subjects. Nevertheless, expansion brought the Greeks face to face with new ideas and made them aware of their own limitations. The result was a new outburst of activity in art, literature, and philosophy which broadened the older Greek culture without destroying its basic features.

The literary output of the Hellenistic Age was massive. The outpouring was in part due to the patronage of wealthy monarchs, officials, and private individuals and in part to the increased demand for literature by a growing reading public needing to develop bureaucratic skills and desirous of keeping in touch with their Hellenic cultural origins. The Greek language became the common tongue of the Hellenistic world of government, commerce, and learning. Not a few Greek subjects learned the language and put it to use, as illustrated by the fact that the Old Testament was translated into Greek (the Septuagint) in Alexandria in the third and second centuries B.C. for the use of Jews living there who had forgotten Hebrew. While the writers of the Hellenistic Age were prolific, they were not especially creative. They imitated the epic and lyric poems, the tragedies and comedies, and the histories of classical Greece. Most of the writers, especially the poets, were chiefly concerned with style. They often worked over old subject matter in an attempt to achieve stylistic perfection. As a consequence, later ages found Hellenistic literature of little interest, and almost none of it has survived. It did, however, serve as a model for the Romans in developing their literary styles in Latin.

The Hellenistic Age also produced a multitude of scholars who spent their lives reconstructing earlier Greek literary masterpieces,

writing extensive commentaries on their meaning, analyzing their grammar, and defining their stylistic features. This patient and somewhat dull labor played an important role in establishing and preserving the texts of the Greek classics that have come down to the present. Intensive scholarship helped to fix the rules of Greek grammar and to identify the basic features of literary forms. Scholarly activity tended to concentrate in a few great cities, of which Alexandria and Pergamum were the most important and Athens the most prestigious. Supported by royal patronage, scholars at Alexandria and Pergamum collected great libraries as storehouses

Aphrodite of Melos (Venus de Milo) demonstrates the changing styles in art in the Hellenistic period: She is more like a portrait of an actual woman than an idealization of the female form. *Photo: Alinari–Art Reference Bureau*

of the wisdom of the entire civilized world. The scholarly establishment provided endless grist for an education system that was expanding in the Hellenistic Age and becoming increasingly literary and formal. Education played an increased role in preparing the Greek ruling elite to discharge its duties and to sustain the cultural brand that was its mark of superiority. Men who wished to become professionals in philosophy, medicine, teaching, science, and even the arts tended to gravitate to the major scholarly centers for training, so that a kind of higher education evolved.

The artists of the Hellenistic period were no less active than the literary men. Again clas-

sical Greek models exerted a powerful influence, completely overshadowing the artistic traditions of the Near East. Architecture enjoyed a great boom because of the numerous new cities built by the Greeks and because of the desire of Greek kings and rich merchants to display their power and wealth. The new cities were filled with the traditional buildings —temples, gymnasiums, theaters, and buildings for conducting public business. There was a tendency to stress size and ornateness in these buildings, although their basic architectural style followed the traditional pattern. Most Hellenistic cities were much better planned than the older Greek cities, with emphasis on wide streets, adequate water supplies, commercial conveniences, and parks. As a result, cities like Alexandria were more impressive than older cities like Athens.

Much Hellenistic sculpture was mere copying of the masters of fifth-century Greece. However, some of this work took on important new features. In place of the classic quest to create idealized perfection in portraying a subject, Hellenistic sculptors tended toward realism. They came down into the streets for their subjects instead of ascending to the abode of the gods. Children, old people, common laborers, and barbarians occupied their attention. In place of the restraint and reasonableness of classic sculpture, Hellenistic artists gave vent to emotions, seeking to portray action and violence, passion, sorrow, and suffering. Often they overdid themselves, but occasionally a Hellenistic artist caught the full spirit of the classical style, as the famous *Winged Victory of Samothrace* or the *Aphrodite of Melos* (more commonly known as the *Venus de Milo*) illustrate so well.

This statue of an old market woman, a second-century Hellenistic marble found in Rome, reflects even more than the Aphrodite an emotionalism and realism far removed from the serene, idealized figures of classical Greece. *Photo: The Metropolitan Museum of Art*

5. PHILOSOPHY AND SCIENCE

The major contributions of the Hellenistic Age were in the fields of science and philosophy, which had been opened by the pioneering Greeks in the sixth, fifth, and fourth centuries. Often the Hellenistic thinkers moved beyond their predecessors, a development that seldom occurred in the fields of literature and art.

The moment was especially ripe for scientific advance. The Greek philosophers of the sixth, fifth, and fourth centuries had posed the big questions about the universe and had made brilliant hypotheses about the natural world. Some of them, especially Hippocrates and Aristotle, had introduced the idea that the natural world could best be understood by observing it and by rationally classifying the results of observation. Some of Aristotle's successors in the Peripatetic School at Athens followed the master's lead by specializing in systematic observation. Many educated men shared a sense of the importance of this approach; Alexander, for example, arranged for the collection of strange natural specimens during his military ventures into the distant east. His conquest put the Greeks in touch with a huge body of data compiled over many centuries by learned men in the ancient Near East. The general use of Greek as the language of learning permitted scientific advances to spread widely. Royal patronage, especially by the Ptolemies, who built a great library and museum at Alexandria, helped to create an interest in science and to provide the necessary facilities. In this favorable climate the quest for knowledge about the natural world was actively pursued.

It will serve our purposes to mention a few of the great scientific names of the age, letting their work illustrate the efforts of the many who worked in science. For instance, geography was of great interest in the Hellenistic period. The new geography was summed up by Eratosthenes (ca. 275–200 B.C.), who worked at Alexandria. Using observations from a variety of sources, he reached many important conclusions. He calculated the circumference of the earth as 24,662 miles, about 200 less than the actual figure. On the basis of his study of tides, he insisted that the Atlantic and Indian oceans were joined and that India could be reached by sailing around Africa. He made maps using lines of longitude and latitude and divided the earth into zones still used by geographers. Seleucus (second century B.C.), along with others, studied the tides and came close to relating them to the gravitational force of the moon.

Astronomy likewise attracted attention. The two greatest names were Aristarchus (ca. 310–230 B.C.) and Hipparchus (ca. 185–120 B.C.). Both men worked from observations, many of which had been made by Mesopotamians of an earlier period. Aristarchus insisted that the earth revolved around the sun. Hipparchus denied this, and his opinion carried the day. Hipparchus compiled an extensive atlas of the stars and from observation of their movement arrived at a calculation of the length of the solar year that was extremely accurate. Both these great astronomers tried to calculate the size of the sun and its distance from the earth, but with little success.

Much was also done to advance mathematics. Euclid (323–285 B.C.) compiled a textbook of geometry that remained standard until the twentieth century. Archimedes (287–212 B.C.) calculated the value of π (the ratio between the circumference and the diameter of a circle). He also devised a system for expressing large numbers, solved the problem of the relative volumes of a cylinder and a sphere, and laid the foundations for calculus. Trigonometry was perfected by Hipparchus, and a fundamental work on conic sections was done by Apollonius of Perga (third century).

Scientific medicine was of great interest to the scholars of this period. Following the lead of Hippocrates, Hellenistic physicians made important progress in anatomy and physiology. Among the chief accomplishments of these men were the discovery of the nerves and the exploration of the function of arteries and the brain. Surgery advanced considerably; so did the use of medicines as a healing art.

Comparatively little work was done in physics, chemistry, zoology, and botany. Archimedes, however, discovered the laws governing floating bodies and developed the theory of the lever; and Theophrastus (ca. 372–287 B.C.) wrote an important descriptive work on botany that summarized most of the knowledge of plants in his day.

Most of the important work of Hellenistic scientists had been completed by the end of the second century B.C. Thereafter interest shifted to magic, astrology, and empty repetition of past accomplishments. The Hellenistic Greeks, like their predecessors in classical Greece, were limited in their scientific progress by lack of proper instruments. And there was still no widespread interest in the practical application of scientific ideas, although a few scientists did distinguish themselves as inventors. Archimedes, for instance, invented the windlass, the double pulley, the endless screw, and several devices for defending his native city, Syracuse, against Roman attack.

The last significant development in ancient science came when certain scholars of the first and second centuries A.D. compiled great encyclopedias summarizing earlier scientific work. Among these works were those of Ptolemy (ca. A.D. 85–160) in astronomy and geography, Strabo (ca. 63 B.C.–A.D. 21) in geography, and Galen (A.D. 130–201) in medicine. The bulk of the material in these manuals was derived from the labors of Hellenistic scientists, so that each is a monument to their accomplishments. These encyclopedias served as scientific guides until the beginning of the great scientific revolution in early modern times; little was added in the nearly two millennia separating the Hellenistic scientists from Galileo and Copernicus. And the information contained in these collections served as the starting points for the work of the early modern scientists. It may be fair to conclude that the Hellenistic Age was the second greatest period of scientific advance in history, surpassed only by the advances of the last four centuries.

For vigor and creativity, Hellenistic science was rivaled by Hellenistic philosophy. The old philosophical interests lived on, as evidenced by the continued activity of Plato's Academy and Aristotle's Lyceum in Athens. However, the basic interests and major accomplishments changed. The older Hellenic quest for absolute truth about the cosmic order gave way to concern with problems of human conduct, ethical principles, and above all the human soul. The individual and his personal destiny became the focus of the philosopher's quest. This trend was already evident among the Sophists of the fifth century B.C. In the Hellenistic Age it was given new impetus by the wrenching experience which projected many Greeks out of the hothouse of the *polis* into a cosmopolitan world where men were on their own among strangers of many kinds. Left with only his own resources, man needed self-knowledge and reassurance.

The search for individual identity and guidance in a cosmopolitan world produced several schools of thought. Some of them caught popular fancy or aroused popular ire for their eccentricity and excess. One such school was that of the Skeptics, who made a principle of doubting everything and argued that men should go about living with no concern for truth or values. The Cynics were more spectacular; they advocated that society should abandon all its civilized conventions, its refinements, and its wealth in order to return to nature. In search of converts, the Cynics took to the streets in filthy rags to deliver their diatribes against the "establishment."

More profound and influential was the teaching of Epicurus (ca. 341–270 B.C.), who taught at Athens. He built his ethical concepts on a strictly materialistic basis. He taught that the universe consisted of atoms, which by chance formed themselves into beings and things. The gods, if they existed, had nothing to do with this process and therefore need be of no concern to men. Given such a world, men should concern themselves only with happiness and pleasure. Epicurus argued that mere physical pleasure is not the path to happiness. Those things that will bring a peaceful, undisturbed mind alone can make a man truly happy. Epicurus pleaded with his disciples to withdraw into themselves, avoid excessive wealth, involvement in politics, superstition, and too great contact with the world. Each individual ought to create a world of his own in which there is a minimum of strife, worry, or concern over the future. This philosophy was welcome to many educated men of the period who saw little use in struggling in a world where great kings and great wealth determined most things. It offered a logical reason for escaping to a refined, enlightened, unburdened privacy. Although some disciples of Epicurus turned his teachings into an excuse for seeking purely physical pleasure, most Epicureans were admirable men, learned and refined, obedient to public authority, calm, and long-suffering.

Even more influential in shaping the moral atmosphere of the Hellenistic Age were the Stoics, whose founder, Zeno (336–264 B.C.), taught in Athens while Epicurus was there, but who was of Semitic origin and thus an interesting product of the Greek impact on the Near East. Stoicism was based on Zeno's conviction that the universe is ruled by a Divine Reason which determines the fashion in which nature operates. For many Stoics this Divine Reason is a great god, overshadowing all other gods and providing a unity within the universe. This Stoic deity had ordained a perfect world; harmony and order would result if the laws of nature were adhered to by all creatures in the universe. Man's moral duty is thus clear. He must use his reason to attune himself and his actions to the unchanging laws of nature arising from Divine Reason. He must bear all misfortune with patience, since everything that happens has been ordained by an all-knowing Providence. And he must bear his good fortune without pride, since he is not responsible for it. The Stoic was schooled to adjust himself to circumstances; his life was a pilgrimage in which he disciplined himself to accept whatever came.

6. HELLENISTIC RELIGION

In at least one realm of life, the Greek way suffered an eclipse. This was in the area of religion. The old civic religion of the Greeks had already been weakened by the blows suffered by the city-states in the fifth and fourth centuries and by the assaults of the philosophers. The old gods and the communal rites in their honor ceased to have any meaning to the Greeks who migrated from the city-states into the Near East. From Alexander's time onward, there was an attempt to encourage the worship of kings as the civic religion, but it took no root among the Greeks.

Permeating the Near East were powerful religious forces rooted deep in the past. These forces had evolved into definable cults that we shall call collectively *mystery religions*. With the passing of time, the Near Eastern mystery religions simply overpowered Greek civic religion and drew increasing numbers of Greeks into their orbits. Many mystery cults flourished in the Near East in the Hellenistic Age: Isis worship, Mithraism, the Earth Mother cult. In fact, the Greeks still had their own mystery cult in Dionysus worship. Whatever their origin, all shared certain fundamental ideas that clashed sharply with the communally oriented, humanistic cults of the *polis*. They centered around the worship of a savior whose death and resurrection provided salvation for each individual. The gods of the mystery cults tended to be universal, appealing to men of all classes and nations. The mystery religions involved elaborate, emotional ritual practices and stressed the moral conduct of each individual believer. In the cosmopolitan atmosphere of the Hellenistic world, ideas from various mystery religions constantly mingled; this syncretism pointed toward the growth of a common faith shared especially by common men throughout the entire Hellenistic world. Here was the seedbed for two new religions soon to arise in the Near East—Christianity and Islam.

The mystery cults powerfully influenced several aspects of thought and expression. Science and philosophy were put to the service of these religions. Scientific astronomy was transformed into astrology, the "scientist" studying the stars in order to know the future rather than to find new information, while the philosopher's quest for an understanding of the universe became an attempt to achieve contact with the powerful deities of the mystery cults. In this sense the peoples of the Near East conquered the Greeks during the Hellenistic period.

As we observe this "religionizing" of culture, we sense that Greek culture and its Hellenistic continuation had come full circle. A culture born out of religion was now being absorbed back into religion. A real possibility existed that some of the finest achievements of the Greeks would be swallowed up and twisted out of shape as a result of their losing encounter with Near Eastern religious ideas. This trend was checked at least temporarily by the emergence of Rome as a new champion of Greek civilization. Under Roman auspices Greek culture in a Latinized form enjoyed a renaissance and increased its geographical sway considerably by spreading to the western Mediterranean world.

Suggested Reading

Political History. The best general survey of this period is Max Cary, *A History of the Greek World From 323 to 146 B.C.* (2nd ed., rev., 1963). There are several excellent recent studies of the always intriguing figure of Alexander the Great. Perhaps best is W. W. Tarn, *Alexander the Great* (2 vols., 1948; Vol. I has been published in a paperback edition by Beacon), which stresses Alexander's importance as the creator of brotherhood and unity. **A. R. Burn, *Alexander the Great and the Hellenistic World* (Collier) is a short, popularly written biography, so well done that it reads like a novel; it ends with a stimulating discussion of Alexander's impact on world history. C. A. Robinson, *Alexander the Great: The Meeting of East and West in World Government and Brotherhood* (1946), is a clear, well-constructed story of Alexander's career, perhaps colored too much by the aspirations of the immediate post-World War II years. A general survey of Hellenistic life in all its aspects is supplied by **W. W. Tarn and G. T. Griffith, *Hellenistic Civilization* (3rd ed., Meridian); the book is organized topically.

Hellenistic Cultural Life. A provocative treatment of the Hellenistic intellectual achievement is Moses Hadas, *Hellenistic Culture: Fusion and Diffusion* (1959). M. Bieber, *Sculpture of the Hellenistic Age* (rev. ed., 1961), is thorough and has excellent illustrations. A rather prosaic outline of Hellenistic literature is provided by F. A. Wright, *History of Later Greek Literature* (1932). Hellenistic science is thoroughly treated by **George Sarton, *A History of Science: Hellenistic Science and Culture in the Last Three Centuries B.C.* (Wiley); and **O. Neugebauer, *The Exact Sciences in Antiquity* (2nd ed., Dover). For Hellenistic philosophy, two excellent although somewhat difficult books are **N. W. DeWitt,

Epicurus and His Philosophy (Meridian); and Edwyn Bevan, *Stoics and Sceptics* (1913).

Sources. A colorful biography of Alexander the Great is provided by **Arrian, *The Life of Alexander the Great,* trans. A. de Selincourt (Penguin); although Arrian lived in the second century A.D., he used materials written at the time of Alexander but now lost in compiling his biography.   Plutarch, *Lives,* contains a short but excellent sketch of Alexander.   W. J.

Oates, ed., *The Stoic and Epicurean Philosophers* (1940), provides a collection of nearly all the writings of the Stoic and Epicurean writers of the Hellenistic period; these philosophers are well worth studying for their importance to the later history of philosophy. **F. C. Grant, *Hellenistic Religion: The Age of Syncretism* (Liberal Arts), brings together an excellent collection of ancient writings dealing with religious movements in the Hellenistic Age.

Chapter 9 🌿 The Rise of Rome to Domination

of the Mediterranean World

The failure of the Greek city-states and the Hellenistic kingdoms to establish permanent order in the eastern Mediterranean opened the way by the end of the third century B.C. for the intrusion of a new power from the West: Rome. Down to about 4000 B.C. there had been few differences between eastern and western Mediterranean peoples, but after that date the West had fallen far behind. The rise of Rome to a position where it could challenge eastern powers marks the first time western Mediterranean peoples were able to play a decisive role in history. Their long preparation for this role is the concern of this chapter.

1. THE EARLY ITALIANS

The city of Rome was the catalytic force which organized the peoples of the western Mediterranean, and especially of Italy, for their new role, but Rome relied primarily on the Italians for the human resources to achieve her greatness. The formation of the Italian people was a long, complex process still badly understood. At a very ancient date Italy was inhabited by paleolithic hunters whose way of life was similar to that of paleolithic peoples all across the Mediterranean basin. During the third millennium B.C., farming culture, strongly affected by influences from the east, spread over Italy. This new culture was probably brought by peoples migrating to Italy, perhaps from North Africa. These stocky, swarthy people were to be the basic population of the future. Between about 2000 and 1000 B.C., successive waves of Indo-Europeans moved into Italy from north of the Alps and were fused with the neolithic stock. The newcomers brought with them superior technical skills, especially the use of copper, bronze, and iron, and superior military and political skills, so that they often imposed their authority on the natives. Especially significant was the emergence of various Indo-European dialects, of which Latin was one, as the prevailing language in Italy. In the second millennium B.C., there was a steady advance in the level of life in Italy, although the population still lagged far behind that of the eastern Mediterranean.

Beginning approximately 800 B.C., the backward western Mediterranean world, including Italy, was powerfully stimulated by the appearance of highly civilized easterners in the West—the Phoenicians, the Greeks, and the Etruscans. The Phoenician impact was slight in Italy but decisive in North Africa, where it was the source for the emergence of the powerful city of Carthage. As we have seen, the Greeks settled in Sicily and southern Italy, where their city-states created a replica of the Aegean world and from whence powerful cultural forces flowed to the Italian mainland. It was the Etruscans, however, who had the most immediate and direct influence on

Italy and especially on Rome. This people is still an enigma to historians, in large part because their language has not yet been deciphered. They probably came from Asia Minor during the eighth century B.C. and established a series of cities along the western coast of Italy north of the Tiber. Although these cities remained politically independent, they were bound together by strong economic, religious, and cultural ties. Within a short time Etruscan influence began to expand so that between about 650 and 500 B.C., they ruled supreme over western Italy from the Po Valley to Naples. After 500 B.C. their power declined as a result of native resistance and opposition from Greeks and Carthaginians. However, during the period of their predominance, the Etruscans transmitted to the peoples of Italy a wide range of political, technological, religious, and cultural influences that were decisive in preparing these peoples for a major historical role. Their most precocious pupils were some villagers living along the Tiber.

2. THE FOUNDATION AND EARLY HISTORY OF ROME TO 509 B.C.

The colorful legends enshrined in the works of the Roman historian Livy—including the story of the founding of Rome by Romulus and Remus in 753 B.C.—are undoubtedly beguiling, but they have little relationship to fact. Rome's emergence was a tortured process that seemed to hold small promise of greatness. The future "head of the world" was initially the creation of simple, backward herder-farmers living in a poor area known as Latium, which lay south of the Tiber and west of the foothills of the Apennines. About 750 B.C. some of these Latins established villages on a cluster of seven hills lying south of the Tiber about 15 miles upstream. Perhaps these settlers were attracted by the convenient ford in the river at this point, but more likely they sought the protection and the pastures offered by the hills. Although the villages grew in population during the ensuing century, each

The origin of the Etruscans is still a subject of debate among scholars, for although their culture bears traces of other influences, it is unique and distinctive. This bronze figure, whose costume is Cretan in origin, shows both Etruscan artistic conventions and skill in metalwork. *Photo: Soprintendenza alle Antichita, Museo Archeologico, Florence*

151

retained its own lands and its own tribal political institutions. The residents ultimately formed a loose league which was probably based on common religious practices and a common burial ground in the swampy land below the hills, the future site of the Forum of Rome. Tradition spoke of a common king in this age, but nothing substantiates this legend.

Shortly after 600 B.C., the several villages were rather suddenly transformed into a single city-state. What brought about this decisive event is not clear, but it was probably the consequence of Etruscan domination. During the last half of the sixth century, Rome was ruled by Etruscan kings; they may have been preceded by Etruscan warrior-lords who seized control of the villages and imposed political unity on them. During this period of Etruscan domination, a single government under a king was established. The king was advised by a council of elders, called the Senate, composed of men of wealth who drew their authority from their headship of families. There was also an assembly of freemen who were grouped into thirty units called *curiae*, but this assembly was severely limited in its power, and did little more than approve the decisions of the king and the Senate. The city-state populace was divided into two distinct classes, *patricians* and *plebeians*, with the former exercising a predominant influence over society. Many plebeians were closely tied to the patrician families by the institution of *clientage*. This institution permitted a plebeian to become a *client* of a noble *patron* who undertook to protect him and to assist him materially. In return, the client performed various services for his patron, including following the political directions of the patron. The shaping of these political and social patterns was rooted in earlier institutions, but was decisively influenced by more sophisticated Etruscan models.

Etruscan domination was even more influential in the economic, cultural, and religious life of the fledgling city-state. Advanced techniques, especially those related to trade and industry, were adopted by the Romans, greatly strengthening their primitive economy. An alphabet was derived from Etruscan models, resulting in the rapid development of Latin as a written language. Etruscan architectural and decorative styles served as models for the temples and public buildings that adorned the burgeoning city. Primitive Latin religious practices took on more sophisticated patterns reflecting Etruscan usages. Rome was rapidly becoming the center of an advanced culture; her people were learning the talents needed for a larger historical role.

Despite their debt to the Etruscans, the Romans chafed under their domination. Shortly before 500 B.C. Etruscan power began to be contested by her dependent subjects everywhere in western Italy, while Greeks and Carthaginians vied with Etruscan forces in the larger setting of the western Mediterranean. The challenge was too much for the Etruscans. In Rome the patricians took the lead in a revolution which dethroned the Etruscan king and established in his place two *consuls* elected annually from patrician ranks to wield the *imperium*, that is, the highest authority of the state. This revolution marked the beginning of the Roman Republic, an episode long celebrated by the Romans as the greatest event in their history.

3. THE EARLY REPUBLIC, 509–265 B.C.

The two and a half centuries following the founding of the republic put the Romans to a severe test. On one hand, they had to face constant attacks from outsiders; on the other, there were serious internal problems concerning the distribution of political power. These pressures were resolved in a way that advanced Rome as a power. She disposed of her many Italian enemies by conquering them and forging them into an entity that supplied her with the strength to conquer the Mediterranean world. Internal tensions were relieved by constant adjustment of the instruments of government in ways which resulted in ever-wider citizen participation and ever-stronger patriotism.

From 509 to about 350 B.C., the Romans were chiefly occupied in Latium defending themselves against a variety of foes. Immediately after the revolt against the Etruscans, the other cities of Latium turned against Rome and forced her to accept a position as their equal in a Latin League. This league fought desperately for years to hold back the Etruscans and the tough, prolific mountain peoples of central Italy. About 400 B.C. a new menace emerged in the form of Celtic invaders from Gaul. After ravaging most of northern Italy, they captured and sacked Rome in 390. But the Romans rebuilt their city and soon put a new army into action. More and more, the peoples of Latium viewed the Romans as their protectors and became increasingly dependent on them.

Rome's growing military prowess and her influence in Latium eventually bred fear among some members of the Latin League. They revolted in 340 B.C., but were subdued within two years. The ancient league was dissolved, and Rome established control over Latium. From this base, she turned her attention to the troublesome mountaineers. In a series of campaigns known as the Samnite Wars, stretching from 326 to 290 B.C., she systematically crushed these tribes and incorporated their territory into her expanding state. In the meantime, Roman influence was expanding northward at the expense of the Etruscans and the Gauls. In fighting these various peoples simultaneously, the Romans showed considerable diplomatic skill and succeeded in keeping their foes isolated from one another. Hardly had the Samnite Wars ended when Rome was drawn into the strife-torn world of the Greek city-states in southern Italy. A series of victories in that area ended in 265 B.C. with the Romans in complete control. All Italy south of the Po Valley was hers, constituting the base for a new—although still unproved—world power.

Many factors combined to bring the tiny city on the Tiber these victories. Its Etruscan masters had provided a good start. Rome's location at the center of the Italian world was fortuitous; it brought the city under constant pressure, yet gave it a prime location from which to resist. The Romans showed considerable talent for military organization and for diplomatic maneuvering. But two factors were crucial to victory: Rome's enlightened treatment of her victims and her ability to adjust her internal political system to retain and deepen the loyalty of her citizens.

The victorious Romans spurned the usual methods of brutal subjugation and exploitation of conquered peoples. Rather, they applied a variety of solutions, usually dictated by the practical demands of the situation, to bring their victims under their direction. To some peoples, especially those in Latium, Rome extended outright citizenship. Others, especially those already organized as city-states, were made partial citizens without rights to participate in Roman public life but with rights to trade and intermarry. These cities continued to govern themselves in most matters, but their half-Roman citizens owed financial and military obligations to Rome. Still other communities were made allies of Rome, each group signing a formal treaty which left it considerable local independence but which deprived it of control over foreign affairs and imposed on it the obligation to provide men and money for Rome's wars. These arrangements for partial citizenship and alliances were based on the assumption that the subject peoples would eventually earn full citizenship when they demonstrated their loyalty and their capability to participate fully in Roman political and social life. Rome moved to hasten the process by planting numerous colonies of her citizens at various places in Italy. This complex set of arrangements meant that by 265 B.C. Rome ruled over a loose confederation of Italians, most of whom enjoyed a considerable degree of independence, but all of whom were tied to Rome by virtue of an obligation to serve in her armies and of a promise to achieve full citizenship. A system that made Rome's yoke relatively light soon paid off richly in her favor.

Italy 265 B.C.

The map legend reads:
- Territory of Roman Citizens
- Roman Territorial Conquests

Scale: 0 25 50 75 100 mi.

The intelligent program for conquered peoples was matched by a constant modification of the Roman constitution which promoted increasing solidarity and deepening allegiance among the citizens. When the Romans threw off Etruscan rule in 509 B.C., power in the newly established republic fell into the hands of a narrow patrician aristocracy who controlled the elective offices, the Senate, and the assembly of *curiae*. During succeeding years, this oligarchy was under constant pressure from the plebeians, whose services were needed to man the Roman armies engaged in a struggle for survival. Besides a desire to gain greater political power, the plebeians were motivated by economic pressures that resulted from patrician control over the agricultural system. The patricians grudgingly surrendered their powers and accepted the plebeians as equals in directing the Roman state. For the most part, changes in the constitution were effected peaceably, although on several occasions the plebeians did secede temporarily to force their demands.

The long evolution of the early republic is referred to as the "Struggle of the Orders." Roman historians recorded the steps in this conflict in great detail and with considerable pride, but essentially the story is one of repeated concessions to the plebeians which gave them greater rights in ruling the city. Perhaps even before 509 B.C. they were given an important role in the army, that role being defined by wealth. A political organism, the *Assembly of Centuries*, emerged from the new military classification, and it increasingly played a crucial role in political decisions. Special officials, called *tribunes*, possessing power to veto the acts of regular officials, were created as a device for protecting the interests of the plebeians. Out of this unique arrangement emerged a plebeian assembly, the *Assembly of Tribes*, to guide the tribunes. The law was codified to protect citizens from arbitrary interpretations by patrician judges. One by one, elective offices of the state were opened to plebeians. Legislation was enacted protecting debtors from unjust interest rates and curbing patrician monopoly over public lands. Intermarriage between patricians and plebeians was legalized. Colonizing ventures were undertaken to provide opportunities for impoverished citizens. The final result of these changes—and of the struggles which brought them about—can best be seen by examining the constitution of the republic in 265 B.C.

Theoretically, Rome was governed in 265 by the decisions of the total citizen body acting through the assemblies, of which two were especially important. The Assembly of Centuries was based on a grouping of the citizenry into military units called centuries; each citizen was assigned to a century according to his wealth. The majority of the centuries were comprised of the wealthier citizens; these same wealthy citizens exerted considerable influence over the centuries made up of less wealthy citizens by virtue of their patronage over these plebeians. The Assembly of Centuries was thus dominated by a numerical minority. However, all citizens could participate in and share its important powers, which included approving all laws and electing all officials. The other important assembly was the Assembly of Tribes, created early in the history of the republic as an assembly of plebeians. It was based on territorial units, called *tribes*, of which there were eventually thirty-five. All male citizens in each of these territorial units were equal. The body was presided over by the tribunes and was originally intended to provide these officials with guidance in the exercise of their powers of veto over the actions of the regularly elected officials. Eventually, the Assembly of Tribes gained the power to enact laws, called *plebiscites*, binding on the entire state. Patrician citizens were also incorporated into it, so that it embraced the whole citizen body.

The will of the citizenry was enacted by elected magistrates. As a consequence of a fear of abuse of power, the Roman magistracy was a collegiate one: With minor exceptions, every office was occupied by a board of at least two members of equal rank, each of whom had the power to veto the acts of his colleagues. The highest executive authority in the state—the *imperium*— was exercised by two consuls who were charged with the management of all civil and military affairs. Next below the consuls were the *praetors*, elected primarily to administer justice, but under special circumstances capable of exercising the *imperium*. The *quaestors* handled the financial matters of the state. The *aediles* managed the policing of the city, the repair of streets and public buildings, the city's food supply, and the conduct of religious ceremonies. Priestly colleges were elected to carry out the actual worship of the civic gods. All these officials were elected for one-year terms. *Censors* were elected every five years to classify the citizens for military service and to judge the moral fitness of citizens for public functions. In times of grave crisis, a *dictator* could be elected for a term of six months with unlimited powers to rule the state. According to law, any citizen was eligible for election to these offices, but since there was no pay for service and electioneering was expensive, few men of humble means aspired to high office and even fewer gained it.

Especially potent in the republican system of government was the Senate, a body of about three hundred men who served for life. New members were recruited almost exclusively from the ranks of ex-magistrates. Election to the consulship and praetorship automatically qualified a man for the Senate. The composition of the body is easier to describe than its powers. Theoretically, the Senate was an advisory body, the receptacle of the political wisdom of the community available to counsel the magistrates and the assemblies in all public matters. But in their capacity as advisers, the senators controlled the state. Decisions relating to finances, war, peace, justice, and all other matters were almost never made without consulting the Sen-

ate. Its deliberations and ultimate decrees were almost invariably accepted by the magistrates and the assemblies—yet such great authority came from the prestige of the senators, rather than from specific powers assigned to the Senate.

Although ostensibly a democracy, the Roman Republic was controlled by a small aristocracy. At the middle of the third century B.C., that aristocracy was still largely hereditary, composed of the descendants of ancient patrician families who protected their good names by carefully arranged marriages with other noble families. The wealth of these ancient families was based chiefly on land ownership. However, changes were beginning to alter the composition of the old aristocracy. Rome's expanding power in Italy (and soon overseas) created opportunities for enterprising plebeians to gain wealth through trading ventures, supplying the armies, and securing land beyond Rome's old boundaries. Their wealth whetted the appetites of these "new men" for power, and the political reforms emerging from the "struggle of the orders" made them eligible for the elective magistracies and for membership in the Senate. The old aristocratic element met the challenge by drawing the new men into their ranks. As a consequence, the basis for aristocratic status began to shift from birth to wealth; new families possessing little more than wealth emerged out of plebeian society to intermarry and to share political power with the old families.

This aristocracy acted consciously to protect and advance its interests by controlling the machinery of government, seldom allowing the total citizen body to exercise the power it theoretically possessed. Men of high rank and wealth were almost always elected to the magistracies and passed from these offices into the Senate, from which they could exercise powerful control over decision making. They carefully managed the elections to control both the candidates and the outcome. They used their wealth and influence to manipulate the assemblies. Especially important in dominating the elections and the assemblies was the institution of clientage, which permitted wealthy men to cluster around themselves large numbers of plebeian clients who acted politically as their patrons directed.

Most Romans were content to entrust the fate of the city to these aristocrats, satisfied that means were at hand to curb them if they abused their power. The history of Rome from 509 to 265 B.C. justified that confidence. The aristocrats led the Romans to mastery over Italy. They were not guilty of prolonged periods of abuse of power, and they were usually responsive to popular demands for change. They not only satisfied the citizenry and commanded obedience, but also proved capable of pursuing a consistent policy to a successful conclusion, especially in the vital areas of war and diplomacy. Seldom did Rome suffer from the indecision that hampered so many of the more democratic Greek city-states.

4. OVERSEAS EXPANSION: THE PUNIC WARS, 264–201 B.C.

Rome's success in establishing mastery over Italy brought about an important change in her position in the Mediterranean world by 265 B.C. Although her people did not fully realize it, she had become a major power. For many decades after 265, her energy was directed toward establishing her place among the other Mediterranean powers; she ended by conquering them and welding them into a vast empire.

The first important Roman encounter with a major overseas power—a clash with the African city of Carthage—was perhaps decisive. Originally a Phoenician colony, Carthage had gone her own way after Phoenicia's defeat by Assyria. She created a thriving commercial empire in the western Mediterranean and by the third century was the greatest power in that area. Until 265, Rome had shown little concern over Carthaginian might. On several occasions Rome and Carthage had signed friendly treaties which recognized Carthaginian dominance in the western Mediterranean while conceding Rome's control over Italy.

The two powers almost blundered into their first encounter. Sicily provided the setting. In 265, the Sicilian city of Messana, seeking to escape domination by Syracuse, appealed to both Rome and Carthage for help. Carthage had long been established on Sicily because of its strategic importance for commercial and sea power. Her main concern lay in containing the Greeks so that she could maintain her position on the island. She thus moved quickly to help Messana. Rome was now faced with a serious dilemma. The Senate was indecisive in disposing of the request for help, apparently reluctant to become in-

Although the Romans used slave labor, there was also a large class of artisans who made goods, carried on trade, or sold their services. This relief, now in the Musée Calvet in Avignon, shows a towboat carrying casks of wine. *Photo: Alinari–Art Reference Bureau* volved in a war outside Italy with a major sea power. When the issue was referred to the people in assembly, they voted for intervention. One ancient historian says they were beguiled by promises of rich spoils, but the matter was probably not that simple. Some Romans apparently felt that a Carthaginian stronghold so close to Italy would give the Carthaginians an opportunity to intervene in the affairs of Rome's recently conquered Greek allies in southern Italy. The decision to become engaged in Sicily was thus an expression of Roman self-interest.

The First Punic War (264–241 B.C.) centered around a struggle for Sicily. In the early stages of the war Rome sent several armies to Sicily but without success, because Carthage controlled the sea routes and the key seaports. Rome was finally driven to build a navy to offset Carthage's advantage— and in this venture she succeeded almost miraculously. So confident did the Romans become that they undertook an invasion of Africa in 255, but this move ended in a disaster that prolonged the war many years. The Romans continued their efforts to dislodge the Carthaginians from the fortress cities in Sicily, suffering a series of naval disasters in the course of the struggle. But they persisted, building fleet after fleet to threaten Carthaginian sea power. Eventually, in 241 Carthage sued for peace, in part as a result of the emergence of a faction at home that wished to reduce Carthage's imperial commitments and to confine her interests to Africa. In the treaty ending the war, Rome gained Sicily and received a sizable money payment as reparation for her losses.

But the issue was far from settled. In the years that followed the peace of 241, the Carthaginians resumed their imperial interests and turned their energies to rebuilding their forces for a new showdown. Under the leadership of Hamilcar Barca, Spain was made the base for the next war. Hamilcar successfully subdued the native Spanish population, collected a huge war chest, and recruited and trained an excellent army of na-

tive Spaniards. After his death in 229, his policy was carried on first by his son-in-law and later by his son, Hannibal. In the meantime, Rome was too involved with other issues to pay much attention to the revival of Carthage. She organized a provincial government for Sicily and then for Corsica and Sardinia, which she seized from Carthage in the aftermath of the first war. Her forces were deeply involved in extending Roman authority into the Po Valley against the bitter resistance of the natives and in curbing the activities of pirates operating along the Dalmatian coast; her horizons were spreading in these years. And so a determined Carthage and a busy Rome headed for a new war, which finally began in 218 B.C., when Hannibal attacked a Roman ally in Spain.

The Second Punic War (218–201 B.C.) was certainly Rome's sternest military test, due in large part to the genius of Hannibal. Hannibal had settled on his strategy before the war began. He decided to invade Italy, hoping to encourage Rome's allies to desert her and to isolate Rome for the final assault. Rome, on the other hand, hoped to end the war quickly by invading Africa and Spain. Hannibal upset these plans by boldly leading an army from Spain across southern Gaul into northern Italy; to counter this move, the Romans were forced to abandon plans for invading Africa, although they did send an army to Spain. Once in Italy, Hannibal proved unbeatable on the field of battle. On three different occasions between 218 and 216 the Romans challenged him with large armies, only to be crushed each time. The last of these battles, Cannae, convinced the Romans that Hannibal was superior in open battle. They therefore adopted a policy of harassing his army, otherwise leaving him free to do as he pleased in Italy. For fifteen years Hannibal maintained an army on Italian soil, spreading destruction up and down the peninsula—a remarkable feat, especially in view of the fact that he received almost no replacements or supplies from Carthage or Spain. But he could not win: He could not persuade a decisive number of Rome's Italian allies to desert so that he could isolate Rome.

While holding Hannibal at bay in Italy, Rome resolutely undertook the long struggle to crush Carthage. She fought on many fronts, and actually won the war outside Italy. Large armies sent to Spain slowly crushed Carthaginian power, and cut off Hannibal's reinforcements. Another Roman force was dispatched to Sicily to choke off a rebellion in support of Carthage. Meanwhile, Roman naval forces patrolled the western Mediterranean and the Adriatic, keeping Carthage from sending aid to Hannibal and preventing him from getting help from his ally, the king of Macedon. At the same time Roman diplomatic efforts encouraged African peoples to attack Carthaginian territories. Rome's counteroffensive culminated in 205 B.C., when a large army under Scipio Africanus was sent to Africa. Scipio had already demonstrated his military genius in Spain; in him, Rome had found a talent equal to that of Hannibal. He soon attacked Carthage, and Hannibal was recalled from Italy in 203 to save the city. But even he could no longer stem the tide: He met Scipio in a battle in 202 at Zama, and suffered a complete defeat.

After Zama, Carthage sued for peace. She was forced to surrender Spain to Rome, to have her navy destroyed, to accept a heavy fine to be paid over the next fifty years, and to agree never again to wage war outside Africa and within Africa only with Rome's permission. Part of her African territory was turned over to Numidia, a state Rome hoped would balance Carthaginian power in Africa. Carthage was reduced to a minor power; victorious Rome was mistress of the western Mediterranean.

5. OVERSEAS EXPANSION: DOMINATION OVER THE EAST, 200–133 B.C.

The peace of 201 left Rome with many problems: new provinces to organize, a ravaged Italy to repair, war weariness, rebellious subjects to subdue. But these matters had to go

This contemporary coin shows Hannibal, the brilliant Carthaginian general whose eventual defeat by Rome gave her control of the western Mediterranean and was a crucial step in her rise to hegemony over the entire Mediterranean Basin. *Photo: American Numismatic Society*

unattended, for her new role as a world power drew her toward the turbulent eastern Mediterranean. Prior to 200, Rome had seldom been concerned with affairs in the Hellenistic world and was woefully ignorant of the situation there. All during the third century B.C. an uneasy balance of power among the three main powers—Macedon, the Seleucid Empire, and Egypt—tenuously safeguarded the independence of a variety of small states, including Athens, the Aetolian and Achaean leagues, Rhodes, and Pergamum. But the balance was breaking down, chiefly as a result of two factors. First, Egypt grew weak under the rule of the Ptolemies. Second, a pair of ambitious kings, Philip V in Macedon and Antiochus III of the Seleucid Empire, sought to capitalize on Egypt's weakness by seizing her territory and subduing the other independent states in the Near East. Each dreamed of reconstituting Alexander's empire. The aggressive pol-

ATLANTIC
OCEAN

GAUL
51

TRANSALPINE GAUL
ca. 100

CISALPINE GAUL
225–110

ITALY

PROTECTORATE
OF
ILLYRIA
229

BLACK SEA

SPAIN

CORSICA
238

Rome

MACEDONIA
ca. 147

BITHYNIA-PONTUS
74–63

NEARER
197

FARTHER
197

SARDINIA
238

BENEVENTUM
275

CANNAE
216

ASIA
129

FARTHER
197

SICILY
241

ACHAEA
146–145

CILICIA
81

Carthage
ZAMA 202

SYRACUSE
212

SYRIA
63

AFRICA
146

CRETE
ca. 67

CYPRUS
58

MEDITERRANEAN SEA

NUMIDIA
46

CYRENAICA
ca. 74

Alexandria

Empire at 197 B.C.

Expansion to 44 B.C.

0   100   200   300   400   500 mi.

The Roman Empire 197– 44 B.C.

icies of Philip and Antiochus frightened their intended victims into a frantic search for help. They turned to the "rising cloud in the West," Rome.

In 200 Pergamum and Rhodes appealed to Rome for help against Philip V. The war-weary Roman populace, speaking in the Assembly of *curiae*, refused to become involved, but theirs was not the final word. The Senate was more bellicose. Many Roman leaders feared Philip of Macedon, who had been an ally of Hannibal in the Second Punic War, as a threat to the peace of Italy. Perhaps more significantly, many Roman aristocrats, including no less a person than Scipio Africanus, had become ardent admirers of the Greeks. They felt a need to do something to save the Greeks and their civilization from Macedonian

aggression. Senatorial power asserted itself, and Rome declared war on Philip V in 200 B.C.

Although her military performance was not brilliant, Rome managed to defeat Philip within three years. He was required to evacuate all Greece and confine his activities to his own kingdom. Rome then proceeded to restore peace in Greece, an undertaking perhaps prompted by noble intentions, but fraught with difficulty. Many cities hailed the settlement as a reaffirmation of the freedom of the Greek city-states, but others were disgruntled when Rome adjusted boundaries against their interests and interfered in local affairs. The Romans finally withdrew from Greece, having imposed no overlordship nor bound the Greeks in any way.

But Roman involvement in the East was hardly over. Antiochus III had sat by innocently while his fellow aggressor, Philip V, was beaten. Once the Romans had left, he returned to his old schemes. Included among his potential victims were many Greek communities who again clamored for Rome's help. In 192 B.C. Antiochus made Rome's decision easy by invading the Greek peninsula at the urging of some of the city-states displeased with the settlement of 196. Rome again sent her troops east, and Antiochus fared no better than had Philip V. Roman legions drove him out of Greece and pursued him into Asia Minor, where a crushing defeat was inflicted on his army in 190. Once again, Rome tried to establish order. Antiochus was required to keep out of Asia Minor. His navy was destroyed, and a staggering fine was imposed. Rome turned over large territories in Asia Minor to Pergamum and Rhodes, sanctioning them as Roman-backed peacekeepers. Most of the Greek cities were again restored to independence, although those who had aided Antiochus were fined and deprived of some territory. Again, the victors took nothing except the fines.

With both Macedon and the Seleucid state reduced to secondary importance, the peace of the East seemed guaranteed. However, the trouble had only started. With the destruction of the old balance of power, all semblance of international order ended. Warfare among the petty states became chronic. Each squabble was eventually called to Rome's attention; the constant clamor bred her distrust and impatience. Even the Greeks whom she admired so much and had "saved" proved treacherous, quarrelsome, and unreliable. The plain truth emerged ever clearer after 188: A new order was urgently needed in the Near East. With a mixture of idealism, fear, and increasing greed, the Romans accepted the only possible solution—Roman rule in the East.

The first evidence of the new policy came in 171–167 B.C., when Macedon provoked another war with the collaboration of a number of Greek city-states. Rome easily crushed this alliance. She now virtually took over Macedon, leaving her only nominal independence. Roman armies marched through Greece, executing pro-Macedonians, deporting hostages to Italy, and enslaving suspected troublemakers. A few years later a minor disturbance in Macedon resulted in the annexation of the whole kingdom as a Roman province under a Roman governor. Persistent trouble in Greece resulted in stern reprisals, culminating in 146 with the complete destruction of Corinth as an example to the Greeks. By that date Rome had managed to force pro-Roman governments on most Greek cities and to cow anti-Romans into submission. Although technically free, most Greek cities were Roman dependencies.

Rome's allies in Asia Minor had proved equally unreliable and troublesome. Such harsh measures had to be taken against them that the most important states, Rhodes and Pergamum, were virtually ruined. Finally, in 133 Rome took over Pergamum as a province. The king of Pergamum had earlier willed his state to Rome, probably in the hope that Roman protection would safeguard it from his numerous foes. Once established in Asia Minor, Rome would obviously have to protect her position. And there was no one to stay her hand: The Seleucid kingdom was in precipitate decline, and Egypt was virtually powerless.

While concentrating her attention chiefly on the East between 200 and 133 B.C., Rome continued to solidify her power in the West. The occupation of Spain was begun, and an attempt was made to organize that land under a provincial administration. The territory in northern Italy between the Alps and the Apennines, called Cisalpine Gaul, was reconquered and reorganized in the wake of the rebellions there during the Second Punic War. Although no longer a serious threat, Carthage continued to haunt Rome as a potential enemy. With politicians shouting "Carthage must be destroyed" as a solution to every problem, it was only a matter of time until Rome vented her fear and vengeance on her old foe. The final blow came in 149, when Rome again declared war on Carthage for no apparent reason. In 146 Carthage was captured after a heroic defense, destroyed completely, and the site sown with salt. Her territory was annexed as a Roman province.

The passing of her most formidable foe was a fitting symbol of Rome's position in the Mediterranean world as the second century B.C. neared its close. She had grown from a tiny village to the dominant power. But her success posed new problems: What would it profit Rome to conquer so large a world? How would she use her new power and authority?

Suggested Reading

Overview. Excellent comprehensive surveys of the grand sweep of Roman history are provided by A. E. R. Boak and W. G. Sinnigen, *A History of Rome to A.D. 565* (5th ed., 1965); F. C. Bourne, *A History of the Romans* (1966); and Max Cary, *A History of Rome Down to the Age of Constantine* (2nd ed., rev., 1954). Two superlative syntheses emphasizing cultural history are Pierre Grimal, *The Civilization of Rome* (1963); and J. C. Stobart, *The Grandeur That Was Rome* (4th ed., 1961).

Early Italy and Rome. The fascinating story of the Etruscans can be read in **Massimo Pallottino, *The Etruscans* (Penguin); **A. Hus, *The Etruscans* (Evergreen); J. Heurgon, *Daily Life of the Etruscans* (1964); and E. H. Richardson, *The Etruscans: Their Art and Civilization* (1964). The complex history of early Rome is well treated by Raymond Bloch, *Origins of Rome* (1960); and Einar Gjerstad, *Legends and Facts of Early Roman History* (1962).

The Republic to 265 B.C. The best detailed history of the early republic is **H. H. Scullard, *History of the Roman World From 753 B.C. to 146 B.C.* (3rd ed., University Paperbacks). The evolution of republican political institutions can be traced in Leon Homo, *Roman Political Institutions From City to State*, trans. M. R. Dobie (1929); or in F. F. Abbott, *A History and Description of Roman Political Institutions* (3rd ed., 1911). Both these works are old but clear and thorough in describing the nature and working of political institutions. Tenney Frank, *Roman Imperialism* (1921), supplies a useful treatment of Roman expansion, especially its motivating forces. **B. H. Warmington, *Carthage* (Penguin), provides a superb treatment of the history of Rome's greatest enemy. The two great military leaders in the Second Punic War are treated by G. P. Baker, *Hannibal* (1929); and B. H. Liddell-Hart, *A Greater Than Napoleon: Scipio Africanus* (1926). H. M. D. Parker, *The Roman Legions* (1928), discusses fully the vital key to Rome's military success.

Sources. Every student should sample the Roman historians who wrote about her early history for some insight into what the Romans believed about themselves and their origins. Three authors provide a good starting point. Most important and engaging is Livy, *History of Rome* (many editions; the most complete is the translation by B. O. Foster in the Loeb Classical Library [14 vols., 1919ff.]). Two convenient selections are available in translations by **A. de Selincourt under the titles *Early History of Rome* (Penguin), and

War With Hannibal (Penguin). Livy wrote his history between 27 B.C. and A.D. 17; his work was inspired by a belief that the Romans had a special mission in history, and he seeks to portray the heroic ventures that launched them on that mission. Plutarch, *Lives* (many editions; a convenient one is that in the Modern Library), provides biographies of many early Roman heroes, including Romulus, Camillus, Coriolanus, Fabius Maximus, Aemelius Paulus, Flamininus, Cato, and Marcellus, all of whom played a role in the events of this period. Polybius, *The Histories* (several editions; the best is the translation by W. R. Paton in the Loeb Classical Library [6 vols., 1922–27]); an abridged version entitled **The Histories*, ed. E. Bedian and trans. M. Chambers, is also available (Washington Square Press). This work provides an excellent account of Rome's expansion during and following the Punic Wars. Polybius was a Greek who lived in Rome for part of his life as a friend of the Scipios. He wrote to explain Rome's rise to the Greeks.

Chapter 10 ⚜ The Failure of the Roman Republic,

133–31 B.C.

Rome's triumphant march to domination of the Mediterranean area prior to 133 B.C. would suggest that her internal regime was sound and her society healthy. But this outward appearance was misleading. The long succession of wars had generated profound problems that inevitably had to be faced. Prior to 133, the problems had been neglected by a populace increasingly intoxicated with military success and power; the century after 133 was dominated by a succession of crises emerging from them. Before that century had passed, the republic, increasingly obsolete and unresponsive, was in ruins.

1. THE BURDENS OF A WORLD POWER

Rome during the century between 133 and 31 B.C. can only be understood in terms of the problems emerging in the years prior to that time. Certain of these were especially dangerous to the established order.

First, Rome's military successes left her with a long frontier to defend and with many territories inhabited by a variety of peoples to govern. By 133 she had not devised an ade-

quate defense system; the citizen armies called to duty for wars of conquest were ill-suited to the tedious task of defense. The danger of destructive attacks by foreigners was ever present. The devices employed to control the provinces annexed between 265 and 133 were largely improvised. In general, the Romans were inclined to view conquered non-Italians simply as subjects to be exploited. They made no effort to apply to them the enlightened program that had been developed earlier in Italy. Provincial administrations were fashioned with absolute military and civil power entrusted to provincial governors who were seldom held accountable for their conduct. The residents of each province were subject to heavy tribute, the collection of which was entrusted to tax farmers who paid the Roman government what it expected from the provinces and then proceeded to extort all they could from the provincials. No serious effort was made to establish a provincial civil service responsible to the Roman government to impose order and justice. Almost from the beginning, the provincials were exploited and abused with impunity by

This relief from a Roman sepulcher shows quite clearly how manual labor was used to perform tasks that in other civilizations have been delegated to animals or mechanical devices. Here (at left) slaves operate a treadmill. *Photo: Alinari–Art Reference Bureau*

Romans who saw them chiefly as a source of wealth and power. The intrusion of the Romans into the lives of Mediterranean peoples inevitably dislocated the established order and raised immense difficulties for the inadequate provincial administrations.

Second, Rome's allies in Italy, who had fought loyally and suffered much in the wars of conquest, were ill-rewarded for their efforts. The prospect of citizenship, implicit in Rome's earlier arrangements with her Italian allies, grew increasingly remote, and the allies became proportionately restless and rebellious.

Third, Rome's economy was subjected to major strains and transformations. The traditional backbone of the republican economy was the small family farm on which independent owners raised grain primarily for their families and, if there was a surplus, for the city market. This style of farming became increasingly unprofitable, chiefly as a result of the competition of cheaper grain imported from more productive agricultural lands in the provinces. Moreover, many small farms were devastated by the wars in Italy and depopulated to fill the incessant demand for soldiers. Better ways were being discovered to use the land. Enterprising Romans with capital began creating large estates (*latifundia*) devoted to raising grapes, olives, and livestock to be sold as cash crops. Increasingly, slaves, a prime prize of successful conquest, provided the labor force on the *latifundia*. Rome's involvement in the larger economy of the entire Mediterranean world provided new opportunities for trade and industry, further upsetting the simple economic order of the early republican era.

These fundamental economic changes created a fourth set of problems of a social nature. Impoverished small farmers abandoned their farms and flocked to Rome. There they became a rootless and restless proletariat, endowed with political rights by virtue of their citizenship but deprived of an opportunity for gainful employment in a city which increasingly lived from tribute and de-

pended on slavery to supply its needs. This city "mob" was forced to depend on the state or on rich patrons for its livelihood; its members "earned" their living by selling their votes and political support. The "new" Rome also produced a new breed of wealthy men who grew rich as contractors for army supplies, provincial tax collectors, bankers, and organizers of trading enterprises. As their wealth grew, the members of this new class, called *equites*, began to agitate for political power.

Finally, Rome's population was profoundly unsettled by new ideological factors impinging on their lives. Roman society was deeply affected by the sophisticated concepts and styles of Hellenistic literature, art, philosophy, and religion, which became irresistibly attractive from the third century onward. The immense wealth that flowed into Rome as a result of conquest bred a taste for comfort and luxury and a lust for more of both. Incessant military involvement engendered a disturbing tolerance for violence and corruption. These currents made men less willing to abide by the moral standards, rustic simplicity, and cultural naiveté that had characterized the early republic.

In many ways, these vast forces of change spelled progress for Rome and Italy—greater wealth, greater sophistication, greater opportunities. But their impact called for adjustments that could only be effected by innovative political action. Here the Romans failed. During the long and difficult era of conquest, the Roman government remained essentially what it had been in 265 B.C. A narrow aristocracy of wealth and family connections dominated the government through control of the Senate and the elective magistracies and through manipulation of the assemblies. In fact, this dominant minority steadily increased its power. Most citizens, little understanding the complicated issues of war and diplomacy, willingly allowed the patricians to decide Rome's fate. Those outside the ruling circle who felt an urge to power by virtue of newly gained wealth were cleverly taken into the patrician ranks. By 133 B.C., the aristocrats had become so accustomed to unquestioned authority that they thought only in terms of their own interests. In the face of mounting problems, the political system was becoming more inflexible; a conservative, narrowly based government, designed to rule a small city-state, was faced with the problems of a world empire. The fuse was set for an upheaval. When it came, it was so violent that the republican form of government was destroyed.

2. THE PARTIES AT WAR, 133–79 B.C.

The first phase in the ordeal of the republic was a violent party struggle for control of the government. In somewhat simplified terms, the opposing forces fell into two camps. On one side was the old ruling oligarchy, calling themselves the *optimates*—the best—and standing for the established order. Opposed was a shifting alliance of the poor and middle class, the *populares*, usually led by strong leaders from the patrician ranks. These leaders were often men moved by a genuine urge to reform in order to safeguard the state, but they were also driven by an urge for personal power denied them by the "establishment." They turned to the people for support and sought to exploit the unrealized potential for democratic action built into the republican constitution as a means of gaining power.

The initial engagement in the struggle between the parties occurred between 133 and 121 B.C. The champions of the *populares* were the brothers Tiberius and Gaius Gracchus. Descended from eminent aristocratic families (Scipio Africanus was their grandfather), well-educated, and filled with a strong political consciousness, the Gracchi were deeply troubled by the decline of Rome's free farmers, the scarcity of military recruits, and the plight of the proletariat. Elected tribune in 133, Tiberius proposed that public land be redistributed in small parcels for the use of the landless populace of Rome. Plutarch's remark that "no milder or gentler program was

ever devised in the face of such injustice and greed" found no backers among the ruling clique. Most of the land to be redistributed was already in the hands of rich patricians by virtue of grants made by the government on highly favorable terms. Although Tiberius' law would have permitted them to retain sizable holdings of public land and would have compensated them for any improvements they had made, they used their powers to thwart him by inducing another tribune to veto the proposal. Tiberius then capitalized on his great popularity to persuade the Assembly of Tribes to oust the offensive tribune and pass his law. Rather than accept the will of the people, the senatorial party, resorting to violence, murdered Tiberius on the pretext that he was trying to be a dictator when he sought reelection as tribune.

Ten years later, Gaius Gracchus took up the same cause, adding more radical proposals to attract a larger following. Elected tribune in 124 B.C., he persuaded the Assembly of Tribes to pass new land laws, to provide cheap grain for the masses, to establish colonies for the resettlement of impoverished Romans, and to extend political privileges to the Italian allies. His legislation also granted extensive privileges in tax collection to the nonnoble capitalists (*equites*), whom Gaius wished to rally to the reforming cause. Although bitterly opposed by the Senate, Gaius was able to enact his program through the Assembly of Tribes. But ultimately he failed to hold together the alliance of poor farmers, *equites*, and city proletariat, and lost his bid for election as tribune in 122. Shortly after, in order to escape senatorial retribution, he commanded a slave to kill him; three thousand of his followers were murdered by the senatorial forces.

Although the careers of the Gracchi ended tragically, their leadership had at a crucial moment reminded the populace of Rome of its potential power. Perhaps their program was naive and idealistic and certainly their reliance on "mob" support was politically dangerous, but at least they had raised the issue of reform and bequeathed a series of "causes" to the future. The Senate was impervious to the demands of the people. Concerned only with saving its power and wealth, it proved willing to resort to violence to remove those who threatened it. Its posture promised bitter days ahead.

The death of Gaius Gracchus left the *populares* leaderless for a decade. The Senate resumed direction of political life. Although not daring to repeal some aspects of the Gracchan program outright, it proceeded by circumvention to impede its application, to the utter frustration of the *populares*. Ultimately, in the face of a new crisis, the Senate revealed its ineptness. Rome became involved in an internal power struggle in the African kingdom of Numidia. This complicated affair led to charges that certain senators had been bribed to favor Jugurtha, one of the contenders for the Numidian throne. An enraged Roman public forced a declaration of war in 111 B.C. The bungling conduct of the Jugurthine War, resulting in the disgraceful surrender of several Roman armies and continued charges of corruption, aroused growing demands that something be done to save Rome's honor.

A new popular hero arose to turn popular fury against the blundering Senate. The man of the hour was a peasant's son, Marius (ca. 155–86 B.C.), who had held elective offices and who had served in the army fighting against Jugurtha. In 108 Marius ran for consul, building his campaign around an attack on the Senate aimed at rallying the *equites* and the city proletariat. Although bitterly opposed by the patricians on the grounds that he was a man of no position or family connection, Marius was elected to serve for the year 107 B.C. He persuaded the assembly to vote him command of the army in Africa despite the fact that the Senate had already assigned another official. Once in office, Marius took a bold and fateful step. He recruited an army of volunteers to fight in Africa, using his personal appeal to attract men and promising to reward them once the war was over. His con-

trol of this personal army virtually put him beyond the reach of the Senate, which could no longer safely rely on assassination as a convenient way of disposing of threats to its power.

Marius quickly justified the trust placed in him by crushing Jugurtha in 105 B.C. He was ably assisted by a young nobleman named Sulla, soon to play a major role in Rome. So great was Marius' reputation that he was reelected consul during the years 104–101 to fight Germanic tribes threatening the Roman position in northern Italy. Again he was successful, "saving" Rome. With the military danger over, Marius turned his attention to Rome's internal politics, and ran for consul for the sixth time for the year 100 as the leader of a powerful faction proposing broad reforms that contained most of the elements of the Gracchan program. Although his popularity, coupled with some coercion from his loyal troops, ensured his election, Marius proved inept as a political leader. Before his term ended, his party collapsed and he lost most of his great prestige. The *optimates* returned to power, having learned what even an unskilled politician could do to control Rome when backed by an army.

The next decade was relatively quiet, perhaps because moderate elements in the Senate made some effort to resolve critical problems. Two issues defied their efforts, however, and provided the fuel for the next crises. One was the situation of the Roman allies in Italy, who had long been pressing for citizenship but were repeatedly frustrated by opposition from most elements in Rome. In 90 B.C. their disillusionment finally generated a great rebellion that threatened Rome's survival. She responded by granting citizenship to the Italians, a momentous act which ended the days of the simple city-state. In order to meet the military threat posed by the rebels, the Senate then entrusted Sulla (138–78 B.C.) with an army; by 87, he had dispersed the rebels, demonstrated his considerable abilities, and greatly enhanced his influence.

The Italian revolt triggered another crisis

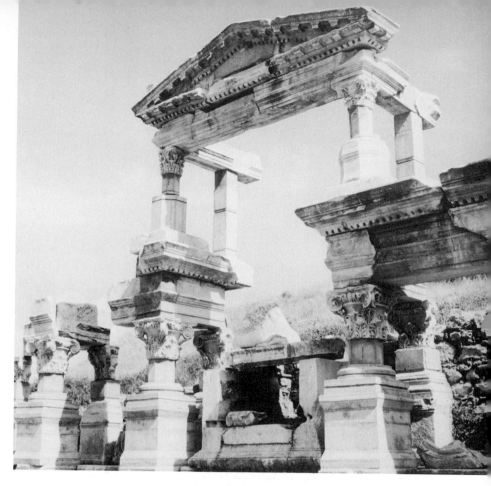

Roman civilization spread with her armies; language, customs, architecture were transported to all parts of the empire. This illustration shows the ruins of Trajan's Fountain, found at Ephesus in modern Turkey.
Photo: Edith Reichmann

which was a byproduct of a second problem, that of a provincial administration which had aroused deepening discontent in nearly every part of the Mediterranean world. In 88 B.C. Mithradates, king of the small state of Pontus in Asia Minor, took up arms against Rome. Because he was widely accepted in Asia Minor and Greece as a liberator, his success endangered the entire Roman hold on the East. Despite the critical situation, there was virtual civil war in Rome over the question of who would command the desperately needed army. The Senate favored Sulla, chiefly because he seemed to offer no threat to its power. The *populares* clamored for Marius. Sulla finally resolved the issue by marching the army he had already commanded in the campaign against the Italians into Rome and securing the command in Asia by force, a procedure that was neither constitutional nor customary, but effective.

Sulla remained in the East until 83 B.C. He disposed of the crisis there by defeating Mithradates and his allies, forcing the king to return to his old kingdom and reestablishing Roman dominance in the eastern provinces. But he made no final settlement of affairs in the East; his eyes were on Rome. Immediately after his departure in 88, the *populares* under Marius forced their way back into power and imposed a reign of terror on the Senate. It was powerless to restrain the Marians now that Sulla's army had left Italy. The *populares* thus ruled supreme until 83, when Sulla and his army finally reappeared in Italy, well fortified with booty seized in the East. Marius himself had died in 86, so that his party suffered from lack of effective leadership. Sulla's battle-tested soldiers easily routed the Marians and assured him complete mastery over the city.

Once in control, Sulla set about a program

aimed at avoiding the violence and illegality that had surrounded Roman political life so often since the Gracchi. His program was conservative: it aimed at preventing anyone from organizing the *populares* faction so as to control Rome and at restoring direction of the state to the Senate. He sought to eliminate *populares* leadership by launching a brutal proscription which led to the execution of thousands of Romans who had been associated with the Marian faction. The powers of the tribunes and the Assembly of Tribes, the chief instruments through which the leaders of the *populares* had gained power, were severely limited. The Senate was enlarged and the new seats given over to *equites*, thus bolstering its depleted ranks with new talent and pacifying an increasingly powerful group in Rome. Sulla settled his loyal veterans at strategic places over all Italy as a counterforce to *populares* agitation among the newly admitted Roman citizens. He took steps to regularize the election procedures for the magistracies, to improve the administration of justice, and to reorganize provincial administration—measures intended to reduce agitation among voting citizens, quiet popular discontent, and avoid provincial revolts. Having restored the ancient constitution with the Senate in charge, Sulla retired from public life in 79 to pursue his intellectual interests and enjoy the great wealth he had accumulated. He obviously hoped that the Senate could find means of resolving Rome's problems now that it was free of rabblerousers who rode to power with the support of Roman citizens.

Although it might seem that Sulla's restoration of the Senate left the situation just where it had been in 133 B.C., his retirement actually ended an era. The Senate was in power in 79 not because of its own virtues, prestige, or accomplishments, but because a successful military leader decreed so. The senatorial oligarchy had earned the hatred and mistrust of many citizens by their bungling, violence, and reactionary attitudes of the past half century. It was clear that bold individuals, properly armed, might topple the Senate as easily as Sulla had restored it. The long, bitter, indecisive clash between the *optimates* and the *populares* favored the emergence of such individuals by encouraging disregard for the law and reliance on force. The republican form of government had suffered a mortal blow.

3. THE ERA OF STRONG MEN, 79–44 B.C.

New opportunities for "strong men" were quick in coming, for the Senate proved itself completely unworthy of Sulla's confidence. Between 79 and 70 B.C. it was faced in quick succession by a revolt in Italy led by a disaffected Roman consul, a revolt in Spain directed by a Roman governor, a slave revolt in Italy led by Spartacus, and a new war with Mithradates of Pontus. A protégé of Sulla, Pompey (106–48 B.C.), was given command of forces to deal with the Italian revolt and then the Spanish insurrection; he did his job well and thus emerged as a key figure. The slave revolt was handled by Marcus Licinius Crassus (ca. 115–53 B.C.), a rich and unscrupulous capitalist who aspired to political greatness. These two ascending political stars were elected consuls for the year 70 largely because both were supported by loyal armies. Both were distinct threats to senatorial authority, not so much because they had positive programs, but because they were ambitious for power.

During their co-consularship, Pompey and Crassus put through a series of acts which negated most of Sulla's legislation—acts that won them the applause of the remnants of the *populares* and raised suspicions among the senators. But neither was yet satisfied. Pompey was the first to move toward more decisive power. By clever manipulation he persuaded the people and the Senate to vote him two important military commands: In 67 he was granted vast powers to clear the Mediterranean of pirates, and in 66 he was given even greater power to deal with Mithradates, who since 74 had again been defying Rome in the East. Pompey hunted down the pirates in a matter of months; in 66 he moved against Mithradates and very shortly eliminated him. This task was not so demanding as it appeared, since a previous Roman general had virtually settled the issue with the king of Pontus. While in the East, Pompey did some things for which he had no authority: He conquered new territories around the eastern end of the Mediterranean, organized new provinces, cleaned up the administration of the old provinces, and put trusted friends in key spots. By 63 B.C. he was virtually the ruler of the East, a position he gained while paying almost no attention to the established government in Rome.

Pompey's success, reminiscent of Sulla's rise to power, caused constant concern in Rome and drove other aspiring politicians to a series of maneuvers to checkmate him. Crassus emerged as a major figure. He found a skilled ally in young Julius Caesar (100–44 B.C.), who proved capable of winning popular support and who demonstrated remarkable talents as a political manipulator. Crassus and Caesar were promoters of various laws to attract popular support. They spent huge sums of money in an attempt to get the people of Rome to vote them armies and authority such as Pompey possessed. They connived both at home and abroad to create a crisis that would call for another protector of Rome. The Senate resisted their maneuvers, although Crassus' immense wealth won him friends even in that august body. A major obstacle was Cicero (106–43 B.C.), a talented, ambitious lawyer who skillfully worked his way to the consulship in 63. Although he had taken many sides in his struggle for prominence, by this time Cicero was openly advocating an alliance between Pompey and the Senate as the solution to Rome's problems. His finest hour came when he foiled a conspiracy by Catiline, a frustrated power seeker and sometime agent of Crassus. Cicero himself proclaimed that he had saved the republic by exposing Catiline, much to the annoyance of Pompey.

All these political gyrations resolved noth-

ing, for Pompey was still the key figure. He brought matters to a climax by returning to Italy in 62. Contrary to expectation, Pompey made no move to seize power; rather, he disbanded his army, and asked only that the Senate reward his veterans and legalize his settlement in the East. Why he acted in this fashion is a mystery. Perhaps he hoped that the Senate would recognize him as Rome's most eminent citizen and seek his counsel in the direction of the state.

Relieved of the prospect of another military dictator, the Senate proceeded to act in a way that drove Pompey, Crassus, and Caesar into a political alliance. It refused to reward Pompey's veterans or ratify his eastern settlement. It took action to restrict the powers of provincial tax farmers, a step which threatened one of the main sources of Crassus' immense wealth. It placed every possible obstacle in the way of the election of Caesar to the consulship. Equally frustrated, the three joined in an informal agreement, the First Triumvirate, designed to ensure that each obtained what he wished. Assured of the support of Pompey and Crassus, Caesar won the consulship for the year 59. Once in office, he took steps to satisfy his fellow triumvirs. The Senate resisted, but to no avail; its own folly had generated an irresistible political coalition that simply disregarded it.

Having finished his term as consul, Caesar went to Gaul as proconsul—his reward from the alliance with Pompey and Crassus. There he remained from 58 to 49, during which time he conquered Gaul and added it to the empire. He also gained experience as a general and strengthened his own power by creating an army fanatically dedicated to him personally. Moreover, his Gallic experience was his making as a statesman. Away from petty politics, he began to see Rome as an imperial power faced with the need to resolve complex problems associated with ruling millions of subjects.

The Triumvirate held together uneasily through these years, due in large part to Caesar's efforts. Acting through a series of henchmen, he managed to keep the Senate from regaining control of political life. The marriage of his daughter, Julia, to Pompey gave him a personal tie with one member of the triumvirate, and his long-standing friendship with Crassus also helped to sustain the alliance. But Crassus was killed in 53 in a futile bid for glory in the form of a war against the Parthians. A showdown between Caesar and Pompey then became inevitable. The Senate increasingly viewed Caesar as its enemy and Pompey as its champion. He was voted an ever-greater range of powers over Rome, Italy, and the provinces that made him a virtual dictator. The climax came at the end of Caesar's proconsulship in Gaul in 49, when he sought to run again for the consulship for 48. Desirous of getting him out of office so that he could be prosecuted, the Senate blocked this move, and called on Pompey to defend the state. Knowing that his political career would end if he gave up public office, Caesar decided to rebel against the government. In 49 B.C. he led his legions across the Rubicon River separating Gaul from Italy and plunged Rome into a civil war between two masters who together controlled most of the Roman world.

Caesar's seasoned veterans, skillfully led by their popular general, made short work of Pompey's forces, although the latter were much larger. First in Italy, then in Spain, and finally in the Greek peninsula, Pompey's armies were smashed. The decisive battle was at Pharsalus in 48 B.C. Pompey fled to Egypt, where he was murdered and his head sent to Caesar, who then used this crime against a Roman citizen as an excuse to intervene in Egyptian politics, where a struggle for control of the crown was in progress between young Ptolemy XII and his sister-wife Cleopatra. Caesar decided to support the claims of Cleopatra against her brother. Perhaps his decision was hastened by the fact that he had become her lover, but he may well have had another motive. Ptolemaic Egypt, fabulously rich, was the last important Hellenistic kingdom still not under Roman control. By putting a young princess attached to him on the throne, he perhaps hoped to control the des-

Detail of a relief showing Cleopatra in the presence of divinities. This is an Egyptian portrait of the queen who enchanted two of the greatest Romans of the period—Julius Caesar and Mark Antony. *Photo: R. Schoder*

tiny of Egypt and to tap its resources. Thus he dallied in Egypt nearly a year, part of the time defending himself against the supporters of Ptolemy XII, and left only when Cleopatra was in control as queen. During 47 and 46 Caesar continued his march through the empire—Asia, Africa, Spain—hunting down the last of Pompey's allies and establishing his agents in control. In 45 B.C. he returned to Rome, undisputed master of the Roman world.

Caesar was now faced with the problem of ruling what he had won. It is not clear whether he had formulated a full-scale program; perhaps he had not yet had time. One thing does seem beyond dispute: He intended to concentrate political power in his own hands. He had himself made dictator, an office which allowed him virtually complete freedom of action. He was also voted simultaneously the offices of consul, tribune, high priest, and censor. The other offices were filled with men of his choice, and the Senate was packed with his appointees. When the need arose, he saw to it that whatever special powers he needed were granted him. It seems very likely, as some ancient authorities claimed, that he intended to make himself king after the style of the divine right monarchs of the Hellenistic world. In any case, he showed little respect for the political system of the ancient republic.

Although not averse to the pleasures of power and glory, Caesar did not gather such vast powers to himself merely for personal gratification. He intended to use them to solve the major problems that had so long plagued the Roman world. He undertook to reduce the number of people in Rome dependent on the dole by extensive public works projects and by sending Romans to the provinces as colonists. He provided a police force for the city, thereby ending the mob violence and gangsterism that had had such a dire effect on political life during the preceding years. Measures were taken to aid the Italian farmers. More orderly institutions of local government were established in many towns throughout Italy. New regulations curbed provincial tax collectors and governors, and ended many of the abuses that had made provincial administration such a disgrace.

Caesar tried always to conduct himself personally so as to appear to be the benefactor of all classes and therefore responsible for the welfare of all. Although he was acclaimed by many who were tired of strife and confusion as a hero, a hard core of conservative senators, aware that his program threatened the existence of the old republican order, was obsessed with the idea of stopping him. Completely helpless to achieve their goal in a legal way, these would-be guardians of the "right" order resorted to assassination. Caesar was killed in 44 B.C. just as he was making preparations for a new military campaign against Rome's enemies in the East. But murder proved no way of stopping the disintegration of the republic.

4. THE STRUGGLE FOR SUCCESSION, 44–31 B.C.

The conspirators who murdered Caesar had no plan of action once they had eliminated the real ruler of the state; they had mistakenly supposed that his passing would somehow result in the restoration of the old republic. The real question, however, was how to find a successor for Caesar's mantle. Fourteen years of civil war were necessary to produce a new master.

Two candidates emerged rather quickly as the main contenders for control of Rome. One was Mark Antony (ca. 83–30 B.C.), who had served Caesar as a military commander and who was an experienced politician. He became powerful immediately after Caesar's death by skillful use of propaganda and of Caesar's troops and wealth. The other was an eighteen-year-old named Octavian, whom Caesar had adopted as his son and legal heir. Octavian entered Rome soon after Caesar's death and immediately began to attract a following, especially among Caesar's veterans. More concerned with Antony, the Senate at

Julius Caesar, who with Cicero and Pompey dominated the Roman political stage between 70 and 44 B.C., is shown here very probably as he actually looked, for Roman sculptors excelled at realistic portraiture. *Photo: Alinari–Art Reference Bureau*

first favored Octavian. (Cicero was especially important in supporting his cause.) But Octavian soon became aware that he was being used as a pawn by the Senate. He therefore entered into an agreement with Antony and another general, Lepidus, to form a Second Triumvirate dedicated to restoring order and punishing Caesar's murderers. This Triumvirate was given legal recognition with virtually absolute powers to last five years. Within a year, most of the senatorial party, including Cicero, had been eliminated by a brutal proscription and by a successful military campaign against the armies raised by Caesar's assassins.

After 42 B.C., Antony and Octavian continued the pose of ruling Rome jointly. Actually each was preparing to eliminate the other, although the final reckoning was delayed for ten years. Antony spent these years in the East on the pretext of restoring order. His sojourn there was a political disaster, especially after he fell into the clutches of

Cleopatra and at least from the point of view of the Romans allowed himself to be used to promote her grandiose schemes for expanding Egyptian influence in the East. By 33, Antony went so far as to marry Cleopatra and give his approval to an ambitious program to establish Egyptian hegemony over the East and to install Cleopatra's children by Caesar and Antony as rulers of Roman lands. It was enough that Antony already had a Roman wife—no less a person than Octavian's sister; to surrender Roman lands to an Eastern queen made him a traitor as well. Antony's efforts to bolster his declining prestige had little effect; in fact, the most serious such effort, a campaign against the Parthians in 36, ended in humiliating defeat.

Octavian made infinitely better use of his time. He skillfully disposed of numerous Italian problems that might have defeated a weaker man. While establishing a solid hold on the western provinces, he conducted a powerful propaganda campaign picturing Antony as a madman, a traitor, and the victim of a crafty Eastern harlot. Gradually he created the impression that he was the upholder of Rome's honor against the wicked schemes of Antony and Cleopatra. Finally, in 32 he refused to continue his joint rule with Antony and declared war on Cleopatra. The decisive engagement was fought at Actium in Greece in 31. Octavian's fleet won an easy victory over the demoralized forces of Antony and Cleopatra. Octavian pursued his enemies back to Egypt, where Cleopatra made one final attempt to entice a Roman to support her. When Octavian would have none of her favors, she committed suicide, as Antony had already done. This left Octavian undisputed ruler of Rome, his sword having raised him to a position comparable to that of Caesar's in 46.

5. CONSEQUENCES OF THE CIVIL WARS

Octavian's victory at Actium ended the civil wars and began an era of peace and order, as we shall see in the following chapter. Before looking to the new age, a word is necessary about the impact of the century of civil war on Roman society, for these years had been revolutionary in the most profound sense of the word.

One result of the turmoil was a social upheaval that especially affected the staunchest supporters of the old order. The incessant warfare, accompanied by proscriptions and confiscation of property, virtually destroyed the old aristocracy. The bids of ambitious politicians for popular support undermined the morale of the city masses, who turned from respect for the old institutions to hope for material reward. It was a golden opportunity for ambitious, ruthless, yet able men, even of low birth, to gain wealth and political power. These men, willing to accept new ideas and institutions as long as their wealth and prestige were recognized, were the greatest beneficiaries of the wars.

Another result was that most Romans lost interest in the old political and social order. They grew weary of war and murder and political intrigue. They became increasingly interested in anything that would give them peace and security. A wave of pessimism and hopelessness spread through Roman society during this period. People turned to pleasure-seeking, to new religions, and to foreign philosophies in search of something to live by in the midst of daily violence. Under such circumstances, fewer men were willing to fight for the old order. New ideas found an increasing audience. The civil wars, involving the whole Roman Empire and its millions of inhabitants, broadened the vision of many Romans beyond the confines of the city walls. The old, narrow Roman patriotism seemed senseless in view of the world within which

Romans now operated and of the millions of provincials upon whom Roman politicians often depended for power. These more broad-minded Romans could hardly be expected to fight to preserve a way of life confined to Rome itself.

The period from 133 to 31 B.C. proved still another thing: The traditional system of government simply could not cope with existing problems. Annually elected officials, a Senate of aristocrats, and a popular assembly attended by small numbers of people living in and around Rome failed on numerous occasions to deal with such problems as defending Rome's extensive frontiers, maintaining peace among millions of subjects, supplying grain to the residents of Rome, and keeping order in the city. In a practical way, the civil wars proved to even the most conservative that the old government was outmoded and must be replaced if Rome was to survive as mistress of the Mediterranean. The wars showed just as clearly that only capable individuals possessing extensive powers could cope effectively with Rome's political problems. In spite of their disrespect for the law and their heavyhanded methods, a Marius, a Sulla, a Pompey, and a Caesar achieved something positive in this wild century, whereas all others failed.

These fundamental changes in the midst of frenzied, brutal struggles for power justify our saying that a revolution had occurred by 31 B.C. The republican form of government, under which a group of aristocratic senators (with the approval of the citizens of Rome) had decided political issues, was replaced by a system of government under which one man guided political life in a vast empire stretching around the Mediterranean.

Suggested Reading

Political Developments. The best detailed history of the period covered in this chapter is F. B. Marsh, *A History of the Roman World From 146 to 30 B.C.* (3rd ed., 1963). Recent scholarship has been especially intrigued with the factors that caused the fall of the republic. The major issues are treated with different conclusions by R. E. Smith, *The Failure of the Roman Republic* (1955); **Ronald Syme, *The Roman Revolution* (Oxford); **F. R. Cowell, *Cicero and the Roman Republic* (Penguin); and **L. R. Taylor, *Party Politics in the Age of Caesar* (University of California Paperbacks, 1961). Syme's book is particularly significant for its analysis of hidden forces in the late republic.

Economic and Social Developments. Tenney Frank, *An Economic History of Rome* (2nd ed., rev., 1927) provides in its early chapters an especially good analysis of the economic problems affecting the Roman Republic. **W. W. Fowler, *Social Life at Rome in the Age of Cicero* (Papermac) presents a well-rounded picture of Roman society at the end of the Republican period, relying heavily on Cicero's letters as a basic source.

Biographies. The lives of the "heroes" help to provide a lively picture of the age. Charles Oman, *Seven Statesmen of the Later Republic* (1902), provides short sketches of the Gracchi, Marius, Sulla, Pompey, Crassus, and Cato the Younger. Also recommended are G. P. Baker, *Sulla the Fortunate: The Great Dictator* (1927); John Buchan, *Julius Caesar* (1936); and **H. J. Haskell, *This Was Cicero* (Fawcett).

Sources. This age produced the most prolific body of contemporary writing on public affairs that has survived from antiquity. Plutarch, *Lives* provides interesting biographies of the Gracchi, Sulla, Marius, Crassus, Pompey, Brutus, Caesar, Cicero, and Cato the Younger: although moralistic in tone, they convey a sense of the personality of the men involved in the struggles of the age. A convenient collection of Plutarch's biographies appropriate to this period can be found in **The Fall of the Roman Republic*, trans. Rex Warner (Penguin). **Suetonius, *Lives of the Twelve Caesars*, trans. R. Graves (Penguin), provides a biography of Caesar filled with many colorful details. The richest source is the writings of Cicero. Especially recommended are **Letters of Cicero: A Selection in Translation*, trans. L. P. Wilkinson (Norton), and **Selected Political Speeches of Cicero*, trans. M. Grant. A briefer selection is supplied in **Cicero, *Selected Works*, trans. M. Grant (Penguin). **Caesar, *Gallic Wars*, trans. S. A. Handford (Penguin), and *Civil War . . .* , trans. J. F. Mitchell (Penguin), provide an insight into the mentality of the greatest figure of the age.

Chapter 11 ❧ The Roman Empire, 31 B.C.–A.D. 180

The eighteenth-century English historian Edward Gibbon wrote that, if he had to choose a period when the condition of the human race was happiest, he would without hesitation name the period between A.D. 96 and 180. During the first and second centuries A.D. the Romans made their most notable contribution to civilization by fashioning out of their past experience and their innate political talents a system of government, known as the Roman Empire, that brought peace and prosperity to the entire Mediterranean Basin.

1. THE FOUNDATIONS OF THE IMPERIAL ORDER: THE WORK OF AUGUSTUS, 31 B.C.–A.D. 14

The victor at Actium, soon to be known by his title, Augustus, was the architect of the Roman Empire, and one of history's greatest statesmen. When Mark Antony and Cleopatra committed suicide after their defeat, Augustus (Octavian) was supreme by virtue of conquest; no one throughout the Roman world was in a position to challenge him. It was clear, however, that open military dictatorship or monarchy could not endure; one-man rule in any form was offensive to the Senate and people of Rome, who for five hundred years had determined their own destiny through a set of institutions which constituted the Roman Republic. But the lesson of the past century was also evident: The only hope for the management of the vast, problem-ridden empire the Romans had created depended on the concentration of power in the hands of one man. Augustus' prime political task was to discover a way to create the reality of monarchy without negating the ideal of citizen control of the state.

His solution, worked out cautiously during his forty-five year rule, was masterful. It involved a series of steps through which the Senate and the people granted sufficient power to permit him to rule the Roman world while retaining the outward forms of the republican constitution. The process began in 27 B.C., when Augustus dramatically surrendered all the powers he then held—largely acquired in the bitter days of his rise to power—to the Senate and the people. Theoretically, the republic was restored; power again rested with the Senate, the elected magistrates, and the popular assemblies. Impressed by this noble gesture, fearful of a recurrence of civil war, and skillfully guided by Augustus, the Senate and people hastened to vote him vast power. He was given the power of tribune for life, the authority of the consuls, command over the armies,

Roman engineering skill has been famous from ancient times, a fame perhaps based on the endurance of the constructions as well as the efficiency and ingenuity of the designs. This aqueduct in Segovia in modern Spain survives intact after almost two thousand years.
Photo: R. Schoder

proconsular authority over most of the provinces, and the highest priestly office. To these powers the grateful citizenry added several honors: first senator, *augustus* ("most revered one"), *imperator* ("victorious general"), and "father of his country." Some even hinted that Augustus was divine. This array of powers and honors so elevated his authority that he was the *princeps*, the first citizen of Rome in every respect. Without a hint of illegality, he could as *princeps* do whatever was necessary to rule Rome. Not as dictator or tyrant or king, but as "first citizen," Augustus was able to effect the reality of one-man rule. Historians have come to refer to this new regime as the *Principate* to reflect its unique blend of republican and monarchical ingredients.

Armed with these great powers, Augustus turned to reconstructing the social order of Rome. His chief concern was the demoralized condition of the Roman citizen body, that relatively small group of Italians who now had no choice but to rule the vast territory of the empire. Adhering to the ancient Roman conviction that a class-structured society was healthiest and most effective, Augustus tried to redefine the old class divisions. He assigned to each class specific functions and responsibilities. Rigid standards of birth, wealth, and conduct were set up for senatorial ranking, and to this elite was assigned a large share in governmental affairs. They were to hold the chief elective offices in the state, to advise the *princeps*, to serve as governors of specified provinces, and to fill high military and civil posts in the provinces. Augustus hoped to make the Senate what it had traditionally been—a loyal, patriotic elite supplying leadership to Rome and sharing decisions with the *princeps*. He was scrupulous in respecting its share in the running of the state, although at times the pride and perversity of the senators tested his patience and political sense.

The equestrian order (*equites*), made up chiefly of rich traders and industrialists, was also clearly defined and given honorable status. New positions in the army, the taxation system, and the judicial system were entrusted to this class; it was to supply bureaucrats to assist the *princeps*.

For the plebeians, Augustus hoped to provide order and security. He concentrated on supplying cheap grain, police supervision, and entertainment for Rome's huge population, and economic security for the farmers of Italy. The plebeians were expected to play a political role by exercising their powers as voters and to serve as volunteers in the armed forces needed to defend the empire. Their response was not always what Augustus ex-

This majestic statue of Augustus, created during his reign, was intended to idealize and exalt Rome's first citizen, the man who had restored peace to the Roman world after the troubled times of the Late Republic. *Photo: Alinari–Art Reference Bureau*

pected, especially in elections; in fact, the populace seemed to prefer a *princeps* who exercised a benevolent mastery over them to one who asked their responsible collaboration in directing the state.

To improve the morale and the patriotism of the citizen body, Augustus encouraged a revival of the ancient Roman religion, patronized writers who turned out masses of propaganda exalting Rome's past greatness and present blessings, and arranged for the passage of numerous laws aimed at checking what he considered softening vices—luxury, sexual irregularities, divorce, childless marriages, gambling, and drinking. He also spent immense sums beautifying Rome and providing public services in the hope that its citizens would feel a resurgence of pride in the capital of the civilized world.

Augustus was no less concerned with the fate of the noncitizens who populated the provinces. Long abused and exploited, the provincials needed attention. To ensure their protection and to minimize the horrors repeatedly perpetrated in the late republican period by uncontrolled armies, he undertook a complete overhaul of the military establishment. The foundation was laid for a professional army by the formation of twenty-five legions recruited from the Roman citizen body for long terms of service. Each legion was complemented by an auxiliary unit composed of noncitizens recruited in the provinces. The total force numbered approximately 300,000 men. Careful discipline, regular pay, and adequate pensions were provided. An elaborate supportive apparatus of roads, supply depots, and military posts was established. The army was commanded by officers responsible to the *princeps* and held in firm check so as to discourage political ambitions. The bulk of this newly constituted army was stationed along Rome's extensive frontier, far from the political center of the empire. Only the Praetorian Guard, a picked contingent of about 9,000 men, was garrisoned in Italy to serve as the bodyguard for the *princeps*. The chief function of the army

was defensive. With the exception of some spirited campaigning on the northern frontier against the Germans, Augustus gave up the idea of offensive warfare and expansion. He began the process of fixing a clear boundary between the Roman and non-Roman worlds. The army's job was to hold that frontier and to strike down elements within the empire who tried to escape Roman domination. The military thus assumed a crucial role as a constructive force in the new order, in sharp contrast with the disruptive part it had played in the political struggles of the declining republic.

Having provided for peace and defense in the provinces, Augustus attempted to improve the Roman administration. By virtue of his proconsular powers he was governor of all but a few provinces that had been entrusted to the Senate, and he began to develop a regular provincial administration that he himself supervised. He selected legates to represent him in each province, and he watched carefully over their conduct. The legates were paid adequate salaries in order to reduce their inclination to build personal fortunes by exploiting the provincial subjects. No legate was given a chance to gain military fame, all military glory being credited to the *princeps*, who was commander of all forces. The task of collecting taxes was completely removed from the legates' hands. Augustus sent into each province a *procurator*, usually of equestrian rank, to collect taxes and render account to the *princeps*. Under the careful eye of Augustus this set of administrative and financial officials almost immediately brought order to the provinces. The notorious corruption, oppression, and violence of the late republican period disappeared, to be replaced by the Roman peace. However, Augustus had no intention of exerting Roman control over every aspect of provincial life. Wherever possible, he encouraged local communities, and especially city-states, to handle as many local affairs as possible.

The complex responsibilities of maintaining the army and administering the provinces generated the need for a central administrative machinery manned by professional civil servants. Under the republic little had been done in this direction, a failure that accounted for a considerable amount of the ineffectiveness of the Roman regime. Augustus began to lay the foundations for a centralized bureaucracy. To an amazing degree, he himself and a circle of confidants directed the far-flung operations of the principate. Slowly, however, there emerged a corps of helpers, comprised to a large degree of freedmen who had no political attachments and who owed everything to the *princeps*. This addition to the political order was immensely important: The efficiency, expertise, and loyalty of its members tended to make the political services of the senators and the citizen population less crucial.

Although one cannot argue that Augustus had a precise economic policy, his new regime produced considerable prosperity, a factor that made his rule more acceptable to citizens and provincials alike. The chief factor in economic revival was the restoration of peace and order. Stability engendered confidence, and the vast reservoir of human and material resources of the Mediterranean world began to be utilized with fresh vigor. Encouraged by a political regime that provided a sound coinage, developed roads, suppressed piracy and brigandage, and imposed an equitable, not-too-heavy tax burden, agriculture, trade, and industry demonstrated new vitality. A wave of prosperity that seemed an intimate part of the Augustan program spread over the empire.

The one remaining problem was for Augustus to ensure the empire a prosperous, stable future. His whole program centered around the concentration of vast powers in the hands of one man; yet he had no legal right to transmit his powers. Only the Senate and people could do so. Augustus began early to try to ensure his succession. He attempted to combine two distinct ideas. First, he hoped to establish the hereditary principle so that the second *princeps* would enjoy the prestige of descent from Julius Caesar and Augustus. Second, he wanted his successor to have gained the practical experience needed to guide the vast empire. Augustus had no sons. His only daughter, Julia, was three times married to potential heirs. Augustus outlived two of her three husbands and her two elder sons. Finally, he chose as his heir his adopted son, Tiberius, whose mother was Augustus' second wife. Tiberius became Julia's third husband and after A.D. 4 was granted ever-greater powers by Augustus. When the *princeps* died in A.D. 14, Tiberius was ready to assume full authority.

This brief summary hardly does justice to Augustus' career, for it makes his efforts seem too simple. True, he seized power in a world that was weary of war and political agitation, a world that was ready for a savior. But this did not mean there were not dangers facing the statesman who tried to improve the situation: the proud, jealous Senate; the irresponsible Roman mob; the restless and distrustful Italians; the sullen, abused provincials; the hostile peoples beyond the frontiers. Augustus' constructive achievements seem almost a miracle. In part he succeeded because he was not a doctrinaire idealist seeking to create a utopian state according to a blueprint; he was a patient, realistic, cautious, hard-working statesman to whom good fortune gave many years to work on his program. He kept central to his political activities certain key ideas: the need to concentrate power in his own hands, the need to honor the ancient political ideals of the Roman citizenry, the need to set positive goals for all elements of a widely diverse population caught up in a common destiny. By working toward these ends, he fashioned a new political order. As it took shape, it elicited from the vital element in the Roman world—the people of Italy—a resurgence of their ancient virtues: patriotism, devotion to public service, loyalty, sobriety. It was this elusive capability for moving men to do what had to be done much more than what he did that best describes the greatness of Augustus.

2. SOLIDIFYING THE AUGUSTAN PRINCIPATE, A.D. 14–96

A laudatory evaluation of Augustus' accomplishments must not beguile us into thinking he had solved all Rome's problems. Between his death and the end of the first century A.D., the principate was tested by severe pressures and by strong opposition. Outwardly this era was marked by the very thing that Augustus wished to avoid: a clash between the *princeps* and the Senate, a struggle between the monarchical thrust of the principate and the republican inertia of the senators. This encounter bred fear, uneasiness, and turmoil, especially in the city of Rome, that threatened to plunge the empire into a new era of disaster.

One of the factors contributing to the tension was the difficulty of finding rulers possessed of the talents needed to run a vast, complex empire while respecting the authority that the Augustan system had entrusted to the Senate and the people. Nearly all Augustus' successors down to A.D. 96 were men of limited abilities who acted in ways that brought accusations of tyranny and that evoked incessant opposition from the Senate. The first four rulers of this era, called the Julio-Claudians, were all related to Augustus, but the family tie did not carry with it wisdom comparable to his. Tiberius (A.D. 14–37) was a cold, suspicious, disillusioned man who repeatedly made brutal assaults on those he suspected of trying to undermine his position. Caligula (A.D. 37–41) was a man lacking completely in political sense; perhaps he was even mad. Claudius (A.D. 41–54) was a scholarly man whose chief interests lay outside Roman aristocratic society; to many he seemed something less than a real Roman and thus enjoyed little respect. Worst of all was Nero (A.D. 54–68). Cruel, vain, wasteful, he kept Rome in a turmoil in his attempts to satisfy his own desires. He was eventually ousted from office, avoiding assassination by killing himself, but only after he had killed his mother and two wives, disposed of numerous senators, persecuted Christians, made a fool of himself posing as an artist, and emptied the treasury in order to indulge his personal whims.

With Nero's passing the family of Augustus was discredited, and the office of *princeps* was forcefully seized by Vespasian (A.D. 69–79), an Italian who had spent most of his life in the army. He and his sons, Titus (A.D. 79–81) and Domitian (A.D. 81–96), were men of considerable ability, but they had little respect for the Senate. The members of this dynasty, called the Flavians, appeared to many aristocrats to be worse tyrants than Augustus' relatives had been.

The unhealthy turmoil of the first century A.D. was also due in large part to the imprecise definition of the powers to be exercised by the *princeps* on one hand and the Senate and people on the other. Often the *princeps* exercised his authority to meet some real need only to find his actions interpreted by the Senate as a usurpation of its authority and a threat to the political system. This posture of suspicion, distrust, and misunderstanding caused the rulers to curb cricitism and resistance with a heavy hand. The circle of misunderstanding and hatred was generated in particular by the problem of the succession. As we have seen, Augustus had established conflicting principles: Theoretically, the Senate and people chose the *princeps* by voting to him the powers and rank of first citizen. Augustus, however, had arranged affairs so that his position was hereditary, and thus it remained until the death of Nero in A.D. 68. Throughout these years there were constant plots against the *princeps*, often engineered by Augustus' numerous relatives and coteries of senators attracted to their cause out of the conviction that the Senate and people had the power to select the *princeps*. These plots ended either in the elimination of the ruling *princeps* or of the plotters (more often the latter); in either case, each one increased the bitterness and suspicion that poisoned Roman political life. At Nero's death, the army again became a participant in politics. In A.D. 68–69 actual war was waged by various legions seeking to elevate a favored general to power.

When Vespasian emerged as the victor, it was obvious the Senate had little to say about the succession. He returned to the hereditary principle of succession, but the old resistance was raised against the Flavians.

In reality, the incessant plots, quarrels, and political murders that loom so large in the records of the first century A.D. were of minor significance compared to developments of a less spectacular nature occurring in the Mediterranean world. The investigations of modern scholars into evidence other than the writings of gossipy, conservative Roman historians have shown that several of the rulers—especially Tiberius, Claudius, and Vespasian—were able statesmen who worked patiently and effectively to increase the power of the *princeps* and to perfect the means of exercising that power to constructive ends. They were worthy successors of Augustus, faithful to his broad policy. But their successes slowly eroded the remaining power of the Senate and people. In large part, this decline was self-caused: Senate and people consistently failed to act effectively and intelligently. Their place was taken by an organized bureaucracy whose members demonstrated an expertise and devotion to public welfare that permitted the rulers to enact and carry out intelligent policies beneficial to the entire empire. They ably defended the frontiers and on occasion extended them; for example, when Claudius conquered Britain. The provinces, far removed from the petty political storms of Rome, were well administered, and their inhabitants grew to respect the imperial regime. Several rulers extended citizenship to many provincials, and thereby drew them into the mainstream of imperial society and added valuable manpower to Roman society. Vast public works were undertaken in Rome, in Italy, and in the provinces, earning for their sponsors the good will of the citizens. Trade, industry, and agriculture were given every possible encouragement. To the majority of men of the Roman world—and increasingly even to the senators—the conclusion that rule by a powerful *princeps* meant order and justice, prosperity and security was inescapable. These were precious gifts, worth surrendering freedom to have.

3. THE EMPIRE AT ITS PEAK: THE "GOOD EMPERORS," A.D. 96–180

With the death of Domitian in A.D. 96, opposition to the principate virtually disappeared, most of the Roman populace having accepted the necessity of one-man rule and having grown to appreciate its advantages. For roughly the next century, the empire enjoyed a golden age that still evokes admiration. From the Atlantic to the Euphrates, from Central Europe to deep inside Africa, the *pax romana* became a reality. It was an era characterized by excellent rulers, just and efficient administration, benevolent concern for the general welfare, internal peace, material prosperity, and stout defense of the frontiers—accolades generally not available to the historian in such combination.

Seldom has any era produced rulers more highly praised than the five men who ruled from A.D. 96–180. Nerva (A.D. 96–98) was an elderly man when chosen to succeed the tyrannical Domitian. Before he died he selected as his heir a native of Spain, Trajan (A.D. 98–117). This forceful, energetic ruler won the admiration of the whole Roman world by his respect for the Roman aristocracy, his brilliant military exploits, and his sound, honest administration. Hadrian (A.D. 117–138) was a cultured humanitarian who spent most of his reign in incessant travel throughout the empire promoting the cause of peace and material well-being. Antoninus (A.D. 138–161), by the excellence of his character and intellect, earned the title of "Pius" from the Senate. The crowning glory of the era was Marcus Aurelius (A.D. 161–180), a noted Stoic philosopher who brought a deep sense of duty, willingness to work, and nobility of purpose to the Roman political scene. So outstanding were these five rulers that later generations referred to them as the "good emperors."

WALL OF ANTONINUS

WALL OF HADRIAN

BRITAIN
43

Londinium

LOWER
GERMANY
89

UPPER
GERMANY
89

NORICUM
ca. 46

DACIA
106

THRACE
46

Rome

LESSER
ARMENIA
72

ARMENIA
114

CAPPADOCIA
ca. 17

OSROENE
ca. 195

ASSYRIA
115–117

MESOPOTAMIA
115–117

ARABIA
ca. 106

Empire at 14

Expansion to 284

Temporarily Controlled Provinces

The Roman Empire A.D. 14–284

The program followed by these emperors was generally consistent. Rather early in his reign each took special care to select a successor. They sought out a man of ability, adopted him as a son, and then slowly increased his power until at the death of the old emperor, the heir was powerfully placed and widely experienced. The succession question was solved. All these emperors were tactful and respectful toward the senatorial class, and avoided any charge of tyranny. The senators, who were given most of the high offices and were continually consulted, became staunch supporters of the principate, even though their independent power was extremely limited. The "good emperors" steadily developed the imperial bureaucracy, creating a disciplined body of administrators who gained by serving the state well. They secured the enactment of legislation affecting all parts of the empire and slowly created a unified body of law for the whole empire. The interests of the provinces were guarded and promoted. Citizenship was granted to an ever-larger number of provincials, and humanitarian projects for the aid of the downtrodden members of the empire were repeatedly inaugurated. Public works—roads, aqueducts, harbor facilities, temples—were built at imperial expense. The army was kept in readiness. These rulers were constantly concerned about the economic welfare of the whole empire. All showed broad tolerance for different segments of the population, allowing local groups extensive freedom as long as that freedom did not threaten the peace. Since the services of the imperial government were costly, the "good emperors" worked tirelessly to establish a sound financial system that would provide adequate income for worthwhile expenditures. All these efforts on the part of the emperors slowly bound the 50 million or so people [1] of the empire into a commonwealth guided from Rome by a benevolent ruler and his disciplined civil servants, enjoying a rule of law, partaking at least to some degree in the general economic prosperity, and safe from war and injustice.

But there was one uncontrollable factor—the frontier question. Rome's army of about 350,000 men was spread too thinly along her long frontier for safety. Trajan tried to safeguard the frontier from the Germans and the Parthians by conquering Dacia and the Tigris-Euphrates Valley. Hadrian reversed this aggressive policy, and trusted to strong defense and diplomacy. But by the time of Marcus Aurelius, however, the problem had still not been solved, and this peace-loving philosopher was forced to spend much of his reign fighting the Germans, who broke across the Danube frontier and penetrated deep into Roman territory. When he died in A.D. 180, a tenuous

peace that was cause for grave concern prevailed along the extensive frontier.

4. IMPERIAL GOVERNMENT IN THE SECOND CENTURY

In its mature form in the second century A.D., the principate was a marvelously effective and enlightened system of government that deserves at least a brief description. Throughout this period the Senate and the Roman people in theory still had final authority in the state. In fact, a large part of the ancient republican machinery of government continued to operate: The Senate met regularly and debated with fervor; elections were held for the traditional offices and the victors enjoyed honorable positions in society; on occasion, the assemblies met to speak the voice of the citizens. All this kept the Roman citizenry solidly in touch with a sacred and meaningful tradition—yet it had little to do with the realities of political life. These venerable organizations had but one function, to approve and legalize the authority of the real wielder of power, the *princeps*.

The *princeps*, or *emperor* (derived from the title *imperator*, the honor voted by soldiers to their victorious general), had assumed a virtual monopoly of executive, legislative, and judicial powers. These powers were legally voted each emperor at the beginning of his reign. His key powers were command over all military forces, control of all revenues, and control of legislation. Most emperors enjoyed even greater authority than that voted by the Senate and the people. Each had a huge personal fortune to be spent as he pleased. Each held various honorary titles that exalted him above all others, and most emperors were believed to be especially blessed by the gods, if not actually divine.

The emperors exercised their vast powers through two agencies: the bureaucracy and the army. The bureaucracy was divided into great departments, each headed by an experienced, able official. Under the chief were numerous grades of officials with carefully de-

---

[1] Population figures for ancient Rome are at best guesses and none too reliable. Some authorities would put the population of the empire as high as 70 million for the second century of the Christian era.

fined functions, ranks, and rewards. The top levels of the bureaucracy were manned by senators and equestrians, while the lower ranks were filled with educated plebeians or freedmen. Romans, Italians, and provincials alike were accepted in the civil service, making it an extremely cosmopolitan body. The "good emperors" maintained close guard over the bureaucrats, ensuring honest, efficient conduct of public business.

The army had changed little since Augustus' time. The total number of men under arms was slightly increased. The bulk of the soldiery was recruited for twenty-five-year terms from the citizen population of Italy, although by the second century more provincials were being drawn into the legions. Every effort was made to get good commanders, to provide adequate training, pay, and pensions, and to sustain morale. On the whole, the performance of the army was superb. The soldiers faced the hard life along the frontiers without complaint; they fought bravely to restrain invaders; and they responded to imperial orders to crush rebels within the empire. They not only played a vital role in defending the empire, but served as transmitters of Roman techniques and skills to backward peoples living along the frontiers and to the barbarians beyond.

The support of these two agencies imposed a tremendous financial burden on the state. Salaries for the civil servants and pay, pensions, and provisions for the soldiers made imperative a large, regular income. Added to these expenses were the costs of public services supplied by the government—roads, public buildings, food for the poor of the cities, police forces, and so forth. The emperors of the first and second centuries A.D. succeeded in meeting these financial demands by developing an elaborate but fair tax system that kept the regime solvent. No small part of the tax burden was borne by the provincials as their contribution to the support of the Italians who protected and governed them. Another notable achievement of the rulers of the first two centuries of the Chris-

tian era was the creation of an effective provincial administration. By A.D. 180 the empire was divided into roughly forty provinces. Some of these were still administered under the authority of the Senate, but most were under the direct authority of the *princeps*. A governor was assigned to each with a wide range of powers to keep order, administer justice, and protect Rome's interests. The emperors exercised great care to select honest and effective men for these crucial posts. In each province the machinery for collection of taxes was maintained under officials called *procurators*, drawn largely from the ranks of the *equites*. They too were carefully selected and rigorously supervised from Rome.

The second-century emperors followed Augustus' principle of allowing as much local freedom as possible, and throughout the empire city-states were encouraged to regulate their own affairs. The emperors tried to create hundreds of small Romes for the purpose of supplying local government. Each city-state and its surrounding territory was ruled by a body of local aristocrats (called *curiales*) who made up a local senate. These senates elected local magistrates, collected local taxes, assumed responsibility for policing and beautifying the city, held courts, and did the many other things necessary for sound government. As a matter of fact, these city-state governments bore the brunt of day-by-day political life, the Roman governors and armies merely standing by to keep order and protect them. There can be little doubt that the Romans were inspired to this policy by the model of the Greeks. They believed the city-state was the ideal political institution and encouraged residents to be patriots concerned with the well-being of their city. Where city-states did not already exist—especially in the Western provinces—the Romans founded as many as possible. The second century was truly the culminating age of city-state polity; the whole vast Roman Empire was becoming a federation of nearly autonomous city-states kept at peace by the mighty *princeps* who ruled in Rome. It must not be thought, however, that the imperial government was totally aloof from local affairs. The emperors themselves sometimes intervened in local affairs and regulated matters contrary to local wishes. Once Rome did intervene, the small cities had little hope of defending themselves. They had no power to match that of the *princeps*.

It is beyond question that by the second century A.D. Rome possessed the essentials of autocratic government. A Trajan or a Hadrian could do virtually anything he desired. However, Roman government of the second century was not despotic; seldom have men with such great power ruled so benevolently or humanely. This calls for a word of explanation: The emperors of the second century were strongly motivated by rather well-defined ideas of what constituted good government and the duty of a ruler. They believed that power entailed duty, that power existed so that humanity could be served. The excellence of government could be judged only by the good it caused. A strong sense of service to humanity thus kept the emperors from abusing their nearly unlimited power. This political philosophy was based to a large degree on the Stoic ideas to which most second-century emperors were devoted, but no less on the theories of men like Plato and on the political practices of men like Alexander the Great. The emperors were also bound by the deep Roman respect for law. The task of an emperor was to operate within the framework of the law, limiting and shaping his powers to fit it. This deep sense of duty and respect for the law gave Roman government an aspect that ought not to be forgotten in evaluating second-century Roman society. A strong idealism literally drove emperors and their thousands of servants: Good government to these men was the first need for civilized life.

5. LIFE IN THE EMPIRE

An elaborate, orderly, powerful government brought peace and stability in which certain patterns of social and economic life flourished. What these patterns were, how they functioned in the second century, and what they augured for the future are questions well worth studying. Emperors could decree and armies march, but unless all those who lived within the system had their needs and wants satisfied at least to a degree, it could not long endure.

For the majority of the people in the empire, farming was still the fundamental means of livelihood, and the level of agricultural prosperity was high in the second century, for the great cities and the Roman army created a large and steady demand. Especially flourishing were the great estates (*latifundia*) owned by men of wealth who had sufficient capital to engage in large-scale commercial production of grapes, olives, livestock, and grain. These estates developed in every part of the empire, often at the expense of small, independent farmers who could not compete successfully. The great estates were nourished by the thriving trade that was the key to imperial prosperity. The reduction of artificial trade barriers, the sound money system, the good roads, and the well-policed seas encouraged the movement of goods to every corner of the empire. The Mediterranean Sea became a busy roadway linking its bordering lands in a common economic system. The traders of the Roman world carried on their activities not only within the confines of the vast empire, but also with India and China. Although a large part of Roman commercial activity involved grain, olive oil, wine, and other agricultural products, some of it was devoted to the exchange of a variety of manufactured goods produced by skilled artisans in the cities. The East had long been noted for its industrial skills, and from that area came high-quality goods universally prized by the affluent. One of the economic developments of the era, however, was the remarkable growth of industry in previously backward areas of the West, especially Gaul, Spain, and Africa. These complex international patterns of agriculture, trade, and industry tended to reduce the economic importance and self-sufficiency of Italy. The Italians, with their monopoly on political power, were able to exploit the economic strengths of the rest of the empire so as to compensate for declining productivity at its heart, but the likelihood of trouble in the future was real. For the present, a sound economy assured a considerable proportion of the population a decent livelihood; a small number of people even amassed vast wealth and lived in splendid luxury. Probably the level of prosperity of the entire Mediterranean world was greater than it had ever been.

The social system, centered on an urban pattern of life, regained its stability. Rome, of course, was the hub of the entire empire, but many other cities—especially the great Eastern centers like Alexandria, Antioch, Corinth, Ephesus, and Athens—were worthy rivals. In these cities life was dominated by an aristocracy made up of wealthy landowners, successful traders, and high state officials. These

aristocrats were recognized by the imperial government as the leaders of society and were supported in their direction of civic life. They used their wealth and social prestige to ensure themselves a full share of the comforts of life —fine houses, expensive food and clothing, abundant servants, good education, costly entertainment. Their conduct defined the essence of civilized life in the Roman world. And although they sometimes indulged their desires to vulgar excess and were always keenly and arrogantly conscious of their status, this aristocracy, moved by civic pride, poured considerable amounts of talent and wealth into the promotion of the welfare of the cities. Furthermore, the aristocracy was never a closed one; members of the lower classes could enter it by attaining wealth or winning favor with the imperial government.

Below the aristocrats was a bewildering array of city-dwellers: shopkeepers, skilled artisans, minor officials, hired laborers, servants, slaves, and throngs of idle poor. Some elements of this populace, especially the shopkeepers, artisans, and officials, fared fairly well economically and socially—but for many in the cities, life was always poverty and misery. These people lived in slums, often dependent upon the largess of the state or the favors of a rich aristocrat for the bare essentials of life. Still, the city had its compensations: its pageants, its public games, its splendid buildings, its religious ceremonies, its constant excitement.

Those who received the least benefit from the *pax romana* were the peasants who spent their lives tilling the soil. Isolated from the cities, they seldom felt the impact of the forces that gave Roman society its vitality. During the first and second centuries A.D., the condition of the free peasants tended to deteriorate. The major trends in agricultural life

This relief shows an everyday scene in a Roman household: Food is being prepared and baked in the oven at right. The panel, now in the Musée de Trier, dates from the third century. *Photo: Alinari–Art Reference Bureau* encouraged the growth of large estates, a process that increasingly engulfed the holdings of the small independent farmers and reduced them to dependency on powerful absentee landlords. These dependent agricultural workers, called *coloni*, were helpless tenants forced to give their labor and a large part of their produce to a landlord who permitted them only a bare subsistence. Their personal freedom was gradually eroded to the point where they had virtually no choice but to serve a powerful, greedy aristocracy. Increasingly, the greater burden of the taxes was shifted onto them as well. In effect, the peasantry supported the other classes in Roman society with very little recompense and less hope for a better life.

Slavery played a prominent role in Roman imperial society. In the cities slaves worked in the households of the rich and in the workshops and stalls of artisans and merchants, performing a great variety of menial, unpleasant tasks. Nearly every agricultural establishment had slave laborers, and some of the large estates depended almost totally on slaves. So also did the mines and the great factories where ceramics were made. Needless to say, the lot of slaves was a hard one and their treatment often brutal, especially in circumstances where great gangs of them were utilized. There is some evidence, however, that their condition tended to improve. Many were given their freedom by masters who in some cases seem to have been moved to this action by moral scruples. Some slaves managed to acquire enough wealth to purchase their freedom and enjoy considerable prosperity practicing trades they had learned as slaves. Numerous funerary inscriptions render praise to slaves for their loyalty and industry, and other literary sources suggest that masters and slaves often associated amicably. Imperial legislation extended several rights to slaves and sought

to assure them humane treatment. Despite these signs of a more enlightened view toward slavery, the institution demeaned labor and justified the idleness of many freemen.

One of the chief social consequences of the Roman imperial order was the degree to which barriers of every kind tumbled to create a cosmopolitan Mediterranean society. The distinction between Roman and non-Roman faded as provincials gained citizenship, wealth, and the opportunity to serve the imperial government. The gulf between national and ethnic groups disappeared as a consequence of the free movement of peoples and the common institutions serving every part of the empire. The distinction between civilized and barbarian lessened in the wake of the effort to bring the basic ingredients of civilized life to all Roman subjects. Religions, philosophies, art forms, and ideas fused in an atmosphere of toleration. Under Roman rule, the Mediterranean basin tended to become one world racially, religiously, culturally, and economically. The Romans provided the synthesizing agency and the chief bond of unity in the form of the imperial government, one of the most humane and beneficent political systems ever devised.

Even a brief description of the Roman world in the second century will elicit admiration for its peace, order, prosperity, and unity. That admiration is warranted, but it must be tempered by certain reservations. The empire had its poverty, its injustices, its oppression, its violence, its greed. The callous disregard shown by the proud, self-satisfied ruling aristocracy for these conditions; the immense power concentrated in the imperial government without any checks; the signs of vulgarization, sterile imitation, and barbarization in the emerging cultural synthesis; the dangerous weaknesses in the economy—all these signs belied the Roman pride and faith that their world was destined to last to eternity.

first sign of decline of empire

Suggested Reading

Political History. A brief but highly effective survey of the history of the Roman Empire from the time of Augustus to its fall is **M. P. Charlesworth, *The Roman Empire* (Galaxy). A detailed treatment, especially good on the evolution of political institutions, can be found in two volumes that constitute successive parts of a series on Roman history: **E. T. Salmon, *History of the Roman World From 30 B.C. to A.D. 138* (University Paperbacks); H. M. Parker, *A History of the Roman World From A.D. 138 to 337* (2nd ed., 1958). Theodor Mommsen, *The Provinces of the Roman Empire From Caesar to Diocletian* (2 vols., 2nd ed., 1909), brilliantly treats the nature and effects of Roman rule over her provinces. Less specialized and more concerned with provincial society is Victor Chapot, *The Roman World*, trans. E. A. Parker (1928). Two rather difficult books, both by the same author, provide a thorough analysis of the political institutions of this age: Mason Hammond, *The Augustan Principate in Theory and Practice* (rev. ed., 1968), and *The Antonine Monarchy* (1959). A stimulating treatment of political ideas and institutions is **F. E. Adcock, *Roman Political Ideas and Practices* (Ann Arbor). Still worth reading for the majesty of its style and its breadth of detail is a classic written in the late eighteenth century by the English historian Edward Gibbon, *History of the Decline and Fall of the Roman Empire* (many editions; the best one is that edited by J. B. Bury, 7 vols., 1909–14, but more easily accessible is a two-volume edition in Modern Library).

Economic and Social History. Perhaps the most readable description of Roman imperial society as a whole is provided by **Jérome Carcopino, *Daily Life in Ancient Rome*, trans. E. O. Lorimer (Yale). Two shorter works, likewise broad in coverage, are **Martin Nilsson, *Imperial Rome* (Schocken); and **Harold Mattingly, *Roman Imperial Civilization* (Anchor). A classic work, well worth the effort needed to master it, is M. I. Rostovtzeff, *Social and Economic History of the Roman World* (2 vols., 2nd ed., 1957). Rather old, but excellent on social conditions, is **Samuel Dill, *Roman Society From Nero to Marcus Aurelius* (2nd ed., Meridian). Also excellent for its picture of society in the city of Rome is H. T. Rowell, *Rome in the Augustan Age* (1962).

Biography. Valuable insights into the history of this period are supplied by excellent biographies of the most important emperors. Especially recommended are John Buchan, *Augustus* (1947); F. B. Marsh, *The Reign of Tiberius* (1931); A. Momigliano, *Claudius the Emperor and His Achievements* (new ed., 1962); Stewart Perowne, *Hadrian* (1960); and A. S. L. Farquharson, *Marcus Aurelius* (1951). Briefer sketches are supplied by B. W. Henderson, *Five Roman Emperors* (1927), dealing with Vespasian, Titus, Domitian, Nerva, and Trajan; and M. P. Charlesworth, *Five Men* (1936).

Sources. Augustus provided a summary of his own activities in a book entitled *Compendium of Roman History: Res gestae divi augusti*, trans. F. W. Shipley (Loeb Classical Library, 1924). The basic works on the history of the first century A.D. are Tacitus, *Annals* and *Histories* (many editions; a good one is by A. J. Church and W. J. Brodribb in **Complete Works of Tacitus [Modern Library Edition]). The **Annals are also available in a translation by M. Grant (Penguin). Although he was a disgruntled conservative not favorably disposed toward the rulers, Tacitus gives a detailed and lively picture of the era. **Suetonius, *The Twelve Caesars*, trans. Robert Graves (Penguin), sets down a gossipy, personalized sketch of each emperor from Julius Caesar to Domitian. **Pliny the Younger, *Letters*, trans. Betty Radice (Penguin) provides excellent information on the activities of a Roman provincial governor in the reign of Trajan.

Chapter 12 ﹰ Roman Culture

As the Romans were perfecting an imperial government that served the entire Mediterranean world, their intellectual and artistic life reached maturity. Rome played a dual role in the cultural history of the Western world. In certain fields, especially in art, philosophy, and abstract scientific thought, the Romans were not creators; their role in these fields was primarily one of borrowing from and adapting the Greek tradition, and then disseminating the synthesis among their subjects, especially those living in the western part of the empire. In this role the Romans helped to keep alive the Greek tradition and to transmit it to peoples incapable of appropriating the treasures of Greece by themselves. However, the Romans were not entirely imitators. They made major contributions stamped with their unique genius in literature, architecture, engineering, and law —contributions sufficient to ensure them an important place in cultural history.

1. THE LONG APPRENTICESHIP

Before 250 B.C. the Romans displayed little interest in cultural pursuits. Their life, strongly influenced by Etruscan models, was simple and conservative. Out of these early centuries, however, emerged a basic orienta-tion toward life which shaped thought and colored cultural achievement for centuries. The Romans became a practical, down-to-earth people, little given to intellectualism or emotionalism. The virtues they admired were sobriety, industry, piety, and a sense of responsibility toward family, state, and gods. Originality, creativity, and individual achievement—all potentially dangerous to stable society but vital to cultural vigor—were little admired or encouraged and seldom made manifest.

This early Roman outlook on life was shaped by four major forces—family life, agriculture, warfare, and religion. The powerfully entrenched family structure was dominantly patriarchal. Fathers, who themselves possessed a strong sense of responsibility toward their kinsmen, impressed on other members of the tightly knit families a sense of discipline, obedience, and respect for authority and tradition. Farm life made the early Romans a practical, realistic people, willing to work and content to live simply and frugally. Constant warfare in defense of Rome deepened the sense of duty and strengthened discipline. But religion had the most profound effect on the thought and actions of the early Romans. Their belief that every aspect of life was controlled by numerous gods and spirits

The Roman way of life was introduced and maintained in all her provinces by the soldiers and administrators who were sent from the capital to distant posts in the empire. This mosaic showing a charioteer in the pose of a proud victor was found in North Africa. *Photo: Bardo Museum, Tunis* instilled in them a deep piety and a sense of dependence on outside forces.

The chief Roman gods at this early date were household and agricultural deities: Janus, the god of the doorway; Vesta, the goddess of the hearth; and the *lares* and *penates*, spirits guarding the productive powers of the family and its lands. Almost as significant were the deities who protected civic life, headed by Jupiter and his wife Juno. Conciliating these spirits was life's chief burden, to which the Romans took a businesslike attitude. They approached the gods with dignity and reserve. Religious worship consisted chiefly of making sacrificial offerings to the various gods and of repeating long-established prayers in their honor. The head of each family led the worship of the family and household gods. The ceremonies in honor of civic gods were conducted by priests who placed great emphasis on the correct performance of traditional ceremonies and the proper utterance of ancient prayers. Even the least deviation from the proper pattern might anger the gods and bring great misfortune on their worshipers. This devotion to formalism discouraged religious speculation and emotionalism; it instilled instead a strong sense of propriety and dignity.

Family, farm, battlefield, and altar thus worked together to establish the early Roman outlook and character. The best Roman was a sensible, unemotional, hard-working, disciplined man, willing to accept the world as it was, not especially eager to seek out new things and usually indifferent to speculation.

2. THE HELLENISTIC TIDAL WAVE

But the early cultural and spiritual world of the Romans was a narrow, simplistic one within which they could not remain forever isolated, especially once their power began to extend over Italy and the entire Mediterranean world. Beginning with the conquest of the Greek cities of southern Italy in the first half of the third century and continuing until the end of the second century B.C., these simple Romans experienced a cultural revolution. As a result of their relationships with the Italian Greeks, their wars in the East, and the importation of many Greek slaves into Italy, the Romans slowly became aware of the cultural heritage of the Greek world, particularly in its Hellenistic phase. They were so impressed that during the third and second centuries B.C., they were literally conquered by the culture of their subject peoples.

One of the consequences of this experience was the adoption of a new educational system. Previously the young Roman had been educated at home by his father. He was taught family customs, the principles of Roman law, farming, civic duties, and religion. Now that system was replaced by the Hellenistic model. In every respectable Roman household educated Greek slaves were employed to teach young men to read Greek, to introduce them to Greek literature and philosophy, and to develop in them the skills needed to express their own ideas. The study of grammar and rhetoric became the touchstones of the new educational system and long remained the instruments through which the young were brought into civilized society.

Their fascination with Greek culture soon spurred the Romans to imitation. Greek influence was clearly evident in literature. Epic poems, comedies, tragedies, histories, and even philosophical tracts were produced in Latin. Most early Roman authors usually copied Greek literary styles slavishly and filled

One of the great achievements of Roman architects was the building of a harmonious group of public buildings called a forum, the center of a city's political and commercial life. This picture shows a portion of the most famous forum, that of Rome itself. *Photo: Harriet Glickstein* their works with Greek subject matter. But in their attempts at imitation, the Romans perfected Latin as a language for literary expression and laid the groundwork for an independent Latin literature.

In art, the Romans were even more deeply impressed by Greek models. During the wars in the East huge numbers of art pieces were pilfered to decorate Roman villas. Those who could not steal what they wanted hired Eastern artists to turn out copies of Greek art objects. Greek styles of architecture were applied to civic buildings in Rome. Private dwellings were built and decorated in styles used in the East. Rome was transformed physically into a Hellenistic city. Her populace became accustomed to seeing beauty in only those things modeled on the Greek style.

Even the masses in Rome felt the impact of Greek influences, but they were touched chiefly through religion. The terrible strain of the wars of conquest left many people intellectually and emotionally lost. The formal, unemotional religion of Rome offered

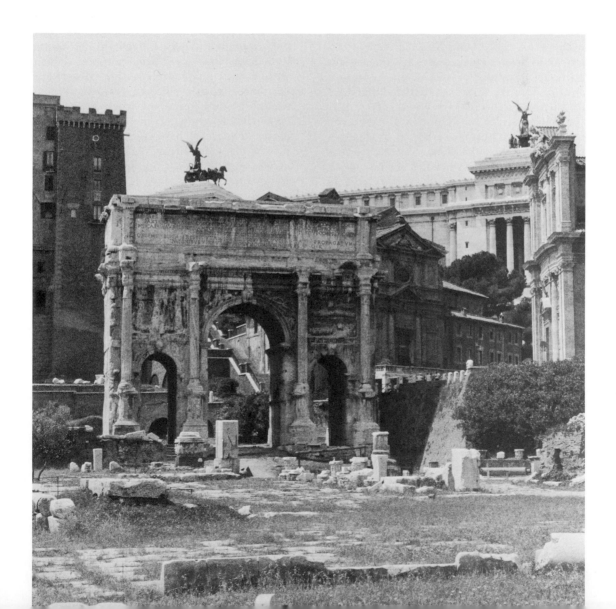

little satisfaction. The Eastern religions did. Throughout this whole period, new gods and new rituals taken from the Greek civic religions were added to public religious life in Rome, but even these additions did not satisfy many Romans. From Eastern slaves they learned about more exciting religions like the worship of Dionysus or Cybele or Isis. These mystery religions were all essentially alike, promising life after death to all, emphasizing personal morality, and involving a highly emotional ritual that furnished an outlet for personal feelings. All over Italy people joined the Greek and Asian cults in large numbers.

By 100 B.C. the Romans had become ardent disciples of Hellenism. The old, simple outlook had been replaced by new ideals and attitudes derived from Greek art, literature, and philosophy. Some Romans, however, fought this intellectual revolution. Typical of the conservatives was Cato the Elder, a second-century statesman who spent his life preaching against the Greek way. He argued that Rome was being ruined by the loss of her ancient virtues—sobriety, industry, respect for the old gods, patriotism. However, Cato was fighting a lost cause. Rome was destined by circumstance and choice to be heir to the magnificent Greek cultural patrimony.

During the first century B.C. the Romans began to put their own stamp on what they had borrowed. Always using Greek forms and ideas as starting points, Roman writers, artists, and thinkers began to add a distinctive Roman touch to their work. Rome's greatest cultural achievements were produced in the years between 100 B.C. and A.D. 180, especially after the accession of Augustus in 31 B.C. Peaceful conditions, imperial patronage, and Augustus' attempt to regenerate Roman society inspired poets, artists, and philosophers to supreme efforts. After Augustus' death there was a brief slackening; the "golden age" had passed. But a second period of considerable activity, often called the "silver age," took place under the "good emperors" (A.D. 96–180). During these three centu-

ries the Romans added enough to what they had borrowed from Greece to permit us to call the product "Greco-Roman culture."

3. LITERATURE

The most impressive and easily appreciated reflection of the Roman cultural genius is found in literature. The chief masterpieces of this literature were produced during the years between about 100 B.C. and A.D. 150, but behind the mature works lay a long period of the formation of Latin as a superb instrument for the clear expression of ideas. The early Latin writers were deeply indebted to Greek models for both style and content, but as the Roman genius developed, authors demonstrated that unique talent that gives Latin literature its own place in history. Roman writers poured into their works a depth of personal conviction, a complete seriousness, a powerful sense of realism, and a passion for instructing and uplifting their readers.

Outstanding among all Roman writers is Vergil (70–19 B.C.). Born in rural Italy, Vergil grew to manhood during the last years of the civil wars. Eventually he attracted the attention of Augustus, whose patronage permitted him to devote the last years of his life to writing. Although much of his great talent was poured out in the service of the new Augustan order, it would be erroneous to overemphasize Vergil's role as a propagandist for the Augustan regime. His support was genuine; what he wrote in praise of the new order welled up out of deep conviction and great enthusiasm. His *Georgics* expressed in beautiful terms a strong feeling for nature and for what involvement in nature and the pastoral life can mean to men—especially to those corrupted by the violence and greed surrounding the last days of the republic. Vergil's masterpiece was an epic poem, the *Aeneid*, which was an attempt to glorify Rome and to show that her rise to mastery of the world was divinely ordered. The plot centers on the adventures of a Trojan hero, Aeneas, who after the fall of Troy was ordered by the gods to establish in Italy a new city destined to rule the world. The noble Aeneas—an ideal Roman—undergoes a series of supreme tests, but obeys the divine order. In recounting the feats performed by Aeneas and his progeny in the creation of the new city, Vergil glorifies the virtues he believed to be responsible for Roman greatness—piety, bravery, self-control, diligence, sobriety. Here is old Roman character being revived so that it might serve as the foundation of the new Augustan order. Never was the Roman ideal of the virtuous patriot portrayed with more force and spiritual intensity.

Two other poets, Catullus and Horace, illustrate another side of the Roman character. Catullus (ca. 85–54 B.C.) was a product of high society in the late republican period. His life was lived amid a dissolute, pleasure-seeking crowd of young nobles. Among his many adventures was a love affair with a noble lady who was already married and who eventually jilted him. His love and disappointment inspired Catullus to pour forth powerful lyric poetry. Horace (65–8 B.C.) was also a lyric poet. He enjoyed the patronage of Augustus and was second in influence only to Vergil, whose intimate friend he was. His best work, the *Odes*, represents his personal reactions to hundreds of situations he met in his lifetime. He expresses every shade of feeling from deep seriousness to light frivolity. Although he lacked the fire and passion of Catullus, Horace spoke to a wider circle, his poems reflecting the reactions of an educated, humane Roman to life as a whole—a great spirit looking at the world about him with sanity, intelligence, and wit. In his own day he was, and still remains, the ideal of a civilized man. Catullus and Horace together represent the Roman individual's ability to see, feel, and appreciate life in all its aspects.

Lucretius (ca. 95–55 B.C.) demonstrated still another aspect of Roman poetic genius. A contemporary of Catullus, he lived through the civil war era. He found his personal sal-

vation in Epicurean philosophy, which he undertook to explain in a long poem called *On the Nature of Things.* With almost missionary zeal Lucretius put poetry to the service of instruction. He made a noble plea to educated Romans to seek in philosophy the bases of moral regeneration. He urged his readers to dedicate their lives to the pleasure of seeking truth about nature and man's place in it. Seldom has a poet shown greater moral earnestness, idealism, and dignity than did Lucretius. His poem was a monument to the moral seriousness that characterized the enlightened Roman.

Among the lesser poets were Ovid (43 B.C.– A.D. 17), who entertained Augustan high society with his *Art of Love*, a frivolous but amusing poem on the art of seduction, and his *Metamorphoses*, an entertaining, lively rendering of Greek mythological stories into Latin; and Martial (ca. A.D. 38–102) and Juvenal (ca. A.D. 55–140), both of whom revealed the shortcomings of Roman society in their brilliant satires. Having found their inspiration in Greek models, the Romans produced poetry filled with idealism, touched with deep insight into human strength and weakness, and dedicated to enlightening humanity. Enshrined in that poetry were the noblest thoughts of the Greeks expressed with the dignity and good sense of educated Romans.

The Romans were equally adept at prose writing. Cicero (106–43 B.C.) was the most famous prose writer in Roman history. Although an active statesman, he found time to produce a wide variety of writing, of which his speeches form a large part. As a lawyer and magistrate, Cicero was constantly engaged in argumentation. Indeed, he made it an art; his polished speeches are masterpieces in the use of words to persuade. In addition, Cicero wrote two important essays on political theory, *Republic* and *Laws*, defending Roman republican institutions, but pleading for the establishment of a first citizen to guide the state. He also wrote several philosophical tracts that made abstract Greek thought understandable to Roman readers. His numerous *Letters* supply a brilliant picture of Roman politics and society in the first century B.C. This eloquent, learned Roman made Latin prose a language capable of expressing any idea. He demonstrated an intellect alive to real problems and confident that the human mind could cope with all situations.

Keenly conscious of their history and deeply respectful of tradition, the Romans generated a considerable body of historical literature. The earliest historical writing in Latin was influenced by Hellenistic models, but the Romans again discovered their own talent. The most influential Roman historian was Livy (59 B.C.–A.D. 17), another of those inspired to creative activity under the Augustan regime. His masterpiece, the immense *History of the Roman Republic*, covered the period from 753 B.C. to A.D. 9. Although a large part of the work has been lost, it is quite clear from what is left that Livy believed Rome had a great historical mission and wished to instruct his readers on the subject. Livy was not a scientific historian, interested only in the truth; his work was a conglomeration of truth and fiction put together to teach a lesson. Nonetheless, it presented with great dramatic impact the men and events that made Rome great over seven centuries. Patriotism, a sense of duty, sobriety, and moral excellence were put forward as the marks of Roman greatness. Livy was the prose counterpart of Vergil.

Less monumental but equally artistic was Tacitus (ca. A.D. 55–117), who wrote about Roman history after Augustus. His *Histories* and *Annals* covered large portions of the period A.D. 14–96. Although Tacitus was a man of senatorial and republican sentiments, prejudiced against the successors of Augustus, he wrote with brilliance and deep moral sense. Another of his works, *Germania*, presented important information about the German barbarians who were soon to play a larger part in Roman life. Suetonius (ca. A.D. 75–150) vividly presented a wealth of interesting material about the Roman emperors from Julius Cae-

sar to Domitian in his *Lives of the Twelve Caesars*. The works of Greek writers swelled the body of excellent histories. One of the greatest Greek historians was Polybius, who lived in Rome from 167 to 151 B.C. as a hostage. During his stay in Rome he became an intimate of the pro-Hellenic Scipionic circle and was greatly impressed by the Romans. He produced a superb work chronicling Rome's rise to world power, a feat he wished to make the Greeks understand. Plutarch (ca. A.D. 46–120), using biography as a means of moral instruction, provided a brilliant series of biographies of Greek and Roman men in his *Parallel Lives*. Several Romans produced personal memoirs that were of the nature of histories. Probably the best examples were Julius Caesar's *Commentaries on the Gallic Wars* and Marcus Aurelius' *Meditations*.

Doubtless the reader has noted that no mention has been made of certain kinds of literature. During the era when Greek ideas and art forms were first sweeping over the Roman world, attempts were made to imitate the magnificent Greek dramatic art. The most outstanding Roman dramatists were Plautus (third century B.C.) and Terence (second century B.C.). But drama failed to take root among the Romans; one suspects they lacked the depth of feeling and the imagination required to respond to or to produce this grand art. Only occasionally did a fiction writer grace the Roman literary scene. Perhaps these gaps in the literary picture tell a great deal. They suggest that the creation of highly imaginative literature was foreign to the Romans, who had to be tied to reality—to history, to current moral problems, to personal experiences.

This review of Roman literature, touching on only a handful of the best writers, should leave no doubt that Rome stands independent in the history of literature, for her writers handled great subjects in a powerful style, and countless generations in Western Europe in the centuries following Rome's fall were to be introduced to a civilized view of life by reading them.

The enormous amphitheater of the Colosseum, built in the center of Rome near the end of the first century, once accommodated 50,000 spectators at the gladiatorial games. Its miles of corridors and stairways were skillfully designed to allow for an orderly flow of traffic, and beneath the floor of the arena (visible in this photograph) were chambers where men, animals, and equipment were kept. *Photo: Bruce Davidson–Magnum*

4. ART

Rome's most impressive and distinctive artistic achievement was in the field of architecture. The style was eclectic, although Greek models predominated. However, the Romans added important elements to what they borrowed. They developed concrete as a building material and used it to form the basic structure of most of the large buildings. They also perfected and put to new uses the arch and the dome, which had been developed earlier in the Near East. These technical advances permitted the Romans to construct larger buildings and to depart from the horizontal lines that characterized Greek architecture.

As builders, the Romans achieved their best results in buildings intended to serve worldly,

public ends. They were not, like the Greeks, great temple builders. Most Roman temples were more ornate versions of Greek models. However, the Romans did effect significant modifications of temple styles. The Pantheon, built in Rome in the second century A.D., is the greatest round temple ever built. Its domed roof, made of stone, is 142 feet in diameter, and is supported by massive concrete walls built around a rotunda under the dome. A rectangular porch, the roof of which is supported by Greek columns, leads into the rotunda, supplying a pleasing mixture of Greek and Roman architectural ideas.

Much more distinctly Roman were the public baths, amphitheaters, aqueducts, bridges, meeting halls (basilicas), and palaces that appeared in Rome and in many provincial cities during the two centuries following Augustus. The famous Colosseum at Rome, about half of which still stands, illustrates the Roman architectural genius. Built to serve the large audiences who loved the games, this concrete structure measures approximately 617 by 512 feet on the outside. The outer wall rises about 160 feet and consists of three tiers of arcades topped by a blank wall. The arcades of each tier are decorated with columns executed in the Greek style; however, these columns are purely decorative, having nothing to do with the structure of the building. Inside is an arena from which rises tier after tier of seats, each giving a good view of the scene of the action. Underneath the structure is an intricate network of arched passageways and rooms.

The Roman basilica, built in great numbers in cities all over the empire, is especially significant in architectural history because it served as a model for early Christian churches and for most Christian architecture for many centuries after the fall of Rome. The basilica was essentially a long hall flanked by side aisles. The walls of the main hall were built higher than the side aisles, allowing windows to be cut in them. The Romans made skillful use of the arch in covering these halls; for instance, in the Basilica of Maxentius (early fourth century A.D.), a concrete roof was put over a main aisle 80 feet wide. In Roman baths, which consisted of a great central court surrounded by numerous smaller rooms, skillful use was made of arched vaults and passageways to achieve great size. All these buildings are especially impressive because of their size; they reflect the power and wealth of the people who built them.

Roman sculpture showed less independent genius than did architecture, for Greek models exerted an especially powerful influence. Although almost every form of sculpture was produced in great quantity everywhere in the empire, the best work done by the Romans was in portraiture and relief work treating historical incidents. In both forms, the Roman artists worked stone into realistic portrayals of a personality or an event. Even statues of emperors were extremely lifelike, accentuating the dignity and manliness of their subjects, but avoiding excessive idealization. The historical scenes carved on triumphal arches or the walls of public buildings are almost photographic. Romans showed little interest in the idealization of reality, the trademark of Greek sculpture. What little we know of Roman painting, used chiefly to decorate buildings, reflects this same sense of realism.

5. PHILOSOPHY, SCIENCE, AND RELIGION

Roman philosophers were chiefly engaged in digesting and explaining those portions of the Greek philosophical tradition that seemed applicable to Roman problems, especially to politics and ethics. They carried on the trend already established in the Hellenistic period of concentrating on the application of philosophical principles rather than on further speculation. Rome's greatest accomplishment was, therefore, the transmission of at least a part of the Greek philosophical tradition to areas where it was unknown, especially Western Europe.

Four figures represent the main currents in Roman philosophy. Cicero was an eclectic philosopher, borrowing from many Greek schools of thought and working out a set of ideas he felt were fitted to Roman society in the first century B.C. Lucretius was a disciple of Epicurus who made a powerful plea for intelligent Romans to adopt an outlook based on a materialistic concept of the universe and to abandon the superstitions propagated by traditional religion. From Epicureanism he sought to justify a life of learning and withdrawal from the world, arguing that this alone was the true source of pleasure. Not all Epicureans, however, followed Lucretius' path; many Romans used Epicurean materialism as an excuse for a life of sensual pleasure.

But most intelligent and sensitive Romans found greater attraction in a more sober and serious philosophy. Stoicism provided them with sensible answers to human problems, and it was the prevailing philosophical force of the first two centuries of the Christian era. Its two most articulate spokesmen were Seneca (ca. 4 B.C.–A.D. 65) and Marcus Aurelius (A.D. 121–180), whose *Meditations* provides a good reflection of Stoic ideas. On the basis of Zeno's teaching that the universe was governed by a super intelligence, Stoics advocated reasonableness as the aim of life. From reasonableness would spring all the Stoic virtues —humanitarianism, tolerance, devotion to duty, humility, and resignation to hardship. By arguing for the need for one state and one law, the Stoics also helped to justify the Roman imperial government.

The Romans did not distinguish themselves in pure science. Their interests were practical and nontheoretical, quite in contrast with the bold speculativeness of Greek thought. In fact, the views of the natural world and the knowledge of natural phenomena prevailing in the Roman world were in the main derived from the Greeks. The Romans "practiced" science by translating Greek concepts into Latin. Perhaps the most significant advance in science in the Roman period resulted from the efforts of "scholars," such as Pliny the Elder (ca. A.D. 23–79), Galen (A.D. 131–201), and Ptolemy (ca. A.D. 121–151), to compile great encyclopedias of scientific information derived chiefly from Greek and Hellenistic sources. Through their compilations a considerable part of Greek science was eventually transmitted to Western Europe. Galen's compilation on medicine and Ptolemy's works on geography and astronomy were standard guides until the scientific revolution of the sixteenth and seventeenth centuries.

In putting existing scientific knowledge to practical use, however, the Romans were expert. Rome's engineers were unequaled in antiquity; her roads, aqueducts, and bridges have withstood the ages. The technical skills developed by engineers and artisans formed a precious heritage handed on to later generations; perhaps this heritage was as important

The Arch of Titus, built to commemorate the victory of the emperor Titus over the Jews in A.D. 70, spans a street in the heart of Rome. It was decorated with reliefs such as this one, which shows Roman soldiers bearing spoils away from Jerusalem after its capture. *Photo: Alinari–Art Reference Bureau* to Western Europe as was the literary, artistic, and philosophical tradition transmitted by Rome.

While the educated upper class of imperial society absorbed and assimilated Greek philosophical and scientific knowledge, the bulk of society continued to find their chief source of satisfaction in religion. The most important development of the era from 100 B.C. to A.D. 180 was the growing popularity of Eastern mystery religions. The ancient Italian religion continued to decline, in spite of Augustus' efforts to revive it. Many intellectuals were atheists and openly scoffed at the old beliefs. Some of the emperors tried to institute a new religion centering around worship of themselves, but this movement did not appeal to most Romans. They preferred the emotional, personal Asian mystery religions, which gave them a savior and promised them a happy life after death. These cults gained an ever-increasing following in the western part of the empire. The imperial policy of tolerance aided their spread immeasurably. As we shall see, Christianity began its conquest of the Roman world during this period. Despite the enthusiasm of the converts, some drastic results accompanied the spread of the Eastern religions. All of them tended to lessen the interest of their adherents in Roman public life and to concentrate attention on personal problems and life after death, thus making it more difficult for Rome to control her citizens. The spread of Eastern religions marked the beginning of Rome's decline.

6. LAW

Perhaps Rome's most enduring cultural monument was her law. Although the evolution of Roman law was not confined to the period between 100 B.C. and A.D. 180, certain developments in this era decided its final character.

The Romans, unable to conceive of a state without a legal basis, had been concerned with law from the beginning of their history. In this respect they were not unique; other ancient political communities, such as the He-

brews, the Mesopotamians, and the Greeks, had a similar idea. Roman law was unique, however, in that it continued to grow century after century. Unwritten custom was constantly modified by the legislation of the assemblies during the republican period. Even more important was the custom of allowing the chief judicial official of the republic, the *praetor*, to pronounce his interpretation of the law at the beginning of his term. There thus developed by the end of the republic a vast body of judge-made law. Moreover, in the republican period the Romans began to develop a body of law for their noncitizen subject peoples. This body of law became a kind of international law (*lex gentium*). Proclaimed by provincial governors and *praetors* elected to judge cases involving foreigners, it was built on legal ideas derived from the laws of the subject peoples, on Roman legal principles, and on the common sense of the judges. By the end of the republic, a huge although somewhat confused body of international law had thus been accumulated.

In the period from 100 B.C. to A.D. 180, an effort was made to codify this law into a single, systematic body. This move was prompted by many forces. The new imperial government, itself moving toward a unified administration, saw in a unified law a means of exercising authority. The general trend toward removing the distinctions between Romans and non-Romans indicated a single law to fit a unified people. The extensive legislation by the emperors tended to create uniformity. Stoic philosophy, with its emphasis on a universal law of nature, prompted men to think in terms of a consistent body of law for all society. These forces produced during the first and second centuries a series of notable legal authorities who devoted their lives to the study and codification of the law, usually with the wholehearted support of the rulers. Their writings became the basis of legal education, so that most lawyers and public administrators adopted a similar view.

While giving Roman law its fundamental features, the great jurists sought to relate human laws to deeper principles of natural law, thus providing the legal system a theoretical basis outside human whim and fancy. Recognizing the need for rational application of general principles to current problems, they sought to make the law consistent but flexible. In effect, the jurists argued that the law was not yet perfect and that a continuous effort must be made to bring it nearer perfection. By the end of the second century A.D., the Roman jurists had by no means completed the unification and standardization of Roman law; that would be done only in the sixth century by the emperor Justinian. But they had established its basic principles. Although law could be derived from many sources, it must be related to the universal order of things, that is, to the natural law. It must be supple enough to bend to changing conditions, yet firmly enough based on principle to avoid manipulation by unscrupulous men. It must serve the needs of all men and not a narrow segment of the population. These principles have survived until the present as the highest ideals of all legal systems.

[margin annotation: Nature of law]

7. THE ROMANS AS SPREADERS OF CULTURE

One final achievement that must be credited to the Romans is perhaps more important than anything else in their cultural history. The Romans developed a special talent for spreading their culture to backward peoples. From the first century B.C. onward, large areas in the western part of the empire were rapidly transformed into images of Rome. This transformation was of inestimable importance for the future of Western Europe. It represented the first step in the elevation of Western European peoples from barbarism and made it possible for them to play a more important role in history.

Rome's way of impressing her civilization on backward peoples was a complicated one. Roman soldiers, officials, and merchants, moving freely about the whole empire, were agents of civilization. The government founded towns in far-flung areas of the empire and encouraged Romans to live there. It urged the establishment of schools in these towns. The study of grammar and rhetoric, literature and philosophy spread a common store of ideas and set of tastes to the far corners of the empire. The government encouraged provincials to familiarize themselves with Roman ways in order to facilitate administrative activities. Latin and Greek, the administrative languages of the empire, soon became known to the barbarians, who thus gained direct knowledge of the Greco-Roman literary tradition. Emperors built roads, aqueducts, temples, and public buildings throughout the provinces, impressing upon even the least advanced the majesty of Rome and prompting them to imitation. The freedom given to scholars, religious missionaries, philosophers, and artists encouraged them to seek out the barbarians. Rome opened her doors to men with artistic and intellectual talents from all corners of the empire, thus turning all eyes toward a common cultural center and providing a channel for the spread of culture.

To trace the spreading circle of Roman culture into the heart of ancient centers of barbarism would require a detailed history of a dozen provinces and a hundred cities. Suffice it to say that the marks of Roman culture remain. The French and Spanish tongues, for instance, are direct descendants of the Latin learned in these areas in the first and second centuries. When the modern traveler comes across an elaborate bath in the city of Bath in western England or a great amphitheater in France or a Roman bridge at one of a dozen places, he is encountering evidence of the extent of the Romanization of the Western provinces. Luckily for the inhabitants of Spain, France, Britain, and North Africa, the Romans did not adopt the Greek attitude of looking down on foreigners. Instead, the Romans gave their best to all, and in the process spread civilization over a large area of the world previously caught in barbarism.

Suggested Reading

General Treatments. Roman culture has not inspired general works of the quality of those on Greek culture. As an introduction, the student might begin with **Edith Hamilton, *The Roman Way* (Norton), which is kind toward the Romans, but leaves the impression that they are distinctly inferior to the Greeks. Another brief survey is **D. R. Dudley, *Civilization of Rome* (Mentor). R. M. Geer, *Classical Civilization: Rome* (2nd ed., 1950), does an excellent and thorough job of detailing the Roman cultural achievement in a chronological framework. Perhaps the best work on the whole subject is Pierre Grimal, *The Civilization of Rome*, trans. W. S. Maguinnes (1963). An older work still of considerable merit is Albert Grenier, *The Roman Spirit in Religion, Thought, and Art*, trans. M. R. Dobie (1926).

Religion. A superlative treatment of Roman religion is Franz Altheim, *A History of Roman Religion*, trans. Harold Mattingly (1938), especially good for making clear the setting out of which Christianity emerged. Considerably shorter and less complex is H. J. Rose, *Ancient Roman Religion* (1948), a work that is especially clear on the Roman concept of deity, the religious duties of man, and the relationship of religion to public life. Another good survey is F. C. Grant, *Ancient Roman Religion* (1957).

Literature. A brief but well-done history of Roman literature is **M. Hadas, *History of Latin Literature* (Columbia). Also brief and sound is **H. J. Rose, *Handbook of Latin Literature* (Dutton). A longer treatment of high quality is **J. W. Duff, *Literary History of Rome: From the Origins to the Close of the Golden Age* (3rd ed., University Paperbacks), and *Literary History of Rome in the Silver Age: From Tiberius to Hadrian* (3rd ed., University Paperbacks). A perceptive evaluation of the major Roman historians is **M. L. W. Laistner, *The Greater Roman Historians* (University of California), who comments on Livy, Sallust, and Tacitus. Related to Roman literature is the story of education in the ancient world; an excellent study is **H. I. Marrou, *History of Education in Antiquity* (Mentor).

Art. A good introduction to Roman art is supplied by **M. Wheeler, *Roman Art and Architecture* (Praeger). Another excellent survey is H. Kähler, *The Art of Rome and Her Empire* (1963). A superlative discussion of Roman architecture is **F. E. Brown, *Roman Architecture* (Braziller). More extensive, but also more demanding, is T. Rice Holmes, *The Architect of the Roman Empire* (2 vols., 1928–31). A perceptive treatment of Roman painting is A. Maiuri, *Roman Painting* (1953).

Law. Perhaps the best treatment of the development of Roman law is Fritz Schulz, *History of Roman Legal Science* (1946). Almost as good is J. Declareuil, *Rome the Law-giver*, trans. E. A. Parker (1927). Considerably more technical is H. F. Jolowicz, *Historical Introduction to the Study of Roman Law* (2nd ed., 1952).

Sources. An excellent sampling of the Roman literary heritage can be gained from a good anthology; recommended is Kevin Guinagh and Alfred P. Darjahn, *Latin Literature in Translation* (2nd ed., 1952). Then the student should turn to Roman authors themselves, and read works in their entirety. In addition to the historical works of Livy, Polybius, Tacitus, and Suetonius cited in earlier chapters, certain others stand forth as representative of Roman literature and thought. Above all is **Vergil, *Aeneid* (many editions; an excellent one is the translation by C. Day Lewis [Anchor]). **Vergil, *Eclogues* and *Georgics*, have also been translated by C. Day Lewis (Anchor). **Horace, *Odes and Epodes*, trans. J. P. Clancy (Phoenix), provides a good sampling of Latin lyric poetry. **Lucretius, the advocate of Epicurean philosophy, sets forth his ideas in *On the Nature of the Universe*, trans. R. E. Latham (Penguin). **Ovid, *The Metamorphoses*, trans. Rolfe Humphries (Midland Books), is a poetic rendering of the chief religious myths of the Roman world.

**Julius Caesar, *Conquest of Gaul*, trans. S. A. Handford (Penguin), will provide a good sample of Roman personal memoirs well spiced with propaganda. A sampling of Cicero's extensive writings can be found in **Cicero, *Selected Works*, trans. M. Grant (Penguin); ***Letters of Cicero: A Selection in Translation*, trans. L. P. Wilkinson (Anchor); and **Cicero, *Nine Orations*, trans. P. Bovie (Mentor). The most important philosophical writings in the Roman tradition, aside from Lucretius, are represented by **Seneca, *Stoic Philosophy of Seneca: Essays and Letters*, trans. M. Hadas (Norton); and **Marcus Aurelius, *Meditations*, trans. J. H. Staniforth (Penguin).

RETROSPECT
A moment's reflection on the long period covered in this section might help to give it a clearer shape. Few millennia in all history reveal a greater achievement than that extending from the time when the Greeks began to emerge from their dark age in about 800 B.C. to the generation which saw the Roman imperial order reach its full maturity about A.D. 160—the epoch from Homer to Marcus Aurelius. We need not list all those magnificent achievements; the intriguing question is *why* this millennium was so fruitful. What was the special quality that gave Greco-Roman civilization its uniqueness and significance in the total stream of history? The answer is at once simple and profound: It was a civilization that made man and his well-being its central concern. Its motto could well be the slogan of Protagoras and the Sophists: "Man is the measure of all things." Socrates formulated its one commandment: "Know thyself." He likewise defined its motor force when he insisted that self-knowledge made men good. The eternal "itch" agitating the Greco-Roman world was human self-consciousness, the effort to know what sort of creature man was and how he fit into the grand order of the cosmos. And the spur to action was the urge to transform self-knowledge into the making of things worthy of man—temples, poems, statues, cities, governments, laws, roads, palaces, schools, baths, agricultural estates.

We cannot help being impressed at how much the Greco-Roman world discovered about man and how great were the energies unleashed by that self-knowledge. At grave risk of oversimplification, we might single out a few of these discoveries as being the foundation stones of Greco-Roman civilization, its value-giving, directive forces. First was the rationality of man. Second was the ordered universe which provided the setting for his activities. Third was rational man's capacity for positive good. Fourth was the capability of man to transcend whatever he was at any instant through knowledge and good action. Last was the political nature of man, which gave him no alternative except to join other men to realize his potential to know, to be good, and to outreach his present condition.

The Greco-Roman quest to know man resulted in the most majestic concepts of humanity ever formulated—concepts immediately subjected to doubt. In fact, a perceptive Roman of the second century A.D. might have had some doubts, all planted in his mind by the very poets, philosophers, and artists who had so effectively defined the confident view of humanity upon which classical civilization was based. The Greeks and the Romans were never quite sure that man was essentially rational; in him lurked an

206

elusive element of the demonic, an untamed capacity for irrationality. Always there was a suspicion that self-knowledge and the power it gave could be turned as easily to evil as to good. Despite the rational demonstration of order in the universe, there were hints of dark forces in nature which lay beyond man's knowledge and control. One had to ask: Was it really sufficient to know oneself? Was it really possible?

Moreover, the kind of society that emerged from the centuries-long effort to create a world fit for reasonable, good, enlightened men had some features that were disturbing. The confidence that political action could achieve perfection had given the state—the Greek *polis*, the Hellenistic monarchies, the Roman Republic, the Roman Empire—a dangerous dominance over men at the expense of other dimensions of their existence. The majestic assumptions about man's rationality and capacity for good had given undue power in society to those who managed to acquire the symbols of rationality and good: an education, offices, wealth, and manners. These aristocrats, seldom quite in the Homeric mold, tended to be oblivious to those who had not been enlightened or blessed with power and prestige. The politicized and intellectualized flavor of classical civilization bred in those who wielded power and participated in the mainstream of cultural life a disdain for other kinds of activity—especially labor—and for other kinds of human behavior—especially that emerging from man's emotional nature. The rationalizing of human conduct and of nature bred an intellectual posture which saw things in terms of absolute, fixed forms and found it extremely difficult to accept or to initiate change.

These insights might well have persuaded men living in the second-century Roman Empire of what now seems fairly evident: Classical men had learned much about human nature and that knowledge had liberated man so that a whole new range of talents were unleashed to enliven and beautify the world, but they had not seen man's whole nature. The civilization they constructed thus had inherent limitations arising from their restricted and distorted view of humanity. Perhaps the end product of the classical world is symbolized by a man who revealed his soul to posterity at the very end of the period—the emperor Marcus Aurelius. Marcus Aurelius was the embodiment of classical man: reasonable, good, serious, politically aware, sensitive to others. As ruler over a marvelous political system, he appeared (by classical standards) to have the power to achieve whatever the good of humanity demanded. Yet in his *Meditations* he emerges as the victim of a cruel joke—a man caught up in a mechanical universe running on forever without change, a man who knew and understood but found nothing to do, a man so good that the nature of evil eluded him, a perfect citizen who was destined to the unappetizing business of fending off stupid barbarians. What was there to do but to resign oneself? One suspects that a kind of bloodless, cold, unemotional resignation in the face of what reason and goodness cannot encompass is what classical civilization finally meant. Something of this attitude is apparent in a Greek statue or in the lines spoken by the chorus in some Greek tragedies. For all its accomplishments, the classical world had still not learned enough about man.

But whatever its limitations, classical civilization had changed the course of history. No nation, no people, no civilization of the future could escape its influence—especially not those inhabitants of Europe who first felt the force of civilized life by being drawn into the Greco-Roman world.

Part Three

The Fall of Greco-Roman Civilization

A.D. 180–500

During the second century A.D. Greco-Roman civilization had established unchallenged sway over the Mediterranean basin, and extended its influence inland from the sea to three continents—Europe, Asia, and Africa. A vast community had been created within which a bewildering variety of peoples were bound together by powerful forces. The political genius of the Romans, expressing itself through the imperial system of government, furnished the most potent bond of community. Almost as important were the widely shared cultural-spiritual concepts that created a common system of values. Derived primarily from the Greeks and finding expression in a remarkable literature, art, philosophy, and learning, this cultural-spiritual force of unity had been adopted by the Hellenistic world and then by the entire Mediterranean world through the Romans. The shared political system and cultural-spiritual values were powerfully reinforced by a common economy which linked together the many parts of the Mediterranean world in an interdependent material existence. The simultaneous operation of these unifying forces produced one of the most magnificent eras in all human history.

However, no human order, however strong it appears, is perfect, and no community of men, however confident they are of their talents, is safe from change and its tensions. As the second century A.D. drew to an end, serious stresses and strains emerged within the splendid Mediterranean community the Romans had put together. The long process leading to the formation of that community was reversed, and the forces of disintegration became dominant. Although Greco-Roman civilization was endowed with great reserves of strength, they were not enough. Within a relatively short time— only about three centuries—a vast transformation occurred in the Mediterranean basin. Greco-Roman civilization was virtually destroyed, eaten away by incurable sicknesses within its body and torn apart by the assaults of barbarians from outside. The disintegration of that civilization has always held a fascination for students of the past, ultimately prompting them to ask why it is that man's greatest achievement—a mature civilization —cannot be made to last. Intriguing as the question might be, however, the more important fact is that the end of classical civilization left the vast population of the Mediterranean world with no alternative but to set out again to construct new and viable patterns of life.

Chapter 13 ❧ The Decline of the Empire and

the Rise of Christianity

The era of change and decline began with dramatic suddenness during the century following the death of Marcus Aurelius in 180. In vivid contrast to the *pax romana* of the second century, this period was characterized by almost incessant civil war that deeply disturbed the internal order of the empire and increased its vulnerability to outside attack. Amid the political crisis, a series of economic and social maladjustments surfaced to add to the stress. And intellectual and spiritual confusion sapped the capabilities of society to respond to the growing problems. In retrospect it is clear that the foundations of Greco-Roman civilization were being eaten away and that a desperate sickness was engulfing the Mediterranean world. The basic causes of the third-century crisis need analysis because they determined the fate of the Roman Empire and of Greco-Roman civilization.

1. THE POLITICAL CRISIS, A.D. 180–284

The peaceful, humanitarian regime of the "good emperors" suffered an astonishing reversal after Marcus Aurelius. The incompetence of his son and successor, Commodus (A.D. 180–192), was in part responsible. But more important was a serious defect in the political order—the succession question. Marcus Aurelius turned his back on the adoptive system utilized by second-century emperors to select

and train their successors far in advance of the end of each reign. He returned to hereditary succession, a choice that brought with it incompetence in the one office that could sustain the *pax romana*. Amid rising dissatisfaction with Commodus' misrule, the military quickly demonstrated that it had the power to resolve the problem. A brutal struggle for the successor to Commodus ended in the victory of Septimius Severus (A.D. 193–211), a general of African origin whose career had been with the army.

The dynasty of the Severi controlled the imperial office until A.D. 235. Wedded to the armies which put them in power, the Severi pursued a policy of favoritism to the soldiers, most of whom were noncitizens recruited from the provinces. Here was another long-standing problem finally coming to bitter maturity. Throughout the second century the Roman citizenry, that is, the populace of Italy, showed an increasing reluctance to bear the military burden, and the government had no choice but to recruit noncitizens. This force, so crucial to the well-being of the empire, was now demanding to be paid. The Severi, following Septimius' advice to pamper the troops and forget the rest of the population, provided the rewards: higher pay, larger pensions, rights of citizenship, new career opportunities in the bureaucracy. The new force challenging the long supremacy of the Italians, especially the aristocratic senators, was hardly gentle or peace-loving.

The immediate effect of the Severan favoritism toward the army was an era of anarchy lasting from A.D. 235 to 284: the era of the "barrack emperors." The anarchy was the product of a struggle within the army for possession of the imperial throne. Encouraged with promises of new favors from ambitious generals, units of the increasingly pampered army repeatedly sought to elevate their favorites to the purple. Civil war, usually ending in the murder of the reigning emperor, became the order of the day. The victorious general, installed as emperor, made it his prime business to reward the soldiers. New revolts, sparked by the ambitions of other commanders and the greed of their troops, followed immediately. The *pax romana* had turned to ashes; the Mediterranean world was in chaos.

Behind the facade of civil war, a fundamental change was occurring in the political structure of the empire. The emperors thrust into power during the third century were a different breed of men than the earlier rulers: By birth products of the frontier provinces and by experience children of the army, they were insensitive to the problems of civil administration and to the needs of the civilian population. Moreover, they had slight sympathy for or understanding of the fundamental principle of the Augustan principate: the sharing of power by the *princeps* and the aristocracies of Rome and the imperial cities. Their instinct was toward a militarized society that vested total power in the hands of the emperor. Their major policy concern was with military well-being—a matter which indeed deserved serious attention. This led them to favor the army and its needs, for they saw clearly that here lay the power that could ensure the emperor complete authority and safeguard the beleaguered empire. Increasingly, administrative posts were filled from the army at the expense of the Italian aristocracy. The emperors moved inexorably toward more thor-

ough regimentation of civilian society and civilian economic productivity to serve military ends. They imposed a heavier and heavier tax burden on the citizenry to support the demands of the army and the enlarged bureaucracy that was required to enact the emperors' expanding role. They intruded ever more decisively into the political affairs of the previously independent city-states, forcing local aristocracies (*curiales*) to muster money and manpower to support the central government rather than local interests. They ceased to respect the privileged role of the Italians in imperial affairs, a policy that culminated in A.D. 212 with the extension of citizenship to all freemen in the empire by Caracalla. Gradually the autocratically inclined rulers of the third century constructed around their office and persons an aura of religious sanctity which added an element of divinity to the ruler. With remarkable speed, the imperial regime was being transformed into a divinely sanctioned military autocracy. The *princeps*, a first citizen on the model of Augustus or Trajan or Hadrian, was becoming a *dominus*, an absolute lord over all Romans after the model of an Oriental despot.

The instability of the new political order during the third century, chiefly a result of the constant civil war, makes it difficult to evaluate its performance. Despite the sickening brutality and violence of this era—contrasting so sharply with the peace and order of the preceding age—the militarization of society was a realtistic response to some crucial problems. The empire was facing a deepening crisis in defense, especially from two of its ancient foes, the Persians and the Germans. In Persia a new dynasty, the Sassanians, proved much more aggressive than their predecessors and soon engaged the Romans in a protracted, expensive, and dangerous struggle for mastery in Asia. Simultaneously, the Germanic pressure increased. Small tribes were coalescing into larger groups much more difficult for the Romans to manipulate and restrain. Other peoples pressed the Germans from behind, driving them ever more strongly to the south and west against Rome's fragile defenses. A vigorously led, well-organized society was needed to face these mounting dangers. Perhaps we can applaud the emergence of autocracy because it broadened Roman citizenship, involved more people in the conduct of political life, and reduced the undue influence of the aristocratic Italians in directing the affairs of a cosmopolitan empire.

Yet the path to autocracy was filled with grave dangers to the established constitution of the Roman Empire. The dominance of the army loosed a pampered caste preying on the populace. The seizure of the imperial office by military leaders narrowed considerably the political vision of the government. The concentration of power in the hands of the central government ruined local governments, long the real backbone of the empire, and entrusted the conduct of public affairs to a ruthless bureaucracy open to every form of corruption. The militarization of society imposed increasing regimentation on every group, with an accompanying reduction of freedom. The insatiable demands of the army and the bureaucracy led to a reckless fiscal policy and a destructive inflation. On balance, we must conclude that the transformation of the Roman imperial government into a military autocracy was destructive of the existing order. Greco-Roman civilization had begun to disintegrate at its most crucial point —the political system.

2. ECONOMIC, SOCIAL, AND CULTURAL DISLOCATIONS

The stresses and strains accompanying the drastic realignment of political forces between A.D. 180 and 284 were accentuated by a broad range of economic and social problems. Most of these problems predated the era of crisis, but all were made more acute by the civil strife and the transformation of political institutions.

The third century was marked, first of all, by decreased economic production. The causes of this depression are too complex and the surviving evidence too scanty to allow for a completely satisfactory explanation. Certain trends do appear clear, however. Most serious was a decline in agricultural production. In part, that decline was a result of the civil wars within the empire and the destructive raids of enemies along the frontiers. The war-bred destruction led to the abandonment of lands in many places, especially along the frontiers, where farms were turned over to barbarian settlers who were not expert farmers. But the major forces restricting agricultural production were deeper. There appears to have been a shortage of agricultural labor, probably caused by a decline in population over the entire Mediterranean world. Agricultural technology did not advance, so that nothing was done to offset the inevitable soil depletion and erosion that ultimately affects any established agricultural system. The increasing prevalence of large estates (*latifundia*) as the basic form of agricultural organization was depressive, chiefly because these estates were increasingly supplied with labor by dependent, exploited tenants (*coloni*).

Trade and industry suffered an even greater depression. Again, the political chaos was a contributing factor. The brigandage, banditry, and piracy that accompanied the civil wars seriously interfered with the movement of goods. The reckless fiscal policy of the emperors of the third century inflicted terrible financial burdens on traders and artisans. A regular policy of debasing the currency as a means of getting money to reward the army caused inflation and removed a basic requirement for vigorous trade—a sound system of exchange. Heavy taxation bore especially hard on the trading class, whose wealth could be most easily seized. State regimentation of the economy to serve military needs limited opportunities for new commercial and industrial ventures. And as in agriculture, basic

Another kind of imperial commemorative monument was the free-standing column, such as the one built in the second century to celebrate the emperor Trajan's victory over the barbarian Dacians. This detail shows Roman soldiers defending their position against a Dacian attack. Such attacks, repeated on all the borders of the empire from the second century on, eventually broke through the frontier. *Photo: Alinari–Art Reference Bureau*

weaknesses in the Roman trading and manufacturing economy now emerged. Trade began to decline in part because of the growing self-sufficiency of those backward parts of the empire that once obtained needed products by exchange with more advanced areas. The development of industry in Gaul and Spain during the second century made it less necessary for those people to depend on the East for manufactured goods. The end of Roman geographical expansion offered no new "backward" areas to generate new trade. Trade and industry always suffered from a lack of new capital, because the directive elements in the Roman world preferred to invest wealth in land or in nonproductive city beautification and luxurious living. Trade and industry likewise never commanded the best talent in the Roman Empire; politics and war were the more respectable careers. Finally, the whole aristocratic cast of ancient society precluded any serious thought of generating commercial and industrial growth by elevating the standard of living of the lower classes.

Thus trade and industry were fragile elements in the classical economy, easily upset by slight changes in the political situation.

The whole texture of society was changing significantly by the third century. Perhaps most serious was the decline of the urban aristocracy. The military autocrats ruthlessly eliminated the aristocrats of Rome and Italy from their ancient places of power in the central administration and the army. In cities throughout the empire, local aristocracies were crushed by the burden of taxation and deprived of their control over local affairs by increasing hordes of bureaucrats representing the central authority. The old imperial order could ill afford the decline of a large, dedicated class that had always carried the burden of government and sustained and promoted the cause of civilized life. Had the lower classes benefited from the decline of the aristocracy, the loss might not have been so serious. But the urban lower classes were increasingly regimented and their social position debased. Artisans and laborers in the cities were forced into compulsory associations (*collegia*) through which their wages and production were tightly controlled in the interests of the state. The peasantry, increasingly driven toward becoming hereditary tenants (*coloni*) on the *latifundia*, lost their freedom and ended owing powerful landlords their labor and their earnings to an extent that made them virtual slaves. These trends in society obviously reduced the benefits of membership in the great Roman community.

Meanwhile, two elements in Roman society drew advantage from the changing social order: the great landlords and the soldiers. The owners of large estates tightened their control on agricultural production and the labor force. The state, interested chiefly in securing revenue and produce from the land, gave the landowners increasing freedom to exploit the peasantry and pass on to them the burden of taxation. As their control over the *coloni* increased, the great estateholders moved inexorably toward independence and the satisfaction of their local self-interest, a process that gravely threatened the unity of the Mediterranean community. At the same time, another elite was born—the soldiery. A soldier of ability could work his way to a high position in society, perhaps to the imperial throne. Even the lower ranks of the army enjoyed all kinds of favors not open to other citizens. This elevation of the military element in society had evil effects. On an ever-increasing scale, soldiers were recruited from the most primitive areas of the empire or from among barbarians willing to serve Rome. These people, little acquainted with Roman ideas and institutions, now moved to the leadership of society. The result was a barbarizing of Roman life. The emerging elite groups—great landlords and soldiers, symbolizing localism and barbarization—offered a threat to unity and to civilized values.

Even more serious was the inability of the Roman world to generate out of its conventional value system intellectual and spiritual energies to combat the political, economic, and social problems. The turmoil of the third century was hardly conducive to vigorous cultural activity, and the period is one of the least productive of the whole classical era. Writers, artists, and thinkers merely imitated the past without any zest or creative power. There seemed nothing new to think or say. The intellectual and the artist were caged in a worship of tradition, but that splendid past did not illumine their way. The world seemed to have lost faith in the humanistic, rationalistic values of the Greco-Roman tradition; man and his vaunted powers at last seemed inadequate to the realities of a troubled world.

But the human spirit was seeking refuge and meaning in a new realm—in religion. The third century was alive with powerful religious currents which together seriously threatened the classical world view. The Oriental mystery religions, with their personal deities, their promises of eternal salvation, and their emotional rituals, won increasing numbers of adherents at all levels of society. The worship of Mithras, of Isis and Serapis, of Cybele the Mother Goddess, and of many other deities became empire-wide. The ancient civic deities of Greece and Rome drew intensified support as well. There was a vast resurgence of interest in astrology and magic. Even the realm of philosophy was permeated by a religious, mystical element, as demonstrated by the great vogue of Neoplatonism in the third century, especially after its tenets were systematized by the Egyptian-born Plotinus (A.D. 205–270). Although immensely complex in the form delineated by Plotinus, Neoplatonism basically denied the importance of the material world, characterizing it as unreal and evil-ridden, and asked its adherents to surrender to a contemplative life that would lead them step by step to an ecstatic mystical union with eternal, nonmaterial Reality. In its essence Neoplatonism symbolized the whole spiritual thrust of this age—the search for knowledge and light through a mystical contact with the divine. In this quest human reason played a small part, and many of the old Greco-Roman values seemed to have small relevance.

One cannot avoid the conclusion that the most momentous change occurring in the third century A.D. was a profound spiritual revolution. One particular spiritual movement, which was destined to reshape history, merits a separate discussion.

3. THE RISE OF CHRISTIANITY: THE BEGINNINGS

The origins of Christianity have been studied intensively, but the numerous interpretations which have resulted indicate that the essential characteristics of the history of the movement will always elude clear understanding. We can at least, however, discern certain aspects surrounding the birth of the new religion that made its adherents a "new people" apart from the mainstream of Greco-Roman civilization.

Christianity at its beginning certainly did not seem a candidate for a major force of change that would sweep the Greco-Roman world. It began as a splinter movement among the Jews, who as a people had already earned a reputation as adherents of unique religious ideas and as threats to any established order. Christianity arose in a Jewish world that was charged with tension born out of repeated frustrations in the effort to recover lost national independence and out of great expectations that eventually the hour would strike when God's promise to the Chosen People would be fulfilled. Since the destruction of the Hebrew kingdom in 586 B.C. by the Chaldeans, the Jews had dreamed of the day when their political freedom would be restored. The Persians had allowed them to rebuild the Temple in Jerusalem and to sustain a religious community, but that was not sufficient to those who cherished the memory of David and Solomon and who were exhorted by the prophets to stand apart in the world. The Maccabean Revolt in 165 B.C. against the Hellenistic Seleucid kingdom had brought the Jews close to independence, but hope vanished when Rome took over Palestine in 63 B.C. The Romans were generous in conceding religious privileges to the Jews, but were suspicious and repressive in the face of any threat of Jewish independence.

The frustration of their national aspiration had by the first century B.C. bred serious division within the Jewish community. Most Jews accepted the idea proclaimed by earlier prophets that a God-sent Messiah would deliver them from their oppressors. But they now disagreed on how to act in the immediate historic setting. One group, the Sadducees, made up chiefly of upper class Jews, tended to favor political compromise with the ruling Romans in the interests of peace and religious freedom which would permit the Jews to live as a religious community according to the Hebraic law. A larger group, enjoying strong popular backing, was the Pharisees, who were inclined to accept adaptation of the law to permit a deeper inner spiritual development of the individual, but were violently opposed to the intrusion of foreign ideas into Jewish life. Smaller groups of radicals opted for more drastic solutions. The Zealots were willing to take up arms against the Romans. The Essenes, whose views have been revealed by the recent discovery of the Dead Sea Scrolls, were spiritual radicals, seeking to break through the letter of Hebraic law to spiritual purity; they sought to realize their ideals by withdrawal from the Jewish religious community into an ascetic life. Added to these groups were innumerable individual prophets, such as John the Baptist, crying out that deliverance was at hand. Of considerable importance were the Jews of the Diaspora—believers in Judaism who had been dispersed by accident or choice to all corners of the Mediterranean world during the centuries prior to Roman rule. Because of their circumstances they had been strongly influenced by the ideas of the Greco-Roman world and tended to incorporate these ideas into their religious views. In many cities they had earned deep respect from the non-Jewish population for their piety and moral earnestness.

Into this complex and highly charged scene came Jesus, born probably in 4 B.C. as the Augustan order was taking shape. His appearance may have indeed been in the "fullness of time" by divine reckoning, but in the particular historical setting he confronted a nervous, divided Hebrew society and suspicious Roman rulers interested in peace at any price. When he reached maturity, he went forth among the Jews preaching a message that was grounded in the Judaic tradition, but had an appealing freshness that attracted immediate attention. He proclaimed that God's promised kingdom was at hand and that men must immediately prepare for it by repentance and spiritual regeneration based on repudiation of the world and on love for God and men. He did not ask his followers to abandon their Jewish heritage, but insisted that they must transcend simple observance of the law and performance of the traditional rituals by opening their hearts to God's grace. To those who repented and accepted his message, he promised eternal salvation. His message attracted an enthusiastic following—but it also earned enemies. His scathing attack on the formalism of Jewish religion and the materialism of religious leaders turned "the scribes and the Pharisees" against him. To them, he was a threat to the whole fabric of historic Judaism. Many of his early followers lost much of their enthusiasm when he made it clear that his mission was not to create or rule an earthly kingdom and that he would not take up the sword to liberate the Jews. This hostility ended with his crucifixion, an act to which the Romans gave assent in the interest of maintaining peace in the Jewish community.

Jesus' death triggered a crucial development. A group of his stoutest adherents were convinced that he had arisen from the dead, returned among them, and commanded them to carry on what he had begun. To these disciples, the Resurrection was proof that Jesus was the Son of God—the Christ, the Messiah—born into the world and sacrificed to ensure human salvation. This conviction set the little band apart from the whole world; in the words of Paul, "We preach Christ crucified, a stumbling block to Jews and folly to the Gentiles. . . ." (I Cor. 1:23). A new religion had been born.

4. THE RISE OF CHRISTIANITY: TO THE END OF THE THIRD CENTURY

The first Christian community in Jerusalem was vigorous but not overpowering; the new message had only limited success against the organized strength of Judaism. The early Christians lived as Jews, observing the Judaic law even while holding to the concepts preached by Jesus. Soon their ideas spread to other cities, where they attracted the attention of Jews of the Diaspora and non-Jews who sympathized with Judaism. Before long, many dispersed Jews who were not strict adherents of Judaic practice and many non-Jews were asking to join the new community and were being received. This development posed a grave question for the foundling movement; its resolution was decisive in the success of Christianity. The basic issue was whether or not new converts were to be held to strict observance of Judaic law. Put in other terms, the question was whether the new religion was to be addressed to all men in a fashion that would deemphasize its Judaic aspects and relieve them of the need for close observance of a variety of Jewish practices. There were those in the primitive Christian community who took a conservative position, but others, typified by Peter, leader of the disciples, increasingly insisted on universalizing Christianity so that it would be acceptable to Jew and Gentile alike.

The major figure in the establishment of the mission to the Gentiles was St. Paul. He was a Jew born at Tarsus, where he gained a considerable exposure to Greco-Roman thought as well as a thorough knowledge of Judaic law. Initially he was a persecutor of Christians, but then was suddenly converted and baptized into the Christian community.

Convinced that he had been marked by the Lord "to carry his name before the Gentiles, and kings, and children of Israel" (Acts 9:15), he began a long career of preaching that took him to Asia Minor, Greece, and eventually Rome. The message he proclaimed emphasized those precepts of Jesus which had universal application—the redemption effected by the Son of God; the need for moral regeneration through faith, love of God and man; salvation as a reward for belief in the Christ; purity of moral life. He insisted that Christians were not bound by the requirements of the Judaic law, observance of which was to him merely an outward sign of piety. By the time of his martyrdom in Rome (perhaps about A.D. 67), the thrust toward making Christianity a universal religion had become dominant. Through his preaching and writing, Paul had established the fundamental points of emphasis in the new faith. Christianity and Judaism had moved irreparably apart.

Once launched in the Pauline direction, Christianity steadily spread over most parts of the Roman world. During at least the first century after Jesus' death, a series of dedicated missionary preachers working under all kinds of conditions were the chief agents of expansion. They concentrated their efforts in the major cities of the empire, so that Christianity developed chiefly as an urban religion. Often these missionary preachers began their activities in the synagogues of the city. Their efforts usually won a small group of adherents, especially from the lower classes in society, although there were always a few aristocrats who accepted the new religion. These "cells" became self-sustaining "churches," the members of which labored to win new followers; thus the steady advance of Christianity was largely the work of devoted Christians acting in the local setting to persuade acquaintances to join their community. By the end of the third century, Christian communities existed everywhere in the empire. The heaviest Christian population was in the cities of the East—Egypt, Syria, Palestine, Asia Minor, Greece—and in Italy. There is no way

of knowing how many Christians there were by A.D. 284, but we are certainly safe in assuming that they formed only a small minority of the total population in all but a few cities. Still, Christianity had become a potent factor in the Roman world, one far exceeding what might have been expected in view of its beginnings.

The progress of Christianity was not, however, painless and automatic. One obstacle was provided by the Roman government, which viewed the Christians with suspicion and from time to time persecuted them. The imperial authorities did not act against the Christians for religious reasons; rather, they were inspired by political motives. The Christian refusal to worship the state gods made it impossible for them to fulfill many of their civic responsibilities, including army service, and caused the state to view them as lacking in patriotism. Usually the persecutions were local and temporary, although in the third century more serious attempts were made to exterminate Christianity. The measures taken against the Christians did produce a series of martyr-heroes whose steadfast refusal to bow before the authorities proved a source of inspiration to the struggling survivors of persecution.

The Christians also met opposition of a less official but more menacing nature from various elements of the Roman populace that in one way or another came into contact with the new communities. Among the masses of people there spread a battery of vile rumors about strange beliefs and immoral, bestial practices, rumors fed by the Christian refusal to participate in public religious rites and by their private, semisecret services. Roman intellectuals scorned Christianity, holding up for ridicule its simplistic, superstitious, illogical concepts. The religious leaders of the state religion and of the Jewish synagogues constantly charged the Christians with false beliefs and debased practices. The menacing posture of these foes of the new religion became especially dangerous during the third-century troubles, when the accusation was often made that Rome's disasters were the result of false worshipers in society's midst, false worshipers whose actions made the gods angry. On occasion, the government itself intervened to protect Christians from violence.

The Christians even made difficulties for themselves. From the very beginning, there were divisions within their ranks on what constituted right belief and proper usage. St. Paul was already warning his audiences about false prophets. The early Christian communities disagreed on the nature of the relationship between Christianity and Judaism. The proper moral posture for a Christian was often a subject for debate, especially because there were those who insisted on a puritanical denial of the world and its pleasures. By the second century, and increasingly in the third, Christians disagreed violently on the exact meaning of certain fundamental doctrines, thus giving rise to what may be called the first heresies. These internal conflicts inevitably set Christian against Christian and diverted the faithful from proselytizing.

5. THE RISE OF CHRISTIANITY: REASONS FOR ITS SUCCESS

Yet Christianity grew. Its success was due to many factors stemming from conditions in the empire and from the nature of Christianity itself. As a religious movement, Christian-

ity showed remarkable flexibility during its early years in adapting itself to the religious needs of the age while retaining its individual character. The developments discussed below were perhaps chiefly responsible for its advance.

Conditions in the Roman Empire were favorable to the growth of a new religion. The empire was so knit together that the movement of ideas was easy. In spite of isolated cases of persecution, an atmosphere of tolerance generally prevailed. The ever-growing power of centralized Roman government and the decline of city-states weakened civic religions and caused individuals to seek personal, individual spiritual satisfaction, while the chaos of the third century made the need for personal fulfillment even more urgent. The emergence of a single state uniting many peoples into one society made a religion that would apply to all men regardless of origin or class seem natural. Admittedly, other religions of the Roman world enjoyed these same advantages; but Christianity came into existence at the right moment.

Another source of Christian strength lay in its appeal as a religion. No matter how far in other directions we push the search for an explanation of its expansion, it is always evident that Christianity won converts primarily because its teachings answered their deepest religious needs. Such ideas as the existence of one almighty, loving, merciful God; his sacrifice of his son to redeem men; eternal salvation based on individual worth; damnation for sinners; and universal brotherhood together supplied a powerful answer to those seeking to know about God's ways toward men. The humanity of Christ, who had lived on earth not long before, gave an intimacy to Christianity that other religions lacked. Moreover, Chris-

This beautiful bas-relief, now in the Museo Aquileia in Rome, shows two major figures of the early Christian Church, the apostles Peter and Paul. *Photo: Alinari–Art Reference Bureau* tian teachings were dramatically and simply presented in the New Testament, which began to take form immediately after Christ's death. No other religion in the Roman world possessed so effective a sacred literature.

Another basic source of strength was the church organization that took shape during the first three centuries after Christ. The earliest organization was simple. Christians in a community met for worship, partook of a common meal, and joined together in prayer and song. Certain individuals, especially those who had been close to Christ, were recognized as natural leaders and served as instructors to others. Some of these leaders, like Paul and Peter, were accepted by many different communities. Later in the first century a few communities began to look to local figures for guidance and leadership, and titles like *bishop*, *presbyter*, and *elder* appeared. With the passage of time, disputes within the Christian body, persecutions, and increasing wealth led to new problems demanding a stronger, more organized structures. Authority began to settle in the person of the bishop, who undertook to settle matters of discipline, doctrine, property, and worship. The establishment of episcopal authority received theoretical justification with the development of the concept of apostolic succession: by virtue of his ordination, each bishop was the spiritual successor to the original apostles sent forth by Jesus to proclaim the faith. The bishop's authority almost always coincided with the boundaries of a city-state, an indication that the Christians were imitating the political organization of the empire. In some of the larger cities, where the burden was too great for one man, subordinates were appointed to assist the bishop. For instance, in a city that had several churches, presbyters, or *priests*, were put in charge of each church, but all priests remained under the authority of the bishop. In effect, the Christian world was evolving toward a structure of self-contained, self-governing units, each of which had a machinery for discipline, uniform instruction, and adequate resources to carry on its activities in an organized fashion.

Christians never lost sight of their bonds of unity, however. While many churches existed, there was an awareness of oneness. Church organization reflected this idea. At first, the great prestige of Christ's disciples and the early missionary leaders served to tie the scattered communities together. Later, bishops from large areas met to decide common problems and to apply these decisions in each locality, thus establishing *church councils* with legislative and judicial powers. Before the end of the third century, there was already a movement to establish a final authority who could lay down doctrine and enforce obedience. Some of the chief bishops, such as those of Jerusalem, Antioch, Alexandria, and Rome, were exerting considerable influence. The bishop of Rome was especially influential. He naturally gained prestige because of Rome's position as capital of the empire. Furthermore, an important doctrine, called the *Petrine theory*, had begun to take shape to buttress the power of the bishop of Rome. According to this doctrine, Christ had granted to Peter a special place as his vicar on earth. Peter had chosen Rome as the seat of that power, and his successors as bishops of Rome exercised the same authority. By A.D. 285, Peter's successors, designated as the *pope* (a word derived from the Latin word for "father"), were turning this claim to spiritual supremacy into active leadership in defining doctrine and prescribing discipline for Christian communities over much of the Roman Empire. And many of these communities were eagerly seeking the pope's guidance, especially in doctrinal matters. The decisions of the popes were already accepted as law in some quarters, especially in the Latin West, where there was no other bishopric with the prestige of Rome. Christians had by no means accepted a single head, but there was every indication that eventually they would. A kind of second Roman Empire was being born, subdivided into well-governed local units.

No other religion could boast such an organization.

Christianity also increased its appeal, especially to the sophisticated upper classes, by developing a systematic, reasoned statement of its fundamental beliefs. This articulation of its doctrine in literary form marked a rather dramatic departure from primitive Christianity. Jesus had preached in Aramaic to an audience that was largely apart from the mainstream of Greco-Roman intellectual and literary life. The early leaders of the new religion were quite open in their rejection of pagan culture, and thus established an anti-intellectual bias in the Christian community. However, this posture did not survive long. As soon as Christians began to convert Gentiles, they had to use other languages—Greek especially, and also Latin. Many of the early converts were adults educated in the modes of thought prevailing in the Roman Empire; the new faith had to be presented to them in terms they could comprehend. Thus the initial barriers between Christianity and classical culture began to crumble. By the second century two particular forces spurred the Christians toward a more intellectualized explanation of their position: the need to answer the accusations of non-Christian intellectuals that the new religion was silly and irrational, and the problem of resolving differences of opinion on basic teachings within the Christian ranks. In answering their critics, the "apologists" sought to express Christian concepts in terms their audience could understand, that is, in the language of Greco-Roman literature and philosophy. In this fashion, Christian thought began to take on a Greco-Roman intellectual complexion. The trend became more pronounced by the third century, when Christian thinkers more consciously set about defining the exact meaning of the faith. These theologians borrowed heavily from Greco-Roman philosophy, especially the Platonic tradition, to state the essence of their belief. The most influential figures in this movement were two scholars from Alexandria, Clement (ca. 150–216) and Origen (ca. 185–254),

both well educated in classical culture. Their writings, especially those of Origen, represent an extensive borrowing from philosophy. This wedding of Christian thought and Greco-Roman culture produced an ever-more elaborate statement of Christianity that was understandable and meaningful to educated, cosmopolitan Greco-Romans. As a body of thought developed, Christianity ceased to be described as simple and irrational. The merger likewise increasingly persuaded Christian thinkers that classical learning had been a preparation for the true revelation and therefore was useful in illuminating the meaning of God's word. The emerging capability to speak on an intellectual level and the growing confidence that classical culture was a source of better understanding of the faith greatly strengthened Christianity.

For those who were not capable of absorbing the lofty ideas of the theologians, Christianity had something else to offer. Growing in a society accustomed to splendid religious pageants, to highly emotional practices of worship, and to the constant round of nonreligious spectacles provided in the circuses, the Christians developed a ritual that could compete on equal terms. To a large extent this involved adapting existing customs. Christian worship, which originally consisted of meetings in private dwellings for a common meal imitating the last supper of Christ and for prayers, gradually became more elaborate. Churches were built and decorated with art inspired by doctrine. Services were conducted by a clergy in elaborate attire. The common meal became the center of a ritual that emphasized Christ's sacrifice (the beginning of the Mass). Prayer and music became more elaborate, and ceremonies were instituted for such events as baptism, marriage, and burial. Holidays commemorating the highlights of Christ's life and the death of early martyrs were celebrated. In short, the development of an elaborate ritual made Christian worship as spectacular and as impressive as that of any other religion or the secular pageants. Although modern men sometimes scoff at this aspect of religious life, there can be little doubt that splendid public ritual increased Christianity's appeal, especially to the vast majority of men for whom religion is more a matter of feeling than of thought. The Christian movement also developed a strong social consciousness. Christ in his teachings and his life repeatedly exemplified the need for charity and kindness in dealing with others. This idea received expression in Christian practice almost from the beginning. Christians poured out their resources to help the sick, the poor, criminals, slaves, orphans, widows, and others of the unfortunate in Roman society. In spite of their belief that happiness came in the hereafter, the early Christians did not close their eyes to earthly affairs. Anyone could find help within the Christian community.

The steady progress of Christianity against major opposition may now be a little more understandable. Impelled by the powerful message transmitted by Christ, the early Christians fitted themselves to their work with amazing skill. In the name of God they turned all things to religious ends. No other agency, religious or nonreligious, demonstrated such vitality during the three centuries after Christ's birth.

Now we can ask some of the questions that prompt us to study the growth of Christianity: Did its growth contribute to the decline of the Roman Empire? Was the Christian of the third century a good Roman? The answers are difficult. In many ways, the Christian was a good Roman. He performed his duties as long as he was not required to deny his god. He paid his taxes and obeyed the emperor. He tried his best to help the unfortunate members of his community. He read books on Christian theology that contained huge portions of Greco-Roman philosophy. He worshiped in a fashion that bore a strong resemblance to non-Christian worship. At least the Christian was not an open rebel, bent on pulling down the established order.

Yet in more important ways, he was not a good Roman. He might be in the Roman Empire, but his allegiance lay elsewhere. He served a god who would tolerate no rivals, including Roman emperors who claimed divinity. Believing that his god disapproved of the ways of non-Christian men, he tended to avoid involvement in worldly affairs. His strong sense of sin led him to regard the world, including the Roman Empire, as hardly worth saving. His belief in the omnipotence of God and in human frailty caused him to distrust human reason and man's ability to build a paradise on earth. He thus found little that appealed to him in the basic premise of Greco-Roman civilization: the conviction that enlightened human activity could create a perfect society on earth. The Christian was a devoted, disciplined member of an organization existing independently of the Roman state. His "citizenship" was in the Church, and the Church served his needs better than did the Roman state. Through art, literature, and religious services, the Church kept constantly before his eyes and his mind a series of symbols and arguments that made him feel his separateness and his uniqueness. Every Christian convert meant one less Roman citizen in the fullest sense of the word.

What has just been said about the Christians applies to a lesser degree to the adherents of the other Eastern religions of the third century. The followers of Mithra, Isis, the Unconquerable Sun, and Dionysus all found new ends to serve and gave all their energies in that service. These new religions ate away at the heart of the worldly, politically oriented thinking of Greco-Roman civilization. When men began serving these deities to gain an eternal reward, they lost interest in serving the emperor for worldly prizes.

As the third century drew to a close, Rome and all it stood for seemed destined for quick destruction. Political chaos, external assaults, economic decline, social turmoil, and desertion to foreign religions all coincided to strain the imperial structure to its limit. There was little sign of eventual recovery, for seldom had Roman leadership seemed less inspired and more selfish and brutal.

Suggested Reading

Overview. A brief general treatment of the period of Rome's decline and fall (A.D. 200–500) is **Solomon Katz, *The Decline of Rome and the Rise of Medieval Civilization* (Cornell). Probably the best treatment is Joseph Vogt, *The Decline of Rome*, trans. J. Sondheimer (1967); this book presumes a considerable knowledge of the details of late Roman history and concentrates on interpretation. Another excellent review of Rome's decline is S. Mazzarino, *The End of the Ancient World*, trans. G. Holmes (1966). The classic work of Edward Gibbon (already cited in Chapter 11) traces in majestic detail the events marking Rome's demise. **Ferdinand Lot, *The End of the Ancient World and the Beginnings of the Middle Ages* (Harper Torchbook), supplies a sensitive analysis of the weaknesses of late Roman society. A vast work pinpointing in detail the problems of the late Roman world is A. H. M. Jones, *The Later Roman Empire, 284–602: A Social, Economic, and Administrative Survey* (3 vols., 1964). The basic conclusions of this magnificent survey are presented in A. H. M. Jones, *The Decline of the Ancient World* (1966). **C. G. Starr, *Civilization and the Caesars* (Norton), presents an excellent discussion of the intellectual revolution accompanying the fall of Rome. Almost every author who treats the subject of Rome's decline discusses the "causes" of that development. Two excellent collections containing representative interpretations on this topic are **Donald Kagan, *Decline and Fall of the Roman Empire: Why Did It Collapse?* (Heath); and **Mortimer Chambers, *The Fall of Rome: Can It Be Explained?* (Holt). F. W. Walbank, *The Decline of the Roman Empire in the West* (1946), and *The Awful Revolution: The Decline of the Roman Empire in the West* (1969), present provocative interpretations from a Marxist perspective. **R. M. Haywood, *The Myth of Rome's Fall* (Apollo), sums up the various approaches to the problem, and offers critiques of many. Well worth examining are the ideas expressed by Arnold Toynbee, *A Study of History* (12 vols., 1934–61), Vol. I, pp. 22–84;

Rome's fall is placed in the larger framework of universal history.

Third-century Crisis. The best general survey of the difficulties of the third century is H. D. M. Parker, *History of the Roman World From A. D. 138 to 337* (2nd ed., 1958). Valuable economic and social material, stressing especially the class divisions developing in this period, is contained in M. I. Rostovtzeff, *Social and Economic History of the Roman Empire* (2 vols., 2nd ed., 1957). **Franz Cumont, *Oriental Religions in Roman Paganism* (Dover), treats the mounting influences of the mystery religions in the late empire. **A. D. Nock, *Conversion: The Old and the New in Religion* (Oxford), helps in understanding the processes by which people in the empire were attracted to new religious ideas. E. Brehier, *Philosophy of Plotinus* (1958), provides an excellent introduction to Neoplatonic thought and its impact on the third century.

Rise of Christianity. The literature on this subject is so immense that any selected list is bound to omit many items of great value. A good starting point might be **Emil Schurer, *History of the Jewish People in the Time of Jesus* (Schocken); Charles Guignebert, *The Jewish World in the Time of Jesus* (1959); and **T. H. Gaster, *Dead Sea Scriptures* (Anchor), which will help to establish the setting out of which Christianity came. The following titles will provide brief, clearly written accounts of early Christianity: E. R. Goodenough, *The Church in the Roman Empire* (1931); **Henry Chadwick, *The Early Church* (Penguin); **Rudolph Bultmann, *Primitive Christianity in Its Contemporary Setting* (Meridian); and **J. G. Davies, *The Early Christian Church* (Anchor). Chadwick's book has a good guide to additional literature. There are several excellent longer histories of the early Church. One of the most recent by two world-renowned authorities on church history is J. Daniélou and H. I. Marrou, *The First Six Hundred Years* (The Christian Centuries, Vol.

I), trans. V. Cronin (1964). **H. Lietzmann, *A History of the Early Church*, Vols. I and II (Meridian), presents a detailed study of the first three centuries from a Protestant perspective. **Jules Lebreton and Jacques Zeiller, in *The Church in the New Testament* (Collier), *Heresy and Orthodoxy* (Collier), and *Triumph of Early Christianity* (Collier), provide the same wealth of detail from a Roman Catholic point of view. **H. Daniel-Rops, *Jesus and His Times* (2 vols., Image), and *Church of the Apostles and Martyrs* (2 vols., Image), presents a lively picture, sometimes marred by the author's personal convictions, but much easier to read than some less personal interpretations. K. S. Latourette, *A History of the Expansion of Christianity* (7 vols., 1937–45), Vol. I, discusses the difficult subject of Christian expansion in the first three centuries. **W. H. Frend, *Martyrdom and Persecution in the Early Church* (Anchor), is a superlative treatment of the relationship between the Roman state and the early Christians. The development of Christian thought can be seen in **A. C. McGiffert, *A History of Christian Thought* (2 vols., Scribners), Vol. I, and perhaps more easily in J. Daniélou, *The Development of Christian Doctrine Before the Council of Nicaea* (1964). Four highly sophisticated and significant works grappling with the all-important relationship between Christianity and classical culture are Werner Jaeger, *Early Christianity and Greek Paideia* (1961); E. R. Dodds, *Pagan and Christian in the Age of Anxiety* (1965); **C. N. Cochrane, *Christianity and Classical Culture* (Galaxy); and Henry Chadwick, *Early Christian Thought and the Classical Tradition* (1966). The development of Christian worship is brilliantly summarized by J. A. Jungmann, *The Early Liturgy to the Time of Gregory the Great* (1959); and Gregory Dix, *The Shape of the Liturgy* (2nd ed., 1945). Fascinating glimpses of the simpler aspects of early Christian society are provided by J. G. Davies, *Daily Life in the Early Church* (1952); and C. J. Cadoux, *The Early Church and the World* (1925).

Sources. The third century produced very little pagan literature that is of value as source material. Perhaps the best reading (but not the easiest) would be *The Ennaeds of Plotinus*, trans. S. Mackenna (2nd ed., 1956). The literature associated with the rise of Christianity is richer. First in importance is, of course, the New Testament. As a guide to this book as a historical source, read R. M. Grant, *Historical Introduction to the New Testament* (1963). An early Christian version of the history of the primitive Church is **Eusebius, *History of the Church From Christ to Constantine*, trans. G. A. Williamson (Penguin); Eusebius wrote in the early fourth century. A collection of Christian writings from the second century can be found in *Early Christian Fathers*, trans. C. C. Richardson (1953). Valuable material on the relationship between the Roman state and the Christian community is collected in P. R. Coleman-Norton, *Roman State and Christian Church* (3 vols., 1966).

Chapter 14 ❧ The Destruction of the Roman Empire,

A.D. 284—500

In A.D. 285 a general named Diocletian seized the imperial throne by force. In itself this was not a startling event; rather, it was a repetition of what had happened during the preceding century when frequent military uprisings had replaced the reigning emperor with a victorious general. However, the accession of Diocletian heralded a new period in late Roman history. He and his most important successor, Constantine, undertook a thorough reform of the empire in an attempt to check the steady decline of the preceding century. In essence, their reforms were a consolidation of major trends that had appeared during the difficulties of the third century. Their work gave the empire a reprieve, but it did not check the basic forces that were eating away the vital centers of Greco-Roman civilization. By the end of the fourth century, the empire was unable to resist the onslaught of the barbarian Germans. During the next century the Germans smashed the empire and brought to an end a whole civilization.

1. THE REFORMS OF DIOCLETIAN AND CONSTANTINE

The way for Diocletian was paved during the years from about 260 to 284, when a series of rulers began the process of curbing the civil wars and pacifying the empire. A Dalmatian by birth and a soldier by experience,

Diocletian fit the pattern of so many previous emperors. He did have, however, considerable political talent and a clear insight into the basic problems facing the Roman world. He acted with decisiveness to restore order, stability, and prosperity to the empire.

Central to his entire program was the concentration of power in the hands of the emperor; but sensing that the task of ruling the empire was too great for one man, Diocletian evolved a system of shared responsibilty. To himself and another he assigned the title *Augustus;* for each Augustus, a subordinate designated as a *Caesar* was established. The empire was divided into four parts, called *prefectures;* each ruler was given the full power to defend and govern the territory assigned to him. Diocletian had no intention of thus destroying the unity of the empire. The Augusti and Caesars ruled jointly, with Diocletian himself providing overall direction. His intention in effecting this change was to make available additional leadership to face the grave problems of the period, especially that of defense. The system was also intended to settle the troublesome succession question. When an Augustus died, his Caesar would succeed and immediately appoint another Caesar as co-ruler and eventual successor.

More significant was Diocletian's effort to solidify the absolute authority of the four co-rulers. His whole regime operated on the assumption that the imperial authority was unlimited and beyond question. No pretense was made of consulting with the Senate and the people. The emperor's pronouncements were assumed to be law. To strengthen this system, Diocletian sought to create a new image of the emperor. Following Oriental precedents, he made every effort to make the imperial office sacred. The emperor withdrew himself from public view as much as possible. An elaborate court ritual was established, designed to envelop the ruler in an aura of mystery and sanctity, to associate him with divine powers in the exercise of his authority. The traditional *princeps*, first citizen, had disappeared in favor of a charismatic *dominus*, lord, whose will must be obeyed without question.

However, Diocletian was too realistic a statesman to think that imperial power would be made effective simply by proclaiming it and by adorning the ruler with the symbols of divine sanction. Thus he also undertook practical measures to tighten and extend the imperial administrative system. At the court of each of the four co-emperors, administrative functions were organized into clearly defined departments, each directed by officials designated by the emperors and each manned by an extensive corps of civil servants. The responsibility of these officials was to see to it that the imperial will was applied promptly and uniformly throughout the empire. Within each of the four prefectures, the provincial administration was more rigorously organized

and made responsive to the central government. The number of provinces was increased, and the provinces were grouped into intermediary administrative units called *dioceses*, of which there were twelve. The building of this bureaucratic hierarchy allowed the central administration to act more directly and more uniformly in local affairs, and it all but ended the active role of local city governments.

Diocletian was especially concerned with the military forces of the empire, so often distracted by civil wars and so severely tested by foreign attackers during the preceding century. He now created two basic elements within the military establishment. One con-

One of Diocletian's solutions for the problems of the empire was to share the office of emperor among four men, two called augustus and two subordinates called caesar. They would rule jointly, and when an augustus died, his caesar would assume his position and in turn appoint a new subordinate. This famous grouping, which stands now outside St. Mark's in Venice, shows the augusti Diocletian and Maximian with their caesars, Constantius and Galerius. *Photo: Alinari–Art Reference Bureau*

sisted of an infantry army settled along the frontier to absorb the chief blows of outside attackers. The second was a mobile cavalry force held as a reserve to move quickly to meet particular dangers. This reorganization considerably increased the size of the army and raised monumental problems of recruitment and support.

The more elaborate imperial courts (now four in number), the enlarged bureaucracy, and the increased military establishment imposed an even greater financial burden on the imperial government than it had had to face during the third century. Diocletian met this challenge by a reorganization of the financial system. A survey of the empire was undertaken which ended in the designation of taxable units of land and in the identification of taxable human beings. Assessments in both kind and money were specified for land and persons. Assessments were also made on the services of certain productive elements in society. On the basis of this elaborate arrangement, the imperial tax collectors exacted from the total populace a huge income in produce, money, and services which was then distributed to feed and equip the armies, pay the bureaucrats, and support the court. The new fiscal measures had the effect of putting the wealth and talent of the total population at the disposal of the state.

Concerned over the economic weaknesses that had manifested themselves in the preceding century and that threatened adequate income for the state, Diocletian also undertook a massive regimentation of the imperial economy. In 301 he decreed a system of fixed prices and economic measures aimed at checking the inflationary pressures. His bureaucracy sought to control production of goods and services by exacting needed produce and services from farmers, artisans, miners, shipowners, caravan operators, and so forth. To keep producers on their jobs—especially where the vital interests of the state were concerned—the imperial government sought to freeze men in their jobs. Peasants, artisans, traders, bureaucrats, and many oth-

ers were forbidden to change their occupations. Sons had to step into their fathers' shoes in many occupations. A kind of hereditary caste system was being shaped under imperial direction. Increasingly, citizens of the Roman Empire had but one end for which to live—service to the state.

Diocletian's expanding autocracy even sought to regiment men's minds and focus their attention on one object—the state. Crucial to this end was the restoration of religious unity. His reign was marked by a major effort to rally the populace around a worship of the old deities, whose agent the divine emperor was. This policy brought Diocletian into conflict with the ever-expanding and increasingly confident Christian community, which steadfastly refused to make obeisance to these gods or the state that honored them. Because their position was intolerable within his frame of reference, Diocletian attempted to suppress them. The last of a series of punitive decrees in 303 and 304 made death the penalty for defiance. His assault on the Christians was the most serious threat they ever faced from the Roman government, and it tried their strength to the utmost. They were to survive and triumph, but Diocletian's persecution symbolized the degree to which religion had come to be viewed as the sustaining force in the Roman imperial regime.

In 305 the aged and ill Diocletian abdicated his power. Although he was judged harshly by his contemporaries, particularly the Christians, his strong measures had proved effective. Internal order was restored, the imperial defenses were holding, the administrative machinery had begun to operate effectively again, and adequate resources were made available to the state. Diocletian had established the pattern of government that was to prevail until the empire collapsed. Immediately after his abdication, however, the new order was seriously threatened, chiefly because Diocletian's scheme to determine the succession did not work. There was another series of civil wars, ended only when Constantine fought his way to complete control over the entire empire, a goal he did not finally accomplish until 324. Constantine was a worthy successor to Diocletian and carried on most of his policies. He strengthened the armies, tightened bureaucratic controls over society, further regimented the economy, improved the financial machinery, and took more power into his own hands. Through his efforts the absolutist, bureaucratic, militaristic state envisaged by Diocletian was made a reality. But it bore little resemblance to the Augustan principate; it was now a dominate.

Constantine added important elements to the new order. Most significant was his religious policy. The direction of that policy was dramatically revealed in 313, when Constantine and his co-emperor issued the Edict of Milan, which decreed that henceforth all religions would be tolerated in the empire. The Edict meant the end of the terrible persecution of Christians that had begun in 303–304. It also meant that Christianity had at last received legal recognition. But there was more to the decree than legal issues. Behind it was an event of immense psychological importance: the conversion of Constantine himself. During the decisive battle of his career, fought at Milvian Bridge near Rome in 311, he had had a vision which promised him that if he would display the cross as the insignia of his army, victory would be his. He did this and smashed his enemy. Although in fact he was not baptized until just before his death in 337, this event gave notice to the world that a Christian ruled the empire. After the edict of toleration, Constantine gave every indication that he was a Christian, intent on promoting Christian causes. He poured out money to assist in building churches. He drew clergymen into the councils of state as advisers and extended a variety of special privileges to them. His legislation increasingly reflected Christian teachings in matters such as slavery and marriage. He directed state authority toward resolving disputes within the Christian community. True, he did not openly attack other religions, but he treated them in a way that little encouraged them. Every sign pointed in one direction: that Christianity was the favored religion and that the empire was becoming a Christian state.

The implications of this profound change in state policy have been endlessly discussed. Contemporary Christians hailed Constantine's conversion as a triumphant fulfillment of God's promise. Constantine became their hero as the first Christian emperor. The evidence suggests, however, that his decision was prompted by powerful political motives. The strength of the Christians had been demonstrated by their resistance to the persecutions of Diocletian; they could obviously be powerful allies to an aspirant for imperial power, as Constantine was when he first moved toward recognition of the new religion. Constantine was seeking—in line with the whole trend of imperial thought in his age—a justification of his authority. If he could become the servant of the god who gave him victory in battle, would not he as servant of the same god be able to unify his subjects and ensure the safety and well-being of his empire? His religious policy therefore was motivated by a desire to put the Christian world view to the service of the state: to make the empire the agency of the Christian god, the emperor his almighty servant, and the citizenry a single community worshipping that god so as to earn his favors. In short, Christianity was to Constantine the most promising instrument for unifying and revitalizing the empire. However, this was not cynical manipulation of religion: It emerged from genuine religious convictions. He was a man of his age, powerfully drawn to religion, and especially to Christianity. His mother, Helen, was a Christian and exerted a strong influence on him. His own writings and the testimony of his contemporaries indicate that he was deeply moved by the kind of religious ideas represented by Christianity. And the evidence used to cast doubts on Constantine's conversion is not very convincing. Deathbed baptisms were usual in his day. His tolerance of paganism reflects the basic fact that he did not have the power to wipe out at will religions that had been practiced for centuries. Constantine was indeed the first Christian emperor both by conviction and in practice. His yoking of the Roman Empire and the Christian community was a momentous event in world history.

Equally momentous was Constantine's decision to build a new capital at the ancient city of Byzantium (now renamed Constantinople) located on the Bosporus. By this action Constantine not only created a rival to "old" Rome, but also shifted the center of imperial power from the West to the East. This great change was no mere autocratic whim. Rome had been declining in importance in imperial affairs for many decades. As early as the second century, men of non-Roman origin had been elevated to the imperial throne; during the tumultous third century, dominated by the "barrack" emperors, the Roman-born emperor was a rarity. The local attachments of these rulers diminished Rome's aura as the source of power and greatness. Also, during the third century the incessant struggles for power and the problems of defending the frontiers revealed that Rome was badly located in terms of strategic demands; other cities served better as centers from which to conduct wars aimed at seizing the imperial throne and at restraining the aggressive Germans and Persians. Diocletian's reorganization of the empire into four prefectures each with its own ruler led to the emergence of new centers of political authority. Diocletian established his own headquarters at Nicomedia in Asia Minor, while his co-rulers established their courts in Milan, Sirmium in the Balkans, and Trier in the Rhineland area, choices dictated primarily by military considerations. After Diocletian's abdication in 305, his divisions of the empire persisted for several years until Constantine was finally able to conquer his rivals and establish himself as the single ruler of a reunited empire. In these struggles Rome did not play a decisive role.

In 324, the year that he won the final battle for supremacy, Constantine began construction of his new capital; it was dedicated in 330. He chose the site in part for very practical reasons. It was admirably situated for defense by land and sea. From it the imperial forces had easy access to the most vulnerable and hard-pressed frontiers—the Danube region and the eastern provinces. The new city was close to the great centers of wealth in the East from whence came the chief resources of the imperial government. And it was situated where Christian strength was greatest, a matter of considerable importance to an emperor who had identified himself with a religion that still commanded the allegiance of only a minority of the imperial population. Aside from these practical considerations, Constantine wished to be free from the restrictive traditions of republicanism and paganism that were entrenched in old Rome as threats to his new autocracy and new religious policy. In the actual construction of Constantinople, the emperor replicated much of old Rome, including a Senate, "bread and circuses," forums, baths, theaters, and even temples in honor of the ancient gods. But Constantinople was not Rome; it was the emperor's city, where all men were his creatures and where Christianity predominated.

The full impact of the founding of Constantinople was not immediately obvious. Old Rome still remained an important city upon which Constantine showered favors, not the least of which was a great Christian church built in honor of St. Peter on Vatican Hill at a site where the bones of the first pope were believed to be buried. Yet the relocation of the capital did have a powerful psychological impact on contemporaries. It turned the attention of the imperial population to the East as the source of authority. What old Rome stood for was now spurned by a despot who preferred to live in the East, to worship an Eastern god, and to be fawned over by Eastern slaves. To many who cherished ancient values, it seemed that Constantine had turned the world around, allowing the East to surpass the West, the Greek to predominate over the Latin. And in the near future, when outsiders threatened to conquer both East and West, the rulers in Constantinople chose to defend "new" Rome and let "old" Rome and the West fall victim to the barbarians.

2. THE FOURTH-CENTURY LULL BEFORE THE STORM

The vast reorganization of imperial forces carried out by Diocletian and Constantine appeared to have saved the empire: The era from Constantine's death in 337 to the end of the reign of Theodosius (379–395) was one of relative calm and order, especially when compared to the third century. There was a fairly regular succession of emperors based on the hereditary principle, with little civil strife. Agriculture, trade, and industry seemed to hold their own, albeit under rigid state control. The armies were supplied and the bureaucrats were paid. Society, carefully manipulated by the emperors, appeared stable and orderly—and even content. The Roman political genius appeared again to have saved the civilized world, as in the days of Augustus.

Yet, as is now evident, this calm was misleading. The old sicknesses persisted. There was no real economic growth. The citizens were more apathetic than ever in supporting the state. Social developments continued to destroy the city aristocracy and depress the peasantry. The menace along the frontiers did not disappear. To these familiar plagues were added new ones. The absolutist, militarized state, which Diocletian and Constantine hoped would resolve all problems, became a monster consuming the wealth of the empire and crushing the spirits of its citizens. The bureaucracy grew more costly, rapacious, corrupt, and inefficient. Regimentation of the economy stifled all enterprise and growth. The army became more barbarized, and its barbaric generals moved into key offices in the direction of the state. The imperial policy of favoring Christianity bred a schism in Roman society by alienating those who still placed trust in the pagan religious tradition and the culture which sustained it. Pagan resentment surfaced during the reign of Julian (360–363), called the "Apostate" by the Christians be-

cause he repudiated Christianity and sought to destroy it in favor of the restoration of a pagan "church" following a doctrine he himself prescribed. His effort failed, but it kept alive a fundamental division in imperial society and thought.

The Julian reaction points up the fact that Christianity did not fulfill the role expected of it by Constantine in unifying the state and stirring the citizens to patriotic fervor. Christianity did continue its triumphant march to dominance, culminating when Theodosius made it the state religion and outlawed all others, but during the fourth century the movement was rent with internal disagreements that promoted disorders. Even during the reign of Constantine, the Christians divided into two warring factions, the Arians and the Orthodox, over the question of the Trinity. The Arians, troubled by the danger of worshipping more than one god and puzzled by the intricate problem of the relation of the Father and the Son, sought to exalt the power of the Father by making the Son subordinate and denying the absolute divinity of Christ. The Orthodox spokesmen insisted that the Son was co-equal with the Father and that the two persons, plus the Holy Spirit, formed a unity. An attempt to settle this bitter quarrel was made at the Council of Nicea in 325. Churchmen from all over the empire gathered under the auspices of Constantine and agreed upon the Nicene Creed as a basic definition of the nature of Christ. The creed was a victory for the Orthodox. In spite of the agreement, however, the quarrel continued to rage for a century, involving the imperial government, setting Christian against Christian, and causing persecutions of one side by the other. The Arian dispute was only one; there were other "heresies" dividing the Christian community and the empire. The involvement of the imperial government in this quarrel was a manifestation of another source of friction in the Christian world. The whole thrust of the Constantinian religious policy was to subordinate the Christian Church to the imperial government. This tendency alarmed many Christian leaders and generated active resistance to imperial domination of religious life, providing still another source of contention and struggle. In a larger sense, Christianity failed to supply the vitalizing force in the "new" empire; it was a movement with its own ends and strengths, not easily bent to other purposes.

All these signs of deteriorating imperial strength and internal friction were extremely ominous, for a crisis was in the making as the fourth century drew to a close. Its source lay in Central Europe, an area beyond the control of the imperial regime. It involved the Germanic barbarians who had for so long plagued the empire and taxed its strength. German pressure on the imperial defenses had been constant throughout the fourth century. Many small groups had actually penetrated the empire, usually as recruits in the Roman army or as settlers on vacant land along the frontier. About 370 a wild horde of Asiatic nomads, the Huns, suddenly swept out of the East across southern Russia toward Central Europe. When they approached the Black Sea area, they encountered two settled Germanic nations, the Ostrogoths and the Visigoths. The former were quickly overpowered by the Huns. The terror-stricken Visigoths begged permission from the imperial government to migrate across the Danube into Roman territory in the Balkan area. Their request was granted. The Visigoths were allowed to keep their own king and were promised lands in return for military service. When the imperial government failed to provide for their needs, the Visigoths revolted. The emperor Valens marched against them, but suffered a smashing defeat at Adrianople in 378. Rome now had a barbarian nation within her boundaries which she could neither control nor destroy.

3. THE BARBARIAN GERMANS

The reckoning which confronted the Roman Empire had to be made with a people known as Germans. What and who were they? They have always been designated as "barbarians," a term that is proper if used to characterize the simplicity of their institutions and culture compared with the sophisticated, advanced life of the Roman world. The basic Germanic political institution was the *tribe*, composed of a number of *clans* and headed by a *tribal chief*. Direction of tribal life was by no means the monopoly of the chief; heads of clans played a vital role in shaping the decisions of the group, and freemen in the clans had a political voice through an *assembly*. The tribal government concerned itself chiefly with war and with religious worship, most other matters being decided by the clans. Every tribe had an extensive body of customary law which was rigorously observed as one of the foundation stones of group life. The Germans were primarily hunters and herders, although by the third century A.D., they were beginning to turn to agriculture. Trade and industry played a minor role. In religion, the Germans were polytheistic; they worshiped especially the forces of nature. They believed that the gods controlled the material welfare of men, and their chief religious concern was to make the gods happy by sacrifices and prayers. There was no written Germanic language; what literature they had, mostly stories about the deeds of gods and heroes, was transmitted orally.

But this pattern of life was not rigid; the Germans were not a "backward" people. By the fourth century their society was undergoing significant changes. Small tribal groups were being unified into *nations* ruled over by elected kings enjoying considerable powers. This political development made it easier for a single Germanic ruler to mount heavy attacks on the Roman frontier and more difficult for the Romans to play small group against small group. The trend toward larger political units and monarchy made the Germans eager learners in the art of politics. Within Germanic society there was also developing a unique institution—the war band (*comitatus*)—composed of tested warriors united by pledges made under oath to follow a military chief, who in turn pledged to lead them in profitable ventures and to share the booty wih his companions in arms. These warriors became a kind of aristocracy, practicing war as a way of life and gaining tremendous proficiency in fighting. Germanic society was moving rapidly toward a more advanced agricultural economy. As a consequence, the Germans had a great hunger for farmland. Since tillable land was short in the heavy forests of Central Europe, many nations and tribes moved south toward the rich lands of the Roman world in search of places to settle. The agricultural economy was transforming Germanic society by creating an aristocratic landowning elite and by bringing elements of the population into economic dependence on these landowners, changes for which the Roman world again supplied a model. These changing conditions made Germanic society dynamic, open to foreign influences, mobile, adaptable. Even though barbarians, the Germans were becoming a potent force in the civilized world.

Between Germans and Romans there was no deep-seated hatred at the moment of their decisive encounter. The Germans were admirers of Greco-Roman civilization, desiring nothing more than to settle within the empire and to become "civilized" so as to enjoy its fruits—especially its material wealth. The Romans on their side respected the Germans for their splendid physical features, their fighting prowess, and their alleged moral excellence. For many centuries, the two peoples had been in close contact—fighting, trading, and living side by side. The Romans had from at least the time of Augustus established a set frontier, and permitted Germans to cross that frontier as long as their movement could be controlled. Large numbers of Germans had entered the empire as soldiers and as farmers. These migrants quickly became Romanized and often rose to high places in Roman society. Influences from the Roman world also sifted across the frontiers into the Germanic world, especially in those areas adjacent to the frontier. For example, during the fourth

century many Goths were converted to Christianity by Ulfilas, himself a Goth educated in Constantinople. Ulfilas provided a Gothic version of the Bible for his converts, a feat that required the creation of a written language. Thus over a long period, many Germans had already been drawn into the orbit of Greco-Roman civilization. And there is some evidence that by the fourth century the Germans were exerting some influence over the Romans, adding a tinge of barbaric coloring to Greco-Roman life.

It would seem that the barbarian Germans were thus moving peacefully into the mainstream of Greco-Roman civilization and might in the long run have been completely transformed, as some were before A.D. 400. However, the relationship which produced this development depended upon Roman strength. The Romans had to be able to prevent too great a flood of Germans from pouring into the empire at once and to dominate those who did enter. Was the Visigothic victory at Adrianople in 378 a sign that Rome had lost that ability? If so, the very existence of the empire and of Greco-Roman civilization would be at stake.

4. THE BARBARIAN INVASIONS AND THE FALL OF THE EMPIRE

The crisis caused by the Visigothic victory was faced by the last great emperor to rule the united empire, Theodosius. He kept the Visigoths in check by establishing them as *foederati* (allies), meaning that they were assigned lands in the empire in return for supplying troops for the Roman army. Theodosius took effective steps to ensure that they abided by the terms of the arrangement, and succeeded in confining them to the Balkan area of the empire. He struggled valiantly with rival contenders for his throne and eventually eliminated most of them. The elaborate machinery of state was kept running, permitting a continued defense of the frontiers.

His passing, however, spelled the beginning

of the end of the uneasy calm lying over the empire since the time of Diocletian and Constantine. Theodosius was succeeded by two sons; one was assigned the western section of the empire and the other, the eastern. Neither had much ability or interest in the problems of state and both allowed the direction of affairs to fall into the hands of powerful generals, most of whom were Germanic in origin and whose power rested primarily on the loyalty of their Germanic troops. This situation set off a series of power struggles in which the generals sought to manipulate imperial policy for their own advantage.

Its directive force caught up in ceaseless intrigue, the empire lost control over the Germanic hordes pressing in on it. As the fifth century opened, the Visigoths, firmly entrenched in the Balkans and effectively led by a capable king named Alaric, were playing a dangerous game of selling their services to either the emperor in the West or the one in the East. Eventually they turned against the West and Italy, having been promised by the emperor at Constantinople whatever new lands they might conquer. To defend Italy against the Visigoths, the real wielder of power in the West, a German general named Stilicho, withdrew troops from the British, Rhine, and Danube frontiers. This fateful decision was to no avail, for the Visigoths captured and sacked Rome in 410—the first time in eight centuries that the city had suffered such a fate. While the civilized world shuddered from the shock of Rome's capture, other Germans poured across the undefended frontiers into the heart of the empire.

The invaders were primarily interested in finding lands upon which to settle; they were not particularly concerned with destroying Roman government and Roman society. The effect of their assault was, however, the dismemberment of the western part of the empire. Wherever they occupied lands of their choice, their kings and warrior nobles became the real rulers over Germans and Romans alike. Often the fiction was maintained that the new settlers were allies of the Roman government, but this meant little in practice. As a consequence of this process, during the fifth century a series of new Germanic kingdoms on Roman soil replaced the previously unified empire. Angles, Saxons, and Jutes wiped out Roman outposts in Britain and established several petty kingdoms. The Vandals crossed Gaul into Spain; from there, their one great king, Gaiseric, led them into North Africa, where a formidable Vandal kingdom was established. It soon developed enough sea power to allow the Vandals to pillage Rome in 455. After a brief sojourn in Italy following the sack of Rome, the Visigoths settled in southern Gaul and soon extended their sway over Spain. The Burgundians created a kingdom in southeastern Gaul straddling the Rhone Valley. Late in the fifth century the Franks, led by a ruthless, able king named Clovis, seized most of Gaul as their base of power, drove the Visigoths into Spain, and overran the Burgundian kingdom. Eventually Italy fell victim to the Germans when the Ostrogoths captured it in 493 and established their king, Theodoric, as ruler. The ferocious Huns under Attila created a huge kingdom north of the Danube from which they harassed the East and then invaded the West in 451–452. Attila's western invasion was repulsed by a coalition of Roman and German forces. Germanic tribes repeatedly ravaged the territory south of the Danube during the fifth century and hurled themselves at the eastern provinces. Unable to bypass Constantinople, they were denied the conquest of the East. Despite this failure, the history of the fifth century really belonged to the Germans. They had won the West; the Alarics, the Gaiserics, the Clovises, the Theodorics were the movers of this era.

The magnitude of the Germanic victory is revealed by the fate of the imperial government in the West. Under the relentless pressure of Germanic attack, the regime slowly dissolved. Some of the generals serving the weak emperors in the West fought valiantly to check the invasions and negotiated desperately to turn German against German. Each

Legend:
← Alemanni
← Burgundians
←-·- Franks
← Huns
←···· Ostrogoths
← Vandals
←-- Visigoths
←-·- Angles
←-- Jutes
← Saxons
←···· Suevians
←--- Lombards

450
376–500
376–500
358
ANGLO-SAXONS
SAXONS
SLAVS
THURINGIANS
FRANKS
Soissons •Reims
486 451
407
LOMBARDS
406
400–500
340
375
VOUILLE ✗
507
Autun
BURGUNDIANS
473
GEPIDS
443
OSTROGOTHS
452
489
375
BULGARS
SUEVIANS
Braga •
BASQUES
507
409
Toulouse
412
Ravenna 397
375
376
VISIGOTHS
Toledo •
418
410
•Rome
455
• Constantinople
395 BYZANTINE
VANDALS
429
Carthage •
EMPIRE

Frankish Kingdom at 486
Areas Conquered by Clovis

0 100 200 300 400 500 mi.

Barbarian Kingdoms 526

Germanic nation was usually persuaded to sign a treaty with the Roman government by the terms of which it accepted the status of *foederatus* and recognized Roman overlordship in a legal sense. In practice, however, Rome's allies became independent in the areas assigned to them. Their kings became the real rulers, taking over the responsibility for maintaining order, collecting taxes for their own use, conducting independent foreign policies, and grasping for more land. The Roman bureaucracy broke down, imperial income dwindled, and the authority of the suc-

cessors of Caesar Augustus disappeared. By 476 the political realities in the West were officially recognized. A German general, Odoacer, deposed the last western emperor and turned the insignia of imperial office over to the emperor in Constantinople with the advice that there was no longer need for a ruler in the West. In theory, this act reunited the empire under the sole authority of the emperor in Constantinople; in practice, the eastern emperor had virtually no control over the West. And perhaps he did not deserve any, for throughout the trying times of the fifth century, the eastern rulers did little to assist in holding the West. They had decided to abandon that area in order to concentrate their resources on the defense of the East and the protection of civilized life there. The West belonged to the Germans by right of conquest.

5. THE FRUITS OF INVASION

The Germanic invasions of the fifth century had consequences much more far-reaching than the political changes traced in the preceding section. Every aspect of life in the empire, and especially in the western part, was affected in a way that spelled the end of Greco-Roman civilization. Although the Germans would have preferred to participate in rather than to destroy that civilization, their presence destined another course of events.

The most obvious and important byproduct of the invasions was the dissolution of imperial administration in the West. Gone were the mighty emperors, their courts, their law, their public projects, their armies, their bureaucrats. Although imperial government had become oppressive and inefficient in the century before the invasions, its destruction could not help but change conditions for the Roman population. The new masters of the West, the Germanic kings and their warriors, were not fitted to conduct government after the fashion of the Roman emperors. Some of

them tried to do so, but with small success. Political chaos settled over the West.

Economically, the invasion was followed by increasing impoverishment. The invaders were not wholly responsible for this depression, which had begun long before their arrival. Nonetheless, the wars they caused and the destruction of the Roman government accelerated the decline. The new Germanic overlords were primarily interested in land, and reversion to an agricultural economy was rapid. Cities suffered an especially disastrous decline, some of them shrinking to a fraction of their old population and most of them being stripped of their functions as cultural, administrative, and economic centers. Their decline meant the end of the urban aristocracies which had sustained Greco-Roman civilization in the West. Roman landholders, although sometimes ousted from their property by German warriors, bent their efforts to enlarge their holdings amid the confusion and usually succeeded. Peasants were glad to serve these great landowners in return for whatever protection the landowners, be they German or Roman, could offer in these perilous times; as a consequence, the ranks of the dependent peasantry swelled everywhere in the West. Most of the owners of large estates sought to achieve self-sufficiency, with the result that the western part of the empire broke up into thousands of tiny self-contained units that had less and less economic interchange with each other. Trade was drastically reduced, and manufacturing centered more and more in the isolated large estates. All these developments drove standards of living inexorably down toward subsistence level.

Culturally, the invasion era was also marked by decline. The new German rulers tried to absorb Roman civilization by learning Latin, by patronizing artists and writers, and by adopting Roman dress and manners. Educated Romans in Italy, Gaul, Spain, and Africa continued to read their classics, to study philosophy, to send their children to schools, and even to write. But their efforts were to no point. No longer was there an opportunity for the cultivated man to serve the imperial court or the local city-state government. The cities, long the centers of civilized life, were dead. The agricultural population, increasingly isolated and barbarized, was too provincial to shoulder the burden of upholding the literary, artistic, scientific, and philosophical traditions of the old order. The content and spirit of that tradition related to few of the real issues of the new day, and thus were cut off from the vitality that comes from the interaction between the world of learning and art and the world of practical life. Try as they might, the new Germanic leadership could do no better than imitate, and all too often their basic barbarism broke through the thin veneer of civilized life.

Finally, the Germanic invasions had created a division between East and West. The new political order in the West was markedly different from the imperial regime still surviving in the East. The simple agricultural economy developing in the West set that world apart from the more stable and sophisticated East, undisturbed by the terrors of the invasion period. The Mediterranean community was ruptured; that fact alone was fatal to Greco-Roman civilization.

We must, however, be cautious in assigning to the Germanic invasions too great significance. Destruction of life and property was not excessive, and in most cases the Germans and Romans settled down peacefully side by side, quite oblivious to the fact that one was conqueror and the other conquered. The Germans were not numerous enough to affect such basic matters as the ethnic composition of the population or language. The chief features of fifth-century history—the disintegration of the imperial government, economic decline, cultural stagnation, and division of the Mediterranean world—had begun before the Germans invaded the empire en masse. What the invasions did was to accelerate these trends and make them irreversible.

6. CHRISTIANITY IN THE LATE EMPIRE

In the face of events bringing virtual ruin to the structure of late imperial society, Christianity showed great resilience and emerged from the ordeal stronger than ever. In some ways this is surprising, for during the fourth century Christianity had become so closely identified with and integrated into imperial society that we might have suspected it would go down to ruin with Rome.

The fourth century was a glorious period in Christian history. Great numbers of converts were made from all levels of society. Christian leaders advanced to prominent positions in society. The wealth of the Christian establishment increased tremendously. The organizational structure became regularized and was extended to embrace virtually the entire Roman Empire, so that a Church in the

As the barbarian tribes pressed into the empire, even Roman culture was engulfed and transformed. This cast of a gilded copper plaque depicts Agilulf, king of the Lombards, surrounded by warriors and spirits of victory; the figures are done in a debased version of the classical Roman style of art. *Photo: Alinari–Art Reference Bureau* sense of a visible organization with its own officials, wealth, regulations, and power had taken its place as a prominent feature of Greco-Roman society. The Roman imperial government of the fourth century gave powerful support to these developments so that the triumphant Church had become to a considerable degree dependent on the caesars. All these successes meant that by 400 the Roman Empire had truly become a Christian Roman Empire, a fact recognized by Theodosius when he legally designated Christianity as the state religion and outlawed all others.

However, success brought new and serious problems. The avalanche of converts, no longer faced with the terrible possibility that baptism might spell martyrdom, diluted the spiritual fervor that had characterized the pre-Constantinian Christian community. Discipline within the growing Christian ranks became more difficult. Wealth and power turned the heads of Christian leaders toward dubious ends; a hostile Christian could even describe a late fourth-century bishop of Rome as a "ladies' ear tickler." Christian practices of worship and Christian doctrine were threatened with obliteration before the flood of Greco-Roman religious practices and ideas still held by many of the inadequately trained and spiritually lax converts. The influx of pagan ideas and practices generated numerous heresies that set Christian against Christian in battles in which no quarter was given. As we have already noted, the rapid advance of Christianity had steeled the pagan world for a final defense of religious concepts deeply rooted in the fabric of society. Perhaps the gravest danger facing Christians was state control of the Church. Faithful to the Constantinian view, fourth-century emperors were prone to use the Christian establishment as an instrument to advance the interests of the state and to interfere in religious affairs to bend developments to political ends. In brief, the advance of Christianity to a central position in late classical society threatened to deprive the movement of its uniqueness, its zeal, and its sense of mission. The Christian com-

munity of the fourth century proved capable of responding to these challenges, of "reforming" itself to meet the realities of the time. This early "reformation" made it a different institution from what it had been in the second and third centuries (a transformation that later Christians often lamented), but it also strengthened the Christian world.

One response to the problems associated with discipline and the intrusion of pagan influences into Christian worship was the strengthening of clerical authority in the Church. There was a considerable increase in the powers of the clergy, especially the bishops, over individual churches. The increasing powers were used to define more rigorously the Christian way of behavior and mode of worship and to compel Christians to obey the rapidly evolving Christian "law." In simple terms, an authoritarian power structure was rapidly taking shape. A major beneficiary of this new power structure was the bishop of Rome. We previously noted that by the end of the third century the successors of St. Peter had begun to exercise considerable spiritual influence over the Christian world. During the fourth century the Christian emperors showered wealth on the popes and relied on them repeatedly to formulate orthodox dogma which the emperors hoped to impose on the whole empire as a means of combating the divisive heresies of the age. The popes responded by asserting their authority more positively and by actively involving themselves in numerous situations where a statement of doctrine or a decision imposing discipline was needed.

During the fourth century Christianity was also able to recapture its spiritual vision. This feat was the work of a new breed of Christian men who called themselves "athletes of Christ"—the *monks*. *Monasticism* was born in the late third and early fourth century in the bosom of the Christian world. It constituted a response to worldliness, moral laxness, and wealth. It originated in the deserts of Egypt, to which pious men fled to seek perfection through prayer and mortifi-

The sixth-century church of S. Apollinare in Classe in Ravenna is a basilica, an adaptation of a Roman architectural style for Christian use. The heavy walls of the central hall (nave) are supported by columns, and the small, high windows of the nave are cut above the roof of the side aisles. Although the exterior is completely unadorned, the interior shimmers with the light and color of marble surfaces and glittering mosaics. *Photo: G. E. Kidder Smith*

cation of the flesh. These men were inspired by Jesus' command to all those who would be saved to leave all worldly things behind and sacrifice themselves for him. The spiritual heroics of the desert fathers, exemplified by St. Anthony, electrified the Christian world. Soon the individualistic hermits began to gather into communities and accept rules which defined the spiritual exercises to be followed in achieving perfection, thus creating the first monasteries. Such rules were defined by St. Pachomius in Egypt and St. Basil in Asia Minor. By A.D. 400, monasticism had

spread over much of the Roman world, and had created a new model of the ideal Christian. Few men were willing or able to follow the way of the "athletes of Christ," but their presence in society was a dramatic reminder of the ancient Christian suspicion of the world and its corrupting influences.

In the face of state control over religious life, many fourth-century clergy began to resist and to back their resistance by articulating statements which sought to define the limits of imperial authority and religious freedom. To recount the full story of this development would involve us too deeply in the details of fourth-century political history. It is enough to note that the many individual cases of defiance of imperial authority added up to a growing conviction that the community of Christians was a separate society that had its own function and must make its own decisions; some were even beginning to argue that the Christian society was more important than secular society and therefore must be supreme. As the concept of the independence of the Church took shape, it raised a related issue—that of the governance of Christian society. This issue gave increased impetus to the problem of where ultimate authority in the Church lay. More and more, many Christians agreed that the bishop of Rome, Peter's successor, was the spiritual leader of the Christian world.

Perhaps the most significant success of the Christian community was its assumption of cultural leadership in the Roman world. The intellectual and artistic vitality of the Christians in this era was in part a response to continued pagan attacks, in part a response to disagreements within the Christian world, and in part an outburst of creative energy to meet the needs of Christian worship and education. Church building provided one of the chief outlets for the talents of architects, sculptors, and painters, who showed great creative powers in developing new modes of conveying the Christian message and in appropriating the classical artistic tradition for Christian purposes. Some of the most inspired poetry of the age flowed from the pens of Christians, who again showed remarkable powers of turning the Greek and Latin languages and the traditional litarary forms to new uses. But the jewel of the period was the theological writing of a remarkable group of intellectuals called the church fathers. The chief fathers —especially the Greeks Athanasius, Basil, Gregory of Nyssa, Gregory Nazianzus—deserve lengthy discussions for their individual achievements. Collectively, they represent a group of men educated in the classical tradition who turned their great talents to the

definition and explication of Christian belief. The fruit of their labors was a massive body of literature destined to provide intellectual guidelines for centuries to come. Beginning with a deep faith grounded in the message of the Scriptures, these fathers borrowed boldly and creatively from the content and methods of Greco-Roman philosophy to build a consistent, logical, articulate statement of Christian belief. In the process they literally redefined human values and reoriented the end of human existence toward the service of God. They effected a massive intellectual revolution which overpowered the Greco-Roman world view. No representative of the pagan tradition appeared to stay their triumph, to match their intellectual vigor, their zeal, their persuasiveness, or their confidence.

A description of one of their number especially important in Western thought will illustrate the role of the church fathers. He is St. Augustine (354–430), the bishop of Hippo in North Africa. Despite his many duties, Augustine produced an immense body of theological writing. Two of his works are especially significant. His *Confessions* recounts the spiritual pilgrimage of an enlightened man through most of the philosophical systems and religions of the ancient world to Christianity as the only satisfying response to spiritual life. The work demonstrates not only the failure of Greco-Roman philosophy and religion, but contains a powerful argument for faith as the only adequate response to life. Even more influential was his *City of God*, written to answer pagan charges that the Visigothic sack of Rome in 410 succeeded because the gods were angry at the Romans for becoming Christians. Augustine sought to demonstrate that this catastrophe was only a step in the unfolding of God's plan for the universe. God, he said, had ordained two cities, that of God and that of men. The true City of God exists only in the other world; membership will be awarded to men who serve the true faith on earth. In this world is the sinful City of Men, of which the Roman Empire was a part. The coming of Christ had established an earthly embodiment of the City of God in the form of the Christian Church. Rome must now pass away so that men could give their allegiance to the more perfect society. Not despair, but joy should greet the fall of Rome, since that event was a preordained step toward a better world planned by the will of God. Almost immediately, Augustine's interpretation of the cosmos and of history replaced the several world views offered by classical philosophers.

Others worked in more practical ways to supplement Augustine's effort to Christianize culture. For example, St. Ambrose (ca. 340–397), bishop of Milan, set forth the basic principles of Christian morality in a powerfully persuasive manner. St. Jerome employed his learning to produce a Latin translation of the Bible called the Vulgate, which ensured that Latin would survive as the language of the Church and as a link to classical civilization.

It was armed with this vitality that the Christian community faced the Germanic invasions and the fall of the imperial government. The Church survived this ordeal amazingly well and emerged from it the most potent force in society, especially in the West. Its basic organization remained almost intact; in many parts of the West, bishops replaced imperial officials as keepers of order, administrators of justice, and caretakers of the unfortunate. Often they remained the only protectors of the stricken cities. Their role is well illustrated in the city of Rome. Pope Leo I (440–461), for example, not only exerted a strong role as spiritual leader of the Christian world, but also served as the virtual governor of the city of Rome and as a forceful diplomat defending Rome against the attacks of the Vandals and the Huns. By 500 most of the Germans had been converted to Christianity, a development that gave them a powerful common bond with the Roman population. The Germanic kings had begun to lend their support to the Church, to favor it with gifts, and to lean on it for assistance in their efforts to rule. As a result, the role of the Church in political, social, and economic life expanded rapidly. As the focus of life shifted toward rural centers, the Church followed and made considerable progress in incorporating the heretofore neglected peasantry into Christian society. As cultural life collapsed, the monasteries provided havens for study amid spreading barbarism. By 500, as civilized men surveyed the wreckage of the era of the invasions, the Church loomed as a pillar of order, stability, and strength. At least in the West, it had fallen heir to the leadership of society.

Suggested Reading

Political, Economic, and Social Developments. The major developments marking the reforms of Diocletian and Constantine and subsequent history are adequately covered in the general works cited in Chapter 13. Some special problems might warrant attention. The chief one is the issue of the conversion of Constantine, which has produced a great deal of literature. A classic on the subject is ****Jacob Burckhardt, *The Age of Constantine the Great*, trans. M. Hadas (Anchor), which plays up the political calculations prompting Con- stantine. More recent discussions include ****A. H. M. Jones, *Constantine and the Conversion of Europe* (Collier); A. Alföldi, *The Conversion of Constantine and Pagan Rome* (1948); and N. H. Baynes, *Constantine the Great and the Christian Church* (1930). A stimulating discussion of the sometimes forgotten power of paganism in the fourth century is A. Momigliano, ed., *Conflict Between Paganism and Christianity in the Fourth Century* (1963). **Samuel Dill, *Roman Society in the Last Century of the Western Empire* (Meridian), presents an excellent picture of fifth-century society.

Church History. The stirring events in fourth- and fifth-century church history are fully covered in the major histories cited in Chapter 13; especially recommended are the histories by Daniélou and Marrou, Lietzmann, Lebreton and Zeiller, and Chadwick. Two books by H. von Campenhausen, *The Fathers of the Greek Church*, trans. S. Godman (1959), and *The Fathers of the Latin Church*, trans. M. Hoffmann (1964), supply a remarkably clear picture of the thought of the patristic age. The role of the Latin fathers as transmitters of a cultural heritage to the barbarian world is developed by **E. K. Rand, *Founders of the Middle Ages* (Dover). The origins of monasticism are colorfully presented in D. J. Chitty, *The Desert a City* (1966); and **Helen Waddell, *The Desert Fathers* (Ann Arbor). C. R. Morey, *Early Christian Art* (2nd ed., 1953), provides an understanding of the way in which Christian art developed.

The Germans. The nature of early Germanic culture is well presented by **Francis Owen, *The Germanic People* (Collier); and E. A. Thompson, *The Early Germans* (1965). Professor Thompson has provided a closer look at a particular Germanic nation in his *The Visigoths in the Time of Ulfilas* (1966). The Huns and their society are colorfully described by **C. D. Gordon, *The Age of Attila: Fifth-century Byzantium and the Barbarians* (Ann Arbor); and E. A. Thompson, *A History of Attila and the Huns* (1948). **J. B. Bury, *The Invasion of Europe by the Barbarians* (Norton), is adequate on the subject, but not as up to date as more recent works in French and German.

Biographies. Helpful in throwing light on the nature of this age are the following biographies: J. Steinman, *St. Jerome and His Times*, trans. R. Matthews (1959); Peter Brown, *Augustine of Hippo: A Biography* (1967); **Frederik van der Meer, *Augustine the Bishop: The Life and Work of a Father of the Church* (Harper Torchbook); **Henri Marrou, *Augustine and His Influence Through the Ages* (Harper Torchbook); F. H. Dudden, *The Life and Times of St. Ambrose* (2 vols., 1935).

Sources. A basic work on the early Germans is the *Germania* of the second-century Roman historian Tacitus; a good version of this often-edited work is **Tacitus, *On Britain and Germany*, trans. H. Mattingly (Penguin). For a student with patience and imagination, there is a great store of information about late Roman society in the Roman law codes; see especially *Theodosian Code*, trans. Clyde Pharr *et al.* (1952). A revealing picture of fifth-century society in the West is provided by Sidonius Apollinaris, *Letters*, trans. O. M. Dalton (2 vols., 1915); and by Salvian, *On the Governance of God*, trans. E. M. Sanford (1930). The vast body of writing by the church fathers is well worth investigating. Much of it is available in good translations in two recently initiated series: *Ancient Christian Writers*, ed. Johannes Quasten and Joseph C. Plumpe (1946ff); and *The Fathers of the Church*, ed. R. J. Defarri *et al.* (1947ff). Two works by St. Augustine ought to be studied to get the basic sense of patristic thought: **Confessions*, trans. E. B. Pusey (Modern Library); and **City of God*, trans. Marcus Dodds (2 vols., Hafner Library of Christian Classics). A work reflecting the Augustinian concept of history is Orosius, *Against the Pagans*, trans. R. J. Defarri (1964). The life of St. Anthony, the founder of monasticism, helps to understand the spirit animating that movement and its impact on Christian society; see Athanasius, *The Life of St. Anthony*, trans. Robert T. Meyer (*Ancient Christian Writers*, No. 10, 1950).

RETROSPECT At some risk of raising objections on a much-disputed question, we can conclude that it was to the years between the deposition of the last Roman emperor in the West (A.D. 476) and the capture of Italy by the Ostrogoths (A.D. 493) that we can assign the end of Greco-Roman civilization. Its descent from the splendid days of the second century had been rapid. The Romans had created a magnificent political order which had brought peace, well-being, and concord to some 50 million people. Why had it not lasted? Within that community an enlightened, sophisticated, esthetically pleasing culture had spread to supply men with a sense of direction, a set of values, and occasion for pleasure. Why was it not sufficient? Any answer to these questions is apt to convince the reader that he has been witness to a great tragedy—almost Greek in character—to be lamented still as it was by some men of the time.

But was the collapse of classical civilization a tragedy? On reflection, we might conclude that Greco-Roman civilization had become a prison for the human spirit by the third and fourth centuries. Autocratic government, regimented economy, and militarized society may have brought peace and order and security, but the price was heavy. The traditional cultural values seemed to be empty forms from which flowed no inspiration capable of breeding new thought or fresh expression.

The world had become filled with parrots endlessly repeating meaningless cant—but with little conviction. The power that came from an effective political system, from a sound economy, and from a sophisticated culture was increasingly monopolized by a few and abused to exploit the many; the aristocratic quality once so productive in the classical world had become a cruel joke.

The emergence of the Germanic barbarians as a potent force in society may from one perspective have been destructive, but from another, their presence infused society with an element of vitality. Here were fresh doers, learners, experimenters. The rapid rise of Christianity accentuated modes of thought and morality that seemed to lack the sophistication of the concepts governing classical civilization. Again, however, Christianity represented a fresh breeze in the Greco-Roman prison, a new vision of man and his destiny that provided a sense of direction and a reason for acting. The barbarians and the Christians held the key to the future. The promise of man did not die with Greco-Roman civilization.

Moreover, to speak of the fall of that civilization is to utter only a partial truth. When the Roman Empire collapsed, it left behind monu-

243

ments that would serve as guides to its heirs—a magnificent literature, a great art, model forms of government, a legal system, economic institutions and techniques, moral precepts, philosophical ideals, scientific knowledge, and countless other achievements. In a sense, Greece and Rome did not really die. Little that has happened in the Western world since 476 or 493 makes much sense outside its Greco-Roman background. We are all children of the classical world.

Part Four

The Early Middle Ages, 500–1000

Struggle Toward a New Order

The fall of the Roman Empire ended the political, economic, and cultural unity of the Mediterranean world. During the centuries that followed Rome's fall, three new civilizations emerged, each absorbing a part of the Roman world and each extending beyond its boundaries into "new" territory. One of these, the Byzantine, had its center at Constantinople, and continued the Greco-Roman tradition almost unchanged. Byzantine civilization exerted its chief influence in Asia Minor, the Balkans, and European Russia. The second new civilization, the Muslim or Islamic, began in the Arabian Desert and spread eastward to India and westward across North Africa into Spain. The third new civilization was created by the Germanic invaders of the Roman Empire. Gaul and Italy formed its center, but its influence eventually reached into Germany, Great Britain, Scandinavia, Spain, and the western portions of the Slavic world.

The basic features of these three civilizations were fashioned during the five hundred years extending from about 500 to 1000. Because of the chaos and barbarism of the period, it has often been called a "dark age" and was in the past given only cursory attention by historians as an unfortunate hiatus in the story of Western civilization. In many ways it deserves this designation, for the birth pangs of the three new societies were often severe, marked by false starts, and accompanied by a variety of convulsions that spelled human misery. But these outward appearances must not veil the fact that seminal processes were at work in this age: new institutions and ideas that were to mold the modern world were appearing in each society. Equally deserving of notice are the differences that set the life styles of the Byzantine, Muslim, and Western European worlds apart.

The dynamism of this age came from various sources. In all three societies powerful vestiges of Greco-Roman civilization persisted to shape the essential features of the new civilizations. In two of them—the Muslim and the Western European worlds—new peoples supplied a leavening agent. But perhaps it was religion that furnished the chief animating force in this "dark age." Two new universal religions dominated the history of the period and provided the matrix within which old cultural values and new peoples interacted. Christianity finally achieved full power after a somewhat painful period of gestation, and became the motor force in the Byzantine Empire and in Germanic Western Europe. Islam, bursting suddenly on the world and becoming established almost immediately as a dominant force by its warlike Arab adherents, affected the destiny of a vast area reaching across southern Asia and North Africa from the Indus Valley to the Atlantic. A meaningful comprehension of the period consequently demands careful attention to the role of religion as a dynamic, creative force in shaping the character of civilizations.

Chapter 15 ❧ Heirs to the Roman Empire:

The Byzantine and Muslim Empires

The complex processes which brought the Roman Empire and classical civilization to an end left the East more affluent and better organized than the West, and the two successor civilizations that developed in this area long remained more powerful and more advanced than the Germanic West. The brief characterizations to which we are limited here are intended to provoke more intensive study, for the Byzantine and Muslim cultures each played a tremendous role in the history of the world.

1. BYZANTINE CIVILIZATION: ITS ORIGINS AND POLITICAL HISTORY UNTIL ABOUT 1100

Byzantine civilization originated in the eastern part of the old Roman Empire, where the established order escaped relatively unscathed from the forces of internal decay and the Germanic invasions. The reforms of Diocletian and Constantine, which led to the creation of an absolutist state, took root most deeply in this part of the empire. As a conse-

quence, the emperors who ruled in the East after the death of Theodosius in 395 were able to hold off the Germanic threat and to sustain the basic features of the late Roman imperial system even as the western provinces were being lost. After the deposition of the last western emperor in 476, the rulers in Constantinople continued to act as if they were masters of the old Roman world. They claimed suzerainty over the newly founded Germanic states by insisting that the empire had remained intact but was now ruled from the "second Rome" at Constantinople. In fact, during these centuries the main features of the old order did continue almost unaltered in the East.

However, by the sixth century there were signs of a transformation in the East. The emerging order has been designated as "Byzantine" civilization to distinguish it from its Greco-Roman predecessor. The watershed between the two worlds can perhaps be placed in the reign of Justinian (527–565), often called the last Roman emperor and the first Byzantine emperor. If this great ruler had

The mosque of the sultan Ahmed (the Blue Mosque) in Istanbul, built by the Turks after the fall of the Byzantine Empire, illustrates how the Byzantine style lived on in the Muslim synthesis of many ancient artistic traditions—classical Greek, Persian, Byzantine, and Arabic. *Photo: A. F. Kersting* been asked to describe himself, he would certainly have claimed to be a Roman emperor: His whole policy was aimed at fortifying and safeguarding the old order. But the end result of his efforts was further and irrevocable change.

Justinian's central concern was the restoration of the unity of the old empire. To this end, he set out to reestablish his authority over the Western provinces held by the Germans, an ambition that involved him in war for the greater part of his reign. However, the best that his armies could do was to recapture North Africa from the Vandals, Italy from the Ostrogoths, and a small strip of southeastern Spain from the Visigoths. Gaul, most of Spain, England, and the Danube provinces remained beyond his reach. More significant than his partial successes, however, was the lesson that had to be learned from them. Justinian's western policy could be carried out only by leaving the eastern frontiers exposed. And the Sassanid Persians took full advantage of this situation to attack Syria and Palestine and to threaten disaster there. By the end of Justinian's reign, it was clear that imperial forces and resources must be concentrated in the East to hold the areas crucial to

the survival of the empire; the Germanic West would have to be abandoned. And the emperors in Constantinople would have to be content with a reduced domain confined to the East.

Concurrent with this historic decision, other developments emphasized the fact that a new pattern of life was emerging in the territory ruled from Constantinople. Justinian took important steps to perfect the system of absolutist, divine right monarchy that had its origins in the reforms of Diocletian and Constantine. His chief effort in this direction was the codification of the Roman law. During his reign he commissioned a corps of legal experts to pull together into systematic form the long tradition of Roman legal development. The result was the *Corpus juris civilis* or Code, one of the great monuments of legal science and a work destined to exert considerable influence on the development of law in the future. In the context of Justinian's own age, the codification of Roman law was important because the Code provided legal sanction for a highly centralized, absolutist form of government which stood in sharp contrast to other contemporary systems of government, especially those in the Germanic West. Thus the eastern Roman or Byzantine world began to stand apart because of its unique political system.

Religious policies were also changing. As we have seen, it was already implicit in the late empire that the state assumed the right to control the Christian religious establishment. Justinian brought this trend to completion by claiming that he as emperor was the religious as well as the political head of society. This policy was articulated chiefly in an effort to end the violent dogmatic quarrels raging in the eastern Christian world. By

A gold medallion struck around 534 to commemorate his early victories shows Justinian the triumphant emperor. Cabinet des Médailles, Bibliothèque Nationale. *Photo: Jean Roubier*

issuing edicts defining orthodox doctrine that would be acceptable to all parties, Justinian laid the foundations for a Byzantine Church whose organization, membership, and doctrines were confined to the boundaries of the Byzantine Empire and whose leader was the secular emperor.

Justinian's reign was also the time of the birth of a distinctive Byzantine culture that was oriented primarily toward the ancient Hellenic tradition. Although Christian values played a prominent role as the matrix channeling interests toward the Hellenic past, Byzantine culture was not a monopoly of the Church; it had deep roots in a sophisticated lay society. In its artistic aspect the culture taking shape in Justinian's day was marked by a merging of Greco-Roman styles with influences from the Near East, especially from Persia. The great symbol of this new culture was the magnificent church of Santa Sophia built by Justinian in Constantinople, a monument characterized by a marvelously impressive blending of Greco-Roman and Near Eastern building and decorative styles.

Byzantine political history from the reign of Justinian until the First Crusade (1095) would fill a thick volume with a rich panorama of wars, intrigues, intricate diplomacy, and great leaders. We can sketch only its simplest outlines. One theme dominates that history: the desperate military and diplomatic struggles of the Byzantine state to survive a succession of attacks from beyond its frontiers. These assaults reduced the size of the Byzantine state and modified the structure of Byzantine society so as to accentuate its uniqueness among its neighbors.

Hardly was Justinian dead when the first blow was struck. In 568 the Lombards, a Germanic nation, invaded Italy and seized a considerable portion of the peninsula, leaving only Venice, a corridor of land from Rome to Ravenna, and the southern portion of the peninsula under Byzantine control. Little could be done to stop this assault because the Byzantine Empire was facing a greater menace

elsewhere. Late in the sixth century the Sassanids mounted their greatest offensive in the East, succeeded in seizing Syria, Palestine, and Egypt, and advanced through Asia Minor to Constantinople. At the same time the Avars, an Asiatic people who established a state composed largely of Slavs north of the Danube, moved into the Balkans and toward Constantinople itself. For a moment in the first years of the seventh century it appeared that the empire would perish between the Persian-Avar pincers. But a savior appeared in the person of Heraclius (610–641), who miraculously regrouped Byzantine strength and flung back the enemies in a war of liberation which permanently weakened both Persians and Avars.

The dynasty of Heraclius soon had to face an even greater challenge in the form of the rampant Arabs, whose rise to power we shall trace later. During the last half of the seventh century the Arabs swept away Byzantine power in Syria, Palestine, Egypt, and North Africa. By the early years of the eighth century they occupied most of Asia Minor, and in 717–718 they placed Constantinople under siege. Again a savior appeared in the person of Leo III the Isaurian (717–741), who rescued the capital and succeeded eventually in liberating Asia Minor. However, the eastern provinces were permanently lost and the Byzantine Empire was reduced in size to its basic shape: a state comprising Asia Minor and the Greek peninsula.

Despite Leo III's remarkable victories, the power of the Isaurian dynasty was soon weakened, chiefly as a consequence of its religious policy, which involved the empire in the iconoclastic quarrel (see p. 253). While the Isaurians struggled with internal crisis, the Franks seriously undermined the Byzantine position in Italy, as we shall see later. And in 800 the Frankish ruler Charlemagne assumed to himself—with the blessing of the bishop of Rome—the title of emperor, a direct challenge to the universalist claims of the heirs to the imperial title, the emperors in Constantinople.

In the ninth century the Byzantine Empire was again threatened by the emergence of the Bulgar state in the Balkans. And again the threat of foreign invaders produced a series of strong rulers, this time the Macedonian dynasty (867–1057). Not only did the Macedonians throw back the Bulgars, but under the greatest Macedonian, Basil II the Bulgar Slayer (976–1025), the Bulgar state was destroyed and Byzantine influence was extended far into the Balkan area and into Russia. Under the Macedonian dynasty Byzantine power was also greatly increased in the East at the expense of the Muslim world. This power reached its acme in the late tenth century, although Byzantium never recovered the territory it had ruled under Justinian.

By the eleventh century the Byzantine state began to suffer decline due in part to internal trouble and in part to still another assault from the outside, this time mounted by the Seljuk Turks, who were joined in attacking Byzantium by the emerging Italian city-states and by the Normans. We must return to that story again, because to save the empire this time, the emperors appealed to the West. This appeal was instrumental in launching the crusades and marked a fateful day in Byzantine history. The empire that had for many centuries withstood repeated attacks which trimmed away its territory and placed tremendous strain on its populace was now beginning to consume the resources that had permitted it to survive and that constituted the essential features of Byzantine civilization.

2. BYZANTINE CIVILIZATION: POLITICAL, ECONOMIC, RELIGIOUS, AND CULTURAL LIFE

The ability of the Byzantine Empire to resist these blows stemmed chiefly from the strength of its government, from its vast economic resources, and from the devotion of its people. The Byzantine government was an absolute monarchy. The emperor in theory possessed complete power to do what he wished with his subjects. At his court in Constantinople, he lived amid splendor and ritual that rivaled those of the great rulers of the ancient Near East. He commanded a horde of civil servants, to each of whom was assigned a specialized function, a rank, and a salary. The empire was divided into a number of districts, called *themes*, where officials representing the emperor recruited troops, collected taxes, maintained order, judged cases, and enforced imperial edicts.

The emperor's power was buttressed by a well-organized army and navy, an efficient system of taxation, and a responsive ecclesiastical establishment. Of crucial importance was the army. During the crises brought on by Persian and then Arab attacks from the East, the imperial government abandoned the long tradition of relying on barbarian soldiers and developed a system of military recruitment that depended on the peasants of Asia Minor. The small farmers of this area were awarded plots of land in return for military service. Command of these peasant-soldiers was entrusted to aristocrats from the same area. For centuries these tough, loyal soldiers stood heroically against repeated attacks on the Byzantine state.

In a real sense, this system of government was a continuation of that of the late Roman imperial regime. The Byzantine emperor was even stronger than the Roman emperors had been, since the Byzantine imperial office had stronger religious sanction. The emperor was looked upon as an agent of God, given his office so that he might maintain peace and order among the Christian population of his state. On many occasions, the efficient operation of this government was impeded by ambitious generals, greedy bureaucrats, dissatisfied churchmen, scheming empresses and courtiers, self-centered landowners, and even the mobs of Constantinople. However, none of them ever completely paralyzed the imperial government; it always had the ability to keep order and defend the empire.

Byzantine economic strength played an

equally vital role in the long struggle for survival. The agricultural system formed the backbone of the Byzantine economy. Large estates, farmed by tenants, existed throughout the empire, but the chief strength of the agricultural system rested with small landowners who were carefully protected by the imperial government. The state took a vital interest in keeping agricultural production at a high level so that taxes could be collected from the farmers, whether large or small, landowner or tenant. Aside from agriculture, the empire enjoyed a tremendous commercial and industrial activity, and for many centuries Constantinople was the world's chief trading and industrial center. Goods entered her markets from all directions, while her shops produced a variety of high-quality products in demand throughout the Mediterranean world. All commerce and industry were rigidly controlled by the state. Wages, prices, and profits were carefully fixed. Artisans and traders were compelled to remain in their trades and hand them on to their sons. The imperial government itself monopolized many lucrative businesses.

A strong government and a prosperous economy do not, however, fully explain the vitality of the Byzantine Empire. Byzantine life was strongly affected by Christianity, which helped to shape nearly every institution and activity. Perhaps most important, Christianity provided the prime bond linking the populace to the imperial regime and thus supplied the basis for the remarkable loyalty of the imperial subjects. In the long run, Constantine had been right: In many important ways, a Christian of the Byzantine Empire was like a Christian anywhere, holding to the same basic beliefs and conducting himself by the same standards of conduct. However, with the passage of time, Byzantine Christianity underwent unique developments that gave rise to what is now called the Greek Orthodox Church.

The Greek Orthodox Church was always more completely allied with and subjected to the state than the church in the West. The emperor was accepted as the divinely ordained director of both spiritual and secular life. As a result of this feature of religious life, called *caesaropapism*, the emperor appointed clergymen, defined dogma, settled theological disputes, imposed discipline on both clergy and laymen, and used the wealth of the Church to serve the purposes of the state. Byzantine religious life was also distinguished by its intense interest in questions of dogma. Quarrels over such problems as the nature of Christ and his relationship to God aroused strong feelings in everyone from the most learned monk to the lowliest artisan and peasant and led to serious political crises on more than one occasion. Greek Orthodox religion placed a tremendous emphasis on rituals, and its adherents felt a deep trust in the efficacy of these rites to ensure the salvation of their souls and to bring God's blessings in earthly affairs. On occasion, attempts were made to curb this tendency. The chief such effort was the iconoclastic struggle that raged from 725 until 843. This quarrel began when Emperor Leo III, backed by part of the clergy, attempted to remove all visual representations (icons) of the deity from the churches and the ritual. The iconoclasts (icon breakers) insisted that Christians were worshipping the statues instead of God and thus were guilty of idolatry. But these "puritans" ultimately failed, and in 843 the icons were restored. From then on, an elaborate ritualism characterized religious life in the Byzantine Empire. A prominent place was also given to mysticism and emotionalism, that is, to those kinds of religious experiences in which believers were convinced that they could reach and commune directly with God. Monasteries were the chief centers of this type of religious life, and a number of monks exercised a powerful influence over every aspect of Byzantine life.

These unique characteristics of the religious establishment emerging in the Byzantine Empire, added to equally unique developments in Western Europe shaping the Roman Catholic Church, led not surprisingly to a growing division in the Christian world. In part, these differences centered in dogma and ritual, but especially divisive was the ever more bitter quarrel over whether the pope in Rome was superior to or coequal with the patriarch of Constantinople as the spiritual head of the Christian world. With the establishment of the capital of the Late Roman Empire in Constantinople, the patriarch of that city enjoyed a rapid rise to prominence. By the end of the fourth century, the patriarchs were claiming an equal voice with the bishops of Rome in pronouncing the final word on matters of faith. This claim was stoutly maintained in succeeding centuries, usually with the support of the emperors, against the constantly expanding claims of the bishops of Rome to supremacy. The slow drift toward separation on this issue culminated in 1054, when pope and patriarch excommunicated each other, and created a schism that to this day has proved irreparable.

The schism between Rome and Constantinople was accentuated and given added significance by the success of the Greek Orthodox Church in missionary affairs. From almost the beginning of Byzantine history, Greek missionaries, strongly backed by the imperial government, began to penetrate the vast world of the Slavs in Central and Eastern Europe. Eventually, most of the Slavs in the Balkan Peninsula and in Russia were converted to Christianity. Although these converts were permitted to organize their own churches and to utilize native languages in their services, Byzantine religious practices, political ideas, and social concepts spread among them. A large portion of the Slavic world was therefore oriented toward Byzantium at a crucial point in the development of Slavic institutions and culture and thus was set apart from Western Europe in a way that created barriers which have not yet disappeared. The Iron Curtain was not entirely a creation of the twentieth century.

The Byzantine Empire itself gradually developed a unique cultural life. Often Byzantine accomplishments in this field have been overlooked, perhaps because Byzantine cultural activity was devoted chiefly to the preservation of the classical tradition, especially the Greek, and to the adaptation of that tradition to Christian teachings. A highly developed educational system based on the study of classical literature provided the chief avenue of contact with the past. It produced a large number of men, both laymen and ecclesiastics, who were conversant with the literary, scientific, and philosophical masterpieces of ancient Greece and the Hellenistic world. This educated group, often associated with the imperial court, the prime patron of cultural life, not only studied the classics, but also collected copies of them, commented on them, and wrote in imitation of them. Their efforts ensured the survival of the Greek classics and provided a source to which others could eventually turn to find examples of Greek literature and learning. For example, the cultural renaissance in fourteenth- and fifteenth-century Western Europe depended almost entirely on Byzantine sources for copies of Greek literature, science, and philosophy. Many centuries earlier, Muslim scholars had looked in the same direction. It is not an exaggeration to say that the works of Homer, Aristotle, Plato, the Greek dramatists, Herodotus, Thucydides, Galen, and Ptolemy might have been lost without the efforts of Byzantine men of learning. The all-pervasive influence of classical Greek models, however, tended to make Byzantine literature and thought imitative. Probably the most creative figures in Byzantine society were the theologians, whose incessant quarrels over dogma produced a huge volume of writing in which philosophical concepts from the classical tradition were applied to Christian teachings in an effort to define the true tenets of the faith. Byzantine historians, influenced by the models of Herodotus, Thucydides, and Polybius, also produced excellent works. The skill of these historians is illustrated by the work of Michael Psellus (1018–1079), a high official in the imperial regime who chronicled the exploits of the Macedonian emperors, and Anna Comnenus (1083–1148), the daughter of Emperor Alexius I, whose *Alexiad* colorfully describes the career of her illustrious father. The Byzantine poetic genius expressed itself most originally in hymns, some of which can still be heard in the liturgy of the Greek Orthodox Church.

Byzantine art demonstrated greater distinctiveness; it is perhaps the best mirror of the spirit of Byzantine culture. Architecture was the preeminent art of the Byzantine world. In its basic features, best illustrated in church building, it represents a fusion of Hellenistic and ancient Near Eastern traditions skillfully turned to Christian purposes. The style was formed during the fourth and fifth centuries in Egypt, Syria, and Asia Minor, and then was elevated to official status by Justinian's building program in sixth-century Constantinople. The great church of Santa Sophia, designed for Justinian by architects from Asia, was based on a floor plan derived from the Greco-Roman rectangular basilica upon which was imposed a great central dome after the Persian manner. The glory of this combination lies in the vast internal spaciousness it permits. The dome of Santa Sophia is more than 100 feet across and rises about 180 feet above the floor of the church. Although it rests on four great arches springing from four massive pillars that form the central square of the nave, the dome indeed seems "to hang by a golden chain from heaven," as a contemporary put it. Justinian, upon viewing the completed church, exclaimed: "I have outdone you, O Solomon." The architectural style represented by Santa Sophia was widely imitated, and in the course of time a variation of this style gained considerable popularity. The ground plan of this new style was based on the Greek cross with its four equal arms. Domes were built over the space created by each arm and over the space where the arms cross. The famous church of St. Mark in Venice is an example of this five-domed structure. Although their greatest genius was poured into religious buildings, Byzantine architects also built huge and splendid palaces,

most of which have unfortunately disappeared except for their foundations.

Byzantine architecture, for all its technical ingenuity in combining diverse traditions into an integrated style and for all its massiveness, is incomplete without its decor. The churches and palaces were immense frames for sumptuous decoration. Santa Sophia, for instance, was decorated with a brilliant array of precious metals, mosaics, paintings, jewels, and fine stone, so that its interior was a blaze of color. The techniques and themes of church decoration were derived from Greco-Roman and Near Eastern traditions, but the latter tended to exert an especially powerful influence. Particularly unique were Byzantine mosaics and frescoes, the best examples of which have survived in the churches built in Ravenna in Italy in the sixth century. The pictorial art of Byzantium centered primarily on portraying in mosaics and wall paintings the great chapters of the Christian epic; the walls of Byzantine churches are a kind of Holy Writ in pictures. In their efforts to express the essence of the Christian message, Byzantine artists made an immense contribution to the development and enrichment of Christian iconography. Their work was never basically concerned with a realistic portrayal of the world; rather they sought to use human, natural, and abstract forms to create a symbolism capable of evoking spiritual understanding. In their effort to achieve this end, color played a crucial role. It is impossible to describe in words the mystical effect of the color combinations achieved by the skillful utilization of stones, metals, jewels, and paints in the total setting of a single church.

Byzantine artists, however, did not concentrate all their talents on religious themes; Byzantium was noted for its skillful jewelers, goldsmiths, silversmiths, manuscript illuminators, and workers in almost all the other minor arts. In every kind of art, the same features predominated—the fusion of Greco-Roman and Oriental motifs and styles, the love of elaborate decoration and color, and the preoccupation with symbolism.

3. MUSLIM CIVILIZATION: ORIGIN AND EXPANSION

No less vital was the second civilization that emerged in the East. This was the Muslim civilization, originally the creation of the nomadic inhabitants of the Arabian Desert. Although in the ancient past the people of this desolate area had powerfully influenced the course of history (the Akkadians, the Assyrians, the Hebrews), no one living about 600 would have guessed that they were soon again to play a major role. Badly divided into numerous competing tribes, the desert dwellers (called Bedouins) lived a poverty-stricken nomadic life dependent upon pasturage of animals. Constantly on the move, always faced with starvation, and quick to take advantage of the weaknesses of others, the Bedouins under their tribal leaders (sheiks) were fiercely independent. Their nonliterary culture and their polytheistic religions, coupled with their simple political organization and backward economic life, made them seem barbaric by comparison with the advanced civilizations of the Byzantine and Sassanid empires that bordered on the Arabian Desert. Influences from these more advanced civilizations had penetrated the Arab world, especially the cities, which served chiefly as trading centers along the caravan routes that traversed the desert. The most important such city was Mecca, a flourishing trading hub and a religious center for many Bedouin tribes who came there annually to worship at the famous temple called the Kaaba. But for all its vitality and its contacts with the outside world, Mecca and its inhabitants seemed to offer little promise of transforming the desert-dwelling nomads into an international power.

Yet in little more than one generation, this is what happened. The catalyst was a religious prophet, Mohammed, who succeeded in galvanizing the Arab world into unity and in jolting it out of its isolation. Mohammed was born in Mecca about 570. Orphaned in his youth, he was brought up by an uncle for a career in trade as a camel driver. Eventually he entered the service of a rich widow whom he married, thereby ensuring himself a more respectable and leisured career. As a trader, Mohammed appears to have traveled abroad and to have been in constant contact with foreign merchants who came through Mecca. These associations probably gave him some familiarity with other cultures and aroused his interest in foreign religions. Despite the cloud of legend that veils his intellectual and spiritual development, there is reason to suspect that the decisive aspects of Mohammed's career were shaped less by these extraneous conditions of his life than by his own introspective, contemplative, brooding, ascetic spirit, which caused him to spend much of his time in prayer and meditation, often in the solitude of the desert.

When Mohammed was about forty, he suddenly made an amazing claim. He insisted that God—called *Allah* in Arabic—had spoken directly to him and had told him that he was Allah's prophet. From then on he dedicated himself to convincing others that Allah had shown him the way to righteousness and truth, and by the time of his death he had won enough converts to change the history of the Arabs and the world.

What did Allah reveal to his prophet? After Mohammed's death some of his associates compiled a book containing what was recorded or could be recalled of the prophet's revelations. This book, called the *Koran*, became the source of truth for Mohammed's followers and serves as the best guide to his teachings. His message was simple and in many ways not especially new to anyone except the Arabs. Many of his teachings were so closely related to Christian and Jewish thought that it is virtually certain Mohammed borrowed ideas from these well-established religions. Mohammed insisted that there was but one god, Allah; he demanded that his followers reject their worship of many gods for monotheism. He taught that Allah had revealed himself bit by bit down through the ages, the Jewish prophets and Jesus all being accepted as his spokesmen. However, Mohammed was the last and greatest prophet, superseding all others. Older religions were therefore inferior, and Mohammedanism was destined to conquer the world. Allah was pictured in the Koran as an almighty deity who required complete submission to his will. The religion is thus called *Islam*, which means "submission to God." Every true adherent of Islam, called a *Muslim*, must regulate his existence to abide completely by the will of Allah. Those who believed in Allah and obeyed his orders would gain a happy life after death, while the disobedient and the wicked would be damned forever.

To these simple articles of faith Mohammed added a list of duties required of all the faithful. All must pray five times daily while facing Mecca. All must give of their wealth to support the poor. Each Muslim must fast during one month of each year. And everyone must, if possible, make a pilgrimage to Mecca once in a lifetime. Mohammed also laid down strict rules regulating diet and marriage, prohibiting drinking and gambling, and demanding of each Muslim honesty, fair play, and respect for others. This code of conduct, strongly reminiscent of the ethical code enshrined in the Old Testament of the Hebrews, injected a strong ethical vein into the new religion. Each man was personally responsible to Allah for his conduct; Mohammed created no church, no clergymen, no sacraments to assist in gaining Allah's favor.

At first, the teachings of the new prophet fell on deaf ears in Mecca; several years of preaching netted only a few converts. In fact, Mohammed won many more enemies than followers. By 622 these foes forced him to flee to Yathrib (later renamed Medina, which means "city of the Prophet"), a city north of Mecca. This flight, called the *Hegira*, marked a turning point in the history of the new religion. Feeling himself spurned and convinced that the will of Allah had been defied by the Meccans, Mohammed began to shape a religious-political community dedicated to the punishment of sinners and to the spread of the true religion by force of arms. He molded his converts, mostly Arab nomads from Medina and its vicinity, into an armed political following, held together and inspired to obedience by the commands of the prophet. More and more Mohammed's revelations took the

Mohammed replacing the Black Stone of the Kaaba, the sacred building in Mecca to which all Muslims come at least once during their lifetime if they are able. Miniature from an Arabic manuscript. *Photo: Edinburgh University Library*

The Expansion of Islam

form of political and social legislation destined to create a holy nation of warriors. By 630 his following was strong enough to recapture Mecca, a feat that impressed many Arab tribes and caused them to join the prophet. During his last years Mohammed also turned his conquering force against other Arab tribes to compel them to join his community. When he died in 632, Mohammed was the leader of a large following of Arabs whose primitive tribalism had been overcome by their willingness to obey Allah and his prophet.

Mohammed's success in drawing together the Arab world was impressive enough, but even more astonishing developments were to

come. Almost immediately after his death, the new Arab "nation" burst out of Arabia and began a series of military conquests that affected most of the civilized world. During the first generation after Mohammed (that is, from 632 to 661), Arab armies won an amazing series of victories that destroyed the Persian Empire and wrested the prize provinces of Syria, Palestine, Egypt, and extensive areas of North Africa from the Byzantine Empire. Before the end of that period, Arab armies were probing India, and Arab sea power was developing to challenge Byzantine control of the Mediterranean. After a brief interlude during which internal problems over leadership of the Muslim community absorbed Arab energies, the advance resumed. During the latter part of the seventh century, all of North Africa was conquered, while Arab forces pushed into the Indus Valley and the outer reaches of China. An offensive was mounted in Asia Minor, and the seemingly irrepressible Arabs moved closer and closer to Constantinople. Before 700 they were in virtual control of the Mediterranean, a development which further threatened the Byzantine position. In 711 Arab forces crossed from Africa into Europe and quickly overran the Visigothic kingdom in Spain. From there they began to conduct raids into Gaul to threaten the Frankish kingdom. But the drive to expand was weakening by this time: In 717–718 Arab forces were defeated at Constantinople by Leo III and soon after were driven out of Asia Minor. In 732—exactly a century after Mohammed's death—the Frankish leader Charles Martel defeated them at the battle of Tours in Gaul and halted their further advance in Europe.

The conquest of this vast empire within a century represents one of the great military feats in all history. Such success must have convinced the Arab warriors that Allah was guiding their efforts, as Mohammed had promised. Other factors, of course, played a part in this remarkable expansion. For one thing, their foes were weak. The Sassanid Empire was exhausted from its long struggle with the Byzantines. Religious disaffection among the Christians in the eastern provinces of the Byzantine Empire caused the people there to welcome the Arabs as liberators freeing them from the religious tyranny of the emperors at Constantinople. As their armies advanced, the conquerors interfered little with local affairs, and thus made their overlordship easy to accept. The Arabs demonstrated great military prowess, and they were brilliantly led; their long training as desert warriors had paid off. Their enthusiasm for their cause was certainly also a factor. Mohammed had said to the faithful: "Fight and fear not; the gates of Paradise are under the shade of the swords." Their wars were thus holy wars and they fought in that spirit. Yet all these factors together do not quite account for the dramatic emergence of Arab power to world prominence. In a sense, that development seems almost a historical accident.

4. MUSLIM CIVILIZATION: POLITICAL, ECONOMIC, AND CULTURAL FEATURES

The rapid expansion of the Arabs of course had a profound effect on the Mediterranean world, for nearly a third of the old Roman Empire had been absorbed by the new power. First of all, the conquering Arabs, despite their limited experience, managed to establish a new political order to direct the destiny of the vast empire they had won by force of arms. Prior to his death Mohammed had made no provision for the future direction of his followers. His close associates therefore proceeded to pick one from among them to serve as *caliph*, or successor to the prophet. Although the role of the caliph was at this early date somewhat imprecise, from the beginning he did interpret and apply the law as revealed by the prophet. This function gave him vast authority over the political and religious activities of the faithful, and assured him immense power. Down to 661, the caliphs were drawn from the ranks of Mohammed's close associates; in 661, however, a military leader in the Arab army seized control and made the office of caliph hereditary. The dynasty he founded, known as the Omayyads, ruled until 750. Its center of power was located at Damascus in Syria. The Omayyads had a strong imperialistic bent; they insisted that Islam was the special religion of the Arabs and that the Arab mission was to conquer the world in the name of Allah. But they were also efficient and able administrators who realized that the task of ruling what the armies conquered demanded well-developed political institutions. Strongly influenced by Byzantine models, the Omayyads created a centralized court, a bureaucracy, an efficient tax system, and a strong army and navy. Under their guidance the office of caliph became more secularized and worldly, although it never lost its religious aspects.

In 750 the Omayyads were overthrown (except in Spain), and the caliphate fell into the hands of the Abbasids, who ruled until 1258. The accession of the Abbasids represented a basic shift in Muslim society. The new dynasty was much more cosmopolitan, and held that all Muslims, whether Arab or non-Arab, were equal. Their rise to power thus marked the end of Arab domination of the Muslim world. The Abbasids shifted their capital from Damascus to Bagdad on the Tigris River, close to the heart of the old Persian Empire. The population of the new capital was soon swelled by men of all races and backgrounds who came to serve the caliph as civil servants and soldiers, to trade in the capital of the Muslim world, or to engage in some cultural or educational pursuit. All that was needed to gain acceptance was adherence to the faith of Mohammed; and so it was elsewhere in the vast empire. In this new atmosphere the militancy which the Arabs represented was greatly diminished, and the energies of the Muslim world were turned inward to develop the potential of the vast empire it had conquered.

The Abbasid dynasty reached its peak in the late eighth and early ninth centuries. Its most famous caliph was Harun al-Rashid (reigned 786–809), immortalized in the *Arabian Nights*. The caliphs of this era ruled in the best style of Oriental despotism, using their governmental machinery and their religious authority to command the obedience of millions of subjects. By the end of the ninth century, Abbasid power began to decline. This weakening of the central government caused a rapid disintegration of the empire. The independent caliphs who established themselves in Spain, North Africa, Syria, and India soon fell to fighting each other. Seeking to protect itself against these rivals, the Abbasid family increasingly placed its trust in Seljuk Turkish mercenary soldiers, who by

1055 had become the real masters of Bagdad. These barbarians from Central Asia became another disruptive element in the Muslim political world. The Muslims were never so well-organized politically as the Romans and their successors, the Byzantines. Neither the Arabs nor the non-Arabs within the empire were capable of fashioning a stable, lasting political order.

The expansion of the Arabs promoted a significant economic revival. The key to this new prosperity was a network of trade routes stretching from Spain to India and China, over which materials and manufactured goods moved freely. Great cities like Cordoba in Spain, Damascus, Bagdad, and Alexandria, whose merchants and artisans were seldom restricted by Muslim governments, became centers of production. The wealth of the Muslim world at this time exceeded even that of the Byzantine Empire and far outstripped that of Western Europe, which still depended upon a backward agricultural economy.

However, neither the political nor the economic changes that accompanied the rise of the Muslim Empire were as significant in establishing the main features of Islamic civilization as were religious and cultural developments. The religion of Mohammed demonstrated an amazing power to win converts. Its success did not usually depend on force, since Arab conquerors seldom insisted that their subjects accept the new religion. At first, most Christians, Jews, Zoroastrians, and Hindus continued to worship as they had in the past. The conquerors demanded only that their non-Muslim subjects pay a special tax for the privilege of retaining their old religion and accept exclusion from government positions. As the years passed, however, most devotees of other religions were converted. Perhaps the tax penalty was too great a burden. Perhaps the exclusion from high positions was unbearable. But perhaps more significantly, Islam had universal appeal as a religion. In time, the overwhelming majority of men in the vast conquered area stretching from Spain to India became Muslims. There always remained important communities of non-Muslims, but they had little influence on the mainstream of life.

Islam itself tended to grow more complex from the ninth century onward as a result of the efforts of theologians and lawyers, who developed a rich body of literature in the form of commentaries on the Koran and on the pronouncements attributed to Mohammed other than those in the Koran. Their work resulted in an orthodox faith rather far removed from that first proclaimed by Mohammed to the Arabs; its adherents were called Sunnite Muslims and constituted the vast majority in the Islamic world. But there were dissenters and heretics, the chief of which were the Shi'ites, who insisted that the true faith was preserved by the blood descendants of Mohammed. Despite these rifts, Islam provided the prime basis for unity in the Muslim world. Its members believed in one God, worshiped in the same fashion, and observed a single moral code. Political divisions might fragment that community at one level, but nothing ever succeeded in destroying the religious ties that held the "sons of Allah" together. Even to this day, Islamic religious unity is a prime factor in world affairs.

Muslim expansion also brought about a tremendous cultural revival and resulted in a cultural unification of the empire. The conquests of the Arabs brought together in a single society nearly all the world's chief cultural traditions: Greco-Roman, Persian, Mesopotamian, Egyptian, Germanic, Jewish, Indian, and Arabic. The semibarbaric Arab conquerors took these diverse traditions and molded out of them a new culture which retained aspects of the old, but which as a synthesis had its own distinct characteristics. The religious convictions of the Muslims again supplied the unifying force. Since Mohammed had forbidden the translation of the Koran into any other language, all Muslims had to learn Arabic; and since the Koran contained the final truth, it was necessary to reconcile the knowledge of older cultures with

Muslim religious teachings. The labors devoted to these tasks resulted in a brilliant outburst of writing and scholarship, for practically all the literature of the empire's many peoples was translated into Arabic. The Muslims could rightly claim to be the cultural heirs of all the ages.

Many historians would agree that the greatest Muslim achievements were in philosophy and science. Muslim philosophers devoted their efforts chiefly to the task of reconciling Greek philosophy with the teachings of the Koran. When the philosophical writings of the Greeks were translated into Arabic, huge commentaries were composed showing how the principles of Greek philosophy explained and enlarged upon the teachings of the Koran. At the same time, philosophers wrestled with the contradictions inherent in the Greek tradition, especially those separating the Platonic and Aristotelian traditions. Their efforts are closely akin to those of the scholastic philosophers of medieval Western Europe. In fact, the speculations of the greatest Muslim thinkers, Avicenna (980–1037) and the Spanish Ibn Rushd (1126–1198), known in the West as Averroës, exercised a direct influence on Western scholasticism.

In science, the Muslim efforts were even more spectacular. Huge collections of scientific information from Greek, Indian, Persian, Mesopotamian, and Egyptian sources were compiled. As a result, Muslim scientists possessed a larger body of reliable knowledge than did scientists anywhere in the world until modern times. And they made this knowledge available to a large circle of educated men by putting it into Arabic, the language of the whole Muslim world. Moreover, Muslim scientists made many original contributions and were amazingly successful in finding practical applications for their new knowledge.

In mathematics, the Indian numerical system was adopted and the use of the zero was added to create the Arabic system of numbers which is used almost universally today. A Muslim, al Khwarizmi (ca. 780–850), combined

Greek and Indian mathematical ideas to create algebra. Astronomy advanced tremendously as a result of joining the knowledge of Greeks such as Ptolemy with that of Persian and Mesopotamian astronomers. The works of great medical writers like al Razi (865–925) and the philosopher Avicenna represent compilations from numerous sources. Muslim doctors studied diseases in hospitals, dissected bodies, and experimented with drugs, thereby adding tremendously to the existing body of medical knowledge. Astronomers, geographers, and physicists followed the same course.

Muslim literature also demonstrated great vigor and variety. The colorful, imaginative, emotional literature is best exemplified by the poetry of Omar Khayyám and the fascinating stories of the *Arabian Nights*. The latter work is especially typical of Muslim literature because it consists of stories collected from nearly all the peoples over whom the Arabs ruled.

Like most of the rest of Islamic culture, Muslim art reflects a creative synthesis of many traditions. The architectural talents of the Muslims were devoted chiefly to the building of mosques and palaces. The mosques were primarily places where individuals could go to render their obligation of daily prayer, not centers of community worship. They were basically simple structures whose inner space was often divided by rows of graceful columns creating aisles covered by arches. As a rule, the mosques were covered by domes similar to those of Byzantine churches, above which rose graceful towers (minarets) from which the call to prayer was issued. Many mosques made effective use of the horseshoe arch to create doorways, windows, and aisles. Before each mosque was an open court containing a purification fountain and surrounded by a covered passageway. In spite of this simplicity, the greatest mosques, such as those at Damascus and Cordoba, are impressive, beautiful structures marked by delicacy and grace. Surviving palaces, such as the Alcazar at Seville and the Alhambra at Granada, reflect the same architectural style as the mosques, although they are much more elaborate.

Most Muslim buildings are rather bare on the outside, but brilliantly decorated inside, especially with paintings and mosaics. Since the use of human and animal forms in religious art was prohibited lest the faithful be tempted to compromise their monotheism, Muslim decorative arts accentuated floral designs and geometric patterns (arabesques), all done in splendid colors and to magically beautiful effect. Muslim artistry also manifested itself with special brilliance in the minor arts. Muslim fabrics, tapestries, carpets, leather work, metal work, weapons, and jewelry were the most prized articles in the medieval world, due in large part to their exquisite worksmanship.

Muslim civilization reached its apogee in the ninth and tenth centuries. Thereafter it began to suffer a variety of internal dislocations which sapped its energies and permitted outsiders to take advantage of it. We shall return to these problems in another connection, especially as they provided an opening for Western European assaults on the Muslim world during the crusades. Despite the afflictions besetting Muslim society after the eleventh century, the immense achievements of the preceding centuries ensured Muslim civilization a permanent place in the history of human accomplishment.

5. WESTERN EUROPE AND HER EASTERN NEIGHBORS

The brilliance and vitality of the Byzantine and Muslim civilizations received little competition from the Germanic-Roman portion of the old Roman Empire, for Western Europe lagged far behind them until at least the twelfth century. Before continuing with the history of the West, let us take a look at the nature of the relationship between the West and her more mature neighbors, a theme that we shall return to in more detail in succeeding chapters.

Outwardly, considerable hostility marked this relationship. During most of the early Middle Ages, both the Byzantine Empire and the Muslim world posed threats to the West, although the Muslim danger was by far the greater. Religious and linguistic differences promoted discord. Christians in the West, who looked upon the Muslims as heathens, believed any atrocity story told about them. And the Byzantine Christians were distrusted almost as much.

One might suspect that because of this hostility, the West was cut off from the Byzantines and Muslims and little influenced by them. Over the gulf, however, passed influences that played a crucial role in shaping the culture emerging in Western Europe during the dark centuries that followed the fall of Rome. From both Byzantines and Muslims, the Western Europeans derived an extensive body of technical knowledge, especially for manufacturing and commercial practices. Almost all the luxury items that added to the refinement of life in Western Europe during the Middle Ages were introduced from one or the other of the civilizations of the Near East.

Western Europe inherited Roman law from the Byzantine Empire in the form of Justinian's Code. The first distinctive architectural style to develop in the West in the Middle Ages (the Romanesque) developed from Byzantine models, as did the sculpture and painting styles used to decorate churches built in the Romanesque style. Throughout the Middle Ages and into the Renaissance, Western European scholars learned about the splendid culture of ancient Greece from those who played a vital role in preserving it in Constantinople. Muslim cultural influences were nearly as strong in medieval Europe. A large body of philosophical and scientific knowledge came to Western Europe as a result of the meeting of Christians and Muslims in Spain. This knowledge provided the chief leaven in the resurgence of Western European culture in the twelfth and thirteenth centuries. Finally, European literature received a priceless heritage in the love poetry of the Muslims.

In short, during these centuries no aspect of Western European civilization escaped the subtle influence of the East. It is a debt often forgotten today, when the West has so far materially outstripped the peoples of the Near East.

Suggested Reading

Overview. There are several broad surveys of the era 500 to 1000 that will provide good introductions to the period: **R. E. Sullivan, *Heirs of the Roman Empire* (Cornell), stressing the unique features of the new civilizations; **H. St. L. B. Moss, *Birth of the Middle Ages, 395–814* (Galaxy), emphasizing Byzantine influences; **A. R. Lewis, *Emerging Medieval Europe, A.D. 400–1000* (Knopf), featuring Western Europe; and **Christopher Dawson, *Making of Europe* (Meridian), stressing the role of the Church. A unique view of the age is provided by D. T. Rice, ed., *The Dark Age— The Making of European Civilization* (1965), which points up the diverse peoples contributing to the new order; the book is beautifully illustrated. The history of the Church is adequately surveyed by **H. Daniel-Rops, *The Church in the Dark Ages* (2 vols., Image). **Robert Latouche, *The Birth of the Western Economy*, trans. E. M. Wilkinson (Harper Torchbook), provides a splendid survey of economic and social developments. Cultural history in the West is dealt with by **M. L. W.

Laistner, *Thought and Letters in Western Europe, A.D. 500 to 900* (Cornell). The history of art is summarized by W. F. Vollbach, *Early Christian Art* (1962).

Byzantine Civilization. Two excellent introductions to Byzantine history and civilization are **J. M. Hussey, *The Byzantine World* (Harper Torchbook); and **Steven Runciman, *Byzantine Civilization* (Meridian). Also valuable but more difficult is **N. H. Baynes and H. St. L. B. Moss, *Byzantium: An Introduction to East Roman Civilization* (Oxford). Broad surveys of Byzantine history include **C. Diehl, *Byzantium: Its Greatness and Decline*, trans. N. Walford (Rutgers); P. Lemerle, *A History of Byzantium* (1964); and **R. Guerdan, *Byzantium: Its Triumph and Tragedy* (Capricorn). **R. Jenkins, *Byzantium: The Imperial Centuries, 610–1071* (Vintage), surveys the period dealt with in this chapter. Longer and more advanced surveys are Georg Ostrogorsky, *History of the Byzantine State*, trans. Joan Hussey (rev. ed., 1969); **A. A. Vasiliev, *History of the Byzantine Empire* (2nd ed., rev., Wisconsin); and **J. B. Bury, *A History of the Later Roman Empire From Arcadius to Irene* (*395 A.D. to 800 A.D.*) (2 vols., Dover). **P. N. Ure, *Justinian and His Age* (Penguin); and John W. Barker, *Justinian and the Later Roman Empire* (1966), provide excellent introductions to a crucial age in Byzantine history. The fascinating role played by the city of Constantinople in Byzantine history is described by Glanville Downey, *Constantinople in the Age of Justinian* (1960); and **D. A. Miller, *Imperial Constantinople* (Wiley). Charles Diehl, *Byzantine Portraits* (1927), discusses representative types from Byzantine society as a means of characterizing the chief features of that civilization. The important relationship between Byzantium and the Slavic world is treated in two works by F. Dvornik, *The Slavs: Their Early History and Civilization* (1956), and *The Making of Central and Eastern Europe* (1949); also valuable are G. Vernadsky, *The Origins of Russia* (1959); and S. Runciman, *The History of the First Bulgarian Empire* (1930). The history of the Eastern Orthodox Church is treated by R. M. French, *The Eastern Orthodox Church* (1951); and G. Every, *The Byzantine Patriarchate, 451–1204* (rev. ed., 1962). J. M. Hussey, *Church and Learning in the Byzantine Empire, 867–1185* (1937), is one of the few good studies in English of post-Justinian Byzantine intellectual history. Byzantine art is splendidly treated in several works: **D. T. Rice, *Art of the Byzantine Era* (Praeger), and *Byzantine Art* (Penguin); A. Grabar, *Byzantine Painting* (1953); and **M. Chatzidakis and A. Grabar, *Byzantine and Early Medieval Painting* (Compass Books). **Spiros Vryonis, *Byzantium and Europe* (Harcourt) is extremely valuable in evaluating the contribution of Byzantium to the West.

Muslim Civilization. The best brief survey of Muslim history is **B. Lewis, *The Arabs in History* (Harper Torchbook). A longer standard history is **P. K. Hitti, *History of the Arabs: From the Earliest Times to the Present* (8th ed., Papermac); Hitti's major points are incorporated in a shorter work entitled **The Arabs: A Short History* (Gateway). Two longer surveys of great value are **Carl Brockelmann, *A History of the Islamic People*, trans. J. Carmichael and M. Perleman (Capricorn); and the splendid work of B. Spuler, *The Muslim World* (3 vols., 1960–69). W. Muir, *The Caliphate, Its Rise, Decline, and Fall* (rev. ed., 1950), provides an understanding of Muslim political institutions. **H. A. R. Gibb, *Mohammedanism: An Historical Survey* (Galaxy), is the simplest discussion of the basic ideas of the Islamic religion; it can be supplemented by **A. Guillaume, *Islam* (2nd ed., Penguin), especially good on the evolution of the religion. **Tor Andrae, *Mohammed, The Man and His Faith* (Harper Torchbook), provides an interesting analysis of Mohammed. A splendid survey of Muslim culture is **G. E. von Grunebaum, *Medieval Islam: A Study in Cultural Orientation* (2nd ed., Phoenix). H. A. R. Gibb, *Arabic Literature: An Introduction* (2nd ed., 1963), provides an adequate introduction. **K. A. C. Croswell, *A Short Account of Early Muslim Architecture* (Penguin) is useful. Three works will help to catch the flavor of Islamic thought and its influences: D. E. O'Leary, *Arabic Thought and Its Place in History* (2nd ed., 1939); **E. A. Myers, *Arabic Thought and the*

Western World in the Golden Age of Islam (Unger); and **P. K. Hitti, *Islam and the West: An Historical Cultural Survey* (Anvil).

Sources. Only a small part of Byzantine literature has been translated. The age of Justinian is represented by the work of Procopius. His main writings, edited by H. B. Dewing, *Procopius* (7 vols., 1914–40), recount in somewhat tedious detail Justinian's efforts to reconquer the West. His **Secret History*, trans. G. A. Williamson (Penguin), gives a gos-sipy, scandal-filled picture of Justinian's court. **Michael Psellus, *Fourteen Byzantine Rulers*, trans. E. R. Sewter (Penguin), gives an interesting picture of the lives and reigns of several members of the Macedonian dynasty. E. Barker, *Social and Political Thought in Byzantium From Justinian to the Last Paleologus* (1957), has collected and translated Byzantine writings on political theory. For Muslim history, the prime source is **The Koran* (many editions; a good one is the translation by N. J. Dawood, 2nd rev. ed., Penguin).

Chapter 16 ❧ Heirs to the Roman Empire:

The Germanic West, 500–750

By comparison with the brilliant Byzantine and Muslim civilizations, the third heir to the Roman Empire presented a sorry picture. After 500, the Germanic West was characterized on the surface by strife, confusion, economic backwardness, and cultural decline. In the midst of rampant barbarism, however, creative forces were at work. By 750 new ideas and institutions destined to play a chief role in Europe's history for many centuries had begun to take shape as the basis for a stable civilization with its own unique features and with an immense potential for future development.

1. POLITICAL DEVELOPMENTS

Much of the outward confusion of the period 500 to 750 in the West resulted from the absence of sound political institutions. As we have already seen, by 500 the conquering Germans, constituting only a small minority of the total population, had established themselves as political masters of the western part of the old Roman Empire. They had divided the imperial territory into several independent states: Visigothic, Ostrogothic, Vandal, Burgundian, Frankish, and Anglo-Saxon. This process of division had ended the political unity characteristic of the Roman imperial regime. It also imposed on the rulers of each of these states the responsibility of building political institutions to replace those of the

Roman Empire. That responsibility was a heavy one for the new lords of the West, who had never ruled states as large as they now possessed and who were faced with diverse populations within their kingdoms. The political chaos almost inevitable under such conditions was aggravated by the fact that by 500, political boundaries in the West were no longer fixed. This fluidity, coupled with the ambitions of the Germanic rulers for new lands and the repeated intrusions of outsiders, led to a succession of conflicts over territories. The warfare resulted in the destruction of some of the weaker Germanic states, and by 750, the political map of the Western world began to take shape in a form highly significant for the future. A new kind of order was being created.

During the first half of the sixth century, two major developments gave this process of recombination a significant impetus. First, large numbers of Slavs moved westward into Central Europe and the Balkan Peninsula to replace the Germans who had left to settle within the Roman Empire. Although still badly organized politically, the Slavs established control over areas they still occupy. The second and more spectacular development was the rise of the Franks in the West. Prior to 500, the Franks had not played a very significant role in history. They occupied a small territory in the extreme northern part of Gaul (modern Belgium) along the lower

Rhine, where they had been allied with the Roman imperial government as defenders of the frontier. However, under the leadership of their first great king, Clovis (reigned 481–511), the Franks were transformed into a crushing military force. Clovis and his immediate successors pursued a policy of ruthless aggression which resulted in the conquest of Gaul by 550. In the course of that conquest, the Burgundian kingdom was destroyed, and the Visigoths driven out of Gaul into Spain; Frankish power was also extended east of the Rhine into areas not previously part of the Roman Empire. Clovis' conversion to orthodox Christianity in 496 greatly aided the advance of his armies, for the other major Germanic nations were Arian Christians and thus viewed as heretics in the West, while the Franks were accepted as "liberators" by the orthodox Roman population of Gaul. Frankish conquests shaped a large kingdom that embraced peoples with both Roman and German backgrounds; and in this kingdom more than anywhere else in the West, the Roman and barbarian cultures were forced to mix. Out of this mixture emerged many of Europe's fundamental political, economic, and social institutions.

Justinian's attempted reconquest of the West in the middle of the sixth century was likewise a decisive step in shaping the new map of Western Europe. His armies destroyed the Vandal kingdom in North Africa and the Ostrogothic state in Italy; Byzantine rule was imposed on these areas. Part of Justinian's work was undone shortly after his death, when the Lombards invaded Italy in 568 and established a kingdom embracing a good part of Italy, but the Byzantines retained their hold on several areas, notably around Venice, Genoa, Ravenna, and Rome. At about the same time, an Asiatic people, the Avars, were imposing their authority over the Slavs in the Danube Basin and in the Balkan area and forming another important new state.

There were no further major changes in the political map of Western Europe until the early eighth century, when Muslim forces began to make their presence felt in the West. They destroyed Byzantine power in North Africa, established their control over the Mediterranean seaways, and in 711 wiped out the Visigothic state in Spain. Except for a few tiny Christian kingdoms in the extreme north, Muslim power was to remain supreme in Spain for centuries. Thus, by 750, only three Germanic groups survived in the West: the Franks, the Lombards, and the Anglo-Saxon kingdoms in what is today England. The Byzantine Empire still had a precarious foothold in Italy, and in Central Europe the Slavs had established their dominance. This general arrangement of the political map was to remain for a considerable time into the future.

As their territories slowly took shape, the rulers of each Germanic kingdom tried to build workable institutions of government within their states. The civil war, violence, injustice, and oppression that were constant companions of the search for this order constituted sure signs that the Germanic rulers at first had little success. However, in the kingdoms surviving in 750, the bases for workable government had been established. A full understanding of the patterns of government painfully evolved in the West would require an examination of the political history of each kingdom. In the long run, only two systems were of importance, that of the Anglo-Saxons in England and the Franks on the Continent. We shall return to the Anglo-Saxon political system in a later section; here we shall concentrate our attention on the Franks.

As the Franks established their power in Gaul in the early sixth century, they sought to establish order by creating an absolute monarchy. Clovis, the first of the Merovingian dynasty that ruled the Franks until 751, claimed for himself the roles of supreme lawgiver, final judge, sole commander of the armies, and religious director of his subjects, whether Frankish or Roman. He was obviously influenced in this view of his office by Roman concepts, for earlier Germanic kingship had been much more limited. To execute these vast powers, Clovis and his immediate successors borrowed heavily from Roman precedents. They created a central court of officials, many of whom bore old Roman titles and were assigned duties comparable to those of Roman bureaucrats. To exercise their authority over their subjects on a local level, they established a system that retained the old Roman territorial divisions of Gaul as the units of local administration. Each district, now called a *county*, was governed by a *count* who was appointed by and responsible to the king. The count was charged with holding regular courts, keeping order, improving public facilities, collecting taxes, and raising army contingents. Outwardly, it appeared that Roman political institutions were being sustained in the Frankish kingdoms—but under new management.

However, the Merovingians never enjoyed the real power of the Roman emperors. The history of the dynasty is one of steady decline from the exalted position established by Clovis, a decline so drastic that the last Merovingians were dubbed "do-nothing" kings. Many factors explain this failure. The Merovingians could not divest themselves of an ingrained habit of using force to gain their ends, so that they appeared to many as bloodthirsty tyrants. They had a very limited sense of public service, so that their government seldom performed a positive function in society. They persisted in following the ancient Germanic custom of treating the state as their private property to be divided among all their male heirs at the end of each reign. This practice led to family quarrels that assumed the proportions of civil wars and brought untold misery to their subjects. By the early eighth century, Clovis' kingdom had split into three distinct subkingdoms as a consequence of repeated division, and the weakening of royal authority allowed other groups to break away to enjoy an almost independent existence. The Merovingians demonstrated such limited managerial ability that their complex administrative machinery degenerated into little more than a group of household officials who concerned themselves with caring for the king's personal needs. They never managed to command sufficient financial resources to conduct good government, a fate imposed on them by the economic difficulties of the age and by their own ineptness. They persisted in the Germanic custom of allowing each man to be judged by the law under which he was

A seventh-century Frankish buckle of bronze, ornamented with incised patterns and applied motifs, seems primitive and rough when compared with the contemporary products of Byzantine craftsmen. *Photo: The Walters Art Gallery, Baltimore*

born, be it Frankish, Roman, Burgundian, Visigothic, or whatever, thereby creating more division among a populace already set apart by differences in custom, language, religious practice, and cultural level. All these royal failures were accentuated by the fact that powerful elements in Frankish society persisted in the ancient Germanic custom of the feud, entire families taking up arms to avenge wrongs done by other families against their members. In the face of this ingrained lawlessness, weak kings were unable to perform even the basic governmental function of maintaining order in the kingdom.

Yet the Merovingian political experience, for all its failures, did establish monarchy as an important and necessary political institution. The Merovingian kings did exercise positive powers as leaders of armies, lawgivers, protectors of the Church, and dispensers of justice. Their activities were part of the slow process of defining the functions of kingship in the new order, a role considerably less exalted than that of the Roman emperors, but considerably more powerful than that of the ancient Germanic chieftains. Furthermore, the royal family served as a visible symbol of unity for a diverse group of people thrown together by conquest. To see the king traveling through the land, to hear of his exploits in war, to witness the ceremonies of court life, offered the Franks, the ex-Romans, the Burgundians, the Visigoths virtually the only tangible sign that they belonged to a state. Monarchy was taking shape as a visible sign of public life at a moment when poor communications, economic fragmentation, and cultural differences created tremendous obstacles to the formation of viable political groupings.

Severely limited in their efforts to create an effective centralized system of government that could provide the basic political needs of society, the Merovingians were eventually forced to share their power with the great landowners, both lay and ecclesiastical. The emergence of the landed nobility as possessors of political power was one of the major developments of the era. The rise of the aristocrats stemmed chiefly from the inability of the kings to sustain an effective taxation system and a professional bureaucracy. Always lacking money income to run their government and skilled personnel to act in their behalf, the kings had to call upon their subjects for personal service to the state. When they needed an army or civil servants, they had to depend on subjects who could and would serve at their own expense. Only the great landowners could afford such service, and in return they exacted from the kings grants of land and the right to govern their private estates as they saw fit. Inexorably, a system of private government evolved with the great nobles controlling affairs in their localities and interposing themselves between the central government and the populace. The kings devoted increasing attention to their relationships with the nobility, seeking whatever means they could find to ensure their loyalty, purchase their support, and limit their independence. The growing power of the nobles was a source of incessant strife in the Merovingian state, for the demarcation between royal authority and noble privilege was imprecise; and the growth of aristocratic control at the expense of royal power was a poor omen for the stability of the monarchy.

This trend was accentuated by a complementary development. Amid the political chaos and economic insecurity characteristic of the period, there was a widespread tendency for the weak in society to seek out the protection of the strong and to accept a position of dependency. At all levels of society, individuals of their own free will subordinated themselves to others by a process known as *commendation*, by which one man pledged under oath to serve another in return for protection and material support. These arrangements meant that strong men in society, chiefly the great landowners, built up private followings over whom they exercised considerable governing powers. Here were the roots of the feudal system operating in a way which created private jurisdictions to rival the public authority, which spread political power widely through the noble ranks of society, and which fragmented the state into many separate entities.

Thus by 750 the political picture in the Germanic West was a somber one. Only slowly—and accompanied by constant warfare—were the boundaries of the chief powers being defined. Within the several states, royal power had been severely circumscribed, chiefly as a result of the inadequacies of the rulers. Powerful landowners were exerting tremendous political influence at a local level, often of an irresponsible and disorder-promoting kind. But these were to be the political institutions that would dominate Western Europe for several centuries: monarchy, private jurisdictions dominated by landowners, personal dependency. The shape of this new order was a poor substitute for Rome's splendid government, but its full potential for orderly existence had not yet been exploited.

2. ECONOMIC AND SOCIAL LIFE

The economic and social conditions prevailing in the Germanic West between 500 and 750 reflect the same backwardness and depression characteristic of political developments and stand as sharply in contrast with the prosperous Byzantine and Muslim worlds. Although modern scholars have demonstrated that the economic and social order in the West was not so depressed and stagnant as was once thought, still the overall picture is one of decreasing wealth and shrinking economic activity. In the main, the economic and social trends of decay evident in the late Roman period continued to predominate.

The most notable development of the period was the progressive strangulation of commerce and the industrial life associated with it. Trade and industry were already moribund in the West by the fourth century, as we have seen. In the period of the Germanic invasions (the fifth and sixth centuries), this decline accelerated. More, the Germans were not interested in trade, and when they as-

sumed political power they did little to sustain it. During the invasion period, trade and industry were especially hard hit in the old frontier zones of the empire, where these activities had supported the huge Roman military and administrative machinery. Commercial and industrial activities located nearer the Mediterranean, especially in southern Gaul, Spain, Italy, and North Africa, did not suffer so much, and commercial contacts with the richer East were maintained. There was perhaps even a slight quickening of trade after the middle of the sixth century as a result of the political stability brought by Justinian's reconquests and the establishment of the Frankish kingdom. But this modest revival did not persist. Toward the end of the seventh and the beginning of the eighth centuries, trade again contracted, perhaps because of the seizure of control of the Mediterranean by the Muslims or because of more restrictive economic policies introduced by the Byzantine Empire. By 750 there was little circulation of goods in the West, the flow of money was small, city life had deteriorated except where the Church sustained it for administrative reasons, and the skilled artisan class had virtually vanished or had retreated to the large agricultural estates to produce for strictly local consumption.

To meet its economic needs, Western Europe's population turned almost exclusively toward an agricultural economy. Possession of land became the measure of a man's social position and power. Its successful exploitation offered the only hope of escaping abject poverty. The organization of agricultural production tended inexorably toward the formation of large self-sufficient estates, called *villas*, a trend that carried over from the later empire and the great *latifundia*. Many of the Roman *latifundia* survived the fall of the empire and the invasions, especially in the areas adjacent to the Mediterranean. Where Germanic settlement was heaviest, the Roman estates often disappeared and were replaced by village settlements inhabited by free landowners who farmed their own lands lying outside the village. But by the eighth century village establishments were being supplanted by the villa, which proved to be more efficient economically and more viable politically in a disordered age.

The early medieval villa was a farming unit of several hundred acres owned by a noble or by the Church. The owner usually reserved part of this land for his own support. His basic need was for labor to work the land and to turn its produce into articles he needed. There were still slaves in this era, but a surer labor supply was provided by tenant farmers. Between 500 and 750 increasing numbers of peasants were legally bound to the great estates, given a piece of land from which to derive their own living, and required to work the lord's land and render him dues in return for their tenancy. This pattern of exploitation laid the groundwork for the medieval manor and for serfdom, institutions that were basic in the future development of Western European civilization.

The villa system is not one that elicits praise; yet in the context of the early Middle Ages, it proved a vital institution. In a time of declining population it allowed an effective concentration of labor. In an age of political chaos it made possible the gathering together of men in a situation where effective direction and fruitful cooperation were possible. It provided the great mass of men with the permanent possession of a piece of land which may not have been theirs legally, but which in fact did become theirs to use as they chose. Even before 750 there was evidence that the villa possessed potential for economic growth. For instance, by 700 new lands were being cleared around some villas, thus reversing a trend toward decreased cultivation that had been in progress for centuries.

The social structure in the West also changed to meet new conditions. The direction of change was toward a simpler system than had been characteristic of the Roman world. In 500 the main features of the Roman social order were still clearly visible in most of the West. In fact, the invasions added new complexities, since in many areas the Germans tried to keep themselves apart from the Roman population and to retain their ancient social order alongside the Roman one. But this situation did not persist. By 750 the urban social groups had disappeared, and the distinctions setting German and Romans apart had also vanished. The main thrust of social development was toward the creation of a new aristocracy composed of men who proved capable of acquiring land, seizing political power, and grouping around themselves dependents who served them in some way. The new aristocrat was a self-made man, usually crude, aggressive, and lacking in refinement; he was more likely the descendant of the Germanic warrior than the Greco-Roman nobleman. Accompanying the emergence of this new aristocracy was that of a large lower class, chiefly peasants, who were legally tied to the great estates and dependent on a powerful overlord. All but a few freemen, both German and Roman, were swallowed up into this class of semifree men. Freedom was a dubious condition in an age of political chaos and economic difficulty; protection by a strong man and the security of a piece of land were far more precious.

3. THE CHURCH

Western society needed more than the reshaping of its political, economic, and social structure, for the passing of Greco-Roman civilization meant the virtual destruction of moral, spiritual, and cultural standards. To the Church fell the struggle against the barbarism that threatened to engulf Western Europe. It was especially fitted for this task because it had survived the fall of Rome better than had any other institution, carrying over into the new age an appealing, satisfying religious message plus large elements of Greco-Roman culture that found their way into its organization, theology, liturgy, and moral code.

But the Church itself faced great adversity in the West between 500 and 750. It lost the beneficial support of the Roman government, and under the influence of recently Christianized German rulers, broke into units that coincided with the boundaries of the Germanic states and that usually disregarded one another. Both the ineptness of the new rulers and the split into local groupings threatened the unity of Western Christendom. Moreover, by 750 differences in theology, ritual, and organization had already separated the Greek and Latin churches, and as the Christian world divided its energies, the assaults of Muslims and Slavs rolled back its frontiers.

Even more dangerous was the decay of religious life within the Western Church. The character of Christian leadership had changed drastically. The bishops, who were the most important Church officials, were especially lax in their religious duties: Most of their energy was devoted to increasing Church lands. As the possessors of large holdings, the bishops had the same political duties as did other landowners. And in the unholy competition for the office of bishop, with its land and political power, the strong usually won over the pious. The typical bishop of the age was a quarrelsome, greedy, worldly figure, forever fighting and seeking power. Seldom did he concern himself with spiritual affairs. As a consequence, discipline in the lower ranks of the clergy also suffered. The typical priest who dealt directly with the people was unlettered, ignorant of the rudiments of doctrine, unfamiliar with liturgy, and lax in moral life.

Religious life in general reflected its inferior leadership. Recently converted pagans mixed their old religious ideas with Christianity to create beliefs and practices of the most amazing kinds. Most Christians had but vague understanding of such ideas as original sin, the Incarnation, the Redemption, free will, and the rewards of the good life; their daily life was dominated by efforts to avoid Satan's hordes, who plagued mankind at every turn and had to be defeated by miracles, magic, and the intervention of the saints. Church writers of the period complained bitterly about sexual promiscuity, crimes of violence, thieving, and general unruliness among Christians. People were in need of instruction and discipline, neither of which was forthcoming from the degraded clergy. Few of these difficulties had been corrected by 750, but a revitalization had begun, chiefly from within the Church itself. In the process of reform, the Church in the West took on a unique character setting it apart from Christian communities elsewhere. And it expanded its role as a dominant directive institution in Western European society.

One of the most significant features of the period was the Church's continued ability to win new converts. We have already noted that some of the Germans accepted Christianity as soon as they came in contact with Roman civilization. After the fall of Rome, Christianity continued to spread among them. Just as this period opened, Clovis and his Franks were converted (496), thus bringing into the Christian camp the Germanic nation destined to dominate the West. Backed by the Franks, missionaries in the sixth and seventh centuries slowly pushed the Christian frontier eastward from the Rhine. About the same time, the Anglo-Saxons in Britain were converted by missionaries converging on England from Rome and from Ireland. Ireland had been converted in the fourth century and had remained a Christian stronghold during the troubled period of the Germanic invasions. In the first half of the eighth century, English missionaries crossed to the Continent to win new converts on the northern and eastern frontiers of the Frankish kingdom—in areas embraced roughly by modern West Germany and the Netherlands. While the Christian frontier was being pushed outward, the less spectacular task of converting the rural population of the West went forward. As new converts were won, a Church organization was set up to serve their needs. Bishoprics were created where they had never before existed. Monasteries grew up. Rural parishes and privately founded churches appeared in numerous places. By 750, the Church had succeeded in supplying the one unifying force in the lives of all men in the

West—Romans and Germans, nobles and peasants, rich and poor.

A second positive achievement of the Church was its growing participation in activities that were not strictly religious. The Church, living in a world of weak governments, often shouldered the burden of caring for the weak in society—widows, orphans, cripples, slaves, prisoners. It maintained the only hospitals and schools available. It injected some of its ideas of justice and mercy into the harsh law codes of the era, and thus powerfully influenced the administration of justice. Each time the Church intervened in these matters, its prestige as a social agency and its influence over society increased. These activities set new standards of social welfare that were to serve as models in reawakening the social consciousness of society in general. The Church's greatest accomplishment in this period was its ability to perfect institutions capable of attacking the weaknesses within its own body—corruptness and worldliness among the clergy, moral laxness, ignorance, and lack of discipline. Especially important were two institutions that evolved rapidly between 500 and 750: the Roman papacy and the Benedictine monastic order.

The remarkable progress of the Roman papacy during the sixth, seventh, and early eighth centuries grew out of the strong position established by the bishops of Rome in earlier centuries. By 400 the popes had come to enjoy a widespread respect in the Christian world as defenders of true doctrine and proclaimers of the right law for Christian behavior. In part, that prominence was a result of the Petrine theory, which insisted that Christ had designated St. Peter as his representative on earth and that that commission applied to Peter's successors as bishops of Rome. Papal power and prestige also owed much to the favors extended the popes by the first Christian emperors. The collapse of the imperial government under the impact of the barbarian invasions deprived the popes of imperial support, but worked in other ways to enhance their role during the fifth century. They had

imposed on them the burden of protecting and virtually governing the city of Rome and the responsibility for holding the Christian forces in the West together in the face of the triumphant Germans. By the end of the fifth century, the popes were generally recognized as the authoritative spokesmen of the Church in spiritual matters in the West. They responded to their growing prestige by developing a theory of their independence from secular authority. A prime example was Pope Gelasius I's (492–496) famous theory of the two swords. He argued that religious and secular power represented two orders of authority, each established by God to achieve different ends and each independent in its own sphere. This doctrine created the ideological basis for further additions to papal authority and for greater independence of the Church from secular governments.

However, conditions in the early sixth century seriously affected the position of the pope. Political chaos in Italy offered the gravest danger. The Ostrogoths, who ruled Italy in 500, were Arians and thus did not recognize the leadership of the pope. When Justinian later destroyed the power of the Ostrogoths, the pope came under the authority of the Eastern emperor, whose Greek orientation tended to reduce the importance of Rome in favor of Constantinople. Still later, in 568, the Lombards seized most of Italy from the Byzantines, and opened up an era of bloody struggle between Lombards and Byzantines that made it nearly impossible for the pope to act positively. Finally, the influence of the pope was diminished in other Germanic kingdoms in the West as kings and bishops seized control of religious life and made it serve their own ends.

The recovery of the papacy was sparked by the genius of the first great churchman of the Middle Ages, Pope Gregory I, the Great (590–604). Descended from a noble Roman family and educated for a political career, Gregory rejected worldly affairs to become a monk. Eventually he left his monastic life to serve as a papal diplomat in Constantinople

This later representation of Gregory the Great shows the pope, inspired by the Holy Ghost (the dove), supervising the copying of Gregorian chants, the religious music form used by the Church for centuries. *Photo: The Bettmann Archive*

and then to become pope. Coupling deep religious fervor with hardheaded business sense, Gregory quickly established himself as one of the truly constructive figures of the age. In essence, his policy was to make the pope politically and economically independent while at the same time asserting the authority of the papal office as the fountainhead of spiritual life in the Christian world.

Gregory was convinced that wealth was necessary for political and economic independence. He therefore devoted himself to the sound administration of papal property in Italy; he took an active part in the management of his estates, collecting everything due him, goading his agents into farming better, and acquiring new lands whenever possible. He used this income to establish full control over the city of Rome, and turned it into a little state ruled by the pope. On the basis of his political power, Gregory began to act as an independent agent in the incessant struggles between the Lombards and Byzantines. By playing one side against the other, he managed to enhance his position in Italy. He had begun the process of creating an independent papal state with resources sufficient to make its power felt in ever-wider circles. Gregory was not, however, simply a wily politician and administrator. His greatest fame came as a spiritual leader with a simple, clear message especially suited for the culturally backward Christians of Western Europe. During his busy pontificate, he found time to write important books on theology and church administration. His powerful sermons, circulated in manuscript form, served as examples to revive the art of preaching in the West. He improved the liturgy. He sought to bestir princes and clergymen to reform their lives. Perhaps his most spectacular achievement as a spiritual leader was his sponsorship of the conversion of England, a program that allowed him to organize the new church in England under papal guidance. Rome took on new glory as the center of Christianity, and the pope's word began to serve in Western Europe as a final guide in spiritual matters.

Gregory's successors continued his policy. As a consequence, papal political independence and economic strength increased. Popes continued to speak out on theological and disciplinary matters, and the papacy became the authority for Western Christendom. Obviously a new force of unity and discipline was emerging, although by 750 it had not yet achieved complete domination of the Christian world in the West.

Monasticism had been imported from the East as early as the fourth century and had received an enthusiastic reception, so that there were many thriving monastic centers by the fifth century. None was more vital than that in Ireland, where the severe ascetic practices of the East took deep hold. The Irish monasteries became cultural centers and incubators for a powerful missionary movement which during the sixth and early seventh centuries took Irish monks to England and the Continent armed not only with great piety, but also with considerable learning. But on the whole, early Western monasticism, perhaps too imitative of the East, failed to sustain its initial vigor. The West needed its own style of monastic life, and another great churchman appeared to answer that need.

Benedict of Nursia (480–543) stands alongside Gregory the Great as a builder. He too was an aristocratic Italian who abandoned his worldly career to become a hermit, but his rigid practices and holiness attracted so much attention that he was forced to create a monastery for the followers who gathered around him. At Monte Cassino, a village between Rome and Naples, he built his monastic house. There he put into practice the Rule he had devised to govern the community of monks. The Rule was so practical, so sensible, and so well fitted to the needs of the period that by 750, the Benedictine monastic system had spread all over the West and had begun to play an important role in revitalizing the whole Christian world.

The Benedictine Rule contained several basic principles that explain its success. It established the idea that a community of men could serve God better than a single individual. Such a community must, however, be made up of selected members. The Rule laid down rigorous tests for the sincerity of prospective members. After a long testing period, each new member was required to take vows promising to renounce all personal wealth, to remain chaste, to obey his superiors, and to remain permanently in the community he entered. These vows created complete loyalty to the monastery and obligated the monk to avoid the chief sins of clergymen

of the era—greed for wealth, luxury, sexual laxity, and disregard for authority. Since some kind of government was necessary for the community, the Rule entrusted absolute authority to an *abbot*, a sensible move in view of the desperate need for discipline in the Church. Probably the most important part of the Rule was its provision for an orderly daily routine. Benedict assigned to his monks three kinds of activity. The most important was the worship of God, and eight religious services were established for each day. Although this seems an outrageous burden to the modern worshiper, it was a sensible requirement when measured alongside some monastic practices of the day, such as spending one's life atop a pole. The second activity required of Benedictine monks was four to eight hours of manual labor a day, depending on the season. That labor included cooking, field work, clerical work, the crafts, and teach-

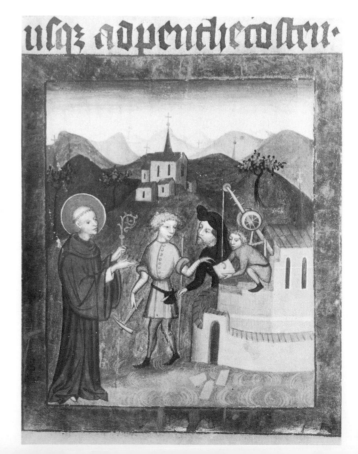

In this German miniature, St. Benedict supervises the building of a monastery. By 750, the Benedictine rule had spread over most of Western Europe. *Photo: Bayerische Staatsbibliothek, Munich*

ing, depending on the talents of each monk. Finally, each monk was required to devote a part of each day to study. Having provided for the selection, discipline, and occupation of his monks, Benedict wrote one final principle into his Rule—moderation. He repeatedly cautioned against too strict discipline, advising the abbot to temper his rule with mercy. This spirit of moderation permitted a flexibility in the typical Benedictine monastery that allowed for nearly every human circumstance.

Benedict's Rule won widespread favor in many parts of Western Europe (and was eventually adopted for women's religious communities), in no small part because of the powerful endorsement given it by Pope Gregory I. By 750 "schools for the service of God," as Benedict called his monasteries, had become the predominant form of monastic life. As their numbers increased, so did their role as shapers of society. These monasteries not only served as places of withdrawal from barbarized society for those Christians who desired to perfect their lives, but also produced large numbers of men and women who stood out as ideal Christians. Their service to society was immense: Monks carved new estates out of Europe's wilderness and made them into the best-managed economic institutions in the West. They taught backward peoples all kinds of technical skills. They showed bewildered Christians the proper performance of Church rituals. They instructed the ignorant in the basic tenets of the faith. Their devotion, charity, and purity of life inspired others to reform. They bore the brunt of missionary work, and they implanted Christianity in many of the more backward areas. They were the preservers and transmitters of culture. In a time of uncertainty, they were a small but stable bulwark against barbarism.

4. INTELLECTUAL AND ARTISTIC ACTIVITY

The general characteristics of the age—decline, narrowing of horizons, simplicity, deterioration of techniques, shrinking of knowledge —were little conducive to creative thought and expression. Yet during these centuries there were developments decisive in determining the cultural future of Western Europe and in directing its cultural energies into unique paths.

In the realm of literature and learning, the chief accomplishment was the preservation of significant elements of classical and patristic Latin literature (the use of Greek had virtually ended in the West). In the sixth century this preservative activity was carried on by both secular society and the Church. Aristocrats in Italy, Gaul, and Spain, still enthralled with classical literature, struggled to maintain the old municipal schools where their sons could learn the traditional Latin rhetoric and grammar and continued to collect and read classical Latin authors. Germanic courts, especially that of the Ostrogoth Theodoric in Italy, actively patronized literature and learning. One of the intellectual luminaries of that court, Boethius, set out to translate the works of Aristotle and Plato into Latin. His famous *Consolation of Philosophy*, written while he was in prison awaiting execution for alleged treason, was a moving defense of learning and rational thought filled with the classical spirit. The Church, still influenced by the great fathers of the fourth and fifth centuries, who had utilized massive elements of classical thought to explain the Christian faith, likewise felt a strong urge to guard that tradition. It was this inspiration that led Cassiodorus, another servant of Theodoric, to devote the last years of his life to collecting a library of classics to serve the monks in a monastery he had founded.

Before the end of the sixth century, secular society ceased to play this role, and the burden of preservation fell to the Church, and primarily to the monasteries. Faithful to Benedict's injunction to serve God by study, the Benedictine monks established schools to teach their neophytes to read and write, tediously copied classical authors and church fathers, compiled textbooks in Latin grammar and rhetoric to keep alive the language of the Church, and wrote simple commentaries on the old texts to make them understandable. The Irish monasteries pursued these goals with an enthusiasm they transmitted to Benedictine monasteries in England. The monastic concerns tended to be narrow, governed by a passion to know God, to understand His word, and to pray well. Thus the monks were selective in their endeavors as preservers. And they felt no compunction about turning the classical heritage to Christian purposes, and sometimes distorted classical thought almost beyond recognition. Nonetheless, they did save much of classical Latin literature and patristic writing.

A few creative figures, almost all churchmen, also managed to transcend merely preservative activities to produce literary works with unique qualities. One of these was Boethius; another was a Visigothic bishop, Isidore of Seville, who compiled the *Etymologies,* an encyclopedia of information (and misinformation) about nature that encouraged interest in science and organized knowledge. Pope Gregory the Great's important works set forth basic theological concepts in direct, simple terms more suited to the age than the sophisticated presentations of the great fathers from whom he borrowed most of his ideas. A Frankish bishop, Gregory of Tours (ca. 538–594), in his *History of the Franks* demonstrated a real ability to compile and organize historical material. The most outstanding intellectual figure of the age was an English monk named Bede (673–735), whose theological, historical, and biographical writings set high standards of style. His *Ecclesiastical History of the English People* is one of the best pieces of historical writing of the entire Middle Ages. If we judge the intellectual temper of this age from these few outstanding men, we would have to say that the era was marked by traditionalism, total concern with religious issues, credulity, a tendency to turn reality into symbols, and suspicion of worldly things. The classical tradition, so painfully preserved in the letter, as

yet had little positive impact on the spirit of its preservers.

During this period, the lay world in the main sank into illiteracy. One wishes he could fathom their unrecorded thoughts and feelings, but it is virtually impossible for us to comprehend the mental processes of those who never read. Perhaps we can guess that lay aristocrats drew their views in part from the Germanic oral tradition. One work that might suggest their patterns of thought has survived this period—the magnificent Anglo-Saxon epic, *Beowulf.* The illiteracy of the laity did create one situation of immense cultural significance in Western European history: the language of learning, literature, and religion became different from the *vernacular,* the language that men spoke. This condition was destined for centuries to make learning and letters the property of an elite, chiefly churchmen, and to necessitate the learning of a foreign tongue in order to join that elite. And it was destined to keep learning and letters somewhat remote from many of the realities of life.

The art of this period reflects a mixture of old and new forms and themes. As in every realm of life, classical Greco-Roman forms persisted in architecture, sculpture, and painting; most of these classical influences had already been appropriated by Christian artists prior to 500 and were simply carried over into the new age. Many of the churches built in the West followed the basilica plan characteristic of Roman buildings. Byzantine architectural forms, given definite shape by Justinian's building program, exerted strong influence in sixth-century Italy and persisted there to affect building styles in other areas of the West. In sculpture and painting, classical and Byzantine influences tended to merge, so that pictorial art increasingly emphasized symbolic representation of religious motifs. The Germans and Celts added an important ingredient to the art of this period: a distinctive decorative style utilizing animal and geometric forms to create fantastic abstract designs which were employed especially to decorate articles of adornment and to illumi-nate manuscripts. All these traits of a youth-ful art style beginning to take shape are splen-didly illustrated by three remarkable illuminated manuscripts that survive from this age, the Irish Book of Durrow (late sev-enth century), the English Lindisfarne Gos-pels (eighth century), and the Irish Book of Kells (early ninth century), and by the innu-merable items of personal adornment that have been recovered from Merovingian graves. On the whole, the art of this period reflected considerable freedom from fixed can-ons and unusual combinations of merging ar-tistic traditions. Artistic expression tended toward abstraction, symbolization, and a search for religious values at the expense of earthly concerns.

By the middle of the eighth century the Western world had by no means emerged from the time of troubles that followed the fall of Rome. The Germanic heirs to Greco-Roman civilization had been marked by their troubled experience. Habits of violence, igno-rance, poverty, and moral decadence had been ingrained into men's lives and were to affect the conduct of Westerners for many centuries. However, out of the experiences of this period had emerged institutions and patterns of life that represented creations unique to the West: monarchy, a new nobility, a stabilized peasantry, a mode of agricultural exploitation, an involved Church, the papacy, Benedictine and Celtic monasticism, a treasury of Greco-Roman learning and literature, new art forms. The potential of these creations had not been realized, but their existence ensured the sur-vival of civilized life in the West and compen-sated to some degree for what had been lost by the fall of classical civilization.

Suggested Reading

Political, Social, and Economic History. The works cited in the Suggested Reading list for Chapter 15, especially Sullivan, Moss, Lewis, Dawson, and Latouche, will be useful for this chapter. Three additional works will help to clarify the confusing history of the period: C. D. Burns, *The First Europe* (1947); **Margaret Deanesly, *A History of Early Medieval Eu-rope, 476–911* (University Paperbacks), a par-ticularly lucid account; and **J. M. Wallace-Haddrill, *The Barbarian West: The Early Middle Ages* (Harper Torchbook). **Sylvia Thrupp, ed., *Early Medieval Society* (Appleton-Century-Crofts), has translated several funda-mental essays by recent European scholars on crucial social problems of the period. Samuel Dill, *Roman Society in Gaul in the Merovingian Age* (1926), although out of date and rather difficult to read, provides a full picture of conditions in Gaul in the sixth century. **Lynn White, Jr., *Medieval Technology and Social Change* (Galaxy), will open new vistas to its readers. Every student should read the seminal work of the Belgian historian **Henri Pirenne, *Mohammed and Charlemagne* (Me-ridian), which advances the thesis that the society of the Merovingian period was a con-tinuation of Roman civilization and that only the Islamic invasions brought a break with the past. This thesis is attacked by **William C. Bark, *Origins of the Medieval World* (Stan-ford), who argues for the creative originality of the age. The great debate raised by the Pirenne thesis is summarized in **A. F. Havig-hurst, *The Pirenne Thesis: Analysis, Criti-cism, and Revision* (Heath).

Church History. The most complete survey is the work by Daniel-Rops, cited in Chapter 15. The evolution of papal ideas of government are treated provocatively by Walter Ullmann, *The Growth of Papal Government in the Mid-dle Ages* (2nd ed., 1962). The role of Greg-ory the Great is fully treated by F. Homes Dudden, *Gregory the Great: His Place in His-tory and Thought* (2 vols., 1905); and P. Batiffol, *Saint Gregory the Great* (1929). The development of monasticism is surveyed adequately by Jean Décarreaux, *Monks and Civilization*, trans. C. Haldane (1964). On the establishment of the Benedictine Order, see J. Chapman, *St. Benedict and the Sixth Century* (1929). **Justin McCann, *St. Benedict* (Image), will also be helpful. More recent is Leonard von Matt and Stephen Hilpisch, *Saint Benedict* (1961). The glorious history of Irish monasticism and its accomplishment is well treated by Ludwig Bieler, *Ireland: Harbinger of the Middle Ages* (1963); J. Ryan, *Irish Monasticism: Origins and Early Development* (1931); and N. K. Chadwick, *The Age of Saints in the Early Celtic Church* (1961) An excellent picture of the missionary and cultural activities of the monks of this age is **E. S. Duckett, *The Wandering Saints of the Early Middle Ages* (Norton).

Cultural History. The basic work of Laistner (see Chapter 15) can be supplemented by Gustav Schnürer, *Church and Culture in the Middle Ages*, Vol. I, trans. G. Undreiner (1956); and **E. K. Rand, *Founders of the Middle Ages* (Dover). A provocative interpretation of the new directions of cultural history is **Jean Leclercq, *Love of Learning and the Desire for God: A Study of Monastic Culture* (Mentor).

Sources. A sampling of the literature of this period will help in understanding the main cultural developments. **Boethius, *The Consolation of Philosophy*, trans. V. E. Watts (Penguin), will illustrate the powerful attrac-

tion of classical civilization to a sixth-century scholar. Pope Gregory the Great's many writings are a good mirror of the intellectual interests prevailing about 600. His *Pastoral Care*, trans. H. Davis (*Ancient Christian Writers*, No. 11, 1965), consisting of his advice to a bishop, reveals the condition of the Church. His *Dialogues*, trans. O. J. Zimmerman (*Fathers of the Church*, Vol. 39, 1959), shows the deep interest in monastic life and its mystical aspects. His letters present a vivid picture of the troubles of the times and a pope's way of coping with them; see *Selected Epistles of Gregory the Great*, in *A Select Library of Nicene and Post-Nicene Fathers of the Christian Church*, 2nd Series, Vols. XII–XIII (1956). Of vital importance in understanding the age is the Rule of Benedict; a good version is Benedict, *Rule for Monasteries*, trans. L. J. Boyle (1949). A dramatic introduction to the Merovingian age is provided by the Frankish bishop Gregory of Tours in *History of the Franks*, trans. O. M. Dalton (2 vols., 1927); Gregory was an eye witness to many of the events he records in his history. Conditions in seventh- and eighth-century England are pictured in **Bede, *The History of the English Church and People*, trans. L. Sherley-Price (Penguin); this is one of the outstanding literary works of the period. A work reflecting the values of Germanic society is the Anglo-Saxon epic **Beowulf* (many editions; an excellent one is the translation by David Wright, Penguin). J. T. Shotwell and L. R. Loomis, eds., *The See of Peter* (1927), is a collection of historical documents relating to the development of the papacy.

Chapter 17 ❧ The First Revival of Europe, 750–900

Prior to the middle of the eighth century, the Germanic West had fashioned a variety of new institutions and viewpoints that gave its society a distinct character. However, in the general setting of chaos and barbarism, these innovations had by 750 borne only modest fruit. Then, rather suddenly and spectacularly, the Western world enjoyed a revival which was brief in duration—hardly more than a century—but of great historical significance because it established the identity of the West and accentuated the sources of its strength. The revival was the handiwork of a narrow segment of society. On the Continent, a new Frankish royal family, the Carolingians, provided the leadership, while in England, the kings of Wessex played a comparable role. These Germanic ruling houses served as focal points around which clustered other dynamic elements in society, especially clergymen and aristocrats. Out of a complex of conscious and unconscious motives, these people worked to unleash society's potential for greater order, wealth, spiritual fervor, and cultural maturity. These efforts were promoted and given direction not only by the ambition and inspiration of a European elite, but also by a vast change in the relationships between the Western world and its neighbors

—Byzantium, Islam, the still-pagan world of the Slavs and the Scandinavians. Although the dreams of this narrow elite were by no means realized, their work had one particularly important result: it made the West visible in the larger world as a coherent unit possessing unique institutions and strengths. And it gave to the West a self-consciousness of its own civilization. The activities of these men created the first "Europe."

1. THE RISE OF THE CAROLINGIANS

The central figures in Western Europe's first revival were the Carolingians. From an inauspicious beginning, this family rose to a position of virtual control of most of continental Europe between about 750 and 900. The Carolingians originated in the northeastern section of the Merovingian kingdom in a subkingdom known as Austrasia. At first they were only one of the ambitious landowning families that joined other nobles in undermining the authority of the ever-weakening Merovingian royal family. Toward the end of the seventh century, the Carolingians gained hereditary control of one of the key offices in the Merovingian political system, the office of *mayor of the palace*. This position gave its holder con-

This tenth-century ivory of the Virgin enthroned is typical of the style of art that flourished during the Carolingian period. The vigorous, vital quality of the carving shows that the barbarian invasions and the new cultural strands that came with them had a marked effect on the plastic arts. *Photo: The Metropolitan Museum of Art* siderable power to control the activities of the royal court and to manipulate royal lands, an opportunity which the Carolingians used to increase family wealth and to build up a powerful circle of dependents. As their power increased, they shifted their ambitions toward strengthening the central government and expanding their control of that government beyond Austrasia to the other Merovingian subkingdoms—where other noble families were also struggling to dominate the royal administration and wealth. The decisive turn of events came in 687, when the Carolingian mayor of Austrasia, Pepin of Herstal, defeated the rival mayor of Neustria and claimed the right to be mayor for the entire Frankish kingdom.

Pepin of Herstal's victory was exploited to the fullest by his successors as mayors of the palace, Charles Martel (714–741) and Pepin the Short (741–751), who became the most powerful men in Western Europe, far overshadowing the Merovingian kings whom they served. Their program was essentially simple, yet it struck directly at the major political evils of the era. Both labored to check the disintegration of the kingdom into regional subkingdoms and to reestablish Frankish unity. Both waged incessant and successful war against the turbulent, greedy nobles. Both defended the frontiers against hostile invaders, and Charles Martel gained undying fame by defeating at Tours in 732 a Muslim army that had invaded the Frankish kingdom from Spain. Both tried to improve the royal administration so that justice might be rendered, taxes collected, and the weak protected. Both tried to recapture for the benefit of the royal government resources in land that had been usurped by the lay and ecclesiastical nobles or given away foolishly by the weak Merovingians. This policy led to the confiscation of large amounts of Church property. Both tried to use the royal lands more wisely so as to make grants only in return for service to the central government. To compensate the Church, Charles and Pepin gave generous support to missionary work, sought to reform the clergy, and encouraged the improvement of the quality of religious life throughout the kingdom.

Despite all they did, however, Charles and Pepin were still only servants of the "do-nothing" kings of the Merovingian dynasty. As the years passed, it became clear that the real power lay in the hands of the mayors of the palace. They raised armies, administered justice, defended the frontiers, appointed officials, and made laws. Finally, Pepin took steps to transfer the Frankish crown from the Merovingian family to his own. Fearing that a forceable deposition of the Merovingians would arouse hostility among the Franks, who still harbored a deep respect for their ancient royal house despite the miserable performance of the last rulers of that blood, Pepin sought the approval of a higher authority to sanction his usurpation. His choice was a momentous one: he turned to the pope. In 751 he sent an envoy to Rome to ask Pope Zachary if it were not right that one who really exercised power should wear the crown. When Zachary approved, Pepin deposed the Merovingian king and had himself elected king of the Franks. The willingness of the Franks to accept the change of dynasty on papal authority was a mark of how greatly the prestige of the papacy had grown. When Pepin was crowned as King Pepin I in 751, a papal legate was present to anoint him; in 754 Pope Stephen reconsecrated the new king. These acts indicated that in the eyes of the Church Pepin was king by the grace of God.

Papal sanction of the dynastic change was dictated in considerable part by new and desperate problems facing the bishops of Rome, problems created by vast changes in the power structure of the Mediterranean world. Since the days of Justinian, Rome had been part of the Byzantine holdings in Italy, and the popes had relied on the Byzantine emperors for protection. Although the relationship between Constantinople and Rome was sometimes stormy, the arrangement had sustained the papacy. During the first half of the eighth century, however, this situation changed drastically. Involved in a desperate struggle to protect itself against the Muslim onslaught, the Byzantine emperors were increasingly unable to defend their position in Italy. Moreover, the iconoclastic policy adopted by Emperor Leo III was viewed as heretical by the papacy, and caused the popes to repudiate the emperors as defenders of the orthodox faith. The decline of Byzantine power in Italy encouraged Byzantium's long-time rivals, the Lombards, to take the offensive. But Lombard expansion threatened to engulf Rome and place the papacy under new and perhaps less lenient "protection." Lombard domination also threatened to deprive the papacy of the independent control it had long exercised over the city of Rome and the extensive papal property in Italy. The popes desperately needed a new ally and protector. Who could serve better than the rising Carolingians, already proven champions of the Church by virtue of the policies of Charles Martel and Pepin the Short.

In 753–754 Pope Stephen II, whose predecessor had helped Pepin acquire his crown, made a journey to the Frankish court to secure a protector. After long negotiation, an agreement, called the Donation of Pepin, was reached. Pepin promised to ensure papal control over specified territories in Italy, some of which the Lombards already held. To establish a legal claim to these territories, Stephen apparently confronted Pepin with a document known as the Donation of Constantine. This document, probably compiled at the papal court just before Stephen's departure, claimed to be a deed in which the emperor Constantine, who died in A.D. 337, granted to Pope Sylvester complete control over the western part of the Roman Empire, especially Rome and Italy. Constantine was allegedly prompted to this action by virtue of the fact that the pope had cured him of leprosy. This forgery established in the minds of the parties involved the right of the pope to claim a "state" over which he possessed complete sovereignty. In return for the aid of the Frankish king, Stephen not only reanointed Pepin as

king of the Franks, but bestowed on him the somewhat vague title of "patrician of Rome," signifying his role as protector of the papacy and of the papal state. Pepin then made two campaigns into Italy and forced the Lombards to surrender some of the territories claimed by the papacy.

The alliance of the Franks and the papacy was truly a landmark. The Frankish kings now ruled by the grace of God bestowed through the papacy. They had assumed the responsibility of safeguarding their realm against all enemies of Christianity and of encouraging their subjects to become more perfect Christians. They had placed themselves under the guidance of the pope, who claimed the power to lead the Christian world toward perfection. At the same time the papacy, now backed by strong protectors, had lifted itself to a new position of authority, and had established its own political area, the Papal States, within which it could operate in total freedom.

2. THE REIGN OF CHARLEMAGNE (768–814)

The preparations made by Charles Martel and Pepin I were brilliantly exploited by Charlemagne (reigned 768–814), who emerges as the first great Western European secular ruler. For centuries he remained the prototype of greatness, elevated to the stature of hero by the rich legend surrounding his name. In his own day he embodied the qualities of greatness: His biographer, Einhard, wrote of an imposing physique that made him a war leader par excellence, a joy for life that drew men to him as loyal friends and boon companions, a powerful intelligence, a strong devotion to family, and a deep piety.

The energetic, talented Charlemagne was first of all a successful war lord. His long reign was highlighted by a series of campaigns that added important territories to the Frankish realm and threw back its enemies. Charlemagne's first notable success came in 774, when he defeated the Lombard king of

Italy and annexed all the peninsula except the Byzantine territories in the south and the Papal States, over which he was already protector. Even before disposing of the Lombards, Charlemagne launched an attack on the Saxons who lived on the northeastern frontier of the Frankish kingdom. He finally subdued them after thirty years of struggle and forced them to accept Christianity. This victory marked the incorporation of the last major remnant of pagan, barbarian Germans into the Christian, civilized world of the West. His armies also drove down the Danube into the land of the Avars and the Slavs, where another large territory was annexed. His attack on Muslim Spain resulted initially in his famous defeat at Roncesvalles, but persistent pressure in that direction led to the creation of a *march*, or militarized border district, known as the Spanish March, south of the Pyrenees near the modern city of Barcelona. This aggressive policy permitted Charlemagne to rule over the largest state in the West since the fall of Rome. In all his wars, Charlemagne managed to create the impression that he was not merely serving his own greed, but rather overpowering barbarians, pagans, and infidels to save his Christian subjects from grave danger. Popes, poets, and nobles addressed him as "the strong right arm of God."

Charlemagne aimed to set up good government as well as to conquer. He made some innovations in the system of government his family had taken over from the Merovingians. He supported himself and his court chiefly by the careful use of royal lands (there was no longer a system of taxation). The king's commands were executed locally by counts and dukes whom he appointed. Charlemagne devoted considerable energy to rigorous supervision of his counts and dukes to prevent them from exploiting their offices for private advantage. His chief instrument in this effort was a corps of special officials, called *missi*, sent out from the royal court periodically with careful instructions to discover how royal officials were conducting themselves. He also made wide use of the practice of *commendation* to bind his officials to him as personal dependents, or *vassals*, obligated by oath to serve him loyally. Often he rewarded his vassals with grants of land to be enjoyed by them as long as they remained loyal.

Charlemagne's great distinction as a ruler lay in what he tried to achieve within this old system of government. More than anything else, he sought to institute a regime of order and justice, the sense of which was derived in large part from Christian ideology. The counts and dukes were instructed to quiet the turbulent nobles and to give protection to the weak and helpless. Tremendous emphasis was placed on safeguarding each man's rights under the law to which he was born. Charlemagne sought to supplement the existing legal systems by issuing edicts (*capitularies*) affecting nearly every phase of life. For at least the length of his reign, Charlemagne once again made monarchy stand for justice, protection, and order.

A silver coin of Charlemagne, issued in the last year of his reign. It is supposed to be the best likeness of the emperor. *Photo: Staatliche Museen, Berlin*

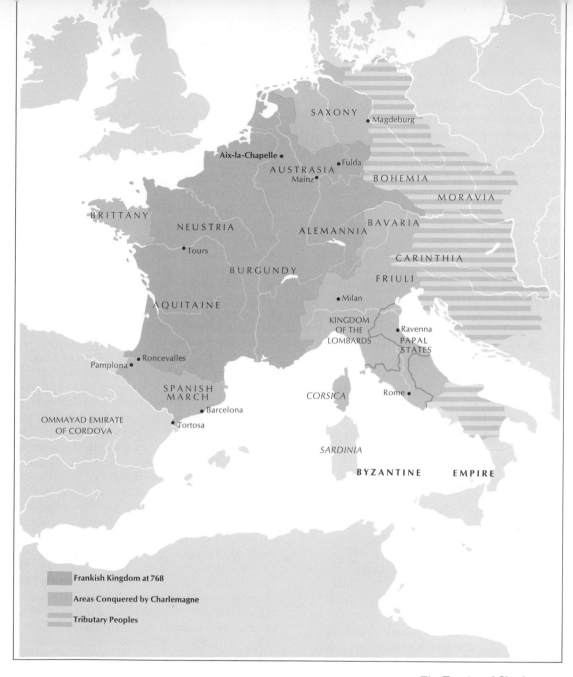

The Empire of Charlemagne

Moved by a deep personal piety and realizing that the only thing all his subjects had in common was religion, Charlemagne was especially concerned with the condition of the Church. He took the position that his divinely sanctioned royal office imposed on him the prime duty to strengthen and sustain the Church in its important task of saving souls. He was an ardent champion of the expansion of Christianity, encouraging missionaries and even using force to compel pagans to accept baptism. He also continued the vigorous reform movement begun by Pepin. With the advice of the higher clergy, he enacted a large body of law aimed at strengthening Church organization, protecting Church property, imposing higher moral and educational standards on the clergy, establishing uniform doctrines and rituals, and destroying pagan superstitions. He poured out his royal wealth to support the activities of the Church and the clergy. Of course, such an active interest led to constant royal intervention in every aspect of religious life—from the outright appointment of church officials to the most mundane problems connected with church property. So exalted was Charlemagne's vision of his religious role that he even felt free on occasion to advise the pope on how to conduct himself. His policy actually differed little from the caesaropapist program of the Byzantine emperors. In formulating and enacting his religious program, Charlemagne relied heavily on guidance from Rome, so that his effort marked a decisive step in imposing the Roman stamp on the religious life of Western Europe; in this sense Charlemagne was a major architect of the Roman Catholic Church. At least on the surface, the Church took on new vigor under his guiding hand.

The high point of Charlemagne's career and, to many of his contemporaries, the culmination of his efforts as warrior, lawgiver, and champion of the true faith came on Christmas Day, 800. While Charlemagne was attending a mass in St. Peter's Basilica in Rome, Pope Leo III placed a golden crown on his head and the crowd hailed him as "Augustus, crowned by God, the great and peace-bringing Emperor of the Romans." Einhard, Charlemagne's biographer, claimed that the king was surprised by Leo's action and did not want the new title. Perhaps this was only polite modesty or perhaps it was a reflection of Charlemagne's displeasure at the fact that Leo III seems to have snatched the initiative in this momentous event. Certainly the elevation of Charlemagne to the emperorship was a logical culmination of Carolingian policy and in keeping with his position. The new title better fitted his role as conqueror, ruler of diverse peoples,

lawgiver, protector of the weak, and champion of the Church and the papacy than did his old title, king of the Franks. It was a fitting tribute for one who had done more than any ruler since the fall of Rome to protect and encourage an ordered world. It helped clarify the heretofore vague position of Charlemagne with respect to the Papal States. And it reflected the conviction widely shared in the West that the emperor in the East (the imperial throne was in fact occupied by a woman in 800) had failed to protect the Christian world and safeguard the orthodox faith.

In a sense the coronation of 800 was an attempt to revive the Roman Empire in Western Europe; Charlemagne was often hailed as a new Constantine. However, the Carolingian Empire was clearly distinct. Territorially, it came nowhere near embracing the old Roman imperial territory, even in the West. It was based on ideas distinct from those underlying the Roman imperial system. Those who instituted the new empire, especially the churchmen who played a key role in advising Charlemagne, were prompted by Christian idealism. They were convinced it was God's will that all Christians should be joined in a single earthly commonwealth under a Christian prince. They argued that a strong prince sanctioned by divine power was the only instrument capable of constructing the *respublica Christiana* and safeguarding it from its enemies. The Carolingians repeatedly turned to the Old Testament for their political models; Charlemagne was the new David ordained by God to ensure the enactment of divine will. The other claimant to this role, the emperor in Constantinople, had failed miserably, and it was now time to renew the ancient covenant between God and the new Chosen People, the orthodox Franks. This was a political vision that owed an immense debt to St. Augustine, whose *City of God* was said to have been one of Charlemagne's favorite books. The translation of Augustinian political idealism into a Germanic context was a crucial step in creating a Western European sense of mission and political consciousness.

Charlemagne ruled fourteen years as emperor, and his actions indicate that he took his new title seriously. He conducted a skillful diplomatic drive that compelled the Eastern emperor to recognize his new title. This was a touchy problem in view of the vaunted claims of the ruler at Constantinople with respect to the West. Charlemagne also legislated more extensively than before, especially in religious matters, and assumed many of the trappings of the imperial office. When he died in 814 he left a large, well-ruled state that had moved far in the direction of unity based on acceptance of one emperor and one religion.

3. THE CAROLINGIAN RENAISSANCE

Perhaps the most lasting achievement of the indefatigable Charlemagne was the cultural renaissance that distinguished his age, a revival brought about chiefly through his personal efforts. We have already noted that the era from the fall of Rome until the middle of the eighth century was on the whole one of cultural decline, but one in which there were efforts to keep alive learning, letters, and the arts. Charlemagne made a concerted effort to give these cultural activities new vitality and succeeded in making considerable progress in that direction by concentrating them, giving them relevance to the issues of his day, and inspiring others to join him in more active support. The motivation behind his cultural policy was pragmatic: he was convinced that the quality of religious and political life could be improved only by developing a more educated group of leaders, especially churchmen.

His chief instrument to this end was the palace school which he began in the 780s and 790s, but which took on special vigor after he built his splendid church and palace at Aachen about 800 and made that city the center of his political activities. To this school he attracted the best minds from all over Europe, so that it became a focal point where the accomplishments of diverse cultural centers of the sixth and seventh centuries min-

gled and matured. By far the most notable luminary of the palace school was the Englishman Alcuin, a product of the energetic English cultural environment that had produced Bede roughly a century earlier. Alcuin became the directing spirit of the palace school and the architect of its development.

In one sense, the palace school was a gathering of intellectuals who encouraged each other to study, to write, and to discuss problems. Charlemagne himself was an active participant in this activity. But a more important function was the development of a sound educational program. Under Alcuin's guidance, its teachers labored primarily to create the tools and methods of instruction. Their main passion was to discover and make available the best possible versions of those books needed to ensure sound Christian education and the proper practice of the true religion. They thus sought authentic versions of Scripture, missals, laws, patristic texts, classical authors, church regulations—all those precious books that would guide men to what the Carolingians often spoke of as "the norms of righteousness" which should define and govern Christian life. Charlemagne even encouraged his scholars to collect Germanic legends as a part of this search for accurate versions of what great men in the past had said. The court scholars also gave special attention to the teaching of Latin in a pure form, and so sponsored the compilation of improved textbooks of grammar and spelling and the search for models of good Latin expression in classical authors. They devoted particular care to the accurate copying of these model works for their libraries. One of the major impediments to the discovery of accurate versions of ancient works was the debased character of Merovingian handwriting. The Carolingian copyists responded to this problem by developing a beautiful script called *Carolingian miniscule*, which provided the base from which all modern scripts and typefaces grew. The workshops where books were produced, called *scriptoria*, likewise developed an impressive style of manuscript illumination that constitutes a major aspect of Carolingian art.

As the tools of education were forged, Charlemagne employed his authority to universalize their use. He insisted that monasteries and bishoprics organize schools and that the books and methods developed at the palace school be employed in them. His efforts led to a significant expansion of education and a greatly increased concern for the quality of teaching in the monastic and episcopal schools. After Charlemagne's death, the palace school declined and cultural leadership passed to these new centers, especially the monastic schools, where throughout much of the ninth century the Carolingian renaissance was sustained.

Although their major energies were consumed in gathering and mastering the models of good thought, style, and language, the leading lights of the court school were soon prompted to try their own skills at writing. They produced a considerable body of poetry, history, biography, letters, and theological tracts. Much of the literary activity showed little originality; its chief distinction lies in the improvement in the use of Latin, the greater mastery of literary forms, the wider range of information, and the greater versatility of mind. Some Carolingian authors, however, did achieve considerable distinction, especially if compared to their predecessors of the era from 500 to 750. As already noted, Einhard produced an excellent biography of Charlemagne. Alcuin compiled several important textbooks of grammar and logic, wrote excellent letters, and composed good Latin verse. An Italian, Paul the Deacon, wrote a well-organized *History of the Lombards*. A Spaniard, Theodulf, was the author of excellent poetry. A succession of theologians prepared impressive commentaries on Scripture and showed considerable talent in synthesizing theological discourses out of a variety of patristic sources. Perhaps the most original mind of the age and the most competent Western theologian since Gregory the Great was an Irishman, John Scotus Erigena, who lived in the Frankish kingdom from 850 to 875. A man of great learning, with a good knowledge of Greek, he was strongly influenced by Neoplatonic ideas and was confident of the power of human reason to discern truth. Although the bulk of the work of these luminaries and many other lesser lights was derivative and timid in the face of new ideas, it was infused with an esthetic sense reflecting a genuine appreciation of classical literature. Thus one may speak of a Carolingian humanism mingling with deeply ingrained Christian values.

A vigorous artistic revival was associated with the Carolingian renaissance. It too grew out of religious concerns. Several fine churches were built, the most splendid of which was Charlemagne's church at Aachen. Considerable effort was made to decorate these churches with mosaics and frescoes. In many ways the best Carolingian art took the form of miniatures: small paintings in illuminated manuscripts, ivory carvings for altar adornment, metalwork, jewelry. All Carolingian art was distinguished by the mixing and mingling of diverse artistic traditions: classical, Byzantine, Germanic, Celtic. Again, the men of this age appropriated past traditions and formed them into new shapes.

4. THE DISINTEGRATION OF THE CAROLINGIAN EMPIRE

Charlemagne's political empire did not survive long. The history of the ninth century is dominated by the painful story of its disintegration and by the reduction of the power of his successors to a level hardly greater than that of the Merovingians from whose misrule the Carolingians had rescued the Frankish kingdom.

Charlemagne had not succeeded in developing governmental institutions capable of surviving him. To secure assistance in carrying out the functions of government, Charlemagne had been forced to grant large blocks of lands to the nobles in return for military service, often conceding authority to exercise governmental powers over the lands he had granted.

Such grants of governmental authority, called *immunities,* were made on the assumption that the nobles would be guided in their actions by the example of the great emperor, and Charlemagne tried to keep these men faithful to him by the device of having them swear loyalty as vassals. But this arrangement could work for the benefit of the emperor only if he were forceful enough to keep his widely scattered, wealthy vassals under close watch. This was a tremendous burden, one that most of Charlemagne's successors could not manage.

Moreover, Charlemagne's empire was never unified in a real sense. Germans, Romans, and Slavs were still divided by language differences; and in spite of all Charlemagne's legislation, numerous law codes still existed within the empire. The different cultural backgrounds to which his subjects were heirs could not be wished out of existence. Neither the Christian religion nor the commands of an emperor were powerful enough to bridge the gap between groups as diverse as the newly conquered and converted Saxons and the residents of Rome. The Church, upon which Charlemagne relied so heavily to inspire and guide his subjects to obey and to serve, was actually a doubtful ally. Its leaders in Rome and in the great bishoprics and monasteries scattered over the empire were uneasy about Charlemagne's interference in Church affairs. While aspiring to the same end that he did, namely, an earthly society dedicated to the service of God, many churchmen preferred to lead society themselves rather than to bend before a layman. Their independence was a harbinger of bitter conflicts between church and state later in the Middle Ages.

The empire was also threatened by powerful external foes. On the south were the aggressive Muslims, especially strong in sea power, against which the Franks had little defense. On the east the Slavs, under the pressure of new invaders from Asia, the Magyars, pushed relentlessly westward. Finally, the Vikings or Norsemen (Danes, Swedes, and Norwegians) threatened on the north. The Vikings, virtually strangers to Western Europe in the early ninth century, quickly became the greatest danger.

The Vikings were still barbarians and heathens. They had long dwelt along the wild coasts of Scandinavia, surviving chiefly by fishing and piracy. These occupations made them skilled seamen. Politically, strong clans played a dominant role, although by 800 loose kingdoms were in the process of formation. In the ninth century, for reasons hard to discern, the Vikings began to expand. Traveling by sea in small groups, they spread over an immense area, touching Ireland, England, the whole Atlantic coast of Europe, the southern shores of the North and Baltic seas, Russia, Iceland, Greenland, and probably North America. Following the rivers, they penetrated far inland in Western Europe, England, and Russia. Wherever they went, they pillaged the land and hauled off vast quantities of loot. In the late ninth and tenth centuries, some of them began to settle permanently in the lands they had been raiding, especially in England, Ireland, France, and Russia, and piracy gave way to trade. The Vikings slowly accepted the religion and culture of Western Europeans. As we shall see later, they became one of the most creative groups in Western Europe, especially in the eleventh and twelfth centuries. However, all this was too late to spare the Carolingian Empire. Charlemagne's successors had to face the full fury of the destructive raids and found no effective defense against the dreaded raiding parties.

Perhaps more Charlemagnes could have offset these immense problems, for the well-being of the Carolingian state depended to a considerable degree on the personal capabilities of its ruler. But the empire suffered from inadequate leadership throughout much of the ninth century. Charlemagne's son Louis (814–840) was an indecisive ruler. His most powerful instinct was to pursue the universalist ideals embraced by the Carolingian political ideology. This inclination carried him toward a close alliance with powerful churchmen, whose gratitude earned Louis the title "Pious," but who were not averse to bending imperial policy to suit their ends. Equally powerful elements in Frankish society resisted the realization of the imperial idea with its implication of strong central government, and Louis on occasion surrendered to their pressures. The major problem of his reign centered around what provision he would make for his four sons (one of whom died before he did). Louis was torn between safeguarding the unity of the empire by designating a single successor and observing the ancient Frankish custom of dividing his empire among his heirs. His efforts to compromise these conflicting ideas led his sons to revolt with the encouragement and support of the enemies of strong government and unity and prompted the supporters of unity to damn him as an enemy of the divinely ordained scheme of things. The stage was set for a bitter struggle destined to distract the rulers from the innumerable other problems of the empire.

Before his death Louis did provide a "kingdom" for each of his three surviving sons and granted to his eldest, Lothair, the title of emperor with a vague authority over the others. Almost immediately the younger sons declared war on Lothair, and in 843 forced him to sign the Treaty of Verdun. This document legalized the division of the empire into three parts: a kingdom embracing most of modern France, a kingdom of Germany, and a kingdom of Lotharingia (Lorraine) consisting of a narrow band between the west and east kingdoms stretching from the North Sea to Italy. The middle kingdom swiftly became a battleground, a prize sought by the rulers of the other two kingdoms. Eventually, there were further divisions that created the kingdoms of Italy and Burgundy.

After 843, Carolingian unity was fatally compromised. Most of the energies of the Carolingians who ruled these several kingdoms were absorbed in snatching bits of territory from their relatives. The resulting petty wars left little time for problems of religion, justice, internal order, and defense against the mounting attacks of outsiders. The later Carolingians continued the practice of buying support by granting new lands to nobles. And the recipients of these favors sought successfully to ensure themselves permanent possession of these grants and the political powers that went with them. This constant diminution of the royal estates and power eventually left the Carolingian rulers powerless to curb the nobility.

High churchmen usually supported the later Carolingian kings and tried to keep alive the old imperial ideal as it had existed under Charlemagne, and the kings showed their gratitude by heaping rich endowments on the Church. But in the long run ecclesiastical support of the Carolingian family worked against the interests of the rulers. The Church became bolder and bolder in its claims to supremacy over the state. By the middle of the ninth century, the pope was openly claiming superior authority over all Christians—including kings. Pope Nicholas I (858–867) actually tried to exercise these claims by interfering in the private lives of the kings, while at the same time carrying on extensive diplomatic negotiations in an attempt to halt the civil wars raging everywhere, legislating for the whole Church, and taking the lead in spreading Christianity. By 900 the Carolingian dynasty was thoroughly discredited and the empire divided beyond repair. Invaders pillaged Western Europe almost at will. Landed nobles tightened their holds on their small principalities and compelled the lower classes to submit to their petty domination. Even the Church, the last bastion of unity, suffered fragmentation. The dream of Charlemagne and his advisers to make Western Europe a single political unit had not been fulfilled; what developed instead was feudalism, a system based on fragmentation.

These obvious failures must not hide the deeper significance of the Carolingian Empire as the first attempt by some Western Europeans to give expression to the uniqueness of the West. Germanic rulers—represented by

Charlemagne—demonstrated a deepened awareness of a responsibility other than conquering lands for their own private profit. It is not without significance that Charlemagne became the hero of numerous legends eagerly read during the centuries following his death. He became the ideal prince for medieval Western Europe. His attempt to unify Europe politically was destined to inspire the actions of numerous later medieval kings. Several of the chief kingdoms of Europe, especially France, Germany, and Italy, traced their origin to the Carolingian period and considered themselves successors of the Carolingian kingdom. Certain Carolingian techniques of government, especially the practice of creating lord-vassal ties to define the relationship between ruler and ruled, long served as the basis for political life in these successor states. Carolingian law codes persisted for many centuries as the basis of justice in some areas of Western Europe. Under its Carolingian champions, the Western Church moved further from dependence on and cooperation with the Greek Orthodox Church, succeeded in imposing a considerable degree of doctrinal and liturgical uniformity throughout the West, and gained important ground in creating an independent state in Italy. The papal role in sanctifying the Carolingians first as kings of the Franks and then as emperors established a significant precedent for the fundamental medieval idea that the state must have the blessing of the Church. The revival of the idea of empire dramatically reaffirmed the tie between Western Europe and classical Rome. The renewed interest in Roman civilization brought about an upsurge of intellectual activity. This Carolingian renaissance was the first of several that brought Western Europeans into more intimate contact with the classical civilizations of Greece and Rome. The true significance of the Carolingian era must thus be sought in the world of ideas: It was a period when some Western Europeans tried to define what they wanted politically, socially, religiously, and culturally. Although few of the ends pursued were attained at the time,

Anglo-Saxon England

much of later medieval history consists of working out the details of ideas developed in the Carolingian period.

5. ENGLAND IN THE EARLY MIDDLE AGES

While the Carolingians were shaping much of Western Europe, the small Anglo-Saxon kingdoms of England were undergoing an important transformation. After a long period of fruitless warfare, these kingdoms began to coalesce, chiefly as a result of two outside forces—Christianity and the Viking menace.

England had been Christianized in Roman times, but the Anglo-Saxon invaders wiped out Christianity in the territories they occupied. Late in the sixth century missionaries began to penetrate England both from Rome and from Ireland. Within a century, the Anglo-Saxons were converted, and a common religion prevailed throughout the different kingdoms. For a brief period in the seventh century, Roman and Irish missionaries clashed bitterly for the right to dominate England. Rome won, assuring uniformity of organization, ritual, and doctrine and putting the English in touch with the mainstream of continental religious life. The second force bringing about unity in England, the terrible threat of the Vikings, was the more important. No area suffered more from their pillaging, especially during the first half of the ninth century. Some Vikings even settled permanently in England, occupying a large territory in the northeast known as the *Danelaw* (that is, the land where Danish law was supreme). Several of the old Anglo-Saxon kingdoms were swallowed up by the invaders.

The kingdom of Wessex became the center of resistance and eventually of counterattack against the Vikings. The reign of Alfred the Great (871–899) was the decisive period. Alfred was a crafty, determined war leader. He not only stopped Viking expansion, but

A page from the Book of Kells, a masterpiece of Irish manuscript illumination, showing Christ being captured in Jerusalem. In the years around 800, Irish monks combined geometric and animal forms and Christian themes to produce a rich array of ornamental designs in a unique style. *Photo: The Board of Trinity College, Dublin*

also laid the groundwork for the reconquest of the Danelaw. His leadership served to revitalize the Church and the dormant English intellectual life, and both these accomplishments helped stir up the English against foreigners. During the tenth century Alfred's heirs rewon the Danelaw, pushing the English frontier to about the present boundary between England and Scotland. All the conquered territory and its peoples, including the Danes, were made subjects of a single king, who was no longer king of Wessex but king of England.

The unification of England necessitated a single governmental system for the whole kingdom. This system of government, based on institutions that had existed in England since the arrival of the Anglo-Saxons in the early fifth century, assumed its final shape by 1000. A single king, claiming to be supreme judge, leader of the army, head of the Church, and lawgiver, ruled over the land. Actually, royal power was limited, since the kings lacked effective means of exercising their authority. The central government consisted chiefly of household officials who cared for the kings' personal needs. Each king supported himself and his court chiefly from the income derived from royal estates. On rare occasions, the king could levy a direct tax on his subjects—for instance, several kings collected the Danegeld, levied first in 991 to buy off Viking raiders—but ordinarily this was not possible. For military support, the kings depended heavily on knights to whom land had been granted, although the king could summon all freemen to serve in the army (called the *fyrd*). The king was advised on matters of great importance by the *Witan*, an assembly of great nobles and churchmen that in a general way was held to represent all freemen. Usually the Witan was taken into the king's counsel on such matters as waging war or enacting new laws. However, a strong king could do any of these things without its help or approval. The whole complex of institutions surrounding the king—household officials, fyrd, royal knights, and Witan—made the central government an institution of considerable importance, but certainly not strong enough to control political life in all England.

Much more significant in tenth-century England was the system of local government that had long been evolving. England was divided into *shires*, of which there were about forty in the tenth century. The king was represented in each shire by three officials—the *earl*, the *sheriff*, and the *bishop*. The earl was most important in rank and prestige, but the sheriff usually conducted most of the royal business. A court was held in each shire twice a year, and all freemen were expected to attend. At this court the king's orders were proclaimed and all civil and criminal cases were handled. Any freeman could bring his complaints to the court. The law administered in these courts was customary law, dating from far back in Anglo-Saxon history and known by the local landowners who sat in the court. Each shire was subdivided into smaller units called *hundreds*, where courts, presided over by a royal official, met monthly to deal with minor cases. The agricultural villages also had their own courts and customs; great landowners usually conducted these courts. As a rule, the business of the Church was conducted in the shire and hundred courts. This network of local institutions, tied to the central government through royal officials but also self-sufficient to a large extent, provided an element of orderly political life in England that was sometimes lacking on the Continent.

The political and social institutions of Anglo-Saxon England were largely a product of Germanic influences implanted at the time of the invasion. With the exception of Christianity, English society was little affected prior to the eleventh century by the ideas and practices of the Mediterranean world that were so important in shaping the continental Germanic kingdoms. This situation gave English society a unique quality that was to persist far into the future. However, by 1000 England's political and social institutions were somewhat archaic due to her isolation and consequently incapable of adjusting to new conditions stirring everywhere in Western Europe. During the eleventh century England was conquered by the Normans from the Continent. As we shall see later (Chapter 21), the newcomers imposed on the strongly Germanic English society new institutional patterns that "modernized" her society and opened a new era of growth. Perhaps the chief importation was feudalism, which during the ninth and tenth centuries had developed on the Continent as a stabilizing force but which had not emerged in late Anglo-Saxon England. We must now turn our attention to feudal society before returning to England's later history.

Suggested Reading

Carolingian History. General treatments of Carolingian history can be found in the works of Sullivan, Moss, Lewis, Dawson, Wallace-Haddrill, Burn, Deanesly, and Pirenne, already cited in chapters 15 and 16. Especially good is **H. Fichtenau, *The Carolingian Empire: The Age of Charlemagne* (Harper Torchbook). Also valuable are F. Ganshoy, *Frankish Institutions Under Charlemagne*, trans. B. and M. Lyon (1968), and Peter Munz, *Life in the Age of Charlemagne* (1969). A splendidly illustrated treatment of the period is Donald Bullough, *The Age of Charlemagne* (1965). The much-debated problem of the coronation of 800 is discussed in **R. E. Sullivan, ed., *The Coronation of Charlemagne: What Did It Signify?* (Heath); F. L. Ganshof, *The Imperial Coronation of Charlemagne: Theories and Facts* (1949); and P. Munz, *The Origins of the Carolingian Empire* (1960). A somewhat popularized biography of Charlemagne is **Richard Winston, *Charlemagne: From the Hammer to the Cross* (Vintage). The work of Daniel-Rops, cited in Chapter 15, treats church history. Aside from the works of Laistner and Schnürer cited in Chapters 15 and 16, Carolingian cultural history is treated in two works by E. S. Duckett, *Alcuin, Friend of Charlemagne* (1951), and *Carolingian*

Portraits: A Study in the Ninth Century (1962). **Roger Hinks, *Carolingian Art* (Ann Arbor) presents a thorough treatment of the major features of art history. The early chapters of K. J. Conant, *Carolingian and Romanesque Architecture, 800–1200* (2nd ed., 1966), show clearly the essential features of Carolingian architecture and relate it to later architectural history.

Vikings. The best history of the Vikings and their culture is **Johannes Bronsted, *The Vikings* (Penguin). Axel Olrik, *Viking Civilization* (1930), provides a brief description of Viking culture, drawing heavily on Scandinavian literature. A recent work, P. Sawyer, *The Age of the Vikings* (1962), supplies some interesting new interpretations of the impact of the Viking raids, but the book is not easy to read.

Anglo-Saxon England. Two excellent introductions to Anglo-Saxon history are **D. Whitelock, *Beginnings of English Society: Anglo-Saxon Period* (Penguin); and **P. Hunter Blair, *Introduction to Anglo-Saxon England* (Cambridge). Longer and much more ponderous, but thorough, is F. M. Stenton, *Anglo-Saxon England* (2nd ed., 1947). An excellent evaluation of Alfred the Great is **E. S. Duckett, *Alfred the Great: The King and His England* (Phoenix).

Sources. Considerable light is thrown on Carolingian society in about 750, especially religious affairs, by *The Letters of St. Boniface,* trans. E. Emerton (1940); Boniface was an English monk who came to the Continent, took up missionary work with papal support, and became the spearhead of the reform of the Church in the time of Charles Martel and Pepin the Short. Indispensable is **Einhard, *Life of Charlemagne,* trans. S. E. Turner (Ann Arbor). A life of Louis the Pious by an anony-

mous author can be found in *Son of Charlemagne: A Contemporary Biography of Louis the Pious,* trans. A. Cabaniss (1961). Contemporary biographies of two powerful ninth-century churchmen can be read in *Charlemagne's Cousins: Contemporary Lives of Adalard and Wala,* trans. A. Cabaniss (1967). **S. C. Easton and H. Wieruszowski, eds., *The Era of Charlemagne* (Anvil), provides a selection of documents, accompanied by perceptive commentaries that throw interesting light on many phases of Carolingian life. D. Whitelock, ed., *English Historical Documents, c. 500–1042* (1955), provides a similar collection for Anglo-Saxon England.

qui est sapientia p[...]
mutat. Explicit p[...]

in illum puale et
a deo. puata[...]

Chapter 18 🍃 The Emergence of the Feudal and Manorial Systems

The idealistic dreams that moved a few men to struggle toward a unified Christian Europe in the Carolingian age were blasted by the events of the last half of the ninth century. It was necessary to return to simpler ways, to discover a broader, more solid base for society, to face the societal realities of the age, and to operate within their limits. Amid the wreckage, two institutions emerged to provide a workable base for society: *feudalism* and *manorialism*. Both were products of forces that had been working at the foundations of political, social, and economic life since the fall of the Roman Empire. By the late ninth and tenth centuries they emerged as the focal points of Western European society.

1. ORIGINS AND NATURE OF FEUDALISM

The essential practices that characterized feudalism by the ninth and tenth centuries had their origins deep in the European past. In very simple terms, feudalism grew out of the merging of two distinct practices: personal dependence and a system of land tenure that involved shared rights in land. Personal dependence probably had its origins in the Germanic *comitatus* and in the Roman system of clientage, both of which involved a pledge on the part of one individual to serve another in return for some kind of reward. The Romans had also developed a system of land usage whereby an owner of land allowed another the use of the land for a specified period in return for a service or payment. The confusion and chaos of Western Europe after the Germanic invasions caused these usages to become widespread by the seventh and eighth centuries. In search of a strong protector, many men were happy to swear allegiance and render service to another, an arrangement called *commendation*. Likewise, those in search of a means of livelihood or of a way to enlarge their holdings were willing to accept the use of another's land in return for service. Many small landholders were even willing to surrender ownership of their land to a more powerful man on condition that he would allow them the use of the *benefice*, as such lands were called. The greatest landowners, especially the Church, were eager to free themselves of the obligation of exploiting their extensive holdings by granting them as benefices to those willing to accept the use of the land in return for some service to the grantor.

A knight receives his sword from his lord, here a king, in this early fourteenth-century initial from a Latin bible manuscript illumination. *Photo: Dean and Chapter of Durham Cathedral, England*

During the Carolingian period these usages spread and were given much more precise legal definition, chiefly because the strongest Carolingian rulers employed them as a means of expanding their power. They required the great men of their kingdom, especially those who served as public officials, to commend themselves to the kings—to become *vassals*, in the terminology of the times—as a means of ensuring faithful service. In turn, these powerful figures bound lesser men to them by the same process. The kings and great lords likewise granted benefices, now called *fiefs*, to their dependents. The most decisive development of the Carolingian period was this merging of vassalage and benefice. The impetus for this crucial step in the evolution of feudal-ism came primarily from a basic change in warfare. For reasons not entirely clear, there occurred in the early eighth century a shift from the use of infantry to that of cavalry, which required that warriors possess horses and heavy armor. Because these tools of war were expensive, the limited resources of the Carolingian monarchs forced them to depend on warriors who could equip themselves. As early as the time of Charles Martel, the central government began to seek out vassals to whom were awarded grants of land on condition that the recipients render military service at their own expense. The royal use of vassalage and benefice for political and military purposes resulted in the spread of these practices among an elite group of governing and fighting men in society and made them vital to the operation of the royal government. The Carolingians added to this thrust by conceding to their vassals certain rights of government over their benefices or fiefs; these grants of *immunity* tended to remove lands and their inhabitants from royal control and to exalt the position of fief holders and vassals in society.

The eclipse of central government after about 850 amid the mounting fury of Saracen (Muslim), Magyar, and Viking raids forced society to depend more and more on these systems to ensure some kind of political stability. Military security was most essential, and the emerging feudal system was especially suited to this end. A resourceful lord and his warrior vassals were the only effective force capable of defending a locality against the quick-hitting, elusive raiders. All who could sought to become vassals under a strong lord; every powerful figure tried to find new vassals to swell his military following. To ensure that such arrangements would persist, vassalage and fiefs were made hereditary. Under these circumstances, the holders of fiefs assumed the right to provide whatever other governmental services needed to be performed, and often usurped political functions formerly exercised by the kings and their agents. By the beginning of the tenth century, considerable areas of Europe, especially the northern parts of the old Carolingian Empire, were fragmented into hundreds of small private jurisdictions ruled by persons who held the land at the moment. The relationships among the people involved were controlled wholly by the terms of their private agreements—by feudal contracts. Public authority was too weak and too remote to be effective.

One important point must be added. Long before the beginning of the tenth century, the bulk of the peasant population had already become associated in a condition of dependency with self-sufficient agricultural estates—the villas or, as they came to be called, *manors*. Their dependency was a condition that bound them to serve a possessor of land in the performance of menial services in return for use of a tenancy sufficient to the needs of a family. As a consequence, the peasants were not, properly speaking, participants in the feudal order. Feudalism involved freemen capable of receiving and giving pledges of loyalty and service. It involved those capable of performing the honorable services of fighting and governing and of managing the fiefs that were granted them in order that they could perform these services. The feudal system was therefore a political, social system embracing a small class of aristocrats. These same feudal lords and vassals ruled over the peasant population through a set of institutions collectively called *manorialism*.

2. THE FEUDAL CONTRACT

The essence of the political bonds involved in the feudal system was defined by the feudal contract. The ritual that evolved to mark the establishment of such a contract provides a convenient key to the nature of these bonds. One man knelt before another, placed his hands between those of the second, and declared himself willing to become his "man." By this voluntary act, involving two freemen, the first became a vassal and the second a lord. This process was called *homage*. The lord lifted up his new "man" and kissed him, signifying that he accepted him as a vassal. The vassal then swore an oath of *fealty*, binding himself in the sight of God to live up to his obligations, and the lord gave him some object like a banner, a clod of dirt, or a ring.

This medieval French fortress, the Chateau du Peyrepertuse, seems almost to grow out of the mountainside on which it is built. Note its advantageous defensive position—the sweeping view of the valley, the steep, difficult approaches from above and below. *Photo: Gilles Ehrmann, Réalités*

This was called *investiture*. It symbolized the granting of a fief, usually a piece of land, by the lord to the vassal. By the three acts of homage, fealty, and investiture, two individuals bound themselves together in a way that gave to each important rights and imposed on each duties that controlled his political and social activities to a large degree.

The relationship between lord and vassal was intended to last until one party died, unless either broke the contract by some illegal act. By the time the feudal system had reached its full development in the tenth century, the whole arrangement had become hereditary. When a lord died, his eldest son took his place, receiving homage and fealty from his father's vassals and investing them with their fiefs. When a vassal died, his lord accepted his son as a vassal and permitted him to retain the fief of his father. Under these arrangements, lord-vassal relationships continued for generations in the same families, adding considerable stability to the entire system.

The exact obligations of each party differed from place to place in Europe and are not easy to describe accurately in generalized terms. Generally, however, there were certain basic duties for each party. The lord obligated himself to protect his vassal and give him justice. In an age when there was no effective central government, this meant that a lord was obligated to use his army to protect a vassal against attack. It also meant that the lord had to maintain a court where the vassal could appear and receive a hearing for any grievances he might have. Put briefly, it imposed on the lord the grave responsibility of running a small-scale government for his vassals.

The vassal's duties can be spelled out somewhat more precisely. In a general way he was obligated to conduct himself honorably and loyally toward his lord so as to bring no disgrace on him—an obligation that generated a total style of living in the feudal world. More specifically, the vassal's first and chief obligation was military service as an armed knight for forty days a year at his own expense. The vassal also owed counsel and advice to his lord, meaning that he had to appear at the lord's court when summoned and to perform any political duties the lord might require. The third obligation of a vassal was to give *aids*—make a specified money payment to his lord under certain conditions. Usually there were three cases when an aid was required: the ransom of a lord who had become a prisoner of war, the knighting of a lord's eldest son, and the marriage of his eldest daughter. A lord might require other aids from his vassals, but usually only with their consent. A fourth duty of a vassal was that of *hospitality*, that is, of entertaining his lord and the lord's party when the lord happened to travel through the fief (this could be a burden when the lord came often with a large following and stayed long). In addition, the vassal was obligated to respect certain privileges pertaining to the lord with respect to the fief. These *feudal incidents* derived from the fact that the lord was the real owner of the fief and thus had rights to it; the vassal had only received it to use. The vassal was obliged to maintain the fief in good condition so that its value would not deteriorate. His heir had to pay an inheritance tax, called a *relief*, when he succeeded to the fief. The lord had the right of guardianship, or *wardship*, over a vassal's minor heir and had to approve of the marriage of his daughter, since her husband might someday become heir to the fief and to the status of vassal. The vassal was obliged to recognize that if he died without heirs, the fief was to revert to the lord.

The operation of the feudal system depended entirely upon the performance of these obligations. The great sin of the feudal world was infidelity—unfaithfulness to the sworn word. How were these contracts (which incidentally were seldom written down) enforced? When a contract is made in our society, the state stands above the parties as the enforcing agency. In the tenth century there was no effective higher authority; enforcement, too, had to be settled by lords and vassals. The chief instrument for this purpose was the lord's court, in which there was applied a customary law that embraced in intricate detail the customs that governed feudal contracts in a given area. A vassal was summoned if he was thought to be guilty of infidelity, judged by his "peers," that is, by other vassals, and punished as custom dictated. To this same court every vassal had a right to bring complaints against his lord; again, his peers judged whether he had redress. These courts did sometimes act as enforcing agencies to adjudicate disagreements, but force was always the final recourse. A lord could call on his other vassals to march against an unfaithful vassal, and a wronged vassal could appeal to his fellow vassals to join him in raising the standard of revolt against an unjust lord who infringed on his rights. Such wars were numerous in the feudal age; in fact, we often equate feudalism and incessant warfare.

It would be wrong, however, to picture feudal lords and vassals as seeking any opportunity to start a brawl. In a society that knew no other workable political system, lords were anxious to keep their vassals and gain their services. And vassals were equally anxious to enjoy the protection of a lord, even though he might not be a paragon of virtue, for it was from him alone that they received protection and justice. Thus it was to the mutual advantage of each party to live up to the terms of the contract. Then too, it must be remembered that the contract was sealed by an oath

of fealty. In an age when men took religion seriously, there was a good deal of reluctance to break a promise sealed in the presence of God.

3. FEUDALISM AND THE STATE

The popular view of feudalism has long been that it was the antithesis of effective government, but such a generalization must be made with caution. At least in theory, feudalism was not contradictory to the good governance of the state, as feudal lawyers from the thirteenth century down to the French Revolution loved to point out. The king was the supreme lord and theoretical owner of all the land in the kingdom. At his own pleasure he had granted out his land as fiefs to men who became his vassals. Each owed him the services previously described. Perhaps the king had also granted his greater vassals rights of immunity, which permitted them to exercise the powers of government over their fiefs. The great vassals of a king could then subdivide their holdings into smaller fiefs and grant them to other men willing to become vassals. This process, called *subinfeudation*, could continue until fiefs had been created that were only large enough to permit a single vassal to support himself and fulfill his obligations. In theory, a vast hierarchy was constructed, with a king at the top and with each rank beneath owing allegiance and services to an authority above (see diagram).

In practice, the feudal system did not work so smoothly. First, the king's authority was only theoretical. If he should grant too much of his land, he had no means at his disposal to enforce his authority over his vassals. Although they owed him services, there was little he could do to force them to render those services if he had no means of backing up his orders The same fate might befall any lord in the feudal hierarchy if he granted away too much of his land to vassals. Second, subinfeudation created contradictory loyalties which disturbed the hierarchy. There was nothing to keep a vassal of one lord from becoming the vassal of and accepting a fief from another. To illustrate the confusion that resulted from this practice, let us return to the diagram. Vassal F, an ambitious, capable man, dissatisfied with his status as a simple vassal of E, also does homage to A, B, C, and D in return for fiefs from each one, owing services for each of these fiefs. Once these agreements had been established, several interesting situations could arise. Suppose A and D went to war. Whom would F serve, since he owed military service to each? We can see clearly that the orderly hierarchy would be broken down. Suppose that by all his deals F acquired control over more land than any of his lords—A, B, C, D, or E. Who would be master of the situation then? Obviously the vassal would be in a position to defy his lords and turn the feudal hierarchy upside down. Subinfeudation, by creating conflicting allegiances and confusing alignments that destroyed the theoretical hierarchy, made it impossible for feudalism to operate effectively for the control of a large state. As feudal institutions matured, attempts were made to counteract the fragmentation of authority resulting from subinfeudation by developing *liege homage*, a system whereby a lord required not only his own vassals but also their vassals and subvassals to pledge their prime allegiance and loyalty to him. But this practice developed too late to prevent the atomization of power in early feudal society.

In view of these considerations, it is evident that the impact of feudalism on the governance of an extensive kingdom depended upon a complex set of circumstances. In the areas of Western Europe where it developed first and spread most widely—that is, in the kingdom of the West Franks (France) and to a lesser degree in the kingdoms of Burgundy (Arles) and Italy—feudalism seriously weakened royal power in the tenth and eleventh centuries. In these areas the kings divided most of their lands into numerous fiefs which were granted to vassals in return for services. Often these royal vassals were conceded immunities or simply usurped the royal rights of government, thereby acquiring extensive political powers over their fiefs. These kingdoms were broken into a confusing array of counties, duchies, viscounties, marches, and other principalities over which the weakened kings had little control. Most of the royal vassals subinfeudated their fiefs to become feudal lords in their own rights. As this process continued, a confusing tangle of relationships blurred clear lines of authority. Some of the great vassals of the kings managed to maintain control over their vassals, thereby creating well-governed feudal principalities functioning on the basis of the rights and obligations governing feudal contracts. However, other great fief holders were just as ineffective as the kings in controlling their fiefs and vassals, so that their principalities suffered considerable fragmentation and confusion.

Feudalism tended to spread outward from France in various ways and with various effects. It penetrated the kingdom of the East Franks (Germany) very slowly and did not take deep hold there until the twelfth century. As it advanced into Germany, it tended to destroy royal power and to create a permanent division of the kingdom into small principalities. Spain became feudalized in the course of the long war to liberate the land from the Muslims; this circumstance provided feudal nobles with an opportunity to become firmly entrenched, but also made them dependent on a king for leadership in the wars of conquest. Feudalism was brought into England by a conquering king from the Continent, but he used it skillfully to increase royal power. As it penetrated the western Slavic world in the later Middle Ages, feudalism tended to weaken the state to the advantage of the nobles.

It is obvious, then, that the long-established generalization that feudalism was destructive to the state cannot be defended. Perhaps all we can say is that feudalism tended to divide large kingdoms into a series of small jurisdictions, each with its own set of interpersonal relationships, its own laws, and its own instruments of government. These entities were tied to the king primarily by a personal contract between the king and the holder of the fief which constituted the jurisdiction. If the king were skillful, careful of his resources, and willing to labor at the task, he could exact what was due him and thus draw strength from the feudal system. If he squandered or in some other way lost his resources and could not act toward his vassals in an effective way, then he had little power and his kingdom was weak and divided. In short, feudalism impinged on larger political entities in terms of how it was utilized. Herein lay its danger and its dynamic potential.

4. FEUDALISM AND THE CHURCH

Feudalism had a drastic effect on another vital institution in Western society: the Church. Under the guidance of the great Carolingian rulers of the eighth and early ninth century, the Church had enjoyed a tremendous upsurge in power and influence, owing to better organization, reform of the clergy, and standardization of ritual and doctrine. The coming of feudalism undid most of this work and pushed the Church into one of its worst periods of decay and inefficiency.

The difficulties of the Church in feudal society stemmed from its position as a great landholder. Much of the Church's land had been acquired in the form of grants from kings (the Carolingian rulers had been especially generous). However, they expected the Church officials who received land to render services as did any other recipient of royal lands. Bishops and abbots had to become vassals of the kings and fulfill their obligations as vassals. Great Church officials were not even averse to receiving fiefs from powerful laymen other than the king and accepting positions as vassals of these lords. Once having acquired large fiefs, these officials acted as did other landholders of the feudal age: They granted their lands out as fiefs, and thus became lords in their own right. And as lords, they had to concern themselves with protecting their vassals, holding courts, and protecting their interests in general.

There is little use in condemning this conduct; in the feudal age, those who had no land had no power. And those who had no lords to protect them or vassals to serve them did not long survive. Churchmen were only adapting themselves to the times. However, the consequences were disastrous in terms of the spiritual well-being of Western Europe. The ruling officials of the Church became completely preoccupied with secular matters at the expense of their religious duties. Laymen who granted fiefs to Church officials wanted to be sure that the fief was in capable hands. They refused to invest any bishop or abbot with a fief unless he had the qualities of a good vassal. In effect, this meant that laymen controlled elections to high offices. These offices came to be filled with good fighters and good administrators who had little interest in religious problems. The whole top level of the Church organization was dominated by men who were laymen and feudal nobles at heart. They neglected discipline, education, charity, moral conduct, and all the other matters properly associated with running a religious establishment. The lower clergy sank into ignorance. Religious life in lay society suffered an assortment of evils worse than in any other age in Christian history. Even the pope, who was the head of the Church, did not escape. During the tenth century the papal office was filled with men chosen by powerful feudal lords in central Italy. Most of these popes were only tools of these nobles and were looked upon with contempt by Christians in the rest of Western Europe.

One must be somewhat cautious, however, in decrying the abysmal condition of the Church in the feudal age. For its feudalization drew it into intimate contact with the basic institutions and practices of the society in which it operated. This more profound involvement with all elements of life prepared the Church for an even more decisive role in society than it had previously enjoyed and gave it a relevance to reality such as it had seldom before had. Perhaps it would not be wrong to say that for the first time since its beginnings, Christianity had become fully engaged in the world and was finally in a position where it could move the whole world by bestirring itself.

5. THE FEUDAL NOBILITY

The emergence of the feudal system brought with it the crystallization of Western Europe's nobility as a distinct class. As we have seen, that class was long in the making; its ancestors included the old Roman nobility, the Germanic warriors, the Merovingian landholder-politicians, the Carolingian royal vassals. The maturing of feudalism drew these strains together into a class of specialists in warfare and government who stood above the rest of society with a definite role to play in the maintenance of that society. As it took shape and found its role, this class developed a style of life impregnated with the usages of feudalism that made it a distinctive, exclusive group almost inaccessible to the rest of Europe's population. Like its fiefs, its style of life became hereditary, so that the feudal nobility was self-perpetuating.

In the ninth and tenth centuries that way of life was rough and crude. No better picture of it can be found than in the epic poems

written to celebrate it, especially the *Song of Roland* or *The Cid*. The great virtues of the class were loyalty, bravery, faithfulness, and generosity. Above all, the feudal noble had prowess—the ability to fight. His life centered in a career of fighting for his lord, his lands, his serfs—and his God. From his youth, a member of the feudal nobility was schooled to be a warrior. He learned his craft as an apprentice in the service of one who already knew the art. The culmination of his education was his knighting, an elaborate ceremony surrounded by religious symbolism which ended with his investment with the tools of war. These made him a noble. Of course, he had to be able to sustain himself as a warrior, so that the management of his ancestral lands constituted a part of his education. And he had a political function stemming from his position as the vassal of another and probably as a lord over still others. Therefore, his education had economic and political dimensions, again the product of practical experience acquired from association from boyhood with the affairs of the feudal world.

The crudeness of the feudal noble's life stemmed in part from the economic limitations of society, but also in part from the fact that the feudal world was a man's world. The typical residence of a feudal noble was a wooden fortress designed for defense rather than comfort. The routine of life centered in pursuits typical of soldiering: heavy eating, drinking, gambling, hunting, dancing, wenching, the mock warfare of the tournament, and often real warfare. The intellectual horizons of the nobles were narrow. Usually they were illiterate, "reading" through their ears by listening to the tales of war sung by bards and to the simple preaching of the priests. Marriage was a utilitarian matter, arranged with an eye toward gaining new lands, new vassals, or new political opportunities; seldom was it marred by considerations of sentiment. But the family was another matter, for a household rich in strong sons and nubile daughters was a great asset in this world of war, land acquisition, and personal relationships. The nobles were religious in a simple, unintellectual way: they believed in God and trusted him to take care of them if they were brave and faithful and generous. Their way of expressing their faith was active, impelling them to do something visible to show their piety—build a church, give land to a monastery, go on a pilgrimage, or fight for God.

Under the impact of improving economic conditions, greater order, and new spiritual impulses, the feudal nobility moved toward greater gentility and refinement, and ultimately developed an elaborate code of conduct known as *chivalry* (see Chapter 19). But even in its harsh, crude form, the ethics of the feudal noble constituted a vital factor in Western European history. It nourished a sense of responsibility and obligation for the security of society. It produced men who possessed skill in fighting and ruling. It engendered independence of action and individual prowess. All these qualities and skills developed leaders with great potential for constructive activity on a scale wider than the fief or kingdom.

6. THE MANORIAL SYSTEM

The feudal nobility was supported by the peasantry, comprising the great bulk of the population and living in a world apart in terms of legal status and social position. By the tenth century, peasant life in most parts of Western Europe was bound up in the manorial system. This institution again was the product of long historical evolution, its origins reaching back to the Roman villas and to the Germanic village communities. The peasants who inhabited the manors were the descendants of slaves, Roman *coloni*, and free villagers forced into dependency in order to find security and a livelihood. By the tenth century, too, the manorial system had a dual aspect. The manor was an economic unit organized and exploited to produce everything needed by its noble possessor and its peasants. It was also a political and social unit providing for the governance of the peasants living there.

As a self-sufficient economic unit, the typical manor was an estate of considerable proportions, its exact size being determined by the requirements of self-sufficiency. A workable manor had to have arable land for raising crops, meadowland for hay and pasture, woodland for fuel and building material, and a natural water supply. Some feudal nobles possessed only enough land to constitute one such unit, while others might possess a fief large enough to enable them to carve out several such self-sufficient units. One third to one half of the manor's tillable soil was reserved as a domain for the lord's support. The rest was divided into small tenancies and allotted to the peasants for their own support. The untillable land, like meadows, pastures, and woods, was exploited in common, the individual's share being determined by custom. In the actual farming of the land, the open field system was widely used. The tillable land was divided into large, unfenced plots that were exploited as units. Each large field was subdivided into strips of about an acre. The lord reserved some of these strips in each large field to himself and assigned others in each field to each tenant. In this way everyone got a share of good and bad land.

Farming techniques were crude. Most labor was done by hand, since few peasants could afford to feed oxen, long the chief beast of burden. Teams of oxen for heavy jobs like plowing and hauling farm equipment were communally owned. Most labor was also performed as a common effort. To protect the fertility of the soil, the three-field system was employed over much of Europe. The arable land of each manor was divided into three open fields, lord and tenants having strips in each. Every year one field lay fallow, a second was planted to wheat in the fall, and a third to barley or rye in the spring. A regular rotation followed in succeeding years. In spite of this system, yields were small. Aside from the crops, each manor produced hay from its meadows and had facilities for pasturing a limited number of animals. Pigs and goats were especially popular because they could live off the woods and wasteland. Most peasants raised vegetables on the small plots surrounding their huts; these gardens were often very productive because they were fertilized with human and animal waste.

Food and animals were not the only things produced on a manor; most manufactured goods had to be made there, since there was little trade. Although specialized artisans such as blacksmiths, carpenters, and masons sometimes plied their trades on the manors, the peasants were generally required to make and repair the equipment, buildings, and furnishings needed to sustain life. Women, including noble ladies, were skilled at making clothing, preserving food, concocting medicine, and a dozen other things. As a result, the manor had little need for the outside world.

The center of a manor was a village containing a manor house, peasant huts, a church, granaries, a mill, a bakery, and the like. This village was more than a collection of buildings; it was a community containing a government and a social system. Its governor was the manorial lord. He was typically a member of the feudal order, caught up in the extramanorial relationships involved in feudal lordship and vassalage. But on his manor he was master, having the power to judge, to punish, and to exact what he wished from his peasant-subjects. Only rarely did an outside force—the king, a feudal overlord, the Church—succeed in intruding into the manorial jurisdiction. If the lord lived on his manor, he usually exercised his power in person with the aid of a few *bailiffs* drawn from the peasant population. If he lived elsewhere, as many of the great nobles who possessed numerous manors did, he entrusted the management of his manor to *stewards* and bailiffs. Each manor had its own governmental institutions —a court, a law, a police force. The law,

consisting of a vast body of custom defining every aspect of the relationship between the lord and the peasants, was of crucial importance in regulating manorial life.

The peasant population of a typical manor was divided into complex legal groupings, the exact status of each group being defined in terms of the obligations its members owed to the lord. On some manors, there were slaves who were simply the property of the lord; there were also freemen who rented land and returned payments in money and produce for its use but were otherwise free to do what they wished. The ordinary peasant was a *serf* or *villein* who was bound to the soil and obligated to provide services to the lord at his will, the most important such service being labor. Serfs almost always held a tenancy from which they could not be dispossessed, making their status a secure one. On some manors, there were peasants who had no tenancy but simply possessed a hut and garden; these *cottars* often owed some kind of service to the lord and sometimes worked for hire, either for the lord or for other peasants. These legal distinctions eventually became meaningless as a result of economic and political conditions on the manors: Because slavery was not economically feasible, most slaves merged into the class of serfs; because the freeman's liberty meant little in a world of limited choices, many of them preferred the security of serfdom.

More important to the peasant than his legal status were the obligations he owed the manorial lord. Although these varied greatly across Europe and even within a single manor, certain types were common. Most vital to the operation of the manor was the *corvée*, the obligation of the serf to perform labor in the tilling of the lord's land. The serf customarily spent three days a week in the service of the lord, although he sometimes had to put in extra time (called *boon work*) on the lord's land at certain seasons, such as harvest. The remainder of the serf's time was devoted to cultivating his own land. Freemen were not usually subject to the *corvée*. In

Medieval peasants at work on the manor, here harvesting a crop. Note the sickle with which the man cuts the grain. These manuscript illustrations, many of them made during the later Middle Ages, are one of the few sources of information about peasant life during the whole period. *Photo: The Walters Art Gallery, Baltimore*

addition to the regular week-work, the lord could impose extra labor obligations on the serfs to keep up the village roads and buildings, to transport produce from one place to another, or to do any other task involved in the operation of a large estate. All the peasants were required to render to the lord certain produce; these impositions, called the *taille*, amounted to a primitive taxation system. And they had to pay *tithes* to the Church, an income that often found its way into the hands of the lord. On most manors, the peasants were obliged to pay fees, called *banalities*, for the use of the mills, ovens, and wine presses over which the lord maintained a monopoly—perhaps because he alone could afford to build these facilities. Almost everywhere, the lord collected a death tax (*heriot*) from peasant families. If a serf wished his daughter to marry outside the manor, he also had to pay a tax (*formariage* or *merchet*). There were, of course, fees and fines to be paid by peasants involved in litigation in the manorial court. These obligations bore heavily on the time and resources of the peasants, who lived at a bare subsistence level despite their long labors.

It is obvious that the manor provided the lord with considerable opportunities to enrich himself; the peasants were as exploitable as the land. There were, however, limits on the exploitation of the peasants. The lord of the manor was dependent on them for one prime ingredient of the manorial economy—labor. There was no substitute for human labor, and there was no source for it except the people who lived on the manor. Extreme cruelty and greed on the part of the lord might affect the performance of these laborers and thereby upset the functioning of the entire manorial economy. If this happened, the lord would lose his income and with it his ability to perform his role in the feudal world. He had to act with some justice and benevolence toward laborers who were legally little more than his slaves if he hoped to get from them efficient and constant labor. In their own crafty way, the peasants could take vengeance on an unjust lord by careless, slovenly performance of their work which permitted the lord's crops to rot in the field, his animals to die, his buildings to·fall down. Thus the life of the peasant was somewhat softened by the benevolence of a paternalistic lord who knew well enough how much he depended on their services. The manorial system also supplied considerable security for the peasant in a so-ciety that tended to be insecure. The little surplus that the collectivity could amass was a hedge against the frequent crop failures and plagues that might have meant death to a peasant on his own. The Church was ever-present on the manors, offering its particular kind of solace in the face of life's hardships. Within his family and among his friends in the manorial village, the peasant found an array of pleasures—beer drinking, gaming, singing, dancing—all capable of making easier long hours of labor and a low standard of living.

Feudalism and manorialism do not usually receive a sympathetic evaluation; one in fact often finds it difficult to try seriously to under-stand them. They were obviously institutions suited to a backward, limited, crude society; by comparison, the political, social, and eco-nomic bases of most other civilized societies seem far superior and considerably more effective. Despite their limitations, however, they deserve our fullest understanding, for their operation in the backward society in which they developed was crucial. Each worked to create small associations of men under circumstances that established stability in an unstable, undisciplined world. Each brought together in simple, integrated cells groups of people from various levels of so-ciety and with various talents. These simple collectivities soon demonstrated an immense potential for development. It is not just coin-cidence that Western European society began a spectacular period of growth *after* feudal-ism and manorialism had emerged; in a fun-damental sense, these institutions caused the growth. They constitute the foundation stones the infant Western European society had been struggling to find since the collapse of Greco-Roman civilization.

Suggested Reading

Feudalism. A simple, straightforward descrip-tion of feudalism is **Carl Stephenson, *Me-diaeval Feudalism* (Cornell). A work stress-ing the legal aspects of feudalism and the evolution of feudal usages is **F. L. Ganshof, *Feudalism*, trans. P. Grierson (Harper Torchbook). The classic treatment of the subject, written with a view toward revealing the sociological aspects of feudalism, is **Marc Bloch, *Feudal Society* (2 vols., Phoenix). **Joseph Strayer, *Feudalism* (Anvil), provides documents illustrative of feudal usages. **Sidney Painter, *Mediaeval Society* (Cornell), presents a brief but engag-ing picture of the feudal nobility. **C. W. Oman, *The Art of War in the Middle Ages, A.D. 378–1515* (rev. ed., Cornell), supplies an excellent picture of the nature of feudal war-fare.

Manorialism. An excellent brief discussion of the manorial system is N. Neilson, *Medieval Agrarian Economy* (1936). **H. S. Bennett, *Life on an English Manor* (Cambridge), pre-sents a dramatic picture of manorial life, stressing especially peasant conditions. Marc Bloch, *French Rural History: An Essay on Its Basic Characteristics* (1966), tries to describe the historical roots of the manorial system and trace its evolution. **Robert Latouche, *The Birth of the Western Economy* (Harper Torchbook), presents in his later chapters a characterization of the manorial system and the forces that changed it. Undoubtedly the best work on the subject, but one not easy to read, is Georges Duby, *Rural Economy and Country Life in the Medieval West*, trans. C. Postan (1968); an excellent selection of docu-ments is included to illustrate Duby's points.

**Eileen Power, *Medieval People* (10th rev. ed., University Paperbacks), presents a delightful picture of medieval society by describing the activities of typical representatives of the major social groups; her portrayal of the medieval peasant is especially effective.

Sources. Every student can read with profit **The Song of Roland* (many translations; the best is by F. B. Luquiens, Collier), for a picture of the ideals and practices of the feudal nobility. Written about 1100 to recount the exploits of Charlemagne and his followers against the Muslims in Spain, it reflects the values of the eleventh-century nobility very accurately. Equally revealing is **The Poem of the Cid*, trans. L. B. Simpson (University of California Press), recounting the adventures of a Spanish noble in the era of the reconquest of Spain from the Muslims.

RETROSPECT

RETROSPECT In a letter written in 593 or 594, Pope Gregory I dolefully asked his contemporaries: "What is there now, I ask, of delight in this world?" He called their attention to the strife, the suffering, the destruction of cities, the depopulation of the countryside, the injustices, the attacks of savages everywhere before their eyes. "See what has befallen Rome, once mistress of the world," he asked. "She is worn down by great sorrows, by the disappearance of her citizens, by the attacks of her enemies, by numerous ruins." In a way, Gregory supplied the key to the history of the period we have called the Early Middle Ages; it was the story of the sad fate that befell Rome, which for so long prior to 500 had been the symbol of civilized society.

In one sense, Gregory's lament contained an important truth. During the Early Middle Ages most of what was characteristic of classical Greco-Roman civilization had been lost, especially in the western part of the old Roman world, and society was the poorer. One can easily write—as many have—the history of the Early Middle Ages in terms of the destruction of classical civilization, and from this perspective the era is indeed a dark age. However, between A.D. 500 and 1000 much happened to replace what had been lost. Three new civilizations had been shaped within the confines of the classical world, each retaining significant elements of the old order. Each of these three had extended its influence beyond the classical world, so that the civilized world was larger than it had been in the days of Greco-Roman glory. Each of these new societies had developed new institutions and ideas to suit its needs and situation. An inventory of what men had created in these difficult centuries to permit the continuation of orderly, civilized life gives ample evidence that these "dark" centuries deserve a decisive place in the continuum of history. A perceptive observer living in 1000 could have pointed to all these things to remind Gregory I that there were still "things of delight" in the world.

As he comes to realize the immensity of the transformation that occurred between 500 and 1000, the modern student might conclude that the most significant development of this era was the emergence of three separate civilizations—Byzantine, Muslim, and Western European—standing in direct contact and confrontation with one another. In addition to the dynamic forces at work within each, there had developed by 1000 a new source of dynamism in the civilized world in the form of the interactions among these civilizations. The Greco-Roman world had tended to absorb all existing civilized societies; it stood facing the barbarian world. By 1000 the lines of stress and tension existed among civilized societies rather than between the civilized and uncivilized worlds. The consequences of this new situation must be kept in mind as a determinant in the course of future historical development.

The period just reviewed belonged to the East; Byzantium and the Muslim world far surpassed the Western European world in every respect. This little-appreciated fact must be remembered, for the superiority which the people of the Byzantine and Muslim worlds established in these centuries gave them a pride and a sense of contribution to the development of civilized life that other societies have often forgotten as the West eclipsed the East in later ages. None benefitted more from the achievements of these leaders in civilization than the struggling Western Europeans. The future glory of the West would certainly have been different had it not been for the existence of the East, with its storehouse of the knowledge and techniques of civilized life.

Part Five

The High Middle Ages, 1000–1300

The Revival of Europe

An eleventh-century chronicler named Ralph Glaber tells us that many Europeans were convinced that, in accordance with ancient prophecy, the world would come to an end at the end of the first millennium of Christian history, that is, in the year 1000. But, wrote Ralph, when that fateful year passed without the appearance of the Antichrist, "it was as if the very world had shaken itself and cast off its old age." Everywhere, he said, men rivaled each other to build better churches and were filled with new ardor for the faith. This bit of medieval legend, whatever its validity in summing up the actual state of mind of Western Europeans in the late tenth century, provides a fitting introduction to this section. In actual fact, Western Europe did enjoy a sudden revival beginning about 1000 and continuing with unabated vigor until about 1300. This era is often referred to as the High Middle Ages. It is the period in which medieval Western European society reached its full maturity.

As our account of these effervescent, creative centuries unfolds, it should become increasingly clear that the revival of Western European civilization was rooted in certain basic institutions that had been forged during the preceding era: feudalism, manorialism, the Church, the precious treasure of learning stored up by Carolingian scholars. Although primitive in many ways, these institutions and ideas provided basic patterns of organization, social control, thought, and belief which permitted men to apply their energies and intelligences constructively. They were suddenly capable of producing new wealth. They found themselves able to construct larger political entities and to form new class relationships. Their spiritual, intellectual, and esthetic capabilities were expanded so that a wide range of cultural achievements was possible. They found themselves able to turn outward from their beleaguered world to make a major impression on wide areas of the world heretofore little known to them. In short, the High Middle Ages was an era of creative activity that made Western European civilization a factor of major significance in the world. The long centuries of painful experimentation that marked the Early Middle Ages had clearly ended.

la postoiles et tout li prelat qui la fu
rent assemble. Atant obeirent a la re
queste le roy. atant se departirent et retor
na chascuns en la contree en loudur et en gra
citat le roi qui regne et regnera p tous les
siecles del siecles. A ———— ω ⨁ 2·

Comment la foire du landit fu translatee
a s. denis en france. par le roi .vii. li. le cha

Chapter 19 ❦ Economic and Social Revival

A prime factor in the resurgence of Western Europe between 1000 and 1300 was a remarkable economic revival which greatly increased wealth and afforded a wide range of new economic opportunities. Economic growth was accompanied by major adjustments of the social order. These economic and social changes had their source at the base of society, far removed from royal courts, ecclesiastical centers of power, and the halls of learning. Modest manorial lords, toiling peasants, peddler merchants, and simple artisans were the agents of these changes. The more spectacular accomplishments of the High Middle Ages in politics, religion, and culture which we shall discuss later owed to these simple members of society a debt that is seldom acknowledged.

1. POPULATION GROWTH

The forces which generate economic growth in any society are so complex that they defy clear description, and so it was in Western Europe in the tenth century. However, one contributing factor is evident: the population was expanding rapidly. This demographic change, representing a reversal of a trend prevailing since late Roman times, probably began in the ninth century. From then on, growth was steady and rapid until about 1350. It was felt not only in Western Europe but also clear across Asia to the Far East. There is no way to provide accurate figures of the amount of growth, but the best estimates suggest that the Western European population grew from 27 million in 700 to 73 million in 1300. The causes of this worldwide growth are obscure. There is some evidence that the Eurasian world was relatively free of killer diseases, especially bubonic plague; that the destructive aspects of warfare were curbed; and that more food was available. Probably there were psychological factors at work: conditions of relative stability and security may have encouraged population growth. The growing population had a double effect on Western European society. It put enormous pressures for greater productivity on the stable, self-sufficient agricultural system. And it provided new hands which could be turned to new economic enterprises. These pressures were not the same in all of Europe, so that the reactions occurred at different levels. Our scanty knowledge suggests that the heaviest population concentrations were centered in the Loire-Seine basins in France, in the Low

This illustration from a fourteenth-century manuscript, the Grandes Chroniques de France, shows the fair at St. Denis, one of those gatherings of buyers and sellers that in the twelfth and thirteenth centuries were major centers of Western European commercial activity. Through the hands of merchants and traders at the fairs passed goods from all over the Continent and from overseas. *Photo: Giraudon*

Countries, in northern Italy, and in the Rhine Basin.

2. AGRICULTURAL EXPANSION

Perhaps the most important source of economic growth in the era from 1000 to 1300 was the expansion of agricultural production. This aspect of medieval economic life is often overlooked, perhaps because the manorial system has too frequently been viewed as an economic institution geared to self-sufficiency production and therefore incapable of expansion. Such was not the case. By the tenth century, the manorial establishment constituted a potent reservoir of managerial ability, disciplined manpower, and technological skills which permitted a considerable expansion of agricultural production and made possible new economic undertakings in trade and industry. And the pressure of a growing population unleashed these latent forces.

The expansion of agricultural production during this period involved four interrelated developments. First, more land was put under cultivation as a result of an immense amount of land clearance and peasant resettlement. Until the tenth century, the typical manor had been a cultivated island surrounded by vast stretches of forest that separated it from other manors. After 1000, the peasants of each manor began to clear these forests and put the soil to the plow. By 1300, the forests had largely disappeared, and the boundaries of the cultivated land of one manor had reached out to touch that of its neighbors. In the meantime, European cultivators had moved into virgin lands to carve out new estates and put new lands under tillage. Usually these settlers were peasants from established manors persuaded to leave their old habitats by crowded conditions, by the promises of landowners interested in putting new lands to work, or by an urge to better their lot. The chief areas of colonization were on the German frontier east of the Elbe River and in Spanish lands being wrested from Muslim control. Although there is no way of being certain, it appears that the area of cultivated lands in Western Europe doubled or trebled between 1000 and 1300; the increase in agricultural productivity was equally great.

Perhaps most of the increase in productivity resulting from land clearance was absorbed by the growing population. However, productivity was also greatly increased by technological advances that freed considerable amounts of human labor for other tasks. Again we are dealing with a development that was given little attention by the literate world of the time. But certain technological advances are clearly evident. More efficient wheeled plows, capable of turning over the heavy soils of northern Europe, were perfected and used more widely. New methods of harnessing animals, especially the shoulder collar, were developed. The collar was particularly significant because it allowed wider use of the speedier, more efficient horse as a draft animal. The iron horseshoe came into wide use to increase the efficiency of the horse. Water and wind mills were greatly improved and their use was spread widely; their application to such time-consuming and onerous tasks as grinding grain permitted human talents to be put to more productive uses.

Third, agricultural production was increased by improved methods of tillage and animal husbandry. Irrigation systems were developed in some parts of Western Europe. Agricultural specialization was made possible by the increasing opportunities for exchange that we shall describe later. Among the prime examples of this specialization were the vineyards of Burgundy, southwestern France, and the Moselle-Rhine area, and the great sheep-raising granges in England. Greater attention was given to fertilization. Of prime importance was the spread of the three-field system of tillage introduced earlier. The three-field system had the advantage of protecting the fertility of the soil while permitting more soil to be tilled each year, allowing more efficient use of labor and equipment, and permitting a greater variety of crops to be grown. Better seeds were developed in many parts of Europe to take advantage of local soil and weather conditions. And there were improvements in animal breeds to produce better draft animals and more animal products, such as meat and wool.

Finally, and implicit in what has already been discussed, agricultural production was expanded as a consequence of increased human ingenuity and inventiveness—perhaps we can say agricultural entrepreneurship. Planning and adaptation of ancient customs were required to free labor to clear new lands around existing manors, to apply new tools and techniques, and to dispose profitably of any excess production. Boldness and foresight were required to organize, transport, and resettle groups of peasants on distant lands, and new modes of operation had to be perfected to sustain these new settlements. Conscious thought and accumulated knowledge had to be mustered to develop new seeds, to breed new animals, and to turn toward specialized production. The entrepreneurship, exercised in small and undramatic ways, was seldom described in the historical record, but it was obviously at work to change the face of rural Europe. Perhaps it provides the key to the greatest agricultural revolution in world history between the neolithic discovery of agriculture and the advent of modern mechanized agriculture.

The expansion of agricultural production between 1000 and 1300 had immense effects on the agricultural economy and the rural population of Western Europe. These cannot be weighed, however, without an understanding of a concurrent and interrelated economic development of equal magnitude and importance: the revival of trade and manufacturing.

3. REVIVAL OF TRADE AND MANUFACTURING

Trade had never entirely vanished from the Western European scene, but it had declined steadily from late Roman times until it reached a low point in the ninth and early tenth centuries. During the late tenth and early eleventh centuries a revival began, and that expansion continued until the mid-fourteenth century. During the era of expansion, commerce became the catalytic force in the European economy, promoting growth and change in all other segments of the economy. The causes of the commercial revival are obscure and complex and have been subject to considerable debate among historians. Among the contributing factors were population growth, agricultural expansion, greater political order, outside stimuli, and Western European political, military, and religious expansion. But to these must be added a human element resulting from the choices and the labors of men whose activities are for the most part unknown to us.

One aspect of European commercial expansion involved long-distance trade with the East. It will be recalled that all during the Early Middle Ages, trade and industry flourished in the Byzantine and Muslim empires. In considerable part, Europe's commercial expansion was a story of the ability of the Europeans to break into that Eastern trading complex and to gain control of a share of it. Western Europeans had always remained in contact with the Eastern trade centers, primarily through Byzantine outposts in Venice and southern Italy. In the tenth century this activity began to quicken. The Venetians took the leading role, steadily enlarging their contacts by sea with Constantinople. The Byzantine government constantly made concessions to the Venetians, allowing them to trade on advantageous terms and to establish depots in Constantinople. By exploiting these opportunities, Venice grew rich, and in the process brought an ever-increasing volume of goods to the West. In the eleventh century Pisa and Genoa began a comparable, although more forceful, intrusion into the Muslim trading complex. Their navies successfully challenged Muslim control over the Western Mediterranean seaways, and their merchants established trading relations with the Muslims in Spain and North Africa. The successes of the early crusading movement allowed the Italian cities to establish important footholds in the Muslim cities of the eastern Mediterranean in the twelfth century, and the conquest of Constantinople in 1204 during the Fourth Crusade gave the Venetians virtual control over Byzantine trade. By the thirteenth century Italian merchants and to a lesser extent those from Mediterranean port cities in southern France and Spain dominated Mediterranean trade and grew rich as the middlemen between Western Europe and the East. The lifeblood of this international trade was luxury items, especially spices and fine cloth. Much of these goods were paid for by European gold, but gradually the Europeans developed products that found a market in the East.

Meanwhile, another trading network stretching toward the East developed on the northern fringes of the Continent. Viking pirates were the pioneers in opening this window to the East. Their seafaring prowess carried them along the northern seaways to far places. By way of the North Sea and the Atlantic, they reached northern France, the Low Countries, the British Isles, and Iceland. Through the Baltic, they reached northern Germany and Russia, whose rivers opened an avenue to the Black Sea and Constantinople. Viking piracy and adventuresomeness slowly grew into organized trade. Northern Europeans began to exploit the sea lanes and the rivers to carry a variety of goods to and from the lands bordering the North and Baltic seas and Constantinople. The focal point of this northern trading complex came to be Flanders and the cities of northern Germany, and to a lesser degree the English port cities. Although the main flow of international trade was between Western Europe and the Byzantine and Muslim East, it is worth noting that by the thirteenth century the Europeans developed a long-distance sea trade linking the lands bordering the Baltic Sea, the North Sea, the Atlantic Ocean, and the Mediterranean Sea. As a consequence, Europe's international trade was not wholly dependent on Eastern connections.

By no means so spectacular as the expansion of international trade, but probably more important, was a steady growth of trade within Europe. The fundamental impetus for this expansion came from two sources: the demand of Europe's lay and ecclesiastical aristocracy for luxury items and the needs of manors and towns for the necessities of life.

The aggressive Italian and Flemish merchants took the lead in distributing luxury items from the East across the face of Western Europe, although they were ultimately joined by merchants from other areas. As early as the eleventh century, Italian merchants began moving out of northern Italy across the Alps into the Rhone and Rhine valleys, and thus into the heart of France and Germany. Flemish traders penetrated England by the Thames, and France and Germany by the Rhine, Scheldt, and Meuse valleys. From these prime arteries an ever-widening network of overland and river routes spread out in all directions. Often the luxury items brought by the Italians were distributed along these secondary routes by local traders. During the twelfth century the great meeting place of international traders was the Fairs of Champagne in France. Here merchants from all Europe came to display their wares to other merchants who in turn carried their purchases to local markets and prize customers. By the thirteenth century the fairs had declined in importance, and their role was increasingly filled by permanent markets established in cities.

Complementing the traffic in luxury items was an ever-growing exchange of goods required to feed, clothe, and equip the inhabitants of the manorial villages and the towns. Few manors were ever entirely self-sufficient, so that local trade in such items as salt, wine, and metals had always existed. This kind of trade grew steadily from the eleventh century onward. The needs of the growing towns provided the prime stimulus for local trade in foodstuffs and raw materials, and the manufactured products of the towns flowed back to the villages in increasing volume. In terms of

Trade Routes, Twelfth and Thirteenth Centuries

volume and of the number of people involved, the local exchange between town and country undoubtedly constituted the largest component of medieval trade.

The expansion of commercial activity in Western Europe promoted the growth of manufacturing. During the eleventh and twelfth centuries European merchants had to rely largely on gold and raw materials to pay for the goods they purchased in the East. The manufacture of goods in the West was largely confined to manorial workshops where simple items were fashioned to satisfy local needs. By the twelfth century the towns began to offer opportunities for skilled artisans who could devote all their time and talent to a single product which they then sold directly to their fellow townsmen and rural buyers or to merchants who distributed them wherever there was a demand. This kind of manufacturing long remained a vital element of the town economy and supplied a vast quantity of commonplace items to be exchanged for money or other items. And in some cases skilled artisans were able to produce high-quality items that found an international market. By the thirteenth century some areas of Europe, particularly Flanders and northern Italy, had developed more complex manufacturing organizations involving merchant entrepreneurs who bought raw materials in quantity and "put out" the material into the households of hired laborers. This system, called the "putting out" system or "cottage" industry, was especially applied to the woollen industry, which became international in scope: raw wool was produced in England and processed into fine cloth in Flanders and northern Italy.

There is no way of ascertaining what the revival of trade and manufacturing meant to the Western European economy in quantitative terms. Surviving records from some of the northern Italian and Flemish cities reveal that in the most active centers of commerce and industry an impressive volume of goods was exchanged and that large numbers of people depended on these operations for their livelihood. For much of Europe, however, the record is too sparse to make a satisfactory judgment. It is probably safe to venture that by the thirteenth century, trade and industry in Western Europe exceeded that of the classical world. Agriculture was certainly the most important element in the total economy, but the added wealth created by exchange and expert craftsmanship was of decisive importance in creating a prosperous Europe.

4. ECONOMIC CONSEQUENCES OF INCREASED PRODUCTION

The impact of increased agricultural, commercial, and industrial productivity on the Western European economy was immense. The most obvious consequence was a new level of prosperity that manifested itself in a hundred ways: better homes and furnishings, bigger churches, more elaborate dress, greater quantities and varieties of food, more art and literature, more leisure. By 1300 the specter of constant poverty and starvation had vanished for most Europeans. But aside from the general increase in wealth, greater productivity had more specific results that need special note.

First, economic growth caused the revitalization of city life. Towns in the sense of physical entities where people lived in close proximity had never disappeared from Western Europe. However, between the fall of Greco-Roman civilization and about 1000, towns for the most part became ecclesiastical, administrative, or defensive centers, sparsely populated and economically dependent on agriculture; the chief exceptions were a few coastal cities in Italy that managed to maintain commercial ties with the Byzantine Empire. Between 1000 and 1300 this situation changed dramatically. Ancient towns grew in area and population, and new towns appeared in many places. Whereas in 1000 most towns had only a few thousand inhabitants at most, by 1300 there were cities of considerable population: Milan had 200,000 inhabitants; Venice, Florence, and Genoa all had at least 100,000 residents; Paris boasted 80,000 people; and London had perhaps 50,000. By that date perhaps 10 percent of Europe's population lived in urban centers. More significant than mere physical growth was the fact that the great bulk of the residents of the towns of 1300 earned their livelihood from trade and manufacturing, thus turning the "new" towns into completely different institutions than the old had been. The urbanization of Western Europe had begun, never to stop until the present.

The formation of medieval towns as commercial and manufacturing centers was a complex process still not clearly understood. In terms of physical growth, most of the important towns of the era were simply enlargements of older episcopal, monastic, administrative, or military centers. Merchants were attracted to these centers as places of settlement for many reasons: security, favor shown them by ruling authorities, access to rivers and roads, availability of buyers. Often they settled haphazardly outside the walls of the old center, their shops, stalls, and households creating a *suburb* (from a Latin term meaning "under the city"). The merchants were followed by artisans, perhaps attracted to the suburbs from the surrounding countryside. As the commercial and manufacturing activity increased, the walls were extended to enclose the suburbs. In many cases the marketplace of the suburb became the real center of urban life. New towns were often established at locations favorable to commerce—good harbors, river junctions, crossroads. Their physical growth resembled that of the suburb emerging around an old population center. However, there was much more to the creation of a medieval town than its physical configurations; we will return later in this chapter to some of the political and social aspects of town evolution.

A second consequence of economic expansion, and especially of commercial revival, was the growth of a money economy. Money had always circulated in Western Europe, but at a very minimal level until the eleventh century. Thereafter its use rapidly expanded to meet the needs of trade. The money economy soon spread to agriculture, where payment in kind had long prevailed as the basis of exchange. Its impact was revolutionary. A whole new form of wealth emerged to challenge the monopoly held by land. New patterns of exchange developed to affect all kinds of transactions. Old economic relationships were dissolved and replaced by new. The exploitation of money shaped a new set of economic values.

A third major effect of economic growth was the transformation of the manorial system. In very simple terms, the growing

towns provided a market for surplus agricultural produce. For this produce, landlords and peasants received money payments, in return for which they could embellish their lives with the products for sale in the town markets. This new potential for profit changed the emphasis on the manors from self-sufficiency to surplus production. And under this pressure, the traditional manorial system began to dissolve.

The dissolution proceeded in two broad directions. In many areas of Western Europe, especially in the twelfth century, landlords began to give up the tilling of their reserved domain on the manor as a means of supplying their needs, preferring to convert their rights into cash payments with which they could buy what they wished. They broke their reserved lands into tenancies which they rented out to peasants for cash. And they commuted the labor obligations of their serfs and the dues owed them in kind to money payments. Serfs could afford to buy off their obligations because the town market offered them a chance to sell produce and save a little money; they were especially favored because the whole era was an inflationary one. As the new arrangement emerged, the peasants could keep whatever profits they derived from their new tenancies and thus could save still more money to expand their operations. But landlords could move in the opposite direction, and many did, particularly in the thirteenth century, after they realized the profits possible from agricultural production. They could expand their domain, and manage its cultivation themselves for profit. A most profitable course was to concentrate on a specialized crop for sale. Lords who did this often displaced peasants from their ancient tenancies, imposed more rigid labor obligations on them, and forced them to work for wages. In either case, the old manorial system with its family-sized tenancies, its lord's domain, its open fields, its common lands, its intricate system of obligations, its cooperative forms of labor, and its self-sufficiency vanished over much of

One of the signs of the growth of a money economy and of more effective government in the Middle Ages was a change in tax collection; as this illustration shows, the officers of the king are collecting taxes in coins rather than in produce or service. Enlarged detail of a drawing from the Canterbury Psalter. *Photo: Master and Fellows, Trinity College, Cambridge*

Western Europe. In place of the self-contained manors there emerged a variety of forms of agricultural exploitation where the concern for profit predominated, an end that could only be achieved by linking the countryside to the towns, their markets, and their money.

The fourth economic change to be noted in this age of expansion will perhaps come as no surprise. The economic activities of Western Europeans were more and more motivated by an urge for profit. No longer were men content with self-sufficiency; they worked and planned in order to gain more worldly goods. Probably the merchants were the first exemplars of this new urge, but as we have just noted, the same spirit penetrated to the very heart of the old economic order—the manorial system. Not only did the urge to accumulate wealth loom larger in men's values, but Western Europeans began to perfect means to achieve this end. Merchants engaged in high-profit overseas trading ventures were often supplied the money needed to buy the goods by a nonmerchant investor under the terms of a contract (called a *commenda*) that provided for sharing the profits after the merchant returned and disposed of the goods. We have already described how landlords consciously manipulated their lands for profit. The business of lending money for profit (called *usury* by the Church and condemned as a sin) was widespread by the thirteenth century. These are only a few of the multitude of practices which heralded a new economic spirit. A protocapitalist economy had developed.

Finally, Western European economic growth reached such a level by 1300 that the Europeans had seized economic leadership in the vast area surrounding the Mediterranean—a leadership that would soon be extended to the world. No longer did Byzantium and the Muslim world stand in the relationship of advanced economic areas to a backward West. As we shall see later, political factors, especially the crusading movement and the expansion of Western European power into the Near East, helped to promote the advance of the Europeans economically, but it is equally obvious that their enterprise, their techniques, and their methods in the economic realm played a vital role in establishing their leadership. It is ironic that the rapid rise of the Western European economy was in large part due to the ability of the Europeans to intrude into the richer economies of the East and exploit them for the benefit of the West.

5. SOCIAL CHANGE: THE EMERGENCE OF THE BOURGEOISIE

The far-reaching economic transformation of the era from 1000 to 1300 had a significant impact on the simple order that characterized the feudal-manorial world of the tenth century. The most important social development was the emergence of a new class, the *bourgeoisie*, which added a dynamic element to the social structure.

The development of the bourgeoisie was a byproduct of the growth of commerce and the revitalization of the cities. Those engaged in commerce and living in towns found themselves in a society that had no place for them: no legal status, no laws governing their activities, no understanding of their needs, no respect for them. One challenge facing them was to compel the feudal-manorial-ecclesiastical world basically foreign to them to recognize and accept them and their unique activi-

ties. Another was to devise rules and techniques that would permit them to conduct their new activities in an orderly, efficient fashion.

As soon as men in the tenth and eleventh centuries began to devote full time to commerce and manufacturing, they felt a basic need for personal freedom. Their need was not abstract in any sense. Their livelihood depended on freedom to move about in a world that fixed men to fiefs and manors. They required the freedom to dispose of their property at will in a world where property was bound up in an intricate network of mutual obligations involving many parties. They needed the liberty to apply their talent and labor to whatever opportunity arose in a world where nobles and peasants were linked together by long-sanctioned customs which dictated the specific ways they spent their time and talent. And so the merchants and the artisans of the towns struggled for personal freedom and were successful in achieving it. Their methods were various: purchase; force; grants won from kings, feudal lords, and bishops; flight to where those who claimed control over them could not find them. By 1300 the townsmen had succeeded so well that simply living in a town meant personal freedom. This freedom constituted a prime legal mark of the new class: its members were nonnoble freemen, legally distinct from both aristocrats and serfs. But personal freedom, although vital, was not sufficient. The merchants and artisans could not operate adequately under the political order that governed the feudal world or the manorial system. They had therefore to shape new institutions of government and new laws to suit their needs.

To meet these political and legal needs, the inhabitants of a particular town often banded together into a voluntary corporation and then sought collectively to gain political privileges which would allow them to create suitable institutions. Usually the object of their corporate action was a *charter* granted by the possessor of political power—a king, a feudal lord, a bishop. Often the charter was not to be had for the asking, and many city communities had to struggle desperately for their privileges. The task grew easier when the power wielders of the old order began to appreciate the advantages of having thriving towns in their kingdoms, principalities, or bishoprics. Charters varied from place to place, but most of them shared certain essential features. The typical charter usually recognized the citizen body of the town as a *corporation* that could act and be treated legally as a person. It almost always granted personal freedom to the residents of the town. Most charters carefully defined what the corporation owed to the granter. Almost always dues were to be paid in money instead of in personal service. Finally, most charters granted some degree of political freedom, thereby giving the townsmen permission to institute their own government. In a few cases, especially in Italy, towns gained complete political freedom. Such towns, called *communes*, were the exception. More commonly, the townsmen had only the right to regulate local affairs while respecting some higher authority in matters not strictly local. This was particularly true of towns chartered by kings, few of whom were willing to let rich cities slip completely from their control.

In shaping political institutions, the townsmen experimented considerably. In most towns there was some degree of popular participation in political life, authority being vested in an elected council that varied in size from town to town. In a typical commune the council usually possessed complete power to legislate, conduct courts, levy taxes, expend money for civic purposes, and negotiate with outside powers. Its only responsibility was to the citizens of the town. There was a tendency in many towns to establish officials, chosen either by the council or by the populace, to carry the chief burden of administration under the supervision of the council. These officials bore various titles—*mayor, burgomaster, podesta.* Judicial affairs were entrusted

to specially trained judges. In towns where the charter granted only limited freedom, the townsmen often had to respect the authority of a royal official or a representative of a feudal lord who exercised many powers in judicial and financial matters. Whatever the form of government, the towns quickly created an elaborate new body of law regulating civic affairs. As a consequence, the bourgeoisie lived in an entirely different legal setting than did feudal nobles, the clergy, and the serfs.

Not all the problems of the bourgeoisie were solved by the establishment of personal freedom and their own city governments. Probably the gravest problem was the regulation of economic activity among merchants and artisans, a problem for which the rest of society had no solution. The usual answer was the establishment of guilds within each town. A *guild* was an association of men engaged in a common commercial or manufacturing enterprise who set up rules governing the conduct of that enterprise. The merchants in each town usually formed a merchant guild while the artisans formed several craft guilds, one for each trade. The merchant guilds existed primarily to protect the interests of merchants from outsiders and to restrain the merchants within a town from taking unfair advantage of one another. Each guild enacted specific rules governing prices to be charged, trading practices to be observed, and the conditions under which trade could be conducted. Most of these rules had one basic purpose—to give each merchant a share in the available trade without permitting anyone an unfair advantage. The craft guilds were not essentially different. They imposed regulations on their members concerning prices, quality of goods, conditions of labor, and quantity of production. The craft guilds also controlled the conditions for entering a trade, a power which gave them a vital role in education. Boys began their preparation for entering a craft by becoming *apprentices* to a master, working from two to seven years under his guidance and living in his household. The apprentice then became a *journeyman* who worked for hire until he had saved sufficient money and developed adequate skill to open his own shop and become a *master*. Before he acquired that rank, he had to submit his workmanship to a rigid examination by the guild. Along with their regulative functions, merchant and craft guilds had purely social functions. Each usually had its own guildhall, where banquets, pageants, and religious affairs were conducted for the entertainment and edification of the members. Each guild also aided its members when sickness or death struck a family.

Obviously, the guilds placed considerable restrictions on their members. Usually they could count on the town governments to enforce their regulations and to oust any merchant or craftsman who refused to obey the rules. In spite of their restrictive, monopolistic bent, the guilds played a vital role in the expansion of commerce and industry. Merchants and craftsmen of the Middle Ages lived in a society ruled by nobles and clergymen who had little sympathy for their activities. The guilds supplied protection and discipline for the merchants and artisans, restraining them from excessive profiteering and preventing them from destroying one another. Until central governments became strong enough to assume these burdens, the guilds were absolutely necessary for controlling and safeguarding the economic life of the merchants and artisans.

New business methods also developed rapidly in the towns. The use of money as a measure of value and a means of exchange became typical of the town economy. Sound systems of coinage were developed, especially among the Italian towns, whose coins were used over much of Europe until royal governments finally took an interest in sound money and began to develop national money systems. Along with a money economy, banks appeared. Banks lent money for interest, supplied bills of exchange to merchants who did

not want to carry large amounts of coins with them, and provided places of deposit. Although the Church strenuously opposed usury and tried to keep it a function confined to Jewish moneylenders, its struggle was not successful. By the thirteenth century several rich Italian merchant families and the great crusading orders, especially the Templars, conducted large-scale lending ventures. They were criticized by the Church but not with any great effect. Gradually the Church began to modify its position on usury, conceding that anyone who lent at great risk ought to be compensated and that a borrower who did not pay his debt promptly ought to be penalized. Indeed, churchmen were among the best customers of Italian bankers, and they paid high rates of interest for the convenience. Insurance was developed to protect merchants against almost any risk. Wholesaling became a regular practice in many cities. Bookkeeping systems were devised. In brief, a modern businessman would have been much at home among his medieval predecessors.

For all its success in carving a place for itself in medieval society, the bourgeoisie was still by 1300 not very exalted. The nobility looked down on the new class as uncultured and boorish, an attitude that often caused the bourgeoisie to spend their riches aping the habits of the nobles. The Church officially disapproved of many bourgeois activities as violations of Christian morality. The peasants were suspicious of the sharp practices of the townsmen; the "city slicker" is no recent invention of the rural mind. Still, the bourgeoisie was solidly established in law and in fact as a dynamic factor in the social order. It is worth noting that neither the Byzantine nor the Muslim world produced a comparable class, although trade, manufacturing, and city life in these societies were older and no less vigorous. The explanation is not clear, but perhaps it was because the state was too powerful in these civilizations. In the final analysis, the rise of the bourgeoisie in Western Europe was a consequence of successful private initiative carried out by men who operated in a setting where there was considerable room for free action.

6. SOCIAL CHANGE: THE FEUDAL ARISTOCRACY AND THE PEASANTRY

While the bourgeoisie was forging a position for itself in medieval society, the older classes were affected by powerful currents of change which altered their condition considerably. A significant development affecting the feudal nobility from the late eleventh century onward was the increasing refinement of its pattern of life. In part this change was a consequence of the greater wealth which afforded aristocrats more luxury and leisure, but more fundamentally, the refinement of noble life involved a transformation of the original life style of the feudal world. The warrior's code stressing loyalty, bravery, generosity, and military prowess expanded into a complex code of behavior that is called *chivalry*—a code of behavior brilliantly celebrated in the literature of the troubadors and the writers of romances. Chivalry tended to place a premium on courtly manners rather than on battlefield prowess. Women became the center of attention as objects of devotion, loyalty, and sentimental attachment, and the modes of conduct pleasing to women were given high value. Even the warrior instinct was transmuted—at least in theory—to a quest for some ideal for which to fight, such as the spread of the true faith or the protection of the weak. The code of chivalry, with its particular manners, modes of conduct, tastes, and ideals, tended to make aristocratic life more exclusive than previously.

While noble life was becoming more complex and refined, the economic and political conditions surrounding the existence of the aristocracy were changing in directions that reduced the real power of that class. The evolving money economy created a new kind of wealth that challenged the monopoly of landed property upon which the power of the feudal nobility was founded. The nobleman's quest for a share of this money wealth led many aristocrats to bargain away their total mastery over the manorial structure in return for cash payments; they thus tended to become simple landlords dependent on rents rather than the directors of agricultural exploitation. In an era of inflation, the rents they were willing to settle for at one moment lost their value in the long run, so that many nobles were in dire economic straits by the thirteenth century. The development of stronger central governments in many parts of Western Europe reduced the nobleman's role in warfare and government. With royal armies, officials, courts, laws, and taxes ever more present, the role of the lord-vassal relationship and its attendant mutual obligations became less important; the feudal relationship increasingly centered on the fief as a source of income. The weakening of the lord-vassal nexus tended to reduce the typical aristocrat's concern with who was above him and below him, and increase his interest in those of his class who shared his refined manners, who were striving with him to turn land to profit, and who wished to check the advance of royal power against aristocratic privilege. By the thirteenth century a nobility of refinement and privilege had evolved out of a class which in the tenth and eleventh centuries was made up of specialists in warfare and governance who largely directed a simple agricultural society.

The peasantry was also affected socially by the currents of change. During the twelfth and thirteenth centuries there was large-scale freeing of serfs, especially in France, England, Flanders, Italy, and western Germany. In part this was a consequence of the peasants' ability to accumulate a bit of wealth with which to purchase their freedom. A more important cause was the willingness of landlords to surrender their rights to a serf's labor services and dues in produce in return for money payments. Some serfs gained their freedom in return for colonizing new lands, and others by leaving the manors for the city.

In much of the West the serf was becoming a tenant farmer, enjoying whatever benefits freedom brought, but also losing the paternalistic protection the manorial lord had often extended. In a general way, the peasant tenants of the twelfth and thirteenth centuries prospered, chiefly due to the fact that in an inflationary age prices for the goods they raised increased faster than rents. However, the economic improvement of the peasant's lot did not elevate his social status; he was still at the bottom of the social scale, perhaps even further removed from the top than ever because of the increasing complexity and refinement of aristocratic life.

Without question, then, the landlords, peasants, merchants, and artisans had combined their productive efforts to enrich Western Europe greatly between 1000 and 1300. And their diverse economic activities produced not only new wealth, but also a battery of economic skills and techniques capable of still more growth. These centuries laid the economic groundwork for the world supremacy of Western Europe. Meanwhile, the social order had been rearranged into more complex patterns which allowed greater flexibility and adaptability in the face of new situations. A solid foundation for collective political effort had been shaped.

Suggested Reading

Overview. The era from 1000 to 1300, the High Middle Ages, is one so complex that it has discouraged works of synthesis. Useful for an orderly narrative survey are two volumes in a series: Z. N. Brooke, *A History of Europe From 911 to 1198* (3rd ed., 1951); and C. W. Previté-Orton, *A History of Europe From 1198 to 1378* (3rd ed., 1951). A brilliant essay, concentrating on certain "silent" changes affecting Western European society between the end of the tenth century and the beginning of the thirteenth, is **R. W. Southern, *The Making of the Middle Ages* (Yale). **Friedrich Heer, *The Medieval World, 1100–1350* (Mentor), is also good; it covers most aspects of the High Middle Ages while trying to demonstrate that Western European society passed from an "open" to a "closed" society. After a student has gained some knowledge of this period, he can achieve a new level of understanding and fresh insights into the nature of medieval society by reading R. S. Lopez, *The Birth of Europe* (1967), a truly masterful interpretation.

Economic History. A perceptive survey of the major economic and social trends of this era, emphasizing especially commercial growth, is

**Henri Pirenne, *Economic and Social History of Medieval Europe* (Harvest), although some of its conclusions need to be updated. A much more detailed and technical work is *Cambridge Economic History* (3 vols., 1952–1963), a cooperative work that includes specialized essays by most of the leading medieval economic historians. To the fundamental works of Robert Latouche, Georges Duby, and Marc Bloch on agricultural history cited in Chapter 18 should be added the excellent survey by B. H. Slicher van Bath, *Agrarian History of Western Europe, A.D. 500–1850* (1963), because it puts medieval agricultural development in a larger historical context. An excellent summary of the growth of medieval commerce, containing a significant collection of source materials, is **H. L. Adelson, *Medieval Commerce* (Anvil). An important collection of documents relating to medieval trade has been made by **R. S. Lopez and I. W. Raymond, eds., *Medieval Trade in the Mediterranean World* (Norton).

Social History. A broad survey of social developments (also containing considerable economic history) is **P. Boissonnade, *Life and Work in Medieval Europe: The Evolution of*

the Medieval Economy From the Fifth to the Fifteenth Centuries, trans. E. Power (Harper Torchbook). The development of the cities and the bourgeoisie is well treated in several works. Although somewhat old, **Henri Pirenne, *Medieval Cities* (Anchor), remains a basic work. C. B. Troedsson, *The Growth of the Western City During the Middle Ages* (1959), provides an up-to-date although not especially stimulating summary. The most recent treatment, based on deep knowledge of the subject, is **Fritz Rorig, *The Medieval Town* (University of California). Brief, but supported by an excellent selection of contemporary documents, is **J. H. Mundy and Peter Riesenberg, *The Medieval Town* (Anvil). **J. F. Benton, ed., *Town Origins: The Evidence From Medieval England* (Heath), presents a selection of modern scholarly opinions dealing with the much-disputed problem of town origins. Summerfield Baldwin, *Business in the Middle Ages* (1937), provides a brief but excellent summary of the evolution of new practices designed to cope with the problems of enlarged commercial activity. Two excellent studies by **Sidney Painter, *Mediaeval Society* (Cornell), and *French Chivalry* (Cornell), are helpful introductions to the nature of medieval society, especially aristocratic society. **U. T. Holmes, *Daily Life in the Twelfth Century* (Wisconsin), provides an intriguing picture of social life in Paris in the twelfth century as seen through the eyes of a university student.

Chapter 20 ❧ Western European Political Revival:

The Holy Roman Empire

While Western Europe's lesser men were producing wealth at an astounding rate and rearranging their social relationships into dynamic new patterns, its kings and feudal lords were rebuilding the political order. The era extending from 1000 to 1300 was characterized by remarkable progress in fashioning strong political entities in which royal governments became a positive directive force in society to a degree that had not been true in the West since the fall of the Roman Empire. These new entities and institutions were to persist far into the future, in some cases even to the present. The political revival was general in Europe, but its basic patterns were established primarily in Germany, Italy, France, and England. We shall therefore concentrate on the political history of these areas, first on the Holy Roman Empire embracing Germany and Italy, and then in the following chapter on France and England. But before discussing these particular cases, a brief review of the general political situation and the direction of political evolution will provide a helpful orientation.

1. POLITICAL PROBLEMS AND SOLUTIONS

Between the fifth and the tenth centuries Western Europe had endured a long period of political instability marked by unsuccessful experimentation in search of a workable basis for political organization. By the tenth century there was a universal trend toward extreme localism that featured a set of political relationships based on feudal contracts and on the rights of landholders to control the dependents attached to their manors. From a political point of view, feudalism and manorialism did provide for defense and a modicum of local order. But the feudal-manorial regime had severe limitations. In a broad sense it militated against the shaping of effective collectivities large enough to permit meaningful common action, and it generated extreme confusion in terms of political obligations and loyalties. Thus in the tenth century Western European society, beginning to stir toward new activity in many spheres, was faced with the problem of creating larger political entities within which some effective authority could coordinate and concentrate the energies of a variety of people.

Despite the triumph of the feudal-manorial regime, there still existed in the minds of tenth-century men possible solutions to this fundamental problem, political concepts which in the main lingered from the abortive experiments of the post-Roman era. Most remote was the faint memory of Germanic "national" groupings—Franks, Lombards, Saxons, Bavarians—remnants of which still survived in law codes, dialects, and legends. More recent, and certainly most vivid in memory, was the Carolingian ideal of a universal Christian empire, relating back to the old Roman Empire. In actual existence were the ineffective kingdoms created by the artificial divisions of the Carolingian Empire in the ninth century. There also existed, especially in France, several large feudal principalities which appeared viable as effective political entities. Finally, there were the examples of large political entities outside Western Europe, the most impressive of which was the Byzantine Empire, which reached its apogee in the tenth century under the Macedonian dynasty.

Given these "models" of large political communities, there remained the problem of discovering an agency capable of redirecting a disintegrating society toward the formation of larger political groupings. Effective political leadership in the tenth century generally lay with feudal nobles, but their political interests and mentality little inclined them to think in terms of larger units. Churchmen were perhaps most intellectually alive to the need for larger political groupings, but their dreams tended toward the impossible ideal of a universal Christian community. The only possible focus for any attempt to shape larger political entities rested with Europe's monarchs. Although woefully ineffective over much of tenth-century Europe, monarchy was an ancient institution everywhere accepted as necessary to right order. Surrounding every royal office was an aura of authority derived from religious ideas, the deeds of past kings, and traditions of royal rights enshrined in laws and customs.

The political history of Western Europe from 1000 to 1300 centers around the efforts of monarchs to create and rule larger political entities. In their struggles they drew on all the religious, historical, and legal precedents that surrounded monarchy. To these they added a crucial new ingredient not available prior to the late ninth and tenth centuries; namely, the exploitation of feudalism as a means of strengthening monarchy. The history of political revival is basically a story of the interaction of the king and the feudal

order, of the struggle of the king as supreme feudal lord to control his vassals, of the efforts of the king to turn feudal usages into monarchical institutions effective in governing extensive realms. We can best characterize the political developments of this era in terms of the growth of feudal monarchy.

2. THE FOUNDING OF THE HOLY ROMAN EMPIRE

The earliest and most spectacular effort at political reconstruction during the period 1000 to 1300 involved the Holy Roman Empire, a political entity embracing Germany and Italy. The chief units that were combined to create the Holy Roman Empire were two kingdoms established by the divisions of the Carolingian Empire. The most important was the kingdom of the East Franks, or Germany, defined by the Treaty of Verdun in 843. A generation later, further divisions of the Carolingian state created the kingdom of Italy. Until the early years of the tenth century, each of these kingdoms was ruled by members of the Carolingian dynasty. In both, royal power steadily declined, and the kingdoms tended to break into smaller principalities. In Germany, disintegration took the form of division into duchies whose boundaries corresponded roughly with those of the ancient Germanic nations that had existed prior to Frankish conquest, boundaries that the Franks perpetuated for administrative purposes. The later Carolingians failed to maintain control over the counts and dukes who had once served as representatives of royal authority. These nobles usurped royal power to create virtually independent principalities, the chief of which were Saxony, Bavaria, Franconia, Swabia, and Lorraine. In 911 the dukes deposed the Carolingian dynasty and elected one of themselves, Conrad, duke of Franconia, as king. A comparable process, but much more violent and confused, was occurring in Italy, where the kingdom was torn to bits by local potentates and where royal power virtually disappeared. To complicate the situation, both Germany

Otto I, Holy Roman Emperor, is shown in this tenth-century ivory plaque offering a model of Magdeburg Cathedral to Christ in majesty. The Holy Roman emperors, so closely linked with the Church, were its great patrons. *Photo: The Metropolitan Museum of Art, Gift of George Blumenthal, 1941*

and Italy suffered terribly from invasions in the late ninth and early tenth centuries. Germany was attacked by the Vikings and by hordes of Asiatic nomads called the Magyars (Hungarians), while Italy felt the lash of the Magyars and the Saracens. Since the only hope of resisting these marauders lay in well-organized local defenses, royal authority and centralized government were further weakened.

In Germany the path toward disintegration and localism was suddenly reversed by a royal dynasty emerging from the duchy of Saxony. When Conrad I died in 918, his greatest rival, Henry, duke of Saxony, was elected king. Henry I (919–936) concentrated his attention chiefly on the governance and protection of Saxony, leaving the other dukes to govern themselves. His leadership in Saxony created a solid base of power for his son, Otto I the

Great (937–973), who made Germany the chief political power in Europe and created the Holy Roman Empire.

Otto I was a man of great vigor and political skill whose political concepts were strongly influenced by Carolingian ideas and practices. Like the early Carolingians, his most pressing task was to curb the forces that were fragmenting his kingdom and to compel respect for the royal office. This policy pitted him against the great dukes, and only after years of struggle was royal authority successfully imposed on them. In the course of the struggle Otto was forced to uproot some of the old ducal families and replace them with more docile vassals, often his own relatives. Again like the great Carolingians, Otto was a warrior king who faced the task of defending his kingdom, especially from the destructive assaults of the Magyars. His efforts were rewarded in 955 at the great Battle of Lech-feld, where the royal armies smashed the Magyar horde so completely that it never again seriously threatened Germany. Otto was hailed as the savior of Germany and Christendom. Not content to trust the safety of his realm to one military victory, Otto launched a policy of military expansion, colonization, and missionary activity into the Slavic world, a "drive to the East" that continued for centuries—in fact, through the end of World War II.

To muster the military resources needed to curb the dukes and defend the frontiers and to find the administrative help required to exercise royal power posed a major problem for Otto. To resolve it, he made a decision that proved successful, but only for the moment. He chose to base his political power on an intimate alliance with the clergy, a decision that involved the feudalization of the German Church and its high officials. Convinced that clergymen were more loyal to the idea of monarchy than lay nobles, he decided to rely to a large extent upon Church officials for the performance of the services required to rule Germany. To secure those services, Otto made large grants of land on what amounted to a feudal basis. Ecclesiastical fiefs were created in every corner of Germany. In return for his grants, Otto collected from churchmen the military and political services he required to sustain his royal authority. To make this policy work, Otto had to be certain of the capabilities and loyalty of the men who filled high ecclesiastical offices. He then had to assume the power to elect the clergymen who were to receive royal lands and to serve the king. In effect, the ecclesiastical establishment became an arm of the monarchy, tied to it by a feudal nexus. Through lay investiture, the king assumed the direction of ecclesiastical life much in the way the strong Carolingian kings had done.

Successful in uniting and defending his kingdom and served well by his ecclesiastical vassals, Otto made German monarchy the strongest in tenth-century Europe. From this position it was an easy step to dreams of greater power and prestige. These dreams pointed in a predictable direction: the renewal of the Carolingian Empire. Such a course meant involvement in Italy, and by the mid-tenth century, Italy was ripe for outside intervention. The kingdom created there by the division of the Carolingian Empire was being torn to pieces by ambitious nobles seeking to create independent principalities. The whole peninsula was scourged by Magyar and Saracen attacks, and the chaos caused many Italians to look beyond Italy for a new protector. Among them were the popes, captives of the local Roman aristocracy. In fact, the papal office had become a pawn of these noble families and was occupied during much of the first half of the tenth century by unscrupulous and profligate representatives of these families whose activities badly tarnished the spiritual authority of the office. Despite their moral lapses, the popes yearned for their old independence and realized that only a powerful outsider could restore it. Otto did not remain aloof from this situation, in part because some of his German vassals were fishing in Italy's troubled waters in an effort to increase their power. His first venture into Italy came in 951 and ended with his assumption of overlordship over the king of Italy. However, troubles in Germany prevented a decisive settlement. He returned in 961 and assumed the title of "king of Italy." Then he marched on Rome, took the city, and in 962 persuaded Pope John XII to crown him emperor, the title the Carolingians had once held.

Carefully avoiding any claim to Byzantine territory in southern Italy and showing his good will toward the empire in the East by marrying his son and heir to a Byzantine princess, Otto proceeded to make his power permanent in Rome and northern Italy. His policy was similar to that which he had followed in Germany. Quarrelsome aristocrats were forced to admit his authority and obey his commands. Great churchmen in Italy were vested with powers as agents of Otto's administration. Especially significant was his policy toward the papacy. John XII had hoped to find an ally so occupied in distant places that he would permit the pope to rule Rome and the Papal States independently. Otto had no such idea; he was lord of Rome and expected the bishop of Rome to serve him as other churchmen did. When John refused to accept a subservient position, Otto deposed him and dictated the election of a more pliant successor. The emperor further imposed the rule that no pope would be elected in the future without the consent of the emperor, thus opening an era of German domination of the papacy. As Otto's Italian policy took shape, it became clear that ruling that troubled land would be a major task; and Otto spent most of his later years in Italy trying to ensure his control over the nobles and the papacy.

This renewed Western empire—usually called the Holy Roman Empire—made the emperor at least in theory the head of all Christian princes in the West. Otto of course was actual master only of Germany and Italy, and his success in counteracting the forces of localism by creating a huge, multinational empire left his heirs a terrible burden. But for the moment, the ruler of Germany was the greatest political figure in Western Europe.

3. OTTO'S SUCCESSORS AND THE GATHERING OPPOSITION

From Otto I's death in 973 until 1056, a succession of five emperors continued and expanded his policies with considerable success. Their basic policy centered around developing monarchical power to a point where it was the unifying force in imperial society. In Germany the independent spirit of the old duchies was virtually eliminated. The Church was skillfully manipulated so as to keep it a docile servant of the rulers; in the main it accepted this role willingly. Its contribution to the administration of the realm was supplemented by the development of a corps of secular administrators (called *ministeriales*) recruited from the nonnoble class and completely devoted to royal service. The rulers

labored to enlarge, consolidate, and exploit a royal domain as the prime source of their support. The emperors kept a firm hold on Italy, acting there chiefly through the powerful bishops. Strong pressures continued to be applied in the east, so successfully that by 1056 Poland, Bohemia, and Hungary all recognized imperial overlordship. On the western frontiers of the Holy Roman Empire, German domination was established over a significant remnant of the Carolingian Empire known as the kingdom of Burgundy.

The Holy Roman Empire remained the most important state in Western Europe, but as it grew, the authority of the emperors was bound to breed opposition. More significantly, some of its foes grew in strength during the eleventh century. Perhaps most ominous was the German aristocracy, whose condition remained unusual. Feudalism had not yet made very extensive inroads into Germany. As a consequence, the aristocracy was composed of freemen who had no feudal obligations to anyone and who admitted no superior except the king. The absence of feudal connections among the aristocrats meant that the rulers were deprived of a powerful means of controlling them, that is, the feudal bonds entailed in vassalage and fief holding. In the eleventh century the free aristocrats were busy consolidating their hold on the peasantry and building their own alliances with the Church by founding monasteries which they controlled. This strength could potentially be turned against the emperors, whose administrative machinery was not yet effective enough to exert sustained direct control over the aristocrats and who lacked the rights over them permitted by the feudal system. The absence of feudalism also prevented powerful overlords from establishing control over lesser nobles so as to create organized feudal principalities which the emperors could manipulate by controlling the overlord.

Italy was also the source of growing opposition. The Italian nobles remained unruly and resentful of imperial authority in any form. More serious was a new force emerging in

Italy: the commercial cities. Waxing richer and stronger from their successful exploitation of growing opportunities in trade, the townsmen disliked being dominated by bishops who acted as imperial agents and who had no appreciation of the problems associated with commercial enterprises. The towns sought an independence that could be gained only at the expense of imperial power.

The strength and aggressiveness of the Holy Roman Empire also bred resistance from outsiders. The French in the West and the Slavic kingdoms in the East were hostile and suspicious. Particularly significant was the emergence of a powerful Norman state in southern Italy and Sicily. We shall return to its establishment later (see Chapter 22), noting here only that by 1050 its ambitious, aggressive leaders began looking to the north as an area of expansion; and this led them to a confrontation with the Holy Roman emperors.

Finally, and most important, was a vast reform movement in religious life which in its ideological aspects led churchmen to repudiate the imperial idea that the emperor was the divinely ordained leader of Christian society and in its practical aspects prompted them to build a "new" Church that would be self-directing and free from secular control over its property and personnel. In essence, the reform movement was directed against the feudalization of the Church and its attendant evils; it involved a revolution against long-prevailing concepts of the relationship between secular authority and the Church. Its origins lay in the tenth-century monastic world, especially the Cluniac movement in France (see Chapter 23). The Cluniac reform movement had as one of its basic principles the idea that monastic communities should be free from lay control over monastic property and personnel; its supporters insisted that spiritual purity could not be achieved unless monks were separated from all secular influences on their lives. As the Cluniac order spread over Europe, its principles found support among other monks, among bishops and even among laymen, so

that by the mid-eleventh century, powerful spiritual currents were surging through European society in support of liberty for the Church, spiritual purity in the clergy, and more intense piety among laymen. Ironically, among the most ardent supporters of religious reform was the saintly emperor Henry III (1039–1056), who was seemingly unaware of its implications for his power.

Ultimately, the reform movement found its leadership in Rome. The German emperors had controlled the papal office since 962, and had rescued it from the corruption it had suffered in the early tenth century. But that very policy prepared the ground for a less docile papacy. The decisive turning point came when Henry III installed a dedicated reformer, Leo IX (1049–1054), as pope. Under Leo's leadership, the reforming spirit took over the papal court. Its driving force was a monk named Hildebrand, later to be pope as Gregory VII, who gave the movement a more radical, political orientation. Hildebrand and his supporters found their guiding principle in the ancient Christian idea that God had created man in order that he might gain salvation. The sole means to that end was the divinely ordained Church, which Hildebrand saw as an earthly corporate body working out God's will. From these premises it followed that the Church must be organized to fulfill its mission. It must become a visible community with its own head, its own law, its own resources, and its own liberty. By divine commission, the headship of the earthly Church was vested in the pope. It was his responsibility to do whatever was necessary to establish the Church in its rightful role. He must clear away the evils that impeded its divine mission: sinful clergymen, lay control over its property, lay selection of its officials. All Christians, even the greatest princes, must be directed by the pope to the proper execution of their responsibilities in the drama of salvation. Herein lay the radical element in the reform ideology: It denied the role of secular rulers as divinely ordained directors of Christian life. The priestly function of properly elected emperors was the essence of the imperial ideology. The emergence of the papal reform program thus laid the groundwork for a struggle centering on the issue of the right order in society.

The ideas of the papal reformers were all rooted deep in Christian tradition. What was now significant was that they were clearly rearticulated, related to the existing political and social order, and given expression in a practical program of reform vigorously pushed by the popes from Leo IX onward. Popes began to legislate against the immorality and corruption afflicting the clergy, especially *simony* (buying and selling Church offices) and violation of clerical celibacy. They began to build a centralized administrative machinery to enforce these rules over all Europe. In 1059 a papal decree provided that henceforth popes would be chosen by the College of Cardinals, a body of key officials who assisted the pope in directing the Church administration. The emperor was deprived of any voice in papal elections except to approve what the cardinals decided. Seeking to strengthen its position, the papacy in 1059 formed an alliance with the Normans in southern Italy and Sicily to ensure itself protection from a source other than the emperor.

This aggressive policy naturally generated resistance in many quarters. Immoral clergymen, especially those guilty of simony, began to squirm at talk of reform. Many sincere bishops and abbots, long accustomed to independence, resented Rome's growing interference in local religious affairs. Laymen were uneasy at the prospect of losing the right to appoint Church officials and with it control over the Church's extensive lands. If the popes were successful, the whole feudal order was endangered. Especially vulnerable was the Holy Roman emperor, who relied on a subservient Church as a chief source of power. This formidable opposition might well have blighted the reform movement had it not been for Gregory VII. A strong, willful man of great political ability and courage, he was not afraid to act to achieve what he

believed right. Once elected pope in 1073, he moved resolutely to carry through the reform program. His legislation against corrupt clergymen was strong, and he began to remove bishops whom he judged unworthy and unfit for high office. In 1075 he decreed that lay investiture was illegal, an act that put him on a collision course with all the secular princes of Western Europe, who had long made a practice of appointing high church officials. This act opened the investiture struggle, which was destined to have an especially great impact on the Holy Roman Empire.

4. THE INVESTITURE STRUGGLE AND ITS CONSEQUENCES, 1076–1152

During the critical period when the papacy was seizing leadership of the reform movement, redefining its ideology in terms that repudiated the traditional relationship between secular rulers and the Church, and formulating specific actions to bring about reform, the imperial forces were temporarily crippled. Henry III died in 1056, leaving as his successor the child Henry IV, who did not reach his majority until 1065. During this interval German and Italian nobles revolted in hopes of weakening imperial authority. When he did finally assume full power, Henry IV had to spend several years restoring order. He demonstrated great political ability and showed repeatedly that he fully intended to follow the policies that had made his predecessors strong. Among other things, he proceeded to appoint men of his choice to episcopal office, despite papal attacks on lay investiture.

But a clash was sure to come, for the German ruler symbolized all that the Gregorian papacy opposed. The break developed in 1075 in connection with a vacant episcopal see in Milan. Dependent on a loyal episcopacy to uphold his power in Italy, Henry IV acted decisively to impose his candidate. Late in 1075, Gregory sent Henry a letter ordering him to do penance for violating Church law and threatening him with loss of his office. With

R ex ROGAT ABBATEM. MAThILDIM SupplicAT ATQ̄ :

The investiture struggle, shown in this miniature from an early twelfth-century manuscript of the life of Countess Matilda of Tuscany. Here Henry IV begs Abbot Hugh of Cluny and the Countess to intercede for him with the pope, Gregory VII.
Photo: Vatican Library

the backing of most of the German bishops, Henry replied by declaring that "the false monk" Hildebrand was not even pope, since his election had been improper. Whereupon in 1076 Gregory excommunicated the emperor, freed his subjects from their vows of obedience, suspended Henry from royal office, and invited the Germans to elect a new king. A considerable number of German nobles and bishops leaped at this opportunity to weaken the king. They commanded Henry to clear himself of excommunication in a personal meeting with the pope to be held in Germany in the near future or face deposition.

Henry IV faced a crucial issue. The specific question of lay investiture was no longer so

critical as was the broader implication that the pope could claim to judge the emperor unworthy of his office and bring about his deposition. This was a threat to the entire rationale behind the imperial office, which rested on the idea that the emperor was God's agent charged with providing order in human society. The pope was claiming that role, and Henry had to offset this claim if he were to save his regime. His next action was tactically brilliant. With his crown in jeopardy, he set out to intercept Gregory before the pope could reach Germany to preside over a meeting of bishops and nobles that would surely lead to the loss of his crown. In January 1077, he found Gregory at Canossa in northern

The Investiture Struggle: A Medieval Revolution?

In writing the history of medieval Western Europe, it is difficult to avoid treating the sequence of events commonly called "the investiture struggle" as *the* decisive event in medieval history. One American medievalist has, in fact, insisted that it was one of four "world revolutions" that shaped the Western world. This may seem a little exaggerated, especially as our readers become more familiar with the many momentous revolutions occurring later in Western European history. However, it is vital to understand the reasons why medievalists argue that the investiture struggle was so crucial in the course of the history of Western Europe.

One school of investigators sees the investiture struggle as a revolt against a deeply imbedded system governing church property and offices. These historians argue that when the Germans established their mastery over the Western Roman Empire during the invasion period, they brought with them a concept of property that made no allowance for corporate property such as the Roman world had evolved. Rather, the Germans insisted that everything connected with a piece of property belonged to the proprietor. As a consequence, they viewed churches built on lands they occupied as private property, totally at the disposal of the possessor. They could not con-

ceive of these churches as belonging to a corporate entity, the Church, as had been the case under Roman law. In subsequent centuries these proprietors, including kings, often were responsible for building and equipping new churches on their lands. In keeping with Germanic custom, they considered these churches as their own (*Eigenkirchen*, private churches) to be exploited, bought, sold, or traded for their private profit. It was but a simple step from viewing the church building and its furnishings as private property to treating the office associated with the church —the priestly, episcopal, abbatial, and even the papal office—as a piece of property to be disposed of by the possessor as he saw fit. This led to control by proprietors over appointments to these offices and to their buying and selling ecclesiastical offices. Thus emerged the feudal Church—a creation based on Germanic concepts of property. The investiture struggle was in essence an attempt to liberate church property and offices from private ownership and to vest that "property" in corporate hands, represented by the bishops and abbots. The revolutionary implications are obvious: the shifting of vast wealth from secular to clerical hands, the possibilities of independence open to the corporate Church, the shift of power from lay to ecclesiastical hands. In short, the investiture struggle was a revolution against a deeply-engrained concept of property in favor of another system, a revolution which threatened to shift control of society from one set of hands to another by shifting control of a major part of the wealth of society from one element of society to another.

Another view emphasizing the revolutionary character of the investiture struggle—not unrelated to the foregoing—centers on its political implications. Many generations of historians of Germany and Italy have viewed the clash as a decisive and fateful episode in the history of the Holy Roman Empire, an event that condemned Germany and Italy to many centuries of internal political chaos and backwardness. These historians argue that during the period from 962 to 1075 the Holy Roman Empire, representing a revival on a limited scale of the Carolingian Empire, had become a viable entity representing the strongest, best-organized political unit in Western Europe. Its basic strength derived from a close and mutually beneficial union between church and state. The emperor based his effective power on the feudal services rendered him by powerful churchmen who were his vassals and whose offices and properties were bestowed on them as imperial fiefs. In return for their services, the emperor offered the clergymen his protection and his favors and bent his efforts to promote the true faith—priceless benefits in a chaotic age. To these historians, the investiture struggle was an assault mounted by Pope Gregory VII on this unique political system. Although not fully agreed on Gregory's motives or goals, these historians insist that his program worked to detach the German and Italian clergy from the unique relationship with the emperor. The ultimate consequence was to destroy the constitutional basis of the Holy Roman Empire and to open the way for the secular nobles to establish their independence from the emperor, fatally weakened by the loss of his ecclesiastical support. In brief, the investiture struggle destroyed a constitution with consequences felt for centuries.

Other historians see the revolutionary nature of the investiture struggle in even more radical terms. They insist that it represented an effort by an ecclesiastical faction led by Gregory VII to apply a revolutionary sociopolitical ideology to late eleventh-century society. For centuries, Western Europeans had accepted the basic idea that the welfare of Christian society depended upon the actions of divinely ordained kings and emperors whose elevation to office gave them God's blessing to subordinate and direct all society, including the clergy, toward salvation. The royal office combined the functions of both *rex* and *sacerdos*, king and priest, to the end that the divine will be accomplished. During the Early Middle Ages, this concept of right order in society, dramatically exemplified by Constantine, Charlemagne, and Otto the Great, led to a clear subordination in theory and practice of the church to the state. The Gregorian party challenged this conception of right order. Pulling together a variety of ideas of Judaic and early Christian origin, they articulated a doctrine that insisted it was God's will that the priests should direct society toward its ultimate destiny. Ordination to the priestly office bestowed on clergymen the highest authority to direct all society, including its secular rulers. The true Christian community—the Church—was a society of the baptized guided by priests whose office gave them the divine grace and wisdom to instruct the faithful according to God's plan. The kings were only agents of the priests, obligated to do the priestly bidding so that right order would be maintained.

The revolutionary aspect of the Gregorian program, including the attack on lay investiture, flowed from its implications for the established order in society: The Gregorians felt compelled by the logic of their ideology to deprive secular rulers, especially the emperors, of the priestly functions through which they claimed the right to control every aspect of society. The investiture struggle was therefore one aspect of a revolution aimed at shearing secular rulers of authority they claimed by divine right and transferring that authority to the pope and his agents, the lesser clergy. It was a struggle to "free" the Church so that it could direct society toward spiritual perfection, a revolution mounted to restore "right order" in a world that for centuries had defied God's will by permitting secular rulers to lay false claims to control of Christian society.

Several scholars are willing to accept as true that the investiture struggle was surrounded by a rhetoric of revolution, but insist that these ideological polemics were not of prime significance in the real world of power and politics. What is more important and truly revolutionary to these scholars is the fact that the Gregorian ideology led to a radical change in the actual governance of the Church. Ideas about the right of the clergy to rule society and about the nature of the Christian community as a corporate entity with its own ends led to a concern about creating a centralized system of government within the Church itself. As a result of the investiture struggle, the papacy turned its energies toward a precise definition of its powers over other elements of the clergy and laity and toward developing techniques for asserting its claims to power. The revolutionary by-product of the investiture struggle was the papal monarchy and the centralized Church that reached its maturity in the thirteenth century and has remained an important ingredient in Western European society to the present.

Still another group of scholars sees the investiture struggle as a turning point in the long history of religious reform. These historians consider it primarily as part of the many-faceted effort in the tenth and eleventh centuries to purge religious life of its corruption and to improve the quality of spiritual life. Prior to the Gregorian epoch, that reforming effort centered chiefly on the monastic idea that the true path to spiritual improvement involved withdrawal from the world to the holy precincts of a monastery where one could concentrate on prayer and contemplation. The investiture struggle marked a revolutionary shift directing holy men—exemplified by Gregory VII—to move out of the cloister into the wicked world in order to attack evil and to persuade sinful kings, nobles, bishops, priests, and ordinary men to "convert" to the true Christian life. The investiture problem and its attendant abuses constituted an issue that reversed the centuries-long tradition idealizing flight from the world and replaced it with an activist ethos that saw improvement of the human condition in terms of involvement in worldly affairs.

Whether these issues constitute the "stuff" of real revolution will depend on one's judgment of what is decisive in human affairs. However, it is difficult to escape the conclusion that when a particular episode in history centers around control of property, the constitution of a powerful political entity, the relation of church to state, the nature of right order in society, the character of ecclesiastical government, and how man acts to change society, then revolutionary issues are at stake. One test might be to watch for the extent to which these issues dominated historical development after the investiture struggle. This test may indeed establish it as one of the great "revolutions" in Western European history.

Italy. In the garb of a penitent, he begged the pope's forgiveness. Although Gregory realized that to grant this request would free a strengthened Henry to return to Germany and continue the imperial policy, he could not abdicate his role as priest. Henry was absolved. The pope had won a moral victory by forcing the most powerful ruler in Europe to admit that he had a superior, but he had apparently lost the war.

Henry moved at once to deal with his most dangerous immediate foes, the German nobility. Although deprived of their advantage by the papal action, they still persisted in their plans to depose Henry and replace him with a ruler of their own choice. The king, however, beat down their resistance by force, a task he completed with remarkable skill and speed. He then turned to Italy, captured Rome, forced Gregory VII into exile (where he remained until his death in 1085), elevated a supporter to the papal throne, and had himself crowned emperor in 1084. By 1085 it appeared that the empire was saved and the papal reformers defeated.

But the victory was a hollow one; the papal challenge had unleashed too many enemies. Henry was unable to hold Rome against the papal allies, led by the Normans. The papal office was returned to strong and independent hands, especially those of Pope Urban II (1088–1099), who rallied anew the reforming forces and the imperial foes. The real damage to Henry's cause was done in Germany, where the nobles kept up their resistance and slowly undermined royal power. As a consequence, Germany and Italy moved ever deeper into chaos and civil war. Although Henry defended his power valiantly, by the end of his reign he was a virtual fugitive from the rebellious nobles, including his own son.

Henry IV's three successors, who ruled until 1152, could not stem the tide against monarchical power. Effective imperial control over Italy nearly disappeared, political power being usurped by independent towns, nobles, and the papacy. The imperial crown tended to become a pawn of warring noble factions,

election going to the prince who seemed least likely to exert effective power.[1] Imperial resources were dissipated or usurped, and the imperial administrative machinery broke down almost completely. In 1122 Emperor Henry V made peace with the Church over the specific issue of lay investiture by signing the Concordat of Worms, which provided that election to ecclesiastical offices be made by the Church, while the lands and secular powers associated with the office be invested by the ruler. This compromise settlement—to which Gregory VII would probably never have agreed—gave the emperor an effective veto over ecclesiastical elections by allowing him to withhold the property of the office. But it also broke the power that the emperor had held over the Church since Otto the Great's day and thus deprived the monarchy of absolute control over its major support.

However, the investiture issue had long since ceased to be the crucial problem from the German monarch's point of view. The real significance of the investiture struggle lies in the fact that it created a situation in Germany (and to a lesser extent in Italy) which encouraged the rapid spread of feudalism. The interminable civil wars drove the weak to seek the protection of the strong and the strong to strengthen their hand by rallying as many followers as possible. As lord-vassal complexes took shape, the lords built castles from which they could defy all authority. With the legitimacy of elected rulers constantly in question by factions in Germany and Italy and by the popes, the nobles usurped public authority and began to build territorial units over which they exercised nearly complete control. The desperate emperors often conceded lands and rights in an effort to buy the support of nobles. The real

---

[1] The two major factions were the Welfs and the Waiblings. The Welfs in general stood for elective kingship, weak central government, liberty for nobles and Church, and support of the papacy. The Waiblings represented the opposite, seeking in the main to return to the old tradition of imperial power. Comparable parties, called Guelfs and Ghibellines, developed in Italy.

victors in the investiture struggle were clearly those nobles who succeeded in creating followings of vassals and in laying claim to political powers formerly exercised by the rulers. The emergence of a feudalized Germany left the monarchy out of the picture, for the emperors had traditionally claimed authority on a basis other than the feudal one. By 1152 the Germany monarchy that had been so successful in the tenth and eleventh centuries had lost touch with the new society which had emerged during the investiture struggle. A kingdom that had escaped feudalization in the tenth century had now acquired a feudal structure, and the monarchy had no means of coping with it.

5. THE HOHENSTAUFENS, 1152–1250

Despite the destructive impact of the investiture struggle, the Holy Roman Empire survived. At mid-twelfth century a new dynasty, the Hohenstaufens, heirs to the Waibling tradition, took up the task of rebuilding the imperial government. The first notable Hohenstaufen was Frederick I Barbarossa (1152–1190). Elected king with a remarkable show of unanimity among the warring nobles, Frederick I began from a position of strength. He knew well enough that he faced a new array of forces: the powerful feudalized German and Italian nobility, the rich Italian towns which had grown accustomed to considerable independence, a papacy that would never forget the essential concepts of the Gregorian reform. Frederick set resolutely about establishing a basis for royal power that would fit the new political world in which he lived. In essence, his policy aimed at turning feudalism to royal advantage in order to build a system of government based on secular rather than theocratic principles, principles that Frederick derived in considerable part from the Roman law then enjoying a revival in Western Europe.

His first task was the establishment of order. To achieve this end, he sought to take advantage of the feudal structure so recently evolved in Germany. He made broad concessions to a few of the greatest nobles and allowed them to curb their troublesome vassals, the lesser nobles. The chief beneficiary of this policy was the leader of the traditionally anti-Hohenstaufen Welf faction, Henry of Saxony, who with royal approval became the master of Saxony and Bavaria. But Frederick was careful in this arrangement to define his regalian rights clearly and to insist that his great vassals respect them. In order to enforce these rights, he gave special attention to increasing his royal domain, much of which was concentrated in Swabia (the Hohenstaufen homeland), and in developing a nonfeudal corps of civil servants to administer his land and to guard the royal prerogative throughout Germany. He continued the old imperial policy of turning the German Church to royal support, a policy that entailed royal control of ecclesiastical elections.

Also true to imperial tradition, Frederick I was soon drawn to Italy. In fact, it seems clear that he counted heavily on exploiting his rights over the rich Italian cities as a complement to his sources of power in Germany, to build a solid base for royal authority in southern Germany and northern Italy. Although his early relations with the papacy were friendly, permitting him to be crowned emperor in 1155, he made it clear that he had no intention of admitting papal supremacy or of allowing the papacy to restrict what he considered to be his rights over the Church. As early as 1158 he demonstrated the essence of his policy in Italy when he summoned representatives of the Italian towns to a meeting at Roncaglia and laid down a new set of rules to govern the relationship between the emperor and the towns. Henceforth, the towns were to pay regular taxes, accept imperial officials as their rulers, and permit the emperor to coin money and regulate commerce. At one stroke, the freedoms the Italian cities had been fashioning for the previous century were to be denied them.

Once Frederick had made clear his policy

with respect to the papacy and the towns, the storm broke. For most of his reign he was forced to fight an imposing array of enemies, led by the papacy. Pope Alexander III (1159–1181), a true heir of Gregory VII, was the main protagonist, battling with great skill to uphold the independence and supremacy of the Church. Frederick sought to offset Alexander's opposition by having another pope elected, but most of Europe supported Alexander. With papal encouragement, the Italian towns formed the Lombard League to resist Frederick, and once again the Norman kingdom of Sicily rallied to oppose the emperor. And the German nobles, still refusing to accept a strong king, used every chance to limit and defy royal authority. Frederick battled this alliance with great skill, yet he failed to emerge victorious. With good sense, he eventually worked toward a compromise that left him in a strong position. In 1176 at the Battle of Legnano he suffered a crushing military defeat at the hands of the Lombard League, a catastrophe brought on in part by the refusal of his great vassals in Germany to supply troops. In 1177 he gave up his attempt to establish a German pope and recognized Alexander III. In 1183, at the Peace of Constance, the Italian towns came to terms, recognizing Frederick's overlordship in return for certain specific rights, such as choosing their own officials and levying their own taxes. In 1186 he arranged for the marriage of his son Henry to the heiress of the Norman kingdom of Sicily, a diplomatic triumph that set the stage for the removal of one of the most persistent foes of imperial power. Frederick had not gained full control of Italy, nor had he subdued the papacy. However, his authority was still extensive there and his position as emperor was still intact. His long-standing policy of trying to live with a few great princes in Germany did not prove completely successful. Eventually he had to smash the chief of these nobles, Henry of Saxony. Thereafter, Frederick decided to break up the large principalities that had long been a feature of Germany, and granted the territory to many lesser no-

bles instead of a few great ones. This step relieved the immediate danger, but in the long run, by further promoting the feudalization of Germany, proved fatal to royal power.

Frederick Barbarossa's illustrious career ended in 1190 when he drowned while leading the Third Crusade. He had established a new base for imperial power, but a steady hand was needed to continue the rebuilding job. His son, Henry VI (1190–1197), began as if he would sustain his father's work, but his attention soon became fixed on Italy at the expense of Germany, where effective power was still needed to maintain control over a restless nobility not yet accustomed to respecting royal authority. Henry's chief concern was with the kingdom of Sicily, which he claimed by virtue of his marriage to the heiress to that kingdom. Intending to incorporate it into the imperial structure, he fought a costly but victorious war to establish his control. But then, instead of confining himself to the hard business of ruling his enlarged empire, Henry became enmeshed in a series of schemes to extend his power over the Mediterranean to the Holy Land, and to France and Spain. As his schemes unfolded, the foes of strong imperial power began to join hands. Only a premature death in 1197 relieved him from paying the full price for too great ambition.

For the next two decades the fate of the Holy Roman Empire was determined by the most powerful of all the medieval popes, Innocent III (1198–1216). Henry VI left a three-year-old son, Frederick, as his heir; in 1198 Innocent III assumed guardianship over this child and in that role took virtual control over the kingdom of Sicily. His basic concern was to prevent a single Hohenstaufen from ruling Germany and Sicily, a policy that would allow him to restore papal power in central Italy. In Germany the nobles remained loyal to the Hohenstaufens, and elected Philip of Swabia as king. Innocent immediately promoted the claims of another candidate, Otto of Brunswick, an heir to the Welf tradition. This led to a civil war which lasted until 1212 and virtually ruined Germany. Not only did papal

Emperor Frederick II, a fascinating medieval king, is shown here as a newborn baby being displayed to the people by his mother, the empress Constance. *Photo: Bürgerbibliothek, Bern*

conniving keep the war going, but French and English interests intervened. Papal diplomacy encouraged the northern Italian towns and the nobles of central Italy to throw off imperial control. The work of Frederick Barbarossa seemed completely ruined; the Holy Roman Empire had become a pawn of the papacy.

In 1212 Innocent decided to use his ward to impose papal control on Germany. Securing the aid of the king of France, he engineered the election of Frederick II to the kingship of Germany and eventually to the Holy Roman emperorship. Frederick paid for papal support by making sweeping concessions that returned control of the German Church to the papacy and fortified papal independence in central Italy. But Frederick II proved to be no docile servant of the papacy. He once again took up the battle to build a strong Holy Roman Empire. To this battle he brought considerable political skill, ruthless ambition, and a set of personal qualities that made him one of the most intriguing figures in all medieval history. His enemies—and they were many—branded him irreligious, immoral, dishonest, cruel, the Antichrist, while his admirers saw him as a new man driven by a secular spirit quite distinct from that of the age in which he lived.

Frederick II took a new view toward the Holy Roman Empire. He was little interested in Germany as the base for imperial power; Sicily was his true homeland, and Italy was the focus of his political concern. After becoming ruler of Germany, he remained there only until 1220. He spent these years surrendering the royal power that his predecessors had so painfully established. We have already noted how he gave up control of the Church to the papacy. He was equally generous to the great feudal princes. Their fiefs were made hereditary, and they were given full rights of government over the fiefs. Little was left for the king; even the strong position the early Hohenstaufens had established in the towns was turned over to the princes.

As he progressively disengaged himself from Germany, Frederick turned his energies to building the kingdom of Sicily into a centralized, bureaucratic state where royal power resembled that claimed by the Byzantine emperors. From this base he sought to extend his control to all of Italy, especially the northern area. But this program reopened ancient hostilities. The papacy felt itself being surrounded, and the Italian cities saw their liberties threatened. For nearly thirty years a series of able popes backed by the cities battled Frederick II in a ruinous struggle. The Hohenstaufen fought skillfully and with great flair, but he did not win. He lacked the resources to overpower his Italian foes. The papal prestige was too extensive in Europe to permit Frederick to form an antipapal alliance. He drew almost no help from Germany; his subjects there were too busy enjoying the privileges he had extended them to render help to their absent king. Frederick II died in 1250 far from realizing his ambitions; in fact, his policy had irreparably damaged any realistic power base upon which imperial authority could be established.

During the period from Frederick's death in 1250 until 1273, known as the Interregnum, the last vestiges of effective imperial power were destroyed. Amid fighting and bickering and foreign intervention, the German nobles did not agree on a new king until 1273, when they elected Rudolph of Hapsburg, qualified chiefly by his lack of strength. In the interval the feudal lords finished appropriating to themselves the last remnants of royal authority. Germany had finally broken to pieces politically. The local princes ruling over small territorial states owed only the vaguest obedience to the king and emperor. Meanwhile, in Italy a French prince, Charles of Anjou, accepted a papal invitation to assume the crown of the kingdom of Sicily, a mission he accomplished in 1266. In the rest of the peninsula each city, each noble, each churchman went an independent way, respecting no higher authority and feeling no attachment to Italy. The Slavic kingdoms that had so long been under strong German influence were also free. In fact, all Europe no longer needed to face the prospect of being absorbed into a single state called the Holy Roman Empire, which at least in theory claimed to be a superior kind of political entity. One of the cherished dreams of medieval men—the dream of a Christian empire in which men who worshiped one god and held one faith would enjoy one ruler and one law—had failed to become a reality.

Suggested Reading

The Holy Roman Empire. A very brief survey of the history of the Holy Roman Empire in this period can be found in Chapter III of **Sidney Painter, *The Rise of Feudal Monarchies* (Cornell). By far the best treatment of the subject is **Geoffrey Barraclough, *The Origins of Modern Germany* (Capricorn), although this masterful synthesis presupposes some knowledge of German history. A classic treatment is that of **James Bryce, *The Holy Roman Empire* (Schocken Books), stressing the idea that the Medieval Empire was primarily a revival of the Roman Empire. The early chapters of Friedrich Heer, *The Holy Roman Empire,* trans. Janet Sondheimer (1968), are stimulating, stressing especially the empire's ideological foundations. Also provocative is G. Falco, *The Holy Roman Republic: A Historic Profile of the Middle Ages,* trans. K. V. Kent (1965). **R. E. Herzstein, ed., *The Holy Roman Empire in the Middle Ages: Universal State or German Catastrophe?* (Heath), brings together a selection of essays by modern authorities which presents varying interpretations of the nature and historical importance of the Holy Roman Empire. Good works in English on medieval Italian history are not plentiful. As a general guide, the best treatment is L. Salvatorelli, *A Concise History of Italy* (1940). W. Butler, *The Lombard Communes* (1906), is old but useful. Peter Munz, *Frederick Barbarossa: A Study in Medieval Politics* (1969) helps clarify the role of the most effective Hohenstaufen. Ernst Kantorowicz, *Frederick II* (1957), is a romanticized yet intriguing study of one of the great figures in the history of the Holy Roman Empire.

The Investiture Struggle. One of the most balanced and comprehensive treatments of the basic ideological issues of the investiture struggle is G. Tellenbach, *Church, State, and Christian Society at the Time of the Investiture Struggle* (1959). **Schafer Williams, ed., *The Gregorian Epoch, Reformation, Revolution, Reaction?* (Heath), is a collection of interpretations of the nature of the investiture struggle by modern authorities. Walter Ullmann, *The Growth of Papal Government in the Middle Ages* (2nd ed., 1962), provides an interesting but debatable interpretation of the papal position in the conflict with the emperors. A good picture of the chief papal protagonist in the investiture struggle is A. J. Macdonald, *Hildebrand: A Life of Gregory VII* (1932).

Sources. For a student who would like to sample what contemporaries thought and felt on the issues of the investiture struggle, there are two works of great importance. *The Correspondence of Gregory VII,* trans. E. Emerton (1932), supplies an insight into the ideas and motives of Gregory VII. *Imperial Lives and Letters of the Eleventh Century,* trans. T. W. Mommsen and K. F. Morrison (1962), provides documents that help make clear the imperial position. An interesting interpretation of imperial destiny by a twelfth-century historian and bishop is Otto of Freising, *The Two Cities,* trans. C. C. Mierow (1928). The same author wrote **Deeds of Frederick Barbarossa,* trans. C. C. Mierow and R. Emory (Norton).

Chapter 21 ❧ Western European Political Revival:

Feudal Monarchy in England and France

While the German rulers struggled valiantly but in vain to create a strong state embracing Germany and Italy, political change progressed less dramatically but more effectively in England and France. In each of these kingdoms the kings, chiefly by exploiting their feudal rights, slowly built their power to the point where they exercised extensive control over states of limited but manageable size. By the thirteenth century their actual power far exceeded the vaunted claims of the Holy Roman emperors, in large part because these kings had created effective institutions of royal government, whereas the emperors had failed to do so. Strong central government developed in England earlier than in France, but during the thirteenth century the powers of the English kings were considerably curtailed. French monarchy was long in becoming established, but its powers were ultimately greater—so great, in fact, that France had become the dominant political power in Europe by the end of the thirteenth century.

1. ENGLAND: THE NORMAN CONQUEST AND ITS CONSEQUENCES

Political institutions in England, as previously noted, evolved in a unique pattern during the

Early Middle Ages. From purely Germanic origins, there had slowly evolved an effective system of central government, a strong set of local institutions, a legal system based on customary law, and a military and financial organization that permitted a king like Alfred the Great to defend his people against the Vikings and to impose his authority on most of England. Anglo-Saxon monarchy reached its peak in the tenth century. The kings of England exercised considerable power directly over their subjects, most of whom were freemen, at a time when royal power was disintegrating and being replaced by the feudal system in many areas on the Continent.

During the eleventh century, Anglo-Saxon monarchy began to show signs of losing its vitality. The rulers no longer demonstrated the military and administrative abilities of Alfred and his immediate successors. Their chief local officials, the earls and the sheriffs, steadily secured rights of private government. The kings began to grant royal lands to *thegns* who pledged military service in return, but often failed to render it. Many freemen were forced to become dependents of the powerful nobles, either as vassals or as serfs. These trends were accelerated by new Scandinavian assaults, chiefly those of the Danes, whose

Aside from the Bayeux Tapestry, few contemporary illustrations of Normans or Anglo-Saxons exist. This fragment from a French manuscript shows a boatload of Norman soldiers carrying the pointed shields and long spears used at Hastings.
Photo: Bibliothèque Nationale, Paris

successes undermined royal prestige and encouraged local independence. The invaders even managed to establish a Dane, Canute, as king of England (1016–1035). Canute dreamed of drawing England into a vast northern maritime empire, but his plans were foiled by his early death and by ineffective successors.

In 1042 a descendant of the old· Anglo-Saxon royal line, Edward the Confessor (1042–1066), took the throne after spending many years as an exile in Normandy. Edward was an ineffective king, and his reign was characterized by a rapid deterioration of royal power to the special advantage of the great earls, of whom Godwin of Wessex was the most powerful. The Scandinavians again began to menace England. In this mounting crisis, a new factor entered in the person of William, duke of Normandy and distant relative of Edward. This ambitious chief of a well-organized French feudal principality and leader of an aggressive expansionist nobility saw England as a potential prize available to him and his followers. Then Edward died without heirs in 1066. The Witan elected as king Harold, son of Earl Godwin, a choice that promised to keep England within her ancient Germanic framework and perhaps promote the forces of localism. The new king was faced with a Scandinavian invasion, led by Harold Hardrada, king of Norway, who intended to establish himself as king and again draw England into the Scandinavian world. And William of Normandy laid claim to the throne as a relative of Edward; his success meant that England would be drawn toward the Continent and its feudal patterns. Both Harald Hardrada and William chose almost the same moment to assert their claims, forcing a settlement on the field of battle in 1066. King Harold crushed the invading Scandinavians, only to meet disaster a short time later in October 1066, at the Battle of Hastings, where William's Norman knights overpowered the Anglo-Saxon forces and made it possible for their leader to assume the English crown as William I (1066–1087).

William's position was far from secure in 1066. He and his few knights were foreigners surrounded by hostile Anglo-Saxons, many of whom were not willing to accept the decision at Hastings as final. Much depended, therefore, on how the new king used his military victory. William made wise choices which laid the groundwork for the rapid growth of monarchical power. One prime decision was his assumption of all the powers that tradition had associated with the Anglo-Saxon monarchy. He made it clear at his coronation that he would observe Anglo-Saxon customs and exercise all the rights belonging to the Anglo-Saxon kings. This gave his office a theoretical base far broader than was the case on the Continent, where feudalism had eroded royal power. And it gave him claims on his subjects far more extensive than those available to Continental kings.

However, William's rights and powers as an Anglo-Saxon king would have been empty if he had not had the strength to exert them. To provide that strength, he introduced feudalism into England as an instrument for bolstering royal power. William claimed all the land of England by right of conquest. He set aside about one-sixth of it as the royal domain, exclusively for the support of the king. Most of the rest he granted out as fiefs to his Norman followers. In return, they became his vassals, owing him services, chiefly military, in proportion to the size of their fiefs. Most of his direct vassals (called *tenants-in-chief* or *barons*) subinfeudated their lands and acquired their own vassals. William, however, by insisting that all subvassals owed first allegiance to the king, thereby established a meaningful feudal hierarchy with the king at the head. As a consequence of the introduction of feudalism, William not only secured a valuable royal domain, but also the military service of about 5,000 knights, enough to ensure his mastery of England. Moreover, through vassalage he laid claim to the obedience of the powerful men in England. In short, the feudal system allowed him to impose a new ruling elite on England in a fashion that gave him as king control over it.

As successor to the Anglo-Saxon kings and chief lord of the feudal hierarchy, William possessed extensive authority and resources which he utilized in capable and constructive fashion. He laid the groundwork for a strong central government able to make its power felt throughout England. The Anglo-Saxon Witan was replaced by a feudal body called the *curia regis,* at whose meetings the lay and ecclesiastical vassals of the king were expected to render court service, judge cases, and advise the ruler. Careful attention was given by the king and his agents to the exploitation of the royal domain, the income from it constituting the chief source of support for the monarchy. William continued to collect the taxes owed the king from Anglo-Saxon times, the chief one being the Dangeld, a tax originally imposed in 991 to provide ransom money to the Danes. In 1086 William's agents compiled Domesday Book, a vast survey of England's wealth manor by manor which permitted the royal government to know what men had and how much they owed the king. No other monarch in Europe was in a position to reach so directly into the affairs of his subjects; and it was the administrative machinery being developed that was the key to the exercise of royal power.

William's royal authority benefited greatly from the system of local government he had inherited, the Anglo-Saxon shires and hundreds. He was careful to retain these units of administration and to see to it that the local officials, especially the sheriffs, served royal purposes. Through the shires and the hundreds the king kept in direct touch with large numbers of the English people in the administration of justice, police regulation, and taxation. This was of vital importance, because the introduction of feudalism had resulted in the establishment of feudal courts where lords and vassals settled their affairs according to feudal law. On the Continent these feudal governments had expanded their activities to replace royal government, but in England the presence of strong local institutions controlled by the king prevented this development, to the distinct advantage of royal authority.

Overlooking no possible source of power and prestige, William acted to attach the Church to his new establishment, a matter of crucial importance at a time when a reformed Church, led by the militant Gregorian papacy, was often hostile to strong states. William won the support of the reformers and the blessing of the papacy by promising at the time of the conquest to undertake the reform of the Anglo-Saxon Church, which indeed was badly corrupted. Once in control of England, he brought in a Norman, Lanfranc, as archbishop of Canterbury. Lanfranc worked hard at the purification and reordering of religious life along lines advocated by the reforming forces and considerably improved conditions in England. William was generous in endowing the Church with property and in permitting it liberty to conduct its own courts. However, he never relinquished real control over the Church, especially in the choice of high ecclesiastical officials. Such a policy risked a quarrel with the Church, but its successful application assured the king of the loyalty and support of key church officials, support that was immensely valuable in building strong monarchy.

The Norman conquest was thus a watershed in English history. A disintegrating, somewhat out-of-date monarchy was given new political vitality by injecting into its structure certain Continental feudal practices that buttressed the power of the king. The combination of royal and feudal powers and resources provided the king-lord with an opportunity to make himself the real master of England. Moreover, the establishment of the Normans as masters of England had opened that island to new, invigorating influences. The manorial system with its potential for great agricultural productivity spread rapidly, although it did have the effect of reducing many Anglo-Saxon *ceorls* (freemen with small individual landholdings) to serfdom. New ideas and styles in theology, literature, and art flooded into England to transform Anglo-Saxon culture. Trade relations with the Continent quickened. All these new forces, championed primarily by the new ruling elite, provided ingredients for a new England where society was focused on the monarchy. Contemporaries sometimes lamented that much was lost as a result of the submersion of Anglo-Saxon society, but on the whole England gained from being drawn into the mainstream of Continental life by her Norman conquerors. Her greatest gain was the foundation of a sound political order.

2. ENGLAND: GROWTH OF THE MONARCHY IN THE TWELFTH CENTURY

William the Conqueror's work might have been wasted had England not enjoyed the good fortune of a succession of energetic, capable kings who worked hard during most of the twelfth century to develop royal power: the rough, brutal William II (1087–1100); the quiet, prudent, and avaricious Henry I (1100–1135); the ambitious, tempestuous Henry II (1154–1189); and the colorful, romantic ideal knight, Richard I the Lionhearted (1189–1199). Only one difficult interlude interrupted this succession of strong kings, that brought about by a disputed succession in 1135 which resulted in two decades of strife centering around the rival claims of Matilda, the daughter of Henry I, and Stephen of Blois, a nephew of Henry. England's twelfth-century kings were men with interests far transcending the governance of England. They managed to expand English influences into Wales, Scotland, and Ireland. William left them with a Continental commitment in Normandy, a commitment that was expanded by Henry II into an "empire" that embraced half of France as well as England. Richard played a leading role in the Third Crusade and at least dreamed of exerting England's influence in the Mediterranean. These activities made England a major power in twelfth-century Europe. But we must neglect these aspects of English history in order to concen-

trate on the successful efforts of the kings to perfect effective monarchical government. The twelfth-century constitutional developments in England ought to be described reign by reign, for to a considerable degree the growth of royal power was a slow, step-by-step building upon prior achievements, but space limits us here to a description of the broad patterns of growth.

One of the major achievements of the twelfth-century English kings was the formation of an effective central administration. The administrative system was fashioned by combining the old Anglo-Saxon household officials and the feudal *curia regis*. From these beginnings, the twelfth-century kings, especially Henry I and Henry II, moved along two complementary lines. On the one hand, they began to draw men from the *curia regis* to serve the king constantly instead of returning to their private affairs after brief meetings of this body. To this core of full-time royal servants they gradually added increasing numbers of permanent civil servants, often of nonfeudal, nonnoble origin. On the other hand, the kings began to assign specialized functions to this body of permanent servants —the beginnings of departments of administration. During the twelfth century four specialized groups had begun to emerge: the *Exchequer*, devoted to financial administration; the *Treasury*, concerned with guarding and dispensing royal money; the *Chancery*, charged with issuing royal orders and composing royal correspondence; and the *royal law courts*. The development of this permanent bureaucracy surrounded the kings with a loyal group of servants whose expertise assured the efficient conduct of royal business. So competent had these bureaucrats become that Richard I was able to spend most of his reign abroad without suffering any loss of power. It hardly need be added that the growth of the royal bureaucracy greatly reduced the dependence of the kings on the political services of their feudal vassals.

The twelfth-century kings were careful to guard the military and financial resources so vital to royal power. Although the feudal nobles played a crucial role in the military establishment, for the kings continued to count on their military service as the backbone of royal armed strength, the kings maintained their ancient right to summon the *fyrd,* the army of all freemen in the realm. And toward the end of the twelfth century they began to use mercenary soldiers, and to allow their vassals to discharge their military obligation by money payments, called *scutage.* The financial support of the growing government still depended chiefly on exploitation of the royal domain, and the king's agents were remarkably efficient and even ruthless in administering these estates. The royal government collected considerable sums in fines and fees, a tribute to the wide range of its activities. Customs duties were imposed on an ever-wider scale, allowing the kings to capitalize on the growing trade. They also devised ways of imposing direct taxes on the income and property of their subjects. The revenue from all these sources, which tended to increase throughout the century, was vital to the expansion of royal activities and helped considerably in freeing the kings from dependence on their vassals.

The kings continued to sustain and strengthen the ancient system of local government. They resisted the ever-present tendency for the sheriffs to usurp royal power for private advantage by using the agencies of the central government to maintain control over the sheriffs and to broaden their activities in support of the king. Henry II was especially effective in providing clearer definitions of the obligations of the sheriffs. Thus the old local institutions of government remained a powerful support of royal authority and a constant barrier against localism.

Beyond all doubt, the most important development of the twelfth century was the formation of a royal judicial system, a development led and fostered by Henry I and Henry II. The existing legal system in England was a bewildering maze: Courts were conducted by the king, by his local representatives, by feudal lords, by manorial lords, by the Church, and by the independent towns. In each set of courts different systems of laws, different procedures of determining guilt, and different systems of punishment were followed. In the twelfth century the kings and their legal advisers took the initiative in ending some of this confusion and in establishing a law common to all citizens.

One of the chief concerns of Henry I and Henry II was to increase the number of royal courts, to man them with expert judges, and to encourage these judges to apply a unified legal code. Henry I began the practice of sending itinerant judges to various parts of England to try cases involving the king's interests, and by the time of Henry II, this had become a regular practice. At set intervals, announced in advance, royal judges appeared in the shire courts to try cases. After making their circuits, these judges returned to the king's court, where they could compare notes. As a result, they were soon deciding cases on the basis of a common set of principles. Henry II established the first of England's great central courts, setting up at Westminster a group of men who sat permanently to handle many cases previously heard by the *curia regis.* Soon this body began to divide into specialized courts, like the *court of common pleas* and the *court of the king's bench.* The decisions of these central courts became a guide for the activities of itinerant judges and contributed greatly to uniformity in the royal legal system. The need for judges caused a tremendous interest in legal education, which had the effect of further standardizing legal concepts and produced an extensive literature reflecting a search for new ideas that centered especially on Roman law.

Both Henry I and Henry II worked to expand the jurisdiction of the king's courts. This required depriving feudal lords, the Church, manorial courts, and town courts of some of their ancient rights of justice. In this battle the kings and their lawyer-servants of twelfth-century England showed the greatest ingenuity. In criminal cases the kings usually increased their jurisdiction by legislation that defined new crimes against the king's peace and ordered royal judges to punish violators. No one complained too loudly, since all society was happy to see violence curbed. In civil cases, chiefly involving disputes over property, the problem of increasing royal jurisdiction was more complicated and met with greater opposition, especially from feudal lords long accustomed to dealing with property disputes in their own courts. Insisting that it was wrong for a man to lose his property unjustly (who would disagree?), the king made it known that anyone who felt he had been unfairly treated could appeal to the king. All he had to do was purchase a *writ* ordering a royal inquiry into his case. The fertile

minds of the royal lawyers soon devised writs that applied to almost every conceivable kind of property dispute. By purchasing a writ, the man with a complaint brought a royal judge to inquire into his case; and on the basis of that inquiry, the judge ordered justice to be done. In effect, purchasing a writ amounted to transferring a civil dispute from feudal or manorial courts to royal courts.

To encourage the use of royal courts, Henry II and his lawyers made important innovations that ensured speedier and more efficient judgments. Well-trained experts who excelled feudal barons in their knowledge of the law served as royal judges and lawyers. Court sessions were held regularly when scheduled. Fees were clearly fixed. Corruption and bribery among royal judges were severely punished.

Even more significant, however, was the introduction of the *jury system* in criminal cases. Long before Henry II's reign groups of men had been called together by the king or his officials and required under oath to tell what they knew about some public question. After 1164 Henry applied this idea to criminal cases by ordering his sheriffs to call together a group of men from an area where a crime had been committed and to question them under oath concerning what they knew about the crime. On the basis of this testimony sheriffs could then proceed to apprehend the suspected criminals and put them to trial. Such a jury, called a *presentment* or *grand* jury, proved efficient in the speedy apprehension of criminals. By the thirteenth century such groups of men, known as *petit* juries, were used to decide guilt or innocence.

The jury system quickly proved superior to the traditional practices which relied on trial by ordeal or by battle to ascertain God's will in proving guilt or innocence. Trial by ordeal

Manuscript illustration showing the murder of Thomas à Becket in the cathedral at Canterbury, the climax of his quarrel with the king, Henry II. *Photo: The Walters Art Gallery, Baltimore*

required one charged with an offense to submit to a physical test, such as being thrown into water, walking through fire, or holding a hot iron for a specified time. The outcome of such tests revealed divine judgment: for example, if the accused sank in the water, he was innocent because the water accepted him, but if he floated he was guilty. Trial by battle involved an encounter between accused and accuser (or their designated champions) with the victor winning the case. The jury system, emphasizing gathering, presenting, and evaluating evidence, proved fairer, more efficient, and more humane. This innovation, together with the other steps taken to improve judicial efficiency, made royal courts popular. Indeed, nothing increased the prestige of the English monarchy more than the expansion of royal justice. A single, common law for all the land, administered in regularly held courts by trained judges according to well-defined procedures, was virtually a fact by the beginning of the thirteenth century.

As one would expect, the feudal barons and the Church chafed under this rapid, aggressive expansion of royal authority. However, during the twelfth century their resistance was sporadic and ineffective. There were occasional revolts by nobles, most of which the kings disposed of with ease. On the whole, the English feudal nobility did more to sustain the growth of strong monarchy than to oppose it, and in so doing gradually learned to identify their interests with those of the whole kingdom. The kings had considerably more trouble with their numerous vassals on the Continent, where effective royal institutions were not so well developed.

The Church proved a stouter foe than the nobility—and paradoxically a stronger supporter of monarchy. Throughout the twelfth century there were sharp clashes between kings and clergy, although the struggle never reached the proportions it did in the Holy Roman Empire. William I set the pattern for his successors by richly endowing the Church and supporting its reforming moves, while insisting firmly on royal control of ecclesiasti-

cal offices and of a portion of the Church's wealth. During the reign of William II the Church, led by Anselm, archbishop of Canterbury, challenged the monarchy on the issue of the royal right to appoint church officials. This struggle was resolved by the Compromise of Bec in 1106, which allowed the Church to elect its own officials, but reserved to the king the privilege of investing the newly elected officials with their lands. A more serious struggle arose during the reign of Henry II, when the king attempted to limit the jurisdiction of Church courts. This effort was challenged by Thomas à Becket, archbishop of Canterbury, who defended the Church's cause so skillfully that an enraged Henry finally cried out for his murder. Thomas' martyrdom forced the king to concede considerable freedom to the Church in judicial matters. On the whole, however, the English kings exercised a powerful control over the Church, and the Church gave its support to the strengthening of monarchy. England escaped the fatal plague of the Holy Roman Empire—an eternal war with the Church.

By the end of the twelfth century a strong, centralized monarchy had been created in England through the efforts of a series of able kings who exploited Anglo-Saxon traditions and their feudal rights to bring most elements of the population under direct royal control. No other kings in Western Europe ruled over a political community which so directly depended upon the king for protection, order, and justice.

3. ENGLAND: THE LIMITING OF ROYAL POWER IN THE THIRTEENTH CENTURY

The remarkable advance of royal power in twelfth-century England ultimately generated a reaction during the thirteenth century. In that reaction feudal nobles, churchmen, and the rising bourgeoisie joined hands to compel the kings to recognize a principle inherent in feudal monarchy: that royal power was limited by the "law" of the feudal contract. The thirteenth-century effort to establish this prin-

A portion of the Magna Carta, engraved from one of the original copies in the British Museum.
Photo: NYPL Picture Collection

ciple marked a major step in establishing constitutional monarchy in England.

The clash between the king and the feudal, ecclesiastical, and bourgeois interests broke into the open during the reign of John (1199–1216). A rash, obstinate tyrant who brought part of his trouble on himself by his inordinate demands on his subjects, John also had the misfortune of having as his enemies two of the most formidable personalities in medieval history, King Philip Augustus of France and Pope Innocent III. By force of arms, Philip deprived John of a considerable part of the territories the English controlled in France in a war that required John to impose a heavy burden of service and taxation on his subjects in a losing cause, a combination that always discredited a medieval king. To complicate his situation, John became involved in a struggle with Innocent III over the appointment of the archbishop of Canterbury. Again he lost to a redoubtable foe, being forced to acknowledge that he was a vassal of the pope holding England as a fief.

These rebuffs, coupled with a series of tyrannical acts on his own part, led to a rebellion in 1214 from which John extricated himself only by signing Magna Carta in 1215. Loudly celebrated by later generations as a charter of liberty, Magna Carta was basically an affirmation in specific terms of the privileges enjoyed by the nobles, churchmen, and

to a lesser degree, the townsmen. The king promised that he would refrain from intruding his authority into certain of these privileged areas, involving chiefly taxation, the administration of justice, and the holding of land. The charter was therefore conservative, seeking to put limits on the expansion of royal power. However, its framers had no thought of destroying effective royal government or of impeding its capability to maintain order. They simply insisted on the principle that there was a point, defined by law and custom, beyond which royal power must not go. Here was a crucial ingredient of feudal monarchy: the principle that not only the lord, but also the vassals; not only the king, but also his subjects, have rights that must be respected.

John's concession in no way resolved the clash between monarchy and the privileged interests. It continued throughout the long reign of his weak, extravagant, foolish son, Henry III (1216–1272), who made problems for himself by relying on Frenchmen for advice, by making outlandish concessions to the papacy, and by involving himself in costly but futile foreign adventures. The nobles resisted him in a variety of ways: forcing him to reissue Magna Carta, using their influence to compel him to dismiss his foreign advisers, and forming a council of nobles to reform and supervise the operation of royal government. When these efforts failed, they resorted to

358

arms in a major uprising in 1264–1265 led by Simon de Montfort. The rebels won the upper hand temporarily, and Simon de Montfort tried to ensure their continued control over the government by summoning the nobles, the clergy, and representatives from the towns and shires to a *Parliament* which would establish control over the monarchy. This effort was thwarted by inability of the rebels to agree and by the actions of Henry's son, Edward, who mustered the royal forces and crushed the rebels. However, the exercise of brute force was hardly an answer to the issues involved in the rebellion; neither was constant rebellion a suitable recourse for disaffected segments of the population.

The astute, capable Edward I (1272–1307) sensed these issues and proved capable of facing them. His reign therefore constituted a culmination of the shaping of medieval English monarchy. Edward was aware that few of the nobles who opposed John and Henry III wished to end strong monarchy or to destroy the institutions which permitted the kings to exercise their powers. Their protest was against the misuse of royal government and the abuse of ancient rights by kings and their officials. They insisted that royal government had to be conducted to serve the interests of at least a portion of England's people and not merely for the pleasure and profit of the king and his cronies. More significantly, within the ranks of those who from time to time opposed the king there had developed some degree of group consciousness. A *community of the realm* had begun to emerge, consisting of great barons, lesser nobles, churchmen, and townsmen, all of whom felt a common interest in the political affairs of England as a nation. This feeling led them to act together in confronting the royal government and to transcend on occasion the narrow confines of feudal contracts, ecclesiastical privileges, and town charters. The community of the realm was the product of English political history since the conquest, of two centuries during which royal power was strong enough to affect all men in a substan-

tial way. Its emergence provided the basis for the modern English national spirit and for the development of political institutions through which the community of the realm could find expression.

Edward I's reign represented an attempt to strengthen the central government by taking these views into account. Edward first of all maintained a watchful eye over the administrative and judicial system he had inherited from his predecessors. Local officials were rigorously supervised, and expert civil servants were chosen to man the chief governmental posts. Effective administration removed many of the complaints that the nobles, clergy, and townsmen had previously raised. Second, a series of fundamental laws was enacted, defining more clearly the rights of the crown and the manner in which it would exercise its powers. In general, this legislation, which earned Edward the honor of being called England's Justinian, further limited the power of feudal lords and the Church, while expanding that of the king and his courts. Edward's aggressive legislation raised protests, but his political skill usually disarmed the criticism before it became dangerous.

Edward's chief means of avoiding opposition and one of the chief developments in English history was the regular use of Parliament as a means of taking the important elements of the population into consideration in ruling England. Advisory bodies, like the Anglo-Saxon Witan and the Norman *curia regis*, had long played a part in English life. These groups, however, represented only those individuals having a feudal obligation to serve the king by advising him. During the reign of Henry III a new practice was instituted when Simon de Montfort, seeking the widest possible support for the reforms he was trying to force on the king, summoned representatives of the shires and the towns to join with the feudal barons and churchmen in a meeting. And later Edward I clearly sanctioned this precedent in his Model Parliament of 1295. He commanded that each county and each town select two representatives to

Parliament to take counsel with the barons and ecclesiastical lords. Such a body was soon accepted as having the power to speak for all Englishmen. Edward called Parliament to serve his own purposes, and especially to get extra money or to have approved some piece of legislation that promised to irk part of the population. At first the organization and the powers of Parliament were vague; not for at least another century did it divide into the Houses of Lords and Commons and establish its rights to approve taxes, to initiate legislation, and to censure or even depose the king. The importance of Edward's innovation in establishing Parliament lay in his recognition of the fact that he had to listen to the demands of his subjects and in his willingness to create an institution that gave his subjects a voice in government.

Edward's death in 1307 heralded the end of one age and the beginning of another. His career, built upon the work of his predecessors, left England with a sound set of political institutions that permitted the king to supply justice and order to all his subjects while still allowing them to retain part of the rights and privileges they claimed. The chaos that threatened to engulf England before 1066 had been replaced by a solidly established monarchy whose authority was widely accepted yet limited by law and ancient custom.

4. FRANCE: ROYAL IMPOTENCE DURING THE TENTH AND ELEVENTH CENTURIES

Monarchical power grew at a slower pace in France than in England and without a decisive turning point comparable to the Norman conquest. In the long run, however, the medieval French kings emerged more powerful than their English counterparts. The kingdom of France was established by the Treaty of Verdun in 843, when the sons of Louis the Pious divided the Carolingian Empire. With the exception of a brief interval, the Carolingians ruled this new kingdom until 987—much longer than they ruled in the other kingdoms carved out of Charlemagne's empire. Royal power declined steadily during this long period, especially as a consequence of Viking invasions and of the general ineptness of the rulers. Political power devolved into the hands of local leaders, and feudalism took root more deeply in France than anywhere else in Western Europe. The kings were still recognized in a vague way as rulers of all France, but real power had settled in the hands of the great vassals who held extensive fiefs from the king and enjoyed the right to govern these lands. Although the royal vassals admitted that the king was their overlord, they seldom rendered to him any of the obligations they owed. The position of the late Carolingians as royal figureheads contrasted sharply with contemporary Anglo-Saxon kings and with the Ottonian dynasty in the Holy Roman Empire.

In 987 the French nobles and churchmen finally ended the Carolingian dynasty by electing as their king one of the chief feudal lords in France, Hugh Capet, count of Paris. Hugh's descendants, called the Capetians, ruled France without interruption until 1328. They were the architects of French monarchy and a strong French state. Capetian success, however, was hardly instant. Under the first four Capetians, who ruled from 987 to 1108, the kings exercised almost no power outside their own royal domain, a territory around Paris known as the Ile de France. Even within this territory, royal power was constantly challenged by petty vassals who established hereditary fiefs and defied the authority of their lord, the king of France. The rest of the country remained divided into a confusing array of feudal principalities, some of them larger and richer than the royal domain. The real political history of France during the eleventh century must be told in terms of the history of each of these principalities, for there was no France as a nation during this period.

The eleventh century was, however, decisive in the political development of certain feudal principalities in France. The dukes, counts, and viscounts who held these principalities as fiefs made remarkable progress in establishing order over their subvassals, in developing institutions that made their power effective, and in concentrating in their hands the military and financial resources needed to perpetuate their supremacy. These powerful royal vassals brought order to their fiefs primarily by utilizing their rights as feudal lords. In brief, they made feudalism an effective instrument for establishing sound government on a small scale. This solidification of the feudal principalities was most notable in the great fiefs of northern France, especially Normandy, Flanders, Anjou, Maine, Champagne, Burgundy, and Blois. Southern France, where feudalism was slower to develop, remained more chaotic; the feudal princes of Aquitaine, Gascony, and Toulouse, for instance, were seldom able to control their subvassals. The establishment of well-governed, disciplined feudal principalities in northern France was ultimately decisive in French history, for this process created ready-made building blocks which the king as supreme overlord eventually took over along with the power created by the feudal princes.

During the period 987 to 1108, however, the Capetians had little role in these decisive developments. They were theoretically the overlords of the great princes, an overlordship which the princes usually admitted because it legalized their rights to their fiefs. Aside from their tenuous authority over the royal domain, the early Capetians succeeded only in keeping monarchy alive, in making the royal office hereditary, and in retaining the support of the Church for the idea of monarchy as an institution common to all who lived in the kingdom of France.

5. FRANCE: THE RESURGENCE OF ROYAL POWER, 1108–1223

The period between 1108 and 1223 saw a decisive upturn of Capetian fortunes and a notable advance in the strength of French monarchy. This revival of monarchy was in part the result of the efforts of intelligent,

industrious, and persistent kings to exercise their rights as feudal lords over the great fiefs of France. It was also in part a consequence of a broader revival affecting French society at many levels to establish French leadership in Western European economic, cultural, and religious life.

The first accomplishment of the twelfth-century Capetians was the establishment of effective control over the royal domain, the Ile de France. Louis VI (1108–1137) was chiefly responsible for this decisive achievement. After the fashion of some of his great vassals who had established firm control over their subvassals during the eleventh century, Louis set patiently about forcing his vassals in the Ile de France to end their lawlessness, compelling them to render their dues to the king, and creating an administrative machinery capable of collecting what was his due. In the main, he was successful; by the end of his reign the king was the real lord of the Ile de France in a sense that was never true of the earlier Capetians. His control of the royal domain gave him greater ability to play a significant role in the affairs of his vassals outside the Ile de France. On occasion he acted as judge in disputes between his vassals, protected weaker ones against the stronger, and played a part in determining the succession to fiefs held from the king. The royal presence was at least being felt—if not decisively—outside the confines of the royal domain. Nowhere was this better illustrated than by the decision of the duke of Aquitaine as death approached to entrust his daughter and heiress, Eleanor, to the protection of his overlord, the king of France. Louis VI promptly married his ward to his son, thereby setting the stage for the annexation of Aquitaine to the royal domain.

Louis VI's successor, Louis VII (1137–1180), tried to continue this policy, but with increasing difficulty. He was a limited man who lacked the energy and clearheadedness to navigate the murky waters of French feudal politics. Thanks to the able work of his father's administrators, especially the great abbot of St. Denis, Suger, Louis VII did keep a firm hold on the royal domain. But his efforts outside the Ile de France were ineffectual. He proved incapable of controlling Aquitaine, where the feudal nobility acted in complete defiance of the king's will. His participation in the Second Crusade not only won him no glory, but cost him a wife and her dowry. The gay, romantic Eleanor accompanied him on the crusade and was rumored to have engaged in amorous adventures with some of the more attractive knights of the crusading army. This scandal was too much for the pious Louis; added to it was the fact that Eleanor had produced no son to assure the survival of the Capetian dynasty. Perhaps Eleanor had had enough too; she is alleged to have said that she discovered she had married a monk instead of a king. In any case, Louis arranged to have the marriage dissolved with consequences that were dangerous to his power.

The king's major difficulties, however, did not stem from his political and marital ineptness. During his reign the Angevin "empire" emerged as a major threat to the very survival of French monarchy. The successful French response to this challenge marked the turning point in the struggle of the Capetians to make their royal office the directive force in France. The Angevin empire came into existence as a consequence of the aggressiveness of the counts of Anjou, one of the powerful fiefs into which France was divided. During the eleventh century the counts of Anjou were ruthless, ambitious men who imposed order on their own territory and vassals and constantly expanded their holdings. By the twelfth century Anjou had become one of the most powerful principalities in France. Count Geoffrey was especially successful in expanding his holdings, managing to establish control over Normandy and Brittany by marrying the daughter of Henry I of England, who was also duke of Normandy. When Geoffrey died in 1151 he bequeathed to his son, Henry, a huge territory consisting of Anjou,

Normandy, and Brittany. In 1152 the same Henry won the hand of Eleanor, recently repudiated by Louis VII; Eleanor brought to Henry as a dowry the duchy of Aquitaine. For all these territories Henry was a vassal of Louis VII, but obviously he was an extraordinary vassal endowed with resources far exceeding those of his lord. Then in 1154 this same Henry became king of England as Henry II, further increasing his power and endangering Louis VII.

The French king could do little to check the building of the Angevin empire or to check the ambitious Henry from aggression against royal territory and authority. But the next Capetian, Philip II Augustus (1180–1223), met the new challenge successfully, ultimately on the field of battle. Philip bided his time as long as Henry II lived, doing only what he could to make Henry's burden in ruling his French territories as heavy as possible. This task was made easier by the fact that Eleanor had blessed Henry II with a brood of unruly sons, among them Richard the Lionhearted and John, who delighted in joining their mother in making trouble for their father and husband. With the accession of Richard I, Philip II began the struggle to break Angevin power. He was finally successful against John, whose conduct alienated many of his Continental vassals and caused them to turn to John's feudal overlord, Philip II, for protection and justice. When John refused to appear to be judged, Philip II declared his fiefs confiscated and proceeded to seize the key territories of Normandy, Anjou, and parts of northern Aquitaine. When John finally tried to retaliate, his effort was crippled by discontent and rebellion in England. Philip's success was sealed in 1214 at the Battle of Bouvines, where he and his allies, Pope Innocent III and Frederick II of Hohenstaufen, crushed the armies of John and his ally, Otto of Brunswick. As a consequence of this victory, Philip II was assured of control of Normandy and Anjou, which were added to the royal domain. The seizure of this vital territory from a diso-

SCOTLAND

DENMARK

POMERANIA

York

WALES   ENGLAND

Lübeck

•Bremen

FRISIA   SAXONY   •Brandenburg

MARCH

OF LUSATIA   POLAND

London   •Goslar

THURINGIA

Clarendon• •Winchester   •Canterbury   Bruges• •Ghent   LOWER   •Cologne

HASTINGS 1066 ✖   FLANDERS   Aix-la-Chapelle   BOHEMIA   •Prague

BOUVINES 1214 ✖   LORRAINE   FRANCONIA   MORAVIA

Rouen•   •Trier   •Mainz

Bayeux•   NORMANDY   Reims•   UPPER   •Worms   AUSTRIA

•Paris   •Verdun   LORRAINE   •Passau

Rennes•   MAINE   CHAMPAGNE   •Toul   BAVARIA

BRITTANY   BLOIS   •Troyes   Freiburg•   •Salzburg

ANJOU   •Orléans   SWABIA

•Nantes   TOURAINE   Dijon   HUNGARY

POITOU   •Poitiers   BURGUNDY   •Besançon

Autun•   KINGDOM   OF

Cluny•   BURGUNDY-ARLES

Clermont•   LOMBARDY   ✖LEGNANO 1176

AQUITAINE   AUVERGNE   •Milan   •Venice

PERIGORD   Pavia•   •Roncaglia

Bordeaux•   Canossa•

GASCONY   TOULOUSE   •Avignon   Florence•   Pisa•

NAVARRE   Toulouse•   Arles•   PROVENCE   TUSCANY   PAPAL

LANGUEDOC   Marseilles•   STATES

ARAGON   Sutri•

Rome•

•Barcelona   Naples•   KINGDOM OF

TWO SICILIES

French Royal Domain

⟨pattern⟩ 987

⟨pattern⟩ 987-1180

⟨pattern⟩ 1180-1328

━━━ **Boundary of English Holdings**
in France 1180

⟨pattern⟩ **English Holdings in France**
1328

⟨pattern⟩ **Holy Roman Empire ca. 1200**

⟨pattern⟩ **Republic of Venice**

Medieval England, France, and Germany

bedient vassal provided the king of France with a well-organized, rich domain that exceeded the territory held by any royal vassal. Almost overnight the king had emerged as the major force in France, a position dramatically different from that of the earlier Capetians.

6. FRANCE: THE CONSOLIDATION OF ROYAL POWER, 1223–1328

Louis VI and Philip II had established the keystones of Capetian policy: careful administration of the royal domain and territorial consolidation. Successful pursuit of these policies characterized the reigns of the later Capetians and account for France's emergence as the strongest state in Europe in the thirteenth century. After Philip II's decisive victory at Bouvines, the French kings added new territories to the royal domain with relative ease. They exploited every possible means to lay hold of territories over which they claimed overlordship: marriage, purchase, confiscation, escheat. No territory was too small to escape their attention and none was too large to defy them. By 1328 most of France had been consolidated under royal control. Those fiefs still not under direct royal administration were no longer any threat to the power of the kings; in most of them the kings made their authority felt in a decisive way. France had in fact become a territorial state ruled directly by a king.

The expansion of the royal domain necessitated more effective royal administration. The later Capetians, especially Philip II, Louis IX (1226–1270), and Philip IV the Fair (1285–1314), responded to this task by constantly increasing the power and activity of the royal government. In broad outlines that government resembled the one fashioned by the twelfth-century English kings; the Capetians borrowed heavily from the English model as well as from the political techniques developed by the feudal princes who had established firm control over their principalities during the eleventh century. The great Cape-

tian constitution builders based their expanding power primarily on their rights and obligations as feudal lords to protect, judge, and demand services from their vassals. These feudal concepts were enriched by ideas borrowed from Roman law and from Christian political ideology. The thirteenth- and fourteenth-century kings increased their power chiefly by expanding and modifying primitive institutions bequeathed to them by the earlier Capetians. First, there was the *curia regis*, the meeting of the king's vassals to give justice and advice to their overlord. Second was the royal household (the *hôtel*), composed of those officials who cared for the personal needs of the royal family and its retainers. Finally, there were the *provosts*, officials who managed the royal estates from which the king derived his living.

One of the chief accomplishments of Philip II, Louis IX, and Philip IV was the shaping of an effective central administration out of these primitive institutions. Philip II began the process by increasing the amount of royal business put before the *curia regis*. Although this body still consisted chiefly of feudal vassals, he began adding nonfeudal administrators (mostly lawyers) as full-time royal officials. The royal household began to merge with the *curia regis* to serve as a single judicial and administrative body. Paris became the fixed seat of royal government. Louis IX and Philip IV continued to enlarge the activities of the *curia regis*, and under their direction, that body began to divide into specialized departments: the *conseil*, a small circle of intimate advisers of the king; the *parlement de Paris*, concerned chiefly with the administration of royal justice; the *chambre des comptes*, which handled financial matters; a *chancery* for producing royal orders and keeping records. By the reign of Philip IV the central administrative system had developed into a complex, sophisticated organism fully informed of activities over the entire kingdom and capable of making royal power felt everywhere.

As the royal domain grew, the kings were

faced with the monumental task of creating a local system of government to carry out royal commands. The French kings were not so fortunate as the English in this respect; local government had long since been monopolized by feudal and manorial lords. Philip II attacked this problem by extensive use of officials known as *baillis* (bailiffs). Usually selected from the nonnoble personnel of his court, these officials were assigned to specific areas in the royal domain. They held courts, collected taxes, and kept order in the name of the king. Succeeding kings expanded the

numbers and the activities of the *baillis* and laid down ever-more precise rules guiding their activities. Louis IX established special officers, called *enquêteurs*, whose job it was to check on the conduct of the *baillis* and report their misdeeds to the central government. The *baillis*, acting in the name of the king, steadily assumed to themselves political functions once monopolized by feudal nobles and churchmen. However, all during the thirteenth century (and far beyond) the nobility continued to perform with royal approval considerable political functions, sharing with the

The institution of parliament grew up in France as well as in England. Here King Philip IV is shown presiding over a parlement; nobles and churchmen sit to the right and left below the king. *Photo: Bibliothèque Nationale, Paris*

royal government the task of governing France. But they were no longer at liberty to do what they pleased.

The growth of the governmental machinery and the broadening range of royal activities, especially warfare, placed a heavy financial burden on the kings, and they responded with an avaricious quest for new sources of income. A prime source remained the exploitation of royal lands. Feudal dues of all kinds were carefully collected. The thirteenth-century kings were usually willing to allow their vassals to discharge their service obligations by money payments. Direct taxes were levied from time to time, and special assessments were exacted from the towns, the Church, the Jews, foreigners, and anyone else the kings could exploit. Philip IV even resorted to confiscating the wealth of the famous crusading military order, the Templars, and to debasing the currency in his effort to keep his government solvent. Although the Capetians had sufficient income to sustain a strong government, they were always short of money. This shortage grew especially acute near the end of the period, when the kings relied less on knight service and more on mercenaries for military activities and when the size of the royal bureaucracy had become extremely large.

While extending their tentacles over all France and perfecting the central government, the Capetians in the early fourteenth century instituted another practice that strengthened their position. They began to summon representatives of various classes (*estates*) from all over their realm to advise them and approve their policies. On three occasions during the reign of Philip IV, townsmen were summoned, along with nobles and clergymen, to meet with the king and discuss serious issues facing the kingdom. These meetings came to be known as *Estates General*. Such meetings always ended in approval of what the king proposed and added tremendous weight to royal power by making it appear that the entire nation approved what the king wished to do. Philip IV was careful to keep the Estates General under control so that it did not develop independent powers, a custom that served many later French kings with absolutist ideas well. Nonetheless, the development of the Estates General was important in uniting the major classes of France under a single government.

Although both the English Parliament and the French Estates General emerged primarily out of a growing political solidarity and greater political unity in each kingdom, the institutions were quite different. The Estates General was much more the tool of the monarchs than was Parliament. This difference stemmed in part from the political reaction of the French nobility to the growth of monarchy. The nobles resented the growth of royal power and often resisted it with force. But these nobles never found a basis for joint action against the kings. They never joined hands to exact a Magna Carta or to claim collectively supervisory powers over the royal administration, as did the thirteenth-century English nobles. Individuals won confirmation of their rights and privileges, but never did they stand as a group ready to resist the king and act in a responsible way to share power. Perhaps this was the fruit of the extreme feudalization in the ninth and tenth centuries that had made the French nobles particularistic and independent. If this be the case, then we have a paradox: the extreme weakness of French monarchy in the face of feudalism opened the way for its ultimate power.

While the Capetians were expanding and consolidating their hold on France, they drew valuable support from the Church. Almost to the end of the Capetian period, kings and Church lived peaceably and mutually supported each other. The kings bestowed considerable wealth on the Church, helped to reform it, supported it in the heat of the investiture struggle, and respected its liberties. In return, the Church supported the claims of the Capetians to greater power, praised the piety and virtue of the dynasty, and lent its wealth and talent to the improvement of royal government. The Capetians often exerted strong control over ecclesiastical elections and tapped church wealth for political purposes, but churchmen seldom protested. The long, happy relationship did not end until the reign of Philip IV, by which time the Capetians had established unquestioned authority in France. Philip IV became embroiled in a bitter quarrel with Pope Boniface VIII (1294–1303) over the extent of the king's power to tax church property and to judge clergymen. When Boniface tried to command Philip to obey papal orders, the king turned French public opinion against Rome and cowed the French clergy into obeying his orders. Philip even sent his agents to Rome to capture the papacy. The mighty head of the Church, so long successful in thwarting the Holy Roman emperors, had suffered a crushing defeat. The explanation is clear: By the early fourteenth century the king of France possessed the kind of power that the pope could not dissolve by simple command; there were no crowds of dissatisfied subjects in France to be turned against the king.

The victory of Philip IV over Boniface VIII points to a final achievement of the Capetians, one hard to describe because it involves a qualitative factor associated with French monarchy. The imposing structure of French monarchy, built on solid administrative, financial, and religious moorings, was buttressed by an immense prestige. The greatest Capetians were surrounded by a quality, a style that made them stand out in thirteenth-century Europe. Their prestige was best reflected by Louis IX, eventually sainted by the Church. He was lauded as a lover of justice for his subjects, ideal Christian, gallant knight, crusader, peacemaker, promoter of morality, ideal son, husband, and father—in short, the ideal prince. This aura of superiority surrounding the Capetians added immensely to their authority. It too had to be created out of the obscurity and ignominy surrounding the beginnings of the dynasty. The Capetians proved as skillful in fashioning an image as they had been in shaping political institutions.

Thus by 1300 in England and France a problem that had persisted since the fall of the Roman Empire, namely, how to create a stable, just political order that would make a contribution to the collective activities of men, had been resolved. The answer was feudal monarchy, a unique system of government in which the king as supreme feudal lord developed the instruments that permitted him to control his vassal subjects. In fashioning his power, however, the feudal monarch learned to respect the rights of privileged groups—vassals, churchmen, townsmen—as partners in the tasks of government. The system of government evolved in England and France between the tenth and the thirteenth centuries gave these kingdoms the strength, order, and stability that ensured for them a central role in the future of European civilization.

Suggested Reading

General. Two works treating the political histories of both England and France will provide a good starting point for additional reading on the issues covered in this chapter. The first, **Sidney Painter, *The Rise of Feudal Monarchies* (Cornell), is brief. More complete and especially good in showing the parallels in the constitutional development of England and France is **Charles Petit-Dutaillis, *The Feudal Monarchy in France and England From the Tenth to the Thirteenth Century*, trans. E. D. Hunt (Harper Torchbook).

England. There is a superabundance of excellent work on medieval England's political development. Especially recommended are three recent, well-written shorter works that are especially valuable because they tie together Anglo-Saxon and post-conquest history; they are **C. W. Hollister, *The Making of England, 55 B.C. to 1399* (Heath); **Christopher Brooke, *From Alfred to Henry III, 871–1272* (Norton); and Christopher Brooke, *The Saxon and Norman Kings* (1963). Somewhat more detailed and directly related to the period covered in this chapter is **D. M. Stenton, *English Society in the Early Middle Ages (1066–1307)* (4th ed., Penguin). The most thorough treatments of English history in all its aspects are successive volumes in the Oxford *History of England:* A. L. Poole, *From Domesday Book to Magna Carta, 1087–1216* (2nd ed., 1955); and F. M. Powicke, *The Thirteenth Century, 1216–1307* (2nd ed., 1962). These two works are hardly light reading, however. A crucial problem in English political development centers around the nature of the Norman conquest. **C. W. Hollister, ed., *The Impact of the Norman Conquest* (Wiley), has collected varying views on the problem. Another work of prime importance on this subject is **H. R. Loyn, *The Norman Conquest* (Harper Torchbook). For provocative interpretations of constitutional developments after 1066, a student might turn to **G. O. Sayles, *Medieval Foundations of England* (2nd rev. ed., Perpetua); and H. G. Richardson and G. O. Sayles, *The Governance of Medieval England From the Conquest to Magna Carta* (1963). Two clear, balanced surveys of constitutional and legal development are Bryce Lyon, *A Constitutional and Legal History of Medieval England* (1960); and **J. E. Jolliffe, *Constitutional History of England: From the English Settlement to 1485* (Norton). The classic treatment of the development of Eng-

lish law is **Frederick Pollock and F. W. Maitland, *The History of the English Law Before the Time of Edward I* (2 vols., Cambridge). **J. C. Holt, *The Making of Magna Carta* (Virginia), is an excellent treatment of an important issue. Valuable for the early history of Parliament is **G. L. Haskins, *The Growth of English Representative Government* (Perpetua). Among many biographies that might be read for this period, the following are especially recommended: **David Douglas, *William the Conqueror: The Norman Impact Upon England* (University of California); **Amy Kelly, *Eleanor of Aquitaine and the Four Kings* (Vintage); L. F. Salzman, *Henry II* (1967); R. Winston, *Thomas Becket* (1962); Sidney Dark, *St. Thomas of Canterbury* (1927); P. Henderson, *Richard Coeur de Lion* (1958); and W. L. Warren, *King John* (1961).

France. The works available in English on medieval French political history are embarrassingly few. Aside from the Petit-Dutaillis work cited above, the only book of substance is **Robert Fawtier, *The Capetian Kings of France* (St. Martin).

Sources. Excellent selections of documents illustrating English constitutional development are provided by Carl Stephenson and F. G. Marcham, eds., in *Sources of English Constitutional History* (1937); and D. C. Douglas and G. W. Greenway, eds., *English Historical Documents, 1042–1189* (1953). An interesting view of a medieval French king is provided by Jean de Joinville, *Life of St. Louis*, trans. René Hague (1955); another edition is *The History of St. Louis by Jean Sire de Joinville*, trans. Joan Evans (1938).

Chapter 22 ✻ The Medieval Expansion of Europe

The agricultural and commercial growth, the social readjustments, and the political solidification of Western Europe's heartland—Germany, Italy, France, England—created the potential for European expansion. The realization of that potential between 1000 and 1300 is another aspect of the revival of Western Europe, an aspect that had immense significance for the future of the world. Prior to 1000 the feeble, poor, disorganized West had been a beleaguered world, constantly assaulted by outsiders and often in danger of succumbing to these blows. After 1000 the situation was reversed. Western Europeans began to move outward and in the succeeding three centuries brought immense territories under their sway at the expense of the Byzantines, Muslims, Slavs, and Scandinavians. The outward thrust took many forms: missionary activity, commercial penetration, colonization, military conquest, all of these sometimes combining in a particular phase of expansion. The ultimate consequence of this expansion was a major step toward the domination of the world by Western Europeans.

1. MISSIONARY EXPANSION

One form of Western European expansion in the High Middle Ages was a sustained effort to bring the pagans into the Christian fold and under the influence of the Roman Catholic Church. The missionary urge had been present in the Christian community in the West even during the darkest hours of the Early Middle Ages, bringing considerable numbers of pagans into the fold prior to 1000; missionary activity after 1000 was but a continuation of that effort. Although almost always intermingled with economic and political factors, the missionary thrust was highly significant in opening new lands to European influence and in providing for the immediate incorporation of new peoples into one prime European institution, the Church.

By the end of the Carolingian period, Christianity was solidly established in the British Isles, France, Italy, and Germany west of the Elbe. It was from this base that missionaries moved into new territories. Already during the ninth century the first effort had been made to convert the Scandinavians. Although abortive, this effort charted one line of expansion that was pursued successfully after the worst fury of the Viking attacks had subsided. The late tenth and eleventh centuries marked the crucial era in the conversion of Denmark, Norway, and Sweden. In most cases the conversion of the kings was the decisive event in implanting Christianity and destroying paganism. The new Christian kings, however, received invaluable help in their work from

This illustration from a fifteenth-century French manuscript shows the siege of Jerusalem during the Crusades. (The dress and weapons, however, are those of the later period.)
Photo: Bibliothèque Nationale, Paris

pious churchmen, especially from England and Germany, who devoted their careers to proselytizing the Scandinavians. Once Christianity was implanted in Scandinavia, an episcopal organization, often closely linked with Rome, developed.

Meanwhile, Christian forces also moved across the Elbe into the Slavic world, usually with German political backing. Again, the first Christian expansion into the Slavic world came in the Carolingian period, but permanent successes were achieved only when the Holy Roman emperors gave their support to German clergymen interested in the Christianization of the Slavs. During the late tenth and eleventh centuries the Bohemians, Poles, and Hungarians were drawn into the Roman Catholic fold, a process marked by revivals of paganism sparked by the fact that conversion often brought with it German political domination. Western Christian forces in these areas were sometimes challenged by Byzantine missionaries who during the same period spread Christianity among the Balkan Slavs, the Bulgars, and the Russians, and drew these peoples into the Byzantine orbit. Over a long period Christian influences, again promoted by the Germans, spread along the Baltic to convert the Wends, the Prussians, the Finns, the Livonians, and the Lithuanians. This missionary activity, often marked by the use of force, brought most of the Baltic world under Christian influence by 1300.

Primarily as a consequence of the crusading movement, Western European Christians even began to dream of more distant missionary fields. In the thirteenth century missionary adventurers, chiefly Franciscan and Dominican monks, sought to win converts in the Mongol Empire and in China. Although their labors were ephemeral, their explorations opened vast new prospects. There were also efforts to spread Christianity among the Muslims of North Africa and the Near East, but the Islamic world proved little susceptible to the Christian message.

Wherever the missionary effort of the High Middle Ages succeeded—Scandinavia, Central Europe, Iceland, the Baltic area—the presence of the Church played a powerful role in drawing new peoples into the orbit of Western European civilization. Along with its organization and practices of worship, the Church brought learning, literature, and art that often represented the first contact of the new converts with higher civilization. The Church was also often instrumental in shaping political and social institutions in these areas along lines similar to institutional patterns in Western Europe.

2. ECONOMIC EXPANSION: COLONIZATION AND COMMERCE

While some Western Europeans thrust outward with the cross, others were driven beyond Europe's old frontiers primarily by economic interests. We have previously discussed this aspect of expansion, and need only allude to it briefly here so that it can be understood in the total context of the Western European offensive against the rest of the world.

One of the great accomplishments of medieval men during the era from 1000 to 1300 was the opening and colonization of an agricultural frontier on the eastern fringes of Europe. During this period large numbers of German landowners and peasants pushed across the Elbe and down the Danube Basin to conquer and colonize an extensive territory previously controlled by the Slavs. Ultimately this mass movement resulted in the Germanization, and therefore the Westernization, of lands extending along the entire southern shore of the Baltic, of the area from the Elbe across the Oder River halfway to the Vistula, and of a broad territory on either side of the Danube to the point where it turns south at Budapest—in today's terms, a territory comprising northern Poland, most of East Germany, large areas of Czechoslovakia, and Austria. This Germanic "drive to the East" had the strong backing of the Holy Roman emperors, but in the main it was carried out by landowners and peasants seeking new lands to exploit. Churchmen gave the movement their support because it assured the Christianization of the occupied territories. As the German tide moved eastward, many Slavs brought under German political, religious, and cultural control tended to merge with the Germans and lose their identity.

Likewise between 1000 and 1300 merchants reached beyond Europe to establish the Western European presence in a much larger world. Italian merchants, powerfully abetted by crusading armies, wrested control of the Mediterranean seaways from the Byzantines and the Muslims, and established trading posts in Constantinople and several Muslim seaports in Syria, Egypt, and North Africa. From these outposts they penetrated inland to reap a rich profit from the flourishing trade of the Byzantine and Islamic worlds. Northern Europeans, spearheaded by the Vikings, pushed through Russia's riverways to the Black Sea and Constantinople. In the process, the Scandinavian pirate-traders established settlements at Novgorod, Smolensk, and Kiev; from these settlements emerged the Kievan principality that constituted the first effective state in Russia. Scandinavian raiders also settled Iceland and drew it into the European world. After the conquest of Constantinople in 1204 by the armies of the Fourth Crusade, Western European merchants established bridgeheads around the Black Sea which opened access to the cities of Central Asia and China. Between about 1225 and 1350, Italian merchants roamed widely across the Asian world, reaping rich profits in trade and learning the potential of that vast area— information conveyed back to the West in travel accounts such as that composed near the end of the thirteenth century by the Venetian merchant Marco Polo to recount his adventures in Peking and other Eastern cities. A few bold Europeans were finding their way toward the waterways along southern Asia leading to India and the Indies, but their progress in this direction was impeded by their inability to break through the Muslim

world at the key spot, Egypt, which was repeatedly but unsuccessfully attacked by crusading armies in the thirteenth century. During this same century, Western European seafarers also began to push southward in the Atlantic along Africa's west coast, drawn in that direction chiefly by the fame of the gold mines of Senegal. These many forays by adventuresome, profit-seeking merchants into strange worlds opened new horizons to end Western Europe's isolation; and they presaged a new age of European expansion.

3. MILITARY EXPANSION: SPAIN AND SOUTHERN ITALY

The most spectacular form of expansion during the High Middle Ages was military conquest, which added considerable territories to the Western European world and gave temporary control over others. Europe's military expansion was one reflection of its growing political and economic strength. Europeans were impelled to use that strength by a variety of motives: land hunger, quest for markets, adventure, religious zeal, fear. Military expansionism manifested itself around the whole rim of the European heartland, but the thrust was aimed primarily at the Byzantine and Muslim worlds, those ancient heirs of the classical world that had so far outstripped Western Europe in the Early Middle Ages.

One of the most important areas of expansion was in Spain. When the Muslims (or *Moors*, as they are called in Spanish history) conquered the Iberian Peninsula in the eighth century, they failed to subdue a few tiny Christian principalities in the mountainous areas of northern Spain. Almost immediately, these principalities began to wage war on the Muslims, beginning the *Reconquista*, a war of liberation that did not end until 1492. Even as early as the Carolingian age, Europeans outside the peninsula were drawn into this conflict.

The reconquest was slow until the eleventh century. The petty Christian states—Leon, Castile, Navarre, Barcelona—had been too

Iberia 1140

weak to make any significant progress against the powerful Caliphate of Cordova, which reached its apogee in the tenth century. At the beginning of the eleventh century, however, the caliphate disintegrated, and Muslim Spain broke into numerous warring principalities. This gave the Christians their opportunity, and they turned their energies to a common assault on the Moors. The kingdom of Castile-Leon (united in 1037) took the lead, and drove as far south as Toledo, which was captured in 1085. Its efforts were supported by forces from Navarre, Barcelona, and the newly established kingdom of Aragon. As the Reconquista gained momentum, large numbers of Christian knights from outside Spain, especially from France, joined the fray in search of new lands and adventure. The pa-

pacy took the lead in propagandizing the holy cause in Spain. After 1085 there was a temporary halt, and the Christian frontier was rolled back as a result of Muslim reinforcements called in from Africa, rivalry among the Christian states, and political dissension within these states. By mid-twelfth century, the Christians renewed their offensive; this time Aragon (now united with Barcelona) took the lead, but Castile-Leon also pushed its frontier southward. A new kingdom, Portugal, emerged as a result of successful aggression in the west. The Muslim defense, bolstered by support from Africa, was stout until the early thirteenth century, but thereafter the Christians advanced with less difficulty, and by 1300 they had occupied all of the peninsula except Granada in the extreme southeast.

The Reconquista created three major new kingdoms—Castile, Aragon, and Portugal. The internal development of these war-born realms constitutes an important chapter in the political revival of medieval Western Europe and warrants a brief description.

Each kingdom developed its own system of government, although all had certain basic similarities. Monarchy was, of course, the basic institution, the various kings claiming extensive powers over society. The Spanish kings steadily gained prestige as a result of their leadership of the Reconquista. The Church championed their cause. The profits they gained at the expense of the Moors supplied them with resources to bolster their power. Newly conquered lands gave them a chance to settle people as farmers or townsmen under conditions that allowed the king to retain his authority. These factors retarded the coming of the feudal system, and Spain was never as thoroughly feudalized as France. Eventually, however, feudal practices not un-

The Christian kingdoms of the Iberian peninsula were gradually enlarged by successful military campaigns against the Muslims, although the last Moorish kingdom, Granada, was not to be conquered until 1492, the year of Columbus' voyage. This manuscript illustration shows Christians being captured by the Muslims. *Photo: Fotografía Autorizada por el Patrimonio Nacional, Madrid* like those of France did develop. Hereditary fiefs were granted to nobles in return for services, and some of the vassals gained a large degree of immunity from royal control. The Spanish monarchs worked incessantly to make their power more effective. Particularly during the thirteenth century, they sought to develop centralized administrations, specialized civil servants, well-organized financial systems, and effective courts. Several thirteenth-century kings of Aragon and Castile legislated extensively in an attempt to define royal powers and rights. Such legislation usually assigned to the kings extensive authority. Local officials of the king, comparable to the French bailiffs, were appointed and put under rigid royal supervision.

Nobles and townsmen resisted royal attempts to monopolize power by every means at their disposal. In the long run, the Spanish monarchy was checked, compelled to admit limitations on its powers and to allow considerable independence to nobles and towns. Still, one must concede that Spanish monarchs retained much authority to check internal disorder, to provide justice, and to protect the whole population. This balance between monarchy and specially privileged groups was symbolized by an institution that became a regular part of government in the twelfth and thirteenth centuries. This was the *Cortes*, a representative body composed of nobles, clergymen, and representatives of the towns. Before the end of the thirteenth century these bodies were being summoned in all the kingdoms to consult with the king. Custom had already sanctioned the right of the Cortes to approve new taxes, to address petitions to the king for redressing wrongs, and to be consulted in matters of war and peace. Nowhere else in Europe, with the possible exception of England, was there such a well-defined institution for curbing the authority of kings and confronting them with the desires of the vested interests in their realms.

This brief outline hardly does justice to Spain's history in the Middle Ages. The complex, troubled relationships among the Spanish states and their involvement (especially that of Aragon) in political and diplomatic activities on the larger European scene are of great importance. Suffice it to say that the base had been laid for the emergence of a major power, capable of rivaling England and France.

Another area of European military expansion was in southern Italy and Sicily. Norman nobles, continuing the ruthless adventuresomeness that had established their Viking forebears in Normandy, were the aggressors here. Early in the eleventh century they intruded themselves into the chaotic Byzantine territory in southern Italy and employed their military and political skills to establish dominance. By mid-century the papacy had recognized their occupation and begun to rely on them for protection. Before 1100 the Normans had snatched Sicily from the Muslims. In 1130 these feats were given formal recognition when the papacy sanctioned the creation of the kingdom of Sicily, embracing southern Italy and Sicily. A strong monarchy was soon shaped, incorporating a mixture of feudal, Byzantine, and Muslim practices that made the king virtually

absolute. A brilliant cultural life developed at this meeting place of the Byzantine, Muslim, and Western European worlds; through this kingdom important Eastern cultural influences flowed into Western Europe. The Kingdom of Sicily passed into Hohenstaufen hands at the end of the twelfth century and continued its brilliance under their control, especially during the reign of Frederick II. In 1266 the papacy invited a French prince, Charles of Anjou, to take over the kingdom. French domination lasted until 1282, when a great rebellion, called the Sicilian Vespers, ousted the French and gave the royal house of Aragon control. These rapid changes of masters, often prompted by outside interests, began to weaken the kingdom and blight its vital cultural and economic life. But at least it remained in European hands, a prime example of Western European military prowess and organizational ability.

4. MILITARY EXPANSION: THE CRUSADES

The expansionist venture that most dramatically symbolizes Western European vitality in the High Middle Ages was the crusading movement, a succession of military operations stretching over two centuries that had as its central objective the restoration of Christian control over the holy places of the Christian religion. The crusading movement was consequently a war against Islam, although as it evolved, its objectives became more diverse and more complex.

The origins of the movement defy easy description. In part, the Western Europeans took up arms because developments in the Near East provided them an opportunity. The vast Abbasid Empire, after reaching its peak in the ninth century, began to disintegrate into independent caliphates bitterly contending with one another for territory. The disintegration of Abbasid power in a general way increased its vulnerability to attack, as witnessed by the success of the Italian cities in establishing their sea power and of the

Normans in seizing Sicily. As this vast internal struggle developed, a major point of weakness in the Muslim armor emerged in Syria and Palestine. When the Abbasid hold on this area deteriorated, the aggressive Fatimid caliphate in Egypt sought to expand in that direction. In the late tenth century the Byzantine Empire also became a serious contender for control over territory that it claimed by ancient right. In an effort to save their power, the Abbasid caliphs in Bagdad relied increasingly on the Asiatic Seljuk Turks, who in turn used their position to gain control of as much territory as possible. By the late eleventh century they too had become rivals for control of Syria and Palestine. Capitalizing on these conflicting claims, local leaders had established several small principalities in Syria and Palestine, and these rulers were willing to make any arrangement that would thwart the efforts of any one of the stronger rivals to establish dominance. In a sense, then, Syria and Palestine offered an enticing target for aggression, a target created out of the weakness of the Muslim political structure.

The Byzantine Empire was also undergoing a crisis in the eleventh century. The emperors of the Macedonian dynasty that followed the great Basil II (died 1025) were ineffectual rulers who failed to sustain the defense of the empire, especially by allowing the aristocracy to subordinate the free peasantry which had long provided the backbone of Byzantine military strength. New enemies took advantage of this situation to attack the empire. The Normans wrested southern Italy from imperial control and began to attack Byzantine territories in the Balkans. More ominous was the advance of the Seljuk Turks in Asia Minor. In 1071 Byzantine forces suffered a crushing blow at the hands of the Seljuks at the Battle of Manzikert, and in succeeding years the Turks conquered most of Asia Minor. Again Byzantium found a savior in the person of Emperor Alexius Comnenus (1081–1118). His primary task was to recover Asia Minor, long the main source of Byzantine strength, a task that appeared more and more

possible as Seljuk power began to disintegrate not long after Manzikert. However, Alexius realized that he needed help and began to appeal to the princes and the pope in Western Europe for troops to join in the struggle.

Thus, Byzantine problems and imperial policies stemming from them directed Western European attention toward military ventures in the East. But there would have been no crusading movement without the coincidence of a variety of factors in the West that persuaded men to take advantage of the situation. There had long existed an animosity toward Islam that was made more active by the eleventh-century wars of conquest in Spain and Italy. The Italian cities were eager to advance their commercial interests in the Muslim world. Western Europe was well supplied with knights whose fighting urge was being curtailed by the advance of effective royal government. The developing code of chivalry among these aristocratic warriors emphasized the turning of the military ethos to some higher cause. The whole thrust of religious reform engendered the idea that the Christian community must work collectively and actively to exalt the cause of the true faith. The chivalric nobility found it easy and appealing to turn this religious impulse into the idea of a holy war against the infidel. The resurgent papacy, enmeshed in the investiture struggle and nourishing dreams of a more effective leadership over Christendom, became the force that turned these many impulses to a specific program. An appeal for help from Alexius in 1095 opened to the papacy the prospect that in return for channeling the militant spirit of the feudal nobility into aiding Byzantium against the Muslims, it could gain Byzantine recognition of papal supremacy over the whole Christian world and could heal the schism that had separated Rome and Constantinople since 1054. While helping the Greeks, the pope's soldiers could rewin the holy places, an act that would be pleasing to God and excellent for papal prestige.

It was Pope Urban II who triggered the holy war of the West against the East. After carefully setting the stage, in 1095 he delivered a stirring speech at Clermont in France calling for Christian knights to join forces in attacking the Muslims, defending the Christians in the East, and liberating the Holy Land. For the next two centuries the goals that Urban proclaimed at Clermont remained the object of European efforts in the East.

Urban apparently intended that a single army of knights under the leadership of agents designated by the pope would form and proceed to the East. Although his appeal to launch a holy war was greeted enthusiastically, especially in France, no single army was formed. Rather, several different feudal potentates (but no kings) gathered separate armies, a development that augured ill for the future. By the summer of 1096 these armies, totaling about 15,000 knights and foot soldiers and a large contingent of hangers-on, began to move toward Constantinople. The several leaders had made no coordinated plans. The main armies had been preceded by an undisciplined horde of peasants and artisans stirred to crusading fervor by overenthusiastic preachers. Before its annihilation, this peasants' crusade aroused hostility along the entire route from the West to Constantinople as a result of the unruly conduct of its participants. Certainly this was hardly what Alexius expected when he requested Western help, and he may have begun to have doubts about the value of European aid in achieving his goals.

The crusading armies converged on Constantinople during the fall and winter of 1096. Protracted negotiations, necessitated by confusion and rivalry among the crusading leaders and by conflicting intentions between the crusaders and the Byzantine government, finally led to an arrangement which allowed the armies to move eastward. Alexius persuaded the crusading leaders to swear an oath of allegiance to him personally and to return to Byzantine control conquered territories that had previously belonged to the empire. In return, Alexius promised to provide supplies and military support.

In the spring of 1097 the crusaders began their march across Asia Minor. One decisive battle at Dorylaeum brushed aside Turkish resistance and allowed the crusaders to pass on toward the Holy Land. Once in Syria, the crusading army began to split up, chiefly because its leaders were anxious to assure their private fortunes. One group left the main body to establish control over Edessa and its surrounding territory. After the key city of Antioch had been captured in June 1098, a Norman prince, Bohemond, refused to leave it, claiming it as his by right of conquest. It was not until July 1099, that Jerusalem was captured by the remaining crusaders, who vented their fury on the Muslims by slaughtering hundreds of natives. This great victory made the First Crusade a success. All Europe was exalted at the news that the valiant Christian warriors had planted the cross once again in the Holy City.

Once in possession of Jerusalem, Antioch, Edessa, and other key cities, the crusaders had to think of instituting a government. Disregarding their pledge to Alexius to serve as his vassals and the papal plan to create a state subordinate to Rome, the crusaders established a feudal monarchy similar to what they had left behind in Europe. In 1100 Baldwin of Edessa was elected king of the Latin Kingdom of Jerusalem. He created a series of fiefs that he granted to men willing to become his vassals. These great fief holders subdivided their holdings and acquired vassals of their own, creating a typical feudal hierarchy. The king ruled this kingdom with the advice of his vassals, who met regularly in a high court at Jerusalem. A Latin patriarch of Jerusalem was installed, subordinating the Christian establishment in the new kingdom to Rome. The native population was disturbed very little. Usually their previous local rulers continued to control them under the supervision of the Latin rulers.

The chief problem of the Latin Kingdom of Jerusalem was defense. The Latins tried hard to strengthen their position. They seized the chief seaports along the Mediterranean with

The Crusades

aid from Italian navies. They built powerful castles at strategic locations in the Holy Land. Before 1130 they established the two great crusading orders, the Knights Templar and the Knights Hospitaler, made up of knights who had taken a vow to defend the Christians living in and coming to the Holy Land. Nevertheless, the Christian position was always weak. For most of the next two centuries, the plight of the Christians "overseas" repeatedly persuaded Western Europeans to go crusading as a way of serving God. Often they went in small groups or individually; on occasion large-scale expeditions were organized to help hold the Holy Land, permitting us to speak of a succession of crusades.

The Second Crusade was prompted by the loss of Edessa in 1144 to a Turkish leader who had imposed his authority over the divided Muslims in Syria and then had turned on the Christians. Proclaimed by the pope and preached by the most influential churchman of the day, St. Bernard, this crusade attracted two kings as its leaders: Conrad III, Holy Roman emperor, and Louis VII, king of France. Despite such prestigious leadership, the crusading armies were virtually destroyed by the Turks in Asia Minor. When the two rulers did arrive in the Holy Land with remnants of their forces, their misdirected military efforts aided little in the defense of the Latin kingdom.

During the years following the Second Crusade, a profound change occurred in the Muslim world. Under the skillful guidance of two leaders, Nureddin and Saladin, a unified Muslim state stretching from Syria into Egypt replaced the many small, quarreling principalities that had existed when the crusaders first attacked the Holy Land. In 1187 Saladin struck against the kingdom of Jerusalem and easily captured all the Christian holdings except Tyre, a few isolated castles, and the northern counties. Europe was deeply shocked. The pope called for a new crusade and received the promises of Henry II of England, Philip II of France, and Frederick Barbarossa of Germany to lead armies against Saladin. Frederick left first but was drowned en route; most of his army turned back after his death. Henry II also died, even before he could begin his march; however, his successor, Richard the Lionhearted, stepped into his place. He and Philip, almost always at odds, made their way to the East by 1191. Philip, anxious to snatch away Richard's French possessions, stayed on the scene only the minimum time. The colorful English king remained for over a year. After several inconclusive engagements with Saladin, he finally agreed to a truce by which the Christians were allowed to visit Jerusalem, although the city remained in Muslim hands. The Third Crusade, which promised to be the greatest, did little to improve the Christian position in the East.

The Fourth Crusade, which ultimately made a travesty of the crusading movement, was initially prompted by Pope Innocent III, who was desirous of enhancing papal prestige and perhaps aware of the weakening of Muslim power that followed the death of Saladin in 1193. However, the pope soon lost control over the forces that were raised. To ensure transportation to the East, the crusading leaders became entangled with the Venetians, who persuaded them to pay their obligations by capturing for Venice the Adriatic port city of Zara on the Dalmatian coast, an act that caused Innocent III to excommunicate the whole army. Then the Venetians and the crusading leaders entered into an agreement with a claimant to the Byzantine throne to put him on the throne in return for trade concessions for Venice and money and troops to be used by the crusading armies for an attack on Egypt. Having succeeded in restoring their Byzantine ally to the imperial office, the Venetians and crusaders found him unwilling or unable to deliver on his promises. The crusading forces therefore decided to take Constantinople for themselves.

Their attack was successful, and the city fell into Western hands in 1204. The victorious crusaders immediately proclaimed a Latin Empire of Constantinople, and elected a Flemish noble as emperor and a Venetian clergyman as patriarch of the Greek Orthodox Church, thus reuniting the Church for the moment. Innocent III forgot his original anger at the crusaders and approved the whole arrangement. The crusading nobles began immediately to carve out rich fiefs for themselves, especially in the European sector of the Byzantine Empire. The Venetians, who assumed control over the chief port cities of the empire and thereby immensely strengthened their commercial position in the East, were the real beneficiaries of the whole undertaking. The Latin Empire of Constantinople survived until 1261. Much of its history was a constant defense of its existence against Greek forces whose leaders kept alive a legitimate Byzantine government in Asia Minor and fought valiantly to oust the usurpers. Thus the Fourth Crusade, aside from turning the crusading spirit to dubious ends, created another Western outpost in the East and inflicted on the Byzantine Empire a crippling blow from which it never fully recovered.

After the Fourth Crusade, the crusading movement lost much of its appeal to Europeans. Innocent III organized a fifth crusade, but he died before it got under way in 1217. The armies of this crusade attacked Egypt, where the chief center of Muslim power had been located since Saladin's time. The result of this attack was the capture of the key city of Damietta, a major Mediterranean port located on one of the main channels of the Nile. The crusaders could have traded Damietta for Jerusalem, but greed led them deeper into Egypt, where they permitted themselves to be trapped by a Nile flood and were destroyed by the Muslims.

Frederick II led the next crusade, chiefly because he wanted to secure possession of the Holy Land, to which he had a legal right by virtue of his marriage to the heiress of the Latin Kingdom of Jerusalem. Frederick's crusade was fraught with difficulties from the very beginning. Because of his refusal to accept papal direction, he was in the bad graces of the papacy when he departed for the Holy Land. Once in the East, he chose to gain his ends by diplomacy rather than by the sword. In 1229 he signed a treaty with the Muslims that restored Jerusalem to the Latins and provided for a cessation of war between Christians and Muslims. This indeed was a great victory, but the way it had been gained outraged many in the Christian West. When Frederick finally occupied Jerusalem, he himself was under a sentence of excommunication, and the city was immediately placed under papal interdict.

After this, the turmoil among the Christians in the Latin Kingdom of Jerusalem steadily increased, and as it did the kingdom grew more vulnerable. In 1244 the Muslims again captured the holy city. This loss prompted the saintly Louis IX of France to organize what amounted to the last major crusade. Louis' forces attacked Egypt in an attempt to get at the major source of Muslim power, but his attempt was another disaster. Although Louis spent four years in the Holy Land, his presence did little to strengthen the Christian position. In fact, his Egyptian campaign increased the danger by providing the opportunity for a strong, aggressive ruling dynasty, the Mamelukes, to establish themselves in Egypt.

The increasing pressure on the Latin Kingdom of Jerusalem was relieved temporarily in the middle of the thirteenth century when the Christians allied themselves with the Muslims against the Mongol threat. Early in the century a great leader, Genghis Khan, transformed the Mongol nomads of Central Asia into a potent military force. For the next half century, the Mongol hordes were the scourge of Eurasia, fashioning a vast empire stretching from China to Central Europe. Faced with this threat, the Muslims in the Near East were willing to ally with the Christians for mutual defense. After 1260, however, when the Mongol threat began to lessen, the old hostilities between Muslim and Christian were renewed. In 1291 the Mamelukes took the last Christian strongholds in the Holy Land. After nearly two centuries, the Latins had finally been ousted from Syria and Palestine; from the whole crusading venture they retained only some Mediterranean islands, especially Cyprus and Rhodes.

So ended the most overt and dramatic manifestation of medieval Western European expansionism. The consequences of the crusading movement have long been debated; in general, modern scholars have tended to attribute to the crusades less importance than did earlier historians. They must not, however, be dismissed as inconsequential acts of folly. Because of them, Western Europeans did rule a crucial area in the Near East for two centuries. This outpost was the scene for an interaction between the East and the West which gave Europeans a broader view of the world and "educated" them to new ideas, products, and styles of life. The crusades played a crucial role in extending Western Europe's commercial power. They decisively affected the histories of both the Byzantine Empire and the Muslim world, weakening the former and provoking the latter to new aggressiveness that was to affect Europe significantly in the later Middle Ages. Perhaps the most significant consequence of the crusading movement was the image of the Western Europeans that it imposed on the peoples of the Near East: the aggressive, greedy, faithless, crude warrior; the crafty, grasping merchant; the ambitious, worldly churchman—all of whom would do anything to acquire land, wealth, and power. This image was not to be transformed easily.

5. WESTERN EUROPE AND THE WORLD IN 1300

By 1300 there were many signs that Western Europe's outward thrust was abating. But certainly the efforts of missionaries, colonizers, merchants, and warriors had caused immensely significant changes in the relationship between Western Europe and the world. First, the basic posture of Western Europe had changed. Whereas in 1000 the West was still reeling from the attacks of Vikings, Magyars, and Muslims capable of penetrating to the very heart of Europe, by 1300 the Europeans were exerting offensive pressures in many directions. Second, the Western European offensive had captured and brought under Western control and influence considerable territory: the Iberian Peninsula, southern Italy and Sicily, the lands between the Elbe and the Oder, much of the Baltic coast, Iceland. Added to these lands won was the vital matter of control of the Mediterranean Sea and its crucial trade routes. Third, European expansion had established outposts in the great trading centers of the Near East: Constantinople, and the ports of Syria, Palestine, Egypt, and North Africa. From these vantage points the traders of the West were able to influence and profit from the major movement of commerce on a world scale. Fourth, the influences exercised by aggressive Westerners had powerfully affected the development of peoples living on the periphery of the European heartland and drawn them into the Western pattern of civilization. The evolution of the Slavic states in Poland and Bohemia, of Hungary, and of the Scandinavian states in Denmark, Sweden, and Norway were to a large extent determined by European religious patterns, literary and art styles, political practices, agricultural and commercial techniques, educational practices, and value systems. To a considerable degree, these influences entered these societies as a result of the presence of European missionaries, traders, colonists, and warriors. To these peoples, the Western European pattern of civilization had become one to be imitated. Finally, the Western Europeans had been able to exert an important influence on the evolution of great powers beyond the areas of their direct control. The histories of the Byzantine Empire and the Muslim caliphate between 1000 and 1300 cannot be told without reference to the impact of the Europeans. This was an amazing turnabout considering the impotence of the West vis-à-vis these civilizations prior to 1000.

Suggested Reading

Missionary, Commercial, and Colonial Expansion. The best general survey of medieval missionary history is K. S. Latourette, *A History of the Expansion of Christianity*, Vol. II: *The Thousand Years of Uncertainty, A.D. 500–A.D. 1500* (1938). Commercial expansion and agricultural colonization are treated in several of the books cited in Chapter 19, especially Pirenne and Duby. Valuable insights into these movements can be found in R. S. Lopez, *The Birth of Europe* (1967), pp. 121–32, 258–66, 284–95.

Territorial Expansion in Spain, Southern Italy, and Sicily. An old but still useful history of medieval Spain is R. B. Merriman, *The Rise of the Spanish Empire: The Middle Ages* (1918). More recent and briefer are the early chapters of Rafael Altamira, *A History of Spain From the Beginnings to the Present*

Day, trans. Muna Lee (1949). Also adequate is **H. V. Livermore, *A History of Spain* (Minerva). A classic treatment of the Normans is **C. H. Haskins, *The Normans in European History* (Norton), which stresses the positive contributions of the Normans.

The Crusaders. A good brief survey of the crusading movement is provided by **R. A. Newhall, *The Crusades* (Holt, Rinehart, and Winston). A popularized version of the movement, filled with colorful details, is Harold Lamb, *The Crusades* (1945). A fuller history, enhanced by provocative interpretations, is **Steven Runciman, *A History of the Crusades* (3 vols., Harper Torchbook); this work shows special sympathy for the Byzantine Empire. *A History of the Crusades*, ed. K. M. Setton, vols. I and II (2nd ed., 1969), represents the beginnings of a projected five-volume treatment of the crusading movement being undertaken primarily by American scholars on a cooperative basis; some of the essays are superb, especially those dealing with the Muslim world in the eleventh and twelfth centuries. A selection of essays interpreting the crusading movement is provided by **J. A. Brundage, ed., *The Crusades: Motives and Achievements* (Heath). D. C. Munro, *The Kingdom of the Crusaders* (1935), gives an excellent account of the history of the Latin Kingdom of Jerusalem. More recent is Bon-Ami (pseud.), *Social Change in a Hostile Environment: The Crusaders' Kingdom of Jerusalem* (1969). R. C. Smail, *Crusading Warfare, 1097–1193* (1956), is a superb description of an important aspect of crusading history. **Zoe Oldenbourg, *The Cornerstone* (Ballantine Books), is a splendid novel on crusading life and the society that produced it. For Byzantine and Muslim history during the crusading period, see the works cited in Chapter 15, especially Ostrogorsky and Vasiliev for Byzantium, and Hitti and Spuler for the Muslim world. Additional valuable studies treating Byzantium are R. J. H. Jenkins, *The Byzantine Empire on the Eve of the Crusades* (1953); and Steven Runciman, *The Eastern Schism: A Study of the Papacy and the Eastern Churches During the XIth and XIIth Centuries* (1955). S. Lane-Poole, *Saladin and the Fall of the Kingdom of Jerusalem* (2nd ed., 1926), helps to appreciate the crusading movement from the Muslim perspective.

Sources. Two important chronicles that will help to shed light on missionary and colonizing expansion into the Slavic world are *The Chronicle of the Slavs by Helmold, Priest of Bosau*, trans. F. J. Tschan (1935); and *The Chronicle of Henry of Livonia*, trans. J. A. Brundage (1961). An unusually large number of sources relating to the crusading movement have been translated into English. A fine selection of materials is provided by J. A. Brundage, ed., *The Crusades: A Documentary Survey* (1962). Another collection of documents narrower in scope is A. C. Krey, ed., *The First Crusade: The Accounts of Eyewitnesses and Participants* (1921). A massive work by a twelfth-century Latin bishop living in the East is William of Tyre, *History of Deeds Done Beyond the Sea*, trans. E. A. Babcock and A. C. Krey (2 vols., 1943). Two works dealing particularly with the First Crusade and written by participants are *Fulcher of Chartres: Chronicle of the First Crusade*, trans. M. E. McGinty (1941); and the anonymous *The Deeds of the Franks and Other Pilgrims to Jerusalem*, ed. and trans. Rosalind Hill (1962). A long poem written by the daughter of Emperor Alexius Comnenus, Anna Comnenus, *The Alexiad*, trans. E. A. S. Dawes (1928), provides a vivid picture of the impression made by the Westerners on the Byzantine court. The Second Crusade is treated by **Odo of Deuil in *De Profectione Ludovici Septimi in Orientem: The Journey of Louis VII to the East*, trans. V. G. Barry (Norton). Ambroise, *The Crusade of Richard Lion-Heart*, trans. M. J. Hubert and J. L. LaMonte (1941), treats the romantic adventures of the most glamorous of all the crusaders. The activities of the Fourth Crusade are dealt with by Robert of Clari in *Conquest of Constantinople*, trans. E. H. McNeal (1936). **Geoffrey de Villehardouin and Jean de Joinville, *Memoirs of the Crusades* (Everyman and Penguin), supply eye-witness accounts of the capture of Constantinople during the Fourth Crusade and the exploits of St. Louis of France during his crusade. Another perspective on the crusading movement is provided by *Arab Historians of the Crusades*, trans. F. Gabrieli (1969).

Chapter 23 ❧ The Revival and Triumph of the Church

While powerful forces were transforming secular society and changing the relationship between Western Europe and the non-European world, equally potent movements were revitalizing religious life. With some justice this movement has been characterized as a "reformation." The resurgence of religious life in the High Middle Ages was so complex and so far-reaching in its consequences that we cannot hope to treat it adequately here. For the sake of clarity our discussion will focus on the two most significant aspects of the medieval reformation: first, the drive to strengthen the Church as an earthly community by perfecting its organization, defining its teaching, and disciplining its members; and second, the drive to probe more profoundly the spiritual meaning of the Christian message. Usually complementing each other but occasionally working at cross-purposes, these two movements resulted in the transformation of the Church into a super-community, a spiritual empire, which directly influenced every member of Western European society. To some at least, the closest approximation of the City of God on earth had been realized by the thirteenth century when the reformation had run its course.

1. ORIGINS OF THE REFORM MOVEMENT

Perhaps we need not seek further for the origins of the reforming movement of the High Middle Ages than the nature of Christianity itself. Throughout its history it had demonstrated a dynamic quality that dramatized men's imperfections and drove them to changing their lives in order to come closer to the perfection symbolized by its founder. This renewal mechanism was certainly at work in the Christian world in the West from the tenth century onward. As has been the case so often in the history of Christianity, the reforming urge was triggered as a reaction against the secularization, immorality, and spiritual insensitivity which engulfed the feudalized Church of the tenth century. However, more specific factors involved in the reforming movement gave it a unique form. At considerable risk of oversimplification, we can give three such sources of the reforming spirit that seem to have been at work as early as the tenth and eleventh centuries generating religious revival and to have continued to operate to sustain the reform movement until about 1300.

First was a powerful ferment within the monastic establishment. Faithful to the historic role of the monastic spirit, the reforming drive arising in the monasteries emphasized denial of and flight from the world, extreme asceticism, contemplation, and mysticism. It tended to produce a succession of spiritual heroes who provided models of religious excellence for men outside the monasteries. The monastic world of the High Middle Ages

The most solemn moment during the celebration of the Catholic mass is the Consecration, when according to Church doctrine, the wafer of bread, here held aloft by the priest, is changed into the body of Christ. *Photo: The Walters Art Gallery, Baltimore*

generated spiritual currents that tended to enrich all of religious life in terms of moral concepts, devotional practices, education, and emotional perceptions.

A second factor promoting reform was a new intellectualism surging through Western European society to touch nearly every aspect of human activity. It was an intellectual trend that emphasized bringing order into things that were previously disordered, that insisted on establishing norms against which particular human endeavors could be judged. This intellectual movement promoted religious reform by encouraging men to collect the rich traditions of the faith, to submit them to logical scrutiny in order to eliminate contradictions, and to formulate vast syntheses that were taken as absolute truths supplying the norms of Christian behavior. The reforms born of this intellectual activity tended to affect church organization, law, doctrine, and discipline.

The third source of religious reform in the High Middle Ages was popular piety. Although not easy to follow in an age that made little effort to record the activities of the great mass of people, there is still sufficient evidence to prove that concepts and practices welling up out of the popular practice of Christianity wrought significant changes in the religion of the High Middle Ages. Reform coming from popular sources tended to represent popular reactions to certain simple elements of the faith: the deeds of Jesus recorded in Scripture, his suffering, the travail of the Virgin, the miracles of the saints, the anticipated pleasures of heaven and the agonies of hell. The popular reform movement often took the form of protest against the power and wealth and misconduct of the great in society, especially the clergy, who in many cases failed to exemplify the perfection of Jesus. Popular reform movements also tended toward excess and often ended in heresy, revolt, apocalyptic preachings, and frenzied emotionalism. Despite these rather negative aspects, this popular force played a vital role in sustaining and

restating Christian idealism in its most exalted form.

Wherever these reforming forces were at work, they all placed a premium on looking back into history as a source for models and ideals. Thus the reformation of the High Middle Ages was deeply rooted in tradition— as perhaps all religious reformations are. Because of the traditionalist spirit surrounding this religious revival, one is sometimes tempted to conclude that there was nothing new in Christian life between 1000 and 1300. In one sense, this is true; every facet of religious change built on the old. But in another sense, everything was new, for the real essence of the reformation of the High Middle Ages consists of the originality with which tradition was viewed and the vigor with which it was applied to the realities of the world.

In a chronological sense, the medieval reformation began in the tenth century. Its origins have traditionally been traced to the new monastic community established in 910 at Cluny in east-central France. The Cluniac movement represented an attempt to purify Benedictinism by restoring strict observance of the Benedictine Rule and freeing monasticism from lay control. The movement spread rapidly over all of Western Europe and was an important influence in promoting reform. But it is too simple to attribute the origin of the reforming movement entirely to the monastic world. In the late tenth and early eleventh centuries, there were powerful religious stirrings in every element of the population: bishops, kings, feudal nobles, simple priests, and peasants all manifested an urge to purify religious life and to rescue the Church from its perilous position. By the eleventh century the movement found a dramatic focus in the papacy, and thereafter until 1300 the popes charted its major direction. In fact, by the thirteenth century reforms had to have papal sanction in order to be undertaken; otherwise, efforts at change often ended as heresy. Again, however, it is an oversimplification to equate reformation totally with the papacy, for throughout the eleventh, twelfth, and thirteenth centuries a bewildering array of reform movements and ideas emerged from monasteries, schools, bishoprics, and lay circles.

2. CENTRALIZATION OF CHURCH ORGANIZATION

A major thrust of the reform movement of the High Middle Ages was toward centralization of the organization of the Church under papal control. This movement toward a monarchical religious organization paralleled and outstripped a comparable movement among secular kingdoms toward centralized control in political life. The roots of this movement date back almost to the beginning of Christian history. Scripture contains allusions to the ideal of a single community of the faithful, to which the fathers of the fourth and fifth centuries gave substance. A succession of ecumenical councils and the activities of a long series of popes provided precedents for central direction of religious life. However, prior to 1000 effective centralization was far from a reality; the Church in the West consisted of a loose confederation of many local churches which recognized a titular head but in fact did what local churchmen—and often laymen—wished.

This situation began to change in the eleventh century. Perhaps the Cluniac movement was a precedent, for as the order spread and new monasteries were created, the abbot of the mother house at Cluny remained in control of all the houses. By the eleventh century the abbots of Cluny were monastic monarchs whose power extended over most of Europe. More crucial, however, was the formulation of an ideology that demanded centralized control. This ideology was the product of the radical papal reformers who came to prominence during the last half of the eleventh century with Hildebrand, later Pope Gregory VII, as their leader. As we noted previously, these reformers envisaged the Church as a visible earthly community made up of those baptized into the Christian faith and joined in

pursuit of a common goal, eternal salvation. This community needed its own head, its own law, its own resources, and its own liberty. On the basis of the ancient Petrine theory (see Chapter 13), it was of course obvious that the bishop of Rome was the divinely commissioned head of this Christian community. The Church as conceived by the Gregorians was a corporation superior to all other human organizations by the nature of its mission. Therefore, it must take precedence over these other organizations, including the state, and its officials must possess the final authority in human affairs. As the Gregorians would have put it, God ordained two kinds of power, spiritual and temporal, each symbolized by a sword. He entrusted these swords to his earthly vicar, the pope, who retained the spiritual sword but entrusted the temporal one to lay princes to be used to promote the quest for salvation. The pope retained full authority to recall the temporal sword and to direct its use by any prince, who was no more than a member of the Christian community.

Impelled by this clearly articulated ideology, Gregory VII acted to convert idea to reality. His efforts led him into conflict with secular rulers over the issue of the supremacy of church over state. We shall not review this struggle, which went on long after his death, except to say that the Church made considerable progress in establishing the principle that the pope was the final arbiter in the world. The Gregorian ideal also pointed in a second direction: toward creating a stronger, more centralized, more universal church organization under papal control. The fundamental ingredients for a centralized ecclesiastical organization already existed; Gregory began to make them function and to add to them. Even before he became pope, his circle established the College of Cardinals as the body responsible for the election of the pope, thereby putting the office beyond lay control. Gregory launched an extensive legislative program, aimed in large part at eliminating abuses distracting his clergy from their pastoral work (simony, marriage, immorality) and practices that limited the full liberty of the Church to control its personnel and property (lay investiture). Papal legates were sent to all parts of Europe to ferret out and correct clerical abuses and infringements on the Church's liberty. Difficult cases were referred back to Rome for settlement. Special attention was given to papal finances, with the intention of regularizing and increasing income.

Gregory VII did not live to see his program succeed. Indeed, he had mapped out an immense task, one made no easier by the fact that it met resistance from many quarters, particularly from the bishops of Europe, who rightly sensed that their ancient freedoms were threatened. Gregory's successors pursued his policy with vigor, skill, and persistence. Step by step through the twelfth and thirteenth centuries an ecclesiastical monarchy was built, making the successors of St. Peter heads of the Church in reality. This centralizing trend reached a culmination during the pontificates of Innocent III (1198–1216) and his powerful successors, Honorius III (1216–1227), Gregory IX (1227–1241), and Innocent IV (1243–1254). Innocent III, for example, lacked none of Gregory VII's conviction about the nature of the Church and the power of the papacy. What made Innocent's position so imposing was that he headed an immense organization capable of wielding that power on a large scale. A brief description of it will reveal one major achivement of this period.

As head of the Church, Innocent III controlled an extensive bureaucracy located in Rome and called collectively the papal *curia*. This body of officials was divided into specialized departments dealing with finances, correspondence and records, judicial cases, and treatment of sinners. A special body, the College of Cardinals, made up of churchmen especially selected by the pope, acted as an elective body, sat with the pope in special meetings (called *consistories*) to decide major policies, and often directed the routine administration of the curia. The curia was manned by well-trained specialists of clerical rank who made careers of papal administration. The papal curia maintained an elaborate communications network reaching all corners of Europe. In many areas, clergymen designated as papal *legates* resided for extended periods to control local affairs in the name of Rome; on numerous occasions, other legates were sent from Rome to perform some specific activity in the interest of the papacy. The legatine system, coupled with the extensive correspondence of the papal curia and the numerous judicial appeals to Rome, kept the popes well informed about local conditions throughout Europe. A huge income, derived from papal property, gifts, fees, assessments on the laity, levies on the lesser clergy, and numerous other sources, sustained this vast organization.

Ranked under the thirteenth-century popes was the age-old hierarchy of archbishops, bishops, and priests. By 1300 the exact functions of each branch of the clerical hierarchy were carefully defined in canon law. In the process of establishing these definitions the papacy had acquired considerable power in determining local elections and confirmations to the higher offices in the hierarchy, so that papal control over archbishops and bishops was extensive. Each archbishop and bishop headed a small-scale model of the papal curia, called a *cathedral chapter*, made up of *canons* who played a significant role in the election of the archbishops and bishops, advised these officials, and directed the administration of the *diocese* over which the archbishop or bishop presided. The bishop and the canons of the cathedral chapter supervised the parish priests who directed the religious life of laymen, conducted judicial proceedings, collected and dispensed considerable diocesan income, and managed the extensive properties attached to every bishopric.

Aside from its sheer impressiveness as a bureaucratic feat, the centralized church organization that had evolved by the thirteenth century was particularly effective in imposing a high degree of uniformity on European religious life. As a consequence of organizational efficiency, Christians participated in the same ceremonies, received the same sacraments, said the same prayers, and were taught the same doctrines. A single code of laws, administered by an efficient, centralized system of courts, imposed a common discipline. The whole thrust of organizational centralization was toward exalting religious conformity and damning heterodoxy. A manifestation of this growing emphasis on conformity was the development in the thirteenth century of a special papal court, called the *Inquisition*, charged with searching out and punishing heretics. Armed with almost total freedom to devise its own methods of inquiry and with authority to impose severe penalties, the Inquisition became a devastating weapon against those who balked at accepting the Church's authority and abiding by its rules.

The powerful, centralized administration that had been shaped by the thirteenth century permitted churchmen to extend their influence far beyond religious affairs. Nothing illustrates this better than the role played by Innocent III in European political life, a story that could be replicated by examining the careers of most of the thirteenth-century popes. To describe all of Innocent's political exploits would demand telling most of the political history of Western Europe in the early thirteenth century. We have already observed how Innocent manipulated affairs in Germany and Italy to weaken the Holy Roman emperor and to make his own candidate, Frederick II, ruler of the empire. This was also the pope who humiliated John of England over the issue of filling the highest church office in England. After a long quarrel Innocent finally compelled Philip II of France to take back his second wife, whom he had repudiated the day after their marriage. Several lesser states were compelled or persuaded to accept the pope as their overlord, their kings becoming papal vassals. Innocent launched the Fourth Crusade and exercised considerable influence in Byzantine affairs when that crusade ended in the capture of Constantinople. The mighty

pope was able to organize a crushing crusade against the heretical Albigensians in southern France by calling on the services of the French king and nobility. In exercising such wide political power, Innocent made no distinction between religion and politics. He used religious weapons to gain political ends and political pressure to impose his spiritual leadership. When he spoke of his right to exercise "the fullness of power," Innocent meant complete mastery over all aspects of life. And while the pope was acting on so broad a stage with such impressive results, the extensive hierarchy of archbishops, bishops, priests, and monks under his authority was exerting a potent influence on European society at the local level, usually in support of the papacy.

3. STANDARDIZATION OF CANON LAW AND DOCTRINE

Organization alone did not solve all the Church's problems. Increasing centralization revealed considerable confusion in the governing regulations and teachings of the Church. Because the success of the whole centralization movement demanded conformity, there was in the eleventh, twelfth, and thirteenth centuries a great surge of activity to standardize law and doctrine, an effort that drew on the major intellectual movements of the era.

One area of progress centered around the canon law. By the eleventh century the Church possessed an immense body of law, much of it dating from earlier periods. Many of the provisions of that law were contradictory, and some no longer applied to current situations. Moreover, new difficulties were constantly arising in this era of reform to demand new legal solutions. Guided by Scripture, papal decrees, the acts of church councils, the writings of the early fathers, and the example of the Code of Justinian, church lawyers worked to create an extensive, consistent, and organized collection of canon law. A decisive figure in the shaping of canon law was Gratian, who in 1140 published his *Decretum*, a collection that treated canon law in a strictly logical fashion to remove contradictions and confusions. It immediately became the standard guide for church administration and discipline. Among many other things, Gratian's work defined the powers of each rank of the clergy, the jurisdiction of ecclesiastical courts, crimes against the Church and their punishments, the proper use of church income and property, and the manner of conducting religious ceremonies. Throughout the work ran one predominant idea—the supremacy of the papacy in the governance of the Church. The extensive commentaries that were made on Gratian's work clarified particular aspects of the law, and eventually led to new codifications, usually made under papal auspices. By the end of the thirteenth century, the canon law had assumed a form that has persisted with little change to the present.

Church doctrines were even more confused than Church law. The teachings of the early fathers were not adequately understood. And, as we shall see later, during the twelfth century Western Europeans began to gain a wider acquaintance with the philosophical and religious teachings of the classical Greeks, which often contradicted Christian teaching. This challenge was answered by the emergence of several theologians who worked successfully to define with precision the basic doctrines of the Church.

Perhaps the decisive figure in the Church's struggle to standardize its doctrines was Abelard, a tempestuous twelfth-century scholar, constantly in trouble for his criticism of other scholars. Abelard's contribution to the development of a systematic theology lay in establishing a method for eliminating confusion and contradiction. He dramatically called attention to the conflicting teachings of Scriptures, the fathers, and tradition on certain key theological questions. He insisted that only by the application of human reason could these differences be resolved. This method of clarifying revealed truth by the use of reason soon came to be known as *scholasticism*. Most theologians quickly adopted the method.

During the thirteenth century a series of great scholastic philosophers, the chief of whom was Thomas Aquinas, worked toward a systematic description of the Church's teachings and eliminated most of the earlier confusion. Not only did Thomas Aquinas and his fellow theologians define doctrines more clearly, but they also tried to weave all human knowledge into a single body related to the Church's teaching, giving the Church a single version of the truth that could be taught to all.

Leaving aside for a moment the larger implications and achievements of the scholastics, let us concentrate on the doctrines concerning salvation and the sacramental system that stood at the heart of the Church's teachings by the thirteenth century. None of these doctrines was new; most of them dated back to the early centuries of Church history. The theologians of the twelfth and thirteenth centuries merely supplied more precise definitions and, with the backing of the ecclesiastical hierarchy, imposed greater uniformity concerning these fundamental questions.

According to the thirteenth-century theologians, God had created man in order that he might eventually be saved, human life being but a testing period during which man proved his worthiness of salvation. Corrupted by nature because of original sin, a Christian could be saved only by virtue of the grace God bestowed on him. Grace was obtained by partaking of the sacraments, instituted by Christ as the essential part of his divine mission. According to Peter Lombard, a twelfth century theologian whose *Sentences* was the most widely read book on doctrine of the age, there were seven grace-giving sacraments. Prior to this there had been considerable disagreement on the exact number of sacraments. Baptism, usually administered at infancy, removed the stain of original sin, which all Christians inherited from Adam and Eve. Confirmation infused into a Christian the Holy Ghost, strengthening his faith and fortifying him against the devil. Extreme unction, administered to those in danger of death, supplied its recipients with grace to strengthen them spiritually at the time when they might face the Almighty and removed from their souls the stain of the minor (or venial) sins they had committed. Marriage sanctified the married state and family life.

Holy orders or ordination, through which a layman was elevated to the rank of priest, supplied the recipient with the special powers required to perform his religious duties. This sacrament was administered by a bishop, whose authority, according to the doctrine of apostolic succession, extended back in an un-interrupted line to the apostles. The Church taught that Christ had handed on to his apostles the powers to teach the faith, to forgive sin, and to consecrate the eucharist. The apostles had in turn conferred these powers on certain bishops who by this act acquired the power to transmit them to their successors. Therefore, each ordained clergyman by receiving the sacrament of holy orders became a valid successor of Christ and the apostles in teaching the faith, forgiving sins, and consecrating the eucharist at mass.

The eucharist was the sacrament by which Christ himself was present to the faithful during the celebration of the mass. The exact nature of this sacrament had long troubled theologians. It was not until 1215 at the Fourth Lateran Council, held under the direction of Innocent III, that the doctrine of transubstantiation was officially pronounced. According to this doctrine, Christ became truly present at the moment of the consecration under the appearance of bread and wine. His real presence was effected by a miraculous change in the substance of the bread and wine, although their external accidents (that is, color, shape, taste, etc.) remained the same. Partaking of this sacrament by attending mass and receiving communion signified the receiving of Christ and the consequent infusion of grace into the soul. No punishment was greater than to be excommunicated, which meant being cut off from receiving the eucharist. The last sacrament was penance, whereby a sinner who confessed his sins to a priest and felt sorrow for them would receive the forgiveness of God. Provided that he made some sacrifice or did some good work assigned by the priest, the penitent sinner who had confessed was relieved of all the punishment for his sins. The Fourth Lateran Council decreed that every Christian must confess at least once a year. These sacraments were administered by the clergy, meaning that the Church held the keys to the kingdom of heaven. No man could thus expect salvation without the services of the Church.

This is but a bare outline of the fundamental doctrines; embroidered on the sacramental system was a rich array of belief that offered to man the help of God in every aspect of his life. There were prayers that invoked God's help in battle, in the harvest, in famine, in sickness, and in any other conceivable human situation. To almost every Christian there were available sacred objects, especially relics, that possessed powers to draw man to God and God to man. An army of saints filled heaven to plead the cause of humanity with God, and an equally numerous horde of devils schemed and labored under Satan's command to ruin mankind. All these concepts were enlarged and enriched through the efforts of the theologians of the High Middle Ages. In a general way, their activities tended to expand the human element involved in Christian teaching. For example, theologians of the period placed much greater emphasis on the human life and suffering of Jesus and the Virgin than had earlier been the case. This humanizing trend in theology, emphasizing compassion, love, and feeling, often had its source in the monastic world, which must be credited with adding depth and warmth and variety to the rather austere and awesome basic concepts of the sacramental system. The Christian world owes the medieval reformation a debt for a considerable part of its most emotionally appealing teachings.

4. MONASTIC REFORM

While great energy was being devoted to a successful effort to perfect an ecclesiastical monarchy and codify its laws and doctrines, other regenerative forces were being produced in the monastic world. Perhaps no other age in Christian history witnessed a more intense monastic life that manifested itself in a variety of new monastic movements, each of which added some new dimension to the quest for spiritual perfection.

The dominant monastic force during the tenth and eleventh centuries was the Cluniac movement, which had sought to restore the primitive purity of the Benedictine Rule. In a spiritual sense, the movement placed heavy emphasis on the performance of an elaborate daily round of religious services as the main duty of the monks. The Cluniac liturgy was a splendid model of externalized religion, appealing especially to the feudal aristocracy and having an impact on the religious ethos of that class. Cluniac concepts of piety and clerical conduct and of ecclesiastical governance had helped to shape the widespread reform movement of the eleventh century which attacked lay investiture and clerical corruption. However, as the eleventh century progressed, the Cluniac Order lost its spiritual leadership. The hundreds of monasteries in the order grew rich and complacent, and the monks became deeply involved in administering the order's wealth. As we have seen, leadership of the reform movement passed to other hands, and especially to the papacy.

More significant in the passing of Cluniac dominance was the emergence of new spiritual movements which turned away from the basic spirit of Benedictinism. Historically, the Benedictine ideal was based on withdrawal from the corrupt world to create holy communities so ordered that men could live in them, serve God, and earn salvation without contact with the world. As things worked out, these holy islands did so well that they became rich and powerful and quite at home in the world. To some, Benedictinism seemed self-defeating; flight from a corrupt world resulted in involvement with the very things the monks wished to leave behind. The spiritual aspirations of some began to turn toward ways of assuring personal perfection and of making monasticism a force that would reshape the world rather than run from it. Out of this disillusionment with the Benedictine approach were shaped the powerful new movements that dominated monasticism during the twelfth and thirteenth centuries.

The urge for personal perfection generated attempts to return to the practice of the hermit life exemplified by the early desert fathers. The most notable example of this style of monastic life was the Carthusian Order, which spread throughout Europe from France, where it was established in the late eleventh century. Selecting the most unattractive locations as sites for monastic houses, the Carthusians celebrated a hermit life filled with extreme ascetic practices. Never very popular as a result of the severity of its regimen, the Carthusian Order did, however, impress upon an admiring world a model of denial of self and the world.

The new spirit circulating in the monastic world found its best expression in the Cistercian Order, founded in 1098 by a Benedictine monk who felt that the ancient Rule was not being strictly observed. The new order was dedicated to extreme poverty, simplicity of worship, complete isolation from the world, hard labor, and rigid discipline. It proved immensely popular, so that by 1300 there were about seven hundred Cistercian monasteries spread over all of Europe. The Cistercians were especially effective in establishing new houses in remote areas which the labor of the monks quickly turned into rich agricultural establishments. As the order spread, it developed a unique organizational pattern that combined local autonomy and centralized direction. The abbot of each house directed local affairs but was required each year to attend a general meeting at the mother house at Cîteaux; these meetings decided policies affecting all houses, and a system of regular visits was developed to see that local houses adhered to general rules.

However, the Cistercian movement was more than just another form of Benedictinism; it represented a potent new spiritual force that exerted powerful influences on all aspects of religious life. Owing largely to the influence of the greatest Cistercian, Bernard of Clairvaux, the order became a militant agency seeking to arouse all men to purity, piety, and devoted action for Christ. Bernard entered the order in 1113, and until his death in 1153, he was the most influential religious figure in Western Europe. As a monastic leader, he insisted that a monk could learn to know God directly only if he deprived himself of physical comforts and prayed long and earnestly. Thus fortified, the monk would be a worthy opponent of the devil and could go into the world to fight sin and spiritual indifference without fear of corruption. This was exactly what Bernard did. During his long career he was involved in nearly every important event in Europe. His preaching was instrumental in launching the Second Crusade; he became the papacy's chief support in hunting down corrupt clergymen (he even turned his blasts against a pope or two); he was a ruthless and relentless foe of any unorthodox or heretical movement; he hounded Europe's kings constantly to improve their lives and their governments. He had no peer as a popular preacher. He and other monks like him— almost an army of puritanical, industrious, sober soldiers of Christ—penetrated every corner of Europe urging men to be better Christians.

Although the Cistercians dominated monasticism during the twelfth century, other movements contributed to the deepening of religious life. Hermitic life in various forms continued to flourish, but especially fruitful were movements seeking to utilize the monastic model as a means of transforming the

The spirit of the great monastic movements that were part of the regeneration of the Church in the twelfth and thirteenth centuries is exemplified in this miniature from a contemporary French bible, which shows a man casting away the demon of worldly desires as he enters the religious life. *Photo: Trustees of the British Museum*

world. An order called the Augustinian Canons was organized for the purpose of improving the moral quality of the clerks who made up the cathedral chapters. The rule of the Augustinians bound the cathedral canons to poverty, prayer, and moral excellence, while allowing them to move about freely as preachers and administrators. In this same century the great crusading orders—the Templars, the Hospitalers, and the Teutonic Knights—were founded. These orders were made up of knights who took special vows fitting their work as warriors against the Muslims. Their rigid discipline, their zeal, and extensive organizations capable of raising men and money all over Europe permitted them to play a decisive role in defending the Christian establishment in the Holy Land. The military orders also organized numerous charitable agencies to help pious crusaders in the difficult journey to the holy places.

The trend toward involvement in the world

which had exercised a strong influence on twelfth-century monasticism became dominant in the early thirteenth century with the establishment of the *mendicant* (begging) orders, the Dominicans and the Franciscans. Both represented a religious response to a new factor in European life, the city with its new class, its new values, and its new problems. Both also represented a search for some means of escaping the blight that success and wealth imposed on earlier monastic movements. The mendicants sought the answer to these challenges by abandoning cloistered life in favor of living in the world and by refusing any form of wealth, either individual or corporate.

The Dominican Order was the product of the fertile mind of a Spanish priest named Dominic (1170–1221). During a tour through southern France, where the Albigensian heresy was rampant, Dominic became convinced that orthodoxy would prevail only on condition that preachers learned in theology and free from all suspicion of excessive wealth mingled with the heretics. In 1215 he presented this idea to Innocent III, who authorized him to organize a new order dedicated to the destruction of heresy by preaching. The rule provided for an austere life to be directed by an all-powerful minister-general who was advised by an annual meeting of delegates representing the various provinces into which the order was divided. Once the constitution of the order was set, Dominic immediately began to recruit members. He required that all of them practice poverty, and insisted that his monks live by begging. Even greater stress was placed on education. Each Dominican was put through a rigorous training program aimed at making him an expert theologian. Armed with their knowledge, the Black Friars of St. Dominic spread over Europe preaching to everyone. The Friars Preachers, as the order was called, very quickly established themselves as one of the strongest arms of papal power, especially useful in directing the Inquisition against heretics and controlling the teaching of theology in the great universities.

The inspiration for the Franciscan Order was supplied by one of the most appealing figures in all history, Francis of Assisi (1182–1226). The son of a wealthy Italian merchant, Francis established in his youth a reputation as a playboy and jovial companion. But while still a young man he underwent a fundamental spiritual conversion that convinced him that he must imitate Christ in a most literal sense. Because of his strange conduct his father disinherited him, whereupon Francis turned to a life of poverty, preaching, and the performance of charitable works. He stressed the need for love and repentance. Francis was especially effective as a preacher because of his personality, which exuded joy, lightheartedness, and a sympathy for all men. To his contemporaries, he was "God's own troubador," filled with happiness and love as a consequence of his disdain for power, wealth, and glory. Almost immediately both men and women were converted by his simple message and his fascinating personality. They surrendered their wealth, worked or begged for a livelihood, and preached a simple message of love for all.

Francis was always an obedient son of the Church. In 1210 he applied to Innocent III for permission to continue his work. Innocent hesitated, feeling that Francis' demands on his followers were too severe, and perhaps concerned lest the simple message of love and repentance would breed a crop of heretics with little regard for the elaborate machinery that the organized Church supplied for saving souls. Finally, however, he consented to Francis' request. Between 1210 and 1226, when Francis died, the order grew rapidly, spreading to nearly every part of Western Europe and even to areas outside Europe. Often the Friars Minor met opposition from local clergymen because of their stirring sermons, their exaltation of poverty, and their ability to attract attention. The Franciscans flourished in spite of this opposition. Their fresh approach to religious life was welcome, especially among the masses.

The mendicant orders of begging friars

were pillars of strength for the thirteenth-century Church. Each order was a controlling influence on the dynamic forces working in Europe and threatening the Church's power. The Dominican Order, emphasizing education and teaching, became the refuge of scholars and preachers, who studied, systematized, and propagated Christian doctrine with a vigor seldom seen in the earlier history of the Church. The simple disciples of Francis, preaching a message of repentance and love, provided an outlet for those dissatisfied with the rigorous, rather formal activities of the organized Church. The friars proved especially useful to the papacy, for they lent themselves to the containment and direction of theological speculation and popular religious life. Because of their flexible organization, which did not confine friars to a fixed residence, the new orders were able to extend the Church's influence to those centers of thirteenth-century life where there was tremendous ferment—the cities, the universities, and the courts of the powerful kings. Their success demonstrated the Church's ability to make an appeal to almost any element of society.

5. POPULAR RELIGIOUS MOVEMENTS AND HERESIES

The urge for new spiritual understanding so evident in the monastic world also stirred lay society and gave birth to a confusing array of popular movements and heresies which added an important dimension to religious life between 1000 and 1300. The factors at work in these new strains are obscure. Probably they were in part a result of a deeper and more profound understanding of the gospel message among the laity brought about by more pious and serious priests and monks. The increasing number of articulate and educated laymen in society produced a leadership for such movements. The struggles over the use of the Church's wealth increased men's awareness of corruption and abuse. Greater social and economic pressures resulting from the

growth of the towns and the changes in the manorial order sensitized laymen to injustices and abuses of power within the Church. Whatever the causes, there developed in lay society in the eleventh and twelfth centuries a powerful urge to live in imitation of the poverty and humility of Jesus and an increasingly critical posture toward the powerful and wealthy clergy who directed Church life.

In the eleventh and twelfth centuries this new spirit produced numerous individual preachers from all levels of the lay world who urged men to abandon their wealth and power and to follow Jesus. Often these preachers succeeded in establishing bands of followers who shared their wealth, engaged in works of charity, cared for the sick, and worshiped after their own style. Some of the leaders of these brotherhoods spiced their exhortations on the gospels with passionate attacks on the clergy and the wealth of the Church, thus making anticlericalism a regular part of popular religious movements. In extreme cases, the enthusiasm produced by the preachers led to overt action against the Church. For example, at mid-twelfth century an Italian monk, Arnold of Brescia, so aroused the populace of Rome by his preaching against the wealth and secular power of the papacy that he was able to drive the pope out of the city and hold it until the pope persuaded Frederick Barbarossa to depose and execute the radical troublemaker. Often popular religious movements that began innocently enough as pious efforts to practice Christianity more perfectly ended as outlawed movements, suffering suppression at the hands of the Church and the established political authorities. Intolerance toward heterodox movements and anticlericalism became greater as the official Church developed a stronger sense of uniformity and the organizational strength to enforce conformity. Two particular movements, the Waldensians and the Cathari (Albigensians), illustrate the nature and fate of many popular reforming movements.

The Waldensian movement grew out of the work of Peter Waldo, a rich French merchant who in 1173 gave away his wealth and took up a life of poverty in imitation of Christ. His dramatic decision attracted a large following. The Waldensians took as their only authority the New Testament, refusing to accept the dictates of popes and bishops, who were only men and who because of their wealth were not good Christians. Living in poverty, the Waldensians went among the people, preaching and praying in vernacular languages, condemning the ordinary clergy, and refusing to admit many of the current teachings of the Church. They developed their own clergy and their own religious services. Among their followers they insisted upon a strict moral life, reflecting many of the ideas about sobriety, temperance, honesty, and simplicity of life that St. Bernard and his Cistercians had preached. Although the Waldensians were permitted to carry on their work for a while, eventually they were accused of heresy and attacked by the papacy and the Church hierarchy. Some Waldensian groups, especially in France, returned to orthodoxy. However, in northern Italy they survived persecution throughout the Middle Ages.

Far more radical were the Cathari, or Albigensians. This heresy originated in the Near East as early as the fourth century, probably as a result of the mixing of Christian and Zoroastrian ideas. It spread slowly westward across Asia Minor, through Bulgaria and Hungary, and finally reached northern Italy and southern France in the tenth century. The movement was most vigorous in southern France, although by 1200 it exerted an influence throughout Europe. The Cathari believed that two powers, one good and the other evil, were constantly in combat for the world and for men. The power of good was spiritual, while the evil force was materialistic. Everything that had to do with the material world was to be avoided. Because the organized Church had wealth and dealt in worldly affairs, it was condemned; its clergy, its sacraments, its services were creations of the devil. The true Church was made up of those who completely denied the world and

the flesh. True Cathari refused to marry, holding that even reproduction was evil. They ate no meat, milk, or eggs, which were the fruits of sexual union. They owned no property and refused to shed blood. The "perfect," as they called themselves, were certain that they were saved. Allowance was made, however, for weaker men. Second-grade Cathari, called "believers," were permitted to indulge more freely, although every "believer" hoped someday to become a "perfect." Since they repudiated the Church, the Cathari developed their own clergy, their own simple services, and their own rules of conduct. Needless to say, they were considered heretics from the beginning, and in the thirteenth century the papacy and the French monarchy delivered a ferocious assault that virtually eradicated the movement.

6. THE CONSEQUENCES OF THE MEDIEVAL REFORMATION: A SUMMARY

This simple, brief attempt to identify and describe the major patterns of religious reform working in Western Europe from 1000 to 1300 should dispel the notion that the medieval Church was a rigid, inflexible giant. Nothing could be less true. In fact, the reformation of the High Middle Ages completely transformed the Christian establishment in the West. It is perhaps not an exaggeration to say that a "new" Church was created. True, many aspects of the new establishment were old, but traditional patterns were reshaped and reapplied so that in their essence they little resembled what they had been. And to them were added new elements that would certainly have been foreign to the apostolic or patristic or Carolingian ages. In essence, the reformation of the High Middle Ages created the Roman Catholic Church that has survived to our day and that is only now beginning to consider alteration of its medieval configurations.

One major consequence of the medieval reformation was to make the Church into an effective European community which possessed an organization that had the power, the resources, and the personnel capable of imposing upon its membership one body of belief, one code of conduct, and one set of religious practices. And not only did this organization have the capability to unify the European population, it also had the intention of imposing conformity; its whole outlook was universal and catholic. The "new" Church therefore worked at achieving conformity and, on the whole, succeeded, so that by the thirteenth century it was chiefly responsible for providing Western European civilization with its integrating element.

A second major consequence was a revolutionary redefinition of the relation between church and state. The traditional relationship had been defined in the Late Roman Empire and had established the Church as an agency of the divinely sanctioned secular ruler. Throughout the period 1000 to 1300 the leader of the Church insisted in a variety of ways that the Church had an independent sphere of activity, an area of liberty into which no other authority could intrude. Moreover, these same leaders insisted that the Church stood superior to all other authorities and could judge their activities and conduct. In the

society of the High Middle Ages this concept of liberty and responsibility gave the Church immense powers to impose its influence on political, economic, social, and cultural life, an opportunity that was seldom missed. In a larger historical perspective the Church's quest for its independence played a role in defining political freedom. And more significantly, it freed the state from the primary responsibility of serving religious ends, thereby opening up to it a new range of activities.

Finally, the medieval reformation articulated an immensely broader range of spiritual possibilities in Christianity. It may be true, as some have insisted, that the totality of Christian spirituality was present from the beginning, but a study of the first millennium of Christian history does not persuade one that believers realized the range of spiritual possibilities available to them. After 1000 the search for meaning in religion produced an amazing array of new insights of a spiritual nature to enrich Christianity. It can be argued that many of the most potent spiritual concepts associated with Christianity date from the High Middle Ages rather than from the apostolic or patristic ages.

Suggested Reading

General. A brief survey of medieval church history that succeeds in highlighting the most important aspects of the Church's activities is **M. W. Baldwin, *The Mediaeval Church* (Cornell). Two other good brief surveys are the appropriate sections of M. Deanesly, *A History of the Medieval Church, 590–1500* (8th ed., 1954); and K. S. Latourette, *A History of Christianity* (1953). A longer history by a renowned Roman Catholic scholar is Philip Hughes, *A History of the Church*, Vol. II (rev. ed., 1949), covering the period from the fourth to the thirteenth centuries. **Henri Daniel-Rops, *Cathedral and Crusade* (2 vols.,

Image), is full of fascinating details, but many of its interpretations are debatable. A useful handbook, providing extensive bibliographies on nearly every aspect of church history, is Karl Bihlmeyer and Hermann Tüchle, *Church History*, Vol. II: *The Middle Ages*, trans. V. E. Mills and F. J. Muller (1963). A particularly stimulating interpretation of religious development is given by **J. B. Russell, *A History of Medieval Christianity: Prophesy and Order* (Crowell).

Organization, Law, Doctrine. Summerfield Baldwin, *The Organization of Mediaeval*

Christianity (1929), is a clear, brief description of the intricacies of medieval church organization. **Geoffrey Barraclough, *The Medieval Papacy* (Harcourt, Brace and World), will help to clarify papal development. More detailed and especially concerned with papal centralization is William Barry, *The Papal Monarchy From St. Gregory the Great to Boniface VIII (590–1307)* (1902). An excellent picture of the papal government in action is supplied by S. R. Packard, *Europe and the Church Under Innocent III* (1968). Varying interpretations of the pontificate of Innocent III are presented by **J. M. Powell, ed., *Innocent III, Vicar of Christ or Lord of the World?* (Heath). D. P. Waley, *The Papal State in the Thirteenth Century* (1961), supplies a detailed picture of the operation of the Papal States in Italy. Interesting insights into the operation of the Church at the local level is E. L. Cutts, *Parish Priests and Their People in the Middle Ages in England* (1914). A good description of the evolution of the canon law is R. C. Mortimer, *Western Canon Law* (1953). Two excellent works on the Inquisition are the classic study of H. C. Lea, *A History of the Inquisition of the Middle Ages* (3 vols., 1888), written from a Protestant point of view; and E. Vacandard, *The Inquisition* (1908), by a Catholic scholar. Works relating to doctrinal development will be found in connection with scholasticism in the following chapter.

Monastic Reform, Popular Religion, and Heresy. The best general survey of monastic history is **H. B. Workman, *Evolution of the Monastic Ideal From the Earliest Times to the Coming of the Friars* (Beacon). For the Cluniac movement, one can turn to L. M. Smith, *The Early History of the Monastery at Cluny* (1920); and Joan Evans, *Monastic Life at Cluny* (1931). The history of the mendicants is well treated by W. H. Hinnebusch, *The History of the Dominican Order*, Vol. I: *Origin and Growth to 1500* (1966); and J. R. H. Moorman, *A History of the Franciscan Order from Its Origin to the Year 1517* (1968). J. B. Russell, *Dissent and Reform in the Early Middle Ages* (1965), presents an excellent account of dissenting movements, many of popular origin, down to the twelfth century. **Norman Cohn, *The Pursuit of the Millennium* (Harper Torchbook), is a brilliant study of messianic concepts and their social implications in Western Europe between the eleventh and the sixteenth centuries. **S. Runciman, *The Medieval Manichee* (Compass), is an excellent analysis of Catharism.

Biographies. The following biographies will be useful in understanding the various aspects of the medieval Church and the role of individuals in shaping religious life: L. E. Elliott-Binns, *Innocent III* (1931); Paul Sabatier, *The Life of St. Francis*, trans. L. S. Houghton (1930); Watkin Williams, *Saint Bernard of Clairvaux* (2nd ed., 1953); Roger Lloyd, *Peter Abélard: The Orthodox Rebel* (2nd ed. rev., 1947); J. Sikes, *Peter Abailard* (1965); **Bede Jarrett, *Life of Dominic (1170–1221)* (Image); and P. F. Mandonnet, *St. Dominic and His World* (1944).

Sources. Some idea of the operation of the papal curia in the thirteenth century can be gleaned from *Selected Letters of Pope Innocent III Concerning England*, eds. C. R. Cheney and W. H. Semple (1953). A remarkable collection of documents treating church-state relationships has been compiled by **Brian Tierney, *The Crisis of Church and State, 1050–1300* (Spectrum). G. G. Coulton, *Five Centuries of Religion* (4 vols., 1923–1950), is a vast collection of source materials illustrating the nature of medieval religious life; although Coulton is not generally sympathetic to the Church, the collection provides a good "feel" for the nature of medieval religious concepts and practices. Materials pertaining to St. Francis of Assisi can be found in *Saint Francis of Assisi, The Little Flowers of St. Francis, The Mirror of Perfection, Saint Bonaventura's Life of St. Francis* (Everyman, 1963); and *The Writings of Saint Francis of Assisi*, trans. P. Robinson (1906). For Bernard of Clairvaux, see *The Life and Works of Saint Bernard*, trans. S. J. Eales (4 vols., 1889–1896); and *The Letters of Bernard of Clairvaux*, trans. B. S. James (1953).

Chapter 24 ✣ Intellectual, Literary, and

Artistic Achievements

The crowning achievement of Western European society in the High Middle Ages was the original and creative work done in thought, literature, and art. After a long apprenticeship, Western Europeans came alive culturally and demonstrated a singular genius in all aspects of thought and the arts. Their performances in these activities were no less important in establishing Western Europe in a preeminent place in the world than were the remarkable advances in politics, economics, religion, and expansion. To complete our picture of the burgeoning of the West in the High Middle Ages, we shall try to capture in this chapter some of the major developments in thought, literature, and art.

1. A CHRONOLOGICAL OVERVIEW

This treatment of cultural life during the High Middle Ages will concentrate on a description of the major accomplishments in certain broad areas of cultural activity. But a brief chronological survey of the cultural history of the period from 1000 to 1300 may be helpful, especially in making us realize that medieval cultural life was an evolving one shaped out of long experimentation.

In 1000 Western European cultural life was at a low ebb. The gains of the Carolingian renaissance had not been lost, but their impact was felt only in the very narrow world of the monasteries. The brutal realities of the ninth and tenth centuries were not conducive to vigorous cultural activity. However, rather suddenly in the eleventh century and extending on into the twelfth, there was a spectacular outburst of cultural activity. One famous American medievalist labeled this surge "the twelfth-century renaissance," rather unabashedly claiming for it accomplishments usually attributed to a more famous renaissance three centuries later.

Whatever we choose to call the renewal of the eleventh and twelfth centuries, it still remains a movement marked by great vigor and freshness. The impetus for cultural revival came from many directions: new religious ideas, economic growth, social change, political developments, and wider contacts with the outside world, all of which placed on society new demands to think, to speak, and to create. The range of cultural activities broadened immensely. New educational institutions in the form of cathedral and municipal schools challenged the monopoly on education held by the

The façade of Saint-Étienne at Caen, which was founded by William the Conqueror soon after his invasion of England. Here are the Romanesque rounded arches, the heavy buttresses, the appearance of weight and solidity almost reminiscent of a fortress. *Photo: Jean Roubier* monastic schools. The content of education was enlarged, chiefly by a new interest in classical learning and literature. Theological speculation quickened, and men began to develop an interest in the study of law and the natural sciences. As their knowledge expanded in these areas, they sought ways of systematizing theology, law, and science, a task that put a premium on logical thought. Literary activity was greatly intensified, and an amazing array of new literary forms appeared: Latin poetry, hymns, history, and drama; vernacular epics, lyric poetry, romances, fables. New artistic concepts found expression in the design and decoration of Romanesque churches and the beginnings of the Gothic style. The twelfth-century renaissance was indeed a remarkably "open" cultural movement, encouraging men to experiment with a wide variety of new ideas, forms, and techniques in order to express their reaction to their world. Its total effect was to expand cultural perspectives beyond the narrow confines of the monastic world and to draw into the world of thought, literature, and art not only more churchmen, but also important segments of the secular world.

Shortly after 1150 the cultural climate began to change. The buoyant, questing spirit of the twelfth-century renaissance lost its edge, and men began to concern themselves more with drawing together and synthesizing their accomplishments. The cultural history of the thirteenth century was dominated by this spirit. This was especially true in the "sciences": theology, law, studies of the natural world. The new universities became the focus of these areas of learning, and the intellectuals who worked in them spent their energies summarizing knowledge into systematic patterns. Their prime objective was to reconcile their knowledge with Christian faith in order to produce statements of an ultimate truth. The literary activities of the age became more stylized and concerned with putting materials into set forms. The thirteenth century was the age of the Gothic in the arts. In a very real way the Gothic style was a

product of synthesis, an attempt to merge all forms of art into a structure that would reflect the great truths of the faith. This age of synthesis, of summing up, of organizing thoughts and feelings produced the most mature expressions of medieval culture: the theological writings of Thomas Aquinas, the poetry of Dante, exquisite Gothic cathedrals, the great romances. But it lacked the spontaneity, the freshness of the twelfth-century renaissance.

2. THE WORLD OF LEARNING: EDUCATION

In discussing medieval cultural history, we must always keep in mind that there were two cultural spheres in Western European society. The line of demarcation between them was a linguistic one. There was one cultural world where Latin was the vehicle of expression. As the official language of the Church, Latin provided the key to the prime sources of the Christian faith: Scripture, the church fathers, the law, the liturgy. When medieval men had something important to say on life's serious issues, they were expected to say it in Latin. But Latin was not the language that men normally spoke; it had to be learned. Thus those who had learned Latin were set apart from the rest of society. They were the "learned men," and the great majority of them were churchmen. Those who had mastered Latin lived intellectually in a world of learning that had its own idiom and ideas. But there was also another cultural world in which the language of the people, the vernacular tongues, prevailed. It too developed its own interests, styles, and values. In general, this cultural realm did not concern itself with the subjects proper to the Latin world of learning—theology, philosophy, law, science, liturgy, political theory. It tended to reflect the lay world, especially that of the aristocracy. The worlds of Latin learning and of vernacular culture were never isolated from one another, but they were enough separated so that ideas and concepts prevailing in one often did not affect the other very seriously.

Our first concern in this chapter will be with the world of Latin learning. Since Latin was a language that medieval men had to learn, education was vital to this cultural sphere. One of the major developments in Western European culture in the High Middle Ages was an impressive expansion of the educational system. And the new patterns of education played a crucial role in shaping the emphases that prevailed in learning and thought.

By 1000 formal education in Western Europe was confined largely to monastic schools, although there were a few modest cathedral schools and, in Italy, some municipal schools. These schools, most of them products of the Carolingian era, touched a very narrow segment of the population and cultivated a very narrow range of interests. In the eleventh and twelfth centuries they underwent an amazing expansion. The impetus for this change came chiefly from the demands of the Church, the royal governments, and the cities for more literate men capable of handling the growing complexities of administration and commerce. The cathedral and municipal schools, best suited to meet these needs, thus expanded at a greater rate than did the monastic schools. The revival expressed itself in part in terms of increasing numbers of schools and students—but perhaps more important was the changing emphasis in what was studied. Especially in the cathedral schools there was a marked intensification of the study of the seven liberal arts. Three of these arts (called the *trivium*)—grammar, rhetoric, and dialectic—especially captured the interest of the era. Many cathedral schools owed their fame to individual masters who specialized in one of these arts and who worked hard to expand the content of the subject and to sharpen the skills associated with it. To a large extent, the subject matter in these disciplines was provided by classical models, so that the schools became centers of a renaissance of classical studies. The other

four liberal arts (the *quadrivium*)—arithmetic, geometry, astronomy, music—were not so central to the interests of teachers, students, and society, but still their content was constantly expanded, again chiefly as a result of contacts with the classical world.

Toward the end of the twelfth century the monastic, cathedral, and municipal schools no longer met the needs of some elements of society, particularly those of the masters and students who were most directly involved in them. The accomplishments of these institutions tended to make them obsolete by opening up intellectual vistas which abbots and bishops—being practical men—had no utilitarian interest in fostering. Moreover, during the last half of the twelfth century Western Europe was flooded by great quantities of new knowledge coming primarily from the ancient Greek world by way of the Muslims. This new knowledge, chiefly philosophical and scientific, posed a challenge to existing religious beliefs that had to be met by more intense study and thought. The response to these pressures was a new educational institution, the university, which in its origin represented a self-generating community of scholars seeking to create a setting that would allow them to devote their energies to the pursuit of truth and knowledge independent of abbots, bishops, kings, or townsmen. The first universities tended to concentrate on one special "science," that is, one area of learning: Salerno and Montpellier, for example, on medicine, Bologna on law, Paris on theology.[1]

Universities were founded by the action of either students or faculty, who organized themselves into corporations or guilds (the general Latin term for "guild" was *universi-*

---

[1] The exact date of the foundation of the earliest universities is difficult to ascertain. Most of them grew out of earlier schools. The University of Paris was granted legal status by the king of France in 1200, although an important institution of learning had existed there at least a century earlier. Bologna became a university in the period between 1150 and 1200. A school of medicine existed in Salerno in the tenth century. Oxford and Cambridge were established early in the thirteenth century.

tas) and assumed powers of self-government. At Bologna the students took the initiative in forming a *universitas* because they felt the need for protection against the townsmen. At Paris, on the other hand, the teachers of the arts in the Paris episcopal school broke away from the control of the bishop and founded a self-governing body, and later faculties of law, theology, and medicine were added. A rector was elected as head of each faculty, the rector of the arts faculty being the head of the university.

Each university had as the basis for its curriculum the study of the seven liberal arts, and maintained a faculty for the teaching of these arts. The presence of several masters in the arts was a factor that distinguished the university from the cathedral school, which usually enjoyed only one master. The arts program, often lasting six or eight years, usually culminated in the grant of a master of arts degree, which entitled its holder to full membership in the teaching profession. Eventually a bachelor of arts degree was instituted, requiring four or five years of study but not entitling its holder to teach. The doctor's degree was taken in theology, law, or medicine. Advanced study in these specialized fields was usually begun after the master's degree had been earned. At Paris the doctor's degree in theology required at least thirteen years of study. The granting of degrees carrying certain privileges was another aspect of the university that distinguished it from earlier educational institutions.

Teaching in medieval universities consisted chiefly of commenting on texts. Students who could afford to buy a manuscript copy of the authority under discussion made notes of the teacher's comments in the margins of the text. Those without a text tried to copy the text as the master read it (thus the origin of the lecture system, since reading from a text was called *lectio*). Examinations, coming at the end of his four or six or thirteen years, depending on the student's curriculum, were designed to test his ability to take a text or thesis and expound on it. Success depended upon a good memory and the ability to reason closely. Often the masters prodded the student to test his ability to think with facility by subjecting him to rigorous questioning.

At first most universities had no buildings. Classes were held in rented halls, while students took lodgings in private homes. During the thirteenth century men of means, perhaps moved by the miserable conditions under which some students lived, began to endow establishments for housing and feeding students. Such establishments, called *colleges*, became the centers of most educational activities. The first such institution was the Sorbonne at Paris, endowed in 1258 by Robert de Sorbon, a rich courtier. University authorities assumed responsibility for disciplining students. Usually students and faculty were considered members of the clergy and thus were under the jurisdiction of church courts. This led to endless conflicts between townsmen (who had to tolerate students without being able to control them) and the university community. Medieval students were a tough, rude lot who demanded much and were willing to use almost any means to get what they wanted; some of their exploits make the modern academician thankful for the serenity of the modern university and the seriousness of modern students.

3. THE WORLD OF LEARNING: THEOLOGY AND PHILOSOPHY

A major portion of the intellectual energies of medieval men of learning was absorbed in a quest for a fuller understanding of the Christian faith. Out of this quest came one of the chief monuments of medieval culture: a body of theology and philosophy that attempted to clarify Christian doctrine and to relate all other branches of knowledge to Christian teaching.

Between the fifth and the eleventh centuries little significant theological work was produced in Western Europe. However, in the eleventh century there was a revival of interest in theology. An ever-increasing amount of attention was devoted to the question of the extent to which human reason could be useful in grasping religious truth. Some conservative thinkers insisted that reason was dangerous and that one must rely on revelation as set forth in Scripture and in the writings of the early fathers for knowledge about God. Others, influenced chiefly by an increasing knowledge of classical thought and advancing skills in formal logic and troubled by the contradictions in Christian doctrine, argued that God had given man reason in order that he might seek the truth. These men began scrutinizing some of the doctrines of the Church in an attempt to find rational justification for them.

One of the early and influential exponents of this approach was Anselm of Bec (later archbishop of Canterbury), whose aim was to provide a logical proof of the existence of God. The attempts of eleventh-century scholars to clarify the use of reason in exploring religious authority reached a decisive point with the career of Peter Abelard (1079–1142). Even as a student, this bold thinker disturbed the intellectual leaders of his generation; according to his own version of his life, he put his teachers at Paris to shame in philosophical dispute. His own career as a teacher was ruined by a love affair with one of his young pupils, Heloise, and he was forced to spend the rest of his days wandering from monastery to monastery. However, certain of his ideas influenced both his contemporaries and later theologians.

Abelard argued that only through the use of reason could man come to a fuller understanding of God. Superbly skilled as a logician, he began to establish a method by which reason could be used to enlarge man's vision of God. In a famous book entitled *Sic et Non* (*Yes and No*) he set down numerous cases in which authorities were in direct conflict on matters of faith. Obviously, only human reason could resolve these contradictions. Abelard also developed new insights into how men know things. He maintained that the truth consisted of concepts formed in the mind as a result of the study of the things

God had created, such mental concepts being the nearest approximation to the perfect knowledge that is God. A philosopher's task is to organize in a logical fashion all that he knows so as to create in his mind an image of God's universe. The opposition to Abelard's rationalism, led by Bernard of Clairvaux, was strong, and some of his teachings were officially condemned by the Church before his death. However, his approach to theology soon became the predominant one, especially after Peter Lombard (1100–1160) produced his book, *Sentences*, which not only set down differing opinions, but also proceeded to resolve them rationally so as to arrive at an acceptable position on any doctrine.

The utility of the new rationalistic approach was powerfully enhanced as a consequence of a vast body of new knowledge that became available in the West during the last half of the twelfth and the early thirteenth centuries. A large number of Greek and Muslim philosophical and scientific works were translated into Latin by scholars working in Spain and Sicily. Particularly significant was the translation of almost the entire body of Aristotle's works; he quickly became the leading authority on logical methods and scientific knowledge. But the new knowledge confronted Western theologians and philosophers with a serious challenge: Not only did they now possess kinds of knowledge heretofore unknown to them, but they also were confronted with logically demonstrated truths that often contradicted basic Christian teachings. Careful, systematic scrutiny of this new knowledge was necessary to reconcile it with the Christian outlook. The major concerns of thirteenth-century thought, especially in the universities, therefore centered around the problem of coping with the implications of this new knowledge. Many scholars, collectively called the *scholastics*, labored at the tasks of mastering the knowledge, organizing it into systems, and seeking to bring it into some kind of relationship with Christian doctrine. A variety of responses were formulated, and scholars fought bitterly over intellectual issues, especially those posed by Aristotelianism. Their intellectual wars belie later widely held notions that the Middle Ages was a time of uniformity and conformity in the world of ideas.

The initial reaction to the new knowledge had been a fear and suspicion so strongly felt that the teaching of Aristotle was forbidden at Paris, but this impossible position was soon reversed, for the new knowledge was irresistible. Its study became a major component of the intellectual fare of the universities. One major positive reaction took the form of a whole-hearted acceptance of Aristotelian rationalism. A group called the Averroists (after a famous Muslim philosopher and scientist; see Chapter 15) stoutly maintained this position throughout much of the thirteenth century, arguing that reason was capable of defining an order of truth that had its own validity irrespective of the tenets of the faith. At the opposite pole was a school of thought that rejected the main elements of Aristotelianism and built a philosophical system that strongly reasserted the Platonic tradition and Augustinianism. The most notable figure in this tradition was a Franciscan, Bonaventura (1221–1274), a teacher at Paris and eventually head of the Franciscan Order. Bonaventura argued that reason could not discover the ultimate truth, which must come to man by a mystical illumination. The natural world which the senses and reason comprehend are but symbols of the reality of the divine order; that reality can only be grasped by an inflow of wisdom that comes from God and not from man.

But the response to the new knowledge and Aristotelianism that was most representative was formulated by a succession of scholars who tried to reconcile reason and revelation. By far the most influential advocate of this approach was Thomas Aquinas (1225–1274), an Italian Dominican who spent most of his life studying and teaching at the university in Paris. Thomas produced a huge body of theological writing during his life, which in one modern edition fills thirty-four large volumes.

His chief work was the *Summa Theologiae*, which is probably the best product of medieval thought. In this and all his works Thomas begins with the assumption that God created the universe in such a way that all its parts fit together and have a single purpose. Every man has the duty to know God and his works. There are two paths to a knowledge of the truth: revelation and reason. The task of the human mind is to seek the truth by applying itself to those things that are the proper subjects for reason while accepting on faith those things that can be learned only by revelation. Thomas accepted on faith the creation, the Trinity, and the Incarnation. However, he applied reason to other problems such as the existence of God, immortality, the operation of the natural world, the nature of government, and ethics. He saw no conflict between revelation and reason, since there is but one truth. If there is a conflict, then it results from faulty reasoning.

Aquinas relied heavily on Aristotle as his authority on subjects proper to human reason, although he always implied that the human mind could learn the truth by observation of the natural world. In his quest to square Aristotle's ideas and his own observations with revealed truth, Thomas' chief tool was logic. Following the rules of thinking formulated by Aristotle, he proceeded step by step through the whole realm of human knowledge and measured item after item against the revealed truth. His method consisted of a rigorously applied series of steps: formulation of a truth, statement of all possible contrary positions, demonstration of the fallacies in these contrary positions, demonstration of the logical validity of the true position. Each single truth in Thomas' system is part of an interlocking structure of thought which relates all things to a perfect truth. The final result of Aquinas' work is a synthesis of all knowledge into one vast structure glorifying God and demonstrating his power. For Aquinas and those who subscribed to his conclusions, the human mind had found its fundamental task; namely, to glorify God by relating all knowledge from whatever source to his divine plan of things.

The Thomistic synthesis perhaps best represents the overall spirit of medieval thought. Moved by a strong belief that all knowledge is one because it stems from God, medieval scholars devoted their energies to the organization of knowledge into a single consistent structure. Not new knowledge, but the organization of existing knowledge was their constant objective. Out of this effort there emerged a bent toward closely reasoned, highly organized thought that was destined to play a major role in the future of thought in Western Europe. During the Middle Ages, however, there was an important limitation on the way rationalism operated: Reason was always controlled, disciplined, and channeled by a conviction that there was a higher, more sacred truth—that which God had revealed to man. Therefore, human reason was not free to wander and seek where it would; it had always to test its findings against the teachings of Christianity.

4. THE WORLD OF LEARNING: SCIENCE, LAW, AND POLITICAL THEORY

Although theology and philosophy were the major preoccupations, medieval thinkers did concern themselves with the natural world, law, and political theory. Since most scholastics conceived theology and philosophy as all-embracing "sciences," their reflections on natural science, law, and politics were often incorporated into their theological works and tied in with religious issues.

The scientific work of medieval scholars seems pale by the standards of our age, and indeed their accomplishments were limited, in large part by the sources from which their knowledge was derived. Their knowledge of the natural world consisted of a considerable but confused body of information derived from Scripture, mythology, popular concepts, and the scientific works of the Greeks and the Muslims. All this information, mixed together uncritically, had given rise to many errors about the natural world and its operation. Even in the thirteenth century, when European thinkers had at their disposal the excellent scientific works of the great Greek and Arab authorities, they made little effort to correct current errors or to advance science. This lack of interest in discovering new scientific knowledge was largely due to the preoccupation of the scholastics with the task of relating all knowledge to revealed truth. Those with any interest in science usually spent their time trying to work that information into the vast summaries of thought that were the chief product of scholasticism.

Occasionally, however, the medieval intellectual world did produce men with a true scientific spirit. An especially important group, most of them Franciscans, centered at Oxford in the thirteenth century; Robert Grosseteste (1168–1253) and his pupil, Roger Bacon (ca. 1214–1294), were its most distinguished members. These men insisted on the necessity of conducting experiments to ascertain the truth about the natural world. Bacon argued that most scholastics put too much trust in ancient authorities and consequently perpetuated errors that a little observation and experimentation would correct. Bacon himself engaged in experimentation, especially in optics. Although his work was far from outstanding, he and his fellow scientists prepared the intellectual ground for the later revolutionary explosion of scientific knowledge.

Actually, during the Middle Ages there was a steady increase in practical knowledge relating to medicine, mechanics, and plant and animal life, but this information was merely accumulated without thought for scientific method as it is conceived today. Typical of this kind of knowledge was that acquired by medieval alchemists. While seeking to change base metals into gold by a variety of magical practices, they managed to learn a great deal about the nature of metals and the way to handle them. These data were regarded as "incidental," and no one thought to change the direction of his work from seeking the formula for gold to looking at what might be done with some of the discoveries that had been made in pursuit of this goal.

The study of law was pursued avidly during the twelfth and thirteenth centuries, especially at the University of Bologna. We have previously noted the work of the canon lawyers, who labored to collect, codify, and explain the diverse and complex body of legal enactments that had developed over many centuries. The crucial figure in canon law was Gratian, who in his *Decretum* not only created a model collection of canon laws, but also demonstrated a logical method for eliminating contradictions and inconsistencies. The chief concern of civil lawyers was the Code of Justinian, which in the eleventh century began to be studied after a long period of neglect in the West and which continued to be of prime interest thereafter. The civil lawyers spent most of their time writing commentaries (called *glosses*) on the Code to try to elucidate its intention and relate its principles to existing society. The work of these lawyers had a great impact on the conduct of the rising monarchies of the age and on the kind of law they administered in their realms.

The High Middle Ages produced a rich harvest of political theory. Political theorists were spurred on by a variety of influences: the Christian concept of the nature of the state and society (especially as articulated by Augustine), the conflict between church and state, the need to justify the powers and actions of the new monarchies, the revival of Roman law, the recovery of classical Greek and Roman works on political theory (notably Aristotle). Overriding their efforts to cope with the issues raised by these diverse forces was a conviction that political and social theories must correspond to what was accepted as God's plan for the universe. In the eleventh and twelfth centuries political thought tended to reassert the Augustinian idea that the state was a divinely ordained organism established to curb man's sinful nature, the ruler being God's agent for the correction of men and the curbing of their evil nature.

Under the impact of classical ideas, this concept gradually changed.

Perhaps Thomas Aquinas represents the typical thirteenth-century view of the nature of political life. He argued that the state was a manifestation of natural law, instituted to fulfill man's nature. The state is therefore necessary, good, and constructive. To function properly, the state must be made up of classes, each with a specific function. Peasants and artisans must work, nobles must rule, and priests must pray and administer the sacraments. Those who refuse to do their duty are guilty of defying God's will. Those who perform their duty are entitled to a fair share of the things of this world. The function of the state and the ruler is to see to it that each does his duty and that each gets his reward; this is justice. A tyrannical king, a merchant who charges unfair prices, a banker who charges interest, and a lazy or rebellious peasant are all guilty of injustice in that they are depriving someone in the community of his due. To the ruler falls the God-given responsibility of seeing that justice is done. Aquinas placed upon the ruler the heavy responsibility of discovering the principles of natural law that God has ordained to regulate human society. No prince is free to do as he pleases; if he acts despotically, he is unfit to rule and may be deposed.

5. LITERATURE

The world of learning, inhabited by teachers and students, theologians and philosophers, lawyers and scientists, produced, of course, a vast body of writing reflecting the values that prevailed at one level of medieval cultural life. There was, however, another kind of writing produced in great quantity to instruct and entertain a much broader audience. This literature was one of the most brilliant products of the cultural revival of the High Middle Ages. Its variety and richness are still a source of pleasure for the modern reader.

A huge body of literature was produced in Latin, most of it by clergymen who learned

Latin as a part of the preparation for the clerical profession. Although classical Latin influences in style and language were strong, there were still fresh and innovative aspects of medieval Latin literature. The vocabulary of the language was constantly infused with new words and meanings, and inherited literary forms were modified considerably. Probably the best Latin literature of the High Middle Ages took the form of lyric poetry written to express personal feelings about religious themes; often these poems were composed to serve the religious liturgy, especially as hymns. The most moving Latin poetry employed a new verse technique based on rhyme and accent rather than the classical technique of using long and short vowels to create the pattern. The new technique gave a freshness and vigor that facilitated the expression of deep emotions. The new style also lent itself well to nonreligious themes. For example, a large number of student songs, called collectively Goliardic poetry, were written in Latin to celebrate the glories of taverns, drinking, sensual love, gambling, and a variety of other worldly subjects to which at least medieval students had an attachment. From 1000 to 1300 there was also a great outpouring of historical literature and biography written in Latin, some of it marked by keen observation of contemporary events, good organization, and excellent style.

Despite the vast quantity of works in Latin, it is vernacular literature, written in the many tongues that Europeans spoke in their daily lives, that represents the best of the High Middle Ages, for here we can see the literary genius of Western Europeans coming to maturity. And it is also in this literature that we find better expressed some of the unique views of life that welled up in the resurgent medieval world.

Most vernacular literature was produced to reflect the values of and to entertain the feudal nobility. One of the earliest forms of such literature was the epic, or *chanson de geste*, so-called because it was a song recounting the deeds of great warriors. The plot of a medieval epic was usually based on an oral tradition rooted in a historical event; to this core a succession of poet-minstrels added materials to create literary pieces that reflected the ideals of the society they entertained. The epic tradition in the Middle Ages is difficult to categorize simply. The great Anglo-Saxon epic, *Beowulf,* is largely rooted in pre-Christian Germanic society. So too are the Scandinavian sagas, the *Poetic Edda* and the *Prose Edda of Snorri Sturlson,* not written down until the twelfth and thirteenth centuries, but reflecting a much earlier society of violence, paganism, and simple organization. The chief Germanic epic, the *Nibelungenlied,* composed about 1200, likewise reflects a tradition dating back to the time of the Germanic invasions. The most representative *chansons de geste* were produced in France, the best known being the *Song of Roland,* written about 1100 by an unknown author of great poetic talent. The subject of the poem is Charlemagne's expedition to Spain in 778 to attack the Muslims, an expedition that ended in the defeat of the Frankish forces at Roncesvalles. However, the author of the *Song of Roland* adorned that event with the ideals and customs of eleventh-century feudal Europe. The hero, a rash, violent man named Roland, becomes a model knight, reflecting the love of battle, the loyalty of vassals, the hatred of Muslims, the physical prowess, the simple religious views that surrounded the feudal nobility. He is an idealized type created by a writer for others to enjoy and to imitate. So too is the Cid, the famous Spanish knight whose deeds fighting the Muslims were recorded in the *Song of the Cid,* the Spanish counterpart of the *Song of Roland.* The world portrayed in the *chansons de geste* is a crude, rough one, filled with proud, arrogant men who know little except fighting and glory in it. The anonymous authors of the epics capture that milieu with great vividness and drama; their works, written in languages which as yet had produced no literature, compare well with the great epics of all ages.

The epic form as a written genre was soon

rivaled by a new vernacular literary form, the lyric, which during the twelfth and thirteenth centuries enjoyed a tremendous vogue in the aristocratic world. The new poetry developed first in Provence in southern France, from where it spread over most of Europe. Its creators, called *troubadors*, were for the most part men of aristocratic origin who found their inspiration in love for a noble lady rather than in the action-filled, bloody world of the *chansons de geste*. Literary historians have long searched for the sources of this new poetry; some have argued that it was an adaptation of classical love poetry, that it derived from Muslim models, and that it marked the emergence of women as patrons of the art in an increasingly leisured feudal society. Whatever its origins, troubador poetry reflected a whole new set of values in the feudal world. The troubador found in love for a beautiful woman, usually married to someone else, the force that transformed his very existence. His poetry, based on his personal emotions—longing for love, suffering from a lack of it, seeking for a sign of recognition from the object of his passion, anticipating the consummation of his love—became an instrument for self-understanding, feeling, and refinement. The rules of "the gay science," as the art of love was called, demanded a mode of conduct from the lover that would be pleasing to the ladies, one emphasizing gentility,

good manners, and refinement rather than battlefield prowess. As the lyric style spread (lyric poets in northern France were called *trouvères* and in Germany *minnesänger*), its forms tended to become highly stylized, the concept of love more ethereal and elevated, and its impact less direct. However, the lyric poetry written in the new style (some four hundred such poets have been identified for the twelfth and thirteenth centuries) left an indelible mark on both the feudal world and Western European literary history. These poets had developed a vehicle for self-identification, for permitting man to look at himself and to report what he saw. Idealized woman as the object of contemplation which revealed man to himself long remained the lyricist's main theme. A new set of values and emotions, quite unknown to the classical world and absolutely anathema to the early Christian view, had been charted in the intense, passionate poetry of the Provençal troubadors and their successors.

Before the end of the twelfth century, the epic and lyric traditions had merged to produce a third type of vernacular literature, the *romance*. Romances were stories combining love with high adventure, written to entertain nobles. The love theme was treated in an exaggerated manner. The adventure element centered around three broad themes: the deeds of Charlemagne, the adventures of King Arthur and his knights, and the actions of Greek and Roman heroes. These basic plots were used with complete disregard for historical accuracy. A reader might find Alexander the Great fighting the Seljuk Turks, attending mass, and engaging in a tournament. Such flights of imagination did not trouble the romance writers, since their aim was to create an idealized and entertaining picture of refined

A woodcut from the title page of the first edition of the Decameron. Boccaccio represents another strain in medieval literature: He wrote in the vernacular, and his themes were secular rather than spiritual. *Photo: NYPL Picture Collection*

feudal society. Many of the romances were run-of-the-mill productions, comparable to the bulk of modern novels and movies. A few writers, however, managed to fashion romances with enduring appeal. Among them was Chrétien de Troyes, a twelfth-century French author whose treatment of the Arthurian material established a powerful picture of the ideal knight. Perhaps even more profound and exalted were the romances of two thirteenth-century Germans, Gottfried von Strasbourg and Wolfram von Eschenbach. Gottfried's *Tristan* is a masterful revelation of the meaning of love in the lives of two who were its prisoners, while Wolfram's *Parzival* represents an appealing picture of a man in pursuit of the object of his desire, symbolized by the Holy Grail.

While the epics, lyrics, and romances were being written, sung, and read by nobles, the middle class produced a literature suited to its tastes and situation. Especially popular in the towns were dramas and *fabliaux*. Medieval drama had its origin as a part of church liturgy. Attempts were made to dramatize certain parts of the services, and eventually the presentation of these plays was moved outside the church into the marketplace. By the thirteenth century the guilds had taken over the responsibility for producing these dramas on the occasion of religious festivals. Several types of plays were popular: mystery plays, enacting scenes from the Bible; miracle plays, treating the highlights of saints' lives; morality plays, teaching a lesson by personifying human virtues and vices. Often the stories dramatized in medieval plays were already familiar to the audience, whose chief interest was in seeing how well the actors could portray their parts as God or Noah or the devil.

The *fabliaux* were short tales recited in public squares for the entertainment of the crowds. The subject matter could be almost anything. Whatever the subject, the *fabliaux* were always close to city life, faithfully representing everyday events in the lives of ordinary people. They were often filled with vulgar humor and satire directed especially at priests and women. The most famous collection of such literature was the *Romance of Reynard the Fox*, made up of many stories in which animals symbolize people and human characteristics.

Of the many writers during the High Middle Ages one genius, Dante Alighieri (1265–1321), towers above all others. He was to the literary world what Thomas Aquinas was to theology. Dante was a product of Florence, actively engaging in political life in that city and eventually suffering exile. It was while in exile that he wrote the *Divine Comedy*, one of the great masterpieces of world literature.

Outwardly the *Divine Comedy* is Dante's account of his journey through hell, purgatory, and heaven. Guided through the first two by Vergil, and through heaven by Beatrice, Dante is permitted to see all things from the depths of hell to God Himself. The poem, however, is much more than a well-written adventure story. Dante is a philosopher, presenting with consummate skill the medieval idea that all things in the universe are ordered under God and according to his will. He is a mystic, yearning to the depths of his soul to catch a glimpse of God. He is a love poet, expressing his sentiments as skillfully as any troubador. (Beatrice, his guide in heaven, is a symbol of human love, which purifies and uplifts man.) Dante is a scientist, weaving into his poem many medieval ideas about the structure of the physical universe. He is a lover of Greek and Roman classics, praising the men of the ancient world who produced them, although he has to condemn them to hell as non-Christians. He is a keen political observer, full of fierce partisanship. His hell is crowded with men guilty of what Dante believes to have been political crimes. During the course of his long journey from the gates of hell to its very pit, where Lucifer chews three great traitors, Brutus, Cassius, and Judas, Dante discusses with Vergil nearly every kind of sin, showing a deep understanding of human nature and its weaknesses. Few artists have grasped human life and human aspirations more fully or written of them with greater artistry. This greatest medieval writer weaves into one masterful poem all the many threads that run through medieval literature.

6. THE ARTS

Medieval artists created monuments to the medieval spirit no less marvelous than did scholars like Thomas Aquinas or writers like Dante. The High Middle Ages marked one of the decisive epochs in the history of art. Two major art styles, Romanesque and Gothic, were perfected between 1000 and 1300. A great spurt in building activity adorned almost every town and village with an impressive array of new structures. Most of these were churches, for the Church was the prime agency inspiring and promoting artistic endeavor in this era. Architecture was queen; the other arts were used and developed to adorn the structures that architects fashioned. Consequently, the churches that have survived from the High Middle Ages are complete museums, filled with sculpture, paintings, wood carving, glasswork, metalwork, and decorative handwriting. The artists who built and adorned the structures and the people of all ranks who gave of their wealth to pay for them built to honor God, to express their understanding of him, and to provide a place to worship him. It is difficult for modern men to comprehend the outpouring of talent and wealth for these ends, but this was an age when religion was a major force in men's lives.

The Romanesque and Gothic styles that bloomed in the High Middle Ages were the fruits of a long artistic evolution. The basic architectural form from which medieval church architecture developed was the Roman basilica, which was simply a rectangular meeting hall with a semicircular *apse* at the rear to provide a place for the conduct of meetings. The early Christians placed their altars in the apse and conducted there the liturgical services centering in the eucharistic feast. The rest of the hall, called the *nave*,

provided seating for the faithful. Aisles were often added along either side of the nave and around the apse. A lateral aisle, called the *transept*, was sometimes built crossing the nave just in front of the apse, so that the early church took the form of a cross. The walls of the nave were built higher than those of the side aisles, permitting windows to be cut high in the nave walls to create a *clerestory* which admitted light. During the Early Middle Ages a variety of architectural features were added to this basic structure; often these additions were imported, especially from Byzantium. The early Christian basilicas were decorated with paintings and carvings that attempted to portray the basic elements of the Christian story and convey the spiritual concepts embraced by the Christian message. Again, classical influences were strong in shaping religious art, but over the centuries, the classic mold of church art was considerably modified by influences from the Byzantine, Germanic, and Celtic worlds and by new creative forces emerging from daily life. Thus the art styles of the West tended to be eclectic as they evolved. During the High Middle Ages artists finally succeeded in blending these many forms into distinctive new styles.

The Romanesque style in architecture first appeared in the late tenth and early eleventh centuries and flourished through most of the twelfth century. Its main features are admirably illustrated by several churches still standing: Notre Dame la Grande in Poitiers, the cathedral of Saint-Sernin in Toulouse, the cathedral at Worms, the abbey church of Maria Laach in Germany, the two abbey churches at Caen in France, and the church of Sant'Ambrogio at Milan in northern Italy. The Romanesque style was characterized both by technical innovations and by a new spirit. The monastic world, especially the Cluniac reformers, played a dominant role in developing and spreading this style, for with their emphasis on elaborate rituals involving large numbers of monks and because of their concern with the veneration of relics and pilgrimages, the Cluniacs needed churches large enough to house a number of chapels and accommodate great crowds. Architects had also long been concerned with replacing the traditional wooden roofs, which so often were destroyed by fire. The solution was a church built entirely of stone.

The distinctive technical feature of the Romanesque style was the construction of immense buildings with stone roofs. This was achieved by the use of round arches to create the support for the roof structure. Barrel vaults were thrown over the full length of the nave and of the side aisles. Cross vaults were evolved to cover the area where the nave and transept crossed. Since the stone roof exerted a tremendous downward and outward thrust, Romanesque churches had heavy walls and a minimum number of windows. Wherever the walls were pierced to create passageways, massive piers had to be constructed; and these piers had to be spanned by equally massive arches to bear the weight from above. The typical Romanesque church tended to be dark, filled with an atmosphere of gloom and mystery which was not dispelled by the decorative paintings on piers, arches, and walls. This atmosphere was not, however, totally a product of the technical aspects of Romanesque; it was a reflection of a religious mentality that viewed the church as God's citadel standing in a world filled with evil forces. The Romanesque church was a sacred fortress into which the faithful could retreat from the howling demons and the frightful forces of nature, a refuge where men could confront in a solemn atmosphere the mighty God who protected them from the mysterious forces of the universe. The Romanesque style reflects the simple faith of men living in the confusions of the feudal world and comprehending their re-

ligion in a mystical, irrational, emotional context.

By mid-twelfth century the European world was changing rapidly under the impact of the economic, political, social, cultural, and spiritual forces we have already discussed. The new environment produced a new architectural style, the Gothic. This style appeared first in the Ile de France, the domain of the

This thirteenth-century Romanesque painted tabernacle panel in the Church of Santa Maria Nuova, Viterbo, shows the characteristics of the style— the stylized figure, the flat planes with no attempt at three-dimensional illusion, the use of folds of drapery as a decorative element. *Photo: André Held*

Capetians; the first full-scale Gothic church was the Abbey Church of St. Denis near Paris, rebuilt 1137–1144 by Abbot Suger, the adviser to kings Louis VI and Louis VII. Gothic architecture was preeminently the product of the new towns, which were the foci of new wealth, new ideas, and new spiritual currents. The bishops of these towns organized the building of Gothic churches as their cathedrals, and the townsmen joined enthusiastically to support the effort, often engaging in an almost unholy rivalry to outdo neighboring towns in the size and beauty of their cathedral. From the Ile de France the Gothic style spread over much of Europe; only Italy was little affected, for there by the thirteenth century a classical revival was creating a Renaissance architecture.

The Gothic style evolved out of a desire for height and light in churches, a desire derived largely from new intellectual and spiritual concepts that fostered a more rational view of God and saw his chief attributes in terms of reason, light, number, and proportion. Those familiar with twelfth-century theology, philosophy, and science can easily point to numerous ways in which these concepts were coming to dominate thought. The Gothic church was an attempt to make visual these new modes of thought, to create a soaring structure that would leave behind the mystery-shrouded, awesome world of the Romanesque in order to move into the light and purity of paradise—the paradise Dante pictured in poetry. Among the Gothic structures that achieve this effect magnificently are Notre Dame at Paris and the cathedrals at Chartres, Rheims, Amiens, Strassburg, and Bourges in France; at Lincoln, York, and Salisbury in England; and at Cologne in Germany.

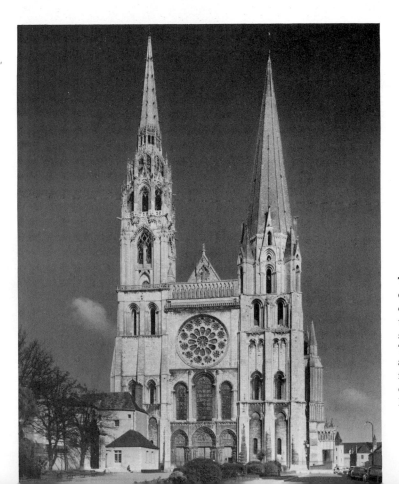

The west façade of Chartres, one of the most glorious of the Gothic cathedrals. Structure and decoration are harmonized to give a soaring, upward-striving effect. The great stained glass windows and the delicate stone tracery still further distinguish the Gothic church from the massive, gloomy Romanesque. *Photo: A. F. Kersting*

A detail from the tympanum of the Cathedral of Saint-Lazare at Autun, carved by
Giselbertus before 1135. Here again, as in the painting shown earlier, are the flat, stylized,
clearly defined figures of the Romanesque style. Christ in Majesty at the Last Judgment was
a subject often chosen for the sculpture above the main portal of most churches built in
the Middle Ages. *Photo: Pierre Belzeaux–Rapho Guillumette*

Technically, this transformation was made possible by the use of the pointed arch and the ribbed vault. The pointed arch had the effect of carrying thrust downward, and the ribbed vault allowed the architect to concentrate the thrust at a few points. Architects were able to combine them to fashion tremendously tall skeletons of stone in which the weight flowed to earth through a series of slender pillars. The outward thrust, greatly reduced and concentrated at a few points by the pointed arches and ribbed vaults, could be offset by thickening the columns at the outside of the building or by building flying but-

tresses, pillars set away from the main structure and joined to it by bracing arches high above the ground. Once the skeletons were constructed, thin walls, supporting nothing but their own weight, could be filled in between the pillars. More important, light could be let into the structure by great windows placed between the members of the structural skeleton. Nothing is more characteristic of the Gothic style than the many arched windows, often interlaced with delicate decorative stonework, which pierce the lofty clerestory and the side aisles, and the majestic round windows at the ends of the

These Gothic figures from the south portal of Chartres illustrate vividly the ability of medieval artists to treat the human figure with a degree of realism while retaining the dignity and solemnity appropriate to a religious subject. *Photo: Jean Roubier*

nave and transept. The windows were often filled with great expanses of many-hued stained glass depicting figures or scenes that suffused the interior with a breathtaking display of colored light. The Gothic church is a structure of light and ordered intelligence, within which an ethereal atmosphere inspires the worshiper to a contemplation of the divine intelligence that is the source of the light that engulfs him.

Nearly every other visual art was put to work to decorate medieval churches. The exterior of a Romanesque church was generally plain except for the facade, where the great doorways leading to the nave and side aisles provided a setting for sculpture. As illustrated by the facades of the church of Saint-Trophime at Arles and the church at Vézelay, these spaces were filled with massive, highly symbolical sculpture portraying human figures, animals, and abstract decorative patterns. The object of this sculpture was to teach something about God, and a favorite subject was the Last Judgment, in which a stern Christ relegated men to heaven or hell. Within a Romanesque church there was more sculpture, chiefly decoration for the massive piers. The large, flat wall spaces were decorated with frescoes portraying scriptural scenes, particularly those that stressed the suffering of Christ and his judgment on men. The style of Romanesque sculpture and painting is a somber one that makes man small, powerless, and dependent; it grips his emotions rather than his mind.

The development of the Gothic style of architecture brought about changes in the other arts. The exteriors of Gothic churches provided innumerable places for decorative sculpture, giving stone carvers an opportunity to experiment with a fantastic array of decorative motifs; one of the main directions of Gothic art was toward greater elaboration in external decoration. Gothic facades continued to be filled with sculptured scenes, but now the emphasis had changed: sculpture tended to be more realistic and humanistic. Its whole spirit was centered more on the human qualities of Jesus, the Virgin, the apostles, and the saints—a reflection of the new spiritual trends. The themes and their treatment blend with the search for light and order and reason reflected in the architectural style. The carvings that adorn the cathedrals at Chartres and Amiens provide especially good examples of the major themes, their mode of treatment, and the technical aspects of Gothic sculpture.

The interior of Gothic churches offered less space for painting and sculpture than did Romanesque churches; what decoration there was was devoted chiefly to the adornment of columns and arches. Not images, but light fills the Gothic church. The painted walls of the Romanesque church were replaced with stained glass windows. These windows are marvelous pieces of workmanship in terms of design and use of color. Most of them were devoted to the portrayal of scriptural scenes, often shown in a way that provides us with a view of the daily activities of medieval men. The stained glass at Chartres and in the beautiful Sainte-Chapelle built by King Louis IX in Paris still enthrall those who view their intricate designs and the light that pours through them. However, the sculptors, painters, and glass workers were never primarily concerned with presenting a picture of man's life on earth. They sought to teach a religious message, to bring man to the presence of God by placing before him a vision of God's creatures engaged in doing his bidding.

Another art associated with religious activity, music, also developed significantly during the High Middle Ages. Church music consisted primarily of melodies to which were sung verses taken from Scripture (especially the psalms) or composed for liturgical events (such great hymns as *Dies Irae* and *Stabat Mater* came from the Middle Ages). A mode of singing these verses, known as *Gregorian chant* (after its alleged inventor, Pope Gregory I) or *plain song*, developed as early as the sixth century. At first, the singing was done in unison, but over the centuries the variations worked on plain song developed into contrapuntal music. The variations required a different scheme of written indications for the music, so that by the eleventh century, the musical notation system still in use today had been developed. An adequate notational system allowed two or three or even more groups of voices to sing either simultaneously or alternately different melodies which were organized so as to harmonize. By the thirteenth century, amazingly complex and moving contrapuntal compositions, rendered by many voices and various instruments, filled the churches with sounds almost as heavenly as

the light that poured through the stained glass windows.

The great cathedrals commanded the best artistic talent and the bulk of the wealth that medieval society had to devote to art. However, there were other lines of artistic pursuit, most of which imitated styles and techniques borrowed from church building. Feudal castles, whose characteristic feature was massiveness rather than elegance or comfort, were built in many places. The Romanesque style was especially suited for such buildings. In the towns, especially from the thirteenth century onward, beautiful town halls and guildhalls were constructed, putting Gothic principles to new uses. None ever rivaled churches in size and beauty, but some of them were impressive signs that the Church never completely absorbed artistic energies.

7. THE UNDERLYING SPIRIT OF MEDIEVAL CULTURE—A SUMMARY

Our attention has ranged far and wide in the preceding pages. Perhaps we ought to conclude by searching for something to tie together the many cultural trends that reached their culmination in the thirteenth century. Certainly it is not easy to find a common denominator for Thomas Aquinas, Dante, the architects and sculptors who built the churches at Poitiers, Amiens, and Chartres, the troubadors, the romance writers, and the authors of *fabliaux*. The cultural life of the High Middle Ages was marked by diversity and variety. One need not search far in medieval cultural life to find signs of nearly every attitude or idea present even in modern society, a fact that increasingly has led scholars to insist that modern Western European culture was born in the eleventh, twelfth, and thirteenth centuries.

However, medieval culture has its own distinctive flavor. Most medieval art and thought are permeated by a quest for truth and light outside and beyond the world in which men live. This ever-present reaching out of the mind and the imagination sprang from the almost universally accepted belief that God controlled the universe and that it was man's duty to know and worship him. The artist and the writer stood in awe of God and used their talents humbly to see, know, and serve him. Medieval culture viewed as a whole, therefore, has an atmosphere of otherworldliness and of surrender to a power beyond human understanding.

Yet, intertwined with this aspiration toward the infinite and with the humble submission to the divine, there is a warm, sympathetic feeling for humankind. Medieval men believed that man was God's finest creation. Artists and writers were never disdainful of human powers and potentialities. They took joy in presenting man as he was and wrestled constantly with the problem of understanding human nature more fully.

The medieval genius shines most brilliantly when it attempts to synthesize these two outlooks. These men never felt that otherworldliness and secularism, spirituality and humanism were exclusive terms. Medieval culture was most clearly distinguished by its attempts to make human knowledge and emotion at one with God. Thinkers and artists respected their own powers enough to believe that they could reach out toward God—by building cathedrals higher or by putting together greater *summae* of knowledge or by flights of poetic fancy. Yet they were men of great enough faith to believe that their quest would lead them to a power infinitely greater than themselves.

Suggested Reading

General. There is an immense body of excellent literature available on medieval culture from which only a few items can be selected here. Perhaps the best way to understand that culture is to read the works of medieval authors themselves; therefore we shall emphasize these works in this list. For a general survey of medieval culture, the best work is still H. O. Taylor, *The Medieval Mind* (2 vols., 4th ed., 1949), written by a nonspecialist with imagination and great sympathy. Another fine work of synthesis, especially good for its bibliographies, is F. B. Artz, *The Mind of the Middle Ages: A.D. 200–1500: An Historical Survey* (3rd ed., 1958). **C. H. Haskins, *The Renaissance of the Twelfth Century* (Meridian), is a classic treatment of the revival of intellectual life in the eleventh and twelfth centuries. This pioneering work can be supplemented by two more recent ones: **Christopher Brooke, *The Twelfth-century Renaissance* (Harcourt, Brace & World); and C. W. Hollister, ed., *The Twelfth-century Renaissance* (Wiley). Three excellent anthologies will provide a sampling of medieval literature:

**J. B. Ross and M. M. McLaughlin, eds., *The Portable Medieval Reader* (Viking); C. W. Jones, *Medieval Literature in Translation* (1950); and Ruth Brantl, *Medieval Culture: The Image and the City* (1966).

Education. The best introduction to the medieval university is **C. H. Haskins, *The Rise of the Universities* (Cornell). More recent are L. J. Daly, *The Medieval University, 1200–1400* (1961); and **Gordon Leff, *Paris and Oxford Universities in the Thirteenth and Fourteenth Centuries* (Wiley). **H. Wieruszowski, *The Medieval University: Masters, Students, Learning* (Anvil), provides a brief description illustrated by a well-selected body of source materials. A delightful and informative picture of university life from the point of view of contemporaries can be found in *University Records and Life in the Middle Ages*, trans. Lynn Thorndike (1944).

Theology and Philosophy. The best brief survey of medieval theological and philosophical development is **D. Knowles, *The Evolution of Medieval Thought* (Vintage); this work perhaps stresses too much the continuity between medieval thought and classical philosophy. Two other brief surveys that are comprehensible to the nonspecialist are **Gordon Leff, *Medieval Thought From St. Augustine to Ockham* (Penguin); and **Paul Vignaux, *Philosophy in the Middle Ages* (Meridian). Larger and more complex but fundamental is Etienne Gilson, *History of Christian Philosophy in the Middle Ages* (1955); Gilson is the greatest modern authority on the subject. Also excellent is **F. Copleston, *History of Philosophy*, Vol. II: *Mediaeval Philosophy*, parts 1 and 2 (Image). **Maurice De-Wulf, *Philosophy and Civilization in the Middle Ages* (Dover), attempts to interrelate thought and society. For anyone interested in a fuller study of the key figure in medieval philosophy, see Etienne Gilson, *The Philosophy of St. Thomas Aquinas*, trans. E. Bullought (2nd ed. rev., 1937); and **F. Copleston, *Aquinas* (Penguin). Also to be recommended are Etienne Gilson, *The Philosophy of St. Bonaventure*, trans. I. Trethowan and F. Sheed (1965); and **E. Bettoni, *Saint Bonaventura*, trans. A. Gambatese (University of Notre Dame). A good representative collection of medieval philosophical writings is **Richard McKeon, ed., *Selections From Medieval Philosophers* (2 vols., Scribners). Another useful anthology is **Anne Fremantle, ed., *Age of Belief: The Medieval Philosophers* (Mentor). A. C. Pegis, ed., *Introduction to Saint Thomas Aquinas* (Modern Library), will provide a sample of the style and content of the scholastics. An insight into the character of the meteoric Abelard can be gained from *The Letters of Abelard and Heloise*, trans. C. K. Scott-Moncrieff (1926).

Science, Law, Political Theory. The best survey of medieval science is **A. C. Crombie, *Medieval and Early Modern Science* (2 vols., 2nd ed. rev., Anchor). R. C. Mortimer, *Western Canon Law* (1953), is the best introduction to an important subject. The work of the civil lawyers is well summarized in P. Vinogradoff, *Roman Law in Medieval Europe* (2nd ed., 1929). An excellent survey of medicval political theory is C. H. McIlwain, *The Growth of Political Thought in the West* (1932). More

recent and excellent are **John B. Morrall, *Political Thought in Medieval Times* (Harper Torchbook), and **Walter Ullmann, *A History of Political Thought: The Middle Ages* (Penguin). A provocative effort to place medieval political theory in a larger context is A. P. d'Entrèves, *The Medieval Contribution to Political Thought* (1939). A fine collection of medieval writings on political theory is Ewart Lewis, *Medieval Political Ideas* (2 vols., 1954). The essence of Thomas Aquinas' political ideas is presented in *Aquinas: Selected Political Writings*, trans. A. P. d'Entrèves (1948).

Literature. The best introduction to this vast subject is W. T. Jackson, *The Literature of the Middle Ages* (1960), which contains a good guide to other literature. Professor Jackson has also prepared a more compact guide entitled **Medieval Literature: A History and a Guide* (Collier). Two other valuable surveys emphasizing Latin literature are **E. R. Curtius, *European Literature and the Latin Middle Ages* (Harper Torchbook); and M. Helin, *A History of Medieval Latin Literature* (1949). There are excellent histories of the literature written in each vernacular tongue; a guide to them can be found in Jackson's works. H. J. Chaytor, *The Troubadors* (1912), will introduce lyric poetry. **W. P. Ker, *Epic and Romance* (Dover), is an excellent interpretation. A sensitive, provocative study of the significance of the literature of courtly love is **C. S. Lewis, *The Allegory of Love: A Study in Medieval Tradition* (Galaxy). A fresh interpretation of the origins of medieval drama is **O. B. Hardison, Jr., *Christian Rite and Christian Drama in the Middle Ages: Essays in the Origin and Early History of Modern Drama* (Johns Hopkins). For the genius of Dante, one might turn to **P. Toynbee, *Dante Alighieri: His Life and Works*, ed. C. S. Singleton (Harper Torchbook); and **T. G. Bergin, *Dante* (Houghton Mifflin).

For those interested in representative works of medieval literature, the following are suggested. For the epic tradition: **Beowulf*, trans. David Wright (Penguin); **Nibelungenlied*, trans. A. T. Hatto (Penguin); **Prose Edda of Snorri Sturlson: Tales From Norse Mythology*, trans. J. I. Young (University of California); and **Song of Roland*, trans. F. B. Luguiens (Collier). For the lyric tradition:

An Anthology of Medieval Lyrics, ed. Angel Flores (1962); J. A. Symonds, *Wine, Women, and Song* (1925); and **H. J. Waddell, *Medieval Latin Lyrics* (Penguin). Representative of the romance tradition: ***Medieval Romances,* ed. R. S. and L. H. Loomis (Modern Library); *Arthurian Romances by Chrétien de Troyes,* trans. W. W. Comfort (1914); ***Romance of Tristan and Iseult as Retold by Joseph Bedier,* trans. H. Belloc and P. Rosenfeld (Anchor); ***Aucassin and Nicolette and Other Medieval Romances,* ed. E. Mason (Dutton); **Wolfram von Eschenbach, *Parzival,* trans. H. M. Mustard and C. E. Passage (Vintage); **Gottfried von Strassburg, *Tristan,* trans. A. T. Hatto (Penguin); and **Guillaume de Lorris and Jean de Meun, *The Romance of the Rose,* trans. H. W. Robbins (Dutton). For the drama: ***Medieval Mysteries, Moralities and Interludes,* ed. V. F. Hopper and G. B. Lakey (Barron), and ***Everyman and Medieval Miracle Plays,* ed. A. C. Cawley (Dutton). If one can choose only one medieval author to read, it should be Dante. A recent translation of his classic, ***Divine Comedy of Dante Alighieri,* trans. J. B. Sinclair (3 vols., Galaxy), is excellent, but in the judgment of some, ***The Comedy of Dante Alighieri,* trans. D. Sayers and B. Reynolds (3 vols., Penguin), is superior.

The Arts. An excellent introduction to the history of medieval art is *Larousse Encyclopedia of Byzantine and Medieval Art,* ed. René Huyghe (1963). For a more sophisticated treatment, every student should know the great work of H. Focillon, *The Art of the West in the Middle Ages* (2 vols., 1963); the illustrations are particularly well chosen. C. R. Morey, *Medieval Art* (1942), surveys sculpture and painting. **P. Francastel, *Medieval Painting* (Dell), is excellent. A classic work that attempts to draw a contrast between the spirit of Romanesque and Gothic and succeeds in providing a provocative interpretation of both is **Henry Adams, *Mont Saint Michel and Chartres* (Anchor). A well-illustrated study of the Romanesque style can be found in François Souchal, *Art of the Early Middle Ages* (1968). K. J. Conant, *Carolingian and Romanesque Architecture, 800–1200* (1959), is a good guide to Romanesque architecture. For Romanesque painting, see either **J. Ainaud, *Romanesque Painting* (Viking), or better still, A. Grabar and C. Nordenfalk, *Romanesque Painting* (1958). A splendidly illustrated treatment of Gothic art is H. H. Hofstätter, *Art of the Late Middle Ages* (1968), but better in terms of the text are M. Aubert, *Art of the High Gothic Era* (1965), and **A. Martindale, *Gothic Art From the Twelfth to the Fifteenth Century* (Praeger). Either **Robert Branner, *Gothic Architecture* (Braziller), or **P. Frankl, *Gothic Architecture* (Penguin), will provide good introductions to the technical features of the Gothic style. **Otto von Simson, *The Gothic Cathedral* (Harper Torchbook), supplies an illuminating analysis of the origins and inspiration of the Gothic style. **Emile Mâle, *The Gothic Image: Religious Art in France in the Thirteenth Century* (Harper Torchbook), is excellent on the intellectual forces that produced the Gothic style in sculpture and painting. Jean Gimpel, *The Cathedral Builders,* trans. C. F. Barnes, Jr. (1961), introduces the reader to the techniques of medieval builders. A stimulating attempt to relate Gothic art and scholasticism is undertaken by **E. Panofsky, *Gothic Architecture and Scholasticism* (Meridian). **H. Hutter, *Medieval Stained Glass* (Crown), is a good introduction to an art unique to the Middle Ages. Gustav Reese, *Music in the Middle Ages* (1940), is an excellent study, although somewhat technical.

RETROSPECT

The events upon which attention has been focused in this section were decisive in world history, for the central development of the era from 1000 to 1300 was the rise of Western Europe. The High Middle Ages was distinguished by the remarkable expansion of the primitive society that had been so painfully and tenuously pieced together atop the ruins of classical civilization. At every level of society and in every phase of life, there was sustained, constructive activity which increased wealth, secured order, changed the social structure, expanded mental horizons, deepened understanding of human existence, and enlarged capabilities for expression. The new institutional patterns and ideas that were fashioned during this remarkable age—the youthful national states, the social structure of nobility, peasantry, and bourgeoisie, the towns, the Church, the universities, the theology and philosophy, the vernacular literature, the art styles, the commercial and agricultural practices, the laws, the technology—have all survived in their essential forms almost to the present. They are developments basic to an understanding of the later history of Western Europe.

But the era has another, equally important, dimension. While gathering strength internally, Western European society began to impinge on the outside world. The High Middle Ages was the period of the first decisive steps toward the establishment of European preeminence in the world. Those who would understand the situation today would be well served by attempting to identify the ingredients which by 1300 had given Western Europeans the capability to determine the destinies of other peoples. Perhaps never in the entire history of humanity has one civilization demonstrated greater capacity to intrude itself into the lives of other societies for so long a period of time and with such an impact: The political, social, and economic forces that move the peoples of the world today were set in motion in the Western Europe of the High Middle Ages.

In our concentration on the remarkable growth of Western European society and its outward thrust toward other civilizations, we have perhaps not given enough attention to an internal development that may well supply the key to its future history. In considering the High Middle Ages, one is constantly struck by the fact that, as Western European society matured, its institutional and ideological fabric was laced with dichotomies and contradictions. Basic to the political order was tension between strong monarchical government and the privileges and rights of feudal nobles, the Church, and townsmen. Political thought and practice was divided by the clash between the universalism represented by the Holy Roman Empire and the localism inbred in the emergent nations. Engrained in Western European civilization were the contrasting aspirations of church and state. The religious structure was riven by the thrust toward universalism represented by the papacy and the local self-determination claimed by the ancient bishoprics existing all over the West. Everywhere some men struggled to impose uniformity and conformity in religious belief and practice, while others reached out toward personal, individualistic varieties of expression. In the economic realm, commercial towns contended with agricultural villages. On the farms, the traditional forms of collective, manorial exploitation stood juxtaposed with specialized, capitalistic exploitation. In the cities, the guilds sought to impose just prices, common standards of production, and equitable division of business opportunities, while resourceful entrepreneurs tried to follow their private ends. A universal Latin culture competed with localized vernacular cultures. The revealed tenets of the faith were challenged by the dictates of human reason. The world-denying spirit of the monastic world confronted powerful secular, humanistic interests. One is almost forced to conclude that as a consequence of its historical development during the High Middle Ages, Western European civilization in a unique way was compounded of contradictory thrusts. It was like a Gothic cathedral in which height was limited by weight, light met dark, color competed with stark bareness, space was confined by structure.

Can we say perhaps that this juxtaposition of opposites that emerged from 1000 to 1300 constitutes the essence of Western European civilization? Dare we suggest that these medieval contradictions have supplied the Western world with its dynamism? Might we suspect that the history of the West after 1300 may be a story of the resolution of these contradictions: central government versus private interests, rights, and privileges; state versus church, reason versus faith; national states versus universal empire? Perhaps when the West has relieved its inner tensions by resolving these medieval issues, it will have lost its vitality.

Part Six

The Late Middle Ages

1300–1500

The historian who seeks to construct a comprehensible account of the long sweep of history sometimes encounters periods that are difficult to describe with a single neat phrase. Such is the Late Middle Ages, the era from 1300 to 1500. In the centuries since, historians have labeled this period "the dawn of a new era," "an age of transition," "the death of medieval civilization," "the age of the Renaissance," "the decline of the medieval world," "the ordeal of transition," "the autumn of the Middle Ages," "the waning of the Middle Ages." These modes of description all suggest that change was the keynote of these two centuries—but they also suggest that historians are not at all agreed on the direction and the significance of that change. Some would emphasize the new forces emerging, holding them to be worthy of greatest attention; others would stress the dissolution of old ways that had been typical of the medieval world, insisting that the temper of the age was set by the transformation of established institutional and ideological patterns.

Perhaps we should let those who lived then tell us what was fundamental. If we spend a little time reading the literature and viewing the art of these two centuries, we will be struck by the strong sense of frustration, bitterness, morbidity, and doubt gripping men's minds. Their comments on their world show they sensed that something was amiss; and with few exceptions, they seemed lacking in confidence and incapable of hope.

These frightened, desperate reactions argue that the dominant theme of the Late Middle Ages must be sought in terms of decline and disintegration rather than in terms of new forces, renaissance, and the onset of modernity. Our description will follow that lead by suggesting that the equilibrium established in the thirteenth century between the numerous dichotomous forces characteristic of Western European civilization failed to survive. Perhaps Thomas Aquinas could reconcile revelation and reason, but his successors could not sustain the balance. The architects who built the Gothic cathedral at Amiens might have found the perfect formula to balance height and weight, but their successors who tried to achieve greater height saw their cathedrals crash to earth. Magna Carta might juxtapose royal authority and baronial right, but that equilibrium could not be maintained. And so it was in most aspects of society. The fragile balance of contradictory forces that had been fashioned during the High Middle Ages failed to last. The fourteenth and fifteenth centuries mark a period when men were acutely aware of this failure; their lives were plagued by maladjustments and imbalances, and their minds were troubled.

425

Our task will be to describe the tensions and stresses that began to alter what had been forged in the High Middle Ages as the essence of civilized life in the West: empires, feudal monarchies, the tripartite class structure, the towns and guilds, the universities, the universal Church, scholasticism, the Gothic style. In this sense, the keynote of our discussion will be the decline of what was typically medieval—but not at the expense of the new forces welling up in society. They were numerous, powerful, and important, and we must return to them in future discussions. Men living during the era from 1300 to 1500 could not, however, sense their existence and promise as well as we can, gifted as we are with the clear vision of hindsight. To those men, the age was filled with the agonies that mark the passing of the known and familiar.

Chapter 25 ❦ Political, Economic, and Social Tensions

Politically, the fourteenth and fifteenth centuries were filled with disorder. Such typically medieval institutions as the Holy Roman Empire, the Byzantine Empire, the feudal monarchies of England, France, and Spain failed to cope with new political problems. Their inadequacies bred civil strife, class struggle, international war, and internal injustice everywhere in Western Europe. Behind much of this political trouble lay economic and social problems arising from the growing failure of medieval agricultural and commercial institutions.

1. THE DECLINE OF THE HOLY ROMAN EMPIRE

The most obvious case of the failure of a medieval political institution was that of the Holy Roman Empire. We have previously traced the efforts made by a succession of German rulers between 950 and 1250 to join Germany, Italy, and the western fringes of the Slavic world into a single state and observed that at least at times they succeeded in establishing the most powerful state in Europe. We have also discussed how their efforts generated powerful opposition, led by the papacy, which constantly thwarted attempts to make the Holy Roman Empire permanent. The death of the last great emperor, Frederick II, in 1250 marked the beginning of the end of the Medieval Empire: Not only did the empire as an institution disintegrate in the Late Middle Ages, but also the political ideal that had given it birth, the concept of a Christian commonwealth binding all men sharing the fatherhood of God and the brotherhood of a common faith into a single state which would provide the setting for their struggle for salvation.

In Germany, Frederick II's death opened a quarter century of civil strife, exacerbated by the incessant intervention of the papacy and of France and England. During this struggle, nobles, clergy, and townsmen successfully established their independence from central authority. In 1273 the long rivalry for the crown ended with the election of Rudolph of Hapsburg (1273–1291), whose chief recommendation was his lack of strength. Rudolph confined his efforts to increasing his family holdings in the area of modern Austria. His success in this venture caused the princes of Germany to repudiate the Hapsburgs in 1308 in favor of a prince from Luxemburg, Henry VII (1308–1313), who succeeded in establishing control over Bohemia, thereby greatly strengthening his family's position. In 1314

This contemporary miniature shows a castle under siege during the Hundred Year's War.
The French besiegers use both bow and arrow and a kind of primitive gun. *Photo: Trustees of the British Museum*

Lewis IV (1314–1347) from the house of Wittelsbach of Bavaria was elected out of fear that the house of Luxemburg was getting too strong. By the attitude they reflected in the election process, the German nobles demonstrated that they would not tolerate a strong ruler. Those who desired to gain the imperial office fully realized the situation; although they used the imperial office to improve the standing of their family and to acquire title to rich provinces, they did little to disturb the independence of other princes.

This trend was finally given legal definition. In 1347 Charles IV (1347–1378) of Luxemburg was elected ruler. His most important act was to promulgate in 1356 the famous Golden Bull, designed to establish a constitution for Germany that would recognize the existing situation. This document provided that in future the Holy Roman emperor would be elected by seven German princes designated as the *electors*. These electors were the archbishops of Cologne, Trier, and Mainz, and the princes of Saxony, Brandenburg, the Palatinate, and Bohemia. The papacy was excluded from the election process, which was now a strictly German affair. Each of the electors was granted almost complete independence within his own territory. In evaluating Charles IV's action, perhaps the words of Lord Bryce are most fitting: "He legalized anarchy and called it a constitution." The Golden Bull made the German crown a pawn in the hands of a select group of independent princes who had the power to demand all kinds of concessions from any individual who hoped to be emperor.

After 1356 Germany progressed rapidly toward decentralization. Other princes demanded and gained the same kind of independence enjoyed by the electors. Germany was not a real kingdom; it was a confederation of roughly one hundred independent states. The emperor had no real power. He could call together the princes, churchmen, and representatives of the towns in meetings called *diets*, but such meetings usually achieved little, since the emperor lacked any means of enforcing decisions. He had no national army, no tax system, and no court system with which to make his influence felt. And as previously noted, most of the emperors devoted their attention to increasing their holdings. For instance, the Hapsburgs, who recovered the imperial throne again in 1438, pursued a dynastic policy which brought vast territories under their rule and made them one of the great royal families of Europe. As rulers of Germany and Holy Roman emperors, however, they enjoyed little effective power. Within their small principalities, many princes created stable, well-organized political systems. Germany was not a lawless, ungoverned land by any means. But she did lack unity, and for this she was to pay a heavy price in early modern times, when she had to meet the competition of the large national states that emerged elsewhere in Europe.

In Italy, the trend toward decentralization after 1250 was even more pronounced. The elected emperor was in theory the ruler of Italy, and from time to time some Italians did seek to have him exert his authority (as Dante's powerful political tract, *On Monarchy*, illustrates), but most Italians cared little. After the early fourteenth century, the emperors seldom even tried to exert any influence. There emerged a welter of independent states of all sizes and descriptions whose histories are almost impossible to summarize. Among them, five stand forth as important, both then and in the later history of the peninsula.

In southern Italy the old Norman state, now called the Kingdom of Naples, continued to exist, but it was now in decline. Throughout most of the Late Middle Ages, its destiny was controlled by outsiders, especially France and Aragon, who contested for it bitterly in order to capitalize on its wealth and strategic position, but with little thought for its inhabitants. In no small way, their machinations were responsible for the misery that has blighted this part of Italy up to the present.

The Papal States dominated central Italy,

their independence firmly established through the efforts of the great thirteenth-century popes. But papal overlordship was bitterly resisted by the local nobility, so that the Papal States were in almost constant turmoil. The political authority of the popes was badly compromised by the long period during which they resided at Avignon in France (1309–1377) and by the Great Schism that followed (see Chapter 26). When the papacy was finally reestablished in Rome early in the fifteenth century, that authority had been all but dissipated. It was restored by a succession of popes ruling during the last half of the fifteenth century, who used all the tactics of power politics and intrigue in order to establish a despotic regime. The activities of these worldly popes, symbolized by the notorious Alexander VI (1492–1503) of the house of Borgia, made them powerful, but ruined the reputation of the pope as a spiritual leader throughout most of Europe.

The three remaining "major" powers in Italy were the northern city-states of Milan, Venice, and Florence. Their histories between 1300 and 1500 are worthy of greater attention than we can give them, for these were the golden years of their renaissance, during which they accomplished much that would eventually exert a major influence on all of Western Europe. The city-states were preeminently the products of commercial and industrial activity, which made them unique in the West. As a consequence of their long struggle to resist the power of the Holy Roman emperors, their populations grew fiercely independent and localistic. After the imperial threat ended with the death of Frederick II, the cities battled one another for land, trading advantages, power, and security. Internally, the city-states tended to move from a political order that allowed for considerable citizen participation toward one-man or oligarchical rule. This trend was encouraged by the pressures of intercity warfare and class strife within each city, for a strong man or group often seemed the only way to restore

order and rally the people to the defense of the city-state. Milan was taken over by a despot early in the fourteenth century when the Visconti family established its power. Visconti domination, which made Milan rich and powerful, lasted until 1447, when the Sforzas replaced them. Florence resisted despotism longer, but after years of incessant factional struggles, a powerful banking family, the Medici, established control in the city shortly after 1430. Venice always remained under the control of an oligarchy of rich merchants, but their political methods did not differ greatly from those of the despots. The turbulent, strife-filled life in the cities called for new political techniques, with the result that these states made notable progress in advancing the arts of war and diplomacy. The new style of politics, described so brilliantly in Machiavelli's *Prince*, tended to stress the absolute sovereignty of the state, its freedom to do what it pleased toward other states, its right to create its own moral sanctions, its superiority over its subjects. Many historians see in these military and political developments the prototypes for modern European diplomacy, power politics, and balance of power theories.

Despite the vitality of the Italian Renaissance states, their history in the Late Middle Ages has a tragic dimension. The fragmentation of the peninsula doomed Italy to weakness in the face of more powerful states— Spain, France, and even the larger German principalities. The kinds of rivalry, diplomacy, and political morality that were generated during the fourteenth and fifteenth centuries led to decisions that were catastrophic. Symbolic of this difficulty was the invasion of Italy by Charles VIII, king of France, in 1494. Charles was called into Italy by the Sforza ruler of Milan in order to gain advantage for his city. The French invasion opened a long era during which domination of Italy was a major objective of the other nations of Europe, and she became a pawn in European power politics.

2. THE FAILURE OF FEUDAL MONARCHY IN FRANCE, ENGLAND, AND SPAIN

After 1300 England, France, and the kingdoms of the Iberian Peninsula encountered troubles nearly as serious as those of the Holy Roman Empire. It will be recalled that up to 1300 these states had developed well-organized feudal monarchies, in which kings shared political power with such vested interests as the nobles, the Church, and the towns. These systems of government had been shaped chiefly as a consequence of the success of monarchs in curbing the anarchic tendencies of feudalism and in creating effective substitutes. As the fourteenth century progressed, these feudal monarchies began to show signs of instability and inadequacy. Kings were not content to share power, a trait clearly manifested by the policies of Philip IV of France and Edward I of England at the beginning of the fourteenth century. Nobles, clergy, and townsmen were unwilling to surrender more of their privileges. Kings lacked the power and the resources to solve the major problems, the wars and economic crises, and the vested interests were not blessed with vision great enough to face them. The result was a heightening of tension in each kingdom, a situation that led to an erosion of effective royal authority and inevitably to civil wars which pitted the crown against the nobles and noble factions against each other. Under unbearable strain, the essential features of feudal monarchy and the concepts that animated the political order of the High Middle Ages slowly broke down. A new situation was created which ultimately permitted kings to lay claim to greater powers and to fashion territorial states in which royal authority stood uncontested and in which the sovereign interests of the state transcended all other considerations.

The evolution of France and England from 1300 to 1500 must be dealt with together because the histories of the two center around a single event, the Hundred Years' War (1337–1453). This struggle was merely an extension of a conflict between England and France that had begun in the twelfth century. The first phase was marked by a decisive French victory won by Philip II over John of century. The treaty of Paris (1259) had left England still in possession of most of the old duchy of Aquitaine, including Guienne and Gascony, in southwestern France. The rivalry continued, and the struggle was renewed as a result of the actions of Edward III (1327–1377) of England. He was uneasy over the steady progress made by the French kings in absorbing royal fiefs and extending their control over France. Aquitaine was vulnerable, since the English kings held it as a fief from the kings of France. So also was the county of Flanders, long the object of royal ambitions. If the French established control over this center of the woollen industry, England's economic interests would be threatened, for she supplied much of the raw wool used by Flemish manufacturers and the king depended heavily on customs duties collected on the export of wool. The English were also annoyed by French support of the Scots resistance, a matter of bitter concern to England after the Scots virtually assured their independence at the decisive battle of Bannockburn in 1314.

Soon after Edward became king, the moment was ripe for a blow against France. In 1328 the last member of the Capetian house died, and Philip of Valois succeeded to the throne as Philip VI. He and his successors were men of little ability who equated kingship with romantic notions about chivalry and showed scant interest in performing the administrative tasks associated with ruling a state. So Edward struck boldly. After careful steps to create a good army and to build up a system of alliances against the king of France, he announced in 1337 that he was claiming the French throne on the grounds that he had a superior hereditary claim to the throne, since he was the grandson of Philip IV while Philip VI was only a nephew: Philip VI answered this claim by pronouncing Edward a rebellious vassal and confiscating his fief.

The first phase of the Hundred Years' War

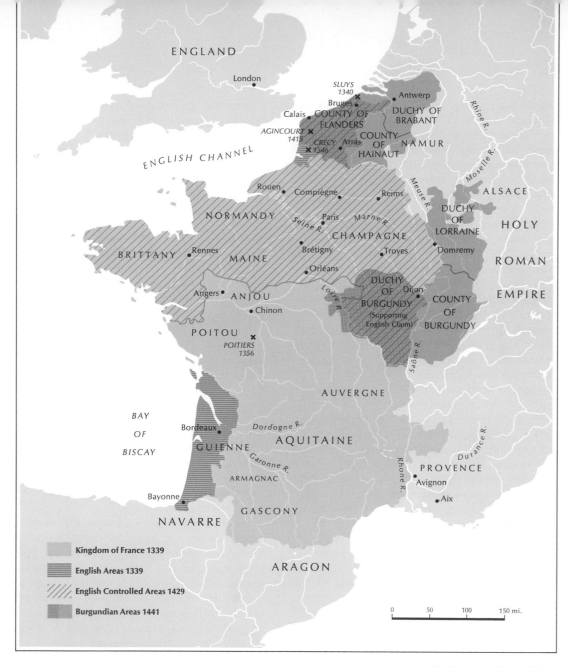

Kingdom of France 1339

English Areas 1339

English Controlled Areas 1429

Burgundian Areas 1441

The Hundred Years' War

lasted until 1360, and was nearly fatal to France. English ships won control of the Channel. English armies, made up largely of nonnoble longbowmen and pikemen, cut to pieces the flower of French feudal nobility in two great battles at Crécy (1346) and Poitiers (1356). Between times English armies rav-

aged French soil and spread chaos through the land. The French monarchy was powerless to check this disaster. The crowning blow came at the battle of Poitiers, when King John of France (1350–1364) was captured and carried off to England.

Without a king, France was plunged into

crisis. John's son, Charles, tried to carry on as regent, but his authority was challenged on every side. The Estates-General, led by a Parisian merchant, Etienne Marcel, undertook extensive reforms aimed at curbing royal taxation, correcting abuses in the royal government, and putting controls on royal civil servants. A peasant revolt, called the *Jacquerie*, broke out in 1358 in protest against taxes and war losses. Bands of soldiers ran wild over France. The nobles sought greedily to extend their privileges. Charles finally crushed the rebellious Estates-General by force, while the terrified nobles smashed the peasants. John bought his release by signing a humiliating peace with the English in 1360, in which Edward III was given full title to Guienne. France had been reduced greatly in power, chiefly because her kings could not ward off a foreign foe and control dissatisfied elements within the kingdom.

The next phase of the war, extending from 1364 to 1415, was marked by little decisive fighting but by tremendous internal dissension in each kingdom. France enjoyed a brief recovery under the rule of Charles V (1364–1380), who succeeded in rebuilding France's military strength and increasing royal income. Using these resources skillfully, he slowly weakened England's hold on Guienne and threatened to drive her out of France. However, his work was not continued by his successor, Charles VI (1380–1422). This pitiful figure became a helpless victim of the French nobility. When Charles VI became king, he was still a minor. A regency, dominated by the young king's greedy uncles, of whom Philip, duke of Burgundy, was the most powerful, was placed in control of the kingdom. Charles succeeded in ridding himself of the influence of his uncles for a brief period after he reached his majority, only to fall under the spell of his brother Louis, duke of Orléans. While still a young man, Charles began to suffer from spells of insanity. Each attack required the reinstitution of a regency. The Burgundians and the

Armagnacs (partisans of the duke of Orléans) competed bitterly for control of the regency and control of the kingdom. By the early fifteenth century their rivalry divided the nobility of France into two great camps engaged in a ruinous civil war. Efficient administration broke down completely. Peasant revolts, civil strife in the towns, and private warfare added to the confusion. Without a strong king to curb them, the feudal nobles plunged France into chaos in an incredible display of violence, greed, and selfishness. The final proof of the political bankruptcy of the nobility came when the Burgundians and the Armagnacs each began to dicker with the English to help destroy the other.

England was hardly less troubled during these years. The old hero of the first years of the struggle against France, Edward III, ruled until 1377 amid increasing trouble. His reign was highly significant for England, however, because of the rapid growth of Parliament. Edward's chief interest was always in waging war against France, but for this he needed money, and the easiest way to get it was to call Parliament. Frequent meetings of Parliament resulted in the rapid development of parliamentary organization.

The *House of Lords*, comprising the great feudal barons and high churchmen, separated from the *House of Commons*, made up of townsmen and of the lesser gentry representing the counties. Each house perfected rules regulating conduct of business and steadily increased its powers. Edward usually agreed to parliamentary demands because he wanted money. Aside from extensive control over taxation, Parliament began to gain a voice in spending money, in controlling royal officials, and in initiating legislation. By the time of Edward's death Parliament had become a vital factor in English political life. However, its future was not yet charted. Obviously it could curb royal power, but no one knew whether Parliament would use its power to weaken monarchy beyond a safe point, and it was not yet possible to tell whether the interests represented in Parliament would cooperate for the common good or would use their power to further private instead of national goals.

Edward's successor, Richard II (1377–1399), certainly felt the new power of Parliament. His stormy reign was filled with civil strife arising from dissatisfaction with royal government. A great peasant revolt broke out in 1381 and had to be crushed by force. The nobles, acting in Parliament, tried hard to limit royal power, and when Richard resisted their efforts, he was charged with tyranny and in 1399 was deposed by Parliament. Henry IV (1399–1413) of the powerful house of Lancaster was elected in his place. This was an event of tremendous importance, since it made the monarch more than ever responsible to Parliament. However, Parliament was neither capable of directing royal government adequately itself nor willing to trust the king to do so. The result was civil war, led by great nobles who refused to recognize Henry IV as king. What these nobles wanted was a ruler who would favor their interests. Parliament became a convenient place to agitate for a change of kings or for control over the present king, although the battlefield might be the final scene of decision. Just as in France, the nobles were making a bid to retain their power, their aim being to achieve this end by controlling the king.

Henry V (1413–1422) hastened both England and France along their troubled paths by reopening the Hundred Years' War. Desirous of giving his nobles something to think about other than curbing his authority and assured that he would find support among France's warring factions, he invaded France in 1415. His avowed aim was to seize the French throne. His campaign opened brilliantly when he crushed a French army at Agincourt in 1415 and then captured a series of key cities in west-central France. Instead of rallying to defend the kingdom, the Burgundians and Armagnacs tried to use the English to destroy one another. Eventually the Burgundians al-

lied openly with the English, permitting Henry V to force the humiliating Treaty of Troyes on Charles VI in 1420. By its terms Henry married Catherine, the daughter of Charles. He or his successor was to become king of France when Charles died; until that time he would act as regent for the mad Charles. Most of France north of the Loire River was in English hands. A great nation seemed about to be exterminated.

Both Henry V and Charles VI died in 1422, leaving Henry's nine-month-old son, Henry VI, to inherit both thrones. But the English were not destined to enjoy dominance over France for long. France made a spectacular recovery from the disasters of the early fifteenth century. A new, hard-to-define feeling was the inspiration for her recovery—the feeling of patriotism, of love for France and hatred for foreigners. The chief beneficiary was the son of Charles VI, soon to be known as Charles VII. After 1420 he had fled to southern France as a virtual prisoner of the Armagnac faction. For some years he lived at Bourges, despairing of ever becoming king of France. It was at this point that there appeared a simple peasant girl, Joan of Arc, claiming God had revealed to her that Charles must free France from the English and assume his rightful place as head of the French kingdom. Her pleas bestirred the dispirited Charles and pumped new confidence into the French soldiers loyal to Charles. Joan herself was present with the French army that captured Orléans in 1429, the first French victory for many years.

From 1429 to 1453 the French won victory after victory, until the English held only the city of Calais in France. But Joan did not live to see these victories. After the victory at Orléans she persuaded Charles that he should brave the English danger to go to Reims to be crowned. The successful accomplishment of this mission galvanized the French people behind their king, the heir to the glorious tradition of the past. In 1430 she was captured by Burgundian troops, turned over to the English, tried by the Church for heresy, and burned at the stake in Rouen in 1431. Yet, the maid of Lorraine lived on as a symbol of France to rally the French population to a common purpose.

However, the French victory was based on more than enthusiasm generated by a peasant girl. During the reign of Charles VII there was a great revival of royal power. A strong, well-trained army, equipped with new weapons, was created and paid for by the king, who thus ended his dependence on the sort of useless feudal army that had been slaughtered at Crécy, Poitiers, and Agincourt. In 1439 the Estates-General voted Charles VII the power to impose a direct tax on persons, called the *taille*, without any consultation or further authorization. And since the king was winning victory after victory, no one was in a position to protest the growth of royal authority. Even the great nobles bowed before royal will. Charles VII became the focal point of political life. The bitter taste of defeat, of disorder, of irresponsibility on the part of great nobles compelled everyone to turn to the king for leadership. Charles VII was not a strong ruler; but he was served by excellent ministers who guided him wisely in making full use of his opportunity. When he died in 1461, his son, Louis XI (1461–1483), inherited a solid base from which to rule: a strong army, the power to tax at will, a patriotic people, and the bitter memory of what royal weakness and feudal selfishness could mean to France. His accession marked the beginning of a new era.

England was in a less happy state. Strife among rival factions of nobles struggling to dominate weak kings finally led to a destructive civil war called the Wars of the Roses. This struggle had its origins during the reign of Henry VI (1422–1461). Because he became king in infancy, there was a long regency. Moreover, the claim of his family, the Lancastrians, to the throne was tainted by virtue of the fact that it had been elevated to power by parliamentary action without the best hereditary claim. When Henry VI did reach his majority, he continued to be dominated by noble factions motivated chiefly by personal ambition. The final blow was an attack of insanity. Two major factions of nobles, the Lancastrians and the Yorkists, locked in a deadly struggle for control of the government. Outwardly, the issue at stake was the rival claims of the two houses to the throne, but actually the basic issue was simply power and the benefits it could bring. While this civil war raged, the regular processes of orderly government were neglected. Tyranny, intrigue, murder, confiscation of property, and pursuit of private ends were the order of the day, perpetrated by nobles acting through the bands of armed retainers they had gathered around themselves. Henry VI and his supporters held the crown until finally defeated by Edward of York, who as Edward IV (1461–1483) tried to restore royal authority. The Lancastrians refused to accept his rule and kept the struggle going.

Edward was succeeded by his twelve-year-old son, Edward V, but within three months the young king's uncle seized the throne as Richard III. Within a year Edward V and his brother were murdered, an act for which their royal uncle still seems the chief suspect, despite innumerable efforts to clear his name. Richard III tried vigorously to restore order in England, but he could neither dispel the view that he was a usurper nor blunt the hatred of the Lancastrians. Finally in 1485, Henry Tudor, a Lancastrian, defeated Richard III in a pitched battle at Bosworth Field and assumed the throne as Henry VII. Although Henry VII's claim to the throne was extremely tenuous, the nation, weary of civil war and disorder, was willing to follow anyone who promised to restore peace and security. The old noble factions had been decimated. Henry was therefore free to do much as he pleased. More significantly, many elements of the medieval government—the royal bureaucracy, the law, the local government, the courts—survived the civil war to provide the king with the basic ingredients for effective government. Henry used the opportunity to end the feudal state and to create a strong central government that united the English people into a nation.

In the Iberian Peninsula the three major kingdoms—Aragon, Castile, and Portugal—shaped out of the territories won from the Muslims between the tenth and the thirteenth centuries, also had their difficulties during the Late Middle Ages. By 1300 the holy war against the Muslims ceased to be the significant factor in Spanish affairs, for they had been confined to the narrow territory of Granada in southeastern Spain. The Christian kingdoms then turned on one another, competing bitterly for territory. Added to these wars was the almost constant civil strife within each kingdom that replicated the struggles in England and France. Spanish nobles, churchmen, and townsmen were as anxious as their counterparts in England and France to curb royal power, and the kings as anxious to expand their authority. Castile was especially plagued by a long series of disputed successions that undermined royal authority. Aragon's internal order was compromised by the aggressive overseas policy pursued by her kings, especially in Italy, a policy seldom favored by the nobility. The kingdom was also rent by conflict between the landed and the commercial interests, which were especially strong in Catalonia. All these senseless quarrels finally began to abate when in 1469 the heiress of Castile, Isabella, married Ferdinand, the heir of Aragon. In 1479, when this couple had succeeded to both thrones, they quickly took steps to end the strife and unify their lands into a single state ruled by a strong government and capable of playing a leading role in European society.

In Portugal, a steady consolidation of power in royal hands occurred in the fifteenth century. Portuguese kings did not meet such violent resistance as did the kings of the other Iberian kingdoms. They gained considerable support within Portugal because of their heroic struggle to prevent Castile from absorbing Portugal. The Portuguese kings also promoted the commercial interests in their kingdom. Throughout the fifteenth century, Portuguese merchants with royal backing expanded southward along the African coast and found lucrative markets.

3. EASTERN EUROPE AND THE MEDITERRANEAN WORLD

In Eastern and Southeastern Europe the decline of the Holy Roman Empire and the collapse of the Byzantine Empire heralded a new political order of immense significance to the future of Europe. The Byzantine Empire never fully recovered from the attacks of the Seljuk Turks in the late eleventh century and the capture of Constantinople by Western Europeans in 1204 during the Fourth Crusade. After the Europeans were finally ousted in 1261 and Greek emperors assumed power, a fatal illness seemed to afflict the empire. Civil strife slowly sapped the strong imperial government. The Italian city-states, led by Venice, deprived the empire of much of its trade, and bit by bit the territory of the Byzantine Empire was pared away, especially by the Ottoman Turks. The emperors of the fourteenth and fifteenth centuries appealed desperately to the West for help but received little, since Western Europeans were too enmeshed in their own rivalries. Finally, in 1453 Constantinople was captured by the Ottoman Turks, ending forever the power that had so long shielded Western Europe and supplied Europeans with inspiration and models in scholarship, the arts, industry, and trade.

The victory of the Ottoman Turks at Constantinople in 1453 signified more than the fall of the Byzantine Empire. It marked the reappearance of an aggressive Muslim force threatening Western Christendom, a danger that had not existed for a long time. We previously noted that the Abbasid dynasty (750–1258) had been incapable of maintaining political control over the vast Muslim Empire. The disintegration of that empire and the resulting internal rivalries removed most of the pressure of Muslim expansion and prepared the way for the European counterattack dur-

ARCTIC OCEAN

FINLAND

KINGDOM OF SWEDEN

BALTIC SEA

L. Onega

L. Ladoga

Novgorod

Moscow

TEUTONIC ORDER

Riga

Königsberg   Vilna

Smolensk

Danzig   DUCHY OF
PRUSSIA

Ob R.

GRAND DUCHY
OF
LITHUANIA

Oder R.

Vistula R.

Warsaw

KINGDOM
OF POLAND

Kiev

Dnieper R.

UKRAINE

Dniester R.

Volga R.

Ural R.

KHANATE OF THE GOLDEN HORDE (TARTARS)

ARAL
SEA

Vienna

Pruth R.

MOLDAVIA

Don R.

Astrakhan

Budapest

KINGDOM OF HUNGARY

WALLACHIA

SEA OF
AZOV

CASPIAN
SEA

Belgrade

Danube R.

BLACK SEA

BOSNIA   SERBIA

BULGARIA   Varna

Kossovo   Sofia   Nicopolis

MACEDONIA   Constantinople

Trebizond

ADRIATIC SEA

Thessalonica

AEGEAN
SEA

MAMELUKES

MEDITERRANEAN
SEA

RHODES

CRETE

CYPRUS

Ottoman Possessions ca. 1355

Byzantine Possessions ca. 1355

Ottoman Possessions ca. 1481

Grand Principality of Moscow ca. 1300-1505

Boundary of Holy Roman Empire

Western Boundary of Mongol
Expansion, 13th Century

Note: Crete, to Venice, 1204-1669;
Cyprus, Crusader Kingdom to 1489, then to Venice until 1571;
Rhodes to Knights Hospitallers, 1309-1523

The Ottoman Empire and Russia to 1505

ing the era of the Crusades. Vast upheavals continued to shake the Muslim world after the crusading movement had subsided, and the chief cause was the intrusion of non-Muslim Asiatics into the Muslim world. In the thirteenth century a Mongol horde led by Genghis Khan and his successors moved westward to build an empire that reached into western Russia, Asia Minor, and Syria. The already-weak Abbasid dynasty disappeared before this avalanche. When by the end of the thirteenth century the Mongol threat began to recede, the Muslim portions of the Mongol Empire broke into rival principalities. One of the most powerful was that of the Ottoman Turks in Asia Minor.

The Ottoman Turks were Asiatic nomads, distantly related to the Seljuk Turks, whose earlier attacks on the Byzantine Empire in Asia Minor played a part in the crusading movement. The Ottomans, uprooted by the Mongols, moved westward and were permitted to settle in Asia Minor in the thirteenth century by the Seljuk Turks, who still maintained an important state there. The newcomers accepted the Islamic faith and adopted many of the ways of Muslim society. Within a short time the Ottomans had established their independence. Their first great ruler was Osman, or Othman (1290–1326), from whence the term "Ottoman." The new state began to expand almost immediately, chiefly at the expense of Byzantine possessions in western Asia Minor. By the end of the fourteenth century the Ottomans had taken over Asia Minor. As early as 1354 the Byzantines had allowed them to enter the Balkans as allies in the Byzantine effort to hold back aggressive Slavs. Soon the newcomers had taken control of most of the Balkans.

Early in the fifteenth century Ottoman power was nearly destroyed by a new threat from the east in the person of Tamerlane, a Mongol warrior who sought to reconstruct the empire of Genghis Khan. However, Tamerlane's death in 1405 was followed by a sudden collapse of his empire. The Ottomans soon recovered from these defeats and returned to their attack on the Byzantine Empire and on the Balkans. Attempts to raise a crusade against them failed, and finally in 1453 they captured Constantinople. Early in the next century they conquered Syria, Palestine, and Egypt, creating a huge state that stretched from the Danube to the Nile. Flying the flag of Mohammedanism, rich in material resources, and possessing an excellent army and navy, the Ottomans loomed as a major threat to Western Europe as the Middle Ages ended.

Central and Eastern Europe began to assume its modern shape in the wake of the decline of the Holy Roman and the Byzantine empires during the Late Middle Ages. During this era the south coast of the Baltic Sea was dominated by Germans, spearheaded by the crusading military order of the Teutonic Knights, who concentrated their efforts in this region now that the Near East was closed to them. The Knights were followed by German traders, missionaries, and agricultural colonists whose presence imposed strong Germanic influences on the area and filled the Slavs of Central Europe with an abiding distrust for and fear of the Germans. The Germanic threat resulted in a union of the ruling houses of Poland and Lithuania under the Lithuanian prince Jagiello, who married a Polish princess and governed both states as King Ladislas II (1386–1434). The house of Jagiello exerted considerable military pressure on the Baltic Germans and on the Russian states to the east during much of the fifteenth century, but they never succeeded in creating an effective government for their huge kingdom. To the south, the kingdom of Hungary continued to develop, but its energies were increasingly absorbed in defending itself against the advancing Ottoman Turks and in holding back ambitious German noble families who would have liked to gain control of the Hungarian throne. Until the Ottoman Turks seized control of the Balkans at the end of the fourteenth century, a flourishing Serbian kingdom dominated that area; after its destruction, the Hungarians stood as Western Europe's outpost against the Ottomans.

In general, all the Central European nations were influenced by the West, but their development was far slower than that of the Western Europeans.

Farther east, the Russians slowly freed themselves from the Mongol invaders who had seized much of Russia during the thirteenth century. The Mongol *khans* (emperors) had made no attempt to establish a system of government in Russia. Instead, they forced the numerous conquered Russian princes to become tribute-paying subordinates of the khans, responsible for collecting tribute from the Russian populace. In the fourteenth century the princes of Moscow gained the privilege of collecting tribute in the name of the khans from all the other Russian princes. Using this right skillfully, the Muscovites began to establish a strong state at the expense of the other Russian principalities. Early in the fifteenth century they rejected the overlordship of the khans, whose power was rapidly deteriorating, and started a series of wars for the purpose of Muscovite expansion and liberation. Under Ivan III (reigned 1462–1505), the Mongol hold on Russia was finally broken, and Ivan was powerful enough to compel most Russian princes to accept his authority. After the fall of Constantinople in 1453, the Muscovites claimed they were the heirs of the Byzantine tradition and the protectors of the Greek Orthodox religion. Ivan III began calling himself *tsar*, which implied that he was the successor of the Roman caesars. This sense of protecting an ancient heritage gave Russia a new mission and a feeling of uniqueness that would help to solidify her people into a powerful nation in the future.

4. ECONOMIC AND SOCIAL TENSIONS

Responsible for a part of the political difficulties we have just traced were basic economic and social problems troubling most areas of Europe. The economic system that had flourished in the twelfth and thirteenth centuries ceased to be entirely adequate and suffered a series of contractions that not only limited growth, but also badly shook men's confidence in their abilities to improve their economic lot. Social disequilibrium and strife often accompanied economic difficulties.

The most vital factor in the prosperity of the twelfth and thirteenth centuries had been *expanding* trade. In the fourteenth and fifteenth centuries many factors combined to cause a leveling off and, in many areas, a decline in commercial activity. The incessant warfare of these centuries upset established trade processes. Europe's population ceased growing, probably because of recurrent famines and the epidemic of bubonic plague, the Black Death, which between 1347 and 1350 wiped out nearly one third of the population and perhaps more in the cities where its toll was heaviest. The rise of the Ottoman power made it more difficult for Western Europeans to penetrate new geographical areas. There was a shortage of capital. The independent cities that had been the sources of medieval commercial growth lacked the manpower, the wealth, and the political power to offset these numerous difficulties. Persistent cooperation among commercial cities proved nearly impossible. The most successful effort of this kind was the Hanseatic League, which linked together about seventy cities in northern Germany, Scandinavia, and the Low Countries. During the fourteenth century, the league acted with considerable effectiveness to provide mutual protection in the North and Baltic seas and to assure its members a monopoly over trade in that area. But ultimately the league declined, chiefly because its members refused to sacrifice local interests for a larger cause. All these limitations on commerce did not mean that the fourteenth and fifteenth centuries enjoyed none of the benefits of trade; however, trade did not grow so fast as it previously had.

Industry experienced a comparable constriction. The existing productive system was the biggest barrier to industrial growth. The guild system, which had once promoted the growth of industry, grew increasingly restrictive. Seeking to protect their monopoly on production in each city, the guilds passed rules excluding the products of outsiders. They barred technical changes that seemed to threaten their members, and they excluded new members or reduced them to inferior rank in the guilds. Often their pricing arrangements were unrealistic. Such practices curtailed production and discouraged expansion into new areas of production.

Agricultural production, the foundation of the European economy, likewise suffered a depression. A variety of forces combined to halt its expansion: Widespread warfare ravaged many lands. There is some evidence that a climatic change occurred which made growing conditions more difficult in many parts of Western Europe. The eastern frontier was closed, limiting areas for colonization and new land clearance. Especially crucial was the impact of the Black Death, which not only decimated the rural labor force, but also sharply reduced the city market for agricultural products. Under these pressures the old manorial system continued to break up. Landowners across much of Western Europe turned their estates into tenancies which they rented to peasants; the latter were increasingly freed of the burdens of serfdom in return for money payments to the landlord. Some landlords also resorted to enclosing their land and using hired labor to keep it in production. Since the landlords were chiefly interested in money income, they manipulated rents and sought to impose on their peasant tenants whatever remnants of the old manorial dues system they could (the *heriot*, banalties, and so forth).

Economic dislocation and contraction led to considerable social tension and disturbance in

the Late Middle Ages. In a general way, the social structure lost its earlier mobility. The dominant social elements closed ranks to protect their advantages and sought to use their power to control and exploit other groups who might threaten their position. Disadvantaged groups chafed under these circumstances and often resorted to violence to better their lot. The social structure of Western Europe continued to be dominated by a nobility whose power and prestige were traditionally based on landowning, feudal ties, mili-

A guild meeting in Germany in the fifteenth century. The guilds during this period were a barrier to economic activity, for in attempting to protect themselves, the guild members set up rules that limited the amount of production and stifled innovation. *Photo: Kupferstichkabinett, Staatliche Museen der Stiftung, Berlin*

tary prowess, and the chivalric code of conduct. That nobility, however, was under
severe stress. Its position as the wealthiest
element in society was challenged by the rising capitalist entrepreneurs in commerce, industry, and finance. Its monopoly on warfare
was destroyed by the nonnoble professional
soldier who fought a new style of warfare
with new weapons. The nobles completely
discredited themselves politically as a result
of their obstructionist attempts to impede the
development of royal government and to seize
political power for their own interests. With
the old bases of social preeminence dissolving,
the nobility of the Late Middle Ages turned
increasingly to ruthless exploitation of its
lands and to costly indulgence in a mode of
life based on an exaggerated version of chivalry. And, perhaps most significantly, the nobles ultimately turned to the monarchs to
sanction and protect their privileges.

Although most peasants in the western
areas of Europe enjoyed improvement in their
social position as a consequence of the virtual
disappearance of serfdom, their status deteriorated in other ways. They were thrown
more and more on their own economically.
As renters they could no longer appeal to a
kindly manorial lord in times of war and
famine. Landlords sought to squeeze every
penny out of their tenants. Taxes levied by
kings to fight expensive wars fell heavily on
the peasants, and the wars that the peasants
thus paid for often ravaged their farms, especially in France, Italy, and Germany. They
were under constant pressure to pay higher
rents and dues at a time when markets were
shrinking and prices declining, and when
there were fewer avenues of escape in the
troubled cities and on the closed frontier.
Thus peasant life was afflicted with economic
hardship, uncertainty, and insecurity. Peasants expressed their discontent by frequent
and violent rebellions, movements that often
reached frightening proportions, for example, the *Jacquerie* in France in 1358 and the
Peasants' Revolt of 1381 in England. The rebels always cried out for justice and acted

savagely to punish their oppressors; but their
fervor was seldom supported by a positive
program, and their angry, passionate outbursts were usually brutally crushed by kings,
nobles, and clergymen acting in concert.

Equally unhappy were certain elements of
the bourgeoisie, especially in Flanders and
Italy, where capitalistically organized industry increasingly dominated the scene. Many
artisans were reduced to the ranks of laborers
for hire, working for the entrepreneurs who
bought raw materials in bulk and produced
finished products in great quantities. These
artisans often lost the political power they
had enjoyed in the twelfth and thirteenth centuries when the towns were struggling for
independence. The rich entrepreneurs more
and more dominated political life in the cities.
The monopolistic guilds tended to exclude artisans from the trades, leaving many people
with little means of earning a livelihood. The
laborers and the unemployed frequently resorted to mob violence, but with no more
success than the peasants. The towns, which
once had made men free, were no longer havens for the oppressed.

The social group making the greatest advance in the fourteenth and fifteenth centuries
was an elite element in the bourgeoisie engaged in capitalistic ventures in commerce
and industry. This was particularly the case
in northern Italy and Flanders, although the
generalization also holds for France, England,
and parts of Germany and Spain. The success of this group is exemplified by the activities of the Medici and the Bardi in Italy, the
Fuggers in southern Germany, Jacques Coeur
of France, and some of the entrepreneurs associated with the Hanseatic League which monopolized trade in the Baltic and North seas.
Often the members of this group refused to
carry on business within the framework of
the old guild structure and felt no need to
confine their activities to a single city. Their
boldness in such fields as banking, moneylending, and the woollen industry netted them
huge fortunes. They seized political control
of most city governments and found increas-

ing favor with kings. Culturally they were able to patronize the advancing cause of the humanists and to set standards of fashion. In a sense, the emergence of this powerful group meant the formation of a new class. Or perhaps it would be more accurate to say that this group now represented the bourgeoisie. Groups that had formerly been counted in this class—simple artisans and small shopkeepers—were emerging as a group apart, a laboring class, increasingly dependent on the economic decisions of the rich merchants and financiers. This new bourgeoisie of successful capitalist entrepreneurs was destined to play a major role in the future of Western Europe.

More and more it became obvious that the solution to the economic and social problems of the fourteenth and fifteenth centuries lay with a stronger central government. Peasants, capitalists, industrial workers—all regarded kings as champions of their cause and pressed central governments to assume more active control over trade, industry, agriculture, and the class structure. In countries such as England and France, kings responded to this pressure and began regulating economic and social conditions on a national scale. This trend was proof of the passing of medieval society, which had been built on social stratification, economic localism, and group protection of vested interests.

By approximately 1450 the worst of the economic and social stresses of the Late Middle Ages were over, and there were signs of recovery everywhere. Aside from the return of political order accompanying the restoration of royal authority, the population had begun to grow again. The new methods evolved by the capitalist entrepreneurs found wider application and ensured more effective conduct of commerce and industry. The agricultural system became increasingly stable, chiefly on the basis of a system of renting which bound landlord and peasant together on a money basis. New technological advances were being made and were being applied more widely—water mills in the textile industry, better mining techniques, printing, improved shipbuilding, the compass, the astrolabe, gunpowder. New frontiers were opening by way of the seas that washed Europe's western shores; the discovery of America in 1492 symbolized that reaching out in new directions. All these forces pointed toward new economic growth in Western Europe. It was obvious, however, that this growth would be achieved in ways different from those that prevailed in medieval Europe.

Suggested Reading

Overview. The best general treatment of the history of the fourteenth and fifteenth centuries is W. K. Ferguson, *Europe in Transition, 1300–1520* (1962). Another survey, somewhat dated on several matters, is **E. P. Cheyney, *The Dawn of a New Era* (Harper Torchbook). Two shorter works spanning the period and strong on interpretation are **R. E. Lerner, *The Age of Adversity: The Fourteenth Century* (Cornell); and **Margaret Aston, *The Fifteenth Century: The Prospect of Europe* (Harcourt, Brace & World). Stimulating interpretations of the major issues of the era are presented in Denys Hay, *Europe in the Fourteenth and Fifteenth Centuries* (1966). Those who seek a detailed history that stresses political developments will find useful successive volumes of a series: C. W. Previté-Orton, *A History of Europe From 1198 to 1378* (3rd ed., 1951), and W. T. Waugh, *A History of Europe From 1378 to 1494* (1932). A classic piece of historical literature dealing with this period is **J. Huizinga, *The Waning of the Middle Ages* (Anchor), which explores the psychological changes affecting Western European society.

The Holy Roman Empire.   The appropriate sections of the books by Barraclough, Bryce, and Heer cited in Chapter 20 provide the best treatments of the fate of the Holy Roman Empire in the Late Middle Ages.   There is no satisfactory guide to the general history of Italy in the Late Middle Ages.   Excellent treatments of particular cities, stressing especially internal social developments, are **Hans Baron, *Crisis of the Early Italian Renaissance: Civic Humanism and Republican Liberty in an Age of Classicism and Tyranny* (rev. ed., Princeton); **Ferdinand Schevill, *Medieval and Renaissance Florence* (2 vols., Harper Torchbook); **Gene A. Brucker, *Renaissance Florence* (Wiley); Lauro Martines, *The Social World of the Florentine Humanists, 1390–1460* (1963); David Herlihy, *Pisa in the Early Renaissance* (1958); and D. Muir, *A History of Milan Under the Visconti* (1924).   A brilliant analysis of intercity relationships and the techniques developed to deal with the problems of war and peace is **Garrett Mattingly, *Renaissance Diplomacy* (Penguin).

England, France, and Spain.   The best treatment of the Hundred Years' War, including considerable information on both French and English internal history, is the fine work of **E. Perroy, *The Hundred Years' War* (Capricorn).   **A. R. Myers, *England in the Late Middle Ages, 1307–1536* (Penguin), is an excellent survey of English development in this period.   Also useful, especially on social and economic history, is **George Holmes, *The Later Middle Ages, 1272–1485* (Norton).   More detailed but tedious are successive volumes in the Oxford *History of England:* M. McKisack, *The Fourteenth Century, 1307–1399* (1959), and E. F. Jacob, *The Fifteenth Century, 1399–1485* (1961).   Two good works on the development of Parliament in this crucial era in its history are **G. L. Haskins, *The Growth of English Representative Government* (Perpetua); and F. Thompson, *A Short History of Parliament, 1295–1642* (1953).   Virtually the only treatment of French political history in this period is P. S. Lewis, *Late Medieval France: The Polity* (1968).   For insights into French politics and society, see Joseph Calmette, *The Golden Age of Burgundy* (1963); and O. Cartellieri, *The Court of Burgundy* (1929).   R. Pernoud, *Joan of Arc, by Herself and Her Witnesses*

(1966), provides an intriguing picture of a key figure in late medieval France.   A classic treatment of the Maid of Orleans is **J. Michelet, *Joan of Arc*, trans. A. Guerard (Ann Arbor).   The works of Merriman, Altamira, and Livermore cited in Chapter 22 will cover the complicated history of Spain in this era.   Excellent for the end of this period is **J. H. Elliott, *Imperial Spain* (Mentor).

The Eastern Mediterranean and Eastern Europe.   The history of the Byzantine Empire in its declining days is well covered by the works of Ostrogorsky and Vasiliev cited in Chapter 15.   S. Runciman, *The Fall of Constantinople, 1453* (1965), gives a splendid dénouement to the history of the empire.   Islamic history is treated in the works of Hitti, Lewis, and Spuler cited in Chapter 15.   A. S. Atiya, *The Crusades in the Later Middle Ages* (1938), provides a good picture of the attempts by Western Europeans to maintain their influence in the East.   An exciting although not always accurate picture of the Mongols is presented by **Harold Lamb, *Genghis Khan, Emperor of All Men* (Bantam).   More reliable is **M. Prawdin, *The Mongol Empire* (2nd ed., Free Press).   P. Wittek, *The Rise of the Ottoman Empire* (1958), is a good treatment of early Ottoman history.   F. Dvornik, *The Making of Central Europe* (1949), and *The Slavs: Their Early History and Civilization* (1956), are the best treatments of Central European history.   The development of Russia in this period is brilliantly treated by G. Vernadsky, *The Origins of Russia* (1959); and Michael T. Florinsky, *Russia: A History and an Interpretation*, Vol. I (2 vols., 1953).

Economic and Social History.   The works of Pirenne, Boissonnade, and Duby, and the *Cambridge Economic History*, Vols. II and III, cited in Chapters 18 and 19, will provide excellent discussions of the major economic developments of this period.   The most thorough work is J. W. Thompson, *Economic and Social History of Europe in the Later Middle Ages, 1300–1530* (1935).   Helen Zimmern, *The Hansa Towns* (1889), is an old but good treatment of the Hanseatic League.   **Johannes Nohl, ed., *The Black Death: A Chronicle of the Plague Compiled From Contemporary Sources* (American Century), provides a graphic picture of the grim consequences of the Black Death. A. B. Kerr, *Jacques Coeur* (1927); **Raymond de Roover, *The Rise and Decline of the Medici Bank, 1397–1494* (Norton); and **Sylvia Thrupp, *The Merchant Class of Medieval London* (Ann Arbor), will all help in understanding the nature of emergent capitalism. A brilliant treatment of social history is **D. W. Robertson, Jr., *Chaucer's London* (Wiley). R. L. Kilgour, *The Decline of Chivalry* (1937), provides interesting insights into the changing conditions of the late medieval nobility.

Sources. **Jean Froissart, *Chronicles of England, France, and Spain* (Dutton), provides a fascinating picture of late medieval society caught up in the Hundred Years' War; it reveals the weaknesses of the nobility with particular clarity. *The Memoirs of Philippe de Commines,* ed. S. Kinser, trans. I. Cazeaux (1969), is also excellent for its portrayal of conditions in aristocratic society in the fifteenth century. **Chaucer, *Canterbury Tales* (many editions; a good one is that of Nevill Coghill, Penguin), provides a broader picture of English society. **William Langland, *Piers the Ploughman,* trans. J. F. Goodridge (Penguin), a fourteenth-century English poem, reflects the bitter resentment felt by the lower classes against the rich and powerful in English society.

Chapter 26 ❧ The Decline of the Church

The tensions that beset Western European political, social, and economic institutions in the fourteenth and fifteenth centuries afflicted the Church even more severely. After 1300 this powerful institution, which had earlier influenced all aspects of human activity and supplied the common denominator for every element of European society, found itself increasingly incapable of guiding men. Its teachings, its system of government, and its leaders were subjected to merciless criticism and to open defiance. And the Church failed to discover new resources with which to meet these criticisms, thereby dooming itself to a reactionary role in society.

1. THE DECLINE OF THE PAPACY

The decline of the Church in the fourteenth and fifteenth centuries was most obvious in the case of the papacy. We have noted that during the thirteenth century the papacy was amazingly successful in taking control of the Church, creating a religious monarchy in which a single man guided the beliefs, the morals, and the worship of most Europeans. The centralization of religious life under a single ruler meant that the vigor of the Church depended to a large extent upon the forcefulness and quality of that leadership.

After 1300 the papacy suffered repeated setbacks, until by 1500 papal prestige was little respected anywhere in Western Europe.

The apogee of papal power came during the pontificate of Boniface VIII (1294–1303), the proud, ambitious heir to the immense prestige that the great popes of the thirteenth century had built up. Symbolic of Boniface's might was the reaction of Western Europe to the jubilee year he proclaimed in 1300. During that year, according to one commentator, "almost the whole world came running to the Roman curia"—no less than 2 million visitors, said some contemporaries. Most of them came to partake of the spiritual benefits that the successor of St. Peter and the vicar of Christ could dispense, reflecting the crucial role that the faithful believed the pope played in the drama of salvation. The pilgrims poured forth their wealth to sustain the papal power that seemed so necessary to the right order of the world.

Perhaps this spectacle inflamed what Dante called Boniface's "prideful fever." For amid his triumph, "the prince of the new Pharisees" was faced with desperate challenges to which he reacted with vanity and exaggerated claims of authority. His first serious setback came at the hands of the powerful kings of England and France, Edward I and Philip IV, both

The decline in the prestige of the papacy in the fourteenth century began with the reign of Boniface VIII, a strong-minded pope who suffered several humiliating defeats in controversies with the kings of France and England. In this detail of a fresco by Ambrogio Lorenzetti, Boniface is shown receiving St. Louis of Toulouse at the papal court. *Photo: Scala* trying to assert maximum authority in their realms. These rulers both proposed to impose new taxes on the Church in their kingdoms in order to fight a war against each other. Boniface insisted that the Church's property was exempt from lay control and issued a papal bull, called *Clericis Laicos*, in which he maintained that only with papal consent could any taxes be laid upon the Church. Edward and Philip defied Boniface and took steps to cut off all revenues from their kingdoms to Rome. Boniface had to retreat from his position, something the bishops of Rome were not accustomed to do.

Before long he was involved in a new quarrel with Philip IV, this time over the question of the proper courts for trying clergymen. Again the strong-minded pope stated his case in a way that outraged Philip. In the bull *Unam Sanctam*, Boniface insisted that the French king and all men must subject themselves to the pope if they were to be saved. Philip counterattacked violently. He turned public opinion in France against the pope by blatantly distorting the papal position, called a meeting of the Estates-General, and finally sent some of his henchmen to Italy to capture Boniface. Philip's agents were successful, and the pope escaped what might have been an even more painful defeat by dying, perhaps as a result of the shock of his capture by Philip's agents. No one could mistake the importance of these events: the pope had suffered a humiliating defeat at the hands of a strong political leader unwilling to accept papal guidance in the running of his kingdom.

Philip IV capitalized on his victory by arranging for the election of a Frenchman as pope. The new pope took up residence at Avignon, a city on the Rhone River lying just outside the boundaries of the French kingdom. In large part this fateful decision was dictated by turbulent conditions in the Papal States in Italy. From 1309 to 1377 this city remained the residence of the papacy. During these years of what the Italian writer and humanist Petrarch called the "Babylonian Captivity" the popes were accused, unfairly as is now obvious, of being pawns of the French kings, and many Europeans regarded them as unworthy of the title of head of the universal Church. The English, for instance, who were engaged in the Hundred Years' War with the French, took steps to abolish papal control over ecclesiastical affairs. The German emperors and the German princes were equally defiant. Many Christians were troubled by the fact that the pope's claim to power was based on succession to St. Peter as bishop of Rome, not Avignon. These critics were not impressed by the plea of the papacy that Rome was not safe; neither had it been for Peter nor for many earlier popes who had suffered by remaining in the holy city. The Babylonian Captivity caused scholars and writers to raise major questions regarding church government and to arrive at answers that challenged papal supremacy.

The Avignon popes were not idle during these years, however. Realizing that papal prestige was being challenged, they worked to increase their command over the organization and the resources of the Church. Several of them were skilled administrators who succeeded in pushing papal control over church organization to its greatest height. They increased the number of offices which they could fill with their own appointees. They collected old taxes with great vigor and even discovered new sources of income. They steadily increased the number of judicial cases that had to be appealed to Rome and derived a huge income from this activity. They enlarged the papal bureaucracy beyond anything previously known. In terms of income, number of subordinates controlled, and amount of business handled, the popes at Avignon were actually the most powerful men in Europe.

However, this emphasis on administrative, financial, and judicial affairs did the papacy more harm than good in terms of prestige. Abuses of the worst kind began to plague the papal government. The increasing horde of papal bureaucrats engaged in every type of corruption, such as selling offices and accepting bribes. Knowing that favors were for sale, crowds of opportunists descended on Avignon. Many buyers of church offices were interested only in income, and never went near the office they purchased. Absenteeism thus became a major problem. Bishops and abbots in all parts of Europe resented papal interference in local church affairs and tried to escape papal control, often by turning to their kings, who gladly protected them—for a price. Papal taxation aroused bitterness everywhere. Edward III of England reflected the dislike for the money-grabbing popes when he said: "The successor of the Apostles was ordered to lead the Lord's sheep to the pasture, not to fleece them." Much of this wealth was spent on luxurious living by the clergymen who managed to get their hands on it, arousing the bitter anger of the many in Europe whose lot was poverty. The popes at Avignon were not entirely responsible for this corruption and moral laxness; any huge organization has to face such a problem. But the popes did nothing to correct it, and as a consequence, they were blamed for it. Religion had become a profitable financial venture; religious leaders appeared to be greedy profiteers, little interested in saving souls. A thorough house cleaning was in order. However, the Avignon popes never found the energy to begin such a reform.

The Babylonian Captivity finally ended in 1377 with the return of the pope to Rome. This move only heralded a greater tragedy for the papacy. The return of the pope to Rome led to the election by a part of the College of Cardinals of a second pope, who continued to live at Avignon. Thus began the Great Schism, which lasted until 1417. For forty years the Church was headed by at least two and sometimes three popes. This intolerable situation upset religious life all over Europe. Two administrative systems, two systems of taxation, two systems of church courts were created, leaving everyone at a loss to know which was the right one. Corruption increased. Rival popes played politics more furiously than ever before, each seeking to gain enough allies to oust the other. Many Europeans—and especially princes—thought in terms of obeying the pope who offered the best political "deal." Few took seriously the papal claim to be spiritual leader of Europe; popes who competed with one another and encouraged the division of Christendom seemed little better than greedy politicians. The schism was a costly chapter in the history of the Church.

Before the schism was many years old, serious men began to search for a way of ending the division. Eventually it was agreed that a general council should be called in which churchmen from all Europe would meet to end the schism and reform the clergy. According to the advocates of the conciliar theory, an assembly of bishops possessed an authority superior even to that of the bishop of Rome. This ancient idea which seemed so revolutionary in the context of the Late Middle Ages threatened the whole concept of papal supremacy and the traditional idea of a Church ruled from the top down.

The attempts to apply the conciliar idea increased the confusion in church affairs during the first part of the fifteenth century. Four councils were held between 1409 and 1449. Each was a stormy affair, marked by interminable negotiations. In general, the conciliar movement was a failure in terms of finding a new way of governing the Church, although the second council, held at Constance (1414–1418) did end the schism and reestablish a single pope. Thereafter the popes generally devoted their energies to controlling the councils and ending this dangerous threat to papal authority. Since the councils were often split by quarrels among clergymen representing different nations, papal control was not too difficult to maintain. Perhaps the most significant part of the papal effort came when the popes began to make concessions to Europe's monarchs in order to win their support for the idea of papal governance of the Church. For example, in 1438 Charles VII of France issued the Pragmatic Sanction of Bourges which, when accepted by the papacy, gave the French monarch extensive rights over ecclesiastical income and the clergy. Comparable agreements worked out with other rulers marked a serious limitation on papal power and hastened a trend toward the creation of "national" churches.

Probably the greatest failure of the councils of the fifteenth century was their inability to institute a meaningful reform movement affecting the whole Church. Although many serious clergymen and laymen desired reform and tried to enact reforming legislation at these councils, they never succeeded in devising a practical program of action. When the last council disbanded in 1449, most people had lost confidence in this means of revitalizing the Church. The greatest influence of the conciliar movement was indirect. It raised the whole question of the Church's organization and caused many to conclude that the papacy was not necessarily sacred.

The popes of the last half of the fifteenth century sacrificed the final bit of papal influence by pursuing policies that were far removed from religious leadership. They concentrated on strengthening their control over the Papal States in Italy and competing in the many power struggles raging in Italy in this period. To all outward appearances each was a secular prince, scheming, bribing, and brawling to get what he desired for himself, his family, and his friends. Each enjoyed a life of luxury rivaling that of any prince in Europe. A few lived in a way that was absolutely scandalous, and several became patrons to Renaissance artists and writers who were openly repudiating Christianity in favor of paganism. Since the political activities and the luxury of the papal court were expensive, causing increased financial exactions and increasingly flagrant abuses to gain wealth, corruption became more rampant than ever before. Any thought of reforming the Church slipped further into the background.

Every activity of the popes of this period pointed to a single conclusion: the papacy ceased to enjoy the respect and veneration of most Christians. No one would deny that the popes were powerful in terms of wealth and political resources. What the popes had lost was the moral authority that had been their chief source of influence in the thirteenth cen-

Although the conciliar movement was a failure in terms of reforming the government of the Church, the second council at Constance (1414–1418) did succeed in ending the schism and the system of rival popes that had torn the Church for forty years. This illustration from a contemporary chronicle shows one of the popes arriving at the council. *Photo: Rosgartenmuseums, Konstanz*

tury, and without that moral authority, the papacy became a liability to the Church.

2. THE DECLINE OF THE CLERGY

Although the prolonged decay of the papacy was a shattering blow to the strength of the Church, it was not the only source of decline. Hardly less significant was the steady decay of the whole body of the clergy. A large part of the vitality of the earlier Church had depended upon the work of disciplined, serious, well-trained monks, priests, abbots, and bishops. After 1300 clergymen in general conducted themselves in ways that brought criticism on the Church and reduced their ability to control their flocks.

Especially pronounced was the decline of monasticism. Before 1300 reform movements had repeatedly begun in the monasteries; very often new monastic orders had been founded primarily for the purpose of purifying the Church. Between 1300 and 1500 not a single new monastic order of any importance was established in Western Europe, and the older monastic institutions became increasingly corrupt. Monasteries were no longer a refuge for the dedicated or a stage from which the zealous could launch their efforts to cleanse and purify religious life.

Except for a few purists, especially among the Franciscans, the most powerful orders of the era, the Franciscans and the Dominicans forgot their ideals about poverty and service and turned instead to the pursuit of wealth and power. Lesser orders followed suit. Strict rules about moral purity and piety were relaxed to the point where monks and nuns openly broke their vows. Little attention was paid to the kinds of recruits entering monasteries; many were populated by aristocratic ladies who could not find husbands, younger sons without land, and commoners who wanted to escape work. Monastic government fell into the hands of absentee abbots who thought only of capturing the monastic incomes. Of course not all monks were guilty of this laxness and this lack of religious fer-

vor. However, the culprits, as usual, got most of the publicity. One needs to read only a little of the literature of the fourteenth and fifteenth centuries to realize that monasticism was held in low repute. No longer did monastic life singnify holiness, zeal, and moral excellence. It epitomized rather laziness, greed, immorality, and hypocrisy. Some of the stories in Boccaccio's *Decameron,* for example, reflect the widespread animosity felt toward the monks.

The secular clergy, charged with the Church's business in the everyday world, was equally plagued by corruption and moral laxness. The tone was set by the powerful officials of the papal curia, especially the cardinals, whose vast entourages, immense wealth, and talent for political machinations indeed made them "princes of the Church." Bishops were better known for their political activities and their wealth than for their interest in administering their flocks. Many of them purchased their offices, paying prices that left them little choice but to spend their time wringing money out of their subjects. Some held several offices at once, making it impossible for them to perform the duties of any. Absenteeism was a common thing, many bishops and priests preferring life at Avignon or at a royal court to life in their episcopal sees or parishes. Absentee clergymen often turned their religious duties over to ignorant clerks who served for a small price but who were incapable of guiding religious activities. Heavy papal taxes tempted bishops and lesser clergymen to devote their energies to shady financial practices. Church services, instruction, confessions, preaching, and counseling were slighted, leaving people with religious problems lost and unhappy.

Although the decay of the clergy called for reform and although many Christians were aware of this need, little was done prior to 1500. The Church was organized in such a way that effective reform had to come from above, but we have already discussed the conditions that made it impossible for the papacy to purge the ranks of the clergymen.

3. OLD PRACTICES AND NEW IDEAS

The Church of the later Middle Ages suffered another setback stemming from its inability to put to its service certain new religious ideas that welled up in Western European society. Prior to 1300 most Europeans had accepted and found satisfaction in a basic set of religious ideas discussed in a previous chapter. Fundamentally, this belief centered around the idea that Christ had instituted a Church that held the keys to heaven in the sacraments it administered. Man's duty was to accept the gift from the Church. By 1300 the theologians and canon lawyers insisted that this was *the* way to salvation. After 1300 few church leaders gave much thought to the meaning of the Christian message. Roman Catholic belief and the religious practices based on it fell into a rather unbending, formal pattern that became increasingly mechanical. Most churchmen were content to equate piety with going through the motions of attending services, receiving the sacraments, and obeying the clergy.

During the last two centuries of the Middle Ages dissatisfaction with this situation was demonstrated in many ways. One of the most important manifestations of discontent was an increase in the number of *mystics*, that is, persons who believe they can experience and know God directly through intuitive powers. Mysticism was present throughout the whole of the Middle Ages; St. Bernard and St. Francis of Assisi were mystics. But the fourteenth and fifteenth centuries produced an especially large number. Many of the most influential were simple men and women who never wore clerical garb. Several of them attracted great attention by recounting their visions of God and by teaching fresh ideas about his will toward men. We have already noted how a French peasant girl, Joan of Arc, impressed those she met by claiming to have heard directly from God. Dozens of comparable figures might also be listed.

None was more prominent than Catherine of Siena (1347–1380). At an early age she

spoke of visions of Christ and vowed to remain unmarried in order to serve Him. For many years during her youth she devoted herself to prayer and physical deprivation, believing that this would bring her closer to Christ. Eventually she turned her energies to helping the poor, the sick, the criminals, and the downhearted. She also found time to agitate for religious reform and to try to conciliate political quarrels in Italy. When death ended her career at the age of thirty-three, many believed her to be a saint possessed with powers to heal and to commune personally with Christ. Although she was never seriously at odds with the Church, Catherine certainly added elements to Christianity with which contemporary bishops, priests, monks, and popes were not acquainted. Nearly every country in Europe produced mystics like her. These figures and their followers, although still Roman Catholics, were going beyond the Church's official cult.

The activities of the mystics led to the development of communal movements that operated almost independently of the official Church. These movements were especially strong in Germany and the Low Countries. Perhaps the best example was the Brethren of the Common Life (and its female counterpart, the Sisters of the Common Life), founded by a lay preacher named Gerard Groote (1340–1384), who was one of the many spiritual heirs of the ideas propounded by the great German mystic, Meister Eckhart (1260–1327). This organization was the outgrowth of the teachings of a long series of mystics whose message centered around a new kind of piety that came from prayer, love, and direct communion with God. Devotees of the *devotio moderna* (new devotion) founded communities where members pooled their earnings, engaged in common prayer, confessed their sins to one another, cared for the unfortunates about them, educated their children, and even produced their own devotional literature. One of the best examples of their literature, still read today as a spiritual guide, was Thomas à Kempis's *Imitation of Christ*.

The many communities of Brethren seldom strayed into heresy, but their piety, their puritanical life, their communal spirit, and their mysticism set them apart from traditional and conventional religious life within the main body of the Church. It is not therefore surprising that some of the most important later reformers of the Church were educated in their schools or that the Brethren were often attacked for spreading dangerous ideas.

More radical than the mystics and the new communal movements were the reformers—usually called heretics by the Church—who spoke forth openly and whose words provoked many to violent action against the Church. Some of these reformers were intellectual figures who devoted their time to writing criticisms of the Church. Typical was Marsiglio of Padua, whose devastating book, *The Defender of the Peace*, appeared in 1324. Its thesis was that the secular state ought to be independent of the Church. The Church was obligated to fulfill certain spiritual duties, but was not entitled to exercise any secular powers. Marsiglio advocated that it be deprived of its wealth and relegated to the role of a branch of government, subservient to the ruler of the state. Perhaps even more revolutionary was his view that the pope's claim to rule the Church was a fiction and not in accord with Christ's instructions. Marsiglio argued that the "Church" as a community of all Christians should be ruled by a council representing all elements in Christian society, not by a hierarchy of officials headed by the pope. This idea was soon to be put into effect in the conciliar movement. But Marsiglio's ideas influenced many other than churchmen. Such thinkers were clearly undermining the older opinion with respect to the place of religious affairs and of the Church in society.

Somewhat later an Englishman, John Wycliffe (1320–1384), delivered an even heavier attack on the Church. This Oxford scholar and teacher entered the ranks of rebellion only during the last part of his life after having spent years studying most phases of Roman Catholic teaching and professing a rather traditional scholastic philosophy. It appears that he was turned into a reformer by a growing tide of anticlericalism and antipapalism emerging in an England troubled by the burdens of the Hundred Years' War and internal social and economic stresses. In his first attacks on the Church he argued that the Church had abused its right to hold property and that all church property should be confiscated by the state. This suggestion was eagerly welcomed by many Englishmen who wanted such property for themselves or who were tired of seeing the papacy milk the English to support the corrupt papal court at Avignon. Later Wycliffe advocated the destruction of the whole clerical hierarchy on the grounds that it was not necessary. He insisted that salvation depended not on clergymen, but upon the power of God. Here, of course, he was striking at the fundamental belief upon which the medieval Church was built.

Holding that every man was his own priest, Wycliffe also attacked many of the religious practices of the Church, including elaborate ritual, prayers to saints, veneration of relics, pilgrimages, and the like. Wycliffe even questioned the validity of the sacraments. He argued that Scripture alone must be the authority for Christian doctrine and practice. In line with this idea, he translated the Scriptures into English and encouraged all men to read them. Running throughout his writings was the argument that the ruler should take religious affairs in hand to bring about necessary reforms.

Although Wycliffe was soon condemned as a heretic and forced to leave Oxford, his teachings attracted many followers, known as the Lollards, and for many years Lollard preachers and writers agitated for their master's ideas in England. In time, however, they came to challenge all authority, and the English kings of the fifteenth century joined the Roman Catholic clergy in hunting them down and destroying their movement.

Wycliffe's ideas had their most dramatic and disturbing effect not in England, but in

John Huss, the religious reformer who became a Bohemian national hero, was tried and executed as a heretic in 1415 by the Council of Constance. The artist here records Huss being burned at the stake. *Photo: Rosgartenmuseums, Konstanz*

Bohemia. The leading disciple there was John Huss (ca. 1373–1415), a priest who taught at the University of Prague. His preaching of Wycliffe's radical ideas raised a protest from the Bohemian clergy and ruling faction. Since most of this element was German and was passionately hated by the native population, Huss became a national hero of the Bohemians. Religious revolt mixed with patriotism proved to be explosive. The teachings of Huss were brought to the attention of the papacy, and the agitator was excommunicated as a heretic. He finally consented to journey to the Council of Constance under a promise of safe-conduct from the German emperor. Once at Constance, Huss was imprisoned, tried, and executed as a heretic in 1415. A tremendous rebellion broke out immediately in Bohemia and raged until 1436. Crusade after crusade was preached by the papacy against the Hussites; several German armies, led by an emperor who was anxious to re-

claim Bohemia, were soundly thrashed by the fanatical Bohemians. Eventually peace was restored by granting certain concessions of a religious nature to the Hussites. However, a faction of the followers of Huss and Wycliffe, called Taborites, was not satisfied by these concessions and became practically a church apart during the last years of the Middle Ages.

These few cases illustrating the ways in which religious thought and practice deviated from the norms defined by the official Church by no means span the full range of religious ferment. During the fourteenth and fifteenth centuries, there were any number of fiery preachers proclaiming to emotional crowds the end of the world and the coming of God's wrathful judgment. Wildly emotional cults, such as the Flagellants, who constantly whipped one another to atone for the world's sins, preyed on men's religious sensibilities, especially in times of great crisis like the Black Death. Repeated cases of brutal massacres of the Jews in the name of Christian righteousness marred the histories of many cities. Witchcraft flourished on an unprecedented scale. Increasingly men sought assurances of salvation by purchasing indulgences, which ensured that the punishment due for sins would be removed. Never was the cult of relics more appealing and more brazenly abused, as illustrated by Chaucer's pardoner with his bag full of "pigs' bones." Preoccupation with death in particularly horrible forms was the identifying characteristic of the literature, art, and sermons of the age.

Clearly, Europe was in a state of religious ferment. Neither the gentle mystics nor the fiery-tongued rebels, neither the adherents of the occult nor the victims of fearful hysteria were at home in the Roman Catholic Church. They had begun to strike out in all directions, questioning ritual, devotional practices, organization, and dogma. But the institution that claimed to care for men's souls either ignored the quest or ruthlessly crushed those who showed signs of discontent. This failure to meet basic religious problems was but another sign of the decay of the Church.

4. THE FAILURE OF INTELLECTUAL LEADERSHIP

The Church suffered another serious blow to its dominant position in society as a consequence of fundamental developments in the intellectual life of Western Europe. It will be recalled that the major thrust of thirteenth-century thought was toward reconciling the truth of God's revelation with the truths discovered by human reason. That reconciliation was apparently achieved by the scholastics of the thirteenth century. Thomas Aquinas' *Summae* created a vast synthesis of religious and philosophical concepts that seemed to prove the Church possessed of unassailable truth and to provide complete justification of its teachings. However, the Thomistic synthesis proved fragile. It had, in fact, left many basic questions unanswered. Even before 1300, thinkers were assailing it and creating intellectual fissures in the West that made it impossible for the Church any longer to monopolize learning.

Outwardly, the life of learning during the Late Middle Ages continued down already established paths. The universities remained the focal points of learning in theology, law, medicine, and the natural sciences and provided the major attraction to most intellectuals. The scholastic method, stressing close logical analysis of theological and philosophical propositions, continued to prevail. What did change was the emphasis in intellectual endeavors. In general terms, many thinkers gave up their effort to reconcile faith and reason and devoted their energies to an attack on the basic proposition that faith and reason were compatible. Synthesis gave way to analysis. Even while the Thomistic synthesis was being hammered out, there were those who refused to accept it; most adamant were the Averroists, with their unqualified rationalism, a position that persisted throughout the Late Middle Ages. Shortly after Aquinas' death in 1274, the attack on his position heightened. The Franciscan scholar John Duns Scotus (ca. 1266–1308) argued with great force that God's

freedom and power were so exalted that all attempts to describe his attributes in rational terms imposed limits on him that were untenable. In effect, Duns Scotus was saying that the knowledge of God—theology—was not a proper matter for rational speculation.

This trend of thought was expanded by William of Ockham (ca. 1300–1349), an English Franciscan who taught at Oxford and served in the court of Emperor Lewis IV of Bavaria until the Black Death claimed his life. A powerful logician, Ockham assailed the basic rational supports upon which Thomistic theology was constructed. In his mind such things as the existence of God and the immortality of the soul were not rationally demonstrable; knowledge pertaining to these kinds of truths came only by intuition and mystical experience. Theology and philosophy thus became separate "sciences," incapable of reconciliation and fundamentally unrelated. In defining the realm of philosophy and reason, Ockham argued that only by sense perception of individual objects could man know; in this respect he was a philosophical nominalist, repudiating the long tradition that insisted that ideas constituted the ultimate reality (philosophical realism). Duns Scotus and William of Ockham gained powerful disciples who followed up the assault on Thomism. Fourteenth- and fifteenth-century scholasticism was dominated by their logical wars. We need not venture into detailed descriptions of these struggles; what is important is that the thirteenth-century confidence in one all-embracing truth had been shattered and with it had been shattered a powerful prop of the Church.

The disarray among the scholastics encouraged and even directed serious thinkers to take new intellectual paths. The assault on the power of human reason to understand God nourished the mysticism we have already described. Since reason was distinct from faith, political theorists like Marsiglio of Padua constructed new concepts of the governance of church and state which were especially destructive to theologically based justifications of the Church's power. The attack on rational theology opened the way for the radical theological concepts of Wycliffe and Huss. Many intellectuals, disillusioned by the barren wastes of scholasticism, found intellectual sustenance in classical literature and philosophy. Most pregnant for the future was the growing interest in science. Since—according to William of Ockham—reason was not capable of discerning religious truths, it must confine itself to the tangible objects of this world. Following this path, scholars, especially at the universities of Paris and Oxford, produced a considerable body of scientific knowledge and provided significant corrections to Greco-Arabic scientific generalizations. Their efforts laid the groundwork for the revolutionary scientific discoveries of Copernicus, Galileo, and others in the sixteenth and seventeenth centuries. These diverging strands of thought pointed clearly to a more pluralistic intellectual climate than had prevailed in the thirteenth century. As intellectual life became more variegated, the potential for intellectual criticism of the Church increased, and the Church's ability to control intellectual activity for its benefit decreased.

5. THE PRESSURE OF NEW FORCES

So far we have noted the sure signs of decay *within* the Church—decline of leadership, corruption, inflexibility in dogma and ritual, lack of strength to reform, and loss of intellectual vigor. But these do not reveal the true dimensions of the crisis enveloping the Church. While the Church was faltering internally, new, nonreligious forces were challenging its leadership. This is not the place to analyze these new forces in detail; they will be discussed later. They must be mentioned here, however, merely to round out the picture of the decline of the Church.

The new, aggressive national states certainly harassed the Church in the later Middle Ages. The rulers of these states were determined to control any institution that challenged their dominance or that might be useful to them. Everywhere the princes, although still Catholic, sought to limit and dominate the Church. In England a series of laws was enacted to exclude the papacy from taxing church property and from controlling church offices. The king and Parliament alike joined in this activity. In France the royal government worked steadily, often with the help of the clergy, to establish a "French" church, independent of the papacy and subservient to the crown. In Spain late in the fifteenth century the monarchs even undertook to reform the Church independently of the papacy. As 1500 approached, "national" churches, dominated by kings, were becoming a reality at the expense of the previously self-sufficient universal Church.

The middle class, accepting a capitalistic philosophy, was likewise challenging the Church's social and economic teachings. Many capitalists would have liked to see church wealth put to a different use. Most of them paid no attention to religious arguments against charging interest or on behalf of fair prices. To these men, the Church was reactionary and deserved to be deprived of its position of power and its wealth. More ominous was their value system, grounded in secularism, the goods of this world, pleasure, individualism, and practicality. These new values did not necessarily or even usually lead to a repudiation of the Church by the bourgeoisie; rather, they combined with economic interests to reduce the claim of the Church on bourgeois energies and wealth.

Finally, a new breed of thinkers, writers, and artists, sometimes called collectively *humanists*, was emerging to criticize, disregard, or repudiate many of the teachings and practices of the Church. The new humanism, developing first and most vigorously in Italy and then spreading to other parts of Western Europe, was oriented toward the joys and wonders of the physical world. It found its major intellectual sustenance in classical thought and its esthetic values in classical art. Its setting was urban, and its patronage came chiefly from the emerging bourgeois elite. Its emphasis was toward realism and naturalism. Its spirit was individualistic and localistic. It generated in its adherents a critical, analytical temper not averse to challenging authority. Wherever the humanistic spirit manifested itself, it was at odds with some of the most profound and basic positions taken by the medieval Church. The progress of humanism thus challenged and weakened the cultural undergirding that had helped sustain the medieval Church.

Seeing the combination of internal difficulties and challenging outside forces that undermined the power and influence of the Church in the late Middle Ages, one can no longer doubt that an epoch was ending. Admittedly, the breakup of the medieval empires, the decline of feudal institutions, the dislocation of the class structure, the failure of manorialism and the guild system—all point toward the passing of medieval civilization. However, the Church had stood above all these as the essential factor in medieval civilization. For centuries it had played the leading role in determining what men thought and how they acted. Without its presence, medieval civilization is inconceivable. The decline of the Church marked the passing of the medieval epoch in Western European history.

Suggested Reading

Decline of the Medieval Church. The works of Deanesly, Latourette, Hughes (Vol. III), and Bihlmeyer and Tüchle listed in Chapter 23 will provide excellent introductions to Church history in the fourteenth and fifteenth centuries. More detailed is A. C. Flick, *The Decline of the Medieval Church* (2 vols., 1930). A detailed treatment of the travail of the papacy in the Late Middle Ages is L. E. Elliott-Binns, *History of the Decline and Fall of the Medieval Papacy* (1934). T. S. R. Boase, *Boniface VIII* (1933), is thorough on the career of a key figure in papal history. **G. Mollat, *The Popes at Avignon, 1305–1378* (Harper Torchbook), presents the case for the Avignon popes in a favorable light. A learned study of the Great Schism is W. Ullmann, *The Origins of the Great Schism: A Study in Fourteenth-century Ecclesiastical History* (1948). The origin and nature of the conciliar movement is skillfully presented by Brian Tierney, *Foundations of the Conciliar Theory* (1955).

New Religious Movements. There is no adequate survey of monastic history in the Late Middle Ages. The development of mysticism is treated with great insight by R. M. Jones, *The Flowering of Mysticism* (1939); and J. M. Clark, *The Great German Mystics: Eckhart, Tauler, and Susa* (1949). A. Hyma, *The Christian Renaissance: A History of the Devotio Moderna* (2nd ed., 1965), gives a sense of the spirit pervading the religious communities that developed in the Late Middle Ages. More radical movements disturbing the established religious order are described by **Norman Cohn, *The Pursuit of the Millennium* (Harper Torchbook); and Gordon Leff, *Heresy in the Later Middle Ages* (1967). There are several valuable studies of John Wycliffe. The most thorough is H. B. Workman, *John Wyclif: A Study of the English Medieval Church* (2 vols., 1926). Stronger in interpretation is **K. B. McFarlane, *The Origins of Religious Dissent in England* (Collier), originally published as *John Wycliffe and the Beginning of English Nonconformity* (1952). A good recent study is G. H. W. Parker, *The Morning Star: Wycliffe and the Dawn of the Reformation* (1965). The Hussite movement is treated by Howard Kaminsky, *A History of the Hussite Revolution* (1967); and F. G. Heymann, *John Žižka and the Hussite Revolution* (1955).

Intellectual Developments: There is little to recommend on the cultural history of this period specifically. The best guides are several of the works cited in Chapter 24: Taylor and Artz for general treatments; Knowles, Leff, Gilson, and Copleston for philosophy and theology; Morrall, Ullman, and McIlwain for political theory; Crombie for science; and Jackson for literary history. Works relating to the cultural aspects of the Renaissance will be cited later.

Sources. Anyone wishing to gain an insight into the concepts of the most influential philosopher of the Late Middle Ages might read **William of Ockham, *Philosophical Writings*, trans. P. Boehner (Liberal Arts Press); however, this master logician is a real challenge. A fundamental work on political theory is **Marsilius of Padua, *Defensor Pacis*, trans. A. Gerwith (Harper Torchbook). An excellent anthology of mystical writings is R. C. Petry, ed., *Late Medieval Mysticism* (1957). The classic piece of mystical literature from this period is **Thomas à Kempis, *Imitation of Christ* (many editions; a good one is the translation of L. Sherley-Price, Penguin). Another piece of mystical writing worth sampling is **Meister Eckhart, A Modern Translation*, trans. R. B. Blakney (Harper Torchbook). Valuable insight into religious thought is provided by V. Scudder, *St. Catherine of Siena as Seen in Her Letters* (1905). M. Spinka, ed., *Advocates of Reform From Wyclif to Erasmus* (1953), contains a good selection of material illustrating how contemporaries viewed the problem of correcting the decaying Church during the fourteenth and fifteenth centuries.

RETROSPECT

By 1500 there were many signs that Western European society stood again on the threshold of a remarkable era of expansion; that date marked a moment comparable in many ways to the year 1000, when Western Europe made its first great leap forward. Yet it is understandable that most men living in 1500 were dimly, if at all, aware of the great promise before them. Like men in most ages, they were better instructed by the immediate past than by the unrealized future. That immediate past had been a troubled one. Our review of it in the preceding two chapters emphasized the multiple stresses and tensions which affected the basic patterns of civilization characteristic of the Middle Ages. Given the magnitude of these difficulties, it is not surprising that men's thoughts were colored by pessimism and despair and that their reactions to life were marked by excess and violence.

In retrospect, the causes of the troubles of the Late Middle Ages seem fairly clear. The major institutions, thought patterns, and value systems that had been created prior to 1300 as essential to medieval Western European civilization had unstable features that began to emerge after 1300. The medieval political ideal of a Christian commonwealth, institutionalized in the Holy Roman Empire, was flawed by fundamental disagreements about the leadership of the ideal commonwealth and by deep-seated localism. The feudal monarchies were beset by conflicts between royal authority and private privilege. The universal Church, with its central leadership, and uniform doctrine, liturgy, and discipline, was challenged by religious localism, new concepts of leadership, and heterodox spiritual visions. Localistic, monopolistic, self-sufficient economic organizations contended with international, profit-seeking, individualistic enterprises. Faith and reason, Latin and vernacular cultures, religious and secular values confronted each other in men's minds. In all these institutional and intellectual contradictions, each opposite side was an integral part of the medieval order. The strength of medieval civilization rested in the balancing of the two. When the balance became unsettled, then strife and turmoil and uncertainty ensued.

In a superficial way, the general situation prevailing between 1300 and 1500 might resemble that which marked the third and fourth centuries of the Christian era, when classical Greco-Roman civilization suffered its fatal decline. In both eras there was violence and tension arising primarily from flaws in the institutions and values basic to their existence. However, a little reflection will reveal that, unlike the situation in the late classical period, the difficulties facing late medieval society arose not from the total exhaustion of an established pattern of civilization, but from the deepening disparity between vital forces vying to establish the dominant tone in Western European civilization. It was not the onset of decreptitude, but the release of vital energies stored up in institutions and concepts that caused the disturbances in the Late Middle Ages. The release of these energies for new growth only awaited the decision to opt for one way or the other between the alternatives posited by medieval Western European civilization: strong central government or private interest, reason or faith, individualistic religious concepts or a universal Church.

By 1500, these contradictions had begun to be resolved. The path toward the future was emerging. Strong monarchy, reason, religious diversity, a pluralistic culture, a capitalistic economy, among other things, were gaining the upper hand. The future of Western European society lay in the development of these patterns as the essence of civilized life; a future that would be spectacular. But as it unfolded, it was never marked by a catastrophic break such as that which signaled the transition from classical to medieval Western European civilization. The wave of Europe's future had already formed in the medieval world. In fact, "modern" Europe was born in the Middle Ages, and its history is unintelligible without a knowledge of the civilization of that period.

Part Seven

The Beginning of Modern Times

Fifteenth and Sixteenth Centuries

In the previous section, we have described the various tensions and weakening institutions that marked the decline of the medieval world during the fourteenth and fifteenth centuries; now we shall see how the institutions that we have come to call modern grew out of the decaying medieval system.

In place of the declining feudal monarchies and empires there arose the national or territorial state, which became the dominant political institution of the modern era. The first of these national states to emerge were Spain, Portugal, France, and England. From then until now, the history of the Western world has been centered around them and the other national states that were patterned after them.

Europe's medieval economy, characterized by subsistence agriculture, monopolistic guilds, and localism, gave way to capitalistic practices and institutions. The landed aristocracy who had dominated the medieval economy now found themselves challenged and threatened by a new middle class of aggressive entrepreneurs, whose ambition and vitality pushed Europeans out of their own small world into the larger one. The end result was the discovery and domination of much of the rest of the world.

The decline of the Western Christian Church in the last two centuries of the Middle Ages had important repercussions not only on religious institutions and beliefs, but also on the nonreligious thought, the literature, and the arts of the Western European world as well. Theology could no longer command the attention of most of the best minds. Increasingly, they turned to humanistic philosophy and to science—natural and political. Artists became obsessed with the beauties of the physical world. In short, there was a *renaissance* (rebirth) of secularism.

The Western Church itself split, and much of Northern Europe became Protestant. This, in turn, provoked or at least hastened a Roman Catholic revitalization or reformation. The breakup of the powerful Roman Catholic Church which had so dominated medieval Western Europe contributed further to the secularization of society.

Since these four great movements—the rise of national states, the rise of a capitalistic economy, the renaissance of secularism, and the Reformation (Protestant and Roman Catholic) occurred primarily during the fifteenth and sixteenth centuries, it may be useful to conceive of the fifteenth as a century of transition and the sixteenth as the first century of the modern era.

Chapter 27 ❧ The Rise of National States

In fifteenth-century Europe, at least four royal monarchs succeeded in creating powerful national states. They did so at the expense of the feudal barons who were unable to adjust to changing conditions, and had lost their former necessary function as the main support of the monarchy. Kings no longer needed them. The longbow and gun powder had begun to destroy the fighting effectiveness of the mounted armored knight as early as the fourteenth century. At the same time, reviving commerce, bringing with it a moneyed economy and a prosperous middle class, undermined the economic monopoly of the land-owning aristocracy. The kings made use of the new, moneyed class and with its support hired standing armies equipped with the new weapons. To legalize their growing power, the kings utilized the principles of Roman law to evade the common law upon which feudal holdings were based. (Roman law considered kings to be sovereigns in whose hands the welfare of all the people was placed.)

Another factor that facilitated the building of nation-states was the rise of a national consciousness based primarily upon language. In each of the lands that are now Spain, Portugal, France, England, Germany, and Italy, one dialect became predominant. Once established, the national vernacular became the instrument for propagating the common traditions, customs, and legends on which national pride and loyalty were built.

Although other factors retarded unification in Italy and Germany until the nineteenth century, Spain, Portugal, France, and England were already well on their way to becoming powerful national states in the late fifteenth century.

1. SPAIN

The most powerful and influential of the new states at the opening of the modern era was Spain. The energy and enthusiasm that Spain displayed at this time may be attributed in part, at least, to her long and finally successful struggle against the Moors. By the middle of the thirteenth century the Moors had been driven out of the entire Iberian Peninsula except for the southernmost province of Granada. Furthermore, the numerous medieval feudal holdings in what is now Spain had been consolidated into four large kingdoms— Castile, Aragon, Granada, and Navarre (south of the Pyrenees). The marriage of Ferdinand of Aragon and Isabella of Castile in 1469 united for all practical purposes the two largest kingdoms. During their reign (1474–1516) [1] Granada and Navarre were conquered. Thus, within a forty-seven-year span from 1469 to 1516 the Spanish national state was created.

Ferdinand and Isabella strove for political and religious unity. In order to suppress further the jealous nobility, they allied themselves with the middle class, leaning heavily upon it for financial and administrative assistance. In return, the joint sovereigns did everything in their power to advance the

---

[1] Isabella ruled Castile from 1474 to 1504, and Ferdinand ruled Aragon from 1479 to 1516.

fortunes of the merchants. Vigorous enforcement of law and order, stabilization of the currency, building of roads and bridges, tariff protection of home industries—all served to advance the economic prosperity of Spain in general and the middle class in particular. The climax of this commercial expansion came in 1492 with the discovery of the New World in the name of Spain. The ensuing profits and loot further strengthened the hands of the Spanish sovereigns by freeing them from dependence upon the Cortes (the representative bodies that had grown up in both Castile and Aragon during the Middle Ages) for funds.

In religious affairs as well Ferdinand and Isabella attained virtually complete unity for their country. Against the two non-Christian groups in their realm, the Jews and the Muslims, the "Catholic Sovereigns" waged a campaign of conversion or extermination. The Jews had long been the object of hatred and persecution in Christian Europe. In part this hatred derived from religious differences, but there was also an economic factor. Church laws against usury had given the Jews a monopoly on moneylending, which high rates of interest rendered very profitable. The envy and hatred of the Christians led to periodic outbreaks of violence. In the late fourteenth century, an outbreak of unusual severity forced many Spanish Jews to seek safety in outward conversion. But these Marranos, as the pseudoconverts were called, were the object of increasing suspicion. Finally Ferdinand and Isabella, yielding to Dominican fanatics, permitted the Inquisition to be introduced into Spain. At the mercy of this dread church court, the Marranos were terrorized by imprisonment, torture, and loss of life and property. In 1492 the remaining Jews were ordered to leave the country. The exiles thus banished (estimated to be in the neigh-

borhood of one hundred and fifty thousand) took much of their wealth and all their economic energy and skills with them.[2]

Shortly afterward the Muslims suffered a similar fate. Upon surrendering their last stronghold in Granada, in 1492, they had been promised religious freedom in return for submission to the political authority of the Spanish crown. However, again the "Catholic Sovereigns" yielded to the increasing pressure of religious intolerance, and in 1502 the Muslims were ordered to accept Christianity or leave Spain. Although thousands did leave, even more thousands remained and went through the farce of outward conversion. But these "converts," called Moriscos, only delayed their fate. In the two succeeding reigns they too were persecuted and expelled. A little later the Inquisition was also used to rid Spain of Protestantism. Spain, then, was unified religiously, but at an economic and intellectual cost that was to blight her future. Nevertheless, territorially consolidated and politically unified by Ferdinand and Isabella, enriched by the wealth of the New World, and inspired by the crusading zeal of a purified

[2] The Jews had earlier been expelled from England, France, and the German states.

A coin of Ferdinand and Isabella, sovereigns of Spain, most powerful of the new national states. *Photo: American Numismatic Society*

NLAND

elsingfors

ONIA

IVONIA
iga

• Novgorod

• Moscow

R U S S I A
(MUSCOVY)

• Vilna

LITHUANIA

L A N D

Kiev •

nberg
LICIA   PODOLIA

MOLDAVIA

Dniester R.

YEDISAN

KHANATE OF THE CRIMEA

NSYLVANIA
Y

CRIMEA

WALLACHIA
Bucharest •

R.

Danube

ofia •

Adrianople •

• Salonica

AEGEAN
SEA

EECE
anto

CHIOS
(Genoa)

• Smyrna

REA

(Venice)

BLACK SEA

• Constantinople

O T T O M A N   E M P I R E

RHODES (Turkish)

CYPRUS
(Venice)

CRETE
(Venice)

0   100   200   300 miles

and triumphant religion, Spain was to be the most powerful and influential of the new national states during the first century of the modern era.

2. PORTUGAL

Next to Spain the most prosperous and energetic national state in the sixteenth century was Portugal. The origins of this state can be traced back to the eleventh century, when, in return for his services in the struggle against the Moors, Count Henry of Burgundy was granted a fief in the vicinity of Oporto by the king of Leon. Count Henry and his doughty successors not only asserted and achieved independence from their Spanish overlords, but by driving the Moors steadily southward, carved out for themselves the sizable state of Portugal. Meanwhile, the Portuguese dialect was developing into a national language somewhat different from Spanish.

Hemmed in by their larger Spanish neighbors on land, the Portuguese turned to the sea. In the fifteenth century adventuresome navigators such as Diaz and Vasco da Gama carried the Portuguese flag around the Cape of Good Hope to India and laid the foundation for a vast empire. As a result of the papal Line of Demarcation (1493) and the Treaty of Tordesillas (1494) with Spain, Portugal obtained a monopoly on trade with the East around the Cape. From this trade she amassed more wealth than Spain extracted from the New World. However, so many of Portugal's able merchants and administrators went out to the East to make their names and fortunes that her sparse reserves of talent were depleted at home.

Like Spain, Portugal persecuted and expelled her Jews, Muslims, and Protestants. And like Spain her brilliance rapidly waned after the sixteenth century.

3. FRANCE

The reign of Louis XI (1461–1483) may be said to mark the beginning of France as a modern

467

This altar relief from the Capilla Real in Granada shows the surrender of the last Moorish kingdom to the Catholic sovereigns in 1492. With the conquest of Navarre, the modern Spanish national state was created. *Photo: Foto Mas*

national state. Louis came to the throne of France eight years after the end of the Hundred Years' War with England. His predecessor had used the war emergency to obtain a permanent tax (*taille*) and a standing army for the crown. During the last phase of the war a great upsurge of French national spirit under the leadership of Joan of Arc made possible, at long last, the expulsion of the English invaders. Louis XI put these inherited advantages to clever use. First of all, he set out to crush the power of the feudal nobility who had taken advantage of the royal distress during the Hundred Years' War to assert their virtual independence of the crown. By craft and by direct military force he broke up the league that the insubordinate nobility formed against him and reduced the individual nobles to submission. In order to

achieve this goal, Louis utilized the rising middle class. In return for its support he placed many member of this class in his councils and in key administrative posts and did what he could to foster commerce and industry. Roads, harbors, and waterways were improved. Shipbuilding, commerce, and industry were encouraged by royal subsidies and protective regulation.

Louis XI virtually completed the territorial consolidation of the French national state. He brought province after province under direct royal control, until by the end of his reign France has acquired all of its modern territory except the northwesternmost peninsula of Brittany (which was acquired by Louis' son) and a few territories along her fluid northeastern frontier. This expansive movement brought Louis XI into conflict with

Charles the Bold of Burgundy. Charles the Bold (perhaps "the Rash" would have been a more accurate title) had inherited rich and strategically located territories that included the Netherlands, the duchy of Burgundy, and the free county of Burgundy. These he hoped to consolidate into a great national state—the old Middle Kingdom of Charlemagne's grandson Lothair—between France and Germany. Had he succeeded in doing so, the course of history might have been changed significantly. However, Charles the Bold and his successor, Mary of Burgundy, were no match for the "spider king." Charles was killed battling the Swiss, and Mary was unable to prevent Louis XI from seizing the duchy of Burgundy, Picardy, and part of Flanders. (The abortive Burgundian "Middle Kingdom" has been a battleground between France and Germany throughout much of the modern period.) Thus consolidated and enlarged, France was to play a dominant role in European affairs in the centuries which followed.

Louis XI's schemes, however, did not include the betterment of the condition of the lower classes. Having paid for his ambitious programs with heavy taxes but having received little in return, the lower classes remained disaffected and discontented.

4. ENGLAND

Modern times, so far as English history is concerned, may be said to have begun with the reign of Henry VII (1485–1509), the first of the Tudor dynasty. The political unity of the English national state had been brought about as early as 1066 by William the Conqueror (aided to a considerable degree by geography). However, the feudal system, with its decentralization of administration and society, the Hundred Years' War with France (1337–1453), and the Wars of the Roses (1455–85) between the rival houses of Lancaster and York, had by the last quarter of the fifteenth century brought England to a state of turmoil bordering on anarchy. Henry

Tudor acquired the English throne by victory on the battlefield over the Yorkish king, Richard III, who was slain. Himself a member of the Lancastrian family, Henry ended the bloody dynastic feud by marrying Elizabeth of York.

The most pressing task confronting the strong-willed new monarch was the suppression of the turbulent nobility. The great feudal barons had taken advantage of the decades of civil war and of the long rule of a weak king prior to the war to defy royal authority. They retained their own private armies and overawed the local courts. At once and with great vigor Henry VII proceeded to enforce the laws against livery and maintenance,[3] thereby destroying the illegal feudal armies. Since the regular local courts were too weak to proceed against the nobility, Henry set up his own Court of Star Chamber, which, backed by the royal army, was able to overawe the most powerful barons and bring them to justice and to submission to the crown.

In these undertakings Henry VII had the wholehearted support of the lesser gentry and the middle and lower classes, all of whom yearned for peace and order. The middle class, particularly, desired stability for the sake of its growing business activities, and it was with this class that the Tudors allied themselves. Henry selected many of his counselors and administrators from the ranks of the bourgeoisie. He made favorable commercial treaties with the Netherlands, Denmark, and even with Venice, the jealous queen of the rich Eastern Mediterranean trade. Navigation acts were passed to protect English shippers. Henry's frugality and careful collection and handling of revenues not only were good business, but freed the king of dependence upon Parliament for funds.

---

[3] So called from the practice of the peasantry wearing the lord's badge or livery, signifying membership in his private army, in return for the lord's promise to maintain (support) them in courts of justice.

Henry VII, unlike Louis XI of France, attempted to protect the interests of the English peasants, who were being forced off the land by the enclosure movement. The landed nobility, taking advantage of the brisk demand for wool, were turning their farming lands into sheep runs. Thousands of dispossessed peasants roamed the countryside as beggars or drifted to the cities looking for work at any price. Laws passed to protect the peasants from dispossession proved to be largely ineffective, however, as anyone traveling through the lush green and largely untilled English countryside can observe today.

Henry VII died in 1509, prematurely worn out by his arduous labors. But he passed along to his glamorous son, Henry VIII, a united and orderly national state and a well-filled treasury. And under his granddaughter, Elizabeth, England rose to a position of first-rate importance in European and world affairs.

5. GERMANY AND ITALY

Although Germany and Italy have played a vital role in modern European history, they did not achieve political unity at the opening of the modern period. That failure, although it did not prevent them from making important contributions to art and science, did create political maladjustments that account for much of Europe's modern turmoil, particularly in the twentieth century.

During the fifteenth century, when the Spanish, Portuguese, French, and English peoples were becoming united under powerful national monarchs, the German-speaking peoples remained split up into more than three hundred virtually independent units. The only political bond between them was the impotent government of the Holy Roman Empire. This ramshackle institution—a survival of the state set up by Charlemagne in 800 and revived by Otto the Great in 962—purported to be a restoration of the old Roman Empire, but it never was. In the Middle Ages,

when the Spanish, Portuguese, French, and English sovereigns were consolidating their territories and their authority, the German emperors were frittering away their time and energy trying to bring Italy under their control. While they were away from Germany on these quixotic ventures, the local feudal barons conspired against them, consolidated their own power, and built up hereditary states of their own within the empire. Meanwhile, territory after territory slipped from under the emperor's control, until by the opening of the modern period, the Holy Roman Empire included for all practical purposes only the German-speaking states (plus Czech-speaking Bohemia).

Eventually seven of the emperors' most prominent subjects gained the right to elect him. This elective feature not only diminished the prestige of the emperor, but forced candidates to bribe the electors and bargain and promise away any chance of strengthening the office. Since the emperor had no sure income, he had no military force with which to enforce his will. Even to defend the empire, he was forced to call upon his subject princes to furnish troops. The lawmaking and taxing power lay in the hands of the Diet, which was composed of three houses: the house of electors, the house of lesser princes, and the house of representatives of the free imperial cities. The Diet had no regular time or place of meeting, and was seldom able to reach agreement on any important question. In the late fifteenth century an imperial court was set up to settle disputes between member states. However, lacking any means of enforcing its decisions, this instrument too proved ineffective.

The one factor that gave any semblance of vitality to the Holy Roman Empire was the Hapsburg family. A Hapsburg was first elected emperor in 1273. After 1438, with only one brief exception, no one but a Hapsburg was elected until the empire finally died at the hand of Napoleon in 1806. By marriage and diplomacy, the Hapsburgs expanded their

THE FIVE GREAT POWERS

Republic of Florence

Duchy of Milan

Kingdom of Naples

Papal States

Venetian Republic

1 MARCH OF MONTFERRAT
2 MARCH OF MANTUA
3 DUCHY OF MODENA
4 REPUBLIC OF LUCCA
5 COUNTY OF ASTI
6 DUCHY OF FERRARA

DUCHY OF SAVOY
Turin
PIEDMONT
Milan
Pavia
GENOA
Genoa
Parma
EMILIA
Bologna
Pisa
Arno R.
TUSCANY
Florence
Siena
SIENA
Perugia
Tiber R.
Rome
Verona
Adige R.
Venice
Padua
ISTRIA
Po R.
Adda R.
ROMAGNA MARCHES
DALMATIA

ELBA
(to Florence)

CORSICA
(to Genoa)

SARDINIA
(to Aragon)

Benevento
Naples
Bari
Brindisi
PUGLIA
CALABRIA

Palermo

SICILY
(to Aragon)

Italy 1454

original Austrian lands until they possessed at the opening of the modern period one of the largest and richest dynastic estates in Europe. Although, therefore, the Holy Roman emperor as emperor was virtually powerless, as head of the house of Hapsburg he was one of the most influential of monarchs. Nevertheless, all efforts of the Hapsburgs to strengthen the central government of the empire foundered on the rocks of German particularism—the local interests of the jealous princes.

Italy's modern history has paralleled to a

considerable degree that of Germany. At the opening of the modern period the Italian peninsula was divided into six major independent states without even the pretense of a Holy Roman Empire to unite them. The six were The Kingdom of the Two Sicilies (sometimes called Naples), the Papal States, Florence (Tuscany), Venice, Milan, and Piedmont. The Kingdom of the Two Sicilies, the poorest and most backward of the Italian states, occupied the southern third of the peninsula and the large island of Sicily. During the fifteenth and sixteenth centuries it was a bone of contention over which France and Spain repeatedly fought. The Papal States occupied the central portion of the peninsula. These states were ruled by the pope not only as supreme pontiff, but also as political head. The popes based their claims to political rule over these states upon the Donation of Pepin, the father of Charlemagne, who drove out the Lombards and gave the territory to the pope in 756. Florence and Venice, republics in name, were dominated by rich banking and commercial families. Milan, another thriving center of commerce, was ruled by an autocratic duke. Piedmont, occupying the northwesternmost portion of the peninsula, was the property of the house of Savoy. This mountainous state, which eventually assumed leadership in the unification of Italy, played a relatively minor role in Italian affairs before the nineteenth century.

An important factor accounting for Italian disunity in the first centuries of the modern era was the presence of the Papal States in the strategic center of the peninsula. Fearing the loss of their territories to a national monarch, the popes vigorously opposed all efforts to set up an Italian national state. A second factor was the long tradition of independence and the great commercial prosperity in the thirteenth, fourteenth, and fifteenth centuries of Florence, Venice, and Milan, where a spirit of local rather than national pride and loyalty was encouraged. Like the Germans, the political division and weakness of the Italians in an age of powerful national states continued to be a standing invitation to aggression against them.

6. INTERNATIONAL RIVALRIES IN THE AGE OF CHARLES V, 1516–1556

The rise of national states failed to bring peace to Europe. The national monarchs, supported by the bourgeoisie, had justified their own aggrandizement on the grounds that it was necessary to end the interminable feudal wars, and they had in fact established a large measure of internal law and order. However, the little feudal wars were followed by big national and dynastic wars. Throughout the first modern century—the sixteenth—international strife centered around the house of Hapsburg.

During most of the first half of the century the house of Hapsburg was headed by Emperor Charles V. Charles V inherited from his parents and four grandparents an array of territories and claims that have been exceeded in history only by those of his son, Philip II. This is Charles' family tree:

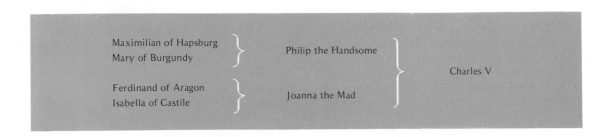

From his grandfather Maximilian he inherited the Hapsburg provinces of Austria, Tyrol, Styria, Carinthia, and Carniola, to which were added in Charles' lifetime Hungary, Bohemia, Moravia, and Silesia. As a Hapsburg, he also inherited a good claim to the imperial crown of the Holy Roman Empire. From his grandmother Mary he inherited the Burgundian lands: the free county of Burgundy (Franche Comté), the Netherlands, Luxemburg, Flanders, Artois, and claims to the duchy of Burgundy and Picardy, which had been seized by Louis XI. From his grandfather Ferdinand he received Aragon, Minorca, Majorca, Sardinia, and The Kingdom of the Two Sicilies. From his grandmother Isabella he received Castile and a claim to the entire Western Hemisphere based upon the papal Line of Demarcation (1493) and the Treaty of Tordesillas (1494). And from Ferdinand and Isabella jointly, he inherited Granada and Spanish Navarre.

The very size of Charles V's far-flung holdings spelled perpetual trouble. The language problem alone was appalling. To this were added differences in local customs, tastes, and eventually religion. Moreover, Charles V was sure to become involved in all the major international conflicts of Europe. Born and reared in the Netherlands, Charles got himself accepted in Spain only after serious opposition and open revolt. His efforts to strengthen the government of the Holy Roman Empire and to raise money and troops there were frustrated by the local German princes. Finally, the Lutheran revolt further split the empire and shattered completely the personal power of Charles in Germany.

Charles V found himself almost continually at war with Francis I of France. Each feared the other's power. Francis vigorously contested Charles' election as Holy Roman Emperor. They fought over conflicting territorial claims in Italy, the Burgundian lands, and along the French-Spanish border. Charles won nearly all the battles, but was never able to make his victories permanent.

The relations between Charles of Hapsburg and England were limited to a personal family quarrel. When Henry VIII sought an annulment of his marriage to Catherine of Aragon, the aunt of Charles V, Charles used his influence with the pope to block the proceedings, thus touching off a chain of events that ended with the separation of England from the Roman Catholic Church. It was under Charles' son, Philip II, that conflict between Spain and England was brought to a climax.

Among Charles V's more constructive achievements were his marriage to Isabella of Portugal, which brought about a brief union of Spain and Portugal under Philip II, and his repulse of the Ottoman Turks. Early in the sixteenth century, the Turks under Suleiman the Magnificent swept across Hungary and laid siege to Vienna, the capital city of Hapsburg Austria. It was feared that all Western Christendom might fall to the Muslims. At this point, Charles V rallied the forces of the empire and the Hapsburg provinces, raised the siege of Vienna, and drove the Turks back into Hungary. He also defeated the Muslim Barbary pirates in the Western Mediterranean.

In 1555 Charles V began to divide his holdings between his son, Philip II, and his brother, Ferdinand. To Philip he gave the Burgundian provinces and Spain, with her appanages in Italy, the Mediterranean, and the New World. To Ferdinand he gave the Austrian provinces and successfully promoted his candidacy to the crown of the Holy Roman Empire. Henceforth there were two branches of the Hapsburg dynasty—Austrian and Spanish—both of which would long continue to play important roles in European and world history.

7. SUMMARY—THE POLITICAL MAP OF EUROPE IN 1500

At the beginning of the modern period, then, four powerful national monarchies, those of Spain, Portugal, France, and England, dominated Europe. Germany and Italy were divided into many small states. The German states and Slavic Czech-speaking Bohemia were in the Holy Roman Empire. The Netherlands, owned by the Hapsburgs, were a part of the empire. Switzerland, nominally in the empire, was in reality an independent confederation of semi-autonomous cantons. Elsewhere in Europe, Scotland was still independent, and England's control over Ireland was only tenuous. Denmark owned Norway and was in temporary union with Sweden, but Scandinavia had too few people and resources to count for much in international politics. Poland, including Lithuania, occupied a large stretch of territory east of Germany, but her anemic government made her impotent at

home and abroad. Russia, under Ivan III, had just freed herself from Tartar overlordship and as yet counted for little in European or world affairs. The Balkan peninsula was a part of the Ottoman Empire. Hungary was a battlefield fought over by the Hapsburgs and the Ottoman Turks. The four new national states which represented the political wave that the rest of Europe and most of the world would eventually follow had been firmly established. But their new internal strength brought not a more peaceful international order, but war on a larger scale, as symbolized by the continental scope of the operations of Charles V.

Suggested Reading

General—The Modern Era. A vast and reliable storehouse of knowledge of modern European history is the *Cambridge Modern History* (14 vols., 1902–12), planned by Lord Acton. The bibliographies are full and excellent, but the writing tends to be dull and specialized, although accurate. It is valuable chiefly for reference. *The New Cambridge Modern History,* under the editorship of Sir George Clark, has been appearing volume by volume since 1957. There are a number of good textbooks on modern Western history that treat much of the material covered by this textbook in fuller detail. The best is probably R. R. Palmer and J. Colton, *A History of the Modern World* (4th ed., 1971). Robert Ergang, *Europe From the Renaissance to Waterloo* and *Europe Since Waterloo* (1954); and Carlton J. H. Hayes, *Modern Europe to 1870* and *Contemporary Europe Since 1870* (rev. ed., 1953 and 1958) are also excellent.

Beginning of Modern Times. **E. P. Cheyney, *The Dawn of a New Era, 1250–1453* (Harper Torchbook) is the first volume in the Rise of Modern Europe series edited by W. L. Langer. This series attempts to cut across national boundary lines and emphasizes cultural his-

tory. All the volumes are now in paperback. A. H. Johnson, *Europe in the Sixteenth Century* (7th ed., 1928) treats the political history of Europe during the first modern century.

The New National Monarchies. R. B. Merriman, *The Rise of the Spanish Empire in the Old World and the New* (4 vols., 1918–34). Volume II of this scholarly and readable work deals with the reigns of Ferdinand and Isabella. A highly readable but somewhat antiquated volume by one of America's finest literary historians is W. H. Prescott, *History of the Reign of Ferdinand and Isabella the Catholic* (4 vols., 1904). Probably the best survey of the history of Spain in English is R. Altamira, *History of Spain From the Beginning to the Present Day,* trans. P. Volkov (1930). The best survey of the history of Portugal in English is C. E. Nowell, *History of Portugal* (1953). The best biography in English of France's first modern king is P. Champion, *Louis XI,* trans. W. J. Whale (1929), written in a popular style. A good survey of French political history in the early modern period is A. J. Grant, *The French Monarchy, 1483–1789* (4th ed., 2 vols., 1920). P. M. Kendall, *Warwick the Kingmaker* (1957) is a vivid biography of one of the last great feudal barons who was a dominant figure in England at a time when feudalism was crumbling and the modern national monarchies were emerging. C. W. S. Williams, *Henry VII* (1937) is a scholarly biography of England's first modern king. Conyers Read, *The Tudors: Personalities and Practical Politics in the Sixteenth Century* (1936) is a scholarly and readable account.

Germany and Italy. The best history of modern Germany is Hajo Holborn, *A History of Modern Germany* (3 vols., 1959–69). For the Germanies at the opening of the modern period, **Geoffrey Barraclough, *The Origins of Modern Germany* (Capricorn) is excellent. James Bryce, *The Holy Roman Empire* (1932) is still the best treatment of that complicated subject. Surprisingly readable. By far the best biography of Emperor Charles V, around whom most of the political history of Europe centered during the first half of the sixteenth century, is Karl Brandi, *The Emperor Charles V: The Growth and Destiny of a Man and of a World Empire*, trans. C. V. Wedgewood (1940). A useful survey of Italian history is J. P. Trevelyan, *A Short History of the Italian People From the Barbarian Invasions to the Attainment of Unity* (1920). An excellent history of Florence, the cultural and financial capital of Italy at the opening of the modern era, is **Ferdinand Schevill, *Medieval and Renaissance Florence*, Vol. II, *The Coming of Humanism and the Age of the Medici* (Harper Torchbook).

Sources. There are a number of good selections of source materials for the history of Western civilization. One of the best is **B. Tierney, D. Kagan, and L. P. Williams, *Great Issues in Western Civilization* (2 vols., Random House). A fascinating eye-witness account of the struggle to decide whether there would be a great French nation or a great "middle kingdom" of Burgundy is Comines, *The History of Comines*, trans. Thomas Danett (1897). Comines was in the service of both Louis XI of France and Charles the Bold of Burgundy. A useful collection of documents for the reign of the first Tudor king is A. F. Pollard, *The Reign of Henry VII* (3 vols., 1913–14).

Historical Fiction. One of the greatest historical novels ever written is **Charles Reade, *The Cloister and the Hearth* (Washington Square). An account of the unwed parents of Erasmus, the novel presents a vivid picture of life in Europe at the dawn of the modern era, based upon excellent historical research. The romantic novel by Sir Walter Scott, *Quentin Durward* (written in 1823, many editions), is set in France during the reign of Louis XI.

Infula hyspana

Chapter 28 A New Economy and

the Expansion of Europe

The rise of the modern national state was closely associated with the rise of a modern capitalistic economy. The royal monarchs who created the national states made great use of the rising middle class in overcoming the feudal aristocracy. The strength of this middle class lay in its capitalistic wealth. The term *capitalism*, stripped to its barest essentials, may be defined as a system of putting money to work to make more money. It involves, among other things, private property, the profit motive, a substantial amount of free enterprise and individual initiative, the hiring of labor, and the lending of money for interest.

1. ROOTS AND BEGINNINGS OF MODERN CAPITALISM

Although we are likely to think of capitalism as a typically modern system of economy, it reached a fairly high development in ancient Greece and Rome. The reader will recall from earlier chapters that trading, banking, and production of certain wares on a capitalistic basis thrived in and among the Greek city-states, particularly in the Hellenistic age. Capitalism developed to a higher degree in the

Roman world. For many centuries all roads and all ship lanes in the Western world led to Rome and were protected by Rome. Interest rates came down, and the standard of living went up.

However, the reader will also recall that, with the breakdown of the Roman Empire, capitalistic practices virtually disappeared. Early medieval economy, like early medieval government, was decentralized. Each manorial estate produced almost all its own needs. Agriculture was collectivist or cooperative. Commerce was a mere trickle of luxuries for the rich, and necessities such as iron, implements, and salt. The Church insisted upon the "fair price" rather than competitive pricing, and since it also forbade the lending of money for interest (usury), only the Jews, who were not bound by these dictates, practiced what small-scale lending of money there was.

During the course of the Middle Ages commercial activities and capitalistic practices began to revive. A slight increase may be observed as early as the eleventh century, and by the thirteenth century a pronounced recovery was under way. The Crusades contributed significantly to this revival. The huge

This illustration is from a letter of Columbus to the treasurer of the King of Spain, published in Basel a year after his first voyage. Here the Spaniards are offering the Indians gifts as they approach the island. *Photo: NYPL Picture Collection* movement of men and supplies from Western Europe to the Holy Land enriched the merchants and shippers of Venice and other Italian cities. Many of these set up permanent trading posts in the Near East and introduced the luxuries of the materially more advanced Muslim and Byzantine worlds to Western Europe. The Fourth Crusade, which the Venetians diverted to the looting of Constantinople, was particularly fruitful for rising Western capitalism. The Venetians seized not only a great hoard of gold and silver in the stricken Eastern imperial capital, but also almost half the territory of the Byzantine Empire itself. This wealth flowed into the stream of Western European commerce.

Foremost among the centers of this newly revived commerce and capitalism were the city-states of northern Italy, such as Venice, Genoa, Florence, and Milan. Venice was the queen of the Mediterranean in the thirteenth, fourteenth, and fifteenth centuries. After her chief rival, Genoa, was eliminated in the fourteenth century, she enjoyed a virtual monopoly over the lucrative trade with the East. At the peak of her prosperity, her merchant marine numbered some thirty thousand sailors. Milan was the starting point of the overland traffic across the Alps to Northern Europe. In the late fourteenth century she gained control of the port city of Genoa. Florence manufactured large quantities of fine woolen textiles on a capitalistic basis, and in the fourteenth and fifteenth centuries was the banking capital of the Western world. The Medici family alone possessed at one time some two hundred branch banks scattered throughout Western and Central Europe.

In Northern Europe, the Hanseatic League, composed of some eighty German Baltic and North Sea cities, enjoyed a brisk trade in such commodities as fish, furs, grain, and timber. In southern Germany and the Rhine Valley, numerous trading centers such as Augsburg, Nuremberg, and Cologne sprang up along the overland route between Italy and Northern Europe. Finally, the Netherlands, Paris, and London shared in this early period of revived commercialism.

By the end of the fifteenth century, however, the further growth of European commerce was threatened by a number of obstacles that little feudal fiefs and independent cities were not able to overcome. One was the expense of the trade routes between Europe and the East, which were partly overland, especially after Muslim middlemen had taken their share of the profits. Another was the inadequacy of the gold and silver supply to serve as a satisfactory medium of exchange. A third was the restrictive practices of the guilds. All these obstacles were soon to be overcome.

2. THE AGE OF DISCOVERY

In the late fifteenth and early sixteenth centuries, European mariners made a series of daring voyages in which they discovered not only the New World, but also new and much better routes to the East. These voyages were promoted by the governments and peoples of the four nation-states along the Atlantic coast. Their principal motive was a desire to bypass the Venetians, the Muslims, and the land barriers that separated them from the riches of the East. But there was also a powerful outward impetus in the spirit of inquiry and adventure kindled by the Renaissance interest in the secular world, and in the Christian missionary zeal that had always been a spur to expansion. The results were momentous. The age of discovery brought an economic boom vaster in scale than anything yet dreamed of and eventually brought most of the rest of the world under the domination of Europe.

The first to begin in the fifteenth century were the Portuguese. Prince Henry the Navigator, who as the younger son of the king was not immediately in line for the crown, devoted his talents and influence to navigation. He set up a school for mariners, and sent sailors down the coast of West Africa until, by the time of

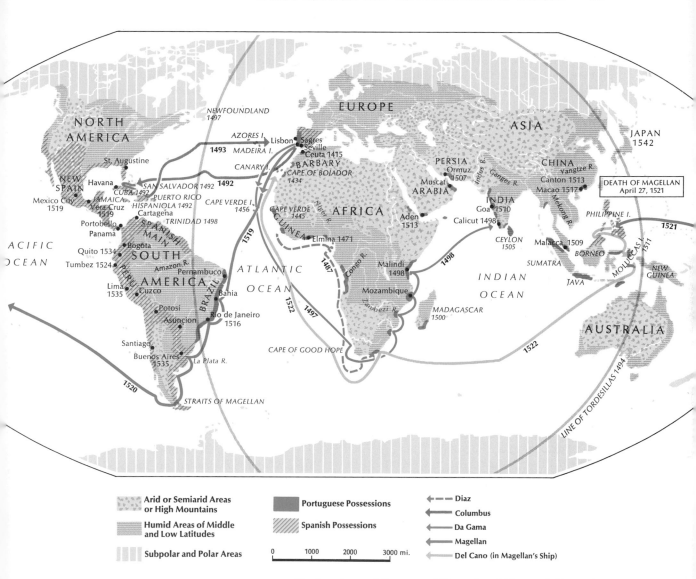

Exploration and Conquest, Fifteenth and Sixteenth Centuries

Henry's death in 1460, they had reached the westernmost bulge at Cape Verde. In 1488 Diaz rounded the cape, soon to be named Good Hope; and in 1498 Vasco da Gama, in what was probably the greatest voyage in the history of navigation, reached India, the object of the quest. Vasco da Gama was out of sight of land 93 days—three times as long as Columbus on his voyage to the New World. That the Portuguese knew what they were up to is proved by the fact that Vasco da Gama's return cargo sold for sixty times the cost of the expedition. These glad tidings sent a host of Portuguese adventurers hurrying to the

East Indies, where they carved out a huge commercial and political empire.[1] One of these adventurers, Cabral, swinging too far westward, touched the eastern bulge of South America, thus laying the basis for Portugal's claim to Brazil. With the discovery of an all-water route to the East, the commerce of the Italian city-states soon withered. So did that along the overland route from Italy across Germany.

Meanwhile, Spain was sending her mariners westward, for by the late fifteenth century most educated people in Western Europe assumed that the earth was round, although they greatly underestimated its size. It was therefore believed by many navigators that the East Indies could be reached by sailing west. The first European to attempt it was Christopher Columbus. (Nothing had come of the tenth-century voyages to Greenland and northern America of the roving Norsemen, Eric the Red and Leif Ericson.) Almost every American schoolboy and schoolgirl knows the story of Columbus. Many even assume that American history begins with Columbus rather than with the civilizations of ancient Egypt and Mesopotamia. Columbus was born in Genoa but moved to Portugal. When, however, Portugal failed to support his proposed westward voyage, he turned to Queen Isabella of Castile, who gave him the necessary backing. His three ships touched a West Indian island on October 12, 1492. Thinking that the West Indies were islands off the east coast of Asia, Columbus made three further voyages in the hope of bypassing these barriers and sailing on to his real goal, the East Indies. Instead he was turned back by the South and Central American mainlands and died disappointed, not having realized the magnitude of his discovery.

But others soon realized it, and in the first half of the sixteenth century, Spanish expeditions to the New World multiplied. As previously noted, the pope in 1493 had drawn a

line of demarcation dividing the non-Christian world between Spain and Portugal. This line was somewhat altered in favor of Portugal the following year by the Treaty of Tordesillas. Since all of the Western Hemisphere except the eastern part of Brazil and Greenland fell to Spain, the Spanish sailors continued to move westward. Ponce de Leon, De Soto, and Coronado explored the southern part of what is now the United States. Balboa crossed the Isthmus of Panama and looked out upon the Pacific Ocean. In 1519 Magellan set out around the world by way of the Strait of Magellan. Although he himself was killed in the Philippines, one of his ships completed the circuit. Also in 1519, Cortez began the conquest of the Aztec Empire in Mexico. In 1531–1532 Pizarro conquered the Inca Indians in Peru.

The other two new national states, England and France, were relatively inactive in discovery and exploration during the fifteenth and early sixteenth centuries. The English crown did, however, sponsor voyages to northern North America by the Italian mariner John Cabot in 1497–1498. These voyages became the basis for England's claims to North America, where she later built a great empire. The French government sponsored Jacques Cartier, who in 1535 sailed up the St. Lawrence to what is now Montreal and claimed Canada for France. Nonetheless, it was not until the seventeenth century that Spain and Portugal were replaced as the world's leading imperial and commercial powers.

3. THE FOUNDING OF THE SPANISH NEW WORLD EMPIRE

Although most of the Western Hemisphere at the beginning of the sixteenth century was sparsely inhabited by primitive and often savage Indian tribes, the Spaniards did find two rich and colorful civilizations: those of the Aztecs in Mexico and the Incas in Peru.

The American aborigines are clearly members of the Mongoloid branch of the human family. They are generally believed to have

---

[1] For conditions in Southern Asia at the time of the European intrusion see pp. 586–590.

come from Asia across the Bering Strait, perhaps as long as forty thousand years ago.

The first of these primitive tribes to build a highly civilized society were the Mayas. They are believed to have come into what is now Guatemala and the Yucatán Peninsula of southeast Mexico from the northwest about 1000 B.C. Their civilization reached its height between A.D. 400 and 600. It was a city-state civilization resembling that of ancient Greece approximately a thousand years earlier. Their writing, most of which has been lost, was a combination of pictures and ideographs. Their best art was brightly colored pottery, gems, gold and silver ware, and sculpture. Probably their most remarkable creations were a system of mathematics based on the decimal (actually vigesimal) system and a calendar based upon astronomy, both of which were in advance of those used in contemporary Europe. Their massively walled stone cities were connected by elaborately paved roads. These cities, however, were continually at war with one another, and in the twelfth century the less-civilized but better-organized Toltecs conquered the Mayan city-states much as Philip of Macedon conquered the Greeks.

In the fourteenth century the warlike Aztecs came down from the north and founded a city on an island in Lake Tezcoco—the present Mexico City. From this base they conquered and organized a military empire or confederacy comprising most of what is now southern Mexico. The Aztecs were the Romans of the New World, and like the Romans they acquired most of their culture from the earlier civilization (Mayas). Theirs was the gift of military and political organization. They developed an elaborate, though stern, system of justice. Their religion was important and highly organized. Several thousand priests, both regular and secular, tended the impressive temple and supervised education and morals. The numerous gods, taken mostly from the Mayas, were headed by the terrible war god, whose unquenchable thirst for blood demanded human sacrifice, usually prisoners

of war. And yet the rank and file Aztecs were gentle lovers of poetry and art. A flourishing commerce, agriculture, and mining added to the wealth obtained by conquest.

An even more colorful civilization was that of the Incas in the Andean Plateau of South America. In the eleventh century the Inca Indians began to extend their sway over their neighbors until their empire covered an area 1500 miles long and 300 miles wide—including present-day Ecuador, Peru, and parts of Bolivia and Chile. An elaborate system of roads and communications tied this vast and lofty empire together. Incan society was a combination of benevolent despotism and socialism. The all-powerful Inca (ruler) was treated as a god. However, he had a body of advisers and administrators chosen from the upper classes. All land and all production were owned and directed by the state. The regimented lower classes did all the work under close supervision and shared from the common stores. A high degree of specialization was practiced. Agriculture was well advanced, and huge terracing and irrigation projects had been developed to overcome the difficulties of the Andean terrain. Religious worship, particularly of the sun god, was a beautiful and important feature of national life. Although Incan writing was backward, its art was well advanced. Outstanding were pottery, architecture, textiles, and gold and silver ornamental objects.

Cortez with a band of some six hundred soldiers and eighteen horses overcame the Aztecs by a combination of treachery and superior weapons. He took advantage of the Aztec belief that the Spaniards were ancient gods whose return had long been expected. Once inside the capital city, the Spaniards were too strong to be expelled. They slaughtered and looted the poorly armed Aztecs without mercy. Even more spectacular was the conquest of the Incas. Pizarro enticed the Incan emperor into a conference. At a given signal Pizarro's small but well-armed band of Spanish soldiers fell upon the splendidly dressed but primitively armed Incan troops and slew them by the thousands. Not a Span-

Although there are many Spanish records of their arrival and explorations in the New World, this Aztec manuscript (ca. 1519–1522) is one of the few surviving Indian versions of the coming of the Europeans. The illustration here shows Cortez arriving in Mexico.
Photo: La Biblioteca Apostolica Vaticana, Rome

iard lost his life. Pizarro promised to free the Incan chieftain in return for a ransom of gold objects sufficient to fill a room seventeen by twenty-two feet to a height of nine feet, plus a larger amount of silver. This ransom was collected and paid, but Pizarro, who never really intended to free the emperor had him put to death anyway. When this gold and silver, an estimated ten million dollars' worth, reached Spain, the money shortage in Europe was over.

Throughout the sixteenth century Spaniards flocked to the New World. By 1607, when the first permanent English colony was founded in North America, a quarter of a million Spaniards had settled in the vast Spanish Empire stretching from what is now Arizona to Cape Horn. A number of distinguished missions and cathedrals had been erected, and several thriving universities had been founded. The native civilizations had been almost wholly destroyed and replaced by the Christian civilization of Spain. Meanwhile, the Portuguese, in addition to reaping a golden harvest from their commerce with the East, were duplicating the Spanish feats on a smaller scale in Brazil.

4. THE COMMERCIAL REVOLUTION

The discovery of the New World and of all-water routes to the Far East resulted in an expansion of European commerce on such a scale that the term *commercial revolution* may accurately be used to describe it. As the main routes shifted from the Mediterranean to the Atlantic, the stranded Italian and German cities decayed, and new commercial centers to the west began to flourish. Contrary to one's expectations, Spain, surfeited with gold and silver from Mexico and Peru, never developed a thriving commercial capitalism. And although Lisbon became the first great terminus of goods pouring in from the East, the Portuguese, like the Spanish, were so preoccupied with their vast overseas empire that they neglected the marketing opportunities in Europe itself.

These lucrative opportunities were first seized by the Dutch. Enterprising Dutch merchants purchased the goods in Lisbon, shipped them to the Netherlands, and sold them at a nice profit throughout Northern and Western Europe. In the sixteenth century Antwerp, with its excellent harbor and location, was the leading commercial center in Europe. In the seventeenth century, following the sack of Antwerp in 1585 by Spanish troops, Amsterdam and London led the commercial world. The Dutch even took advantage of their newly won independence from Spain and of Portugal's temporary conquest by Spain in 1580 to seize the best part of Portugal's Eastern Empire, the area of present-day Indonesia.

Another phase of the commercial revolution was the advent of more bounteous supplies of commodities. Spices, coffee, tea, sugar, dyes, tropical fruits, fine textiles, tapestries, and precious stones, long known but in scarce supply and too expensive for all but the very rich, now came into Europe in ever-increasing volume. From the New World came potatoes, corn, tobacco, and chocolate (all of which were previously unknown in Europe), new dyes and medicines, gold and silver.

A different kind of new product—Negro slaves—also helped to swell the rising stream of commerce. This most nefarious traffic of modern times was first begun by the ship captains of Prince Henry the Navigator. It was later taken over by the Spaniards to supply labor for their empire in the New World. When the Spaniards discovered that the native Indians were poor slave laborers, they turned to tropical Africa. Thousands of Negroes were captured or bought from local chieftains and crowded into the holds of ships. Many of them died during the crossings, but the survivors were sold like cattle for a high price in the New World markets. So heavy was this immensely profitable traffic that the racial and social complex of the New World society was quickly and drastically altered.

New types of business organization were developed to accommodate the expanding volume of commerce. *Chartered companies* were organized to bypass the medieval guilds, which were unable or unwilling to meet the new demands. The first chartered companies were called *regulated* companies. A group of merchants would voluntarily band together under a government license or charter for the purpose of exploiting a certain market. While cooperating to the extent of limiting competition and providing mutual protection, the individual members of the company carried on their own private operations. Since one member could take advantage of the others and since reorganization was required upon the death or defection of a member, a more efficient type of organization was sought.

In the early seventeenth century the *joint stock* company began to replace the regulated company. The members of a joint stock company pooled their resources, hired or elected their management, and shared in the profits in proportion to the amount of stock owned. In this way competition within the company was eliminated and permanence was achieved by selling or buying the stock of changing personnel. Moreover, unlimited amounts of capital could be raised by selling stock. This type of business organization has never been improved upon for large-scale efficiency, as present-day joint stock companies such as General Motors, Standard Oil, and United States Steel demonstate.

Two of the earliest joint stock companies were the British East India Company, founded in 1600, and the Dutch East India Company, founded two years later. The British company was given not only a trading monopoly over British India, but political control as well. The Dutch company was given a monopoly over all Dutch trade east of the Cape of Good Hope. Annual profits of 300 percent were not uncommon for these giant companies. The annual profits of the Dutch East India Company never fell below 12 percent over a period of two hundred years.

Although there was some expansion of industrial capitalistic activity in this period, it was relatively slight until means had been found to overcome or evade the obstruction of the monopolistic craft guilds. Wherever the production of goods was done on a capitalistic basis, the domestic or "putting out" system was generally used. Entrepreneurs would purchase the raw materials and distribute them to craftsmen, who would do the piecework in their cottages. Then the entrepreneur would collect the finished products, pay the cottagers for their work, and market the goods at a profit. While this system had certain advantages, it limited the volume of production. Until the coming of the machine and the factory system in the late eighteenth and early nineteenth centuries, therefore, large-scale capitalism was to remain commercial rather than industrial.

Banking expanded in proportion to commerce. In the sixteenth century the Fugger family of Augsburg occupied the place in the financial world that the Medicis of Florence had held in the fifteenth. Jacob (the Rich) Fugger loaned Charles V the money with which he bribed his way to the emperorship of the Holy Roman Empire. He also loaned the Archbishop of Mainz the money with which he purchased his archbishopric; and it was the selling of indulgences by this archbishop in order to repay the loan that was one of the sparks which touched off the Protestant Reformation. In the seventeenth century the Bank of Amsterdam and the Bank of England were founded on a seminational basis. Both of these banks were really private joint stock companies, but in return for certain monopolies, such as the handling of government funds and the issuance of currency, they were obliged to accept a degree of government regulation. Banks of this size were able to mobilize sums of money and credit sufficient not only to launch and control large-scale commercial ventures, but to influence government and religion as well.

5. A NEW COMMERCIAL POLICY—MERCANTILISM

Governments attempted to exercise some control over economic developments. From the beginning of the Age of Discovery in the late fifteenth century until the end of the eighteenth century, all the governments of Western Europe except the Dutch Netherlands pursued a policy that has come to be called *mercantilism*. Mercantilism was, in essence, economic nationalism. While the monarchs of the new national states were consolidating their political power, they were also attempting to unify and centralize their national economies. Efforts were made to standardize national currencies and weights and measurements. Internal commerce was encouraged by improving communications and reducing or removing internal tariff barriers. These efforts, however, were only partially successful. More attention was paid to the aggrandizement of each nation's economy at the expense of its neighbors. The basic assumption of mercantilist theory was that gold and silver are the true measure of national prosperity and power. Gold and silver, the mercantilists believed, in addition to being convenient mediums of exchange, could purchase anything— consumer goods, armies, navies, and administrative personnel. Spain's good luck in Mexico and Peru and her sixteenth-century brilliance and influence undoubtedly strengthened this view.

Spain alone was fortunate enough to come upon the gold and silver directly. All the other states had to devise more roundabout means of acquiring the precious metals. The favorite device was to seek a *favorable balance of trade*. The importation of expensive manufactured goods was discouraged by high tariffs, whereas the exportation of manufactures was encouraged, if need be, by subsidies. The reverse was true of inexpensive raw materials. The national aim was to buy low and sell high. Colonies were sought as sources of raw materials and markets for manufactured goods. But the colonies were not to be permitted to compete with the manufacturers and shippers of the mother country. Navies were advocated for the protection of the colonies. Sometimes the mercantilists closely regulated a nation's manufactures with a view to maintaining a reputation abroad for high quality. This phase of mercantilism reached its highest development in France in the seventeenth century under Louis XIV's economic minister, Colbert. It was not until the latter part of the eighteenth century that the British economist, Adam Smith, and the French physiocrats began to undermine public faith in the validity of mercantilist principles and to prepare the way for an era of *laissez faire*, or free trade.

6. POLITICAL AND SOCIAL CONSEQUENCES

The immediate political consequence of the rise of modern capitalistic economy in Western Europe was the strengthening of royal absolutism. The monarchs made use of the merchants and bankers in order to increase their own power at the expense of the rival nobility. More money was now available for the royal treasury and the royal army. The middle classes, of course, shared the benefits of their alliance with the royal monarchs. Many members of the bourgeoisie were appointed to key positions in the royal administrations. With their increased wealth came increased social and political influence. The strongholds of their influence were the towns and cities whose growth paralleled the expansion of commerce. Western European society was becoming more urban—yet another change from the medieval pattern.

As the power of the national monarchs and the middle classes grew, the position of the nobility declined. Their wealth and power were based upon land, and now money was more important. A severe inflation brought on by the great influx of gold and silver into Europe further hurt the nobility in relation to the moneyed bourgeoisie. Not overnight, but slowly and with occasional setbacks over the decades and centuries, the nobility of Western Europe were displaced by the middle classes in political and social influence. Only in England and the Netherlands did they avoid disaster by openly engaging in business operations.

The triumph of the middle class did not bring an immediate improvement in the condition of the lower classes. Indeed, the *nouveaux riches* often proved to be harsher taskmasters than the older aristocracy, who had had time to learn that power brings responsibility. The urban wage earners, no longer protected by the guilds, were especially hard hit by the inflation. In France and England some peasants who had converted their feudal dues to money payments profited, but most of the peasants in Western Europe and all of those in Central and Eastern Europe suffered from the inflation and the general loss of feudal security. The distressed landlords were likely to pass their hardships along to the peasantry. Peasant revolts were common throughout Europe in the sixteenth century. However, the rise of the middle class and the disappearance of feudal class lines produced a more fluid social structure and made possible the future growth of democracy. Money is more easily acquired by the commoner than is blue blood or title.

7. EUROPEAN DOMINATION OF THE GLOBE

Europe's Age of Discovery and the rise of modern capitalistic economy were as momentous for the rest of the world as they were for

Europe itself. Much of the Western Hemisphere, Southern Asia, and the coastal areas of Africa were quickly brought under European domination. This amazing expansion continued until by the end of the nineteenth century practically the entire world was dominated by Europe and European civilization. Spanish, Portuguese, English, French, and Dutch colonists, followed later by the nationals of all the other European countries, flocked to the New World, taking their Western Christian culture with them. The brilliant Aztec and Incan civilizations of Mexico and Peru were destroyed. The more primitive tribes of American Indians were exterminated, absorbed, or confined to reservations.

The Muslim, Hindu, Buddhist, and Confucian civilizations of Asia and Africa were virtually enslaved by the aggressive European imperialists. Modern European history is therefore world history, and the details of European expansion (and eventual contraction) constitute a considerable portion of the history of Western civilization in the modern era.

Thus we see Europe's static, agricultural, collectivist, "fair price" economy transformed into a dynamic, urban, competitive, profit-motivated economy. The rise of capitalism not only changed the nature of European society; it also provided much of the explosive force that enabled tiny Europe to dominate most of the rest of the world.

Suggested Reading

General. An excellent general survey of European economic history is Herbert Heaton, *Economic History of Europe* (1948). Also good is S. B. Clough and C. W. Cole, *Economic History of Europe* (1952). Another useful survey is S. B. Clough, *Economic Development of Western Civilization* (1959).

The Age of Discovery. There are many good books on the voyages of discovery. Sir Percy Sykes, *A History of Exploration: From the Earliest Times to the Present Day* (3rd ed., 1950) is a good comprehensive treatment of the whole subject. Another excellent survey is C. E. Nowell, *The Great Discoveries and the First Colonial Empires* (1959). **B. Penrose, *Travel and Discovery in the Renaissance* (Atheneum), and **J. H. Parry, *Establishment of the European Hegemony, 1415–1715* (Harper Torchbook), are also good. The fabulous voyages of the Portuguese to the East Indies are well told by E. Sanceau, *Henry the Navigator* (1947); and H. H. Hart, *Sea Road to the Indies* (1950). By far the best account of Columbus is S. E. Morison, *Admiral of the Ocean Sea* (2 vols., 1942). Before writing the book, Morison sailed the route followed by Columbus on his first voyage to America. A handy, brief account by the same author is **S. E. Morison, *Christopher Columbus* (Mentor). **J. B. Brebner, *The Explorers of North America 1492–1806* (Meridian) covers the English, French, and Dutch explorers as well as the Spanish and Portuguese.

Overseas Empires. The best work on the Spanish Empire as well as on Spain itself at the peak of her power is R. B. Merriman, *The Rise of the Spanish Empire in the Old World and the New* (4 vols., 1918–38). Briefer and also excellent is **C. H. Haring, *Spanish Empire in America* (Harbinger). **W. H. Prescott, *The Conquest of Mexico* (Modern Library) and **The Conquest of Peru* (Dolphin), although written a century ago, combine good historical scholarship with excellent writing. The same thing can be said of Francis Parkman, *France and England in North America* (many editions). The numerous books written under this title about a century ago are considered by many historians to be the finest of American historical writing.

The Commercial Revolution. The best introduction to this subject is the brief and lucid **L. B. Packard, *The Commercial Revolution, 1400–1776* (Berkshire). An excellent brief introduction to the history of capitalism is H. E. See, *Modern Capitalism, Its Origin and Evolution,* trans. H. B. Vanderblue and G. F. Doriot (1928). J. H. Parry, *Europe and a Wider World, 1415–1715* (1949), analyzes the effects of overseas expansion on Europe itself. An excellent account of the Medici banking house is **R. deRoover, *The Rise and Decline of the Medici Bank, 1307–1494* (Norton). The Fuggers have been treated in equally scholarly fashion by R. Ehrenberg, *Capital and Finance in the Age of the Renaissance: A Study of the Fuggers and Their Connections,* trans. H. M. Lucas (1928). The best introduction to the theory and practice of mercantilism is J. W. Horrocks, *A Short History of Mercantilism* (1925).

Sources. Probably the most interesting and available contemporary account of the major voyages and discoveries is **Richard Hakluyt, *Principal Navigations, Voyages, Traffiques and Discoveries of the English Nation* (Everyman).

Historical Fiction. **T. B. Costain, *The Moneyman* (Permabooks) is the story of Jacques Coeur, France's leading merchant and financier in the last years of the Hundred Years' War. This is a vivid and, on the whole, reliable picture of the times by a popular American historical novelist. A classic novel depicting the spirit of the times of Queen Elizabeth I and Philip II is **Charles Kingsley, *Westward Ho!* (Everyman).

Chapter 29 🌿 The Renaissance: Italy

The term *renaissance* means rebirth, and in the development of Western civilization it designates particularly the rebirth of a secular civilization that was inspired in large measure by the civilizations of ancient Greece and Rome. However, *rebirth* implies too sharp a change with the immediate past. Secular interests had never completely died out, even at the peak of the Church's prestige in the Middle Ages; and the revival of secular interests was a gradual process. Furthermore, the Renaissance was not merely a return to pre-Christian culture; new elements that had not existed previously were added. It would be better to regard the Renaissance as an intensification of the secular spirit in Western European thought, literature, and art during the fourteenth, fifteenth, and sixteenth centuries. The key word here is *secular*, meaning that which pertains to this physical world as contrasted with the religious emphasis on the spiritual. The Renaissance began in Italy, where many physical reminders of the glory that was Greece and the grandeur that was Rome had remained.

1. GENERAL NATURE

Probably the most basic of the secular attitudes that characterized the Renaissance was humanism—the focusing of interest on man rather than God. In a period dominated by humanistic concepts, the arts, the sciences, and all forms of intellectual and practical activity tend to be directed toward the scrutiny of man. The emphasis on theology, concerned with the nature of God, changes to one on a philosophy centered around the nature and condition of man. During the Renaissance man, not God, was enthroned as lord of the universe. In this respect, Renaissance thought was like that of pagan Greece and Rome and unlike that of the Christian-dominated Middle Ages. The medieval Christian theologians distrusted the flesh as an enemy of the spirit, and human wisdom as a frail thing unable to perceive divine truth by rational processes unless guided by Christian inspiration. But men of the Renaissance, like their Greek and Roman kinsmen, glorified the human form as a thing of beauty and the human intellect as capable of discovering all truth worth knowing.

Humanism extols not only mankind in general but also individual man. Individualism, therefore, was another important facet of the secular spirit of the Renaissance. In this respect, the difference between the medieval and the Renaissance spirit was primarily one of degree. Probably no influence in history has done more than Christianity to elevate the dignity of the individual soul and the individual personality. Christianity taught that even when a sparrow falls God sees and is concerned. How much more then is he concerned for every man, made by him in his own image and for his own glory. But the medieval churchmen feared pride as the deadliest of all the sins. Therefore, they taught that the individual ego must be carefully held in check. Medieval monasticism went so far as to attempt to suppress the individual ego altogether and submerge it in the group. In practice, then, medieval Christianity, like medieval economy, tended to be collectivist. Church artists and writers usually did not sign their names to their work, which was supposed to contribute only to the greater glory of God. Renaissance individualism, like that of Rome, was of the lusty variety. One could hardly imagine a Machiavelli or a Boccaccio hiding his identity. This kind of individualism also gave rise, as in ancient Rome, to excessive men. No more egotistical individual can be found in history than Benvenuto Cellini, liar, thief, murderer, rapist, and one of the most gifted artists of the Renaissance era.

That a Cellini should be not only tolerated but also honored by his contemporaries may be further explained by the fact that he represented another cardinal principle of the Renaissance ideal—versatility. We are reminded of Pericles' all-round man of Athens of the fifth century B.C. and of the broadly educated Roman patrician. The educated man of the Middle Ages was usually a specialist—a theologian or a church artist or administrator. But the most renowned Renaissance schoolmasters taught many subjects in addition to the traditional formal ones—dancing, fencing, poetry, and vernacular languages, to mention a few. Many of the Renaissance universities secularized and broadened the old theology-oriented seven liberal arts and made much greater use of pagan classical literature and philosophy in the curriculum. One of the most popular books in Europe in the sixteenth century was Castiglione's *Book of the Courtier*. The ideal courtier, said Castiglione, is not only a gentleman and a scholar, but also a man of action—a soldier and an athlete. Probably the best illustration of versatility in any age is Leonardo da Vinci. This revered Renaissance figure, one of the most celebrated painters of all time, was also an able sculptor, architect, mathematician, philosopher, inventor, botanist, anatomist, geologist, and engineer.

Finally, the secular Renaissance civilization was urban—again like that of ancient Greece and Rome, but unlike that of the Middle Ages, which was rural. Renaissance writers and artists were more often than not sustained by rich merchants and bankers, first in the revived commercial cities of Italy and later in those of Northern Europe.

2. LITERATURE

These secular characteristics of the Renaissance spirit are richly illustrated by the Italian literature of the fourteenth century. The best of that literature was produced by the Tuscan Triumvirate—so called because it consisted of three men who lived in Florence in the old Etruscan province of Tuscany. The first was Dante Alighieri (1265–1321). In an earlier section (see Chapter 24) we discussed Dante as the greatest of the late medieval writers. His masterpiece, the *Divine Comedy*, is so full of medieval Christian lore and theology that it has been called a *Summa Theologiae* in poetry. Nevertheless, there is so much of the secular spirit in the *Divine Comedy* and in Dante's other writings that he belongs also to the Renaissance. In the "Inferno" of the *Divine Comedy*, Dante paints vivid, sensuous word pictures that smack of this world rather than the next. The blazing fires and sulphurous fumes of hell, the cries of lament and curses of the damned come alive in our imagination. Furthermore, the author venerates such pagan classical writers as Vergil and Cicero to a much greater degree than had the medievalists (although a number of medieval writers had tried to make Vergil a Christian).

Dante's other major writings are entirely secular. His love lyrics, written in his native Tuscan vernacular and addressed to Beatrice, are among the most beautiful in any language. In fact, Dante's writings greatly enriched the Florentine dialect and raised it eventually to the status of the national language of Italy.

Dante was also versatile; he was a man of public affairs as well as of letters. An active participant in the turbulent politics of Renaissance Italy, he was exiled from his native Florence when his faction lost out. Dante even went so far as to fill hell in the *Divine Comedy* with his political enemies. His political treatise, *On Monarchy*, argues for a united Italy under the leadership of the Holy Roman Emperor.

Petrarch (1304–1374), the second of the Tuscan Triumvirate, like Dante wrote beautiful love lyrics in the Tuscan vernacular. His exquisite odes and sonnets were poured out for Laura, a noble lady whom he saw at mass and loved from afar. He goes on rapturously about Laura's bosom, arms, face, and feet with most unmedieval abandon. The sonnet is Petrarch's own invention.

Boccaccio (1313–1375) did for Italian prose what Dante and Petrarch did for Italian poetry. In his *Decameron*, a collection of one hundred tales or novelettes, Boccaccio makes no pretense of using Christian restraint. He relates bawdy romances with skill and grace, condoning and even glorifying the seamy side of human nature. Here we have open revolt against the medieval ideal.

3. HUMANISM

Toward the end of the fourteenth century, the original Italian Renaissance literature was stifled by the rise of humanism. Italian humanism was a movement consisting of two rather distinct phases. One was the passionate quest for Greek and Latin literary manuscripts; the other was the development of a many-sided secular philosophy of life.

The search for classical literary manuscripts conflicted with the creation of original Italian literature by siphoning off the interest and energy of the writers. This conflict is illustrated by Petrarch, who rather early in life ceased writing what he called his "worthless" lyrics in order to discover lost classical manuscripts and to copy their style. He did succeed in bringing to light many priceless classical literary gems, but his epic *Africa* (relating the exploits of Scipio Africanus), written in Latin after the style of Vergil's *Aeneid*, is all but forgotten.

Petrarch interested Boccaccio in the recovery of Greek and Latin manuscripts, and the search soon became a fad. Popes, princes, rich merchants, and bankers subsidized the humanists, so-called because the pagan Greek and Latin literature dealt with human rather than divine affairs. (Studies concerned with classical literature and language, philosophy, and history came to be called the humanities.) In the fifteenth century, Italy was busy with professional humanists hunting, copying, translating, and editing ancient manuscripts. Many of them were distinctly second-rate scholars. Spurning the use of the beautiful vernacular in favor of Latin and slavishly imitating the classical authors in both form and content, these men set a style devoid of creativity or spontaneity. But in time the tendency of the Italian humanists to adopt the pagan vices without their accompanying virtues, and their snobbish scorn of the less learned, caused them to lose favor. The use of the printing press, which became commonplace by the end of the fifteenth century, ended most of their careers.

Meanwhile, the content of the classical masterpieces was influencing the growth of a secular philosophy of life. This phase of humanism had many facets, such as the rise of the concept of the nonmoral state, the development of a critical or scientific attitude, and the revolt in private and social behavior against Christian moral restraints. Machiavelli, in his celebrated *The Prince*, suggested that Christian morals have no place in government. Since men are self-seeking animals, the prince (or ruler or governing officials), to be effective, must be both amoral and ruthless. The prince must assume that his own lieutenants, like all rival princes, are conspiring for his crown. Therefore, his own chief subjects must be set against each other and maneuvered into impotence. Foreign rivals must be deceived and treacherously attacked at the most favorable moment before they can do the same. While Machiavelli was trying to remedy the deplorable reality of a divided Italy overrun and pillaged by more powerful foreign enemies, he also reflected the thinking of a man-centered, secular age. Few books have had more influence on, or been more descriptive of, modern political thought and practice.

Another facet of the humanistic or secular view of life was the development of an analytic or scientific attitude. When Lorenzo Valla proved by linguistics that the Donation of Constantine was a forgery, the scholarly and secular-minded pope raised no objections, although this was one of the documents upon which the papacy had based its claims to temporal power in the West. In fact, Pope Nicholas V made Valla his secretary. By making this discovery, Valla established himself as the father of modern critical historical scholarship. This spirit of critical inquiry was to bring about the first flowering of modern natural science in the seventeenth century.

A third product of the rise of a secular philosophy of life—the revolt against Christian restraints on private behavior—is a facet of humanism illustrated by the fabulous career of Benvenuto Cellini. This gifted Florentine—some say the greatest gold- and silversmith of all time—boasts loudly in his *Autobiography* of his lies, thefts, illicit loves, even of rape and murder. Admittedly Benvenuto Cellini is an extreme case, but the fact that such a character should have been honored in early sixteenth-century society indicates the degree to which Italian Renaissance society had departed from the medieval Christian ideal.

4. ART

The renaissance of secularism is vividly illustrated in the Italian visual arts of the fourteenth, fifteenth, and sixteenth centuries. Medieval painting in Europe had been closely allied with the Church. Human flesh was deliberately penalized in order that the spirit might shine forth unimpeded. The figures, nearly always saints, were stiff, haggard, flat, and elongated. The physical world too was blanked out with solid gold backgrounds. The styles were stereotyped.

In the early fourteenth century Giotto, a contemporary of Dante, began to break this medieval mold of artistic custom by humanizing his figures and painting functional landscape backgrounds. Although his magnificent frescoes in the church of St. Francis at Assisi depicting the life of St. Francis were still rather flat, with diffused lighting, this did not make them less decorative—an artistic principle known to ancient Egyptian artists. True, Giotto's subject matter was almost entirely religious, but his treatment of it was such that the secular spirit made definite advances at the expense of the sacred. In the early fifteenth century, Masaccio greatly developed the trend begun by Giotto a century earlier. He increased the illusion of depth by introducing atmospheric perspective and by further developing linear perspective. He also introduced the principle of the known light source, which thereafter replaced diffused light in painting. His nude human forms were further rounded and humanized. His landscape backgrounds were realistic and detailed. With Masaccio, the transition from medieval to Renaissance painting was completed and the stage set for such towering geniuses of the Italian High Renaissance as Leonardo da Vinci, Michelangelo, Raphael, and Titian.

It would be difficult to find a more representative figure of the Italian Renaissance than Leonardo da Vinci (1452–1519). All the colorful facets of the secular spirit are richly illustrated by the career and work of this versatile genius. As a painter, he is probably unsurpassed in any age. Leonardo was an illegitimate child, as were a number of the famous figures of the Renaissance. He was born near Florence and began his career there, but some of his most productive years were spent in the employ of the duke of Milan. He finally followed King Francis I to France, where he died. Like most Renaissance artists, Leonardo dealt primarily with religious subject matter, but, also like the others, his treatment of it was invariably secular and human. In his *Virgin of the Rocks*, for instance, Leonardo creates with exquisite grace and beauty the Virgin Mary and the Christ child. The

The breaking of medieval artistic traditions that was to culminate with the glorification of the human form in the great works of the Renaissance began in the fourteenth century with Giotto, whose figures were far more human and who introduced perspective and naturalistic backgrounds. In this fresco, *The Flight into Egypt*, the subject matter is religious, but the spirit is secular.
Photo: Alinari–Art Reference Bureau

Virgin, however, is the loveliest of women, and the Christ child is a plump and playful baby boy. The characters are human, not divine. The background is a strange rock formation, naturalistic enough to reveal a keen interest in this material earth, and yet arrestingly abnormal. The plant forms in the background are actually identifiable. Leonardo's *The Last Supper* depicts the reactions of the twelve disciples to Christ's words, "One of you shall betray Me." This celebrated fresco, exhibiting the artist's complete mastery of technique and draftsmanship, is essentially a study in human psychology—a subject in which Leonardo showed a special interest. The famous *Mona Lisa* is not religious in subject matter; it is the portrait of a real woman. (Portrait painting, which was begun by Renaissance artists, reflects clearly the humanistic spirit of the time.) The mysterious half-smile—the mouth smiles but the eyes do

not—so captivates the viewer that he is likely to overlook other features of the picture, including the hands, which are said to be the most sensitive ever painted. In the *Mona Lisa*, Leonardo, who appears to have been little interested in women in real life, is believed to be probing the universal human nature of womanhood.

Michelangelo (1475–1564) is second only to Leonardo da Vinci as a versatile Italian High Renaissance genius. Since Michelangelo was primarily a sculptor, his painting is sometimes called "painted sculpture." His favorite subject was the virile, muscular male nude. Although a Florentine, much of his life was spent in Rome, where he labored in the service of the popes. His greatest painting—some say the greatest single painting of all time—was the ceiling fresco in the Vatican Sistine Chapel. The hundreds of individual figures, representing nine scenes from the book of

Genesis, marvelously blend together into one harmonious whole. A subdued, blond cast adds to the religious atmosphere of the work. And yet the figures are all vibrant human beings. Later Michelangelo painted the *Last Judgment* as an altarpiece for the same chapel. The Christ in this picture is actually a terrifying, pagan giant, hardly the Jesus of Nazareth of the New Testament and the Christian Church.

Some critics believe Raphael (1483–1520) to be the greatest painter of all time; others say that he merely synthesized the original work of others. The output during his brief life was enormous. His favorite subjects were religious, but his Madonnas were feminine, gracious women and his Christ childs pudgy and mischievous. His best-known paintings, the *Sistine Madonna* and the *Madonna of the Chair*, both in oil, well illustrate this secular

With Leonardo da Vinci (1452–1519), Renaissance painting reached its peak. In The Virgin of the Rocks, the Virgin is a beautiful woman, and the Christ Child is a playful, pudgy boy. The rock formation is authentic, and the plants are identifiable specimens. *Photo: Archives Photographiques, Paris*

treatment of a sacred theme. Many of his vivid portraits are of lay princes and tycoons. His monumental fresco *The School of Athens* reveals the veneration that Renaissance man felt for the pagan glory of Greece.

The fourth of the great painters of the Italian High Renaissance was Titian (1477–1576). A citizen of Venice, the most prosperous commercial city of the fifteenth century, Titian reflected the secular spirit of the Renaissance to an even greater degree than his three renowned contemporaries. Although a considerable portion of his painting was of religious subjects, his focus was nearly always the pomp and pageantry of the Church rather than its teachings. But a large part of his subject matter was purely secular. The wealth and brilliance of Venice, overflowing with cargoes of luxurious fabrics, tapestries,

and gems from the East, provided a challenging array of sensuous and colorful material for the artist to depict. And in the use of color, particularly vivid yellows, reds, and blues, Titian had no peer. He always painted the hair of his women a reddish-gold hue that has come to be called Titian. His portraits of some of the great lay personages of the sixteenth century, such as Francis I of France, Emperor Charles V, and Philip II of Spain, are masterful character studies.

With Titian, the break with medieval painting, begun by Giotto and Masaccio, was completed. Space has limited us here to a bare outline of the High Renaissance and to brief descriptions of only its giant figures. There were, of course, many other brilliant painters in this period, such as Fra Filippo Lippi, Fra Angelico, Botticelli, and Tintoretto.

In sculpture, the artist without peer in any age is Michelangelo. It is true that he had Roman copies of the sculpture of Hellenic Greek masters such as Praxiteles and Scopas to guide and inspire him. But the gifted Florentine was no mere copier. The Greek masterpieces, for all their beauty and grace, were idealized types—half gods, half men. Michelangelo and his lesser-known immediate predecessors and contemporaries added a typically Renaissance characteristic to sculpture: individuality. The statues of the Italian Renaissance are not only human beings, but human individuals. Even Michelangelo's *Pietà*, which represents the mother of Jesus holding the dead body of her son as she looks down piteously, is a study in human emotions. His *Moses* portrays the fierce and rugged strength of man, not God. Moses' beard, as crude as icicles beneath a water tank in January, displays the sculptor's ability deliberately to distort for effect. The three-dimensional

The genius of Michelangelo, master sculptor of the Renaissance, is exemplified in this work, the Dying Slave, now in the Louvre, which glorifies both the human form and the human spirit. *Photo: J. B. Harrison*

The largest Christian church in the world, St. Peter's basilica in Rome, was built in the sixteenth and seventeenth centuries at enormous cost. The secular-minded Renaissance architects of St. Peter's were influenced by the styles of pagan Greece and Rome. *Photo: Alinari–Art Reference Bureau*

medium of marble enabled Michelangelo to exploit to the full his favorite subject, the masculine nude. Numerous statues of David are used to convey not only the virile muscular power, but also the agile grace of the male animal. His *Dying Slave* is a sublime portrayal of both the human form and the human spirit. Some critics think that the great sculptor's finest genius is displayed in the companion statues of two members of the Medici family—Lorenzo, the contemplative type, and Giuliano, the man of action. In these two pieces the master craftsman and artist exhibits every technique of sculpture. The work of Michelangelo is probably our

best example of the Renaissance glorification of man as lord and master of the universe.

The subject of Renaissance sculpture cannot be dismissed without brief mention of the work of Benvenuto Cellini. His work in gold and silver was of an exquisite delicacy that has never been equaled. His most famous larger work is the bronze statue of Perseus holding up the Gorgon's head. In this amazing conglomeration of unrealities, Cellini showed complete disregard of all accepted traditions and standards, yet with happy results. Such bold and original pioneering was typical of the self-confident, secular nature of the Renaissance mind.

Renaissance architecture, like Renaissance sculpture, drew heavily from Greek and Roman sources. From Greece by way of Rome came columns (now merely decorative) and horizontal lines; from Rome came the dome, the arches, and the massiveness that characterized Renaissance buildings. All of these features (except massiveness) represented a revolt against the Gothic architecture of the later Middle Ages, although the Gothic style had never gained much of a foothold in Italy. The two greatest monuments of Italian Renaissance architecture are the cathedral at Florence and St. Peter's basilica in Rome. St. Peter's cannot be called a cathedral, since it has never been the seat of a bishop. The Florentine cathedral, with its gigantic octagonal dome and ornate rectangular facade and bell tower, reflects the influence not only of ancient Rome but of Byzantine and Islamic art as well. But the most grandiose achievement of Renaissance architecture is St. Peter's. This magnificent structure was to the Renaissance era what the Pyramids, the Parthenon, the Colosseum, and the Gothic cathedrals were to their respective epochs. It was built during the sixteenth and early seventeenth centuries at a cost that shook all Western Europe religiously and politically. Its numerous architects drew primarily upon pagan Greek and Roman sources for their inspiration. Even seventeenth-century baroque features eventually entered into its design. Raphael served for a time as chief architect, and Michelangelo designed the dome. One has to step inside St. Peter's to appreciate the breathtaking grandeur of this awesome structure. Its lofty proportions and gigantic pillars, its brilliant paintings and sculptures, its gold, marble, and mosaic decorations all glorify the material things of this world rather than the spiritual aspects of this world and the next. Built by the popes of the Western Church, St. Peter's is really a temple dedicated to the sensuous beauty, earthly pride, and confidence in man that characterized the secular spirit of the Renaissance.

Music was another field of art in which the Italian Renaissance made many original contributions. The chief developments in Renaissance music occured in the sixteenth century. Instrumental music became popular, and great improvements were made in the instruments. The harpsichord, forerunner of the piano, and the violin family of instruments came into existence. Musical techniques such as major and minor modes, counterpoint (the blending of two contrasting melodies), and polyphony (the interweaving of several melodic lines) rapidly developed. The most illustrious musician of the sixteenth century was Palestrina, chief musician to the pope, and probably the greatest master of polyphonic music of all time. Although most of the music of the Renaissance still centered about the Church, it was now more sensuous and versatile. Moreover, new and entirely secular forms appeared. The madrigal, popular throughout Europe in the late sixteenth century, was a musical rendition of stanzas of secular lyrical poetry. Renaissance musicians laid the foundations for modern classical music in all its major forms—concerto, symphony, sonata, oratorio, opera.

5. SCIENCE

It was almost inevitable that a renewed interest in the physical world, combined with optimism and confidence in the wisdom and self-sufficiency of man, should have resulted in scientific inquiry. Although the flowering of

The range of interests and the versatility of the men of the Renaissance are superbly exemplified by Leonardo da Vinci, whose inventions, drawings, and scientific hypotheses are amazing even today for their accuracy and ingenuity. This drawing from one of his notebooks shows a giant crossbow that could be operated mechanically. Leonardo wrote backwards; you will need to use a mirror to read his notes. *Photo: The Bettmann Archive* natural science did not occur until the seventeenth and eighteenth centuries, that blossoming sprang from the seedbed of the Renaissance. Leonardo da Vinci, for example, made accurate observations and pondered deeply on such subjects as geology, anatomy, botany, and applied mechanics. His inventions, drawings, and scientific predictions are impressive even today.

In 1543 two of history's most original and provocative scientific works—Copernicus' *Concerning the Revolutions of Celestial Orbs* and Vesalius' *Concerning the Structure of the Human Body*—were published. Both were in large measure products of the free atmosphere of the University of Padua. Copernicus was a Pole, and Vesalius was a Fleming. Both were attracted by the intellectual climate of Renaissance Italy, and both attacked long-accepted theories. Copernicus challenged the

geocentric theory of Ptolemy (A.D. second century) that the earth is the center of the universe in favor of the heliocentric theory, according to which the sun is the center of the solar system, the earth being only one of many planets revolving around it. Vesalius assaulted the theories of Galen (also second century) concerning the structure of the human body, particularly the heart. Both books raised a storm of opposition, and both were popularly rejected. However, after a century of controversy, Copernicus was to become the father of modern astronomy, Vesalius the father of modern anatomy and physiology. This spirit of scientific inquiry completely supplanted medieval scholasticism. More important, the beginnings made by Leonardo, Copernicus, and Vesalius were to bring forth in the seventeenth century and after an incredible expansion of scientific knowledge.

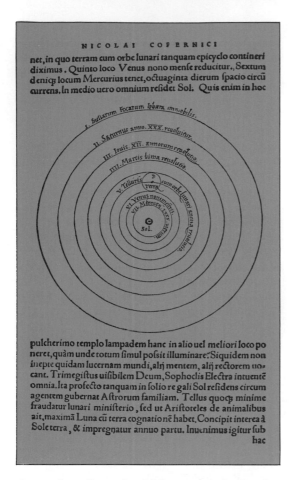

A page from Copernicus' "Concerning the Revolution of Heavenly Bodies." *Photo: Rare Book Division, New York Public Library, Astor, Lenox, and Tilden Foundations*

6. DECLINE

The Italian Renaissance slowly changed and then declined, as the center of Renaissance activity shifted from Italy to Northern Europe. This shift closely paralleled that of commerce from the Mediterranean to the Atlantic. When Venice, Florence, and Milan were the most prosperous commercial and banking centers in Europe, they were at the same time the most vigorous seats of Renaissance culture. As their economy stagnated with the shifting of the trade routes to the west, their cultural vigor likewise declined, although Italian art, heavily patronized by the Church, kept its momentum for several generations longer. Literature had declined by the end of the fourteenth century, and humanism by the end of the fifteenth; by the end of the sixteenth century, art too had lost its vigor.

Another factor that undoubtedly contributed to the decline of the Italian Renaissance was the revival of interest in religion, a result of the Protestant and Roman Catholic reformations. Italian humanism, which was more secular and pagan than Northern humanism, was particularly hard hit by the religious revival. It must be remembered also that the Renaissance was in large measure of, by, and for the elite only. The Italian humanists were particularly contemptuous of the masses. Other causes of the decline of the Italian Renaissance are obscure. One frequently reads that the invasion of Italy by the French, Spanish, and German armies and the general military and political instability of the period constituted important factors in the decline. This proposition, however, is difficult to prove. The ancient Greeks and modern Germans—to cite two parallel cases—produced their greatest cultural achievements while they were split up into many political units, and often under adverse conditions such as foreign invasion or civil war. The causes of the decline of brilliant civilizations and epochs remain a challenge to the student of history.

Suggested Reading

General. **M. P. Gilmore, *The World of Humanism, 1453–1517* (Harper Torchbook) is the second volume in the excellent Rise of Modern Europe series. It is a good analysis of various interrelated forces operating during the period of the Italian High Renaissance. **W. K. Ferguson, *The Renaissance* (Berkshire) is an excellent brief survey by a leading contemporary authority. Probably the most influential book that has yet been written on the Italian Renaissance is **Jakob Burckhardt, *The Civilization of the Renaissance in Italy* (2 vols, Harper Torchbook). The original edition was written over a hundred years ago. Another classic work on the Italian Renaissance is J. A. Symonds, *The Renaissance in Italy* (7 vols., 1875–86). Burckhardt, Symonds, and other important writers on the Renaissance are analyzed in W. K. Ferguson, *The Renaissance in Historical Thought: Five Centuries of Interpretation* (1948).

Literature, Humanism, Science. J. B. Fletcher, *The Literature of the Italian Renaissance* (1934) is a scholarly treatment of that subject. J. H. Robinson and H. W. Rolfe, *Petrarch, the First Modern Scholar and Man of Letters* (2nd rev. ed., 1914) is a study of Petrarch's letters. E. H. Gibson, *Dante the Philosopher* (1949) is a good study of the leading literary figure of the Italian Renaissance. **F. Chabod, *Machiavelli and the Renaissance* (Harper Torchbook) is a sound approach to the controversial political theorist of the Renaissance period. A standard detailed treatment of the beginning of modern science in the Renaissance period is **A. Wolf, *A History of Science, Technology, and Philosophy in the Sixteenth and Seventeenth Centuries* (Harper Torchbook).

The Arts. Two excellent works on Italian Renaissance art are **B. Berenson, *Italian Painters of the Renaissance* (Meridian); and **H. Wölfflin, *The Art of the Italian Renais-sance* (Schocken). F. B. Artz, *From the Renaissance to Romanticism: Trends in Style in Art, Literature, and Music, 1300–1832* (1962) is a good discussion of cultural developments in Europe during and after the Renaissance. A good study of Leonardo da Vinci, in many ways the most fascinating of all the Renaissance artists, is **K. Clark, *Leonardo da Vinci* (Penguin). A good approach to developments in music during the Renaissance period is P. H. Láng, *Music in Western Civilization* (1941). Láng attempts to relate music to its cultural environment.

Sources. **P. Taylor, *The Notebook of Leonardo da Vinci: A New Selection* (Mentor) reproduces scores of drawings, sketches, and designs of this versatile genius. Giorgio Vasari, *Lives of the Most Eminent Painters, Sculptors, and Architects*, trans. A. B. Hind (4 vols., 1927), is a major source for Renaissance art. Vasari was himself a sixteenth-century artist. The textbook for gentlemanly behavior throughout Western Europe during the Renaissance period was **B. Castiglione, *The Book of the Courtier* (Anchor), written by an Italian courtier. **Benvenuto Cellini, *Autobiography* (Bantam) is the artist's own account of an adventuresome life. **Dante Alighieri, *The Divine Comedy* (Rinehart) is the greatest literary masterpiece of the Italian Renaissance. **Machiavelli, *The Prince* and *the Discourses* (Modern Library) are the two chief works of the foremost political theorist of the early modern era.

Historical Fiction. **D. Merejkowski, *The Romance of Leonardo* (Modern Library), although fictional in form, is based upon excellent historical research and is a good approach to Leonardo and the spirit of the Italian Renaissance. The same can be said of Irving Stone, *The Agony and the Ecstasy* (1961), a novel based upon the life of Michelangelo.

Chapter 30 ✿ The Renaissance: The North

The Northern Renaissance was in large measure an importation from Italy. Northern European scholars such as Chaucer had gone to Italy as early as the fourteenth century, by the late fifteenth century, such inspirational journeys to Italy were commonplace. The rapid increase of commercial and capitalistic activity in Northern and Western Europe, following the shift of trade routes from the Mediterranean to the Atlantic, facilitated the development of the Northern secular spirit.

1. GENERAL NATURE

Not only was the Northern Renaissance later than the Italian Renaissance, but it was also somewhat different in nature. Painting, sculpture, and architecture played a much less prominent role; humanistic philosophy and literature, on the other hand, were relatively more important. Northern humanism itself, though an importation from Italy, was markedly different in nature. Whereas Italian humanism very frequently represented an open revolt of pagan secularism against Christian ideals, Northern humanism sought, for the most part, to humanize Christianity and thereby to reconcile the sacred and the secular.

2. NORTHERN HUMANISM

The trend to secularism as a basic attitude toward life began in earnest in Northern Eu-

rope in the late fifteenth century. One of the first evangelists of the new man-centered faith was Johann Reuchlin, a German scholar. After a sojourn in Italy during which he became imbued with the ideas of the Italian humanists, Reuchlin undertook to introduce the new classical learning into Germany. Specifically, he sought to broaden and enrich the university curriculum by establishing the study of the "un-Christian" Hebrew and Greek languages and literature. The Church and university interests vested in the medieval order of things attempted to thwart him, invoking the Inquisition to try him on grounds of heresy. Reuchlin fought back courageously and enlisted a large and enthusiastic following. Eventually the pope condemned him to silence. However, the victory really lay with Reuchlin and his humanist supporters. The tactics and self-centered motives of the churchmen and scholastic pedagogues disgusted most of the genuine scholars and students of the day, and during the first few decades of the sixteenth century the new humanistic curriculum became established in all the major universities of Germany.

Meanwhile, in England a group of Oxford professors was accomplishing with less opposition what Reuchlin had fought for in Germany. John Colet was the most prominent member of this group. He, too, visited Renaissance Italy. In true Northern humanistic fashion he gave a rationalistic slant to his preaching and teaching of the Scriptures at

This woodcut of the Four Horsemen from his Apocalypse series (ca. 1497–1498) shows Albert Dürer's skill as a master of delicate, graceful line. Note the artist's signature at center bottom. *Photo: Marburg–Art Reference Bureau*

Oxford. Probably the greatest of Colet's contributions to the new learning was the founding of St. Paul's grammar school in London, with a curriculum devoted largely to the pagan classics. To guarantee its secular orientation, he chose as trustees a guild of London merchants. St. Paul's soon became a model for many other such schools throughout England.

The most famous of all the early sixteenth-century English humanists was Sir Thomas More, Lord Chancellor of the Realm. More's *Utopia*, like Plato's *Republic*, blueprinted an earthly, not a heavenly, paradise. In pictur-

ing his ideal commonwealth, More indicted the social, religious, and political evils of his own time. Utopia was a socialistic society where private property and profits were unknown. Much attention was given to public health and education. The economy was planned and cooperative. Iron was more valuable than gold because it was more useful. War was outlawed except in self-defense. Religious freedom was granted to all but atheists. Although More eventually was to accept death by beheading rather than to recognize Henry VIII as head of the English church in place of the pope, his ideal society was en-

The "prince of the humanists,"
Erasmus, is shown in this fine portrait by the northern Renaissance
painter Hans Holbein. *Photo: Archives
Photographiques, Paris*

tirely secular. Man through his own wisdom would create his own perfect world here on earth.

Towering above all the other Northern humanists was Desiderius Erasmus (1466–1536), the intellectual dictator of the sixteenth century. In his efforts to humanize Christianity itself, the "Prince of the Humanists" presented the fundamental issue of Western civilization: Are the basic faith, ideals, and standards of Western civilization human or divine? Erasmus was born in Rotterdam in the Netherlands, the illegitimate son of a priest. Reared as an orphan, he was educated in a school run by the Brethren of the Common Life, a pietistic order of laymen that taught the Greek and Latin classics and emphasized simple inner piety rather than ritual and formal creed. (It is interesting and probably significant that Martin Luther, the great contemporary and adversary of Erasmus, also attended a school of the Brethren of the Common Life.) At the age of twenty-one Erasmus entered an Augustinian monastery (again like Luther) and was eventually ordained. Instead of serving as a priest, however, he spent every possible moment studying his beloved classics—a pursuit he was to continue at the Sorbonne and for the rest of his life.

Erasmus' vast erudition combined with his great personal charm made him a much-sought-after man. He was a popular figure around Paris. On a trip to England he added to his growing band of friends and followers many of the important personages of that land, including John Colet and Sir Thomas More. They persuaded him to begin writing. His first book was *Adages*, a collection of wise sayings of the Greeks and Romans together with his own comments. It was an immediate success, and other books soon followed. His greatest work was the *Praise of Folly*, in which he ridiculed with subtle humor and delightful satire the ignorance, superstition, credulity, and current practices of his day, particularly those connected with the Church. The folly which he praised was man's very human light-heartedness, his sense of humor.

Wherever Erasmus went—France, England, Italy, Switzerland, Germany, the Netherlands—he was received with admiration and awe. No man so advanced the cause of Northern humanism by popularizing the study of the pagan Greek and Latin classics. He ended his career in Basel, Switzerland, as editor and adviser of the Froben press.

In addition to popularizing the new humanistic learning north of the Alps, Erasmus is significant in history for at least two other reasons—his influence on religious and social reform, and his efforts to humanize and intellectualize Christianity. He was at his best when laughing to scorn the abuses and superstitious practices of the Roman Catholic Church. The taking of money from the poor and ignorant masses by wealthy and corrupt churchmen, veneration of relics, and unquestioning belief in the miraculous were in the eyes of Erasmus beneath the contempt of enlightened men. But he was clever enough to sheathe his barbs with humor, thus making them more subtle and effective. Erasmus, however, was no Protestant. When Martin Luther first began his attacks on the Roman Catholic Church, Erasmus thought that he was merely seeking to correct glaring abuses and hailed him as a fellow spirit. But when Erasmus discovered that the German reformer was primarily interested in doctrinal reform and that the Protestants were as dogmatic as the Roman Catholics (actually more so in the early sixteenth century), Erasmus would have nothing more to do with him. The great humanist, uninterested in religious dogma, found it more comfortable to remain in the Roman Catholic Church. The two men ended hurling epithets at each other. Nevertheless, Erasmus' incessant attacks on the abuses in organized Christianity undoubtedly encouraged both the Protestant and the Roman Catholic reformations.

Erasmus' efforts to humanize Christianity, however, are far more significant historically than his campaign to eradicate religious and social abuses. Since the fall of the Roman Empire the great common denominator of

Western civilization has been the Christian religion. The vast majority of the members of Western society have subscribed even if they have not lived up to its creeds, ideals, and moral standards. Furthermore, the vitality of these creeds, ideals, and moral standards has derived, in large measure, from the belief that they are of divine origin and sanction. Indeed, it is difficult to conceive of Western civilization as it has developed thus far without this basic faith at its center. This is why Erasmus' questioning of the divine origin and nature of the Christian religion—his efforts to humanize it—is of such deep significance. Although the "Prince of the Humanists" never did specifically say so, the implication running through his writings is that Jesus was a human being—the greatest, best, and most charming man who ever lived, the man we should all try to emulate, but nevertheless man, not God. Erasmus would bypass formal creed, dogma, ritual, organization, and seek the "historical" Christ. Now, all this is quite appealing to the rationalistic humanist, but it is not quite so simple as it first appears. The historical Christ is a most elusive figure. As a matter of fact, the only documentation we have for Christ is in the New Testament, and if we apply to it the same standards of critical analysis used for other historical documents, its evidence is by no means conclusive. And yet the secondary evidence—the word of mouth and written tradition—is overwhelming. Few historians today would deny the existence of Jesus of Nazareth. However, all we have to go on for the "historical Christ" is the New Testament and the early tradition, and the Christ of both these sources is not the Christ of Erasmus. He is a miracle-working Christ who claimed to be the son and image of God, to have the gift of eternal salvation, who "spake as no other man ever spake." Far simpler to reject Christ as did many of the Italian humanists than to humanize him. Erasmus' attempt was not only the ultimate in the renaissance of secularism, but the beginning of a controversy that has endured until today.

3. THE NATIONAL RENAISSANCE LITERATURES

The national literatures that flourished during this period reflected the secular spirit in all its phases; they also reflected the rapidly growing national interests and traits. In both respects they constituted a sharp departure from the literature of the Middle Ages, which in the main (with noteworthy exceptions, of course) centered around religious subjects and was international in viewpoint. Although the national literatures of the Northern Renaissance owed a great deal to the Italian literature of the fourteenth century, they reached their prime much later—in the sixteenth and early seventeenth centuries. The most important literary developments in this era were in England, France, and Spain.

English Renaissance literature began with Chaucer (1340–1400), who traveled to Italy, became acquainted with Boccaccio, and brought back to England the spirit and much of the technique of the early Italian Renaissance writers. His *Canterbury Tales* are almost an Anglican *Decameron* in charming verse. Salty and very earthy characters from all walks of life parade past us on their way to Canterbury, their human frailties and sins of the flesh forgiven them by the author. Only hypocritical churchmen get the censure of the English Boccaccio, and even they with a light and subtle touch. Chaucer's use of the Midland dialect helped to establish it as the national language of all England. As in Italy, however, the century following Chaucer was rather barren in a literary sense; it was not until the mid-sixteenth century, the time of Queen Elizabeth I, that his plantings suddenly burst forth in full flower.

The reign of Elizabeth I (1558–1603) was a period of great energy and optimism in England. To the rediscovery of the achievements of ancient Greece and Rome were added the discovery of the New World and of new routes to the riches of the Far East. English seamen such as Drake, Gilbert, Hawkins, Grenville, and Howard first plundered the Spanish treasure ships, and then crushed the "Invincible Armada" of the world's chief military power, making England mistress of the seas for the next three centuries. English explorers boldly laid the foundations for a future empire in the East and in the West. England's commerce increased, and the standard of living for the middle and upper classes rose sharply. The Queen herself knew how to stimulate national pride centered around her own person. England became "a nest of singing birds" such as the world has never seen or heard. Edmund Spenser's *Faerie Queen* glorified the versatile man of the Italian humanists, particularly the ideal set forth by Castiglione in his *Book of the Courtier*. Christopher Marlowe in his brief life wrote man-centered plays of such caliber that some critics think he would have achieved the stature of Shakespeare had he lived. His *Tamburlaine the Great* and *Edward II* treat of the worldly drama of royal ambition. The central figure in *The Jew of Malta*, a forerunner of Shylock, is a product of the revived commercial capitalism. *Doctor Faustus* dramatizes the theme, later immortalized by Goethe, of the intellectual who in true Renaissance fashion sold his soul to the devil in return for earthly knowledge and pleasure.

Mightiest of all the artists of the English Renaissance was, of course, William Shakespeare (1564–1616). Shakespeare was born in the same year that Michelangelo died, a fact which ought to remind us that virtually the same set of circumstances that stimulated the Italian artists of the sixteenth century to design St. Peter's and paint the *Sistine Madonna* spurred the English artists to write the *Faerie Queen* and *Hamlet*. So little is known of Shakespeare's life that there is still controversy over whether or not he is actually the author of the poems and plays we know as his. Shakespeare wrote some of the world's most beautiful lyrical poetry. His most important work, however, was in the field of drama. Here he was heavily indebted to his contemporary, Christopher Marlowe, as well as to the ancient Greek and Roman dramatists. Marlowe developed the blank verse form, which Shakespeare perfected. In plays such as *Hamlet, Macbeth, Othello, King Lear, Merchant of Venice, As You Like It, Henry IV, Romeo and Juliet*, and *Julius Caesar*, Shakespeare displayed a mastery of every known technique of the dramatic art.

More important for the student of history, he exemplified and dramatized every facet of the secular spirit of the Renaissance. Secular man is Shakespeare's subject matter. Rugged, distinctive human personalities are the heroes and villains of his plays. No human emotion, aspiration, or psychological conflict escapes his eye. On the whole, Shakespeare, unlike the Greek dramatists, makes man the master of his own fate. In addition to making man the center of his universe, Shakespeare illustrates the Renaissance spirit and times in other ways. Admiration for pagan Greece and Rome, a keen interest in new-found lands, the first stirrings of modern natural science, the commercial revolution and social problems arising from the emergence of the capitalistic middle class, the rise of national monarchy and a national patriotic spirit—all enter into the fabric of the plays. In spite of the fact that both the Protestant and the Roman Catholic reformations loomed large in the affairs of England and the rest of Western Europe just before and during Shakespeare's time, he showed little interest in matters of religion. In this respect, too, he was a true child of the Renaissance.

One of Shakespeare's most important contemporaries was Sir Francis Bacon. Though not Shakespeare's peer as an artist, Bacon was nonetheless an intellectual giant. His father, Sir Nicholas Bacon, was one of the chief administrators and advisers of Queen Elizabeth, and Francis spent much of his life seeking political fortune. Finally he succeeded, becoming Lord Chancellor of England, only to be convicted of dishonesty, stripped of his powers, and for a time imprisoned. That his reputation and his own self-esteem could survive such misfortune is indicative of the moral relativism of the Renaissance era. Bacon's intellectual interests were broad, and his knowledge encyclopedic. His *History of the Reign of Henry VII* is still an important source. His *Novum Organum* is one of the first important treatises on modern natural science. Bacon preached the absolute necessity of accurate and unbiased observation in acquiring scientific truth. His major contribution to Renaissance literature is his *Essays*, which he continued to polish and refine as long as he lived. The final result is fifty-eight gems of pithy, salty, practical, and very human wisdom.

The last of the giants of Elizabethan literature was Ben Jonson. This robust personality, a familiar figure in the bohemian taverns of London, could serve as a trooper in the English army and also write "Drink to me only with thine eyes." Jonson was first a connoisseur of classical literature. With exquisite plays reminiscent of the Greek dramatists, he attempted unsuccessfully to reverse the trend toward cheap popularization and sensationalism that had characterized the English stage after the death of Shakespeare. Jonson's death in 1637 marked the end of the most glorious epoch in the history of the world's literature—England's greatest contribution to the Renaissance and the Renaissance spirit.

The two chief figures in French Renaissance literature were François Rabelais and Michel de Montaigne, both of whom lived in the sixteenth century. Rabelais was a renegade priest, a bored physician, and a loving student of the classics. Although he stumbled quite by accident and late in life upon his gift for writing, he turned out to be one of the greatest creative geniuses in the history of literature. His masterpieces are *Pantagruel* and *Gargantua*. They are fantasies about two completely unrestrained giants who wallow and revel unashamedly in all the sensuous and sensual pleasures known to man. These works are an open assault upon Christian moral standards and restraints. The wit is coarse, lewd, and sympathetic toward the frailties of human nature. Rabelais' rich imagery, his marvelous gift of expression, and his graceful artistry combine to make him one of the founding fathers of modern French prose. He shares that honor with his contemporary, John Calvin, whose lucid and incisive Protestant writings Rabelais hated no less than the works of the Roman Catholic theologians and the scholastic philosophers.

Montaigne was a prodigy born of a wealthy family. By the age of thirty-seven he had received a university education, practiced law, served as a magistrate in his native Bordeaux, and retired to spend the rest of his life in study, contemplation, and writing. Like Rabelais, he was an ardent lover of the classics. This, together with the fact that his mother was Jewish and his father Roman Catholic, probably accounts for his skepticism in matters of religion. The result of his life of study and reflection was his *Essays*. Montaigne was a skeptic and an Epicurean. To arrive at reliable truth, he believed, one must rid himself of all religious prejudice. He was a moral and spiritual relativist, rejecting all absolutes. Unlike his successors of the eighteenth-century Enlightenment, he distrusted the authority of human reason. Unable to replace the authority of Christian dogma with any other firm conviction, Montaigne was nearly always negative in his conclusions. But he immensely enjoyed this game of intellectual hide-and-seek. In fact, Montaigne believed that the chief purpose of life is pleasure —not the "eat, drink, and be merry" pleasure of Rabelais, but urbane, sophisticated, restrained, intellectual pleasure. The influence of Montaigne has been enormous—obviously upon essayists from Bacon to Emerson and later, but also upon the development of modern thought in general.

Standing out above all others in Spanish Renaissance literature are Miguel de Cervantes and Lope de Vega. Cervantes was a contemporary of Shakespeare, the two dying within a few days of each other in 1616. Cervantes' early life is also obscure. In time he became a soldier of fortune, fought heroically and was wounded in the great naval battle of Lepanto with the Turks, suffered a five-year imprisonment in Algeria, and finally served as a quartermaster for Spain's Invincible Armada. In poverty-stricken later life he settled down to write *Don Quixote,* called by some critics the greatest novel ever written. This masterpiece of Spanish literature relates with urbane grace and humor the adventures of a slightly addled knight who filled his noble head too full of the lore of chivalry, and of his groom, Sancho Panza. Sancho, a squat plebeian on a donkey, and Don Quixote, an emaciated knight on a tall, lean horse, go about Spain from one delightfully charming adventure to another. It is altogether necessary to read a few pages, almost any few pages, of this rollicking fantasy to appreciate the genius of Cervantes. Since all types and classes of people in all parts of Spain are lucidly portrayed, *Don Quixote* is the most valuable historical source in existence for life in sixteenth-century Spain. But Cervantes does not stop with sixteenth-century Spain; he probes the depths of human nature. All of us are Don Quixotes—at least all of us who are not Sancho Panzas. Cervantes' more immediate purpose was to laugh out of existence what was left of medieval chivalry. He therefore did to feudal society what Erasmus and Rabelais were trying to do to medieval Christianity, and in much the same manner.

Lope de Vega was a contemporary of Ben Jonson. In sharp contrast with Cervantes, whose literary life and genius were centered on one masterpiece, Lope de Vega wrote a fabulous number of works in practically every known genre. His plays alone exceed in number those of any other writer, whether we accept the writer's own claim to twenty-two hundred or recognize only the seven-hundred-odd plays that can be accounted for today. Secular man, pictured in every conceivable dramatic situation, is the hero of the great Spanish playwright. Lope de Vega was an ardent Spanish nationalist; he sailed with the Invincible Armada. Like the Elizabethans and other Northern Renaissance writers, he thought that his country and the sixteenth and early seventeenth centuries were an exciting place and time to live.

Thus the writers of the Northern Renaissance had much in common. Their chief interests were contemporary man and the exciting, rapidly expanding material world around them. Their chief inspiration was the pagan classics of Greece and Rome. They were on the whole nationalistic, and wrote in the new national vernaculars. Although the Protestant and Roman Catholic reformations were tearing Western European society apart throughout the sixteenth century, the men of letters were in the main either apathetic or, as in the case of Rabelais and Montaigne, hostile to theology in general and to Christianity in particular.

4. NORTHERN RENAISSANCE ART

Northern Renaissance art did not equal either the Northern literature or the Italian art after which it was largely patterned. It was, however, excellent in a relative sense. The best Renaissance painters outside Italy were the Flemings (Belgians) and the Germans. The Van Eyck brothers, Hubert and Jan, lived in Ghent in the Flemish Netherlands in the early fifteenth century. Like Masaccio, their Italian contemporary, they brought to near completion the transition from medieval to Renaissance painting. Their greatest joint work is *Adoration of the Lamb.* Not the least of their contributions to painting was the development of oil as a medium. It was from them that Leonardo da Vinci learned to work in this medium, which he perfected in such masterworks as the *Mona Lisa* and the *Virgin of the Rocks.*

In sixteenth-century Germany, Albert Dürer

An illuminated page from the Gutenberg Bible, after a facsimile. *Photo: Rare Book Division, New York Public Library, Astor, Lenox, and Tilden Foundations*

of Nuremberg and Hans Holbein the Younger of Augsburg were the leading painters. Dürer was primarily a master craftsman of delicate and graceful line. Probably for this reason, his woodcuts and engravings are better than his paintings, and in these media he is without peer in any age. Holbein was a skillful sketcher and woodcutter, but he made his greatest contributions in the field of portrait painting. He painted several portraits of Erasmus and illustrated Erasmus' *Praise of Folly* with pen-and-ink drawings. Many of his most productive years were spent in England in the employ of Henry VIII. Among his greatest portraits are those of Henry VIII, Edward VI, Mary Tudor, and Sir Thomas

More. Both Dürer and Holbein were interested primarily in the contemporary things and people of the material world around them.

Renaissance artists did not produce many architectural monuments outside Italy, probably because commercial capitalism had not yet developed sufficiently in Northern Europe to finance this more costly type of undertaking. The largest Renaissance structure outside Italy is the vast Escorial near Madrid, which Philip II of Spain built as a royal palace and mausoleum. Its rugged massiveness, rectangular shape, and horizontal lines typify the Renaissance style. Some of the best examples of Northern Renaissance architecture are the Renaissance wing of the Louvre in Paris, which is the world's largest and probably greatest art gallery, and some of the largest chateaux along France's Loire River. This architecture was essentially derivative; the French Renaissance chateaux were really fortresses being played with.

5. PRINTING WITH MOVABLE TYPE

A major Renaissance contribution to the world of intellect and literature was the invention of printing with movable type. In ancient and medieval times manuscripts were written and copied in longhand on parchment or papyrus, a slow and costly process that greatly retarded the dissemination of knowledge. In the fourteenth century printing from carved wooden blocks came to Western Europe from China by way of the Mohammedan world and Spain. This process too was tedious, costly, and limited. Also from China came paper, made of various fibers, silk, cotton, or flax. Paper was a great improvement over parchment or papyrus for purposes of mass production. (Even the art of printing by movable type itself was a Chinese invention, although this is not believed to have influenced its invention in the Western world.)

John Gutenberg set up the first practical printing press using movable type in Europe at Mainz in western Germany. The Gutenberg forty-two-line Bible printed in 1454 is the earliest known book to be printed by the new process. The invention was an immediate success and spread quickly to all the other countries of Western Europe. It is estimated that by the end of the fifteenth century more than twenty-five thousand separate editions and nearly ten million individual books had been printed. To appreciate the significance of the new invention in making knowledge available to the masses, the reader need only reflect for a few moments on the probable cost of this book if it were copied in longhand on parchment or printed from nine hundred hand-carved wooden blocks at present-day wages. As a result of Gutenberg's invention and later improvements few people in the Western world today can excuse their ignorance of literature on the grounds that it is unavailable.

6. SIGNIFICANCE OF THE RENAISSANCE IN HISTORY

In retrospect, then, it is apparent that the Renaissance was a transition from the God-centered civilization of the Middle Ages to the man-centered, secular civilization of the modern period. In some measure it was a rebirth of the classical civilization of pagan Greece and Rome, but it was not merely that. There was much in the Renaissance that was fresh and original. The rediscovery of the brilliant culture of antiquity and the rising secular spirit with its confidence in man, versatility, egotism, materialism, and individuality combined to produce some of the most beautiful art and literature the world has ever known. In addition, the foundations were laid for the later rise of science. The Renaissance was also a serious challenge to Christianity, directly in Italy and somewhat indirectly in Northern Europe. That it did not destroy or palsy Christianity as a dynamic force in Western civilization is due in some measure to the Protestant and Roman Catholic reformations, which revitalized Christianity. To these great movements, which paralleled the Renaissance in its later stages and which were in part provoked by it, we must now turn.

Suggested Reading

General. An excellent overall view and interpretation of an outstanding present-day authority is W. M. Ferguson, *The Renaissance in Historical Thought: Five Centuries of Interpretation* (1948). A highly readable and influential intellectual history of modern Western civilization from its medieval roots to the twentieth century is J. H. Randall, *The Making of the Modern Mind* (1940). Science is the hero; Christianity the villain.

Northern Humanism. Northern humanism is well analyzed by a distinguished scholar, E. H. Harbison, in *The Christian Scholar in the Age of the Reformation* (1956). A lively, brief survey of Northern humanism and its leading figure is M. M. Phillips, *Erasmus and the Northern Renaissance* (1950). Probably the best all-round biography of the Prince of the Humanists is **Johan Huizinga, *Erasmus and the Age of Reformation* (Harper Torchbook).

Literature. By far the best way to get acquainted with the literature of any period is to read some of its masterpieces, such as those mentioned below. Three good guides to the literature of the sixteenth century are **H. O. Taylor, *Thought and Expression in the*

Sixteenth Century (5 vols., Collier); E. C. Dunn, *The Literature of Shakespeare's England* (1936); and A. Tilley, *The Literature of the French Renaissance* (2 vols., 1904).

Art and Printing. An excellent guide to Northern Renaissance art is O. Benesch, *The Art of the Renaissance in Northern Europe: Its Relation to the Contemporary Spiritual and Intellectual Movements* (1945). For Flemish art, Sir Martin Conway, *The Van Eycks and Their Followers* (1922) is good. A scholarly treatment of German Renaissance art is H. A. Dickinson, *German Masters of Art* (1914). The story of printing and the printing press is well told by D. C. McMurtrie, *The Book: The Story of Printing and Bookmaking* (3rd rev. ed., 1911); and Pierce Butler, *The Origin of Printing in Europe* (1940).

Sources. Some of the great Northern Renaissance literary masterpieces available in inexpensive editions are **Erasmus, *The Praise of Folly* (Ann Arbor); ** Sir Thomas More, *Utopia* (Appleton); **François Rabelais, *Gargantua and Pantagruel* (Penguin); **Michel de Montaigne, *Autobiography* (Vintage); and **Miguel de Cervantes, *Don Quixote* (Modern Library). A delightful source depicting one aspect of sixteenth-century European society is **G. T. Matthews, ed., *News and Rumor in Renaissance Europe* (Capricorn). It is a collection of reports of the agents of the Fuggers, who succeeded the Medicis as Europe's greatest bankers.

Chapter 31 ❦ The Protestant Reformation

The Protestant and Roman Catholic reformations, which split Western Europe into two hostile religious camps, virtually completed the destruction of the medieval synthesis, for this synthesis had centered around the Church. (Russia and the Balkans with their Orthodox Church had never been a part of this synthesis.) The Protestant Reformation had strong political, economic, and intellectual overtones; nevertheless, it was primarily a religious movement. Western Europeans of the sixteenth century were intensely interested in religion. The Church was still at the very center of their lives, and even the unlettered masses knew a good deal about matters of doctrine and ritual. The leaders of both the Protestant and the Roman Catholic reformations were certainly men whose lives were dedicated to religion.

1. BACKGROUND

In the later Middle Ages there developed within the ranks of the Roman Catholic Church a growing dissatisfaction with some of its fundamental doctrines (see pp. 452–454). Some had come to believe that the Roman Catholic Church had departed so far from the spirit and practices of the apostles and early fathers that it could no longer be considered God's appointed custodian of the Christian religion. They began to define *The Church* to mean the sum total of all those who put their faith in Christ, not any one specific institu-

tion.[1] The Scriptures alone, not the decisions and traditions of an organized church, became for these reformers the sole authoritative source for Christian dogma. Their growing conception of the Christian religion as a direct relationship between man and God tended to lessen the importance of the professional clergy and the sacraments of the Roman Catholic Church. They spoke of the priesthood of all believers. These ideas the reformers believed to be in harmony with those of St. Augustine and the early Church, as well as with those to be found in the Scriptures. They clashed sharply, however, with the beliefs and practices of the Roman Catholic hierarchy of the Late Middle Ages. This doctrinal split within the ranks of organized Western Christendom was the most fundamental of all the causes of the Reformation.

Other factors, however, contributed to the break within the Roman Catholic Church.

---

[1] The reformers disputed the Petrine doctrine upon which the popes based much of their claim to headship over the Christian Church. The popes claimed that, as bishops of Rome, they inherited the authority of St. Peter, the first bishop of Rome, whom Christ designated to head his Church. (". . . thou art Peter and upon this rock I will build my church . . . ," Matthew, 16:18.) The reformers maintained that in the original Greek the word for Peter is *petros*, meaning an individual stone, and that the word for rock is *petra*, meaning a large body of stone. Therefore, they assert, Christ did not mean to say that he would found his Church upon Peter, but upon the faith that Christ was the son of the living God, which Peter had just affirmed.

Quite apart from matters of doctrine, many abuses had arisen in the Church during the fourteenth and fifteenth centuries when the Church was torn by the Babylonian Captivity, the Great Schism, and the struggles between the popes and the councils (see pp. 447–451). Ignorance and worldliness of the clergy, the sale of Church offices and services (simony), the favoring of relatives for lucrative Church offices (nepotism), the holding by one man of more offices than he could adequately serve (pluralism)—all were subjects of loud and growing complaint. Many of the higher clergy, even the popes, became infected with the secular spirit of the Renaissance. Often they displayed greater interest in humanistic pleasures and pursuits than in feeding their flocks. Eventually the Church hierarchy came to realize the seriousness of these abuses and took drastic steps to remedy them, but not until much of Western Christendom had left the Roman fold.

Politically the rise of national states and of local loyalty to them clashed with the international character of the Church. The national monarchs became increasingly jealous of the claims of the pope over their subjects, and in many cases they supported native Protestant leaders and movements.

Economic motivation undoubtedly played a significant part. Church taxes drained away to Rome much wealth from the local economy. The rich tax-exempt lands of the Church all over Western Europe excited a great deal of envy. The Church's opposition to usury and its close alliance with the landed aristocracy antagonized the rising capitalistic classes.

Finally, the intellectual activities of the humanists weakened the hold of the Church on many minds. Erasmus and other humanists heaped ridicule on what they considered to be the superstitious beliefs of the Church. Their scholarly translations and critical textual studies exposed errors in the sacred documents upon which the Church based its claims. It must not be assumed, however, that the Protestants were more humanistic than the Roman Catholics. As a matter of fact, the sixteenth-century humanists found

This cartoon shows John Tetzel, the papal dispenser of indulgences in Germany in 1517. It was in opposition to the doctrine of indulgences that Luther posted the ninety-five theses and advocated open debate of Church policies. The last lines of the jingle at upper left read: "As soon as gold in the basin rings, Right then the soul to heaven springs." *Photo: Lutherhalle, Wittenberg*

the Protestant leaders even more dogmatic and uncongenial than the Roman Catholic hierarchy. However, the humanists unwittingly helped to bring about the Reformation by weakening the position of the Church.

As early as the fourteenth century such reformers as John Wycliffe in England and John Huss in Bohemia had voiced their protests against the Church. By the opening of the sixteenth century the religious, political, economic, and intellectual opposition to the Church had reached explosive proportions. All that was needed for revolt was a dynamic personality to lead it and an incident to set it off.

2. LUTHERANISM

The Protestant Reformation was composed of four major distinct but related movements— Lutheranism, Calvinism, Anglicanism, and Anabaptism. From these four main stems have sprung the hundreds of Protestant denominations that exist today. The Lutheran revolt was first in point of time.

Martin Luther (1483–1546), who was the son of an ambitious ex-peasant miner of central Germany, was chosen from among his numerous brothers and sisters to be educated. At a boarding school run by the pietistic Brethern of the Common Life he, like his contemporary Erasmus, was introduced to a type of Christianity that emphasized simple piety rather than dogma and ritual. Later at Erfurt University he received a traditional liberal arts education. He was an excellent student. However, upon the completion of his undergraduate course and just as he was ready to begin study of the law, he suddenly renounced the world and entered an Augustinian monastery. This decision was no passing whim. As a child, Luther had been much concerned over the fate of his soul, and throughout his university days, his religious yearning had increased.

But the young friar found no satisfaction in the monastic life of the sixteenth-century Church. He scourged himself, donned beggar's garb, and went out among his former fellow students with sunken cheeks and gleaming, feverish eyes. It was not until, on the advice of a perceptive supervisor of his monastic order, he began to read the writings of St. Augustine and St. Paul that Brother Martin found the answer to his lifelong quest. On reading in Paul's Letter to the Romans (1:17) "the just shall live by faith," it began to dawn on Luther that here was the true means of salvation—not good works, sacraments, and rituals, but simple faith in Christ. Over a period of years he developed a theology based on this fundamental concept. Gradually he regained his old radiance and energy.

In the meantime Luther had become a member of the faculty of the newly founded University of Wittenberg in Saxony, where he was to remain for the rest of his life. For several years he taught philosophy and theology, quite unaware that his belief in salvation by faith alone was in fundamental conflict with the dogma of his church. Students flocked from afar to listen to him.

One day a friar named John Tetzel came into the vicinity of Wittenberg selling indulgences. According to the doctrine of indulgences, which had grown up in the late Middle Ages, Christ and the saints, by their good works while on earth, had accumulated in heaven a treasury of excess merit which the pope could apply to the credit of penitent sinners, thereby shortening for them or their loved ones their stay in purgatory. By the opening of the sixteenth century the dispensing of this extra sacramental means of grace had become nothing less than a money-making venture. Huge sums, taken from the credulous all over Europe, were brought to Rome for the construction of St. Peter's or for other costly papal projects.

On October 31, 1517, Martin Luther posted on the church door in Wittenberg ninety-five theses or propositions concerning the doctrine of indulgences, which he proposed to be debated publicly. It did not once occur to him that this event would mark the beginning of an upheaval to subside only after almost half of Western Christendom had broken away

This print shows Luther being questioned by Emperor Charles V and the Archbishop of Mainz at the Diet of Worms in 1521. *Photo: Prints Division, New York Public Library, Astor, Lenox, and Tilden Foundations*

from the Roman Catholic Church. He was astonished and at first dismayed to find himself suddenly the national hero of all the various disgruntled elements throughout Germany. When, however, two years later in a public debate at Leipzig Luther finally realized that his position was hopelessly at odds with that of the Church, he lost no time in making the break clean. He published a series of pamphlets in which he violently denounced the pope and his organization, and called upon the German princes to seize the property of the Church and make themselves the heads of the Christian Church in Germany.

A papal bull of excommunication (which Luther publicly burned) soon followed. A few months later Emperor Charles V called the troublesome monk to appear before the Diet of the Holy Roman Empire at Worms (1521). There Luther boldly refused to recant and was outlawed by the highest civil authority in Germany. Although Luther remained under this death sentence with a price on his head for the rest of his life, he was protected by his prince, the elector of Saxony, and by German public opinion.

By this time all Germany was in religious and social turmoil. Nearly everyone with a grievance of any kind was looking to Luther for leadership. Religious zealots, many of them calling themselves Anabaptists, began preaching individualistic and more radical doctrines in his name, and he found it necessary to repudiate them. Taking a somewhat more conservative stand, he decided that only those features of the Roman Catholic Church that were opposed to the Scriptures ought to be rejected. In the early stages of the conflict Erasmus and many other humanists thought they saw in Luther a kindred spirit, but this alliance was short-lived. Erasmus soon found Luther to be as dogmatic and uncompromising in matters of doctrine as the Roman Catholic theologians, if not more so. Erasmus was primarily interested in matters of the intellect, and Luther in those of religious faith. Erasmus found it more convenient and comfortable to remain in the Roman Church, which he had done so much to discredit. He and Luther ended their days hurling recriminations at each other.

Luther also found it necessary to break with a group of rebellious peasants in south Germany. The condition of the peasants was bad and growing worse. The landed aristocracy, themselves losing ground to the rising middle classes, were depriving their peasants of long-established manorial rights such as free use of meadows and woodlands. In 1524 widespread disturbances broke out in southwestern Germany. The next year the peasants published a list of moderate demands; when these were refused, the peasants rebelled in the name of Luther, whom they believed to be against all oppressive authority. Luther, although sympathetic, pleaded with them to refrain from violence. This the peasants refused to do, and when they went on a bloody rampage, killing and burning in Luther's name, he repudiated them and called on the civil authorities to suppress the revolt by force. The alarmed authorities did so with a vengeance.

In the end both sides blamed Luther for the

revolt and its painful results. South Germany has remained a Roman Catholic stronghold to this day. Luther was in favor of peaceful social reform, but he believed that successful reform depended upon a change of heart. In short, the first Protestant leader found it necessary quite early in the revolt to make it clear that Protestant Christianity was neither a humanistic philosophy nor a materialistic social reform movement, nor yet a free-for-all for everyone to believe and preach anything he chose.

Luther's new religion, as he eventually formulated it, made the Scriptures the sole authoritative source of Christian dogma. That all might have access to the Bible, he translated it into German.[2] He conceived of the Church as the whole body of believers in Christ, not the Roman Catholic Church or any other specific organization. He abolished the hierarchy of pope, cardinals, and bishops, and reduced the importance of the clergy in general, proclaiming the priesthood of all believers. He made the various secular rulers the heads of the Christian Church in their territories. He abolished monasteries and the celibacy of the clergy. Luther himself married an ex-nun. The ritual of worship was made much simpler. Of the seven sacraments of the Roman Catholic Church, Luther kept only the two he found mentioned as sacraments in the Bible: baptism and the eucharist. He rejected the Roman Catholic doctrine known as transubstantiation.[3] Luther interpreted the Scriptural passages that refer to the Holy Eucharist, or Lord's Supper, to mean that during the administration of the sacrament Christ's body somehow enters into the bread and the wine, but the bread and wine remain. He denied the Roman Catholic belief that a sacrifice is involved.

---

[2] Luther's translation was in such excellent German that it had great influence on the standardization of the modern literary German language.

[3] The New Catholic Dictionary defines transubstantiation as "the marvellous and singular changing of the entire substance of the bread into the entire substance of the Body of Christ and of the entire substance of the wine into His Blood."

The Emperor Charles V was greatly distressed by this religious revolution, which further divided his scattered and chaotic empire. Although determined to suppress the Protestants, he was too busy with his wars against the French and the Turks to make much headway. Nine years of indecisive fighting between the Roman Catholics under Charles V and the Protestants ended in 1555 with the compromise Peace of Augsburg. Each of the more than three hundred German princes was left free to choose between Lutheranism and Roman Catholicism; his subjects were to abide by his choice. Luther himself died in 1546, just before the fighting began. Lutheranism triumphed in the northern half of Germany and soon spread to Denmark, Norway, Sweden, and most of the Baltic provinces (now Latvia, Estonia, and Finland), which were then under Swedish control. In addition, Lutheranism heavily influenced all later Protestant movements.

3. CALVINISM

Calvin shares with Luther the position of first importance in the founding of Protestant Christianity. Born in France in 1509, John Calvin was twenty-six years younger than Luther. He was the son of a lawyer who was secretary to the bishop of Noyon in Picardy. Young Calvin had a radiant personality that made for warm friendships. Long association with aristocratic friends probably accounts for his elegant manners. His father sent him first to the University of Paris for a thorough grounding in the humanities and theology, and then to the best law schools in France, where Calvin ruined his health by overwork. Upon finishing his legal training, he entered upon a humanistic literary career and quickly showed signs of becoming a second Erasmus. Suddenly, at the age of twenty-four, he was converted to Protestant Christianity, probably as a result of reading Luther.

The zealous young reformer soon aroused the ire of Roman Catholic authorities in France and of the French government, and was forced to flee for his life. Calvin then spent the next two years in hiding writing the first edition of *The Institutes of the Christian Religion*. Published in Basel, Switzerland, when Calvin was only twenty-six years of age, this theological treatise was to become the most influential writing in the history of Protestantism. Its precise and forceful logic reveals not only the fine legal training of the author, but also one of the most powerful intellects in history. Its lucid and facile style had much the same influence on the formulation of modern literary French that Luther's translation of the Bible had on German. It immediately made Calvin an important name in literary and theological circles.

Probably Calvin's most significant contribution to Christian theology is his sublime concept of the majesty of God. To the author of the *Institutes*, the Divine Creator is so majestic and awe-inspiring and man so insignificant by comparison that salvation by election, or *predestination*, as it is more often called, seems to follow logically. According to Calvin, God in the beginning planned the whole universe to the end of time. For unfathomable reasons of his own, God selected those human beings who would be saved and those who would be damned. He planted in the minds of the elect a saving faith in Christ and an insatiable desire to live the Christian life and to bring about the Kingdom of God on earth. In no other way could men acquire this faith and this desire. Calvin based this doctrine upon the Scriptures (particularly the writings of St. Paul), which he considered to be the sole authoritative source for Christian theology. St. Augustine, the most influential of the early Church fathers, and Luther also believed in salvation by election, but neither they nor anyone else had ever spelled out the doctrine so precisely.

Shortly after the publication of the *Institutes*, Calvin went to Geneva. That city, like most of the rest of Switzerland, was in the throes of religious and political revolt brought on partly by the influence of Luther and the native Swiss reformer, Ulrich Zwingli (1484–1531). The Protestant leaders in Geneva immediately recognized in Calvin a natural leader and with difficulty persuaded the gifted but modest young man to remain there and make Geneva a model city of God on earth. Calvin, by sheer force of personality and intellect, soon rose to a position of virtual dictatorship over the city. He brought the town council, which was remarkably democratic and representative for the sixteenth century, under the dominance of a consistory composed of Protestant pastors and laymen. In other words, Geneva became a theocracy. Under Calvin's leadership, the town council

An anonymous portrait of Calvin as a young man. Calvin's The Institutes of the Christian Religion, published in 1536 when he was only twenty-six, became the most influential writing in the history of Protestantism. *Photo: Société du Musée Historique de la Réformation, Genève*

and the consistory set up a strict system of blue laws. Churchgoing was compulsory. Dancing, card-playing, theatergoing, drinking, gambling, and swearing—all were forbidden. Enforcement was vigorous, and penalties severe, even for the sixteenth century. The most famous penalty was the burning of Michael Servetus, an eccentric amateur scientist and theologian whom the Roman Catholic Church had already condemned to death for heresy.[4] Servetus escaped his Catholic persecutors and came to Geneva for the purpose of destroying Calvin and his works. Calvin had warned him to stay away on pain of death; when Servetus arrived, he was seized, tried, convicted, and burned at the stake.

A strong minority in Geneva had no use for Calvin, his theology, or his blue laws. To them Calvin was a kill-joy, a bigot, and a tyrant, a verdict that has found its way into many textbooks. The majority of the Genevans, on the other hand, practically worshiped their leader; they considered him the most brilliant, inspiring, sympathetic, kindly, and gentle of men. Protestant Christians came from many countries to sit at the feet of Calvin and to study at the University of Geneva, which he founded. John Knox, who came from Scotland to study under Calvin, called the Genevan theocracy "the most perfect school of life that was ever on earth since the days of the apostles."

Calvinist ritual was even simpler than that of the Lutherans. The worship service consisted of preaching, praying, and psalm-singing. Like Luther, Calvin retained only two of the seven sacraments—baptism and the Holy Eucharist, or Lord's Supper. But to Calvin, Christ was present only in spirit in the bread and wine, and only for the elect. Calvin patterned his system of church government after that of the very earliest church as described in the Bible (Acts of the Apostles). The local churches were governed by laymen called *elders* who were elected by the congre-

gations. A measure of unity in faith and practices was maintained by means of a hierarchy of representative assemblies.

Calvinism became dominant in most of Switzerland (Swiss Reformed), the Dutch Netherlands (Dutch Reformed), Scotland (Presbyterian), and the German Palatinate. It also had a strong minority following in England (the Puritans), and a smaller but vigorous following in France (the Huguenots), Bohemia, Hungary, and Poland. The Calvinists played an important part in the founding of the United States, particularly the Puritans in New England, the Dutch Reformed in New York, and the Scotch-Irish Presbyterians along the frontiers of all the original states. Such well-known denominations in present-day America as the Congregationalists, the Presbyterians, and the Baptists are Calvinist in origin. The Calvinists were the most zealous and evangelical of all the major early Protestant groups. In later years they made a strong appeal to the rising middle classes. Wherever they were found, they were a powerful influence for the growth of democracy and for public education.

4. ANGLICANISM

The occasion, though not the cause, of the beginning of the Reformation in England was the desire of Henry VIII (1509–1547) for a male heir. Catherine of Aragon, to whom he had been married for eighteen years, had given him only a daughter, Mary. When it became apparent that Catherine would have no more children, Henry decided to ask the pope to annul the marriage. The pope, however, was in no position to grant the annulment. Catherine was the aunt of the Emperor Charles V, whose troops were at that very moment in control of the city of Rome. When Henry finally realized the pope was not going to accommodate him, he took matters into his own hands. At his bidding a subservient Parliament passed the Act of Supremacy, making the king of England, not the pope, head of the Church in England. Later the monasteries,

---

[4] The most serious of Servetus' heretical views was his denial of the Trinity, which cast doubt on the divinity of Christ.

strongholds of papal influence, were dissolved. Meanwhile, Thomas Cranmer, whom Henry made archbishop of Canterbury, had granted the annulment, and Henry had married Anne Boleyn. (He was to marry six times in all.) Henry was, of course, excommunicated by the pope.

But Henry VIII was no Protestant. In the days before the annulment controversy the pope had given him the title "Defender of the Faith" for his anti-Lutheran writings. Now he had Parliament pass the Six Articles reaffirming the Catholic position on all controversial doctrinal points except that of papal supremacy. Protestants, on the one hand, and Roman Catholics who refused to acknowledge the headship of Henry VIII in place of the pope, were persecuted with equal severity. Death was the penalty for both.

It was during the reign of Henry VIII's young son, Edward VI (1547–1553), that the Anglican Church first became Protestant. Archbishop Cranmer drew up a *Book of Common Prayer* and Forty-two Articles of faith that were definitely Calvinist in flavor. Edward VI was succeeded by his elder sister, Mary (1553–1558), who was the daughter of Catherine of Aragon and a devout Roman Catholic. Mary's ambition was to restore her kingdom to the Roman Catholic fold. Her first step was to marry her cousin, Philip II of Spain, the most powerful champion of resurgent Roman Catholicism in all Europe. Next she asked and received papal forgiveness for her wayward people. Finally, "Bloody Mary" burned at the stake some three hundred Protestants, including Archbishop Cranmer. But Mary's marriage to the man soon to be king of England's most dangerous rival and her persecutions were extremely unpopular in England; in the long run her policies hurt rather than helped the Roman Catholic cause there.

Elizabeth I (1558–1603), the Protestant daughter of Anne Boleyn, followed Mary on the English throne. This high-spirited, cynical, and politically minded queen found theology tiresome. Her chief interest was to find a satisfactory compromise that would unify her people. During the course of her long reign the Anglican Church became definitely, but moderately and conservatively, Protestant. Cranmer's *Book of Common Prayer* was readopted with slight alterations. The Forty-two Articles were changed to the Thirty-nine. Some of the more controversial doctrinal points which seemed to prevent the various Protestant sects from uniting were left purposely vague. Although celibacy of the clergy was abandoned, the episcopal system (government of the church by bishops and archbishops) was retained. A rather elaborate ritual was adopted. Two of the sacraments, baptism and the eucharist, were retained.

Although the great majority of the English people appear to have accepted Elizabeth's compromise settlement, two groups remained dissatisfied. An extreme Calvinist element sought to "purify" the Anglican Church of all remaining traces of Roman Catholicism. These Puritans were to increase in strength until under Oliver Cromwell's leadership in the next century they gained temporary control of the country. The Roman Catholic minority, on the other hand, lost steadily in numbers. The support that some Roman Catholics gave to Philip II's attempt to conquer England and to the effort of Mary, Queen of Scots (a Roman Catholic) to overthrow Elizabeth (see Chapter 32) tainted all of them with the suspicion of treason and played into Elizabeth's hands. By the end of her reign, England was one of the Protestant countries of Europe.

5. THE ANABAPTISTS

Some reformers believed that Luther, Calvin, and the Anglican leaders had not gone far enough. They would break more sharply with all the existing institutions of the early sixteenth century—political, economic, and social as well as religious. Hence the term *radical* is usually applied to them. Since these "radi-

What Is the Meaning of the Protestant Reformation?

Most historians agree that the breakup of the all-powerful medieval Church was probably the most significant factor in bringing the Middle Ages to an end and that the Reformation was, therefore, of major importance in the rise of modern Western civilization. But there the agreement ends. Was the Protestant Reformation spiritual, as its leaders firmly believed, or was it something else—intellectual, political, economic? As the modern Western world has become more and more secular, so have interpretations of the Reformation.

The historians of the Enlightenment of the eighteenth century tended to think of the Protestant Reformation as the religious aspect of the Renaissance. They liked to believe that the early Protestants were seeking intellectual freedom and individualism in their search for theological truth. Whatever might be said about the trend of Protestantism in later centuries, this interpretation of early Protestantism, with the possible exception of certain minor sects, is certainly based upon faulty information. It did not take Erasmus very long to discover that the early Protestant leaders were more dogmatic and less compatible with his humanistic approach to Christianity than was the Roman Catholic hierarchy.

From the mid-nineteenth century to the present day, many historians have thought of the Protestant Reformation in political terms. They have viewed the various religious movements of the sixteenth century as adjuncts of nationalism. They believe it to be significant that the Protestant Reformation began in Germany, where there was no strong central government to protect the German people from exploitation by the Italian papacy. Luther strongly and openly appealed to German nationalism against Rome, and there can be little doubt that his nationalistic appeal gained many followers. By contrast, the strong rulers of France and Spain were able to extract such concessions from the pope as to create what amounted to a Gallican Church and a Spanish Catholic Church. The various Calvinistic churches were generally set up along national lines, such as the Swiss, Dutch, German, and Scottish Reformed churches. And of course the Anglican Church was a national church. All this was in striking contrast to the medieval Church, which had encompassed all of Western and Central Europe. Another popular twentieth-century interpretation has been that of the Freudian psychologists, who have used the theories of Freud to analyze the personalities of the early Protestant leaders, particularly Luther.

Most popular of the secular interpretations of the Protestant Reformation from the late nineteenth century to the present has been the economic interpretation. Those who emphasize this line of thought point out the hunger for the rich lands held by the Roman Church, the resentment over the tax exemption of these lands and over the draining away of money to Rome, and the opposition of the commercial class to the Church's ban on usury. From this viewpoint, Protestantism seemed to promise an end to all these "abuses." The ultimate in economic approaches to explaining the Reformation is that of the Marxists, who regard all religion as the "opiate of the people"—a trick of the "haves" to keep the "have nots" quiet and obedient.

A widely accepted interpretation of the Reformation is that of Max Weber, a German sociologist who was strongly influenced by Karl Marx. The Weber thesis was first published in 1904–1905 in two articles entitled "The Protestant Ethic and the Spirit of Capitalism." Weber believed that Protestantism, particularly Calvinism, contributed to the rise of capitalism. It removed the ban on usury, and made possible unlimited profits. The doctrine of salvation by election encouraged its believers to work hard, each in his appointed calling, for the glory of God and for the assurance that he is one of the elect. This hard work, coupled with the asceticism Calvin preached, resulted in growing surpluses which were reinvested in capitalistic enterprises. Weber also offers as evidence the capitalistic successes of the Calvinistic Dutch and Swiss and the Puritans of England and New England. Weber's thesis has won the support of thousands of readers. His critics, however, have demonstrated his surprising unfamiliarity with the actual writings of the early Protestants. Calvin devoted only 50 out of some 30,000 pages of his published writings to economic matters; Luther devoted about twice as many pages to this topic out of a similar total. Both Calvin and Luther repeatedly warned against the danger of riches and admonished lenders not to take advantage of the poor and distressed. Nowhere did they consider prosperity as a sign of election. The voluminous writings of the seventeenth-century English Puritans continue in a similar vein. Critics of Weber point out that capitalism is much older than Calvinism, and wonder why Weber did not cite the early modern commercial prosperity of Roman Catholic northern Italy, southern and western Germany, or the Belgian Netherlands, or the lack of capitalistic activity in Calvinistic Scotland. Weber's most influential disciple was R. H. Tawney, a British economic historian active in Labour party politics. His *Religion and the Rise of Capitalism*, published in 1926, reveals a great deal more knowledge of history than does Weber, and more subtlety and sophistication, but adheres essentially to the Weber thesis.

It would appear that writers and readers of history tend to impute their own motives to the makers of history—to read the prevailing spirit of their own times into the spirit of earlier epochs. This is particularly true in the field of religious history, where it is impossible to know the hearts of the proclaimers of the various faiths. Historians very frequently reveal their own times more than the times of the period about which they write.

cals" were highly individualistic in their approach to religion, it is difficult to generalize about the many sects with their widely differing views and points of emphasis. One of the most commonly held beliefs was their opposition to infant baptism. The true Christian, they believed, was one who was "born again" and baptized as an adult according to Scripture. Those who had been baptized as infants must be rebaptized. Anabaptism means *re-*baptism. The Anabaptists believed that the true church of Christ on earth is a gathered church composed only of born-again Christians (in contrast with the territorial or state churches of the Roman Catholics, Lutherans, Calvinists, and Anglicans which of necessity contain many who are not genuine Christians). The Anabaptists attempted to live lives of uncompromising holiness as dictated by the Bible or by the Holy Spirit speaking directly to each individual. All human institutions are evil. These sects refused to recognize or participate in civil government, take oaths of allegiance, recognize titles, or serve in armed forces. Some practiced a shared or communistic economy. Most of them were poor. They were feared and cruelly persecuted, of course, by all organized secular society, and by Roman Catholics, Lutherans, Calvinists, and Anglicans alike.

A few of the early Anabaptist leaders were violent activists, such as Thomas Müntzer, who inflamed the peasant rebels of southwest Germany, and John of Leyden, who set up a violent dictatorship in Münster in northwest Germany. This bizarre "heavenly Jerusalem" held out for more than a year against besieging Lutheran and Roman Catholic armies. The leaders were then tortured to death and their bodies hung in iron baskets from a church tower for three hundred and fifty years. But the great majority of the Anabaptist leaders were pious and gentle—in fact, pacifists. Conrad Grebel, the first prominent Anabaptist leader, was a humanist from an upper class family of Zurich, Switzerland. Probably the most successful and influential

of all the Anabaptist leaders was the convert Menno Simons, a gentle Roman Catholic priest from the Dutch Netherlands. His followers, the Mennonites, spread throughout much of Western Europe and later the United States. Also in the Anabaptist tradition was the Society of Friends, commonly known as Quakers. Founded by George Fox in England in the mid-seventeenth century, this pietistic and pacifistic sect has spread to many parts of the world. It has furnished two presidents of the United States.

6. SUMMARY

By the end of the third quarter of the sixteenth century, then, Protestantism had triumphed in the northern half of the Germanies, in Scandinavia, in most of the Baltic provinces, in most of Switzerland, in the Dutch Netherlands, Scotland, and England. In addition, it had gained a strong minority following in France, Poland, Bohemia, and Hungary. And, no matter how much the various Protestant denominations might disagree among themselves on minor details, they presented a solid front against the Roman Catholics. All Protestants rejected papal supremacy, the divine sanction of the Roman Church, the celibacy and indelible character of the priesthood, monasticism, and such other characteristic Roman Catholic doctrines as purgatory, transubstantiation, invocation of saints, and veneration of relics. These doctrinal differences between the Protestants and the Roman Catholics were fundamental, and no middle ground for a compromise was ever found. Nor was the Roman Church, notwithstanding its strong comeback, ever able to reconquer the territories in which the Protestants had gained a definite majority. The Reformation split Western Christendom into two sharply defined and hostile camps. In place of the two major divisions into which Christianity had been separated since the early Middle Ages (Eastern Orthodox and Roman Catholic), there were now three.

Suggested Reading

General. Probably the most useful single volume on the Reformation is **G. R. Elton, *Reformation Europe 1517–1559* (Harper Torchbook). It is scholarly and objective, but for some reason does not cover the English Reformation. Another good up-to-date text is H. J. Grimm, *The Reformation Era* (1954). This work has an extensive and excellent bibliography. An older but still very useful treatment of the Reformation era is P. Smith, *The Age of the Reformation* (1920). This comprehensive work is erudite and readable, but is strongly prejudiced against Calvin and Calvinism.

Lutheranism. An excellent and recent study of the historical setting for the Reformation in Germany is Hajo Holborn, *A History of Modern Germany: The Reformation* (1959). The two best biographies of Martin Luther are **R. H. Bainton, *Here I Stand: A Life of Martin Luther* (Mentor), a delightful book combining scholarship with a good journalistic style; and E. G. Schwiebert, *Luther and His Times* (1951).

Calvinism. A good brief biography of Ulrich Zwingli, Calvin's forerunner in Switzerland, is O. Farner, *Zwingli the Reformer, His Life and Work*, trans. D. G. Sear (1952). There are no biographies of Calvin in English comparable to the two of Luther mentioned above. One of the best is still Williston Walker, *John Calvin, the Organizer of Reformed Protestantism* (1906). Two more recent studies of Calvin and Calvinism that are scholarly and judicious are J. T. McNeil, *The History and Character of Calvinism* (1954); and **Georgia Harkness, *John Calvin, the Man and His Ethics* (Apex). The great biography of Calvin, surpassing all others by far, is unfortunately available only in French. It is E. Doumergue, *Jean Calvin* (7 vols., 1899–1927). Doumergue has a pro-Calvin bias, in contrast with the great majority of writers on the subject. The classic work on Calvin's followers in France, the Huguenots, is H. M. Baird, *History of the Rise of the Huguenots in France* (2 vols., 1907). Two books on Protestantism, particularly Calvinism, that have had tremendous influence are **Max Weber, *The Protestant Ethic and the Spirit of Capitalism* (Scribner), originally published in 1904; and **R. H. Tawney, *Religion and the Rise of Capitalism* (Mentor), originally published in 1926. Unfortunately, neither Weber nor Tawney bothered to find out very much about what Calvin and Luther and their chief followers believed about economics and how relatively little interest they had in economic matters. These weaknesses are well pointed out by A. Hyma, *Christianity, Capitalism, and Communism* (1937).

Anglicanism. The best survey of the English Reformation is **A. G. Dickens, *The English Reformation* (Schocken). By far the best biography of the English king who played the decisive role in breaking with Rome is J. J. Scarisbrick, *Henry VIII* (1968). A scholarly study of Archbishop Cranmer, the chief English theologian in setting up the Anglican Church, is A. F. Pollard, *Thomas Cranmer* (1904). An excellent study of the reign of Elizabeth I when the English Reformation settlement was finally made is **J. E. Neale, *Queen Elizabeth I* (Anchor).

The Anabaptists. The best study of the Anabaptist movement is F. H. Littell, *The Anabaptist View of the Church* (1952). This is the work of a first-rate scholar about a subject that has been too long neglected. A more recent and detailed, but perhaps less inspired, study is G. H. Williams, *The Radical Reformation* (1962).

Sources. A useful and handy selection of excerpts from the writings of important Reformation figures is **R. H. Bainton, *The Age of the Reformation* (Anvil). Many important documents pertaining to the Reformation may be found in H. S. Bettenson, *Documents of the Christian Church* (1947). Of course, see Martin Luther, *Three Treatises: An Open Letter to the Christian Nobility, The Babylonian Captivity of the Church, The Freedom of a Christian*, trans. C. M. Jacobs, *et al.* (1960). John Calvin, *The Institutes of the Christian Religion*, trans. J. Allen (7th rev. ed., 1936) contains Calvin's famous dedication to King Francis I.

Chapter 32 ❧ The Roman Catholic Reformation

The loss of almost half of Western Christendom by the Roman Catholic Church and the threatened loss of the rest touched off a reform movement within the Church. By the middle of the sixteenth century the Roman Catholic reform movement was well under way. The Church was revitalized, and a counteroffensive was launched against the Protestants—one that not only prevented their further encroachment on the Roman Catholic domain, but pushed them back a bit.

1. THE RISE OF A REFORM MOVEMENT

Long before the revolt of Luther and Calvin, there had been a demand for reform by many loyal Roman Catholics. In Spain, around the turn of the sixteenth century, Cardinal Ximenes had forestalled a possible protest movement by enforcing strict discipline upon the clergy and waging bitter warfare against heresy. However, in the rest of Western Christendom, the secular interests of the Renaissance popes and prelates and the popes' fears that a reform council might again challenge the absolute authority of the Holy See prevented effective action. Now, with area after area becoming Protestant, countermeasures of a rather drastic nature became imperative. There were two schools of thought concerning the proper course of action. One,

led by the liberal Cardinal Contarini of Venice, advocated compromise and conciliation. Contarini eventually went so far as to meet with Melanchthon, a close friend of Luther and an important figure in the Lutheran revolt, in earnest quest of an acceptable compromise. They were unsuccessful; the two religions appeared to be incompatible. The other school of thought was led by the conservative Cardinal Caraffa of Naples. Caraffa believed that many corrupt practices in the Church needed to be reformed, but that no compromise whatever should be made in the dogma. He believed that the Protestants were heretics and could reunite with the Roman Catholic Church only by recanting and submitting to the pope. This is the school of thought that triumphed, and Caraffa became Pope Paul IV. The upshot of this line of thinking was the calling of a Church council at Trent, an imperial city in northern Italy.

2. THE COUNCIL OF TRENT

The Council of Trent, which was in session off and on for eighteen years from 1545 to 1563, was probably the most important council in the history of the Roman Catholic Church. The popes skillfully controlled its membership and voting procedure. The ultimate decisions of the council were in two categories: dog-

The Great Armada, with which Philip II intended to conquer England, was defeated and scattered by the English fleet in the Channel. This defeat tarnished the prestige of Spain and of Roman Catholicism throughout Europe. *Photo: The Bettmann Archive* matic and reformatory. In matters of faith or dogma, all the traditional doctrines of the Church were reaffirmed and redefined, especially controversial ones such as the sacraments, transubstantiation, auricular confession, celibacy of the clergy, monasticism, purgatory, invocation of the saints, veneration of relics, and indulgences. The dogmatic canons and decrees of the council concluded: "Anathema to [accursed be] all heretics! Anathema! Anathema! Anathema!" The council also took stern measures to stop corrupt practices. Simony, nepotism, pluralism, and immorality and ignorance among the clergy were condemned. Schools for the education of the clergy were called for. Bishops were admonished to exercise closer supervision and discipline over the lower clergy. To implement its canons and decrees, the council endorsed the Inquisition, which had recently been set up in Rome to combat heresy, and inaugurated the Index of Forbidden Books to prevent the reading of heretical literature except by authorized persons. Both instruments were placed under papal control and supervision. The Index, periodically revised, proved to be particularly effective. Thus the Roman Catholic Church at last spoke out, selected its weapons, and girded itself for more effective battle against the Protestants. At its service were the militant new Jesuit order and the greatest military power of the sixteenth century, Philip II's Spain.

3. THE SOCIETY OF JESUS

The founder of the Society of Jesus, Ignatius Loyola (1491–1556), was the equal of Luther and Calvin as a dynamic personality, organizer, and leader. He was a member of the Spanish lesser nobility, and until early middle life was an obscure and ignorant soldier. In a battle with the French his leg was crushed by a cannon ball. Without benefit of anesthetic, he had it set and, when it grew crooked, twice broken and reset. He remained a cripple for the rest of his life. During the months of agony and convalescence Loyola read lives of the Christian saints and underwent a deep spiritual conversion. He determined to devote his tremendous energies and latent talents to the service of the Roman Catholic Church—to become a soldier of Christ, the Virgin Mary, and the pope. Since his first efforts only revealed his ignorance and got him into trouble with the clerical authorities, he set off for the University of Paris to begin his education. Loyola was, however, not a scholar or theologian, but a man of action. He soon began to attract a band of followers, with whom he organized the Society of Jesus.

The Jesuit Order, as the Society of Jesus is commonly known, was founded along military lines. A general, elected for life and residing in Rome, issues orders that are transmitted through a hierarchy of officials to the rank and file. Absolute and unquestioning obedience is the first requirement. Loyola admonished his followers, ". . . if she [the Church] shall have defined anything to be black which to our eyes appears to be white, we ought in like manner to pronounce it to be black." Members are urged to cut all earthly ties, even with family and friends, that might divide their loyalties or impede their wholehearted devotion to the work of the order. Applicants for membership are carefully screened. Only those of superior intelligence, sound health, and attractive appearance are chosen. Then follows a two-year testing time, a sort of officer-training school, during which the novices are severely tried and examined for signs of weakness of will or purpose. Those who survive are next given a long and rigorous education as scholastics in preparation for their specialized work. When found to be ready, they are admitted to full-fledged membership as coadjutors. They may now serve as priests, teachers, medics, diplomats, or in almost any other capacity suitable to their talents and training. Whatever their work, it is "all for the greater glory of God," which to the Jesuit means for all practical purposes the Roman Catholic Church. After years of service a few of the most outstanding are admitted to the highest circle. These select few take, in addition to the three Benedictine vows of poverty, chastity, and obedience, a fourth vow of special obedience to the pope. It is from this inner circle that all the high officers of the order are chosen.

For the spiritual guidance and inspiration of the members of the Society, Loyola wrote the *Spiritual Exercises*. Revealing the author's deep understanding of psychology, the *Exercises* guide the member through a solid month of concentrated meditation, a week each on the horrors of sin, the life of Christ to Palm Sunday, his suffering and crucifixion, and his resurrection and ascension. This remarkable work has proved to be a powerful stimulant in time of flagging zeal.

Loyola's high standards, far from deterring applicants, served as a challenge and an attraction. The Society of Jesus grew rapidly. As priests, the Jesuits were nearly always the best trained, the most popular, and the most influential. As teachers, they were usually more highly educated, devoted, and attractive than their competitors. They have always been keenly aware of the power of education, especially for the very young. "Give me the child, and I care not who has the man." The Jesuits soon got control of all education in most Roman Catholic countries.

These dedicated soldiers of Christ also made the best missionaries. In North and South America the dauntless Jesuits went among the Indians, risked and in many cases lost their lives, learned the languages of the natives, lived with them, and converted most of them to Roman Catholic Christianity. In the Far East, Francis Xavier, second only to Loyola himself in Jesuit history, converted tens of thousands.

Not the least important of Jesuit activities was that of gaining the confidence of kings, princes, and other high political personages, and thereby influencing state policy. This militantly zealous order was a powerful stimulant to the wavering cause of Roman Catholicism. In Italy, Spain, Portugal, and Ireland, where Protestantism had only a weak foothold, the Jesuits stamped it out altogether. In France and Belgium they helped to turn the tide against the Protestants. In southern Germany, Poland, and the Austrian Hapsburg lands, all of which seemed to be on the point of going Protestant, the Jesuits reversed the trend and made those lands the strongholds of Roman Catholicism they are today.

4. THE CRUSADE OF CATHOLIC SPAIN

Also at the service of the Roman Catholic Church in its counteroffensive against the Protestants was the world's greatest military power of the sixteenth century—the Spain of Philip II. Emperor Charles V had bequeathed the greater part of his vast empire to his son Philip II (1556–1598). In addition to Spain, Philip's inheritance included the Netherlands, Franche-Comté, Milan, The Kingdom of the Two Sicilies, Sardinia, the Balearic Islands, holdings along the west coast of Africa, and the Western Hemisphere. When in 1580 Philip conquered Portugal in the name of his Portuguese mother and became master (at least in name) of Portugal's huge Eastern empire, he exercised legal rule over more of the earth's surface than any other man in history.[1] Philip II, unlike his father, was a native Spaniard. The gold and silver now flowing in a steady stream from the New World and the lucrative commerce of the East Indies and of the busy Netherlands he utilized in the interests of Spain. The soldiers of the Spanish infantry were the best foot soldiers of the sixteenth century. Philip II was also a firm believer in the divine rights of monarchy. Ignoring the Cortes and the local rights of Aragon and tending personally to the myriad details of government, the meticulous and stubborn Philip brought Spain under his sway to an extent that Ferdinand and Isabella and Charles V had never been able to do. Little wonder that the king of Spain was the most feared man in Western Christendom.

More important even than Spain in the

---

[1] Sixty years later Portugal regained her independence.

The Netherlands 1578–1609

mind of Philip II, however, was the Roman Catholic Church. He conceived it to be his chief mission in life to use the great wealth and power of Spain to restore the dominion of the Roman Church over all of Western Christendom. In the Netherlands, in England, and in France, Philip II threw the might of Spain on the side of the Roman Catholics in their counteroffensive against the Protestants.

Religion was only the chief among many causes of the revolt of the Netherlands against Spanish rule. Philip II, unlike his father, Charles V, was considered by the Netherlanders to be an unsympathetic foreigner who taxed their prosperous commerce and industry for the benefit of Spain. The absolutist monarch and his Spanish administrators also overrode the traditional political privileges of the nobles and the cities in the Netherlands. Nonetheless, religion was the foremost cause of dissension. By midsixteenth century, nearly half the people in the

Netherlands had become Protestant. Most were Calvinists, but a considerable number were Anabaptists. Philip II, who would tolerate no heresy in his empire, took stern measures to stamp out Protestantism. The Inquisition was used to enforce the laws against heresy, and twelve new Roman Catholic bishoprics were added. In 1566 four hundred of the leading noblemen of the Netherlands presented a list of grievances to Philip's regent. When no relief was forthcoming, bands of Protestants began to deface Roman Catholic churches. Philip thereupon dispatched the Duke of Alva with 10,000 Spanish soldiers to reduce the Netherlands to submission. A six-year reign of terror followed, in which thousands were put to death.

Far from being cowed, however, the Netherlanders resisted fiercely. They found a brilliant leader in William of Orange, or William the Silent, as he came to be known. They took to the sea, playing havoc with Spanish commerce and communications. When, in 1580, Philip conquered and annexed Portugal, the hardy Dutch "Sea Beggars" seized the richest parts of the Portuguese Empire in the East Indies. The Spanish infantry quickly overran the ten southern (Belgian) provinces, but against the seven northern (Dutch) provinces, made up largely of islands and peninsulas and skillfully defended by the Dutch fleet, Spain's armies could make little headway. Most of the Protestants soon fled north from the Spanish-occupied southern provinces. Likewise, most of the Roman Catholics fled south from the Protestant-dominated north. In 1579 the ten Roman Catholic southern provinces, fearful of the growing power of the Protestant northern provinces, submitted to the Spanish yoke. The seven northern provinces, however, banded together in the Union of Utrecht and continued the struggle for independence. When in 1584 William the Silent was assassinated by a hireling of Philip II, other able leaders arose to take his place. Finally in 1609, eleven years after Philip's own death, Spain agreed to a twelve-year truce, and in 1648 Spain recognized the complete independence of the Dutch Netherlands, as the seven northern provinces are commonly called. In the seventeenth century the little Dutch republic led the world in commerce and in painting and was second to none in science and philosophy.

Thus Philip II's crusade in the Netherlands was only partly successful. He saved the southern provinces for Spain for another century, and for the Roman Catholic Church, but the Dutch provinces were lost both to Spain and to the Church.

Most grandiose of all Philip II's crusading efforts was his attempt to restore wayward England to the Roman Catholic fold. His first move was to marry England's Roman Catholic queen, Mary Tudor. This was done in 1554, two years before he began his own rule over the Spanish Empire. However, Mary's marriage to the king of a feared and hated rival power and her persecution of English Protestants only increased her own unpopularity and that of the Roman Catholic cause in England. Moreover, the marriage failed to produce an heir. When Mary died in 1558, Philip sought to continue his influence in England by trying to marry her successor, Elizabeth. But Elizabeth, a Protestant and a high-spirited English patriot, refused. Not to be deterred in his scheme to gain control of England, Philip, some years later, plotted the assassination of Elizabeth. Next in line for the English throne after Elizabeth was Roman Catholic Mary Stuart (Queen of Scots). Having been driven from Scotland by her Calvinist subjects, Mary had thrown herself on Elizabeth's mercy and was kept under detention. Only Elizabeth, then, stood between the English throne and another Roman Catholic queen. When Elizabeth was convinced that Mary Stuart was an accomplice to Philip II's assassination plots, she had her Scottish cousin beheaded. Meanwhile, Elizabeth was aiding the Dutch Protestant rebels and encouraging English sea dogs to plunder Spain's treasure ships sailing from her New World colonies— indeed, to plunder the colonies themselves.

When Philip II learned of the death of Mary Stuart, he undertook to conquer England by direct military action. In 1588 his "Invincible" Armada sailed forth—130 ships, many of them great galleons. Aboard was a formidable Spanish army. The Armada was to go first to the Netherlands and pick up additional Spanish veterans. In the English Channel it met the somewhat larger English fleet, composed mostly of smaller but swifter and more heavily armed ships. The Spaniards fought well until finally their formation was broken by English fire ships sent into their midst. Once scattered, the Spanish ships were no match for the English fleet. Storms added to the catastrophe. Only about half the ships ever reached Spain by way of northern Scotland, whither they had fled. It was at this point that England began to wrest control of the seas from Spain. Philip II had not only failed to exterminate Protestantism in England, but the Roman Catholic cause there was now tainted with treason, and Protestantism was stronger than ever.

Philip found it more profitable to crusade against the Muslim Turks than against the Protestants. In fact, one of the few clear-cut successes of his career was the great naval victory over the Turks at Lepanto. Under the urging of the pope, Venice, Genoa, and Spain amassed a fleet of more than two hundred vessels under the command of Philip's illegitimate half brother, Don Juan. In 1571 this fleet caught and annihilated the somewhat larger Turkish fleet off Lepanto on the coast of Greece. Never again were the Turks to menace Christendom by sea.

5. THE RELIGIOUS WARS IN FRANCE

In France and Germany the Roman Catholic counteroffensive against Protestantism resulted in bitter religious wars in the late sixteenth and early seventeenth centuries. Crusading Spain participated in these wars, but here her role was relatively minor and indecisive. In France, Calvinism had made slow but steady progress during the reigns of Francis I (1515–1547) and Henry II (1547–1559) in spite of vigorous persecution by those Roman Catholic monarchs. By 1559 the Huguenots, as the French Calvinists were called, numbered possibly a tenth of the total population. However, since their ranks included many of the prosperous bourgeoisie and some of the greatest families of France, their influence was far greater than their numbers would indicate. Enmity between the Huguenots and the Roman Catholics, which had smoldered under the strong rule of Francis I and of Henry II, broke into open and consuming flame under Henry II's three weakling sons, who ruled in succession from 1559 to 1589. All three were dominated by their unscrupulous and ambitious mother, Catherine de Médicis. This situation invited political as well as religious faction and intrigue, and in the civil wars that followed politics and religion were intertwined.

The leadership of the Roman Catholic faction was assumed by the powerful Guise family; that of the Protestants by the influential Bourbon family, who were related to the royal line. The first eight years of fighting were ended in 1570 by an uneasy truce. However, Catherine de Médicis, fearful of the growing influence of the Huguenots, decided to exterminate them all. She was, of course, supported and urged on by the Guises. At a given signal at midnight, August 24, 1572 (St. Bartholomew's Day), the Roman Catholics in Paris fell to slaughtering the Protestants. The massacre soon spread to the provinces and went on for weeks. Thousands of Huguenots were slain. When news of the Massacre of St. Bartholomew reached Madrid, Philip II, who seldom smiled, smiled.

The ablest of the Huguenot leaders, young Henry (Bourbon) of Navarre, escaped and rallied the remaining Protestant forces for the war that was now renewed in earnest. The wealth and energy of the numerous bourgeois and noble members of the Huguenot faction, plus the brilliance of their dashing young leader, offset the superior numbers of the Roman Catholics. Eventually Henry III, the third son of Catherine de Médicis to rule

France, organized a moderate Roman Catholic faction to stand between the uncompromising Guise faction and the Protestants. The struggle now became a three-cornered "War of the Three Henrys" (Henry, duke of Guise, Henry of Navarre, and Henry III, king of France). Philip II of Spain threw his support to Henry, duke of Guise. Henry III, now regarding Henry, duke of Guise, as the greater menace to his own royal authority, had him assassinated in 1588. The next year an agent of the Guises assassinated Henry III. This left Protestant Henry of Navarre, by right of succession, King Henry IV of France. However, it was only when he abjured Protestantism four years later and went through the formality of becoming a Roman Catholic that the great majority of his subjects, who were Roman Catholics, allowed him to enter Paris and be legally crowned. "Paris is worth a Mass," he is alleged to have remarked. Five years later (1598) he issued his famous Edict of Nantes (see p. 543), which by gaining toleration to the Protestant minority, ended religious strife in France for nearly a century. Once again the crusade of Philip II had stalled.

6. THE THIRTY YEARS' WAR IN GERMANY

The Peace of Augsburg (1555), which had brought to a close the first armed conflict in Germany between the Roman Catholics and the Lutherans, proved to be only an uneasy truce. Since the signing of the treaty, which recognized only Roman Catholics and Lutherans, the Calvinists had made strong headway in several states of the Holy Roman Empire and demanded equal recognition. Furthermore, lands of the Roman Catholic Church were constantly being secularized in Protestant areas in violation of the treaty. On the other hand, the Roman Catholics, becoming more aggressive as a result of the clarification of their position by the Council of Trent and the activities of the militant Jesuits, dreamed of exterminating Protestantism in the Holy Roman Empire and recovering all their lost

State Religions in Europe ca. 1560

Lutheran
Anglican
Calvinist Established Churches
Calvinist Minority Groups
Anabaptist
Roman Catholic

—— Border Between Protestant State Churches and Roman Catholic Church
–––– Approximate Eastern Border of Western Christianity

lands and souls. The Protestants in alarm formed a defensive league. The Roman Catholics countered by forming a league of their own.

The increasing tension finally erupted into the Thirty Years' War (1618–1648). In this war the religious issue was complicated and often confused by political and dynastic issues. The individual princes of the empire were struggling to maintain or even increase their independence of the emperor. The Hapsburg dynasty, both Austrian and Spanish, threatened to become so powerful that the apprehensive Bourbons of France entered the war against them. The upshot was that eventually the Roman Catholics, the Holy Roman Emperor, and the Hapsburg dynasty (the emperor was an Austrian Hapsburg) formed one faction against which were arrayed the Protestants, most of the individual princes of the empire, and the Bourbons.

The long-brewing Thirty Years' War began in 1618 when a group of Bohemian noblemen, mostly Calvinists and fearful of losing both their religious and their political rights, declared their Hapsburg ruler deposed and

This print shows Magdeburg, where in 1631 one of the battles of the Thirty Years' War was fought. The last and bloodiest of the religious wars that accompanied the Roman Catholic Reformation, the Thirty Years' War devastated much of Germany and exhausted the participants. *Photo: NYPL Picture Collection*

chose the Calvinist elector of the Palatinate as their king. The Hapsburg Holy Roman Emperor, aided by the Roman Catholic League and by Hapsburg and Roman Catholic Spain, took the field and easily crushed both Bohemia and the Palatinate. Hundreds of Calvinist Bohemian noblemen were executed and their property confiscated. Protestantism was outlawed in Bohemia. The Calvinist Palatin-

ate was annexed to Roman Catholic Bavaria. This quick and crushing victory by Roman Catholic and imperial forces frightened not only the Protestant princes of northern Germany, but also the Protestant neighboring states.

In 1625 Lutheran King Christian IV of Denmark, who held numerous bishoprics in Germany that had been illegally secularized, en-

Wallenstein's army, together with the regular imperial and Roman Catholic forces, defeated Christian IV and drove him out of Germany. The Danish king was deprived of all his German holdings except the duchy of Holstein. Upon the conclusion of this phase of the war in 1629, the victorious emperor issued the Edict of Restitution, restoring to the Roman Catholic Church all the lands illegally secularized since the Peace of Augsburg—more than a hundred tracts, large and small.

The whole Protestant world was now genuinely alarmed at the resurgent power of the Roman Catholics. The German princes were faced with the loss of their powers to the Holy Roman Emperor. The French Bourbons were concerned about the rapidly growing strength of the Hapsburgs. At this juncture another Protestant champion stepped forward—Gustavus Adolphus of Sweden. This Lutheran "Lion of the North" was a military leader of great ability. Furthermore, he was well backed by French gold; Cardinal Richelieu, who was then at the helm of the French government, placed the interests of his Bourbon masters above those of his church. Gustavus Adolphus marched and fought victoriously through the Germanies, gaining allies among the Protestant princes as he went. The Hapsburg emperor hastily recalled the ambitious Wallenstein, whom he had dismissed upon the conclusion of the Danish phase of the war. Two of the ablest military commanders of early modern times now faced each other. In the battle of Lützen (1632) Wallenstein was defeated, but Gustavus Adolphus had been killed and the victory was far from decisive. Fortunately for the Protestants, Wallenstein was dismissed and assassinated two years later. Since the Swedes had failed to turn the tide of the war, Richelieu in 1635 threw the full weight of France's military might directly into the fray. For thirteen more years the war dragged on until all participants were exhausted. The Treaty of Westphalia in 1648 finally brought the struggle to a close.

In general, thanks largely to the intervention of France, the Roman Catholics, the Holy

tered the war against the Roman Catholic and imperial forces. Christian IV was aided by English subsidies and numerous German Protestant princes. At this critical juncture a brilliant soldier of fortune, Albrecht von Wallenstein, offered his services to the emperor. This military genius raised a volunteer army of 50,000 adventurers of various nationalities whose only motivation was hope of plunder.

Austrian Habsburgs

Spanish Monarchy

Swedish Dominions

Brandenburg-Prussia

Church Lands

—— Boundary of the Holy Roman Empire

0   100   200   300 miles

SHETLAND I.

ORKNEY I.

NORWAY

SWEDEN

Bergen

Stockholm

SCOTLAND

Edinburgh

KINGDOM OF
DENMARK AND NORWAY

NORTH SEA

DENMARK

(TO SWEDEN 1658)

Copenhagen

BALTIC SEA

IRELAND

Belfast

SCHLESWIG

BRANDENBURG-PRUSSIA

Dublin   Liverpool

HOLSTEIN
Hamburg

SWEDISH
POMERANIA

Danzig

DU
PR

Lübeck Stralsund

ENGLAND
(COMMONWEALTH
1649-1660
UNITED KINGDOM
1707)

Bremen

Elbe R.

Stettin

POMERELIA

Vistula R.

ATLANTIC OCEAN

Bristol

London

UNITED
PROVINCES

Amsterdam
Ryswick
Utrecht

HANOVER

BRANDENBURG

Berlin

GREAT
POLAND

Warsaw

ENGLISH
CHANNEL

SPANISH
NETH.

Brussels

Rhine R.

Münster

Cologne

MINOR
GERMAN STATES

Leipzig

SAXONY

Oder R.

Dresden

Breslau

SILESIA

LITT
POLA

Rouen

Trier

Mainz

Prague

BOHEMIA

MORAVIA

Cra

Rennes

Paris

Metz PALATINATE

Strasbourg

BAVARIA

Augsburg

AUSTRIA

Vienna

KINGDOM OF HUNGARY

HUNG

Nantes

Orléans

LORRAINE
ALSACE

FRANCE

FRANCHE
COMTÉ

SWISS CANTONS

SLAVONIA

La Coruña

Bordeaux

Lyons

SAVOY

PIEDMONT

Milan

REP. OF VENICE

Venice

BOSNIA

Belgrad

SER

Oporto

León

Montauban

Parma

Genoa

Zara

ADRIATIC SEA

MONTENEGRO

NAVARRE

Avignon

Marseilles

Florence

TUSCANY

PAPAL
STATES

Valladolid

PORTUGAL
(TO SPAIN
1580-1640)

Escorial Madrid

CASTILE

SARAGOSSA

ARAGON

CATALONIA

PYRENEES

Barcelona

CORSICA
(Genoa)

Rome

Aquila

Bari

Lisbon

Mérida Toledo

S P A I N

Valencia

BALEARIC I.

MINORCA

MAJORCA

SARDINIA

Naples

NAPLES

ALB

Seville

Murcia

KINGDOM OF THE
TWO SICILIES

IONIA
(Veni

Cadiz

Malaga

GIBRALTAR

Tangier
(Portugal)

Ceuta (Spain)

MEDITERRANEAN

Palermo

SICILY

SEA

Algiers

Oran (Spain)

Tunis

MALTA (Spain)

FEZ AND MOROCCO

ALGERIA

TUNISIA

B A R B A R Y   S T A T E S

The map shows labels including: FINLAND, Helsingfors, INGRIA, TONIA, LIVONIA, Riga, Moscow, RUSSIA, LITHUANIA, Minsk, OLAND, Kiev, Lemberg, ALICIA, PODOLIA, RPATHIANS, Dniester R., YEDISAN, MOLDAVIA, Y, RANSYLVANIA, BESSARABIA, CRIMEA, WALLACHIA, Bucharest, DOBRUJA, BLACK SEA, TTO, Danube R., BULGARIA, O, M, A, N, RUMELIA, Constantinople, Salonica, EMPIRE, AEGEAN SEA, EECE, Athens, Smyrna, RHODES (Turkish), CYPRUS (Turkish), CRETE (Venice)

Europe 1648

Roman Emperor, and the Hapsburgs suffered a setback. Not only were the Roman Catholics thwarted in their efforts to exterminate Protestantism in Germany, but the Calvinists now gained equal status with the Lutherans and Roman Catholics in the Holy Roman Empire. The Edict of Restitution was nullified. The Holy Roman Empire practically fell apart. According to the terms of the Treaty of Westphalia, each of the more than three hundred individual princes could now make his own treaties. Three of the most important princes, the rulers of Brandenburg, Bavaria, and Saxony, made sizable additions to their territories. Sweden gained strategic territories along the German Baltic and North Sea coasts. France gained the important bishoprics and fortress cities of Metz, Toul, and Verdun, and the province of Alsace except for the free city of Strasbourg. These former imperial territories gave both Sweden and France a vote in the Diet of the Holy Roman Empire and a say in German affairs. The complete independence of Switzerland and the Dutch Netherlands was officially recognized. The Austrian Hapsburgs retained their hereditary possessions but lost prestige as emperors of a disintegrating Holy Roman Empire. Also, their relative position declined as that of France rose. The Spanish Hapsburgs fared worse. After eleven more years of fighting with France they yielded a strip of the southern Netherlands and the Spanish border province of Roussillon to France. Spain's days of greatness were finished.

The immediate effect of the Thirty Years' War on Germany was disastrous. For three decades hostile German and foreign armies had tramped back and forth across Germany, killing, raping, and looting the defenseless inhabitants. In the wake of Wallenstein's army of 50,000, for instance, swarmed 150,000 camp followers bent on plunder. To the usual horrors of war was added religious fanaticism. Many years would be required for Germany to recover from these wounds.

The Thirty Years' War was the last and the

bloodiest of the religious wars that accompanied the Roman Catholic Reformation. Although there would still be much religious strife and controversy, the religious map of Europe henceforth would change very little. In a real sense, then, 1648 marked the end of the era of the Protestant and Roman Catholic reformations. The Roman Catholic Church, by closing ranks, setting its house in order,

and availing itself of the militant Jesuit Society, had checked the further spread of Protestantism in Europe, but had been able to win back relatively little that had been lost. Western Christendom was now definitely split into two irreconcilable camps—Roman Catholic and Protestant. After 1648, political rather than religious affairs would occupy center stage in the Western world.

Suggested Reading

General. A good brief survey of the Roman Catholic Reformation, is B. J. Kidd, *The Counter-Reformation, 1550–1600* (1933). A scholarly and more detailed account by a Roman Catholic historian is P. Janelle, *The Catholic Reformation* (1949).

The Council of Trent. A good brief survey of the Council of Trent is R. B. Littledale, *A Short History of the Council of Trent* (1888). The great work on the Council of Trent will be the multivolume history by H. Jedin, *History of the Council of Trent*, of which twelve volumes have appeared, and two have been translated into English (1957 and 1960).

Index and Inquisition. Literature on the Index is neither plentiful nor good. Probably the best book available is G. H. Putnam, *Censorship of the Church of Rome and Its Influence on the Production and Distribution of Literature* (2 vols., 1906–07). The classic work on the Inquisition is H. C. Lea, *History of the Inquisition in Spain* (4 vols., 1906–07).

The Jesuits. An objective brief survey of the history of the Jesuits is H. Boehmer, *The Jesuits*, trans. P. Strodach (1928). The best biography of Loyola is P. Dudon, *St. Ignatius of Loyola* (1949). Dudon is a Jesuit priest, but is objective and scholarly.

The Crusade of Philip II. The best volume on the reign of Philip II is Volume IV of R. B. Merriman, *The Rise of the Spanish Empire in*

the Old World and the New (4 vols., 1918–34). A good brief account is ** R. T. Davies, *The Golden Century of Spain* (Harper Torchbook). A monumental history of the successful struggle of the Dutch against Philip II is J. L. Motley, *The Rise of the Dutch Republic* (3 vols., 1877). More up-to-date and objective, though far less exciting, is **P. Geyl, *The Revolt of the Netherlands 1555–1609* (Barnes & Noble). The best account of Philip II's attempt to conquer England and the impact of his failure on the course of the Roman Catholic Reformation all over Western Europe is **G. Mattingly, *The Armada* (Sentry). An excellent brief account of the complicated religious wars in France is Franklin Palm, *Calvinism and the Religious Wars* (1932); a more detailed account is J. W. Thompson, *Wars of Religion in France* (1909).

Thirty Years' War. By far the best volume on the Thirty Years' War in Germany is **C. V. Wedgwood, *The Thirty Years War* (Anchor), although the author tries a little too hard to prove that the damage caused by the war has been exaggerated.

Sources. The canons and decrees of the Council of Trent are contained in J. Waterworth, *History of the Council of Trent* (1948). **E. M. Burns, *The Counter Reformation* (Anvil) contains many interesting documents. E. A. Fitzpatrick, *The Spiritual Exercises of St. Ignatius Loyola*, trans. J. Rickaby (2nd ed., 1923) is a good reflection of the mind and the methods of Loyola.

RETROSPECT

RETROSPECT During the fifteenth and sixteenth centuries, medieval civilization did not abruptly end and modern civilization begin. As a matter of fact, lords and ladies still exist in Western Europe; people still revel in the symbols and pageantry of chivalry; agriculture is still a necessary part of Western economy; and the Christian religion still holds the allegiance of millions. Nevertheless, the world of 1600 was very definitely not the world of 1400.

During these two centuries, the first four national states had come into being, shattering once and for all the theoretical political unity of Western Europe under the Holy Roman Empire and ending the actual independence of thousands of feudal fiefs by bringing them under the authority of the national monarchs. In each of these new political units, a national vernacular triumphed over the common Western European language, Latin, further fragmenting the Europe of the Middle Ages.

The revival of commerce and the development of capitalistic practices and institutions ended the monopoly of medieval Europe's agricultural economy and of the land-owning class, the nobility. The nobility now faced competition for influence from the new middle class, from merchants, bankers, lawyers. It is true that the bourgeoisie sought most of all to enter the ranks of the nobility, and did so whenever possible, and that the nobility held the upper hand politically and socially for two or three more centuries. But by 1600 class lines had become more fluid. European civilization had become definitely urban. Furthermore, much of the rest of the world had come under European economic and political domination.

Even in the fourteenth century, a secular trend in Western European literature and art could be observed. This turning (or returning) from the sacred, God-centered ideals of the Middle Ages to the secular, man-centered interests of the modern world continued and accelerated during the fifteenth and sixteenth centuries. Western European man had become more self-centered, proud, versatile, and materialistic. These humanistic Renaissance qualities produced, as in the ancient Greece and Rome after which they were largely patterned, some of the world's greatest literature and art. They also laid the basis for an era of modern natural science.

Finally, by 1600 the Christian Church, which in 1400 still monopolized religious life and strongly influenced the intellectual, political, and economic life of Western Europe, was split asunder. This may have been the most important of all the developments that brought the medieval system to an end and ushered in the modern era, for nothing so characterized medieval

537

civilization as the dominance of the Church. By 1600 the Western Christian world had become fragmented, to a considerable degree along national lines. On the other hand, the Protestant and Catholic Reformations revived interest in and allegiance to the Christian religion at a time when Western man appeared to be turning his attention to secularism, nationalism, and capitalistic enterprises. Christianity, though its position of dominance had been lost, continued as a major force in the modern world.

Part Eight

The Age of Royal Absolutism

Seventeenth and Eighteenth Centuries

As we have seen, the kings of Spain, Portugal, France, and England gained the ascendancy over the feudal nobility in the late fifteenth century and welded the first four national states around their own persons. In the sixteenth century, Spain and Portugal were at the peak of their power and affluence. They acquired vast and lucrative colonial empires in the West and in the East. During the reigns of Charles V and Philip II, Spain was the dominant military power in Europe. After Philip's death in 1598, however, Spain's decline was as rapid as had been her rise a century earlier. Although her huge empire in the New World was still intact and although her greatest outpouring of literature and art was yet to come, her military and political power and influence were spent. Portugal's decline was equally precipitous. When in 1580 she was annexed to Spain, the Dutch, then fighting the Spanish for their independence, took advantage of Portugal's misfortune to seize the richest part of her Eastern empire. Although Portugal regained her independence in 1640, she never recovered her sixteenth-century wealth and influence.

The decline of Spain and Portugal left France in a favorable position to dominate Western Europe. Henry IV, the first of the Bourbon line of kings, who ascended the throne in 1589, brought the three decades of religious and political turmoil in France to an end. The Bourbon kings set out to make themselves supreme in France, and France supreme in Europe. France's only real military and political rival in Western Europe at the opening of the seventeenth century was England. Under the vigorous Tudor dynasty, royal absolutism had reached its peak during the sixteenth century. By the opening of the next century, Parliament was ready to challenge the royal authority—and the kings were the politically inept Stuarts. Meanwhile, the French, the English, and the Dutch were preparing to replace the Iberian nations as the leading commercial and colonial empire builders.

In Central and Eastern Europe two vigorous new dynasties—the Hohenzollerns of Prussia and the Romanovs of Russia—began to assert themselves. Their natural enemies were the Austrian Hapsburgs, the Ottoman Turks, the Poles, and the Swedes.

Chapter 33 ❧ The Dominance of France:

The Age of Louis XIV

France was the dominant nation in Europe throughout most of the seventeenth and eighteenth centuries, and the reign of Louis XIV represented the height of royal absolutism. All other monarchs strove to emulate the "Sun King." The well-lighted stage across which he strode was set for him by three able predecessors—Henry IV, Richelieu, and Mazarin.

1. THE RISE OF FRANCE UNDER HENRY IV, RICHELIEU, AND MAZARIN

When Henry IV became king of France in 1589, his country was torn and bleeding from several decades of bitter religious war. Respect for law and order had broken down. The feudal nobility had in many cases reasserted its own authority. The finances of the central government were in chaos. Roads and bridges were in disrepair. French prestige abroad was at a low ebb; even the city of Paris was garrisoned by the Spanish troops of Philip II.

Henry of Navarre, the first of the Bourbon dynasty to rule France, set out to change all this. The new king, in his prime at the age of thirty-six, was debonair and witty, courageous, generous, optimistic, and democratic in his social life. His slogan, "A chicken in the pot of every peasant for Sunday dinner," was

more than an idle phrase; it is little wonder that *Henri Quatre* became the most popular monarch in French history. The romantic Henry had in the Duke of Sully an able, methodical administrator to serve and to steady him. The most urgent task was to restore the authority of the central government. This he set out to do by vigorously suppressing brigandage and enforcing the law. The lesser nobility was brought to heel directly and quickly. The powerful nobility was dealt with more gingerly, but by the end of Henry's reign real headway had been made toward reducing the nobles to obedience to the central government.

Henry and Sully launched a comprehensive program of economic reconstruction. Agriculture and commerce benefited from the increased security of life and property, from the repair of roads, bridges, and harbors, and from the freeing of internal and external commerce of many obstructions and tariff barriers. Marshes were drained for farming. Better breeding methods were introduced. The peasants' livestock and implements were protected against seizure for debt or taxes. New industries producing glass, porcelain, lace, tapestries, and fine leather and textiles were subsidized and protected by the state. Silk culture, which brought vast wealth to France, was introduced. The building of France's overseas empire began in 1608 when

Champlain founded Quebec, the first French colony in the New World.

When Henry IV came to the throne, only about one-fourth of the heavy taxes, from which the clergy and the nobility were largely exempted, ever reached the national treasury. The rest went into the pockets of corrupt officials and tax farmers, that is, the collectors who bid a fixed sum for the privilege of collecting the taxes and were permitted to keep anything over and above the contracted amount. Sully was unable to change this vicious system, but by means of careful bookkeeping, efficient administration of expenditures, and elimination of corruption, he was able to show a surplus for the first time in many years.

Another major achievement of Henry's reign was the granting of religious toleration to the Huguenot minority. Although Henry abjured Protestantism in order to gain acceptance as king of an overwhelmingly Roman Catholic nation, the sympathy and probably the faith of this former leader of the Huguenots remained with the Calvinist minority. The Edict of Nantes, which Henry IV issued in 1598, granted not only complete freedom of conscience and limited public worship to the Huguenots, but also civil and political equality. Moreover, they were given military control of some two hundred fortified cities and towns as a guarantee against future oppression. The Edict of Nantes stands as a handsome monument in the bloody and endless struggle for religious freedom—probably the most precious possession of civilized men. It antedates the work of Roger Williams in Rhode Island by thirty-eight years.

Having laid the foundations for royal supremacy, economic health, and religious toleration, in the last years of his reign Henry IV devoted an increasing amount of attention to foreign affairs. He talked vaguely from time to time about a sort of league of nations for perpetual peace, but nothing came of it. His specific goal was to make France first secure and then supreme in Europe by weakening the power of the Spanish and Austrian Hapsburgs. In 1610 he readied his armies for a campaign, but just as he was preparing to join them he was assassinated by a fanatical Roman Catholic who doubted his orthodoxy.

After fourteen years of retrogression under Henry IV's Italian wife, Marie de Médicis, and their young and inept son Louis XIII, Cardinal Richelieu gained active control over the government of France. Although technically a mere servant of the fickle Louis XIII, the masterful cardinal made himself so indispensable that for eighteen years (1624–1642) he held firm control over French affairs. Handsome, arrogant, and calculating, Richelieu was a true Machiavellian. His twofold policy, from which he never veered, was to make the royal power supreme in France and France supreme in Europe.

Believing the high nobility and the Huguenots to be the chief threats to royal absolutism, Richelieu crushed them both. He boldly destroyed the castles of the nobles who remained defiant, disbanded their private armies, and hanged a number of the most recalcitrant. The special military and political privileges that the Huguenots enjoyed under the Edict of Nantes were considered by Richelieu to be intolerable, giving them the status of a state within a state. After a bloody two-year struggle, he stripped the Huguenots of these privileges, although he left their religious and civil liberties intact.

In order to bypass all local political influence, which in some provinces was still strong, the dynamic minister divided all France into some thirty administrative districts called *généralités*, each of which was placed under the control of an *intendant*,[1] who was an agent of the crown. So absolute was the power of the *intendants* over local affairs, even of the most minute nature, that they soon came to be called the "thirty tyrants of France." They were chosen from the ranks of

---

[1] The *intendants* existed before Richelieu's time, but he greatly increased their power and functions.

the bourgeoisie and were shifted around frequently lest they become too sympathetic with the people over whom they ruled. The royal will was thus extended to every nook and cranny of France.

Although Richelieu was a cardinal in the Roman Catholic Church, he did not hesitate to plunge France into the Thirty Years' War in Germany on the side of the Protestants. His purpose, of course, was to weaken the Hapsburgs, chief rivals of the French Bourbons for European supremacy. As a result of Richelieu's intervention, Protestantism in Germany was probably saved from extermination, but the Hapsburgs were humiliated. When Richelieu died in 1642, he had gone far toward bringing to fruition Henry IV's policies of royal supremacy in France and French supremacy in Europe. Richelieu, however, did not share Henry IV's concern for the common people. Their lot became harder under the imperious and ruthless cardinal, at whose death they rejoiced. Twentieth-century France is still saddled with an excessively centralized and bureaucratic administrative system whose agents are entrenched and often self-seeking—a system that owes much of its origin to Richelieu.

Richelieu was succeeded by his protégé, Cardinal Mazarin. Louis XIII's death in 1643, one year after that of his great minister, left the throne to Louis XIV, a child of five. Mazarin played the same role in the early reign of Louis XIV that Richelieu had played during most of the reign of Louis XIII. From the death of Richelieu in 1642 until his own death in 1661, Mazarin vigorously pursued the policies of his predecessor. The Thirty Years' War was brought to a successful conclusion. All who opposed or challenged the absolute authority of the crown were summarily crushed.

Although the policies were the same, the methods of carrying them out were quite different. Whereas Richelieu was bold and forthright in dealing with even his most formidable enemies, the Italian-born Mazarin was treacherous, deceitful, and devious. He was hated even more intensely than Richelieu. The most noteworthy events during his administration were two uprisings, known as *Frondes*, against his tyranny. The Frondes were revolts of the disgruntled nobility, supported by various other rebellious elements, against the ever-increasing authority of the central government. At times it looked as if the rebels might succeed, but the crafty Mazarin was too much for them. The failure of the Frondes marked the last overt resistance to royal absolutism in France until the French Revolution in 1789. When Cardinal Mazarin died in 1661, he passed along to young Louis XIV a royal power that was at last absolute and a national state that was easily the first power of Europe.

2. LOUIS XIV AND HIS GOVERNMENT

Louis XIV was twenty-three years of age when, in 1661, he stepped forth as the principal actor on the world's gaudiest stage. Young Louis was well fitted for the part. He had a sound body and a regal bearing. His lack of brilliance and of deep learning were more than offset by a large store of common sense, a sharp memory, a sense of responsibility, and a capacity for hard, tedious work. From his Spanish mother, from Mazarin, and from his tutors he had gained the conviction that he was God's appointed vicegerent for France. In Bishop Bossuet he had the most famous of all theorists and exponents of royal absolutism. Bossuet in numerous writings argued that absolute monarchy is the normal, the most efficient, and the divinely ordained form of government. Furthermore, the royal monarch, the image of God and directly inspired by God, is above human reproach and accountable to God alone. These ideas were the culmination of the thinking of James I of England a half century earlier (see the next chapter). As acted out by Louis, they gained and held the ascendancy throughout the continent of Europe—and indeed far beyond its confines—during the late seventeenth and most of the eighteenth century.

Louis XIV, under whom royal absolutism and splendor reached unparalleled heights, is shown here greeting his father-in-law, Philip IV of Spain, on l'Ile de Faisans. Louis' family loyalty was not strong, for France was to be one of the attackers whose determined and continuous assaults in the seventeenth century reduced Spain to a second-rate power. **Painting by Lausmonier in Le Musée Tessé.** *Photo: Giraudon*

Absolute though he might consider himself (the words *"L'état, c'est moi"* [I am the state] are often attributed to him), Louis could not possibly perform all the functions of government personally. Actually, the great bulk of the decisions and details of government were handled by a series of councils and bureaus, and administered locally by the *intendants*. The functions of the chief councils, such as those of state, finances, dispatches, and the privy council, appear on paper to have been overlapping and ill-defined. As supervised by the industrious Louis XIV, however, the administrative machinery worked smoothly and efficiently. In fact, it was the envy of his fellow monarchs and probably constituted his most constructive achievement. In the government of Louis XIV there was no semblance of popular participation. The role of the people was to serve and obey; in return, they enjoyed reflected glory and received such benefits as the monarch might be willing and able to bestow upon them. The Estates-General was not called once during the seventy-two years of Louis XIV's reign or the fifty-nine-year rule of his successor.

3. THE KING AND HIS COURT: VERSAILLES

In line with Louis XIV's concept of divine right absolutism, he believed that he should have a palace worthy of God's chief vicegerent on earth. Hating tumultous Paris, congested and crowded with vulgar tradesmen, he selected Versailles, 10 miles southwest of the city, to be the new seat of government. There as many as thirty-five thousand workmen toiled for thirty years, turning the marshes and sandy wastes into the world's most splendid court. The cost was so staggering that Louis destroyed the records. The greatest art-ists in the land were employed in the creation of the palace and the grounds. The most costly marbles, glass, tapestries, paintings, and inlaid woods were used in profusion in the ornate Baroque style of the period. Hundreds of acres of gardens, parks, walks, canals, and artificial lakes were laid out with mathematical precision. Playing fountains and myriad marble statues formalized the landscape.

Around his court Louis XIV gathered the great nobles of France. Henry IV, Richelieu, and Mazarin had broken their power; Louis XIV turned them into court butterflies. The inevitable jostling for the king's attention,

There were hundreds of rooms and halls in the palace of Versailles, each exquisitely and lavishly decorated, lighted with crystal chandeliers containing thousands of candles. The epitome of royal splendor, Versailles was duplicated on different scales by other monarchs all over Europe. This is the Queen's Room. *Photo: French Government Tourist Office*

which was the one source of preferment, and the conflicting claims of so much titled rank necessitated the drawing up of an elaborate code of etiquette. The king was dressed and undressed, bathed, and fed by the highest noblemen in the land—all in strict ritual. The household personnel consisted of ten thousand soldiers in brilliant uniforms and four thousand civilians. Little wonder that all the world's other monarchs were awed and that many attempted to imitate Louis' incredible style. Nor was the pageant of Versailles mere glitter alone. Louis XIV subsidized or gathered around himself the leading French artists and literary figures. Mansard the architect and Lebrun the painter were the chief designer and decorator, respectively, of the palace. Corneille, Racine, Molière, La Fontaine, La Rochefoucauld, Saint-Simon, and Madame de Sévigné made Louis XIV's reign the golden age of French literature. (Their work will be discussed in Chapter 37.)

But there was a reverse side to the coin. Versailles was a showplace, not a comfortable home for the king. It was cold, drafty, and inconvenient. The balls, parades, hunts, and social ritual were not sufficient to absorb the energy of the vivacious and ambitious nobility of France. The court seethed with gossip, scandal, and intrigue. Nor did the hard-toiling, heavily taxed French masses, who were supposed to enjoy the reflected glory of the monarch, always appreciate such extravagant glamour. Indeed, expressions of discontent were heard with increasing frequency.

4. COLBERT AND THE FRENCH ECONOMY

Louis XIV was fortunate to have at his command during the first half of his reign a prodigious financial manager. Jean Baptiste Colbert was an inordinately ambitious social climber who realized that, because of his bourgeois origin, his only means of advancement was through indispensable service to the king. An engine of efficiency, he toiled end-lessly, supervising the myriad details of the French economy.

Colbert's first and probably his most difficult task was to balance the national budget, which had become badly unbalanced under Richelieu and Mazarin. The careful accounting of receipts and expenditures that Sully had inaugurated three quarters of a century earlier was resumed. Some of the debts that the government had contracted at exorbitant rates of interest were canceled; on others the rates were reduced. Colbert, however, like Sully before him, was unable to change the pernicious system of tax farming. He had to be content with discharging and punishing dishonest tax collectors. Neither was he able to abolish all internal customs duties, although he did free a large block of territory in northern France from these crippling barriers to commerce.

With Colbert, mercantilism reached its peak. French industries were protected by prohibitive tariffs, while exports and new industries were subsidized. Raw materials, however, were strictly husbanded. Imperial and commercial activities in India and the vast interior of North America were vigorously promoted. It was at this time that Marquette, Joliet, and La Salle explored the Great Lakes and the Mississippi Valley for France. To protect this growing empire and the commerce with it, a large navy was built. But Colbert did not stop with these traditional mercantilist practices. In order to gain a world-wide reputation for the uniformly high quality of French products, all manufacturing was subjected to the most minute regulation and supervision. So many threads of such and such quality and color must go into every inch of this textile and that lace. A veritable army of inspectors enforced the regulations. This extreme phase of mercantilism, the economic adjunct to royal absolutism, has come to be called Colbertism. It achieved its immediate end so far as quality and reputation were concerned, but it stifled initiative and retarded future industrial development. That Colbert was able to balance the budget and achieve general economic prosperity in the face of Louis XIV's lavish expenditures, including the building of Versailles, was a remarkable feat. It is well, however, that Colbert died in 1683, for Louis' wars of aggression eventually wrecked most of the great minister's work. With the exception of the Netherlands, practically all of Europe copied Colbert's policies and techniques during the latter part of the seventeenth and most of the eighteenth centuries.

5. ABSOLUTISM AND RELIGION

It was virtually inevitable that Louis XIV's concepts of divine right monarchy would have religious repercussions. First of all, they ran counter to the claims of the pope. All his life Louis considered himself to be devoutly loyal to the Roman Catholic faith, as were the majority of his subjects. But when it came to matters of church administration—matters so important in French government and society —Louis was not willing to have his royal authority limited, even by Rome. Numerous conflicts between king and pope led to the calling of a great council of the French clergy in 1682. This council, under the domination of Bishop Bossuet, faithful servant of Louis XIV and famed exponent of the theory of royal absolutism, drew up a statement of Gallican Liberties, special privileges or freedoms of the French church from Roman domination. These were in essence: 1. A church council is superior to the pope. 2. The pope's jurisdiction is supreme only in matters of faith, and his rulings even here are applicable in France only after they have been accepted by the French clergy. 3. The traditional customs and practices of the French church shall be respected. The Gallican Liberties brought the French church to a position close to that of the English church under Henry VIII. They might even have led to eventual separation from Rome had not Louis XIV in later life fallen increasingly under the influence of the Jesuits and his pious mistress, Madame de

Maintenon, who were able to rekindle his loyalty to the pope.

Louis' absolutism also ran afoul of the Jansenists, so-called because they were followers of a Belgian bishop, Cornelius Jansen. This group represented a Puritan movement within the Roman Catholic Church. The Jansenists had no intention of breaking away from the Church, to which they considered themselves entirely loyal. It was their wish to return to the teachings and practices of the Church in the days of St. Augustine. They emphasized predestination, inner piety, and the ascetic life. A number of intellectuals and people of means were attracted to their ranks, including the dramatist Racine and the mathematician and philosopher Blaise Pascal. At Port Royal near Versailles a group of prominent Jansenists practiced a communal life and established an excellent school that attracted much favorable attention. It was probably fear for the reputation of their own schools that aroused the jealousy of the Jesuits, militant watchdogs over Roman Catholic orthodoxy and papal supremacy. After a long and bitter controversy, the pope was persuaded to declare Jansenism heretical, though no bill of particulars was ever presented. Eventually the Jesuits also aroused against the Jansenists the animosity of Louis XIV, who could tolerate no deviation from his own views even in matters of religion. He outlawed the sect and destroyed its buildings. But he was unable to destroy Jansenism itself, which has continued to exist to the present time.

The chief religious victims of Louis XIV's absolutism were the Huguenots. Ever since Richelieu had removed the military and political privileges they had enjoyed under the Edict of Nantes, the Huguenots had lived quietly as good French citizens, clinging unobtrusively to their Protestant faith. Although the Huguenots numbered not more than one-tenth of the total population of France, many of them were industrious, prosperous, and educated members of the middle class. The Jesuits had little difficulty kindling the ire of Louis XIV against these heretical subjects who had the audacity to consider the king's religion not good enough for themselves. The Huguenots were subjected to one of the cruelest persecutions in the bloody history of religious intolerance. Barbarous regular army troops were quartered in Huguenot homes and instructed to live licentiously. Students familiar only with twentieth-century civilian armies will need to reflect a little to realize the significance of this move. Whole Huguenot communities would abjure their faith at the approach of the troops. Finally, in 1685 the Edict of Nantes was revoked and the Protestant religion outlawed. Although Huguenots were forbidden to emigrate, many—probably a quarter million—succeeded in doing so, taking much of their wealth and all their economic knowledge and skills with them. Not only were these industrious citizens, the backbone of French commercial and industrial life, lost to France, but they greatly strengthened some of France's rivals and enemies, such as England, the Dutch Netherlands, and Brandenburg, who welcomed them. Forbidden to enter the under-populated French colonies, many Huguenots helped to people the English colonies in America.

6. LOUIS XIV'S WARS OF AGGRESSION

The Sun King was not content to remain merely the most awesome single monarch in the world. France was not big enough to satisfy his vanity, ever inflated by the constant flattery of his courtiers. He coveted a wider domain. Louis' immediate and expressed goal was to extend his rule to France's natural frontiers. Since the French boundaries were already delimited by mountains and sea on every side but the northeast, it was in that direction that Louis looked for expansion. He claimed that only the Rhine River would provide France with an adequate natural strategic boundary on that side. This was, of course, pure fiction. River valleys unite rather than separate people; nor have rivers ever proved to be effective military barriers. A glance at the map (p. 550) will

quickly reveal that an advance to the Rhine would involve France in war with most of Europe. Between the French frontier and the Rhine lay the Spanish Netherlands, much of the Dutch Netherlands, imperial territory belonging to the Austrian Hapsburgs, and many German states, including some holdings of Brandenburg. England, too, would be threatened, and the balance of power upset. Nevertheless, Louis XIV felt himself equal to the task of challenging and defeating all these powers.

Louis' war minister, Louvois, is often considered the father of modern militarism. Louvois organized France's huge military establishment on a scientific and businesslike basis, replete with supply depots and hospitals. He introduced strict discipline, uniforms, and marching drill. Louis had other distinguished military aides. Vauban was one of the great designers of fortifications and of siege operations. It was a common saying that a city defended by Vauban was safe and that a city besieged by Vauban was doomed. Condé was an able and dashing military leader, and Turenne a masterly planner of campaigns and battles. No combination of enemies could match this array of talent, and no single adversary could come close to France in wealth and resources.

Between 1667 and 1713, Louis XIV fought four wars of aggression. The first is known as the War of Devolution. Trumping up the ridiculous claim that, in accordance with local inheritance laws, the Spanish (Belgian) Netherlands devolved upon his Spanish wife, Louis unceremoniously sent French armies in to conquer those rich provinces. Since Spanish power had declined rapidly since the days of Charles V and Philip II, Louis' armies captured one fortress city after another. The Dutch, however, took alarm and formed an alliance with England and Sweden to check the French menace. This array of power in addition to Spain caused Louis to accept a peace that granted him only a slice of the Spanish Netherlands.

The frustrated Grand Monarch determined

The Wars of Louis XIV

to punish the upstart Dutch. In the seventeenth century the Dutch Netherlands possessed the largest and the most profitable commerce of any nation in the world. Having won their independence from Spain early in the seventeenth century and having taken advantage of Portugal's temporary conquest by Philip II to seize the best part of the Portuguese Empire in the East, the Dutch soon became the envy of all their neighbors. The seventeenth century was also the century of Rembrandt, Grotius, and Spinoza—the golden age of Dutch artistic and intellectual achievement (see Chapter 37). It required an all-out effort of the English by sea and of the French by land to end this amazing Dutch

France's territorial ambitions are satirized in this cartoon, which shows the French king, the German emperor, and Cardinal Richelieu in a game of cards; the stakes, of course, are various pieces of territory in Europe. The caption says, "It is the Cardinal who runs the game." *Photo: Bibliothèque Nationale–Estampes*

supremacy. The interference of the Lowland-
ers in French affairs, the great wealth of the
Dutch Netherlands, and their location straddling the Rhine were sufficient in Louis XIV's
mind to justify attack. Having detached
Charles II of England and the king of Sweden
from the Dutch alliance with lavish bribes,
Louis sent the huge French armies under
Condé and Turenne into the Netherlands. The
cause of the Dutch seemed hopeless, and in
desperation they opened their dikes. Large
portions of their land were flooded, but the
French were held at bay. Meanwhile, the
power of France frightened Spain, the Holy
Roman Emperor, Brandenburg, and several
small German states into joining the Dutch in
alliance. Louis XIV won many victories over
the allies, but when the English Parliament
forced Charles II to break his agreement with
the French king and join the alliance against
him, Louis XIV decided to make peace. Again
hapless Spain was the loser, giving up to
France the long-coveted Franche-Comté (free
county of Burgundy) and another strip of the
Spanish Netherlands.

At the end of the Dutch War (1678) Louis
XIV stood at the peak of his power. He had
defeated all the greatest military powers on
the Western European continent and had
gained valuable territories. But the tide was
about to turn. Turenne was killed near the
end of the Dutch War, and the aged Condé
retired at the end of war. No comparable
generals were found to replace them.
Colbert's hard-won surplus and balanced
budget were now things of the past, and
France's economy was suffering. All Europe
had become alarmed by the French aggression. Louis XIV, however, was not statesman
enough to perceive the realities of the present.
His ever-growing appetite for power and glory
had hardly been whetted.

No sooner had the Dutch War ended than
Louis began trumping up claims to various
territories in Alsace and Lorraine and sending
in his armed forces to occupy them. The
result was another defensive alliance against
Louis composed of the Dutch Netherlands,
Spain, Sweden, the Holy Roman Emperor,
and a number of small German states. The

heart of the alliance was William of Orange, stadholder of Holland, and when the redoubtable Dutchman became King William III of England after the Glorious Revolution of 1688, England, too, was brought into alliance against Louis. The alliance was called the League of Augsburg, and the war that followed is known as the War of the League of Augsburg. After nine years of exhausting and fruitless struggle, Louis XIV was forced to accept a peace that gave him only the city of Strasbourg.

But the Sun King, still blinded by pride and greed, was not about to give up. Before the last monarch of the Hapsburg line in Spain died in 1700, Louis XIV persuaded him to choose one of Louis' grandsons as king. The prospect of Spain and the Spanish Empire joined to the already inordinately powerful French monarchy frightened the other powers of Western Europe into once more forming an alliance against France. This alliance, known as the Grand Alliance, was also engineered by William III; it consisted of England, the Dutch Netherlands, Austria, Brandenburg, several small German states, Savoy, and Portugal. The ensuing War of the Spanish Succession lasted eleven years (1702–1713) and was the most destructive of all Louis XIV's wars. The allies, led by the brilliant duke of Marlborough (John Churchill, a direct forebear of Winston Churchill), administered to the French and Spanish armies a series of severe defeats. In 1713 Louis XIV, beaten and exhausted, was forced to accept the Treaty of Utrecht. Although Louis' grandson was permitted to retain the Spanish throne, France yielded Newfoundland, Nova Scotia, and Hudson Bay to Great Britain.[2] Spain gave up Gibraltar and Minorca to Great Britain, and ceded the Belgian Netherlands, Naples, Sardinia, and Milan to Austria. The duke of Savoy received the title of king and the Spanish island of Sicily (which he later exchanged with Austria for Sardinia). The Hohenzollern margrave of Brandenburg was granted the title "king in Prussia," and henceforth his state was called Prussia. Thus the houses of Savoy and Hohenzollern, which later were to create the Italian and the German nation, respectively, added greatly to their prestige. France was somewhat humbled. She was beginning to lose ground overseas to Great Britain, and in Europe she had been halted short of the Rhine. But she was still the most powerful single nation in Europe.

Louis XIV lived only two years after the signing of the Treaty of Utrecht. He had long outlived his popularity. As the body of the grandest of all the absolute monarchs was drawn through the streets of Paris, some of his abused people cursed in the taverns as the coffin passed. A faint scent of revolution was already in the air.

---

[2] The term *Great Britain* replaced the term *England* in 1707 when England and Scotland were united.

Suggested Reading

General. **G. N. Clark, *The Seventeenth Century* (Galaxy) is a good brief survey of Europe during the seventeenth century that emphasizes cultural aspects. The three volumes in the excellent Rise of Modern Europe series that cover the seventeenth century are **C. J. Friedrich, *The Age of the Baroque, 1610–1660;* **F. L. Nussbaum, *The Triumph of Science and Reason, 1660–1685;* and **J. B. Wolf, *The Emergence of the Great Powers, 1685–1715* (all Harper Torchbooks). All the books in this series cover political, social, and economic matters as well as cultural aspects.

Rise of France Under Henry IV, Richelieu, and Mazarin. The best biography of Henry IV is still P. F. Willert, *Henry of Navarre* (1902). An excellent brief study of France under Richelieu is **C. V. Wedgwood, *Richelieu and the French Monarchy* (Collier). A scholarly but ponderous history of France under Mazarin is J. B. Perkins, *France Under Mazarin* (2 vols., 1886).

Louis XIV and His Court. **L. B. Packard, *The Age of Louis XIV* (Berkshire) is a brief but excellent survey. **W. H. Lewis, *The Splendid Century* (Anchor) is a delightful study of French society during the age of Louis XIV. Superseding all other biographies of the grand monarch is **J. B. Wolf, *Louis XIV* (Norton), a scholarly masterpiece published in 1968.

Economic and Religious Affairs. C. W. Cole, *Colbert and a Century of French Mercantilism* (2 vols., 1939) is a scholarly, detailed treatment of this major aspect of Louis XIV's reign. A. J. Grant, *The Huguenots* (1934) is a brief and highly readable study of one of Louis XIV's major problems and mistakes.

Sources. Two major sources that provide the historian with much valuable material on the reign of Louis XIV are Duc de Saint-Simon, *The Age of Magnificence: The Memoirs of the Duc de Saint-Simon,* ed. and trans. Sanche de Gramont (1963); and Marie de Sévigné, *Letters From Madame la Marquise de Sévigné,* ed. and trans. Violet Hammersby (1956). These two works make highly interesting reading for the nonprofessional student of the period. The writers were both participants in the court life of Versailles during the reign of Louis XIV.

Historical Fiction. One of the most popular novels ever written, **Alexandre Dumas, *The Three Musketeers* (Penguin), presents a vivid picture of France in the time of Richelieu. Francis Steegmuller, *The Grand Mademoiselle* (1956) is a novel about the richest woman in Europe (the cousin of Louis XIV and heiress of the vast Orleanist fortune). It is based on sound historical research and brings the reader close to the spirit of the time.

Chapter 34 ❧ The Climax and Decline of Absolutism in England

While Henry IV, Richelieu, Mazarin, and the Sun King perfected royal absolutism in France and set an example for other Continental powers, absolutism passed its peak and received a setback in England. Most of seventeenth-century English history centers around the struggle between absolutist monarchy and the partisans of limited monarchy, the latter eventually winning. This constitutional change played an important part in strengthening England's position as one of the great European powers toward the end of the seventeenth century. The English Revolution also exerted a significant influence on other parts of the world for it long served as a model in the struggle against absolutism.

1. TUDOR ABSOLUTISM

Royal power reached its pinnacle in England during the Tudor period (1485–1603). The greatest Tudors, Henry VII, Henry VIII, and Elizabeth I, successfully concentrated the control of English society in their own hands. They brooked little criticism of their policies and summarily checked any efforts to weaken their domination over English political life.

In its essential features, Tudor absolutism was not much different from that of Louis XIV. Although the great Tudor rulers seldom talked much about their power, they assumed that it was their prerogative to guide every phase of English society. As we saw above (see pp. 469–470), Henry VII established the pattern of Tudor government. He strengthened a centralized administration manned by advisers of his own choice, paid careful attention to financial matters so that his government had adequate resources, monopolized the military resources of the state, perfected local institutions of government, and established special courts to serve royal dictates. Henry VIII and Elizabeth continued to work within this framework. Their chief accomplishment was to expand the range of governmental activity and to enlarge the machinery of government. Religious life in England was placed under royal control. The nation's economic life was more thoroughly regulated. New financial resources were exploited to permit the government to expand its activities. A large part of the success of the Tudors was due to their ability to raise money without having to go to Parliament. The hard-working Tudor rulers, with the help of loyal and skilled advisers, had gained nearly complete control over England by 1603.

Tudor absolutism demanded a tremendous amount of skill on the part of the rulers. From the Middle Ages England had inherited a tradition of limitations on royal power. These limitations had taken shape in two highly significant institutions: Parliament and the common law. By never assaulting these institutions openly, the Tudors managed to avoid the charge of tyranny. However, they worked with infinite patience and skill to get around the restrictions these institutions might have imposed. For instance, Parliament was consulted whenever any important and controversial legislation needed to be enacted. By personal persuasion, bribery, skillfully applied compulsion, and patronage the Tudors always managed to get Parliament to do exactly what they wanted. A good part of Tudor success sprang from the fact that their ideas for the good of England happily coincided with the interests of their subjects. Internal peace, religious reform, success in foreign wars were all popular; Englishmen did not think too seriously about how these goals were achieved. Few rulers have been more popular than Queen Elizabeth I, and it was easy for her to exercise tremendous power.

As the Tudor period neared its end, however, there were increasing signs of tension, discontent, and change. Parliament was restive under royal manipulation; many of its leaders were acutely aware that they were being managed. The general consensus which had once approved religious change was giving way to a realization that the initial changes involved in the Tudor reformation had engendered deep-seated differences on religious issues. Especially significant was the growing number of Puritans who believed that the newly established Church of England needed further reform and who were zealous in their conviction that their vision of godliness and the right religious order must prevail. New economic interests, bent on profit-seeking and capitalistic modes of exploitation, were advancing rapidly in the prosperous setting of Tudor England. Most notable was the new country gentry, whose control of land and vigorous economic activity permitted them to replace the old medieval aristocracy as the dominant element in England. This group was impatient with the ancient feudal restraints that still surrounded economic and political life. Equally aggressive and anxious for a larger voice were the burgeoning commercial interests, eager for England to take a more aggressive position in developing overseas trade and in supporting policies that would promote commercial activities at home. Finally, the lessening of the Spanish threat after 1588 removed a unifying bond among Englishmen and reduced their dependence on the crown as the protector of the realm. A major change was in the making in England as the seventeenth century opened; it was not completed, however, until she had passed through a deep political crisis that radically changed her political structure.

2. THE FIRST STUARTS (1603–1649)

Despite mounting problems, "Good Queen Bess" ended her reign a beloved ruler. Because there were no immediate heirs, the throne fell to a cousin, James Stuart, king of Scotland. James I (1603–1625) came to England with definite ideas about the royal office; he was a convinced absolutist, believing that God had set him on the English throne with full authority to do as he pleased. Not only did he openly claim absolute power, but he was quick to make an issue of the matter whenever anyone challenged him. But he was woefully ignorant of political realities in England. He gave no evidence that he realized the intricate maneuvering, the hard work, and the many compromises that the Tudors had devoted to the task of making royal power a reality. The combination of rigid absolutist convictions and political ineptitude on the part of the king led to a polarization of political forces in England and to the elevation of practical issues to the realm of principle.

James I began his reign by alienating the Puritans, who had had great hope for sympathetic treatment because the new king had been ruler of Presbyterian Scotland. In fact, James was an avowed Anglican, not inclined to bend any longer before what he considered to be religious radicals. When the Puritans confronted him with their demands, he threatened to harry them out of the country if they did not abide by the regulations of the Church of England. The Puritans were made more desperate by his refusal to become involved in the Thirty Years' War, a policy that appeared to abandon the cause of Protestantism at a moment when its fate was threatened in all of Europe by resurgent Catholic forces. James further aroused religious fears and outraged patriotic sentiments by making peace with Spain, that bastion of Catholic strength which within the memory of men had tried to invade England. As a practitioner of autocratic government, James was a failure. He surrounded himself with incompetent wastrels as councillors and permitted the royal administrative machinery to become ridden with corruption and venality. His constant need for money forced him to turn to Parliament, but he grew angry at parliamentary criticisms of his policies, his conduct, and his advisers. His encounters with Parliament usually ended with its dismissal, and caused many to feel that the king refused to abide by ancient constitutional customs. Without grants of money from Parliament, James turned to means of raising funds that were viewed as illegal. When the courts declared as much, James retaliated by dismissing judges, further confirming the belief that he refused to respect the constitution and the law.

Perhaps the decisive development of James' reign was the tendency for these disagreements and discontents to focus in Parliament, especially in the House of Commons. Theoretically representing all Englishmen, the House of Commons was dominated by well-to-do country gentry, lawyers, and businessmen. Historians have bitterly debated what these men stood for and what they wanted and still do not agree. On the whole, they were patriotic, religious, conservative men who seem to have had no idea of triggering a revolution. But they were also men of political experience, intent on sharing with the king the governance of England because they believed that this was the nature of the "constitution." James could not accept the outrageous idea that his power must be shared; each of his acts dramatized his aversion to

ancient custom and confirmed the growing opinion that he was defying the established order. He never learned the subtle art of using Parliament as the Tudors had done. As a consequence, his reign was marked by repeated confrontations between crown and Parliament into which religious, administrative, financial, foreign policy, and class issues began to enter.

Under James' successor, Charles I (1625–1649), the conflict developed into civil war. Charles I was one of a large number of kings in history whose inflexibility and incompetence have bred revolution. During the first years of his reign he was forced to summon several Parliaments because of his financial needs, only to dismiss them for demanding that he alter his policy or dismiss his detested advisers. Royal efforts to raise money without parliamentary consent led to new clashes with the courts and the alienation of those upon whom the illegal levies fell. A blundering foreign policy resulted in costly wars but no victories. The sharpening antagonisms led the leaders of Parliament to frame the Petition of Right, which was presented to the king in a session of Parliament he summoned in 1628 in order to raise money. This bold document charged that Charles had acted illegally by imposing martial law in peacetime, taxing arbitrarily, imprisoning citizens without trial, and quartering soldiers with private citizens. It clearly posited the principle upon which Parliament was ready to stand: that even the king must be bound by the law. Desperate for money, Charles accepted the Petition of Right, perhaps without realizing its implications for his autocratic concepts. But when the next Parliament, meeting in 1629, renewed the demand that the Petition be respected, he dissolved it over the bitter protests of its leaders.

For eleven years, Charles ruled without Parliament. Money was his gravest problem. Only by the strictest economies, by refraining from war, and by exploiting every source of revenue did he manage to survive. And without being able to meet in Parliament, the opposition was largely paralyzed. However, Charles' policies continued to make new enemies. His financial exactions, many of which were illegal or of questionable legality (unless one assumed with the king that anything he did was legal), outraged nearly everyone. The courts tried to check his attempts to gain money, but Charles used pressure to intimidate the judges and limit the independence of the courts. Perhaps he might have survived the consequences of his brand of absolutism had it not been for his religious policy. Under the guidance of his chief adviser, William Laud, archbishop of Canterbury, the royal government mounted a concerted effort to compel strict adherence to a rigid Anglicanism and to bring an end to every form of Protestantism that did not conform to Anglican concepts of doctrine, liturgy, and church organization. This policy was especially detestable to Puritans of all persuasions; they saw their most cherished convictions threatened with destruction. Many of them sought refuge in the New World in order to escape the tyranny they believed to be engulfing England. Even many Anglicans resented Laud's policy, which in their view smacked too much of Roman Catholicism.

Charles' attempt to rule without Parliament finally failed when Laud tried to force his religious ideas on Presbyterian Scotland, where Charles was also king. In 1639 the Scots leaped to arms to defend their religion. Charles had to have money to resist; the only place to get it was from Parliament. So in 1640 he called a new Parliament.

The first Parliament of 1640, called the Short Parliament, lasted only three weeks. Its leaders angered the king by their threats against his policy, and so the king dissolved it. However, as the Scots continued to press, Charles had to abandon the hope of ruling without Parliament. He summoned the so-called Long Parliament. Once seated, the Long Parliament proceeded to legislate an end to Stuart absolutism. It forced Charles to sacrifice his chief ministers, including Laud. It abolished all the extraordinary courts, including the Star Chamber and the Court of High Commission, which had long been tools with which absolutist kings had dodged the common law. An act was passed requiring the king to call Parliament every three years and curbing his power to dismiss Parliament. Severe limits were imposed on royal taxing power unless Parliament was consulted. To all these assaults on his concept of royal government Charles acceded, chiefly because he realized the inability of his government to face the rebellious Scots without the money which only Parliament could supply.

Up to this point, Parliament had succeeded brilliantly in legislating what amounted to a bloodless revolution. Yet its success did not stay a rapid drift toward more extreme measures. The past record of the Stuarts did not inspire great trust among parliamentary leaders that Charles would respect the new style of government. There were strong suspicions, cleverly played upon by radical Protestants, that the rigid Anglicanism of Laud was merely a cover for a return to Catholicism. Religious feelings ran especially high when the Roman Catholic Irish rebelled in 1641. When the king asked for troops and money to meet this problem, parliamentary leaders responded with legislation that stripped the crown of much of its military power. This act was symptomatic of a rising spirit of radicalism among some elements of Parliament. Not only did the assaults on monarchy become more violent, but parliamentary leaders moved rapidly to end Anglicanism "root and branch" in favor of some form of Puritanism. This mounting radicalism cooled the ardor of many influential men who had previously supported the limitation of royal power and drove them toward support of Charles as the symbol of the established order. The division in the parliamentary ranks caused the king to try to restore his control; he went so far in early 1642 as to seek to arrest the leaders of Parliament as a means of ending their meddling in matters that were the royal prerogative. His action was a call to arms, a challenge perhaps not unwelcome to the elements of English society that had for a generation been resisting royal absolutism in all its forms.

Historians have long debated the causes of England's descent into civil war. Some have argued that the issue was a clash between two political philosophies: autocracy versus parliamentary government. Others have seen the issue in terms of the blind, stupid blunders of men in power. Still others are convinced that the struggle was basically religious—an attempt to carry the Reformation beyond the Tudor settlement. Of great vogue in recent years has been the view that the civil war was the political side of an economic revolution which involved the transformation of England from a feudal, agricultural society into a capitalistic, commercial society; the outbreak of armed conflict in 1642 simply marked the final chapter in the effort of the new landed gentry and the commercial class to seize political power to match their economic supremacy. All these issues were involved; yet in the final analysis, the struggle that began in 1642 is best understood as a clash between elements of a ruling class which had lost its community of interest, so long centered in the king. England was about to endure a civil war, but not a revolution.

3. THE CIVIL WAR (1642–1649)

The lines of division that marked the opening of the civil war have not yet been clearly defined. Charles represented himself as the champion of the established political and religious order against the radicals in Parliament. His position won him a considerable following, soon known as Cavaliers, from many elements in society. The backbone of his support came from the great noble families and their extensive clientele and from the country gentry living in the more economically backward areas of northern and western England. The opposition, called the Roundheads, proclaimed their cause as liberty from tyranny, protection of the law, and the safeguarding of the principles of Protestantism. Roundhead support came from lawyers, the gentry of the south and the east, and the commercial interests; great numbers of these groups were Puritans. To this core was soon joined radical elements from the poor and the oppressed, especially those living in London. Into the intricate matter of choosing sides went a complex array of personal elements—family ties, friendship, personal loyalties, and so forth— much after the fashion of the American Civil War.

The first phase of the war lasted through 1646. In the beginning neither side was prepared militarily, but the royal forces had the upper hand for the moment. Some initial defeats did not, however, deter the Roundheads. The navy sided with them. More significantly, they controlled the richest part of England, including London. And they were in possession of the regular organs of administration, which gave them the great advantage of being able to vote and collect money. In 1643 the Roundhead cause was bolstered by an alliance with the Scots that brought Scottish military forces into the struggle against the king in return for the establishment of Presbyterianism as the religious system for England and Scotland. But Scottish support was not decisive; the outcome of the war ultimately hinged on the ability of the Roundheads to create an effective army. The chief architect of the victorious army was Oliver Cromwell. A farmer with strong Puritan convictions, Cromwell organized a cavalry regi-

This contemporary cartoon satirizes the conflict between Cavaliers and Roundheads, between royal absolutism and parliamentary government, that led to civil war, the execution of the king (Charles I), and eleven years of experimentation in governing England without a king. *Photo: Historical Pictures Service, Chicago* ment of disciplined, deeply religious recruits who proved more than a match for the Cavalier forces they faced. His ideas were soon applied to the entire Roundhead force. The result was the New Model Army, made up of selected troops paid and equipped in a businesslike fashion. Upon this force was imposed a strict discipline, strongly colored by Puritan ideas of godliness and sobriety. The New Model Army was deeply imbued with enthusiasm for the Puritan cause. It quickly proved itself superior to the Cavalier army; by 1646 Charles' forces were crushed, and the king himself surrendered to the Scots.

With victory in their grasp, the Roundheads split into factions. The events of the war tended to transfer Roundhead leadership from fairly moderate parliamentarians with a leaning toward Presbyterianism and a willingness to accept limited monarchy to more radical leaders strongly devoted to religious independence and the abolition of the state church. These radicals were centered in the New Model Army, which was the decisive source of power. Religious radicalism nourished political radicalism in the New Model Army, where there was an increasing clamor for more democratic elections, the abolition of monarchy, and the redistribution of property. Fearful that the radicals would assume complete control, the moderate group turned back toward the king, who suddenly discovered considerable enthusiasm for parliamentarianism and Presbyterianism now that the path seemed opened for his return to power. The Independents, with Cromwell in firm control, ended Charles' hope in a single battle in 1648. Convinced of the righteousness of his cause and backed by the victorious New Model Army, Cromwell acted swiftly to ensure the position of the Independents. He forceably purged Parliament of all members not dedicated to his cause, and created the Rump Parliament as chief authority in the land. The Rump Parliament immediately legislated out of existence the Anglican Church, the House of Lords, and the monarchy. More momentous was the decision to try Charles for treason. Chiefly at Cromwell's urging, the king was judged "a tyrant, traitor, and murderer" and beheaded in 1649, a culmination of the civil war that shocked many Englishmen who had little love for the king but had not contemplated an England without a king.

Oliver seeking God while the K. is murthered by his order.

The deep religious fervor of the Puritans and the taint of regicide that lingered throughout the Commonwealth and the Protectorate is satirized here as Oliver Cromwell is shown at prayer while Charles I is being executed. *Photo: NYPL Picture Collection*

4. EXPERIMENTATION IN GOVERNMENT: COMMONWEALTH AND PROTECTORATE (1649–1660)

For eleven years after Charles I's death, Cromwell's party sought to rule England without a king, experimenting desperately but unsuccessfully to establish a stable order. From the beginning, the Cromwellians represented a minority, and they never gained additional support. Their main strength was concentrated in the army, a fact that was destined to make many Englishmen suspicious.

The first experiment centered around establishing a republican form of government called the Commonwealth. The office of king and the House of Lords were abolished. A one-house Parliament was made the supreme authority. It was to be aided by a council of state made up of about forty men who were charged with conducting the daily affairs of government. The men who dominated the Commonwealth were far from radical; in fact, one of their first decisive acts was to silence the ever-more strident voices of the political and religious extremists in the army. Led by Cromwell, the Commonwealth government optimistically began the onerous tasks of reestablishing order and prosperity in England. In different circumstances, Cromwell's policies might have won approval. Somewhat unexpectedly, he showed considerable toleration toward all varieties of Protestantism. He sent his armies into Ireland to crush a long-festering rebellion with such ferocity that the Irish never forgave him. Scotland was likewise brought under firm English control. An aggressive foreign policy, aimed at promoting English commercial and colonial interests, was undertaken. Navigation acts were passed to ensure that trade in England's emerging empire would be monopolized by England. War was waged on the Dutch, and to some extent, England's commercial position vis à vis her chief rival was improved. None of these policies, however, helped to popularize the Commonwealth; resistance and criticism grew steadily. The Cromwellian faction never escaped the charge of being regicides, nor were their puritanical religious ideas acceptable to more than a small minority of Englishmen.

Cromwell blamed much of the trouble on what he considered the self-seeking leaders of the Rump Parliament. With characteristic vigor and self-righteousness, he dissolved the Rump by force in 1653. The army and its officers were now completely in power. Cromwell tried appointing a Parliament to lead the Commonwealth. This hand-picked body (called Barebones Parliament in honor of Praise-God Barebones, the first name on the roll) failed to distinguish itself except by a series of extremely radical proposals and was likewise dissolved before the end of 1653. Now even the instrument that had originally stood against tyranny was gone. The tide of revolution had peaked.

Left in complete power, Cromwell and his friends then produced a written constitution entrusting power to a protector. The protector was to be advised by a council and guided by a one-house Parliament elected by property holders from districts of approximately equal population. Cromwell became the first protector late in 1653. When the new Parliament met in 1654 and began to criticize the protector, Cromwell dismissed it. Thereafter he assumed the role of virtual dictator. Although he called later parliaments, he seldom heeded their advice. He repeatedly found that the parliaments he called reflected political and religious concepts that ran contrary to the convictions of those who alone could sustain him in power, the "godly" men of the New Model Army. Despite his realization that civilian control of the state alone would assure stability, Cromwell was forced to rely on the army.

To curb disorder, he imposed martial law on England, and placed army officers in full authority in several areas. The rule of these puritanical soldiers was detested by most Englishmen, and so was the man responsible for their actions. Opinion began to run in favor of a restoration of monarchy. In 1657 a majority of the members of Parliament asked Cromwell to become king. Although he refused this honor, he did agree to changes in the constitution that made him protector for life. When he died in 1658, Cromwell had approached as nearly as possible to being king of England without having the formal title. The wheel had come almost full circle since the day Cromwell and his soldiers thought that they had abolished monarchy by executing Charles I.

Perhaps no figure in England's history has caused more debate than Oliver Cromwell. He has been called everything from a religious bigot and bloody tyrant to a champion of democracy. No simple description will ever fit him. Unquestionably he was a man of great talent, especially capable in warfare and administration. He was driven by strong religious compulsions that made him feel that whatever he did was godly; he felt obligated to purify Englishmen of those things he considered sinful—gambling, drinking, swearing, ostentatious living, enjoying themselves on Sunday, and staying away from church services. Yet, a tolerant man by the standards of his day, he favored a religious settlement that would allow broad freedom to many groups. Although he frequently resorted to force as a means of solving his problems, he believed in parliamentary government and tried until his dying day to establish it. Certainly England has had few greater patriots. Seldom did Cromwell do anything for his personal gain; his life was lived for England. His failure was largely due to the fact that only a minority of Englishmen were willing to accept Puritanism and republicanism.

At Cromwell's death his son, Richard, became lord protector. This weak figure was soon swept aside by more powerful forces. By 1660 elements of Cromwell's army, backed by considerable segments of the men of property and influence in the realm, brought pressure to bear for restoration of the Stuarts as rulers of England. A new Parliament was elected and negotiations were opened with Charles Stuart, the son of Charles I. By May 1660 all parties were satisfied, and Charles appeared in London in triumph, greeted by a happy people tired of Puritanism and radicalism.

5. THE RESTORATION (1660–1688)

The Restoration of the Stuarts left unresolved the great questions that had been so bitterly fought over since 1603. Neither king nor Parliament had established its supremacy.

In a reaction to the repression of the Puritan years, the theater bloomed during the Restoration. Here is the title page of John Dryden's **All for Love**. *Photo: Rare Book Division, New York Public Library, Astor, Lenox, and Tilden Foundations*

Religious division had not been wiped out, nor had any principle of toleration been discovered. For twenty-eight years after 1660 these problems continued to disturb England. However, the struggles of the Restoration era proved to be more moderate. Most Englishmen had learned between 1640 and 1660 the bitter price of dogmatism, violence, and tampering with ancient institutions. Moreover, they were weary of struggle, of the flouting of the law, and of the burden of saintliness. They were ready for "a very merry, dancing, drinking, quaffing and unthinkable time." For all his faults, Charles II proved to be a king who won the hearts of his subjects, something the austere, godly Cromwellians had never done.

When Charles became king in 1660, he seemed genuinely interested in working with Parliament. Both he and Parliament were eager for an end to radicalism and experimentalism. In a spirit of compromise and forgiveness, together they repealed the acts of the Commonwealth and the Protectorate. Only a handful of the Cromwellian faction were punished by execution; the spirit of vengeance was in part slaked by digging up and hanging Cromwell's body. Included in the arrangements surrounding Charles' restoration was a generous return of property confiscated during the era of the civil war to the original owners. The whole spirit of this settlement centered in the reestablishment of the wealthy landowners in control of England. The king was assured of a sizable income on a regular basis, but he was deprived of many of the ancient feudal rights which had allowed earlier kings to exact taxes without approval of Parliament. Not only was control of taxation reserved to Parliament, but the Triennial Act was passed to ensure that Parliament would meet at least every three years whether or not the king so wished.

The one matter that defied a satisfactory compromise settlement was religion. Parliament was forced to enact a religious settlement that again bred discord. The settlement was embodied in a series of acts passed in 1661 and 1662 and known as the Clarendon Code, after Charles II's chief adviser, the Earl of Clarendon. These laws reestablished the Anglican Church and threatened to destroy the Independents and Presbyterians. The Act of Uniformity required all clergymen to abide by the Book of Common Prayer or to surrender their livings. The Corporation Act provided that all members of city governments worship in the Church of England. The Conventicle Act made religious meetings other than Anglican illegal, and the Five Mile Act forbade all preachers who were not Anglicans to come within five miles of any city.

The Clarendon Code raised immediate dissension within the ranks of the nonconformists, who were once more treated as criminals.

As important as it was in restoring order, the settlement accompanying the restoration of the Stuarts generated its own problems, which continued to keep England agitated. The exact powers of the king and Parliament were still not clearly defined, and religious sentiments were deeply offended by the Clarendon Code. These deep-seated sources of trouble were exacerbated by a series of disasters that befell England shortly after Charles returned to power. Charles became involved in a war with the Dutch, during which the Dutch fleet humiliated the English. In 1665 a plague struck England, and the next year a large part of London was destroyed by fire. Charles II's court became notorious for immorality, and the king earned a reputation as its most profligate member. One member of Parliament, in an obvious reference to Charles' many illegitimate children, proposed that cradles be bought by the government in wholesale lots.

In the minds of some people, England's misfortunes were divine retribution for royal immorality. Public wrath fell on Charles' chief minister, Clarendon, and Parliament forced him out of office. Parliament also grew stingier toward the king, who then turned to Louis XIV of France. In an alliance of 1670, Louis promised him a sizable subsidy provided that Charles join France in a war on the Dutch and work for the restoration of Roman Catholicism in England. But when in 1672 Charles tried to set aside laws against Roman Catholics, Parliament was so outraged that it passed the Test Act (1673), excluding Roman Catholics from all public offices in England. And when Charles joined France in a war against the Dutch in 1672–1674, Parliament again blocked him by refusing financial aid.

By the middle of his reign Charles seemed determined to end the deadlock between crown and Parliament either by dispensing with Parliament altogether or by controlling it. He continued to rely on Louis XIV for money. He succeeded in building a court party devoted to monarchy and Anglicanism. The opposition scornfully dubbed the members of this party *Tories* (a term previously used to designate Irish bandits). An opposing party, committed to parliamentary supremacy and the tolerance of all Protestant groups, was also formed. Members of this party were called *Whigs* (after a term used to designate Scottish horse thieves and murderers). By skillful use of the Tories and with French money, Charles managed to enjoy a great deal of freedom during his later years. Fear that he would use his power to restore Roman Catholicism, however, steadily increased, fanned whenever possible by the Whigs, who used every possible occasion to persuade the English that a "popish plot" was afoot to restore Catholicism. The Whigs centered their efforts in Parliament chiefly on trying to pass an Exclusion Act that would have barred Charles' brother, James, from the throne. Charles kept the bill from passing, but his methods convinced the despairing Whigs that tyranny had returned to England.

Charles' successor, James II, inherited a strong position, based in large part on a parliamentary majority controlled by the king. However, he acted with such reckless abandon that his following soon melted away. His chief mistake was open avowal of Roman Catholicism, the one thing that neither the Tories, the king's supporters, nor the Whigs, his enemies, would tolerate. Early in his reign James was forced to call the army to crush a rebellion. When the danger had passed, he kept the army and began to appoint Roman Catholics as officers, acts that seemed to threaten a forceful imposition of Catholicism. Increasing numbers of Catholics were appointed to high offices in the royal government, and several clergymen favorable to Rome were installed in the chief religious posts. In 1687 James issued the Declaration of Indulgence, which relaxed the restrictions on all religious groups, Dissenters and Roman Catholics alike. Protestants interpreted this act as favorable to Roman Catholics. Finally, in 1688, a son was born to James by his Roman Catholic wife, ensuring that his regime would be perpetuated by a Catholic successor.

This was the last straw. A group of prominent Tories and Whigs, usually bitter political rivals but drawn together by their conservative concerns for property, Anglicanism, and aristocratic domination of politics, invited James' daughter, the Protestant Mary, and her husband, William of Orange, the rulers of the Netherlands, to accept England's throne. William, eager to ensure England's support against the French threat to his country, accepted. When he invaded England late in 1688, the great majority of the people rallied to his side, and James fled to France. For a second time the unhappy Stuarts had been forced off England's throne.

6. THE GLORIOUS REVOLUTION

The flight of James II, unlike the death of Charles I, was not followed by a period of radical political experimentation. Instead, the Glorious Revolution was carried through without bloodshed and recrimination. A series of laws was passed that pacified England and established the basis for her future political development.

The major laws were enacted immediately after the accession of William and Mary. Parliament declared James deposed by virtue of abdicating his office. A new coronation oath was devised requiring William and Mary to swear to abide by decisions of Parliament as well as by the ancient laws of England. The Bill of Rights was passed in 1689. This charter spelled out in detail the laws to which the king must adhere. It laid down Parliament's authority to depose a king and choose a new one. It assured the members of Parliament the right of free speech, immunity from prosecution for statements made in debate, and freedom from royal intervention in elections. It declared illegal a whole series of acts: taxation without consent of Parliament, dispensing with laws, maintaining a standing army in peacetime, requiring excessive bail,

depriving citizens of trial in the regular courts, interfering with jurors, and preventing people from petitioning the king. The Toleration Act was also enacted, allowing religious freedom to Puritans and Independents, although still keeping non-Protestants out of public office.

Accepting the crown on the basis of these laws and conditions, William and Mary acted with vigor to dispose of other sources of difficulty. In 1689–1691 William led an army into Ireland, where James was attempting to stir up a rebellion that would put him back on the throne. William crushed the rebels and instituted a policy of depriving Irish Catholics of their land in favor of English landlords. Ireland was thus placed on a colonial status, to be exploited by England. Hard as this policy was for the Irish, it did deprive political rebels of a convenient base of operations against England.

William also conducted long negotiations to solve the problem of Scotland. These negotiations bore fruit after his death, when Parliament passed the Act of Union (1707), which joined the two kingdoms, gave Scotland a liberal number of seats in Parliament, and guaranteed her Presbyterian religious organization. The Act of Union created a political unit known thereafter as Great Britain.

Probably William's most significant act was to give England a new orientation in foreign affairs. A dedicated enemy of the schemes of Louis XIV to dominate Europe, William threw all of England's resources into the struggle against France. His action was decisive. Not only were Louis XIV's ambitious plans upset, but through these wars England became a great power and was well on the way to acquiring a great empire.

Still another significant issue remained to be settled—the succession problem. Mary died in 1694 and William in 1702, leaving the crown to Anne (1702–1714), another daughter of James II. Even before William's death it was apparent that Anne would have no heirs. To avoid the return of the Roman Catholic Stuarts, Parliament in 1701 passed the Act of

Settlement. This law provided that none but Protestants would inherit the English crown. In line with this principle, Parliament designated Sophia of the German state of Hanover, granddaughter of James I, and her heirs as successors to Anne. In spite of strong sentiment in favor of restoring the dynasty of James II, this act was honored in 1714, when George of Hanover became King George I of England.

7. THE EMERGENCE OF THE CABINET SYSTEM

The establishment of parliamentary supremacy in the wake of the Glorious Revolution left unsolved one more major political problem—that of the executive power. How would the daily affairs of government be conducted? Many were afraid to trust this task to the king, fearing that he would regain control over political life. Yet Parliament, composed chiefly of landowners and businessmen, was in no position to take up this burden. During the half century after 1688 a solution was found that permitted Parliament effectively to control the executive branch of the government while still assuring the skillful conduct of state business. The answer lay in the emergence of the cabinet.

English kings had long employed advisers to conduct government affairs and to shape policy. Up to 1688 these ministers had usually been chosen by the king and were responsible to him alone. After 1688 it became absolutely necessary for the king to gain parliamentary support for every phase of government policy. From William III's reign onward, therefore, royal ministers were increasingly chosen because of their influence in Parliament. Since Parliament tended to divide into parties that controlled large blocs of votes, it proved wisest for the king to seek out party leaders for posts as ministers and advisers.

After the accession of Anne, this trend developed rapidly. Since Anne and the first Hanoverians, George I (1714–1727) and George II (1727–1760), were unfit for the rigorous job of administering the state, the direction of the government and the formulation of policy fell into the hands of royal ministers who could get the approval of Parliament. This group of ministers slowly learned to accept mutual responsibility for the total operation of the government, which required that they all be members of the same party and stand together in Parliament. While their party held a majority in Parliament, they could enact their program; when they lost control over Parliament, they had to give way to a new cabinet that could control Parliament. One member of the cabinet, the *prime minister*, came to be recognized as the leader and spokesman of the whole group.

Anne relied heavily on the advice of John Churchill, duke of Marlborough, to conduct her government. However, a minister of the first two Georges, Robert Walpole, was the first real prime minister and the first to observe the principles of cabinet government. A Whig member of Parliament for many years, he learned well the potential power of a disciplined party. In 1721 he became George I's chief minister, primarily because of his power in Parliament, and he virtually ran England until 1742. He surrounded himself with men who could control votes in Parliament and followed policies suitable to the interests of his party. A coarse, hard-drinking squire, Walpole was not above bribery and the shameless use of patronage to keep his party strong. His strength in Parliament made him the real ruler of England; even the king could not control or check his dominance. Walpole lost control of Parliament when he tried to keep England out of war with Spain, a policy that was not popular with most Englishmen. Having lost his control of Parliament, Walpole resigned as prime minister in 1742. However, the king had little choice but to appoint another prime minister who could command a majority vote in Parliament. The cabinet, under a prime minister, had taken over the executive branch of the government, exercising that power through a group of parliamentary leaders who devoted themselves to administration but who had to render account for their conduct of state affairs before Parliament.

The Glorious Revolution and the settlement that followed were a turning point in England's history. Two burning issues had been settled to the satisfaction of most Englishmen. Parliament, representing the landed and moneyed interests, replaced the king as supreme authority. Religious toleration was established for all Protestant sects, thus putting an end to religious uniformity. (Roman Catholics, Unitarians, Jews, and atheists were not given the right to worship freely or to exercise fully their rights as Englishmen.) Although much blood had been spilled deciding these issues, England emerged from her revolution with no deep scars. She had managed to hold her own in competition with other powers, especially France, which at the time enjoyed a more stable political system. In fact, England had raised her prestige and power in world affairs during the seventeenth century and entered the eighteenth even stronger than she had been at the death of Elizabeth in 1603. With her political quarrels settled, she was able to increase her world power rapidly during the next two centuries. Her revolution against absolutism and her new constitutional monarchy were destined to serve as models for other nations ready to discard royal absolutism.

Suggested Reading

General Treatments. The entire period treated in this chapter is dealt with brilliantly by Roger Lockyer, *Tudor and Stuart Britain* (1964). More exciting to read is an older work by **George Macaulay Trevelyan, *England Under the Stuarts* (21st ed., University Paperbacks), deeply sympathetic with the parliamentary cause and anti-Stuart, but filled with valuable insights into the social history of this era. **M. Ashley, *England in the Seventeenth Century* (Penguin), is adequate. **J. F. Kenyon, *The Stuarts* (Wiley), treats the major personalities of the era with deep insight. **Christopher Hill, *The Century of Revolution, 1603–1714* (Norton), interprets the seventeenth century from a Marxist perspective; his account will open new insights into the age, especially in terms of economic forces. The fullest treatment of the Stuart period is provided by successive volumes in the Oxford History of England: G. Davie, *The Early Stuarts, 1603–1660* (2nd ed., 1959), and G. N. Clark, *The Later Stuarts, 1660–1714* (2nd ed., 1955); but these are works that will try the reader's patience. The major constitutional problems of the age are treated by **David L. Keir, *Constitutional History of Modern Britain Since 1485* (Norton); and **J. R. Tanner, *English Constitutional Conflicts of the Seventeenth Century* (Cambridge). A lively treatment of the political concepts that gripped the age is Harold J. Laski, *Political Thought in England From Locke to Bentham* (1920). **Crane Brinton, *An Anatomy of Revolution* (rev. ed., Vintage), provides fresh insight into England's age of revolution by comparing it to the American and French revolutions.

The First Stuarts and the Civil War. **D. H. Willson, *King James VI and I* (Galaxy) is the best biography of an often mistreated figure. A masterful description of the crucial years of Charles I's reign is provided by **C. V. Wedgwood, *The King's Peace, 1637–1641* (Collier), and *The King's War, 1641–1647* (Collier). Two studies covering Charles' reign in detail and from a strongly royalist point of view are Esmé Wingfield-Stratford, *Charles King of England, 1600–1637* (1949), and *King Charles and King Pym, 1637–1643* (1949). A representative selection of views on the hotly disputed issue of the causes of the Civil War is **Philip A. M. Taylor, ed., *The Origins of the English*

Civil War: Conspiracy, Crusade, or Class Conflict? (Heath). **William Haller, *The Rise of Puritanism* (Harper Torchbook), provides a brilliant treatment of the religious forces at work in seventeenth-century England.

The Age of Cromwell. The activities and significance of the intriguing Oliver Cromwell can best be appreciated by reading one or all of these biographies: C. H. Firth, *Oliver Cromwell and the Rule of the Puritans in England* (3rd ed., 1924); **C. V. Wedgwood, *Life of Cromwell* (Collier); S. R. Gardiner, *Oliver Cromwell* (1925); and **Maurice Ashley, *The Greatness of Oliver Cromwell* (Collier). Firth's study is the fullest; Wedgwood's is probably the best. A summary of various views of Cromwell's achievement is provided by **Richard E. Boyer, *Oliver Cromwell and the Puritan Revolution: Failure of a Man or a Faith?* (Heath).

The Restoration, the Glorious Revolution, and the Aftermath. Good surveys of this period are **D. Ogg, *England in the Reign of Charles II* (Oxford), and *William III* (Collier). **George Macaulay Trevelyan, *The English Revolution, 1688–1689* (Galaxy), provides a penetrating account of the political events of 1688–1689. **Gerald Straka, ed., *The Revolution of 1688: Whig Triumph or Palace Revolution?* (Heath), draws together a representative collection of differing interpretations of the Glorious Revolution. **Peter Laslett, *The World We Have Lost* (Scribner), evokes a remarkable picture of English society about 1700. The early chapters of Dorothy Marshall, *Eighteenth-Century England* (1962), provides the best introduction to the immediate post-revolutionary period; also useful is **J. H.

Plumb, *England in the Eighteenth Century, 1714–1815* (Penguin). A great deal about crucial constitutional developments can be gained from John Morley, *Walpole* (1889), and the masterful two-volume work of J. H. Plumb, *Sir Robert Walpole* (2 vols., 1956–61), and *The King's Minister* (1960). But perhaps best of all is the magnificent classic of Thomas Babington Macaulay, *A History of England From the Accession of James II* (many editions; the best is by C. Firth, 6 vols., 1913–15); originally published in 1849–61, this work is one of the great pieces of historical literature in the English language, given flavor by the author's magnificent style and his firm sympathy for limited monarchy and parliamentary government.

Sources. An excellent collection of constitutional documents, including the Petition of Right and the Bill of Rights, is included in Carl Stephenson and Frederick George Marcham, eds., *Sources of English Constitutional History* (1937). A fascinating picture of English life in the Restoration period is provided by **Samuel Pepys, *Diary* (many editions; a good one is Harper Torchbook). **John Locke, *Two Treatises of Government* (many editions; a good one is by T. I. Cook, Hafner), supplies the best statement of the political ideas that inspired the Glorious Revolution. *The Political Works of James I*, ed. C. H. McIlwain (1918), supplies a statement of the absolutist concepts of government behind Stuart rule and against which many Englishmen reacted in the seventeenth century. **John Milton, *Areopagitica: Of Education* (many editions; a good one is by George H. Sabine, Appleton), is a classic argument for free speech by the great seventeenth-century poet.

Chapter 35 ❧ The Rise of Prussia and Russia

The most significant political developments in Central and Eastern Europe during the seventeenth and eighteenth centuries were the rise of Prussia and Russia. At the opening of the seventeenth century, the two chief powers in Central and Eastern Europe were the Ottoman and Hapsburg empires. Although the Muslim Ottoman Turks had been restrained by the Hapsburgs in the sixteenth century on both land and sea, they were about to renew their effort to conquer Christian Europe. The Austrian Hapsburgs, in addition to disputing the control of Southeastern Europe with the Turks, dominated the Holy Roman Empire, which included all the German states. In Northeastern Europe, Sweden, Prussia, Poland, and Russia competed for hegemony. Among all these powers, Prussia and Russia had hitherto been the least conspicuous in world affairs.

1. THE EARLY HOHENZOLLERNS

The history of Prussia is in large measure the history of the Hohenzollern family. This aggressive and prolific dynasty was first heard of in the tenth century. At that time the Hohenzollerns were obscure counts ruling over the castle of Zollern and a tiny bit of surrounding territory in southwest Germany just north of the Swiss border. In the twelfth century they became burgraves of Nuremberg, an important commercial city in Bavaria. Early in the fifteenth century the Holy Roman Emperor, looking for an able ruler for the mark of Brandenburg, a military province near the exposed northeastern border of the empire, chose the head of the house of Hohenzollern. Although its ruler was one of the seven electors of the Holy Roman Emperor, Brandenburg was a bleak and thinly populated little province. Yet around this nucleus the Hohenzollerns built the important state of Prussia, and later the German Empire—the world's most powerful and feared nation.

From the time the Hohenzollerns became margraves of Brandenburg (1415) until they were finally overthrown at the end of World War I in 1918, they followed a threefold policy from which they never veered: militarism and territorial aggrandizement; paternal despotism; and centralized bureaucracy. No state in modern times has been so wedded to militarism as a cardinal feature of national life and policy as that of the Hohenzollerns, and few modern states have been more autocratic in their government.

Early in the seventeenth century Brandenburg began to expand. In 1609 the Hohenzollerns inherited three little provinces in and near the Rhine Valley far to the west, and nine years later they inherited East Prussia, a

---

This illustration from a history of the reign of Frederick the Great shows one of the assets that Frederick developed and used to make Prussia a great power: her trained, disciplined army. Prussian militarism was, from this time on, an element to be reckoned with in European politics. *Photo: The Metropolitan Museum of Art, Harris Brisbane Dick Fund, 1935*

The Growth of Prussia 1417–1807

fief of Poland on the Baltic far to the east. In 1640 Frederick William, the Great Elector, one of the ablest of all the Hohenzollerns, became margrave and began filling in the territorial gaps. His first move was to take Brandenburg out of the Thirty Years' War, which had been devastating the Germanies for the past twenty-two years. While the other adversaries, France, Sweden, the Hapsburgs, and many of the small German states, exhausted themselves in eight more years of struggle, Brandenburg recouped her strength and resources. Reentering the war shortly before its end, she was in a position to demand and get valuable territories. According to the terms of the Treaty of Westphalia (1648), Brandenburg received Eastern Pomerania, a sizable strip of territory that gave her valuable frontage on the Baltic, the large bishopric of Magdeburg, which straddled the Elbe, and several smaller bishoprics. Shortly afterward Frederick William gained the independence of East Prussia from Poland.

The Great Elector centralized and administered the governments of his scattered territories with energy and skill. He protected the native industries, improved communications, and aided agriculture. In a most intolerant

age he followed a policy of religious toleration. When Louis XIV revoked the Edict of Nantes in 1685, Frederick William welcomed thousands of industrious Huguenots to Brandenburg. At the death of the Great Elector in 1688, Brandenburg was on the road to becoming a great power.

The next Hohenzollern, Frederick I (1688–1713), acquired the title of king for the dynasty. The Hapsburg Holy Roman Emperor in 1701 granted Frederick the title in return for aid against Louis XIV in the War of the Spanish Succession. Frederick I chose Prussia rather than Brandenburg for the name of his kingdom, since Prussia was outside the Holy Roman Empire and a free sovereign state. Hence Brandenburg became Prussia.

From 1713 to 1740 Prussia was ruled by a vigorous militaristic autocrat, Frederick William I (since he was the first Frederick William to be king). Unquestioned absolutism, machinelike centralized bureaucratic administration, and above all militarism were his obsessions. He built the Prussian army into the most efficient and one of the largest fighting forces in Europe. And yet Frederick William was so efficient and miserly that he was also

THE CONQUEST OF SILESIA BY 1748

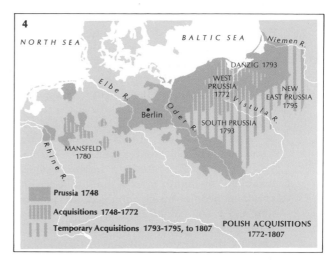

POLISH ACQUISITIONS 1772–1807

able to pass along to his talented son a well-filled treasury.

The talented son, the future Frederick the Great, was a "problem" child. An ardent lover of music, literature, and philosophy, young Frederick hated militarism and governmental details. He even attempted to flee the country to escape the stern discipline of his disgruntled father. Arrested, he was forced to undergo exceptionally rigorous training from the bottom up in the army and the government services. Eventually Frederick became enamored of both, and Frederick William I died happy, sure that the Hohenzollern state would pass into good hands.

2. THE EMERGENCE OF PRUSSIA AS A GREAT POWER UNDER FREDERICK THE GREAT, 1740–1786

In the same year that Frederick II became king of Prussia (1740), the beautiful and gracious young Maria Theresa became archduchess of the Austrian Hapsburg dominions. These dominions included, in addition to the Austrian lands, the Kingdom of Hungary and the triune crown of Bohemia, Moravia, and Silesia. Maria Theresa's father, Emperor

Charles VI, had spent much time in his last years attempting to safeguard his daughter's accession to the Hapsburg throne. He succeeded in obtaining the signatures of virtually every European sovereign, including the king of Prussia, to a document called the Pragmatic Sanction, which guaranteed the integrity of Maria Theresa's crown and territories. Two months after Charles VI died, however, Frederick II, without a declaration of war, marched his troops into and seized Silesia, one of the richest of the Hapsburg provinces. This Machiavellian act of the young Prussian king plunged most of the major European states into a series of wars for the mastery of Central Europe. Bavaria, Saxony, France, and Spain rushed in to despoil Maria Theresa of her territories. Only Great Britain and the Dutch Netherlands took the side of Austria. Great Britain was a bitter rival of France in India and North America, and she was also concerned for the Austrian Netherlands, with which she enjoyed a profitable trade, and for Hanover, whose ruling family now sat on the British throne. The Dutch were fearful of renewed French aggression in their direction.

The War of the Austrian Succession lasted for eight years (1740–1748). Maria Theresa successfully repelled the Bavarians, Saxons, French, and Spaniards, but she was unable to dislodge Frederick II from Silesia. Frederick, on his part, cynically deserted his allies as soon as he had achieved his own purposes. The Treaty of Aix-la-Chapelle in 1748 brought the hostilities to an end. Frederick retained Silesia, and Maria Theresa's husband, Francis of Lorraine, was recognized as Holy Roman Emperor. The only real gainer from the war was Frederick II. Silesia, a fertile province inhabited by more than a million German-speaking people, nearly doubled the population and resources of Prussia.

The Hapsburgs, however, had no intention of being thus despoiled of one of their fairest provinces by the upstart Hohenzollerns. Proud rulers over territories many times the size and population of Prussia and for centuries emperors of the Holy Roman Empire, of which Prussia was but a member state, they viewed the Hohenzollerns with condescension. Maria Theresa's able diplomat, Count Kaunitz, was soon at work lining up allies. Saxony, Sweden, Russia, and even France were won over. Spain, now ruled by the Bourbons, later followed France into the alliance. This time, however, Great Britain took the side of Prussia. She did this in order to oppose her arch-enemy France, with whom she was already at war in India and North America, and to safe-guard Hanover. This double shifting of alliances came to be called the Diplomatic Revolution. Since Great Britain was Prussia's only ally and since her aid was limited to subsidies and to tying down French forces overseas, the opposition was certain of victory over Frederick II. They were already dividing up his territories, leaving him only the little original Hohenzollern province of Brandenburg.

But Frederick was not one to wait for his enemies to strike first. As soon as he became aware of their designs, he opened hostilities by overrunning Saxony. Thus began the Seven Years' War (1756–1763), the bloodiest war in history up to that time. Frederick, with his slender resources, soon found himself at bay; the four greatest military powers on the conti-

nent of Europe were closing in on him from all directions. The Austrians advanced from the south, the Russians from the east, the Swedes from the north, and the French from the west. Hurling his disciplined but ever-dwindling army against first one and then another of his enemies, Frederick held them off for seven years. His lightning marches, tricky maneuvers, and indefatigable tenacity in the face of seemingly hopeless odds won for him the title, "the Great." But after six years the end appeared to be near. His treasury was empty, his manpower exhausted, much of his territory laid waste. The Russians even captured and burned his capital, Berlin. Then suddenly fortune changed. In 1762 the Russian Tsarina Elizabeth, one of his bitterest enemies, died and was succeeded by the weakling Peter III, who was an ardent admirer of Frederick II and who put Russia's forces at the disposal of Prussia. Although Peter III was soon murdered by a group of his own officers and court nobility and Russia withdrew from the war, the remaining allies had no further stomach for the fight. The Peace of Hubertusburg in 1763 left things as they were at the beginning of the war, Prussia retaining the controversial Silesia. In the same year the Treaty of Paris brought to a close the colonial struggle between Great Britain and France in India and North America, leaving Great Britain master of both.

Having so narrowly escaped destruction, Frederick the Great spent the remaining twenty-three years of his life reconstructing his war-ravaged territories. His career as an enlightened despot will be surveyed in Chapter 38. He encouraged agriculture, subsidized and protected industry, and invited immigrants into his well-governed territories. At no time, though, did he neglect his war machine. In 1772 he joined Austria and Russia in the first partition of Poland. Frederick took West Prussia, thus joining East Prussia with the main body of the Prussian state. When Frederick II died in 1786, Prussia had been raised to the status of a great power, sharing equally with Austria the leadership of

Central Europe. During his reign Prussia's size and population had more than doubled, and her military exploits pointed to a spectacular future.

3. RUSSIA BEFORE PETER THE GREAT

While Prussia was becoming a great power in Central Europe, Russia was rising to prominence to the east. The first shaping of some of the Slavic tribes of Eastern Europe into what eventually became the Russian national state was begun by Viking invaders in the ninth century. These intrepid seamen moved out from their Scandinavian homes in all directions—across the Atlantic, into the Mediterranean, and up the rivers of what are now England, France, Germany, and Russia (the word *Russia* is apparently derived from the Swedish word for rower). Their most important commercial and political center in Eastern Europe was Kiev, which became Russia's first capital. Eventually, however, the Norse adopted the Slavic culture of their subjects.

In the tenth century Christianity was brought to Russia by missionaries from Constantinople. This is probably the most significant development in Russian history, for through the influence of the Greek Orthodox Church, whose headquarters were in Constantinople, Russia became a semi-Oriental Byzantine civilization and was cut off from the Greco-Roman and Roman Catholic culture common to the countries of Central and Western Europe. English, Spanish, Polish, and Swedish churchmen were constantly traveling to Rome, where they associated with churchmen from Italy, Hungary, France, and Germany. Russian churchmen, on the other hand, traveled to Constantinople, where they met only Greek, Serbian, Bulgarian, and Rumanian churchmen of the Balkan Peninsula.

Second in importance only to Greek Orthodox Christianity in the infusion of Oriental influence into Russian civilization was the Tartar conquest of the thirteenth century. Around the turn of the thirteenth century the Mongol conqueror Genghis Khan (1162–1227)

had established a vast empire in Eastern Asia. Shortly after his death the Golden Horde, as the Mongol warriors were called, swept westward into Christian Europe. The thirteenth-century Europeans were no match for the Tartars. Russia was easily overrun, and in 1241 a combined German and Polish army was defeated at Liegnitz in the heart of Central Europe. All Christian Europe appeared to be at the mercy of the invaders. At that moment, however, the great khan died in Eastern Asia, and the Tartar commander withdrew his forces to Russia and hastened back to seize his share of the spoils. The Golden Horde never resumed its triumphal surge westward, but for two and a half centuries it inundated Russia. Although there was little mixing of blood between the Mongol Tartars and the Caucasian Russians, there was considerable mixing of cultures. When the Mongol tide finally receded near the end of the fifteenth century, a deposit of such characteristically Oriental traits as backward-looking conservatism, fatalism, female seclusion, and absolutism in government had been added to the Byzantine cultural influence.

During the Tartar occupation the grand dukes of Muscovy managed to ingratiate themselves with their Mongol masters and build up their own influence and power. Moscow replaced Kiev as the political center of Russia. The first of the grand dukes of Muscovy to consider himself to be tsar of Russia was Ivan III (1462–1505). In 1480 Ivan III defeated the rapidly declining Tartars and limited their power in Russia to the southeastern area. Ivan greatly extended his sway both to the north and to the west by military conquest. A momentous event in Ivan III's reign was his marriage to Sophia Palaeologus, heiress to the now-defunct Byzantine (Eastern Roman) Empire. Ivan immediately declared himself successor to the Eastern Roman Caesars—hence the title Tsar. When he died, the foundations of a Russian national state had been laid.

Ivan IV (1533–1584) the Terrible added both to the authority of the Russian tsars and to

The Growth of Russia in the West

Map legend (left): Muscovy in 1462 / Acquisitions 1462–1682

Map legend (right): Russia in 1682 / Acquisitions of Peter the Great, 1682–1725

the territories over which they ruled. He destroyed the remaining power of the Tartars in southeastern Russia and annexed most of their territory. The Ottoman Turks, however, seized the strategic Tartar territory north of the Black Sea. Although Ivan IV established trade relations with England by way of the White Sea and the Arctic Ocean, his efforts to gain a foothold on the Baltic were frustrated by Sweden and Poland. It was during Ivan IV's reign that Russia's conquest of Siberia was begun. Half a century later the Russian flag was planted on the shores of the Pacific.

The twenty-nine years following the death of Ivan IV are known as the Time of Troubles (1584–1613). Weak rulers and disputed successions resulted in such anarchy that the Poles were able to capture Moscow and hold it briefly. To end the political chaos, a group of leading nobles in 1613 chose Michael Romanov as tsar. The Romanov dynasty was to rule Russia until the Communist revolution of

1917. Throughout the seventeenth century, Russia under the early Romanovs slowly but gradually established commercial and cultural contacts with the West. Increasing numbers of traders, craftsmen, and adventurers from Central and Western Europe, particularly Germany, came to Russia to seek their fortunes. Thus the stage was set for Peter the Great at the end of the century to Westernize Russia and make her a first-rate European power.

4. RUSSIA UNDER PETER THE GREAT, 1689–1725

Peter I (1689–1725)[1] was a physical giant full of mental vitality and primitive animal instincts and emotions. At the age of seventeen

---

[1] In 1682 Peter I, at the age of ten, technically became joint ruler with his elder brother, Ivan V, who was mentally incompetent. Until 1689, however, his rule was only nominal, and that date is usually considered to be the beginning of his reign.

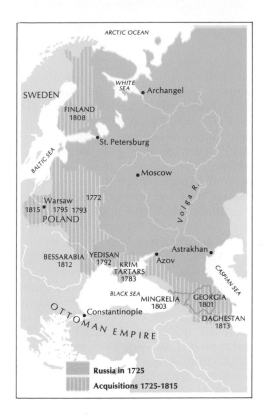

Russia in 1725
Acquisitions 1725-1815

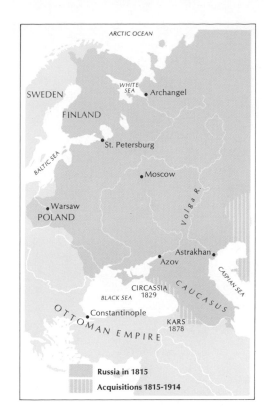

Russia in 1815
Acquisitions 1815-1914

he seized the reins of government from his elder sister, after he had firmly established his control over the government. For the next thirty-six years he devoted his boundless energy to the twofold policy of Westernizing Russia and of gaining windows to the West on the Baltic and Black seas.

During Peter's youth he had come in contact with foreign craftsmen in Moscow and had become enamored of Western technology, particularly shipbuilding. In 1697 the twenty-five-year-old tsar made a grand tour of Western Europe, seeking allies against the Turks and firsthand knowledge of Western ways. He failed to gain any allies, but he learned a great deal about Western customs and techniques, which he proceeded to introduce into Russia. In the Hohenzollern province of East Prussia, Peter studied one of the world's most efficient military organizations; in the Dutch Netherlands, shipbuilding; in England, shipbuilding, commerce, and finance.

On his way to Italy from Vienna he was suddenly called home by the revolt of his bodyguard. Slicing off hundreds of heads by his own hand, he crushed the revolt with a ruthlessness that cowed all potential troublemakers. To make his authority as absolute as that of the most autocratic Western European monarchs, he adopted their bureaucratic system in both central and local government. Western technicians were brought to Russia in large numbers, and new industries were subsidized and protected by mercantilist policies. Western, particularly French, social customs were introduced to the upper and middle classes of Russian society. Women were brought out of seclusion, and the long beards and flowing Oriental robes of the men were banned. These reforms hardly touched the peasant masses, who were increasingly tied down in a system of serfdom bordering on slavery—a process that had been going on in Russia throughout the sixteenth and seven-

With boundless energy and enthusiasm, Peter the Great set about Westernizing Russia and the Russians. Not only were Western institutions to be adopted, but Western attire and appearance as well. In this gently humorous woodcut, Peter is snipping off the beard of an unhappy noble. *Photo: The Bettmann Archive*

teenth centuries. When the patriarch of the Russian Orthodox Church opposed the tsar's authority and some of his Westernizing policies, Peter abolished the patriarchate. He placed at the head of the church a Holy Synod composed of a committee of bishops and presided over by a lay procurator-general, all appointed by the tsar. Henceforth, the Orthodox Church was a powerful instrument of the Russian government. But Peter the Great's

chief concern was always his military establishment. He built a navy and patterned his conscript army after that of Prussia. By the end of his reign, Russia had one of the major fighting forces of Europe.

When Peter became tsar, Russia had no warm water access to the West. Sweden held the coveted shores of the Baltic Sea, and the Ottoman Turks occupied the territory north of the Black Sea. Peter's efforts to dislodge these "natural" enemies were only partly successful. He did manage to seize Azov on the Black Sea from the Turks and hold it for fourteen years, but the Turks were still too strong for the Russians and blocked them off from the Black Sea for another half century. Against Sweden Peter was more successful. In 1697 the fifteen-year-old Charles XII came to the throne of Sweden, which since the reign of Gustavus Adolphus in the early seventeenth century had been the greatest military power in Northern Europe. Hoping to take advantage of Charles XII's youth, Peter formed an alliance with Denmark and Poland for the purpose of despoiling Sweden of valuable territories. Charles, however, proved to be a first-rate military genius. Not waiting for his enemies to ready their plans, he struck first at Denmark and forced her to sue for peace. Marching rapidly into Russia, he crushed a Russian army much larger than his own at Narva. Instead of pursuing the demoralized forces of Peter, however, he turned to Poland, defeated the Polish army, and placed a puppet king on the Polish throne. After spending seven years rearranging the affairs of Poland, Charles, known as the "Madman of the North," at last turned his attention once more to Russia. But Peter had used the seven years of grace to rebuild his forces. He retreated before the advancing Swedes deep into the vast interior of Russia, scorching the earth

Catherine the Great's territorial ambitions are satirized in this cartoon, which shows her leaping toward a coveted goal, Constantinople, as the pope and other European leaders look on in dismay. *Photo: NYPL Picture Collection* behind him. In 1709 the forces of Charles XII, decimated by hunger and disease, were brought to bay and shattered at Poltava, in southern Russia. Charles escaped with a remnant of his army to Turkey, but the military strength of Sweden was spent. Nine years later Charles XII was killed fighting in Norway. By the Treaty of Nystad in 1721, Russia received the Swedish Baltic provinces of Livonia, Estonia, Ingria, and Karelia. On the Neva River near the Baltic Peter built a new modern capital, St. Petersburg, facing the West. At his death in 1725, Russia was a great and growing power ready to play a major role in European affairs.

5. RUSSIA UNDER CATHERINE THE GREAT, 1762–1796

Peter the Great was followed by a succession of weak or mediocre rulers who undid much of his work. After an interval of thirty-seven years, Catherine the Great (1762–1796) ascended the Russian throne. Catherine was an obscure princess from one of the little German states. She had been married for political reasons to young Peter III, grandson of Peter the Great, while he was still heir to the Russian crown. After he became tsar, Peter III, a weakling, quickly alienated all classes of his subjects. The astute Catherine, meanwhile, was becoming a good Russian, popularizing herself with all her people. She was also reading widely from classical and French eighteenth-century authors. Less than a year after her husband became tsar, Catherine conspired with a group of aristocratic army officers, who murdered Peter and declared Catherine tsarina of Russia.

The Machiavellian tsarina prided herself on being an enlightened despot, as was fashionable in the late eighteenth century. She carried on a lively correspondence with Voltaire, D'Alembert, Frederick the Great, and other leading members of the eighteenth-century intelligentsia. She invited Diderot to St. Petersburg and became his friend and patron. She talked learnedly about freedom, education, and reform, and soon after her seizure of the throne, she called a commission to study the question of reforms. All this made good salon talk, but none of it was translated into deeds. No one knew better than Catherine, as she admitted to a confidant, that an enlightened populace would endanger the position of all despots. The desperation of the peasants led to one of the greatest "slave" insurrections in history. Under the able leadership of a Don Cossack, Pugachev, hundreds of thousands of peasants rose against their masters. The rebellion was put down with difficulty. The cruel repression left the Russian serf really a slave.

The chief significance of Catherine the Great in history lies in her aggressive foreign policy. Peter the Great had reached the Baltic by despoiling the Swedes. Catherine reached the Black Sea, the Balkan Peninsula, and the heart of Europe by defeating the Turks and destroying Poland. In two major wars between 1768 and 1792 Catherine defeated the Turks (something that Peter the Great had never been able to do) and seized all of their territory north of the Black Sea as far west as the Dniester River. Russia also gained a vague protectorate over the Christians in the Ottoman Empire, which gave her a standing opportunity to meddle in the internal affairs of the Turks. But Catherine fell short of her real goal, Constantinople. So certain was she of winning the old Byzantine capital on the Bosporus, which the Russian tsars had coveted since the days of Ivan III, that she named her second grandson Constantine. However, turning aside to join Prussia and Austria in the partitioning of the remainder of the Polish state, Catherine died before she could resume her drive on Constantinople. Already in 1772 Russia, Prussia, and Austria had seized strips of Poland. In 1793 Russia and Prussia enlarged their holdings, and in 1795 the three powers divided among themselves the remainder of the once-huge Poland. Catherine's share, which was about two-thirds of the total, brought Russia's western boundary deep into Central Europe. The second and third partitions of Poland and concern over the French Revolution, which began in 1789, absorbed Catherine's energies during the last years of her life. When she finally died in 1796, Russia was a nation ominous in size and power, and a major factor in European and world affairs.

6. THE DISAPPEARANCE OF POLAND AND THE DECLINE OF SWEDEN AND THE OTTOMAN EMPIRE

Poland, at the opening of the eighteenth century, was the third largest country in Europe, exceeded in size only by Russia and Sweden. In the sixteenth and seventeenth centuries it had appeared that she would become a major power. At the beginning of the seventeenth century the Poles had taken advantage of Russia's internal difficulties to capture Moscow. In the latter part of the century they had saved Vienna from the Turks.

Actually, however, the Polish nation was far from strong. Sprawling over a large area between Russia and the German states, she enjoyed no natural boundaries either in the east or the west. The eastern half of her territory was inhabited by Russian-speaking people. Her northern provinces were peopled largely by Latvians, Lithuanians, and Germans. There were also many Germans in the west. Religious cleavages followed the language lines. The Poles themselves were militantly Roman Catholic under strong Jesuit influence. Some of the Russians were Orthodox and some were Uniates (orthodox Christians who recognized the headship of the Roman pope). The Latvians and Germans were mostly Lutherans, as were some of the Lithuanians. In the cities lived many Jews.

Moreover, there was no strong middle class to vitalize Poland's economy. In the Late Middle Ages a flourishing overland commerce between the Black and the Baltic seas had flowed across Poland. But with the shifting of commercial routes and centers to the west in the early sixteenth century, Poland's commerce had withered like that of Italy and the German states. Furthermore, the Polish nobility, jealous of its own power and fearful of an alliance between the bourgeoisie and the king, deliberately penalized commerce with severe restrictions. The great mass of the people were serfs, tilling the soil of the powerful nobility.

In the face of so many divisive forces, only a strong central government could have made Poland a stable national state. But here lay Poland's greatest weakness. The kingship was elective, and the great nobles who held the elective power saw to it that no strong king ever came to the throne to threaten their own position. During the eighteenth century the kings were all foreigners or puppets of foreign powers. The legislative Diet was completely monopolized by the nobility. In order to safeguard each nobleman's rights, unanimity was required for the passage of every measure. This meant that any nobleman could veto any proposed law (*liberum veto*). In addition, any nobleman could disband ("explode") the Diet and cancel all its acts. This system guaranteed virtual political anarchy. National spirit was practically nonexistent. The all-powerful nobles were far more concerned for their own private interests than for the well-being of the nation.

It would have been surprising had such a power vacuum as eighteenth-century Poland

Aging Empires (Holy Roman Empire, Poland, Ottoman Empire) and New Powers (Austria, Prussia, Russian Empire)

not invited the aggression of her ambitious neighbors. In 1772 Catherine the Great and Frederick the Great bargained to take slices of Polish territory. The somewhat less greedy Maria Theresa of Austria, fearful of being outdistanced by Russia and Prussia, joined them, although her slice was beyond the Carpathian Mountains. Russia took a strip occupied by White Russians, and Prussia took West Prussia, joining up East Prussia with Brandenburg. This aggression at long last stirred the Poles to action. Sweeping reforms were passed improving the condition of the peasants and the bourgeoisie and giving the king and the Diet power to act effectively. But it was too late. Russia and Prussia were determined to prevent the emergence of a vigorous Polish nation. In 1793 they marched in and seized additional slices of territory. The Poles, under the leadership of Thaddeus Kosciusko, now flew to arms, although the arms were often only agricultural implements. They were no match for the professional armies of Russia, Prussia, and Austria, who in 1795 divided the remainder of Poland among themselves. Russia's share of Poland, about two-thirds of the total, was inhabited largely by Russian-speaking people. Austria's share was inhabited by Roman Catholics, as was Austria itself. Prussia's share, however, except for part of West Prussia, was inhabited by people who were neither linguistically nor religiously akin to the Prussians and who proved to be a fruitful source for future trouble.

Poland was not the only victim in Eastern Europe of the rise of Prussia and Russia. Sweden and the Ottoman Empire declined, both relatively and actually. Sweden had become the dominant military power in Northern and Eastern Europe under Gustavus Adolphus in the early seventeenth century. At the opening of the eighteenth century she was second only to Russia in size among the nations of Europe, holding large areas east and south of the Baltic in addition to the homeland. However, her population and resources were too small to hold for long such far-flung territories, which were coveted by ambitious and growing Prussia and Russia. Charles XII made a spectacular effort to hold them, but in the end he lost all his trans-Baltic territories except Finland, and dissipated Sweden's strength in so doing. Sweden has never been a major power since.

The Ottoman Turks, after reaching the gates of Vienna early in the sixteenth century and again late in the seventeenth century, weakened rapidly. The Treaty of Karlowitz in 1699 limited their power in Europe to the Balkan Peninsula and a strip of territory north of the Black Sea. Their two serious defeats at the hands of Catherine the Great marked the beginning of the breakup of the Ottoman Empire. By the end of the eighteenth century, the three dominant powers in Central and Eastern Europe were the relatively static Austrian Hapsburg Empire and the two rapidly rising military despotisms—Prussia and Russia.

Suggested Reading

General. The appropriate volumes in the indispensable Rise of Modern Europe series with their excellent bibliographies are **J. B. Wolf, *The Emergence of the Great Powers, 1685–1715;* **P. Roberts, *The Quest for Security, 1715–1740;* **W. L. Dorn, *Competition for Empire, 1740–1763;* and **L. Gershoy, *From Despotism to Revolution, 1763–1789* (all Harper Torchbook).

The Early Hohenzollerns. **S. B. Fay, *The Rise of Brandenburg-Prussia to 1786* (Berkshire) is a brief but excellent survey of the Hohenzollern state to the death of Frederick the Great. A much fuller account is Hajo Holborn, *A History of Modern Germany 1648–1840* (1966), which is the second volume of a three-volume scholarly history of modern Germany. Ferdinand Schevill, *The Great*

Elector (1947) is a good biography of the first great Hohenzollern. The eccentric father of Frederick the Great is soundly portrayed by Robert Ergang, *The Potsdam Führer: Frederick William I of Prussia* (1941).

Prussia Under Frederick the Great. Probably the best all-round biography of Frederick the Great is G. P. Gooch, *Frederick the Great, the Ruler, the Writer, the Man* (1947). Frederick the Great's military prowess in the Seven Years' War is emphasized and soundly presented by W. F. Reddaway, *Frederick the Great and the Rise of Prussia* (1904). The best biography of Frederick's chief adversary, Maria Theresa of Austria, is still J. F. Bright, *Maria Theresa* (1897).

Russia to the Death of Peter the Great. The best general survey of the history of Russia before 1917 is M. T. Florinsky, *Russia: A History and an Interpretation* (2 vols., 1953). G. P. Fedotov, *The Russian Religious Mind* (1946), analyzes the impact of Christianity upon earlier Russian paganism. A sound biography of the ruler Ivan III is J. Fennell, *Ivan the Great of Moscow* (1961). Probably the best biography of Peter the Great is **V. Klyuchevsky, *Peter the Great* (Vintage). Briefer but also excellent is **B. H. Sumner, *Peter the Great and the Emergence of Russia* (Collier).

Russia Under Catherine the Great. A brief but scholarly treatment of Russian expansion in the latter part of the eighteenth century is **G. S. Thomson, *Catherine the Great and the Expansion of Russia* (Collier). Still the best biography of Catherine the Great is Kasimierz Walizewski, *The Romance of an Empress* (1894). A recent scholarly treatment of one of the major aspects of Russian history that constituted a critical problem during the reign of Catherine the Great is Jerome Blum, *Lord and Peasant in Russia From the Ninth to the Nineteenth Century* (1961).

Disappearance of Poland and Decline of Sweden and the Ottoman Empire. Two good histories of Poland that cover the eighteenth-century partition are **O. Halecki, *A History of Poland* (rev. ed., 1956); and W. F. Reddaway *et al.*, eds., *Cambridge History of Poland* (2 vols., 1941–1950). The best biography of Charles XII, during whose spectacular but disastrous reign Sweden began to decline, is J. A. Gade, *Charles the Twelfth* (1916). A brief but sound account of the decline of the Ottoman Empire in Eastern Europe during the eighteenth century may be found in L. S. Stavrianos, *The Balkans Since 1453* (1958).

Chapter 36 ❧ Overseas Colonization and
Competition for Empire

During the age of royal absolutism, the European nations increased and intensified their competition for overseas possessions and commerce. Whereas Spain and Portugal had led the way beyond the Atlantic frontier during the sixteenth century, England, France, and the Netherlands threw themselves vigorously into colonizing and commercial expansion in various quarters of the globe during the seventeenth and eighteenth centuries. The newcomers indeed outstripped their older rivals and established themselves as the leading European imperial powers. As large as the world beyond Western Europe was, the competition for it led to struggles among the leading European powers; the outcome of these struggles decisively affected the power relationships among the competing nations. And while the Europeans colonized, traded, and competed around the globe, European civilization spread with them. The seventeenth and eighteenth centuries marked a decisive turning point in the establishment of Western European domination over much of the world.

1. THE NEW WORLD: THE ENGLISH

One of the areas attracting the English, French, and Dutch was the New World, where all three nations established thriving colonies during the seventeenth century and eventually became embroiled in bitter rivalry for dominance. The Northern European nations certainly had their appetites whetted by the vast profits reaped from the New World by the Spanish and the Portuguese during the sixteenth century. These two powers retained their vast empires in Central and South America during the seventeenth and eighteenth centuries and continued to earn a rich reward from their enterprises. But the days of vast gold and silver hauls were over, and the Spanish and Portuguese turned their energies toward creating large plantations worked by oppressed natives and imported slaves to produce products marketable in Western Europe. Their presence in South and Central America turned the attention of the English, French, and Dutch toward North America and the Caribbean area. Into this vast region the

The arrival of the colonists in Virginia, where the first successful English colony was established, is shown here in an illustration to the diary of Thomas Harriot, one of the colonists. Note Roanoke Island in the left foreground. The text on the same page begins, "The sea coasts of Virginia arre full of ilands, wehr by the entrance into the mayne land is hard to finde. . . ." *Photo: Rare Book Division, New York Public Library, Astor, Lenox, and Tilden Foundations*

Northern Europeans came in considerable numbers, pushed aside the native Indians, and turned extensive parts of North America into an annex of Europe.

The English were the most successful colonizers in North America. England had shown increasing interest in the New World throughout the sixteenth century, but had been curbed by Spanish strength. That barrier was removed in 1588 with the destruction of the Spanish Armada, and England soon capitalized on her opportunity. The first English colony was established at Jamestown, Virginia, in 1607 by a joint stock company chartered by James I. After a period of great difficulty, the Virginia colony took root and great rapidly. It attracted a large population and produced a good return economically, though the return was increasingly based on a tobacco economy in which imported African slaves played an important role. In the meantime, a small group of Puritans, inspired by a quest for religious freedom and increasingly disenchanted with the idea of finding it in Stuart England, had on their own authority planted a colony at Plymouth in 1620, drawing up their own "constitution" in the form of the Mayflower Compact and battling magnificently against the harsh environment.

The Plymouth Colony was soon overshadowed by the colonization undertaken by another joint stock company, the Massachusetts Bay Company, controlled largely by Puritans. In 1626 the company established a colony in Salem; soon thereafter Boston was established and became the headquarters of the company, which moved from England. A steady stream of emigrants moved to Massachusetts in the following years. Several new colonizing ventures were undertaken by the company from its American headquarters. In 1636 a group migrated to Connecticut, soon to be followed by others, most of whom resented the strong-handed tactics of the governors of the Massachusetts Bay Company. In 1636 Roger Williams led a group to Rhode Island in hopes of escaping the religious dictates of the Puritan masters of Massachusetts, who liked Williams and his ideas on tolerance even less than he liked them. Both Connecticut and Rhode Island were eventually recognized as independent colonies. Other settlements were established in New Hampshire and Maine, although these did not become independent colonies.

Other colonies were established by proprietors, that is, persons to whom the English king gave large grants of land. Maryland was established in 1632 through the efforts of Lord Baltimore, who tried to make his colony a refuge for Catholics. In 1663 eight English gentlemen were given proprietary rights over Carolina, and two centers of colonization were established shortly thereafter. In 1664 the English captured the Dutch colony of New Netherland, whereupon Charles II made his brother, the duke of York, its proprietor. Thus New York came into existence as an English colony. In 1681 William Penn received a grant from which grew the colony of Pennsylvania, where Penn hoped Quakers would find refuge. New Jersey and Delaware grew out of grants to various other proprietors. When in 1733 a colony was established in Georgia, England controlled the Atlantic seaboard from Maine to the Spanish colony in Florida. Her seaboard colonies, established under a variety of circumstances, very quickly began to enjoy a considerable independence that permitted them to take advantage of local circumstances and to develop a stable, prosperous order which showed remarkable potential for growth.

The English were also active elsewhere in the Western Hemisphere. English explorers and traders, seeking to establish a profitable trade in furs, penetrated into the Hudson Bay area in Canada. Flourishing colonies were established in the West Indies, the chief ones being Barbados, Jamaica, and Bermuda. In this area the English concentrated on developing highly profitable sugar plantations utilizing Negro slaves as a labor supply. At first, these Carribean colonies probably appeared more valuable than did the seaboard colonies to the north.

The new environment, the mixing of peoples, experimentation in government, different economic conditions, and numerous other factors combined to make it impossible for the English colonists to re-create the English way of life on this "frontier." Eventually this situation was to cause England trouble, but for a century and a half her colonial subjects remained loyal Englishmen, and her New World colonies supplied valuable wealth for the benefit of the mother country.

2. THE NEW WORLD: THE FRENCH AND THE DUTCH

Although no less interested and ambitious, France was not so successful as England in colonizing North America. Her first American colony was established by Samuel de Champlain at Quebec on the St. Lawrence River in 1608, only a year after the founding of Jamestown. Although Champlain explored the whole St. Lawrence Valley to the Great Lakes, settlers were slow to come from France to live in Canada. Most of those who did leave France preferred to settle in the West Indies, where France had also established colonies. Not until the reign of Louis XIV did the French turn to a more vigorous policy. Colbert, Louis's economic minister, put all of New France under royal administration and sent the Comte de Frontenac off to the New World as governor. Frontenac exerted every effort to increase France's possessions. During the last quarter of the seventeenth century, explorers and missionaries such as La Salle, Joliet, and Marquette explored the Mississippi Valley, allowing France to claim a huge territory, called Louisiana, which stretched from the Great Lakes to the Gulf of Mexico and included extensive lands on either side of the Mississippi. Territorially, the French holdings in North America were much larger than those of the English.

Efforts to attract settlers to this rich territory were unsuccessful. Although the population grew after about 1675, New France remained badly underpopulated. France closed her empire to non-Catholics, thus excluding the element that had been so important in populating England's colonies—the religiously dissatisfied. The French government, by making extensive grants to aristocrats, made it difficult for the lower classes to get land overseas. The excellent trading opportunities in the fur business attracted more attention than the less profitable pursuit of agriculture. French settlements were thus few and far between in the territory stretching from New Orleans to the mouth of the St. Lawrence. When England seized France's American empire in 1763, perhaps no more than eighty thousand people lived in New France, and most of these were in the St. Lawrence Valley.

Even this sparse population left its mark. The Roman Catholic Church was established firmly in New France. Missionaries were active converting the Indians. The French language was spoken everywhere. Larger communities, such as Quebec and New Orleans, imitated the ways of French society. Even today the influence of these early French colonists can be seen along the St. Lawrence Valley and in Louisiana.

The Dutch attempted to join the other powers in colonizing the North American wilds. In 1621 the Dutch West India Company was chartered to undertake colonization and commerce in the New World. In 1624 a colony was planted on Manhattan Island. Soon other Dutch communities were established in the Hudson Valley and on the Connecticut and Delaware rivers. The Dutch enjoyed only limited success, since Dutch interest and effort were concentrated chiefly on the more profitable East Indies. And in 1664 the English seized New Netherland during a war with the Dutch, ending Dutch colonization in North America.

3. EUROPEAN PENETRATION OF THE FAR EAST

The nations that colonized North America in the seventeenth and eighteenth centuries—England, France, and the Netherlands—were equally aggressive in the Far East. Portugal had established her supremacy there in the sixteenth century, building a commercial empire based upon control of a few key ports. Spain had sought to enter the Far East, but had not progressed beyond the Philippines.

By 1600 Portugal had begun to lose her dominant position. Conquered by Spain in 1580 and held for sixty years, she was unable to protect her empire. The enterprising Dutch, who were successfully freeing themselves from Spanish control, were the chief beneficiaries. Early in the seventeenth century all the competing Dutch companies interested in Far Eastern trade were joined into a single Dutch East India Company, to which the Dutch government gave almost complete freedom of action. The company soon drove the Portuguese out of the Spice Islands, which became the center of the Dutch Empire. In 1641 Malacca on the Malay Peninsula was seized, giving the Dutch control of the seas around the East Indies. Ceylon and the Celebes were captured. The English tried to seize a share of this rich area, but were driven out by the Dutch as early as 1623. To safeguard the sea route to the Indies, the Dutch established a colony at the Cape of Good Hope in South Africa. To watch its interest in the Indies, the Dutch East India Company established a governor-general in Java, who in turn set up several other governmental centers in the island empire.

For years after, the Dutch continued to profit from their holdings in the Indies. They demonstrated remarkable skill in utilizing the native agricultural economy to produce commodities such as spices that were in great demand in Western Europe. Consequently, their presence disturbed very little the existing patterns of life in the area. The Dutch also made attempts to penetrate China and Japan, but both countries refused to deal with them and were too strong to permit entrance by force.

The English, although shut out of the East Indies by the Dutch, made rapid progress toward replacing the Portuguese in India. The English East India Company was chartered in 1600 and given a monopoly of English trade in the East. This company concentrated chiefly on India, slowly forcing the Portuguese to let English traders into that rich land. The company founded its own "factories" (trading posts) at key locations—Surat, Madras, Bombay, and Calcutta. For a long time the East India Company was content to exploit the trading opportunities available in these cities; the merchants interfered little with Indian affairs and had little influence on Indian society.

Rather belatedly, the French entered the competition in the Far East. Again it took the farsighted Colbert to see what France was missing. He organized a French East India Company (1664), which soon established a French outpost at Pondicherry in India. From this center the French company built up a prosperous trade that returned large profits.

When one has seen how various European powers established trading depots in the seacoast cities of India and the East Indies, one knows almost the whole story of European penetration of the Far East during the seventeenth and eighteenth centuries. Except in the Philippines, the existing patterns of life were barely disturbed by the arrival of the Europeans. In contrast with the New World, most areas of the East were not rapidly Europeanized. Few Europeans went as colonists. An explanation for this contrast is not hard to discover. In the Far East the Europeans encountered ancient cultures, solidly founded and not inferior to that of Western Europe. A brief discussion of Indian civilization will illustrate why Europeans had to conduct themselves differently in the East than in the Americas and why European influence penetrated the Far East only slowly.

4. INDIAN CIVILIZATION

When the Europeans first began their penetration of India, they were confronted by a situation rare in her long history: the presence of a unified political system embracing the entire subcontinent. Political unity had been imposed by the Moguls, a branch of the Mongol horde of Tamerlane that had begun to penetrate India about 1500. By the reign of Akbar (1556–1605), the Moguls had subdued most of the petty principalities into which India had long been divided. Muslim by faith and the bearers of a foreign culture, the Mogul emperors held their power throughout the seventeenth century chiefly because of their tolerant attitude toward native Indian civilization. But their success represented a relatively rare episode in Indian history. Since the beginnings of Indian civilization in the third millennium B.C., foreign invaders had repeatedly tried to unite the peninsula, only to be frustrated by the racial, linguistic, and geographical barriers that fragmented this vast and populous land. For long stretches of time, Indian political life was dominated by numerous petty princes. A tradition of strong political organization was therefore not a decisive element in Indian civilization. Its strength lay elsewhere, in institutions and beliefs that were affected very little by the presence of outsiders, including Europeans.

Indian society in the sixteenth and seventeenth centuries gained its cohesion primarily from three interrelated and very ancient institutions—the village, the family, and the caste system. With the exception of a small minority of the population living in the coastal cities, the great mass of Indians lived in self-sufficient agricultural villages under the authority of the Brahmins (priests), whose role we will examine in a moment. Each village was made up of several families. Every family was a tightly knit unit held together by blood ties, common ownership and

exploitation of the land, and religion. Each village had its own government, amazingly democratic in its operation. The villages sometimes had to pay taxes to a faraway central authority, but seldom did that authority significantly influence the course of village life.

Even more fundamental in the life of each Indian was the caste system. Its origins were ancient and are still poorly understood. Long before the beginning of the Christian era, Indian society had been stratified into groups, each with its own customs, responsibilities,

The flowering of Indian civilization under the Mogul emperors is revealed in splendid architectural monuments such as the Taj Mahal, in glorious poetry, and in exquisite painted miniatures such as this one, which shows the emperor Akbar on a hunt. *Photo: The Victoria and Albert Museum, London*

and rights. The system steadily became more complicated and more rigid. In ancient times there were four broad castes: the priests, the aristocratic warriors, the small landowners and artisans, and the laborers. The untouchables were those having no caste. As the centuries passed, numerous subgroups were created within each broad caste, and the rules regulating the conduct of each group became constantly more elaborate. By the time Europeans became acquainted with Indian society, there were hundreds of caste groups. Almost every occupational group in India constituted a special caste. Elaborate rules defining every detail of life within the caste and of relationships with other groups had been evolved. A member of a caste had his life clearly cut out for him from birth. Education, marriage, occupation, manners, dress, and nearly everything else were clearly defined. Obviously, this institution gave the individual little freedom, but just as obviously it provided him with a definite place in society and established a remarkably stable and unchanging social order.

The strength of the Indian caste system lay in the religious sanctions that stood behind it; every Indian accepted the system that bound him to his present lot because he believed that that system was the earthly embodiment of the divine order of the universe. More than anything else, religion gave Indian civilization its distinctive qualities and made most Indians immune to Western influences.

That religious system was already ancient when the Europeans first began settling in India. Several religious traditions, some dating back to the beginnings of Indian civilization, had merged to create the main body of Indian religious thought. By 500 B.C. a basic set of assumptions had been clearly formulated by religious and philosophical leaders and set down in a body of philosophical literature called the Upanishads. From the Upanishads later developed the chief religious systems of India (except Mohammedanism, which entered India from the outside). A brief description of the basic ideas contained in the Upanishads is the best starting place for an understanding of Indian religion.

The ancient Indian thinkers agreed that the universe is permeated by a spiritual force that creates and animates everything. This spiritual force is the only thing that is real. The world that man sees and experiences is merely an illusion, representing the spirit entrapped in material things. The destiny of spirits born to the flesh is to escape back to the perfect world of pure spirit.

At a certain stage on their way to perfection spirits are born into the material world. Once made flesh, spirits become excessively attached to earthly existence, piling up a record of activities not befitting a pure spirit. This record must be atoned for before a spirit achieves its ultimate perfection. When death parts the spirit from its earthly prison, the soul carries its record with it. Therefore, the spirit must be reincarnated in some earthly form to continue its purification. The form that rebirth takes depends on the record of a spirit's previous activities; forces beyond man's control assign him to a status in this world and demand that he keep that status. Rebirth may occur many times, each time putting the spirit in a different shape and presenting it with new tests. Eventually the spirit will end its dependence on the material world and be freed from reincarnation. Toward that perfect state all things are destined.

Hinduism was by far the most significant religion that grew out of the concepts discussed above. The great spiritual force, which the philosophers said directed the universe, became gods. Most Hindus worship many gods, although three predominate: Brahma the Creator, Vishnu the Preserver, and Siva the Destroyer. No matter how many different gods are worshiped, the Hindu believes they are all part of a single spiritual order and thus in no sense competitive. To honor these gods, an elaborate set of rituals has developed over the centuries, chiefly under the guidance of the Brahmins, or priests, who play a leading role in Indian society because they are necessary to approach the gods in the proper way.

Hindus take literally the idea that a part of the divine spirit dwells in every creature. This has led to the development of a complicated list of prohibitions against killing and eating animals, doing violence to other men, and mistreating one's own body. Since detachment from the world is a way of freeing the spirit, Hindus are strongly ascetic, often withdrawing from daily life for fasting, prayer, and chastisement of the flesh. All Hindus believe in reincarnation, and consider the caste system to be the earthly form of this truth. Each caste is a kind of religious order representing a stage into which spirits are born on the path to perfection. It becomes every Hindu's religious duty to accept his caste and fulfill all the obligations attached to it. In the ascending structure of the caste system, each grade represents a step nearer to spiritual perfection and liberation from the material world. The untouchable is the least pure of all humans and must suffer burdens equal to his impurity. The Brahmin at the top of the caste system is nearest to perfection and is about to end the cycle of rebirth, a status that gives Brahmins the wisdom to control earthly society. The orthodox Hindu therefore accepts the established social system in India as a vital part of his religion and feels that to change it would be to tamper with the divine order.

Hinduism places a heavy emphasis on acceptance of one's lot and upon close observation of all the rituals and laws connected with one's earthly station. The good Hindu believes, worships, observes the law, and waits until repeated reincarnation delivers him. It is one of the most formalistic religions in the world.

However, the powerful stream of Indian religious life did not confine itself to that one channel. Buddhism, for example, illustrates how the basic set of beliefs which we have just noted could produce a different religion. Buddhism drew its original inspiration from the teachings of Gautama Buddha (ca. 563–483 B.C.). Buddha, the son of a prince, was well educated in the philosophical ideas of the Upanishads. Rejecting his princely heritage to become a religious leader, Buddha preached a doctrine according to which men freed themselves from the suffering of this world by moral activity. He believed that all suffering was caused by the desire for things that did not befit human beings. To help men free themselves from such desires, Buddha laid down an enlightened moral code, called the Eightfold Path, which stressed love of others, good works, and rejection of sensual pleasures. By following this code Buddha felt that a man could help himself along the road to spiritual freedom. Buddha did not reject reincarnation; he taught merely that a morally strong man could speed up his own deliverance.

Buddha's teachings, originally an ethical protest against Hindu religious practices, were soon turned into a religion. His disciples, organizing themselves into monastic groups, turned Buddha into a god, began worshipping his statues, and devised rituals to give expression to his teachings. The new religion took deep roots in India and flourished for many centuries. Eventually it fell into decline and by 1500 virtually disappeared there. In part this was due to the fact that several foreign invaders of India were converts to Buddhism, causing it to gain a reputation as a foreign religion. However, before it died in India, Buddhism had gained a foothold abroad, especially in China. In its new home it flourished and spread, until today it is one of the major religions of the world, practiced nearly everywhere in the Far East except India. Buddhism left its mark on India despite its disappearance there. Its moral earnestness, its explanation of suffering, and its denial of this world all became part of the Indian religious tradition.

Indian religion accounted for many things

about the civilization that the Europeans met in India in the early modern period. Indians were inclined to accept this world passively, feeling that the individual's destiny lay elsewhere. Progress, competition for wealth, and the search for new things were not attractive to them. The good Indian took what life gave him reverently and humbly. He was not impressed by the Europeans, for he was convinced that he had reflected as keenly and deeply as they about human problems and had arrived at answers superior to theirs. He could point to a remarkable art and literature to prove (to his own satisfaction, at least) the superiority of his way of life. Nothing the European could bring him would, in his mind, improve upon his institutions and ideas. He therefore refused to be agitated by the advent of the Europeans. They, in turn, found that a few hundred soldiers and a few cannon could not shake the Indian's confidence in his village and family life, his caste system, and his religion. Only slowly and almost imperceptibly did the European way of life make any significant impression on the East.

5. THE STRUGGLE FOR OVERSEAS EMPIRE

In spite of nearly empty continents to occupy in the New World and rich trading opportunities to exploit in the highly civilized East, the aggressive European nations could not keep out of one another's way in their overseas expansion. In the sixteenth century the competition had begun with Dutch and English assaults on the Spanish and Portuguese empires. By the end of the seventeenth century the struggle for overseas empires had entered a critical phase and progressed rapidly toward a decision in the eighteenth.

This struggle did not arise because the world overseas had become too crowded with Europeans. As mercantilists, the colonial and commercial powers of the eighteenth century believed that their wealth and self-sufficiency depended on absolute control of territories overseas and that they could strike a mortal blow at their European foes by depriving them of their colonies. Every European war was, therefore, extended overseas, and every major settlement of a European war included a redistribution of overseas possessions.

The Dutch were the first to engage in serious competition with other European powers. As we have previously noted, they began to dismember the Portuguese Empire in the Far East in the sixteenth century. England soon followed the Dutch lead. Although her attacks on the Spanish Empire in the New World were not especially profitable, England did succeed in seizing most of Portugal's Indian holdings during the seventeenth century.

By the middle of the seventeenth century, the rivalry between the English and the Dutch began to increase. As early as 1651 England passed her first Navigation Act, providing that all goods coming to and from England and her overseas possessions would be carried in English ships. This struck a blow at Dutch commercial power, which concentrated on providing shipping services for other nations. It also encouraged the growth of the English navy, badly neglected by the first two Stuart kings. On three different occasions between 1651 and 1688 England engaged the Dutch in warfare. In general, these wars were not decisive. England did annex New Netherland in 1664, but gave the Dutch territory elsewhere. Probably the chief result of the wars was to add to the growing strength of the English navy. Eventually the English and the Dutch began to see that France was the chief danger to both. The result was an alliance in 1689, when William of Orange became king of England. By that time the Netherlands was no longer the major sea power in Europe. The Dutch were content to keep their already-established holdings, letting the other nations compete for the rest of the world.

The Dutch and the English had real cause for alarm. Louis XIV threw France wholeheartedly into the competition for overseas possessions in Canada, Louisiana, the West Indies, and India—all areas near to England's centers of operation. From 1689 until 1763

This engraving shows ships being built in Europe by the Dutch East India Company for use in the great competition for world trade and overseas possessions in which the English, the French, and the Dutch were engaged in the sixteenth and seventeenth centuries.
Photo: Historical Pictures Service, Chicago

England and France fought each other regularly in Europe, and each engagement had its repercussions abroad.

Several times during the War of the League of Augsburg (1688–1697), the English and the French engaged forces in North America, where the war was called King William's War. Neither in Europe nor in America was the action decisive, and no changes were made in the holdings of either combatant. England had more success during the War of the Spanish Succession (1702–1713). In North America, where the struggle was called Queen Anne's War, England captured Arcadia (Nova Scotia) and received recognition of her claims to Newfoundland and Hudson Bay. From France's ally, Spain, she received Gibraltar and Minorca, assuring her entrance into the Mediterranean. Spain also granted to England the right to supply Spain's colonies with slaves (the *asiento*) and the privilege of sending one ship a year to the Spanish colonies in America. These concessions ended Spain's long effort to close her empire to outsiders and gave England the advantage over other nations in exploiting Spanish overseas holdings.

From 1713 to 1740 England and France remained at peace. During this calm neither nation was idle in overseas matters. France,

The World in 1763

Map labels:

ALASKA, GREENLAND, ICELAND, SWEDEN, RUSSIA, Tobolsk, Tomsk, Irkutsk, Yakutsk

HUDSON'S BAY, GREAT BRITAIN, DEN., NETHERLANDS, H.R.E. POLAND, FRANCE, AUST. HUNG., ASIA, JAPAN

NORTH AMERICA, QUEBEC, Louisburg, Ft. Duquesne, PORTUGAL, SPAIN, PERSIA, CHINA, Canton, PAC OCE

FLORIDA (Britain, 1763-1783), MEXICO, ATLANTIC OCEAN, BENGAL (Britain), INDIA, PHILI (S

PACIFIC OCEAN, Dakar (France), GUINEA, AFRICA, CEYLON (Dutch)

GUIANA (Dutch & French), ASCENSION (Britain), ST. HELENA (Britain), INDIAN OCEAN, DUTCH EAST INDIES

PERU, SOUTH AMERICA, EUROPEAN SLAVE TRADING STATIONS, REUNION (France), MAURITIUS (France), Cape Town (Dutch)

Legend:
- Spanish Empire
- Portuguese Empire
- French Empire
- British Empire
- Dutch Empire
- Ottoman Empire
- Russian Empire

WEST INDIA
CUBA (Spain), SANTO DOMINGO (France), HISPANIOLA (Spain), PUERTO RICO (Spain), JAMAICA (Britain), GUADALOUPE (France), MARTINIQUE (France), CARIBBEAN SEA, CURAÇAO (Dutch), BARBADOS (Britain), TRINIDAD (Britain), VENEZUELA (Spain)

EAST INDIA
Sutlej R., HIMALAYAS, Brahmaputra R., Ganges R., Delhi, Agra, Plassey, Chandernagor (France), Calcutta (Britain), Bombay (Britain), INDIA, Hyderabad, BAY OF BENGAL, Goa (Portugal), Madras (Britain), ARABIAN SEA, CARNATIC, Pondicherry (France), CEYLON (Dutch), British Sphere, 1763

realizing the weakness of her position, was especially active in North America. She tried to protect her holdings from English sea power by building a strong fort at Louisburg at the mouth of the St. Lawrence. She also began constructing a series of forts designed to keep the English colonists pinned to the Atlantic seaboard. England concentrated her efforts on widening the commercial breach she had made in Spain's empire in 1713. A new European war in 1740, the War of the Austrian Succession, led to a sharp conflict between England and France in America (King George's War) and in India. At the end of the war in 1748 each power restored its spoils to the other, England giving up Louisburg and France restoring Madras.

An eight-year truce ensued in Europe, each side preparing desperately for the struggle that everyone knew would soon reopen. In North America, France went back to her policy of building a barrier against the westward expansion of the English colonies. Already the colonists were pushing across the Appalachians into the Ohio Valley, claiming the territory as part of their original grants from the English crown. The inevitable clash came in 1755, when the British tried to stop the French from occupying Fort Duquesne at the present site of Pittsburgh. The issue was clearly joined; one power must destroy the other in America.

In India a no less dramatic struggle was shaping. France had entered the scene later than England but had made steady progress up to 1740. Growing English sea power then made France's position precarious. To offset this disadvantage, the French governor of Pondicherry, François Dupleix, decided to take advantage of the internal chaos in India resulting from the decline of Mogul authority. In return for concessions favorable to France, he supplied troops and made promises to whatever political faction in India gave him the best advantage. The policy netted France a claim to most of southern India. Dupleix soon found his match in a lowly clerk of the British East India Company named Robert Clive, who began to fight fire with fire. Spending money liberally and making even greater promises to the Indians, Clive built a counteralliance of Indian princes and wrung generous concessions from them for his company. Soon an undeclared war was on in India. Dupleix was recalled to France in 1754, chiefly because his company did not trust his high-handed methods. The showdown began in 1756, when an Indian prince attacked the British garrison in Calcutta. Having captured the garrison, the prince put 146 Englishmen into a tiny cell; by the next morning 123 were dead in this "Black Hole" of Calcutta. Clive decided to avenge this atrocity.

Thus, at the opening of the Seven Years' War (French and Indian War in America) in 1756 France and England were pitted against each other on three continents. We have previously examined the course of that war in Europe (see Chapter 35). England, led by William Pitt, threw her chief efforts into the naval and colonial war and won a smashing victory. In North America the French held their own until 1757. The superior British forces, supported by the navy, overpowered the French outposts one by one. The decisive blow came, in 1759, when the British captured Quebec, opening all Canada to the British. British naval units captured the chief French holdings in the West Indies. In India, Robert Clive gave the British as great a victory as

Quebec. Using his military resources brilliantly and gaining invaluable help from the navy, he smashed France's Indian allies and captured her trading centers. When Pondicherry fell in 1761, France was ruined in India. Perhaps even more important, Clive had added large territories to England's sphere of influence by conquering several native Indian states.

The Seven Years' War ended in 1763 with the Treaty of Paris. France surrendered Canada and all Louisiana east of the Mississippi (except New Orleans) to England. Spain, who had been an ally of France, ceded Florida to England. By a special treaty France compensated Spain for this loss by giving her the rest of Louisiana (west of the Mississippi). All French possessions in the West Indies except Guadeloupe and Martinique also fell to England. France's empire in India likewise went to Britain. The French were permitted to enjoy trading privileges in India and to keep Pondicherry, but Britain controlled the chief centers of trade, ending any hope of a French recovery of power there.

The Treaty of Paris closed an era in European expansion. Although the Dutch and the Spanish still had extensive holdings abroad, Great Britain had fought her way to supremacy in colonial and commercial affairs. She could now turn to the exploitation of her empire.

Since Columbus' voyage the Europeans had wrought an important change around the world. Energetic colonizers had planted European civilization on the soil of the New World. Enterprising merchants had begun to tap the wealth of a considerable part of the East. European history never again ceased to have a world-wide scope.

Suggested Reading

Overseas Colonization. The best general treatment of the colonizing effort of the European nations is **J. H. Parry, *The Establishment of the European Hegemony, 1415–1715: Trade and Exploration in the Age of the Renaissance* (Harper Torchbook). To understand the concepts that motivated Europe's outward thrust, a student must comprehend the nature of mercantilism; for a definitive treatment of this subject, see E. Heckscher, *Mercantilism* (rev. ed., 2 vols., 1955). H. E. Bolton and T. M. Marshall, *The Colonization of North America, 1492–1783* (1924), provides a thorough study of the colonizing efforts of the European powers in North America. A splendid description of the Spanish role in the New World is **C. H. Haring, *The Spanish Empire in America* (Harbinger). W. B. Willcox, *Star of Empire: A Study of Britain as a World Power, 1485–1945* (1950), is a well-written, balanced account of British imperialism. A good study of the British in India is P. E. Roberts, *History of British India* (3rd ed., 1952). H. B. Priestley, *France Overseas Through the Old Regime* (1939), is a thorough, although rather dry description of France's imperial activity. The Dutch overseas empire in the Far East is discussed in A. Hyma, *A History of the Dutch in the Far East* (1953); and in J. J. van Klaveren, *The Dutch Colonial System in the East Indies* (1953). An illuminating effort to put the expansion of Europe into a larger historical context is provided by **W. H. McNeill, *The Rise of the West* (Mentor).

Non-European Cultures and the Europeans. In order to better comprehend the impact made by the Europeans on the world in the early modern period, the student should take time at this point to absorb some of the history of the major non-European cultures which the Westerners encountered in the sixteenth, seventeenth, and eighteenth centuries. Such understanding can only be achieved by studying the long histories that shaped these cultures; some of them had origins more ancient than those of the Western Europeans. A sympathetic introduction to the Far Eastern civilizations can be found in the appropriate sections of Will Durant, *Our Oriental Heritage* (1935). More substantial is the work of one of the great American authorities on the Far East, K. S. Latourette, *A Short History of the Far East* (4th ed., 1964). A longer general survey by a renowned scholar is René Grousset, *The Civilization of the East* (4 vols., 1931–34); this work is enhanced by excellent illustrations. A brief history of India is provided by W. H. Moreland and A. C. Chatterjee, *A Short History of India* (4th ed., 1957). Fuller in details are R. C. Majumdar, H. C. Raychaudhuri, and K. K. Datta, *An Advanced History of India* (2nd ed., 1961); and **R. Thapar and Percival Spear, *A History of India* (2 vols., Pelican); both have excellent bibliographies. **H. G. Rawlinson, *India: A Short Cultural History* (Praeger), and R. Mukerjee, *The Culture and Art of India* (1959), will provide useful introductions to India's rich intellectual and artistic history. A good treatment of the complex problem of the caste system is J. H. Hutton, *Caste in India: Its Nature, Functions, and Origins* (4th ed., 1963). **K. M. Sen, *Hinduism* (Penguin), is a standard work on one of India's main religions, while **C. Humphreys, *Buddhism* (Penguin), and **E. Conze, *Buddhism: Its Essence and Development* (Harper Torchbook), will provide adequate introductions to Buddhism. K. S. Latourette, *The Chinese: Their History and Culture* (4th ed., 1964), is an excellent introduction to Chinese history. More recent is **Wolfram Eberhard, *A History of China* (University of California). Paul Radin, *The Story of the American Indian* (rev. ed., 1944), supplies a good orientation to a neglected subject.

Imperial Rivalry. Several of the works already cited treat the rivalries of European powers for overseas possessions and commercial advantage. A splendid work devoted more directly to this theme during a decisive period is **Walter L. Dorn, *Competition for Empire, 1740–1763* (Harper Torchbook). Still the most exciting treatment of the Anglo-French rivalry is provided by the late nineteenth-century American historian, Francis Parkman; especially recommended are his **Half-Century of Conflict* (Collier), and **Montcalm and Wolfe* (Collier). Henry Dodwell, *Dupleix and Clive: The Beginning of Empire* (1920), is old but still excellent on Anglo-French rivalry in India. The British victory is treated in Kenneth Feiling, *Warren Hastings* (1954).

Chapter 37 ✥ Classicism, Baroque, Pietism

The spirit of royal absolutism, with its exaltation of kings, princes, and attendant nobility, and also its concern for order and form, was reflected in the literature, the arts, and certain religious movements of the seventeenth and eighteenth centuries. The prevailing styles were Classicism in literature and music, and Baroque in painting and architecture. Pietistic religious movements passively accepted royal absolutism as a form of government. Absolutism had its direct apologists in the field of political theory.

1. THE PHILOSOPHY OF ABSOLUTISM

In our twentieth-century concern for popular government we sometimes forget the service performed in early modern times by the royal monarchs. It was they who suppressed feudal turbulence, established law and order, and molded the first national states. Some were incompetent and some were predatory. However, the tragic example of Poland and the Holy Roman Empire, where the monarchs were dominated by the nobility and the local princes, would seem to indicate that in the first three centuries of the modern era, the absolutist kings generally served a useful, and possibly necessary, function. Their role was appreciated and defended by many of their subjects. We have already encountered Bishop Bossuet's eloquent defense of Louis XIV's claims to be God's duly ordained vicegerent on earth, and James I's espousal of divine right monarchy.

The seventeenth-century thinker Thomas Hobbes, dismayed by the civil strife then raging in England (the Puritan Revolution), decided that only absolute government could maintain law and order. In his *Leviathan* (1651), Hobbes theorized that basically selfish men for their own protection contracted with a prince to rule them; but, once having made the compact, they could not revoke it.[1] To be effective, the prince must be all-powerful, controlling even the religion of his subjects. The great Dutch political theorist Hugo Grotius argued not only for absolute governmental authority within the state, but also for absolute sovereignty and equality of all states large and small. His chief work, *The Law of War and Peace* (1625), was one of the earliest and probably the most influential of all treatises on international law. It was the outgrowth of Grotius' experiences during the revolt of the Netherlands against Spain and of his observation of some of the horrors of the

---

[1] While proffering the social-contract theory of government, Hobbes did not believe that it actually occurred as a historical event.

This photograph of the interior of the church at Ottobeuren, Munich, shows the elaborate, gaudy splendor of the baroque style, the hallmark of the age of royal absolutism and affluence. *Photo: Hirmer Verlag*

Thirty Years' War in Germany. Both Hobbes and Grotius believed royal absolutism to be in accordance with the natural law.

2. THE GOLDEN AGE OF FRENCH LITERATURE

The reign of Louis XIV (1643–1715), which marked the apogee of royal absolutism in France and indeed in all Europe, was also the golden age of French literature. The elegance, the sense of order, and the formalism of the court of the Grand Monarch were all reflected in the literature of the period, sometimes called the Augustan or the classical period of French literature. It was in the field of the drama that the French writers attained their greatest success. Corneille wrote elegant tragedies, of which *The Cid* and *Polyeucte* are among the best known, in the style of and

often on the same subjects as the ancient Greek tragedies. The struggles of man against himself and against the universe furnish the dramatic conflicts. Corneille's craftsmanship and style are handsomely polished, though often exalted and exaggerated.

Even more exquisitely polished were the perfectly rhymed and metered couplets of Racine's tragedies. *Andromaque* relates the tragic story of Hector's wife after the death of her husband at the hands of Achilles and the ensuing fall of Troy. *Phèdre* is about the wife of the legendary Greek king Theseus who falls in love with her stepson. This story had also been the subject of plays by Euripides, Sophocles, and Seneca. As with the Greek and Roman dramatists, abnormal love was a favorite theme with the French playwrights of the seventeenth century. Racine, an ardent Jansenist, turned later in life to religious subjects. *Esther* and *Athalie* are biblical plays of serene beauty.

One of the greatest of all the French dramatists was Molière. In his charming and profound comedies—such as *Tartuffe*, *Le Misanthrope*, and *Les Femmes Savantes* (*The Learned Ladies*)—Molière devastatingly portrays and satirizes the false, the stupid, and the pompous among men: egotists, pedants, social climbers, false priests, quack physicians. The tragic conflicts and the personality types of Corneille, Racine, and Molière are universal and eternal.

Other major French writers of the age of Louis XIV were Blaise Pascal, the scientist and mathematician who also wrote the marvelously styled *Provincial Letters* against the Jesuits and the deeply reflective *Pensées* (*Thoughts*); Madame de Sévigné, who wrote

LE TARTVFFE

The frontispiece from the 1669 Paris edition of Molière's Tartuffe. Molière's works, witty and profound, helped to make the reign of Louis XIV the Golden Age of French literature. *Photo: Rare Book Division, New York Public Library, Astor, Lenox, and Tilden Foundations* almost two thousand letters to her daughter, each a work of art; and the Duke de Saint-Simon, who spent the latter part of his life writing forty volumes of *Mémoires*. Madame de Sévigné and the Duke de Saint-Simon, both of whom were eyewitnesses of the court of Louis XIV, constitute two of the most important sources we have for the history and the life of that period.

The common denominator among all these writers is their emphasis upon and mastery of elegant and graceful form. In this they reflect the spirit of royal absolutism at its height. However, the form is valued not merely for its own sake, but as an artistic clothing for subtle and critical thought. It is little wonder that French literature in the late seventeenth century overshadowed that of all other countries of Europe, much as did French military and political influence. The lucid and graceful French language became the fashionable language of most of the royal courts and courtiers on the European continent.

French literature in the eighteenth century continued for the most part in the classical vein. Voltaire wrote dramas and poems carefully tailored to the dictates of classical formalism. His prose works exalted logic and the ideals of Greece and Rome. Only Rousseau among the major eighteenth-century French writers departed from the classical spirit to anticipate the romanticism of a later era. Voltaire and Rousseau, however, are much more important for the philosophic content of their works than for their literary artistry, and will be more fully examined in the following chapter, "The Intellectual Revolution."

3. THE ENGLISH CLASSICAL WRITERS

Next to France, England produced the most important literature in the seventeenth and early eighteenth centuries, and like the French the English authors generally wrote in the classical vein. The giant of English letters in the mid-seventeenth century was John Milton. This learned Puritan was steeped in the litera-ture of ancient Greece and Rome. His exquisite lyrics *L'Allegro* and *Il Penseroso* and incomparable elegy, *Lycidas,* are thickly strewn with references to classical mythology. The conscientious Milton contributed much of his great talent and energy to public affairs. During the Puritan Revolution he went blind working as pamphleteer for the Puritan cause and as secretary for Oliver Cromwell. The chief literary product of this period of his life is *Areopagitica,* probably the noblest defense of freedom of the press ever penned. Milton's masterpiece is *Paradise Lost,* written in his blindness and after the restoration of the Stuart kings had ruined his public career. *Paradise Lost* is a poem of epic proportions based on the Genesis account of the rebellion of Satan against God and the temptation and fall of man. This most ambitious of themes is treated in stately blank verse of formal elegance. Even in this deeply religious work, holy writ is interwoven with classical pagan myth.

The two greatest poets to succeed Milton were John Dryden in the late seventeenth century and Alexander Pope in the early eighteenth century. Both were satirists, both displayed a massive knowledge of Greek and Roman lore, and both wrote chiefly in the formal rhymed couplets typical of the classical period. In the precision of their form, as in the sharpness of their satire, their appeal was to reason rather than to emotion. In these respects they resemble the great French classicist Voltaire, whom they preceded by a few decades.

The eighteenth century in English literature was an age of great prose. Following the great upheavals of the seventeenth century, the Puritan and Glorious revolutions, it was a time of political and religious bitterness and bickering. In pungent and incisive prose Jonathan Swift, in his *Gulliver's Travels* and political essays, and Richard Sheridan in his numerous dramas, pilloried the fops, pedants, bigots, and frauds of the day, much as Molière had done a century earlier across the channel. It was in the eighteenth century that the English novel was born. Samuel Richardson, in *Clarissa Harlowe,* and Henry Fielding, in *Tom Jones,* used this medium to analyze human personality, emotions, and pyschology, just as Corneille and Racine had used the poetic drama in France for the same purpose.

In the eighteenth century several writers—Robert Burns in Great Britain, Rousseau in France, Schiller and Goethe in Germany—anticipated romanticism (see pp. 737–739). But the prevailing spirit in eighteenth as in seventeenth century literature was classical. Precision, formalism, and ofttimes elegance marked the style. Pagan Greece and Rome furnished the models. The appeal was generally to reason. The royal monarchs and their courts had little to fear from this literature, even from the poetic and dramatic works of Voltaire. They could derive comfort from its formal order and laugh with the rest of the world at its satire, which was aimed at mankind in general rather than at ruling regimes.

4. BAROQUE PAINTING AND ARCHITECTURE

If the literature of the seventeenth and eighteenth centuries did not offend the absolutist kings and their aristocratic courtiers, the visual arts of the period usually glorified them. The dominant style of painting and architecture was the baroque, which was an elaboration of the classical style of the Renaissance. The baroque style was originally a product of the Roman Catholic Reformation and reflected the resurgence of a revitalized Roman Catholic Church led by the militant Jesuits. Later its massive and ornamental elegance reflected the wealth and power of the absolutist monarchs and their courts, then at the peak of their affluence.

The most popular of the baroque painters

of the early seventeenth century was the Fleming Peter Paul Rubens. After studying the work of the Italian High Renaissance masters, Rubens returned to Antwerp and painted more than two thousand pictures, many of them huge in size. He operated what amounted to a painting factory, employing dozens of artists who painted in the details designed and sketched by the master. Rubens, a devout Roman Catholic, first painted religious subjects. His sculpturesque and sensational *Descent from the Cross* undoubtedly reveals the influence of Michelangelo. His later subjects were pagan mythology, court life, and especially voluptuous nude women—all painted in the most brilliant and sensuous colors. All these subjects appear in his most ambitious work—twenty-three colossal scenes (mostly imaginary) from the life of Marie de Médicis, widow of King Henry IV of France. Seldom, if ever, has a dull and colorless woman been more glamorized in paint.

Spain boasted two of the greatest seventeenth-century baroque painters: El Greco and Velásquez. El Greco, whose real name was Domenikos Theotokopoulos, was a native of the Greek island of Crete (hence "The Greek"). After studying the Italian Renaissance masters, he settled down in Toledo and developed a style of his own, usually called mannerism or expressionism. By deliberate distortion and exaggeration he achieved sensational effect. *View of Toledo, St. Jerome in His Study,* and *Christ at Gethsemane* illustrate his genius. El Greco's favorite subject was the reinvigorated Church of the Roman Catholic Reformation. Considered to be a madman by his contemporaries, he is now regarded as the forerunner, if not the founder, of several schools of nineteenth- and twentieth-century painting. Velásquez was a painter of great versatility. Although much of

Rembrandt's **The Polish Rider** (ca. 1655), a work of the later life of this great baroque artist, has a moving depth and subtlety: The rider, alert to dangers we can only imagine, seems about to move past our view as he follows a curving path across the canvas.

Photo: Copyright The Frick Collection, New York

his earlier work was of a religious nature, he also painted genre subjects (depicting the life of the common people) and, later, portraits. He is considered one of the greatest of portrait painters. As official court painter, he exalted and glorified the Spanish royalty and ruling classes at a time when they had really passed their peak in world affairs. Velásquez was one of the chief pioneers of modern art; it was from him that the nineteenth-century impressionists and realists received much of their inspiration.

France's chief contribution to baroque painting was Nicolas Poussin, who spent most of his life in Italy studying the Renaissance masters. Although his biblical and mythologi-

cal scenes are much more serene and subtle than the works of Rubens and El Greco, they are more vibrant and pulsating than the Italian Renaissance paintings that inspired them. They must, therefore, be classified as baroque in style. Some critics think that Poussin's magnificent landscapes have never been surpassed.

In eighteenth-century Great Britain Reynolds, Gainsborough, Romney, and Lawrence (who lived and painted well into the nineteenth century) vied with each other for commissions to paint the portraits of royalty and aristocracy. The result was plumes, jewels, buckles, silks, brocades, and laces in dripping profusion. This flattering of royalty and aris-

Tiepolo, Venetian by birth and training, a master of light and color, was famous for his skill at illusionistic ceiling decoration, one of the hallmarks of the baroque and rococo styles. This painting of Perseus and Andromeda shows the grace and delicacy of his work. *Photo: Copyright The Frick Collection, New York*

tocracy, however, did not go unchallenged. Hogarth in Great Britain and Goya in Spain in the eighteenth and early nineteenth centuries pitilessly satirized the excesses and abuses of aristocratic society. Their brushes matched the pens of Swift and Sheridan.

Only in the Dutch Netherlands did the age of the baroque fail to reflect the ascendancy of royalty. Here in the busy ports and marketplaces commerce was king, and the great Dutch painters of the seventeenth century, notably Frans Hals and Rembrandt van Rijn, portrayed the bourgeoisie and the common people. Hals was one of the first great realistic genre painters. Rembrandt is universally

recognized as one of the greatest artistic geniuses of all time. One of his favorite subjects was the Dutch bourgeoisie. He was not a popularizer, however, and he suffered many personal hardships rather than compromise the sincerity of his art. The tragic toll of these hardships is strikingly revealed in a series of magnificent self-portraits. As a portrayer of character he has never been surpassed, perhaps not even equaled. His mastery of light and shade (*chiaroscuro*) made it seem as if the very souls of his subjects were illumined. *Syndics of the Cloth Guild, Night Watch*, and *Anatomy Lesson of Dr. Tulp* are among his most powerful portrait studies.

These three paintings also vividly depict the commercial prosperity, the festive urban life, and the growing interest in natural science, respectively, in the seventeenth-century Dutch Netherlands. Rembrandt's glowing idealization of people and landscapes anticipates the age of romanticism of the early nineteenth century.

Baroque architecture, like baroque painting, was an elaboration and ornamentation of the classical style of the Renaissance, and a product of the Roman Catholic Reformation. In the late sixteenth, seventeenth, and eighteenth centuries Jesuit churches sprang up all over the Roman Catholic world. The most important and one of the best examples of the baroque style is the Jesuit parent church, Il Gesù, in Rome. Also, like the painting, baroque architecture was later used to represent the gaudy splendor of the seventeenth- and eighteenth-century absolute monarchs and their courts.

Towering over all other monuments of baroque architecture, much as did St. Peter's over all other Renaissance structures, was the Versailles palace of Louis XIV. The exterior of Versailles is designed in long, horizontal classic lines. The interior is lavishly decorated with richly colored marbles, mosaics, inlaid woods, gilt, silver, silk, velvet, and brocade. Lebrun painted many of the ceilings. The salons and halls are lighted with ceiling-to-floor windows and mirrors and crystal chandeliers holding thousands of candles. The palace faces hundreds of acres of groves, walks, pools, terraces, fountains, statues, flowers, and clipped shrubs—all laid out in formal geometric patterns.

So dazzling was this symbol of royal absolutism that many European monarchs attempted to copy it. The most successful attempt was Maria Theresa's Schönbrunn Palace in Vienna. As late as the mid-nineteenth century, mad King Ludwig of Bavaria was building three palaces in the style of Versailles. One, Herrenchiemsee, is a remarkable duplication.

Two other notable examples of baroque architecture, seen by thousands of tourists in Paris, are the Hôtel des Invalides (Old Soldiers' Home) with its magnificent dome, and the Luxembourg Palace and Gardens. In England Sir Christopher Wren was the greatest architect of the baroque period. The great fire that destroyed most of the heart of London in 1666 provided Wren with an opportunity to build numerous baroque structures. His masterpiece is St. Paul's Cathedral, with its lofty dome and columns.

In the eighteenth century, architecture tended to become more feminine and less massive, relying heavily upon multiple curves and lacy shell-like ornamentation. This style is usually referred to as rococo One of the best examples is Frederick the Great's Sans Souci Palace at Potsdam. The rococo style, like the baroque, represented an age of aristocratic affluence.

5. THE GREAT AGE OF CLASSICAL MUSIC

The classical spirit pervaded the music of the seventeenth and eighteenth centuries as it did the literature and the visual arts; and, like the literature and the visual arts, seventeenth- and eighteenth-century music was an outgrowth of Renaissance developments.[2] The piano and the violin family of instruments, whose forebears appeared in the sixteenth century, developed rapidly in the seventeenth. In the late seventeenth and early eighteenth centuries, three Italian families, the Amati, the Guarnieri, and the Stradivari, fashioned the greatest violins ever made. The seventeenth century was also marked by the rise of the opera. Alessandro Scarlatti in Italy, Lully in France, and Purcell in England popularized this grandiose combination of music and drama. The eighteenth was the great century of classical music—the age of Bach, Handel, Haydn, Mozart, and Beethoven.

Johann Sebastian Bach (1685–1750) was a

---

[2] Some music historians designate the music of the seventeenth and early eighteenth centuries, including that of Bach and Handel, as baroque, which was a forerunner of the classical.

member of a German family long distinguished in music. Noted in his own lifetime chiefly as an organist, he composed a vast array of great music for organ, harpsichord and clavichord (forerunner of the piano), orchestra, and chorus, much of which has been lost. Most of Bach's compositions were religiously inspired, and he holds the same position in Protestant music that the sixteenth-century Palestrina does in music of the Roman Catholic Church. Bach was not widely appreciated in his own day. It was not until Felix Mendelssohn in the nineteenth century "discovered" him that he became widely known. Today Bach is considered one of the greatest creative geniuses of all time—comparable to Leonardo da Vinci, Shakespeare, and Cervantes.

George Frederick Handel (1685–1759) was born in central Germany in the same year as Bach and not many miles distant. He studied Italian opera in Germany and Italy, and wrote forty-six operas himself. He became court musician of the elector of Hanover, and when the elector became King George I of England,

Handel followed him there. Handel wrote an enormous quantity of music, both instrumental and vocal. All of it is marked by dignity, formal elegance, and melodious harmony—fitting for and appreciated in an age of royal splendor. His best-known work is the majestic oratorio *The Messiah*, heard every Christmas season.

Franz Joseph Haydn (1732–1809), unlike Handel, was primarily interested in instrumental music; he was the chief originator of the symphony. During his long career in Vienna, which he helped to make the music capital of the world, he wrote more than a hundred symphonies in addition to scores of compositions of other forms of music, particularly chamber music. It was in his hands that orchestral music really came into its own. All his work is in the formal, classical style. As a friend of the younger Mozart, Haydn probably learned more than he taught.

Wolfgang Amadeus Mozart (1756–1791) is regarded by many students as the greatest musical genius of all time. Born in Salzburg, he spent most of his adult life in Vienna. Mozart began composing at the age of five (possibly four), and gave public concerts on the harpsichord at the age of six. At twelve he wrote an opera. Before his untimely death at the age of thirty-five, he wrote more than six hundred compositions in all the known musical forms. Symphonies, chamber music, and piano sonatas and concertos were his favorite forms. His best-known operas are *The Marriage of Figaro, Don Giovanni,* and *The Magic Flute.* In the masterful hands of Mozart the classical style reached the peak of its perfection. Never was music so clear, melodic, precise, and logical. However, Mozart's material rewards in this world were few. Although the courts of many kings, princes, and aristocrats were graced by his marvelous music, whose spirit accorded with the formalism and authoritative orderliness of an age of absolutism, his opulent patrons gave him little money or honor. Even their servants looked down on him, and he was buried in a pauper's grave.

Upon the stage set by Bach, Handel, Haydn, and Mozart emerged the greatest figure in the history of music, Ludwig van Beethoven (1770–1827). Beethoven's dynamic genius overflowed the bounds of any school or style. However, his training, his earlier work, and his fundamental style and form were classical. Beethoven, like Michelangelo, lived a tempestuous, trouble-filled life. He was born in Bonn in the German Rhineland of Flemish ancestry (hence the "van"). High-strung, poor, unsocial, and frustratingly ambitious, he suffered in his early prime the greatest calamity that could befall a musical genius—deafness. At the age of twenty-two, he went to Vienna, where he lived the rest of his life. Although Beethoven studied under Haydn, the greatest influence in his life was Mozart, to whose work his earlier compositions bear a marked resemblance. To the classical style,

however, the mature Beethoven added spontaneous and sometimes noisy emotion, thereby becoming the founder of the romantic style of a later generation. Beethoven lived through the upheavals of the French Revolution, Napoleon, and the surge of nationalism that overthrew the Napoleonic dictatorship. His keen interest in these dramatic events is revealed in his music (see p. 741). Beethoven did not write voluminously; however, his nine symphonies, chamber music, and numerous piano sonatas and concertos constitute the greatest and best-loved music in history.

6. PIETISM IN RELIGION

Royal political authority was passively accepted by a number of pietistic religious sects which arose during the seventeenth and eighteenth centuries.

We have already observed the Jansenist movement within the Roman Catholic Church in France in the seventeenth century (see p. 548). Although the Jansenists were by no means oblivious to the political and social issues of the day and actually participated in the Fronde uprising against Mazarin's tyranny, they were fundamentally a Puritanical pietistic group, seeking communion with God through prayer, meditation, and mild asceticism. Early in the eighteenth century Louis XIV, under the influence of the Jesuits, outlawed the Jansenists and destroyed their buildings. At the same time the pope declared them to be heretics. However, the spirit of Jansenism continued to exist.

In Germany Philipp Spener (1635–1705) and Count Zinzendorf (1700–1760) became leaders of pietist movements of considerable dimensions. Spener, a Lutheran pastor, recoiled from the formal officiousness that his church had fallen into after the heated religious strife of the sixteenth and early seventeenth centu-

This painting of the Mozart family shows the great musical genius as a boy with his parents. Original in Mozart's Wohnhaus, Salzburg. *Photo: Internationale Stiftung Mozarteum, Salzburg* ries. He minimized dogma and external forms in favor of inner piety and holy living. His largely Lutheran following included some of the leading intellects of Germany. Count Zinzendorf, a well-to-do Saxon nobleman, undertook to restore the Bohemian Brethren, the persecuted and scattered followers of the early fifteenth-century reformer John Huss. He called his group the Moravian Brethren. The Moravians, too, shunned intricate dogma and formal ritual. They set up model communities based upon brotherly love, frugal living, hard work, and inner piety. Count Zinzendorf migrated to America and founded Moravian communities at Bethlehem and other Pennsylvania towns. Later many Moravian ("Pennsylvania Dutch") Germans migrated southward along the Appalachian piedmont as far as Georgia, planting settlements, such as Winston-Salem in North Carolina, along the way.

In Lutheran Sweden, Emanuel Swedenborg (1688–1772), a distinguished scientist, inventor, and public servant, founded a movement somewhat like the Moravian Brethren, based upon his visions, which he took to be direct revelations of God. Swedenborg wrote several learned theological works stressing inner and outward piety and individual communion with God. His followers, who called themselves the Church of the New Jerusalem, also came in considerable numbers to America.

England, however, was the seat of the most widespread and influential pietistic movements of the seventeenth and eighteenth centuries. The first was the Society of Friends, or the Quakers, as they were generally called, founded by George Fox (1624–1691). Fox, a man of great energy and stubborn independence, detested formalism in religion as well as in society and government. He believed that true Christianity is an individual matter—a matter of plain, pious living and of private communion with God under the guidance of divine "inner light." Opposed to war, to rank, and to intolerance, the Quakers refused military service, the use of titles, and the taking of oaths. In these respects the Quakers were different from most of the other pietists. They were considered dangerous to the established order and were severely persecuted. Probably the most prominent of the early Quakers was William Penn, a wealthy aristocrat, who in 1682 founded Pennsylvania as a refuge for members of the sect. Pennsylvania and the Quakers both prospered.

A more moderate and much more popular pietist movement was Methodism. The prime mover in Methodism was John Wesley (1703–1791). While studying for the Anglican ministry at Oxford, John Wesley and a little band of his fellow students became disillusioned at the coldness and spiritual emptiness that had fallen upon the Anglican Church following the exciting religious controversies of the seventeenth century. They also deplored its subservience to the government and to the aristocracy. Wesley's little group began holding prayer meetings and visiting the poor and the sick. Their lives were such examples of piety and moderate regularity that their fellow students branded them "Methodists" in derision. After leaving Oxford, John Wesley and his brother, Charles, spent two years in the newly founded American colony of Georgia, trying unsuccessfully to convert the Indians. In Georgia they came in contact with some German pietists and became converted to a more fervent, evangelical type of Christianity. This they took with them back to England. When the Anglican churches closed their doors to John Wesley, he preached emotional sermons to huge throngs in the streets and fields. A tireless and dynamic soul-stirrer, he rode horseback from one end of England to the other until well into his eighties. Charles Wesley wrote more than 6,500 hymns. George Whitefield, the most eloquent of all the early Methodists, electrified tens of thousands in England and America and converted many to pietistic Christianity. The real founder of Methodism in the American colonies was Francis Asbury (1745–1816), who duplicated in many respects the work of John Wesley in England. The Methodists played a prominent part in the two "Great Awakenings" in America—the first in the 1730s and 40s and the second at the opening of the nineteenth century. In both England and America the Methodists grew rapidly in numbers, mostly among the middle and lower classes.

The various pietist groups were definitely not political revolutionaries. They were intensely interested in social reform—in education, health and sanitation, temperance, penal reform, and abolition of the slave trade. But they hoped to achieve these reforms by private charity rather than political action. They tended to accommodate themselves to absolute monarchy in the belief that spiritual and social conditions could be improved within that framework of government. John Wesley, for instance, though deeply interested in social reform in the American colonies, did not sympathize with their struggle for independence. It was not the pietists, but their contemporary rationalistic philosophers of the Enlightenment (see the following chapter), who helped to bring on the revolutionary era that toppled the thrones of many absolute monarchs and chastised or frightened the rest.

Suggested Reading

General. For the cultural aspect of the seventeenth and eighteenth centuries, the student will find the volumes in the Rise of Modern Europe series described in the bibliographies to Chapters 33 and 35 indispensable. These volumes are all oriented toward cultural history. They contain full and critical bibliographies and are available in paperback (Harper Torchbook). Another excellent study of seventeenth-century cultural history is A. Guérard, *The Life and Death of an Ideal: France in the Classical Age* (1928).

Philosophy of Absolutism. One of the chief proponents of the divine right of kings was James I of England. A selection of his writings on the subject may be found in C. H. McIlwain, ed., *The Political Works of James I* (1918). A good secondary study of the principles of royal absolutism is J. N. Figgis, *The Divine Right of Kings* (2nd ed., 1922). Autocratic government in Prussia is examined by Hans Rosenberg, *Bureaucracy, Aristocracy and Autocracy, the Prussian Experience 1660–1815* (1958).

Classical Literature. English literature in the seventeenth century is well surveyed by R. F. Jones, *The Seventeenth Century* (1951). The standard treatment of French literature in the "golden age" of Louis XIV is C. H. C. Wright, *French Classicism* (1920). A good biography of probably the greatest of the French classical dramatists is Brander Matthews, *Molière* (1926).

Baroque Art. An excellent history of Western art is D. N. Robb and J. J. Garrison, *Art in the Western World* (3rd ed., 1953). The best biography of the greatest of all the baroque painters is Jacob Rosenberg, *Rembrandt* (2 vols., 1948).

Classical Music. Two excellent books for laymen by learned musicologists are E. J. Stringham, *Listening to Music Creatively* (2nd ed., 1959); and P. H. Láng, *Music in Western Civilization* (1941). Both authors interpret the music in the various eras in the light of the other facets of culture of the time. A good biography of probably the greatest figure in the history of music, who composed in both the classic and the romantic styles, is J. M. Burk, *The Life and Work of Beethoven* (1943).

Pietism. A scholarly but popularly written biography of one of the great eighteenth-century pietists is **F. J. McConnell, *John Wesley* (Apex). W. C. Braithwaite, *The Beginnings of Quakerism* (1912), explores the origins of another continuingly important pietistic group. An unexpected pietistic influence is treated by K. S. Pinson, *Pietism as a Factor in the Rise of German Nationalism* (1934).

Sources. Some masterpieces of classical literature in paperback edition are **Molière, *Eight Plays* (Modern Library); **Racine, *Three Plays* (Phoenix); **Fielding, *Tom Jones* (Modern Library); **W. H. Auden and N. H. Pearson, eds., *Restoration and Augustan Poets* (Viking). This is an anthology of English poetry from Milton to Goldsmith.

RETROSPECT

RETROSPECT The seventeenth and eighteenth centuries were the apogee of royal absolutism as a form of government in the Western world. With few exceptions, it was the nations ruled by absolutist kings which achieved the greatest successes during those two centuries. The most noteworthy exception was England.

Under Henry IV, Richelieu, Mazarin, and Louis XIV, the Bourbon monarchy achieved a degree of absolutism in France that was virtually complete and a hegemony in Europe that has seldom, if ever, been equaled. European history during the years 1661–1715 has come to be called the age of Louis XIV. Louis and his court were the envy of all other monarchs, who sought to emulate them. France possessed a military strength so great that the major states of Western and Central Europe working in combination held her in check only with difficulty.

France's only real rival for European and world hegemony in the seventeenth century was England. There royal absolutism had reached its peak during the sixteenth century under the vigorous and politically crafty Tudor rulers. The Stuart kings, who came to the throne in 1603 when Elizabeth I died childless, were full of fine absolutist theories but were politically inept. They soon found themselves in a running fight, mostly over money matters, with Parliament, stronghold of the landed and commercial interests. In a showdown—the Puritan Revolution—the parliamentary forces, under the able leadership of Oliver Cromwell, triumphed. Before the century had ended one Stuart king had been executed, another invited to the throne on terms, and a third driven out of the country. During the course of the seventeenth and eighteenth centuries England's parliamentary and cabinet system gradually took shape. The landed and commercial interests now in control of the English government, however, were no less aggressive in foreign and colonial affairs than had been the royal monarchs. In fact, they were more so.

The most significant political developments in Central and Eastern Europe during the seventeenth and eighteenth centuries were the rise of two military despotisms—Prussia and Russia. The Hohenzollerns of Prussia, consistently pursuing the policies of royal absolutism, militarism, and territorial aggrandizement, more than doubled their territory and population and challenged Austria for the leadership of the German-speaking world. Russia under Peter the Great and Catherine the Great became Westernized, decisively defeated Sweden and the Ottoman Turks, and gained valuable territory facing the West. Poland disappeared from the map, carved up by Russia, Prussia, and Austria.

While Prussia, Russia, and Austria were struggling for the mastery of Central and Eastern Europe, the French, the English, and the Dutch were competing for dominance in North America and Asia. In this contest the English emerged victorious in North America and India, and the Dutch in the East Indies. The English found it relatively easy to drive the primitive Indians out of eastern North America and colonize the continent with Europeans. In Asia the English and the Dutch easily defeated the technologically backward natives, but found it next to impossible to Europeanize peoples steeped in cultures and religions more ancient than those of the West.

The Baroque and the Classical styles prevailed in literature and the arts in Western Europe throughout most of the seventeenth and eighteenth centuries. These styles generally harmonized with and often exalted the absolutist monarchs and their courts. And the numerous pietist and quietist religion sects which arose during this period passively accepted, for the most part, the political authority of the absolutist governments.

Part Nine

The Era of the French Revolution

1776–1830

The late eighteenth century was an era of revolution in the Western world, both in Europe and in America. Although the royal monarchs had reached the apogee of their power during the seventeenth and eighteenth centuries —everywhere in Europe except England, where Parliament had gained the ascendancy over the king—European society remained essentially feudal. The feudal nobility were still powerful in government, and their social supremacy remained virtually complete.

The Christian churches, too, were still powerful in the late eighteenth century. Although the Roman Catholic Church had suffered a loss of influence as a result of the renaissance of secularism and had lost much of its territory as a result of the Protestant Reformation, it still had a powerful voice in government and society in predominantly Catholic countries, and had lost none of its spirit of intolerance. The various Protestant churches had adopted quite similar poses wherever they were established. In Eastern Europe, the Orthodox Church had not been touched by either the Renaissance or the Reformation. The clergy there, particularly the upper clergy, like the nobility, enjoyed unchanged the privileged position they had had for hundreds of years.

Meanwhile, new forces were rising to challenge those privileged positions. The nobility in Northern and Western Europe felt increasing pressure from the bourgeoisie as the tempo of commerce, capitalistic enterprises, and urban growth steadily increased. The peasantry, too, and even the wage earners were becoming increasingly restive. The clergy found their theological and intellectual influence undermined during these centuries by the rise of natural science and of rationalistic and empiricist philosophies based upon science.

When the privileged classes steadfastly refused to yield or even to bend to these new forces, a series of revolutionary upheavals ensued—the American and the French revolutions, and the career of Napoleon. The whole Western world was involved, and the changes brought about by these upheavals reached every area and every level of society.

Chapter 38 ❧ The Intellectual Revolution

The so-called intellectual revolution of the eighteenth century marked the triumph of a philosophy of materialistic rationalism and empiricism known as the Enlightenment. This philosophy was based largely upon a scientific attitude brought on by the rise of natural science.

1. THE PIONEER SCIENCE: ASTRONOMY

The first branch of modern natural science to attract systematic attention was astronomy. The founder of modern astronomy was Nicholaus Copernicus (1473–1543), a German-speaking native of Poland whose real name was Kopernik. Like so many other Northern European scholars in the fifteenth century, he crossed the Alps to study in an Italian Renaissance university. It was from his Italian teachers that he received the ideas which led to his revolutionary concept of the structure of the universe. After returning to Poland, he spent the rest of his life in an attempt to prove that the sun, not the earth was the center of the solar system and that the earth and all other planets revolved around the sun while rotating on their own axes. Although this idea had been held by a number of Greek astronomers of the third and second centuries before Christ, it had never gained wide acceptance. For at least thirteen hundred years the Western world had accepted the conclusions of the Hellenistic astronomer Claudius Ptolemy (A.D. second century). The Ptolemaic system, which placed the earth at the center of the universe, satisfied the senses and

seemed to agree with certain statements in the Bible. The medieval Christian theologians, therefore, had come to regard the Ptolemaic system as the Christian view of the physical universe.

Copernicus was quite aware that his startling conclusions would arouse both the ridicule of laymen and the ire of churchmen. It was only near the end of his life that he could be persuaded to publish his views, and the first copy of his book, *Concerning the Revolutions of Celestial Orbs*, reached him on the day of his death. Roman Catholic and Protestant leaders alike denounced the Copernican system as illogical, unbiblical, and unsettling to the Christian faith.

But the new idea could not be suppressed. Nearly a century after Copernicus, a German astronomer, Kepler, with the benefit of additional data, showed convincingly that Copernicus was fundamentally right. However, the exact movements of the heavenly bodies, Kepler discovered, were not quite what Copernicus had believed them to be: the planets revolve around the sun in elliptical rather than circular orbits. Shortly thereafter Galileo (1564–1642), one of the truly great heroes of science and the first to use the telescope in astronomical observation, won over most contemporary scientists to the Copernican theory. Nonetheless, Galileo too was ridiculed and suffered much persecution from the clerical authorities.

The uphill trail blazed by Copernicus, Kepler, and Galileo was continued on to its lofty peak by Sir Isaac Newton (1642–1727).

Newton was a frail boy, the son of a poor English farmer. As a student at Cambridge University he was distinguished enough in mathematics to be chosen to stay on as professor after his graduation. Shortly thereafter, while still in his early twenties, Newton came forth with some of the most tremendous discoveries in the history of science, or indeed of the human intellect. He is probably best known for the law of universal attraction, or gravitation. The concept matured and was refined in Newton's mind over a period of years. As it finally appeared in his *Principia* (*The Mathematical Principles of Natural Knowledge*), the law is stated with marvelous simplicity and precision: "Every particle of matter in the universe attracts every other particle with a force varying inversely as the square of the distance between them and directly proportional to the product of their masses." This law, so simply expressed, applied equally to the movement of a planet and a berry falling from a bush. The secret of the physical universe appeared to have been solved—a universe of perfect stability and precision. The modest Newton was so overcome by the grandeur of this law that he was unable to complete the confirming calculations, a task that he turned over to a trusted assistant. Two centuries were to elapse before Albert Einstein would raise grave doubts about the truth of Newton's theory.

Newton, in addition to his teaching and his prodigious scientific achievements, found time to perform public service. He became a member of Parliament and served for many years as active director of the royal mint. Knighted by Queen Anne, he was one of the few scientists before the nineteenth century to receive prominent public recognition in his own lifetime.

2. OTHER SCIENCES

Astronomy was only the first of many fields of modern natural science that came into being as Western man shifted the center of his interest from spiritual and moral matters to material things. In the seventeenth and eighteenth centuries such a galaxy of great names and discoveries appeared in the various branches of natural science that we can mention here only a few of the most significant.

In the sixteenth century Vesalius, a Fleming living in Italy, wrote the first comprehensive textbook on the structure of the human body to be based on careful observation. Because he dissected many human bodies in order to

Galileo is shown here in dialogue with the duke of Tuscany and other learned men in 1632, arguing the merits of the Ptolemaic versus the Copernican theories of the structure of the universe. It was Galileo who, despite considerable persecution by the Church, established the Copernican system as the true one. *Photo: NYPL Picture Collection*

make his observations, he ran into serious opposition from clerical authorities. In disgust he gave up his scientific studies and became the personal physician of Emperor Charles V. In the seventeenth century William Harvey, an Englishman who also studied in Italy, discovered the major principles of the circulatory system, thus making it possible for surgeons to operate on the human body with somewhat less fatal consequences than had previously been the case. Vesalius and Harvey are regarded as the founders of the science of anatomy.

The founding fathers of biological science were Linnaeus, the Swedish botanist, and Buffon, the French zoologist, both of whom lived in the eighteenth century. Since the varieties of plant and animal life are so enormous, one of the major problems in this field of knowledge is that of classification and nomenclature. Linnaeus worked out a system of names for the various species in both the plant and animal kingdoms that is still in use. He also worked out a system of classification of plant life that is partly used by botanists today. Buffon made important contributions to the classification of the animal kingdom and wrote a vast natural history in forty-four volumes.

An Irish nobleman, Robert Boyle (seventeenth century), laid the foundations for the modern physical sciences by attacking many false assumptions inherited from the ancients and by beginning the systematic search for the basic physical elements. He discovered the law of gases, which still bears his name. Following Boyle's lead, Lavoisier in France (eighteenth century) discovered twenty-three of the basic elements. He also discovered the secrets of combustion and formulated the law of the conservation of matter. Lavoisier is generally considered to be the father of modern chemistry. (He was beheaded by the terrorists during the French Revolution on a false political charge.) Probably the most important developments in the founding of modern physics were the discoveries connected with electricity. A number of men, including

Benjamin Franklin, contributed bits of knowledge concerning electricity, but it was the Italian physicist Volta (1745–1827) who first harnessed electricity by inventing the storage battery. The versatile Newton discovered the basic secrets of light, thereby founding the science of optics. He also made important contributions to hydrostatics and hydrodynamics and formulated the three laws of motion (which had been conceived earlier by Galileo). James Hutton, a Scottish farmer in quest of better agricultural techniques, made observations that led him to the conclusion that the earth's surface has been undergoing gradual changes over eons of time. His *Theory of the Earth*, which appeared toward the end of the eighteenth century, is the first systematic treatise on geology.

3. THE TOOLS OF SCIENCE

Meanwhile, the tools necessary for the ever more rapid progress of natural science were being invented. The language in which science is expressed is mathematics. In the early seventeenth century a Scotsman, Sir John Napier, invented logarithms, by which the process of multiplying and dividing huge numbers is greatly simplified. Shortly afterward the system was applied to the slide rule. About the same time, René Descartes, a Frenchman, adopted the symbols now used in algebra, and devised analytic geometry, a method of combining and interchanging algebra and geometry. In the latter part of the seventeenth century, sometimes called the century of genius, Newton and the German Wilhelm Leibnitz, working independently, invented calculus, upon which many of the most intricate processes of advanced science and engineering are dependent.

During the seventeenth and eighteenth centuries some of the basic physical scientific instruments were invented. Both the telescope and the microscope were products of the Dutch Netherlands. However, it was Galileo who first used the telescope in systematic astronomical observations. Leeuwenhoek, a

Dutchman, was the chief pioneer in the use of the microscope. He discovered bacteria two hundred years before Pasteur learned how to combat them; he also observed the cellular structure of plant and animal tissue, the structure of the blood, and its circulation through the capillary system. Another Dutchman, Huygens, invented the pendulum clock, making possible for the first time in history the precise measurement of small intervals of time. A German, Fahrenheit, greatly improved the thermometer and adopted the scale that bears his name.

It is interesting that the universities played little or no part in this great drama. Nearly all of them were controlled by the churches, either Roman Catholic or Protestant. They looked askance at science. It was the scientific academies that played a significant role in the advancement of science. The earliest and most important of these were the Royal Society in England, chartered in 1662 by Charles II, and the Académie des Sciences in France, founded by Colbert four years later. These organizations and others patterned after them furnished laboratories, granted subsidies, brought scientists together to exchange ideas, published their findings, and encouraged scientific achievement generally.

4. THE ENLIGHTENMENT

The discovery of so many marvelous new truths concerning the physical universe could hardly have failed to have a strong impact upon the direction of the thinking of Western man. From the fifth century A.D. to the fifteenth, Christian theology and its various ramifications had engaged the best minds in the Western world. Christian spiritual and moral concepts pervaded the philosophy, letters, arts, and customs of Western civilization, and set it off from all other civilizations. In the fifteenth and sixteenth centuries, the Renaissance had rediscovered the secular pagan civilizations of Greece and Rome and popularized them in the West. Western philosophy and literature became humanistic, and its art sen-

This eighteenth-century English engraving shows some of the new physical tools for scientific study being developed during this period. *Photo: NYPL Picture Collection*

suous. In the seventeenth and eighteenth centuries, Western man's interests, now predominantly secular, began to focus on science. Not only, as we have seen, did one spectacular discovery follow another, but eminent scientists such as Sir Francis Bacon, René Descartes, and Sir Isaac Newton devoted much thought and writing to scientific methodology and theory. The scientific attitude began to replace the Christian religion as the distinguishing characteristic of Western civilization.

But Western thinkers did not limit their attention exclusively to science. They began to speculate on the broader meaning of science—its ethical, political, social, and economic implications. These speculations gave rise to a philosophical movement which in the eighteenth century came to be called the Enlightenment. Many thinkers contributed to the philosophy of the Enlightenment. Three of the most influential and illustrious of the thinkers who contributed to the Enlightenment were René Descartes and John Locke (both of whom were really forerunners of the movement), and Voltaire.

Descartes (1596–1650), in addition to his major contributions to mathematics, was, as we have seen, one of the first to ponder and write on scientific theory and methodology. His *Discourse on Method* was a landmark in the rise of the scientific spirit. It is an eloquent defense of the value of abstract reason-

ing. He would question all authority no matter how venerable—be it Aristotle or the Bible. From a few simple and self-evident truths he would derive further truths by a process of deductive reasoning. "I think, therefore I am," he believed to be a safe starting point. Descartes thought the whole material universe can be understood in terms of extension and motion. "Give me extension and motion," said Descartes, "and I will create the universe." Only mind and spirit are exempt from the mechanical laws. Though either commonplace or outworn and discarded today, the basic ideas of Cartesian philosophy were revolutionary in the seventeenth century. By challenging all established authority, by accepting as truth only what could be known by reason, and by assuming a

His friend the Genevan painter Huber made these sketches of the head of Voltaire, the great figure of the Enlightenment who played much the same role in the intellectual world of the eighteenth century as did Erasmus in the sixteenth. *Photo: Bibliothèque Nationale–Estampes*

purely mechanical, physical universe, Descartes clashed head on with the prevailing Christian concepts of divine revelation and divine Providence.

John Locke (1632–1704) went a step further. This rugged English thinker would not exempt even the mind from the mechanical laws of the material universe. In his *Essay Concerning Human Understanding*, Locke pictured the human brain at birth as a blank sheet of paper on which nothing would ever be written except by sense perception and reason. This concept ruled out innate ideas as well as revelation. Thus the mechanization of the whole universe was complete. Locke was the first behavioristic psychologist. Although Descartes' rationalism (pursuit of truth through reason) and Locke's empiricism (pursuit of knowledge through observation and experience) were by no means the same, they were one in rejecting divine revelation and authority. Both contributed heavily to the philosophy of the Enlightenment.

Of all the leading figures of the Enlightenment, Voltaire (1694–1778) was the most influential. It was his skillful pen that popularized the deep and original ideas of Locke. Voltaire, the son of a Paris lawyer, became the idol of the French intelligentsia while still in his early twenties. His versatile mind was sparkling; his wit was mordant. An outspoken critic, he soon ran afoul of both church and state authorities. First he was imprisoned in the Bastille; later he was exiled to England. There he encountered the ideas of Locke and Newton and came to admire English parliamentary government and tolerance. Slipping back into France, he was hidden for a time and protected by a wealthy woman who became his mistress. Voltaire's facile mind and pen were never idle. He wrote poetry, drama, history, essays, letters, and scientific treatises—ninety volumes in all. The special target of his cynical wit was Christianity. Few men in history have dominated their age intellectually as Voltaire dominated the eighteenth century. He became the chief spokesman for the *philosophes* or philosophers of the Enlightenment.

Although the *philosophes* differed widely among themselves in matters of detail, the basic elements of their philosophy may be summarized briefly as follows:

EMPIRICAL KNOWLEDGE. All we know and all we can ever know is what we perceive through our senses and interpret with our reason. There are no such things as innate ideas or revealed truth.

MECHANISTIC UNIVERSE. The whole universe and everything in it, including man, are governed by a few simple and unchangeable laws. Anyone who thinks he can change one of these laws—can by praying, for instance, bring down the rain on his parched crops and perchance on his neighbor's unroofed house— is a dupe of his own egotism.

PERFECTIBILITY OF MAN. Man is naturally rational and good, but the proponents of mystic religions have distorted his thinking and given him guilt complexes by preaching false doctrines of original sin and divine moral laws. Rid man's mind of this rubbish, said the philosophers, and he can and will build for himself a perfect society.

GOODNESS OF NATURE. Nature is good and beautiful in its simplicity. Man has corrupted it with his complex political, social, and religious restrictions. A move back to nature would be a move toward wholesome vigor and freedom.

DEISM. This wonderful mechanism called the universe could not have come into being by accident. Some infinite Divine Being must have created it and set it in motion. However, the finite mind of man cannot comprehend the infinite. Therefore, God is unknowable. Furthermore, God, having set his perfect mechanical laws in motion, will never tamper with them nor interfere in the affairs of man. He is impersonal.

In the eighteenth century these ideas came to be generally accepted by the intelligentsia throughout the Western world. A host of French philosophers joined Voltaire in contributing to Diderot's *Encyclopedia*. This gigantic work undertook to explore the whole world of knowledge. It was not objective, however, for the articles were interlarded with the rationalistic and empiricist views of the writers.

Somewhat different from the other philosophers of the Enlightenment, though second only to Voltaire in influence on eighteenth-century thought, was Jean-Jacques Rousseau (1712–1778). One of the most original thinkers and charming writers of all time, Rousseau crusaded for a return to nature—beautiful, pure, simple nature. The message struck home to a society weary of arbitrary and often corrupt governmental bureaucracy and an oppressively artificial and elaborate code of social etiquette. Rousseau was lionized. Great ladies, including the Queen of France, began playing milkmaid. In his novel *La Nouvelle Héloïse*, Rousseau extolled the beauties of free love and uninhibited emotion. In *Emile* he expounded the "natural" way of rearing and educating children. He would let children do what they like and teach them "practical" knowledge. Although Rousseau agreed with his fellow philosophers of the Enlightenment on deism, the mechanistic universe, the perfectibility of man, and the goodness of nature, he differed sharply with them on the matter of reason. Rousseau placed his faith in emotion, feeling, and intuition, rather than in reason. In this he was a forerunner of the romantic spirit and expounded its principles nearly a century before that movement reached its peak.

5. CONFLICT BETWEEN THE PHILOSOPHERS OF THE ENLIGHTENMENT AND THE CHRISTIAN THEOLOGIANS

It is readily apparent that the beliefs of the philosophers of the Enlightenment were diametrically opposed to the doctrines of the Christian churches—Roman Catholic, Protestant, and Orthodox alike. In contrast to the unknowable, impersonal God of the deists, Christian theologians taught that God took on human form and revealed himself to the finite mind of man in the personality of Jesus Christ. Furthermore, they maintained that God is interested in each one of his special creatures—that not a sparrow falls but that he sees and is concerned. To the empirical knowledge of the materialistic rationalists Christian theologians would add divine truth revealed by God, either through Christ, the Bible, and the Church or directly, as in the case of the saints, the prophets, and sometimes even ordinary Christians. They would make the mechanistic universe subject to a miracle-working, prayer-answering Creator. They argued that, if God could create the laws of the material universe, he certainly could change them or set them aside if he so desired. Christian theologians regarded the concept of the natural goodness of man as erroneous. They taught instead that man is a fallen creature, that all inherit Adam's original sin, that man must be "born again" of the spirit in order to attain eternal life. Some theologians argued that the philosophy of the Enlightenment was itself a religion, based on faith. Since it has never been demonstrated that man is naturally good or that if freed from the influence of mystic religion, he can and will build for himself an earthly paradise, these things must be taken on faith—faith that in others the philosophers were so quick to scorn.

Unfortunately the eighteenth-century battle for the minds of men was not limited to honorable debate. Both sides resorted to the tactics of smear and persecution. It is difficult, if not impossible, to determine which side struck the first low blow. The philosophers, often on the flimsiest of scientific evidence and with little knowledge of the Christian religion, would ridicule the miraculous and mystic teachings of the Bible and the churches. Pleading for tolerance, they proved themselves most intolerant of Christian doctrines they did not accept or understand. Voltaire devoted much time and space to pointing out scientific errors in the Bible. *"Ecrasez l'infâme"* ("Crush the infamous thing") was his life motto. The "infamous thing" was, of course, Christianity. Christian theologians, on the other hand, found it much easier to denounce the materialistic rationalists than to answer their arguments. In countries like France and Italy, where the churchmen were strongly entrenched in government, they did not hesitate to persecute the philosophers of the Enlightenment, censor their writings, or even to interrupt the work of scientists. The churchmen were often so ignorant and so corrupt that they laid themselves open to the attacks of their enemies and almost invited the defeat they suffered in the struggle for intellectual leadership.

The materialistic rationalists won, and the French Revolution was in large measure an attempt to translate their ideas into practical institutions. It was not until the late nineteenth century that Christian theologians began to realize the true strength of their religion, to concentrate on spiritual and moral issues, and to rally their forces for a stronger stand (see Chapter 47).[1]

6. POLITICAL AND ECONOMIC ASPECTS OF THE ENLIGHTENMENT

The philosophers of the Enlightenment devoted a good deal of thought to matters of government. If man is by nature a rational and good creature, then surely, if given the opportunity, he can quickly devise for himself efficient and benevolent political institutions. Corrupt tyrannies were no longer tolerable. Of the numerous "enlightened" thinkers in the

field of political science, three stand out above the others in influence. They are Locke, Montesquieu, and Rousseau. Locke's most eloquent plea was for the natural rights of man, which are life, liberty, and property. He theorizes, in his *Two Treatises of Civil Government*, that to safeguard these rights man voluntarily contracted to surrender a certain amount of his sovereignty to government. The powers of the government, however, whether it be monarchical or popular, are strictly limited. No government may violate the individual's right to life, liberty, and property. If it does, the people who set it up can and should overthrow it. These ideas were fundamental in the thinking of the makers of both the French and the American revolutions. Jefferson wrote many of Locke's ideas into the Declaration of Independence, frequently using his exact words. They likewise appear in the American Constitution and in numerous French declarations of liberty.

Baron de Montesquieu (1689–1755) was less a theorizer than a discerning student of history and shrewd analyst of political systems. His masterpiece is *The Spirit of the Laws*. Although a great admirer of the English government after the Glorious Revolution, Montesquieu came to the conclusion that different types of government are best suited to various conditions. For instance, absolute monarchy is best for countries of vast area, limited monarchy for countries of moderate size like France, and republics for small states like Venice or Switzerland. Not only did he approve of Locke's doctrine of limited sovereignty, but he specified how it can best be secured—by a separation of powers and a system of checks and balances. The powers and functions of government should be equally divided among king, lords, and commons, each one beng checked by the other two. This was probably Montesquieu's greatest practical contribution to the science of government. The principle was incorporated into the American Constitution—kings, lords, and commons becoming executive, judicial, and legislative branches of government.

[1] The pietists, of course, concentrated on spiritual and moral issues. For the most part, however, they made their impact upon the lower classes rather than the intelligentsia, who were the chief protagonists in the debates over the philosophy of the Enlightenment. And only in England did the pietists gain a mass following even among the lower classes.

The real father of the theory of modern democracy was not Locke or Montesquieu, both of whom distrusted rule by the masses, but Rousseau. This morbid, erratic genius based the conclusions in his *Social Contract* and in his *Second Discourse* upon pure imagination. Man in his state of noble savagery was free, equal, and happy. It was only when some men began marking off plots of ground saying "this is mine" that inequality began. In order to restore their lost freedom and happiness, men entered into a compact, each with all the others, surrendering their individual liberty to the whole. Since sovereignty is indivisible, the general will is all-powerful. Although Rousseau never made it clear just how the general will would actually operate in practice, he apparently assumed that the individual would be free by virtue of being part of the general will. Rousseau's influence on the leaders of the second and more radical phase of the French Revolution was great. But since it is only a short step from this kind of unrestrained government to state-worshipping dictatorship, the influence of Rousseau is also clearly seen in the Fascist and Communist systems of the twentieth century.

Some of the eighteenth-century planners of the better life through reason turned their thoughts to economics. Since the late fifteenth century, mercantilism had been the dominant economic theory and practice in Western Europe. This system of regulated nationalistic economy reached its peak in the seventeenth century. Only the Dutch Netherlands held out for free trade. But if, according to the fundamental assumptions of the Enlightenment, the universe is run by a few simple mechanical laws, why should there not be a similar natural order in the field of economics? A group of French Physiocrats, led by Quesnay, personal physician to Louis XV, began to teach that economics has its own set of natural laws, that the most basic of these laws is that of supply and demand, and that these laws operate best when commerce is freed from governmental regulation. This

doctrine came to be known as that of *laissez faire* (or free trade and enterprise).

The chief formalizer of the theory of laissez faire was Adam Smith, a Scottish professor of philosophy who associated with the Physiocrats while sojourning in France. His *The Wealth of Nations*, published in 1776, has remained the bible of laissez-faire economics ever since. The ideas of the French Physiocrats and Adam Smith strongly influenced the leaders of the American and French revolutions.

7. THE ENLIGHTENED DESPOTS

The philosophy of the Enlightenment was by no means a monopoly of the intelligentsia. By the middle of the eighteenth century, it had become a fad. Many members of the nobility prided themselves on being followers of Voltaire (probably in most cases without realizing the practical implications of his philosophy). And nearly every country on the European continent was ruled by an "enlightened despot." As a matter of fact, Voltaire, who held the ignorant populace in contempt, believed enlightened despotism to be the most effective form of government.

The most sensational of the enlightened despots was Frederick the Great of Prussia (1740–1786). Frederick had from boyhood loved music, poetry, and philosophy. At the end of the Seven Years' War (1756–1763), the second of his two wars of aggression, he settled down as a model philosopher-king and attempted to apply the laws of reason to statecraft. Frederick was an avid reader of the French philosophers. He even invited Voltaire to visit him at Potsdam, but Prussia was not big enough to hold two such egos at once. The two quarreled and, after several years, parted.

The philosopher-king, who was, of course, a deist, made much of religious toleration. However, he continued to penalize the Jews and never ceased to ridicule Christians of all denominations. He was a strong advocate of public education, although he spent very little on it in comparison with what he spent on his army. The centralized Prussian bureaucracy became the most efficient government in Europe. True to the prevailing thought of the Enlightenment, however, he had no faith in popular self-government. Nor did he make a move to free the serfs or to end the feudal system in Prussia. Probably the most lasting of Frederick's contributions to Prussia were his codification of the law and improvements in the administration of justice. In the field of economy, Frederick was a mercantilist, although he did share the Physiocrats' appreciation of the importance of agriculture. Prussia's economy prospered increasingly during the last two decades of his reign. All in all, Prussia under Frederick the Great seemed to vindicate the contention of the philosophers of the Enlightenment that the rule of reason will quickly and painlessly usher in the good life.

The most sincere of all the enlightened despots was Joseph II of Austria (1780–1790). Unfortunately, he lacked the practical sagacity of Frederick the Great. His well-meaning but ill-conceived efforts to centralize the administration of the far-flung Hapsburg territories, to replace the numerous languages of his subjects with German, to secularize the strongly entrenched Roman Catholic Church,

and to free the serfs in a society still based upon feudalism, all backfired.

More successful were the enlightened despots of Sweden, Tuscany, Sardinia, Spain, and Portugal. Even in Russia, Catherine the Great talked and played at enlightened despotism, although she did nothing to put the theories into practice. Significantly, France alone of the great powers on the continent failed to produce an enlightened ruler. Upon attaining the French throne in 1774, the well-meaning Louis XVI appointed the Physiocrat Turgot as minister of finances. Turgot, a friend of Voltaire, initiated a program of sweeping reforms that might have forestalled the French Revolution. However, within two years' time the powerfully entrenched vested interests persuaded the weak-willed king to dismiss him.

Although enlightened despotism achieved enough spectacular successes to gladden the hearts of some of the philosophers of the Enlightenment, the system soon exhibited two fundamental weaknesses. One was the egotism of the ambitious monarchs, which kept Europe in a state of almost constant war. The second was the uncertainty of hereditary succession. In every case, the benevolent despots were succeeded by despots less benevolent, if not outright malevolent or degenerate. And in any case the people had no choice. Europe's feudal society was not to be thus easily and painlessly reformed.

Suggested Reading

General. Again, the appropriate chapters in the volumes in the Rise of Modern Europe series are invaluable. These are the volumes by Friedrich, Nussbaum, Wolf, Roberts, Dorn, and Gershoy (see the bibliographies at the ends of Chapters 33 and 35). Two useful general intellectual histories of modern Western civilization are J. H. Randall, *The Making of the Modern Mind* (1940); and **P. Smith, *A*

History of Modern Culture (2 vols., Collier). Randall is written in a popular vein; Smith is more erudite.

The Rise of Natural Science. The best general history of science is still W. C. Dampier, *A History of Science and Its Relations with Philosophy and Religion* (1949). Two other good accounts are **H. Butterfield, *The Origins of*

Modern Science, 1300–1800 (Free Press); and F. S. Taylor, *A Short History of Science and Scientific Thought* (1949). A perceptive analysis of the philosophical implications of the rise of modern natural science is **E. A. Burtt, *The Metaphysical Foundations of Modern Science* (Anchor). **A. N. Whitehead, *Science and the Modern World*, is another basic work for the interested reader.

The Enlightenment.   The best and latest study of the Enlightenment is Peter Gay, *The Enlightenment*, Vol. I, *The Rise of Modern Paganism* (1967), and Vol. II, *The Science of Freedom* (1969). Both volumes are available in Vintage paperback editions. Good biographies of the three most important figures of the Enlightenment are N. L. Torrey, *The Spirit of Voltaire* (1938); R. Shackleton, *Montesquieu: A Critical Biography* (1961); and F. C. Green, *Jean-Jacques Rousseau: A Critical Study of His Life and Writings* (1955). Of course, every student of history should read the delightful and provocative little volume, **Carl Becker, *The Heavenly City of the Eighteenth-century Philosophers* (Yale).

Sources.   **René Descartes, *Discourse on Method* (Liberal Arts) reveals the mind of one of the first scientists to speculate philosophically about the implications of science. **John Locke, *Essay Concerning Human Understanding* (Gateway), and **John Locke, *Two Treatises on Government* (Hafner), are the two most important works of one of the chief founding fathers of the Enlightenment. **Montesquieu, *The Spirit of the Laws* (Hafner) is the principal work of the most influential political theorist of the Enlightenment. Voltaire, *Letters on the English* (*Harvard Classics*, vol. XXXIV [1910]) is the best of the more than ninety volumes that Voltaire wrote for an understanding of his fundamental philosophy. **B. R. Redman, ed., *The Portable Voltaire* (Viking) is a well-chosen sampling of Voltaire's voluminous writings. **Rousseau, *Social Contract* (Hafner) is an inexpensive and available edition of Rousseau's most influential work. Rousseau, *Emile* (many editions) has had great influence on twentieth-century Western concepts of education and child rearing.

Chapter 39 ✿ The American Revolution

The political and social ideas of the Enlightenment received their first test and their first application in a somewhat unexpected quarter —the British colonies in America. The American Revolution was a highly significant step in a series of events that altered the political structure of the Western European world by striking down the absolutist concepts of government that had prevailed since about 1500. The bold experiments of the Americans in justifying their rebellion and in shaping new political institutions served as an inspiration and a model for other nations. Placed in its proper setting, the American Revolution was one of the major events in modern world history.

1. AMERICAN COLONIAL SOCIETY

The American Revolution was a complex movement, but behind all its complexity lay one fundamental fact. During the century and a half prior to 1776, American society had become different and separate from British and European societies. America was in the process of becoming independent long before 1776; the revolution was the culmination of this process.

To the American of 1776, probably the most obvious sign of living in a world apart from Europe was the bustling economy that had been created in a wilderness, an accomplishment that had to be attributed to hard work and ingenuity on the part of the colonists. The British, like other mercantilist nations, viewed colonies only as sources of wealth for the mother country.

The backbone of the colonial economy was the diversified agricultural system. The small, independently owned farms of New England and the middle colonies were complemented by the great plantations of certain areas of the South worked by slaves. Between them they produced a large variety of crops: grain, tobacco, rice, indigo, vegetables, fruit, and many others. This system not only fed the rapidly growing population of the colonies, but also supplied a surplus for export. Off to the west lay vast areas of land yet unexploited, an economic opportunity unknown in Europe.

The Americans had by no means neglected commerce and industry. Colonial merchants, especially in New England and the middle colonies, did a thriving business within America. They also reached across the seas to Great Britain, to the West Indies, and to the continent of Europe. The bulk of the overseas trade was in colonial raw materials, such as tobacco and lumber, which were shipped to Britain and Europe in exchange for manufactured goods and slaves. However, by 1776 the

The quarrel of the American colonists with Great Britain was marked by violence and violent propaganda on both sides. This rendering of the shooting of Americans by British troops in Boston in 1770 was engraved, printed, and sold by Paul Revere. *Photo: The Metropolitan Museum of Art, Gift of Mrs. Russel Sage, 1910* colonists were producing manufactured goods in spite of British protest. Numerous fortunes were made in New England by producing rum from West Indian molasses. A thriving shipbuilding industry also existed. Of course the colonists were not self-sufficient, but neither were they absolutely dependent on Great Britain and Europe. American entrepreneurs were intent on protecting and expanding their own interests. Already most Americans were economically comfortable and confident that the future was bright, provided that they were free to pursue their own economic ends.

America's population—about 2.5 million in 1776—was organized in a class structure outwardly similar to that of Great Britain. An aristocracy of rich merchants and planters, which dominated economic life, politics, religion, and manners, was conscious of its position and sought to retain it. A large, enterprising group of independent farmers, shopkeepers, artisans, and professional men was ranked below the aristocrats. There were some day laborers, tenant farmers, and indentured servants, who were condemned to the lower rank of society. And there were the Negro slaves. But this class structure was not nearly so inflexible as that of Europe. Almost none of Europe's aristocracy emigrated to America; the family trees of most of the aristocratic colonial families would not stand close examination. American aristocracy was based on wealth rather than on blood. It was possible for an enterprising and lucky man of the lower classes to attain aristocratic rank by amassing a fortune. The frontier also offered an escape to men of humble origin who resented aristocratic dictation. Colonial conditions thus loosened the bonds of aristocratic society and supplied a large measure of freedom for men of lesser rank and means.

Probably the sharpest differences between the new and old worlds were in political life. Although each American colony had its own government, a common pattern had developed by 1776. Each colony had a governor who represented the authority of the British crown and who was usually chosen by the crown. In theory, the governor had extensive powers to direct colonial affairs and to curb colonial freedom. Each colony (except Pennsylvania) had a two-house legislature. The lower house was elected by property owners, while the upper house was usually appointed by the British king or by the governor. The powers of the colonial legislatures were never clearly defined, but in general they were extensive in local affairs and in taxation. The governors had nearly absolute powers of veto over these bodies, but since they were at the mercy of the legislatures for salaries and funds, they were not usually in a position to exercise these powers. The colonists had a system of courts patterned after British courts and enjoyed the rights of Englishmen as incorporated in English common law.

In actual operation, colonial governments grew accustomed to a wide range of freedom, and the colonists increasingly felt that it was their right to decide their own political fate. Prior to 1776 the colonists would have admitted that the British government had authority over them; yet when it came to specific issues, they would have argued that their own governments must have a voice in making decisions. The feeling was emerging that the colonial governments carried a weight equal to that of the British government. One hundred and fifty years of experience in self-government had created a breach wider than the Atlantic between Great Britain and her colonies.

Colonial religious life was unique. In spite of the fact that the colonies paid taxes to support churches that were often intolerant and dictatorial, there was still greater religious freedom than in most of Europe. Puritanism flourished more vigorously in colonial New England than in Europe. Alongside such established religions as Puritanism and Anglicanism, there was room for Presbyterians, Quakers, Lutherans, Dutch Reformed, Roman Catholics, and Jews. And during the Great Awakening in the eighteenth century, a number of evangelical religions such as Methodism took root.

Prior to 1776 the colonists distinguished themselves least in cultural activities. They did establish colleges and lower schools in an attempt to prepare men for careers in colonial society. Newspapers appeared in many areas. The rudiments of a distinctly American architectural style emerged. But little was produced in literature and art that is worthy of note; and in the final analysis colonial cultural life was still tied to that of Europe. Perhaps the most astounding development in colonial America was the ability of the colonists to keep abreast of Europe's chief cultural movements. Neither the sea barrier nor language nor the rigorous life in the colonies prevented Americans from absorbing the ideas of the Enlightenment and the implications of the new science.

Although there were by 1776 wide differences between American and British society, these differences did not spell revolution. Most Americans were still Englishmen and still closely attached to a European tradition. Their economic ideas, their political system, their religion, and their social concepts were fundamentally European, adapted to fit a new environment, but not magically transformed into something new. Their revolt was inspired by the conviction that Britain was violating the very tradition the colonists had inherited from her. The revolution was not a case of the Americans repudiating Europe; it was more nearly a case of the Americans seeking to put into practice some of Europe's most prized and most advanced concepts in order to fulfill the promise of the society they had planted and nourished in the New World.

2. THE QUARREL WITH GREAT BRITAIN

The numerous forces working to create a unique society in colonial America were little understood in Great Britain. Throughout most of the seventeenth century, the British were completely occupied with the painful struggle to decide the seat of authority and the nature of the political system. During the next century, England became a complacent nation, ruled by a narrow aristocracy not especially sensitive to new ideas and the need for change. The ruling forces in Great Britain subscribed fully to mercantilist principles with respect to colonial possessions: A great power should try to export more than it imported. Colonies were valuable in realizing that goal insofar as they could supply raw materials which the mother country would otherwise have to buy elsewhere and could furnish markets for the manufactured goods produced by the more advanced economic system of the mother country. America was thus to England a source of scarce products, such as lumber, furs, cotton, tobacco, and so forth, and a market for cloth, iron, tea, and other such items. The major question from the English point of view was how to ensure that America served these ends. The essence of England's policy was spelled out in the Navigation Acts, passed originally in 1650 and 1651 and then renewed in 1660 and 1663. These laws required that certain "enumerated" items produced in America had to be sold in England, that the colonists must purchase manufactured goods only in England, and that all shipping from the colonies had to be carried in British or colonial ships. In a broad way, these acts implied that the mother country would control the colonial economy and determine the direction of its growth to suit her own interests. There was no intention on the part of the English to pillage the colonies; rather, the assumption was that the colonists would benefit from conformity to British direction.

For a long time, Great Britain's policy caused little friction with the Americans. The early colonial economy, rich in raw materials and lacking much manufacturing, benefited by having a ready outlet for colonial products and a sure source of manufactured goods. The British were extremely lax in administering colonial policy, with the consequence that many enterprising colonials found themselves in an advantageous position. They enjoyed a privileged position in the British economy, while finding ample opportunity to trade directly with other nations in total disregard of British regulations. During most of the first half of the eighteenth century, many colonials, especially New Englanders, ignored the laws requiring the purchase of manufactured goods and the sale of raw materials in England and built up a far-reaching trading enterprise chiefly profitable to themselves. British laxity and American enterprise combined to promote the development of strictly American economic interests that had little relevance to England's interests and needs.

The long succession of eighteenth-century wars that pitted England against France, culminating in the Seven Years' War, brought a change in England's policy after 1763. England's success in these wars greatly enlarged her holdings in America and awakened her to the potential of her vast holdings. A subtle change was affecting imperial thinking everywhere in Europe, one that stressed the importance of possessing territory rather than the older concept of exploiting trade as a source of power and wealth. The events of the Seven Years' War in America, marked by a refusal of the Americans to raise troops and money, by their blatant trafficking with the enemy, and by their open defiance of royal authority, made England realize how inadequate her system of colonial control was. The long struggle with France also left England with a huge debt, incurred in part to save Americans from the French and the Indians; in the minds of English taxpayers, it was time for the ungrateful colonials to pay up. An overhaul of colonial policy, aimed at more effective control in support of England's interests, was in order. However, the colonials were hardly in a mood to comply after so long enjoying the freedom to do what they wished. Very quickly after 1763 a bitter struggle developed that led the colonials to rebellion, a declaration of independence, and victory.

The strife began when Britain enacted the Grenville (1764–1765) and Townshend (1767) acts, named after the British political leaders who steered them through Parliament. These measures were inspired by a desire on the part of England to raise money and to tighten colonial administration. The laws closed the trans-Allegheny frontier to further settlement, laid duties on numerous imports into the colonies, provided taxes on business documents (the Stamp Tax), prohibited various kinds of manufacturing in the colonies, imposed regulations on colonial money, and established British military and naval forces in the colonies at the expense of the colonial citizenry. Along with these new regulations went an enlargement of the policing forces in the colonies that seriously impeded the ability of the Americans to flout British regulations.

The Americans immediately began to fight back with fiery speeches, boycotts, protest meetings (such as the Stamp Act Congress), and violence. From the American perspective, the British victory in the wars of the first half of the eighteenth century had stemmed largely from the colonial contribution, and therefore it was unjust to force the colonials to pay the cost. The Americans complained bitterly that they were being taxed without representation in Parliament and that their own legislatures, long the chief source of governing regulations, were being completely disregarded. Britain's new imperial policy was broad enough to affect nearly all the colonists and thus drove them to greater unity than had previously existed. A depression following the Seven Years' War exacerbated American anger and discontent.

The vigor of American resistance forced England to modify some of the more inflammatory provisions of the new colonial policy, but did not basically change the thrust of her effort to tighten her control over the colonies and reap a larger profit from them. By 1768 she was compelled to send troops to America to enforce her will, and she had empowered her officials to seize property in ways that paid little heed to British law. Clearly, England's conduct suggested that she considered her colonists less than full British citizens. The Americans likewise grew more radical in their position; one suspects that John Adams was right when he said that the revolution was effected in the minds and hearts of men before the war commenced. Many Americans became convinced that the British were bent on depriving them of their traditional English liberties while stealing their wealth through taxation enacted without their consent. Increasingly in the American mind such an assault on liberty and property was a violation of the fundamental laws of nature and cause enough for resistance of any kind. Independence and self-government appeared to be the only alternative to the policy of a government that seemed less appreciative of its own sacred principles than did the Americans. Reinforcing the political sentiments of the Americans was their concern over the economic cost of Britain's new policy as it bore on American society.

After 1773, the incessant quarreling quickened in tempo to the point of crisis. Angered by the conduct of the Boston "Indians," who destroyed a cargo of tea belonging to the British East India Company, Parliament passed the "Intolerable Acts." This legislation closed the port of Boston, placed Massachusetts under the control of a military commander, quartered troops in Boston homes, and threatened those suspected of a major crime with transportation to Britain for trial in the English courts. As if this were not serious enough, Parliament then passed the Quebec Act, which provided for joining all the territory north of the Ohio River and west of the Alleghenies to the province of Quebec, establishing a nonrepresentative royal administration for this province, and granting toleration to French Catholics. More than ever, Americans were convinced that Britain considered them second-class citizens.

This new legislation provided the leaders of the colonial resistance—men such as Samuel Adams, long an advocate of radical measures—with an opportunity to organize an impressive display of protest and to convert discontent into action. At the instigation of some Virginia legislators at odds with the royal governor of Virginia, the First Continental Congress was summoned in 1774 to meet in Philadelphia. Inspired by radical leaders, the delegates adopted a bold statement that proclaimed the Intolerable Acts illegal, stated that Parliament had violated men's natural rights, and recommended resistance to England. The increasing reference to "natural rights" in the arguments of the colonists was momentous. It signified that many colonials believed in a natural law superior to English law and in a right, perhaps even an obligation, to revolt if the English violated that natural law. Here was a principle that could breed revolution. The ties with England were not yet broken, but they were under an extreme strain.

In England, a few statesmen realized the danger of the situation, but they could not muster enough parliamentary support for conciliatory policies aimed at reassuring that considerable segment of the colonial population still unready to break with England. Rather, the English government showed a determination to enforce the Intolerable Acts; in fact, new measures were enacted to increase English control. Both England and the colonists began to prepare for war. Hostilities opened in April 1775 with skirmishes at Lexington and Concord. In May 1775 the Second Continental Congress, led by men ready to declare independence, took steps to organize the war that had already started and appointed George Washington as commander of the American armies.

Colonial opinion had heretofore lagged behind the radical leaders who wanted a break with England, but once the shooting started it rapidly caught up. There was a rising cry for independence. The most potent statement to that effect was delivered by Thomas Paine in his pamphlet *Common Sense*, which appeared early in 1776. His stirring assault on monarchy and its evils and his scathing denunciation of British greed fired the growing appeal of republicanism and fed the expanding national pride of all manner of men who had once thought of themselves just as Englishmen living in America. Only independence could satisfy these sentiments. The English helped by pushing their war plans vigorously and by declaring the colonists rebels. The English pressure inevitably forced the colonial leaders to realize that foreign aid was needed; and that help could only be gained if the Americans broke with England and stood as an independent nation.

Popular sentiment in favor of independence finally made itself felt in 1776, when various colonies instructed their delegations to the Second Continental Congress to break with Britain. On July 4, 1776, Congress issued the Declaration of Independence, the work of Thomas Jefferson, one of the radical leaders. Its magnificent preamble, leaning heavily on the political philosophy of John Locke and the European disciples of the Enlightenment, stated in strong words the doctrines of natural rights and government by contract. The British government had violated these rights and thus had no claim on the allegiance of its subjects, who were entitled to form a new contract to ensure their rights. The Declaration of Independence elevated the struggle above a petty rebellion against legally constituted authority. It made America's struggle that of all "enlightened" men. Not only did it clarify the issues of 1776, but it inspired later generations to strike for liberty in the name of rights so fundamental that they were beyond the authority of any government.

3. THE AMERICAN REVOLUTION

Only a few words can be devoted to the American struggle for independence. Although Britain's power seemed overwhelming, her advantage was offset by poor leadership, distance, and commitments elsewhere. The chief problem of the Americans was overcoming disunity. Many loyalists, or Tories, did not approve of the war against Great Britain. And those in favor of the revolution often disagreed about the course that the new nation should take. These divisions were almost miraculously set aside long enough to press

the cause of independence to a successful conclusion. In no small way success rested with the leadership provided by men like George Washington, Thomas Jefferson, Benjamin Franklin, and John Adams, who demonstrated unsuspected talents in leading armies, organizing resources, solidifying popular support, and negotiating with foreign powers.

When the war opened in 1775, the British were unprepared and had to withdraw from Boston to gather their resources, an event the Americans interpreted as a victory. Pushing their initial advantage, the Americans undertook an unsuccessful campaign against Canada in late 1775. By July 1776, Britain was ready to attack, and seized New York as a base of operations. The following months marked the darkest hours of the revolutionary cause. Washington's pitifully small army, poorly fed and armed, was hounded through New Jersey and Delaware; only the caution of the British commander, General Howe, saved it from destruction. Washington did manage to strike blows at Trenton and Princeton in the winter, but these victories were valuable chiefly in keeping up American morale.

The turning point came in 1777, when the British attempted to split the colonies by capturing the Hudson Valley. Their strategy consisted of driving down from Canada and up from New York. General John Burgoyne led the British armies from Canada. Under constant attack from the Americans, his progress was anything but spectacular. No help came from the south. Howe occupied himself in the useless capture of Philadelphia. While he enjoyed that victory, Burgoyne's effort turned into a disaster. Finally, in October 1777, he surrendered at Saratoga.

American spirits rose rapidly as a result of this victory. Its chief effect was to swing the French to the American cause. France, moved by a desire to see Great Britain defeated and by a genuine sympathy for America's cause, had unofficially been offering help to the colonists since 1775. However, she had not committed herself fully, fearing that the Americans would either patch up their quarrel with the British or would be defeated, leaving France in a war from which nothing could be won. The victory at Saratoga convinced France that America had a chance for victory. In 1778 a formal alliance was agreed upon, and France began to supply needed money, ships, and troops. In the wake of Saratoga and the French commitment, other European powers showed increasing friendliness toward America and hostility toward Britain. Spain and the Dutch eventually declared war on Britain. The British now had a world war on their hands; the pressure on America was considerably relieved.

After 1777 fighting in America was spread over a wide area. The British withdrew from Philadelphia and concentrated large forces in New York. Washington's army was chiefly engaged in containing these forces. The British threw their offensive effort into a campaign in the South, trying in 1780–1781 to capture the Carolinas and Virginia. This campaign ended in a disastrous defeat at Yorktown, Virginia, in October 1781, Americans and French both sharing in the victory. This was the last major battle of the war, although hostilities officially continued until 1783. By 1781 Britain was anxious to end a war that threatened her position all around the world.

Peace negotiations were conducted in Paris. The American delegation, led by Benjamin Franklin, was sent with instructions to follow French leadership and to make no separate treaty with Britain. However, France, eager to deliver Britain a few more blows, was in no hurry to conclude the war. Moreover, she had hopes of reannexing the territories in North America that she had given up in 1763, since the new American nation as yet had no legal claim to these lands. Having detected the French intentions, the American delegates disregarded their instructions and made a separate peace with the British. By the terms of the Treaty of Paris, 1783, Britain recognized America's independence and ceded to her all territories east of the Mississippi from the Great Lakes to Spanish Florida. The Ameri-

Revolutionary War Campaigns

cans agreed to honor all debts owed Britain and to make restoration to the Tories who had suffered during the war. The French, unwilling now to continue the war on their own, also agreed to these terms. The new American nation had won a magnificent victory.

4. REVOLUTION AND THE DEMOCRATIZATION OF AMERICAN SOCIETY

The American Revolution involved more than a successful war against Great Britain. Some Americans had drawn back in 1775–1776 at the prospect of dissolving the existing social and political order and building a new one. However, once the decision for independence was taken, there was no turning back. As the war progressed, moves were made to construct new institutions for America. In the years following 1776 the Americans showed a genius for combining traditional patterns of life with radical new ideas. Their revolution did not uproot the old social order completely in the name of any radical doctrine; yet it did incorporate into the new order some of the most advanced ideas of the Enlightenment.

The first important efforts at reconstruction were made on the state level (as the colonies were called after July 4, 1776). New state governments, based on British principles of government and on colonial political experience, were created in all the colonies. The framers of these governments sought to create a political order that would protect men's liberties without becoming tyranny. Nearly every state drew up a written constitution carefully defining the structure and functions of government. Elaborate bills of rights, stressing traditional English liberties, were included in the constitutions. Since sovereignty rested with the people, elections were provided for all officials. Two-house legislatures were established, the lower houses being controlled by property-holding voters and the upper houses being selected by the lower chambers. Legislatures were armed with extensive powers to control and check executive officials, who were universally suspected of being the chief instigators of tyranny. Independent judiciaries were almost universally adopted. The whole philosophy of separation of powers was thereby incorporated into the new state governments, signifying a strong conviction that the powers of government must be limited by constitutional safeguards. Taken as a whole, the state constitutions framed between 1776 and 1780 inaugurated a degree of popular control over government unknown in the contemporary world, although none of them was completely democratic.

The revolution affected changes in other areas of life as significant as those altering the political structure. Several states took steps to disestablish state-supported churches, to institute religious toleration, and in general to separate political and religious life. Many states passed new land laws that tended to make it easier to gain ownership of property. Especially significant was the abolition of primogeniture, which required that the eldest son receive all his father's land. Slavery was abolished in some Northern states, in part at least because this institution seemed out of place in a society dedicated to the principles of the Declaration of Independence. All these liberalizing movements pointed toward greater freedom in the future.

Quite accidentally, the revolution had an important leveling effect in terms of the distribution of wealth. An inflation, caused by the efforts of the Americans to pay for the war with paper money, wiped out fortunes, aided debtors, and allowed new fortunes to be built. Many established merchants suffered heavy losses from the disturbance of foreign trade, but new opportunities in trade and industry emerged once America was free from the British commercial system. Small farmers flourished during the war, bolstered by easy money and high prices. Under these varied pressures, the prerevolutionary social order did not survive intact. Again, a greater degree of social equality and personal freedom emerged to characterize life in the new nation.

5. LAUNCHING THE NEW NATION

Even more challenging to the Americans was the problem of creating a central government capable of organizing the struggle for independence. Perhaps there were some who accepted in theory the Enlightenment dream that the best government was a small republic, but the realities of a war for survival, the dangers inherent in a world of large and ambitious nations, and the bonds of unity existing among the people who had carved a new destiny out of the wilderness of the New World compelled the Americans soon after the opening of the war to begin thinking of fashioning a common government. Movement in this direction always had to contend with the existence of the thirteen separate states, each commanding a considerable loyalty and each the proud possessor of a long tradition of independent action in the face of the English government.

The first attempt at forming a national government was the work of the Second Continental Congress, dominated by the radical leadership that had framed the Declaration of Independence. These men had a deep distrust for strong government over which the populace had no control. On the basis of this conviction, they shaped the Articles of Confederation in 1777 and secured its acceptance by all the states by 1781. A national congress in which each state had one vote was created and given considerable authority to conduct foreign affairs, declare war, issue money, raise armies, fix weights and measures, and borrow money. The executive branch of the government was entrusted to a committee of thirteen, selected by congress. However, congress lacked the essential powers to tax and to regulate commerce, and on most vital issues its decisions had to be submitted to the states for final approval. The Articles of Confederation thus established a loose union of thirteen nearly independent states headed by a central government that could not compel them to do anything but could only encourage them to cooperate.

The Articles of Confederation survived until 1789. The central government made some decisions of lasting importance, such as provisions for the use of the public lands west of the Alleghenies. On the whole, however, the government was weak and indecisive, especially after the victory over England removed

the cohesive force of war as the reason for its existence. Little was done to curb the aggressive policies of Britain and Spain to the west. The grievous economic problems of the new nation were unresolved. The states, free to pursue their individual policies in economic affairs, often worked at cross-purposes. Some of them seriously threatened property rights, but the most dangerous action of the states was their issuance of nearly worthless paper money that inflated prices, benefited debtors, and nearly wiped out the fortunes of the wealthy.

In the face of the mounting evidence of the inadequacies of the confederation, there was rising sentiment for a stronger central government. Many grew certain that too little government was as bad as too much. And many began to think "continentally," as Alexander Hamilton put it, seeing issues that far transcended the selfish provincialism so often manifested in the government established by the Articles of Confederation. This new feeling, constantly challenged by the old fears of too-strong central government and the pride of the states, finally led in May 1787 to the summoning of a convention to consider revising the Articles of Confederation. Those present were chiefly men of wealth and position, not a little disturbed by some of the radical moves being taken in the states they represented. This fact has sometimes led to the conclusion that the American constitution was framed by men bent on creating an instrument to safeguard the interests of the privileged few. Although there may be some truth in this position, the delegates were also patriots interested in safeguarding all Americans and men with firm convictions, drawn chiefly from the philosophy of the Enlightenment, about what government ought to be.

The convention immediately decided to scrap the Articles of Confederation and to write a new constitution. Once this task was undertaken, the delegates found themselves in broad agreement on many vital matters. They agreed that a written constitution enumerating the powers of the central government was necessary, that there must be popular control over the central government, and that every government must have built-in checks, necessitating the separation of powers of the various branches. No one believed that the states should be stripped of all power, yet all were convinced that the central government must have certain powers to deal independently with matters affecting national interests.

Working from these premises, the delegates quickly arrived at a basic framework for a new government. A two-house legislature, a president, and a national judiciary were to be established. Each branch was provided with specific functions, and an elaborate system of internal checks was provided to prevent any branch from exercising too much power. The powers of the national government as a whole in certain specific areas were enumerated, while all other matters were reserved to the states. The federal government was given clearly stated authority to coerce the states in those matters over which it had jurisdiction, and to ensure a degree of flexibility, provisions were made for amending the constitution.

In spite of broad agreement, there were a few crucial points over which the delegates long debated. One centered around finding a way to safeguard the interests of the small states against the large. This issue was settled by providing that seats in the House of Representatives would be apportioned according to population (with slaves counting three-fifths as much as freemen), while the Senate would be made up of two senators from each state, whatever its size. Another problem was the method of choosing the president. Many wanted a strong executive but were fearful of allowing the populace to select him. It was finally agreed that the president would be chosen for four years by a special electoral college, the members of which were to be chosen by the states.

The new document was handed over to the states for ratification with the provision that when nine states approved, the new government would go into effect. The constitution aroused stormy discussion within the states. However, one by one they fell into line. On June 21, 1788, the ninth state, New Hampshire, approved the constitution, and the new government was officially in existence. In the next month the crucial states of Virginia and New York accepted the constitution, and thus ensured that it would be put into actual operation. Rhode Island held out until May 1790. Several states added a condition to their acceptance of the constitution, asking that a bill of rights guaranteeing fundamental liberties be added. This condition was filled shortly after the government was set up by the addition of the first ten amendments to the constitution (1791).

The new government began operation in 1789 with George Washington as President and with men who were committed to the new Constitution (Federalists) in control of Congress. During the next decade the new government proved its worth. Congress provided legislation which filled in many crucial details of the governmental system that had been touched on in only a general way in the Constitution: a bill of rights, a system of federal courts, and executive departments to assist the President in discharging his responsibilities. Taxes were levied and collected, and public credit was established when the central government assumed state debts and funded its obligations on a sound basis. Although not gifted with great political wisdom, George Washington conducted himself in a way that gave dignity and independent stature to the

executive branch of the government, thus ensuring effective direction of national affairs while allaying deep-seated fears of executive tyranny. Two of his cabinet members, Alexander Hamilton, Secretary of the Treasury, and Thomas Jefferson, Secretary of State, proved to be skilled and devoted servants of the new nation. Hamilton's economic policies helped to restore prosperity, and Jefferson's foreign policy permitted the new nation to steer a perilous path of neutrality through the stormy international waters disturbed by the French Revolution.

Despite the successes of the new government under Washington and his successor, John Adams, there was mounting discontent with the Federalists who dominated it. The Federalists made it increasingly clear, especially through the policies promoted by Alexander Hamilton, that they intended to make the central government as strong as possible. Aristocratic in his political philosophy, Hamilton was convinced that what the new nation needed most was order and that only a powerful central government based on the support of men of wealth could provide that order. He fashioned a national economic policy intended to favor the wealthy and to tie their interests to a strong central government. His policy aroused opposition not only from economic self-interest on the part of those not favored by it, but also from philosophical principles rooted in fear of strong government, belief in human equality, and trust in the political wisdom of common men—ideas powerfully reinforced by the issues raised by the French Revolution. Those who opposed the Federalists began to rally around Thomas Jefferson, likewise an aristocrat but almost always at odds with Hamilton, especially on philosophical issues. A new political party, called the Republicans (not to be confused

George Washington and the Federalists are satirized in this cartoon, which illustrates the controversy that soon developed in the new nation over the issue of the extent of the central government's power. *Photo: Brown Brothers*

with the present Republican party, founded in 1854), took shape under Jefferson's leadership. The emergence of political parties added an element to the new government that the constitution makers had not foreseen. Although the Republican challenge to the Federalists failed in 1796, when John Quincy Adams was elected president, the new party won in 1800. In a close and bitter contest, Jefferson won the presidency in what he called the "Revolution of 1800." Perhaps it would be more accurate to say that this election completed the revolution begun twenty-five years earlier. It furnished the final proof of the workability of the new government, since it demonstrated that the voters controlled the government and that they did not have to rebel to make their voices heard. If the founding fathers thought they had created a government to serve the interests of the few (which they probably did not) and if the Hamiltonian Federalists felt that only the few could adequately run the new nation (which they probably did not),

they were disabused of that idea by Jefferson's victory in 1800.

Between 1775 and 1800 the Americans had put on an impressive display for the world. They had asserted their rights against tyranny by force of arms, and demonstrated that no government was sacred once it began to oppress men. They had then proceeded in a rational fashion to establish thirteen state governments and a national government that were capable of action yet were restricted from abusing the inalienable rights of men. Furthermore, an ingenious federal system was worked out whereby state and national governments coexisted. These governments proved sensitive to popular control and made the exercise of popular sovereignty a fact. Everywhere liberal, enlightened men saw their dreams becoming a reality in America. Here was inspiration and guidance for those who might like to change society elsewhere. The revolutionary era was launched in practice as well as in theory.

Suggested Reading

Colonial Society. The literature on the American colonial experience is immense; consequently, any selection has serious limitations. Perhaps a good starting point on the subject is Curtis Nettels, *The Roots of American Civilization: A History of American Colonial Life* (2nd ed., 1963). Also good are **L. B. Wright, *Atlantic Frontier: Colonial American Civilization (1603–1763)* (Cornell), and *Cultural Life of the American Colonies (1607–1763)* (Harper Torchbook). Provocative for their fresh interpretations of the unique nature of the colonial period are **D. J. Boorstin, *The Americans: The Colonial Experience* (Vintage); **Max Savelle, *Seeds of Liberty: Genesis of the American Mind* (University of Washington); and **V. L. Parrington, *Main Currents in*

American Thought, Vol. I: *The Colonial Mind, 1620–1800* (Harvest). But these works provide only an orientation; numerous historians of colonial America would not agree with their general views.

The Revolution. The forces that produced the American Revolution have been the subject of a long and bitter debate. A brief introduction to some of the conflicting viewpoints is a collection by **J. C. Wahlke, ed., *The Causes of the American Revolution* (Heath). Another excellent summary of conflicting views is **E. S. Morgan, *American Revolution: A Review of Changing Interpretations* (Service Center for Teachers of History).

A basic work that marked the beginnings of

much of the debate on the causes of the revolution is Carl Becker, *The Eve of the Revolution* (1921), which advanced the thesis that the revolution was a struggle to decide what element of colonial society would rule in America rather than a revolt against British rule. This view has been severely challenged on a wide variety of fronts. Perhaps the best summaries of this vast literature are **E. S. Morgan, *The Birth of the Republic, 1763–1789* (University of Chicago); **J. C. Miller, *Origins of the American Revolution* (Stanford); and **Bernhard Knollenberg, *Origins of the American Revolution, 1759–1766* (rev. ed., Free Press). Each of these works digests major conflicting views and ends with a positive view of what was crucial. Bernard Bailyn, *The Ideological Origins of the American Revolution* (1967), provides a brilliant analysis of the ideas that created a revolutionary spirit in America. An important view of the beginning of the revolution from the British perspective is **L. H. Gipson, *The Coming of the Revolution, 1763–1775* (Harper Torchbook). Also helpful in seeing the revolution from the British viewpoint is **Lewis Namier, *England in the Age of the American Revolution* (Papermac). A fine history of the revolution from a military point of view is **Howard Peckham, *The War for Independence: A Military History* (University of Chicago). Also useful are **W. M. Wallace, *Appeal to Arms: A Military History of the American Revolution* (Quadrangle); and **J. R. Alden, *The American Revolution, 1775–1783* (Harper Torchbook). **S. F. Bemis, *The Diplomacy of the American Revolution* (3rd ed., Midland Books), is the best survey of the diplomacy involved in the revolution. For a challenging view of the consequences of the revolution, one not shared by all historians, see **J. F. Jameson, *The American Revolution Considered as a Social Movement* (Princeton), which argues that the revolution greatly democratized American society. Two brilliant studies placing the American Revolution in the larger context of European history are R. R. Palmer, *The Age of Democratic Revolution: A Political History of Europe and America, 1760–1800* (2 vols., 1959–64); and **Crane Brinton, *The Anatomy of Revolution* (rev. ed., Vintage). **Carl Becker, *The Declaration of Independence: A Study in the History of Political Ideas* (Vintage), presents a brilliant analysis of the political ideals involved in the American Revolution.

The Constitution. A good treatment of the new nation under the Articles of Confederation is **Merrill Jensen, *The New Nation: A History of the United States During the Confederation, 1781–1789* (Vintage); this work casts a favorable light on the Articles. Clear descriptions of the Constitutional Convention are **Carl Van Doren, *The Great Rehearsal* (Compass); and **Max Farrand, *The Framing of the Constitution of the United States* (Yale). A highly influential interpretation of the Constitution is **C. A. Beard, *An Economic Interpretation of the Constitution of the United States* (Free Press). Originally published in 1913, this work maintained that the Constitution was made by a minority of wealthy men seeking to protect their interests. For powerful critiques of the Beard "thesis," see **R. E. Brown, *Charles Beard and the Constitution* (Norton), or **Forest McDonald, *We the People: The Economic Origins of the Constitution* (Phoenix).

The New Nation. Excellent surveys of the early decades of the new nation are **J. C. Miller, *The Federalist Era, 1789–1801* (Harper Torchbook); and **Marcus Cunliffe, *The Nation Takes Shape: 1789–1837* (University of Chicago). H. J. Ford, *Washington and His Colleagues* (1921), provides a feel for the leading personalities of the early years of the Republic. Also excellent are **C. G. Bowers, *Jefferson and Hamilton* (Sentry), which is pro-Jefferson; and L. M. Hacker, *Alexander Hamilton in the American Tradition* (1957), which defends Hamilton. **Joseph Charles, *The Origins of the American Party System* (Harper Torchbook), treats an important subject well. Alexander de Conde, *Entangling Alliances: Politics and Diplomacy Under George Washington* (1958), and Paul A. Varg, *The Foreign Policies of the Founding Fathers* (1963), provide good views of the major issues in foreign policy facing the new nation. For a broad view of American society in the early national period, see J. A. Krout and D. R. Fox, *The Completion of Independence, 1790–1830* (1944).

Chapter 40 ❧ The French Revolution, 1789–1799

During the long reign of Louis XV (1715–1774), French prestige declined steadily from the lofty heights it had reached under his predecessor. Louis XV was a lazy, selfish, and cynical man who lavished more time and money on his mistresses, Madame de Pompadour and Madame du Barry, than on affairs of state. His participation in the War of the Austrian Succession and the Seven Years' War resulted only in disgraceful defeats and the loss of France's empire in India and North America to Great Britain. His successor inherited an unbalanced budget and a discontented populace. Young Louis XVI (1774–1792), though well-meaning, reasonably intelligent, and of good moral character, was not the man to restore the prestige of the throne. He was awkward, shy, and weak-willed when the situation called for decision. His reign was ended by one of the greatest and most far-reaching upheavals in the history of Western civilization—the French Revolution.

1. THE LAST DAYS OF THE OLD REGIME IN FRANCE

France at the succession of Louis XVI, though somewhat weakened, was not in dire distress. She was still the richest and most influential nation in the world. During the reign of Louis XV, in spite of defeats and the loss of

most of her empire, her commerce and prosperity had steadily increased. Half of all the specie in Europe was to be found in France. With the possible exception of Great Britain, she enjoyed the highest standard of living of any of the great powers. It is not, therefore, to desperation born of poverty that one must look as an explanation for the French Revolution, but rather to frustration caused by existing institutions—social, religious, political, economic—that had failed to adjust to changing conditions.

French society on the eve of the French Revolution was divided into three distinct classes or *estates*. The First Estate was the clergy, numbering approximately 100,000 out of a total population of some 23 million. The Roman Catholic Church in France owned about 10 percent of the land—the best land—and from its lands and tithes and fees enjoyed an income probably half as large as that of the government itself. It controlled all educational institutions and censored the press. It monopolized public worship and continued to harass all other religious groups at a time when the spirit of religious tolerance was rising throughout most of the Western world. The clergy itself was sharply divided. The upper clergy—the bishops and the abbots— were rich and powerful. They were drawn exclusively from the ranks of the aristocracy

The women of Paris march on Versailles, October 5, 1789, and capture the King and Queen. Reproduction from a contemporary print. *Photo: Historical Pictures Service, Chicago*

and were generally looked upon by most of the lower clergy and the common people as parasites. The lower clergy—the priests and the monks—came from the lower classes. The income of the priests was modest. They shared the lives of the people they served, but they had almost no influence on Church policy.

The Second Estate was the nobility, numbering approximately 400,000. Since the death of Louis XIV in 1715, the French nobility had recouped its power and influence at the expense of the king and of the bourgeoisie. All the high government posts were now held by the nobility. These offices, many of them just meaningless titles, carried handsome salaries and pensions. The nobility owned approximately 20 percent of the land of France, but was exempt from all direct taxation. The richest of them lived at Versailles as absentee landlords, where they hunted, intrigued, made love, and read the books of the philosophers of the Enlightenment. They were reputed to possess the best manners and the worst morals of any class in Europe. The most haughty of the nobility—the most jealous of their rights—were the newcomers, the *noblesse de la robe* (nobility of the gown). These were former rich bourgeois who had purchased judgeships in one of the high law courts.

The Third Estate was composed of the commoners—the bourgeoisie, the proletariat, and the peasantry—and comprised nearly 98 percent of the total population. Of all the social and economic groups in France in 1789, the bourgeoisie were probably the most frustrated. These were business and professional people, the bankers, merchants, shopkeepers, lawyers who had grown into a middle class between the nobility and the peasantry. By the late eighteenth century, the upper French bourgeoisie had gone as far as their wits and energy could take them. They had become richer by far than most of the nobility, only to find the highest levels of government and society closed to them.

The proletariat—the city wage earners—were not a class-conscious group such as we find in modern industrial society. Many of them were servants of the rich and even tended to identify with their masters. Nevertheless, there was enough distress among the proletariat to create tensions—tensions that would increase with the maladjustments caused by the revolution. During the course of the eighteenth century, the price of bread had risen three times as fast as wages. Paris was the only city in France with a proletariat large enough to make its influence strongly felt. There, about 300,000 citizens (about half the total population of the city) could be classified as proletarians, and there they would play a significant role in the Revolution.

At least 90 percent of the French people in 1789 were peasants, tillers of the soil. Although they were probably better off than the peasants of any other country in Europe (they owned at least 30 percent of the land, and serfdom had virtually disappeared), they were on the whole discontented. Most of the peasants owned land that was subject to feudal dues or were landless sharecroppers who gave up 50 percent of their produce to the lord in addition to the feudal dues (the fees paid by the peasant for use of the lord's mill, oven, wine press, and breeding stock, death taxes, inheritance taxes, sale of property taxes). Not only was the peasant forbidden to hunt; he could not even protect his crops from the lord's hunting parties—nor, for that matter, from the game itself. Although the French peasant no longer had to donate his labor to the lord, he still was required to furnish so many days' labor for roads and public works. On him fell nearly all the direct taxes levied by the national government.

The life of the peasant too had not changed much since the Middle Ages, except that he was no longer a serf. He lived in little rural villages, the houses close together and the livestock frequently under the same roof. The house usually consisted of one room, with a dirt floor, thatched roof, and neither chimney nor glass windows. His daily diet was made up almost entirely of dark bread and wine; meat was reserved for special occasions. Entertainment centered around the Church. On Sundays and holy days, of which there were many, his attire and attitude were festive and gay. Unlike most of Europe, however, there were opportunities for advancement—the ambitious young French peasant could buy some land, become a priest or the lord's steward, a blacksmith or innkeeper, or try his fortune in the city—but only relatively few would succeed.

The government of France was arbitrary. The king's decree was law. The Estates General, the French counterpart of the British Parliament, had not met for nearly two centuries. Justice was capricious and corrupt. There were 237 different codes of law to confuse the litigants. There were no juries as in Great Britain. The king could arrest and imprison at will (although Louis XV and Louis XVI seldom did). The judges of the thirteen superior courts, called *parlements*, purchased or inherited their titles. Torture was still used. The arbitrariness and inherent injustice of this system, which had long been taken for granted, seemed intolerable to the readers of Voltaire and Rousseau.

The breakdown of the old regime in France began in the field of finance. Louis XVI had inherited a large and constantly growing national debt. It was not excessive for a rich nation like France; Great Britain and the Netherlands had higher per capita debts. But, when combined with the exemption of the nobility and the clergy from direct taxation and the extravagant cost of maintaining the military establishment and servicing the national debt (most of which had been incurred by past wars), it spelled eventual bankruptcy. Furthermore, France was still burdened with the corrupt system of tax collection that allowed much revenue to be diverted from the treasury into private pockets.

Upon assuming the throne, Louis XVI appointed the Physiocrat Turgot, a friend of Voltaire, as minister of finance. Turgot initiated a series of sweeping reforms designed to clean up the mess. However, those with vested interests in the old system brought about his dismissal at the end of two years, and his reform measures were rescinded. A succession of ministers then tried all kinds of palliatives, such as borrowing, pump-priming expenditures, better bookkeeping, but to no avail. By 1786 the debt was 3 billion livres,[1] and the annual deficit had reached 125 million. In a desperate effort to save his regime, Louis called an Assembly of Notables in 1787 in an attempt to persuade them to consent to be taxed. But the privileged orders refused, and demanded, instead, a meeting of the Estates General, thinking that they could control it and thereby save their privileges. Pressured by a virtual revolt of his own nobility, the king gave in.

2. THE TRIUMPH OF THE THIRD ESTATE

During the early months of 1789 elections were held for members of the Estates General. All France was agog with excitement. Voltaire and Rousseau had done their work; it was generally believed that man could construct an earthly paradise if given a chance.

Since the Estates General had not met for a hundred and seventy-five years, no one quite knew the procedure. Hundreds of pamphlets appeared, and there was widespread public debate. By tradition, each of the three estates, the clergy, the nobility, and the commoners, elected their own representatives. All males who had reached the age of twenty-five and paid taxes were permitted to vote. Since the Third Estate, including the bourgeoisie, the peasantry, and the proletariat, comprised more than nine-tenths of the total population, it was given as many seats as the other two combined. This large representation for the Third Estate was not believed to be especially significant at the time, since

[1] The livre was technically worth about 20 cents, but its purchasing power in the eighteenth century was much greater than that of the mid-twentieth-century American dollar.

again by tradition the three estates sat separately, and each group had one vote.

By April 1789, the delegates began to arrive at Versailles. Good will prevailed. Violent revolution was far from anyone's mind. The delegates came armed only with *cahiers*, the lists of grievances that had been called for by the king. Of the six hundred representatives of the Third Estate, not one was a peasant. Except for a handful of liberal clergy and nobles who were elected to the Third Estate, they were all bourgeois. Nearly all the members of the Third Estate, as well as many members of the two privileged estates, were fully acquainted with and enamored of the philosophy of the Enlightenment.

The first formal session was held on May 5. Immediately a sharp debate began over the method of voting. The two privileged estates demanded that, according to custom, the three estates meet separately and vote by order, that is, each estate cast one vote. This would mean that all attacks on privilege and inequality would be defeated by a vote of two to one. The Third Estate, already becoming disillusioned by the snobbish attitude of the royal court and of some of the members of the first two estates, demanded that the voting be by head. The three estates would meet jointly, each individual member casting one vote. This would mean that all measures for fundamental reform would pass, for not only did the Third Estate have as many members as the other two combined, but a certain number of liberal clergy and noblemen sympathized with the common people and the cause of reform. Both sides realized that the outcome of this issue would be decisive.

On June 17, after six weeks of fruitless haggling, the Third Estate declared itself to be the National Assembly of France and invited the other two estates to join it in the enactment of legislation. Three days later, on June 20, when the members of the Third Estate arrived at their meeting hall, they found it locked and guarded by royal troops. Adjourning to a nearby building used as an indoor tennis court, they took the "Tennis Court Oath," vowing never to disband until France had a constitution. It was the Third Estate's first act of defiance. On June 23 the king met with the three estates in a royal session at which he commanded them once and for all to meet separately and vote by order. The king, his ministers, and members of the first two estates filed out, but the representatives of the Third Estate defiantly remained seated. When the royal master of ceremonies returned to remind them of the king's orders, Mirabeau, a liberal nobleman elected by the Third Estate, jumped to his feet and shouted, "Go and tell those who sent you that we are here by the will of the people and will not leave this place except at the point of the bayonet!" When the startled courtier repeated these words to his master, Louis XVI, with characteristic weakness, replied, "They mean to stay. Well damn it, let them stay." A few days later he reversed himself and ordered the three estates to meet jointly and vote by head.

The Third Estate had thus won the first round. However, alarming news soon began to arrive that the king was calling the professional troops of the frontier garrison to Versailles. It appeared that he was at last preparing to use force. At this critical juncture, the Parisians countered the threat of force with force. On July 14, a riotous mob marched on and destroyed the Bastille, a gloomy old fortress prison in the working-men's quarter that symbolized the arbitrary tyranny of the old regime. (July 14 has long been celebrated as the French national holiday.) This show of force stayed the king's hand.

Throughout the remainder of July and August the spirit of violence spread from Paris to the rest of France, where it had been only desultory hitherto. Many nobles fled from France for their lives (the *émigrés*), and feudalism, for all practical purposes, came to an end. Since the peasants feared reprisals from the nobility and believed a widespread rumor that the nobles were raising brigand bands against them, this period is known as the

This engraving commemorates the storming of the Bastille, hated symbol of arbitrary government and royal and aristocratic tyranny. The day of its destruction by the Parisian mob, July 14, has long been celebrated as the French national holiday. *Photo: Bibliothèque Nationale–Estampes*

Great Fear. The legal end of feudalism came on August 4, when, during a hysterical night session of the National Assembly, one nobleman after another stood up and renounced his feudal rights and privileges.

Three weeks later, August 27, the National Assembly proclaimed the Declaration of the Rights of Man and the Citizen. This document, which followed the English Bill of Rights by an even hundred years and preceded the American Bill of Rights by two years, was replete with the phrases of the philosophers of the Enlightenment. "Men are born and remain free and equal in rights." The natural rights of man were declared to be "liberty, property, security, and resistance to oppression." Liberty of opinion "even in religion," freedom of the press, and freedom from arbitrary arrest were all proclaimed. Thus, within a span of three weeks' time, August 4 to August 27, 1789, two of the most constructive achievements of the revolution—or of modern history, for that matter—were proclaimed: the end of feudalism and the individual freedom and legal equality of all Frenchmen.

The forces of privilege and reaction, however, still had to be brought to terms. The king not only refused to sign the August decrees, but began once more to assemble troops around Versailles and Paris. In answer to this new threat of force, a huge mob of Parisian women on October 5 and 6 marched the 10 miles out to Versailles, surrounded the palace, and forced the king to accompany them to the city, where he became a virtual prisoner of the populace. As the carriage bearing the royal family rolled toward Paris, the surrounding mob shouted jubilantly, "We have the baker, the baker's wife, and the little cook boy! Now we shall have bread!" A few days later, the National Assembly moved its sessions to Paris, where it came increasingly under the influence of the radical populace of the great city. The Third Estate had triumphed.

3. MAKING FRANCE AN "ENLIGHTENED" MONARCHY

The National Assembly could now at last settle down to the task of making France over in the image of Voltaire and Montesquieu. During the next two years it passed a series of sweeping reforms that may be conveniently classified as follows:

JUDICIAL. The *parlements*, and the manorial and ecclesiastical courts with their arbitrary procedures and overlapping jurisdictions were swept away. An orderly system of lower and higher courts was established. The administration of justice was decentralized and democratized. Judges were to be elected for six-year terms. Torture was abolished. In criminal cases juries were to be used for the first time in French history.

ECONOMIC. In accordance with the doctrine of laissez faire, guilds, labor unions, and trading associations were abolished. All occupations were declared open to all classes. Feudal obligations, including labor on the public roads, had already come to an end on the night of August 4. Internal tolls and customs were abolished.

FINANCIAL. The complex and unequal taxes, direct and indirect, were swept away. They were replaced by a tax on land and a tax on the profits of trade and industry. Both were uniform, and no one was exempt. Tax farming was, at long last, abolished. Expenditures were henceforth to be authorized only by the national legislature. To meet the pressing financial needs of the government, the National Assembly issued paper money called *assignats* to the value of 400 million livres. To back up this paper money, the property of the Roman Catholic Church, valued at approximately that amount, was confiscated.

RELIGIOUS. The seizure of property was the first step toward the nationalization of the Church. Monasticism was abolished. The secular clergy was to be elected by the people (including non-Roman Catholics) and their salaries paid by the state. The bishops were reduced in number, wealth, and power. They were no longer to be invested by the pope. These measures were incorporated in the Civil Constitution of the Clergy, to which all the members of the clergy were required to take an oath of allegiance in order to perform their functions and draw their salaries. The pope, whose control over the organization and the clergy of the French church would have been broken, declared the Civil Constitution of the Clergy to be founded upon heretical principles and ordered the clergy to refuse to take the oath of allegiance. A majority of the clergy, including nearly all the bishops, followed the pope's command. The defection of the "nonjuring clergy" and of thousands of their devoted parishioners was the first serious split in the ranks of the revolutionists.

POLITICAL. Under the new constitution, which was completed in 1791, the central government was patterned after the ideas of Montesquieu. Judicial, legislative, and executive powers were separated. Lawmaking was given to the single-chamber Legislative Assembly of 745 members elected for two-year terms. Voting, however, was limited to males at least twenty-five years of age who paid taxes equivalent to three days' wages. It is estimated that some 4 million adult males ("active" citizens) could meet these qualifications and that some 2 million remained "passive" citizens. Actually to sit in the Legislative Assembly required the payment of taxes amounting to 54 livres. Only some 70,000 Frenchmen could meet this qualification, and the weight of power fell to the bourgeoisie. The king was granted a suspensive veto over all but financial and constitutional measures, but three successive legislatures could pass a bill over the king's veto. The conduct of foreign relations was left in the hands of the king, but he could not declare war or make treaties without the consent of the Legislative Assembly. The king's expenditures were limited to a sum voted by the legislative body. France was greatly decentralized. For purposes of local government and administration, the country was divided into eighty-three departments, each of which was administered by a small elected assembly. The execution of the national laws was placed almost entirely in the hands of the local authorities.

In October 1791, the National Assembly, having completed its work, gave way to the Legislative Assembly, which had recently been elected under the new constitution. Had Voltaire and Montesquieu been alive, they would have had every right to say, "I told you so." Within a brief span of two years and with very little bloodshed, France had been made over. The monarchy had been limited and "enlightened." The Roman Catholic Church had been subordinated to the state. Feudalism had come to an end. Individual rights and liberties and legal equality had been defined and established. But would Rousseau have been happy? Did the general will now prevail?

4. FOREIGN WAR AND THE FAILURE OF THE MODERATE REGIME

The new government so optimistically launched was expected to last forever. Actually, it lasted less than a year. Although the Legislative Assembly, elected under the restricted suffrage provisions of the new con-

stitution, was made up largely of moderate men, it probably represented the wishes and interests of the great majority of the French people. The chief gainers in the French Revolution thus far had been the bourgeoisie and the peasants. The bourgeoisie had gained political control over the country and social equality with the nobility. Most of the peasants, who constituted the bulk of the French population, could now vote, and all of them were at last free from feudal obligations. To the many peasant landowners who owned their land before the revolution were now added a few others who had seized the lands of émigré nobles or had purchased confiscated Church lands. Most of the bourgeoisie and the landowning peasants were satisfied and wished to see the revolution stop where it was, lest they lose their sacred property and their political dominance.

However, there were other groups that were quite dissatisfied. The royal family, the aristocracy, most of the clergy, and the army officers yearned for the restoration of their privileges. On the other hand, the city proletariat and some of the poorest peasants wished to see the revolution continued in a more radical way. They had gained little except theoretical rights and legal equality. Owning no property, they could not vote. Yet they had supplied much of the physical force that had saved the Third Estate and made the moderate reforms possible. Leadership for these disgruntled groups was found among the intelligentsia who were disciples of Rousseau. These intellectual radicals would be satisfied with nothing less than the overthrow of the monarchy and extension of the revolution.

The radical groups, although a definite minority of the French people, were well organized and ably led. In the Legislative Assembly itself, the most liberal or radical group was the Girondins, so-called because many of their leaders came from the vicinity of Bordeaux in the department of Gironde. Outside the assembly numerous clubs, of which the Jacobin Club became the most influential, were formed to debate and plan political matters. Although the Jacobins were and remained predominantly intellectual bourgeoisie and were moderate at first, they gradually became the most radical group in France. Three Jacobin leaders came to tower over all others. Jean Paul Marat, Swiss by birth, was an inordinately ambitious and frustrated physician and scientist turned popular journalist. His was the gift of rabble-rousing journalism. He incessantly demanded the beheading of all those leaders who opposed the further extension of the revolution. Georges Jacques Danton, a former lawyer in the king's council, was a thundering orator of great energy and ability. Maximilien de Robespierre was also a lawyer. This eloquent and sincere man was a fanatical disciple of Rousseau, bent upon the establishment of a deistic republic.

Events soon played into the hands of the radicals. The kings of Austria and Prussia, fearful of the spread of revolutionary ideas to their own lands and urged on by the French émigrés, began to make threatening moves and to issue meddlesome warnings to the French revolutionaries. In France the reactionaries believed that a successful war would enhance the prestige and power of the throne and that a defeat would result in the restoration of the old regime. Most of the radicals believed that war would expose the inefficiency and disloyalty of the king and bring about his downfall. When, therefore, in April 1792 Louis XVI appeared before the Legislative Assembly to request a declaration of war against Austria and Prussia, only seven negative notes were cast. Thus lightly was begun a war that was to last twenty-three years and affect most of the Western world.

The French armies, leaderless since nearly all the high-ranking officers were members of the nobility and had either fled or been de-

posed, were badly defeated. As the Austrian and Prussian armies advanced toward Paris, there was panic in the city. The king, who had already forfeited his popularity when he attempted to flee the country in June 1791, was now rightly suspected of being in treasonable communication with the enemy. On August 10, 1792, a huge Parisian mob advanced on the king's palace. The royal family fled for its life to the Legislative Assembly. The interior of the palace was wrecked, and several hundred of the Swiss guard were slain. The Legislative Assembly suspended and imprisoned Louis XVI and called elections for a national convention to draw up a new constitution to take the place of the one that had just failed.

5. THE TRIUMPH OF THE RADICALS AND THE REIGN OF TERROR

The elections to the constitutional convention took place in an atmosphere of panic and violence. During the interim between the overthrow of the limited monarchy and the meeting of the convention, Danton assumed emergency leadership of the nation. Feverishly he superintended the gathering of recruits and rushed them to the front. As the recruits were preparing to leave Paris, rumors spread that their wives and children would be murdered by the reactionary clergy and nobles. Violent elements began murdering members of the non-juring clergy and reactionary nobles who were being held in the prisons of Paris. During the first three weeks of September 1792, more than a thousand such victims were massacred. In the elections to the National Convention, held amid this hysteria, the radicals won a sweeping victory. Most of the conservative elements prudently stayed away from the polls.

In the Legislative Assembly the Girondins

The execution of Marie Antoinette in Paris, October 1793. The deaths of the members of the French royal family and of many of the nobility frightened the French opponents of the Revolution into supporting the radical regime against the foreign invaders.
Photo: Bibliothèque Nationale–Estampes

had been the Leftist group.[2] In the National Convention they found themselves on the extreme Right. The new Left was made up of the Jacobin followers of Marat, Danton, and Robespierre, mostly from the city of Paris. They came to be called the Mountain, since they occupied the highest seats in the convention hall. This radical convention, elected for the purpose of drawing up a new constitution, was to rule France for the next three years (1792–1795)—the most exciting years of the revolution.

The first act of the National Convention was to declare France a republic. The next move was to dispose of the king. After a fair trial he was found unquestionably guilty of treasonable communication with the enemy and sent to the guillotine—an instrument adopted by the revolutionists for the more scientific and humane beheading of the condemned.

[2] The present political connotation of the terms "right" and "left" derives from this period. In the revolutionary assemblies the conservatives sat quite by chance on the speaker's right, the liberals and radicals on his left.

The execution of Louis XVI, accompanied by proclamations of world revolution by the evangelical Jacobins, sent a shudder of horror through the royal courts of Europe. Furthermore, the hastily recruited French revolutionary armies, which had checked the Austrians and Prussians at Valmy in September 1792, had taken the offensive and overrun the Austrian Netherlands.

Austria and Prussia were now joined by Great Britain, the Dutch Netherlands, Spain, Portugal, Sardinia, and Naples in a great coalition bent upon the destruction of the French Revolution and the restoration of the old regime. The French armies were unable to stand up to such an array of armed might. But the defeats and invasions were not the worst disasters to confront the revolutionary government. The ignorant peasants of the Vendée region in western France, who had been stirred up by the non-juring clergy, rebelled against the radical government. The rebellion spread until some sixty of the eighty-three departments were affected. Major provincial cities such as Bordeaux, Lyons, and

Marseilles were in revolt. Toulon, the chief French naval base on the Mediterranean, invited in the British fleet. Inside the convention itself, many of the moderate Girondins were sympathetic to the rebels.

Faced with what seemed to be inevitable disaster to their radical cause and indeed to the revolution itself, the leaders of the Mountain decided on drastic action. Since the Paris Commune, as the city government was called, was already completely controlled by the radicals, the Mountain leaders conspired with it to incite a mob. On June 2, 1793, the National Convention, now dominated by the left wing and surrounded by a threatening Paris mob, voted the expulsion and arrest of twenty-nine Girondin leaders. Having thus silenced all opposition within the convention, the radical leaders and their followers inaugurated a reign of terror against their political enemies. Their goals were to unite France and to save and extend the revolution.

For efficiency, the National Convention delegated unlimited powers to a Committee of Public Safety, composed of twelve men working in secret. The most influential member of this all-powerful committee was Robespierre. At its call was the Committee of General Security, a national police force. A Revolutionary Tribunal was set up to try, condemn, and execute suspects without the usual legal procedure and as quickly as possible. Members of the National Convention were sent out in pairs to carry the Terror to every nook and cranny of France. Although tens of thousands of persons, possibly half a million, were imprisoned during the Reign of Terror, only some 16,000 are believed to have been executed. The drastic policy was remarkably successful. The disaffected elements were quickly silenced, and the rebellions quelled. The defense of the republic was entrusted to Lazare Carnot. A *levée en masse* was ordered. All men, women, and children were called to the colors. The able-bodied young men were rapidly trained and rushed to the front. Everyone else contributed his bit to the war effort on the home front. This common activity for defense of country produced a high state of morale—the first mass national patriotism in history. Able new officers were found. The armies of the coalition were defeated on every front and hurled back beyond the frontiers.

6. ROBESPIERRE'S UTOPIA OF ROUSSEAU

While Robespierre and his associates were saving the revolution, they were also busy extending it to more radical ground. A fanatical disciple of Rousseau, Robespierre was determined to make France a deistic utopian republic where virtue and fraternity would

This well-known painting by the French artist David shows the death of Marat, with Robespierre and Danton one of the leaders of the radical second phase of the Revolution. *Photo: Musées Royaux des Beaux-Arts de Belgique, Brussels*

reign supreme. During the emergency of 1793 a maximum price was placed upon the necessities of life for the protection of the consumer, particularly the city proletariat. Efforts were made to force people to accept the badly inflated *assignats* at their face value. The lands of the *émigrés* were confiscated and sold in two- or three-acre farms to the peasants. Since these farms could be paid for over a long period of time, almost every French peasant could now become a landowner, and most of them did. France became a nation of peasant proprietors. The metric system was adopted; the Louvre Palace was turned into an art gallery; the national library and the national archives were founded; a law (never implemented) provided for a comprehensive national system of public education. Women adopted the flowing robes and hair styles of ancient Greece. Silk knee breeches, the symbol of aristocracy, gave way to trousers. Rich and poor alike took pride in being *sans culottes* (without knee breeches). Titles of all kinds were discarded for Citizen and Citizeness.

One of Robespierre's greatest ambitions was to replace Christianity in France with the deistic religion of the Enlightenment. A group of his followers, mistakenly thinking him an athestic, set up an actress of questionable morals in Notre Dame as goddess of reason. Robespierre, however, was planning the establishment of the worship of the Supreme Being in the fashion of Rousseau. In an elaborate ceremony, Robespierre, wearing a sky-blue coat and carrying a bouquet of red roses, led a procession across Paris to the scene of the closing festivities. Thus was inaugurated the "Republic of Virtue." Thousands of Christian churches were closed. Even the calendar was de-Christianized by eliminating Sundays. The months were made equal and named after the seasons. The year I was dated from September 22, 1792, the date of the declaration of the republic.

Meanwhile, discontent with Robespierre and his policies was increasing. The defeat of the invading armies of the coalition and the suppression of the internal rebellion appeared to most people to remove the justification for the Terror, yet the Terror was intensified. Robespierre felt that the republic of virtue for which he yearned had eluded him. When Danton counseled moderation, Robespierre sent even him and his most prominent followers to the guillotine. No one, not even the members of the National Convention, felt safe any longer. Finally, in July 1794, the convention found the courage and the leadership to overthrow Robespierre and send him to his own guillotine.

7. REACTION AND THE RISE OF NAPOLEON

Since Robespierre was overthrown on July 27, which was 9 Thermidor by the revolutionary calendar, the reaction that followed is known as the Thermidorian Reaction. The propertied bourgeoisie, who quickly gained control of things, had been frightened and angered by the restrictive measures of Robespierre's regime. All such measures still in force were repealed. The Terror was brought to an end, and the chief terrorists executed. Armed bands of bourgeois hirelings went around for some time beating or killing Jacobins. In 1795 the National Convention finally got around to the task for which it had been elected three years earlier: the drawing up of a new constitution. The constitution reflected the conservative reaction. Only property owners could vote for members of the legislative bodies. Members of the Council of Elders, 250 in number, had to be forty years of age and married. Members of the Council of Five Hundred had to be thirty years of age. Executive functions were placed in the hands of five directors, who were chosen for five-year terms by the two legislative councils. The directors must be forty years of age and married. In October 1795, the National Convention turned over its powers to the Directory, the name that was given to the new government.

The most significant development of the period of the Directory, 1795–1799, was the rise to power of Napoleon Bonaparte. The directors, though men of reasonable competence, were unable to restore peace and political and social tranquility. Though peace had already been made with Spain and Prussia, war with Great Britain, Austria, and Sardinia dragged on. Government finances were chaotic, and brigandage was rife. More and more people longed for a strong man who could bring peace abroad and order at home. Napoleon proved to be the man, and the story of his rise to power will be told in the next chapter. When in November 1799 Napoleon overthrew the Directory and made himself dictator, the French Revolution had run full cycle from absolute Bourbon monarchy to absolute Napoleonic dictatorship. France had failed by popular democratic processes to establish the utopia promised by Voltaire, Montesquieu, and Rousseau. She would now try to achieve it by the dictatorship of a genius.

Suggested Reading

General. Good literature on the French Revolution is enormous. The finest single study of the whole French revolutionary era is R. R. Palmer, *The Age of Democratic Revolution: A Political History of Europe and America, 1760–1800* (2 vols., 1959–64). This brilliant work shows that the French Revolution was a phenomenon of the Western world—not just of France. Another excellent study of quite a different nature is **Crane Brinton, *The Anatomy of Revolution* (Vintage). This is a fascinating comparative analysis of the English, American, French, and Russian revolutions. The volumes in the Rise of Modern Europe series that cover the Old Regime and the French Revolution are **L. Gershoy, *From Despotism to Revolution, 1763–1789* (Harper Torchbook); and **C. Brinton, *A Decade of Revolution, 1785–1799* (Harper Torchbook). **A. Mathiez, *The French Revolution* (Universal Library) is a lively volume by one of France's ablest scholars of the revolution. G. Lefebvre, *The French Revolution* (2 vols., 1962–64) is probably the best all-round history of the revolution. The best textbook on the French Revolution is L. Gershoy, *The French Revolution and Napoleon* (rev. ed., 1964). It is factual and detailed and has an excellent up-to-date bibliography.

Last Days of the Old Regime. **A. de Tocqueville, *The Old Regime and the Revolution* (An-chor) is an astute analysis by one of France's leading intellectuals of a century ago. E. J. Lowell, *The Eve of the French Revolution* (1892) is a great old classic, somewhat out of date in places, but well worth reading. **F. Ford, *Robe and Sword: The Regrouping of the French Aristocracy After Louis XIV* (Harper Torchbook) is a scholarly study of the French nobility on the eve of the revolution. **G. Lefebvre, *The Coming of the French Revolution* (Vintage) is a little gem by one of France's greatest historians.

First Phase of the Revolution. This period, of course, is covered by the general histories listed above. Lefebvre's little book on the coming of the revolution continues on to the signing of the "Declaration of the Rights of Man," August 1789. Good biographies of two of the most prominent leaders during the early part of the revolution are L. Barthou, *Mirabeau* (1913); and G. Van Deusen, *Sieyès: His Life and His Nationalism* (1932).

Second Phase. Again, the general histories of the revolution listed above cover this period. By far the best history of the Reign of Terror is **R. Palmer, *Twelve Who Ruled: The Committee of Public Safety During the Terror* (Atheneum)—a combination of fine scholarship and writing. The outstanding biographer of Robespierre is J. M. Thompson; **Robes-

pierre and the French Revolution (Collier) is a briefer and handy version of his two-volume biography.

Sources. Madame de Campan, *Memories,* ed. J. H. Rose (2 vols., 1917) presents a vivid picture of the court of Louis XVI, by the lady-in-waiting to Marie Antoinette. J. Stewart, *A Documentary Survey of the French Revolution* (1951) is an excellent collection of important source materials. E. Higgins, *The French Revolution As Told by Contemporaries* (1938), skillfully weaves together the story from eye-witness accounts.

Historical Fiction. **Charles Dickens, *A Tale of Two Cities* (Collier), and **Anatole France, *The Gods Are Athirst* (numerous editions) are two famous novels based on the French Revolution. One of the best historical novels ever written is **D. Du Maurier, *The Glassblowers* (Pocket Books). It is based upon fine historical research and brings the revolution very close to the reader.

Chapter 41 ꧁ The Era of Napoleon, 1799–1815

No individual in modern times has enjoyed a more meteoric career than Napoleon Bonaparte, the modern counterpart of Alexander the Great and Julius Caesar. He was essentially a product of the Enlightenment and the French Revolution. His mission was to consolidate the revolution in France and to spread its "enlightened" concepts and many of its institutions to most of the rest of Europe.

1. NAPOLEON'S RISE TO POWER

Napoleon was born on the French island of Corsica in 1769. Corsicans speak Italian, and Napoleon never learned to speak French without an accent. At the age of nine he was sent to a military school in France. Here he was made fun of by his schoolmates because of his foreign accent and his small size. Already suffering from megalomania, he withdrew into himself, studied history, geography, and mathematics, and dreamed of future greatness. At sixteen he received his commission as second lieutenant of artillery. During several years of boring garrison duty he stuffed his photographic mind full of history, the classics, and the philosophy of the Enlightenment, particularly that of Rousseau. Had it not been for the French Revolution, his humble, foreign birth would probably have made it impossible for him to have risen very far.

Napoleon's first big chance came in 1793 at the siege of Toulon, France's Mediterranean naval base, which had gone over to the side of the British. Since most of the regular army officers were nobles and had fled the country or been deposed, the young Napoleon was given an opportunity to try his plan for the recapture of the base. It worked brilliantly, and he attracted the attention of some important people, including General Paul Barras, who was to become one of the five directors. These contacts paid off two years later on 13 Vendémiaire (October 5, 1795). When the National Convention completed the constitution setting up the government of the Directory, the members of the convention, fearful of losing power after so much bloodshed, decreed that two-thirds of the members of the new legislative bodies must be chosen from among themselves. This decree angered a great many disgruntled people who, for one reason or another, wished to see an entirely new government come in. Royalist leaders seized the opportunity to arouse a huge Paris mob against the convention. In the emergency the convention appointed General Barras to defend it. Barras, in turn, called upon Napoleon, whose prowess with artillery he had observed at Toulon. Although the details of the fracas are uncertain, it would appear that Napoleon masterminded the defense of the

The popular image of Napoleon as "the man on horseback" is found in hundreds of representations. This one is a detail of a hand-colored poster issued about 1805.
Photo: The Bettmann Archive

convention. (Barras and Napoleon in their memoirs both claim the leading role and belittle the part played by the other.) An artillery expert with no love for the French people, the ambitious Corsican had long before decided that the way to handle a mob was to let it have a "whiff of grapeshot." A few such whiffs from his skillfully placed artillery dispersed the mob, and Napoleon became the hero of the convention.

The day of 13 Vendémiaire made Napoleon a prominent figure. Although he was now only twenty-six, he demanded and got the command of the Army of the Interior. However, as an astute student of history, he realized that glamour and power could be won only in the field. Therefore, he requested and received command of the Army of Italy—the French army still fighting the Austrians and Sardinians in northern Italy. Napoleon's dynamism and skill quickly galvanized the lethargic French forces, who defeated the Austrians and Sardinians and forced them to sue for peace. Nor was the young general any less skilled in diplomacy and propaganda. He personally negotiated a favorable peace with Austria (a function that really belonged to the newly created French Directory), and sent back glowing reports of his exploits.

Soon the name Napoleon Bonaparte was on everyone's lips. The Directory, grappling with the unheroic problems left by the preceding revolutionary bodies, was concerned for its own existence. Fearing the presence of a popular and ambitious young general in France, it was only too glad to accede to Bonaparte's request to lead an expedition to Egypt as a means of striking at the British Empire. Napoleon's chief purposes in going to Egypt were personal and psychological. He sensed that the time was not yet ripe to overthrow the government, that exploits far away in the mystic East would greatly enhance his reputation, and that during his absence from France crises would arise enabling him to play the role of the returning savior. He was right. His victories in Egypt were of no military importance, but they did add to his personal glamour. (For example, an army officer discovered the Rosetta Stone, which unlocked the secrets of the ancient Egyptian language and history.)

Meanwhile, Great Britain persuaded Austria and Russia to join her in a second coalition against France. This was what Napoleon was looking for. His fleet having been destroyed by the British squadron under Lord Nelson, Napoleon deserted his army in Egypt and slipped back to France with a few chosen followers. The timing was perfect. General Bonaparte conspired with various members of the government, and with the additional support of armed forces under his command, overthrew the Directory, setting himself up as dictator. This coup d'état occurred on 18 Brumaire (November 9, 1799). Napoleon was only thirty years of age.

2. THE CONSULATE—PEACE AND REFORM, 1799–1804

Having seized absolute power by conspiracy and force, Napoleon drew up a constitution to conceal his dictatorship under the cloak of parliamentary forms. He gave himself the title of First Consul with the power to appoint key civilian and military personnel (giving him control over the armed forces), declare war and make treaties, and initiate all legislation through a hand-picked Council of State. Two other consuls without any significant powers served as camouflage. A self-perpetuating Senate selected a Tribunate of one hundred members and a legislative body of three hundred members from a list of candidates elected by all adult French males. The Tribunate discussed proposed legislation drawn up by the Council of State, and the Legislative Body voted on it without discussion. Thus the voters were led to believe that they were participating in the government, whereas in reality their voice was but faintly heard. Local government was again brought under the strict control of the central government by placing each of the eighty-three departments into which France was divided under the control of a powerful agent of the central government called a *prefect*.

The First Consul's initial project was to restore law and order at home and peace abroad. The Directory had never been able to suppress brigandage. Life and property were not safe. Napoleon sent out military detachments that quickly put an end to lawlessness and restored the authority of the government, much to the satisfaction of law-abiding citizens. He lost no time in making a treaty (1800) with the United States, bringing to an end a two-year undeclared naval war that had grown out of French seizures of American vessels and the pro-British and anti-French policies of John Adams' administration. Slipping over the Alps with a French army, the First Consul crushed the Austrian army in northern Italy in the battle of Marengo, knocking Austria out of the Second Coalition. Tsar Paul of Russia was cajoled with flattery and promises into making peace. Even Great Britain was persuaded to sign the Peace of Amiens in 1802, which, however, was to last little more than a year.

The young dictator next proceeded to create by enlightened despotism the permanent institutions that the revolutionary leaders had been unable to establish by the processes of popular government. Of all Napoleon's reforms, the one of which he was the most proud was his Civil Code. The National Convention had set up a commission of lawyers to reduce to order the 237 different legal codes in use in France, but this commission had been unable to complete its work. Shortly after seizing power, Napoleon appointed his own commission of legal experts to draw up a uniform code. When his experts proved to be unequal to the task, Napoleon threw himself into the project. The result was the Code Napoleon, which has been adopted by most of the nations that have since come into existence throughout the world. Later codes set in order criminal and commercial law. These achievements won for Napoleon the title "the Second Justinian."

The First Consul proved himself to be an astute financier. The numerous government notes, bonds, and obligations, all depreciated, were called in and uniformly refunded. Efficient agents of the central government fairly assessed and collected the taxes. Strict economy in expenditures made it possible to balance the French budget for the first time since the early days of Colbert. Napoleon capped France's financial structure with the Bank of France, a seminational bank privately owned but regulated by the state. The bank handled government funds and was given certain monopolistic privileges such as the issuing of paper money. It established branches all over France and grew so strong that it later became a powerful influence on the government itself. During the great world depression of the 1930s it was able to remain on the gold standard longer than either the United States Treasury or the Bank of England. French businessmen, however, never quite trusted Napoleon; they always felt uneasy about what the dictator's next arbitrary move might be.

Napoleon was keenly aware of the importance of religion. "Always treat the pope," he counseled his diplomats, "as if he had 200,000 men." He himself was a Voltairian deist and a cynical moral relativist, believing that God was "always on the side with the most cannon." One of his first steps was to make peace with the pope and end the ten-year struggle between the French revolutionary governments and the Roman Catholic Church. After arduous negotiations, the First Consul and the pope signed the Concordat of 1801, which was to govern the relations between the French state and the Roman Catholic Church until the beginning of the twentieth century. The Roman Catholic religion was declared to be the religion of the majority of French people. The state was to appoint the bishops, but only the pope could invest them in their offices. The bishops were to appoint and discipline the lower clergy, thus restoring the traditional episcopal principle of the Roman Church. The salaries of the clergy were to be paid by the state, and the clergy were to take an oath of allegiance to the state. The pope, in turn, accepted the permanent loss of church property seized by the National Assembly. Once the pope's signature was on the document, Napoleon, in his characteristic manner, violated its spirit by adding "organic articles" that further subordinated the church to the state. According to these articles, the state was to pay the salaries of Protestant as well as Roman Catholic clergy, and all clergy were placed under the "police powers" of the state. Nevertheless, the pope gained firmer control over the Gallican Church than he had enjoyed since the Late Middle Ages. Napoleon, on the other hand, ended the religious cleavage that had harassed France since the early days of the revolution.

Napoleon was also interested in pedagogy. All French schools were brought under the control of a national board of education called the University of France. One of the most important elements in his educational system was the *lycée*, an institution that combined what in the United States would be the last two years of high school with the first two years of college. In addition, professional and technical schools were established. Napoleon had a low opinion of female education and of feminine mentality in general. Actually, he was chiefly interested in educational institutions as agencies of propaganda for the molding of loyal and efficient soldiers and citizens. However, the educational institutions created by Napoleon have served France well.

Napoleon's one outstanding failure during the period of the Consulate was his effort to restore France's lost empire in North America. He successfully pressured the weak Spanish government into returning the vast Louisiana territory to France. But his plans to secure the approaches to Louisiana miscarried when yellow fever and native resistance wrought havoc with a costly French expedition to Santo Domingo. Realizing that war with Great Britain was about to be renewed and that he could not hold Louisiana, he offered to sell it to the United States. President Jefferson eagerly accepted the offer, paying some $16 million for what is now a third of the United States.

With the exception of the overseas imperial venture, the first five years of Napoleon's dictatorship were spectacularly successful. The dictatorship itself was mild. Law and order at home and peace abroad had been attained. Financial stability, equal and efficient justice, religious tranquillity, and the foundations of an effective educational system had all been achieved. Public morale was high. In 1804, as in 1791, the worshippers of Voltaire's materialistic rationalism must have felt vindicated. The benevolent genius on horseback seemed to have ushered in the utopia of human reason that the National Assembly appeared to have achieved a little more than a decade earlier. However, 1804 like 1791 was only a prelude to an era of war, violence, disillusionment, and reaction. Napoleon was not satisfied with his accomplishments. He yearned for more glory. In 1804 he crowned himself Emperor of the French and sought further fields to conquer.

3. THE EMPIRE—WAR AND CONQUEST

Great Britain, France's inveterate foe, had become increasingly alarmed at Napoleon's growing strength. The French dictator had not only continued to build up his military forces, but had taken advantage of the Peace of Amiens to further his commercial and imperial schemes at Great Britain's expense. Before the end of 1803 the British government declared war and the next year joined with Austria and Russia to form a third coalition against France. This was what Napoleon expected and wanted. He soon appeared at the English Channel at the head of a force sufficient to conquer the British Isles, if only the 22-mile water barrier could be crossed. In the Channel, however, lay the world's mightiest fleet, commanded by the greatest of all Britain's admirals, Lord Nelson. Napoleon was unable to lure the British fleet away from the Channel or to figure out any way to get past it. Meanwhile, he was watching the

By 1808, when this Gillray cartoon called "The Valley of the Shadow of Death" was published in England, Napoleon had remade the map of Europe and was the object of mass resentment: From the left, King Joseph sinks in the Ditch of Styx as the Spanish avenger leaps across with the Portuguese wolf; the British lion and the Sicilian terrier attack from the front and the Russian bear from behind; and from the Lethean Ditch in the foreground, the Rhenish Confederation of starved rats crawl out, Dutch frogs spit out their spite, the American rattlesnake shakes his tail, and the Prussian scarecrow attempts to fly. From above, the "Roman Meteor" descends in bolts of lightning, the "Turkish New Moon" rises, the spirit of Charles XII of Sweden descends with raised sword, and the "Imperial Eagle" (Germany) emerges from the clouds. *Photo: Prints Division, New York Public Library, Astor, Lenox, and Tilden Foundations*

movements of the Austrians and Russians and readying his own army. When the time was ripe, he suddenly marched his army eastward, surrounded an exposed Austrian army at Ulm in southwest Germany, and forced it to surrender. But the day after Ulm, Lord Nelson sighted the combined French and Spanish fleets off Cape Trafalgar on the southwest point of Spain and annihilated them (October 21, 1805). Although Nelson was killed early in the battle, his victory saved Great Britain

from the menace of a Napoleonic invasion and limited the scope of the French emperor's conquests to the continent of Europe. Trafalgar was one of the decisive battles of all time.

On land, however, Napoleon seemed invincible. Moving his army eastward from Ulm, he met and crushed the oncoming combined forces of Austria and Russia at Austerlitz. Austria immediately sued for peace, and the demoralized Russians retreated toward their

Napoleon's Russian Campaign June to December, 1812

BALTIC SEA
Riga
COURLAND Vitebsk
Vilna
Tilsit Kovno Borisov
Königsberg
Warsaw
Moscow
Borodino
Smolensk
RUSSIAN EMPIRE
Brest-Litovsk

NORWAY
SWEDEN
FINLAND
St. Petersburg
ESTONIA
Stockholm
LIVONIA
KINGDOM OF DENMARK AND NORWAY
COURLAND
Memel
Tilsit
Niemen R.
Königsberg
Friedland
Vilna
Danzig
Eylau

SCOTLAND
Edinburgh
NORTH SEA
DENMARK
Copenhagen
SWEDISH POMERANIA
HELIGOLAND (Britain)
Lübeck
Hamburg
MECKLEN-BURG
Bremen
PRUSSIA
Posen
Warsaw
Berlin
Brest-Litovsk
Oder R.
GRAND DUCHY OF WARSAW
Vistula R.

IRELAND
GREAT BRITAIN
ENGLAND
London
Dover
Amsterdam
KINGDOM OF HOLLAND
BERG
Rhine R.
K. OF WESTPHALIA
K. OF SAXONY
Breslau
Elbe R.
Leipzig Dresden
GALICIA
Cracow
Tarnopol

ATLANTIC OCEAN
Plymouth
ENGLISH CHANNEL
CHANNEL I. (Britain)
Boulogne
Brussels
Antwerp
Amiens
Cologne
Auerstadt
Erfurt Jena
CONFEDERATION OF THE RHINE
Prague
BOHEMIA
Austerlitz

Cherbourg
Seine R.
Versailles Paris
Fontainebleau
Valmy
Mainz
Metz
BADEN
Strasbourg
WÜRTTEM-BERG
Ulm
Munich
Hohenlinden
K. OF BAVARIA
Wagram
Vienna AUSTRIA
Budapest
HUNGARY

Nantes
Loire R.
Orléans
FRENCH EMPIRE
Rochefort
Basel
SWITZERLAND
Danube R.
AUSTRIA
Drave R.

CAPE FINISTERRE
La Coruña
GALICIA
Oporto
Douro R.
Burgos
Bordeaux
Caronne R.
Toulouse
Ebro R.
Lyons
Rhone R.
SAVOY
PIEDMONT
Genoa
VENETIA
LOMBARDY
Milan
Po R.
KINGDOM OF ITALY
Trieste
ILLYRIAN PROVINCES
SLOVENIA
CROATIA
Save R.
BOSNIA
Belgrade
SERBIA
WALLACHIA
Danube R.

Almeida
Ciudad Rodrigo
PORTUGAL
Tagus R.
Lisbon
Elvas
Talavera
Madrid
Ocaña
SPAIN
Saragossa
Marseilles
Nice
Toulon
LUCCA
Leghorn
Florence
ADRIATIC SEA
DALMATIA
MONTENEGRO
OTTOMAN EMPIRE

Albuera
Guadiana R.
Baylen
Seville
ANDALUSIA
Cadiz
TRAFALGAR ×
Tangier
Gibraltar (Britain)
Valencia
Barcelona
BALEARIC I. (Spain)
MINORCA
MAJORCA
IVIZA
CORSICA
ELBA
KINGDOM OF SARDINIA
Cagliari
Rome
Naples
KINGDOM OF NAPLES
Bari
Taranto
CORFU
IONIAN I. (Britain)
ALBANIA
Salonica
MOREA
CERIGO

MOROCCO
Algiers
ALGERIA (Turkish)
Tunis
TUNISIA (Turkish)
Palermo
KINGDOM OF SICILY
STRAIT OF MESSINA
MALTA (Britain)
MEDITERRANEAN SEA

French Empire
Grand Empire
Allied with Napoleon

0   100   200   300 miles

Europe 1810

home country. At this juncture Prussia declared war on Napoleon. The time was inopportune, and the Prussian army, which under Frederick the Great had held most of Europe at bay, was no match for Napoleon. At Jena and Auerstädt Napoleon overwhelmed and virtually destroyed the Prussian forces (1806). Two weeks later the French emperor was in Berlin. Hearing that the Russian troops were re-forming in Poland, Napoleon moved eastward to meet them. After being held to a draw by the Russians in a blinding snowstorm at Eylau, he defeated them decisively a few months later in the great battle of Friedland (1807). Tsar Alexander I now sued for peace. Although the Treaties of Tilsit (July 1807) were technically between equals, they actually left Napoleon master of the European continent and Alexander I only a junior partner. Russia was given a free hand to deal with Turkey in Eastern Europe, but was not permitted to take Constantinople, the prize the Russians most desired. In return for a dominant hand in Eastern Europe, Alexander promised to join Napoleon against Great Britain, and to force Sweden to do so. Tilsit recognized the changes that Napoleon had already made in Central and Western Europe and left him free to make any others he wished.

Between 1806 and 1808 Napoleon remade the map of Europe. The puppet Duchy of Warsaw was created out of part of Prussia's (and later, part of Austria's) Polish territory. Prussia's territory west of the Elbe was made a part of the kingdom of Westphalia, over which Napoleon's youngest brother, Jerome, was made king. Prussia was thus virtually halved in size. The Holy Roman Empire was at long last abolished, and its hundreds of little principalities greatly consolidated. A strip of German territory along the North Sea was annexed outright to France. The rest of German territory west of the Elbe was brought into the Confederation of the Rhine, with Napoleon as protector. Napoleon's younger brother, Louis, was made king of Holland, but when Louis began to favor the interests of his Dutch subjects over those of the French

Empire, Napoleon deposed him and annexed his territory to France. The whole Italian Peninsula was brought under French dominance. Northwestern Italy down to and including Rome was annexed outright. Marshal Murat and Napoleon's sister Caroline were made king and queen of Naples. The northeastern third of the peninsula was made into the kingdom of Italy, with Napoleon as king and his stepson, Eugene, as viceroy. The coastal areas along the northeastern Adriatic Sea were detached from Austria and annexed to France. In 1808 Napoleon overthrew the weak Spanish royal house and made his elder brother, Joseph, king of Spain. Shortly before, the Portuguese royal family had fled to Brazil at the approach of a conquering French army. Denmark (including Norway) became Napoleon's most faithful ally.

Thus, by 1808, all Europe except the British Isles was under French control or French influence. No other conqueror has so dominated Europe. In all those territories under direct French control, Napoleon's "enlightened" institutions and administrative efficiency were introduced. The rest of Europe, impressed with the effectiveness of the French revolutionary ideas and institutions, adopted many of them voluntarily. And yet this mighty Napoleonic empire was to last less than five years.

4. DECLINE AND FALL OF THE EMPIRE

A number of factors contributed to the decline and fall of the Napoleonic empire. One of the most obvious was British sea power. Because of it, Great Britain alone of the European powers was able to withstand the Napoleonic military onslaught. After Trafalgar dashed Napoleon's hopes of invading the British Isles, he sought the destruction of "perfidious Albion" by economic pressure. In order to wreck the economy of the "nation of shopkeepers," he attempted to blockade the entire continent of Europe against British shipping. All British goods were confiscated. French privateers were set upon British merchant ships. These measures, known as "the Continental System," did cause Great Britain grave distress. However, with her control of the sea, she was able to apply a more effective counterblockade against the Napoleon-dominated Continent. She was able even to hold her own in the War of 1812 with the United States, which attempted to resist the British maritime restrictions. Since Europe was almost entirely dependent upon Great Britain for manufactured goods and tropical products, the Continental System created ever-increasing resentment against Napoleon's rule.

Another factor that undermined the Napoleonic empire was the rise of a national spirit among the subject peoples. The mass spirit of intense patriotism or nationalism, which had its origin in France during the *levée en masse* of 1793, spread to the rest of Europe in the wake of Napoleon's conquering armies. The first people to rebel openly against the French yoke were the proud Spaniards. Hardly had Napoleon's brother Joseph been placed on the Spanish throne when his unwilling subjects rose up and chased him out of Madrid. The superior French armies, even when led by Napoleon himself, were ineffective against the hit-and-run guerrilla tactics invented by the Spaniards. The British government, observing Napoleon's predicament in Spain, sent an army under Arthur Wellesley, the future duke of Wellington, to exploit the situation. Spain became a running abscess that drained away much of Napoleon's military strength. Meanwhile, Prussia, after the humiliation of Jena, had begun a rejuvenation under the leadership of Baron vom Stein. Partly in secret and partly in the open, the Prussians modernized their army and their civil institutions and prepared for the day of liberation. In 1809 Austria declared war on Napoleon in a premature effort to free herself from subservience to the French emperor. Although Austria was once more defeated, the heroic valor with which her armies fought served notice of the rising spirit of national pride and resistance. Napoleon could no longer enjoy the advantage of fighting with soldiers fired with the heady wine of nationalism against lethargic professional armies.

A third factor in the decline of the French colossus was Napoleon himself. He began to slow down—to lose his magic touch. Symptoms of the stomach cancer or ulcer from which he is believed eventually to have died began to appear. As his enemies one after another adopted his winning tactics, he failed to come up with better ones.

The beginning of the end was a disastrous campaign against Russia in 1812. When Alexander I wearied of the hardships of the Continental System and opened his ports to the British, Napoleon, against the advice of his closest associates, decided to conquer Russia. Amassing an army of 600,000, the mightiest army ever assembled up to that time, he plunged into the vastness of Russia. Many of his troops, however, were unwilling conscripts from the puppet states. The Russian army retreated into the interior of the huge country, following a scorched-earth policy and drawing Napoleon ever farther from his base of supplies. Finally, after the bloody battle of Borodino about 75 miles from Moscow, Napoleon's hosts entered the city. However, Alexander I refused to make peace. A fire destroyed much of Moscow, leaving the invaders without shelter in the face of approaching winter. Napoleon began his retreat too late. The Russian winter caught his forces burdened down with loot. Tens of thousands froze or starved. Russian Cossacks, riding out of the blizzards, cut down or captured other thousands. Of the 600,000 men who marched into Russia, only some 20,000 escaped.

Napoleon dashed back to France to raise fresh conscripts, but the flower of French manhood was gone. One nation after another rose up to join the Russians in a war of liberation. At Leipzig in eastern Germany, in October 1813, Napoleon was at last decisively defeated. The next year the allies entered Paris and exiled Napoleon to the island of Elba, off the coast of Italy. When the allies began to squabble over the peace settlement,

Who Was Napoleon?

No man in modern times—if indeed, in all history—has displayed more military and political genius than Napoleon Bonaparte. He was a dreamer and planner of grandiose projects and yet the master of exact practical detail. His memory was photographic; his energy seemed inexhaustible. He possessed charisma—that combination of personal dynamism and charm that enabled him to dominate and lead virtually all those with whom he came in contact. The French Revolution, by pulling down the pillars of a venerable society, presented him with a building opportunity, the like of which would not have happened again, as he himself admitted, in another thousand years. To what ends did he use this unparalleled talent and opportunity?

This is a difficult question to answer. Napoleon made it more difficult by spending much of the last six years of his life on St. Helena dictating his reminiscences, in which he dressed up his record for the historian. According to him, he was a true child of the Enlightenment and heir to the French Revolution—to the principles of liberty, equality, fraternity. His loyalty was to France, but at the same time he loved all mankind. Above all, he was a man of peace. His wars were all in defense of France and of the principles of the Revolution. There can be little question that there is some truth in these assertions, but unfortunately there is so much untruth that it is by his deeds rather than his words that we must judge him.

Napoleon cannot be rightly accused of destroying a popular constitutional regime that had been set up during the course of the revolution. The Directory, which Napoleon overthrew, had already violated the constitution upon which it was based. It had refused to accept the results of every election that had been held during the course of its existence. Moreover, it had failed to achieve either law and order in France or peace abroad. It had been unable to balance the national budget or to stabilize the currency. In short, it had not been able to consummate the revolution. Public opinion, as revealed by all the elections held during the Directory, showed a strong preference for monarchy. A powerful group of conspirators was already looking for the right man to lead a coup d'état when Napoleon returned from Egypt. If Napoleon had not overthrown the Directory, somebody else would have, and the ensuing dictatorship probably would have been harsher and certainly less efficient. On the other hand, there was no widespread popular clamor for Napoleon, as he would have us believe. His fame among the masses at that time was not that great.

Napoleon's best claims to greatness in history lie in his constructive reforms during the period of the Consulate, 1799–1804. He was the last and by far the greatest of the enlightened despots. His achievement of peace, law and order, administrative efficiency, prosperity, and social tranquillity, his legal codes, the Concordat of 1801, his educational institutions, his sound financial measures constitute a record of political and social reform probably unparalleled in history. They vividly reflect the influence of the Enlightenment. Nor should the fact that many, if not all, of these reforms were already under consideration or under way and that other men played an important part in bringing them to fruition detract from Napoleon's role. It was his energy, imagination, sense of the practical and the possible, and political skill that were primarily responsible for bringing them into being.

The Empire is another matter. It was a decade of almost constant war, and all but the last few months of it was on soil other than French. It is difficult to accept Napoleon's claim that his wars and conquests were solely defensive. It is true that many of Napoleon's reforms, such as the Code Napoleon, administrative efficiency, religious toleration, and the weakening of feudalism followed in the wake of his conquering armies. But these benefits were offset by heavy exactions of conscripts and property for the benefit of the French. Likewise, the emperor's boast of creating a European state or confederation was more than nullified by the nationalism that he aroused everywhere in emulation of that of the French. Finally, the Napoleonic empire illustrated a weakness of all dictatorships—dependence upon a mortal man. There was no one to take the great man's place.

So what of Napoleon? Was he a great genius? He was. Did he achieve any lasting humanitarian reforms? He did. Was he a child of the Enlightenment and the heir to the French Revolution? In some measure he was —especially in his youth. But being human, he grew old and fell victim to the great truth that Lord Acton has so well stated, "power corrupts and absolute power corrupts absolutely." The great enemy that Napoleon could never conquer was his own ego.

Napoleon escaped back to France and raised another army, but he was finally defeated by the duke of Wellington and the Prussians under Marshal Blücher at Waterloo in Belgium, June 1815. This time he was imprisoned on the island of St. Helena in the South Atlantic, where six years later he died.

5. NAPOLEON'S IMPACT ON LATIN AMERICA—REVOLUTION AND INDEPENDENCE

One vast area outside Europe upon which the impact of Napoleon was strong and immediate was Latin America. During the eighteenth century, discontent with colonial rule had been steadily mounting in the Spanish and Portuguese colonial empires in North and South America. Like the thirteen English colonies in North America, resentment was directed primarily against economic and political restrictions. As the native-born "Creoles" had come to outnumber the Spanish- and Portuguese-born settlers, the ties of loyalty to the mother countries had become more and more tenuous. The liberal writings of the French and British philosophers of the Enlightenment were smuggled into Latin America and made their converts, particularly among young intellectuals. These liberal Latin American intellectuals could not help being impressed by the successful revolt of the English colonies to the north and the setting up of a liberal New World republic. The French Revolution had an even more profound influence on them. When, therefore, Napoleon overthrew Ferdinand VII of Spain and placed his own brother, Joseph Bonaparte, on the Spanish throne, the sentiments of loyalty on the part of the colonies for the mother country, which were already weak, quickly became quite confused.

By 1810 the colonies were in open revolt. As with the English colonists three decades earlier, the cause of the Latin American revolutionists seemed hopeless. In addition to the regular Spanish troops, they had to struggle against most of the wealthy Spanish settlers and the local Roman Catholic hierarchy. Eventually, however, two brilliant young leaders, Simón Bolívar and José San Martín, emerged to overcome the seemingly impossible obstacles and to lead the South American revolutionists to success. By 1822 the independence of Spanish South America was won. In the same year the issue was decided in Spain's Central American colonies and in Mexico, which then included the southwest quarter of what is now the United States. In all the former Spanish colonies, republics were established, although a long period of troubled apprenticeship preceded the establishment of reasonably stable popular governments. As a matter of fact, real stability has continued to be a problem for Central and South American nations.

In the huge Portuguese colony of Brazil, the independence movement was delayed by the flight of the Portuguese royal family to Brazil in 1807. However, the return of the king to Portugal six years after Napleon's fall and the efforts of the Portuguese government to reimpose the colonial status on Brazil quickly fanned the embers of revolt into flame. In 1822 the Portuguese king's son, Pedro, whom he had left behind as regent, yielded to native pressure and declared himself king of independent Brazil. In all of independent Latin America the Code Napoleon was adopted as the basis of civil law, and the impact of the Enlightenment on political institutions was clearly visible.

6. SIGNIFICANCE OF THE FRENCH REVOLUTION AND NAPOLEON

The French Revolution and its Napoleonic sequel had a profound effect upon the course of history. Like Pandora when she lifted the lid of that fateful box, they let loose forces and ideas that have influenced and ofttimes shaken the world ever since, especially the revolutionary ideals of *Liberty, Equality, Fraternity*. Originally conceived in the eighteenth century by the philosophers of the Enlightenment, they were born materially in the American and French revolutions, and developed and spread by Napoleon.

Liberty, of course, has been one of the chief quests of the human race from its beginning to the present and has never at any time been perfectly attained. In the era of the French Revolution, the ideal of liberty meant freedom from arbitrary authority—political, religious, economic, or social. It meant freedom of speech, press, conscience, assembly, person, and profession, and the sacredness of property. During the moderate first phase of the French Revolution, a great deal of progress toward these goals was made; in the tumultuous and bloody second phase, a good deal was lost. Under Napoleon's dictatorship there was no political liberty. However, he claimed that the efficiency, prosperity, and honor of his regime more than made up for

the lack of popular government, for which, he believed, the world was not yet ready.

Equality meant essentially equality under the law and equality of opportunity for gain and advancement. It was only during the brief dominance of Robespierre that the absolute social equality of all citizens became a cult. Its impracticability was soon evident. Napoleon's law codes were a great boon to the more moderate and practical kind of equality.

Fraternity manifested itself in the mass movements (sometimes violent) for reform, in the comradeship in the conscripted armies, and above all in the new popular and dynamic spirit of nationalism. These forces, released by the American and French revolutions, spread first to the rest of Europe, then to Latin America, and eventually to the rest of the world. Much of the history of the world since the era of the French Revolution has centered around these forces at work.

Suggested Reading

General. The literature on Napoleon, like that on the French Revolution, is so enormous that one has to pick and choose. The volume in the Rise of Modern Europe series that covers the Napoleonic Era is **G. Bruun, *Europe and the French Imperium, 1799–1814* (Harper Torchbook). Probably the best one-volume biography of Napoleon is F. M. Kircheisen, *Napoleon*, trans. C. Philips (1932). This is a translation and an abridgment of the nine-volume original in German. Two other major biographies are J. H. Rose, *Life of Napoleon* (2 vols., 1902); and A. Fournier, *Napoleon the First, a Biography* (1903). **G. Lefebvre, *Napoleon* (2 vols., Columbia University Press), is a recent translation by H. F. Stockhold of a great biography. A good brief biography of Napoleon is **H. Butterfield, *Napoleon* (Collier). An interesting and valuable study, **P. Geyl, *Napoleon: For and Against*

(Yale), analyzes the views about Napoleon, pro and con, of French historians since 1815.

Napoleon's Rise to Power. **G. Lefebvre, *The Directory*, trans. R. Baldick (Vintage) is an excellent treatment of the setting in which Napoleon rose to power. Napoleon's youth and military education are well told by S. Wilkinson, *Rise of General Bonaparte* (1930). A standard work on Napoleon's early life is O. Browning, *Napoleon, the First Phase, 1769–1793* (1905).

The Consulate. Scholarly studies of three of Napoleon's numerous nonmilitary domestic activities which are often neglected are H. H. Walsh, *The Concordat of 1801* (1933); H. Cachard, *The French Civil Code* (1930); and R. B. Holtman, *Napoleonic Propaganda* (1950).

The Empire. A good biography, perhaps too sympathetic, of Talleyrand is **C. Brinton, *The Lives of Talleyrand* (Norton). Napoleon's naval strategy and activities are brilliantly portrayed by A. T. Mahan, *The Influence of Sea Power on the French Revolution and Empire, 1793–1812* (9th ed., 2 vols., 1898). This scholarly work by an American admiral has had great influence on the world's military strategists ever since it was published. The best study of Napoleon's Continental System is E. F. Heckscher, *The Continental System: An Economic Interpretation* (1922). A scholarly study of Napoleon's impact on Germany is G. S. Ford, *Stein and the Era of Reform in Prussia, 1807–1815* (1922). E. Tarlé, *Napoleon's Invasion of Russia* (1942) is an excellent account by a Russian historian. A popular biography of Wellington, the conqueror of Napoleon, is Philip Guedalla, *The Duke* (1931). Two good books on the impact of the French Revolution and Napoleon on Latin America are **W. S. Robertson, *The Rise of the Spanish-American Republics* (Collier); and Hildegarde Angell, *Simon Bolivar, South American Emancipator* (1930).

Sources. The great scholar F. M. Kircheisen has put together many of Napoleon's own words under the title *Napoleon's Autobiography*, ed. F. Collins, (1931). Another work similar in nature is R. N. Johnston, *The Corsican* (1910). A more recent and popularly written selection of Napoleon's quoted words is **J. C. Herold, *The Mind of Napoleon* (Collier). J. M. Thompson, *Napoleon Self-revealed* (1934) is a collection of three hundred of Napoleon's letters. An important primary source for Napoleon's Russian campaign is the vivid and lively memoirs of one of Napoleon's aides-de-camp, **A. de Caulincourt, *With Napoleon in Russia* (Universal Library).

Historical Fiction. Probably the greatest historical novel ever written is **Leo Tolstoy, *War and Peace* (Penguin). This gigantic work is based upon excellent historical research.

Chapter 42 ❧ Aftermath: Restoration and Reaction,

1815—1830

The overthrow of Napoleon in 1815 brought to an end, in Europe at least, the heroic and tumultuous epoch that had begun in 1789 with the meeting of the Estates General. The intervening twenty-six years had been filled with great expectation, experimentation, turmoil, and war. Now there was mass disillusionment and weariness. The European royalty and aristocracy, at long last triumphant over revolutionary France, were determined to put an end not only to the Mirabeaus, Robespierres, and Napoleons, but also to the ideas of Voltaire and Rousseau. To achieve this goal, to redraw the mutilated map of Europe, and to set the clock back as far as was practically possible, the leaders of the victorious powers gathered at the Austrian capital of Vienna in the autumn of 1814. To this conference also flocked representatives of every state in Europe, hundreds of dispossessed princes, agents of every conceivable interest, and adventurers.

1. THE CONGRESS OF VIENNA (1814–1815)

The Congress of Vienna, which never actually met in formal session, was dominated by the four major victors over Napoleon. Great Britain was represented by her able foreign minister, Lord Castlereagh. Prussia's mediocre king, Frederick William III, headed his own delegation, as did Russia's tsar, the idealistic young Alexander I. Austria's emperor, Francis I, played host to the assembled great.

However, the real leader of the Austrian delegation, and, indeed, the dominant figure of the whole congress, was the Austrian chancellor, Prince Klemens von Metternich. As a guiding principle upon which to base their decisions, the conferees decided upon "legitimacy." This meant that in redistributing various territories, attention would be paid not to the desires or interests of the people concerned, but to the legal claims of the former and future sovereigns. Many of the decisions formalized at Vienna had already been made by the four major powers shortly before and after Napoleon's overthrow in April 1814.

Thanks in no small measure to the presence of the clever and able Talleyrand, France, the cause of all the turmoil, got off very lightly. Prussia would have severely punished and weakened France, but her three major colleagues were fearful of upsetting the balance of power. Already saddled with the restored Bourbons, France was merely reduced to the boundaries she had possessed before her annexations during the wars of the revolutionary era. The Congress of Vienna had originally imposed no indemnity upon France. However, because of Napoleon's return from Elba in the midst of the congress and his hundred-day fling that ended at Waterloo, the four great powers compelled France to cede the Saar Basin to Prussia, to pay an indemnity of $140 million, and to return the art treasures stolen by Napoleon from the various galleries of Europe. To contain France within her frontiers and to discourage future French aggression, Prussia was given a sizable block of territory along the Rhine, the Austrian Netherlands (Belgium) was annexed to the Dutch Netherlands, and Piedmont was enlarged by the annexation of the city-state of Genoa.

To safeguard her empire, Great Britain sought a balance of power on the Continent and the acquisition of certain strategic territories. Because of her complete mastery over the seas, she could have helped herself to any of the colonial possessions of France or the Napoleonic puppet states that she desired. However, she limited herself to Helgoland in the North Sea, Malta, and the Ionian Islands in the Mediterranean, several small French and Spanish territories in the West Indies and the Indian Ocean, and the Dutch colonies of Ceylon off the tip of India, the Cape of Good Hope, and part of Dutch Guiana in South America.

Prussia, in addition to her valuable gains in the Rhineland, annexed Westphalia and Swedish Pomerania. In return for a portion of her Polish territory, including the city of Warsaw, which she ceded to Russia, she annexed two-fifths of Saxony. These changes considerably strengthened and consolidated Prussia's territories and made her more homogeneously German and Western. However, her Rhineland territory was not contiguous to the homeland—a situation that invited further aggression.

Russia received Finland from Sweden. Sweden got Norway from Denmark in return. Russia's acquisition of most of Prussia's Polish territory made the great majority of the Polish-speaking people subjects of Russia and brought Russia farther into the heart of Central Europe.

Austria, in exchange for the Belgian Netherlands, took the two rich Italian provinces of Lombardy and Venetia. Austrian princes were placed on the thrones of three other Italian states: Modena, Parma, and Tuscany. This preeminence in Italy, together with the presidency over the German Confederation, made Austria the dominant power in Central Europe. Her mastery over Italy and Germany was made possible by their political division and weakness. The Italian Peninsula was left divided into eight separate states with no common political ties. In the words of Metternich, Italy was "only a geographical expression."

The Holy Roman Empire, which Napoleon had destroyed, was not restored, but in its place was erected the equally weak and ineffective German Confederation. Napoleon's consolidation of the more than three hundred German states into thirty-nine was allowed to stand, bringing the German people that much more political unity. However, Metternich saw to it that the government of the German Confederation was powerless and under the permanent presidency of Austria. Nevertheless, as future developments were to demonstrate, the overall settlement consolidated and strengthened the position of Prussia in relation to that of Austria.

Thus were the peoples and territories of Europe moved about by the great powers at Vienna like pawns on a chessboard, in complete disregard for the wishes of the people or for the spirit of nationalism that was now an increasingly virile force.

2. THE CONCERT OF EUROPE—FIRST RIFTS IN THE METTERNICH SYSTEM

Metternich and his colleagues, pleased with their work, set up machinery for perpetuating it. Conveniently at hand was the Holy Alliance, conceived by Alexander I to establish and safeguard the principles of the Christian religion. Russia (Orthodox), Austria (Roman Catholic), and Prussia (Protestant), representing the three major branches of Christendom, were to form the nucleus of the alliance. All the Christian states of Europe were invited to join, and only Great Britain and the Papal States did not. Metternich considered the Holy Alliance a "sonorous nothing," but saw in it an opportunity for influencing the tsar.

Boundary of the German Confederation

0   100   200 miles

FINLAND
(Russia, 1808)

KINGDOM OF NORWAY
AND SWEDEN

St. Petersb

Oslo

Stockholm

Reval   Novgorod

Smol

Riga

NORTH SEA

BALTIC SEA

LITHUAN

SCOTLAND

Edinburgh

Copenhagen
DENMARK

EAST
PRUSSIA

Niemen R.

UNITED KINGDOM
OF GREAT BRITAIN AND IRELAND

IRELAND   Dublin

ENGLAND

WALES

SCHLESWIG
HELIGOLAND
(Britain)
HOLSTEIN

Danzig

I
A

Hamburg

S
S

Vistula R.

KINGDOM OF THE
NETHERLANDS

HANOVER

Elbe R.

U

Berlin

Warsaw

London

P

R

KINGDOM OF
POLAND
(1815-1831)

Oder R.

GALICIA

ENGLISH CHANNEL

BELGIUM
(Ind. 1831)

Cologne

HESSE

SAXON
STATES

SAXONY

Breslau

Cracow

Dniester

BESSA
(Russia)

ATLANTIC OCEAN

Rouen

Seine R.

LUX.

Rhine R.

Prague

Paris

Metz

LORRAINE

BADEN

WÜRT-
TEMBERG

BAVARIA

AUSTRIA

Vienna

Pressburg

MOLD
(Autonom

Tu

Loire R.

Strasbourg

ALSACE

Munich

AUSTRIAN EMPIRE

Tours

Berne

TYROL

Budapest

FRANCE

SWITZERLAND

HUNGARY

TRANSYLVANIA

Lyons

Rhone R.

SAVOY

LOM-
BARDY

VENETIA

CROATIA

WALLACHIA
(Autonomous 182

Bordeaux

Milan

Po R.

Belgrade

SERBIA
(Autonomous
1829)

Danube R.

O
T
T
O
M

Toulouse

PYRENEES

Marseilles   Nice

PIEDMONT

PARMA
Genoa
LUCCA

MODENA

BOSNIA

DALMATIA

Sofia

BULG

Ebro R.

Toulon

KINGDOM OF SARDINIA

TUSCANY

PAPAL
STATES

MONTE-
NEGRO

Salonica

PORTUGAL

Madrid

Barcelona

ELBA

CORSICA
(France)

Rome

ADRIATIC SEA

IONIAN I
(Britain)

AEGE

Lisbon

Tagus R.

SPAIN

Naples

Ather

Valencia

BALEARIC I.
(Spain)

SARDINIA

KINGDOM OF THE
TWO SICILIES

GREECE
(Independent 1829)

Seville

Cadiz

Gibraltar (Britain)

Palermo

SICILY

Algiers

MEDITERRANEAN SEA

MOROCCO

ALGERIA   (France, 1830)

TUNIS
(Turkish)

MALTA
(Britain)

C

TRIPOLI

TRIPOLI

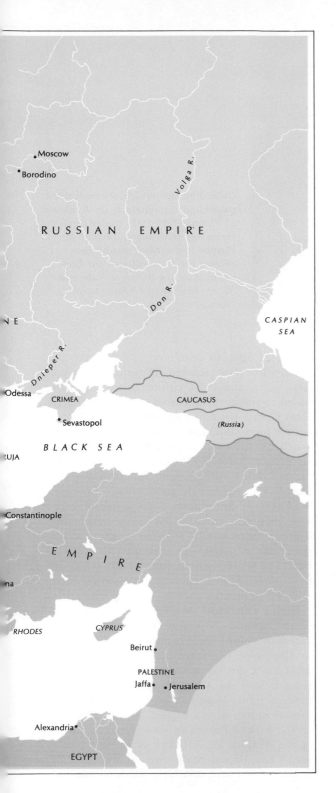

Europe 1815

Intended by Alexander I as a bulwark of Christianity, the Holy Alliance became under Metternich's influence a symbol of reaction and repression.

Much more earthly an agency for perpetuating the Vienna settlements was the Quadruple Alliance. This was a military alliance of Austria, Russia, Prussia, and Great Britain created in November 1815, for the purpose of guaranteeing for twenty years the territorial boundaries established by the Vienna settlement. Metternich was determined to make of the alliance an international military police force that would spy out and suppress any liberal or national movements. It was arranged that the four member powers should hold periodic congresses to carry out the purposes of the alliance.

The first congress was held at Aix-la-Chapelle in northwest Germany in 1818. The purpose was to arrange the withdrawal of occupation forces from French soil. Since France had demonstrated good behavior under the restored Bourbon king, Louis XVIII, she was not only freed of occupying forces, but was admitted to the Quadruple Alliance, which thereupon became the Quintuple Alliance. Congresses at Troppau in 1820 and at Laibach in 1821, both on Austrian soil, concerned themselves with an insurrection that had broken out in Naples against the tyrannical Bourbon king, Ferdinand I. An Austrian army was authorized to put down the insurrection and reestablish the hated Ferdinand I upon his throne. The Neapolitan liberal volunteers, no match for the Austrian regulars, were soon defeated, and their leaders executed, imprisoned, or exiled. What turned out to be the last of the congresses met in 1822 at Verona, in Austria's Italian province of Venetia, to deal with a liberal revolt in Spain against Ferdinand VII. This reactionary Bourbon tyrant, who had spent seven years of captivity in France, had been restored to his throne upon the defeat of Napoleon. With the sanction of the Congress of Verona a French army crossed the Pyrenees and easily put down the rebellion.

671

Guided by Metternich, the assembled rulers and diplomats at the Congress of Vienna (1814–1815) traded territories and rearranged the map of Europe in a cynical great-power contest for dominance of the Continent after the defeat of Napoleon. *Photo: Historical Pictures Service, Chicago*

The bloody vengeance that Ferdinand took upon the liberal rebels revolted the French soldiers who had restored him. However, the first of the alliance powers to repudiate the Metternich system was not France but Great Britain. At the Troppau congress, she clearly indicated her opposition to interfering in the internal affairs of other states. When the Verona congress decided, over her protest, upon intervention in Spain, Britain's representative withdrew from the congress. It was the first sign of dissension within the concert of Europe.

The Metternich system soon received further blows, some from unexpected quarters. At the Congress of Verona, the like-minded Austrians, Russians, and Prussians had been alarmed not only by the rebellion in the Spanish homeland, but also by the revolt of Spain's New World colonies. The brilliant success of the thirteen English colonies was bad enough; it must not be repeated in Latin America. When the corrupt government of Ferdinand VII proved incapable of putting down the revolt, Alexander I, with Metternich's blessing, proposed to send a Russian fleet to help coerce the colonies. Great Britain, however, enjoyed a lucrative trade with the rebellious colonies and did not wish to see them restored to Spanish dominion and commercial monopoly. Her foreign minister, Canning, who had succeeded Castlereagh in 1822, proposed to the government of the United States that Great Britain and the United States issue a joint statement against interference by the "Holy Alliance" in the affairs of the Western Hemisphere. To President Monroe and to his confidants, ex-Presidents Madison and Jefferson, this seemed a good idea. However, Secretary of State John Quincy Adams foresaw that the time might come when the United States would wish to invoke such a policy alone, perhaps even against Great Britain. The British would support the policy of the United States anyway because of their own self-interest.

Adams convinced Monroe that the United States should proclaim the policy alone. When, therefore, the President in his message to Congress, in December 1823, announced what has come to be called the Monroe Doctrine, it was the Adams rather than the Canning version. Monroe stated simply that the United States would regard any interference on the part of European powers in the affairs of the Western Hemisphere as an "unfriendly act." The United States was at the time, of course, a new and relatively weak nation, but

Canning's immediate support of the American policy killed any further thought of "Holy Alliance" intervention in the New World, for Great Britain was the unchallenged mistress of the seas. The Monroe Doctrine was, however, more than a blow to Metternichism in Europe. It guaranteed the independence of Latin America and marked the beginning of active participation by the United States in affairs beyond her own immediate shores.

The next successful blow at repressive tyranny was struck by the Greeks against their Muslim Turkish overlords. The Greek revolt of 1821–1829 is an excellent example of the influence of the past in world affairs. The Greeks had been treated no worse by their Turkish masters than the rest of the Christian European subjects of the Sultan—the Serbs, the Bulgarians, or the Rumanians. However, the Greeks had the memory of a glorious past, which the others did not have, to spur them on to heroism. But the valiant efforts of the Greeks were not sufficient to resist the power of the whole Ottoman Empire. By 1827 they were on the point of being hopelessly crushed.

Meanwhile, the sympathies of the great powers were being aroused for the courageous Christian Greeks, who were being cruelly massacred by the Muslim Turks. Russia, Great Britain, and France in particular displayed a growing concern over the events in Greece. Russia's Orthodox Christian religion was the same as that of the Greeks. Furthermore, the Russians had long desired Constantinople, which controlled her natural strategic and commercial outlet to the Mediterranean. Great Britain was concerned over the possibility of Russia's dominance in the Near East. In addition, the ruling classes in Great Britain and France were steeped in the classical culture of ancient Greece. Lord Byron, the most popular literary figure in Europe, lost his life fighting as a volunteer for Greece.

In 1827 these three powers, over Metternich's protest, intervened in the Greek revolt and defeated the Turks on land and sea. The Treaty of Adrianople in 1829 granted independence to most of the Greeks on the home peninsula and local autonomy to the Serbs and Rumanians. The successful revolt of the Greeks was a victory for the resurging revolutionary principles of liberalism and nationalism. The intervention of Russia, Great Britain, and France demolished the already-battered concert of Europe. The Treaty of Adrianople also hastened the disintegration of the once-powerful Ottoman Empire.

The year 1830 was a bad one for Metternich. Successful revolutions in France and Belgium undid two of the settlements at Vienna. News of the revolution in France (which will be described in the next section) set off the revolt in Brussels. The union forced upon Belgium and the Netherlands at Vienna had never been a happy one, and Belgian discontent with Dutch rule had been mounting for fifteen years. In addition to differences in language, the Belgians were Roman Catholic, whereas the Dutch were predominately Calvinist. The Belgian economy was based on industry, the Dutch on commerce. Belgium, more populous than the Netherlands, was not given her fair share of representation in the government. When the halfhearted efforts of the Dutch failed to suppress the revolt, Austria and Russia threatened to intervene in the interests of legitimacy and tranquillity. However, they were deterred by British and French support of Belgian independence. By 1830, then, Metternich's international system of reaction and repression was definitely breached. In that year even France, the reactionaries' greatest concern, threw off the Bourbon yoke that had been imposed upon her.

3. THE BOURBON RESTORATION IN FRANCE

When the victorious armies of the coalition powers entered France and deposed Napoleon in the spring of 1814, they brought "in their baggage" the members of the Bourbon royal family who had fled the revolution. In their wake trooped the émigré nobility. A younger brother of the guillotined Louis XVI was placed on the throne as Louis XVIII. (The son of Louis XVI, who had died in prison in 1795, without having ruled, was considered to be Louis XVII.) The "restored" Bourbon king was now fifty-nine years of age and too fat and gouty to walk unassisted. He had traveled much and unwillingly during the long, lean years of his exile. When Napoleon returned from Elba in 1815, Louis XVIII had to flee once more. After Waterloo he returned to his throne, which he considered "the most comfortable of armchairs," determined to do nothing that might force him to leave it again.

Upon assuming the throne, Louis XVIII issued a charter, or constitution, that retained Napoleon's administrative and legal system, and civil and religious liberty. Law-making was placed in the hands of a two-chamber legislature. The upper house was made hereditary, and the lower house was elected by a highly restricted electorate. Only those who paid direct annual taxes of 300 francs ($60) could vote; this limited the suffrage to about 100,000 out of a total population of nearly 30,000,000. The lower house could be prorogued or dissolved by the king. Since the king also appointed and controlled his own ministers and the host of civilian and military officials, carried on foreign relations, controlled the military forces, and enforced the laws, his power was only slightly limited by the charter.

Louis XVIII set out to use his powers with moderation in order that tranquillity might be restored. There were no wholesale punishments of revolutionary leaders. The peasant and bourgeois purchasers of church and noble lands were not dispossessed. However, most of the returned émigrés were of a different spirit. They came back from their unhappy exile angry and vengeful, demanding their old privileges and indemnification for their lands. Their leader was the king's younger brother, the Comte d'Artois—a typical Bourbon who had "never learned anything and never forgotten anything." The reactionaries controlled both houses of the national legislature, since even in the lower elected house, suffrage restrictions limited the voters to the aristocracy and the *nouveaux riches*. Louis XVIII found it increasingly difficult to hold these fire-eating reactionaries in check. Shortly before he died in 1824, he warned his incorrigible brother of the danger to the Bourbon dynasty if he did not adopt a more moderate attitude.

Unfortunately, Charles X, as the Comte d'Artois now styled himself, was a stranger to moderation. He quickly aroused animosity against his regime to an explosive pitch. The Napoleonic generals who had brought so much glory to France were immediately retired from duty. An indemnity was voted the émigrés for their confiscated lands, the money to be raised by reducing the interest on government bonds from 5 percent to 3 percent. This angered the upper bourgeoisie, who were the chief bondholders. The peasants were alarmed by a proposed establishment of primogeniture, which seemed to endanger the principle of equality and the security of land titles. The Jesuits were brought back to France, and favors were bestowed upon the Roman Catholic Church. Opposition mounted rapidly. By 1827 Charles X had lost his majority in both houses of the national legislature. Totally blind to the political realities of the day, he twice dissolved the lower chamber and attempted to force the election of a friendly majority by censoring the press and using official pressure on the electorate. The hostile majorities only increased in number.

Finally in July 1830 the king decided to end the parliamentary regime and rule as a dictator. In a set of ordinances he dissolved the newly elected chamber, called for new elections, restricted the suffrage so drastically that only about 25,000 very rich citizens could vote, and abolished completely the freedom of the press. These tyrannical measures set off an uprising in Paris. The Parisian proletariat erected barricades in the streets that the disaffected rank and file of the army were "unable" to break. After three days of desultory fighting, the insurgents had the upper hand, and the last Bourbon king of France was on his way to exile in England. A group of moderate opposition members of the lower chamber now set themselves up as a provisional government and named a new king: Louis Philippe, head of the house of Orléans and a cousin of the departed Bourbon. Louis Philippe, a well-known moderate liberal and friend of the middle class, was accepted by the great majority of the people of France. The French people in July 1830, therefore, showed Metternich and the rest of the world that the spirit of the French Revolution was not dead, but for fifteen years had been only dormant.

4. RESTORATION AND REPRESSION IN THE GERMANIES

In Central and Eastern Europe, particularly in the Germanies, Italy, and Russia, the Metternich system was more secure. The Germanies in 1815 consisted of thirty-seven little states and two large ones—Prussia and Austria. In all of them the influence of Metternich was strong. At the Congress of Vienna the Austrian prime minister had seen to it that the Germanies were reconstructed in such a way that German nationalism and liberalism would be thwarted. The German Confederation was an improvement over the old Holy Roman Empire, which Napoleon had destroyed, only in the sense that Napoleon's consolidation of the more than three hundred states down to thirty-nine was allowed to stand. The boundaries remained the same. The Diet was only a gathering and debating place for the representatives of the rulers of the thirty-nine states. The confederation had no treasury and no army at its command. There was not even a flag to symbolize its German national character. Reactionary Austria enjoyed a permanent presidency over it.

The German nationalism and liberalism that existed in 1815 centered primarily in the little states, some of whose rulers defied Metternich by granting liberal constitutions. The national and liberal activities here were largely the work of university students and professors, who shortly after 1815 began to form *Burschenschaften*, or brotherhoods, for the purpose of promoting German nationalism, liberalism, and the Christian religion. In 1817 in commemoration of the three hundredth anniversary of Luther's publication of his ninety-five theses, the *Burschenschaften* staged a giant festival at Wartburg, where Luther had hidden and had begun his translation of the Bible. Although the festivities were primarily religious in character, enough enthusiasm for German nationalism and liberalism was displayed to fill Metternich with anxiety. The murder two years later of a reactionary propagandist by a fanatical student gave Metternich his opportunity to strike. Calling together the princes of the leading German states at Carlsbad, he joined them in drawing up a set of harsh decrees designed to crush the embryonic national and liberal movements. The *Burschenschaften* were outlawed. Strict censorship was established. Classrooms and libraries were supervised. Liberal students and professors were terrorized by spies and police. The Carlsbad Decrees succeeded in suppressing for a number of years this first outcropping of the revolutionary spirit in Germany since the overthrow of Napoleon. The spirit, however, was not really suppressed; it was merely driven underground.

In Prussia the militaristic, paternalistic, despotic Hohenzollerns reigned. Behind them stood the equally reactionary landed aristocracy, the *Junkers*. In fact these sword-bearing, monocled Junkers, who ruled feudal-fashion over their peasants, officered the Prussian army, and filled the key posts in the civil service and administration, constituted the dominant factor in Prussian history in the nineteenth century. These military lords hated not only liberalism in any form, but also German nationalism. They did not wish to see virile, martial Prussia contaminated by association with the German states that were now infected with the French disease of liberalism. The *Burschenschaften* made slight headway in Prussia. It was only in the economic field that German unity received any encouragement from Prussia. Because her territory was separated into two non-contiguous segments, Prussia in 1819 began making commercial treaties with her smaller German neighbors, providing for the free flow of trade among them. By 1834 nearly all the states of the German Confederation except Austria had joined the Prussian-sponsored *Zollverein* (customs union). Though it was not so intended, the *Zollverein* proved to be a forerunner of German political unity under Prussian leadership.

As was to be expected, Metternichism reached its height in Austria. The spirit of the French Revolution and Napoleon, with the one exception of nationalism, had hardly touched the Hapsburg state and its feudal society. In addition to the natural conservatism of the Hapsburgs and their chief minister, Austria had a language problem that caused her rulers to fear liberalism and its companion nationalism like the plague. Austria proper is German-speaking, but during the sixteenth, seventeenth, and eighteenth centuries the Hapsburgs had annexed territories inhabited by Hungarian (Magyar), Czech, Slovak, Ruthenian, Polish, Rumanian, Serb, Croat, and Slovene language groups. In 1815 two Italian-speaking provinces were added. Before 1789 these various language groups remained quiet under their' feudal lords, the Hapsburg dynasty, and the Roman Catholic Church. However, with the mass nationalism, based largely on language, that followed in the wake of the French Revolution, they began to stir with national consciousness.

Metternich saw clearly that if this new force were not suppressed, the Hapsburg state would fall apart. Furthermore, nationalism unchecked would cause Austria to lose her dominance over Germany and Italy. The various German and Italian states would be drawn together into powerful national states from which Austria would be excluded, for most of the people in the Hapsburg state were neither German- nor Italian-speaking. When these facts are considered, it is not surprising that Austria in 1815 was the most reactionary state in Europe save Russia. In the Hapsburg provinces Metternich's police and spies were everywhere. Permission to enter or to leave the country was made very difficult, lest dangerous ideas be brought in from the West. Classrooms, libraries, bookstores, and organizations of all kinds were supervised with suspicion. Censorship covered even music (in the country of Mozart and Beethoven) for fear that musical notes would be used as a cryptic code for conveying revolutionary ideas. On the surface, these policies appeared for some time to succeed. Nevertheless, Metternich was aware that the Hapsburg state stood on shaky ground.

5. RESTORATION AND REPRESSION IN ITALY

Austria's domination over Italy was even more complete than over Germany. Lombardy and Venetia were annexed outright. Modena, Parma, and Tuscany were ruled by Austrian princes. The Papal States and Naples were under Austria's protection and guidance in both domestic and foreign affairs. In all these states the deposed aristocracy and clericals trooped back, full of hatred for French institutions and for the Italian liberals who had cooperated with Napoleon. Nearly all the Italian intelligentsia were soon in prison or in exile. In the Papal States the Inquisition and the Index were restored, and such Napoleonic innovations as street lighting

This illustration shows Italians being shot for reading Mazzini's writings; it epitomizes the spirit of reaction and repression that characterized the years after the defeat of Napoleon, when the great powers of Europe tried to restore the old order and stifle the new currents of liberalism and nationalism. *Photo: Historical Pictures Service, Chicago* were done away with. Of all the Italian states, only Piedmont in the extreme north-west was free of direct Austrian control, but even here the restored heads of the house of Savoy were so reactionary as to cause Metternich only pleasure.

In considering Italy to be "safe," however, Metternich failed to reckon with the influence of history. Italy had had a glorious past. As the seat of the Roman Empire, it had ruled the Western world for many centuries. During the Middle Ages all roads still led to Rome, which was then the head of Western Christendom. In the fourteenth and fifteenth centuries Italy held the economic and cultural leadership of the West. Venice was queen of the seas and Florence was the center of the banking world. Both were fabulously rich in money and in culture.

The extraordinary brilliance of Venice, Florence, Milan, Rome, Pisa, Siena, Ravenna, and many other Italian city-states in the Renaissance period tended to develop a local rather than a national pride. This local state patriotism was in large measure responsible for Ita-

ly's division, weakness, and decay in early modern times. However, the French Revolution and Napoleon brought to Italy a new kind of nationalism and reawakened memories of past exploits. Very soon after 1815 Italian liberals began to form secret societies, called *Carbonari* (charcoal burners), which met at night around charcoal fires to plot freedom from Austrian and local tyranny and to plan for national unification. In the early thirties a romantic young intellectual, Giuseppe Mazzini, organized the Young Italy society, which was dedicated to the task of achieving a free, united, and liberal Italian nation. Although the first uprisings inspired by the Carbonari and Young Italy were crushed by Austrian arms, the Italian national movement once aroused could not so easily be suppressed.

6. REACTION AND REPRESSION IN RUSSIA

Even primitive, autocratic, semi-Asiatic Russia had not escaped the influence of the

French Revolution and Napoleon. She had joined in the second, third, fourth, and fifth coalitions against France, had been invaded and ravaged as far as Moscow in 1812, and had played a major role in the wars of liberation against Napoleon in 1813–1814. Meanwhile, her young tsar, Alexander I, and many of his aristocratic young army officers had picked up romantic and liberal ideas from the West. Russia, however, was not yet ripe for Western liberalism. She was a vast agricultural nation with a feudal social structure and a very small urban bourgeoisie that could serve as a liberal base. The Orthodox Christian Church, dominated by an upper clergy drawn from the aristocracy, was a handy governmental agency for controlling the masses. The unstable Alexander I soon fell under the influence of Metternich and of his own reactionary boyar magnates, and repented of his liberalism. He sought atonement for his sins by volunteering to stamp out liberal movements in Naples, Spain, and Latin America. He did, however, remain a romantic idealist as long as he lived.

There was no trace of romanticism whatever in Nicholas I, Alexander's younger brother, who succeeded him in 1825. Nicholas was a handsome, dignified, austere autocrat whose military career wedded him to the concepts of discipline and authority. A quixotic revolt by a group of young liberal officers on the occasion of his ascension to the throne and a full-scale revolt against Russian tyranny by his Polish subjects in 1831 further embittered him against liberalism in any form. Both revolts were crushed with an iron hand. For thirty years (1825–1855) Nicholas I was to stand as the perfect symbol of absolute reaction and the armed guardian of the Metternich system. Russia, of all the great powers of Europe, was the least affected by the spirit of the French Revolution. When at the end of the nineteenth century she did begin to yield to liberal and revolutionary forces, it was with disorder and violence.

But in Western and Central Europe it was obvious by 1830 that the liberal and national forces created or released by the Intellectual and the French revolutions and spread by Napoleon were not dead, but only temporarily repressed. Greece, Belgium, and most of Spain's New World colonies had gained their freedom. The restored French Bourbons had been overthrown. In Great Britain the Reform Bill of 1832 opened a new liberal era (see pp. 701–702). The fifteen years of restoration, reaction, and repression that followed the overthrow of Napoleon proved, therefore, to be only a brief interlude. By 1830 the revolutionary forces of liberalism and nationalism were once more on the march.

Suggested Reading

General. The volume in the Rise of Modern Europe series that covers the fifteen years of restoration and reaction that followed the overthrow of Napoleon is **F. B. Artz, *Reaction and Revolution, 1814–1832* (Harper Torchbook). An excellent briefer study is **A. J. May, *The Age of Metternich, 1814–1848* (Berkshire). A strong apology for Metternich and the principle of conservatism is **P. Viereck, *Conservatism Revisited* (Collier). A more objective study of early nineteenth-century conservatism is E. L. Woodward, *Three Studies in European Conservatism: Metternich, Guizot, the Catholic Church in the Nineteenth Century* (1930).

The Congress of Vienna. The two best histories of the Congress of Vienna are **Harold Nicolson, *The Congress of Vienna: A Study in Allied Unity 1812–22* (Compass); and C. K. Webster, *The Congress of Vienna, 1814–1815* (1934). Webster is the more factual and detailed and Nicholson the more readable. A good discussion of the leading personalities at the congress is J. G. Lockhart, *The Peacemakers, 1814–1815* (1932). A scholarly and sympathetic biography of Talleyrand, who played such a vital role in the post-Napoleonic diplomacy, is **C. Brinton, *The Lives of Talleyrand* (Norton).

The Concert of Europe. In praise of the work of the Congress of Vienna is **Hans A. Kissinger, *A World Restored, Metternich, Castlereagh, and the Problems of Peace, 1812–1822* (Universal). The successful struggle of the Greeks for independence against the Turks is told by William Miller, *The Ottoman Empire and Its Successors, 1801–1927* (1928). The story of the harsh repression in Spain and the rebellion against it, so momentous in both hemispheres, is covered by H. B. Clark, *Modern Spain, 1815–1898* (1906). **Dexter Perkins, *Hands Off! A History of the Monroe Doctrine* (Little, Brown) is a popularly written account of the first successful blow against the Metternich system, by America's foremost authority on the subject.

Bourbon Restoration in France. A scholarly and detailed history of France during the Bourbon restoration is F. B. Artz, *France Under the Bourbon Restoration, 1814–1830* (1931). Also of value is N. E. Hudson, *Ultraroyalism and the French Restoration* (1936).

Reaction in Central and Eastern Europe. An excellent survey of modern German history with brief but good coverage of the period 1815–1830 is K. S. Pinson, *Modern Germany: Its History and Civilization* (1954). J. C. Legge, ed., *Rhyme and Revolution in Germany: A Study in German History, Life, Literature, and Character, 1813–1850* (1918), lives up to its title. It is scholarly and entertaining. **A. J. P. Taylor, *The Hapsburg Monarchy, 1809–1918* (rev. ed., Harper Torchbook), is one of the better books of this brilliant British historian. For Italy during the age of Metternich, **R. Albrecht-Carrié, *Italy From Napoleon to Mussolini* (Collier), is a brief survey by a leading authority. A scholarly treatment of Russia during the two decades following the overthrow of Napoleon is **A. G. Mazour, *The First Russian Revolution, 1825* (Stanford).

Sources. Probably the best single source for the period of restoration and reaction is the memoirs of the leading international figure of the period, Metternich, *The Memoirs of Prince Metternich* (5 vols., 1880–82).

RETROSPECT

RETROSPECT The era of the French Revolution was a period of one of the greatest—some historians think *the* greatest—political and social upheavals in history. It was a time of high expectation and excitement. In a matter of weeks, and sometimes days, the kind of fundamental changes that usually require centuries took place. Time-honored institutions, privileges, and customs toppled. Wealth, power, and rights were redistributed. Specifically, the story begins with Copernicus and ends with Metternich.

The French and American revolutions were preceded and in part, at least, induced by an intellectual revolution—the triumph of the philosophy of the Enlightenment. The Enlightenment, in turn, was based upon the concepts of modern natural science. When, therefore, Copernicus in the sixteenth century attacked the long-accepted beliefs concerning the structure of the solar system, he set off a chain reaction. The Christian churchmen who had allowed their theology to become enmeshed in ancient theories of astronomy and physics, which were now questioned, tried to silence Copernicus and his disciples. But they could not. During the course of the seventeenth and eighteenth centuries, the new science prevailed. Indeed, the intellectual world of the West became fascinated with the scientific attitude.

Thinkers like Descartes, Locke, and Voltaire, armed with the new discoveries of science, developed and popularized the philosophy of the Enlightenment. The materialistic, rationalistic, humanistic, deistic concepts of the Enlightenment clashed with the theology of the Christian theologians of the eighteenth century, who were no match for their adversaries. The philosophy of the Enlightenment also advocated limited constitutional government and laissez-faire economics. The widespread acceptance of these ideas played a major role in bringing about the American and the French revolutions.

The American Revolution was primarily a matter of the thirteen English colonies winning their independence from the mother country. A great deal of political and social equality already existed in the colonies—probably more than anywhere else in the world. Nevertheless, there were some further political and social changes. The revolutionary leaders like Franklin, Jefferson, and John Adams were ardent disciples of the Enlightenment. As a result of the revolution, loyalist lands were redistributed, and the royal governors and their aristocratic councils gave way to the more democratic legislatures. The new constitution was filled with the ideas and phrases of Locke, Montesquieu, and Rousseau.

The influence of the Enlightenment on the French Revolution is even more obvious. French society on the eve of the revolution was still essentially feudal, with its privileged clergy and nobility. Government was arbitrary. The Church was intolerant and oppressive. The crisis of the old regime in France, however, occurred in the field of finance. Because the two privileged estates refused to surrender any of their exemptions from direct taxation, the government was forced to declare bankruptcy. And it was the calling of the Estates General for the first time in one hundred and seventy-five years in an attempt to solve the financial problem that triggered the French Revolution.

The French Revolution began modestly enough, but when the two privileged estates refused the demands of the bourgeois-dominated Third Estate for equal representation, the king sided with them and threatened to use force. At this juncture the lower classes rose up with a display of violence of their own and stayed the king's hand. The result was a victory for the Third Estate. A series of sweeping reforms ensued—the end of feudalism, the Declaration of the Rights of Man, and the drawing up of a liberal but moderate constitution.

But the nobility and the clergy were not willing to see their privileges so easily lost. Nor were the radical disciples of Rousseau convinced that the revolution had gone far enough. They wished to see the principles of Liberty, Equality, Fraternity extended not only throughout France, but throughout the world. When Austria and Prussia intervened in behalf of the French royalty and nobility, the radicals deposed and beheaded Louis XVI. All the great powers of Europe except Russia now formed a coalition for the purpose of ending this threat to the established order. The revolutionary radicals, now in control, inaugurated a Reign of Terror for the purpose of uniting and mobilizing the nation. It was remarkably successful; the internal enemies of the revolution were terrorized into silence or support, and the foreign enemies were defeated and driven back beyond the frontiers. The radicals, led by Robespierre, were now able to make France over into what they believed was the image of Rousseau.

But no one seemed able to consummate the revolution and restore tranquillity. Robespierre and his faction were overthrown by the bourgeois moderates, and the terror ended, but the moderates, too, proved unable to bring peace at home and abroad. That task remained for Napoleon Bonaparte, one of the greatest political geniuses of all time. His mission was to build practical institutions to conserve and apply the ideas of the Enlightenment and the reforms of the revolution and to spread those ideas and institutions abroad. After achieving these goals in large measure during his spectacular fifteen-year dictatorship, he was finally defeated and overthrown by a combination of all the great powers of Europe. These powers, under the leadership of Metternich, now undertook to push the historical clock as far back as they could, but their efforts met with only partial and temporary success. The ideas of the Enlightenment and the French Revolution were resurgent within a very few years and have remained powerful forces in the world ever since.

Part Ten

The Industrial Revolution

First Phase:
The Dominance
of the Middle Class
1830–1871

While the French Revolution was releasing upon the world the explosive forces of liberalism and nationalism, the Industrial Revolution was introducing to the Western world new techniques of working and living. Indeed, most of world history in the nineteenth and twentieth centuries has centered around these three forces—liberalism of various hues, nationalism first moderate and then aggressive, and industrialism with its manifold facets and problems. And if we broaden our concept of the Industrial Revolution to include the onrush of science, with which it was closely associated, we may venture to give it first place among all the forces that have influenced Western civilization since the era of the French Revolution. Beginning in Great Britain near the end of the eighteenth century, the Industrial Revolution spread first to Belgium and France, then to the United States, and eventually to most of the rest of the world. Everywhere it drastically changed the pattern of life.

The industrial bourgeoisie, who owned and benefited from the new power machines, rose to a position of great wealth and power, justifying their good fortune with theories of laissez-faire economics. The proletariat, on the other hand, unable to compete with the machines, found themselves insecure and perplexed. Their distress eventually led the masses to organize, take up new theories of economics, and demand and get an increased share in government and in society. From approximately 1830 to 1871, the bourgeoisie were generally in control in the industrialized countries. From 1871 to 1914, the masses were moving toward the top. Meanwhile, science and technology were reshaping life and thought.

Without, therefore, minimizing such dynamic forces as liberalism and nationalism, what better title can be given the history of the nineteenth century than "The Industrial Revolution—First Phase: The Dominance of the Middle Class, 1830–1871; Second Phase: The Emergence of the Masses, 1871–1914"? In this first section we shall examine the bourgeois-dominated first phase of the Industrial Revolution. Our examination, of course, will not be limited to matters of technology and economics. It will include the development of those two great forces unleashed by the French Revolution —liberalism and nationalism, together with a look at the prevailing trends in the arts and letters during the period 1830–1871.

Chapter 43 ❧ The Industrial Revolution

The term "Industrial Revolution" has come into general use to indicate the shifting of production from hand tools, powered by muscles, wind, and water to machinery powered by steam, combustion, electricity, and atomic fission. This, of course, was not an abrupt change. An increase in the tempo of technological development can be observed in Western Europe as early as the seventeenth century. The tempo is still accelerating, and the technology is still spreading to the rest of the world. This shift in the means of production first occurred in significant measure in Great Britain during the last few decades of the eighteenth century and the first few of the nineteenth. Great Britain possessed an abundance of coal and iron and of liquid capital which her merchants and wool growers had amassed from her lucrative commerce. She also possessed the world's greatest merchant marine and the navy to protect it. During the course of the eighteenth century and the era of the French Revolution, Britain's colonial empire had become the world's largest, supplying the mother country with abundant markets and sources for raw materials. Also during the course of the eighteenth century, an agricultural revolution in Britain (described later in this chapter) drove thousands of small farmers from the land to the cities where they provided the industrial entrepreneurs with a cheap supply of labor. Furthermore, since 1688, Great Britain had enjoyed a stable government dominated by the capitalistic classes—landowners, merchants, bankers. Finally, the demand for more manufactured goods was strong. For reasons not clear, the population in Europe and Asia began to increase markedly about the middle of the seventeenth century. Thus, by the middle of the eighteenth century, there were new millions of people to be fed, clothed, and housed.

1. THE COMING OF THE MACHINE

The textile industry was the first to become mechanized. In 1733 John Kay invented the flying shuttle, which doubled the speed of weaving cloth. In 1764 James Hargreaves, a humble English carpenter, hit upon the idea of hitching eight spindles to his wife's spinning wheel, instead of one. The result was the spinning jenny (named after his daughter Jenny). The number of spindles was soon multiplied. Five years later Richard Arkwright, a barber, patented the water frame, a system of rollers driven by water power which spun a much finer and firmer thread than the jenny. In 1779 Samuel Crompton, combining the principles of the spinning jenny and the water frame, produced the hybrid spinning mule—a great improvement over both. In 1785 an Anglican clergyman, Edmund Cartwright, invented the power loom.

The mechanization of both spinning and weaving greatly increased the demand for cotton. The meeting of this demand was made possible by a young American, Eli Whitney, who in 1793 invented the cotton gin. Removing the lint from the seeds by hand was a tedious process; one man could separate only five or six pounds a day. Cotton was therefore grown only in small patches. Whitney's gin not only made possible an adequate supply of cotton for Britain's mills, but also brought into existence the huge cotton plantations, worked by Negro slaves, in the American South.

Meanwhile, a new source of power was found to help water drive the new machines. In 1769 James Watt, a University of Glasgow repairman-mechanic, invented the first steam engine that could be used to drive machinery. The power that could be generated by the steam engine was almost unlimited. Constant improvements in the making of iron and the mining of coal led to the production of still-better machines and guaranteed a sufficient supply of fuel to drive them.

Man now had the capacity to produce a practically boundless supply of goods. The enormous significance of these and other inventions for the future could not, of course, be seen at the time they were made. And today we have become so accustomed to them it is easy to forget their importance. However, the fact is that the inventors of these basic machines and processes were responsible for the coming of a new era. It is true that most of the principles and some of the processes were known in ancient and medieval times, but it was men like Hargreaves and Watt, aided by the favorable political and social setting (and by earlier experimenters), who developed the practical working machines. Most of these inventors were humble amateurs who endured discouragement, scorn, and sometimes bankruptcy and persecution. One of the few exceptions was Richard Arkwright, who rose from barbering to wealth and knighthood.

2. THE REVOLUTION IN TRANSPORTATION AND COMMUNICATIONS

An integral and necessary part of the Industrial Revolution was the improvement of transportation and communications. Otherwise, sufficient quantities of raw materials to feed the hungry machines and adequate markets to absorb the finished products would not have been available. The last decades of the eighteenth century and the first decades of the nineteenth were a time of road and canal building in Great Britain, France, and the United States. Roads had long been good

The steamship and the locomotive revolutionized transportation in the nineteenth century, and were integral parts of the Industrial Revolution, for they allowed the swift movement of the great quantities of raw materials and finished products necessary for large-scale industrialization. This contemporary woodcut (1835) shows the Eisenbahn, one of the first railroads in Germany.
Photo: Ullstein

in France, but in Great Britain and of course in the sprawling, young United States they were notoriously poor. Around the turn of the century Thomas Telford and John McAdam in Great Britain pioneered in the construction of well-drained and surfaced roads. In America Albert Gallatin inspired the construction of the Cumberland Road, or Old National Pike, which, begun in 1811, reached from Maryland to Illinois by 1852. In Great Britain canals were particularly useful in the transportation of coal. However, the most important canal constructed in this period was the Erie, completed in 1825. The Erie Canal opened up the Great Lakes region to lucrative world communications and assured the primacy of New York City as America's chief port and metropolis.

Nevertheless, the real revolution in transportation came with the application of Watt's steam engine to locomotion. In 1807 Robert Fulton, capitalizing on the failures and partial successes of others, steamed his *Clermont* the 150 miles up the Hudson from New York to Albany in thirty-two hours. Twelve years later the *Savannah* crossed the Atlantic in twenty-nine days, using part steam and part sail. This was by no means record time, but in 1838, when the *Great Western* crossed the Atlantic in fifteen days entirely by steam, the last doubts as to the practicability of the steamship were dispelled.

Meanwhile, George Stephenson in Great Britain was developing the first successful locomotive. In 1825 he made his first convincing demonstration by hauling a train of thirty-four cars 25 miles at 12 miles an hour. Five years later his *Rocket* was pulling cars at the rate of 29 miles an hour. The horse was on the way out.

The middle decades of the nineteenth century were a period of great railroad building in Northwestern Europe and the United States. Construction of the Baltimore and Ohio was begun in 1828, and two years later a few miles were opened for traffic. In 1855 Chicago, soon to become the world's leading railroad center, was reached by the New York Central system. By 1869 the Union Pacific had connected the Atlantic with the Pacific. All the while speed and efficiency were rapidly increasing.

Communications were developing faster yet. Until 1844 communications were no speedier than transportation except for a special courier service by horse or a crude system of signaling by semaphore. In that year, however, Samuel F. B. Morse sent a message by wire forty miles from Baltimore to Washington. The telegraph, transmitting messages instantaneously from one end of any length of wire to the other, caught on rapidly. In 1866 a telegraph cable was laid across the Atlantic, enabling news to travel from New York to London as quickly as from New York to Brooklyn. Ten years later Alexander Graham Bell, an American born in Scotland, invented the telephone, and in 1895 Guglielmo Marconi, an Italian, sent the first message by wireless telegraphy.

It is difficult for us today to realize to what degree or how quickly these inventions in the field of transportation and communications shrank the world. Julius Caesar could move his armies as rapidly as George Washington or Napoleon (actually a little more rapidly, thanks to the Roman roads), and Plato could gather news as quickly as Jefferson. Now, in the nineteenth century, far-off places suddenly became near, and strange peoples remained strange only to the primitive, the dull, or the lazy. More and more people, first the rich and then the poor, began to travel and to move their domiciles. The first important effect of the revolution in transportation and communications was to accelerate the Industrial Revolution by greatly facilitating the large-scale mobilization of capital, raw materials, and markets.

3. THE FACTORY SYSTEM

Another basic aspect of the Industrial Revolution was the rise of the factory system.

Before the coming of the power machines, goods were produced either by the non-capitalistic craft guilds or under the domestic, or "putting out," system. It is true that some factories, notably the woolen-manufacturing establishments in Florence, came into existence as early as the fourteenth century when commerce and capitalism were reviving, but they were few and small in comparison with those of the machine age. Under the domestic system entrepreneur capitalists would purchase the raw materials and distribute them to numerous craftsmen who would spin, weave, sew, cut, carve, or mold the products by hand in their own cottages. The entrepreneur would then collect the finished products, pay the craftsmen by the piece for their work, and market the wares. The workers under this system enjoyed the advantages of doing as much or as little work as they wished without supervision. They usually carried on farming operations in addition to their craft-work. On the other hand, since they were scattered throughout the countryside, they were unable to bring any group pressure to bear upon the employers or to achieve any uniformity of wage. The smarter and more aggressive entrepreneur could easily cheat them, and wages were very low. The capitalists, too, were limited by this system. The operations were necessarily on a small scale, much time was lost distributing the raw materials from cottage to cottage and collecting the finished products, and uniformity of quality was virtually impossible to attain.

The coming of the power machines made the domestic system of manufacturing not only antiquated, but practically impossible. The handcraftsmen discovered that it was hopeless to try to compete with the machines, and since they were unable to buy them, they had to go wherever the machines were located. Thus factories, housing both the machines and the workers, came into existence. Crowded around the factories soon appeared living quarters for the workers and their families, hastily and cheaply built. This was the origin of the modern mill town and industrial city. The rise of the factory system eventually completed the process, begun six or seven hundred years earlier with the revival of commerce, of changing civilization in the industrialized areas from rural to urban.

4. THE AGRICULTURAL REVOLUTION

During this same period agriculture also was undergoing revolutionary changes in Western Europe and northern America. In the early eighteenth century Charles (Turnip) Townshend, grandfather of the author of the Townshend Acts that had helped to precipitate the American Revolution, began mixing diplomacy and statecraft with agriculture. He demonstrated that increased yields could be obtained through crop rotation and the use of root crops like turnips and clover. His contemporary and compatriot Jethro Tull invented the seed drill, which made it possible to plant seed in rows and thereby ensure better fertilization and cultivation of the soil. Later in the eighteenth century another Englishman, Robert Bakewell, greatly improved the existing types of sheep and cattle by artificial breeding. These new methods were popularized in the late eighteenth century, largely through the efforts of Arthur Young in Britain and the French Physiocrats. The mechanization of agriculture first began with the reaper, which the American inventor Cyrus McCormick patented in 1834. These improvements in agriculture accelerated the enclosure movement in Great Britain, which had been going on since the sixteenth century. The increased efficiency achieved by the application of the new methods and the consolidation and enclosure of scattered strips and farms meant that larger harvests could now be produced by fewer laborers. The result in the most advanced of the industrialized countries was a surplus of farm laborers, who drifted off to the cities to seek jobs in the new factories. The industrial and the agricultural revolutions thus interacted upon each other while

In this photograph, an immigrant family makes cigars in their tenement apartment in New York. The whole family, including the children, worked long hours in austere conditions just to survive. *Photo: Jacob A. Riis, The Jacob A. Riis Collection, Museum of the City of New York*

they produced an ever-increasing abundance of material goods.

5. THE TRIUMPH OF THE BOURGEOISIE AND THE DISTRESS OF THE PROLETARIAT

With the exception of a relatively few capitalists and well-to-do consumers, the benefits of the Industrial Revolution were not immediate. The first to profit from the mechanization of industry were the owners of the new machines, the industrial bourgeoisie. Ever since the revival of commerce and capitalism in the eleventh and twelfth centuries, the capitalistic middle class had been gaining ground at the expense of the landed aristocracy. It had been a long, slow process with occasional setbacks. In the fifteenth and sixteenth centu-

ries the middle class had formed an alliance with the national monarchs against the feudal lords. In the seventeenth and eighteenth centuries, first in England and then in America and France, the middle class had turned on the king and sharply curtailed his power.

Nonetheless, at the opening of the nineteenth century, the aristocracy in Great Britain and France were still powerful, and everywhere else, except in the United States, they were dominant. But the coming of the power machines gave the industrial middle class such a monopoly over the fabrication and transportation of goods in the industrialized countries that they were able now to establish their supremacy over the upper and lower classes alike. Driving the handcraftsmen out of business and hiring them on their own terms, the industrial bourgeoisie eventually amassed fortunes vaster than those of the merchant princes before them. With such wealth at their command they gained control not only over their nations' economies, but over government and society as well.

The triumph of the industrial bourgeoisie did not, of course, occur overnight, nor did it occur simultaneously in all countries. It followed the course of the Industrial Revolution —coming first in Great Britain, next in Belgium and France, a little later in the United States, then in Germany, and near the end of the nineteenth century in Central and Eastern Europe, and Japan. By the middle of the twentieth century it was reaching most of the rest of the world. After 1871, when the Industrial Revolution had its full impact in Germany and was beginning to reach the rest of the world, the masses were on the move and the heyday of bourgeois, laissez-faire economics had passed its peak. In those areas, therefore, the industrial bourgeoisie never gained complete mastery.

In Great Britain, Belgium, and France, the years approximately from 1830 to 1871 represent an era of industrial middle-class dominance. In the United States, where the growth of industry was a little slower, the industrial bourgeoisie did not gain control until the Civil War (1861–1865) and was not seriously challenged until the turn of the century. The next few chapters will deal primarily with the policies, struggles, and achievements of the industrial middle class in these countries.

By the same measure that the bourgeoisie gained in the first phase of the Industrial Revolution, the proletariat lost. Men have never been equal since the beginning of organized society. The strong, the clever, the aggressive, and the fortunate have always enjoyed an advantage over their weaker, meeker, or less fortunate fellow-men. Nevertheless, before the coming of the power machines, when workingmen lived by the strength of their muscles, there was a modicum of equality. One man's muscles are not too much stronger than another's. The will-

ing worker, with reasonable luck, could hew out some kind of living in competition with his neighbors. No man, however, could compete with steam-driven machines that could do the work of hundreds of men.

The defeated craftsmen and the surplus or dispossessed agricultural workers had no recourse but to flock to the factories to seek employment tending the machines. The rapid increase in population, which had been going on since the middle of the seventeenth century, also swelled the ranks of the industrial proletariat. The owners, under these circumstances, were able to state their own terms. Wages were bid down to the barest subsistence level—sometimes the equivalent of 50 cents for a week of seven eighteen-hour days. Since women and children could tend many of the machines as efficiently as men and could be hired more cheaply, men were often replaced by their wives and children. Contracts were made with orphanages for the employment of the children. Little tots too small to dress themselves were marched off before daybreak to work all day in the factories. If they fell behind the pace, they were beaten. Sometimes they were chained to their machines. Crying could be heard at all times in the factories, particularly toward the end of the day. The factories and mines were dark, dirty, and dangerous. The dwellings of the workers were likely to be hovels clustered around smoky, noisy mills or mine entrances. The workers were frequently compelled to spend the pittance they did receive at company stores, paying monopoly prices arbitrarily set by the owners.

Work lost its dignity. The dull, monotonous, robot-like repetition of a single operation on a machine brought the worker none of the satisfaction and pride of skilled craftsmanship. It is true that in the most highly mechanized industrial systems, there was still a considerable amount of skilled craftsmanship left, but even that became tainted with the connotation of the mill. This loss cannot be repaid with any amount of wage increases. Numerous investigations have shown that factory workers are more interested in personal and social dignity and recognition than in wages, hours, and working conditions. These sentiments, of course, were expressed in more recent years when wages and hours were less cruel.

During the first phase of the Industrial Revolution there was virtually no opportunity for the workers or their children to get an education. The picture of the mid-nineteenth-century industrial proletariat is one of the most dismal in recorded history. Western man, after struggling toward freedom against various forms of tyranny for some six thousand years, was now threatened with a new kind of slavery—slavery to the machine and the machine owner.

Some historians and social scientists maintain that this picture of the distress of the proletariat during the early days of the Industrial Revolution is false, or at least distorted. They undertake to prove by statistics that the early factory workers received higher real wages and enjoyed a better standard of living than they ever had as agricultural workers. There can be little doubt that numbers of workers did move upward in industry and improve their lives. Nor can it be denied that the conditions of work and life among the agricultural poor had always been hard. But statistics often fail when they try to measure human well-being and happiness. The insecurity, the frequent unemployment of the uprooted slum-dwelling factory worker of the early nineteenth century does not appear in statistics. Is a mill hand working seven fourteen-hour days for 50 cents better off than a man plowing, sowing, and reaping, or doing craft work in his own cottage the same num-

This woodcut by Gustave Doré portrays the squalor of a London slum in the early nineteenth century. While the middle class grew wealthy from the Industrial Revolution, the industrial working class was more and more mired in poverty. *Photo: Prints Division, New York Public Library, Astor, Lenox, and Tilden Foundations* ber of hours for 25 cents? The question cannot be answered with certainty, but in history, which deals with human beings, statistics need to be supplemented by imagination.

One of the industrial proletarian's first reactions was violence. Throughout the winter of 1811–1812, when the pressure of the Napoleonic war and the blockade against British commerce was added to the maladjustments of the Industrial Revolution, a wave of personal violence and machine-smashing swept throughout Great Britain (the Luddite riots). This type of reaction to the machine, of course, had no future. Parliament, composed entirely of members of the property-holding classes, quickly made sabotage a capital offense and suppressed violence with a heavy hand. Several dozens of offenders were hanged. Sporadic outbreaks of violence, however, continued for several years. This story was repeated in other countries as the Industrial Revolution spread. In the United States in the middle decades of the nineteenth century, violence broke out among the Irish immigrants working in the anthracite coal mines of eastern Pennsylvania. The exploited miners formed secret terror societies called Molly Maguires. For a number of years they intimidated, even murdered, unpopular bosses and uncooperative nonmembers. They were eventually ferreted out by civil authorities and ruthlessly suppressed.

More peaceful efforts of the industrial proletariat to bring group pressure upon their employers by organizing unions also at first met with defeat. In 1799 and 1800 the British Parliament passed the Combination Acts, which outlawed all labor combinations organized for the purpose of securing better wages, hours, or working conditions. The French and Belgian governments did likewise. In the United States the owners themselves organized for the purpose of breaking up labor unions. Private detectives and police were set upon labor leaders, who were beaten, fired, and blacklisted. It was not until the latter part of the nineteenth century that labor un-

ions were able to make any significant headway. Therefore, during the first phase of the Industrial Revolution, as power machines belched and crunched and ground out ever more and more goods for those able to buy them, and fortunes for their owners, they blighted the lives of tens of thousands of workers, robbing them of the dignity of their labor, and threatening them with a new kind of slavery.

6. NEW ECONOMIC THEORIES—CLASSICAL, LIBERAL, AND UTOPIAN

CLASSICAL THEORY. It was inevitable that the Industrial Revolution should set men thinking about economics. Most of the industrial bourgeoisie of the early nineteenth century were self-made men of limited means who had worked hard and risked their possessions in order to succeed. They were likely to feel rather insecure and self-righteous. Though probably not cruel or inhuman, they would have little sympathy with those who might upset their methods and perhaps lower their profits. Seeking intellectual support and justification for their good fortune, they found perfectly suitable the doctrine of laissez faire, which had been developed during the Enlightenment of the eighteenth century. This doctrine had been best stated by the Scottish philosopher Adam Smith in his classic *Wealth of Nations* (1776). The essence of Smith's theory is that economics, like the physical world, has its own natural laws. The most basic of the economic laws is that of supply and demand. When left to operate alone, these laws will keep the economy in balance and in the long run work to the benefit of all. If the sanctity of property and contracts is respected, competition and free enterprise will provide incentive and keep prices down. Government regulations and collective bargaining only impede the workings of the natural laws of economics and destroy incentive. Government therefore should limit its activities in the economic field to the enforcement of order and of contracts, public education and health, national defense, and in rare instances the encouragement of necessary industries that private enterprise does not find profitable. Here was a theory ready-made for the machine owners at a stage in the game when they held all the trump cards. Later, when competition became more severe and complex, the machine owners were to demand and receive a great deal of government protection. But in Great Britain in the early nineteenth century, all that the industrial bourgeoisie needed was an opportunity to exploit its advantage. Little wonder that the *Wealth of Nations* became its bible.

A strong boost was given to laissez-faire thinking by a young Anglican clergyman, Thomas Malthus, who in 1798 published his *Essay on Population*. Malthus argued that, since population increases by a geometric ratio whereas the food supply increases only by an arithmetic ratio, it is a basic natural law that population will outstrip the food supply. This alleged law has two important implications. One is that nothing can be done to improve the lot of the masses. If their condition is temporarily bettered, they will immediately produce children in such numbers that the food supply will be outstripped and starvation will threaten all. Only poverty and privation hold them in check. The second implication is that the rich are not to blame for the misery of the poor; the poor are themselves responsible because of their incontinence. These ideas were so soothing to so many of the book-buying upper classes that Malthus quickly attained fame and wealth.

David Ricardo supplied further ammunition for the free-enterprise economists. Having made a fortune in stock market speculation, Ricardo purchased a seat in Parliament and spent the rest of his life thinking and writing on economics. In *The Principles of Political Economy and Taxation* (1817), he propounded the law of rent and the iron law of wages. Rent is determined by the difference in productivity of land. Take off all restrictions and subsidies, and the poorest land goes out of cultivation, reducing the rent on the more

productive lands proportionately. He argued for this idea so forcefully that it played an important part in the repeal of England's corn laws, which had maintained the price of grain at an artificially high level. More important in economic thinking was Ricardo's iron law of wages, according to which the natural wage is the subsistence level and the market wage tends to conform to it. Raise the market wage and the workers will multiply so rapidly that soon the law of supply and demand will bring the market wage down below the subsistence level. Then the workers will die off from malnutrition and disease and slow down their reproduction rate. Eventually they will become so scarce as to be able to bid the market wage up above the natural wage. Always, though, the pull is toward the subsistence level. This again was music in the ears of the industrial capitalists.

These thinkers came to be called the classical economists, since they were the first to grapple philosophically with the economic problems of the Industrial Revolution. Their general attitude and assumptions were well expressed by the British Utilitarian philosopher Jeremy Bentham as early as 1789, in his *Principles of Morals and Legislation*. Bentham was an eighteenth-century materialistic rationalist who lived on until 1832, bridging the eighteenth and nineteenth centuries with his life and thought. The Utilitarians believed that the useful is the good and that the chief purpose of government and society is to achieve "the greatest good to the greatest number." But since every individual is the best judge of his own best interests, the surest way to achieve general happiness is to allow each individual to follow his own enlightened self-interest. Individualism, then, is the best safeguard of the general welfare.

LIBERAL THEORY. The early nineteenth-century classical economists who advocated free enterprise and individualism called themselves liberals. However, a new type of liberal, more like the liberal of the twentieth century, soon appeared. The new type of economic liberal, while adhering to the sanctity of private property and to a large measure of individualism, believed that the Industrial Revolution had brought about the need for certain restrictions on both. In fact, Bentham himself came to see the necessity for the state to protect the common weal against overly aggressive individuals. One of the first of the new type of liberal economists was the Swiss historian and philosopher Simonde de Sismondi. In his *New Principles of Political Economy* (1819), Sismondi challenged Bentham's fundamental assumption that the self-interests of the individuals promote the best interests of the common weal. He believed that power machines were interfering with the operation of Adam Smith's laws by glutting certain markets, oppressing labor, and creating monopolies. The true wealth of a nation, Sismondi believed, lay in the equitable distribution of goods and benefits among its citizenry. Therefore, he favored laws that would restrict the amassing of monopolistic fortunes, and divide great estates. He also advocated practices such as profit sharing and long-term job contracts that would give protection and security to the workers.

Probably the most influential of all the new type of economic liberals was John Stuart Mill (1806–1873). Mill, a child prodigy, was brought up to be a good Benthamite. However, he was too sensitive and humanitarian to remain in the hard materialistic camp of the Utilitarians. Moreover, living a generation after Smith, Malthus, Ricardo, and Bentham, he was able to see some of the evil effects of the Industrial Revolution. Although Mill in no wise rejected private property, capitalism, and free enterprise, he believed that in the machine age, restrictions must be instituted by the state for the protection of the poor. Although production is bound by the iron laws of supply and demand, the distribution of goods is not. Public utilities such as railroads and gas and waterworks are natural monopolies and should be owned by the state. The state should provide free compulsory education for all and regulate child labor. He

favored income and inheritance taxes as economic equalizers. Mill's chief work on economics, *Principles of Political Economy*, was published in 1848. In his later years he considered himself a socialist, but would hardly be so regarded today. His are the views of many twentieth-century liberals.

UTOPIAN SOCIALISM. During the first phase of the Industrial Revolution, the economies of the industrialized countries belonged to the bourgeoisie in thought as well as in deed. The theories of the classical economists enjoyed complete ascendancy. Even such an advanced liberal thinker as John Stuart Mill believed resolutely in private property and the capitalistic system. The hard-pressed proletariat, though increasingly disconcerted, was hardly capable of formulating new economic theories. However, as early as the opening of the nineteenth century, a number of intellectuals began to question the fundamentals of the existing system, such as private property and private enterprise for profit. Since the ideas of these intellectuals were only speculative dreams and offered no practical course of action for the immediate present, their advocates came to be called Utopian Socialists. One of the first Utopian Socialists was the French nobleman Henri de Saint-Simon (1760–1825). He and his followers believed that society should be reorganized on a "Christian" basis, that all should work, and that the inheritance of private property should be abolished. His ideal society would be run according to the formula "from each according to his capacity, to each according to his deserts." Saint-Simon would reward the superior artists, scientists, engineers, and businessmen according to their merits. But he laid down no plan of action for achieving his ideal society.

Charles Fourier (1772–1837), a Frenchman of middle-class origin, would do away with economic competition, the source of so much evil. Production, both agricultural and industrial, would be carried on by voluntary cooperatives whose members would pool their resources and live in communal apartment houses. Distribution of goods and profits would be based upon the formula: workers, five-twelfths; capitalists, four-twelfths; management, three-twelfths. Fourier's elaborate plans included many quixotic ideas and some others that have found their way into practice.

A step forward in socialistic thinking was taken by Louis Blanc (1811–1882), another middle-class Frenchman. Louis Blanc would abolish the evils of selfish competitive capitalism by setting up a system of social workshops. The government would lend money to voluntary workingmen's cooperatives, which would establish and run the workshops. Distribution of the proceeds would be according to the formula, "from each according to his ability, to each according to his need," the formula later adopted by Karl Marx.

A different kind of Utopian was Robert Owen (1771–1858). Born in Wales, Owen quickly made an industrial fortune in Manchester and bought large cotton mills in New Lanark, Scotland. In partnership with Jeremy Bentham, he set out early in the nineteenth century to make New Lanark a model socialist utopia. Wages were raised, hours shortened, working conditions improved, child labor abolished, educational and recreational facilities provided, sickness and old-age insurance established. Owen spent the rest of his life and fortune drawing plans for and setting up model socialistic communities. Several were set up in America, notably New Harmony, Indiana. All failed; nor was Owen's benevolent example followed by other industrialists. Obviously, mankind, after thousands of years of competing for private gain, was not yet ready suddenly to start living and working for the common weal.

The Utopian Socialists were all strongly influenced by the materialistic rationalism of the eighteenth-century Enlightenment. All were vigorously opposed to existing organized religion, although Saint-Simon believed that his ideal society should be dominated by a new social Christianity—a brand of Christianity that had never yet been tried. None of the Utopian Socialists had any real influence on his own time. They did, however, start a trend of economic thought that was to become influential later.

It was not until the second phase of the Industrial Revolution (1871–1914), when the masses began to stir and to move, that a virile type of socialism would arise. This later socialism would be a state socialism for the most part and would bear the stamp of Karl Marx. Meanwhile, the industrial bourgeoisie established its control over the economy, the government, and society in the industrialized countries—a control that until 1871 was not seriously challenged.

Suggested Reading

General. Herbert Heaton, *Economic History of Europe* (rev. ed., 1948) is one of the best surveys on the subject, with valuable chapters on the Industrial Revolution. The classic economic history of modern Britain is J. H. Clapham, *An Economic History of Modern Britain* (3 vols., 2nd ed., 1951–59). Equally valuable is his **The Economic Development of France and Germany, 1815–1914* (4th ed., Cambridge). The standard history of British agriculture, which covers the agricultural rev-

olution of the late eighteenth and early nineteenth centuries, is R. E. Prothero, *English Farming Past and Present* (5th ed., 1936). Also valuable are **W. W. Rostow, *The Process of Economic Growth* (Norton); and **A. Toynbee, *The Industrial Revolution* (Beacon).

The Coming of the Machine. **Abbott Usher, *A History of Mechanical Inventions* (Beacon) is still the best single volume on the subject. Well illustrated. The story of the coming of the first machines is told by P. Mantoux, *The Industrial Revolution in the 18th Century* (rev. ed., 1929). A popularly written survey of the rise of technology and its social influence is **Louis Mumford, *Technics and Civilization* (Harbinger).

Social and Political Consequences. J. L. Hammond and B. Hammond, *The Bleak Age* (rev. ed., 1947), is one of the many books that the Hammonds have written depicting the horrors for the industrial workers of the first phase of the Industrial Revolution. **T. S. Ashton, *The Industrial Revolution: 1760–1830* (Galaxy), repudiates the Hammonds. Ashton plays down the hardships to the working classes caused by the Industrial Revolution and attributes what hardships there were to other factors. J. T. Ward, *The Factory Movement, 1830–1855* (1962), tells the story of the efforts of the English workers to obtain the regulation of working conditions in factories during the first half of the nineteenth century. The impact of the agricultural revolution on the agricultural workers in England is depicted by G. E. and K. R. Fussell, *The English Countryman: His Life and Work, A.D. 1500–1900* (1955).

New Economic Theories. A popularly written history of socialistic thought during the first phase of the Industrial Revolution is **Louis Mumford, *The Story of the Utopias* (Compass). H. W. Laidler, *A History of Socialistic Thought* (1927) has good chapters on the early (Utopian) Socialists.

Sources. An excellent selection of source materials, many of them covering the first phase of the Industrial Revolution, is A. E. Bland, P. A. Brown, R. H. Tawney, eds., *English Economic History: Select Documents* (1915). The masterpieces of two of the founding fathers of classical economic theory are **Adam Smith, *The Wealth of Nations* (Modern Library); and **T. R. Malthus, *An Essay on the Principles of Population As It Affects the Future Improvement of Society* (2 vols., Everyman). The basic writings of the great mid-nineteenth-century English liberal John Stuart Mill are collected under the title **J. S. Mill, *On Liberty: Representative Government; Utilitarianism; Autobiography* (Liberal Arts). Writings of two of the Utopian Socialists are C. H. de Saint-Simon, *Selected Writings*, ed. F. M. H. Markham (1952); and Robert Owen, *The Life of Robert Owen, by Himself* (1920, originally published in 1857–58).

Historical Fiction. **Charles Dickens, *Hard Times* (Everyman) describes conditions in an early nineteenth-century English mill town.

Chapter 44 ❧ Triumph of Bourgeois Liberalism

Liberalism is a very difficult term to define. It is of various hues, and from time to time changes its complexion. In general, the term "liberalism" implies a belief in a wider distribution of this world's goods and privileges. During the first three quarters of the nineteenth century, liberalism was closely associated with the middle classes, particularly the industrial bourgeoisie. It was usually strong in those areas where the Industrial Revolution was advanced, and weak where the Industrial Revolution was retarded. In addition to the industrial and commercial bourgeoisie (both great and small), intellectuals and professional people were likely to be liberal. The voice of the industrial proletariat, which after 1871 would be demanding a more radical kind of liberalism, was as yet scarcely heard. The chief wellsprings of this early liberalism were the philosophy of the Enlightenment and the English, American, and French revolutions.

1. GENERAL NATURE OF NINETEENTH-CENTURY LIBERALISM

The middle-class liberals of the nineteenth century prior to 1871 believed in popular government limited by a restricted suffrage and by constitutional guarantees of the rights of the individual. The role of the government should be that of a passive policeman, enforcing laws and contracts. Government should interfere in economic life as little as possible, leaving that realm to private enterprise. The nineteenth-century liberals were also anticlerical; that is, they opposed the interference in government by organized religion. Sometimes, reflecting the influence of the Enlightenment, they were not only anticlerical, but antireligious. Until 1871 the liberals were usually nationalists, since nationalism at that time was primarily concerned with freeing peoples from alien rule and uniting them under one flag, or, where this had already been accomplished, defending the nation's interests. The chief opponents of the nineteenth-century liberals were the vested interests of an earlier day—the aristocracy, the clergy, the military—seeking to retain their favored positions. The peasantry (a term and status applicable in Europe but not in the United States) was still generally conservative, strongly influenced by the clergy and sometimes by the aristocracy, and not very active in politics. The French peasants, most of whom owned their own land, were extremely conservative.

The citizens of Naples joined most of the other states of Italy in rebellion and even sent troops to aid the northern areas—Venetia and Lombardy—in revolt against their Austrian overlords. This drawing showing a barricade on a Naples street in May 1848 just before an attack appeared that year in the Illustrated London News. *Photo: Historical Pictures Service, Chicago*

After 1871 the nature of liberalism was to change. The industrial bourgeoisie, having acquired wealth and power, had by now become a vested interest itself and was hostile to further political and social changes. Its members joined, for the most part, the ranks of the conservatives. Their place in the liberal ranks was taken by the bulk of the industrial proletariat, which was at last becoming politically active. The new liberals (now chiefly the lower middle classes, the intelligentsia, and the proletariat) began to advocate a greatly increased amount of government interference in economic affairs in behalf of the masses. They also adopted a somewhat different attitude toward nationalism. After 1871 nationalism in the West, having in large measure attained its goals of achieving free and united national states, tended to become aggressive and militaristic. This type of nationalism posed a threat to the liberal democracy of the lower middle classes and the proletariat, now the chief liberal groups. After 1871, therefore, liberalism tended to be internationalist, although in times of international crisis and war, nationalism continued to rally the loyalty of all classes.

The period from 1830 to 1871, then, was a time of triumph for bourgeois liberalism in Great Britain, the United States, and France, the first major countries to become industrialized. In Central Europe, where the Industrial Revolution was more retarded, this period marked middle-class liberalism's rise but not its triumph. In Eastern Europe the Industrial Revolution and bourgeois liberalism did not appear until after 1871.

2. POLITICAL AND SOCIAL REFORM IN GREAT BRITAIN, 1832–1867

In Great Britain, the cradle of the Industrial Revolution, the industrial bourgeoisie began to bid for power soon after the Napoleonic wars came to an end. Although Great Britain had been since the thirteenth century the home of the rule of law and of representative government, her government in 1815 was far from democratic. The suffrage was so severely restricted by property qualifications that only about 5 percent of the adult males could vote. Furthermore, the industrial cities of the north, which had grown up since the last distribution of seats in Parliament, were not represented at all. Both houses of Parliament were therefore monopolized by the landed aristocracy. It must be remembered, however, that the cleavage between the middle class and the aristocracy was not so sharp in Great Britain as on the Continent. The law of primogeniture in Great Britain granted the eldest son the entire landed estate and permitted him alone to assume the title. The younger sons sought careers in the church, in the military, or in business. This brought about much intermingling between the upper and the middle classes. The long-sustained prosperity of British commerce had produced a merchant class wealthy enough to purchase respectability, lands, and sometimes titles. The aristocracy frequently invested in commercial enterprises and later in industry. Before 1830 the two great political parties, the Whigs and the Tories, were hardly more than two rival groups of noble families. These facts help to explain why the great political and social struggles in nineteenth-century Britain, though sometimes bitter, lacked the violence of those on the Continent.

A period of economic depression and unrest in Great Britain followed the ending of the Napoleonic wars in 1815. For twenty-two years, with only one brief interruption, Britain had been engaged in a desperate struggle with France, a struggle that was economic as well as military. Meanwhile, her industrial expansion had gone on apace. The war's end found British warehouses piled high with unsold goods. Thousands of returning veterans found no jobs. Strikes and riots, which had begun during Napoleon's blockade, increased. The conservative Tory party, which had seen the country through the war, was strongly entrenched in power. Both the Tories and the slightly more liberal Whigs were still badly frightened by the specter of French revolutionary Jacobinism. The government therefore took strong measures against the restless workers. The writs of habeas corpus were suspended. The climax came in 1819, when troops fired upon a proletarian throng that had assembled outside Manchester to listen to reform speeches. A number were killed and hundreds injured in this "Peterloo Massacre."

Within a few years, however, as the postwar crisis of depression and unrest eased, the Tory government yielded slightly to the pressure for reform. We have already seen how Foreign Secretary Canning by 1822 had deserted Metternich's reactionary concert of Europe and aided independence movements in Latin America and Greece. During the 1820s the navigation laws were somewhat relaxed and the tariff slightly lowered. The Combination Laws were partially repealed, permitting laborers to organize unions, though not to strike. The civil disabilities against nonconforming Protestants and Roman Catholics were removed, permitting them to participate in political life on an equal basis with Anglicans. These measures, however, welcome as they were, did not get at the fundamental issue: broadening popular participation in the government. The pressure for suffrage reform continued to mount, particularly from the industrial bourgeoisie, which was gaining rapidly in wealth. Finally in 1830 the Whigs, long out of power, made common cause with the bourgeois liberals and drove the Tory government from office.

The new prime minister, Earl Grey, immediately introduced and forced through Parliament the Reform Bill of 1832. This bill redistributed the seats in the House of Commons, taking away many from the "rotten boroughs" (once-important towns that had dwindled in population or even disappeared) and giving them to the industrial cities of the north. The suffrage was extended to all those who owned or rented property with an annual value of £10 ($50). It is estimated that the number of voters was thereby increased from approximately 450,000 to 800,000 out of a total popula-

tion of some 16,500,000. The great majority of the newly enfranchised were members of the urban middle class. Although on the surface the Reform Bill of 1832 appears rather innocuous, it represents a great turning point in British history. The long era of dominance of the landed aristocracy had ended and that of the industrial bourgeoisie had begun. The supremacy of the House of Commons over the House of Lords, which had opposed the Reform Bill, was established. A new period of political and social reform had opened.

Both political parties recognized the new era. The Whig party, dominated by the industrial bourgeoisie but containing a right wing of liberal aristocrats and a left wing of intellectual radicals, changed its name to the Liberal party—liberal of course in the pre-1871 sense. For the next half century the Liberals were dominant, under the leadership of such personalities as Lords Grey, Russell, and Palmerston, and eventually William E. Gladstone. The Tory party was still predominantly the party of the landed aristocracy, but it contained some bourgeois elements, and its more liberal wing, led first by Sir Robert Peel and later by Benjamin Disraeli, was now in the ascendancy. The somewhat discredited name "Tory" was changed to Conservative.

Both parties, conscious of the rising importance of public opinion, supported a series of reforms. In 1833 slavery was abolished in the British Empire with compensation for the owners. This achievement was made much easier by the fact that there were no slaves in Britain itself. The Municipal Corporations Act applied the principles of the Reform Bill of 1832 to local government. The barbarous penal code was reformed, reducing the number of capital offenses to three and generally softening the punishment of criminals. The penny post increased the circulation of mail and literature. Parliament granted small but gradually increasing subsidies to the schools, most of which were run by the Anglican Church. Between 1833 and 1847 Parliament passed a series of laws that prohibited the employment in textile mills of children under nine and limited the hours of older children and of women to ten hours a day. The employment of women and children in underground mines was prohibited. In 1846 the Corn Laws (the import tariff on grain) were repealed, greatly reducing the price of bread.

It must be remembered that these reforms were not the work of the masses but of the bourgeois liberals in conjunction with a liberal minority of the aristocracy and a few intellectual radicals. The only reform movement initiated by the proletariat in this period of bourgeois domination came to naught. This was the Chartist movement. The hard-pressed industrial proletariat, keenly aware that it had been bypassed by the Reform Bill of 1832 and that it was not sharing in the unprecedented national prosperity, was dissatisfied with the reforms of the bourgeois liberals. In 1838 proletarian leaders drew up a People's Charter, which demanded (1) universal manhood suffrage, (2) the secret ballot, (3) removal of property qualifications for members of Parliament, (4) pay for members of Parliament, (5) annual elections, and (6) equal electoral districts. The charter was twice presented to Parliament and twice summarily rejected. In 1848, when much of the European continent was ablaze with revolution, the Chartists planned a monster petition and demonstration in London. The frightened government prepared to use force. However, only a few mild disorders followed the third rejection, and the movement came to an end. Nevertheless, the Chartist movement had its influence. Before many decades had passed, all the demands in the charter had been enacted into law except that for annual elections. The most immediate result was to make both political parties aware of the growing influence of the proletariat and of the advisability of winning its favor.

This awareness increased as the numbers and the restlessness of the proletariat increased. During the 1860s William E. Gladstone, a more advanced type of liberal, rose to the leadership of the Liberal party. In 1866 he introduced a reform bill that would have enfranchised large numbers of the proletariat. Although the bill was defeated and the Liberal ministry was forced to resign, the narrowness of the defeat plus the agitation of the workingmen, which now reached ominous proportions, convinced the rising young leader of the Conservatives, Benjamin Disraeli, that the reform was inevitable. The shrewd Disraeli decided to seize credit for the inevitable. The result was the Reform Bill of 1867, which, as amended by the Liberals, gave the franchise to the great majority of the urban proletariat. The Reform Bill of 1867, which doubled the electorate, marked the beginning of a new era in British history. Henceforth, the industrial bourgeoisie would have to share power with the industrial proletariat. Liberalism now took on a new and more radical meaning. It is a tribute to British moderation and to Britain's long tradition of the rule of law that such a revolutionary change should have taken place with so little violence.

3. JEFFERSONIAN AND JACKSONIAN DEMOCRACY IN THE UNITED STATES

The march of liberal democracy in the United States did not follow the European pattern. In America there was never any entrenched aristocracy that had to be overcome as in Europe. The European immigrants who peopled the United States were almost entirely from the middle and lower ranks of society, and they were determined to prevent the rise in America of a class system such as the one from which they had fled. The rough frontier situation in America aided them in their efforts. In the primitive American forests and

Andrew Jackson, frontier fighter and popular hero, on his way to Washington after his election to the Presidency in 1828. This engraving was done by Howard Pyle for an issue of Harper's Weekly in 1881. *Photo: Library of Congress*

prairies, blood and title counted for little; muscle and energy counted for much. These factors, in addition to the British heritage of the rule of law, which most of the early settlers brought with them, and the able leadership they developed within their own ranks, sent democracy in America racing on ahead of that in Europe. Nor was American democracy so closely associated with or dependent upon the Industrial Revolution as in Europe. Although the first factory was set up in America by Samuel Slater in Rhode Island, as early as 1791, the growth of machine industry was at first quite slow. French and British blockades during the Napoleonic wars and the War of 1812 with Britain cut the United States off

from British manufactures and caused much American commercial capital to be diverted to manufacturing. Nevertheless, it was not until after the Civil War (1861–1865) that industrialism in the United States became so advanced that the industrial bourgeoisie was able to gain dominance in politics and society.

The advance of democracy in the young American republic received a great boost with the election of Thomas Jefferson as president in 1800. The coming to power of this democratic theorist—the chief author of the Declaration of Independence—ended an era of the ascendancy of the well-to-do under Presidents Washington and Adams. Although the rich and the well-born raised a cry of anguish at the triumph of Jefferson, he was really a moderate man. It was not so much his radical acts as president as it was his democratic attitudes and principles that made his administration significant. The third president was a scholarly philosopher of liberty and democracy, not a rabble rouser. The toiling masses never felt comfortable around the elegant Virginian.

The first real man of the people to take the helm of the young republic was Andrew Jackson. A rawboned dueler, Indian fighter, and militia commander, Jackson rose from poverty to leadership on the Tennessee frontier. He emerged as the hero of the War of 1812. Without formal education, "Old Hickory" possessed qualities of leadership and a flair for vote-getting. His election to the presidency in 1828 is often referred to as a revolution. However, the revolution of 1828, like that of 1800, was not so much a matter of deeds as of attitudes and spirit. The people's champion did attack and destroy the greatest concentration of private capital in the country, the national bank. He also tackled and crushed such formidable political giants of a more conservative nature as John C. Calhoun and Henry Clay. But there were no radical measures. In the Jacksonian era, democracy was advancing as new states without property qualifications for voting were rapidly being admitted to the Union and as the older states were eliminating property qualifications from their voting requirements. However, the property requirement had never been a serious limitation to democracy in America, since land was so plentiful and cheap that almost everybody was a property owner. The revolution of 1828 was a revolution only in the sense that for the first time a man came to the White House whom the common people could consider one of their own number. Henceforth, if undemocratic men or causes should triumph in the United States, it would not be because of the system, but because free men would fail to take the time and trouble to inform themselves of the issues and to go to the polls to vote.

Industrialization never constituted the threat to the laboring man in the United States that it did in Europe. Although one could find mill and mine conditions in America that rivaled those in Europe, there was too much free land in nineteenth-century America to permit the machine owners to exploit the workers too much for too long. Therefore, when the industrial bourgeoisie gained the political ascendancy in the late 1860s as a result of the Civil War and the rapid growth of industry, it was able to establish the bourgeois liberalism of the European variety in only a limited way and for only a few decades.

The real blight on democracy in the United States was the existence of Negro slavery in the Southern states. This curse not only cast a shadow over the whole American scene, but threatened the life of the nation itself. But this story belongs to the next chapter.

4. THE BOURGEOIS MONARCHY AND THE REVOLUTION OF 1848 IN FRANCE

The rise of liberalism on the continent of Europe was much more turbulent than in Great Britain and the United States. Here industrialization occurred later than in Great Britain, and the forces of privilege and reaction were more strongly entrenched than in the United States.

The Industrial Revolution came to France during the reign of Louis Philippe (1830–1848). This member of the house of Orléans had been placed on the throne by the Parisian middle classes after the tyrannical Charles X, the last of the Bourbons, had been overthrown in the Revolution of 1830. Louis Philippe, recognizing that a new era of middle-class dominance had come to France, catered to this class. He assumed the role of the "Citizen King," casting aside the trappings of royalty and donning those of the Parisian bourgeoisie. His eighteen-year reign came to be called the bourgeois monarchy. His two-fold policy, from which he never veered, was order and prosperity at home and peace abroad. One of his first acts was to lower the tax-paying requirements for voting from 300 francs ($60) to 200 francs ($40) per year. This raised the electorate from approximately 100,000 to 250,000 in a nation of some 32,000,000 people and placed political control firmly in the hands of the middle class. Louis Philippe's chief minister during the last eight years of his reign was François Guizot, one of the most eminent historians and teachers France has ever produced. Guizot was entirely to the liking of Louis Philippe in his domestic and foreign policies. He was a thoroughgoing liberal of the pre-1871 bourgeois variety. He believed in government by the property-owning classes, particularly the bourgeoisie. He therefore opposed any further extension of the suffrage, even to members of the intelligentsia like himself. Meanwhile, France continued to prosper, as the government pursued its policy of order and peace and encouragement to growing industry.

Beneath the surface, however, things were not going so smoothly. The national prosperity was not shared by the industrial proletariat, who suffered the usual hardships, insecurity, and maladjustments that always accompanied the advent of industrialization. Slums mushroomed in Paris and the industrial cities of the northeast. The distressed proletariat clamored for the right to vote and the right to organize unions, but got neither. The growing discontent centered around the chief minister. Guizot, a Protestant, was busily establishing a system of secular education in a Roman Catholic country. Even the policy of peace was becoming tiresome to a people used to national glamour and heroics. By 1847 the mounting discontent began to express itself in a series of reform banquets, at which orators demanded parliamentary and electoral reforms. Still almost no one anticipated a revolution.

The climax came in February 1848, when the government prohibited the holding of a banquet of ominous proportions. Street brawling broke out in Paris. Louis Philippe attempted to quiet the mob by dismissing the hated

Guizot, but the appeasement failed. A shot fired during a brawl between a mob and the troops guarding the residence of Guizot unnerved the troops, who fired a murderous volley into the mob and set off a full-scale insurrection. Barricades flew up all over Paris, and when the disaffected national guardsmen began going over to the rebels, Louis Philippe followed Guizot into exile in England.

The Paris proletariat had triumphed, but only for a fleeting moment. A group of bourgeois liberals hastily set up a provisional government in which the only prominent radical member was the Socialist Louis Blanc. The provisional government immediately called for the election by universal manhood suffrage of an assembly to draw up a new constitution. Under the pressure of the Paris proletariat, the provisional government admitted the workingmen to the national guard, thereby arming them, and set up emergency-relief national workshops. The workshops, however, were a parody on those outlined by Louis Blanc, who cried that they were deliberately planned so as to ensure their failure. Workers of all kinds were paid the equivalent of 40 cents a day to work on hastily arranged projects, and when more workers enrolled than could be used, the surplus workers were paid 30 cents a day to remain idle. Loafers and unemployed of all kinds, of course, rushed in by tens of thousands to receive the 30 cents. The resulting demoralization of labor and the cost to the taxpayers thoroughly frightened all property owners, the peasants as well as the bourgeoisie. The elections held in April 1848 resulted in an overwhelming victory for the conservative republicans and limited monarchists, thanks to the conservatism of the landowning peasants, who constituted the great majority of the French population. The Socialists were crushed. Even in Paris, their only real stronghold, they won a mere handful of seats.

One of the first acts of the newly elected constitutional assembly was to abolish the national workshops. The workers were told

In Central Europe in 1848, liberal sentiment emerged in the form of public demonstrations by the intelligentsia—particularly the university students. Here in June of 1848 German students convene at Wartburg. *Photo: Copyright Staatsbibliothek, Berlin*

either to join the army or to go look for work in the provinces. The desperate Paris proletariat flew to arms and the barricades. "Better to die from bullets than from starvation!" For four days all-out war raged in the streets of Paris between the proletariat, armed with national guard rifles, and the regular army of the conservative constitutional assembly, using artillery in addition to small arms. When the last barricade had been destroyed, some fifteen hundred, mostly workingmen, had been killed. Several hundred were sent overseas to French colonial prisons. Louis Blanc fled to Great Britain. The bloody "June Days" widened the cleavage between radical urban Paris and conservative rural France—a cleavage that has long complicated France's public life.

The inexperienced constitutional assembly hurriedly drew up a constitution establishing the Second French Republic. (The First French Republic had been declared by the revolutionists in 1792 and had been overthrown by Napoleon in 1804.) Legislative power was given to a single-chamber legislature elected by universal manhood suffrage. All executive and administrative powers were placed in the hands of a president, also elected by universal manhood suffrage. The April elections had shown that in nineteenth-century France, with her millions of conservative landowning peasants, private property need not fear universal suffrage. No system of checks and balances between the two branches of government was provided. The first presidential election, in December 1848,

706

resulted in a sweeping victory for Louis Napoleon Bonaparte, nephew of Napoleon Bonaparte, as president. It took this ambitious and clever politician only three years to destroy the weak constitution and to establish himself as dictator. As dictator, however, and later as emperor, Louis Napoleon would carefully nurture the interests of the property-owning bourgeoisie and peasantry.

The Revolution of 1848 in France was the first violent reaction of the industrial proletariat against bourgeois liberalism. The proletariat was too small as yet to make any headway outside of Paris. The revolution shattered against the solid mass of landowning peasantry allied with the propertied bourgeoisie. Its bloody suppression left a heritage of proletarian bitterness that would cloud the future of France.

5. THE REVOLUTION OF 1848 IN CENTRAL EUROPE

The February explosion in Paris set Central Europe aflame with revolt. However, the Revolution of 1848 in Central Europe was quite different from that in France. The Revolution of 1848 in France was a revolt of the Paris industrial proletariat led by intellectual radicals against the bourgeois liberalism that had been dominant since 1830. The Revolution of 1848 in Central Europe was a rising of the intelligentsia and the middle classes with a little support from the proletariat against the aristocracy and royalty. In 1848 the Industrial Revolution was just coming to Central Europe; the industrial bourgeoisie and proletariat were both few and weak. Their role in the liberal movement was secondary to that of the intelligentsia—chiefly university professors, students, and journalists. Furthermore, in 1848 the cause of liberalism in Central Europe was mixed up with that of nationalism. The two forces frequently conflicted with each other, nationalism proving to be the more virile of the two. Both causes failed for the time being, and the story of

their failure can be told here only in brief and general terms.

The most crucial center of revolution was Vienna. This beautiful metropolis was the seat of the Hapsburg government, which not only ruled over the various language groups of the Austrian Empire, but dominated both the German Confederation and Italy. When early in March 1848 news of the events in Paris arrived in Vienna, the long-repressed student liberals began rioting in the streets and clamoring for an end to the Metternich system. As the uprising gained in momentum, Metternich was forced to flee for his life. The Hapsburg emperor, Ferdinand I, hastily abolished the repressive laws and promised constitutional representative government. However, he too was soon forced to flee his own capital. Meanwhile the Magyars in Hungary, under the leadership of the eloquent Louis Kossuth, set up a liberal autonomous Hungary. The Czechs did the same in Bohemia and called for a Pan-Slavic congress to meet at Prague. In Austria's Italian provinces of Lombardy and Venetia the rebellious populace drove the Austrian garrisons into defensive fortresses and declared their independence. Most of the other Italian states adopted liberal constitutions and prepared to dispatch troops to the aid of Lombardy and Venetia. By June 1848, it appeared that the Hapsburg Empire would become liberalized, fall apart along national (language group) lines, or both.

In Berlin, the capital of Prussia, the news from Paris and Vienna set the liberals demonstrating in the streets. The well-meaning but vacillating Hohenzollern king, Frederick William IV, promised a liberal constitution and support for German national unity. As in Paris, an unauthorized volley into the mob set off bloody street fighting, which the king ended by making further concessions to the liberals. Hohenzollern Prussia, like Hapsburg Austria, appeared for the moment to be on the road to liberal popular government.

Meanwhile, in the rest of the German states,

a group of self-appointed liberals called for a popularly elected assembly to meet at Frankfurt for the purpose of constructing a liberal German nation. This was a task so formidable that no one then or since has been able to accomplish it.[1] The drawing up of a code of individual rights and liberties for a people who had never known any was itself a time-consuming undertaking. The two questions confronting the Frankfurt Assembly were whether the German-speaking portions of the multilingual Hapsburg Empire should be included in the projected German nation, and who should head the new nation. Tied in with the Austrian question was that of religion. With Austria (and Bohemia, which was alleged to be predominantly German), the Roman Catholics would predominate, and without Austria and Bohemia, the Protestants. For eleven precious months these knotty problems were debated. Eventually Austria virtually excluded herself by refusing to consider coming into the new German nation without her non-German provinces. By a narrow margin it was decided to offer the emperorship to the king of Prussia. But now it was too late. The situation in Vienna and Berlin had drastically changed.

In Austria the inexperience and weakness of the liberals and the rivalries and conflicts among the various language groups played into the hands of the Hapsburgs. Skillfully playing off one language group against another, the Austrian rulers beat down the liberal and national revolts one after the other. In Hungary they had the help of the reactionary Nicholas I of Russia, whose army crushed the rebels. In Italy a united effort of the various states failed to materialize. Only the kingdom of Sardinia sent significant aid to Lombardy and Venetia. Austrian arms easily prevailed. Everywhere in Italy except in the kingdom of Sardinia, liberalism and nationalism were crushed.

In Prussia, too, the liberals were weak and inexperienced. The unstable Frederick William IV, after his first uncertainty, gradually fell under the influence of his militaristic and reactionary Junker advisers. Further stiffened by the news from Vienna that the Hapsburgs had regained their autocratic position, he spurned the German crown offered him by the Frankfurt Assembly, and replaced the constitution drawn up by Prussian liberals with one that was a travesty of liberalism. The Hohenzollerns' rejection of the crown of a united liberal Germany blasted the hopes of the Frankfurt Assembly. When a few of the most determined attempted to continue their efforts, they were dispersed by Prussian troops. Many of the discouraged German liberals fled to America and became known as the Forty-eighters. Some of them, like Carl Schurz, played a distinguished role in liberal causes in America. The failure of the liberals to unite Germany in 1848 may be explained in large measure by the weakness of the industrial bourgeoisie and proletariat, who were as yet few in number. When the Industrial Revolution did make its influence seriously felt in Central Europe after midcentury, nationalism rather than liberalism would be its chief beneficiary.

6. EMANCIPATION IN RUSSIA

Russia remained untouched by the Industrial Revolution and bourgeois liberalism in the period 1830–1871, when these two forces were triumphing in Western Europe and emerging in Central Europe. Her few liberal reforms at this time came at the hands of the benevolent tsar, Alexander II (1855–1881). Most noteworthy of his acts was the emancipation of the serfs, who constituted a majority of Russia's population. This was done in 1861—one year before President Lincoln issued his Emancipation Proclamation in the United States. The serfs did not get their lands free, however.

---

[1] The Weimar Republic, 1919–1933, was liberal, but it was virtually forced upon Germany by the victorious World War I Allies, who refused to make peace with the Hohenzollern Empire, and it lasted little more than a decade. (See Chapters 54 and 56.)

The land was given over to collective groups called *mirs*, and the ex-serfs were compelled to pay the government redemption dues for a period of forty-nine years. Since they received only the poorest lands, their economic condition was really worse than before. Alexander decreed some legal and administrative reforms, but for the most part these became dead letters in the hands of hostile administrators. In the absence of political and social liberalization such as that which could be seen in Western Europe, Russia's intelligentsia tended to become defeatist and vi-olent. The resulting nihilism and terrorism were direct antecedents to Russia's twentieth-century upheavals.

The first phase of the Industrial Revolution, 1830–1871, then, was marked by the continued advance of democracy in the United States, the triumph of bourgeois liberalism in Great Britain and France, and the beginnings of moderate liberalism in Central Europe. Eastern Europe and the rest of the world were not yet directly affected by industrialization or the bourgeois liberalism that followed in its wake.

Suggested Reading

General. Two textbooks with good coverage of the nineteenth century are R. R. Palmer and Joel Colton, *A History of the Modern World* (4th ed., 1971); and Gordon Craig, *Europe Since 1815* (1961). Two excellent studies of liberalism are **J. S. Schapiro, *Liberalism: Its Meaning and History* (Anvil); and **Guido de Ruggiero, *The History of European Liberalism*, trans. R. C. Collingwood (Beacon). W. L. Langer, *Political and Social Upheaval, 1832–1852* (1969) is the latest volume in the Rise of Modern Europe series. It is ably written by the editor of the series.

Reform in Great Britain. A brief and highly readable history of nineteenth-century Britain is G. M. Trevelyan, *British History in the Nineteenth Century and After, 1782–1919* (rev. ed., 1937). A scholarly and more detailed account is E. L. Woodward, *The Age of Reform, 1815–1870* (1930). W. P. Hall, *Mr. Gladstone* (1931), is a well-written biography of the great liberal British leader. A popular biography of Disraeli is **H. Pearson, *Disraeli: His Life and Personality* (Universal).

Jefferson and Jackson. An excellent survey of American history with good coverage of the Jefferson-Jackson period is S. E. Morison, H. S. Commager, and W. E. Leuchtenburg, *The Growth of the American Republic* (6th ed., 2 vols., 1969). A delightful study of the liberal Jefferson is **Claude G. Bowers, *Jefferson and Hamilton, the Struggle for Democracy in America* (Sentry). Jefferson is clearly the hero. **A. M. Schlesinger, Jr., *The Age of Jackson* (Little, Brown) is scholarly and well-written. **Alexis de Tocqueville, *Democracy in America* (Vintage) is the observations of a brilliant mid-nineteenth-century French visitor. **Frederick Jackson Turner, *The Frontier in American History* (Holt, Rinehart, and Winston) is the world-famous study that analyzes the influences of the frontier on the growth of American democracy.

The Bourgeois Monarchy in France. Two good surveys of French history in the nineteenth century are **D. W. Brogan, *The French Nation, From Napoleon to Petain* (Colophon); and **J. B. Wolf, *France: 1814–1919: The Rise of a Liberal Democratic Society* (Harper Torchbook). Brogan is the more sophisticated; Wolf the more factual. Albert Guérard, *French Civilization in the Nineteenth Century* (1914) is a thoughtful and gracefully written brief analysis. J. M. S. Allison, *Thiers and the French Monarchy, 1797–1848* (1926) is a scholarly study of one of the dominant personalities of the Bourgeois Monarchy.

The Revolution of 1848. The best single volume on the Revolution of 1848 is **Priscilla Robertson, *The Revolutions of 1848: A Social History* (Harper Torchbook)—a scholarly and lucid book. An interesting study of the leading personalities in the 1848 upheaval is Arnold Whitridge, *Men in Crisis, the Revolutions of 1848* (1949). An up-to-date account of the Revolution of 1848 in the Germanies by a foremost scholar of modern German history is Hajo Holborn, *A History of Modern Germany*, vol. III (3 vols., 1959–69). Another study of the 1848 upheaval in the Germanies by an eminent scholar is **L. B. Namier, *1848: The Revolution of the Intellectuals* (Anchor). Namier finds nationalism to be the wrecker of the liberal movement. A scholarly study of a major aspect of the Revolution of 1848 in France is D. C. McKay, *The National Workshops: A Study in the French Revolution of 1848* (1933).

Emancipation in Russia. The reign of Alexander II, the emancipation tsar, is well-covered by M. T. Florinsky, *Russia: A History and an Interpretation* (2 vols., 1953). **W. T. Mosse, *Alexander II and the Modernization of Russia* (Collier) is a good brief account.

Sources. J. F. Scott and A. Baltzey, *Readings in European History Since 1814* (1934) contains many interesting selections from original sources for the history of early nineteenth-century Europe.

Historical Fiction. Two of the world's great novels depicting life in mid-nineteenth-century Britain and Russia, respectively, are **Charles Dickens, *David Copperfield* (Modern Library); and **Ivan Turgenev, *Fathers and Sons* (Modern Library).

Chapter 45 ❦ The Development of Nationalism in

France and the United States

One of the most dynamic forces in the world of the nineteenth and twentieth centuries is nationalism. The variety of nationalism that we have known in the last century and a half was born in the French Revolution and nurtured by the Industrial Revolution. Until around 1871, it was relatively moderate and closely associated with liberalism; since 1871, it has tended to become malignant and aggressive, ofttimes at war with liberalism. Before 1871 it was limited for the most part to Europe and America; since 1871 it has spread to Asia and Africa without losing its vigor in the West.

1. THE NATURE OF NATIONALISM

Nationalism may be defined as a feeling of loyalty to one's country. What are the essential factors that contribute to this feeling? What makes a German a German or a Pole a Pole even when there is no German or Polish national state?

By far the most important factor is language. Language is so basic to a people's culture that it is often mistaken for race. For instance, one sometimes hears of the various races of the Austrian Empire, and the language groups there themselves often considered themselves racial groups, although it is impossible to establish anything more than a cultural identity based largely on language. Language brings people together in under-standing and separates them from those they cannot understand. Probably second in importance is a historical tradition of unity. The Belgians with their two languages and the Swiss with their three languages and two religions illustrate the importance of this factor. Religion can be a powerful factor, too, though not so important as language. The German Empire with its common language came and held together in spite of a serious religious cleavage, and the Austrian Empire fell apart along language lines in spite of a common religion and a long tradition of unity under the Hapsburgs. (In the long run, of course, religion may prove to be a more enduring force in history than nationalism itself.) Territorial compactness and natural boundaries are frequently contributing factors in nationalism.

The first group loyalty was probably to family, tribe, and clan, and to the territory occupied by them; then to language dialect groups. Loyalty to one's own kin and close associates and to the scenes of one's childhood is a natural thing. Loyalty to a large group or area like France or the United States requires conscious education. In Europe in the thirteenth, fourteenth, and fifteenth centuries, the kings of France, England, Spain, and Portugal, aided by the rising middle class and by the ascendancy of one dialect over the others, created by conquest and consolidation the first four national states. Until the French

From 1848 to 1870, Napoleon III was the most influential man in the world. As he grew older and his health failed, he came more and more under the influence of his Spanish wife, the elegant Eugénie, who strongly favored the 1870 war with Prussia which proved disastrous to the Second Empire. *Photo: The Bettmann Archive*

provincial boundary lines, brought the masses of people into direct partnership with the national government. Universal conscription into the revolutionary armies, which were raised first to save France from the invaders and later to spread abroad the blessings of the French Revolution, gave the people a sense of fraternity in a righteous cause—a crusade. Nationalism became a religion. Such mass dynamism made the revolutionary and Napoleonic armies irresistible. Nationalism soon spread to the other peoples of Europe. Since the French Revolution, nationalism has been an ever-expanding force, increasing in scope as more and more people become aware of and participate in national affairs, and increasing in power as science and technology provide the national patriots with the tools to achieve their nationalistic purposes.

2. THE SECOND EMPIRE OF NAPOLEON III: YEARS OF SUCCESS, 1852–1859

Nationalism was both used and advanced by Napoleon III of France, the most influential figure in world affairs from 1848 to 1870. Louis Napoleon Bonaparte was the nephew of Napoleon. His father was Louis Bonaparte, younger brother of Napoleon and king of Holland, his mother was Hortense, daughter of Napoleon's first wife, Josephine Beauharnais. After the overthrow of his father and his uncle, young Louis Napoleon lived in Switzerland, Germany, and Italy, a political exile from France. Very early he developed ideas of grandeur, particularly after the death of Napoleon's only son in 1832 left him the head of the Bonaparte dynasty. On two occasions, in 1836 and again in 1840, the ambitious young adventurer attempted revolutions against the government of Louis Philippe. Both attempts were ludicrous failures. After the second, he was placed in prison, where he spent six years writing propaganda tracts. In 1846 he escaped to Britain. The Revolution of 1848 presented the tireless schemer with his great opportunity. Using his illustrious name with

Revolution, however, national loyalty was chiefly centered upon the ruling monarch or dynasty and was limited for the most part to the educated upper classes who participated in the government of the nation. The French Revolution gave birth to a new and more virile kind of nationalism. The establishment of equal rights and popular representative government, together with the abolition of old

712

consummate skill and appealing to all classes of Frenchmen, he was overwhelmingly elected president of the Second French Republic. The first eleven of his twenty-two years of prominence were years of spectacular success. Everything "the man of destiny" touched seemed to turn to gold. Then he lost his magic touch. The last eleven years of his reign were years of decline, culminating in disaster for himself and for France.

No sooner had Louis Napoleon taken the oath as president, swearing to uphold and defend the constitution of the republic, than he started working to destroy it and make himself emperor. A gifted politician, he managed to take credit for all popular measures and to push the blame for all unpopular acts of government onto the reactionary and leaderless legislative body. By judicious appointments and dismissals, he soon filled all key military and civilian administrative offices with his own supporters. A master showman, he posed as a friend of the urban and rural masses. The bourgeoisie liked his stand for law and order. He made a particularly firm alliance with the Roman Catholic Church by sending French troops to restore the pope to

his throne, from which he had been driven by the Italian revolutionists of 1848, and by helping the Church regain control of French education. After three years of careful preparation, Louis Napoleon seized dictatorial powers for himself in an almost bloodless coup d'état on December 2, 1851. The few courageous liberals such as Adolphe Thiers and Victor Hugo, who attempted to save the republic, were quietly arrested and deported. Exactly one year later, the French president had himself crowned Emperor Napoleon III. (Napoleon Bonaparte's son, who died in 1832 without having ruled, was declared to be Napoleon II.) It would appear that a great majority of the French people approved the deed.

Napoleon III considered himself heir to the spirit of Napoleon Bonaparte, who, he claimed, was a true child of the French Revolution. The new Napoleon believed in government by a powerful tribune (himself) based upon the popular will. This tribune would rise above all parties and rally all factions in a vigorous and benevolent program. Napoleon III was a supreme nationalist, seeking at all times to enhance the prestige of the French

Languages of Europe

nation at home and abroad. The government of the Second Empire was actually a veiled dictatorship. All power, civilian and military, judicial and legislative, as well as executive, resided in the emperor. The veil was a legislative body elected by universal manhood suffrage. By manipulating the electoral machinery, by official pressure, and by a system of official candidates, Napoleon III was able to control the elections. The legislative body had no control over the ministry. It could not even initiate legislation, this function being performed by the Council of State, appointed by the emperor. On occasion the emperor would seek the "advice" of the people by means of a plebiscite. In many ways, Napoleon III was the first dictator of the kind we have come to know in the twentieth century.

The second Napoleon was an economic liberal in the pre-1871 sense. He encouraged and dramatized the rapid expansion of the Industrial Revolution in France. Two giant investment banking corporations, the Crédit Mobilier and the Crédit Foncier, mobilized huge amounts of capital that were poured into industry, railroads, and real estate. The Bank of France was expanded until each of the country's eighty-six departments (three in Algeria) had at least one branch. The emperor's free-trade policies culminated in the Cobden Treaty with Great Britain, 1860, which lowered the tariff on British manufactures in return for lower British rates on French products, of which wine was the most important. This was the heyday of the French industrial and financial bourgeoisie, which amassed great fortunes, sometimes, as in other countries, by means that would not bear inspection.

The urban proletariat was not overlooked by the benevolent dictator. Hospitals, nurseries, and homes for the aged were built. Although prices were rising steadily with the general prosperity, the price of bread for the wage earners was kept low by government subsidies. A system of voluntary social insurance was instituted for workingmen. Cooperatives were encouraged, and labor unions with limited rights to strike were partially legalized for the first time. The peasants were aided by free trade, more and better roads, railroads, canals, the draining of swamps, and the study and practice of scientific breeding. The landowning farmers liked the law and order and sacredness of private property.

All classes, except the liberal republicans, loved the return of court pageantry. Banquets, parades, balls, and spectacles kindled memories of a glorious Gallic past—of Louis XIV and the first Napoleon. Under the guidance of Baron Haussmann, Paris was rebuilt into the world's most beautiful city. In Napoleon III's reign its population increased from approximately 1 million to 2 million. At the center of the court of the Second Empire was the glamorous Empress Eugénie. When Louis Napoleon usurped the French throne, his prospects were held in such low esteem that no royal family in Europe would furnish him a wife. In 1853 he married the Spanish Eugénie de Montijo, of noble but not royal rank. Although she was never popular with the French people, the world of fashion and royalty was soon deferring to her. Paris has remained the world leader of style and elegance ever since. In 1855 thousands of Europe's great, including Queen Victoria, attended Napoleon's Paris Exposition to view the marvels of the Second Empire.

The peak of France's revived national prestige was reached during the Crimean War, 1854–1856. Like his uncle, the second Napoleon was not satisfied with spectacular domestic achievements. He yearned for farther fields to conquer. His opportunity came when Tsar Nicholas I of Russia attempted to dismember the Ottoman Empire, "the sick man of Europe," and to achieve Russia's historic goal: Constantinople and access to the world through the Turkish Straits. France did not relish the prospect of an ambitious new rival in the Mediterranean. (Great Britain, with her vast holdings and interests in the Near and Far East, was even more sensitive to this threat than was France.) A second

At the height of its splendor and vitality in 1855 the Second Empire drew the major personages of Europe, including Queen Victoria, to the great Paris exhibition of French scientific and industrial progress held by Napoleon III. This engraving published in the Illustrated London News that year shows the interior of the industrial exposition building being prepared by workmen. *Photo: NYPL Picture Collection*

source of Franco-Russian conflict arose when the tsar, as the great champion of Orthodox Christianity, attempted to gain a protectorate over all Christians in the Ottoman Empire and over the Christian holy places in the Turkish province of Palestine. France had been since the Crusades the leading champion of Roman Catholic interests in the Near East, including the Christian shrines in the Holy Land. And Napoleon III's strongest ally in France was the Roman Church. The Crimean War is sometimes spoken of as a purely useless and trivial war. In a sense all wars are useless, but in Russia's quest for an outlet through Constantinople, the rivalry of the great powers for control of the strategic Middle East, and the conflict between Orthodox and Roman Catholic Christianity, we have three of the most enduring issues in history— issues that are still with us. A fourth issue was personal and national. Nicholas I alone of the European monarchs had refused to recognize the French usurper as an equal.

In 1853 the Russian army and navy suddenly attacked the Turks. Early the next year Great Britain and France sent their naval and military forces into the Black Sea and laid siege to Russia's naval base, Sebastopol, on the Crimean Peninsula. Sardinia came into the war to gain the friendship of France and Great Britain. Austria maintained a hostile, and Prussia a friendly, neutrality toward Russia. The war was fought with gross inefficiency on both sides. The only real hero was the British nurse Florence Nightingale, whose efforts helped to inspire the creation of the International Red Cross a few years later (1864). Nicholas I died in 1855, humiliated by the knowledge that his creaking military machine was going to fail. The Peace of Paris in 1856 prohibited Russia's naval forces on the Black Sea and maintained the integrity of the Ottoman Empire. The autonomy of Serbia and the Rumanian provinces of Moldavia and Wallachia under the suzerainty of Turkey was guaranteed by the great powers. The Roman

Catholics were left in control of their shrines in the Holy Land. Great Britain at long last agreed to neutral rights on the high seas. The chief immediate beneficiary of the Crimean War was Napoleon III. His troops had fought better than the Russians or the British. He played host to the peace conference, which, of course, he made a colorful spectacle. French national patriotism was now at fever pitch and French prestige abroad at its highest point since the days of the Sun King, Louis XIV. Nationalism itself received a real boost as other peoples observed its success in France.

3. THE SECOND EMPIRE OF NAPOLEON III: YEARS OF FAILURE, 1859–1870

By 1859 the second Napoleon had obtained not only the loyalty of the great majority of his own people, but also a clear hegemony in the affairs of the European continent. France was prosperous and powerful. Then things began to go wrong. Suffering from a painful physical ailment (diagnosed as a stone in the bladder), he aged prematurely. The dynamic force of nationalism, which he understood and used so well in France, he greatly underestimated abroad. In his efforts to control the Italian and German national movements he failed dismally—in the latter case fatally.

The first serious blunder came in 1859, when he made war on Austria in behalf of Italian freedom. (The details of this war belong to the following chapter.) The defeat of Austria set off a frenzy of Italian nationalism that threatened to dispossess all the rulers of the local states of Italy, including the pope. This alarmed and angered the French Roman Catholics, who blamed Napoleon. But when the French emperor deserted the Italian nationalists in the midst of the campaign, with the agreed-upon job only half done, he further alienated the French liberals, who were already unsympathetic to him.

The booming prosperity subsided after 1860. The Cobden Treaty, signed in that year, flooded France with cheap British manufac-

tured goods with which the less advanced French industries could not compete. The French textile industry also suffered heavily as a result of the American Civil War, which cut off its cotton supply. Both the industrial bourgeoisie and proletariat were hard hit. Overexpansion and speculation began to take their toll.

One of Napoleon's most grandiose projects, one that brought much woe to France then and later, was the restoration of an overseas empire. The French have been conspicuously inept at colonial imperialism. For one thing, the French people have always shown a marked disinclination to leave *la belle France* and make their homes elsewhere. The few who have gone to the French colonies have usually gone not as colonists, but as governors, adventurers, and exploiters. And more often than not they have been royally hated by the natives. During the Second Empire the conquest and annexation of Algeria, first begun by Charles X, was completed. French influence was extended in Syria, Senegal, and China. The seizure of Indo-China was begun. Numerous islands in the Southwest Pacific were acquired. These aggrandizements, though adding to the national ego and prestige, brought France little immediate profit and much trouble.

By far the most ambitious of Napoleon's imperial schemes and the most momentous failure was the attempted conquest and annexation of Mexico. In 1855 the corrupt Mexican dictator, Santa Anna, backed by the military, the big landowners, and the Roman Catholic Church, was overthrown by the democratic liberals under the leadership of the gifted native Indian, Benito Juárez. The Juárez regime instituted sweeping reforms in behalf of individual civil liberties. It attacked all special privilege, particularly the privileges of the Roman Catholic Church, whose vast lands were confiscated. And as an emergency measure it suspended for two years the payment of interest on foreign debts.

This last act presented Napoleon III with his opportunity. Joining with the other two chief creditors, Great Britain and Spain, he seized several Mexican ports in 1862, ostensibly to collect the debts. As soon as the British and the Spaniards saw that Napoleon had more ambitious plans in mind, they withdrew. The French armies then marched on to Mexico City, drove the Juárez government into the hinterland, and set up a Hapsburg prince, Maximilian, as puppet emperor for France. The government of the United States protested vigorously in the name of the Monroe Doctrine, but, embroiled in its own Civil War, it could do no more. As soon as the Civil War ended early in 1865, the American government dispatched victorious Union troops to the Mexican border. Napoleon III, now hard-pressed at home, agreed to withdraw his troops. No sooner had the last French soldiers left Mexico City in 1867 than the Juárez forces captured and shot the well-meaning puppet, Emperor Maximilian. The Mexican fiasco greatly added to the growing unpopularity of Napoleon III with the French people.

More serious was the fact that the Mexican venture tied Napoleon's hands while events of grave consequence to France were occurring across the Rhine. The story of Bismarck's creation of the mighty German Empire will be told in the following chapter. Here it is necessary to relate only that Napoleon completely misjudged the situation, and was repeatedly outmaneuvered by Bismarck. When he attempted to retard the rapid growth of Prussia and to offset it by annexing Luxemburg, Belgium, and the left bank of the Rhine, he was helpless in the face of Prussian military power, since the best part of his own military force was in Mexico.

The distracted emperor attempted to allay the mounting discontent of the liberals. Beginning in 1859, he made one concession after another to liberal parliamentary government, until by 1870 the Second Empire was, on paper, at least, a limited constitutional monarchy similar to that of Great Britain. But 1870 was too late. The showdown with Bismarck's rapidly forming German nation was at hand. The sick and discouraged Napoleon III blundered into a war with Germany for which his armies were woefully unprepared (see pp. 730–732). He was defeated and captured, and his government was overthrown.

4. THE RAPID EXPANSION OF THE UNITED STATES

Between 1800 and 1870 the United States was the most rapidly growing nation in the world, both in area and in population. The purchase of the Louisiana Territory by Thomas Jefferson from Napoleon in 1803 for some $16 million doubled the original area of the United States. In 1819 Florida was purchased from Spain for $5 million (after two little chunks of west Florida had been seized in 1810 and 1813). Texas, which was even bigger then than now, was annexed in 1845. The next year the Oregon Country, including the present states of Oregon, Washington, and Idaho, was annexed after the settlement of a long-standing dispute with Great Britain. The annexation of Texas resulted in a war with Mexico, 1846–1848. After a quick and easy victory, the United States took a huge block of Mexican territory, comprising the present states of California, Arizona, New Mexico, Nevada, Utah, and parts of Colorado and Wyoming. This territory was enlarged to the south in 1853 by the Gadsden Purchase from Mexico ($10 million). These additions within a period of fifty years more than trebled the original territory of the young American nation.

Meanwhile, the growth in population was keeping pace with the increase in area. Between 1800 and 1870 the population of the United States increased from approximately 5 million to 40 million. Added to the high rate of natural increase was an ever-increasing tide of immigration from Europe. After 1840 the largest immigrant groups were the Irish, most of whom settled in the cities of the Northeast, and the Germans, most of whom pushed on to the fertile lands of the Middle West. The absorption and Americanization of these millions of people of varied background are one of the miracles of nineteenth-century nationalism.

The War of 1812 with Great Britain, sometimes called the Second War for Independence, resulted in an upsurge of American national spirit. A new crop of nationally minded statesmen arose, the ablest of whom were Henry Clay, John C. Calhoun, and Daniel Webster. Even more dramatic was Andrew Jackson, symbol of the rugged American frontier. The Western frontier itself was one of the greatest of the nationalizing influences. To it came people from all the seaboard states and from abroad who looked to the national government rather than to the states for protection, for roads and canals, and for land titles. Chief Justice John Marshall and Justice Joseph Story handed down from the Supreme Court bench opinion after opinion establishing the authority of the national government over the states.

It was in this period also that American culture began to free itself from strictly European influences. The American Indian began to be idealized by Henry Wadsworth Longfellow and James Fenimore Cooper. Washington Irving's pen made the legends of American colonial days enchanting. Gilbert Stuart and Charles Willson Peale made idealized portraits of American heroes. Probably the greatest nationalist influence of all was the little red schoolhouse, where rich and poor, German and Pole mingled and learned the American version of civilization and world affairs.

5. THE STRUGGLE OVER SLAVERY

Over the world's most democratic and rapidly growing nation, however, hung a dark cloud that grew more menacing until it produced a destructive and well-nigh fatal storm. This cloud was the growing national cleavage over the existence in the Southern states of Negro slavery. Slavery was totally incompatible with American ideals and traditions. By the beginning of the nineteenth century, it had been banished from European society, although serfdom remained in the Hapsburg territories until 1848 and in Russia until 1861.

The first boatload of Negroes was brought to Virginia in 1619, one year before the Pilgrims landed at Plymouth Rock. Because of the tremendous amount of labor required to clear the American wilderness, the African slave trade flourished throughout the colonial period. By the time of the American Revolution, Negro slaves constituted approximately one-fifth of the total population of the thirteen colonies. Slavery was recognized and protected by the national constitution. Because of the climate and the diversified economy, however, slavery was proving to be unprofitable in the Northern states, and between 1777 and 1804 all the states north of Maryland passed emancipation laws. South of the Mason and Dixon line (the boundary between Maryland and Pennsylvania), where agriculture reigned supreme, slavery continued to be profitable and prevalent. But by 1789 most Americans, in the South as well as in the North, detested the institution. After the Revolution scores of antislavery societies were founded, the great majority of them in the South. It appeared that slavery in America was on its way to an early and peaceful end.

Some unforeseen developments, however, changed the attitude of the South toward emancipation, and a sharp line was drawn between the North and the South over the slavery issue. The first of these developments was Whitney's invention of the cotton gin in 1793. This machine made the raising of cotton so profitable that soon large cotton plantations worked by Negro slaves grew up throughout the South. The American South became the chief supplier of Britain's textile mills. Whereas in 1793 cotton exports from the United States were a mere trickle, by 1800 they had risen to over 30,000 five-hundred-pound bales valued at some $5 million. By 1859 they had risen to some 4,500,000 bales valued at over $200 million—well over half the total value of American exports. At the same time the Negro population increased from some 700,000 in 1790 to nearly 4,000,000 in 1860, nearly all of it slave and all the slaves in the South. By the mid-nineteenth century, the Negro slaves outnumbered the whites in South Carolina and Mississippi, and in the rest of the deep South slaves were about equal in number to the whites. By 1830 the Southern economy had become so wedded to cotton and to Negro slavery that the Southern antislavery movement faltered, and the defense of slavery gained momentum. Even more important than economic considerations in the development of proslavery sentiment in the South was the social problem. The Southern whites did not believe that they could absorb into their society or even live alongside so many free Negroes. Opposition to emancipation was even stronger among the poor whites than among the slaveowners.

This serious North-South cleavage over slavery was greatly aggravated in 1831 by the appearance in the North of a violent abolition movement under the leadership of William Lloyd Garrison and by an alarming slave insurrection in Virginia under the leadership of a Negro preacher, Nat Turner. By coincidence, both events occurred in the same year. As Garrison's abolition movement gained momentum in the North, although not without widespread opposition, the South became increasingly frightened and angry. Every conceivable argument—from the Bible, history, Plato, Shakespeare, and the Constitution—was advanced to justify slavery. John C. Calhoun, the South's leading statesman and former extreme American nationalist, assumed the leadership of the Southern defense.

The critical issue was the extension of slavery to the Western territories. The population of the Northern states, with their growing industry, was rapidly outstripping that of the South. The immigrants pouring in from Europe avoided the slavery-ridden South almost to a man. The vast and fertile Northwest was filling up much more rapidly than the more limited Southwest; and whether the settlers in the Northwest came from north of the Mason-Dixon line or from Europe, they were determined to have none of slavery. As the Northwestern territories clamored for statehood, the Southerners took alarm. Already they were hopelessly outnumbered in the House of Representatives, whose membership is based upon population. Their only security in the national government lay in the Senate, where each state has two members. The Southerners did everything in their power to slow down the settlement of the West and insisted that the admission of every free state must be accompanied by the admission of a slave state in order that equality in the Senate be maintained. Henry Clay managed to stall off an open break by his Missouri Compromise in 1820 and by his compromise of 1850. But both measures were only makeshift. Time and tide were on the side of the North. Geography, population, the growth of industrialization, and the march of liberalism in the Western world were irresistible.

By 1852 the statesmen of moderation, Clay, Calhoun, and Webster, were dead, and younger and more uncompromising men came to power on both sides. In 1854 the Republican party was founded as a strictly Northern party committed to the restriction and ultimate extinction of slavery. In 1860, with Abraham Lincoln as its candidate, it won a sweeping victory over the Democrats, now split between North and South over the question of slavery. Lincoln's assurance that he would never molest slavery where it already existed but would only oppose its further extension offered the South little comfort. The violent abolitionists were growing stronger in the North every day. The strictly Northern Republican party was now in power. What guarantee would the South have, once it lost its last stronghold, that of equality in the Senate? Who would succeed Lincoln? Rather than accept an inferior status in the nation and face the prospect of eventually having some 4 million Negro slaves forcibly freed in their midst, eleven Southern states, constituting about half the territory of the Union and a third of its population, seceded and set up their own independent government.

When it became clear that the Southern Confederacy meant to make the separation permanent, Lincoln proceeded to restore the Union by military force. The North had an overwhelming preponderance in population, wealth, industry, transportation, and naval power. But the South enjoyed brilliant military leadership and the further advantage of fighting on its own soil for what it believed to be the survival of its white civilization.

The war lasted four bloody years. For three of the four years it looked as if the Union could not be restored. Indeed, but for the genius, the character, and the personality of Lincoln, it is possible that it might not have been restored. But after numerous discordant elements in the North were brought together, Great Britain and France tactfully neutralized, and the winning commanders and strategy found, the Southern armies were finally crushed.

Slavery was abolished and the Union restored, never to be seriously threatened since. However, the war left a legacy of sectional bitterness that was greatly deepened by the harsh policy of reconstruction followed by the victorious North. The conciliatory Lincoln was assassinated just five days after the war ended. The radical Republican congressional leaders, who now gained control of the government, treated the defeated and devastated South as a conquered province, forcing upon it twelve years of military occupation, political and economic exploitation, and Negro supremacy. In time, however, these wounds too healed over, but not entirely.

The victory of the North in the American Civil War was another great victory for nationalism. It was also a victory for the pre-1871 variety of liberalism, since it brought into power the Northern industrial bourgeoisie, who upon the death of Lincoln gained control of the now dominant Republican party. Thus in the United States, as in France, moderate nationalism and bourgeois liberalism joined hands during the first phase of the Industrial Revolution.

Suggested Reading

General. **R. C. Binkley, *Realism and Nationalism, 1852–1871* (Harper Torchbook) in the Rise of Modern Europe series covers the Europe of the period of the Second French Empire. Two works by Carlton J. H. Hayes, leading authority on the question of nationalism, are *Historical Evolution of Modern Nationalism* (1931), and *Nationalism: A Religion* (1960). One of the best histories of France in the nineteenth century is Emile Bourgeois, *A History of Modern France, 1815–1913* (2 vols., 1919). An excellent survey of American history with good coverage of the mid-nineteenth-century decades is S. E. Morison, H. S. Commager, and W. E. Leuchtenburg, *The Growth of the American Republic* (6th ed., 2 vols., 1969).

The Second Empire of Napoleon III. An excellent brief and sympathetic biography of Napoleon III is Albert Guérard, *Napoleon III: An Interpretation* (1943). Probably the best two studies of the Second Empire are Octave Aubry, *The Second Empire*, trans. A. Livingston (1940); and J. M. Thompson, *Louis Napoleon and the Second Empire* (1965). **Roger L. Williams, *The World of Napoleon III, 1851–1870* (Collier) is a series of well-written biographical sketches depicting the various aspects of the Second Empire—political, social, and cultural. Two good studies of the Crimean War, which brought Napoleon III to the peak of his prestige, are G. F. MacMunn, *The Crimea in Perspective* (1935); and **Cecil Blanche Woodham-Smith, *The Reason Why* (Compass). The latter is a brilliantly written analysis of the Crimean War centered on the charge of the Light Brigade. The author has also written an excellent biography of Florence Nightingale. An up-to-date sympathetic biography of Empress Eugénie is Harold Kurtz, *The Empress Eugénie, 1826–1920* (1965).

Expansion of the United States. Two scholarly studies of the nineteenth-century expansion of the United States by leading authorities on the subject are R. A. Billington, *Westward Expansionism* (1949); and R. I. Riegel, *America Moves West* (rev. ed., 1947). Written in a more dramatic and popular vein, but also excellent, is **Bernard De Voto, *Across the Wide Missouri* (Sentry).

The Struggle Over Slavery in the United States. William E. Dodd, *The Cotton Kingdom* (1919) is a little gem—a brilliant picture of life and thought in the American slave states. **D. L. Dumond, *Anti-slavery Origins of the Civil War* (University of Michigan) stresses the role of the abolition movement in bringing on the Civil War. George Fort Milton, *The Eve of Conflict: Stephen A. Douglas and the Needless War* (1934) is a scholarly and well-written study of the role of partisan politics in causing the American Civil War. A very scholarly and perceptive study of the Civil War and its sequel is J. G. Randall, *The Civil War and Reconstruction* (1937). The best biography of Lincoln is Benjamin Thomas, *Abraham Lincoln* (1952).

Sources. A good selection of original sources for mid-nineteenth-century Europe is J. F. Scott and A. Baltzley, *Readings in European History Since 1814* (1934).

Historical Fiction. Emile Zola, *The Downfall* (1902) is a novel about the defeat and overthrow of Napoleon III's Second Empire, written by one of France's leading realistic novelists.

Chapter 46 🌿 The Triumph of Nationalism in

Italy and Germany

The failure of the Revolution of 1848 in Central Europe and the harsh repression that followed appeared to dash the hopes of liberalism and nationalism in both Italy and Germany. The forces of nationalism, however, were only stung to greater energy. Within a surprisingly short time after the disappointments of 1848, both the Italian and the German people were moving rapidly toward national unity.

1. CAVOUR PLANS ITALIAN UNITY

Before 1848 three different plans for uniting Italy into a sovereign state had been proposed; each had its own following. One plan was to make Italy a liberal democratic republic. This was the plan of Giuseppe Mazzini, an inspiring speaker and writer but not a very practical organizer or man of action. His movement was called Young Italy. The second plan was to form an Italian confederacy under the leadership of the pope. The third plan was to make Italy a limited monarchy under the leadership of the house of Savoy, the ruling dynasty in the kingdom of Sardinia. During the Revolution of 1848 the first two plans were discredited. Mazzini's

chaotic Roman Republic, which he set up after the rebellious populace had driven out the pope, outraged the Roman Catholic world and was overthrown by a French army of Louis Napoleon. After this experience the pope bitterly opposed the unification of Italy, fearing that it would mean the loss of his political control over the Papal States.

On the other hand, the heroic role played by the kingdom of Sardinia in battling the Austrians against hopeless odds won for the house of Savoy the devotion and confidence of most Italian nationalists. However, the powerful Austrians were still in Lombardy and Venetia, the unsympathetic pope was still in the Papal States, and the rest of the Italian states were weak and divided. Despite the new prestige of Sardinia, therefore, the task of uniting Italy required the work of a genius. He soon appeared: Camillo Benso, Count di Cavour (1810–1861).

Cavour was a member of a well-to-do noble family of Piedmont in the kingdom of Sardinia. (The kingdom of Sardinia was composed of Piedmont, the large island of Sardinia, and the little French-speaking provinces of Savoy and Nice.) Young Cavour showed such liberal tendencies that he was soon in

Giuseppe Garibaldi, the most colorful of all the makers of the Italian nation, is shown in this painting, made from a sketch drawn on the spot, during the siege of Rome in the first abortive attempts at Italian unification between 1848 and 1850. *Photo: Prints Division, New York Public Library, Astor, Lenox, and Tilden Foundations* trouble with both military and civilian authorities. Resigning his commission in the army, he traveled widely in Great Britain and France, where he developed great admiration for liberal constitutional monarchy. Back in Piedmont, Cavour proved himself to be an able businessman. He turned his ancestral estates into models of scientific agriculture and organized successful railroad and steamship companies and chemical and fertilizer factories. Shortly before the Revolution of 1848, he founded a newspaper called *Il Risorgimento* (*The Resurrection*), which never ceased to preach Italian unity, even through the discouragements of defeat. In 1850 the tireless Italian patriot was made minister of commerce and agriculture, and two years later prime minister of Sardinia.

From the moment Cavour became prime minister in 1852, he devoted all his prodigious energy to the seemingly impossible task of driving Austria out of Italy and creating a liberal Italian national monarchy. For seven years he strove to make Sardinia a model state that the others would be proud to follow. Though often sorely vexed by the self-interest of political factions and tempted to use dictatorial methods, he carefully respected the liberal constitution that had been drawn up in 1848. On the economic front, he applied his own private business efficiency to the economy of the state. Cavour was particularly interested in building railroads that ran through the various Italian states, believing that economic unity would facilitate political unity. The budget was balanced. Although taxes were high, the taxpayers were prosperous and confident that the money was being put to good use. The religious problem was a difficult one for Cavour. The numerous and powerful Roman Catholic clergy in Sardinia strongly opposed his liberal reforms and his plans for uniting Italy. Cavour, a nominal Roman Catholic, believed in "a free church in a free state." Special legal privileges for the clergy were abolished. The Jesuits were banished from Sardinia. Most of the monastic establishments were abolished and their properties confiscated. The remaining Church property was made subject to taxation. Cavour, of course, could not have survived the clerical storm that followed had he not been sustained, as he was in all his measures, by his sovereign, King Victor Emmanuel II. Finally, the great minister built an efficient and, considering the size of the country, a large army.

Cavour saw clearly that Sardinia, a state of less than 5 million people, could never defeat Austria alone. It must be done in alliance with a great power. Since Napoleon III's Second Empire was the only great power that might be interested, Cavour sent the efficient Sardinian army into the Crimean War in the hopes of winning French sympathy. The plan worked, and at the Paris Peace Conference in 1856, he was given an opportunity to state impressively to the world Italy's case against Austria. Also of help was Orsini, a fanatical Italian patriot who attempted to assassinate Napoleon III in 1858. At his trial Orsini declared that other such attempts would be made in the future unless Napoleon helped Italy become united. The romantic French emperor, himself of Italian stock, was impressed. A few months later, Napoleon met the Sardinian prime minister at Plombières, a French spa, and there Cavour persuaded him to fight Austria. Sardinia would provoke Austria into a declaration of war; France would come in and help Sardinia drive the Austrians out of Lombardy and Venetia, which would then be annexed to the kingdom of Sardinia. In payment, Sardinia would cede the two little French-speaking provinces of Savoy and Nice to France. Cavour left Plombières satisfied that his life's ambition was about to be accomplished.

2. THE MAKING OF THE ITALIAN NATION

When everything was in readiness in April 1859, Cavour easily provoked unsuspecting Austria into a declaration of war. To Austria's surprise, French armies poured across the Alps to fight alongside the Sardinians. In the two bloody battles of Magenta and Solferino, the Austrians were defeated and driven out of Lombardy. But, to the dismay of Cavour, Napoleon suddenly made a separate peace with Austria (the Agreement of Villafranca) on condition that Sardinia receive Lombardy but not Venetia. Napoleon appears to have been motivated by the surprising bloodiness of the battles, the threatening attitude of Prussia, who mobilized troops in the Rhineland, and the anger of the French Roman Catholics, who feared that the wild outburst of nationalism all over Italy follow-

ing the victories over Austria threatened the independence of the Papal States.

Cavour, his hopes apparently dashed with victory within grasp, lost his poise for the only time in his life. He wanted to carry on the war alone to certain defeat but was restrained by King Victor Emmanuel. He resigned as prime minister, but was soon recalled to direct the complex and fast-moving events. News of Magenta and Solferino set all Italy agog with nationalistic fervor. Early in 1860, under Cavour's behind-the-scenes direction, Tuscany, Modena, Parma, and Romagna (the northernmost of the Papal States) joined the kingdom of Sardinia, bringing together all of northern Italy except Venetia. However, with Austria in Venetia and French troops protecting the pope in central Italy, it looked as if the unification movement must now come to a halt.

At this juncture, the rawboned Giuseppe Garibaldi, the most colorful of all the makers of the Italian nation, performed a daring exploit. With a thousand civilian warriors dressed in red shirts and slouch hats, he sailed aboard two little Piedmontese ships for southern Italy. His goal was the conquest of the kingdom of the Two Sicilies, the largest and most populous of the Italian states, with a regular army of 124,000 men and a sizable navy. Cavour officially condemned the seemingly foolhardy expedition of the thousand, but secretly aided it. Garibaldi's exploits read like a fairy story. He conquered the large island of Sicily, including Palermo, once the largest city in Europe, crossed the Strait of Messina, and entered triumphantly into Naples. The opposing troops, of course, had little heart for their cause and deserted to Garibaldi by the thousands after his first victories. Moving northward in the direction of Rome, Garibaldi defeated the last Neapolitan forces.

Fearful that the daring but undiplomatic Garibaldi would march on Rome and bring down the armies of all of Roman Catholic Europe on the rapidly forming Italian nation, Cavour made the last and most difficult great

The Unification of Italy

decision of his life. He sent the Sardinian army southward and seized all the pope's remaining territory except the Patrimony of St. Peter (Rome and the territory immediately surrounding it). When Victor Emmanuel at the head of his army approached the forces of Garibaldi, the gallant warrior and patriot submitted to his king and retired to the rocky island of Caprera. The kingdom of Italy was formally declared in March 1861, with Victor Emmanuel II as king and the liberal Sardinian Constitution of 1848 as the national charter. The red, white, and green Sardinian flag now flew over all of Italy from the Alps to Sicily except Venetia and Rome. Those two provinces were not joined to the Italian state until 1866 and 1870, respectively, when, as we shall soon see, first Austria and then France was defeated by Prussia.

Cavour did not live to enjoy the fruits of his labors. Less than three months after the birth of his beloved Italian nation, he was dead, exhausted by his prodigious efforts and achievements. Paunchy, with ill-fitting glasses and a myopic stare, he was anything but impressive in appearance. Neither was he an orator. "I cannot make a speech," he once truthfully said, "but I can make Italy." The new nation was a monument to his genius and to the spirit of liberal nationalism.

3. THE HOHENZOLLERNS ASSUME THE LEADERSHIP OF A GERMAN NATIONAL MOVEMENT

During the decade of the 1850s, both liberalism and nationalism began to make rapid headway in the German states. It was then that industrialization in this area became more rapid. In Prussia the rise of an industrial bourgeoisie and an industrial proletariat, both classes imbued with liberalism (of different hues) and nationalism, challenged for the first time the dominance of the Junker aristocracy, who abhorred liberalism of any hue and whose national loyalty was limited strictly to Prussia. It was also in the decade of the 1850s that the "Prussian School" of

historians, Droysen, Sybel, and Treitschke, began to write ponderous works setting forth the German version of history. They were strongly influenced by the philosophy of Hegel (1770–1831), who had preached eloquently a version of history based on national cultures. Every epoch is characterized by a dominant spirit, said Hegel. The modern era belongs to the German spirit of liberty through disciplined order. Hegel, in turn, was undoubtedly influenced in part by the earlier German philosopher Herder (1744–1803). This was the beginning of the German master-race concept.

The flowering of this superior German national culture required the political unity of the German people. However, the experiences of 1848–1849 had demonstrated that, without the support of Prussia and her autocratic rulers, the Hohenzollerns, a German national movement could not succeed. The conversion of the Hohenzollerns and the Prussian Junkers to German nationalism was facilitated by the "Humiliation of Olmütz" in 1850. Shortly after the vacillating Frederick William IV had spurned the German national crown offered him by the Frankfurt Assembly in the spring of 1849, he attempted to reorganize the German Confederation under Prussian leadership. The Hapsburg government of Austria, now completely recovered from its embarrassments of 1848–1849, mobilized its superior army and ordered him to cease. At the town of Olmütz in Austrian territory, he abjectly yielded. After this, the Hohenzollerns and more and more of the proud Junkers sought an opportunity to avenge the national insult to Prussia and replace Austria as leader of the Germanies.

In 1858 the unstable mind of Frederick William IV gave way, and his younger brother, who three years later became King William I, assumed the headship of the Prussian government as regent. Unlike his romantic and idealistic brother, William I was a militarist. His first move was to rejuvenate and greatly strengthen the Prussian military machine. As minister of war he appointed an able organizer, Albrecht von Roon; and, as chief of staff,

Helmuth von Moltke, one of the greatest strategists and tacticians of modern times. But their plans to make the Prussian army the most powerful military force in the world required large sums of money. The liberals, now strong in the Prussian Landtag, began to take alarm. Might not this all-powerful military machine be used to suppress liberalism? The liberals hoped that by holding up the military budget, they might bargain for a stronger role for the legislature in the Prussian government. After several years of haggling, the liberals in 1862 finally defeated the military budget. Liberalism and nationalism had collided head-on. William I, unskilled in and unsympathetic with parliamentary government, threatened to resign. As a last resort, on the advice of Roon and Moltke, he called to the chancellorship the one man who could and would force through the military program, Otto Eduard Leopold von Bismarck.

4. BISMARCK WELDS THE NORTH GERMAN CONFEDERATION

The man thus called to the head of the Prussian government at this critical time was to remain there for the next twenty-eight years. He stamped his iron will and his domineering personality not only on Prussia and Germany, but also to a considerable degree on the rest of Europe and the world. Bismarck was a typical Prussian Junker. A blond giant with boundless energy, he was a firm believer in militarism and autocratic government. He had been a dueling, drinking university student, too restless for the academic life. Administrative work in the Prussian government had also failed to challenge him. Back on his ancestral estates he was a hard-riding, hard-drinking country squire, lording it over his peasants and his neighbors. He detested liberalism in any form. He also detested German nationalism, which until 1849 was closely associated with liberalism. His loyalty was to Prussia alone. The other German states he considered weak and effeminate, unfit for union with manly, militaristic, autocratic

Prussia. He had deplored Frederick William IV's temporizing with the liberals in 1848 and was pleased at his humiliation at the hands of reactionary Austria. Bismarck's views on liberalism never changed as long as he lived. However, his attitude toward German nationalism underwent a sudden and complete reversal when, as Prussia's delegate to the Diet of the German Confederation at Frankfurt, he saw at first hand how Austria dominated Prussia. He became an ardent German nationalist —an enthusiast not for a union of German states, but for a Prussianized Germany from which Austria would be banished. As ambassador to Russia and to France, he gained valuable experiences for the key role he was to play in Germany.

Upon assuming the chancellorship of Prussia in 1862, Bismarck, with the backing of the king and the army, defied the liberal opposition in the Landtag, violated the constitution without hesitation, and collected illegally the funds necessary for the military program. "Not by speeches and majority resolutions," said Bismarck, "are the great questions of the time decided—that was the mistake of 1848 and 1849—but by blood and iron." He came to be known as the "Iron Chancellor." Prussian liberalism was crushed. Bismarck declared that a few glorious victories won on foreign soil would turn the Prussian liberals into fervent German nationalists. This prediction soon came true.

The new army created by Bismarck, Roon, and Moltke was the most scientifically efficient military machine that had ever been devised. Behind it was a state and a people long conditioned mentally and physically to military discipline. The Junker officers were used to command; the tow-headed privates and noncoms, mostly from the peasantry, were accustomed to obey. The latest and best equipment was provided. The whole machine worked with clocklike precision under the direction of a general staff. The subordinate officers were well versed in tactics and strategy and could be trusted to use their own judgment in local situations. The privates were well trained to fight in scattered, loose-order formations that made poor targets for the enemy. For the next three quarters of a century, this army was first the envy of, then the model for, the military machines of the other great world powers.

Bismarck lost little time in putting his new military machine to work. An opportunity soon presented itself in the form of a dispute with Denmark over the long-standing and complex Schleswig-Holstein question. Schleswig and Holstein were two little provinces lying between Prussia and Denmark. Their population was partly German-speaking and

partly Danish-speaking. Since 1815 they had been ruled by the king of Denmark, though they had not been incorporated into Denmark. In 1863 the Danish king suddenly annexed Schleswig outright. Bismarck, seeing an opportunity to test the Prussian army, to annex some territory, and also to embroil Austria, declared war on Denmark (1864). Since Holstein was a member of the German Confederation, Austria dared not hold back lest the leadership of the confederation pass to Prussia. The string of Danish fortresses across the narrow peninsula, expected to block any invader for two years, was carried

The German Question 1815–1871

German Confederation, 1815-1866

Prussia, 1815-1866

Annexed to Prussia, 1866

Joined with Prussia in North German Confederation, 1867

South German States Joined in German Empire, 1871

Alsace-Lorraine, Ceded by France to German Empire, 1871

Austrian Dominions Excluded From German Confederation, 1866

Bismarck's German Empire, 1871

0   100   200 miles

by the Prussian army in two weeks. Denmark sued for peace. Bismarck made the peace settlement as complicated as possible. By the terms of the Convention of Gastein, to which he persuaded Austria to agree, Schleswig and Holstein were to be ruled jointly by Prussia and Austria. Schleswig, however, was to be occupied by Prussia; Holstein by Austria. This unworkable arrangement Bismarck soon used to stir up trouble with Austria.

Confident now that the Prussian army was all that he had hoped and expected, Bismarck devoted the two years following the Danish War to feverish preparations for war with Austria. His first task was to obtain the support or the neutrality of the other three continental powers, Italy, Russia, and France. Prussia had been the first great power to recognize the new kingdom of Italy. Now, promising her Venetia, Bismarck drew her into an alliance against Austria. It was always a cardinal principle of Bismarck to maintain friendly relations with Russia (at Prussia's back door). When Russia's Polish subjects revolted once more in 1863, Prussia alone of the great powers supported Russia. Of course Prussia had several million Polish subjects of her own to worry about. Bismarck neutralized Napoleon III by personal persuasion and deception. Visiting the French emperor at Biarritz, he dangled all sorts of vague possibilities before him, such as the annexation by France of Belgium and Luxemburg. Napoleon completely misjudged the military power of Prussia. He believed either that Austria would win the coming war or that an exhausting stalemate would enable France to arbitrate the peace to her own advantage. Bismarck encouraged him in these misconceptions. By the spring of 1866, with everything in readiness, Bismarck created by threats and maneuvers a state of alarm in Austria. Finally, the Austrian government, realizing that it would require Austria twice as long as Prussia to mobilize her forces and fearing a sudden knockout blow, mobilized her army. Pretending that this was an act of

war, Bismarck sent the Prussian army into Holstein, from which the Austrian forces were compelled to flee. Austria thereupon declared war.

In the Austro-Prussian War, most of the little German states supported Austria. Their military forces, however, were quickly crushed beneath the Prussian steamroller. The world was astounded by the rapidity and ease with which Moltke's armies overwhelmed Austria, a nation of twice the size and population of Prussia and long the dominant power in Central Europe. Although the war is sometimes called the Seven Weeks' War, the issue was really decided in less than three weeks. Quickly taking the offensive, the Prussians soon brought the Austrians to bay in northern Bohemia. The Battle of Königgrätz (or Sadowa, as it is sometimes called) was one of the most decisive battles in history. The Austrians fought bravely, but, standing in close formation, they were mowed down by the Prussian infantry, which lay on the ground and fired from behind rocks and trees. The Prussians' breech-loading needle guns fired six times to the Austrian muzzle-loaders' once. As the Prussians marched rapidly toward Vienna, the Hapsburg government sued for peace. William I, Roon, and Moltke wanted to crush Austria, but Bismarck was looking into the future. He saw that Austria was now harmless to Prussia and would make a valuable ally or at least friend in Prussia's future wars. Restraining his king and his generals, he made the terms of the Treaty of Prague extremely lenient. Austria was to pay Prussia a very small indemnity and to accept the rearrangement of Germany by Prussia. She was also forced to cede Venetia to Italy as Italy's reward for fighting on the side of Prussia.

Following the victory over Austria, Bismarck reorganized Germany. Hanover, Nassau, Frankfurt, and Hesse-Cassel were annexed to Prussia outright, bridging the gap between Rhenish Prussia and the main body. The remaining twenty states north of the Main River were bound to Prussia in a North

German Confederation. The confederation was completely dominated by Prussia, which alone constituted four-fifths of its area and population. Prussia's king and prime minister were made president and chancellor of the confederation, for which Bismarck drafted the constitution.

Its government was, of course, fundamentally autocratic. The chief administrative officer was the chancellor (Bismarck), who was responsible only to the king of Prussia as president, by whom he was appointed. The legislative body was composed of the Bundesrat, whose members were really ambassadors of the twenty-two state governments, and the Reichstag, whose members were elected by universal manhood suffrage. All new laws required the approval of both bodies. The Bundesrat was the more influential of the two. The Reichstag had no control over the chancellor and his cabinet, as in Great Britain, and little control over the budget and the army and navy. If the Reichstag failed to vote a new budget, the old one automatically continued in force. This undemocratic document later became the constitution of the German Empire.

Meanwhile, the former liberals in the Prussian Landtag, caught up in the nationalistic fervor following the victory over Austria, repented of their sins of having opposed Bismarck and voted him exoneration for having violated the constitution. The four predominantly Roman Catholic states south of the Main River (Bavaria, Württemberg, Baden, and part of Hesse-Darmstadt) were left out of the North German Confederation at the insistence of Napoleon III and because Bismarck preferred to have them come in later by their own choice. He would not have long to wait.

5. THE FRANCO-GERMAN WAR AND THE CREATION OF THE GERMAN EMPIRE

From the time Bismarck took up the nationalist cause, he anticipated that France would have to be defeated before the German nation could emerge full-grown. France, he reasoned, long the dominant power on the European continent, would not stand idle while a potentially more powerful rival grew up overnight across the Rhine.

Napoleon III had been badly deceived as to the outcome of the Austro-Prussian War. Too late he realized his error and attempted to safeguard French security. He demanded that the four predominantly Roman Catholic German states south of the Main River be left out of the new German nation and that France receive some German territory west of the Rhine to offset Prussia's sudden expansion. As we have seen, the first proposal suited Bismarck's purposes; he was certain he could get the south German states at a convenient time later. But he stood adamant against the cession of any German territory to France. He pointed out to Napoleon the hard truth that, whereas the victorious Prussian army was nearby and ready for action, the best part of the French army was in Mexico. Both powers began to prepare for a showdown that appeared to be inevitable and not too far in the future. The Prussian army was refitted and enlarged, and the forces of the other twenty-one states in the North German Confederation integrated with it. Mistakes revealed in the Austrian war were noted and corrected. Napoleon III, for his part, recalled his army from Mexico and made efforts to renovate and enlarge the French military machine. These efforts, however, were crippled and delayed by the liberals in the Chamber of Deputies, who feared that Napoleon would use the strengthened army to crush the reviving French liberalism. Only a watered-down army-improvement bill was passed.

By 1870 Bismarck was eager for a military confrontation with France. The army of the North German Confederation was at its peak. William I was getting old, and his more liberal son, the future Frederick III, had little use for Bismarck. The French army reforms, on the other hand, were just beginning and would not be completed until 1873. Bismarck's opportunity came when the Span-

This rare photograph shows Otto von Bismarck, the "Iron Chancellor," on his way to the palace at Berlin as an elderly man. The German Empire bore in large measure the stamp of his personality and ideals. *Photo: The Bettmann Archive*

ish crown was offered to a Hohenzollern prince. Bismarck persuaded the reluctant prince to accept the Spanish offer, and the French immediately took alarm at the prospect of being surrounded by Hohenzollerns. Heavy French pressure was exerted on Prussia, to which both the prince and King William I yielded. However, the French ministers were still not satisfied. They had only the spoken word of the aged king of Prussia. Foreign Minister Duc de Gramont ordered the French ambassador to demand assurance from the Prussian king that a Hohenzollern would never sit on the throne of Spain. William I politely refused this unreasonable

demand. He wired a detailed account of this interview, which took place at Ems, to Bismarck in Berlin. The chancellor saw an opportunity to provoke the French into war. Cleverly editing the Ems dispatch so as to make it appear that the French ambassador and the Prussian king had insulted each other, he published it to the world. The French government, walking into Bismarck's trap, declared war.

The prevailing world military opinion was that this time Prussia had overreached herself and that Bismarck's work would be undone. But, as in the case of the Austro-Prussian War, the military might of Prussia was grossly un-

731

derestimated. That of France was overestimated. The sordid character that underlay the surface glamour of Napoleon III's long dictatorship was quickly revealed. The usurper had surrounded himself with conspirators and adventurers like himself. Graft and corruption had robbed the army of its vital necessities. There was confusion everywhere. Men could not find their units; horses were without saddles, guns without ammunition. The French were able to mobilize only 300,000 troops to face the 800,000 fully trained and equipped veterans and reservists of Moltke. The four predominantly Roman Catholic South German states, far from joining Roman Catholic France as Napoleon III had hoped, threw in their lot with Protestant, German-speaking Prussia as Bismarck had anticipated.

The issue of the war was decided in a matter of weeks. With scientific precision, Moltke's superior hosts moved into France. The French fought heroically but were overwhelmed. One French army was surrounded at the fortress city of Metz, where it surrendered three months later. Another French army under Marshall MacMahon and Emperor Napoleon III was surrounded at Sedan and surrendered on September 2. Napoleon III himself was one of the captives. When this news reached Paris two days later, the liberals overthrew the government of the Second Empire and declared the Third French Republic. Within a matter of weeks, Paris was surrounded by the Germans. For four months the great city held out; starvation forced it to surrender on January 28, 1871.

Bismarck forced upon stricken and helpless France a treaty designed to cripple her beyond recovery. The Treaty of Frankfurt required France to pay an indemnity of 5 billion francs ($1 billion) in gold. German troops would remain on French soil until this amount was paid in full (which Bismarck mistakenly hoped and expected would take a long time). The province of Alsace and most of Lorraine were ceded to Germany. Although most of the inhabitants of these two border provinces speak a German dialect, their religion is Roman Catholic, and they had long been associated with France, to which they were unquestionably loyal. And since these provinces contained much of France's vital iron reserves, the seizure of Alsace and Lorraine long poisoned Franco-German relations.

On January 18, 1871, while the big German guns were still battering Paris, the heads of the twenty-five German states at war with France met on Bismarck's call at Versailles (behind the German lines) and in the Hall of Mirrors proclaimed William I emperor of the German Empire. The constitution that Bismarck had drafted for the North German Confederation became the constitution of the German Empire. Bismarck, of course, became its chancellor, and, unlike Cavour, he lived to rule over his creation for the next nineteen years. The German Empire had now replaced France as the dominant power on the European continent and the chief rival of Great Britain for world hegemony.

The venturesome career of the totalitarian, glory-seeking Second Empire of Napoleon III and to a greater extent the rise of Bismarck's militaristic Prussianized German Empire marked the transition from moderate to malignant nationalism. After 1871 nationalism in the Western world would be less a matter of freeing language groups from alien rule and uniting them under one flag (although some of that still remained) than a matter of military aggrandizement on the part of language groups already free and united. This kind of nationalism was a dangerous foe, rather than a friend, of liberalism.

Suggested Reading

General. **R. C. Binkley, *Realism and Nationalism 1852–1871* (Harper Torchbook) in the Rise of Modern Europe series covers the period of the making of the Italian and German nations. Two good textbooks that treat the period more briefly are R. R. Palmer and Joel Colton, *A History of the Modern World* (4th ed., 1971); and Gordon Craig, *Europe Since 1815* (1961).

The Making of the Italian Nation. Two excellent surveys of modern Italian history are **A. J. B. Whyte, *The Evolution of Modern Italy* (Norton); and **R. Albrecht-Carrié, *Italy From Napoleon to Mussolini* (Columbia). A good biography of the "soul" of Italian nationalism is G. O. Griffith, *Mazzini: Prophet of Modern Europe* (1932). A great biography of the chief maker of the Italian nation is W. R. Thayer, *The Life and Times of Cavour* (2 vols., 1911). Briefer but also excellent is A. J. B. Whyte, *The Political Life and Letters of Cavour, 1848–1861* (1930). The dramatic exploits of Garibaldi are brilliantly told in three volumes by G. M. Trevelyan: *Garibaldi's Defence of the Roman Republic, 1848–1849* (1907), *Garibaldi and the Thousand* (1909), and *Garibaldi and the Making of Italy, June–November, 1860* (1911). The second volume in the series is an especially good example of fine historical writing.

The Making of the German Nation. The best up-to-date survey of modern German history that covers the period of unification is Hajo Holborn, *A History of Modern Germany*, Vol. III (3 vols., 1959–69). Briefer but excellent surveys are **A. J. P. Taylor, *The Course of German History* (Capricorn); and **F. Meinecke, *The German Catastrophe* (Beacon). Taylor, an Englishman, is harsh, and Meinecke, a German, is sympathetic toward the German people. For the more ambitious student, the monumental study of German unification by Heinrich von Sybel, *The Founding of the German Empire by William I*, trans., M. L. Perrin (7 vols., 1890–98) is surprisingly readable. An excellent biography of Bismarck is **Erich Eyck, *Bismarck and the German Empire* (Norton), which is based on the author's three-volume work in German. A scholarly study of Bismarck's crushing of liberalism in Prussia is E. N. Anderson, *The Social and Political Conflict in Prussia, 1858–1864* (1954).

The Franco-German War of 1870–1871. A scholarly study of the origins of the Franco-German War is R. N. Lord, *The Origins of the War of 1870* (1924). Lord makes a convincing case that the chief responsibility lies with Bismarck. Another study of the same interesting subject is L. D. Steefel, *Bismarck, the Hohenzollern Candidacy, and the Origins of the Franco-German War of 1870* (1962).

Sources. I. Silone, ed., *The Living Thoughts of Mazzini* (1939) is a collection of the writings of a leader of Italian nationalism. G. Garibaldi, *The Memoirs of Garibaldi*, trans. R. S. Garnett (1931) is a valuable source. *Bismarck, the Man and the Statesman* (2 vols., 1898) is the title of Bismarck's published memoirs. They are disappointing, but an important source. G. Bonnin, ed., *Bismarck and the Hohenzollern Candidature for the Spanish Throne* (1957) is a good collection of documents pertaining to the Franco-German War of 1870–1871.

Chapter 47 🝆 Romanticism in Philosophy, Literature, and the Arts

Schools of thought and art do not fall neatly into chronological patterns. Nevertheless, one is frequently able to observe a prevailing vogue that characterizes the culture of a given era. Thus, although romanticism began in the eighteenth century, the prevailing style in that century was still undoubtedly classical. Similarly, although classicism has continued on through the nineteenth century and into the present day, romanticism was unquestionably the dominant spirit in the first three quarters of the nineteenth century.

1. THE NATURE OF ROMANTICISM

The romantic spirit had many facets. Essentially, however, romanticism was a reaction against the rationalism and formalism of the classic spirit. Whereas classicism extolled reason and perfection of form, romanticism appealed to the emotions, to feeling, and to freedom and spontaneity of expression. Whereas the classicist was interested in the natural order and the laws of man and the universe, the romanticist loved to sing of woods and lakes and lovers' lanes and daffodils and to dream of faraway or imaginary times and places.

Romanticism was associated with and was in large measure a product of the French Revolution and Napoleon. Many classicists had been interested in peacefully reforming society in accordance with the natural law. They did not anticipate the violent upheaval that came, although many of the radical revolutionary leaders and Napoleon believed themselves to be in the tradition of classical Greece and Rome. It was the romanticists, breaking sharply with past forms and traditions and with bold abandon trying the new, who reflected the revolutionary spirit. This does not mean that all romanticists were political radicals, or even liberals. Some, like Shelley and Heine, were. Others, like Edmund Burke and Sir Walter Scott, were conservatives representing a reaction against the excesses of the revolution.

Nationalism was another facet of romanticism. Whether liberal or conservative, the romanticist was likely to be an ardent nationalist of the moderate pre-1871 type. The great poet Lord Byron lost his life fighting for

Greek national independence against the Turks. The dreamer and orator Mazzini was called the soul of Italian nationalism. He spent most of his adult life in exile because of his labors for a free and united Italy. Herder, as early as the eighteenth century, had pleaded eloquently for a German national culture. The fraternity and the freedom so common to the national movements before 1871, no less than pride in real or imagined national achievements, gave outlet to the emotions of the romanticist.

Romanticism also represented in the main a reaction against the rationalistic deism of the eighteenth century and a return to mystic religion. With the exception of the Reformation of the sixteenth century, this was the first reversal in the general trend toward secularism, which began as early as the fourteenth, or possibly the thirteenth, century. The

Roman Catholic Church had received hard blows in France at the hands of the Voltairian rationalists and the French Revolutionists, but after 1815 it made a strong comeback both in official status and in popularity. To a generation weary of war and violent change, the Church seemed a rock of stability. In Great Britain the Methodist movement, which had begun in the middle of the eighteenth century, grew rapidly. In the United States much of the antislavery movement sprang from moral and religious sources. The revival of religion as part of the romanticism of the early nineteenth century brought about a renewed interest in the Middle Ages. The classicists, almost without exception, had drawn their inspiration from pagan Greece and Rome. Now the Knights of the Round Table and Siegfried and Brunhild came back in style once more. No more perfect example of the romantic spirit can be cited than the novels and verse of Sir Walter Scott, whose subject matter was primarily medieval. Gothic architecture enjoyed a revival. The "Dark Ages" were transformed into the "Age of Faith."

Romanticism was a godsend to the societies of the industrialized countries during the first phase of the Industrial Revolution. Its optimism, its moral and religious idealism, and its nationalism constituted a ready-made justification of life for the prosperous industrial bourgeoisie. For the hard-pressed industrial proletariat, inasmuch as they were able to partake of such cultural luxuries, it provided escapism and spiritual food. If the factory workers dully tending their machines had had nothing but the mechanical universe and the impersonal deistic God of the classicists to sustain them, their lives would have been bleak indeed. Now at least they could dream and hope.

2. THE PHILOSOPHY OF IDEALISM

Any discussion of romantic thought must, almost of necessity, begin with Rousseau (1712–1778), even though this French genius lived during the heyday of rationalistic classicism and almost a century before romanticism came into full flower. Rousseau, like most of his fellow philosophers of the Enlightenment such as Voltaire, Diderot, Montesquieu, was a deist, believing in the mechanical universe of natural laws. However, he differed sharply with them over the place of reason. Far from believing that man can know only what is perceived through his five senses and interpreted by reason, Rousseau placed his main reliance in feeling, instinct, and emotions. He also anticipated the romantic movement in his inordinate love of nature. He would stretch himself out on the ground, dig his fingers and toes into the dirt, kiss the earth, and weep for joy. This mad genius was a true romanticist in his revolt against the rules of formal society. Free love, undisciplined childhood and education, the noble savage—all were features of Rousseau's revolt.

His influence on later generations has been enormous.

It seems a far cry from the rough genius of Rousseau to the exquisitely ordered mansions of thought of Immanuel Kant (1724–1804), but the German philosopher was admittedly indebted to Rousseau. Kant, who was partly of Scottish ancestry, was a native of Königsberg in East Prussia. A frail and insignificant-looking little man who never traveled more than 50 miles from the place of his birth, he slowly developed into one of the most powerful and influential thinkers of modern times. He was often in difficulty with the Prussian government because of his liberal and unorthodox views. Kant started out as a scientist and always respected the methods of natural science. He was also steeped in the philosophy of the Enlightenment. However, he was not satisfied with the conclusions of the eighteenth-century materialistic rationalists. Eventually he thought on beyond them. Kant came to believe that there are in reality two worlds, not one—the physical realm and the spiritual realm, or the realm of ultimate reality. The first he called the realm of phenomena; the second the realm of noumena. In the physical realm of phenomena the approach to truth of Descartes, Locke, and Voltaire—sense perception and reason—suffices. However, in the spiritual realm of noumena, these methods fail. Ultimate spiritual truth may be attained only by faith, conviction, and feeling. Truths in the realm of the noumena, such as the existence of God or the immortality of the soul or the existence of good and evil, cannot be proved by reason. And yet we are justified in believing them because they reinforce our moral sense of right and wrong. His principal work, *Critique of Pure Reason*, was a metaphysical answer of the highest intellectual order to the philosophers of the Enlightenment. These ideas came to be called the philosophy of idealism. Kant and his early nineteenth-century followers represented a sharp reversal in the philosophical trend toward rationalism and materialism, which in a sense began in the thirteenth century with the efforts of Albertus Magnus and Thomas Aquinas to rationalize Christian doctrines.

The most influential of Kant's disciples was Georg Wilhelm Hegel (1770–1831). Hegel's chief interest was the philosophy of history. Like his master, he rejected the mechanistic amoral universe of the Enlightenment. He believed, rather, that a benevolent but impersonal God created and runs the universe, making human society better by a process of purposeful evolution. This is achieved by a dialectical system of thesis, antithesis, and synthesis. Any given system or civilization (thesis) is challenged by its opposite (antithesis). From the struggle emerges a new system containing the best elements of both (synthesis). This synthesis then becomes a new thesis, which when it has served its purpose is challenged by a new antithesis, and so on. Hegel believed that every historical epoch is dominated by a *zeitgeist* (spirit of the time). The zeitgeist of the nineteenth century was German civilization, whose greatest contribution was freedom through disciplined order. Hegel exalted the state. Only in and through the state can the individual find meaning and be free. Hegel's influence on romanticism and on the early nineteenth century in general was probably greater than that of any other thinker. It can readily be seen that he also provided inspiration for some of the "isms" of the twentieth century, such as fascism and communism.

3. ROMANTIC LITERATURE

The spirit of romanticism can be made to come alive in no better way than by a study of the British romantic poets. A number of British writers began to break with classicism during the course of the eighteenth century. The best-known and probably the most representative of these writers was Robert Burns (1759–1796). Born in a humble clay cottage, the Scottish poet lived a carefree life, as undisciplined as if he had been reared in accordance with Rousseau's *Emile*. Burns idealized

nature and the rustic rural life with which he was intimately acquainted. In spontaneous verse written in his native Scottish dialect, he wrote an ode to a field mouse, "Wee, sleekit, cow'rin', tim'rous beastie," which he had turned up with his plow. In *The Cotter's Saturday Night* we are given a charming and sympathetic picture of village life among the poor of Scotland. "Auld Lang Syne" is sung with nostalgia every New Year's Eve by millions throughout the English-speaking world. *John Anderson My Jo* could never have been written by Racine or Alexander Pope.

The romantic spirit, early reflected in the poetry of Robert Burns, reached maturity with William Wordsworth (1770–1850) and Samuel Taylor Coleridge (1772–1834). The two were warm friends. Both were closely associated with the beautiful lake country of northwest England, Wordsworth by birth and Coleridge by adoption. They took a trip to Germany together, where they fell under the influence of Kant. Both, as young men, were ardent social reformers. The two collaborated on *Lyrical Ballads*, which appeared in 1798. *Lyrical Ballads* contains some of the best work of these gifted poets, such as Wordsworth's *Tintern Abbey* and Coleridge's *Ancient Mariner*. Both men were masters of versification and poetic expression. They were also lovers and students of nature, and both of them, particularly Wordsworth, were keenly aware of the brooding, mystical presence of the divine. Wordsworth's *Intimations of Immortality* is sublime in its spiritual depth and insight. In their ardent love of nature, their introspective concern for the individual, their preoccupation with the spiritual rather than the material, and their greater attention to substance than to form, Wordsworth and Coleridge broke distinctly with the spirit of classicism.

Once the vogue of romanticism was dignified and popularized in Great Britain by Wordsworth and Coleridge, a host of romantic writers appeared. A younger trio of poetic geniuses of the highest order, Byron, Shelley, and Keats (all of whom lived briefly and died between the years 1788 and 1824), are known and loved wherever the English language is understood. All three gave spontaneous and unrestrained vent to their emotions. Byron and Shelley combined an exquisite esthetic sense with irrepressible revolutionary zeal, defying the forms and customs of society. Keats was a gentler soul, who after a lifelong quest for the beautiful died at the age of twenty-five.

Meanwhile, Sir Walter Scott in novel and verse was devoting his longer life (1771–1832) to glorifying the Middle Ages and his native Scotland. Scott, unlike Bryon and Shelley but like Wordsworth and Coleridge in their mature and mellow later years, was conservative in his attitude toward public affairs.

The last of the British romanticists were Alfred Lord Tennyson (1809–1892) and Robert Browning (1812–1889), who lived on and wrote well into the Victorian era. The young Tennyson's ardent nationalism, exaltation of the Middle Ages in *Idylls of the King*, interest in religion, and essential conservatism were all typically romantic. Browning, deeper and more subtle in thought though less lyrical than Tennyson, paralleled him in many ways.

Across the Atlantic, Longfellow, Cooper, and Irving, as we have seen, were founding an American national literature. In their subject matter, their style, and their attitudes, they reflected the European romantic spirit. In fact, Irving divided his time and his interests between Europe and America. Many other American writers in the early nineteenth century wrote in the romantic vein. We can mention here only a few of the most illustrative. Ralph Waldo Emerson (1803–1882) was considered a religious radical and skeptic in his day. He gave up his Puritan pastorate (by then Unitarian) at Boston's Old North Church because of his heterodoxy. However, in his essays and poems it was the romantic philosophy of Kantian idealism, not the rationalism of the Enlightenment, that he introduced into America. Edgar Allan Poe (1809–1849), short-story writer, literary critic, and romantic poet of a high order, was in a sense an American

Shelley, though less ethereal and more morbid. Henry David Thoreau (1817–1862) took Rousseau's back-to-nature idea more seriously than did its author. Rousseau, for all his passion for nature, would never have withdrawn from society for two years to live by Walden Pond in introspective solitude. Emerson, Poe, and Thoreau were all individualists to the point of being mild social revolutionaries. Thoreau preached civil disobedience and allowed himself to be put in jail rather than pay taxes for what he considered to be unworthy causes. The sensitive Poe, enduring oblivion and poverty, turned to drink and an early grave. Emerson weathered a storm of hostility from organized religion and society for his nonconformist views.

Romanticism came to German literature in the latter half of the eighteenth century, partly under the influence of the early British romanticists and partly as a result of the conscious effort of the Germans, led by Herder, to free themselves from bondage to French classical culture. Foremost among all German writers is Johann Wolfgang von Goethe (1749–1832). Like Shakespeare, Leonardo da Vinci, and Beethoven, Goethe is a genius of such proportions that he cannot be confined to any single cultural school or movement. However, insofar as it is possible to classify him, he belongs more nearly to the romantic tradition than to any other, both in time and in spirit. His prodigious energies were devoted essentially to a lifelong (eighty-three years) search for the secrets of happiness and wisdom. His encyclopedic mind delved fruitfully into literature, philosophy, science, and public affairs. His novels, lyrics, essays, scientific and philosophical treatises, and dramas fill a hundred and thirty-two volumes. No writer except Shakespeare has had so many of his lyrics set to music. Goethe's masterpiece is *Faust*, a philosophical drama written in exquisite verse. It is about a medieval scholar who, dissatisfied with the fruits of knowledge, sells his soul to the devil in return for earthly pleasure and wisdom. Goethe explores the depths of human experience and aspiration. *Faust* was sixty years in the making. In his medieval interests, his fresh emotional spontaneity, his love of nature and of individual personality, and his courageous, robust, pioneering spirit, Goethe was a romanticist.

Goethe's friend and protégé, Friedrich Schiller (1759–1805), was more popular in his own day than the master himself. Schiller drew heavily upon the Middle Ages and upon nationalism (when national aspirations were associated with freedom) for his dramas, histories, and lyrics. *William Tell*, a drama based upon the Swiss struggle for freedom from Hapsburg tyranny, is probably Schiller's best-known work. Neither Goethe nor Schiller can be considered a German nationalist in the narrow sense; both were universal in their interests and their appeal.

Heinrich Heine (1797–1856) was considered to be Goethe's successor as a writer of German lyrics, though not of Goethe's stature. Most of Heine's voluminous writing was in the field of romantic lyrical poetry. One of his most representative works was an ode to the Silesian weavers who rose up against the hardships caused by the Industrial Revolution, which was just coming to Germany, and were shot down by Prussian troops. Because of the hostility of the various German governments in the age of Metternich to his radical political ideas, Heine exiled himself from Germany. The last twenty-five years of his life were spent in Paris. Many of his later lyrics show a touch of the light gaiety of the French.

One would expect France, the home of Rousseau, the French Revolution, and irrepressible individualists, to be the seat of a flourishing literary romanticism. While this was true in a way, France produced only one romantic writer (Victor Hugo) of the stature of Wordsworth or Shelley. (Goethes, of course, come along only every two or three centuries or so.) Neither did French romanticism attain the glories of French classicism of the seventeenth and eighteenth centuries. François René Chateaubriand (1768–1848), a disillusioned nobleman who began writing during the reign of Napoleon I, was one of the first writers of influence to react against the rationalism of the Enlightenment. His *Genius of Christianity* is a return to mystic religion. He also dreamed and wrote of glorified Indians in faraway tropical America. Honoré de Balzac (1799–1850), the greatest of French novelists, set out to imitate Scott. However, he soon changed his setting from the Middle Ages to contemporary France of the early nineteenth century, becoming one of the first to write about the new industrial bourgeoisie. In forty-seven novels, called collectively *The Human Comedy*, he attempted to depict the whole gamut of human nature. Some two thousand characters, many drawn with shrewd insight, parade before us. He foreshadows the realism of a later era. Alexander Dumas the elder (1802–1870) has continued to delight young and old alike with his romantic and melodramatic *The Three Musketeers* and *The Count of Monte Cristo*, painting the haunting afterglow of medieval chivalry. Victor Hugo (1802–1885) in his long and tumultuous life wrote a vast quantity of exquisite lyrics, dramas, essays, and fiction—all in the romantic tradition. His *Hunchback of Notre Dame* is medieval in setting. In *Les Misérables*, sometimes called the greatest of novels, he immortalizes and idealizes the masses of underprivileged mankind, preaching redemption and purification not by planned social reform, but through suffering. We probably should not leave the subject of French romanticism without mentioning Jules Michelet (1798–1874), romantic French historian. In his *History of France* in seventeen volumes he tells the thrilling story of France's long and glorious achievements, usually with skillful historical craftsmanship and always with matchless grace.

The first great figure in Russian literature was the romantic poet Alexander Pushkin (1799–1837). The chief inspiration for his great lyrics, dramas, histories, novels, essays, and tales came from French and British writers, particularly Byron. Because of his revolutionary radicalism (of the French variety),

Another aspect of the arts and literature in the early nineteenth century was a renewed interest in medieval ideals and artistic forms. The Houses of Parliament in London, which were built at this time, were done in a Gothic style. *Photo: A. F. Kersting*

he was for a while exiled by the Russian government to southern Russia. Later he became a Russian nationalist, and took many of his themes from Russian history. His tragic drama *Boris Godunov* (patterned after Shakespeare) is considered to be his masterpiece. Probably Russia's greatest contribution to romantic literature was the work of two of the world's greatest novelists—Ivan Sergyeevich Turgenev (1818–1883) and Feodor Dostoevski (1821–1881). Both were ardent Russian nationalists, but their real love and loyalty were for the Russian common people, particularly the peasants. Because of their radicalism both were arrested. Dostoevski was exiled to Siberia for five years. Turgenev, after eighteen months of house arrest, spent the rest of his life abroad, mostly in Paris. In his masterpiece, *Fathers and Sons*, Turgenev grapples powerfully with the problems of the older conservative Russian generation versus the modern, sophisticated, and radical younger generation. Dostoevski's two greatest novels are *Crime and Punishment* and *The Brothers Karamazov*. In them he delves psychologically and mystically into the problems of evil and purification through suffering. He was deeply religious, but not in any formal or orthodox sense.

4. THE ROMANTIC SPIRIT IN THE ARTS

Words fail miserably to convey the messages and the meanings expressed in the visual and musical arts. This is particularly true of art whose appeal is primarily to the emotions. Brevity, then, will be the soul of our treatment of romantic art.

The leading painters glorified nature, religion, and nationalism. John Constable (1776–1837) in Great Britain, Camille Corot (1796–1875) in France, and George Inness the elder (1825–1894) in the United States painted dreamy, misty landscapes beautiful enough to have illustrated the moods of Wordsworth or Thoreau. Their idealizations of rural life would have delighted Rousseau and Burns. J. M. W. Turner (1775–1851) in England caught the romantic mood in his eerie impressions of seascapes and mythological subjects. Jean François Millet (1814–1875) idealized both the French rural life (*The Sower* and *The Gleaners*) and mystic religion (*The Angelus*). His compatriot, Eugène Delacroix (1798–1863) depicted on canvas Byron's *The Prisoner of Chillon*. On great murals in the Louvre, the library of the Chamber of Deputies, and the Hôtel de Ville he portrayed glorious scenes from the national history of France.

The romantic movement was less pronounced in the field of architecture. Its chief manifestation was a revived interest in Gothic style. The French, after several centuries of apathy if not scorn for anything associated with medievalism, suddenly showed a renewed interest in their magnificent Gothic monuments. It is significant that the Houses of Parliament constructed in London in the early nineteenth century, when England was rapidly becoming industrialized, were built in the Gothic style.

The romantic spirit was caught and expressed by a host of great musicians. First and foremost was Beethoven (1770–1827), who was not only one of the greatest of classic composers but also the first of the romanticists. His earlier work was in the spirit of his idol, Mozart. In maturity his originality overflowed the bounds of classic forms, becoming freer, more individual and emotional. Beethoven lived through the upheavals of the French Revolution and Napoleon, and his keen interest in these dramatic events is reflected in his music. His Symphony No. 3 ("Eroica") was dedicated to Napoleon, whom Beethoven at first regarded as the embodiment of the democratic ideals of the French Revolution. His Fifth and Seventh symphonies were inspired by the German nationalistic upsurge, which helped to overthrow the French tyrant. Karl Maria von Weber (1786–1826), Franz Schubert (1797–1828), Felix Mendelssohn (1809–1847), and Robert Schumann (1810–1856) carried on in the spirit of the great Beethoven.

These gifted and youthful Germans expressed in their melodic music the same spontaneous and emotional spirit that their contemporaries Byron, Shelley, and Keats were expressing in English verse. A German by adoption was the colorful Hungarian-born Franz Liszt (1811–1886). Liszt is believed to be probably the greatest concert pianist of all time. His glamorous personality and sensational, emotional compositions greatly popularized romantic music. Although Liszt was an international figure, his Hungarian folk music was characteristic of the growing national sentiment of the time. He befriended the youthful Richard Wagner, who later married one of Liszt's illegitimate daughters.

The romantic spirit is nowhere better illustrated than in the work of the Polish-French pianist-composer, Frédéric Chopin (1810–1849). Chopin could express his sweet sorrows in lilting nocturnes, his sunny gaiety in bright waltzes and mazurkas, his national patriotism in stirring polonaises, or his deeper, dramatic moods in more formal ballades and concertos—all with equal skill and all in the romantic tradition. Meanwhile,

This lithograph by Delacroix, a famous French Romantic painter of the first half of the nineteenth century, is an illustration for Goethe's masterpiece, Faust. *Photo: Prints Division, New York Public Library, Astor, Lenox, and Tilden Foundations*

other notable Frenchmen were writing romantic symphonies and operas. Gounod's *Faust* is an operatic version of Goethe's great theme. The haunting melodies of Bizet's (1838–1875) *Carmen*, for example, are known wherever music is loved. The greatest Italian romantic composer was Giuseppe Verdi (1813–1901). His operas *Aida, La Traviata, Il Trovatore,* and *Rigoletto* are still sung every season in opera houses all over the world. Verdi was Italy's national cultural hero during the long, uphill fight for freedom and unity.

Richard Wagner (1813–1883) brought to a dramatic close the romantic era in music. Wagner's tempestuous life, like his music, illustrates and marks the transition from the romantic, moderately liberal and nationalistic early nineteenth century to the more violent, cynical, and materialistic spirit of the late nineteenth and early twentieth centuries. In his youth Wagner was a radical, and was exiled from Saxony in 1849 for his revolutionary activities. Later he became an extreme German nationalist—even a German "master racist" of the type that has brought so much violence to the twentieth-century world. His operas, though containing some of the world's greatest music, are in the main grandiloquent, strident, and extremely nationalistic. *Tannhäuser, The Meistersingers, Siegfried, Götterdämmerung, Lohengrin,* and *The Ring of the Nibelungs* are an important part of opera repertory today.

Since man is always a complex, emotional, and religious creature and only sometimes rational, the romanticists played a significant role in the eternal quest for an understanding of the mystery and beauty of life.

Suggested Reading

General. A good survey of the romantic period is R. B. Mowat, *The Romantic Age: Europe in the Early Nineteenth Century* (1937). Jacques Barzun, *Classic, Romantic, and Modern* (1962) is a spirited defense of romanticism against some of the ridiculous things that have been said about it in recent years. C. Brinton, *Political Ideas of the English Romanticists* (1926), and O. Walzel, *German Romanticism*, trans. A. L. Lussky (1932) analyze British and German romanticism.

The Philosophy of Idealism. Three good intellectual histories of Europe and the West that deal with the philosophy of idealism of the romantic period are: **C. Brinton, *The Shaping of Modern Thought* (Spectrum); **J. Bronowski and B. Mazlish, *The Western Intellectual Tradition: From Leonardo to Hegel* (Harper Torchbook); and **E. Weber, ed., *Paths to the Present* (Dodd).

Romantic Literature. G. Brandes, *Main Currents in Nineteenth-century Literature* (6 vols., 1901–05) is a classic work by a brilliant Danish scholar. H. Beers has written two scholarly works on English romanticism—*A History of English Romanticism in the Eighteenth Century* (1932), and *A History of English Romanticism in the Nineteenth Century* (1929). Good surveys of literary romanticism in the United States, France, and Germany, respectively, are: Hervey Allen, *Israfel: The Life and Times of Edgar Allen Poe* (1949); N. H. Clement, *Romanticism in France* (1939); and L. A. Willoughby, *The Romantic Movement in Germany* (1930).

Romanticism in the Arts. Maurice Raynal, *The Nineteenth Century: Goya to Gauguin* (1951) is a beautifully illustrated history of nineteenth-century painting. **K. Clark, *The Gothic Revival* (Penguin) relates the visual art of the early nineteenth century to romantic literature. Two excellent histories of music that relate the music of the various eras to the other aspects of the culture of the time are: Paul H. Láng, *Music in Western Civilization* (1941); and Hugo Liechtentritt, *Music, History and Ideas* (1938). An excellent survey of music in the romantic period is A. Einstein, *Music in the Romantic Era* (1947). H. Weinstock, *Chopin: The Man and His Music* (1949) is an authoritative study of perhaps the most typical of all the romantic composers.

Sources. **T. V. Smith and M. Grene, eds., *Philosophers Speak for Themselves: Berkeley, Hume, and Kant* (Phoenix) is a handy approach to Kant. A good anthology of romantic literature is **H. Hugo, ed., *The Romantic Reader* (Viking). Handy editions of some of the works of three of England's greatest romantic writers are **T. Hutchinson and E. de Selincourt, eds., *Poetical Works of William Wordsworth* (Oxford University Press); **E. H. Coleridge, ed., *The Poems of Samuel Taylor Coleridge* (Oxford University Press); and **Sir Walter Scott, *Ivanhoe* (Pocket Books). A good selection of the works of one of America's greatest romanticists is **Mark Van Doren, ed., *Portable Emerson* (Viking). The celebrated masterpiece of France's foremost romanticist is **Victor Hugo, *Les Miserables* (Washington Square). A good anthology of German romantic literature is F. E. Pierce and C. Schreiber, eds., *Fiction and Fancy of German Romance, 1790–1830* (1927). Three of the immortal masterpieces of Russian romantic literature are **Feodor Dostoevski, *The Brothers Karamazov* (Harper Torchbook); **Ivan Turgenev, *Fathers and Sons* (Rinehart); and **Alexander Pushkin, *Eugene Onegin* (Dutton).

RETROSPECT Four forces dominated the Western world during the half century that followed the era of the French Revolution. They were the Industrial Revolution, liberalism, nationalism, and romanticism. Only the first was a new force, the other three were a product of or a reaction to the Enlightenment and the French Revolution.

The Industrial Revolution was a shifting from hand tools to power machinery as a means of production. This sounds rather innocuous, but it is doubtful if any development in history has so changed man's pattern of living. From earliest times to the mid-eighteenth century, this pattern had hardly changed at all. Man had lived and worked by means of his muscles and hand tools. Then man invented spinning and weaving machines and the steam engine to drive them. Once the process began, one invention begat another in rapid order. The Industrial Revolution began in Great Britain, and by 1830 it had proceeded far enough to noticeably affect the social and political order.

The first beneficiaries of the Industrial Revolution were the industrial bourgeoisie—the owners of the machines. Joining the bourgeoisie of an earlier day (the merchants, the bankers, the professional men), they gained control of the government of Great Britain in 1832, as a result of the Reform Bill of that year. In France, the Revolution of 1830 brought in the bourgeois monarchy of Louis Philippe. Since industrialism developed a little more slowly in the United States, the industrial bourgeoisie did not gain control until the Civil War, 1861–1865.

The liberalism of the period 1830–1871 reflected the interests of the bourgeoisie. It also reflected the influence of the Enlightenment and the French Revolution. It advocated constitutional government, civil rights, limited suffrage, and laissez-faire economics. The government was to limit its interference in economic matters to maintenance of law and order, the enforcement of contracts, and protection of property. In Great Britain and France, the first phase of the Industrial Revolution was the heyday of bourgeois liberalism. The United States enjoyed a much more democratic government and society—the most democratic in the world. East of the Rhine, where the Industrial Revolution was slow to spread, liberalism was largely in the hands of the intellectuals before 1871. And they had little to show for their efforts.

Nationalism proved to be a more powerful force than liberalism during the years 1830–1871. The mass nationalism of this period was a product of the French Revolution and Napoleon. The colorful and adventuresome

744

Second Empire of Napoleon III was a manifestation of this type of nationalism. Both French and British nationalism found an outlet in the Crimean War. Nationalism in the United States expanded her boundaries to the Rio Grande River and to the Pacific Ocean. It also beat down the effort of the Southern slave states to secede and split the nation. In Southern Europe and east of the Rhine, where liberalism was still weak, nationalism succeeded in creating the Italian nation and the German nation.

Romanticism, which was the prevailing style in arts and letters during the first phase of the Industrial Revolution, was in large measure a reaction against the classicism of the period of the Enlightenment. It, too, owed a great deal to the French revolutionary upheaval, which smashed old forms and institutions and popularized the quest for the new.

Part Eleven

The Industrial Revolution

Second Phase:
The Emergence of the Masses
1871–1914

The Industrial Revolution, which in the years 1830 to 1871 was still in its youth and limited primarily to Western Europe and the United States, grew to burly manhood between 1871 and 1914 and greatly expanded territorially. In its second phase, sometimes called the Second Industrial Revolution, the industrialized world became obsessed with technology and science, and time-honored moral and spiritual values were called into question.

The industrial proletariat who were so bewildered and oppressed during the first phase of the Industrial Revolution were now numerous enough and experienced enough to make their influence felt. Liberalism, which in the first phase was of the moderate bourgeois variety, began to reflect this proletarian influence, but not enough to satisfy some of the more radical economic thinkers and proletarian leaders.

Nationalism, too, underwent a great change after 1871. Having achieved, in large measure, its constructive purpose of freeing language groups from alien rule and uniting them under one flag during the period 1830 to 1871, it now became more aggressive. The great powers of Europe took advantage of their technical superiority to impose their will on most of the rest of the world that was not already under their domination. This new thrust of imperialism, in turn, precipitated new rivalries among the European powers which played an important part in bringing on World War I.

The arts and letters during the second phase of the Industrial Revolution reflected the preoccupation of the masses with the marvels of science and technology and reflected also the rapidly changing values of the period. Many old forms and styles were discarded. There was much experimentation and great emphasis on the quest for the new—almost anything new.

The year 1871, then, opened a period of ferment that began with great promise and ended in 1914 with the greatest holocaust in history up to that time.

Chapter 48 ❧ The Onrush of Technology and Science

The period 1871–1914 was a time of technological and scientific advancement such as the world had never known. Since the sixteenth century, interest in technology and science had been steadily growing in Western Europe. By the late nineteenth century, discovery and invention begat discovery and invention in geometric ratio. Industry mushroomed, pouring forth an ever-increasing volume of the comforts of life for increasing numbers of people. Transportation and communications were speeded up, making easier the development of huge and far-flung corporate empires. Scientists seemed to be on the verge of solving the last mysteries of the physical universe.

One might assume that theory (science) would precede practice (technology). And today, as technology grows more and more complex, this is largely the case. In the past, however, the opposite has been true more often than not. Man was using the wheel long before he understood the mathematics of the circle. We shall therefore begin this chapter by discussing the growth of technology.

1. THE RAPID GROWTH AND SPREAD OF INDUSTRY

The first phase of the Industrial Revolution has often been called the age of iron; the second phase, the age of steel. Certainly steel has been the chief sinew of industry and transportation since the latter part of the nineteenth century. Until the mid-nineteenth century, steel was hard to make and very expensive. The discovery of the Bessemer process (1856) and the Thomas-Gilchrist process (1878) of removing impurities from molten iron greatly speeded up and cheapened the production of steel. In 1871 the total annual steel production in the entire world was approximately 1 million tons, of which about half was produced by Great Britain, a fourth by Germany, and an eighth by the United States. By 1914 the world's annual production had increased more than fiftyfold; the United States was producing approximately half the total, Germany a fourth, and Great Britain an eighth. Out of this steel were made tools and machines that constantly increased in numbers and efficiency. By 1914 in the industrialized countries, these increasingly automatic machines fabricated most of the metal, textile, leather, and wood products and produced and processed much of the food.

The power to drive the steel machines was increasing in like proportion. In 1914 probably nine-tenths of the world's industrial power was still provided by the steam engine, which had been vastly improved since the Watt-Boulton model had made its appearance. Other and more efficient power generators, however, were rapidly coming to the fore. Between 1831 and 1882 the dynamo for generating electricity was developed by a number of inventors, the most important of whom were Michael Faraday (British), the Siemens brothers (Germans), and Thomas A. Edison (American). In 1888 the electric motor was invented by Nikola Tesla, a naturalized American born in Croatia. The first practical internal-combustion engine was invented by Gottlieb

Daimler (German) in 1886. One year later he put it to work in the first automobile. In 1892 the diesel engine, efficiently burning cheap crude oil, was invented by Rudolf Diesel (German). The invention of these two engines gave birth to the vast oil industry. Sir Charles Parsons (British) patented the steam turbine in 1884. The turbine proved to be so efficient that it was soon used to drive the largest ships, and eventually to generate most of the world's electric power.

In the last decades of the nineteenth century, pure science was playing an increasingly vital role in industry, and both science and industry were being applied to agriculture. Physics contributed most heavily to the rapidly growing electrical industry. Chemistry made possible such important industries as synthetic dyes, wood pulp, paper, plastics, synthetic fibers, photography, and motion pictures. The electrical and chemical industries were most highly developed in Germany. The mechanization of agriculture made its first big advances in the great grain-growing areas of the United States, Canada, and Australia, although Western Europe was also steadily increasing its agricultural yields through the use of farm machinery and scientific farming techniques.

The Industrial Revolution also spread geographically in this period. In 1871 Great Brit-

ain produced more industrial goods than the rest of the world combined. Besides Great Britain, only Belgium and France were well developed industrially. In the United States and Germany, the Industrial Revolution was still in its youth. Between 1871 and 1914, the United States and Germany surpassed Great Britain. By 1914 the Industrial Revolution had penetrated Central and Eastern Europe, Japan, Canada, Australia, and New Zealand; even India had a small textile industry. However, it was still in Western Europe and the United States that most of the world's industry was to be found, and the greater part of Asia, Africa, and Latin America was still not industrialized.

2. THE SPEEDING UP OF TRANSPORT

Between 1871 and 1914 a large part of humanity became mobile. Whereas before 1871 relatively few people had ever seen more of the world than could be seen on a single day's journey by foot or on horseback, by 1914 millions of people were traveling considerable distances, often by rapid conveyance. Even in places like China, Turkey, and Brazil, trains chugged along, hauling people for distances and at speeds unknown before.

This was the greatest era of railroad building in history. There had been a rather lively

This illustration shows the apparatus for making steel by the Bessemer process. Invented in 1856, the Bessemer process (and the Thomas-Gilchrist process, 1878), increased the rate of production and lowered the cost of producing steel, a metal stronger and more versatile than iron, and the chief sinew of industry and transportation since the late nineteenth century. *Photo: Historical Pictures Service, Chicago*

building of railroads before 1871 in Western Europe and the United States. However, between 1871 and 1914 the world's mileage more than quintupled. In fact, there has been relatively little railroad building since. The increase in speed and efficiency was proportionate to the increase in mileage.

At the same time, the steamship was making comparable progress, although it had stiff competition from the sailing ship until near the end of the nineteenth century. Steel hulls of great size, turbine engines, and screw propellers, however, were too much for the beautiful sails. The opening of the Suez Canal in 1869 and the Panama Canal in 1914, together with the increase in the size and speed of ships, brought the world and its peoples, commodities, and markets much closer together. Events would soon prove, however, that the world's peoples had not yet learned to live together.

During the last three decades of the nineteenth century, the humble bicycle became a common and important means of locomotion, especially in Europe. Millions of people found this a cheap and pleasant means of stepping up their speed and radius; many depended upon it to get to and from their work. But the bicycle was not fast enough for the industrial age. When Gottlieb Daimler attached his little combustion engine to a wagon in 1887, the automobile was born. It quickly captured the imagination of daring and skillful pioneers. Daimler sold his patent to a French company, and until the end of the century the French led the field in automobile development and production. Leadership passed to America with the founding of the Ford Motor Company in 1903. Henry Ford, who started out as a bicycle mechanic, was the father of two momentous ideas that revolutionized not only the automobile industry, but industry in general. The first was that high wages and cheap products would create markets and profits hitherto undreamed of while permitting the common man to share in the fruits of technology and science. The second was the assembly-line method of mass produc-

tion (Eli Whitney had introduced the idea of interchangeable parts a century earlier). The rapid growth of the automobile not only made the masses much more mobile, but created vast new industrial empires in oil, rubber, and concrete. Its social and psychological effects are still unfathomed.

Another invention of this period was the airplane. The first successful heavier-than-air flying machine was flown by Wilbur and Orville Wright in 1903 over the sand dunes at Kitty Hawk, North Carolina. Aviation was still in its infancy in 1914, but the use of airplanes in World War I, largely for reconnaissance but also for fighting and bombing, gave promise of its tremendous future.

The new technology of steel and power and speed created a myriad of machines and gadgets to satisfy the material wants of those who could afford to buy them. But it also created restlessness among those who could not.

3. THE GROWTH OF CORPORATE BUSINESS AND MONOPOLY

At the same time that industry was growing, individual companies were growing larger and combining to form monopolistic mergers or trusts. Such undertakings as railroads, shipping lines, and iron and steel mills were too large for all but a very few individuals to finance. As a rule, therefore, enterprises of this scope were carried on by joint stock companies. Entrepreneur capitalists would raise the necessary capital outlay by organizing a corporation and selling stock in it to other capitalists. The actual operation of the larger industries would be carried on by hired managers, while the owners of the great industries were far removed from the day-to-day operations. The managers, who hired and fired and supervised the workmen, were working for the absentee owners, and their jobs depended on the amount of profit they could show. They were under constant pressure to pay the workers as little as possible and get from them as much work as possible. The capitalistic owners, often as not banks or insurance

John D. Rockefeller, shown here with his son, John D., Jr., on Fifth Avenue in New York, built the first huge business monopoly, the Standard Oil Trust, which was to serve as the model for big business all over the world. *Photo: United Press International*

companies, rarely came in contact with the workers and their problems. This situation is what later gave rise to the term "soulless corporations."

The giant corporations were equally "soulless" in dealing with each other. In this era of unrestrained competition, the big and strong frequently destroyed the small and weak. The premium was on size and strength. The result was combines, mergers, and monopolistic trusts. The organizer of the first monopolistic trust was an American, John D. Rockefeller. Rockefeller began refining oil during the Civil War, and in 1870 organized the Standard Oil Company in Ohio. By shrewd efficiency and ruthless competition, he gained control over so much of the oil-refining business in Ohio and western Pennsylvania that he was able to bargain with the railroads

for a lower rate than they charged his competitors. With this advantage he was able either to drive most of his competitors out of business or force them to sell out to him on his own terms. In 1882 he organized his dozens of affiliated companies into the Standard Oil Trust, so-called because the member companies surrendered their stock to nine trustees who made the policies and distributed the profits. This trust dominated the oil business of the entire United States. It could crush smaller competing companies by price cutting. It could fix prices and set wages. It could influence state and national legislation. It could produce more and better oil. It could produce cheaper oil—if it chose. And it could compete with foreign corporations more advantageously than numerous little companies.

The spectacular success of Rockefeller's Standard Oil Trust soon made it the model for many others, particularly in the United States, in Germany, in Japan, and to a lesser extent, in Great Britain. The German monopolistic combinations such as the giant I. G. Farben Industries (chemicals and dyes) were called *cartels*. They received government encouragement and support, particularly in their operations abroad. In Japan three-quarters of the nation's industry was controlled by five giant family corporations.

Although the United States began restricting some of the predatory practices of the trusts in 1890, all the industrialized countries encouraged the investment of capital in corporations by passing laws that limited the liability of stockholders to the amount of money invested (hence the "Ltd." usually seen after the name of a British corporation or combine). By 1914 most of the world's industry was controlled by a few great corporations and trusts. Although their stockholders were numbered by the thousands, they were really controlled by a relatively few banks and wealthy individuals. And between the owners of these corporations and the millions of workers, there lay a great gulf.

4. THE ONRUSH OF NATURAL SCIENCE: PHYSICAL AND BIOLOGICAL

Theoretical or "pure" science advanced hand in hand with technology and applied science. The greatest advances in the field of the physical sciences in the nineteenth and early twentieth centuries had to do with discovering the nature of matter, energy, and electricity. John Dalton (1766–1844), a gifted British scientist and teacher of humble origin, started a fruitful line of inquiry by reviving the theory that all matter is composed of atoms. The atomic theory had been introduced by the ancient Greeks, and others had speculated about it from time to time. Dalton got on what turned out to be the right track when he came to the conclusion that what distinguishes the various chemical elements is the weight of the atoms of which each element is composed. Building on Dalton's theories, the Russian chemist Dimitri Mendeléev (1834–1907) worked out around 1870 a periodic chart showing the atomic weight of all the known elements and indicating by gaps in the chart that others remained to be discovered. Both Dalton and Mendeléev thought that the atom was an indivisible solid. However, in the 1890s the British physicist Joseph Thomson (1856–1940) and the Dutch physicist Hendrik Lorentz (1853–1928) independently discovered that atoms are composed of still smaller particles, which Lorentz named electrons. Also in the 1890s the German physicist Wilhelm von Roentgen (1845–1923) discovered X-rays, and the French physicist Pierre Curie (1859–1906) and his Polish wife discovered radium and more about radioactivity.

These were marvelous discoveries, but there were still many fundamental secrets concerning the nature of matter yet to be learned. Thomson's theories were further developed early in the twentieth century by another British physicist, Sir Ernest Rutherford (1871–1937). Rutherford conceived of each atom as a miniature solar system, the nucleus being the sun, and the electrons the planets. Furthermore—and this was most startling—Thomson and Rutherford suggested that the neutrons and electrons might not be matter at all but merely positive and negative charges of electricity.

Meanwhile, Albert Einstein (1879–1955), a German physicist who later fled to America, and one of the greatest scientific geniuses of all time, was assailing time-honored concepts not only about the stability of matter, but also about time, space, and motion. The amazing Einstein came up with a formula equating mass and energy: $E = mc^2$ (E = energy in ergs; m = mass in grams; c = the speed of light in centimeters per second). According to this startling formula, the atomic energy in a lump of coal is some three billion times as great as the energy obtained by burning the coal—a truth that was proved several decades later with the development of the atomic bomb. In 1905 Einstein proposed his theory of relativity, which made time, space, and motion relative to each other and to the observer, not the absolutes they had always been conceived to be. These are only a few of the most basic achievements in the physical sciences in the period 1871–1914. It is little wonder that the intellectual world was fascinated and ordinary men shaken in their beliefs.

The intellectual world, however, was even more interested in and influenced by developments in the biological sciences. Evolution, like the atomic theory, had been suggested by the ancient Greeks and from time to time afterward. With the revival of scientific interests and attitudes in the seventeenth and eighteenth centuries, the thoughts of a number of men turned to the problem of the origin of the present world and its phenomena. By the mid-nineteenth century, the concept of a slow and gradual development of the earth's crust and its inhabitants was not at all uncommon among intellectuals. The time was ripe for a first-rate scientist to supply the evidence. The man who did so was Charles Darwin (1809–1882), the Einstein of the biological sciences.

Darwin was of a distinguished British family. The study of medicine at Edinburgh and theology at Cambridge failed to challenge him. The world of plants and, to a somewhat lesser extent, animals was his first love—or, rather, his consuming passion. In spite of frail health, he turned his prodigious energy and powers of observation and reflection to the amassing of biological knowledge. Gradually he developed his concept of evolution. Of great influence on his thinking was Malthus' *Essay on Population* (1798), which described the struggle of human beings for food and survival, and Sir Charles Lyell's *Principles of Geology* (1830–1833), which was the first really scientific treatise on geology. Lyell demonstrated by the study of fossils the likelihood of a gradual evolution of the earth's crust and of plant and animal forms over eons of time. Darwin published *The Origin of Species* in 1859. In this historic work he de-

Contemporary cartoon by Thomas Nast.

"Gorilla: 'That Man wants to claim my Pedigree. He says he is one of my Descendants.' "

"Mr. Bergh [founder of the A. S. P. C. A.]: 'Now, Mr. Darwin, how could you insult him so?' "

A contemporary drawing by the famous American cartoonist Thomas Nast illustrates the controversy stirred up by Charles Darwin, whose theory of evolution changed man's whole conception of himself. *Photo: NYPL Picture Collection*

scribed with an impressive array of factual data, convincing reasoning, and lucid prose, the long, slow evolution of present plant and animal species from simpler forms through a process of natural selection. In the struggle for survival in nature's jungle, the fittest survived. Those specimens that possessed the more useful characteristics—for instance, the horse with the longer legs—survived to produce more offspring and to transmit their superior qualities, both inherited and acquired, to future generations.[1] Twelve years later (1871) in his *Descent of Man*, he under-

---

[1] The chief apostle of the transmission of acquired characteristics was the French naturalist Jean Baptiste de Lamarck (1744–1829). Darwin was unhappy with this theory, but he did not have sufficient knowledge of the laws of genetics to be able to refute it. The theory was generally accepted in Darwin's time. Darwin did relegate it to a secondary position in his evolutionary hypothesis, however.

took to show how man himself evolved from more primitive species by the same process. Although Darwin's work leaves many fundamental questions unanswered and his belief in the transmission of acquired traits has been pretty well discredited by the German scientist August Weismann and the Austrian monk Gregor Mendel, his main thesis quickly gained general acceptance in the scientific world.

Few books in history have had so much influence as *The Origin of Species* (the religious storm it created in the Western world will be discussed in Chapter 52). The industrial bourgeoisie seized upon Darwin's theory as an explanation and a justification of its own success. Rulers and dominant groups everywhere derived comfort from it. Philosophers, notably Herbert Spencer, undertook to broaden the principle of evolution to make it the key to all truth. Meanwhile, Darwin's brilliant work not only popularized, but significantly contributed to the advancement of the biological sciences.

5. THE DEVELOPMENT OF MEDICAL SCIENCE

Medical science lagged far behind the physical and biological sciences at the opening of the nineteenth century. The seventeenth- and eighteenth-century scientists had made great progress in discovering the secrets of the stars, of the elements, and of plants and animals, but where the ailments of the human body were concerned, they were still holding to theories of the Greek physician Galen, of the second century A.D. The medical profession was a lowly one. George Washington was bled to death in 1799 by a physician who was following the standard practice of the time.

Much groundwork had been laid, however, for medical progress. In the sixteenth century Vesalius made great advances in the study of human anatomy. In the seventeenth century Harvey discovered the circulatory system, while Leeuwenhoek and Malpighi were using the newly invented microscope to explore the structure of human tissue and to discover the existence of microbes. By the late eighteenth century the British physician Edward Jenner was successfully inoculating against smallpox, though he did not understand the secret of its success. During the 1840s anesthesia was discovered and used successfully. However, the whole field of germ diseases and infections was still a mystery.

The secrets of bacteria, their nature and their control, began to be discovered first by the French chemist Louis Pasteur (1822–1895). During the 1860s Pasteur, after indefatigable and imaginative research, discovered that fermentation is caused by bacteria that move through the air and can be destroyed by boiling (or by pasteurization). Later he discovered that many diseases of man and animals are also caused by bacteria and that some of them can be prevented by vaccination. His spectacular services to French agriculture and to mankind made him the most honored man in France. Robert Koch (1843–1910), a humble country doctor in Eastern Germany, hearing of Pasteur's first discoveries, picked up the trail and discovered the germs causing anthrax (a deadly disease of cattle), tuberculosis, sleeping sickness, and many other diseases. He became a professor at the University of Berlin and was awarded the Nobel prize. Also building on Pasteur's foundations was the renowned British surgeon Joseph Lister (1827–1912), who applied the new knowledge of bacteria to the use of antisepsis and eventually asepsis in surgery. His amazing success in controlling infection opened a new era in surgery, and Lister was raised to the peerage by the British government. The honors bestowed upon Pasteur, Koch, and Lister, in contrast with the persecutions suffered by so many of the sixteenth- and seventeenth-century scientists, are striking evidence of the triumph of science and the scientific spirit in the nineteenth century. In the last decades of that century, the governments of the European and Europeanized countries began to recognize that health is a public matter by passing health and sanitation laws.

6. THE RISE OF SOCIAL SCIENCE

The spectacular successes of the natural sciences in the nineteenth century encouraged scholars to attempt to apply the techniques and principles of natural science to the study of man and society. The result was the birth of two new sciences, psychology and sociology, both of which soon became popular. The functioning of the mind has, of course, long been a matter of great interest to man. During the vogue of materialistic and mechanistic concepts of the universe in the eighteenth and again in the late nineteenth centuries, the tendency was to make the human brain mechanical in its operations. This mechanistic approach to psychology came to be called behaviorism. John Locke (1632–1704) had laid the foundations for behavioristic psychology by maintaining that man's mind operates mechanically, as does Newton's universe. Locke believed that the human brain at birth is a blank sheet of paper on which nothing would ever be written except by the perceptions of the five senses as interpreted by reason. The first behaviorist to bring psychology into the laboratory was Wilhelm Wundt (1832–1920). In his famous laboratory at Leipzig he and his enthusiastic students tested human reactions and tried all sorts of carefully controlled and measured experiments on cats and dogs, assuming that the findings would also be applicable to human beings.

The Russian scientist Ivan Pavlov (1849–1936), pursuing Wundt's line of attack, excited the intellectual world with the discovery of the conditioned reflex. Pavlov showed meat to a hungry dog and the dog's mouth watered. Then Pavlov rang a bell while showing the meat. Eventually the dog's mouth watered when only the bell was rung. The immediate and fascinating implication was that many of our human responses are purely mechanical reflexes produced by stimuli of which we are often unaware. This was a big step toward the concept of the mechanization of the mind and body of man. The Italian Cesare Lombroso (1836–1909) argued that criminals are born with mental and physical aberrations and are therefore not morally responsible for their acts. The Frenchman Alfred Binet (1857–1911) devised tests for measuring intelligence; variations of his tests are still used today in schools.

The greatest stir of all in the rapidly growing field of psychology was created by the Austrian scientist Sigmund Freud (1856–1939). Freud believed that much neurosis and abnormality are the result of suppressed and frustrated drives of early life, particularly the sex drive—frustrations that then fester in the subconscious. He came to the conclusion that the correct therapy for such neurosis was to bring to the consciousness of the sufferer the facts and circumstances of the original frustration. Freud achieved some remarkable cures, and founded psychoanalysis. His influence on the development of modern psychiatry has been great. The implications of Freud's theories had a profound effect upon pedagogy in the twentieth century, especially in the United States. Many parents and teachers refused to discipline children for fear of frustrating them and giving them Freudian complexes.

It was not psychology, however, but sociology that in the nineteenth century claimed the title, "queen of the social sciences." This new study was founded and named by Auguste Comte (1798–1857), an eccentric Frenchman of great energy and imagination. The history of mankind, said Comte, may be divided into three epochs. The first was religious, when mystical or supernatural explanations were assigned to all phenomena. The second was metaphysical, when general laws and abstract principles were taken as explanatory principles. The third, which man was on the point of entering, was the specific or positive, when the truth would be discovered by the scientific gathering of factual data. Comte had utter scorn for the first, and little respect for the second epoch. He believed that man and society are as susceptible to scientific investigation as minerals, plants, and the lower animals. His religion was the worship of humanity, and he had great faith in the future of mankind. These ideas are called *positivism.* Comte's followers, eager and numerous, placed great faith in statistics. They amassed vast arrays of statistical data on every conceivable social problem. They tended to scorn supernatural religion of all kinds, morals and ideals, chronological history, and individual biography.

Second only to Comte in importance in the founding and promotion of sociology was the Englishman Herbert Spencer (1820–1903). Spencer shared Comte's scorn for mystical religion and denied that morals should be based upon religion. He also shared Comte's faith in the progress of man. In his ten-volume *System of Synthetic Philosophy,* Spencer undertook to synthesize all human and social phenomena into one grand evolutionary system.

Man's natural interest in himself and in human society, together with the scientific spirit of the times, guaranteed for the social sciences great popularity. Anthropologists and archeologists dug feverishly into man's physical and cultural past. Political scientists and economists tended to forsake theory for the statistical and "practical." Strenuous efforts were made to make history a social science. Leopold von Ranke (1795–1886) strove to make history coldly scientific and morally neutral. History, he insisted, should be based upon an exhaustive accumulation and analysis of documentary evidence. Ranke's historical attitude and methodology were imported from Germany into the United States. They became the standard in both countries. Efforts were also made to make history topical and statistical, rather than chronological, and to focus upon social trends and forces rather than individuals. During the late nineteenth and early twentieth centuries this approach was very popular, particularly in Germany and the United States.

To a visitor from Mars it must have appeared that the Western world in 1914 was on the brink of Utopia. Better and better machines, driven by greater and greater power, were turning out more and more goods and labor-saving devices every day. Natural scientists appeared to be solving the last mysteries of the material universe. Medical scientists appeared to be banishing pain and disease from the earth. Social scientists were amassing voluminous knowledge about man's mind and his social relationships. The cult of progress enjoyed wide popularity. And yet we now know that the half-century which followed turned out to be the bloodiest period in the history of the world, more fear- and hate-ridden than any previous era.

Suggested Reading

General. The period 1871–1900 is covered by **Carlton J. H. Hayes, *A Generation of Materialism, 1871–1900* (Harper Torchbook) in the Rise of Modern Europe series. This excellent volume contains a wealth of factual information and thoughtful analysis in a graceful style. In a more popular vein, **Louis Mumford, *Technics and Civilization* (Harbinger) attempts provocatively to show the social influence of the rise of technology.

Rapid Growth of Industry. An excellent general survey is Herbert Heaton, *Economic History of Europe* (rev. ed., 1948). More detailed standard accounts are J. H. Clapham, *An Economic History of Modern Britain* (3 vols., 2nd ed., 1951–59) and **The Economic Development of France and Germany, 1815–1914* (4th ed., Cambridge). The best volume on the coming of the machine is still **Abbott Usher, *A History of Mechanical Inventions* (Beacon). A good background source is **W. W. Rostow, *The Process of Economic Growth* (Norton).

Growth of Business and Monopoly. Two good studies of business combinations and monopolies are H. Levy, *The New Industrial System: A Study of the Origins, Forms, Finance, and Prospects of Concentration in Industry* (1936); and Ida M. Tarbell, *History of the Standard Oil Company* (2 vols., 1904). The latter book, written in a popular style, did much to arouse public opinion and to inspire congressional antimonopoly legislation. On a broader front, E. Hexner, *International Cartels* (1945) is a good study.

Onrush of Natural Science. An excellent general history of science in the nineteenth century is W. P. D. Wightman, *The Growth of Scientific Ideas* (1951). Among the best studies of the rise of the physical sciences in the nineteenth century are C. T. Chase, *The Evolution of Modern Physics* (1947); **Leopold Infeld, *Albert Einstein* (Scribner); **Eve Curie, *Madame Curie: A Biography* (Pocket Books);

and Arthur Compton, *Atomic Quest* (1956), a lucid account of the making of the first atomic bomb by one of the chief participants. A good account of the major developments in the field of biological science in the nineteenth century is **G. Himmelfarb, *Darwin and the Darwinian Revolution* (Anchor). An excellent survey of the rise of medical science is D. Guthrie, *A History of Medicine* (1948).

Rise of Social Science. The best biography of Sigmund Freud is **E. Jones, *The Life and Work of Freud*, a one-volume abridgment of the three-volume original (Anchor). For the chief developments in nineteenth-century sociology, see J. E. McGee, *A Crusade For Humanity, the History of Organized Positivism in England* (1931).

Sources. Two of the most influential books ever written are **Charles Darwin, *On the Origin of Species by Natural Selection* and *The Descent of Man* (Modern Library). They are lucid and fascinating. Another book which has had enormous influence on late nineteenth- and twentieth-century thought is **Sigmund Freud, *An Outline of Psychoanalysis* (Norton). A good example of Herbert Spencer's voluminous writing is **Herbert Spencer, *Study of Sociology* (University of Michigan).

Chapter 49 ✎ The Movement of the Masses[1]

The first phase of the Industrial Revolution brought the industrial bourgeoisie to power in the industrialized countries. The industrial proletariat was too small, too impoverished, and too bewildered to make its influence strongly felt. It is true that it had stirred on occasion, as in 1830 and 1848, but it had been suppressed with relative ease. During the second phase of the Industrial Revolution, however, not only the industrial proletariat, its numbers greatly augmented by the rapid growth of industry, but the masses in general began to assert themselves.

1. THE GROWTH OF POPULATION AND THE GREAT MIGRATIONS

Prior to the Industrial Revolution, the population of Europe was largely rural, relatively stable in size, and immobile. During the course of the nineteenth century, it changed drastically in all three respects. The total population of Europe, which had begun to increase moderately but definitely about the middle of the seventeenth century, is believed

---

[1] For many of the facts and figures in this chapter the authors are gratefully indebted to Carlton J. H. Hayes, *A Generation of Materialism, 1871–1900* (New York: Harper & Brothers, 1941).

to have more than doubled during the nineteenth century. At the same time there was a great movement of people from country to city and from Europe to overseas areas, chiefly the United States. These changes were at their peak between 1871 and 1914. For a time it was believed that the world's birth rate had suddenly jumped. It would now appear that this was not true and that, in Europe at least, the birth rate actually declined after 1871. The revolutionary advances in medicine brought the death rate sharply down; technology and science greatly increased the production and distribution of food; the humble potato fed additional millions as it came into wider use. The movement to the city was brought about by the opportunities in industry and commerce, the growing attractiveness of urban life, and the application of mechanization and science to agriculture, which now required fewer workers to produce greater yields. Urban population exceeded rural in England by 1850, in Germany by 1914, and in the United States by 1920. It is estimated that in the period 1871–1914 more than a hundred million Europeans moved from the country to the city. By 1914 Western civilization was definitely urban.

The overseas migration of Europeans be-

In the years between 1871 and 1914, more than 30 million Europeans migrated from their homelands to settle overseas, most of them in the United States. This photograph of immigrants arriving in New York shows the conditions under which they traveled— jammed together in a small space for a long and sometimes rough sea voyage. *Photo: Museum of the City of New York* tween 1871 and 1914 was phenomenal. Ever since the first settlements in the New World, there had been a sizable trickle of Europeans to the Americas. This trickle had become a flowing stream in the mid-nineteenth century. During the second phase of the Industrial Revolution (1871–1914), it swelled into a rushing torrent. In this brief span of forty-three years, more than 30 million Europeans left their homelands and migrated to the New World or to the British dominion territories. The great bulk of them came to the United States. Never in history had there been such a movement of peoples. The great folk migrations of ancient and medieval times were puny by comparison. These mass migrations were made possible, of course, by the improvements in transportation—railroads and steamships. In addition to the migrations, many more people were now traveling for pleasure. With the coming of the automobile at the turn of the century, so much of mankind took to wheels that tourism eventually became one of the world's biggest businesses. The masses were truly on the move, but not just physically; they were on the move politically, socially, and economically as well.

2. THE MARCH OF DEMOCRACY IN THE UNITED STATES AND GREAT BRITAIN

The period 1830–1871 was marked in most of the Western world by the increasing vogue of liberal, constitutional, and limited government under the domination of the bourgeoisie. The period 1871–1914 was characterized by a surge toward democracy—government of, by, and for the masses. The most democratic nations in the world in 1871 were the United States, Great Britain, France, and Switzerland.

In the United States the great majority of white males had enjoyed the ballot long before the colonies had gained their independence. In 1870 the Fifteenth Amendment granted the recently freed Negroes political equality with the whites, although most of them were illegally denied the ballot in the Southern states. Between 1890 and 1914, eleven Western states gave the ballot to women, and in 1920 the Nineteenth Amendment granted women equal political rights with men. But universal suffrage does not in itself guarantee real democracy. From the death of Lincoln in 1865 until Theodore Roosevelt took office in 1901, the government and the economy of the country were dominated by big business interests that controlled the dominant "Old Guard" wing of the Republican party. Although this was a period of enormous overall economic development, wealth was very unequally distributed. Western and Southern farmers clamored for public regulation of the railroads, upon which they were dependent. Small business, labor, and the consumer demanded protection against the monopolistic practices and prices of the great trusts, which were protected by a prohibitively high tariff. Millions deplored the city slums, the corrupt spoils system in the civil service, and the squandering of natural resources by private interests.

The first great political leader to rally the discontented to a crusade for reform was William Jennings Bryan (1860–1925). Although the silver-tongued Democrat electrified the masses with his eloquence and made three tries for the Presidency, he failed to break the grip of the Republican Old Guard. The next great reform crusader to appear on the American political scene was the liberal "progressive" Republican Theodore Roosevelt (1858–1919), who adopted much of Bryan's philosophy (with the appearance of Bryan and Theodore Roosevelt, the term *liberal* took on the post-1871 meaning in America).

No public figure had ever so caught the imagination of the American people as the youthful, swashbuckling, "roughrider," hero of the Spanish-American War, Teddy Roosevelt. After assuming the Presidency in 1901 upon the assassination of McKinley, "T.R.," as he was popularly known, immediately launched a vigorous program of reform. The Interstate Commerce Act of 1887 and the Sherman Anti-Trust Act of 1890, which had lain dormant, were activated. Organized labor was given support in its unequal fight with organized capital. Pure food and drug acts restricted the corporations and safeguarded the public health.

Roosevelt was a strong believer in conservation of natural resources. More than 200 million acres of forest and mineral lands and water power sites were withheld from private exploitation. He also continued to work for the strengthening of the merit system in the federal civil service. Many of his reform efforts were blocked by Congress and the federal courts, which were still controlled by the Republican Old Guard. Roosevelt firmly believed in the capitalistic system, but he was convinced that the time had come when the superiority of the government over business must be asserted.

When Roosevelt's hand-picked successor, William Howard Taft, exhibited a disappointing lack of zeal in pushing the Progressive reform program and joined hands with the reactionary wing of the Republican party, T.R. ran against him in 1912 with the support of the Progressive Republicans. The split in the Republican ranks gave the Democrats, under the leadership of Woodrow Wilson (1856–1924), their first clear-cut victory since the Civil War. In fact, many of the Old Guard are believed to have voted for Wilson, whom they did not know, in preference to the "terrible Teddy," whom they did know. Wilson, however, proved to be more liberal than Roosevelt. With the Democrats in control of both houses of Congress, Wilson's administration sharply lowered the tariff, passed the Clayton Anti-Trust Act, gave further encouragement to organized labor, and set up the Federal Reserve Banking System, which removed control of the nation's financial policies from the hands of private interests on Wall Street and placed them in the hands of the federal government. After woman suffrage was granted in 1920, the biggest flaw remaining in American democracy was the refusal of the Southern states to allow blacks to exercise their constitutional right to vote.

Politically, if not socially, Great Britain, the mother of parliamentary government, kept pace with the United States in the march toward liberal democracy. Britain still had her royalty (though her sovereign was now a figurehead), her lords and ladies, an established Church, and a people very respectful of law and tradition. However, the Reform Bill of 1867 had enfranchised the bulk of the industrial proletariat, and William E. Gladstone's Reform Bill of 1884 enfranchised most of the rural males. After 1884 virtually every male householder or renter in Great Britain could vote. Woman suffrage came in 1918. The Parliamentary Reform Act of 1911 stripped the House of Lords of most of its former power and made the popularly elected House of Commons supreme. Yet until the end of the nineteenth century, both the Conservative and Liberal parties were controlled by the aristocracy and the wealthy bourgeoisie. Although both parties were fairly benevolent toward the working classes, the large and discontented industrial proletariat wanted its fair share in the government. Between 1881 and 1906 it turned to a program of moderate Socialism, and with the aid of a number of intellectual radicals, notably George Bernard Shaw, H. G. Wells, and Sidney and Beatrice Webb, the Labour party was formed.

In 1906 the rejuvenated Liberal party came to power under the actual, if not official, leadership of the fiery young Welshman David Lloyd George, who also had the backing of the Labour party. Between 1906 and 1911 Lloyd George put through Parliament a revolutionary program of accident, sickness, old-age, and unemployment insurance. To meet this and other increased costs to the government, he forced through the reluctant House of Lords his famous budget of 1909, which shifted the "heaviest burden [of taxation] to the broadest backs." A steeply graduated income tax and high taxes on unearned increment, inheritances, idle parks of the landed aristocracy, and mining royalties struck heavily at the rich. By 1914 Great Britain was well on the road to social and economic as well as political democracy.

Between 1867 and 1909 she granted self-governing dominion status to Canada, Australia, New Zealand, and the Union of South Africa. In 1914 she at long last even granted self-government to Ireland, although the outbreak of World War I in that year delayed its implementation until 1922.

3. DEMOCRATIC ADVANCES ON THE CONTINENT AND EUROPE

During the second phase of the Industrial Revolution, liberal democracy was much less secure in France than in the United States and Great Britain. With the end of the Second Empire of Napoleon III in the Franco-German War of 1870–1871, the Third French Republic was proclaimed. The first elections, however, held in February 1871, after the surrender of Paris, resulted in a sweeping victory for the monarchists. This somewhat surprising result may be explained by the fact that the republican leaders wanted to continue the unpopular and hopeless war with Germany. The city of Paris, made up largely of the liberal bourgeoisie and the radical proletariat, was unwilling to submit to the domination of conservative rural France. It declared its independence from the rest of France and set up its own city government, or commune. Two months (April–May 1871) of fighting, culminating in a week of all-out warfare in the streets of Paris, were required for the rest of the French nation to subdue the Paris Commune. Some 20,000 Parisians were executed and 7,500 were deported. This tragedy further frightened the conservatives.

However, the royalist majority was split into a Bourbon faction and an Orléanist faction, neither of which was willing to yield to the other. Meanwhile, the liberals grew in strength. Finally, in 1875, the frustrated and frightened monarchists consented (by a single vote) to the adoption of a republican constitution. The constitution provided for a Chamber of Deputies elected by universal manhood suffrage, a Senate elected by a complicated indirect method, and a rather powerless president to be elected by the two legislative bodies. Most of the executive functions of the republic were to be carried on by a cabinet of ministers dependent upon the Chamber of Deputies. It was not until four years later, however, that the liberal republicans under the leadership of the eloquent Léon Gambetta gained actual control of the republic.

But the Third French Republic, so furtively born, was still not safe. Powerful groups were hostile to it. The chief of these were the various factions of monarchists (Bourbons, Orléanists, and Bonapartists), the professional military, the Roman Catholic hierarchy, and large numbers of peasant proprietors. In the late 1880s these factions rallied around a handsome man on horseback, General Boulanger, who became so popular that he might have overthrown the republic had he been bolder and more skillful or had the republican leaders been less courageous. As it turned out, when he was summoned to answer charges of treason against the republic, he fled the country and committed suicide. In the 1890s the antirepublican forces rallied again around a group of army officers who had falsely accused a Jewish army captain, Alfred Dreyfus, and sent him to prison on Devil's Island. This time the enemies of the republic were aided by a rising militant nationalism and anti-Semitism. It required twelve years for the republicans, inspired by the novelist, Emile Zola, to get Dreyfus acquitted and the army officers who had imprisoned

This rare photograph shows Captain Dreyfus just after his conviction. He would spend a dozen years on Devil's Island and France would nearly be split in two before the accusations against him would be revealed as false and the antirepublican army officers who had conspired to imprison him punished. *Photo: United Press International* him punished. The Dreyfus case strengthened the republic and discredited its enemies.

Democratic government did not work so smoothly in France as in the United States and Great Britain. The Voltairian tradition of extreme individualism, the animosity between clericalist and anticlericalist, the sharp cleavage between radical urban Paris and conservative rural France, lingering provincial loyalty, and a historic suspicion of strong government and high taxes—all contributed to the formation of a multiplicity of political parties. This meant that the cabinet was forced to rely on the support of a precarious combination of parties (a *bloc*) in order to carry on the executive functions of government. In France the

Chamber of Deputies could overthrow a cabinet without having to risk an immediate national election, as was the case in Great Britain. As a result, there was a rapid turnover of French ministries. During the forty-three years from 1871 to 1914, no fewer than 51 ministries attempted to govern France. However, the French government was not so unstable as it might appear. As cabinets rose and fell, the actual details of administration were carried on with relatively little interruption by a stable civil service, firmly built in the tradition of Richelieu and Napoleon I. Unfortunately, this low-paid but securely intrenched army of civil servants has often been haughty and self-seeking.

As the twentieth century opened, democratic government in France appeared to be firmly established and increasingly responsive to the will of the masses. Factory laws were giving the workers increased protection. Between 1905 and 1910, a limited program of unemployment, old-age, accident, and sickness insurance was inaugurated. This program of social legislation, however, was only a modest beginning, and the French masses, becoming more politically conscious and active, expressed their discontent in strikes and increased votes for the Socialist party.

Switzerland is a shining example of what democratic government can do. Surrounded by dangerous potential enemies, split into three language groups (German, French, and Italian) and two major religions (Calvinist and Roman Catholic), she has nonetheless enjoyed peace and political stability ever since the overthrow of Napoleon in 1815. In 1848 she set up the Swiss Federal Republic, with authority neatly balanced between the central government and the twenty-two cantons, and universal manhood suffrage—the first permanent universal manhood suffrage in the world. Under this democratic government the Swiss have been prosperous and progressive.

The peoples of the smaller countries of Northern Europe also witnessed the triumph of democratic government during this period. Belgium adopted universal manhood suffrage in 1893. Here the weighted vote was established, men of wealth and education getting two or three additional votes. The Dutch Netherlands extended the suffrage in 1887 and again in 1896; in 1917 the suffrage was made universal. Norway adopted universal manhood suffrage in 1898, Sweden in 1909, and Denmark in 1914. In 1913 Norway became the first European country to grant the vote to women. In these five nations, the traditional respect for government and the relatively high degree of literacy made democracy a vigorous reality.

In Spain and Austria universal manhood suffrage was granted in 1907, in Italy in 1912,

and in all the Balkan states except Serbia and Rumania by 1914. In these areas, however, the illiteracy, poverty, and political inexperience of the people combined with a traditional suspicion of all government to make democracy unstable. In Austria, the clashes among the various language groups further hamstrung the functioning of democracy. In Hungary, there was no progress at all.

Even in authoritarian and disciplined Germany and autocratic Russia, the increasing clamor of the people for active participation in the government was heard. In order to lessen the appeal of the Socialists to the German workingman, Bismarck in the decade of the 1880s inaugurated a program of social insurance (see pp. 777–778). In the German elections of 1912, the Social Democratic (workingmen's) party polled four and a half million votes and became the largest party in the Reichstag. Universal manhood suffrage had existed since the setting up of the empire in 1871, but the popularly elected Reichstag, although its approval was required for all new laws, lacked the prestige and power of the lower houses in the United States, Great Britain, and France. Nor was the cabinet responsible to it, as in Great Britain and France. In Russia the liberals, taking advantage of Russia's defeat in the Russo-Japanese War of 1904–1905, forced Tsar Nicholas II (1894–1917) to set up a representative Duma, although it too had no real control over the government. However, in both Germany and Russia between 1871 and 1914, authoritarian government and militaristic nationalism were much stronger forces than was liberal democracy. Therefore, their history will be examined in the following chapter.

Also conspicuously lagging in the march toward democracy in this period was Latin America. Most of this vast area is made up of lofty mountains, arid wastes, or steaming jungle, and the Industrial Revolution had made little headway there. Its masses were poverty-stricken and illiterate. Although its twenty governments were all republics in form (Brazil after 1891 and Cuba after 1900), they were really dictatorships of strong and often violent men.

4. POPULAR EDUCATION AND JOURNALISM

If democratic government was to function effectively, the electorate had to be literate and reasonably well informed, for a democratic government cannot rise and remain very long above the level of the voters who sustain it. Fortunately for democracy, therefore, the second phase of the Industrial Revolution was also a period of great advances in popular education in the industrialized areas. Contributing to this development were urbanization, improvements in transportation, the increase in wealth, and the growing confidence and ambition of the masses.

In 1871 northern Germany and Scandinavia were the only places where practically everyone could read and write. In the United States most of the states had free public elementary schools, but a fifth of the total population was still illiterate (a figure so high because it included the large Negro population in the South). In Great Britain a third of the people were still illiterate, in France and Belgium a half, in Spain and Italy three-fourths, in Russia and the Balkans nine-tenths, and in Latin America all except a very few. Between 1868 and 1881 national systems of free and compulsory public education were established in nearly all the nations of Western and Central Europe and the United States. For the most part, the systems were as yet limited to elementary schools. Nevertheless, by 1914 illiteracy had practically ceased to exist in Scandinavia, Germany, Great Britain, and the Netherlands. The illiteracy rate was less than 10 percent in the United States, Canada, France, and Belgium. In Italy it had been reduced to 50 percent, in Spain, Russia, and the Balkans to a little more than 50 percent. In Latin America, Argentina and Chile had made noteworthy inroads on the mass

illiteracy. Literacy, of course, is only the first step toward education. The enormous and difficult task of really educating the masses remained.

Hardly less potent than public education as an influence on the minds of the restless masses was popular journalism. In 1871 newspapers were relatively few, small, expensive, and written for a limited educated clientele. The London *Times*, probably the world's most influential newspaper, had a daily circulation of some fifty thousand. However, the second phase of the Industrial Revolution—with its improved machinery, transportation, and communications; the growth of liberalism, which stood for freedom of the press; and above all the growing literacy of the masses—brought forth a new kind of newspaper, one that was cheap, sensational, and popular in its appeal. One of the pioneer popular journalists was Joseph Pulitzer (1847–1911), a Hungarian immigrant to the United States. Pulitzer founded the St. Louis *Post Dispatch* and bought and built up the New York *World* until it became the country's biggest newspaper. With screaming headlines, flag-waving patriotism, easy catchy style, sensational news, popular causes and features, and, above all, comics, he made a fortune and became a great influence in politics. His comic strip *The Yellow Kid* was so popular and sought after by other newspapers that it gave the name "yellow journalism" to the new type of publication. In the 1890s William Randolph Hearst built a great newspaper empire patterned after Pulitzer's. In Great Britain Alfred Harmsworth founded the halfpenny popular *Daily Mail*, made a fortune, became Lord Northcliffe, and bought the London *Times* itself. Before the end of the century five newspapers—two in London, two in Paris, and one in Berlin—had a daily circulation of more than a million each. *Le Petit Journal* in Paris had a circulation of more than two and a quarter million. This type of newspaper not only catered to the masses, but also became a powerful molder of public opinion. Hearst boasted, with a modicum of truth, that he manufactured the Spanish-American War. Since the popular newspapers made their money chiefly from advertising rather than from sales, they came increasingly to reflect the viewpoints of their chief advertisers, the great corporations. The big newspapers were themselves, of course, big business. Although they catered to the masses, they did not always represent their interests.

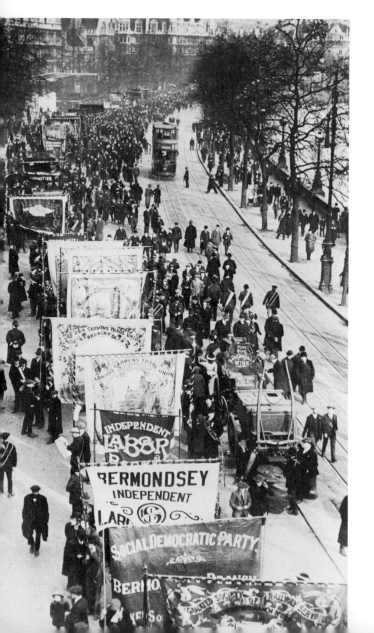

5. LABOR UNIONS AND COOPERATIVES

One of the most important manifestations of the movement of the masses in the second phase of the Industrial Revolution was the formation of labor unions and various types of cooperatives. Democratic legislation, public education, and popular journalism were, for the most part, things done *for* the masses, not *by* them. Labor unions and cooperatives, however, represented direct action by the masses themselves. Wherever industrialization occurred, distressed laborers almost immediately attempted to protect themselves by banding together. However, until around 1871, inexperience, poverty, hostile governments, and unfavorable public opinion caused most of their efforts to fail. Anti-labor-union laws were not fully repealed in Great Britain until 1875. In France they were not fully repealed until 1884. In Germany, Bismarck persecuted labor unions until his dismissal in 1890. During the 1870s and early 1880s, the union movement in Europe was limited chiefly to skilled workmen, organized by crafts, who were moderate in their aims and methods.

In the late 1880s unionization spread rapidly to unskilled workmen, cut across craft lines, and adopted socialistic programs (often Marxist) and more violent methods. In Great Britain the labor unions formed the national Trades Union Congress in 1868, and later they became identified with the Labour party, which was founded between 1881 and 1906. In Germany the individual unions formed in 1890 a national organization that was frankly Marxist. In France in 1895 the various unions banded together in the giant CGT (Confédéra-

Socialism and the union movement spread together all over the industrialized world in the late 1880s. This photograph shows an early demonstration of the Social Democratic party in London; note the union banners. *Photo: The Bettmann Archive* tion Générale du Travail—General Confederation of Labor) with an extreme Marxist (syndicalist) program. In the United States the unionization of labor was retarded by the abundance of free land (until the 1890s), and by the influx of cheap labor from Europe. It was not until 1886 that Samuel Gompers, an immigrant from Great Britain, organized the American Federation of Labor, the first successful national labor organization in America. The AFL was a federation of craft unions of skilled workers. It was nonpolitical in its aims and relatively moderate in its methods, and it grew rapidly. By 1914 the proletariat in the industrialized countries was sufficiently large and organized (though only a minority was as yet unionized) to make itself a power to be reckoned with, both in the factories and mines and at the polls.

Meanwhile, a much bigger portion of the masses was participating in the milder cooperatives of various types. In 1910 in Great Britain membership in cooperative retail stores, fraternal insurance (friendly) societies, and credit associations is estimated to have been some 14 million, the great bulk of whom were wage earners. These organizations also provided much-needed social fellowship for the proletariat. In the 1880s Denmark became the home of the agricultural cooperative movement. By 1914 nearly all of Denmark's agricultural commodities were cooperatively produced and marketed, and the movement had spread to most of Northern Europe, to Italy, and to the United States.

6. MARXIAN SOCIALISM

The most radical movement of the masses during the second phase of the Industrial Revolution was Marxian socialism. Strictly speaking, Marxism was not really a movement of the masses, but rather a movement for the masses begun and carried on by small groups, usually intellectuals. Nevertheless, its influence on the masses between 1871 and 1914 was significant, and since 1914 it has been an enormous factor in world history. It was a product and a compound of various nineteenth-century forces—industrialism, materialism, science, Hegelian philosophy, Darwinian concepts, and the momentary confusion and decline of Christianity. Nor should the influence of the eighteenth-century Enlightenment and the French Revolution be overlooked. Its founder, Karl Marx (1818–1883), was a brilliant Prussian Jew who, having attained his Ph.D. in philosophy and history, was denied an academic position. Exiled from Prussia and later from France because of his radical ideas, he spent the last thirty-four years of his life in London. Marx collaborated with his friend Friedrich Engels, son of a wealthy German manufacturer, in writing the *Communist Manifesto* (1848) and *Das Kapital*, the first volume of which appeared in 1867. These two works present the chief fundamentals of the Marxist philosophy, which in the twentieth century is known as communism. Although Marx's ideas continually evolved and frequently contradict themselves, the salient points of his philosophy are as follows:

ECONOMIC INTERPRETATION OF HISTORY. The good things of life are material. "Religion is the opiate of the people," an ideological veil behind which the "haves" achieve their selfish purposes. The dominant characteristic of a historical epoch is its prevailing system of production, which determines every phase of human culture.

CLASS STRUGGLE. "The history of all hitherto existing society is the history of class struggles"; in ancient times freeman versus slave; in medieval times landlord versus serf; in modern times capital versus labor. The bourgeoisie, having overcome the aristocracy, will in time be displaced by the proletariat.

SURPLUS VALUE. The one fundamental law of capitalist economy is the law of surplus value. The worker, who is paid only a subsistence wage, creates, by his work, value in excess of his wage. This excess value is the source of profit for the capitalist.

INEVITABILITY OF COMMUNISM. The working of the law of surplus value makes it impossible for wages ever to catch up with prices. If wages should be raised, the profit differential working in an accumulative manner will raise even higher the price of the commodity that the worker has to buy back from the capitalist. The capitalists will become richer and fewer; the workers will become poorer and more numerous. Furthermore, the capitalistic system is characterized by alternating periods of prosperity and depression and wars resulting from the rivalries of economic imperialism. Under capitalism, then, the law of surplus value plus boom, bust, and war will finally produce such misery that someday, in a time of depression or war, the workingmen will stage a giant revolution, destroy the capitalistic system, and set up a classless society. Meanwhile, the proletariat must fan the flames of class hatred, sabotage capitalistic governments, and work constantly for their final destruction.

INTERNATIONALISM. Workers in all countries have more in common with each other than they have with the capitalists of their own country. They should unite and obliterate national boundary lines in their struggle against the common enemy—the bourgeoisie.

After Marx's death, his followers, though they split into various groups, tended to regard him as a religious prophet. Indeed, Marx appears to have regarded himself somewhat as a prophet, for he spoke in dogmatic absolutes and in grandiose and stirring, though often vague, phraseology. The most important figure to arise among Marx's orthodox followers was the Russian intellectual Nikolai Lenin (1870–1924). Lenin, a much more effective organizer and leader than Marx, advocated a more positive and violent type of revolutionary activity carried on by a small, highly trained, and constantly purged group of dedicated men. Lenin's greatest influence came after 1914 (see Chapter 55). The chief development in Marxism from the death of Marx in 1883 to 1914 was a moderate revisionism, led by the German socialist Eduard Bernstein. The revisionists became tired of working and waiting for the total collapse of capitalism. Things were not going as Marx had predicted. The rich were not becoming fewer nor the poor poorer. In fact, the condition of the workingmen was steadily improving. Bernstein advocated cooperation with the capitalistic classes to obtain all the practical benefits possible for labor here and now and a gradual approach to socialism.

In Germany, where socialism had its greatest success before 1914, the Social Democratic party adopted in practice, if not in theory, this more moderate type of Marxism during the 1890s. By 1914 it was able to poll some 4½ million votes and had become the largest party in Germany. The French Socialists were more radical and violent than the Germans. In 1905 the orthodox and revisionist wings of the French Socialists joined to form the United Socialist party under the leadership of the scholar-orator Jean Jaurès. By 1914 they numbered a million and a half voters and had 110 seats in the Chamber of Deputies. Contrary to the expectations of Marx, socialism in Great Britain was weak and mild. Among the earliest British Socialists were George Bernard Shaw, H. G. Wells, and Sidney and Beatrice Webb. These intellectual radicals formed the Fabian Society, which was committed to moderation and gradualism. The Labour party, founded between 1881 and 1906, was also mild and grew slowly before 1914. Neither the Fabian Society nor the Labour party could be called Marxist, although both were influenced by Marx. In the United States, too, the socialist movement was relatively weak and (in retrospect) mild. The first prominent American Socialist, Eugene V. Debs, did manage to poll nearly a million votes in 1912 and again in 1920. In 1920 he conducted his campaign from a jail cell, where he had been placed because of his opposition to America's participation in World War I.

Marxism probably set back the rise of the masses by many decades. It frightened the propertied classes, intensified class hatred, and played into the hands of demagogues and dictators at a time when the masses were beginning to gain a greater voice in government, educational advantages, and a larger share of this world's goods and privileges.

7. ANARCHISM

A radical and violent movement that has been falsely associated with Marxist socialism in the minds of many people is anarchism. The two movements are alike in that they are anticapitalist and violent, but they seek opposite goals. Although Marx talked vaguely about the eventual "withering away of the state," Marxists in reality have always striven to make the state omnipotent. Anarchists, by contrast, would do away with the state entirely.

The most influential contributor to anarchist thought and action was Michael Bakunin (1814–1876), a Russian nobleman. Exiled from Russia, he would turn up wherever in Europe anti-establishment violence was brewing. He believed that mankind is by nature good. He would destroy all institutions that restrict man—the state, the capitalistic system, the church, the family. And he would do this by direct action—strikes, sabotage, assassination.

The anarchists and their fellow terrorists provided cartoonists with bearded, wild-eyed, bomb-throwing stereotypes. But they were not a laughing matter; among their victims were Tsar Alexander II of Russia in 1881, President Carnot of France in 1894, King Humbert of Italy in 1900, and President McKinley of the United States in 1901.

Suggested Reading

General—Growth and Movements of Population. **Carlton J. H. Hayes, *A Generation of Materialism, 1871–1900* (Harper Torchbook) in the Rise of Modern Europe series has an excellent, fact-filled chapter on the "Emergence of the Masses." Two scholarly studies of the problem of the growth of population are **Carlo Cipolla, *The Economic History of World Population* (Penguin); and H. P. Fairchild, *People: The Quantity and Quality of Population* (1939). The movement of people to the cities is treated by R. E. Dickinson, *The West European City: A Study in Urban Geography* (1951). The great migrations of Europeans in the late nineteenth century are surveyed by W. F. Wilcox, *et al.*, *International Migrations* (2 vols., 1929, 1931); and H. P. Fairchild, *Immigration: A World Movement and Its American Significance* (1933).

Democratic Advances in the United States and Great Britain. Good biographies of the two most important figures in the struggle to extend democracy in the United States during the second phase of the Industrial Revolution are **Henry Pringle, *Theodore Roosevelt* (Harvest Books); and Arthur Link, *Woodrow Wilson: The New Freedom* (1956), the second volume of Link's projected eight-volume biography. An excellent study of democratic advances in Great Britain is R. C. K. Ensor, *England, 1870–1914* (rev. ed., 1949). Good biographies of Britain's two chief liberal leaders of the period 1871–1914 are W. P. Hall, *Mr. Gladstone* (1931); and T. Jones, *Lloyd George* (1951).

Democratic Advances on the European Continent. The best volume in English on the Third

French Republic is D. W. Brogan, *France Under the Republic* (1940), written in an urbane and sophisticated style. An excellent study of the Dreyfus case is **L. Derfler, *The Dreyfus Case: Tragedy of Errors?* (Heath). This is one of the best volumes in the Heath problems series. Italy in the period 1871–1914 is well covered by R. Albrecht-Carrié, *Italy From Napoleon to Mussolini* (1950). D. Verney, *Parliamentary Reform in Sweden, 1866–1921* (1957) well describes the growth of democracy in one of the smaller states of Europe during the second phase of the Industrial Revolution.

Popular Education and Journalism. P. Monroe, *A Textbook in the History of Education* (rev. ed., 1932) is a good brief survey of that huge subject. A study of a very significant aspect of education in the period 1871–1914 is E. H. Reisner, *Nationalism and Education Since 1789* (1923). Good chapters on popular journalism in the period 1871–1914 may be found in C. F. Carr and F. E. Stevens, *Modern Journalism* (1931); and W. G. Bleger, *Main Currents in the History of American Journalism* (1927).

Labor Unions and Cooperatives. The best general survey of labor movements is W. Galenson, ed., *Comparative Labor Movements* (1952). Excellent studies of the British and French labor movements are H. Pelling, *A History of British Trade Unionism* (1963); and V. R. Lorwin, *The French Labor Movement*

(1954). A scholarly study of the cooperative movement is G. D. H. Cole, *A Century of Co-operation* (1944). W. H. Dawson, *Social Insurance in Germany, 1883–1911* (1912) is a sound treatment of that significant subject.

Marxism. A good survey of the history of socialism in general is **N. I. Mackenzie, *Socialism: A Short History* (Harper Torchbook). An excellent brief biography of Karl Marx is **Isaiah Berlin, *Karl Marx: His Life and Environment* (Galaxy). A good brief history of Marxism is **A. G. Meyer, *Marxism Since the Communist Manifesto* (Macmillan). **Sidney Hook, *Marx and the Marxists* (Van Nostrand) shows the divergencies in Marxism as it spread. The volume also includes some interesting basic Marxist documents. **J. Barzun, *Darwin, Marx, Wagner* (Anchor) is a lively study of the similarities among these seemingly divergent thinkers.

Sources. **Karl Marx and Friedrich Engels, *Communist Manifesto* (Gateway) is the original statement of the essence of Marxist philosophy. It should be read by every student. **Marx and Engels, *Basic Writings on Politics and Philosophy* (Anchor) contains well-chosen excerpts from the writings of the fathers of what we today call communism. A fascinating and widely read work by a late nineteenth-century American socialistic thinker is **Edward Bellamy, *Looking Backward 2000–1887* (Modern Library).

Chapter 50 🦢 Malignant Nationalism: Militarism

Between 1871 and 1914 much of the enthusiasm and energy of the masses was channeled into the rapidly swelling stream of national patriotic fervor. From its birth during the French Revolution until 1871, mass nationalism had been for the most part relatively mild, constructive, and often defensive. It was usually associated with liberalism and concerned with the achievement of national freedom and unity. After 1871, it became more aggressive and militaristic. Politicians and journalists used it to manipulate public opinion. Generals used it to invigorate their armies. It became in its totality (including militarism, wars, and imperialism) the world's biggest business. Although the new nationalism was a strong and important force in Great Britain, France, and the United States during the second phase of the Industrial Revolution, it was somewhat overshadowed in those countries by the growth of political and economic democracy. In Germany, Russia, and Southeastern Europe, just the reverse was true. There progress toward liberalization and democratization was overshadowed by militaristic nationalism.

1. GENERAL NATURE OF THE NEW NATIONALISM

The chief model and inspiration for the new nationalism was Bismarck's Prussia. At a time when the whole Western world seemed to be moving toward liberalism and democracy, Bismarck had crushed liberal opposition at home. He had also defeated Austria, which had long overshadowed Prussia in the Germanies, and then France, long the foremost military power on the continent of Europe and a nation with a liberal tradition. The autocratic, militaristic German Empire which he welded together was the world's most powerful and seemingly most efficient nation. The Prussian exploits appeared to bear out the evolutionary teachings of Darwin and Spencer with respect to the survival of the fittest. Most of the Prussian liberals who had first opposed Bismarck now repented and sought and received forgiveness. The rest of the world was dazzled and awed by the Prussianized German Empire. Philosophers began to develop new theories to fit the new facts.

Probably the two most influential thinkers in the development of the new nationalistic concepts were Georg Wilhelm Hegel (1770–1831) and Friedrich Nietzsche (1844–1900). We have already seen (see p. 737) how Hegel influenced the Prussian school of historians and the formation of the German Empire through his belief that individual freedom depends upon ordered discipline under a strong state and that the *Zeitgeist* (spirit of the time) of the nineteenth century was the spirit of German civilization. However, Hegel,

While Germany was powerful on land, it was the British navy that ruled the seas. Britain's sea power enabled her to control an empire that included one-fourth of all the world's territory and population. Here the fleet is shown on patrol. *Photo: The Bettmann Archive* a disciple of Kant, considered himself a liberal and an idealist and undoubtedly would have disapproved of the excesses to which later German nationalists went in his name. Nietzsche, on the other hand, though neither a nationalist nor a racist, had no use for liberalism and exerted an even more powerful influence upon German nationalists. Nietzsche frankly discarded all liberalism and idealism and considered the Christian religion fit only for slaves. He preached naked force, unbridled self-assertive egotism, the will to power, and the doctrine of the superman. This philosophy was declared to be realism, and its application in statecraft, realpolitik. Most German historians after 1871 shifted from Hegel's moderation to Nietzsche's extremism. Heinrich von Treitschke, the most influential German historian of the time, proclaimed that Germany's victory over France demonstrated the superiority of military autocracy over liberalism. Only strong states ought to exist. Dissident minorities, individualism, and parliamentary inefficiency must not be tolerated.

The new nationalism was by no means limited to Germany. The French historian Hippolyte Taine blamed France's defeat in 1870–1871 on the corrupting influence of liberalism born in the French Revolution and bred during the nineteenth century. He would take France back to the days of the old regime. In Great Britain, Thomas Carlyle in thunderous prose exalted heroes and hero worship, specifically the Prussian variety. Rudyard Kipling, in rhyme if not poetry, sang of the glorious British Empire and the "white man's burden" of ruling and civilizing backward peoples. Slavophilism, the cult of the superiority of Slavic culture and Slavic peoples, became popular in Russia. In the United States the new nationalism was symbolized by rough-riding Teddy Roosevelt and his "big stick" diplomacy. Roosevelt was an admirer of the virile German Empire.

The most extreme feature of the new militant nationalism was racism. People of every nation began to think and talk of themselves as a distinct and superior breed. Language was more than ever confused with race. Thus one spoke of the various "races" in the Austro-Hungarian Empire. By far the most popular and serious of all the racial cults was the Aryan myth. The term *Aryan*, which was originally a linguistic term referring to the ancient Persians (Iranians) and later to all peoples speaking Indo-European languages, was now applied to the Germanic- or Teutonic-speaking peoples or to the Nordic (tall blond) type of Northern European. After Germany's spectacular military triumphs and economic developments under Bismarck, the term *Aryan* came to be applied more specifically to Germans and to the energetic, aggressive, military qualities they were supposed to possess. Oddly, the two chief formulators of the Aryan myth were a Frenchman, Comte de Gobineau, and the renegade Englishman Houston Stewart Chamberlain, who deserted his homeland and became a German citizen. Their ideas, however, were taken much more seriously in Germany than in France or Great Britain. Richard Wagner became a leading racist, repenting of his earlier liberalism to write violent propaganda tracts and to compose grandiose operas stridently extolling the virtues of the early Nordic (German) supermen—Siegfried and the Nibelungs.

The chief immediate victims of the new nationalism were various linguistic minority groups, particularly in Germany, Russia, and Hungary, who were subjected to heavy pressure to give up their native languages and become good Germans, Russians, or Hungarians. The Jews, though not a linguistic group, were also hard hit. In Germany an anti-Semitic party founded in 1887 polled 285,000 votes eleven years later. In Russia during the 1880s the Jews were subjected to such persecutions, including bloody pogroms, that more than a quarter million of them fled, mostly to the United States, in spite of strenuous efforts to prevent their leaving. Another bitter and dangerous fruit of the new nationalism was a series of "pan" movements, particularly pan-Germanism and pan-Slavism. These were moves to bring all German-speaking people under the German flag and all Slavic-speaking people under the Russian flag. If implemented, these programs were certain to lead to wars on a continental if not global scale. In fact, militarism was one of the cardinal features of the new nationalism. After 1871, every nation in Europe except Great Britain undertook to copy the German military system, including universal conscription. Great Britain poured a proportionate amount of faith, effort, and money into her navy. Generals and admirals became ever more popular and influential, and Europe became an armed camp.

2. THE GERMAN EMPIRE UNDER BISMARCK AND KAISER WILHELM II

The center of this new and militant type of nationalism and in many ways its cause was the German Empire. The blood-and-iron method by which it was created by Bismarck and the Prussian military, its autocratic constitution, and its strong-handed leadership, first by the Iron Chancellor and then by Kaiser Wilhelm II, guaranteed that the German Empire would be an enlarged Prussia—a military autocracy. The German Empire possessed the world's most powerful army; a large, energetic, and disciplined population; a rapidly growing industrial machine; and a fervent and restless national spirit. At first it excited the awe and envy, but eventually the fear and hatred, of much of the rest of the world. Bismarck ruled over his creation as chancellor for almost twenty years.

His first concern after the defeat of France and the declaration of the empire in 1870–1871 was to complete the consolidation and the nationalization of the German states and people. The law codes, the currencies, and the military forces of the twenty-five lesser states were brought into conformity with those of Prussia. Banking and railroads were brought under the control of the national government. The empire's spawning industry was protected against British competition by a high tariff. The French in Alsace-Lorraine, the Danes in Schleswig, and the more than 3 million Poles in the eastern districts were subjected to severe pressure to give up their language and traditions and to become good Germans. However, Bismarck learned that loyalty was one thing that could not be achieved by force.

Two groups in Germany excited Bismarck's suspicion and wrath: the Roman Catholics (the Black International) and the Socialists (the Red International). Any German who had a foreign loyalty was intolerable to the imperious Junker. From 1872 to 1878, Bismarck waged an unrelenting campaign against the Roman Catholics which he termed the *Kulturkampf* (battle for civilization). The Jesuits were expelled, civil marriage was made compulsory, and all education, including that of Roman Catholic priests, was brought under state control and largely secularized. When the Roman Catholic clergy and most of the laity, which constituted approximately one-third of the total German population, resisted and rallied to the pope, hundreds of priests and six bishops were arrested. However, it was all to no avail. The Roman Catholic Center party in the Reichstag became stronger, and by 1878 Bismarck needed its support for what he considered to be a struggle of greater importance—that against the Socialists. In 1878 upon the accession of a more conciliatory pope, Leo XIII, Bismarck "went to Canossa" and had the most severe of the anti-Catholic legislation repealed.

In the same year he began a twelve-year crusade against the internationally minded Socialists. He outlawed their publications, their organizations, and their meetings, and set the brutal German police force upon them. But he only drove them underground. Throughout the decade of the 1880s, Bismarck sought to undercut the Socialists' appeal to the workingman by setting up a comprehensive system of social insurance. Accident, sickness, and old-age insurance was provided for the industrial proletariat, the funds being raised by compulsory contributions from the

Most awesome of the military powers in the years between 1871 and 1914 was the German Empire, whose armies nearly conquered Europe in World War I. Here Kaiser Wilhelm II (center) confers with Generals von Hindenburg and von Ludendorff (left and right).
Photo: The Bettmann Archive

workers, the employers, and the state. These laws antedated similar legislation in Great Britain and France by twenty years. Although Bismarck's motives were not benevolent or humanitarian and the payments were mere pittances, his measures represented a momentous new departure in the history of labor relations. Nevertheless, the Socialists were not appeased, and Bismarck continued to fight them as long as he remained chancellor.

Bismarck's foreign policy after 1871 was one of security and retrenchment. He knew that France would be unforgiving and revengeful, forever seeking an opportunity to regain Alsace and Lorraine. Of France alone he had little fear, but France in league with other powers, particularly Russia and Great Britain, would be formidable. Therefore, his consistent policy was to maintain a close military alliance with Austria-Hungary and cordial relations with Russia and Great Britain. He

carefully nurtured British friendship by refraining from naval and imperial rivalry. It is true that Bismarck eventually yielded to the German expansionists and annexed some large chunks of worthless territory in Africa and some islands in the Southwest Pacific, but Britain apparently did not want them. In 1873 Bismarck formed the Three Emperors' League among Germany, Austria-Hungary, and Russia. When the interests of Austria-Hungary and Russia proved to be incompatible, this league was replaced in 1879–1882 by the Triple Alliance among Germany, Austria-Hungary, and Italy. A separate "reinsurance treaty" of friendship and neutrality was made with Russia. Of course Bismarck did not depend wholly upon diplomacy. Throughout this period, the German military machine was made ever more powerful.

Bismarck's policies provided security for Germany, but only insecurity for France and later other nations. As the industry and wealth of the German Empire came to match and complement the strength of her army, the rest of the world became increasingly uneasy. To make matters worse, the imperious chancellor bullied France and manufactured war scares whenever the military budget was being voted on by the Reichstag. The bitter fruit from these seeds would be harvested later.

Kaiser Wilhelm I died in 1888 in his ninety-first year. After the ninety-nine-day reign of his son, Frederick III, his grandson, Wilhelm II, became Kaiser. Wilhelm II (1888–1918) was twenty-nine years of age when he ascended the throne of the most powerful nation in the world. He had been brought up in the army, which was his first love. Egotistical and bombastic by nature, he disliked both his father and his mother, the daughter of Queen Victoria. It may be that a withered left arm gave him a sense of inferiority for which he was attempting to compensate. He was a dabbler in theology, history, and the arts, and gave advice and instructions freely to the leading figures in those fields. He was also an eloquent and willing speaker. Soon after ascending the throne he announced, "Everyone who is against me, I shall crush!" In a speech to some young inductees into the army he stated, "In the presence of the socialist agitation it may happen—though God forfend—that I shall order you to shoot down your relations, brothers, yes even parents—but you must obey my commands without murmuring." Nevertheless, Wilhelm II possessed considerable charm and had his generous and humanitarian moments.

The young Kaiser's personality and policies soon clashed with those of Bismarck. In 1890, just two years after he became emperor, Wilhelm II accepted Bismarck's reluctant resignation as chancellor. The immediate cause of the break was a disagreement over the control of the ministry and the repeal of the anti-Socialist laws, which Bismarck wished to be continued. The real reason, however, was that there was simply not room enough in Germany for two such prima donnas.

Bismarck's foreign policy was quickly reversed. The reinsurance treaty with Russia was immediately allowed to lapse, as the Kaiser assumed a keen interest in extending German hegemony over the Balkans and the Ottoman Empire, areas the Russians considered to be vital to their own interests and ambitions. In 1894 Russia formed an alliance with France, the very thing that Bismarck had worked so hard to prevent. Wilhelm II also soon alienated Great Britain. His extension of German influence in the Near East, particularly his Berlin-to-Bagdad railroad project (see pp. 792–793), threatened an area in which Great Britain had many vital interests and through which ran her "life line" to India and the Far East. In China, too, German interests began to rival those of the British.

It was the Kaiser's naval policy, however, that alarmed the British the most. Wilhelm was an ardent and lifelong navalist. "The waves beat powerfully at our national gates," he cried, "and call us as a great nation to maintain our place in the world. . . ." Germany's "place in the sun" was a favorite phrase of the Hohenzollern emperor. In 1897 Admiral von Tirpitz was made minister of marine. His purpose was to create a German navy equivalent to the army built by Roon and Moltke a generation earlier. He projected, and the Reichstag voted, an enormous naval building program that was steadily increased until in 1908 it called for twenty-eight new battleships of the biggest and latest design. The purpose of this program, which was freely and officially admitted, was to give Germany a battle fleet so great that "a war against the mightiest naval power would endanger the supremacy of that power."

Great Britain, whose food supply as well as her empire depended upon naval supremacy, took utmost alarm. Failing in her efforts to reach an understanding with the Kaiser's government, she launched a huge and costly naval building program of her own. In 1904 she joined France, and in 1907 Russia, in the Triple Entente, which was in reality a defensive military alliance. The interests and policies of Great Britain, France, and Russia had long been so discordant that nothing less than maximum alarm could have brought them together. Thus in seventeen years Wilhelm had undone Bismarck's work and brought about the "encirclement" of the Fatherland by three of the world's greatest powers.

Germany's economic exploits under Bismarck and Wilhelm were no less phenomenal than those in the military realm. In 1871 Great Britain was the world's leading power in manufacturing and commerce; Germany counted for little in either. By 1914 Germany was a clear second to Great Britain in industry and commerce; in many areas, such as the production of steel and machinery, she had far outstripped her. In the up-and-coming chemical and electrical industries and in scientific agriculture and forestry, Germany was far in advance of all other nations. She was also first in the application of science to industry and in industrial and scientific research. By 1914 her merchant marine had captured the lion's share of the lucrative transatlantic passenger traffic. The Hamburg-American and the North German Lloyd lines (in which the Hohenzollerns were said to be heavy investors) were the biggest steamship companies in the world.

At a time when other industrial nations, particularly the United States, were beginning to restrict the giant monopolistic trusts, the German imperial government was encouraging and subsidizing its cartels in order that they might compete more effectively with foreign companies. More and more of the world's market was captured by German business. "Made in Germany" became a familiar mark from the Andean plateau to the Congo jungles. Germany's population, keeping pace with her economy, increased from 41 million in 1871 to 65 million in 1914. Meanwhile, her heavy emigration (which had reached a peak in the 1880s of some 250,000 a year, most of it to the United States) dwindled to a mere trickle. In 1914 the number of German emigrants was less than the number of workers coming into Germany from neighboring countries. Only the United States was keeping pace with Germany in overall economic advancement.

The industrialization of Germany, although accompanied by the growth of a large and prosperous bourgeoisie and a numerous proletariat, did not produce a tide of liberalism as it did in the other Western industrialized nations. The capitalistic classes, imbued with militaristic nationalism after 1866, allied themselves with the autocratic government. Only the Social Democratic party (workingmen) and the small and weak Progressive party (intellectuals, professionals, and small businessmen) advocated responsible democratic government. But even the Social Democratic party, by 1914 the largest party in the empire, was inundated by the flood of militant nationalism that welled up during the international crises that preceded World War I.

Germany's spectacular achievements between 1871 and 1914 excited the awe and admiration of the rest of the world. However, her continuingly autocratic government in a world where democratic liberalism was on the march, her overweening military power and rapidly growing naval strength, her venture into imperialism, her inordinate nationalism, and her irresponsible, egotistical monarch aroused increasing fear and resentment abroad. Germany's militarism and aggressive nationalism had the effect of intensifying the same forces in the other great powers of Europe.

3. RUSSIA UNDER ALEXANDER III AND NICHOLAS II

Another great power whose malignant nationalism helped to strangle liberalism during the second phase of the Industrial Revolution was the empire of the Russian tsars. A strong wave of dissatisfaction arose during the later years of the long rule of Alexander II (1855–1881). The ex-serfs had been cruelly disappointed by the fruits of emancipation (decreed in 1861). In many ways, their economic condition was worse than before. Another revolt of Russia's Polish subjects in 1863 made Alexander II more reactionary. His failure to follow through with more sweeping reforms after the emancipation of the serfs disappointed the liberals, who were mostly intellectual young aristocrats. In despair over the possibility of reforming the huge, semi-Oriental Russian Empire by orderly methods, these young intellectuals became radical and negativist. They set out to destroy Russia's society, government, and church in order to build a new and modern Russia from the ruins. They called their movement *nihilism* (nothingness). When their efforts were spurned by the illiterate masses whom they were seeking to uplift, a more violent wing of the Nihilists turned to terror and assassination to achieve their ends. Numerous bureaucrats and police officials were slain by terrorists, and Tsar Alexander II himself was killed by a Nihilist bomb just as he was preparing to liberalize the government.

The new tsar, Alexander III (1881–1894), was a harsh, reactionary autocrat. Blaming his father's death on softness, he set out to exterminate all liberalism in Russia. The ruthless Plehve was made head of the secret police, whose agents were soon everywhere. Thousands of liberal suspects were arrested. Some were shot or exiled to Siberia. In his sweeping reactionary program of Russianization, Alexander III relied heavily upon his former tutor Pobedonostsev, whom he made procurator-general of the Holy Synod. As an antidote to Western liberalism, Pobedonostsev invoked the most extreme form of Russian nationalism, Slavophilism (love of Slavic culture). According to this cult, the Slavic "races" had a culture of their own, which was different from and superior to that of the West. The salient features of this culture were autocratic government under an omnipotent tsar, a feudalistic agrarian society, and the Orthodox Church. Since Russia was the greatest Slavic power, it was her mission to keep the culture pure and to serve as a model for the lesser Slavic nations and peoples. The censored press, the closely supervised schools,

and, above all, the clergy of the Orthodox Church became potent agencies for the propagation of the cult. The great novelist Feodor Dostoevski had been an important proponent of this Russian counterpart to Germany's Aryan myth. Non-Orthodox religions were persecuted. Language minority groups—the Poles, the Baltic peoples, the Finns, and even the Ukrainians—were forced to use the Russian language. We have already observed the treatment of the Jews, for whom the harshest persecution was reserved. Associated with Slavophilism was pan-Slavism, the belief that all the other Slavic-speaking groups (Poles, Czechs, Slovaks, Ruthenians, Serbs, Croats, Slovenes, and Bulgarians) should be brought either under direct Russian control or into federation with Russia. This would result in the dismemberment of the German, Austro-Hungarian, and Ottoman empires, all of which contained Slavic minority groups.

Alexander III was succeeded by Nicholas II (1894–1917), a well-meaning but weak man who was strongly influenced by his neurotic German wife and eventually by the mystic charlatan monk Rasputin. Although Nicholas attempted to continue the policies of his father, he was unable to make them work. During the decade of the 1890s, the Industrial Revolution finally reached Russia, and an industrial bourgeoisie and proletariat emerged. Liberalism and radicalism reappeared among these new classes, and now there was no strong-handed Alexander III to check them. Of the various liberal and radical parties that emerged, the one of greatest significance for the future was the Social Democratic party. This was a Marxist party whose leadership was made up almost entirely of intellectual radicals. Their chief concern was for the industrial proletariat. In 1903 the Social Democrats split into a moderate, gradualist wing called the Mensheviks (minority) and a violent revolutionary wing called the Bolsheviks (majority). The Bolsheviks were led by the brilliant and dynamic Nikolai Lenin, who was living in exile in Switzerland.

Taking advantage of the embarrassment of

the tsar's government because of Russia's defeat by Japan in 1904–1905 (see p. 791), the various liberal and radical groups clamored for reform. In July 1904 the hated Plehve was assassinated. In January 1905, some fifteen hundred peaceful demonstrators were shot down in front of the royal palace in St. Petersburg by the tsar's guard. This bloody event, known as Red Sunday, fanned the flames of discontent. In October 1905, a general strike, in which the Menshevik Leon Trotsky played a prominent role, completely paralyzed the country for ten days. Nicholas II, yielding at last, issued a manifesto that promised civil liberties and a popularly elected Duma. However, before the Duma could be elected, the return of the Russian troops from the Far East and a huge loan from Russia's ally, France, strengthened the hand of the tsar. During the next two years he and his advisers succeeded in reducing the Duma to an undemocratically elected body that had no real control over the government. Nevertheless, a break had been made in Russia's autocratic system, and it appeared that the voice of the people was beginning to be heard.

However, as in Germany between 1905 and 1914, a series of international crisis engulfed the rising liberalism in a torrent of nationalism, militarism, and war. The eventual winners in Russia were not the liberals but the hardy Bolsheviks.

4. NATIONAL MOVEMENTS IN SOUTHEAST EUROPE

While nationalism between 1871 and 1914 was crushing minority language groups in the German and the Russian empires, it was pulling the Austrian and the Ottoman empires apart along language lines. After Austria's defeat by Prussia in 1866, the dominant German minority in Austria felt obliged to take into partnership the aggressive and restless Magyars of Hungary. The *Ausgleich* (compromise) of 1867 set up the Dual Monarchy of Austria-Hungary. Each country had its own separate parliament. But the two were united under a common ruler, the head of the house of Hapsburg; common ministries of war, finance, and foreign affairs; and joint delegations from the two parliaments whose duty was to coordinate policies wherever possible. This arrangement was essentially an alliance between the Germans of Austria and the Magyars of Hungary against the Slavic, Rumanian, and Italian language groups, which constituted a majority of the total population of the Dual Monarchy. In effect, the Germans said to the Magyars: "You take care of your minorities [mostly Slavs] and we will take care of ours."

Austria followed a relatively moderate policy in dealing with her subject language groups. Cultural autonomy was granted, and the suffrage was gradually extended until in 1907 all adult males were given the vote. However, the subject peoples were more interested in nationalism than in democracy. The various language groups resurrected traditions of a glorious cultural and political past —much of it pure fantasy. The prosperous Czechs of Bohemia were especially adamant. The problem was confounded by the fact that many of the language groups had kinsmen outside the Dual Monarchy whom they wished to join and who deliberately stirred up their disloyalty. Such groups were the Italians, the Poles, the Ruthenians (Ukrainians), the Serbs, and the Rumanians. Parliamentary sessions in Austria frequently degenerated into screaming, inkstand-throwing melees among the various language groups.

Hungary made no pretense of conciliation. The Magyar aristocracy ruled over their Slovak, Rumanian, Serb, and Croat minorities with an iron hand and refused participation in the government to their own Magyar masses. The nationalist discontent in Hungary was even greater than it was in Austria; the Croats and Serbs, desirous of joining their independent Serb kinsmen in the formation of a Yugo (southern) Slav state, were particularly troublesome. When explosive nationalism finally blew Austria-Hungary apart in 1914–1918, much of the world was drawn into the conflict.

The Balkan portion of the Ottoman Empire

between 1871 and 1914 was a hornets' nest of militant nationalism. The hatred of the Christian Balkan language groups for their Muslim Turkish masters was equaled only by their hatred for each other. The once-potent Ottoman Empire crumbled throughout the course of the nineteenth century, and one Balkan language group after another, now aflame with national pride and ambition, emerged as an independent nation. Meanwhile, all the great powers of Europe became involved in the strategic and troubled area of the Near East. Russia, Austria-Hungary, Great Britain, France, Germany, and Italy had important imperial, economic, and military interests in the Balkans. In addition, Russia and Austria-Hungary had serious nationalistic interests there. Russia considered herself as the big brother and protector of the Slavic-speaking Serbs and Bulgarians. Austria-Hungary's large Rumanian and Yugoslav populations desired union with their free kinsmen in Rumania and Serbia. Between 1829 and 1913 first the Greeks, then the Serbs, Rumanians, and Bulgarians, and finally the Albanians gained their independence from the Ottoman Empire. In each case a major crisis occurred among the great powers. These Balkan crises became progressively more severe and finally culminated in World War I (see Chapters 51 and 54).

5. THE NEW NATIONALISM IN GREAT BRITAIN, FRANCE, AND THE UNITED STATES

Malignant nationalism appears to beget malignant nationalism. Great Britain, long the unchallenged mistress of the seas and of the world's commerce and markets, did not relish the appearance of a dangerous rival. In the face of Germany's swift rise to power and prestige, the British took renewed pride in their dominant navy and in their empire, which contained one-fourth of all the earth's territory and people. Many well-to-do Britishers thought themselves to be so superior to the other peoples of Europe that they became the most unpopular of all travelers on the Continent. To some observers, it appeared that Great Britain was as big a bully on the seas and overseas as Germany was on the continent of Europe.

French pride was only intensified by France's defeat at the hands of Germany in 1870–1871. The statue dedicated to the city of Strasbourg in the Place de la Concorde in Paris was draped in perpetual mourning as a constant reminder of the day of revenge. France greatly speeded up her overseas empire building and increased the size of her armed forces until they were larger in proportion to her population than those of the German Empire. She sought and found military allies. When a general strike in 1910 threatened the nation's military security and war preparations, Aristide Briand, himself a radical and former Socialist, did not hesitate to use the armed forces to break it up.

The United States was the slowest of the great powers to catch the new spirit. She had an ocean between herself and the militant nationalism of Europe, and she was still busy exploiting the richest of the continents and absorbing and Americanizing the millions of European immigrants pouring through her gates. Nevertheless, Theodore Roosevelt's "big stick" policy in dealing with the little neighbors to the south, particularly his seizing Panama from a friendly neighbor and afterward boasting of it, smacked of the power politics of Europe. The European powers could see no justification for the claims of the United States to sovereignty over the whole Western Hemisphere. In Latin America, the big Yankee to the north was the most unpopular nation in the world.

When the first shots of World War I sounded in 1914, all groups, including the internationalist socialists (except for a mere handful), rallied to the flags and trumpets of their respective nations. Many promising liberal and democratic movements came to an end, some of them permanently. Aggressive nationalism proved to be a stronger force during the second phase of the Industrial Revolution than liberalism or democracy.

Suggested Reading

General. A. J. P. Taylor, *The Struggle for Mastery in Europe, 1848–1918* (1954) is a spirited account of the new nationalism at work. Barbara Tuchman, *The Proud Tower* (1966) is a brilliant study of the belligerently nationalistic ruling classes in Great Britain, France, Germany, and the United States on the eve of World War I.

General Nature of the New Nationalism. Carlton J. H. Hayes, *Essays on Nationalism* (1926) is an excellent survey by the leading authority on the subject. A scholarly study by another leading authority is H. Kohn, *The Idea of Nationalism: A Study in Its Origin and Background* (1944). J. Barzun, *Race, a Study in Modern Superstition* (1937) is a thoughtful examination of the most extreme aspect of nationalism.

The German Empire. The most up-to-date treatment of the German Empire by a first-rate scholar is Hajo Holborn, *A History of Modern Germany*, vol. III, 1840–1945 (1969). Also scholarly and detailed is W. H. Dawson, *The German Empire, 1867–1914* (2 vols., 1919). Two briefer and more lively accounts are L. L. Snyder, *From Bismarck to Hitler: The Background of Modern German Nationalism* (1935); and **A. J. P. Taylor, *The Course of German History: A Survey of the Development of Germany Since 1815* (Capricorn). Good biographies of the two leading figures in the German Empire are **Erich Eyck, *Bismarck and the German Empire* (Norton); and S. C. Hammer, *William the Second* (1917).

Russia Under Alexander III and Nicholas II. The best general history of Russia in English is M. Florinsky, *Russia: A History and an Interpretation* (2 vols., 1953). Briefer but also excellent is Sidney Harcave, *Russia: A History* (6th ed., 1969). Two additional brief accounts of Russian history during the years 1871–1914 by leading experts are **M. M. Karpovich, *Imperial Russia, 1801–1917* (Berkshire); and **H. Seton-Watson, *The Decline of Imperial Russia, 1855–1914* (Praeger). The

Pan-Slavic movement is expertly examined by H. Kohn, *Pan-Slavism: Its History and Ideology* (1953).

Southeast Europe. A lively account of the multilingual Hapsburg empire is **A. J. P. Taylor, *The Hapsburg Monarchy, 1809–1918: A History of the Austrian Empire and Austria-Hungary* (rev. ed., Harper Torchbook). More detailed is the scholarly study by R. A. Kann, *The Multinational Empire: Nationalism and National Reform in the Hapsburg Monarchy, 1848–1918* (2 vols., 1950). **Oscar Jászi, *The Dissolution of the Hapsburg Monarchy* (Phoenix) is the story of the tearing apart of the Austro-Hungarian Empire by the various national language groups. Two scholarly studies of seething nationalism in the Balkan Peninsula before World War I are H. Kohn, *Nationalism and Imperialism in the Hither East* (1932); and W. Miller, *The Ottoman Empire and Its Successors, 1801–1927* (4th ed., 1926).

The New Nationalism in Great Britain, France, and the United States. **Carlton J. H. Hayes, *A Generation of Materialism, 1871–1900* (Harper Torchbook) has excellent chapters which show that malignant nationalism before World War I was not limited to Germany and Russia. American nationalism and militarism before World War I are examined by **Walter Millis, *The Martial Spirit* (Compass Books); and Harold Sprout and Margaret Sprout, *The Rise of American Naval Power, 1776–1919* (1939).

Sources. Bismarck's memoirs published under the title *Bismarck, the Man and the Statesman* (2 vols., 1898), though somewhat disappointing, constitute an important source for the history of the first two decades of the German Empire. Wilhelm II, *My Memoirs, 1878–1919*, trans. T. R. Ybarra (1922) are another important source. W. B. Walsh, *Readings in Russian History* (1948) contains both primary and secondary sources.

Chapter 51 ⁂ European Imperialism in Asia and Africa

Imperialism went hand in hand with the new aggressive type of nationalism. During the second phase of the Industrial Revolution, European power and influence were extended to those portions of the globe which had not previously been affected: the Near, Middle, and Far East, the remaining coastal regions and the whole vast interior of Africa. Europeans even staked out claims over the frozen wastes of Antarctica. This new wave of imperialism was accompanied by increasingly severe friction between the European imperialists and the "native" peoples, and bitter rivalry among the European imperial powers themselves.

1. A NEW BURST OF EUROPEAN EXPANSION

We have already seen that from the fifteenth to the eighteenth centuries, the national monarchies of Europe "discovered" and conquered most of the Western Hemisphere, the west coast of Africa, and Southern Asia. Then from 1763 until 1871 there came a lull in expansion; Europe was busy with revolution and counterrevolution, industrialization, and nation building. The period 1871–1914, however, witnessed a new burst of European expansion that brought practically all the remaining portions of the earth's surface under European influence or domination.

One of the chief impulses behind the new thrust was undoubtedly economic. The rapid expansion of industry in Europe and the United States created a demand for greater markets, new sources for raw materials, and investment outlets for surplus capital. Until Henry Ford demonstrated in the 1920s that low prices and high wages would develop an almost limitless home market, it was generally assumed that the exploitation of home and foreign markets by high prices and low wages was the only way in which industry could succeed. This idea resulted in the acquisition of more and more technologically backward areas by the industrial powers. Furthermore, science and technology gave the industrialized nations such a military advantage that the conquest and control of the nonindustrialized areas was relatively easy.

Probably an even greater impulse to the new imperialism was the new nationalism. Much of the territory seized by the great powers between 1871 and 1914 had no economic value whatever; some, in fact, was an economic liability. However, it flattered the national ego to see its colors spread over the map. It also provided military and naval bases and manpower for the hungry military machines that were an integral part of militant nationalism. In Europe the conservative parties based upon the landed aristocracy were even more imperialistic than the liberal parties based upon industrial and commercial interests. Many of the imperial governors, generals, and admirals came from the conservative aristocracy. National egotism also gave the citizens of the great Western powers a sense of mission; they were bringing the blessings of civilization to backward peoples. Rudyard Kipling expressed the genuine belief of many Westerners when he sang in rhyme of the "white man's burden" to hold in tutelage and to civilize the "lesser breeds" of the earth. The heady wine of nationalism gave the Westerners during the second phase of the Industrial Revolution the same advantage over the Asians and Africans that the French Revolutionists and Napoleon had enjoyed over the rest of continental Europe. It was an advantage that would not last.

Another motivating factor in the new imperialism was the evangelizing zeal of the Christian religion. Christianity has always followed its founder's command, "Go ye into all the world and preach the gospel to every creature," and it has been the most aggressive of all religions. At the very time that it was wavering under attack in its homelands in the West, it was carrying on foreign missionary activity of unprecedented scope and intensity. And it was gaining millions of converts in Asia and Africa. Much of the work of the Christian missionaries was undone by their association in the minds of the natives with economic and nationalistic imperialistic exploiters; but how much it is impossible to say.

2. THE EXPLOITATION AND AWAKENING OF CHINA

One of the most important scenes of European imperialism during the second phase of the Industrial Revolution was China. This huge and populous country was the seat of the oldest continuous civilization in the world. For some five thousand years China had been a vast melting pot, absorbing invading peoples and cultures and welding them into a tough but resilient civilization. The military conquerors were always themselves swallowed up or conquered by Chinese culture. By far the greatest influence in molding Chinese civilization was Confucianism. Confucius lived five hundred years before Christ. He was reared in poverty, the son of a youthful mother and an aged father. A prodigy both in scholarship and personality, he attracted a body of devoted disciples who wrote down his sayings. Although he himself never held high political office, he was revered as a learned man and

ARCTIC OCEAN

ALASKA
(Purchased by U.S.A.
from Russia, 1867)

ALEUTIAN I. (U.S.A., 1867)

BERING SEA

KAMCHATKA

SEA OF
OKHOTSK

Lena R.

Yakutsk

SAKHALIN

KURILE I.
(Japan, 1875)

KARAFUTO
(Japan, 1905)

S I B E R I A

AMUR PROVINCE
1858

Yenisei R.

Ob R.

AN   EMPIRE

Tobolsk

Omsk   Tomsk

TRANS-SIBERIAN RAILROAD

L. Baikal
Irkutsk

Chita

Amur R.

MANCHURIA

Khabarovsk

MARITIME
PROVINCE
(Russia, 1868)

Vladivostok
1860

SEA OF
JAPAN

JAPANESE EMPIRE

Tokyo

UROPE

ASIA

Urga

Harbin

OUTER MONGOLIA
(Autonomous, 1912   Russian Sphere)

INNER MONGOLIA

Mukden

JEHOL

KOREA
(Japan, 1905, 1910)

PACIFIC OCEAN

L. Balkhash

73

1854

1864   Tashkent   1860-65

4

BOKHARA   1876
1868

5   1895

SINKIANG

Kashgar

Peking

Tientsin

Huang Ho

Port Arthur
(Japan, 1905)

Kiao-chow
(Germany, 1898)

Nanking

Shanghai
(Britain, 1842)

Ningpo
1842

EAST
CHINA
SEA

RYUKYU I.

Kabul

GHAN-
TAN

CHISTAN
1883

chi

KASHMIR
1846

PUNJAB

Delhi

C H I N A

Hankow

Chungking

Yangtse R.

Foochow

Amoy

Canton
(Britain, 1842)

FORMOSA (Japan, 1895)

PESCADORES (Japan, 1895)

MARIANA I.
(Germany, 1899)

GUAM
(U.S.A., 1898)

Indus R.

T I B E T

HIMALAYAS

Lhasa

NEPAL

BHUTAN

Ganges R.

Brahmaputra R.

YÜNNAN

KWANGSI
(French Sphere)

Hong Kong (Britain, 1842)

Maçao (Portugal, 1557)

Kwang-chow
(Lease to France, 1898)

Diu
(Portugal)

Bombay

Hyderabad

Goa
(Portugal)

Madras

Pondicherry
(France)

Karikal (France)

CEYLON

INDIA

Calcutta

BRITISH   INDIA

Yanaon
(France)

BAY OF BENGAL

ANDAMAN I.
(Britain)

BURMA
(Britain, 1852, 1885)

1852

Rangoon

1826

Hanoi

ANNAM

Mekong R.

HAINAN

SIAM

Bangkok

FRENCH
INDOCHINA
1884, 1907

Saigon

SOUTH
CHINA
SEA

Manila

PHILIPPINE I.
(U.S.A., 1898, 1899)

YAP

CAROLINE I.
(Germany, 1899)

PALAU I.

NEW GUINEA

KAISER WILHE
(Germany,

BRITISH
NORTH BORNEO
1888

SARAWAK
1888

BORNEO

CELEBES

MALAY STATES
(Britain, 1800, 1824)

Singapore
(Britain, 1819)

D U T C H   E A S T   I N D I E S

SUMATRA

(Portugal, 1859)

TIMOR   Darwin

INDIAN OCEAN

Batavia

JAVA

AUSTRALIA

was the teacher of many who did become officials in government.

The teachings of Confucius really belong to the realm of philosophy rather than religion. The flavor of his life and thought is much more closely akin to that of Socrates, who lived in Greece only a hundred years after Confucius, than to that of the mystic religious leaders such as Christ, Buddha, or Mohammed. Confucius was only vaguely concerned with the Deity, who, he assumed, governs the universe and is on the side of righteousness. On the other hand, he was very much concerned with and very optimistic about man and his ability through reason to build the good life here on earth. Wisdom, reason, patience, tolerance, and gentleness were the virtues taught by Confucius. These could be developed by the ruling classes and transmitted to the masses by example and persuasion. Confucius was history-minded and held in high esteem the lessons that can be learned from the experiences of the past. He also emphasized family loyalty and filial piety.

Needless to say, the practice of Confucianism, as in all religions, fell far short of the ideal. The use of force was never absent from Chinese government or society. Respect for the past and for family was corrupted into backward-looking ultraconservatism, and an elaborate ritual was built around ancestor worship. Nevertheless, the teachings of Confucius served as a standard that, like Christianity in the West, was at least tacitly accepted by the great majority. The scholar was exalted, not the soldier as in the West. In fact, in no other civilization has the scholar been so revered. For centuries, examinations for the civil service, which was the chief avenue for advancement, were based largely upon the Confucian classics. This guaranteed that the best minds and the ruling classes of China would be steeped in Confucianism.

Considering themselves superior to all other peoples, the Chinese gradually isolated themselves. A great wall (never completed) was constructed along the borders in an effort to retain the old and keep out the new. Although they admitted some European traders and Christian missionaries in the sixteenth and seventeenth centuries, they closed their doors rather tightly thereafter. As science, technology, and dynamic capitalism and nationalism developed in the West, China fell far behind in strength and energy. By the nineteenth century her medieval society, under the corrupt and declining Manchu dynasty, constituted a power vacuum that tempted exploitation by the West.

The first Europeans to force themselves upon the Chinese were the British. Going to war in 1839, when Chinese officials interfered with their sale of opium in China, the British, with their modern weapons, easily defeated the Chinese, who were still using medieval arms. By the terms of the Treaty of Nanking (1842), the Chinese ceded Hong Kong to the British, opened many of their ports to foreign trade free of restricting tariffs, and granted the foreigners extraterritorial rights, such as trial by their own courts, on Chinese soil. This was the first of a series of unequal treaties and the signal for all the great Western powers to rush into China and seize what they could. In the ensuing scramble it was the rivalry among the great powers themselves rather than Chinese resistance that saved China from complete loss of independence.

The British got the lion's share. In addition to Hong Kong and concessions in the Canton area of the southeast, they gained a virtual trading monopoly in the Yangtze Valley, which was the richest and most populous part of China. In the north they gained footholds in the capital city of Peking and its port city of Tientsin, in the Shantung Peninsula, and in Manchuria. They gained dominion over Tibet. In the 1880s they annexed Burma, which owed a tenuous allegiance to China. The French took Southeast China and the large Hainan Island as their sphere. In the 1880s they completed the detachment of Indo-China from Chinese sovereignty. The Russians took Manchuria as their sphere, annexed a large strip of China's northeast coast, including the port

American troops scale a wall in China during the Boxer Rebellion in 1899 in this contemporary photograph. The rebellion was quickly put down with troops from a number of countries interested in keeping China exploitable: Britain, France, Germany, Russia, Italy, Japan, and the United States. *Photo: Brown Brothers*

of Vladivostok, and became active in Korea. The Germans carved out for themselves much of the strategically located Shantung Peninsula and built a powerful naval base at Kiaochow. In 1894 the rejuvenated and modernized Japanese went to war with China. They easily defeated her and not only took away Formosa and Korea, but forced China to pay a huge indemnity. Even the United States got into the act. The United States had launched upon an imperialist program in the Far East in 1898 by seizing the Philippine Islands and Guam from Spain. Now, fearful for her growing trade with China, she attempted to gain a sphere of influence in Fukien Province and demanded an Open Door policy in China with equal trading opportunities for all. Little if

anything came of either of these projects, however.

Meanwhile, Chinese nationalism was being aroused by the Western and Japanese aggressions against the "Celestial Empire." The first overt reaction was the Taiping Rebellion of 1853 against the corrupt Manchu dynasty. The reforming rebels were finally put down eleven years later by Manchu armies, organized by an American military adventurer, Frederick Ward, and led by a British general, Charles (Chinese) Gordon. In 1899 a serious uprising against the foreign exploiters, known as the Boxer Rebellion, took place. Thousands of Chinese Christians and a number of foreigners were slain. This, too, was put down by the Chinese officials with the aid of British, French, German, Russian, Italian, Japanese, and American troops. The rebels were severely punished, and China was forced to pay the foreign governments a large indemnity.

Meanwhile, a more far-reaching revolutionary movement aimed not only at freeing China from foreign exploitation, but also at modernizing and democratizing her society and government was being organized by Dr. Sun Yat-sen (1866–1925). Sun Yat-sen, the son of a Chinese coolie, studied in a British mission school in Hawaii, became a Christian, and later graduated from the British medical school at Hong Kong. Eloquent and dynamic, he organized his followers into the Kuomintang party, which was committed to a three-point program: (1) national independence, (2) democratic government, (3) social justice. In 1911 the reformers launched a revolution against the Manchu dynasty, declared a republic, and elected Sun Yat-sen as provisional president. The revolution swept all southern China. The following year the Manchu officials in Peking, attempting to save themselves, set aside the six-year-old puppet emperor, declared a republic, and elected as provisional president an ambitious, self-seeking war lord, General Yuan. The foreign powers supported the Yuan government, and the idealistic Sun Yat-sen, in behalf of national unity, yielded to General Yuan. However, the two movements were incompatible, and the union lasted only nine years. When World War I opened a new era in 1914, China was torn with revolution and division—convulsions that would rock the world in the decades to follow. Western imperialism in China was soon to backfire with a vengeance.

3. THE EMERGENCE OF JAPAN

Japan's reaction to Western intrusion was quite different from that of China. The Japanese people inhabit four large islands and some three thousand small ones stretching along the eastern coast of Asia for a distance of about two thousand miles. Their culture had been greatly influenced by that of the Chinese mainland. However, Buddhism and emperor-worshipping Shintoism, rather than Confucianism, were the two chief religions. Like China, Japan had admitted the sixteenth- and seventeenth-century European traders and Christian missionaries, but had evicted them and closed her doors after observing what was happening everywhere in Asia where Europeans were admitted. At mid-nineteenth century, the Japanese were living in isolation. Their stage of technical knowledge and their feudal society ruled over by military chieftains were quite similar to those of Europe five hundred years earlier.

In 1853, eleven years after the Treaty of Nanking opened up China, an American navy commodore, Matthew C. Perry, steamed into Tokyo Bay and so overawed the Japanese that they opened their ports to shipwrecked American sailors and to American trade. The alert Japanese were much impressed by the technological superiority of the Americans. In 1868, just fifteen years later, a group of forward-looking young Japanese overthrew the existing government and began reorganizing the Japanese government and society along modern Western lines. Taking what they considered to be the best from the various Western nations, they patterned their business methods after those of the United States, their legal system after the French, and their navy after the British. However, it was Bismarck's Germany that impressed the Japanese the most. They built a military machine and an authoritarian government and education system on the model of the German Empire.

In an incredibly short time Japan became a modern, industrialized, military, and, on the surface at least, a Westernized power. In

A ship passes through the Suez Canal soon after its opening in 1869. By drastically shortening the sailing distance between Western Europe and the Far East, the canal made the Near and Middle East an area of supreme strategic importance. *Photo: Brown Brothers*

1894, as we have already observed, she attacked China, defeated her with ease, and forced her to pay a large indemnity and to give up Korea (which Japan annexed in 1910) and the island of Formosa. In 1902 Great Britain became the first Western power to treat an Oriental nation as an equal by entering into a military alliance with Japan. Thus strengthened and reassured, Japan attacked Russia in 1904 and, to everyone's surprise, defeated her on land and at sea. As her reward, she took the southern half of Sakhalin Island and Russia's railroad and port concessions in southern Manchuria, thereby becoming the dominant power in that large and valuable section of China. By 1914 Japan was a first-rate Europeanized power—industrialized, militaristic, imperialistic. And as in the autocratic European nations, liberal democratic trends in Japan were overshadowed and weakened by aggressive nationalism.

4. COMPETITION FOR THE STRATEGIC NEAR AND MIDDLE EAST

The term *Near East* usually refers to the area at the eastern end of the Mediterranean: Egypt, the old Ottoman Empire, and the Balkan Peninsula. In the period 1871–1914, the term *Middle East* usually meant the area of the Persian Gulf, the territory northwest of India, and sometimes Tibet. (By the middle of the twentieth century the term *Middle East* was generally used to designate the whole area from and including Egypt and Turkey to the western borders of India.) Before the development of its oil resources after World War I, this area (with the exception of the Balkan Peninsula) was relatively barren, poor, and sparsely settled. It was inhabited chiefly by Muslims who were hostile to Europeans. The main. importance of the area, therefore, was stategic. It is the land bridge between the world's two largest land masses—the continents of Eurasia and Africa. The opening in 1869 of the Suez Canal, which shortened the sailing distance between Western Europe and the Far East by 5,000 miles, doubled the strategic value of the Near and Middle East. Indeed, Suez quickly became probably the most vital single commercial and military focal point in the world.

The Suez Canal was built by a French company between 1859 and 1869. However, in 1875 Great Britain, taking advantage of the Egyptian government's financial distress, purchased the khedive's controlling portion of the canal stock. Seven years later, to quell an anti-European insurrection, the British occupied Egypt with their military forces. The French acquiesced in the establishment of Britain's control over Egypt and the Suez Canal in return for British support of French dominance in Morocco.

Serious competition for the British in the Near East soon came from an unexpected source. Wilhelm II, upon becoming kaiser of the German Empire in 1888, immediately began to show a keen interest in the Ottoman Empire. Sultan Abdul Hamid II (1876–1909) was such a cruel slaughterer of his Christian subjects that he was called in the Western world "Abdul the Damned." Nevertheless, Wilhelm II in 1889 paid Abdul Hamid a visit in Constantinople and declared himself to be the friend and benefactor not only of the Turks, but of all the Muslims. Friendship was followed by economic concessions and German investments in the Ottoman Empire. A second visit by the Kaiser in 1898 led to a concession to Germany to build a railroad from the Bosporus to the Persian Gulf. This, with its European connection, was the famous Berlin-to-Bagdad railroad. The British took alarm. The Bagdad Railroad, with a fortified terminus on the Persian Gulf, would undercut Britain's longer water route to the East and threaten India, Britain's richest colonial prize. A projected branch running down through Syria and Palestine to Hedjaz would menace the Suez Canal itself.

Russia was equally concerned. Since the days of Ivan III in the fifteenth century, one of Russia's major ambitions has been to gain a warm water outlet to the world through the Turkish Straits at Constantinople. As a matter of fact, since the tenth century Russia has looked to Constantinople as the seat and legitimate capital of her Orthodox religion and Byzantine culture. As we have seen, the decay of the Ottoman Empire in the nineteenth century encouraged Russia to try for Constantinople, and only the intervention of Great Britain and France in the Crimean War (1854–1856) prevented her from attaining her goal. Again in 1877–1878 Russia defeated Turkey and threatened to dominate the whole Balkan Peninsula. This time Great Britain and Austria-Hungary forced Russia to submit to a general settlement by the European powers. At the Congress of Berlin, 1878, Russian ambitions in the Near East were once more thwarted. Bismarck's support of Austria-Hungary and Great Britain at the Congress of Berlin marked the beginning of German-Russian estrangement. Russia's defeat by Japan in 1904–1905 caused her to intensify her pressure toward the Middle and Near East. Her southward expansion from Siberia so menaced India that Great Britain in the late nineteenth century and the beginning of the twentieth extended the northwest Indian frontier to the Khyber Pass and crossed over the Himalayas to checkmate Russian influence in Tibet, Afghanistan, and Persia.

The new German threat in the Near and Middle East, however, caused the British and the Russians to settle their long-standing differences. In 1907 they neutralized Tibet and Afghanistan and divided Persia into three spheres of influence—a Russian sphere in the north, a British sphere in the south, and an "independent" sphere in the center. Great Britain, Russia, and France, now diplomatic allies, prevented the sale of Bagdad Railroad bonds in their respective countries in an effort to embarrass the financing of the costly undertaking. Germany went right ahead, however, with the extension of her influence in the

Balkans and the Ottoman Empire. In 1913 Germany dispatched a military mission to Constantinople to reorganize and instruct the Turkish army. The Ottoman Empire's friendship and eventual alliance with Germany was undoubtedly motivated by her greater fear of Russia. By 1914 the area of the Near and Middle East was a giant powder keg with fuses leading to St. Petersburg, Berlin, and London.

5. THE SCRAMBLE FOR AFRICA

At the opening of the nineteenth century, Africa was not the seat of ancient and highly developed civilizations, as was Asia. The brilliant civilizations of Egypt, Carthage, and Rome had long since disappeared. The Muslim religion still existed throughout North Africa, but the once-vigorous Muslim civilization was now squalid and tribal except for a few rich potentates. The Portuguese, Spanish, British, and French had trading posts along the gold, ivory, and slave coast on the west. The Dutch and Portuguese had posts and settlements around the southern cape. But most of the huge continent still lay dark and mysterious. By 1871 the African scene had still not changed very much. During the middle decades of the nineteenth century, the interior was explored for the first time, notably by David Livingston, a Scottish missionary, and Henry Morton Stanley, a British journalist. The French had conquered Algeria and made it a part of France, and had pushed up the Senegal River in the west. The British had taken the Cape Colony from the Dutch by the Treaty of Vienna in 1815, and the Dutch settlers had moved northward into the interior. After 1871, however, the tempo of European activity changed drastically. The explorers' tales of strange wild animals and primitive peoples, of jungles, ivory, and gold, excited the imagination of Western European adventurers and evangelical Christians. The new burst of industrialism and nationalism supplied much of the impetus.

After 1871 there took place such a mad scramble for Africa among the powers of Western Europe that by 1914, the only independent areas left were Ethiopia in the east and Liberia in the west. Ethiopia, with French aid, had repulsed an invading Italian army, and Liberia had been sponsored by the United States as a hoped-for receptacle for liberated Negro slaves. The rest of the huge continent had been seized by France, Great Britain, Germany, Portugal, Belgium, Italy, and Spain (listed in the approximate order of size of territory held). (See map p. 794.) The treatment of the primitive natives was very similar to that accorded the New World Indians in the sixteenth and seventeenth centuries.

The looting of so much territory did not occur, of course, without serious international incidents and crises. One such incident occurred at Fashoda in the Sudan in 1898. A French expedition under Major Marchand, bent on establishing an all-French axis across Africa from west to east, arrived at Fashoda and hoisted the French flag. The British, however, claimed the Sudan as an appendage of Egypt. Furthermore, they were interested in a Cape to Cairo railroad running through all British territory even though they were already blocked by German East Africa. Lord Kitchener therefore hurried down from the north with a superior British force and compelled the French to withdraw.

In South Africa the British fought a major war with the Dutch settlers (1899–1902). When British settlers began to move into Cape Colony after the Congress of Vienna had ceded it to Great Britain in 1815, the Calvinist Dutch Boers (farmers) who had settled there in the seventeenth century and who wished to live a biblical, patriarchal life trekked northward far into the interior. Eventually the British recognized the independence of the two Boer states, Transvaal and Orange Free State. When, however, the richest gold mines in the world were discovered in the Transvaal in the 1880s, British immigrants (Uitlanders) flooded in. The unwelcome Uitlanders were badly treated by the Dutch Boers. The British empire builder Cecil Rhodes, with the support of powerful interests back home, was determined to brush aside the two little Boer republics. When the able Boer president, Paul Kruger, saw the British intent, he opened hostilities. What the world expected to be an easy victory for the British took three years of all-out military effort involving severe casualties and enormous costs. Britain's treatment of the defeated Boers, however, was lenient. They were taken into partnership in the Union of South Africa; and their war hero, General Botha, was elected the Union's first prime minister. During the course of the struggle, a telegram of congratulation from

the German kaiser to President Kruger and the British seizure of a German ship attempting to violate the British blockade caused great tension between Great Britain and Germany. Only the superiority of the British navy, as the Kaiser admitted, prevented him from going to war.

The British navy also proved decisive in two crises over Morocco. In 1905 France, with the approval of Great Britain, Italy, and Spain, began the conquest of Morocco. She claimed that it was necessary because of continual raids by wild Moroccan tribesmen on French Algeria. The German kaiser, seeing an opportunity to assert his own power and possibly to

Africa 1914

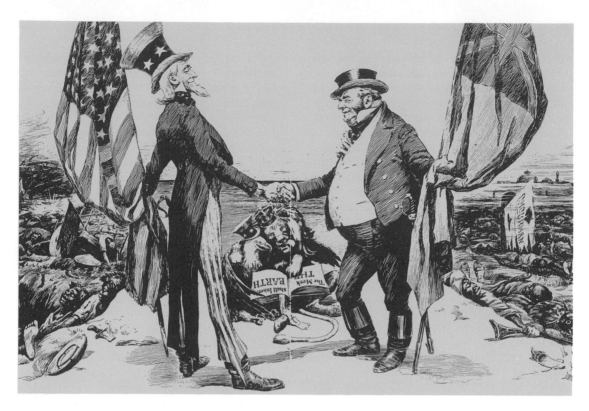

This cartoon, which appeared in Life in 1899, satirizes the attitudes of smug righteousness and superiority with which the Americans, the British, and the European nations extended their dominance over Africa and Asia. *Photo: NYPL Picture Collection*

break up the Triple Entente, which France, Great Britain, and Russia were then forming, appeared at the Moroccan port of Tangier on a German warship and indicated his support of Moroccan independence. Great tension followed. At an international conference at Algeciras, France, supported by her own ally, Great Britain, and by Germany's ally, Italy, won a limited control over Morocco. Disorder continued, however, and in 1911 France sent a conquering army into Morocco, at which point Germany dispatched a cruiser to the Moroccan port of Agadir. Again tension mounted. In the face of Germany's threat to France, Britain's Chancellor of the Exchequer, Lloyd George, talked loudly of war. Again Germany backed down. Between Germany and Morocco stood the British navy.

These two efforts of the Kaiser to drive a wedge between the Entente powers had the effect of driving them closer together. Moreover, his own ally, Italy, had proved uncertain. These two crises growing out of imperialism hastened the coming of World War I.

6. THE BRITISH EMPIRE

Of all the European overseas empires, the British was by far the most successful. Indeed, it was the dazzling size and wealth of the British Empire that helped to excite the other European powers to greater imperialistic activity. By 1914 the British Empire included one-fourth of all the land and people of the earth. In addition to Britain's spheres of influence in China and her African territories, which we have just mentioned, the empire included four great self-governing dominions: Canada, Australia, New Zealand, and the Union of South Africa. It also included British Honduras in Central America; British Guiana in South America; numerous islands in the West Indies; strategic steppingstones along her Mediterranean–Red Sea life line such as Gibraltar, Malta, Cyprus, and Aden; scores of islands in the Atlantic, Pacific, and Indian Oceans; Malaya; Burma; Ceylon; parts of New Guinea and Borneo; and, above all, India. Nor should we forget the English-speaking United States—Britain's prodigal son who made good and who would return more than once in time of need to rescue the mother country.

Great Britain's commerce with her empire was enormous. In 1914 her foreign investments, most of which were in the empire, totaled $20 billion—one-fourth of the total wealth of the homeland. (By comparison, France had $9 billion invested abroad; Germany, 6. The United States was a debtor nation.) The empire, furthermore, provided lucrative and often glamorous careers for thousands of British governors, army and navy officers, diplomats, and civil servants of every description.

In the latter part of the nineteenth century, Great Britain adopted the policy of granting self-government to the English-speaking portions of her empire. Canada, which had gained self-government in 1849, was granted dominion status in 1867. With dominion status, the only remaining effective bond was allegiance to the British crown. The British governor-general was only a figurehead like the king at home. Australia was made a self-governing dominion in 1901, New Zealand in 1907, and the Union of South Africa in 1910. The policy was successful. All the dominions rallied to the mother country in both world wars.

Great Britain's richest imperial prize was India. India's more than 300 million inhabitants accounted for at least three-fourths of the total population of the whole empire. India was nearly twenty times as large as Great Britain and more than seven times as populous. She was the mother country's best customer and supplied many minerals and raw materials. Until 1858 India was governed by the British East India Company, a private joint stock company. However, the great Sepoy Mutiny of 1857, the first large-scale uprising of the Indians against British rule, caused the British government to take over the government of India from the company. Between 1858 and 1914 Great Britain spent millions of dollars in India on railroads, industries, education, and public health. The enormous growth of India's population, which more than doubled during the period, is testimony to the improvement in the conditions of life under British rule. However, the British took out of India more than they brought in, and they showed no inclination to grant self-government. Indian dissatisfaction with British rule mounted steadily. In the late nineteenth century, nationalism, which had provided so much aggressive energy for Europe, was coming to Asia—to India as well as to Japan and China. In 1885 the All Indian Congress party was formed for the purpose of achieving Indian independence. By 1914 it was becoming obvious that India would not remain a placid and profitable colony much longer.

The European world's technology, its dynamic capitalism, and above all its aggressive nationalism had enabled it between 1871 and 1914 to subject most of the rest of the world to its domination. The tail wagged the dog. By 1914 the European world had come to look upon this as a normal and permanent thing. Near the end of the nineteenth century and early in the twentieth century, however, those same forces were coming to Asia and Africa as they had come to Japan a bit earlier. Asia and Africa would soon begin to free themselves from European domination, but not without struggles that would rock the twentieth-century world.

Suggested Reading

General. Two scholarly and detailed studies of European imperialism during the years 1871–1914 by distinguished authorities are W. L. Langer, *The Diplomacy of Imperialism, 1890–1902* (2 vols., 2nd ed., 1951); and P. T. Moon, *Imperialism and World Politics* (1926). E. M. Winslow, *The Pattern of Imperialism: A Study in Theories of Power* (1948) attempts to demonstrate that imperialism is more political than economic in motivation. J. A. Hobson, *Imperialism: A Study* (1902) is a strong condemnation of imperialism. A good, brief survey of one important aspect of imperialism is **D. E. Owen, *Imperialism and Nationalism in the Far East* (Berkshire).

The Exploitation and Awakening of China. K. S. Latourette, *The Chinese: Their History and Culture* (3rd ed., 1940) is a lucid survey by one of America's leading experts. The story of European penetration and exploitation of China is well told by G. F. Hudson, *Europe and China* (1930); and E. R. Hughes, *The Invasion of China by the Western World* (1938). Two excellent studies of the role of the United States in the awakening of China are **J. K. Fairbank, *The United States and China* (Compass); and F. R. Dulles, *China and America: The Story of Their Relations Since 1784* (1946). Fairbank's book brings the story down to quite recent times. A good account of the beginnings of the reform movement in China is M. E. Cameron, *The Reform Movement in China 1898–1912* (1931). **L. Sharman, *Sun Yat-Sen: His Life and Its Meaning: A Critical Biography* (Stanford University) is one of the few good biographies of China's great liberator.

The Emergence of Japan. Two lucid, brief histories of Japan by leading American authorities are K. S. Latourette, *The History of Japan* (1947); and **E. O. Reischauer, *Japan: The Story of a Nation* (Knopf). A scholarly and more detailed account is C. Yanaga, *Japan Since Perry* (1949). The classic account of the awakening and the Westernization of Japan is by G. B. Sanson, *The Western World*

and Japan: a Study in the Interaction of European and Asiatic Cultures (1950).

Competition for the Near and Middle East. Two good general histories of the Middle East are S. N. Fisher, *The Middle East: A History* (2nd ed., 1969); and G. E. Kirk, *A Short History of the Middle East* (rev. ed., 1957). A scholarly and well-written account of the most spectacular of the big power imperialistic clashes in the Middle East during the years 1871–1914 is E. M. Earle, *Turkey, the Great Powers, and the Bagdad Railway* (1923).

The Scramble for Africa. A scholarly survey of African peoples and culture is G. P. Murdock, *Africa: Its Peoples and Their Culture History* (1959). Good brief general surveys of European imperialism in Africa are **H. L. Hoskins, *European Imperialism in Africa* (Berkshire); and H. H. Johnston, *The Opening Up of Africa* (1911). A good biography of Livingston is G. Seaver, *David Livingston, His Life and Letters* (1957). The dramatic story of South Africa is told in scholarly fashion by C. W. de Kiewiet, *A History of South Africa: Social and Economic* (1946); and Basil Williams, *Cecil Rhodes* (1921). Detailed studies of French and German imperialism in Africa are H. T. Priestley, *France Overseas* (1939); and M. E. Townsend, *The Rise and Fall of Germany's Colonial Empire, 1884–1918* (1930). The notorious story of the exploitation of the Congo is told by **R. Slade, *The Belgian Congo* (Oxford).

The British Empire. A scholarly study of the British Empire is P. Knaplund, *The British Empire, 1815–1939* (1941). G. E. Elton, *Imperial Commonwealth* (1946) is a spirited defense of the British Empire and Commonwealth. A brief but scholarly study of Britain's biggest colonial prize is **T. W. Wallbank, *India: A Survey of the Heritage and Growth of Indian Nationalism* (Berkshire). More detailed is P. J. Griffiths, *The British Impact on India* (1952). An excellent history of Canada is **G. W. Brown, *Building the Canadian Nation* (2 vols., McFadden Books).

Chapter 52 ❧ The Challenge to Christianity

Whatever one's religious faith may be—Christian, Jewish, Buddhist, or rationalistic; orthodox or skeptic; evangelistic or apathetic—he can hardly deny the tremendous influence of religion in history. In the Middle East empires rise and fall, conquerors come and go, but Islam remains, setting the pattern of ideals and thought and, to a considerable degree, the life of the people. The same is true of Hinduism in India and Confucianism in China. In Western civilization the great religious base, the great commonality, is Christianity, with its roots of Judaistic ethics and monotheism. Before the nineteenth century Christianity had withstood many assaults: the Arian heresy in its formative years; conflict between pope and emperor, conflict between the Western and the Eastern churches, and various heresies in the Middle Ages; the Great Schism in the fourteenth and fifteenth centuries; the Protestant Revolt in the sixteenth century; and the rationalistic assault in the eighteenth century. In the latter part of the nineteenth century, however, the Christian religion underwent a challenge more serious and fundamental than any of these.

1. THE VARIOUS FORCES AND INFLUENCES OPPOSED TO MYSTIC RELIGION IN THE PERIOD 1871–1914

Of the various factors and developments during the second phase of the Industrial Revolution that were hostile to mystic or supernatural religion, undoubtedly the most direct and challenging was the rapid growth of science and the scientific spirit. However, there were others. Let us recall a few of the most important that we have observed in the four preceding chapters.

The phenomenal growth of technology and industry was in many ways inimical to religious faith and practices. In the industrialized areas it began to appear that the power machines would soon supply all man's material needs and banish grinding toil from the earth. Preoccupation with creature comforts and pleasure gadgets undreamed of a few years earlier now tended to overshadow interest in the sacred and the spiritual. Dazzling speed did not seem to be conducive to meditation and devotion. The Industrial Revolution also brought about a mass migration of people, from farm to city and from country to country, tearing them loose from old social patterns and institutions, of which the church had long been one of the most important. Members of the flocks became separated from their pastors. And in the growing industrial cities, with their movement and relative excitement, many of the newcomers seemed no longer to need the church for their social life and entertainment.

The liberal and radical political movements of the late nineteenth century were for the most part anticlerical and often antireligious. The established churches in Europe, particularly the Roman Catholic Church, had long been allied with the conservative aristocracy and royalty. Liberals, when they came to power, usually proceeded to attack the powers, the privileges, and the property of the established church. France is a good example. After the revolutionary era had ended with the overthrow of Napoleon, the Roman Catholic Church made a comeback. It allied itself with the Bourbon regime and with Napoleon III's Second Empire and opposed liberal movements, including the setting up of the Third French Republic. The liberal leaders of the Third Republic immediately adopted anticlerical policies. During the 1880s, the Ferry Laws loosened the hold of the Church on education by setting up a rival and favored system of public secular schools, in which the teaching of religion was banned. In 1901 the Associations Law virtually destroyed the Church's schools by outlawing the Roman Catholic teaching orders or associations. In 1905 church and state were completely separated. In all the industrialized countries in this period, public secular education made great strides, usually under the sponsorship of liberal parties. Marxist socialism, which began to make headway between 1871 and 1914, was militantly materialistic and atheistic.

A third factor inimical to supernatural religion during the second phase of the Industrial Revolution was the growth of malignant nationalism, which afflicted all the great industrialized powers. Nationalism became itself a religion and drew the allegiance of millions away from their traditional faiths. International Roman Catholicism and international Judaism were particularly hard hit. Between 1872 and 1878, Bismarck waged an unrelenting *Kulturkampf* (battle for civilization) against the Roman Catholic Church in Germany. Bismarck regarded as intolerable the allegiance of millions of German citizens to a non-German pope and the formation of a Roman Catholic political party in Germany. The anti-Semitism that raised its ugly head in many countries at this time may be attributed in part to the resentment against the international character of Judaism and also to rac-

ism, which is an extreme form of malignant nationalism. The Dreyfus case in France is an example. Bloody pogroms in Russia drove tens of thousands of Russian and Polish Jews to America. Many Jews themselves, after centuries of dispersion, became nationalistic and started a movement (Zionism) to set up a Jewish national state in Palestine. Although Bismarck lost his battle against the Roman Catholics in Germany, manifestations of extreme nationalism such as these generally represented serious setbacks to supernatural religion either from direct assault or from transfer of allegiance.

2. THE CONFLICT BETWEEN NATURAL SCIENCE AND CHRISTIANITY

With the exception of the evolutionary hypothesis, the challenge to Christianity by natural science was more indirect than direct. The marvelous achievements of the scientists caused many to place great faith in man and in his ability to do for himself whatever needed to be done. The scientific attitude ran counter to the traditional attitude of religious faith. The discovery of more and more of the secrets of the material world made it possible to attribute to natural causes many phenomena that previously had been attributed to divine intervention. Disease germs, for instance, now appeared to be doing things that had long been ascribed to God. In fact, there appeared to many at the end of the nineteenth century to be less and less place and need for God.

The greatest issues between natural science and the Christian religion to be raised in the nineteenth century grew out of Darwin's evolutionary hypothesis. The publication of *The Origin of Species* in 1859 created an immediate religious storm. The proposal of a long, gradual, and seemingly mechanistic evolution of all present species from simpler forms appeared to contradict the account of divine creation given in the first chapter of Genesis. If Darwin should prove to be right and Genesis wrong, what faith could be put in the divine inspiration and the reliability of the rest of the Bible, upon which so much of Christianity depends? The whole process of evolution as suggested by Darwin appeared to leave God out of the affairs of the universe entirely. Any doubt concerning Darwin's place for man in his evolutionary hypothesis was removed twelve years later, when he published *The Descent of Man.* Man, like all other living things, evolved from more primitive species. This appeared to refute not only the biblical account of man's creation, but also God's purpose, according to the Bible, of creating man in his own image as a temple of the Holy Spirit. According to Darwin's hypothesis, in the view of many, man seemed to be just another animal, albeit the highest.

Churchmen throughout Christendom raged against Darwin and his hypothesis. His character and his motives were assailed. His thesis was attacked and ridiculed. Some of the criticism was sound; for example, there is still no empirical evidence for the existence of many of the hypothesized evolutionary stages. A good bit of the theorizing done by Darwin and his contemporaries has since been generally repudiated by most biologists. And although there is abundant evidence of evolution within a given species, neither Darwin nor anyone else has ever demonstrated the evolution of one species out of another—the origin of a species. However, most of the criticism of the churchmen sprang from ignorance, fear, and habits of thought growing out of the uses and abuses of unquestioned authority. Efforts were made, sometimes successful, to suppress the reading of Darwin's books and the teaching of the evolutionary hypothesis in the schools.

Darwin himself, a gentle and modest scholar of the highest order but not a controversialist, refrained for the most part from attacking the churchmen. He merely defended his thesis when he considered it to be incorrectly or unfairly attacked. However, he was not lacking in doughty champions able

and willing to assail the forces of religion with the religious forces' own techniques. Thomas Huxley (1825–1895), a biologist, surgeon in the British navy, and president of the Royal Society, popularized Darwin's work in dozens of vigorous and lucid books and pamphlets and heaped withering scorn upon the churchmen. He called himself "Darwin's bulldog." Herbert Spencer was carried away with Darwin's thesis and built a whole system of philosophy around the idea of evolution. Spencer considered evolution the key to all truth and all progress. He was vitriolic in his denunciations of the ideals and practices of the Christian religion, which he regarded as the major enemy of both truth and progress. Ernst Haeckel (1834–1919), a prolific German scientist and popularizer, made great and sometimes ridiculous claims for evolution and for science. He claimed that scientists would very soon be solving all the remaining mysteries of life and even creating life. The conflict between the evolutionists and the Christian churchmen that raged in Western Europe in the last four decades of the nineteenth century did not reach its climax in the United States until the 1920s. We shall examine its outcome presently.

3. THE ASSAULT OF SOCIAL SCIENCE ON CHRISTIANITY

The assault of social science upon Christianity was very much more direct and severe than that of natural science. Social science deals specifically with man and society, as does religion. It was inevitable that two approaches to the same subject from diametrically opposite points of view should come into head-on collision. Also, social science is much less exact than natural science, and social scientists are more given to generalizing and philosophizing on complex subjects with less precise data.

Anthropologists dug into man's distant past to unearth the primitive origins of his culture, of which religion is always an important part.

Nearly all of them concluded that religion is based upon primitive superstition. In 1890 Sir James Frazer (1854–1941) published *The Golden Bough*, a vast and fascinating history of early myths, superstitions, and cults from which he believed that present-day religions, including Christianity, are derived. For instance, he shows that it was customary among many primitive tribes to eat their grain god and drink their wine god, hoping thereby to partake of their strength. *The Golden Bough* went through edition after edition, each bigger than the one preceding, until it reached twelve volumes. It is still a good seller in abridged form.

The behavioristic psychologists attempted to mechanize man's mind and his emotions, including religious faith (or "ecstasy," as they sometimes called it). They had man creating God in man's own image in order to have a big brother to lean on in time of need. Some of them saw God as man's creation as a ready answer to the unanswerable.

Historians, many of whom in the period 1871–1914 attempted to make history a social science, assigned natural, usually economic, causes to all religious developments and institutions. The famed German historian of religion Adolf von Harnack (1851–1930) believed Christianity to be an outgrowth of Greek philosophy. Historians of the warfare between science and religion in this period nearly always made science the hero and religion the villain.

It was the sociologists, however, who of all the social scientists in the period 1871–1914 were the most persistently and pointedly hostile to religion. Supernatural religion had no place whatever in Comte's positivism, humanity itself being the object of worship. Through volume after volume of Herbert Spencer's sociological writings ran a vein of hostility to mystic religion in general and to Christianity in particular. Mechanical evolution became, for Spencer, the key to all social progress. Even morals evolved. Religious faith retarded social progress and obscured

man's vision of the evolutionary social process.

4. THE HIGHER CRITICISM

Finally, the scientific spirit of the second phase of the Industrial Revolution brought forth a number of biblical scholars who subjected the Bible to searching scrutiny and analysis—some for the purpose of establishing its exact meaning, and others for the purpose of detecting error or fraud. This type of scholarship is called "higher criticism."

The first prominent nineteenth-century "higher critic" of the Bible was David Strauss (1808–1874), a Lutheran theologian at the University of Tübingen in Germany. After long years of laborious work, Strauss brought out a *Life of Jesus* in two volumes that stripped Christ of his divinity and undertook to explain in natural terms the miracles and prophecies recorded in the New Testament. Strauss asserted that the New Testament was a very unreliable document, that the authorship of the four Gospels could not be proved, and that the four accounts of the life of Jesus were contradictory.

Much more popular and influential was the charming one-volume *La Vie de Jésus* by Ernest Renan (1823–1892), a French scholar and a Roman Catholic. Renan pictured Christ in solely human and natural terms. Christ was the gentlest, wisest, best, and most charming creature who ever lived. We should all worship him and follow his example. But he was man, not God. Renan attributed Christ's belief in his own divinity to hallucinations. But it was these psychological aberrations that gave him his power and drive and much of his appeal. Renan's *Life of Jesus* was greeted with immediate and continuing enthusiasm by the intellectual world of the late nineteenth and early twentieth centuries. Here at last seemed to be the solution to the most stubborn mystery of all—the answer that the humanistic "scientific" philosophers had long been looking for. It was the rationalization and the humanization of the most influential figure of all time. The work of Strauss and Renan and the numerous other "higher critics" appeared to many to bring religion within the compass of onrushing science.·

5. THE CHRISTIAN RESPONSE

The reaction of Christianity to the various nineteenth-century challenges and assaults may be classified under three broad headings: (1) uncompromising rejection, (2) surrender to the challenges and assaults, (3) moderate compromise, or accommodation of the fundamentals of the faith to proved new truth and new conditions. On the whole the Roman Catholics were able to meet the challenge more quickly and easily than the Protestants. This is because the Roman Catholics were more centralized and authoritative in their organization than the Protestants and were less dependent upon the Bible (now under attack) for doctrinal authority. The Roman Catholic Church could achieve by papal decree and clerical discipline what the various Protestant denominations, with their less authoritative and sometimes democratic procedures, required years to accomplish. The Eastern Orthodox Christians were not much affected by the nineteenth-century challenges, since they were located mostly in Russia and the Balkan Peninsula, where science and technology arrived only in the last decade of the century, and then very slowly.

The first reaction of Christianity to the new challenges was angry rejection of the new ideas and forces. In 1864 Pope Pius IX (1846–1878) issued a *Syllabus of Errors,* errors that Roman Catholics were to avoid. These errors, eighty in all, included separation of church and state, civil marriage, secular education, freedom of speech and press, religious toleration, liberty of conscience, liberalism, and materialism. This list was strengthened and brought up to date by Pius X (1903–1914), who issued another *Syllabus* in 1907 specifically condemning all those Christians who

would compromise their doctrines. In 1870 Pius IX called the Vatican council (the first general council since that at Trent in the sixteenth century), which pronounced the doctrine of papal infallibility. According to this doctrine, the pope, when speaking *ex cathedra* (that is, officially *from the chair* of St. Peter) on a matter of faith or morals, is not subject to error. This was the most authoritarian position that the Church and the pope had ever taken, and it came at a time when the intellectual, political, and religious trends seemed to be in the opposite direction. (The pope has used this power only once, as of 1970). In the late nineteenth and early twentieth centuries, the Roman Catholic hierarchy excommunicated numerous members and several priests who had compromised the official doctrines of the Church. By 1914 discipline appeared to have been fairly well restored.

The Protestants had no such disciplinary means and weapons at their disposal. Their difficulties in this respect are illustrated by the failure of the Anglican hierarchy in Great Britain to discipline certain heterodox clergymen. The cases were appealed to the highest secular court; the established Anglican Church, which is subordinate to the British government, was overruled. In Germany, Wilhelm II freely interfered in the affairs of the official Lutheran Church in behalf of compromise (modernist) doctrines. In general, fundamentalism in the Protestant churches was a local or individual matter. However, fundamentalist sects were by no means rare. They interpreted the Bible, including the first chapter of Genesis, literally, and denounced all scientific beliefs that did not accord with it. As science and technology rushed on, the fundamentalist position became harder and harder to maintain.

The second reaction of Christianity to the nineteenth-century challenges and assaults was surrender to them. Many Christians, Roman Catholics and Protestants alike, lost their faith, left their church, and became atheists or agnostics. But many more who lost the traditional faith remained in their church and attempted to change its doctrines. They granted the claims of science and the "higher criticism," and they sympathized with the materialism, liberalism, and extreme nationalism of the day. They continued to go to church, to sing the hymns, to say the prayers, and to recite the creeds, but they did not believe what they sang, said, and recited. They would reject the supernatural and deny the divinity of Christ. They would make the Bible a book of good literature and high ethical ideals; Christ, a great social reformer; and the church, an instrument for the promotion of good will, wholesome fellowship, racial tolerance, temperance, charity, patriotism, and so on. These Christians came to be called *modernists*. The Roman Catholic Church, as we have seen, declared officially against modernism in 1907, and by 1914 it appeared either to have suppressed the modernists in its ranks or driven them under cover. In the various Protestant churches modernism competed with fundamentalism, both extreme and moderate, and by 1914 modernism tended to gain the upper hand. In the United States modernism in the Protestant churches did not reach its peak until the 1920s and 1930s.

The third reaction of Christianity, the one that appears to prevail today, was moderate compromise: a cheerful acceptance of proved scientific facts and reasonable deductions therefrom together with attempts to harmonize the findings of science with the fundamentals of the Christian faith. This involved the interpretation figuratively of certain passages in the Bible, particularly in the first chapter of Genesis, and the admission of a few errors in various versions of the Bible. On the other hand, it was soon found that many of the anti-Christian claims of the scientists and higher critics had been hasty and ill-founded. Many of the higher critics of this period were anything but scientifically objective, setting out deliberately to debunk the Bible. And the belligerently anti-Christian scientists were, for the most part, not first-rate scholars like Darwin, but second-raters—popularizers and publicists who knew as little about the Christian

religion as the militant fundamentalists knew about science. When first-rate men of good will on both sides moved in on the problem, it was discovered that little, if any, conflict existed between the proved facts and principles of science and the fundamental doctrines of the Christian faith. An important feature of this harmonizing Christian reaction was an increased awareness of the responsibility of the Christian churches to participate actively in the social and political problems of the day.

The Roman Catholics were the first to reach this middle position. From 1878 to 1903 the Roman Church was headed by the ablest pope since the thirteenth century, Leo XIII. This elderly, frail, and scholarly man was elected pope at one of the most critical times in the Church's history. It was not thought that he would live long, and he was expected only to hold the rival factions together during his few remaining years, after which a strong pope would be elected. Instead, he lived for twenty-five more years and proved himself to be a brilliant and vigorous theologian, administrator, and statesman.

Leo XIII quickly removed any doubts concerning the willingness of the Roman Catholic Church to compromise its historic doctrines. He proclaimed Thomas Aquinas the official Roman Catholic theologian and philosopher and established numerous centers of higher learning for the study and propagation of Thomistic theology and philosophy. He invited all Protestants and Eastern Orthodox Christians to accept papal supremacy, Roman Catholic doctrines and practices, and to return to the Roman fold. He demanded a privileged status for the Roman Catholic Church in all states, independent of the secular government when in a minority and superior to the secular government when in a majority. On the other hand, Leo XIII welcomed new scientific beliefs on condition that they be proved, opened the Vatican's archives to research scholars, and brought a number of first-rate physicists and the latest scientific equipment to the Vatican observatory. As to the evolution controversy, Leo

XIII and his successors gradually took the position that natural science was not the province of the Church and that the Church, therefore, would not make official pronouncements on it; that the evolutionary concept was not in itself repugnant to the doctrines of the Church; that evolution could be taught in the Church's schools as a hypothesis, and, when and if satisfactorily proved, it could be taught as fact; that the first chapter of Genesis should be taken figuratively; and that within these premises belief in evolution was a private and individual matter.

Leo XIII also faced up squarely and boldly to the economic and social challenges of the second phase of the Industrial Revolution. In 1891, in the most famous of all his encyclicals, *Rerum Novarum* (new things), he denounced materialism and Marxian socialism and proclaimed the sanctity of private property. He did, however, declare limits to the use of private property. Labor must not be treated as a commodity; workers must be paid a fair living wage and protected against too long hours, injury, and disease. Leo XIII advocated a wider distribution of property, labor unions for collective bargaining, and farming cooperatives. Roman Catholic labor unions were soon organized to challenge the socialist-dominated unions.

Protestantism groped its way slowly, and often painfully, toward a position similar in general to that of Leo XIII. However, Protestantism never claimed so exalted a place for the church within the state, nor was it ever so firm in its stand on capital and labor.

Early in the twentieth century a number of developments strengthened the hands of the theologians. The discovery by Rutherford and Einstein that the atom is really composed of particles of electricity or energy and Einstein's theory of relativity underminded belief in the stability of matter and confidence in materialism. Natural scientists were no longer so sure of themselves. Many things in the material world, long regarded as certain, suddenly became less certain. The two world wars, the great depression, and the violence of

Fascist and Communist dictatorships raised grave doubts concerning some of the optimistic tenets of the social scientists and the modernists.

Shortly after the close of World War I, the brilliant Swiss Protestant theologian and philosopher Karl Barth (1886–1968) began to beckon many disillusioned Western Christians to return to an enlightened fundamentalism. The time had come, said Barth, for the Christian churches to concern themselves less with social and political problems, which he called the worship of and reliance upon man, and to concern themselves more with the worship of God and reliance upon Divine Providence. A neo-Calvinist, Barth believed that God still rules the universe and that the Scriptures are his word to man. Barth's fundamentalism differed from the earlier fundamentalism in that it was propounded in the full light of recent science and philosophy and with an impressive display of intellectualism. Probably Barth's most illustrious follower is Reinhold Niebuhr (1892——) in the United States. However, Niebuhr believes that the Christian churches should be actively engaged both in the worship of God and in humanitarian political and social endeavors.

As to evolution, the eminent French scientist Pierre Lecomte du Noüy expressed the views of many intellectual Christians, both Protestant and Roman Catholic, in his *Human Destiny* (1947). Lecomte du Noüy argued impressively that evolution could not have occurred by blind chance, that it must have been divinely guided. The millions of years that God took to create man did not trouble Lecomte du Noüy. Just as a day is long for an insect that has a life span of one day, but short to man, so time that seems long to man would be short to a timeless being like God. Lecomte du Noüy believed that with the appearance of man, evolution ceased to be physical, so far as man was concerned, and became spiritual, Christ being the perfect model. This is a far cry from the fulminations of Huxley and the early fundamentalists. By the time of World War II, the trend in Protestantism appeared to be definitely toward a moderate and somewhat intellectualized fundamentalism.

Protestantism, like Roman Catholicism under Leo XIII, assumed a more direct and organized interest in social problems. The Anglican clergyman, novelist, and historian Charles Kingsley (1819–1875) became so outraged at the lot of the industrial proletariat that he advocated Christian socialism. An English Protestant clergyman, William Booth (1829–1912), founded the Salvation Army, which concentrated on rescue mission work in the industrial slums. The Young Men's Christian Association specialized in wholesome recreation for underprivileged youth; the Quakers, in charities.

Although Eastern Orthodox Christianity was not so seriously challenged in the period 1871–1914 as were Roman Catholic and Protestant Christianity in the more materially advanced West, Orthodox Russia produced one of the foremost Christian social reformers of the time—Count Leo Tolstoy (1828–1910). This wealthy and aristocratic but sensitive literary artist became greatly disturbed by the condition of the wretched poor in Russia's cities. In his book *What Shall We Do Then?* Tolstoy advocates Christian socialism, which he believed to be taught in the four Gospels. The rich should share their goods with the poor and also the physical toil of the poor. Tolstoy practiced his own preaching. Divesting himself of his great wealth, he lived the life of a common laborer and still found time and inspiration to continue his writing.

Judaism was affected by the various challenges of the second phase of the Industrial Revolution in much the same way as Christianity. Many Jews drifted away from their religious beliefs and practices entirely. Many others became Reformed Jews (modernists). Those who remained true to the old religion were called Orthodox Jews. With the exception of Japan, it was not until the mid-twentieth century that Mohammedan, Hindu, Buddhist, and Confucian lands began seriously to feel the impact of technology, science, political liberalism and radicalism, and aggressive nationalism. The responses of those religions are not yet clear.

It is an interesting fact that Christianity, so beset on its home grounds by challenges, assaults, and internal divisions during the period 1871–1914, was never more zealous in sending out missionaries to propagate the faith abroad. Roman Catholic, Protestant, and Eastern Orthodox missionaries vied with one another in converting the heathen in Asia and Africa. Probably the most renowned Christian missionary of the early twentieth century was the French Protestant Albert Schweitzer (1875–1965). An eminent philosopher, historian, musician, and surgeon, Schweitzer in 1913 went into the jungles of French Equatorial Africa to spend the rest of his life ministering to the medical needs of

One of the most prominent of the many Christian missionaries active during this period was the French Protestant Dr. Albert Schweitzer, eminent scholar, musician, and physician, who in 1913 at the age of thirty-eight chose to devote the rest of his life to medical missionary work in the jungles of French Equatorial Africa. *Photo: United Press International*

the primitive tribesmen and teaching them the Christian message by the example of his life,

By 1914 more than 40 million people outside Western Christendom professed the Christian faith. However, since the Christian missionaries also brought Western technology, science, and liberal political ideas to Asia and Africa and since they were often associated in the minds of the native peoples with Western imperialism and exploitation, the overall influence of Christianity on the two largest continents is extremely complex and obscure. The scope and intensity of this Christian missionary activity, however, is striking evidence of Christianity's continued vitality in the West. Nevertheless, in 1914 Christianity in the West was still on the defensive.

Suggested Reading

General. **Carlton J. H. Hayes, *A Generation of Materialism, 1871–1900* (Harper Torchbook) is one of the few studies by a major scholar that treat the various nineteenth-century challenges to the Christian religion objectively. Hayes is better in dealing with the Roman Catholic response than with the Protestant. Arnold Toynbee, *An Historian's Approach to Religion* (1956) is challenging and provocative. Toynbee draws much of the material in this interesting book from his major twelve-volume work, *A Study of History.* J. H. Randall, *The Making of the Modern Mind* (1940) is a popular and influential work that equates intellectual progress with the triumph of science over mystic, particularly Christian, religious faith. Two good studies of the problems of the Christian churches in modern times are J. N. Figgis, *Churches in the Modern State* (1914); and J. H. Nichols, *A History of Christianity, 1650–1950* (1956). Nichols gives special attention to twentieth-century Protestantism.

The Challenge of Science. A. D. White, *A History of the Warfare of Science with Theology in Christendom* (1955) first published in 1896, long considered a classic, is typical of the late nineteenth-century students of science and religion who made science the hero and religion the villain. White was a co-founder and first president of Cornell University and a distinguished American diplomat. **C. C. Gillespie, *Genesis and Geology: The Decades Before Darwin* (Harper Torchbook) examines the challenge that the Bible received from science on the eve of the evolution controversy. Thomas Huxley, *Lay Sermons* (1870) is an eloquent and sometimes vitriolic defense of Darwin against his contemporary Christian adversaries. **William Irvine, *Apes, Angels, and Victorians* (Meridian) is a study of the evolution controversy in the late nineteenth century, written in a popular and humorous style. A more scholarly treatment of the controversy is H. de Dorlodot, *Darwinism and Catholic Thought* (1914). **Sir James Frazer, *The Golden Bough* (Macmillan) is an abridgment of the original twelve-volume work which first appeared 1890–1915. This influential book is a fascinating collection of religious myths that purports to prove Christianity evolved from primitive myths and superstitions.

The Higher Criticism. David Strauss, *A New Life of Jesus* (2 vols., authorized trans., 1865) is the work of one of the first nineteenth-century higher critics of the Bible who sought to strip Christ of his supernatural deity. Probably the most influential masterpiece of higher criticism of the nineteenth century is **Ernest Renan, *Life of Jesus* (Modern Library). Renan analyzes Jesus in human psychological terms. Another very influential work of higher criticism is **Albert Schweitzer, *The Quest for the Historical Jesus* (Macmillan). Friedrich Smend, *Adolf von Harnack* (1927) is a good biography of the great nineteenth-century historian of religion who believed that Christianity is an outgrowth of Greek philosophy.

The Christian Response. **E. E. Y. Hales, *Pio Nono* (Image) is a sympathetic biography of the pope who sternly resisted the various nineteenth-century challenges. R. Fülöp-Miller, *Leo XIII and Our Times: Might of the Church-Power in the World* (1937) is an excellent study of the pope who sought to harmonize the teachings of the Church with the challenges of the new era. An authoritative handbook of the doctrines of the Roman Catholic Church is G. D. Smith, ed., *The Teaching of the Catholic Church: A Summary of Catholic Doctrine* (2 vols., 1949). A brilliant analysis of the evolutionary hypothesis by a distinguished twentieth-century scientist and Christian layman is **Pierre Lecomte du Noüy, *Human Destiny* (Mentor). Important works by two of the major twentieth-century Protestant theologians are **Karl Barth, *The Word of God and the Word of Man* (Harper Torchbook); and **Reinhold Niebuhr, *The Nature and Destiny of Man* (2 vols., Scribner). An excellent handbook of Protestant doctrines is **W. Hordern, *Layman's Guide to Protestant Theology* (Macmillan). Volumes V and VI of K. S. Latourette, *A History of the Expansion of Christianity* (7 vols., 1929 ff.) deal with the nineteenth century, when Christianity, severely challenged at home in the West, made its greatest conquests abroad. A good history of the Jews is J. W. Parkes, *A History of the Jewish People* (1952).

Chapter 53 ❧ Disenchantment, Realism,

Impressionism, Modernism

The materialism of science and technology, the cynicism that accompanied the challenged and wavering religious and moral values, and the restlessness of the masses are reflected in the thought and art of the second phase of the Industrial Revolution, 1871–1914. There was no sudden or drastic breaking away from the spirit of idealism and romanticism that prevailed in the thought and art of the bourgeois-dominated first phase of the Industrial Revolution, 1830–1871. Both idealism and romanticism continued on into the second phase, and beyond. Indeed, there were so many divergent trends and schools of thought and art during this period that the term *eclectic* is sometimes used to characterize its culture. Nevertheless, we may detect certain trends that stand out as significant. It is doubly important that we identify these trends, for many of them have continued to the present.

1. THE GENERAL NATURE OF THOUGHT AND ART DURING THE SECOND PHASE OF THE INDUSTRIAL REVOLUTION, 1871–1914

The prevailing idealism and optimism that characterized the thought of the early nine-teenth century tended after 1871 to give way to materialism, pragmatism, and pessimism—in spite of material progress never before dreamed of. During the second phase of the Industrial Revolution, literature was characterized by realism of various types. The arts tended first toward Impressionism and then toward more open revolt against the standards of the past. In music, however, there was a much stronger carry-over of traditional styles and values than in the rest of the arts.

The chief influences behind the new trends were undoubtedly the intellectual and sociological problems created by science and technology. Darwinism, Freudian psychology, and the discontent of the industrial proletariat run through the literature and art of the period like a refrain. Darwinism appeared to many to make man an animal, a brute, struggling for survival in a heartless, competitive world governed by blind chance. This was a sharp break with the romantic idealism that saw man as a child of God, and the world as a thing of beauty governed by a benevolent Divine Being.

The new psychology made man's mind as well as his body mechanical and animal-like. Furthermore, it discovered in the dark subconscious recesses of the mind selfish and

Claude Debussy, innovator and musical Impressionist, sits in a park with his daughter Claude-Emma, in a photograph that evokes a whole period of Western cultural life. *Photo: The Bettmann Archive*

brutish desires. These disenchanting concepts represented a radical departure not only from those of the romantic idealists of the early nineteenth century, but also from the ideas of the eighteenth-century philosophers of the Enlightenment, who believed in the essential goodness of nature and the perfectibility of man. The rapid development of technology during the so-called Second Industrial Revolution made the proletariat so numerous and so restless that it could no longer be ignored, either by the bourgeois capitalists or by the writers and artists. The smug all's-right-with-the-world attitude that the writers and painters expressed in the bourgeois-dominated early and mid-nineteenth century tended to give way to sordidly realistic writing and painting about the slums and the uprooted.

George Bernard Shaw, cynic, Socialist, materialist —and author of urbane novels, essays, and plays that are known and played all over the world still —in front of his home in his later years. *Photo: The Bettmann Archive*

Finally, Einstein's relativity theory and the startling ideas of the physicists with respect to the stability of the atom, that is, of matter itself, which came toward the end of this period, heightened the wave of cynicism, disillusionment, and revolt. Nor did the Christian religion, then wavering under heavy assault, give out the guiding light that it had long provided in the Western world. It should be noted, however, that the pessimism that tended to prevail among the thinkers and artists of the second phase of the Industrial Revolution did not always reflect the attitude of the masses, who were at last on the move toward a greater share of this world's material goods and privileges.

2. THE PHILOSOPHY OF DISENCHANTMENT

Although the Darwinian concept of evolution by natural selection made some of the philosophers of the late nineteenth century, such as Thomas Huxley, Herbert Spencer, and Ernst Haeckel, extremely optimistic about man and society evolving ever onward and upward, it had the opposite effect on others. A forerunner of the pessimistic type of materialism that was to have so much influence on the twentieth century was Arthur Schopenhauer (1788–1860). In *The World as Will and Idea*, published in 1819, forty years before *The Origin of Species*, this German thinker set forth the idea that one force governs and motivates the whole world of animate life, and that force is will—the will to survive. The world, therefore, is a cruel and heartless place full of struggling and competing creatures, a place where the strong and fierce devour the weak and gentle. The only possible happiness to be found in it is by ascetic denial and withdrawal. They suffer least who participate least in the hard, competitive world.

This line of thinking (at least a variation of it) was carried to its ultimate by an admirer of Schopenhauer, Friedrich Nietzsche (1844–1900). Nietzsche was a disillusioned German theological student turned philosopher. A pain- and nerve-racked genius, he finally went completely insane. Two of his most influential works are *Thus Spake Zarathustra* and *Beyond Good and Evil*. Like Schopenhauer, he believed that the greatest force in the animate world is will. However, this will is not only to survive but, in the strong at least, to achieve power. "The will to power" was Nietzsche's key phrase. If a superior society was to emerge, it would have to come about through the efforts of strong and gifted individuals who would rise to power because of their superior strength, will, and intelligence. Anything that contributes to power is good, be it brute strength, will, boldness, cunning, or intelligence. Whatever leads to weakness is bad, be it gentleness, modesty, generosity, or compassion. The two greatest enemies of the good society are democracy and Christianity. Democracy is the rule of the mediocre masses, cattle. But it was against Christianity that Nietzsche hurled his sharpest invective; he believed Christianity to be the greatest curse of Western civilization: a slave religion that extolls the vices of slavery, such as meekness, compassion, sacrifice, and charity, to compensate for actual weakness. Needless to say, Nietzsche was not very popular with the late nineteenth-century masses, who were obsessed with the marvels and promises of science and technology. However, his influence upon the twentieth century was great. Malignant nationalism, militarism, and fascism drew heavily on his ideas.

Less pessimistic than Schopenhauer's and Nietzsche's cult of the will but equally as materialistic was the philosophy of pragmatism. The chief expounder of this school of thought, which has been so potent and widespread in the twentieth century, was William James (1842–1910), a professor of psychology and philosophy at Harvard University. Pragmatism reflected the uncertainties aroused by atomic physicists around the turn of the century. James rejected all absolutes of logic and religion. Truth is relative depending upon the individual and the circumstances. A thing is true if it works and is useful. We cannot know ultimate religious or moral truths, for instance, but if a particular religious faith gives an individual confidence and peace of mind, then it is practical and therefore true for him. Thus spiritual, moral, and human values become as relative in the minds of William James and the pragmatists as the physical world in the mind of Albert Einstein.

One of James' most influential disciples was John Dewey (1859–1952), a professor of philosophy at Columbia University. Dewey introduced the principle of pragmatism into the classroom. If, for instance, experimentation proved that children found modeling a bust of Julius Caesar more interesting than learning Latin grammar, as indeed many did, much of the latter was discarded in favor of the former. Or if statistical studies showed that woodwork or typing was more often used in later life than algebra, then places were found for these useful skills, if necessary, at the expense of algebra. Everyone must be educated both for practical living and for citizenship. Dewey's pragmatism did much to enliven and democratize mass education in an age when the masses were moving to the fore. Unfortunately, in the hands of some of his more extreme disciples who possessed more enthusiasm than wisdom, thousands of twentieth-century classrooms became amusement centers for unrestrained children, large and small. It was in these classrooms that the philosophy of disenchantment—of relativism, cynicism, materialism, pragmatism—was likely to be disseminated by word and example to the masses.

3. REALISTIC LITERATURE

Much of the literature of the second phase of the Industrial Revolution, like the philosophy, reflected the materialism, the cynicism, and the pessimism of the age. However, there was a strong carry-over of romanticism beyond 1871 and into the twentieth century. The romantic poets Victor Hugo, Robert Browning, and Alfred Tennyson lived on until 1885, 1889, and 1892, respectively. Although Browning was a rugged and analytical realist when probing the depths of human psychology and emotions, he tended at times to be an idealist and an optimist, believing that "God's in his heaven, all's right with the world." And although in 1850 the young Tennyson in his *In Memoriam* revealed a religious skepticism bold for the time, in 1889—well into a cynical age—he hoped to see his "Pilot face to face" when he had "crossed the bar." Nevertheless, the prevailing and most significant trend in literature in the period 1871–1914 was realism. It was expressed most generally in the novel and drama rather than poetry. Realism tended to depict the seamy, sordid side of human nature and society. It villainized the smug, *nouveau riche* industrial bourgeoisie and its religious and moral hypocrisy without idealizing the uprooted and distressed proletariat.

France took the lead in realistic literature. Balzac, who died in 1850, though essentially a romantic novelist, had foreshadowed realism. In his forty-seven novels he subjected the dominant middle class to increasingly exact and severe scrutiny. The first French novelist to catch the full flavor of realism was Gustave Flaubert (1821–1880). His *Madame Bovary* related the illicit sex life of the wife of a small-town French physician in such full and unblushing detail that it scandalized a public not yet accustomed to such unrestrained "realism." *Madame Bovary* became a model to other novelists. Emile Zola (1840–1902), though interested like Flaubert in individual personality, was more concerned with social problems, particularly those created by indus-

trialization. Zola was a bold and radical republican who, it will be remembered, bearded the French military lion and played a prominent role in finally securing justice for Dreyfus. In twenty penetrating but sometimes tedious novels he depicted and analyzed the problems of a changing society. His sympathy was with the industrial proletariat, but he suffered no illusions as to the natural goodness of man, including the distressed lower classes.

The greatest and most influential of the French realistic novelists was Anatole France (1844–1924), whose real name was Jacques Thibault. Anatole France was essentially an Epicurean. With a light touch he satirized the bourgeois society and the Christian religion and morals of the second phase of the Industrial Revolution. The volume and the influence of his lucid writings were enormous. Three of his best-known novels are *Penguin Island*, *The Garden of Epicurus*, and *The Revolt of the Angels*. In later life he took an active part as a Socialist in the struggle to improve the status of the lower classes.

Charles Dickens (1812–1870) in Great Britain, like Balzac in France, combined romanticism and realism. In his sentimentality, his moralizing, his optimism, and his spontaneous gush of words he was a romantic. In his zeal for social reform, his pillorying of bourgeois arrogance and corrupt bourgeois institutions, and his graphic and often sordid detailing of the life of the urban proletariat, he was the first of the British realists. In *David Copperfield*, *Oliver Twist*, *The Pickwick Papers*, a galaxy of characters of the middle and lower walks of life in industrial Britain parade realistically before us. Thomas Hardy (1840–1928), unlike Dickens, had a completely pessimistic view of the universe. His vivid characters—ordinary English countryside folk —struggle Darwin-like against fate, environment, and their own frail natures without any help from God or Hardy. *The Return of the Native*, *The Mayor of Casterbridge*, and *Tess of the D'Urbervilles* are some of the best examples in any language of the realistic novel.

H. G. Wells (1866–1946) placed his faith in materialistic science, technology, and social reform. He fascinated a science-obsessed age with novels that made a world of scientific marvels and supermen seem real and at hand. High on Wells' list of outworn institutions that must be discarded before a scientific and socialistic utopia could be created was supernatural religion.

Probably the greatest of all the British realists was George Bernard Shaw (1856–1950). Of Irish birth, Shaw early crossed over to London, where he long remained the gadfly of bourgeois society. In scores of urbane and sophisticated novels, essays, and plays, he charmingly but caustically taunted Christianity, capitalism, and democracy. Shaw was a cynic, a Socialist, and a stark materialist. He was the epitome of late nineteenth-century and early twentieth-century realism.

In the United States, the era of the realistic novel began with the works of Theodore Dreiser (1871–1945). Dreiser was a member of a large German immigrant family who moved about in poverty from place to place in the Middle West, the Roman Catholic father trying unsuccessfully to keep the restless children in line. Dreiser's novels depicted in hard, rough detail the life and the philosophy of the disenchanted and uprooted proletariat, living in a materialistic, industrial world of changing values. His first novel, *Sister Carrie*, which appeared in 1900, was an American industrial version of *Madame Bovary* told with raw unrestraint. To escape poverty, Carrie became the mistress of a succession of men. The progressive degeneration of the characters constitutes the theme of the novel. Editors were so shocked at the frank and open presentation of lurid details that Dreiser had great difficulty getting the book published. The success of *Sister Carrie* was immediate, and other novels in a like vein followed. His masterpiece was *An American Tragedy*, published twenty-five years later. It was not only Dreiser's narrative that startled the generation of the early twentieth century, but his philosophy as well. He pictured an amoral world of materialistic science and technology where human animals struggle for survival, motivated by unedifying Freudian drives. Dreiser's brand of realism, or naturalism, as the more extreme form of realism is sometimes called, became the dominant trend in American fiction as the century progressed.

One of the most influential of the realists was the Norwegian playwright Henrik Ibsen (1828–1906). A frustrated artist embittered by youthful poverty, Ibsen ridiculed bourgeois society in his popular dramas. In what is probably his best-known play, *A Doll's House*, one of his heroines rebels against the "doll's house" that her stodgy, hypocritical, middle-class husband created for her. In *An Enemy of the People*, Ibsen reveals the fickleness of the masses and their unfitness for democratic government. *Ghosts* deals with the social and personal problems of syphilis.

Ibsen had a wide international following. He was the chief inspiration for the youthful George Bernard Shaw. In Germany, Gerhart Hauptmann (1862–1946) dramatized the dislocation of the proletariat during the early stages of the Industrial Revolution. In Russia, Dostoevski and Turgenev (see p. 740) combined realism with romanticism in much the same manner as did Balzac in France and Dickens in Great Britain. Leo Tolstoy (1828–1910) was more of a realist and dedicated his life and writing almost exclusively to social reform. His masterpiece is *War and Peace*. In this gigantic novel, scores of personalities along with more impersonal social forces so interlace with and influence each other that not even the strongest individual— not even Napoleon—can work his will alone. In his later years Tolstoy sought to combine Christianity with socialism, giving up his great inherited wealth to set a good example. Anton Chekhov (1860–1904) wrote polished but realistic and pessimistic plays about Russian peasant life. Maxim Gorky (1868–1936), up from the proletarian ranks, analyzed the social problems of the Russian masses in his dramas and novels. He was a revolutionary and later a Communist.

Realistic literature, with all its differing varieties, had many things in common. It reflected almost invariably the social dislocation brought about by the Industrial Revolution, particularly in its more advanced second phase. It reflected the materialism of an age of science and technology. It displayed over and over again the influence of Darwin and of Freud. It was increasingly concerned with the disillusionment and cynicism brought about by changing religious and moral values. This last factor is probably the most fundamental and significant of them all.

4. IMPRESSIONISTIC AND MODERN PAINTING AND SCULPTURE

France, the birthplace of realistic literature, was also the chief seat of the Impressionistic and modern painting and sculpture that predominated during the second phase of the Industrial Revolution. Impressionism was a mild and sophisticated revolt against the artistic standards that had prevailed since the late fifteenth century. It reflected the intellectual challenge to traditional values and institutions that arose with the startling advances of science in the late nineteenth century. It took its chief inspiration from the seventeenth-century Spanish painters Velásquez and El Greco, from Japanese art, which was rediscovered after 1853, and from new scientific knowledge concerning the nature of color and light. Impressionistic painting was informal, unposed, and random-angled. It sought to convey by studied casualness the impression of a view one gets at a glance. The chief founder of the Impressionistic style of painting was the Frenchman Edouard Manet (1832–1883). Among his more illustrious disciples were Claude Monet (1840–1926) and Auguste Renoir (1841–1919) in France, and James McNeill Whistler (1834–1903), an Ameri-

Pablo Picasso, Three Musicians (summer 1921), collage Cubism, oil on canvas, 6′ 7″ x 7′ 3¾″. Probably the most influential of all the artistic revolutionaries, Picasso during his long career experimented with many different styles and produced an immense oeuvre that spans both his own personal growth and most of the twentieth century. *Photo: Collection, The Museum of Modern Art, New York, Mrs. Simon Guggenheim Fund*

can expatriate in Europe.[1] These artists painted sunlit parks and landscapes, shimmering lakes and rivers, and subtle, sophisticated portraits. They omitted much detail, painting in only suggestive shapes, forms, and colors as first impressions, and leaving the rest to the imagination. Their work was sensuous, decorative, and mildly iconoclastic.

The breach that the Impressionists made with the long-established traditions was greatly widened near the end of the nineteenth century and early in the twentieth by

more radical modern painters. The new trend was led by Paul Cézanne (1839–1906), a lifelong friend of Emile Zola. Cézanne distorted freely in order to achieve a more powerful effect, and applied thick paint to attain the appearance of solidity and roundness. Going far beyond Cézanne, the gifted but eccentric Frenchman Paul Gauguin (1848–1903) and Dutchman Vincent van Gogh (1853–1890) broke openly with every artistic standard of the past. Gauguin was not interested in painting the literal document of his subject, but only what the subject meant to him. He painted patterns formed in his mind by objects rather than the objects themselves, using the most violent reds, yellows, and greens. He finally went primitive, deserting Western civilization for the South Sea islands.

---

[1] There were, of course, many other great Impressionist painters, such as Hilaire Degas and Henri Toulouse-Lautrec. The interested reader should consult the suggested readings at the end of the chapter for a fuller treatment of this subject.

Paul Cézanne, Still Life with Apples (1895–1898), oil on canvas, 27 x 36½ inches. *Photo: Lillie P. Bliss Collection, The Museum of Modern Art, New York*

Gauguin's friend, Van Gogh, would squeeze out paint directly from the tube on to the canvas to achieve weird but striking effects. Like Gauguin, Van Gogh was an Expressionist, freely distorting the images of nature to make them express his own feelings. Cézanne, Gauguin, and Van Gogh were the forerunners of many iconoclastic schools, such as Cubism and Futurism, that marked twentieth-century painting.

Two of the most influential of the revolutionary modern painters were the Frenchman Henri Matisse (1869–1954) and the Spanish-born (French by adoption) Pablo Picasso (1881–   ), both of whom received their chief inspiration from Cézanne. In some of their work they carried distortion to great extremes. Matisse became enamored with primitive culture. Picasso's figures during one phase of his long career became geometric (hence cubism) and disjointed. He occasionally gave up color entirely for black and white.

It is characteristic of an age of intellectual revolt and crumbling values (the Hellenistic period was such an age) that the artists turn inward. During the second phase of the Industrial Revolution, painting became highly individualistic. The artists tended to paint such objects as fruit, still life, and mandolins. Furthermore, they turned to figures on the periphery of a disintegrating society, such as prostitutes, solitary drinkers, blind beggars, and circus performers. The figures were separate, not joined. This disjointedness and the symbols of science, machinery, and speed, which were so prominent in this painting, surely represented an age of intellectual revolt against traditional values, of materialistic science and technology, and of mass movement. Unfortunately, much of this painting was so technical and highly specialized that it could be appreciated only by a relatively few, at a time when the many were seeking enlightenment.

The rapid growth of cities and of wealth during the second phase of the Industrial Revolution was responsible for the production of a large quantity of sculpture to decorate the new public buildings, squares, and parks. Most of it was patterned after the styles of the past, either classical or baroque, more often the latter. Probably the two sculptors of the period who most truly reflected the spirit of their own time and of future trends were Constantin Meunier (1831–1905) in Belgium and Auguste Rodin (1840–1917) in France. Meunier was the first great sculptor to recognize the importance of the industrial proletariat. Among his rugged and realistic statues are *The Hammersmith*, *The Puddler*, *The Mine Girl*, and *The Old Mine Horse*.

Auguste Rodin, Heroic Head (Pierre de Weissart), 1889, bronze. Rodin's powerful figures represent both a new departure in sculpture and a bridge from the nineteenth century to the twentieth, for he brought the impressionistic spirit to sculpture and was the forerunner of much of the abstract and symbolist work of the years between and after the world wars. Norweb Collection, The Cleveland Museum of Art. *Photo: J. Ciliotta*

Rodin introduced Impressionism into sculpture. His most famous statue, *The Thinker*, illustrates not only impressionistic art, but also the influence of the classical, Renaissance, baroque, and romantic styles. Rodin was the forerunner of much of the modern, abstract, and symbolist sculpture of the twentieth century.

5. FUNCTIONAL ARCHITECTURE

The architecture of the period 1871–1914, like the sculpture, combined the old with the new. The prevailing style in the numerous and increasingly large public buildings continued to be classical or baroque. Gothic architecture, which enjoyed a revival in the early part of the nineteenth century, was now limited primarily to university buildings and to churches. Even Byzantine, Moorish, and Oriental models appeared here and there throughout the West as the world was brought closer together by rapid communications.

The first great architect to develop a style appropriate to an age of steel, science, and speed was the American Louis Henry Sullivan (1856–1924). Sullivan pointed out that "Form follows function." That is to say, the style of buildings is determined by their intended use and by the materials used in their construction. This has always been true; Greek, Roman, Gothic buildings served utilitarian purposes, both secular and religious. Furthermore, the columns, posts and lintels, arches, vaults, and heavy walls that characterized these styles were the only known means of supporting massive or lofty structures. But in an age of structural steel this was no longer true. The architectural devices of the past had lost their utility, were purely decorative. And in fast-moving, crowded, and growing New York and Chicago, what sense did horizontal Greek or Moorish lines make? Sullivan designed the steel-supported skyscraper.

But Sullivan and his followers were not satisfied with the principle "Form follows function." They decided that function is the

The American architect Louis Henry Sullivan (1856–1924) was the first to determine that function is the sole purpose of the style of a building. It was he who first designed the steel-supported skyscraper that is the hallmark of twentieth-century cities all over the world. One of his buildings, the Carson-Pirie-Scott Department Store in Chicago, is in use today. *Photo: Hedrich-Blessing*

sole purpose of architecture. The application of this principle came to be known as "functional architecture." Structural steel, reinforced concrete, and glass brick made it possible for the functional architects to achieve unbroken horizontal lines impossible to the Greeks, and towering heights combined with gracefulness and light that the medieval Gothic builders never dreamed of.

Furthermore, the spirit of intellectual revolt against the standards and values of the past gave the architects a freedom to experiment never before enjoyed. Finally, unprecedented wealth and technological advances provided them with the means to execute their ideas. Some of the massive utilitarian structures of this and later periods, such as a number of the railway stations, some of the American skyscrapers like the Philadelphia Savings Fund Society Building and the United Nations Building, and the Firth of Forth, Brooklyn, Golden Gate, and Straits of Mackinac bridges are creditable monuments to an age of materialism.

6. MUSIC OLD AND NEW

Of all the arts, music showed the least responsiveness to the materialistic and scientific spirit of the second phase of the Industrial Revolution. Some of the greatest romantic composers of the first phase lived well on into the second. Wagner lived until 1883, Verdi until 1901. Their ranks were joined in the late nineteenth century by such great romanticists as Camille Saint-Saëns (1835–1921) in France and Peter Tchaikovsky (1840–1893) in Russia. Nor was there any lessening in the spirit of nationalism in music, which was such an important ingredient of romanticism. We have already seen (Chapters 47 and 50) how Wagner's nationalism became more militant after 1870. Tchaikovsky combined Russian nationalism with his romanticism. More strictly nationalist in their themes and folk tunes were the Russian Nicholas Rimsky-Korsakov (1844–1908); the Czech Anton Dvořák (1841–1904); the Norwegian Edvard Grieg (1843–1907); and the Finn Jean Sibelius (1865–1957). Not only romanticism but also classicism was carried over into the late nineteenth century by the great German composer Johannes Brahms (1833–1897). Spending the last thirty-five years of his life in the Hapsburg capital of Vienna, Brahms became an ardent Hungarian nationalist without giving up loyalty to his native Germany. Probably more than any other musician, Brahms resem-

bles Beethoven in style. Like Beethoven, he combined the classical spirit with the romantic.

The most important innovator in music in the period 1871–1914 was the French composer Claude Debussy (1862–1918). Debussy was the father of impressionistic music. Experimenting with subtle and sophisticated dissonances, he was to music what Manet and Renoir were to painting. Meanwhile, in Germany Richard Strauss (1864–1949) was startling and scandalizing his pre-World War I audiences with his complex and sometimes harshly dissonant "realistic" tone poems. He is often said to have ushered in the "modern" period in music. In Russia Igor Stravinsky (born 1882) was beginning his long career of composing music that was still more iconoclastic and abstract. He is called the father of the expressionist school. Stravinsky, with his more violent and impetuous dissonances, bears somewhat the same relationship to Debussy as does Picasso to Renoir in painting.

The radical, dissonant, and often noisy music of the followers of Debussy surely reflected the spirit of an age of materialistic technology and science, of cynical disenchantment, and of intellectual revolt against traditional values. We must not forget, however, that in any typical concert in the Western world in 1914—or in 1970 for that matter—Mozart, Beethoven, and Schubert would still predominate over Debussy and Stravinsky. The new grew up alongside but did not replace the old.

Meanwhile, looming ever larger in the materialistic, cynical, restless mind of the West from 1871 to 1914 was the spirit of nationalism. The character of the nationalism of this period was ominous, now that the aggressive nations were peopled by the "animal masses" of Darwin and Freud—animal masses whose claws and teeth were made ever so much sharper by science and technology. In 1914 Western man appeared to be on the threshold of a materialistic utopia, free from disease, grinding toil, and want. And yet the haunting pessimism of the time proved to be warranted.

Suggested Reading

General. **C. Brinton, *The Shaping of the Modern Mind* (Spectrum) is the latter part of Brinton's excellent work, *Ideas and Men.* A good intellectual history of Western Europe during the last two centuries is G. L. Mosse, *The Culture of Western Europe, the Nineteenth and Twentieth Centuries* (1961). Another useful study is **R. Williams, *Culture and Society 1780–1950* (Anchor).

The Philosophy of Disenchantment. A good biography of one of the most influential thinkers of the late nineteenth century is **W. Kaufmann, *Nietzsche: Philosopher, Psychologist, Antichrist* (Vintage). An excellent biography of the leading American pragmatist is R. B. Perry, *The Thought and Character of William James* (rev. ed., 1948). John Dewey, *Democracy and Education* (1916) is a major work by the philosopher who introduced the idea of pragmatism into American education.

Realistic Literature. The classic work on nineteenth-century literature by a brilliant Danish scholar is G. M. Brandes, *Main Currents in Nineteenth-century Literature* (6 vols., 1901–05). Realistic English literature is examined by J. W. Cunliffe, *English Literature During the Last Half Century* (1919). M. Geismar has written two scholarly books on twentieth-century American novelists—*Writers in Crisis* (1942) and *The Last of the Provincials* (1947). Two good histories of French and Russian literature are G. E. B. Saintsbury, *A Short History of French Literature* (7th ed., 1937); and M. Slonim, *The Epic of Russian Literature From Its Origins Through Tolstoy* (1950).

Impressionism, Functionalism, Modernism in the Arts. M. Raynal, *The Nineteenth Century: Goya to Gauguin* (1951) is an excellent treatment, beautifully illustrated. The chief French painters of the nineteenth century are briefly but expertly examined by R. E. Fry, *Characteristics of French Art* (1932). A good general survey is W. H. Wright, *Modern Painting* (1930). A. Hauser, *The Social History of Art* (1952) is a fruitful attempt to relate art to the society that produces it. Functional architecture is treated by **J. M. Richards, *An Introduction to Modern Architecture* (Pelican). Music since 1871 is explained in layman's language by two learned musicologists —C. Sachs, *Our Musical Heritage* (1948) and E. Stringham, *Listening to Music Creatively* (2nd ed., 1959).

Sources. Masterpieces of some of the leading thinkers and writers since 1871 that may be found in paperback edition are: **W. Kaufmann, ed. *The Portable Nietzsche* (Viking); **G. Flaubert, *Madame Bovary* (Modern Library); **H. Ibsen, *Ghosts, An Enemy of the People, A Doll's House, The Master Builder* (Modern Library); **E. Zola, *Germinal* (Dolphin); **A. France, *The Revolt of the Angels* (Crown); **T. Hardy, *The Return of the Native* (Pocket Books); **G. B. Shaw, *Man and Superman* (Penguin); **T. Dreiser, *Sister Carrie* (H. M. Riverside Literature series).

RETROSPECT

The growth of technology and science was so rapid in the industrialized countries during the period 1871–1914 that it influenced or overshadowed all other developments. Industrialization also spread during these years from its early base in Western Europe and the United States to Central and Eastern Europe, Japan, and the British dominions. Steel, oil, and electricity joined or superseded the iron and steam of the preceding age. This was the great era of railroad building. The automobile and the airplane appeared. Communications were revolutionized by the telegraph, the telephone, and wireless telegraphy.

Science kept pace with technology. The nature of matter was discovered and it proved to be as shockingly unstable as the old "absolutes" of time, space, and motion. Darwin's evolutionary hypothesis seemed to unlock most of the secrets concerning life on the planet. Medical science had its beginning in this period and the preceding decade. Psychology, sociology, and history made valiant efforts to be scientific. The people in the industrialized countries became fascinated by all this—the masses with the marvels and promises of technology, the intelligentsia with the wonders of science.

The first phase of the Industrial Revolution had belonged to the bourgeoisie. During the second phase, the industrial proletariat, now much more numerous and concentrated in the industrial cities, demanded and got many benefits. Liberalism became much more liberal. By 1914, practically every country in Europe enjoyed universal manhood suffrage. Liberals abandoned laissez-faire doctrines in favor of government protection for the poor and the weak. Public education and journalism became mass-oriented. But the masses were not waiting for the rather slow processes of government action alone to achieve their demands. By forming cooperatives and labor unions, they were exerting greater pressure on the capitalists by direct action than at the ballot box. The most extreme effort on behalf of the industrial proletariat during the years 1871 to 1914 was that of the Marxists: Marx and his followers set out to destroy the capitalistic system completely, and create a classless society.

Nationalism also underwent a drastic change during the second phase of the Industrial Revolution. It became much more aggressive and militaristic; it also became the foe of liberalism. Although all the great powers became infected by this new malignant nationalism, it was particularly strong in Germany and Russia, where liberalism had never gained a firm foothold. This new nationalism was the chief impetus behind the new burst of imperialism which by 1914 had brought most of Asia and nearly all of

Africa under the domination of Europe. The masses so rapidly gaining their freedoms at home, however, were eager to answer the first sound of the trumpet of the new nationalism to go fight the foreign foe.

Meanwhile, the Christian religion, which had for so long been the great commonality—the chief moral and spiritual guide—of Western civilization, underwent its severest test. It was challenged by science, technology, liberalism, and nationalism. And its influence appeared to be on the wane.

The arts and letters during the second phase of the Industrial Revolution also reflected the materialism and the social ferment of the period. The idealism and romanticism of the first phase were, in large measure, replaced by disenchantment, pragmatism, realism, and modernism.

Part Twelve

The Era of the Two World Wars

1914–1970

To many observers in 1914 it must have appeared that Western man had finally reached the gates of Utopia. Most of the things for which he had been struggling for thousands of years had finally been achieved. First of all, he appeared to have gained his freedom. Practically everywhere in the Western world males had obtained the suffrage. With the exception of Austria-Hungary, the major language groups had for the most part been consolidated into independent nations, and national pride was at its peak. Furthermore, the Western nations had gained virtually complete domination over the non-Western world.

Technology had reached a stage of development in the Western world (with the exception of Latin America) by 1914 that promised in the not too distant future freedom from material want, hunger, and grinding toil. Most glamorous of all the achievements of Western man by 1914, perhaps, was science. The last secrets of matter, life, man, and society seemed to be on the point of being solved by the natural and social scientists. In fact, man with his mastery of technology and science seemed to be ready to take the place of God—to be able to do all the things that had formerly been expected of God.

We now know, of course, that these were vain or exaggerated hopes and expectations. Western man did not enter the gates of Utopia in 1914, but into the bloodiest and most fear-and-hate-ridden half century in history. This half century was dominated by two world wars and the fear of a third and final atomic world war. Violent fascist and communist dictatorships challenged the disarrayed forces of liberal democracy. Western empires in Asia and Africa crumbled.

How and why did these things happen? Let us keep these questions in mind as we proceed to examine the latest epoch in the history of Western civilization.

825

Chapter 54 ❧ World War I, 1914–1918

The first blow that rocked the twentieth-century world was World War I. To most of mankind, busy with its daily tasks, it seemed to be a sudden and unforeseen disaster. To statesmen and informed students of world affairs, it was the snapping of long-developing tensions.

1. ORIGINS OF THE WAR

World War I began as a showdown between two hostile alliances of European powers: the Triple Alliance, composed of Germany, Austria-Hungary, and Italy; and the Triple Entente, composed of Great Britain, France, and Russia. This system of alliances was begun by Bismarck shortly after his defeat of France and the creation of the German Empire in 1870–1871. In 1873, as a safeguard against a revengeful France, or indeed against any hostile combination against Germany, Bismarck formed the Three Emperors' League, composed of Germany, Austria-Hungary, and Russia. When the interests and ambitions of Austria-Hungary and Russia proved to be incompatible, Bismarck replaced Russia with Italy (1882) to form the Triple Alliance. However, so long as he remained at the head of the German government, he carefully nurtured cordial relations with Russia and also

with Great Britain. This policy left France isolated and subject to repeated German bullying.

Bismarck's diplomatic work was quickly undone by Kaiser Wilhelm II, who ascended the German imperial throne in 1888 and forced Bismarck's resignation two years later. Wilhelm II immediately dropped the friendship pact with Russia and began to antagonize Great Britain by his grandiose schemes in the Near and Far East and by his huge naval building program. France was now able to form an alliance with Russia (1894) and an entente (understanding) with Great Britain (1904). In 1907 the Triple Entente was formed after Great Britain and Russia had settled their long-standing differences in Asia. Only an intense fear of Germany could have reconciled the sharply divergent interests that had long existed among these three powers.

Suspicion, hatred, and fear between the two power combinations mounted steadily. A ruinous armaments race ensued; the powers of the Triple Entente strove desperately to overcome Germany's long lead in land forces, while Germany sought to erase Great Britain's naval advantage. Rivalries and conflicts among the various members of the two alliances cropped up all over the world, threatening to embroil all the other members. In

World War I smashed the world of the nineteenth century and changed the "art of war" from carefully staged land or naval battles limited in area to chaotic, endless, and bitter fighting along miles and miles of "fronts" and over whole oceans. This photograph shows American soldiers in France in 1918. *Photo: United Press International*

1905–1906 and again in 1911 two such clashes occurred in Morocco between France and Germany. Two occurred in the Balkan Peninsula between Russia and Austria-Hungary. In 1908 Austria-Hungary suddenly annexed two provinces, Bosnia and Herzegovina, which were inhabited by Serbs and Croats. Serbia had planned to annex these territories, peopled by her own linguistic kinsmen. She appealed to her big Slavic brother, Russia. Russia threatened Austria-Hungary, whereupon Germany rattled her mighty sword and forced Russia to back down. A second Balkan crisis occurred in 1912–1913. The various Balkan states defeated Turkey and then fought among themselves over the spoils. Victorious Serbia threatened to expand. Austria-Hungary not only thwarted Serbia's expansion to the Adriatic Sea, but threatened to annihilate her. Again Serbia appealed to Russia and again Germany forced Russia to back down. Each of these crises brought the world close to war, increased international tension, and speeded up preparations for a final showdown.

It was in the Balkans that the fatal explosion finally occurred. Here the interests of Russia and Austria-Hungary clashed head-on. The Serbs, Bulgarians, Rumanians, and Greeks were religious (Orthodox) and cultural (Byzantine) kinsmen of the Russians. The Serbs and Bulgarians were also linguistic (Slavic) kinsmen of the Russians. Moreover, the Balkan Peninsula was of great economic and strategic interest to Russia. Since the days of Ivan III in the fifteenth century, Russia had sought control of the Bosporus and Dardanelles (the Turkish Straits) as a water outlet to the West. Austria-Hungary's interests in the Balkans were, perhaps, even more vital than those of Russia. The Dual Monarchy's chief interest in the area grew out of the polyglot nature of its empire. It was composed of numerous language groups, some of which, particularly the Serbs, Croats, Slovenes, and Rumanians, had linguistic kinsmen in the Balkans.

As the Ottoman Empire in the Balkan Peninsula disintegrated in the nineteenth and early twentieth centuries, the various Balkan language groups emerged as independent nations. These free peoples constituted a strong attraction for the members of their language

Language Groups, Austria-Hungary

SLAVS
Germans
Italians
Magyars
Rumanians

Croats and Serbs
Czechs and Moravians
Poles
Slovaks
Slovenes
Ruthenians

groups in Austria-Hungary, who wished to break loose and join them. This was particularly true of Serbia, which attracted the Hapsburgs' Yugoslav subjects (the Serbs, Croats, and Slovenes). But if the Yugoslavs should join Serbia, Austria-Hungary's other language minorities—Italians, Czechs, Slovaks, Poles, Rumanians, and Ruthenians—would also demand their freedom from Austrian and Hungarian rule and the Dual Monarchy would fall apart. Austria-Hungary therefore felt that she must control the Balkan Peninsula in self-defense. It was also the only direction in which she could expand, particularly after her exclusion from Germany in 1866. And the militancy that characterized nationalism after 1871 caused all nations to feel that they must expand.

Overlying the clashing interests of Russia and Austria-Hungary in the Balkans were those of Germany and Great Britain. Germany felt she must maintain the integrity of the Dual Monarchy, which was her only effective and reliable ally. Then, too, her own ambitions in the Balkans and the Near and Middle East were great. One of Kaiser Wilhelm II's chief imperial projects was the Berlin-to-Bagdad railway (see pp. 792–793), which would make German power dominant in the Ottoman Empire if not the whole Near and

This well-known photograph of the Archduke Franz Ferdinand, heir to the thrones of Austria-Hungary, and his wife was taken as they entered their carriage in Sarajevo on June 28, 1914, just a few minutes before they were assassinated by a Serbian nationalist. *Photo: United Press International*

Middle East. This scheme gravely menaced Great Britain's own imperial life line running through Suez as well as her immediate interests in the Near and Middle East. Germany's project threatened to blight permanently Russia's hopes of gaining an outlet through the Turkish Straits and to cut Russia off strategically from her allies. And France and Italy had interests in the Balkans and in the Near and Middle East, although their primary concern was their commitments to their respective allies.

When, therefore, a third crisis occurred in the Balkans in the summer of 1914, all the great powers of Europe were automatically involved. The two Moroccan crises, the two Balkan crises, and the feverish armaments race had brought the tension in Europe to the breaking point. All that was needed was an incident.

2. THE FATAL EXPLOSION

The incident was the shooting at Sarajevo of the Austrian Archduke Francis Ferdinand by a Serb on June 28, 1914. The assassination was a deliberate plot involving numerous Serbian army officers. Francis Ferdinand, heir to the Austro-Hungarian throne, was singled out because the Serbs feared that his liberal policy toward the Yugoslavs in Austria-Hungary would allay their discontent, thereby lessening their desire to break away and join Serbia. After the assassination, the government of Austria-Hungary decided to crush Serbia and establish her own dominance in the Balkans once and for all. This would require the backing of Germany, for clearly Russia would not stand aside and allow her Serbian kinsmen and allies to be so treated or her own national interests to be thus violated. At a fateful conference in Berlin eight days after the shooting, Kaiser Wilhelm II gave Austria-Hungary Germany's "blank check." He urged Austria-Hungary to act quickly while world opinion was still outraged by the assassination and promised to support her in any emergency. This promise by the German Kaiser greatly intensified the crisis. Russia would not allow

Austria-Hungary to destroy Serbia; Germany would not allow Russia to defeat Austria-Hungary; and France and Great Britain would not allow Germany to defeat Russia, whose support they felt to be indispensable in future dealings with Germany.

Armed with Germany's blank check, Austria-Hungary presented Serbia with an impossible ultimatum. When Serbia failed to yield to all of its terms, Austria-Hungary declared war and invaded Serbia. Russia mobilized her forces against Austria-Hungary and Germany. Germany sent harsh ultimatums to Russia and to France. When Russia failed to reply and France gave an unsatisfactory reply, Germany declared war on Russia on August 1, and on France two days later. The next day, August 4, when German troops violated Belgian neutrality on their way to attack France, Great Britain declared war on Germany. Thus, by August 4, 1914, all the great powers of Europe except Italy were at war. Italy claimed that she was not obligated to aid her allies, Germany and Austria-Hungary, since they were the aggressors. The following year, she entered the war on the side of the Entente powers. To the side of Germany and Austria-Hungary came Turkey and Bulgaria; these were referred to as the Central Powers. To the side of the Entente powers, who came to be called the Allies, eventually came much of the rest of the world—some thirty-two nations in all. This was truly a world war.

In following the tragic events just related, one can hardly fail to be impressed by the great role played by the spirit of malignant nationalism. It was aggressive nationalism that destroyed much of the spiritual unity of Western Christendom, that motivated much of the revived imperial competition, that energized the massive armies, that refused to yield or compromise in times of crisis, that made international law impossible, and produced international anarchy instead.

3. GERMANY'S NEAR TRIUMPH

In a long-drawn-out war, the advantage would appear to lie with the Allies in view of their

The Central Powers

Occupied Areas

Areas of Major Land Fighting

superior manpower and resources and their control of the seas. However, Germany had no intention of fighting a long war, and few world observers saw much possibility of the Allies preventing the superior German army from winning a quick and crushing victory on the mainland of Europe. The German high command had long anticipated the military situation that confronted it in August 1914, and had developed a plan of operation known as the Schlieffen plan. This plan called for a holding action against the slow-moving Russians while the main German forces concentrated on a quick knockout of France, which possessed the only army in the world that gave the Germans any real concern. The main German blow would be a surprise thrust through Belgium, despite a treaty guaranteeing Belgian neutrality, which was signed by all the great powers, including Germany.

Pouring through Belgium, the German army would capture Paris and encircle and destroy the French armies in eastern France. It was calculated that no more than six weeks would be required to crush France. Then the Germans would concentrate on and destroy Russia and with relative ease. Great Britain, her allies gone, would sue for peace.

The Schlieffen plan came near succeeding. Stubborn Belgian resistance held up the Germans long enough for the French to redeploy their forces to the north and for the British to throw their small army across the Channel. Nevertheless, the seemingly irresistible German juggernaut crunched ahead; by the first week in September, it was outside Paris ahead of schedule. At this juncture, the desperate French and British armies turned on the Germans and in the bloody seven-day Battle of the Marne not only defeated them, but drove them back a few miles. Both sides extended their lines from the Swiss border to the North Sea and entrenched. The First Battle of the Marne was one of the decisive battles in history, for it forced on the Germans a long war of attrition that made possible their ultimate defeat.

An important factor in the German defeat at the Marne was the detachment at the critical moment of 100,000 of their best troops for use against the Russians, who had invaded Germany with unexpected speed. Generals von Hindenburg and Ludendorff, with several divisions, were hastily dispatched to the eastern front. Under their command the reinforced German armies trapped the Russians at Tannenberg and administered a crushing defeat that sent them reeling back into Russia. Meanwhile, the British navy swept the Germans from the surface of the seas and set up a blockade of Germany. However, the Germans quickly discovered Britain's Achilles' heel with a new weapon: the submarine.

In 1915 the Germans staged a holding operation in the west while they delivered a series of hammer blows upon the Russians, driving deep into Russia and inflicting immense casualties. A major Anglo-French effort to come to the aid of the hard-pressed Russians by breaking through the Dardanelles was beaten back by sea and by land with heavy losses. In 1916 Germany returned to the assault in the west. In the nine-month Battle of Verdun, the French held the Germans back, but at an enormous cost in men and supplies. The four-month Battle of the Somme between the British and the Germans was even bloodier. Like Verdun, it ended in a stalemate. In the Battle of Jutland, the biggest naval battle in history up to that time, the British fleet thwarted the effort of the German fleet to break the blockade, but suffered serious losses.

By 1917 Germany and her allies, though beginning to show signs of strain, appeared to be close to victory. French morale dropped at the front and behind the lines; numerous units of the battered army mutinied. The Germans launched an unlimited submarine campaign against Great Britain that soon brought her near starvation. The combined German and Austro-Hungarian forces administered a crushing defeat to Italy. In November 1917, Russia, suffering unbearable hardships at the front and behind the lines, succumbed to the Communist Revolution and soon thereafter withdrew from the war. (The story of the Russian Revolution will be told in the following chapter.) And although the harsh terms forced upon helpless Russia by the Germans in the Treaty of Brest-Litovsk strengthened the resolve of the remaining Allies to fight to the finish, the Germans were now able for the first time in the war to concentrate their full strength on the weary French and British. The prospects for the Allies seemed dim. It was at this critical juncture that the United States entered the war.

4. THE ENTRY OF THE UNITED STATES AND THE VICTORY OF THE ALLIES

When the war had begun in 1914, President Woodrow Wilson had admonished the American people to remain neutral in thought as well as in deed. However, from the beginning, public opinion in the United States, as indeed in the entire world, was that Germany and her allies were the aggressors. As Germany came nearer and nearer to victory, most Americans, Republicans and Democrats alike, came increasingly to fear that a German victory would be a world calamity in which the United States would be an eventual victim. To the holders of this view, it would be clearly in the self-interest of the United States to help prevent the fall of France and Great Britain rather than have to face a victorious Germany alone. But the German government eventually gave the United States little choice. Early in the war, the Germans violated American neutrality by using their embassy in Washington as a center for spies and saboteurs to prevent the sale of munitions to Great Britain and France. Early in 1917, the German government, anticipating war with the United States, offered Texas, New Mexico, and Arizona to Mexico as a reward for attacking the United States. Apparently, California was to be offered to Japan. The Zimmermann Note, making this offer, was intercepted by British intelligence and turned over to the United States. For some strange reason, the German government admitted its authenticity.

The sinking of American ships by German submarines, however, provided the immediate impetus for the entry of the United States into the war. When the Germans first began large-scale sinkings of merchant and passenger ships in 1915, President Wilson had protested so vigorously that the Germans finally agreed to desist. Great Britain and France, it is true, had seized some American ships attempting to evade the blockade of Germany, but no lives had been lost and damages had been paid. Early in 1917, the German high command decided to launch an unlimited submarine campaign against enemy and neutral shipping alike. The German leaders fully expected that this course would bring the United States into the war, but they believed that Great Britain and France would be crushed before any appreciable American

weight could be brought to bear in Europe. Upon the announcement of this policy, the American government immediately broke off diplomatic relations with Germany. After several American ships had been sunk, on April 6 Congress, at the request of President Wilson, declared war, not on the German people, but on the German imperial government. The vote for war—82 to 6 in the Senate and 373 to 50 in the House of Representatives—probably reflected the opinion of the American people.

Although a full year elapsed before American troops were able to play an important role at the front, the boost in Allied morale was immediate, and the Americans lost no time supplying financial, material, and naval aid. And although the total contribution of the United States to Allied victory was relatively small as compared to that of France and Great Britain, America's role, coming as it did when both sides were approaching exhaustion, was probably decisive. At the beginning of 1918 the race was between Germany and the United States. Germany transferred troops from the Russian front to overwhelm Great Britain and France before large numbers of American troops could arrive, while the United States strove to raise, train, and transport to France sufficient forces to stem the German tide. Again the advantage appeared to lie with Germany.

In March 1918, Field Marshal Ludendorff, now in command of the German armies, launched the first of a series of massive blows on the western front designed to end the war. The British and French were driven back with heavy losses. In desperation, they at long last agreed to a unified command under France's General Ferdinand Foch. The Americans, under General John J. Pershing, also accepted his command. By the middle of June, Ludendorff had launched four great drives, and the Allied lines had been battered so thin that, when the climactic fifth drive began along the Marne River in mid-July 1918, Ludendorff wired the Kaiser: "If the attack succeeds, the war will be over and we will have won it."

When Foch heard the opening German barrage, he wired his government: "If the present German attack succeeds, the war is over and we have lost it." The Germans were stopped by a narrow margin. Foch, now receiving a swelling stream of fresh American troops and armaments, immediately ordered a counterattack. In the Allied counterattack, the tank, developed by the foresight of young Winston Churchill, then First Lord of the British Admiralty, proved to be the breakthrough weapon. German strength and morale waned rapidly; the war was lost.

The first of the Central Powers to go out of the war was Bulgaria, which at the end of September 1918 surrendered to French, British, and Serbian forces operating from the Greek port of Salonika. A month later Turkey surrendered to British imperial forces in the Near East. Austria-Hungary, her various language groups in revolt, surrendered on November 3 to Italian, British, and French forces driving in from Italy. The following day, a full-fledged mutiny which had been brewing for several days broke out in the German navy and quickly spread throughout Germany. On November 11, the German commanders, their armies hopelessly beaten and in full retreat from France and Belgium, accepted Foch's armistice terms, which amounted to outright surrender.

5. THE PEACE SETTLEMENT

The Allied statesmen who gathered in Paris in January 1919 to try to make a lasting peace were confronted with a formidable task. Much of Europe had been shattered by a war of unprecedented scope and destructiveness. Nine million men had been killed in battle. A much larger number had died of diseases traceable to the war. Twenty-one million had been wounded. The financial and material losses were incalculable. No Western power was solvent. (Even the United States, the most fortunate of the Western powers, was saddled with a huge national debt that she has never been able to reduce significantly.)

The German, Austro-Hungarian, Ottoman, and Russian empires had collapsed. The British and French empires were seriously weakened. A tenth of the richest part of France had been laid waste. Hate and disillusionment poisoned the atmosphere.

Although all thirty-two of the victorious Allies were represented at the Paris Peace Conference, the great decisions were really made by the leaders of the Big Three: France, Great Britain, and the United States. The French delegation was headed by Premier Georges Clemenceau, the aged "Tiger of France." As host to the conference and head of the nation that had done the most to defeat Germany and that had suffered the most, he expected to dominate the decisions. Leading the British delegation was the eloquent and fiery "Little Welsh Attorney," Prime Minister David Lloyd George. As spokesman for the British Empire, which comprised one-fourth of all the land and people in the world, he also expected to dominate the conference. At the head of the American delegation was President Woodrow Wilson. A fundamental and bitter clash immediately developed between Clemenceau, who wanted a hard peace that would mutilate Germany and make her harmless in the future, and Wilson, who wanted a "just" peace free of vindictiveness of any kind. Specifically, Clemenceau demanded the detachment from Germany of all her territory west of the Rhine and its annexation or control by France. Only by this means, he believed, could the power balance be tipped in favor of France and French security safeguarded against another German assault. Wilson would not tolerate another "Alsace-Lorraine in reverse." In the end he proved to be more eloquent and stubborn than Clemenceau, and to his side eventually came Lloyd George. Great Britain needed the trade of a recovered Germany and did not wish to see France become too dominant on the Continent. The Treaty of Versailles with Germany reflected Wilson's ideas in fundamental principles though not in every detail.

Six months of hard work and bitter wrangling were required to draw up the treaty. Its most important terms were, in brief, as follows: Germany and her allies were forced to accept full responsibility for the war. Germany was compelled to give up all her overseas colonies and concessions. Alsace and Lorraine were returned to France. Three tiny districts were ceded to Belgium, and the Danish-speaking portion of Schleswig was returned to Denmark. The Polish-speaking areas of eastern Germany, most of which had been seized by Prussia in the eighteenth century, were ceded to the resurrected Polish state. With one exception, wherever doubt existed as to the wishes of the people in the affected areas, plebiscites were held to determine their desires. The exception was the Polish Corridor, which was cut along the Vistula River to give Poland an outlet to the sea. Although this territory had been seized from Poland by Frederick the Great and approximately half its population was still Polish-speaking, its cession to Poland severed East Prussia from the main body of Germany and gave Hitler his excuse for beginning World War II.

Germany's army was cut down from the most powerful military machine in history to 100,000 officers and men, who were to be long-term volunteers to prevent a rapid turnover of trained personnel. Her navy was reduced from the world's second greatest to six small battleships, six cruisers, and a large number of auxiliary vessels. She was permitted no submarines, no military aviation, no poison gas (which she had introduced during the war), and no offensive weapons such as tanks and heavy artillery. Germany's Rhineland was to be permanently demilitarized, and her munitions industries were made subject to Allied inspection. Her general staff was to be dismantled and her top war leaders tried for violations of the rules and customs of war and, if found guilty, punished. (The Kaiser fled to the Netherlands just before Germany collapsed, and the Netherlands refused to give him up.) Germany was prohibited from making economic reprisals against her neighbors

and her former enemies. Finally, Germany was held liable for an indemnity that in 1921 was set by an Allied reparations commission at approximately $33 billion. Wilson and Lloyd George believed these terms to be just. Clemenceau considered them to be suicidally lenient.

The treaties with Germany's allies were actually more severe than the Treaty of Versailles because the principle followed in territorial rearrangements was freedom or union of all national language groups, and Germany was more homogeneous linguistically than were her allies. The polyglot Austro-Hungarian Empire was split up along language lines. The Czechs and Slovaks were formed into the new state of Czechoslovakia, which unfortunately also included sizable German and other minorities. The Poles were joined to Poland, the Rumanians to Rumania, the Italians to Italy, and the Serbs, Croats, and Slovenes to Serbia, which now became Yugoslavia. Thus the Dual Monarchy was cut down from a nation of 50 million second in area only to Russia among the nations of Europe to an Austria of 6.5 million German-speaking Austrians and a Hungary of 8 million Magyars. Austria was forbidden to unite with Germany. Bulgaria lost her territory along the Aegean Sea to Greece and became one of the smallest Balkan states. Turkey was shorn of her far-flung non-Turkish territories. The new Turkey included only the Anatolian plateau in Asia and the city of Constantinople and its immediate hinterland in Europe. The new national boundaries, in spite of the painstaking care with which they were drawn up, left many pockets of discontent to breed future conflicts.

6. THE LEAGUE OF NATIONS

Wilson, quite aware of the impossibility of making perfect treaties, placed his chief hopes for peace in an association of nations that would settle peaceably the tensions and conflicts that were certain to arise in the future. Fearful that, if left to future negotiations, the

ARCTIC OCEAN

NORTH CAPE

Murmansk

Reykjavik **ICELAND**
(Denmark)

Narvik

FAEROE I.
(Denmark)

NORWAY

SWEDEN

FINLAND

Archangel

L. Onega

L. Ladoga

Volgoda

Helsinki
Reval
ESTONIA

Leningrad

Moscow

S O V

ORKNEY I.
SCAPA FLOW

Oslo

Stockholm

Riga
LATVIA

Edinburgh *NORTH SEA*

DENMARK

Copenhagen

Memel
LITHUANIA

Kaunas
Vilna

WHITE
RUSSIAN
S.S.R.

ULSTER
IRISH
FREE STATE **GREAT BRITAIN**

Dublin Liverpool

Danzig
*POLISH
CORRIDOR*

EAST
PRUSSIA

Hamburg
Bremen

BALTIC SEA

POLAND

Warsaw
Brest-
Litovsk

Kiev

London

NETHERLANDS
Amsterdam

Berlin

*ATLANTIC
OCEAN*

Rhine R.

GERMANY

UKRAINIAN
S.S.R.

Brussels
BELGIUM

RUHR

WEIMAR REPUBLIC

Weimar

Dresden

Prague

GALICIA

Dniester R.

Cologne

Frankfurt

Versailles

Paris

Metz

LUX.

SAAR

Strasbourg

CZECHOSLOVAKIA

Stuttgart

FRANCE

SWITZERLAND

Munich

Vienna

Budapest

AUSTRIA

HUNGARY

BUKO-
VINA

BESSARABIA

CRI

Geneva Locarno

Trent

Trieste
Fiume

TRANSYLVANIA

RUMANIA

Sevasto

Bordeaux

Bilbao

YUGOSLAVIA

Zara
(Italy)

Belgrade

DOBRUJA

BLA

Bucharest

Marseilles

ADRIATIC SEA

Danube R.

PORTUGAL

Madrid

Florence

SERBIA

Sofia
BULGARIA

Lisbon

S P A I N

Barcelona

*CORSICA
(France)*

Rome **ITALY**

ALBANIA

(Turkey) Istanbul

Seville

BALEARIC I.
(Spain)

Naples

GREECE

AEGEAN SEA

Smyrna

T U

Cadiz

Gibraltar *(Britain)*

Tangier

SPANISH
MOROCCO

Algiers

SARDINIA

SICILY

Athens

DODECANESE
(Italy)

MOROCCO
(France)

ALGERIA
(France)

TUNISIA
(France)

MALTA (Britain)

M E D I T E R R A N E A N

S E A

CRETE (Greece)

0 100 200 300 miles

Europe 1923

Areas Lost by Germany
Areas Lost by Russia
Areas Lost by Ottoman Empire
Austria-Hungary 1914

Sverdlovsk

SOVIET UNION

Orenburg
Samara
Volga R.
Saratov
KAZAK S.S.R.
Tsaritsyn
Astrakhan
CASPIAN SEA
CAUCASIA
GEORGIAN S.S.R.
Tiflis
Baku
AZERBAIJAN S.S.R.
Batum
ARMENIAN S.S.R.
Tabriz
IRAN
Mosul
SYRIA AND LEBANON
Baghdad
Tigris R.
Euphrates R.
CYPRUS (Britain)
IRAQ
LEBANON
TRANS-JORDAN
PALESTINE
SAUDI ARABIA
TURKEY

forming of such an association might be shunted aside or put off indefinitely, he insisted that its framework be incorporated in the treaty with Germany. The first twenty-six articles of the Treaty of Versailles therefore constitute the covenant of the League of Nations. Aware also that the United States and some of the other great powers were not yet willing to surrender their absolute sovereignty to a world government, Wilson felt it necessary to settle for a league that lacked the power to compel the major nations to obey its decisions. He hoped and believed that the United States and the other great powers could be persuaded to join such a league and that it would become a steppingstone to eventual world government.

The central body in the League of Nations, which served as a general clearinghouse and forum for discussion, was the General Assembly. All members of the league were represented in the General Assembly and each member had one vote. In addition to serving as a discussion forum, the General Assembly supervised the work of numerous specialized agencies and participated in the choosing of members of all the other bodies in the league. The nearest thing the league had to an executive organ was the Council. This was made up of five permanent members and six nonpermanent members chosen for three-year terms on a staggered basis by the General Assembly. The five permanent members were to be the United States, Great Britain, France, Italy, and Japan. The Council was empowered to make decisions and recommendations relative to the prevention of war. Its decisions required unanimity, which meant that all the permanent members possessed a permanent veto over its work. Carrying on the day-to-day business of the league was the Secretariat, headed by a secretary-general. Closely associated with the league was the Permanent Court of International Justice, with headquarters at The Hague in the Netherlands. The World Court, as it was generally called, was to settle international legal, but not political, disputes.

The League of Nations had no military

837

The "Big Four" as they posed for newsreels at Versailles in 1919. Left to right, Lloyd George, Vittorio Orlando, Georges Clemenceau, Woodrow Wilson. *Photo: United Press International*

forces at its command. Its only teeth, so to speak, were Article X and Article XVI. Article X stated that every member undertook to guarantee the territorial integrity of every other member. This meant that in case one member was attacked, all the other members were morally obligated to come to its aid. However, there was no way to compel them to do so. Article XVI stated that, if a nation went to war in violation of a decision of the league, all the members of the league were to boycott the aggressor. This weapon (economic sanctions) could have been a potent deterrent if faithfully applied. In the last

analysis, however, the success of the League of Nations depended primarily upon its support by the Big Three victorious democracies —the United States, Great Britain, and France.

The refusal of the United States to join the League (see pp. 864–865) was a body blow. Great Britain and France immediately lost faith in it and began to pursue their traditional nationalistic aims. Nevertheless, for twelve years the league achieved some noteworthy accomplishments. Sixty-two nations joined it. Germany was admitted in 1926, and the Soviet Union in 1934. The league supervised the carrying out of many of the terms of the treaties, aided tens of thousands of war refugees, gave financial aid to insolvent nations, settled numerous international disputes, promoted international good will, and supported many humanitarian measures.

However, in no case did it undertake to discipline a great power, and many observers feared the outcome of such a test. The test came in 1931, when Japan invaded Manchuria. The league's failure to pass it marked the beginning of its end and of the return to war.

Suggested Reading

Origins of World War I. **W. L. Langer, *European Alliances and Alignments, 1871–1900* (Knopf) is a scholarly, detailed study of the web of diplomatic intrigue that preceded World War I. A lucid and much briefer account is **B. E. Schmitt, *Triple Alliance and Triple Entente* (Berkshire). **S. B. Fay, *Origins of the World War* (Free Press) is scholarly and well written. It is favorable to Germany and did much to fuel the flames of isolationism in the United States between the two world wars. B. E. Schmitt, *The Coming of the War, 1914* (2 vols., 1930) is a detailed documentary analysis of the chain of events immediately preceding and leading to World War I. It, too, is very readable. It is more critical of Germany's role than is Fay. Probably the most objective of all the major studies of the origins of World War I is L. Albertini, *The Origins of the War, 1914* (3 vols., 1952–57). This is a masterpiece of historical scholarship. A more recent study by a German scholar, **Fritz Fisher, *Germany's War Aims in the First World War* (Norton), first published in 1961, shows Germany's aims and motives to have been much more aggressive than Fay, Schmitt, and Albertini had supposed.

The War. A brilliant account of the immediate background and the opening campaigns of World War I is **B. Tuchman, *The Guns of August* (Dell). The journalistic style belies the painstaking research that went into this excellent work. The best two single-volume histories of World War I are **C. Falls, *The Great War, 1914–1918* (Capricorn) and C. R. M. Cruttwell, *A History of the Great War, 1914–*

1918 (2nd ed., 1936). They are strictly military histories, but are written in nontechnical language for the layman. A much more detailed history of the war is J. Buchan, *A History of the Great War* (4 vols., 1922). A highly interesting account of the war's most fabled battle is **A. Horne, *The Price of Glory: Verdun, 1916* (Colophon). Russia's disastrous role in the war and the collapse of her government are ably portrayed by **M. T. Florinsky, *The End of the Russian Empire* (Collier). A good account of the harsh settlement that Germany forced upon Russia is J. Wheeler-Bennett, *The Forgotten Peace* (1939). The best account of the circumstances of the entry of the United States into the war is C. Seymour, *American Diplomacy During the World War* (1942). This is a work of first-rate scholarship on a controversial subject. Another excellent work on this subject is E. F. May, *The World War and American Isolation, 1914–1917* (1959). B. Tuchman, *The Zimmermann Telegram* (1958) is a scholarly monograph about a serious German blunder that helped to ensure the entry of the United States into the war. F. Chambers, *The War Behind the War, 1914–1918* (1939) tells the often-neglected story of the home fronts in the various countries.

The Peace Settlement. The classic monumental history of the Paris Peace Conference, 1919, containing many of the official documents, is H. W. V. Temperley, *A History of the Peace Conference of Paris* (6 vols., 1920–24). Excellent briefer histories of the peace conference are F. S. Marston, *The Peace Conference of 1919: Organization and Procedure* (1944);

and P. Birdsall, *Versailles Twenty Years After* (1939). A very good brief account of Wilson's predominant role in the making of the peace by the foremost authority on Wilson is **A. Link, *Wilson the Diplomatist: A Look at His Major Foreign Policies* (Quadrangle). An interesting eye-witness account of the conference by Col. E. M. House's private interpreter is Stephen Bonsal, *Unfinished Business* (1944). An influential and controversial book is J. M. Keynes, *The Economic Consequences of the Peace* (1920). Keynes, the famous British economist, condemns the allegedly harsh treatment of Germany. Keynes is strongly repudiated by the Frenchman **Etienne Man-taux in *The Carthaginian Peace—or the Economic Consequences of Mr. Keynes* (Pittsburgh). A well-written history of the League of Nations is F. P. Walters, *A History of the League of Nations* (2 vols., 1952).

Historical Fiction. Three celebrated novels that bring World War I close to the reader are: Jules Romains, *Verdun* (1940); **E. M. Remarque, *All Quiet on the Western Front* (Crest), bringing home to millions of readers the realities of trench warfare; and **E. Hemingway, *A Farewell to Arms* (Scribners), based upon the author's experiences on the Italian front.

Chapter 55 ❧ The Triumph of Communism

in Russia

One of the most important and ominous of the immediate fruits of World War I was the triumph of communism in Russia. In the postwar years, when the statesmen of the Western democracies were attempting to restore the shattered world of 1914, the Russian Communist leaders were striving to destroy not only Russia's capitalistic, semifeudalistic society, but indeed all Western civilization, based upon Christianity, liberalism, and capitalism, and to create an entirely new civilization based upon the blueprints of Marx and Lenin.

1. THE BOLSHEVIK REVOLUTION OF 1917

The violent Russian upheaval of 1917 was the result of maladjustments and discontent that had been long developing. Russia, except for a handful of intelligentsia, had been virtually bypassed by the great liberalizing movements, such as the Renaissance, the Enlightenment, and the French Revolution, which had influenced Western Europe. The Industrial Revolution, which brought in its wake bourgeois liberalism and proletarian radicalism, reached Russia only in the 1890s. While Western and parts of Central Europe and the United States were becoming industrialized and increasingly liberalized, Russia remained a land of primitive and illiterate peasants, feudal aristocracy, and tsarist autocracy. Many of the frustrated

Russian intelligentsia in the latter half of the nineteenth century turned to terroristic nihilism and then to Marxism (see pp. 781–782). The violent wing of the Russian Marxist party, the Bolsheviks, boycotted the abortive liberal revolution of 1905–1906, seeking instead the total destruction of Russia's existing institutions. The Bolshevik leaders were hunted down by the state police and shot, imprisoned, or exiled. Those who escaped bided their time, many of them abroad, plotting the eventual overthrow of the tsar's government.

The Bolsheviks' opportunity came in 1917. During the first three years of World War I Russia suffered staggering losses at the hands of the superior German armies. Behind the lines the suffering of the civilian population, much of which could be attributed to the corrupt bureaucracy of the tsar, was acute. By 1917 many Russians felt that they had suffered enough. In March of that year a mild revolution in Petrograd [1] overthrew the government of the well-meaning but incompetent Nicholas II and set up a moderate bourgeois regime, in which Alexander Kerensky came to be the leading figure. The Kerensky regime attempted to liberalize the Russian government and to continue the war against

---

[1] At the beginning of World War I the Russians changed the name of St. Petersburg, which was a German name, to Petrograd, its Russian form. When Lenin died in 1924, it was changed to Leningrad.

Germany in cooperation with the Allies. Both tasks appeared to be beyond the capacity of the inexperienced new government. At the front, morale was low, weapons and munitions were nearly spent; at home there was spreading anarchy.

In order to increase the chaos and remove Russia from the war, the German government, in April 1917, transported the top Bolshevik leader, Nikolai Lenin, from his place of exile in Switzerland to the Russian border. This brilliant and dynamic leader quickly organized the radical forces against the moderate government. A clever phrase-maker, Lenin knew how to appeal to all the disaffected elements. "Peace to the army, land to the peasants, ownership of the factories to the workers!" To Lenin's side in Petrograd flocked the other Bolshevik leaders whom the Kerensky regime, in a conciliatory effort, had released from their various prisons and exiles: Leon Trotsky, Joseph Stalin, and the rest.[2] In November 1917, the Bolsheviks, under Lenin's skillful direction and with perfect timing, overthrew the moderate Kerensky government and set up a Communist dictatorship.

[2] Lenin, Trotsky, and Stalin are assumed names, but these are the names they were and are known by.

2. EARLY COMMUNIST EXPERIMENTS AND THEIR FAILURE

In order to free the new regime for the enormous task of refashioning Russian society, Lenin immediately opened peace negotiations with the Germans. (The Russian troops were deserting in droves to grab lands and jobs in the new utopia). The Germans, realizing Russia's helplessness, demanded the harshest of terms. Lenin attempted to stall them off, but when the Germans threatened to march on Petrograd and Moscow, he was forced to sign the Treaty of Brest-Litovsk (March 1918). Russia lost Finland, Estonia, Latvia, Lithuania, the Ukraine, Bessarabia, her Polish provinces, and some of her Trans-Caucasian territory. These lands contained one-third of Russia's European population, three-fourths of her iron, and nine-tenths of her coal. In addition, she was compelled to pay a heavy indemnity.

But these hard terms were not the end, or the worst, of Lenin's woes. Two years of bitter civil war followed the peace with Germany. The aristocracy, including most of the higher army officers, faced with extermination, flew to arms against the Bolshevik regime. These "white" forces were aided by various other disaffected groups and by French, British, Polish, Japanese, and a few American troops. It was with the greatest of difficulty that the "red" armies, hastily organized by Trotsky, finally liquidated the "whites." In doing so, the Bolsheviks regained the Ukraine. However, a large additional strip of territory was lost to Poland, thanks largely to French armed intervention on the side of the Poles.

In the midst of these disasters, Lenin's Bolshevik regime undertook to create a pilot Marxist state out of the wreckage of the Russian Empire. (For Marxist theory and Lenin's amendments to it, see Chapter 49.) In place of the tsarist hierarchy, a pyramid of people's councils, or *soviets*, each dominated by a few Communist Party members, was set up. Capitalism (including even the use of money) was abolished. All industry and commerce were placed under the management of committees of workers responsible to Party commissars. The land, far from being distributed to the peasants, as they had been led to believe, was nationalized and turned over to the management of local peasant committees, who distributed it to individual peasants to be worked by their own labor. All crop surpluses were expropriated by the state.

Russia's war-torn economy was soon in shambles. The workers did not know how to run factories and trains, nor did they know how to distribute goods. When the peasants saw that their surpluses would be seized by the government, they refused to raise more than they needed for themselves. By 1921, some 30 million Russians were threatened with starvation, and in spite of considerable foreign relief, particularly from the United States, many hundreds of thousands did starve. Lenin, a realist, saw the necessity for retreat. In 1921 he launched the NEP (New Economic Policy), which was a temporary compromise with capitalism. In order to provide incentive, industries employing fewer than twenty workers were permitted to operate under private ownership. These little industrial capitalists were called *nepmen*. Enterprising peasants, called *kulaks*, were permitted to own and rent land and hire laborers. Money and credit were restored. This small-scale capitalistic activity was closely supervised and regulated by the state. However, the NEP provided enough incentive to pull the Russian economy out of chaos. In 1923, just as the new policy was beginning to function, Lenin suffered a paralytic stroke, and died the following year.

A view of Moscow's most famous shopping street (the huge GUM building is in the foreground) during the revolution in 1917. *Photo: United Press International*

This rare photograph, taken in 1923 at a Party meeting, shows the beginning of the feud between Stalin and Trotsky that ended with Trotsky's murder in Mexico in 1940. As the brilliant, eloquent Trotsky speaks, the taciturn Stalin, son of ex-serfs, eyes him coldly from his seat at the right. *Photo: United Press International*

3. STALIN AND THE FIVE-YEAR PLANS

Lenin's death precipitated a power struggle among his chief associates. The world assumed that his successor would be Leon Trotsky, who had been the chief organizer of the Red Army and had planned its victory over the Whites. A brilliant and eloquent Communist theorist, Trotsky was an apostle of world revolution, and such an uncompromising Communist that he opposed the NEP. At the time of Lenin's death he was the People's Commissar of War. Trotsky and the world, however, underestimated Joseph Stalin, executive secretary of the Communist Party. This unobtrusive and taciturn little man was an un-

scrupulous behind-the-scenes operator. Stalin was the son of poverty-stricken ex-serfs. Expelled from an Orthodox seminary because of his Marxist views and activities, he became a professional revolutionist and terrorist. ("Stalin" is a pseudonym meaning "steel.") He was repeatedly arrested and imprisoned and repeatedly escaped. World War I found him in a Siberian prison. Taking advantage of the amnesty granted to all political prisoners by the Kerensky regime in 1917, Stalin hastened to Petrograd, where he became a devoted and undeviating associate of Lenin. He played a prominent role in the civil war against the Whites and became executive secretary of the Communist Party. In this key position he made himself master of the all-important party machinery. Lenin, in his last will and testament, declared that Stalin was "too hard, too cruel" to be fit for the headship of the government. Nevertheless, the astute Stalin soon maneuvered himself into absolute dictatorship over Russia. Conspiring with one prominent group of Bolsheviks after another and playing off one faction against another, Stalin crushed Trotsky, had him expelled from the Party, and exiled him from Russia. In 1940 Trotsky was murdered in Mexico, presumably by an agent of Stalin. Eventually Stalin executed all his top Bolshevik associates and rivals. By 1928 his dictatorship over Russia was complete.

In that year Stalin launched the first of a series of five-year plans. These were units of planned economy with certain specific goals or objectives to be achieved every five years. They marked the end of the NEP, which had served its purpose of pulling the Communist economy through its first major crises. The objectives of the first five-year plan were: (1) the elimination of the last remnants of capitalism, (2) the industrialization of the Soviet Union, (3) the collectivization and mechanization of agriculture, and (4) national defense.

Achievement of the first goal meant the liquidation of the nepmen and the kulaks. When tens of thousands of the independent peasant-proprietor kulaks resisted collectivization, Stalin ruthlessly exterminated them. The consolidation of their farms into mechanized collectives and the organization of giant state farms went on apace. The state farms were huge outlays up to 300,000 acres in size run by Party managers and hired laborers. Every effort was made to mechanize them. Vast tracts of land in southeast Russia and Siberia were brought under cultivation for the first time. The collective farms were of various types, the most common of which was the *artel*, which the kulaks were first encouraged and later forced to join. In this type of collective, independent farmers surrendered their lands and horses but retained their houses, gardens, cattle, pigs, and chickens for

their own private use. The artel was run by elected managers who were instructed and supervised by Party officials. Elimination of the tiny individual tracts, each one of which had been surrounded by ditches or hedgerows, made mechanization possible. A certain amount of the harvest was set aside for taxes, insurance, improvements, and feed. A large part had to be sold to the state at a fixed price. The rest was distributed to the peasant members in proportion to the amount of their original contribution to the collective in land and horses and to the amount and quality of their work. The mechanization of Russia's primitive agriculture required the construction of huge quantities of tractors and farm machinery.

Since the Industrial Revolution was still in its infancy in Russia in 1928, industrialization meant building from the ground up and concentration on producer goods. Western engineers and technicians were lured to Russia with high salaries. Capital was obtained by exporting scarce supplies of wheat, often at ruinously low prices. At the cost of much privation, enormous strides were made. Steel mills, power plants, foundries, mines, refineries, and railroads were built all over the Soviet Union. At Dnepropetrovsk on the Dnieper River, the world's largest dam and hydroelectric power plant were constructed. At the end of 1932, it was announced that all the goals of the first five-year plan had been reached several months ahead of time.

The second five-year plan, which was launched immediately, called for greater production of consumer goods: the gadgets and comforts of life that are usually referred to as the standard of living. These were the things the Russian masses had never had and were now striving for. But hardly had the second five-year plan begun when Hitler came to power in Germany with a program calling for the conquest and enslavement of Russia. Stalin immediately shifted the chief emphasis from production of consumer goods to production of weapons of defense—and not a minute too soon. Russia only narrowly es-

The world's largest dam and hydroelectric power plant at Dnepropetrovsk on the Dnieper River at its opening in 1932. It was one of the successfully met goals of the first of the Five-Year plans. *Photo: TASS from Sovfoto*

caped total conquest by Nazi Germany (see p. 879).

The economic achievements of Communist Russia have been beyond doubt phenomenal. When the Bolsheviks took over in 1917, Russia was a defeated, war-torn, primitive, agricultural country. Twenty-four years later, when the Germans invaded her in 1941, she was the fourth-greatest industrial power in the world; in a number of categories, she had surpassed both Great Britain and Germany and was second only to the United States. She could never have withstood the German assault had this not been true. Russia's agriculture was no longer primitive but largely mechanized. By the mid-1930s new crop records were established almost every year. Food rationing was

abandoned. Most of these achievements had been made since 1928. They were made, of course, at the cost of total loss of individual freedom (although there had never been much freedom in Russia under the tsars), the liquidation of tens of thousands who sought to retain some measure of freedom, and the privation and forced labor of the rest.

4. THE SOVIET POLITICAL SYSTEM

The Bolsheviks, on coming to power, broke the Russian Empire into eleven socialist republics: Russia proper and ten other language or dialect areas. In 1939–1940 five more were added from territories seized by Russia at the outbreak of World War II. Thus the

Soviet Union is in theory a union of sixteen autonomous republics. (U.S.S.R. stands for Union of Soviet Socialist Republics.) Actually, however, Russia itself constitutes at least four-fifths of the total area and population, and the so-called Union is in reality a monolithic police state.

The Soviet system of government as originally set up consisted of a pyramid of elected councils—village, district, county, and provincial—culminating in the Union Congress of Soviets, which met once every two years and chose executive and administrative boards. Voting was by show of hands in mass meetings. The urban vote was given more than double the weight of the rural vote, since Bolshevism's chief concern was the industrial proletariat. In 1936 Stalin promulgated a new constitution, which appeared to be more democratic. Voting was to be by secret ballot, the differential between the urban and the rural vote was abolished, and the members of the various soviets in the pyramid were to be elected directly by the local districts. The member republics in the union were allegedly granted complete autonomy.

When one examines the actual functioning of the soviet system, however, it quickly becomes apparent that the new constitution, like the old, is entirely farcical as far as democracy is concerned. Only the Communist Party is permitted to engage in organized political activity. It names the official candidates, makes all political policies and platforms, and conducts all election promotion and propaganda. Opposition to the Party's official candidates and program is considered to be disloyal and is ferreted out and crushed by the state police, both secret and regular. The all-powerful Communist Party is organized on an authoritarian basis. The Politburo,[3] eleven men meeting in secret and responsible only to themselves, makes all decisions, which are transmitted without question down through the chain of command to the local cells.

Blind and unquestioning obedience to superiors is demanded of all Party members. Party members are carefully selected and trained. As set up by Lenin, the total number has been kept relatively small, never more than 7 million out of a total population of nearly 200 million. Those of questionable loyalty or zeal are constantly purged. During the late 1930s a series of purges liquidated hundreds of Party members, including a number of the top military and civilian officials in the Soviet Union. Thus constitutions, elections, and elected governmental bodies in Communist Russia are a sham. There is no democracy and no political or civil liberty. The Soviet Union is a dictatorship and a police state.

5. SOVIET EDUCATION, ARTS, AND RELIGION

In 1917 more than 60 percent of the Russian people were illiterate. It was Lenin's belief that a Communist state requires an educated populace in order to succeed. Nearly all the top Bolsheviks themselves were educated men —in fact, they would be considered members of the intelligentsia in almost any time or place. Little could be done in the educational field in the first turbulent years of the Communist regime, but education received major attention in Stalin's five-year plans. In 1928 the Communists launched the vastest program of free compulsory secular education in history. The program covered all levels—elementary, secondary, and higher—for both the young and adults. It included a comprehensive system of technical and on-the-job training. Science and engineering were particularly stressed. By the middle of the twentieth century, Soviet universities and institutes were graduating more than twice as many engineers as were those of the United States, the most materially advanced and technology-conscious capitalistic country. All Soviet engineers were receiving five years of training instead of the four usual in the United States. Of course, Soviet education was interlarded with Communist propaganda, but its stand-

---

[3] The name of the Politburo was changed to Presidium after World War II.

ards were high, and it turned out the kinds of trained people who were needed. In 1941 Stalin announced that illiteracy had been banished from Russia. The quality of Soviet education is difficult to assess. It is certain that much of it was crude and makeshift and that the truth was often deliberately distorted. On the other hand, Western assumptions that Soviet science and engineering were too shoddy to produce tanks that would run and planes that would fly, not to speak of nuclear fission, proved to be dangerous miscalculations. Another facet of Soviet education was the emphasis upon physical education. The results of this emphasis became apparent in international athletic competition.

Nor were advanced scholarship and the arts neglected in the Soviet Union. The world's most extensive program of scholarships, prizes, and institutes was inaugurated for the purpose of encouraging and subsidizing superior talent. Soviet musicians, architects, painters, and dancers more than held their own in international competition. American visitors to the Soviet Union were repeatedly surprised at the great interest of the people in the arts and in classical literature. Yet even the arts ran afoul of the Communist police state. All liberal, bourgeois, or capitalistic literature (which was most of it) was heavily censored. In 1958 Boris Pasternak was officially rebuked for his novel *Doctor Zhivago*, which portrays the Communist revolution in a rather unfavorable light. Under pressure, he declined the Nobel prize for literature. Such world-renowned composers as Prokofiev and Shostakovich occasionally fell into official disfavor because of their modern "bourgeois" music. When some powerful commissar decided that the Mendelian law of genetics, which is generally accepted in the world of science, ran counter to the Party line, Soviet geneticists were forced to disclaim it. Such incidents lead one to wonder how long the arts and pure science can flourish in a police state.

Of all the facets of communism and of its clash with Western Christian civilization, one of the most fundamental is the difference in outlook on religion. The weakening of Christianity in the late nineteenth century in the face of onrushing science, technology, and malignant nationalism was undoubtedly a major factor in the rise of Marxist materialism. Marx and Lenin both were keenly aware of the importance of religion. They considered it "the opiate of the people"—a concoction of the "haves" to quiet the "have nots" lest they demand and seize their share of this world's goods. But communism is itself a religion. Stark materialism and class hatred are its basic doctrines. Marx and Lenin are its major prophets, and their writings are its scriptures.

The religious policy of the Bolsheviks, upon gaining power in Russia, was quite similar to that of the French Revolutionists in 1789–1794. All church property was confiscated. The churches themselves were turned into museums or clubs of various kinds, although they were sometimes leased to religious congregations for purposes of worship. No religious instruction whatever was permitted in the schools, which were all public and secular. The churches were forbidden to give organized religious instruction and even to maintain seminaries for the training of their own clergy. On the other hand, the schools were flooded with Communist propaganda. An oath of atheism is required for membership in the Communist Party. Physical attacks on the clergy and the faithful occurred from time to time, and of course active participation in religious activities was certain to blight a young Russian's career under the Communist regime.

The Communist leaders have always claimed that their harsh treatment of the churches was necessitated by the active opposition of the churches to the Communist government. They claim that when they first came to power they granted religious freedom for the first time in Russian history, but that the churches immediately used this freedom to advocate the overthrow of the very government that granted it. They further claim that churches have always been the tools and agents of capitalistic governments and interests. Whatever truth there may be in these claims, it would appear that religion has remained a great problem and danger to the Soviet regime. Mankind is inherently religious, and churches have nearly always thrived under persecution. Religious groups with international connections, such as the Roman Catholics, Lutherans, and Jews, have attracted sympathy abroad and projected the question of religion into Russia's foreign affairs.

6. SOVIET FOREIGN POLICY

It is Soviet foreign policy that is of greatest concern to the rest of the world. Were the Soviet Union an isolated island, the rest of the world might look upon it as an interesting and perhaps exotic experiment and wish it well. But it is very much in and of the world, to which it has always loomed as an ominous threat. It occupies one-sixth of the land surface of the earth, including the strategic heartland of the world's greatest land mass. It has great physical resources. Its population of some 200 million is rapidly increasing. The Marxist ideology, as modified by Lenin, is activist and violent. What is the foreign policy of the Soviet Union? The rest of the world wants, indeed demands, to know. Is it world conquest, world revolution, or both? These questions are as difficult as they are pressing, partly because of the secretiveness and callous duplicity of the Soviet police state and partly because of the hysteria that has so often accompanied the quest for the answers.

When the Bolsheviks first took over in 1917, they confidently expected most of the capitalistic governments in the war-weary world to collapse and follow Russia along the path of communism. To encourage them to do so and to avoid fulfillment of the harsh terms of the Treaty of Brest-Litovsk, the Communist leaders began an active campaign of revolutionary infiltration and subversion abroad, particularly in Germany. Although some headway

was made in Germany, Bavaria falling under Communist control for a brief time, the only country to go Communist was Hungary, where in 1919 Béla Kun set up a Communist dictatorship that lasted four months. To guide and aid the Communist parties in other countries in the common cause of world revolution, the Bolsheviks set up the Comintern (Communist International) with headquarters in Moscow.

The Western capitalistic powers were as antagonistic to the Soviet Union as was the Soviet Union to them. Thinking that the Bolshevik regime would soon collapse, France, Great Britain, Japan, and the United States landed troops on Russian soil in 1918 and aided the counterrevolutionary White forces. France helped the Poles to seize a large strip of Russian-speaking territory. Great Britain and France organized the anti-Soviet regimes in the countries of Eastern Europe bordering the Soviet Union into a *cordon sanitaire* (health or quarantine belt). For several years, no Western power would recognize the Bolshevik regime. The Soviet Union was refused admission to the League of Nations until 1934, eight years after Germany had been admitted and one year after she had withdrawn under the guidance of Hitler. Even then the Western powers steadfastly refused to cooperate with the Soviet Union in any collective action against the rising Fascist menace.

Nonetheless, the failure of the Communist movements abroad and of the Bolsheviks' early efforts to communize Russia overnight caused the Soviet leaders to adopt a more conciliatory attitude toward the capitalistic powers. The NEP needed foreign commerce and foreign capital in order to function. However, as long as Lenin lived, his inveterate hatred of capitalism kept the spirit of conciliation at a minimum. As noted previously, after his death in 1924 a momentous struggle for top place ensued between Trotsky and Stalin. Trotsky, an uncompromising apostle of pure communism and of world revolution, opposed the NEP and all accommodation to the capitalistic world. Stalin, on the other hand, was a practical realist and compromiser. His prime interest was in making the Communist regime a going concern in the Soviet Union; in Marxist terminology, he advocated "communism in one country." No sooner had Stalin begun to gain the ascendancy over Trotsky than he offered trade concessions to trade-hungry capitalistic powers in return for recognition of the Soviet regime. Great Britain and France yielded to these inducements in 1924. (Germany had recognized the Soviet Union in 1922 in order to frighten her Allied conquerors.) Following the lead of Great Britain and France, one capitalistic state after another recognized the Soviet Union. The United States, which held off until 1933, was the last one to do so.

The five-year plans, which began in 1928, required much Western capital and technical assistance, and by that time Stalin's triumph over Trotsky was complete. Therefore, the next ten years represented the high tide of Soviet tractability toward the capitalistic Western democracies. Stalin showed little or no interest in the Comintern, which was allowed to languish. His foreign minister, Maxim Litvinov, became a respected and even popular figure in Geneva, Paris, London, and Washington. Of course, the Soviet Union's fear of the growing Nazi German menace after 1933 was a significant factor in her conciliatory attitude toward the capitalistic democracies. It was impossible to know whether Stalin was sincere or whether he was merely using the capitalistic democracies until the Soviet Union was strong enough to go it alone and possibly turn against them. At any rate, the honeymoon ended in 1938 with the Munich crisis (see pp. 872–873). From that time, Stalin was apparently convinced that real cooperation with the Western democracies was impossible. The cooperation forced upon the Soviet Union and most of the capitalistic world by the menace of the Axis during World War II lasted only until victory was assured. Meanwhile, after Hitler came to power in 1933, the greatest threat to both the Soviet Union and the capitalistic democracies was Nazi Germany.

Suggested Reading

The Bolshevik Revolution of 1917. The most detailed and authoritative history of the Soviet Union is the multivolume, still-unfinished work by E. H. Carr, *A History of Soviet Russia* (7 vols., 1950 ff.). The first three volumes cover the Bolshevik revolution 1917–1923. Carr does not allow his sympathy for the aims of the revolutionists to interfere with the quality of his scholarship. A good brief account of the revolution by a leading scholar is **G. Vernadsky, *The Russian Revolution, 1917–1931* (Berkshire). A highly readable account, written in a journalistic style for the nonspecialist, is **Alan Moorehead, *The Russian Revolution* (Bantam). Another excellent account for the nonspecialist is **B. Wolfe, *Three Who Made a Revolution* (Delta), which emphasizes the roles of Lenin, Trotsky, and Stalin. Two good studies of the intervention of the capitalistic powers, including the United States, in the civil war are **G. F. Kennan, *The Decision to Intervene* (Atheneum); and J. A. White, *The Siberian Intervention* (1950). A brilliant comparison of the Russian, American, French, and English revolutions is **C. Brinton, *The Anatomy of Revolution* (Vintage).

Soviet Political System and History. The best two biographies of Lenin are **L. Fisher, *Life of Lenin* (Colophon); and **D. Shub, *Lenin* (Mentor). **I. Deutscher, *Stalin: A Political Biography* (Vintage) is not only a scholarly biography of the Soviet dictator, but a good history of the whole Communist movement in Russia. The government of the U.S.S.R. is explained by S. N. Harper and R. Thompson, *The Government of the Soviet Union* (1949); and M. Fainsod, *How Russia Is Ruled* (1963). Police state tactics in a totalitarian dictatorship are described by Z. K. Brzezinski, *The Permanent Purge: Politics in Soviet Totalitarianism* (1956); and W. G. Krivitsky, *In Stalin's Secret Service* (1939). Krivitsky was the former head of Soviet intelligence. The best history of the Comintern in English is H. Seton-Watson, *From Lenin to Khrushchev: The History of World Communism* (1960).

Soviet Economy, Education, Arts, Religion. H. Schwartz, *Russia's Soviet Economy* (1954) was written by a *New York Times* reporter after spending many years in the Soviet Union. J. Maynard, *Russia in Flux* (1948) favorably compares the life of the Russian peasant under communism with his condition before the revolution. N. Jasny has written two important books about the Soviet economy, *The Socialized Agriculture of the U.S.S.R* (1949), and *Soviet Industrialization, 1928–1952* (1961). M. Gordon, *Workers Before and After Lenin* (1941) is an interesting study of that subject. Two good studies of religion in the Soviet Union are N. S. Timasheff, *Religion in Soviet Russia, 1917–1942* (1943); and J. S. Curtiss, *The Russian Church and the Soviet State, 1917–1950* (1953). Worthwhile studies of education in the Soviet Union are M. J. Shore, *Soviet Education: Its Psychology and Philoso-*

phy (1947); B. King, *Changing Man: The Education System in the U.S.S.R.* (1936); and G. S. Counts and N. Lodge, *The Country of the Blind: The Soviet System of Mind Control* (1949). A good history of Russian literature, before and after the revolution, is D. P. Minsky, *A History of Russian Literature* (1949). **B. Pasternak, *Doctor Zhivago* (Signet) is the most noteworthy novel yet written in the Soviet Union. It is a vivid portrayal of life under communism and a stinging if subtle rebuke of its regimentation of life. It was originally published in 1957.

Soviet Foreign Policy. **L. Fischer, *The Soviets in World Affairs* (Vintage) is a lucid analysis by an astute observer of Soviet and world affairs. E. H. Carr, *The Soviet Impact on the Western World* (1947) is a sympathetic account. Much less sympathetic is G. F. Kennan, *Russia and the West Under Lenin and Stalin* (1961). M. Beloff has written two scholarly works on Soviet foreign policy, *The Foreign Policy of Soviet Russia, 1929–1941* (2 vols., 1947–52), and *Soviet Policy in the Far East, 1944–1951* (1953).

Life in the Soviet Union. Three excellent studies of Soviet man and the conditions of life in the Soviet Union are E. Crankshaw, *Russia and the Russians* (1948); **K. Mehnert, *Soviet Man and His World* (Praeger); and A. Inkeles and R. Bauer, *The Soviet Citizen: Daily Life in a Totalitarian Society* (1960).

Chapter 56 ❧ The Triumph of Fascism in Italy,

Germany, and Japan

A fruit of World War I more bitter and poisonous even than communism was fascism. We cannot yet know which of these violently antiliberal forces will prove to have the more enduring vigor, but there is no question that fascism constituted the more immediate threat to liberal democracy. It was fascism that broke down the peace settlement and brought on World War II. The first Fascist dictatorship was set up by Mussolini in Italy. However, it was Fascist Germany and Japan that became the most virulent threats to world peace.

1. MUSSOLINI CREATES THE FIRST FASCIST STATE

Italy emerged from World War I battered and humiliated. Although she was one of the victorious Allies, her armies had made a poor showing and she had realized few of the grandiose ambitions for which she had entered the war. In the Paris peace settlements she had been awarded the adjacent Italian-speaking areas of Austria-Hungary, but had been denied further acquisitions east of the Adriatic and the Turkish and German provinces in Asia and Africa, some of which she ardently desired. These frustrations were severe blows to Italian national pride. Italy's weak economy emerged from the war acutely maladjusted. The national debt was huge, and the treasury empty. The inflated currency, together with a shortage of goods, raised prices ruinously. Hundreds of thousands of demobilized veterans could find no jobs. In the summer of 1919, there was widespread disorder. Veterans began seizing and squatting on idle, and sometimes on cultivated, lands. Sit-down strikes developed in the factories. During the winter of 1920–1921, several hundred factories were seized by the workers. Bolshevik agents arrived from Russia to exploit the distress. The Italian government, torn by factions, seemed too weak to prevent the disorder and protect private property. Although the strife diminished and the Communist threat waned before the end of 1921, the landords and the factory owners were thoroughly frightened. Many of them, and indeed many small business and professional men, longed for vigorous leadership and a strong government. The vigorous leader who stepped forward was Benito Mussolini. The strong government was his Fascist dictatorship.

During the 1930s, Hitler's main concern was to rearm and remilitarize Germany. Men and matériel were trained and built, and the nation and the world were frequently reminded of Germany's growing strength by public displays such as this one. *Photo: United Press International*

Benito Mussolini speaks to a great crowd in Rome after a victory of the Italian forces in Ethiopia, which was conquered as a first step in the Fascist dream of a restoration of the ancient Roman Empire. *Photo: United Press International*

Mussolini was a dynamic organizer and leader. The son of a humble blacksmith, he became first a teacher and later a radical journalist and agitator. Before World War I he was a pacifistic socialist, but during the war he became a violent nationalist. After the war he began organizing unemployed veterans into a political action group with a socialistic and extremely nationalistic program. During the labor disturbances of 1919–1921, Mussolini stood aside until it became apparent that the radical workingmen's cause would lose; then he threw his support to the capitalists and the landlords. Crying that he was saving Italy from communism and waving the flag of nationalism, Mussolini or-

ganized his veterans into terror squads of black-shirted "Fascisti," who beat up the leaderless radical workingmen and their liberal supporters. He thereby gained the support of the frightened capitalists and landed aristocracy. By 1922 Mussolini's Fascist party was strong enough to "march on Rome" and seize control of the faction-paralyzed government. Appointed premier by the weak and distraught King Victor Emmanuel III, Mussolini quickly turned his premiership into a dictatorship. All opposition was silenced. Only the Fascist party (like the Communist Party in the Soviet Union) could engage in organized political activity. The press and the schools were turned into propaganda agencies. The secret police were everywhere. Eventually, the Chamber of Deputies itself was replaced by Mussolini's hand-picked Fascist political and economic councils.

Italy's economic life was strictly regimented, but in such a way as to favor the capitalistic classes. Private property and profits were carefully protected. All labor unions were abolished except those controlled by the Fascist party. Strikes and lockouts were forbidden. Wages, working conditions, and labor-management disputes were settled by compulsory arbitration under party direction. An elaborate system of planned economy was set up for the purpose of modernizing, coordinating, and increasing Italy's production of both industrial and agricultural goods. The very complicated economic and political machinery that Mussolini created for these purposes was called the corporate state. Under the whip and drive of Mussolini, remarkable increases in production were achieved. Trains began to run on time, the budget was balanced, and the currency was stabilized. But taxes were the highest in the world, and labor's share in the fruits of increased production was small.

Fascism, however, was primarily political in character, not economic. The essence of its ideology was nationalism—malignant nationalism run wild. Mussolini understood the dynamic, energizing quality of this kind of nationalism. His writings and speeches rang with such words as "will," "discipline," "sacrifice," "decision," and "conquest." "The goal," he cried, "is always—Empire! To build a city, to found a colony, to establish an empire, these are the prodigies of the human spirit. . . . We must resolutely abandon the whole liberal phraseology and way of thinking. . . . Discipline. Discipline at home in order that we may present the granite block of a single national will. . . . War alone brings up to the highest tension all human energy and puts the stamp of nobility upon the people who have the courage to meet it." The Fascists adopted the trappings and symbols of ancient Rome. The word "fascism" itself comes from the word "fasces," meaning a bundle of rods surrounding an ax borne by Roman magistrates as a symbol of authority. Here we have the arrogant militaristic nationalism of the late nineteenth century, including the "superman" theory of Carlyle, Wagner, and Nietzsche, come to full flower.

Fascism, of course, clashed head-on with Christianity both in spirit and in deeds. In fact every fundamental principle in Fascist philosophy has its opposite in Christian doctrine: love thy neighbor—hate and conquer thy neighbor; blessed are the meek—blessed are the strong-willed and arrogant; blessed are the peacemakers—blessed are the warmakers. Nevertheless, Mussolini realized the advantage of coming to terms with the powerful Roman Catholic Church and made a treaty with the pope—the Lateran Treaty of 1929. The pope recognized Mussolini's regime. (Since the pope had been despoiled of his territories, 1860–1870, he had refused to recognize the Italian government.) In return, Mussolini paid him nearly $100 million in cash and government bonds from a hard-pressed national treasury and allowed the teaching of religion by Roman Catholic clergy in the public schools. This seeming accord, however, was uneasy and quarrelsome from the start.

The building of a powerful army and navy and the recovery of Italy's national prestige were always uppermost in Mussolini's thoughts. Fascist Italy's militarism, self-assertiveness, and expansive ambitions played an important part in the breakdown of the peace settlement and the return to war. Before we examine these activities, however, we must trace the rise and triumph of fascism in Germany and Japan, both of which were more powerful and dangerous to the rest of the world than was Italy.

2. GERMANY REFUSES TO ACCEPT THE PEACE SETTLEMENT

Germany emerged from World War I defeated, humiliated, and angry. As late as July

1918, she had seemed to be invincible; four months later she had been forced to surrender, hopelessly beaten. Then, she was compelled to sign a dictated peace treaty, the terms of which she considered unjust. Furthermore, she was virtually forced to change her form of government by Woodrow Wilson, who refused to negotiate with the Hohenzollern regime. The Weimar Republic (so-called from the city famous for Goethe and Schiller, where its constitution was drawn up), which the Germans set up in 1919, was, on paper, a model of liberal democracy. However, it was lacking in historical precedent and in genuine popular support. The German people, never before having had a democratic government, were inexperienced in its practices. Even worse, the Weimar Republic was set up under the pressure of the victorious Allies and its leaders forced to sign the hated Treaty of Versailles. That it was able to function for ten years with reasonable effectiveness was due more to necessity than to inherent strength.

Germany violated many of the disarmament clauses of the Treaty of Versailles from the start. Old military units and organizations continued to function under assumed names. Weapons were hidden away, and many war plants were not dismantled. The 100,000-man army permitted her became the world's best-trained officer corps, which could be quickly expanded into a powerful army. Forbidden weapons such as tanks and artillery were perfected and tested on Russian and Swedish soil. Denied an air force, Germany became the world's leading nation in civil aviation. Her airfields, aircraft factories, and trained pilots and technicians could, of course, easily be converted to military purposes. When the British, in accordance with the treaty, tried to take possession of the German battle fleet interned at Scapa Flow in the British Isles, the German sailors scuttled their ships. Swift and powerful pocket battleships within the 10,000-ton treaty limit were constructed to serve as commerce raiders in the next war. Two prominent German leaders, Walter Rath-

enau and Matthias Erzberger, who were accused of advocating conciliation with the Western democracies, were assassinated by members of the professional military. The assassins were widely acclaimed as national heroes. When the German people went to the polls for the first time in 1925 to elect a president, their choice was their top military hero, Field Marshal Paul von Hindenburg.

The first overt clash between recalcitrant Germany and the former Allies occurred over reparations. In 1921 the reparations commission that had been established at the Paris peace conference set Germany's reparations bill at approximately $33 billion, to be paid over a long period of time. Although the Germans had been compelled by the Treaty of Versailles to accept in advance liability for whatever figure was set, they received the announcement of this amount with indignation. German governmental and financial leaders boasted both in public and in private that they would never pay it. The Weimar Republic refused to tax heavily the wealth of the great industrialists, and much of their wealth was permitted to leave the country. Germany defaulted on the very first annual payment. To the exasperated French, who were trying desperately to repair the ravages of the war, this was the last straw. Early in January 1923 French and Belgian troops occupied the Ruhr Valley, Germany's richest industrial area. The Germans fought back sullenly with passive resistance. The French countered by trying to stir up a secession movement from Germany in the Rhineland. Bloodshed between the occupying troops and the civilian population was frequent. Although the occupying forces were unable to collect any reparations, Germany's economy was paralyzed and a wild inflation swept the country. Thus more seeds of bitterness were sown.

After seven months of struggle, the German leaders realized the futility of resistance. In August 1923, Gustav Stresemann became head of the German government and offered conciliation. An international commission headed by Charles G. Dawes of the United States drew up a plan for the withdrawal of the occupying forces, for an international loan to Germany, and for the orderly payment of Germany's reparations installments. Her economy quickly recovered. From 1924 to 1929 Germany was the most prosperous nation in Europe and made her reparations payments as scheduled. In 1929 another international commission headed by Owen D. Young, an American financier, reduced Germany's total liability to the equivalent of a cash payment of $9 billion. However, the world depression struck Germany in that year, and after 1931 no further payments were made.

Meanwhile, under Stresemann's leadership Germany sought a *rapprochement* with her former enemies. In 1925 she signed the Treaty of Locarno with France, Great Britain, Italy, and Belgium, guaranteeing Germany's existing frontiers with France and Belgium. In 1926 Germany was admitted to the League of Nations, and Stresemann was elected president of the Council. This apparent good will, however, was deceptive. The old German militarism and nationalism, made more malignant by the sting of defeat, were still strong. The spirit of sullen hatred and revenge toward the former Allies filled the hearts of many Germans. Even Stresemann, we now know from his memoirs, was merely biding his time until Germany was strong enough to reassert herself. He was constantly deceiving the Western democracies and playing one off against the other. However, a far more sinister force was at work in postwar Germany, capitalizing on the economic and social maladjustment and the frustrated militarism and nationalism. This force was National Socialism, organized and led by Adolph Hitler.

3. THE RISE OF HITLER AND NATIONAL SOCIALISM

Adolph Hitler was the neurotic and maladjusted son of a petty Austrian customs official and a young, sensitive, unhappily married mother. As a child he already suffered delusions of grandeur. Of an artistic temperament, he went off to Vienna at an early age to seek an artist's career. Denied admission to the art academies for lack of training and too proud to work as a laborer, he lived for years in poverty and squalor. He fed his ego with German master-race theories and filled his heart with hatred of the Jews. At the outbreak of World War I Hitler was in Munich, Germany, eking out a living at crude art work such as making posters. The ardent young German nationalist threw himself eagerly into the war, which he considered to be a righteous crusade for the beloved fatherland. Attaining the rank of corporal, he got his first taste for command. When the war ended, he was in a hospital, a victim of poison gas. This is believed to account for the strange, hoarse resonance in his voice that unnerved the listener.

After the war, Hitler frequented beer cellars, haranguing demobilized and unemployed troops and organizing them into violent political action groups. He soon discovered his magnetic powers of oratory and of leadership. The disgruntled and the disenchanted, particularly the frustrated young intellectuals and demobilized lesser army officers, began attaching themselves to Hitler in increasing numbers. He organized them into the National Socialist (Nazi) party. Among his most important early followers were Hermann Goering, who became second in command; Rudolph Hess, who became head of the political section of the party; and Paul Joseph Goebbels, who became the chief Nazi propagandist. As early as 1923 Hitler, in league with the popular war hero Field Marshal Ludendorff, made his first grab for power. It was premature, however, and Hitler was jailed for nearly a year. While in jail he wrote *Mein Kampf* (*My Struggle*), which became the Nazi bible.

National Socialism, as outlined in *Mein Kampf*, was the German brand of fascism. In fact, the Nazis were heavily indebted to Mussolini for both ideology and methodology. At the center of its basic philosophy is the German master-race concept. The old Nordic myth of Gobineau and Chamberlain was revived. The terms "German," "Nordic," and "Aryan" were used interchangeably without regard to scientific fact. It was held that the Germans, the only pure representatives of the tall, blond Nordic "race," are superior to and destined to conquer and rule all other peoples. Militarism, indomitable will, pride, aggressiveness, and brute strength were held to be virtues; gentleness, peacefulness, tolerance, pity, and modesty, vices.

As a specific program of action, National Socialism was primarily concerned with foreign affairs. It called for repudiation of the Treaty of Versailles; all-out rearmament; the recovery of all territories, including colonies, lost at the end of World War I; and the annexation of all neighboring German-speaking territories such as Austria, the Netherlands, and most of Switzerland. Then the master race must have *Lebensraum* (living space). This was to be obtained by driving to the east (*Drang nach Osten*), particularly by conquering and enslaving the Soviet Union. There can be little question that in the Nazi mind, world domination was the ultimate goal.

The domestic program was vague and contradictory. Trusts and department stores were to be nationalized. Unearned income was to be abolished. Communism was to be destroyed, and labor unions rigidly controlled. Finally, persecution of the Jews was always part and parcel of the Nazi program. Persecution was later changed to extermination. The capitalistic classes never took the socialistic aspects of Hitler's program seriously. As in Italy, they looked to the Fascists to provide strong government, protect property, and control the working classes.

Hitler copied many of Mussolini's techniques. The rank and file of Nazi party members, wearing brown shirts, were organized along military lines as storm troopers. They marched, sang, and intimidated and beat up the opposition. An elite corps of black-shirted "SS" troops supervised and policed the brown shirts. Pagan symbolism was adopted—appropriately, since Nazism represented the antithesis of everything that Christianity stands for. All party members swore unquestioning and undying allegiance to Hitler.

4. THE TRIUMPH OF HITLER

At first National Socialism grew slowly but steadily. From 1925 to 1929, when Germany under Stresemann's leadership was the most prosperous nation in Europe and was being wooed by her former enemies, Nazi party membership grew from 27,000 to 178,000. After the great depression of 1929, which struck Germany along with the rest of the capitalistic world, the Nazis gained rapidly. In the parliamentary elections of 1930 they obtained several million votes and increased their seats in the Reichstag from 12 to 107. They were now strong enough to disrupt the orderly functioning of parliamentary government, and President Hindenburg resorted to ruling by presidential decree. In the presidential election of 1932 Hitler ran as the Nazi candidate. The moderate and liberal parties, which in 1925 had feared and opposed Hindenburg, now persuaded him to run again as the only man who could stop Hitler (Hindenburg was now eighty-five years old). Hitler got enough votes to force a runoff election against the popular and venerable idol. In the runoff election Hindenburg was elected, but Hitler received more than 13 million votes. In parliamentary elections a few months later, the Nazis obtained 230 out of 608 seats in the Reichstag, the largest number ever held by any party under the Weimar Republic. Hindenburg now offered to make Hitler vice-chancellor, but Hitler, sensing complete dictatorship in the offing, refused.

As the democratic nations stood passively by, the Nazi plans for expansion went into operation in the 1930s. Here German troops are cheered in Salzburg as they overran Austria with no opposition. *Photo: United Press International*

Meanwhile, the Nazis, under Hitler's instructions, paralyzed Germany's economic and political life with violence. When the chaos threatened to play into the hands of the Communists, in January 1933, Hindenburg offered and Hitler accepted the chancellorship. Franz von Papen, head of the militaristic Nationalist party, was made vice-chancellor. It was the great industrialists who finally gave the Nazis the necessary support to come to power. Hitler, determined to have nothing less than complete dictatorship, immediately called for parliamentary elections, to be held on March 5. Now in official control of the state police and the agencies of information and propaganda in addition to their own highly disciplined party machinery, the Nazis made full use of the intervening five weeks to frighten and confuse the people. Like the Fascists in Italy, they exaggerated and exploited the Communist threat. Five days before the elections, they made use of the burning of the Reichstag building, blaming the Communists. The elections themselves, however, were by secret ballot and were relatively free. The Communists polled 4.8 million votes, the Center (Roman Catholic) party 5.5 million, the Social Democrats (workers and small business and professional men's party) 7.2 million, the Nazis 17 million, and von Papen's Nationalists 3 million. The Nazi and the Nationalist vote combined gave Hitler 52 percent of the seats in the Reichstag. A few days later, Hitler, wearing his Nazi party uniform, appeared before the newly elected Reichstag, from which the Communists were excluded, and demanded dictatorial powers for four years. They were granted with only 94 opposing (Social Democratic) votes. Long before the four years had expired, the moderate parties had been destroyed, and the Nazi dictatorship was complete.

5. NAZI GERMANY

The Reichstag, having voted Hitler dictatorial powers, adjourned, to meet henceforth only on the call of the *Führer* (leader) for the purpose of voting approval of his acts. Hitler disbanded all political parties except the National Socialist party. Administration and local government were placed in the hands of Nazi officials. Freedom of speech, press, and assembly was abolished. An elaborate and all-powerful secret police, the Gestapo, was established under the direction of Heinrich Himmler to spy out and destroy opposition. Concentration camps with their torture and gas chambers soon held thousands of victims. Hitler's most intense hatred was vented upon the Jews, who were subjected to every conceivable humiliation. As fast as their services could be dispensed with, they were driven out of public and professional life. Eventually, the Nazis embarked upon a program to exterminate all the Jews under their control. It is estimated that by the end of World War II, the Nazis had murdered 6 million Jews out of a world total of 15 million.

The control and molding of thought always held high priority in Nazi activities. Indeed, this appears to be an absolute necessity for any totalitarian dictatorship. Under the direction of Goebbels, minister of propaganda, the German press and radio spewed forth a constant stream of false or distorted information. To read or listen to foreign newspapers or broadcasts was made a crime. An incessant hate campaign was waged against the liberal democratic world. The schools were, of course, Nazified. Only Nazi party members could be school administrators. Un-

sympathetic teachers were dismissed and punished. Members of Nazi youth organizations were set to spy on their teachers and parents. Textbooks were rewritten to conform to German master-race theories. The burning of liberal books, sometimes even those of Germany's greatest literary figures, such as Goethe and Schiller, became a national fad. The Nazi minister of education admitted that the sole function of education was the creation of Nazis. Hitler wrote in *Mein Kampf* that the German youth's ". . . entire education and development has to be directed at giving him the conviction of being absolutely superior to the others . . . the belief in the invincibility of his entire nationality." The arts were Nazified, only party members or sympathizers being permitted to publish, exhibit, or perform.

Since National Socialism was essentially an anti-Christian religion, the Nazis realized the necessity of controlling the religious establishment. The Lutheran Church, which was the official state church and included more than half the German people in its membership, was easily brought under Nazi domination. Nazi officials turned it into a powerful propaganda agency. The few Lutheran pastors like Martin Niemöller who resisted were thrown into concentration camps. The smaller Protestant denominations met the same fate. Hitler found it much more difficult to deal with the Roman Catholic Church, whose higher authority lay outside Germany. Although he soon signed a concordat with the pope, the terms proved to be unworkable. Roman Catholic clergy, churches, and schools were subjected to constantly increasing pressures, indignities, and physical abuse.

The Nazis rejuvenated and regimented Germany's economic life. The property and the profits of the capitalistic classes were given special consideration. Labor unions were brought under Nazi control, and a system of enforced arbitration of disputes between labor and management was set up along the lines that Mussolini had established in Italy. Strikes and lockouts were forbidden. The entire German economy was forced into the overall pattern and policies of the Nazi government. The vast rearmament program gave employment to millions. Superhighways, airfields, hospitals, and apartment houses were built all over Germany. The most intricate financial trickery was resorted to, but the Nazis expected eventually to finance their huge undertakings out of the spoils of victorious war.

All other activities were subordinated to the prime purpose of making a military comeback. Shortly after assuming power, Hitler took Germany out of the League of Nations and out of the disarmament conference that was in progress in Geneva. Rearmament was pushed as rapidly as possible, and in 1935 Hitler openly repudiated the disarmament clauses of the Treaty of Versailles. In 1936 Hitler remilitarized the Rhineland and sent decisive aid to General Franco's fascist rebels in Spain (see Chapter 57). The following year he made an alliance with the two other fascist powers, Italy and Japan. This Berlin-Rome-Tokyo Axis was aimed specifically at the Soviet Union. In reality, it was an aggressive alliance against the nonfascist world. Before tracing the fascist aggressions that plunged the world into World War II, however, we must examine briefly the triumph of fascism in the third member of the Axis—Japan.

6. THE TRIUMPH OF FASCISM IN JAPAN

We have already observed (see p. 790) Japan's remarkable modernization and emergence as a great power between 1853 and 1914. She participated in World War I on the side of the Allies and received Germany's island possessions in the Pacific north of the equator as her reward. At the Washington Naval Conference in 1922 she gained a 5:5:3 naval ratio with the United States and Great Britain. That is, for every five capital ships of the United States, Great Britain would have five and Japan three. This represented a significant gain for Japan. Of greater importance, Japan

gained a military monopoly in East Asia and the Western Pacific when Great Britain agreed not to fortify anything east of Singapore and the United States agreed not to fortify anything west of Pearl Harbor. Japan in the early 1920s stood at the crossroads. She could use her great energies and skills either to develop her own institutions and raise her standard of living or to become a predatory military state. She could hardly stand still. On her three thousand islands, with a total area no greater than that of the state of California, lived a rapidly increasing population of 60 million. Only 14 percent of Japanese land is arable, and she possesses very few natural resources. Her quickly built industries had overexpanded during the wartime prosperity, and the postwar deflation and sharp competition from her former allies brought severe economic stresses.

Three divergent groups competed for the leadership of postwar Japan. The dominant group was made up of the great industrialists. Seventy-five percent of Japan's industry and capital was concentrated in the hands of five great families, called the *zaibatsu*. This handful of industrial giants had such a stranglehold on the Japanese economy that it was also able to control the highly restricted government. The *zaibatsu*, enjoying such an economic and political monopoly, wished to see no fundamental change in Japan's undemocratic society, but advocated instead the peaceful economic penetration of Asia.

The liberals constituted the second group. This group, with university professors and students providing much of the leadership, set out to broaden the suffrage, which was restricted to the well-to-do, to encourage the more effective unionization of labor, and to diminish the power of the military. Because of the political inexperience and the long tradition of passive submission to authority on the part of the Japanese masses, these were difficult undertakings. They were made more difficult by the activities of a small group of Communists directed from Moscow, who confused liberal reform movements and tainted them with the suspicion of treason. Nevertheless, encouraging progress toward liberal democracy was made. In 1925 the suffrage was broadened. Soon afterward, two liberal political parties appeared. The military budget was reduced. The prestige of the professional military declined to such an extent that many officers ceased wearing their uniforms in public.

The professional military, however, was determined to strengthen and exploit its own traditional power. In the late 1920s a group of restless and ambitious young army officers began to accuse their leaders of softness and plotted to seize control of both the armed forces and the government. When a coup planned for early 1931 was exposed and blocked, the conspirators decided on a bold move to throw the country into such hysteria and confusion that they could seize power. In October 1931 the Japanese army stationed in Manchuria made an unauthorized attack on the Chinese forces and began the conquest of all Manchuria. The next year, 1932, Japanese forces attacked Shanghai, the chief port of China. Once fighting began with huge and potentially dangerous China, war fever and

patriotic hysteria swept Japan, just as the army plotters had foreseen. They now assassinated the premier and numerous other government officials and civilian leaders, and cowed the rest into submission. Once in control, the military immediately turned to the destruction of the liberals. Liberal university professors were accused of disloyalty and silenced, dismissed, or imprisoned. As in Italy and Germany, the schools and the press and radio were made organs of propaganda. All democratic processes of government and civil rights were destroyed. The military and state police were given unlimited authority. The *zaibatsu* were corrupted and won over with lush military contracts.

Meanwhile, Japanese armies overran all of Manchuria, which was made into the puppet state of Manchukuo. When the League of Nations declared Japan an aggressor and ordered her to withdraw from Manchuria, she defied the league and instead withdrew from that organization. In 1937 Japan joined the Berlin-Rome Axis. In the same year she began an all-out assault on China proper. By 1937, therefore, the Fascist powers were on the march.

Suggested Reading

Mussolini Creates the First Fascist State. H. W. Schneider, *Making the Fascist State* (1929) is a useful study of the origin of fascism and the sources of its ideology. Another good study of the rise and triumph of fascism in Italy is A. Rossi, *The Rise of Italian Fascism, 1918–1922* (1938). The best biography of Mussolini is I. Kirkpatrick, *Mussolini: Study of a Demagogue* (1964). Two reliable works on Fascist Italy by well-known scholars are W. Ebenstein, *Fascist Italy* (1939); and H. Finer, *Mussolini's Italy* (1935). A good eye-witness account of Italian fascism in action by a *New York Times* reporter is H. L. Matthews, *The Fruits of Fascism* (1943).

Postwar Germany. The post-World War I period in Germany is examined with up-to-date scholarship by Hajo Holborn, *A History of Modern Germany*, Vol. III (1969). Another great German historian has told the tragic story sympathetically: **F. Meinecke, *The German Catastrophe: Reflections and Recollections* (Beacon). Holborn came to the United States and became president of the American Historical Association; Meinecke weathered the Nazi storm in Germany. Two excellent accounts of the ill-fated Weimar Republic are **S. W. Halperin, *Germany Tried Democracy* (Norton); and **E. Eyck, *A History of the Weimar Republic* (2 vols., Science). H. W. Gatzke, *Stresemann and the Rearmament of Germany* (1954) shows that the allegedly most peaceful statesman in pre-Nazi Germany was not so peaceful after all.

Rise and Triumph of Hitler. The best biography of Hitler is **A. Bullock, *Hitler: A Study in Tyranny* (Harper Torchbook). Another important biography by an eye-witness to the Nazi rise to power is K. Heiden, *Der Führer: Hitler's Rise to Power* (1944). An excellent, if often underrated, account of the Nazi era is **W. L. Shirer, *The Rise and Fall of the Third Reich* (Crest). This gigantic work is written in a lucid, graphic style. **J. W. Wheeler-Bennett, *Nemesis of Power* (Compass) reveals the decisive role of the German professional military in bringing the Nazis to power. **E. Fromm, *Escape From Freedom* (Avon) is a brilliant study of the universal psychological urge to accept dictatorship.

Nazi Germany. A fascinating eye-witness account of Nazi Germany on the eve of and during the first year of World War II by an American reporter is **W. L. Shirer, *Berlin Diary* (Popular). Various aspects of the Nazi regime are competently examined by the following studies: **T. Taylor, *Sword and Swastika: Generals and Nazis in the Third Reich* (Quadrangle); E. Crankshaw, *Gestapo: Instrument of Tyranny* (1956); O. J. Hale, *The Captive Press in the Third Reich* (1964); G. A. Ziemer, *Education for Death: The Making of a Nazi* (1942); A. Frey, *Cross and Swastika: The Ordeal of the German Church* (1938); A. Schweitzer, *Big Business in the Third Reich* (1964).

Triumph of Fascism in Japan. Two excellent histories of Japan are K. S. Latourette, *The History of Japan* (1947), and the more factual and detailed C. Yanaga, *Japan Since Perry* (1949). Three good studies of Japanese militarism and imperialism are D. M. Brown, *Nationalism in Japan* (1958); R. Benedict, *The Chrysanthemum and the Sword* (1956); and A. M. Young, *Imperial Japan, 1926–1938* (1938). The role of the *zaibatsu* is covered by G. Allen, *Japanese Industry* (1940).

Sources. An excellent selection of source material containing many Italian, German, and Japanese fascist documents is A. Baltzly and A. W. Salomone, *Readings in Twentieth-century European History* (1950). The two most revealing and self-incriminating Nazi documents are **A. Hitler, *Mein Kampf* (Sentry); and P. J. Goebbels, *The Goebbels Diaries 1942–1943*, ed. and trans. L. P. Lochner (1948).

Chapter 57 ✖ Paralysis of the Democratic West

The fruits of World War I in the democratic West were economic instability, political and social unrest, and intellectual disillusionment. These weaknesses paralyzed the democracies at a time when Western civilization was being seriously challenged by communism and fascism. The efforts of the distraught and disunited democratic powers to appease the fascist aggressors culminated in World War II.

1. ISOLATIONISM, BOOM, AND BUST IN THE UNITED STATES

The United States emerged from World War I the world's richest and most influential nation. Although her entry into the war at its most critical phase was probably decisive in determining the outcome, she suffered far less war damage than any of the other major participants. President Wilson assumed the leading role in the making of the peace settlements and in the creation of the League of Nations. The rest of the world then looked to the United States to play the major role in supporting the league and maintaining the peace.

When President Wilson returned from Paris in the summer of 1919 and sought to persuade his country to join the League of Nations, he found his political enemies in power. Acceptance by the United States of the league's covenant, which was incorporated into the Treaty of Versailles, required the ratification of the United States Senate by a two-thirds vote. By virtue of a Republican majority of one in the Senate, the chairmanship of the Foreign Relations Committee, through which the treaty must first pass, was held by Wilson's bitterest personal enemy, Henry Cabot Lodge. Lodge was determined to destroy Wilson's handiwork. Indeed, before the exact nature of the league was known and while Wilson was consulting Republican opinion concerning it, Lodge obtained the signatures of thirty-nine senators, more than enough votes to defeat the treaty, to a round-robin agreeing to vote against whatever proposal Wilson brought back from Paris. Since it appeared that a majority of the American people favored the league in 1919, Lodge decided to defeat the treaty by a flank attack. He therefore attached fourteen amendments that Wilson could not ask the other members of the league to accept. (Some of these deliberately offended Great Britain, and some demanded a privileged position for the United States.) As a matter of fact, had Wilson accepted the obnoxious amendments, Lodge probably would have found other means of defeating the treaty. Wilson set out on a speaking tour to rally American public opinion to the treaty, but suffered a paralytic stroke in the midst of the campaign. As he was unable thereafter to lead the fight for the

Jobless and homeless men wait in line for a free meal in New York in 1930. These depression breadlines are part of the reason for the seeming impotence of the democratic nations in the face of the growing Fascist menace. *Photo: United Press International* treaty and was unwilling to give the leadership to others, his opponents easily defeated ratification in the Senate.

Since the American people were never given an opportunity to vote on the league, it is impossible to know what their verdict would have been. Such national organizations as the Federal Council of Churches, the American Bar Association, the American Federation of Labor, and the American Bankers Association declared themselves in favor of the league. Some Republican elder statesmen, such as A. L. Lowell, Charles Evans Hughes, and ex-president William Howard Taft, had worked for America's entrance into the league. The league was not an issue in the Presidential election of 1920. However, the victor, Warren G. Harding, announced that the league was now a dead issue. And during the cynical and disillusioned decade of the 1920s, American public opinion became overwhelmingly isolationist. When, therefore, during the international crises of the 1930s the harassed British and French governments sought the support of the United States against the fascist aggressors, they sought in vain.

The decade following World War I was a period of unprecedented prosperity in the United States. The all-out war effort brought about a great expansion of American industry and unleashed huge quantities of money and credit. Prices and wages soared. In 1914 the United States had been a debtor nation. She emerged from the war a creditor to most of Europe to the amount of $10 billion, a figure that doubled during the next ten years. Her chief economic competitors came out of the war battered and shaken. Between 1919 and 1929 American production, profits, and purchasing power reached heights never before attained anywhere in the world. However, it was an uneven and unsound prosperity.

Agriculture was depressed with surplus commodities and low prices, which meant low purchasing power for great stretches of the South and the Middle West. Nor did wages climb as rapidly as profits and prices in the industrial Northeast. These facts, plus increasing automation, meant growing unemployment and industrial surpluses. Labor unions declined in membership and bargaining power. Foreign markets were killed off by a policy of higher and higher tariffs designed to protect American industry from foreign competition. The government's philosophy of noninterference with free enterprise (except for tariffs) permitted unlimited speculation in the soaring stock market, often with other people's money and with unrestrained use of credit.

The stock market crashed in October 1929. Values tumbled. Thousands of banks and businesses failed. Millions were thrown out of work. The economic depression spread over the entire capitalistic world. For four years the Hoover administration, confident of the essential soundness of laissez-faire economy, refused to permit large-scale government relief measures, hoping and expecting that the natural economic laws would soon bring back prosperity. But the depression only deepened.

In the presidential election of 1932 the Democratic candidate, Franklin D. Roosevelt, defeated Hoover by some 7 million votes, ending twelve years of Republican rule. The Roosevelt administration immediately launched a series of sweeping economic and social reforms that came to be called the New Deal. The New Deal was not a radical, new departure, but rather a further advance along the line charted by Theodore Roosevelt's Progressivism and Woodrow Wilson's New Freedom. First of all, emergency measures were taken to relieve the suffering of the 12 million unemployed and their families. The chief of these was the setting up of the huge Public Works Administration, which undertook to avoid the humiliation of the dole by providing useful work of at least some dignity. The

Wagner Act strengthened the position of the labor unions by guaranteeing the right of collective bargaining. Old-age and unemployment insurance was inaugurated. For the desperate farmers, measures were passed that granted debt relief, commodity loans, price supports, and payments for acreage reduction. Deflation was checked by a devaluation of the dollar. Investments and deposits were protected by strict government supervision. Steps were taken to conserve the nation's natural resources against wasteful private exploitation. Gradually, popular confidence was restored and the nation's economy began to prosper again, though far below the boom proportions of the roaring twenties. However, many members of the business community believed that the New Deal discouraged free enterprise and incentive. They thought it was making the United States into a socialistic "welfare state" and argued that the depression eventually would have ended of its own accord through the working of the natural laws of laissez-faire economics. The depression appears to have had no appreciable effect upon the prevailing mood of isolationism in the United States.

2. THE HARASSED BRITISH EMPIRE

Great Britain emerged from World War I a victor. Her greatest prewar military and economic rival was defeated and apparently eliminated. The British Empire still included one-fourth of all the land and people on the globe. But her economy, her empire, and her world position were shaken beyond recovery. Britain's far-flung possessions in Asia and Africa were beginning to stir restlessly, as the spirit of nationalism, which long had provided the European world with so much of its expansive energy, spread eastward. Great Britain found it advisable to grant freedom to her self-governing dominions, hoping to retain their loyalty. The Statute of Westminster in 1931 gave complete independence and equality with the mother country to Canada, Australia, New Zealand, the Union of South Africa, Newfoundland, and the Irish Free State (free since 1922). These former colonies had been free in reality ever since they had gained dominion status (1867–1922). Now the only remaining legal tie was loyalty to the British crown. The British Empire was thus transformed into the British Empire and Commonwealth. Although the dominions remained loyal (with the exception of Ireland, which severed all relations in 1939), Great Britain could no longer count upon their material support in her world policies, nor could she count upon her restless colonies. Furthermore, Britain was now clearly second to the United States as an industrial and financial power. (It would require many years, however, for British statesmen to readjust their thinking to the reality of their country's reduced position.)

At home, postwar Britain was harassed with acute economic problems. Her national debt had quintupled during the war. She owed the United States more than $4 billion. German submarines had taken a toll of 9 million tons of her ships with their cargoes. Her exports met sharply increased competition in the world markets, particularly from the United States. Rising protective tariffs all over the world hindered her commerce. Her mines and industrial plants were antiquated and in disrepair. Returning servicemen found few jobs. Unemployment hovered around 3 million, a figure that came to be accepted as normal. Government support for the unemployed, sick, aged, and destitute proved to be the most staggering of all Britain's financial problems.

These chronic economic ills were reflected in Great Britain's troubled postwar politics. In 1922 the Conservatives broke up Lloyd George's wartime coalition government of Liberals and Conservatives and won the ensuing parliamentary elections. Under first Bonar Law and then Stanley Baldwin, they sought to restore classical nineteenth-century capitalism by means of rigid retrenchment of government spending, particularly for social services. This policy was so hard on the dis-

tressed masses that in 1924 a Labour-Liberal coalition headed by the Labour party leader, Ramsay MacDonald, ousted the Conservatives. The Labour party was now stronger than the Liberal party, and as times grew harder and feelings more bitter, the once-great Liberal party was virtually crushed between the more extreme parties—Labour on the left and Conservative on the right.

MacDonald's ministry lasted less than a year. Dependent upon the Liberals for his majority, he was forced to follow a moderate course. When he recognized the Soviet Union and made a commercial treaty with her, the Conservatives were able to capitalize on public suspicion and drive him from power. From 1925 to 1929 the Conservatives wrestled with rising discontent, strikes, and the steady growth of the Labour party. In 1929 a Labour victory, supported by the much-dwindled Liberals, again brought Ramsay MacDonald to the head of the government. His moderation in the face of the deepening economic depression, however, caused the majority of his Labour followers to repudiate him two years later. In 1931 MacDonald therefore formed a National coalition of right-wing Labourites, Liberals, and Conservatives to deal with the mounting domestic and foreign crises. This National coalition, which was really dominated by the Conservatives, ruled Great Britain until the end of World War II, fourteen years later. Before the outbreak of World War II, it was on the whole ineffective in dealing with both economic and social maladjustments at home and Fascist aggressions abroad. The Conservative prime ministers Stanley Baldwin and Neville Chamberlain, who followed Ramsay MacDonald as head of the National government in 1935 and 1937, respectively, appeared still to be living in the nineteenth century.

3. FRUSTRATED FRANCE

Although France enjoyed the advantage of being more self-sufficient economically than Great Britain, she had suffered greater wounds in World War I than had her island neighbor. Most of the fighting had taken place on her soil. A tenth—the most productive tenth—of her land area had been devastated. The retreating Germans had deliberately laid waste much of what had not been destroyed in battle. Orchards were chopped down, and mines were wrecked, many beyond repair. Even more tragic was the loss of life. France, with the lowest birth rate of any major nation in the world, suffered by far the heavist casualties per capita of any of the combatants. Out of a population of less than 40 million, she suffered almost 1.4 million battle deaths and 1.7 million wounded. These casualties were suffered largely by France's most productive male age groups. The civilian death rate from direct and indirect causes had also been high. France had fewer people in 1918 than in 1914, even after the return of Alsace and Lorraine.

Postwar France was confronted with a staggering job of economic reconstruction and an equally staggering war debt. In addition to her domestic debt, France owed the United States and Great Britain approximately $4 billion each. To meet these obligations and to finance the reconstruction, the French government counted on German reparations, but, as we have already seen, practically nothing was forthcoming. Inflation became a chronic headache. A more basic and long-range problem was French industry, which was rapidly falling behind its competitors. The highly individualistic French had not gone in for large-scale corporate industry, as had the Americans, British, and Germans. The little French family industries could not compete with mass production. A like situation prevailed in French agriculture, most of which was carried on on thousands of little family farms too tiny to use machinery profitably. Industrial and agricultural production per worker was lower in France than in any other major Western nation.

Considering the serious plight of France's postwar economy and the habitual disorderliness with which her multiparty democracy

traditionally functioned, one is impressed by the remarkable stability of the French government during the decade of the 1920s. From 1919 to 1924, a bloc of conservative parties was in power. It followed an antilabor, probusiness policy. It also favored the Roman Catholic Church and pressed hard for collection of German reparations. Meanwhile, discontent among the laboring classes was mounting. In 1924, the year of MacDonald's first Labour ministry in Great Britain, the parties of the Left under the leadership of Edouard Herriot were victorious. Like MacDonald, Herriot pursued a prolabor policy, advocating an increase in social service, and soft money. He was also conciliatory toward Russia and Germany. But, also like MacDonald, he lasted less than a year.

From 1926 to 1929, a strong right of center National bloc under the leadership of Raymond Poincaré was in power. Poincaré checked the inflation by rigid retrenchment. Upon his retirement in 1929, however, the increasing pressure of discontent threw the country into political turmoil. No leader or political combination seemed to be capable of dealing with the economic crisis brought on by the world depression, the growing menace of fascism, or the unrest in the French colonies. Ministry followed ministry in rapid succession. Scandals and riots occurred, and Fascist groups appeared. In 1936 the Popular Front, consisting of left-wing parties under the leadership of the mild Socialist Léon Blum, came to power. The Blum ministry obtained a forty-hour week and two weeks' annual vacations with pay for the workers. It also nationalized the Bank of France and the great munitions industries. This was too much for the powerful propertied interests, who drove Blum from office the following year. The Rightist parties who regained control, however, were unable to agree upon firm policies, domestic or foreign.

Thus France, like Great Britain, in the face of resurgent Nazi Germany, swashbuckling Mussolini, and militaristic Japan, could summon little strength or unity. The propertied classes were unwilling to share their wealth or privileges or to change their nineteenth-century practices. They feared and hated Léon Blum more than they feared Hitler. The working classes felt that they had little to work or fight for. The army was basking in past glory. Seeking to maintain the status quo, the French were defense-minded. They constructed the Maginot Line fortifications along the German border, and formed defensive alliances with Poland, Czechoslovakia, Yugoslavia, and Rumania. These alliances were no stronger than the faith those small countries had in France's ability to defend them, which by the late 1930s was very little.

When the League of Nations looked to the three formerly potent democratic powers for support in halting Fascist aggression, it found them weak in body and will.

4. THE BREAKDOWN OF THE LEAGUE OF NATIONS

The only international agency that existed for the maintenance of the peace was the League of Nations, which after the defection of the United States was largely dependent upon Great Britain and France for support. For twelve years the league supervised the implementation of the peace treaties, administered relief to tens of thousands of war victims, promoted international good will, and settled numerous international disputes. None of these settlements, however, involved the disciplining of a major power, and thoughtful observers dreaded the time when the league would be called upon to do so.

The first major power to challenge the league was Japan. It will be recalled (see p. 862) that in 1931 the Japanese militarists began the conquest of Manchuria, partly to create a war fever preparatory to setting up a Fascist dictatorship in Japan and partly as the first step in a vast program of conquest. China, the legal owner of Manchuria and a member of the League of Nations, appealed to the league for protection. The league appointed a commission headed by Britain's

Earl of Lytton to make an on-the-spot investigation. The Lytton Commission reported that Japan was guilty of aggression, having violated her solemn obligations both as a league member and as a signatory of the Kellogg-Briand Pact of Paris (1928), which outlawed war as an instrument of national policy. Forceful league action, however, would be largely dependent upon Great Britain and France, who were unwilling to act without American support.

The British and French governments realized the seriousness and significance of this first major challenge to the league and to the peace of the world. Soon after the beginning of Japan's aggression, they sought the support of the United States. Secretary of State Henry L. Stimson, fully aware of the significance of the crisis, wholeheartedly approved of joint measures by the three democracies. However, President Hoover, reflecting the isolationist sentiment of American public opinion, would not consent to the use of force, the threat of force, or even economic pressure by the United States. Stimson could offer the British and the French only words of disapproval of Japan's acts. The British and French governments, harassed by their own domestic economic and political problems and the rising menace of fascism in Europe, could not bring themselves to act alone. The league, without their backing, did nothing. It had failed its first major test and was on the way out as a potent force for peace. Japan's successful defiance of the League of Nations convinced Mussolini and Hitler that they could safely launch aggressions of their own.

The deathblow was struck by Mussolini. Late in 1935 the Italian dictator invaded Ethiopia, a large, undeveloped country in East Africa. This was to be the first step in the restoration of the ancient Roman Empire. Ethiopia was a member of the league and appealed to it for protection. Great Britain, concerned for her numerous interests in the Near and Middle East and for her life line to the Far East, now became greatly agitated. Under the leadership of Great Britain and

After several years of terrific slaughter, Franco and his German and Italian allies beat down the last of the Loyalists and established a Fascist dictatorship in Spain. Here victorious rebel troops enter a just-conquered Loyalist stronghold in 1937. *Photo: United Press International*

France, the league declared Mussolini to be the aggressor and invoked economic sanctions (Article XVI) against him. A list of commodities that league members were not to sell Mussolini was drawn up. However, the list did not include oil, and it soon became apparent that this was the commodity upon which the success of his aggression depended. But it quickly became apparent that, to be effective, an embargo on oil would require the cooperation of the United States. American exports of oil to Mussolini had trebled since the beginning of his campaign against Ethiopia. When the British and French governments requested the cooperation of the United States in withholding excess oil from Mussolini, Secretary of State Cordell Hull and President Roosevelt were sympathetic. Roosevelt requested the American oil companies to refrain voluntarily from selling Mussolini oil in excess of the normal peacetime amount. The

oil companies, however, refused to comply. Roosevelt then asked Congress to pass legislation restricting the excess sales. A battle ensued between the President and the oil companies for the support of Congress. The oil companies won. The press and public opinion were overwhelmingly isolationist, and Congress, in denying Roosevelt's request, reflected that view. Mussolini got his oil. Britain and France, unwilling to resort to the only other means of stopping him, a shooting war, gave up the league struggle. Mussolini conquered Ethiopia. The League of Nations, for all practical purposes, was dead.

5. APPEASEMENT OF THE FASCIST AGGRESSORS

The most serious consequence of the demise of the League of Nations was the unleashing of Nazi Germany. Since the triumph of the

Nazis in 1933, Germany had been feverishly preparing for a military comeback. In March 1936, Hitler ordered his armed forces into the Rhineland, which, according to the Treaty of Versailles, was to be permanently demilitarized. France, recognizing this move as the gravest threat and challenge to herself, called for Great Britain's support. The British offered none. The French fretted and fumed, but in the end did nothing. Hitler had won his gamble. It was France's last opportunity to save herself; a year or two later, Nazi Germany had become too strong.

Fascism's next triumph was in Spain. Modern liberal and industrial civilization had bypassed Spain. Until 1931, she was dominated by the landed aristocracy, a few rich capitalists, aristocratic army officers, and the Roman Catholic Church. The mass of the people were poverty-stricken, illiterate, and landless peasants. Since the turn of the century, however, and particularly since 1918, the pressure of discontent had been rising. In 1930 the dictatorial king yielded, restored the constitution, and granted elections. The liberal and radical groups won such a sweeping victory that the king fled the country. The reformers then proceeded to make over the Spanish nation. They drew up a democratic constitution, granted local autonomy to Catalonia, began a sweeping program of public education, started to modernize the army by placing promotions on a merit basis, granted religious freedom, seized the lands and schools of the Roman Catholic Church, and planned to break up the great estates into peasant-owned farms.

There was much violence—riots, and attacks on priests, nuns, and private property. After two years, the conservative propertied interests, with the vigorous support of the pope, won the elections by a narrow margin and began to undo the reforms. Early in 1936, however, the liberal and radical parties won again and resumed their drastic reform program. The privileged classes were now desperate. In July 1936, a group of generals led by General Francisco Franco launched an armed rebellion against the government. Although the Rebels enjoyed the advantage of professional military leadership, the regular army, and most of the country's wealth, they were unable to make headway against the Loyalists, who enjoyed the support of the majority of the rank and file of the people.

The Spanish Civil War soon became a battlefield in the world struggle of fascism, liberalism, and communism. Hitler and Mussolini, seeing in it an opportunity to advance the cause of fascism, gain a like-minded ally and a strategic military position, and test their new weapons, sent abundant arms and troops to aid Franco. The Loyalists appealed to the democracies for aid but received none, although a few volunteers from the democracies fought as individuals in the Loyalist cause. The only nation that supported the Loyalists was the Soviet Union, but the amount of aid she could send was quite small and probably did more harm that good, since it tainted the Loyalist cause with the suspicion of communism. After three years of terrific slaughter, Franco and his German and Italian allies beat down the last organized Loyalist resistance. A typical fascist dictatorship was established over Spain. Liberalism was shattered. The Communist cause in Spain, on the other hand, was strengthened. At the beginning of the civil war, the Communists constituted only a small minority on the Loyalist side. Not a single member of the Loyalist cabinet was a Communist. However, thanks to limited support from the Soviet Union and to the Communists' skill at underground activity, they fared much better in defeat than did the liberals. The world prestige of Fascist Germany and Italy rose while that of the democracies declined further.

The year 1937 was the year of decision—the point of no return on the road to war. As noted previously, in that year the three great Fascist powers formed the Berlin-Rome-Tokyo Axis, which was aimed specifically at the Soviet Union, but was in reality an alliance of these powers against the rest of the world. In that year the military strength of the Axis powers—their war plants running day and night—forged ahead of that of the rest of the world. They were now out of hand. In that year the Nazis blueprinted their timetable of conquests, and Japan began her all-out assault on China.

Early in 1938 the Nazis' timetable began to function. In March they overran Austria without opposition, annexing the 6½ million Austrians to the German Reich (Empire). Great Britain and France denounced this open aggression and violation of the Treaty of Versailles but did nothing.

Almost immediately Hitler turned his big propaganda guns on his next victim, Czechoslovakia. In constructing this little country out of Austro-Hungarian territory at the end of World War I, the Allied peacemakers had left 3½ million German-speaking people on the Czech side of the border. Although these Sudeten Germans had never been a part of Germany and were separated from Germany by the Sudeten Mountain wall, Hitler now claimed them. His main consideration in attacking Czechoslovakia was military. The Czech republic was allied with France and Russia, and in the coming war that Hitler was planning against those two countries, she could be a threat to the German flank. The "Bohemian bastion" has long been a vital strategic position in Central Europe. Furthermore, the Czech defenses were patterned after those of the French. Possession of them would give the Germans a blueprint of the Maginot Line.

As early as May 1938, Hitler threatened Czechoslovakia. The Czechs, however, surprised him by rushing to their defenses. Hitler spent the next four months arousing his people to readiness for war and softening up the democracies by keeping them in a constant state of tension and alarm. This psychological warfare culminated in a giant Nazi rally at Nuremberg in mid-September. There Hitler screamed to his frenzied followers that if the Sudeten areas were not surrendered to him by October 1, he would march. With France and the Soviet Union standing firm in their alliance with Czechoslovakia, the world anxiously awaited the beginning of a major conflict that was likely to become World War II.

At this juncture, the British Prime Minister Neville Chamberlain took it upon himself to fly to Hitler's retreat at Berchtesgaden and plead for a compromise. The upshot was a conference at Munich on September 29, 1938. The participants were Hitler, Mussolini, Chamberlain, and Premier Edouard Daladier of France. Chamberlain persuaded Daladier to yield to Hitler's demands for the Sudeten areas of Czechoslovakia. Czechoslovakia and the Soviet Union, France's allies, were not consulted. This was one of Hitler's greatest triumphs. By enticing Great Britain and France to abandon France's allies, Czechoslovakia and the Soviet Union, Hitler had driven a wedge between the Soviet Union and the Western democracies. The Soviet leaders never trusted the Western democracies again. Neither did many of the other countries of the world that were watching to see where their greatest safety lay. The Munich "sellout" represented the lowest ebb to which the cause of liberal democracy had ever sunk.

6. THE RETURN TO WAR

Although the four participating powers at Munich had agreed to become joint protectors of what remained of Czechoslovakia, in March 1939, Hitler overran without warning the remainder of the stricken little republic. This

The chief participants at the Munich Conference pose for the photographer in September 1938. Left to right: Chamberlain, Daladier, Hitler, Mussolini.
Photo: United Press International

crass act of betrayal opened the eyes even of Neville Chamberlain to the fact that fascism could not be appeased. When, therefore, immediately following the rape of Czechoslovakia Hitler threatened Poland, Great Britain and France decided to draw a line. In April 1939, they made a guarantee to Poland that they would come to her aid if she were attacked and resisted the attack. The fat was now in the fire. Hitler, however, was not deterred. He was demanding among other things the return to Germany of the Polish Corridor, which separated East Prussia from the rest of Germany, and the city of Danzig, which was governed by the League of Nations. By now, however, it was apparent to almost everybody that specific Nazi demands were merely excuses for unlimited aggression. Throughout the summer of 1939 the Germans

made feverish preparations for war and kept up a drumfire of vilification of Poland and the democracies. Meanwhile, both sides were bidding for the support of the Soviet Union. But after Munich, Stalin had no confidence in the integrity of the capitalistic democracies. He decided to try to make his own peace with Hitler.

On August 23, 1939, the world was stunned by the signing of a ten-year peace pact by Hitler and Stalin. In return for the Soviet Union's neutrality while Germany conquered Poland, Hitler gave Stalin a free hand to reannex the territories in Eastern Europe, including eastern Poland, that Russia had lost at the end of World War I.

With the Soviet Union safely neutralized, Hitler readied the attack on Poland as quickly as possible. At the last moment the British government instructed its ambassador in Berlin to ask Hitler what concessions by Poland he would accept to refrain from war. Hitler informed the ambassador that he was not interested in concessions, that his army and his people were ready and eager for war and that he could not disappoint them now. The wires between Warsaw and Berlin were cut, lest the Poles make a last-minute peaceable surrender to Hitler's demands. At dawn on September 1 the Germans launched an all-out attack on Poland by land, sea, and air. Two days later Great Britain and France declared war on Germany, Hitler having ignored their ultimatum to desist. World War II had begun.

Suggested Reading

Isolationism, Boom, Bust in the United States. S. E. Morison, H. S. Commager, and W. E. Leuchtenburg, *The Growth of the American Republic* (6th ed., 2 vols., 1969) presents an excellent survey of the United States between the two world wars. **F. Allen, *Only Yesterday* (Bantam) is a vivid account of the roaring twenties in the United States, written in a witty journalistic style. **J. K. Galbraith, *The Great Crash, Nineteen Twenty-nine* (Sentry) is by a distinguished American economist. The prolonged consequences of the Great Depression are examined by D. Wecter, *The Age of the Great Depression, 1929–1941* (1948). Two excellent biographies of Franklin Roosevelt are J. Burns, *Roosevelt: The Lion and the Fox* (1956); and **R. Sherwood, *Roosevelt and Hopkins* (2 vols., Bantam). W. L. Langer and S. Gleason, *The Challenge of Isolation, 1937–1940* (1952) is a scholarly study of the response of the United States to Fascist aggression in Europe and Asia.

The Harassed British Empire. A study of the crippling wounds Great Britain suffered during World War I is F. Hirst, *Consequences of the War to Great Britain* (1934). A good brief survey of Great Britain in the twentieth century is D. Thomson, *England in the Twentieth Century, 1914–1963* (1964). A more complete account by a first-rate British historian is C. L. Mowat, *Britain Between the Wars, 1918–1940* (1955). A vivid and witty picture of the British ruling classes between the two wars is **R. Graves and A. Hodge, *The Long Weekend: A Social History of Great Britain,* *1918–1939* (Norton). The history of the British Empire and Commonwealth between the two world wars is expertly told by P. Knaplund, *The British Empire, 1815–1939* (1941).

Frustrated France. A good brief survey of French history since World War I is **E. Knapton, *France Since Versailles* (Berkshire). **H. Luethy, *France Against Herself* (Meridian) is an astute analysis of the various factors that account for the paralysis of France in the face of the Nazi menace. Another perceptive study of French weakness during the turbulent nineteen-thirties is A. Werth, *The Twilight of France, 1933–1940* (1942). The best biography of Léon Blum is J. Colton, *Léon Blum, Humanist in Politics* (1966). Blum in his prison cell in Germany during World War II wrote his own brilliant analysis of the weaknesses that led to France's fall: Léon Blum, *For All Mankind* (1946). Also valuable for an understanding of France's weakness in dealing with Nazi Germany is C. Micaud, *The French Right and Nazi Germany, 1933–1939* (1943).

Appeasement of Fascist Aggression—The Return to War. Excellent surveys of the decade of appeasement that led to World War II are D. Lee, *Ten Years: The World on Its Way to War, 1930–1940* (1942); F. Schumann, *Europe on the Eve: The Crisis of Diplomacy 1933–1939* (1939); G. Craig and F. Gilbert, *The Diplomats, 1919–1939* (1953); and **A. Rowse, *Appeasement* (Norton). Rowse was a bitter eye-witness of British appeasement efforts. An excellent account of the Manchurian Crisis of 1931 by the chief American participant is H. L. Stimson, *The Far Eastern Crisis: Recollections and Observations* (4th ed., 1936). The best history of the Spanish Civil War is **H. Thomas, *The Spanish Civil War* (Colophon). The story of the triumph of fascism in Spain is told more dramatically but less objectively by the American ambassador to Spain at the time, C. Bowers, *My Mission to Spain* (1954). Bowers was strongly pro-Loyalist. A scholarly study of the Munich sellout is **J. Wheeler-Bennett, *Munich: Prologue to Tragedy* (Compass). The story of the last faltering months of appeasement and the beginning of World War II is brilliantly told by **W. Shirer, *The Rise and Fall of the Third Reich* (Crest); and **Winston Churchill, *The Gathering Storm* (Bantam), which is the first volume of Churchill's magnificent six-volume history of World War II. K. Feiling, *The Life of Neville Chamberlain* (1946) is a biography of the greatest of all the appeasers.

Chapter 58 ❦ World War II, 1939–1945

To much of the disillusioned and paralyzed democratic world, the outbreak of World War II seemed the beginning of the end of liberal Western civilization. What instruments of destruction science and technology had developed since World War I, nobody knew. The Nazis boasted that the German air force was capable of destroying all the cities of the non-Fascist world. For two years these dire fears and threats appeared to be justified. The seemingly invincible German and Japanese military machines swept on to victory after victory.

1. TWO YEARS OF AXIS TRIUMPH

The mechanized might of Nazi Germany overwhelmed Poland in a matter of days. Striking without official warning at dawn, September 1, 1939, the German air force caught the Polish air force on its various airfields and destroyed it on the ground. Thereafter the German *Luftwaffe*, by ravaging Polish cities and communications centers and harassing troop movements, prevented the complete mobilization of the Polish army. Meanwhile, Nazi tanks and infantry poured into Poland from the north, west, and south. Within two weeks' time, Warsaw was surrounded and being pounded to rubble by German artillery. At this juncture, the forces of the Soviet Union, in accordance with the August 23 pact with Hitler, moved into eastern Poland and occupied the Russian-speaking areas seized from her after World War I (see p. 843).

From the beginning of the invasion, the Poles, fighting courageously but hopelessly, cried for help from France and Great Britain. The French and the British mobilized their armies along the German West Wall fortifications, and the British fleet blockaded Germany by sea. But that was all. At that time no fighter planes had the range to fly from French or British bases to Poland and back, and the French and British understandably did not wish to provoke the lightning by bombing German cities. Western military leaders, basing their views on the experiences of World War I, believed it to be suicidal to attack elaborate fortifications. They thought that sooner or later Hitler would be forced to attack the French Maginot Line and would then be destroyed. This thinking was little consolation to the Poles. Warsaw surrendered on September 27, less than a month after the fighting began.

The Soviet Union, in accordance with her agreement with Hitler, proceeded to reannex the remaining territories in Eastern Europe that she had lost at the end of World War I. Shortly after Poland surrendered, the Soviet Union demanded military bases in Estonia, Latvia, and Lithuania. The three little Baltic republics appealed to Hitler, but were told to comply. The following spring they were absorbed politically into the Soviet Union. In October 1939, the Soviet Union demanded three strategic little strips of Finnish territory: the Karelian Isthmus, which put the Finnish border within artillery range of the great city of Leningrad; a strip of territory near the Russian Arctic port of Murmansk;

and the naval base of Hangö, which guarded the sea approaches to Leningrad. The Soviets wanted a thirty-year lease on Hangö; the other territories were to be ceded outright. When the Finnish government refused, the Soviet Union attacked Finland and took these territories by force. In June 1940, while Hitler was busy in Western Europe, the Soviet Union demanded and procured from Rumania the return of Bessarabia. With Bessarabia she also took the little province of northern Bukovina, which she had never previously owned.

Early in April 1940, the Germans suddenly overran Denmark and Norway. The British fleet, attempting to intercept the invasion of Norway, was beaten off with heavy losses by the German air force. Denmark and Norway provided the Nazis with important food, timber, and mineral resources, sea and air bases, and a safe route for vital iron ore coming from Sweden.

On May 10, 1940, the German armies assaulted Luxemburg, the Netherlands, Belgium, and France. Luxemburg offered no resistance. The Netherlands fought heroically, but was overwhelmed in six days. Belgium lasted nineteen days, but when she fell, the French and British armies in Belgium fell with her. Trusting to the Maginot Line to hold along the German border, the British army and a large part of the French army moved into Belgium to support the hard-pressed Belgian forces. In a surprise move through the Ardennes forest, powerful German mechanized forces on May 14 smashed through the French defenses at Sedan and drove quickly to the English Channel, cutting off the Belgian, British, and French armies in Belgium. Although some 300,000 British and a few French troops escaped by sea from Dunkirk, all the Belgian troops, the bulk of the French troops together with their weapons and supplies, and the British weapons and supplies were captured.

Only five more days of fighting, June 5–10, were required for the Germans to crush the remaining organized French resistance and turn the French retreat into a disorderly rout. On June 10 Paris was declared an open city.

And on that day Mussolini, thinking it safe, declared war on France and Great Britain. On June 16 Marshal Philippe Pétain replaced Paul Reynaud as premier of France, and the following day dispatched a surrender team to Hitler. On June 25 the "fighting" ceased. The collapse of the French military machine after five days of fighting was the most colossal military debacle in history. It was the one military machine in the world thought to be able to stand up to the Nazis. Hitler forced upon the helpless French a harsh treaty. The northern half of France and all the Atlantic coastal area were placed under German occupation. The unoccupied portion was compelled to disarm and cooperate with Germany. Some 2 million French prisoners were held as hostages to ensure French good behavior. In unoccupied France, Marshal Pétain and Pierre Laval set up a semi-Fascist regime, with headquarters at Vichy, and undertook to cooperate with Hitler.

All Frenchmen did not accept defeat. Many resisted the German army of occupation courageously throughout the war, suffering heavy casualties in so doing. General Charles de Gaulle, having unsuccessfully attempted to warn his superiors of the unreadiness of the French army, escaped to Great Britain and declared himself leader of the Free French. With energy and skill he strove to rally Frenchmen both inside and outside the homeland to resist the Germans and the Vichy collaborators and to restore the dignity and honor of France.

The collapse of France left Great Britain to face the Axis fury alone (except for the Chinese Nationalist forces still holding out against the Japanese in the Chinese interior). Hitler now demanded that she surrender or suffer annihilation. Her situation was desperate. Nearly all her land armaments had been lost at Dunkirk. Against the nearly one hundred and fifty battle-tried Nazi divisions, she had only one fully-equipped division. And although Great Britain did have the English Channel and the world's greatest navy, the fighting around Norway had demonstrated

A view of London in 1941 from the top of St. Paul's Cathedral. During the first three years of World War II, the superior German air force bombed scores of cities in enemy countries, leaving wreckage such as this in its wake. *Photo: United Press International*

that navies could no longer control narrow waters dominated by a hostile air force. Britain's chief weapon of defense was her relatively small but efficient air force. Not the least of her assets was Winston Churchill, who on May 10, 1940, had at last replaced Neville Chamberlain as prime minister. The dynamic and eloquent Churchill defied Hitler. "We shall fight on the beaches; we shall fight on the landing grounds; we shall fight in the fields and in the streets; we shall fight in the hills; we shall never surrender."

Throughout the month of July 1940, Nazi invasion forces gathered along the French coast opposite Britain, 24 miles away. To make the crossing, however, absolute control of the air over the Channel was required.

Early in August, therefore, swarms of German bombers and fighter escorts flew over the Channel, seeking to destroy the British air force and its landing fields. In the ensuing air battles, the British pilots in their swift Spitfires and heavily armed and maneuverable Hurricanes knocked down German planes at the ratio of 2 to 1. Nevertheless, by the end of August the British air forces were facing annihilation by sheer weight of numbers. At this critical juncture, the Nazis suddenly shifted to massive daylight attacks on London, the world's largest city. The destruction and the suffering were immense, but the toll of German planes taken by the British fighters was so great that early in October the Nazis began less effective night attacks. Although the destructive air raids on Great Britain's cities, together with the even more menacing submarine attacks on British shipping, continued until the end of the war, the immediate threat of invasion had now passed; the Battle of Britain had been won.

While the Battle of Britain was at its height, Mussolini set in operation his grandiose schemes for conquering an empire. Upon entering the war in June 1940, he had closed the Mediterranean to British shipping. In September his armies moved on Egypt and the Suez Canal from Libya to the west and from Ethiopia to the south. In October his armies attacked Greece from Albania. To meet this threat, Churchill made one of the most daring and farsighted military moves in history. Believing Suez to be the most strategic spot in the world in a global war, he sent half Britain's scarce supply of tanks and artillery around Africa to Egypt while the Nazis stood poised across the Channel for the invasion of Great Britain. Mussolini's forces met disaster everywhere. The Greeks defeated them and drove them back into Albania. A squadron of British torpedo planes delivered a lethal blow to the Italian fleet at its Taranto base. During the winter of 1940–1941, the Fascist armies moving on Egypt were completely destroyed by light, mobile British forces. Mussolini's bubble had burst with a feeble plop; henceforth he was hardly more than a prisoner of the German forces that were sent to save him.

When in October 1940 it became evident that Great Britain could not be invaded that year, Hitler ordered his planners to complete blueprints for the earliest possible invasion of the Soviet Union. The conquest of the Soviet Union had always been uppermost in Hitler's thoughts, but he had hoped first to dispose of the French and British threat to his rear. The plans called for an assault date not later than May 15, 1941. But first the Balkan flank was to be secured. Hungary and Rumania joined the Axis Alliance in November 1940, Bulgaria, in March 1941. Immediately, Nazi forces poured into those countries. Yugoslavia and Greece, however, refused to yield, and the Germans attacked them in April 1941. Yugoslavia was overrun in eleven days, Greece in three weeks. British forces that Churchill had dispatched to Greece were driven out of the peninsula and also off the island of Crete. Suez now appeared to be doomed. It was open to attack from the north; to the west Rommel's Afrika Korps had driven the British back to the border of Egypt; pro-Nazi movements had broken out in Iraq, Iran, and French Syria. At this point, however, Hitler hurled his legions against the Soviet Union, giving the British a breathing spell to recoup their strength in the Near and Middle East.

On June 22, 1941, the Germans launched against the Soviet Union the most massive assault in history. They were joined by the Hungarians, the Rumanians, and the Finns. There were one hundred sixty divisions in all (eventually the figure rose to two hundred fifty). And although Stalin was able to throw an equal number of divisions against the invaders, his troops were not so well trained or equipped. Hitler expected to crush Soviet resistance in six weeks; the top British and American military leaders were of the same opinion. The Russians fought with unexpected skill and determination, but the Nazi war machine crunched ever forward until by December 1, it was within sight of Moscow. Leningrad was surrounded, and Rostov, the gateway to the Caucasus oil fields, was captured. The richest and most productive part of the Soviet Union was in German hands. The Russians had suffered such staggering casualties that Hitler announced that the Soviet Union was destroyed and would never rise again. The Japanese, taking him at his word and thinking the golden hour had struck, attacked the United States on December 7, 1941. By that time, however, the Arctic winter and the Soviet counterattacks had forced the Germans to retreat. The Soviet Union was still alive, and the United States was now in the war.

2. THE ENTRY OF THE UNITED STATES INTO THE WAR

The entry of the United States into the war—the one thing that might conceivably have turned the tide—was not a sudden but a gradual involvement. We have already observed the refusal of the American people to cooperate with the League of Nations in checking Japan in 1931 and Italy in 1935. To make assurance doubly sure, an isolationist Congress in 1935, 1936, and 1937 had passed a series of neutrality laws limiting the powers of the President to carry out his constitutional functions of conducting the nation's foreign relations. At the same time, Congress steadfastly refused to increase the military budget in the face of the rising Fascist menace. During the Munich and Polish crises, President Roosevelt pleaded with Hitler and Mussolini not to plunge the world into war, but the dictators scorned his pleas, realizing that his hands were tied. The outbreak of the war in Europe caused hardly a ripple in the isolationist sentiment of the American public and of Congress. The French army and Maginot Line and the British navy were believed by most of the isolationists to be capable of containing the Nazis.

But suddenly in May–June 1940, the picture totally changed. The French army and Maginot Line ceased to exist, and the British navy was in grave danger. Much of it would be used up in the defense of Britain in case of invasion. The American people, now seized with consternation, cried for drastic action. Roosevelt promptly came forward with a three-point program: (1) all-out rearmament, (2) bipartisanship in foreign affairs, (3) all aid to those fighting the Axis (which at the moment meant Great Britain) short of war. There was no opposition to the first proposal, and Congress quickly voted a generous military appropriation. Although there were a few partisan murmurings, Roosevelt activated the second proposal by appointing two prominent internationalist Republicans, Henry L. Stimson and Frank Knox, as secretary of war

and secretary of the navy, respectively. Over the aid-to-Britain proposal, however, powerful opposition arose, led largely by stalwart Republican isolationists such as Senator Robert Taft, Colonel R. R. McCormick (publisher of the Chicago *Tribune*), and Charles A. Lindbergh, although a few Democratic isolationists also participated.

The victory of Wendell Willkie, an internationalist Republican, over Robert Taft for the Republican Presidential nomination in July 1940 made it easier for Roosevelt to implement his aid-to-Britain proposal. He immediately dispatched a quantity of World War I arms and ammunition to Britain, and in September 1940, he exchanged fifty World War I destroyers for eight British air and naval bases in the Western Hemisphere. These weapons played an important role in the Battle of Britain. By the end of the year, however, Churchill informed Roosevelt that Britain was nearing exhaustion. Thereupon Roosevelt proposed, and in March 1941 Congress passed, the Lend Lease Act, which authorized the President to sell, lend, lease, or give any commodity to any nation whose defense he deemed necessary for the safety of the United States. Congress also voted funds to finance the measure.

The British navy, stretched thin over the world's sea lanes, however, was unable to guard Britain's Lend Lease ships from German submarines. It soon became apparent that if Lend Lease was to achieve its purpose, the ships carrying the goods would have to be convoyed by the American navy. The sinking of an American ship in the South Atlantic by a German submarine led the American government in June and July 1941 to close all Axis consulates and freeze all Axis assets in the United States and begin convoying Lend Lease goods as far as Iceland. Meanwhile, Lend Lease was extended to the Soviet Union when that country was attacked by Germany. In October 1941, two American destroyers on the Iceland convoy run were torpedoed by German submarines with a loss of 126 American lives. Roosevelt stated that "the shooting war has started. And history has recorded who fired the first shot."

In August 1941, Roosevelt and Churchill had met at sea and drawn up the Atlantic Charter, a joint statement of ideals and war purposes. In it appeared such pregnant phrases as: ". . . their countries seek no aggrandizement, territorial or other; . . . they respect the right of all peoples to choose the form of government under which they will live; . . . after the final destruction of the Nazi tyranny, . . . the establishment of a wider and permanent system of general security. . . ." The Soviet Union subscribed to the Atlantic Charter shortly afterward. Thus, by October 1941, the United States was engaged in a shooting—but not yet official—war with Germany and was in a virtual alliance with Great Britain, one of the belligerents. The American people's eyes were on the Atlantic, where at any moment some new German act of aggression might make war official and total.

It was not in the Atlantic, however, but in the Pacific that the history-changing blow was struck; and not by Germany, but by Japan. Early in 1939 the Japanese, having conquered all the populous coastal areas of China and having driven Chiang Kai-shek's forces far into the Chinese interior, turned southward toward the territories of Southeast Asia and the Southwest Pacific. These territories, rich in rubber, tin, rice, copra, and oil, belonged (with the exception of independent Thailand) to France, the Netherlands, Great Britain, and the United States. Since the French, Dutch, and British had their hands full in Europe with the growing Nazi menace, President Roosevelt transferred the American fleet from the Atlantic to Pearl Harbor in Hawaii as a deterrent to further Japanese aggression. He also gave the Japanese the required six months' notice of the termination of the commercial treaty of 1911. These moves appear to have given the Japanese pause.

In 1940, however, after Hitler's conquest of France and the Netherlands and threatened conquest of Great Britain, the Japanese became much bolder. They took advantage of France's helplessness to occupy northern French Indo-China and threatened the Dutch East Indies. The Roosevelt administration, seeking to restrain the Axis with all pressure short of war, now embargoed the shipment of all commodities to Japan except petroleum, and made a loan of $75 million to Chiang Kai-shek. Oil was left out of the embargo for fear the Japanese would immediately strike the oil-rich Dutch East Indies. Again the Japanese halted. But in the following year, 1941, when the Germans overran the Balkans and launched what promised to be a lethal attack on the Soviet Union, the Japanese leaders decided that the day of Axis world triumph was at hand. In July 1941, therefore, they greatly stepped up their war preparations, poured troops into southern Indo-China for an obvious assault on the Dutch and British East Indies, and launched an all-out propaganda campaign against the United States in the army-controlled press.

The Roosevelt administration, deciding that further conciliation was hopeless, froze all Japanese assets in the United States, which had the effect of embargoing oil. On November 25 the Japanese fleet was ordered to sail for its attack position. The next day the United States, having intercepted and decoded the order, made a final conciliatory offer, which the Japanese government spurned. Roosevelt, realizing that an attack was in motion but not knowing where, sent Emperor Hirohito a last personal plea, which was intercepted and withheld by Japanese army officials. Early Sunday morning on December 7, 1941, a large squadron of Japanese bombers and torpedo planes took off from carriers in a position north of Hawaii and caught by surprise the American fleet anchored in Pearl Harbor. With little loss to themselves, the Japanese planes crippled the American navy in the Pacific, and destroyed the air force in Hawaii on the ground. Later in the day Japan declared the existence of a state of war with the United States. The next day, December 8, the United States Congress declared war on Japan. Three days later, December 11, Germany and Italy, making good their promise to Japan, declared war on the United States. The same day, December 11, the United States replied in kind.

3. CLIMAX AND TURNING POINT OF THE WAR, JUNE–AUGUST 1942

The entry of the United States with her enormous resources and industrial potential, changed the whole complexion of the war. It made possible the turning of the tide. However, many months would be required to mobilize America's resources, and the Axis was determined to win decisively before that mobilization could be achieved. To bring about Allied solidarity, Churchill hastened to Washington, where on January 1, 1942, he and

Roosevelt launched the United Nations Alliance. Twenty-six nations, of which the United States, Great Britain, and the Soviet Union were the Big Three, promised to give their all to the common effort, to make no separate peace, and to abide by the principles of the Atlantic Charter. By the end of the war, the number of member nations had risen to forty-seven.

The now-global war was fought in three major theaters: (1) Russia, (2) the Mediterranean and Western Europe, and (3) the Pacific. The Axis powers made their climactic bid for victory on all three fronts between June and August 1942. The biggest front in terms of numbers of men, weapons, and casualties involved was that in Russia. The Germans, after having been stopped in December

1941 by the Russian winter and the counterattacks, resumed their forward thrust in June 1942, this time in the southern sector. Refreshed and reequipped, they seemed irresistible. By August they had reached the outskirts of Stalingrad on the Volga. Here Stalin ordered a stand: The battle of Stalingrad raged for six months. In February 1943, the Russians, having closed a pincer behind the Germans in Stalingrad, captured all who had not been killed of an army of almost 300,000 men. This was the turning point; the Germans began a slow but general retreat.

The critical battle on the Mediterranean and Western European front was fought in Egypt. General Rommel's tough Afrika Korps in its first drive on Suez in 1941 had been stopped and pushed back into Libya by the British. In June 1942, Rommel, greatly strengthened, struck the British desert forces a shattering blow and chased them in near rout to El Alamein, only 65 miles from Alexandria. Suez seemed doomed, and the British fleet prepared to evacuate the Mediterranean before it could be bottled up. Churchill rushed to the scene and put in a team of winning commanders: Sir Harold Alexander in overall command and Sir Bernard Montgomery as field commander. In August, Rommel assaulted the British positions at El Alamein and was stopped. A race to build up men and supplies ensued; the British, with massive aid from the United States, won. Late in October 1942, Montgomery's superior Eighth Army attacked Rommel's forces, and after a desperate battle drove them back across the desert in defeat. Suez and the Middle East were now saved from the Axis, and for the first time Great Britain and the United States were in a position to assume the offensive.

The war in the Pacific was predominantly naval in character. Three days after Pearl Harbor, Japanese carrier-based torpedo planes struck the British Asiatic fleet a crippling blow in the Gulf of Siam. Now, with unchallenged mastery of the Pacific, the Japanese were able to conquer with relative ease a vast area in the Southwest Pacific and Southeast Asia in the space of a few months. The American islands of Wake, Guam, and the Philippines; British Hong Kong and Malaya; and the Dutch East Indies were overrun. The great British bastion, Singapore, fell on February 15, 1942. Burma was conquered in May. In May a strong Japanese fleet was turned back by the American fleet in the Battle of the Coral Sea, northeast of Australia. However, the main Japanese fleet was preparing a major thrust at Hawaii, which could have been taken easily immediately after Pearl Harbor. The United States navy, which was in possession of the Japanese code, massed for an all-out battle. Early in June 1942, just as the Stalingrad and El Alamein campaigns were beginning, the two fleets came within carrier-plane range of each other off Midway Island, a thousand miles west of Hawaii. The climactic Battle of Midway was fought at long range entirely by aircraft and submarines. American planes sank all four of the Japanese carriers, while the Japanese were able to destroy only one of three American carriers. Pounded from the air and without air cover, the Japanese commander ordered a retreat, never to become so bold again. In August 1942, the Americans assumed the offensive by attacking Guadalcanal in the Solomon Islands northeast of Australia. By that time, the tide was beginning to turn on all three fronts.

4. VICTORY ON THE RUSSIAN FRONT

Although the greatest crises had passed by the end of 1942, two and a half more years of bloody fighting were required to subdue the

Early in the hours of Sunday, December 7, 1941, the Japanese attacked Pearl Harbor, Hawaii, and destroyed the Pacific fleet in the harbor and the air force on the ground. This photo shows the U.S.S. California as she went down following the attack. Note the men swarming over the side. *Photo: United Press International*

Axis. In fact, the defeat of the Axis could not have been achieved at all without a high degree of cooperation among the Big Three allies. President Roosevelt, with his winsome personality, played an important part in maintaining mutual confidence and cooperation among the Allied powers, which were so divergent in their ideologies and specific interests. The chief planners of the coordinated global strategy were Churchill for Great Britain, Stalin for the Soviet Union, and Army Chief of Staff George Catlett Marshall for the United States.

The Battle of Russia was the greatest and most destructive battle in history. Some 9 million men (five hundred divisions) were engaged. For two and a half years after Stalingrad, the Germans were slowly beaten back, doggedly contesting every foot of ground. At last, in April of 1945, the Russians entered Berlin. Along the 1,500 miles between Stalingrad and Berlin lay the wreckage of the greater part of Hitler's war machine, the most powerful engine of destruction the world had ever seen. But the richest and most productive part of the Soviet Union lay devastated. At least 15 million Russians had been killed—possibly many more.

5. VICTORY ON THE MEDITERRANEAN AND WESTERN EUROPEAN FRONT

Early in November 1942, just as the Germans were beginning to retreat from El Alamein, a combined Anglo-American force under the command of General Dwight D. Eisenhower landed in French North Africa. By February 1943, the converging forces of Eisenhower and Montgomery cornered the Afrika Korps in Tunisia, where it surrendered in May. Rommel himself, on Hitler's orders, had flown back to Germany. In July 1943, Eisenhower's troops, now including those of Montgomery, conquered the island of Sicily. Early in September the Anglo-Americans invaded the southern tip of Italy. Mussolini had already been forced to resign (July 25), and Italy surrendered. However, the peninsula was

Hitler's "Empire"

Allied With Germany

Occupied by the Axis

At War Against the Axis

Relations between the Axis and Vichy France were governed by the Armistice of June 1940, but Germany occupied the whole of France in November 1942.

0   100   200   300 miles

ARCTIC OCEAN

NORTH CAPE

Murmansk

NORWAY

Narvik

WHITE
SEA

FINLAND

Archangel

SWEDEN

SHETLAND I.
(Britain)

Bergen

Oslo

L. Onega

L. Ladoga

Leningrad

Helsinki

Stockholm

ESTONIA

Farthest Axis Penetration
—— December 1941
.... November 1942

NORTH
SEA

DENMARK

Copenhagen

Riga

LATVIA

LITHUANIA

Memel

Danzig

EAST
PRUSSIA

SUWALKI

BALTIC SEA

Hamburg

NETHER-
LANDS

Rotterdam

Elbe R.

Berlin

GERMANY

Essen

BELGIUM

Cologne

LUX.

Nuremburg

SUDETEN-
LAND

Breslau

POLAND

Warsaw

BYELO-RUSSIA

Smolensk

SOVIET   UNION

Moscow

Tula

Kuibyshev

Volga R.

Stalingrad

Astrakhan

Kiev

Kharkov

Donetz R.

Don R.

UKRAINE

Rostov

Maikop

Grozny

CASPIAN SEA

Baku

BOHEMIA

Rhine R.

Munich

MORAVIA

SLOVAKIA

Vienna

AUSTRIA

Budapest

HUNGARY

Dniester R.

BESSARABIA

SWITZERLAND

FRANCE

Toulon

CORSICA
(Vichy France)

ITALY

ADRIATIC SEA

Rome

Anzio

Cassino

SARDINIA
(Italy)

Salerno

Taranto

CROATIA

Belgrade

SERBIA

RUMANIA

Bucharest

Danube R.

Sofia

BULGARIA

ALBANIA

Sevastopol

Yalta

BLACK SEA

Batum

TRANSCAUCASIA

Tabriz

IRAN

Istanbul

Ankara

T U R K E Y

Palermo

Bizerte

SICILY

AEGEAN SEA

Athens

GREECE

CRETE

CYPRUS
(Britain)

SYRIA

Baghdad

IRAQ

MALTA (Britain)

MEDITERRANEAN

SEA

LEBANON

TUNISIA
(Vichy France)

PALESTINE

TRANS-
JORDAN

SAUDI ARABIA

This photograph of the Axis leaders taken in July 1944 shows them no longer jubilant. The tide of war had long since turned against them; within the year, both Hitler and Mussolini would be dead, their countries ruined and defeated. Left to right (foreground): Mussolini, Martin Bormann, Admiral Doenitz, Hitler, Field-Marshal Goering. *Photo: United Press International*

held by strong German forces. By December 1943, the Allies had reached Cassino Pass, about 75 miles south of Rome. At this point, the major objectives in the Mediterranean area had been achieved, and Eisenhower, along with most of his forces, was transferred to Great Britain to command the main Anglo-American thrust across the Channel.

This thrust came on June 6, 1944. Thanks in large measure to complete Allied mastery of the skies, successful landings were made on the Normandy coast. After a rapid buildup, the Anglo-Americans broke out of the beachhead, and before the end of the year cleared practically all of France. Germany, meanwhile, was being pulverized from the air. Early in 1945 the American and British forces, now joined by French units, broke through the German West Wall, crossed the Rhine, and joined hands with the Russians on the Elbe. Germany surrendered on May 8, ending the

war in Europe. Near the end, Hitler and several other top Nazis committed suicide, and Mussolini was shot by Italian partisans.

6. VICTORY ON THE PACIFIC FRONT

Early in 1943 American forces under the command of General Douglas MacArthur began with a strong naval escort an island-hopping campaign northwestward from their base in Australia. At the same time, the main American fleet under the command of Admiral Chester Nimitz, now definitely superior to the Japanese fleet, thrust westward from Hawaii toward Japan, capturing the numerous Japanese-held islands in its path. Although the islands, many of them covered by jungles, were bloodily defended, the American forces moved steadily toward Japan itself. In October 1944, the American forces made a bold landing on Leyte Island in the Philippines

The Pacific War

which brought the Japanese fleet out for a last desperate effort. In history's greatest naval battle, the Battle of Leyte Gulf, the Japanese fleet was annihilated. Cut off, uncovered, and subjected to ceaseless air and sea attacks, Japan was doomed. After Germany surrendered in May 1945, American, British, and Russian troops that had been engaged in the European theater were deployed rapidly to the

Far East. In mid-July the atomic bomb, which American and British scientists had been developing for several years, was successfully completed and tested. In order to avoid the heavy and useless casualties that a direct assault on the Japanese home islands would cause, the United States decided to use the bomb to shock Japan into surrender. On August 6, 1945, the first atomic bomb to be used in warfare destroyed the Japanese city of Hiroshima. Two days later, the Soviet Union declared war on Japan and began to overrun Manchuria and northern Korea. The next day, August 9, the second and last atomic bomb then in existence demolished the industrial city of Nagasaki. The Japanese surrendered five days later, August 14, 1945.

World War II had ended. At least 22 million people had been killed, and 34 million had been wounded. Property and moral losses were beyond calculation. Among the casualties was President Roosevelt, who died on April 12, 1945, only a few months before he could have seen the defeat of the Axis, which he had done so much to bring about.

Suggested Reading

General. **Winston Churchill, *The Second World War* (6 vols., Bantam) is the best history of World War II that probably will ever be written. Churchill naturally exaggerates the role played by Great Britain in relation to that of the other Allies, particularly the Russians, but any intelligent reader will understand and discount that. **Charles de Gaulle, *Complete War Memoirs* (3 vols., Clarion) is as brilliantly written and more subtle than Churchill's masterpiece. A useful brief survey of World War II is L. L. Snyder, *A Concise History: The War, 1939–1945* (1960). Erich von Manstein, *Lost Victories* (1958) is a history of the war in Europe from the German viewpoint by one of Hitler's ablest generals. **H. Feis, *Churchill, Roosevelt, Stalin: The War They Waged and the Peace They Sought* (Princeton) is a scholarly study of World War II diplomacy among the Big Three Allied powers. A thoughtful analysis of World War II and its significance is **G. Wright, *The Ordeal of Total War, 1939–1945* (Harper Torchbook).

Two Years of Axis Triumph. The surprising collapse of France in 1940 is shrewdly analyzed by Pertinax, *The Gravediggers of France* (1944) and Marc Bloch, *Strange Defeat: A Statement of Evidence Written in 1940* (1949). Pertinax was the pen name of A. Géraud, a French journalist. Bloch, one of France's most distinguished historians, became a Resistance leader and was executed by the Germans. **Winston Churchill, *Their Finest Hour* (Bantam) is the second volume of his

great history and covers the battles of France and Britain, 1940. It is the best of the six volumes. A. Clark, *Barbarossa* (1964) is a history of the war on the Russian front.

The Entry of the United States. A brief survey of the decade of weak and vacillating American foreign policy that finally led to the Pearl Harbor disaster is R. Devine, *The Reluctant Belligerent: American Entry Into World War II* (1965). A more scholarly and detailed study of the events that led to the entry of the United States into the war is W. L. Langer and S. E. Gleason, *The Undeclared War, 1940–1941* (1953). The best account of the events that led to Pearl Harbor is the scholarly **H. Feis, *The Road to Pearl Harbor: The Coming of the War Between the United States and Japan* (Atheneum). This book should dispel much of the nonsense that is written and talked about this subject. Another good book on Japanese-American relations before Pearl Harbor is J. Grew, *Ten Years in Japan* (1943). Grew was United States Ambassador to Japan immediately before Pearl Harbor. The best book on Pearl Harbor itself is **R. Wohlstetter, *Pearl Harbor: Warning and Decision* (Stanford).

Allied Victory. An excellent account of the role of the United States in World War II is H. L. Stimson and McGeorge Bundy, *On Active Service in Peace and War* (1947), which is the autobiography of the American Secretary of War during World War II. *The War Reports of General of the Army George C. Marshall,*

General of the Army H. H. Arnold, Fleet Admiral Ernest J. King (1947) is the official account of the American military operations in World War II by the Army, Air Force, and Navy chiefs of staff. Marshall's second report is particularly lucid. **Dwight D. Eisenhower, *Crusade in Europe* (Dolphin) is a popularly written account of the Anglo-American military operations in the European theater by the commanding general. **B. L. Montgomery, *Memoirs* (Signet), by the commander of the British forces under Eisenhower's command, is quite critical of Eisenhower's strategy. One of the best of the numerous accounts of individual battles and campaigns in World War II is **C. Ryan, *The Longest Day* (Crest), which is a popularly written account of the Anglo-American landings in Normandy. Another scholarly and highly interesting monograph is **H. R. Trevor-Roper, *The Last Days of Hitler* (Berkeley). The best account of United States naval operations in World War II is S. E. Morison, *The Two-Ocean War: A Short History of the United States Navy in the Second World War* (1963), an abridgment of Admiral Morison's fifteen-volume classic. A scholarly account of the final defeat of Japan is H. Feis, *Japan Subdued: The Atomic Bomb and the End of the War in the Pacific* (1961).

Chapter 59 ✎ The Cold War in Europe

In 1945 the leaders of the victorious nations were once again confronted with the task of restoring a shattered world and making a lasting peace. The existence of atomic weapons now made the question of peace a matter of utmost necessity. To act as a watchdog over the peace, the world's leaders, as in 1919, set up an international organization: this time, the United Nations. However, from the beginning, the work of the UN was seriously hampered by hostility between the United States and the Soviet Union. This hostility, which came to be called the "cold war," pervaded and poisoned every area of postwar international relations.

1. THE UNITED NATIONS

The chief moving force behind the founding of the United Nations was Franklin Roosevelt. Determined to avoid two major mistakes that Wilson had made in creating the League of Nations, Roosevelt (1) saw to it that the UN was born before the war ended and the postwar squabbling among the Allies began, and (2) gave leading roles in the creation of the UN to several important Republicans, so that it would not become a political issue in the United States. The formal launching of the organization took place at a conference in San Francisco in April 1945, a few days after Roos-

evelt died and less than a month before Germany surrendered.

In structure and procedure, the UN bears a close resemblance to the League of Nations. The General Assembly, in which each member state has one vote, serves as a general clearinghouse and supervisor over the work of all other UN bodies and agencies. Any matter that endangers world peace may be brought to its attention at any time. The UN body that was given special guardianship over the peace is the Security Council. It is composed of five permanent and ten nonpermanent members. The five permanent members are the United States, the Soviet Union, Great Britain, France, and Nationalist China. The nonpermanent members are elected by the General Assembly for two-year terms.

The fundamental character of the Security Council and, indeed, of the whole UN is really determined by the voting procedure in the Security Council. Any action involving the use of force or the threat of force requires nine votes, including those of all five permanent members. This means that each of the permanent members of the Security Council has a perpetual veto over forceful actions of the UN and cannot be acted against by that body. This crippling veto was incorporated into the charter because the Big Three sponsoring powers—the United States, the Soviet

The United States representative, Arthur Vandenberg, signs the United Nations Charter in San Francisco in 1945, as President Truman and other members of the United States government look on. *Photo: The Bettmann Archive*

Union, and Great Britain—all were unwilling to submit to the UN's authority. The Soviet Union, finding herself in a constant minority, used the veto to block action to which she was opposed more than a hundred times during the first twenty years of the UN's existence.

The Social and Economic Council supervises the work of a number of specialized agencies such as the International Labor Organization (ILO), the United Nations Educational, Scientific, and Cultural Organization (UNESCO), the World Bank, and the International Monetary Fund. The Trusteeship Council is designed to supervise the rule of peoples held under control or trusteeship by other nations. The International Court of Justice decides international legal disputes. The day-to-day detailed work of the UN is done by the Secretariat, composed of several thousand full-time professional employees presided over by the Secretary-General, who is appointed by the Security Council and the General Assem-

bly. This important post has been held by Trygve Lie of Norway, by Dag Hammarskjöld of Sweden, and by U Thant of Burma—all able men. As a permanent headquarters, the UN chose a site in New York City donated by John D. Rockefeller, Jr.

The United Nations has done an enormous amount of work in the economic, cultural, and humanitarian fields, most of which has failed to make the headlines. It has assisted in arranging cease fires in three conflicts between Israel and the Arab states (1949, 1956, and 1970) and has stopped wars between India and Pakistan, and the Netherlands and Indonesia. It played an important role in checking Communist military aggression in Korea, 1950–1953 (see pp. 915–916). Its biggest failure to date has been its inability to ease the tension between the Soviet Union and the United States, which has threatened to undo the achievements of the UN and engulf the world in atomic war.

2. THE YALTA AGREEMENTS

Soviet-American postwar disagreements first began over the Yalta Agreements. Indeed, the disagreements began even before the fighting in Europe had ended. In February 1945, Roosevelt, Churchill, and Stalin, with their top military and civilian advisers, came together at Yalta in southern Russia for the purpose of coordinating the last Allied blows against the Axis and laying the groundwork for postwar cooperation. The conference marked the culmination of wartime good will and cooperation among the Big Three powers. At the time of the conference, victory was in sight, barring unforeseen disasters; but victory was not so near or so certain that it could be guaranteed without the continued cooperation of the Big Three.

The questions of military strategy were harmoniously worked out by the three military staffs present. The four chief areas of discussion among Roosevelt, Churchill, and Stalin were (1) the UN Charter, (2) Germany, (3)

Eastern Europe, and (4) the Far East. Agreements were quickly reached on questions concerning the UN Charter, the veto being the chief one. The three conferees also found themselves in close agreement concerning Germany. They agreed on stern measures, including complete de-Nazification with severe punishment for the top Nazis, total demilitarization, the division of the country into four occupation zones, and a long period of occupation by the Allies. Further details were left to a later conference following Germany's surrender.

A sharp cleavage developed over the areas of Eastern Europe that had just been liberated from German control by the Soviet armies. Stalin announced that the territories he had recovered in 1939–1940 (eastern Poland, Lithuania, Latvia, Estonia, strips of Finland, and Bessarabia) were really Russian territories that had been taken from her by force at the end of World War I and that under no condition would they be the subject of discussion. Roosevelt and Churchill did not formally concede these points, but they did not make an issue of them. They were primarily concerned over the fate of western Poland, Hungary, Yugoslavia, Bulgaria, and Rumania —all of which were behind the Soviet lines. (For some reason, the Soviets never overran and occupied Finland, which was a defeated enemy country.)

Roosevelt and Churchill insisted that in accordance with the principles of the Atlantic Charter, to which the Soviet Union had subscribed, these countries must be given complete independence. Stalin argued that these countries had been the doors through which Russia had been invaded in both world wars and that they were vital to the Soviet Union's security. He pointed out that Rumania, Hungary, and Finland had attacked Russia as Hitler's allies, that Bulgaria had cooperated with Hitler as his ally, and that the Soviets' military lines to Germany and Austria ran through Poland, Rumania, and Hungary. Therefore, he asserted, the Soviet Union's security demanded that she maintain a measure of control over these countries. Roosevelt and Churchill were adamant and somehow persuaded Stalin to yield to their position. The official protocol signed at Yalta by Roosevelt, Churchill, and Stalin called for free elections as soon as possible for these liberated peoples of Eastern Europe, with all non-Fascist parties participating. Such elections were almost certain to result in democratic, anti-Communist, and anti-Russian victories.

In regard to the Far East, Roosevelt was guided by the advice of the top American military authorities. It was their purpose to bring the Soviet Union into the Japanese war as soon as possible, thereby saving, it was believed, a million and possibly two million American and British casualties. As payment for the Soviet Union's entry into the Japanese war not later than three months after Germany's surrender, Roosevelt offered Stalin the return of the southern half of Sakhalin Island and the railroad and port facilities in Manchuria that Japan had taken from Russia in 1905 (Generalissimo Chiang Kai-shek readily agreed to the Manchurian concessions). Also, the Soviet Union was to regain the Kurile Islands, which Japan had obtained from Russia in 1875. Korea was to be given her independence. However, the United States was to conquer the Japanese in Korea south of the thirty-eighth parallel, and the Soviets were to liberate the portion of Korea lying north of the thirty-eighth parallel. Stalin agreed to these terms, and the Yalta Conference ended with warm cordiality. Within two weeks after the conference adjourned, however, disputes arose over the agreements, and the United States and the Soviet Union have been in conflict over them ever since.

3. THE SOVIET-AMERICAN CONTROVERSY OVER EASTERN EUROPE

It was over Eastern Europe that Soviet-American accord first broke down. On February 24, 1945, exactly thirteen days after the Yalta Conference adjourned, the American and British representatives on the Allied Council in Bucharest began to press for the democratization of the Rumanian government, which was a puppet of the Soviet occupying forces. Whereupon the Soviet deputy foreign minister arrived from Moscow and browbeat the Rumanian government into setting up an all-Communist regime. The Soviet government then announced that the Rumanian question was settled. This, of course, was a crass violation of both the spirit and the letter of the Yalta Agreements. A week later the American ambassador to Moscow reported to President

At the Yalta Conference, February 1945, Churchill, Roosevelt, and Stalin, representing the Big Three Allied Powers, made a series of agreements concerning the major postwar problems. At the time of the conference, victory over the Axis was in sight. *Photo: United Press International*

Roosevelt that the Soviets were refusing to proceed with the implementation of the Yalta Agreements in regard to Poland.

Whether Stalin had deliberately deceived Roosevelt and Churchill at Yalta or whether he had changed his mind after returning to Moscow is not certain (Stalin's suspicions were aroused by the proposals of certain American and British officials in Europe to violate the Yalta Agreements in regard to Germany). It was now clear, however, that the Soviet Union was determined to keep a tight control over the areas of Eastern Europe that its armies had liberated from the Germans. These Soviet violations of their solemn agreements were a source of great disappointment and worry to Roosevelt, whose physical condition was rapidly worsening. He counseled patience and firmness in dealing with the Soviet Union. There was really nothing else to be done at the time, since the war with Germany and Japan was still in progress and the areas in Eastern Europe in question were behind the Soviet lines.

President Truman, who succeeded Roosevelt on April 12, 1945, was in favor of a much tougher policy toward the Soviet Union. As soon as the war in Europe had ended, the United States began to press the Soviet Union to sign treaties with the liberated countries of Eastern Europe. After months of haggling, the Soviet Union finally agreed to withdraw her occupying forces from Rumania, Hungary, and Bulgaria within ninety days after the formal signing of the treaties, which took place on February 10, 1947. Long before the expiration of the ninety days, however, Soviet-American relations had drastically worsened.

General George Catlett Marshall, America's forceful wartime army chief of staff, became secretary of state soon after the signing of the treaties. Both Truman and Marshall believed that the time had come for the United States to adopt a tough policy toward Russia. The immediate occasion for the inauguration of the new policy was the situation in Greece and Turkey, both of which were under severe Soviet pressure. In February 1947, the British government, which had been supporting both Greece and Turkey with troops and money since the end of the war, announced that after March 31 it would be unable to continue to do so. On March 12, 1947, President Truman appeared before Congress and requested authorization to send American military and civilian personnel into Greece and Turkey. "I believe," he said, "that it must be the policy of the United States to support free peoples who are resisting attempted subjugation by armed minorities or by outside pressures." He asked for $400 million to implement the new program, and warned that this was only a starter. Congress greeted this announcement with a standing ovation.

The new policy, which was soon called the Truman Doctrine, meant that the United States would draw a military ring around the Soviet Union and its satellites from Manchuria to Norway. It was the policy of military containment. All real diplomatic negotiations between the United States and the Soviet Union, of course, ceased immediately. The Soviet Union made no further pretense of withdrawing from the areas of Eastern Europe occupied by her troops; instead she tightened the iron curtain that she had drawn around them.

In June 1947, Secretary of State Marshall supplemented the Truman Doctrine with the Marshall Plan. This was an offer of comprehensive economic aid to all European countries (except Fascist Spain) who would improve their economies, stabilize their currencies, and cooperate with each other in bringing about general economic recovery. All the countries of Europe except the Soviet Union and her satellites hastened to accept Marshall's terms and American aid. The Soviet Union regarded the Marshall Plan as an American scheme to shore up Europe's and her own tottering capitalism, to lure away the Soviet satellites, and to make the European countries economic dependencies of the United States. She therefore forbade the countries of Eastern Europe under her control or influence to participate. Congress

President Truman is shown here with two wartime leaders, Generals Omar Bradley and George C. Marshall. In 1947 the President appointed Marshall as Secretary of State to implement the Truman Doctrine, which the Secretary supplemented by sponsoring the Marshall Plan for European economic assistance. *Photo: United Press International*

voted $5.3 billion as the first of four installments totaling some $17 billion for Marshall Plan aid. The later installments were trimmed somewhat.

In the fall of 1947 the Soviet Union began a series of vigorous moves to counter the Truman Doctrine and the Marshall Plan. In September 1947, she set up the Communist Information Bureau, or Cominform, the better to coordinate policies of the Soviet Union, Poland, Hungary, Rumania, Bulgaria, Albania, Yugoslavia, and Czechoslovakia. This was in reality a restoration of the old Comintern, which was the Communist International working for world revolution. The following year the Cominform was supplemented by the Council for Economic Mutual Assistance. This was a Soviet Marshall Plan of her own. At the same time the Soviet Union severely tightened her grip on her satellites. The local Communist parties were rigorously purged of moderates and national patriots.

One tragic victim of the stepping-up of the cold war was Czechoslovakia. This little re-

public, lying geographically between the two armed camps, had tried to remain on friendly terms with both sides. In February 1948, a Soviet-inspired and supported Communist coup overthrew the liberal regime of President Eduard Beneš and drew Czechoslovakia behind the Iron Curtain. Soviet efforts to tighten the reins on Yugoslavia, however, backfired. In March 1948 Communist dictator Marshal Tito severed his ties with Moscow and established relations with the capitalistic West.

After the death of Stalin in 1953, the Soviet government, under the leadership of Nikita Khrushchev, head of the Communist Party, made overtures to the United States to end the cold war. At the same time, it relaxed somewhat its iron grip on the satellites. Some observers optimistically called these overtures and this relaxation the end of the cold war. Unfortunately, this was far from the case. The United States, frustrated and angered by continuing tensions in Germany (see the following section), by the Communist takeover of China, and the costly Korean War (see Chapter 60), quickly spurned the overtures. In the same year that Stalin died, John Foster Dulles became United States Secretary of State in the new Eisenhower administration. It was his belief that communism was a Moscow-directed conspiracy bent upon world conquest. The Truman Doctrine was too tame. The time had come, he proclaimed, to pass over from containment to liberation.

In Eastern Europe itself, long-suppressed discontent in the satellites soon manifested itself. In October 1956, the Polish people elected a native Polish Communist regime to replace the Soviet-endorsed one. At the same time, a massive anti-Communist nationalist revolt broke out in Hungary, only to be bloodily suppressed by the Soviet army. The Rumanian Communist leaders took a more cautious but definitely independent line.

But now the Soviet government was confronted with another serious problem. Early in 1956 Khrushchev had denounced before startled Communist leaders in Moscow the crimes of Joseph Stalin. This touched off an ideological dispute with the Chinese Communists, who were younger and more evangelical in the Marxist faith than the Russians (see p. 914). They accused the Soviet government of heterodoxy and softness toward the capitalistic, imperialistic West. A rivalry sprang up between the neighboring Communist giants, intensified by the cutting off of desperately needed Soviet economic and technological aid to Peking. The Soviet Union and China share the longest international boundary in the world, much of it subject to dispute. Concern over Red China may have influenced Khrushchev to adopt a still more mellow attitude toward the West. Nevertheless, he blundered into a showdown with the United States in 1962 by attempting to set up Soviet nuclear missiles in Cuba and was forced to make a humiliating retreat.

In October 1964, Khrushchev was suddenly ousted from power by his colleagues in the Party's Central Committee. Leonid Brezhnev replaced him as Party Secretary and Aleksei Kosygin as Premier. The new regime rebuked the fallen leader only for his ineffective methods—not his objectives. When the Communist regime in Czechoslovakia attempted to pursue a more liberal and independent course in 1968, the Soviet army marched in and occupied the country. Thus, after twenty-five years, the cold war, so far as Eastern Europe was concerned, had not ended.

4. THE SOVIET–AMERICAN STRUGGLE OVER GERMANY

The biggest prize over which the Soviet Union and the United States struggled in the years immediately after World War II was Germany. The Soviet Union, fearing above everything else a revived and rearmed Germany, was determined to keep her permanently weak and as much as possible under Soviet domination. The United States, on the other hand, having little fear of Germany and seeing in her a valuable potential ally against the Soviet Union, soon set out to restore and rearm her. Fear of a rearmed Germany in alliance with the United States undoubtedly greatly strengthened the Soviet Union's determination to keep Eastern Europe under Soviet control.

The policies and principles to be followed in the government of Germany were agreed upon by the United States, the Soviet Union, and Great Britain at a conference held in Potsdam outside Berlin, in July 1945, shortly after Germany had surrendered. Truman, Stalin, and Clement Attlee, whose Labour party had just defeated Churchill's Conservatives, represented the Big Three. The cordiality that had prevailed at Yalta five months earlier had vanished; suspicion and self-interest reigned instead. On most issues, Truman and Attlee lined up against Stalin.

The Potsdam Agreements tentatively set the eastern boundary of Germany, pending a formal treaty settlement, at the line of the Oder and Neisse rivers (see pp. 898–899). The portion of Germany lying east of this line, the home of some 6 million Germans, was awarded tentatively to Poland except for the port city of Königsberg in East Prussia and its immediate hinterland, which were awarded to the Soviet Union. The rest of Germany was divided into four occupation zones: American, Russian, British, and French. Berlin, which was in the Russian zone, was divided into four sectors and made the headquarters of a four-power coordinating commission. The four occupying powers were to remove from their zones as reparations war plants and peacetime industrial plants in excess of Germany's peacetime needs. Since the Soviet Union's zone was primarily agricultural, it was agreed at Potsdam that she should have in addition to removals from her own zone, 25 percent of the reparations removed from the three Western zones. The principles agreed upon as the policy to be followed by the four occupying powers in the governing of Germany were the five D's: demilitarization, deindustrialization, de-Nazification, democratization, and decentralization.

In the implementation of the Potsdam Agreements for governing the four zones, sharp cleavages soon developed among the occupying powers, particularly between the United States and the Soviet Union. The only major question over which there was substantial agreement was that of punishment of the top Nazis. A court consisting of judges and prosecuting attorneys from the four occupying powers was set up at Nuremberg for the purpose. Twelve of the leading Nazis were condemned to death by hanging, seven to long prison terms. But there the four-power unity ceased. The Soviet Union was determined upon a long, hard occupation of Germany. She dropped an iron curtain in front of her zone, proceeded to communize its government and economy, and enforced the five D's (except for democratization) to the letter. The United States, on the other hand, pursued a lenient policy. The commander of the Ameri-

can zone during the first four years was General Lucius D. Clay. Clay was a great admirer of the German professional military officers and refused to punish them. He was also a believer in free enterprise and big business and soon took steps to restore Germany's private industry. The problem of de-Nazification he soon turned over to the Germans themselves.

The British Labour government believed that socialization of German industry would be an adequate safeguard against remilitarization and aggression. The French agreed with the harsh policy of the Soviet Union, as indeed did virtually all of Europe. Since, however, the French and the British economies had been wrecked by the war and they were heavily dependent upon the United States, France and Britain were eventually persuaded to support the American policy.

After the inauguration of the Truman Doctrine and the Marshall Plan in the spring of 1947, relations between the United States and the Soviet Union in Germany worsened rapidly. In August 1947 Clay announced a sharp stepping-up of the economy of the American and British zones, which had been merged the previous year. This raised the level far above that prescribed by the Potsdam Agreements and was made possible only by Marshall Plan aid. In December 1947 Secretary of State Marshall, reflecting the new get-tough policy with Russia, walked out of the London Conference of Foreign Ministers, thereby breaking up the four-power arrangement for governing Germany. France, faced with an open East-West break in Germany, reluctantly agreed to merge her zone with those of the United States and Great Britain. The American authorities were now able to set in motion their plans for the creation of an independent West German State.

To the Soviet leaders, this was the last straw. They attempted to dissuade the Western powers from going ahead with the project by blockading the three Western zones of Berlin in the hope of starving them out. For

Europe 1970

0   100   200   300 miles

ICELAND

ARCTIC OCEAN

L A P L A N D

NORWAY

Trondheim

SWEDEN

FINLAND

GULF OF BOTHNIA

FAEROE I.
(Denmark)

SHETLAND I.

Bergen

Oslo

Viborg

Helsinki

Leningrad

ORKNEY I.

Göteborg

Stockholm

Tallinn

ESTONIAN
S.S.R.

Skagerrak

Kattegat

BALTIC SEA

Riga

LATVIAN S.S.R.

SCOTLAND

ATLANTIC OCEAN

Edinburgh

NORTH SEA

DENMARK

Copenhagen

Klaipeda

LITHUANIAN
S.S.R.

NORTHERN
IRELAND

UNITED
KINGDOM

IRELAND
(EIRE)

Dublin

Liverpool

Hull

WALES

ENGLAND

NETHERLANDS

Amsterdam

Hamburg

GERMAN
DEMOCRATIC
REPUBLIC

Szczecin

Kaliningrad *(East
Prussia)*

Gdansk
(Danzig)

Minsk

BYELO-RUSS

London

HANOVER

Berlin

Oder R.

Warsaw

POLAND

*PRIPE
MARS*

ENGLISH CHANNEL

Brussels

BELGIUM

Cologne

Bonn

Elbe R.

Dresden

Vistula R.

(Silesia)

Wroclaw

Lvov

Dniest

NORMANDY

Rouen

LUX.

GERMANY

Prague

MORAVIA

CZECHOSLOVAKIA

CARPATHIAN MTS.

RUTHENIA

BRITTANY

Paris

Seine R.

LORRAINE

Strasbourg

GERMAN
FEDERAL
REPUBLIC

BOHEMIA

SLOVAKIA

Loire R.

Tours

ALSACE

BADEN

Munich

BAVARIA

Vienna

Budapest

TRANSYLVAN

MOLDA

BAY OF BISCAY

FRANCE

Berne

SWITZERLAND

AUSTRIA

HUNGARY

RUMANIA

La Coruña

Bordeaux

Geneva

Lyons

Milan

LOMBARDY

Trieste

VENEZIA

Venice

CROATIA-
SLAVONIA

BANAT

WALLACHIA

Bucha

GALICIA

Rhône R.

PIEDMONT

Po R.

BOSNIA

YUGOSLAVIA

Belgrade

Danube

Oporto

Bilbao

GASCONY

LANGUEDOC

PROVENCE

Genoa

Florence

Sarajevo

SERBIA

BULGAR

PORTUGAL

Duero R.

LEÓN

OLD CASTILE

Ebro R.

NAVARRE

ARAGON

ANDORRA

Marseilles

Toulon

TUSCANY

*CORSICA
(France)*

MONTE-
NEGRO

Sofia

Saragossa

CATALONIA

Barcelona

Rome

CAMPANIA

APULIA

Tirana

Salonica

Tagus R.

Madrid

Valencia

Palma

ADRIATIC SEA

ITALY

ALBANIA

Lisbon

SPAIN

NEW CASTILE

LA MANCHA

Palma

*BALEARIC I.
(Spain)*

*SARDINIA
(Italy)*

Naples

AEG

GREECE

Cordoba

Seville

ANDALUSIA

Malaga

Gibraltar *(Britain)*

Ceuta *(Spain)*

Palermo

SICILY

Athens

Tangier

Rabat

Melilla
(Spain)

Oran

Algiers

Tunis

MALTA

MEDITERRANEAN SEA

Casablanca

Fez

MOROCCO

ALGERIA

TUNISIA

Tripoli

Bengazi

TRIPOLITANIA

LIBYA

Archangel

Dvina R.

ITE
A

L. Onega

doga

Moscow

Kuibyshev

Uralsk

Smolensk

Volga R.

Saratov

KAZAK S.S.R.

ARAL SEA

Kursk

S O V I E T   U N I O N

Ural R.

Astrakhan

UZBEK S.S.R.

Volgograd
(Stalingrad)

Kharkov

Kiev

Don R.

UKRAINIAN S.S.R.

Dnepropetrovsk

Rostov

TURKMEN S.S.R.

Dnieper R.

OLDAVIAN
S.S.R.

Odessa

SEA OF
AZOV

C A U C A S I A

CASPIAN SEA

Grozny

Krasnovodsk

AFGHANISTAN

CRIMEA

GEORGIAN   Tiflis
S.S.R.

AZERBAIJAN
S.S.R.

Baku

Sevastopol

ABA

DOBRUJA

BLACK SEA

Varna

Sinop

Batum

Ardahan

ARMENIAN
S.S.R.

Kars

Yerevan

Bosporus

Istanbul

Ankara

L. Van

Tabriz

L. Urmia

Teheran

I R A N

U   R   K   E   Y

rdanelles

Izmir

Tigris R.

Kirkuk

Isfahan

Adana

Aleppo

Euphrates R.

Baghdad

Adalia

SYRIA

I R A Q

CYPRUS

Beirut

Damascus

Basra

Abadan

Bushire

LEBANON

P E R S I A N   G U L F

KUWAIT

TE (Greece)

ISRAEL

KUWAIT

Tel Aviv-Jaffa

Amman

Jerusalem

Gaza

JORDAN

BAHRAIN

QATAR

TRUCIAL
OMAN

OMAN

Alexandria

NILE DELTA

Nile R.

El Alamein

Suez Canal

Cairo

*SINAI
PENINSULA*

Aqaba

S A U D I   A R A B I A

GULF OF SUEZ

GULF OF AQABA

UNITED ARAB REPUBLIC   (EGYPT)

Population Density
Persons per Square Mile

Under 5

5 to 100

101 to 250

Over 250

eleven months, June 1948 to May 1949, the Soviets stopped all land traffic across their zone from the West to Berlin. The Western powers defeated the blockade by means of a giant air lift. However, the tension was great.

Meanwhile, the United States proceeded undeterred in the setting up of the German Federal Republic, which began to function in September 1949. It was a liberal democratic government similar to the Weimar Republic. The Christian Democratic party, a slightly right-of-center party with Roman Catholic leanings, won the first election, and its leader, the elderly and pro-Western Dr. Konrad Adenauer, became the first chancellor. The Western powers replaced their military governors with civilian commissioners and relaxed their control over Germany. One month later (October 1949) the Soviet Union set up the German Democratic Republic in its zone. It was a Communist Soviet puppet state. The United States and the Soviet Union feverishly set about to rearm West and East Germany, respectively. However, a fearful France delayed the rearmament of Western Germany until 1955. Severe labor riots against the Communist dictatorship in East Germany in 1953 demonstrated that the Soviet Union could hardly depend on her East German satellite in a showdown. Meanwhile, West Germany's industrial economy recovered by leaps and bounds. By 1957 she had regained her former industrial supremacy in Western Europe.

The Soviets' fear of a powerful rearmed Germany in alliance with the United States was so great that Khrushchev arranged two conferences with President Eisenhower (1955 and 1960) and one with President-elect Kennedy (1961) to try to convince them of the seriousness of the matter in Soviet eyes. When the Americans proved to be adamant, the Communists threatened to resume the Berlin blockade, and in late 1961 constructed a great wall sealing off Communist East Berlin from democratic West Berlin. Scores of would-be escapees died in their attempt to cross the barriers.

In 1963 Konrad Adenauer finally stepped down (at 87) as chancellor of West Germany. His successors, Ludwig Erhard and Kurt Kiesinger (in 1966), vigorously pursued his policies of strengthening West Germany's military ties with the United States, demanding the reunification of Germany and the recovery of lost territories in Eastern Europe, and a place in the family of nuclear nations. In 1969 Willy Brandt, a Social Democrat, became chancellor.

His government quickly signed a nuclear nonproliferation treaty that had been long pending, and entered into bilateral talks with East Germany and the Soviet Union. In August 1970 Chancellor Brandt and the Soviet Premier Kosygin signed a treaty renouncing force or the threat of force in international relations, and accepting the existing boundary lines of Eastern Europe including the Oder-Neisse line between East Germany and Poland. An official accompanying letter specified that the treaty left open the possibility of the future reunion of the two Germanies. This possibly momentous treaty was accompanied by trade agreements which promised a greatly stepped-up commerce between West Germany and the Soviet Union. If fully implemented, these agreements could mean a significant turning point in the history of the post-World War II world. They could strengthen both Germany and the Soviet Union economically and diplomatically.

5. THE ATLANTIC COMMUNITY

As the tempo of the cold war between the United States and the Soviet Union increased, the United States undertook to organize the Atlantic community of nations into a formal alliance. The military effectiveness of the alliance, however, was uncertain because of the war-torn condition of the major European members.

In Great Britain the Labour party swept to victory in elections held in July 1945, just as the war was coming to an end. Clement Attlee succeeded Churchill as prime minister. The problems confronting Britain and the Labour government were indeed formidable. More than half of Great Britain's merchant marine had been sunk; a third of her buildings had been destroyed or damaged; her foreign investments had been liquidated and used up; she owed the United States $18.5 billion; her empire was crumbling. To distribute the burden fairly, the Labour government strictly rationed the short supplies, raised taxes on the rich, and lowered taxes on the poor. It nationalized (1) the Bank of England, (2) the coal mines and the electrical and gas industries, (3) inland transportation, and (4) the steel industry. Altogether, some 20 percent of Britain's economy was socialized. A vast program of social security, public education, public housing, and national health insurance was launched. Steps were taken to bring an end to British imperialism. The six years of Labour rule were years of austerity for the middle and upper classes. However, the general morale of the people was high, and Britain made a more rapid recovery than any other war-ravaged country. By 1948 her production and exports were higher than before the war, and the masses of the people were enjoying more security, services, and material goods than ever before. Millions of British citizens, for instance, were enjoying excellent medical care for the first time in their lives. Of course, there was much discontent among the former privileged classes, who now had to share these goods and services.

In 1951 Churchill and the Conservatives returned to power. With the exception of denationalizing the steel industry and inland transportation, they tampered little with the Labour party's program, which the great majority of the British people now clearly favored. The liquidation of the British Empire went on apace (see Chapter 60). Britain's economic recovery and growth continued, though at a rate somewhat slower than that of Germany, Japan, France, and a number of other countries. The foreign affairs of Britain under Conservative rule followed the somewhat traditional British policies of close align-

ment with the United States and with the Commonwealth members, seeking trading opportunities wherever they might be found. In the election of October 1964, the Labour party won a narrow victory, and its leader, Harold Wilson, became prime minister. This time the advent of a Labour government produced no drastic new policies, either foreign or domestic. In 1970 the Conservatives won a close election and Edward Heath became prime minister. It continued to be difficult to balance the budget and stabilize the currency. Many of Britain's mines and factories were antiquated. It was obvious that Great Britain was now far outdistanced as a world power by the United States and the Soviet Union. This fact was dramatically underlined by the death of Sir Winston Churchill in 1965. The funeral of Britain's great World War II leader and champion of the British Empire, which may never again be equaled in pomp and pageantry, reminded millions of television viewers all over the world that only yesterday Great Britain was the world's dominant power. Churchill's death marked, in a real sense, the end of an era. Governing colonies, commanding battleships, and playing polo in India are very much more colorful than administering medical care to the poor.

France emerged from the war not only ravaged but, unlike Britain, defeated and demoralized. General Charles de Gaulle returned to France in 1944 with the American and British liberators, who gave official recognition to the government he set up in Paris. However, the first postwar elections, held in October 1945, resulted in a sweeping victory for the parties of the Left, with which the authoritarian De Gaulle could not cooperate. Early in 1946 he went into temporary retirement. The Leftist coalition, suspicious of authority, drew up a constitution very similar to that of the Third Republic, with its weak executive. The Fourth Republic, like the Third, was plagued by a multiplicity of parties. In 1947, just as the Leftist coalition was preparing to launch a socialistic reform program similar to that of the British Labour government, France became enmeshed in the sharply intensified Soviet-American cold war. The Communists, constituting about one-fourth of the electorate, deserted the Leftist coalition and supported the Soviet Union. The United States gave strong support to the capitalistic classes and exerted heavy pressure on the Fourth Republic to take the American side in the cold war. The result was a slight swing to the right in French politics and the adherence of a reluctant, frustrated, and divided France to the American cold war camp.

Although the Fourth French Republic experienced a strong, if uneven, economic recovery, it was unable to cope with the problem of the disintegrating French Empire. After suffering several humiliating defeats, France in 1954 granted independence to Indo-China (Vietnam). Two years later, she granted independence to Morocco and Tunisia. Her inability to solve the Algerian problem, however (see p. 923), led to the mutiny of the French army in Algeria in May 1958, which brought about the fall of the government and the recall of Charles de Gaulle from his twelve-year retirement. The problems confronting him were formidable—a mutinous army, a disintegrating empire, a seemingly endless war in Algeria, a disgruntled working class, an inflated currency, governmental weakness amounting to anarchy, widespread cynicism.

De Gaulle was probably the only man in France who could have reestablished civilian control over the mutinous army. This he deftly proceeded to do. He drew up a new constitution which greatly strengthened the executive branch of the government, and in December 1958 he was elected first president of this Fifth French Republic by an overwhelming majority. He immediately granted independence to all of France's colonies except Algeria with its large French population. (Algerian independence was granted four years later. All the other colonies except Guinea voted to remain with the French Union.) He undertook to strengthen France's capitalistic economy by means of an austerity program. In spite of widespread strikes and sabotage by the working classes, much of it Communist-inspired, France's economy was soon operating at its highest level in history, and the French masses were enjoying the greatest prosperity they had ever known.

In foreign affairs, De Gaulle set out to restore France's "greatness"—her prestige in world affairs and her hegemony in Western Europe. He also sought to make Western Europe a "third force" independent of both American and Soviet domination. To achieve these ends, he created at great cost an independent nuclear striking force, cultivated cordial relations with Germany, withdrew France's military forces from NATO (see p. 904) because of its domination by the United States, and vetoed Great Britain's entry into the European Common Market (see p. 904) because of her close ties to her Commonwealth associates and to the United States.

For eleven years, these policies worked with remarkable success. France regained much of the stability and prestige she had lost in 1940. De Gaulle's strong role, of course, en-

Two of the great postwar European leaders— France's Charles de Gaulle and Germany's Konrad Adenauer—are shown here during a visit of Adenauer to France in 1962. *Photo: United Press International*

countered much opposition, mostly from the extreme Right and the extreme Left. His position and that of France's economy were weakened by massive student and labor union strikes and riots in 1968. When, in early 1969, De Gaulle asked for a vote of confidence from the French people and lost by a narrow margin, he resigned. His successor was Georges Pompidou, who for many years had been De Gaulle's premier.

The story of postwar Italy has been somewhat similar to that of France, except that she was much poorer, the corrupting hand of fascism had lain upon her for eighteen years longer, her Communists were more numerous, and no Charles De Gaulle came forth to lead her with a strong hand. By 1948 she appeared to be definitely in the cold war camp of the United States.

Of the Western powers, only the United States emerged from the war virtually unscathed materially. The war had forced billions of dollars into circulation, ended the long depression, and destroyed much of her foreign competition. Under Presidents Truman (1945–1953), Eisenhower (1953–1961), Kennedy (1961–1963), Johnson (1963–1969), and Nixon (1969——), she enjoyed an economic prosperity such as no nation in history had ever experienced. A family without an automobile and television set was looked upon as very poor or eccentric indeed. This material prosperity stirred the nation's some 20 million blacks to seek their share. In 1954 the United States Supreme Court outlawed segregation in the public schools. Official resistance to the carrying out of this decision in Arkansas and Mississippi was crushed by federal troops. Bloody and destructive riots in the black ghettoes terrorized several big northern cities in the summer of 1964 and recurred every summer until virtually every sizable city in the United States was stricken. In 1965 Congress passed a civil rights act outlawing racial discrimination in private business and services.

Violence in the United States was by no means limited to the blacks. During the dec-

ade of the 1960s, youth all over the world was in revolt. However, violence and the crime rate were higher in the United States than in any other country and were increasing constantly. President Kennedy was assassinated in 1963 and his brother Robert, a major candidate for the Democratic Presidential nomination, in 1968—both by disgruntled youths. In the latter year Martin Luther King, the influential black civil rights leader, also was assassinated. Colleges and universities were scenes of increasing protest, often violent. Some of the contributing factors to this unrest were, undoubtedly, continued racial inequality, widespread poverty alongside great wealth, inflation, pollution and destruction of natural resources, and growing dissatisfaction with American involvement in the war in Vietnam (see p. 919).

The prosperous American people were seized, from the very beginning of the postwar era, by a morbid fear of the Soviet Union and of communism. Many journals, politicians, and business and professional men exploited this fear. During the early 1950s, Senator Joseph McCarthy of Wisconsin fanned this fear into hysteria. In the eyes of McCarthy and his millions of followers, the American government, defense industries, armed forces, and educational system were honeycombed with Communists and fellow travelers. The word *liberal* became synonymous with *Communist*. Thousands lost their jobs. Neighbor suspected neighbor.

In October 1957, just as McCarthyism was subsiding, the American people were shocked by the news that the Soviet Union had orbited a satellite—Sputnik. The implication was that the lean and eager Russians had forged ahead in nuclear weapons and delivery systems while the soft and contented Americans had slept. This time, the ensuing excitement centered on and in the American educational system. Many teachers suddenly observed for the first time in their teaching careers an intense eagerness on the part of the students to listen and to learn. The chief beneficiary of this happy situation was science. Billions were gladly spent on crash programs of scientific research and teaching. Science and technology threatened to smother all other fields of learning, particularly the humanities. The United States had, of course, for some time been working on a satellite of her own, and in 1958 successfully orbited one. In 1960 the Soviet Union and the United States sent men into space and began to race each other to the moon. This race was won by the United States in 1969 at a cost of some $40 billion.

Many Americans were badly frightened by a Communist takeover in Cuba in 1959. Its leader, Fidel Castro, overthrew an American-supported Rightist dictatorship. The American government in 1961 encouraged and aided an unsuccessful attempt by Cuban refugees to overthrow the Castro regime, and the following year, by heavy threats, forced the Soviet Union to dismantle missile bases that she had constructed in Cuba. This widespread American fear of the Soviet Union and of communism during the first postwar decade was undoubtedly the chief motivating influence behind the costly efforts of the American government to build a Western system of collective security and a strong Atlantic Community.

After four years of cold war tension and billions of dollars of American military and economic support, the countries of Western Europe began to set up a more formal relationship with each other and with the United States. In 1949 the United States took the lead in creating the North Atlantic Treaty Organization (NATO). This was a defensive military pact signed by the United States, Canada, Great Britain, France, Italy, Portugal, Belgium, the Netherlands, Luxemburg, Denmark, Norway, and Iceland. Greece and Turkey were admitted in 1951, and West Germany in 1955. According to the terms of the pact, all the members were committed to come to the military aid of any member that was attacked. Also in 1949, under the leadership of Winston Churchill, the Council of Europe was established with headquarters at Strassburg.

Its members were Great Britain, France, Italy, Ireland, Belgium, the Netherlands, Luxemburg, Denmark, Norway, and Sweden. West Germany was admitted two years later. Although the functions of the council were only consultative, it was designed as a step toward the political integration of Western Europe.

In 1950 France's Foreign Minister Robert Schuman astonished the world by offering to pool the French coal and steel industries with those of Germany and other Western European countries. Under French leadership, the European Coal and Steel Community was set up the following year. Its members were France, West Germany, Italy, Belgium, the Netherlands, and Luxemburg. In 1958 these six nations broadened the scope of the cooperation by establishing a Common Market which abolished tariff and immigration barriers among them and sought closer coordinating of their economies. The real author of the Coal and Steel Community and the Common Market was France's Jean Monnet. Considering the venomous hatred and bloody conflicts engendered by selfish nationalism that had for centuries torn the European nations, these were historic achievements. They were undoubtedly aided by the threat of the Soviet Union and of international communism.

But malignant nationalism was not to be easily harnessed. The slackening of the cold war tensions that followed the death of Stalin in 1953 weakened the appeal of the NATO alliance. The phenomenal prosperity and industrial expansion of the Common Market members created new rivalries. In 1963 Great Britain's belated bid for membership in the Common Market was vetoed by President de Gaulle. He apparently feared Anglo-American domination of the European economy. And finally fascism—the most extreme form of nationalism—continued to raise its ugly head here and there throughout the Western world. What would its role be in the stresses and fears of the future?

Suggested Reading

General. An excellent brief survey of world affairs since World War II is **H. Gatzke, *The Present in Perspective: A Look at the World Since 1945* (3rd ed., Rand McNally).

The UN. Two good histories of the United Nations, its origins, structure, and functioning, are A. Vandenbosch and W. Hogan, *The United Nations* (1952); and S. Fenichall and P. Andrews, *United Nations* (1952). A more detailed study of ideas and the diplomacy that went into the making of the UN is R. Russell, *A History of the United Nations Charter* (1958).

The Yalta Agreements. Probably the best account of the Yalta Conference and agreements is to be found in **R. Sherwood, *Roosevelt and Hopkins* (2 vols., Bantam). Sherwood used notes that Hopkins, Roosevelt's closest adviser, had taken at the conference. An eye-witness account by the American Secretary of State is E. Stettinius, Jr., *Roosevelt and the Russians: The Yalta Conference* (1945). Another eye-witness account by Roosevelt's personal military aid is Admiral W. Leahy, *I Was There* (1950). Winston Churchill, a leading participant, discusses the conference in his ***Triumph and Tragedy* (Bantam), volume 6 of his great history of World War II.

Soviet–American Controversy Over Eastern Europe. Three Americans who played prominent roles in formulating the get-tough-with-Russia policy of the United States after World War II have written memoirs detailing the controversy over Eastern Europe, where the Cold War began: Harry S. Truman, *Memoirs* (2 vols., 1955); G. Kennan, *Memoirs, 1928–1950* (1967); and James F. Byrnes, *Speaking Frankly* (1947). Kennan was U.S. Ambassador to the Soviet Union and the chief author of the Truman Doctrine and the Marshall Plan. Byrnes was Secretary of State 1945–1947. D. Fleming, *The Cold War and Its Origins, 1917–1960* (2 vols., 1961) places a considerable amount of blame on the United States. The

Communist takeover of Eastern Europe is best related by H. Seton-Watson, *The East-European Revolution* (1956). Another useful study of Soviet-dominated Eastern Europe is **Z. Brzezinski, *The Soviet Bloc: Unity and Conflict* (Praeger). A good brief history of the Soviet Union since World War II is **H. Schwartz, *The Red Phoenix* (Praeger). **M. Djilas, *The New Class* (Praeger) is a strong criticism of the ruling bureaucracy in the Soviet Union, by a former Yugoslav Communist bureaucrat. A delightful and impressive study of people in the Soviet Union and their outlook is **K. Mehnert, *Soviet Man and His World* (Praeger, 1967). A valuable picture of life in the Soviet Union is Svetlana Alliluyeva, *Only One Year* (1969). The author is Stalin's daughter, who escaped to the United States in 1967.

Soviet–American Struggle Over Germany. H. Feis, *Between War and Peace* (1960) is a scholarly study of the Potsdam Conference that established the four-power occupation and policies for governing postwar Germany. L. Clay, *Decision in Germany* (1950) is an account of the Soviet-American conflict over Germany by the commander of the American zone during the first four years of military occupation. A more objective and scholarly account is E. Davidson, *The Death and Life of Germany: An Account of the American Occupation* (1959). H. Wallich, *Mainsprings of the German Revival* (1955) is a good account of the German "economic miracle." An excellent study of Soviet-occupied East Germany is J. Nettl, *The Eastern Zone and Soviet Policy in Germany, 1945–1950* (1951).

The Atlantic Community. **T. Jarman, *A Short History of Twentieth-Century England 1918–1962* (Mentor) has some excellent chapters on Britain since the end of World War II. Two good studies of Britain's postwar Labour government and its policies and achievements are F. Williams, *Socialist Britain* (1949); and R. Brady, *Crisis in Britain: Plans and Achievements of the Labour Government*

(1950). Charles de Gaulle, *The War Memoirs of Charles de Gaulle,* Vol. III, *Salvation, 1944–1946* (1960) is a graphic account of the liberation of France and the setting up of the Fourth Republic. **D. Pickles, *The Fifth French Republic: Institutions and Politics* (3rd ed., Praeger) is a scholarly study of De Gaulle's France. Two excellent studies of the foreign policy of the United States since World War II are **N. Graebner, *Cold War Diplomacy* (Anvil); and **H. Kissinger, *Nuclear Weapons and American Foreign Policy* (Anchor). The quality of American intellectual life since World War II is sharply examined and condemned by **J. Barzun, *The House of Intellect* (Harper Torchbook). An excellent study of the problems and forces of European unity is E. Haas, *The Uniting of Europe* (1958). **M. Shanks and J. Lambert, *The Common Market Today—and Tomorrow* (Praeger) is a useful, brief study. A keen analysis of the problems of prosperity in the Western world since World War II is **J. K. Galbraith, *The Affluent Society* (Mentor).

Chapter 60 ❧ The Challenge of the Non-Western World

Asia was an important area of conflict in the cold war between the United States and the Soviet Union. But it is a serious mistake to think of mid-twentieth-century Asia as a mere pawn in the Soviet-American world struggle. The vast and populous Asian continent was at last astir and out of the control of either the United States or the Soviet Union. Japan, in the latter part of the nineteenth century, had been the first Asian country to adopt Western technology and aggressive nationalism. In the twentieth century the rest of Asia began to move in the same direction. The movement was sharply accelerated by the two world wars. Africa, too, was astir after World War II. She was the last of the continents to throw off the yoke of European imperialism.

1. JAPAN BETWEEN EAST AND WEST

Japan emerged from World War II defeated on sea and land, the shocked victim of history's first two atomic bombs used for military purposes. Since the United States had played by far the major role in the defeat of Japan, she refused to share the occupation and government of the Japanese islands with her for-

mer allies. President Truman appointed General Douglas MacArthur Supreme Commander of the Allied Powers in Japan and gave him absolute authority. To advise MacArthur, an Allied Council composed of representatives from the United States, the Soviet Union, Great Britain, and China was set up in Tokyo. To formulate policy, a Far Eastern Commission composed of representatives from the eleven nations most interested in Far Eastern affairs was set up in Washington. However, the final decision to accept or to ignore the advice of these two bodies lay with MacArthur.

When the Soviet Union, which had used seventy divisions in crushing the Japanese forces in Manchuria and North Korea and was a next-door neighbor to Japan, realized that she was going to be denied a real part in the control of Japan, she refused for four months to participate in the advisory commissions. MacArthur's only directives came from the United States government, which shortly after the Japanese surrender drew up a four-point policy for postwar Japan: (1) Japan was to be limited to the four "home" islands and some small ones in the immediate vicinity. (2)

On the first anniversary of the founding of the People's Republic of China, October 1, 1950, workers carry hundreds of portraits of Mao Tse-tung in the National Day Parade. *Photo: Eastfoto*

Japan was to be completely demilitarized. (3) Civil, political, and religious rights and liberties for the Japanese people were to be encouraged. (4) Japan's economy was to be developed for her peacetime needs.

For a year and a half General MacArthur ruled Japan with a firm but liberal and benevolent hand. He was fortunate to have the support of Emperor Hirohito, who urged his people to obey the American commander. A democratic constitution similar to that of Great Britain was drawn up and put into effect. In the first elections under the new constitution, the Social Democrats, who were somewhat similar to the British Labourites, won the largest number of seats in the national legislature. The activities of Japanese labor unions were encouraged, and they became effective for the first time. The five great families who had monopolized Japan's industry and finance disbanded their great business combinations under pressure from the occupation authorities. Demilitarization was carried on apace, including the trial and execution or imprisonment of a number of top war leaders.

Of greatest significance was MacArthur's land-reform program. The great mass of Japanese farmers were poverty-stricken landless sharecroppers, giving up from 50 to 70 percent of their yield to absentee landlords. Laws sponsored by MacArthur forced the landlords to sell to the government all land in excess of 7½ acres (more in less fertile areas). The government, in turn, sold the land in plots of 7½ acres to the tenant farmers, who were given thirty years to pay for them. By the end of 1946 Japan appeared to be on the way to becoming a liberal democracy.

Early in 1947, when the cold war was being stepped up in intensity, General MacArthur suddenly reversed his liberal policy in Japan. He first cracked down on the newly formed labor unions. Industrial decentralization ceased, and land redistribution slowed down. Obviously, the United States was now interested in making Japan, like Germany, a link in the containment chain that she was forging around the Soviet Union. By 1949 the conservative parties were firmly in control of the Japanese government once more. On the other hand, a number of left-wing liberals, in cynical disillusionment, began turning to communism.

In 1951 the United States drew up a formal treaty with Japan. The terms granted the United States military bases in Japan and a protectorate over the Ryukyu Islands (including Okinawa) and Japan's former mandated islands in the Pacific. Japan was to pay no indemnity, and was to be free to rearm and to make her own alliances. Although forty-eight nations signed the treaty, India, Burma, the Soviet Union, and the Soviet satellites refused. China was not invited to sign. The Soviet Union complained bitterly that Japan's closest neighbors, the Soviet Union and China, were allowed no part in the making of the treaty and accused the United States of sowing the seeds of future wars by unleashing Japan.

During the 1950s and 1960s Japan made an astounding economic recovery that surpassed even that of West Germany, and like West Germany she received massive American aid. In rebuilding her ruined industries, she adopted the most modern and scientific labor-saving devices. By the mid-1960s her people were enjoying a prosperity and a standard of living such as they had never known before. But some observers were apprehensive. Japan has few natural resources. In an area smaller than California, of which only 14 percent is arable, lived more than 90 million people. The large Socialist party was hostile to Japan's close subservience to the United States and to American military bases in Japan and Okinawa. It was also hostile to the renewed concentration of Japanese industry and finance in the hands of the former *zaibatsu* families and to steps leading to the remilitarization of Japan.

2. THE RISE OF COMMUNIST CHINA

Across the Sea of Japan a very different and even more exciting drama had been enacted in

China. Here, a massive upheaval involving one-fourth of the world's population took place. Sun Yat-sen, after launching his mighty revolution against both China's foreign exploiters and her own reactionary and conniving government (see pp. 786–790), died in 1925, in the very hour of success. His place at the head of the revolutionary Chinese government was taken by his young and vigorous supporter, General Chiang Kai-shek. Chiang Kai-shek, a professional soldier, was much more interested in making China a powerful and independent nation than in liberalizing her government and society. Under him, the revolutionary Kuomintang party, then dominant in China, swung definitely to the right. When the Chinese Nationalist armies were defeated by the Japanese in 1937–1938 and driven deep into the interior, Chiang Kai-shek and the Kuomintang party were cut off from the chief bases of their liberal support, which were the great coastal cities. Heavily dependent then upon the war lords and landlords of the interior, they swung still further to the right. The long years of relative inactivity at Chungking (1939–1945) had a demoralizing effect not only upon Chiang Kai-shek's military forces, but upon the Kuomintang party leaders themselves.

Meanwhile, a rival movement very different in nature and purpose from Chiang Kai-shek's Kuomintang made rapid headway in China. This movement was communism. During the 1920s, when China's Confucian civilization was crumbling faster than Sun Yat-sen's Western Christian liberalism could replace it, another Western influence moved into the vacuum: Marxist materialism. The hostility that the Western democracies showed to Sun Yat-sen's revolutionary liberal movement greatly encouraged the Chinese Communists. In 1927 the Communists found an able leader in the scholarly and shrewd Mao Tse-tung. This dedicated revolutionary from well-to-do peasant stock had risen to leadership by sheer force of intellect, personality, and energy. Chiang Kai-shek exerted every effort to crush

the Chinese Communists—much more, in fact, than to drive out the Japanese invader. During the years 1939–1945, when the Kuomintang forces were inactive in Chungking and getting further and further out of touch with the Chinese masses, Mao Tse-tung's Communists were waging incessant guerrilla warfare against the Japanese and gaining a greater following among the Chinese people.

Following the surrender of Japan in August 1945, a bitter struggle for the control of China ensued between Chiang Kai-shek's Kuomintang forces, now known as the Chinese Nationalists, and the Chinese Communists. In this struggle the United States supported the Nationalists. The American army and navy transported Chiang Kai-shek's forces and seized and held strategic places until Nationalist forces could arrive. Chiang Kai-shek was supplied with American money and weapons. However, the Communists won the support of ever-increasing numbers of the Chinese people. Tens of thousands of people in the populous coastal areas who had endured the Japanese invaders for eight years were outraged when Kuomintang landlords and politicians, having sat the war out in Chungking, returned demanding back rent and back taxes. Morale in the long-inactive and graft-ridden Nationalist armies was low, while that in the Communist armies, toughened by the continuous fighting against the Japanese, was high.

It was in Manchuria that the tide first turned in favor of the Communists. Using Japanese weapons that had been left behind by the Russians, and American weapons and munitions that were surrendered by the Nationalists, the Communists began to gain the upper hand in 1947. During 1949 the victorious Communists swept over the entire Chinese mainland. Chiang Kai-shek, with a remnant of his Nationalist forces, mostly officers, fled to the island of Formosa, where after June 1950, they were protected by the United States navy. In 1949 Mao Tse-tung proclaimed the People's Republic of China and the following year formed an alliance with the Soviet Union. With Soviet aid, he

Asia 1970

ARCTIC OCEAN
SPITZBERGEN (Norway)
FRANZ JOSEF LAND
BARENTS SEA
SEVERNAYA ZEMLYA
NOVAYA ZEMLYA
KARA SEA

ATLANTIC OCEAN

NORWAY
SWEDEN
FINLAND

Igarka
Vorkuta
Archangel

E U R O P E
POLAND
RUMANIA
BULGARIA

Leningrad

Moscow
Kiev

S O V I E T

S I B

Sverdlovsk
Tomsk
Kuibyshev
Omsk
Karaganda

Yenisei R.
Ob R.

MEDITERRANEAN SEA

Istanbul
BLACK SEA
Ankara
T U R K E Y
CYPRUS
Batum

Astrakhan
CASPIAN SEA
AR AL SEA
L. Balkhash

Urumchi

LEBANON
ISRAEL
Cairo
Suez Canal
SYRIA
IRAQ
Baku

Tashkent
Bukhara

SINKIANG
LOP N

JORDAN
Baghdad
Basra
Teheran
I R A N

AFGHANISTAN
Kabul

C

UNITED ARAB REPUBLIC
(Egypt)

SAUDI ARABIA
KUWAIT

PERSIAN GULF

JAMMU AND KASHMIR

Indus R.

TIBET

SUDAN

RED SEA

Mecca
BAHRAIN
QATAR
TRUCIAL OMAN
Riyadh

WEST PAKISTAN

Karachi

NEPAL
SIKKIM
New Delhi
Ganges R.
E
PA

ERITREA

Muscat
OMAN

INDIA
Calcutta

AFRICA

YEMEN
SOUTHERN YEMEN (Aden)
Aden

ARABIAN SEA

Bombay
Hyderabad

BAY OF BENGA

Djibouti
FRENCH TERRITORY OF AFARS & ISSAS
ETHIOPIA

SOCOTRA (Britain)

LACCADIVE I. (India)

Goa
Madras
Pondicherry

SOMALI REPUBLIC

KENYA

MALDIVE ISLANDS

Colombo
CEYLON

TANZANIA

States Recognized as Independent After World War II

0   500   1000 miles

INDIAN OCEAN

ARCTIC OCEAN
WRANGEL I.
NOVO SIBIRSK I.
Bering Strait
ALASKA (U.S.A.)
ALEUTIAN I.

Kolyma R.

Anadyr

BERING SEA

R I A
Lena R.
Yakutsk
Okhotsk
KAMCHATKA

U N I O N
SEA OF OKHOTSK

Amur R.
SAKHALIN
KURILE I.

L. Baikal
Chita
Sovetskkaya Gavan
Khabarovsk

Irkutsk
MANCHURIA
Harbin
HOKKAIDO

SEA OF JAPAN

Ulan Bator
INNER MONGOLIA
Vladivostok
JAPAN

ONGOLIAN REPUBLIC
Mukden
NORTH KOREA
HONSHU

JEHOL
Peking
Lü-Ta Seoul
SOUTH KOREA
Tokyo

Huang Ho
Tientsin
SHIKOKU
KYUSHU

I N A
Tsingtao
EAST CHINA SEA

Nanking
RYUKYU I.

Hankow
Shanghai
OKINAWA

Chungking
Yangtse Kiang

Amoy
FORMOSA
(Nationalist China)

Kunming
Swatow
Canton
Hong Kong
KWANGSI
Macao
HAINAN

BURMA
Mekong R.
Hanoi
NORTH VIETNAM
LUZON
PHILIPPINE REPUBLIC
Manila

Vientiane
LAOS
THAILAND
goon
SOUTH VIETNAM

Bangkok
CAMBODIA
Phnom Penh
Saigon
SOUTH CHINA SEA
MINDANAO

NDAMAN
(India)
NICOBAR I.
(India)

NORTH BORNEO
BRUNEI
(Britain)
FEDERATION OF MALAYSIA
SARAWAK
BORNEO

Singapore
SUMATRA
I N D O N E S I A
Djakarta
JAVA
FLORES
TIMOR
(Portugal)

CELEBES
CERAM
WEST IRIAN
NEW GUINEA
PAPUA
(Australia)

BISMARCK ARCHIPELAGO
TERRITORY OF NEW GUINEA
(Australia)
SOLOMON I.
(Britain)
GUADALCANAL

CORAL SEA
AUSTRALIA

PACIFIC OCEAN
WAKE
IWO JIMA

MARIANA I.
MARSHALL I.

U.N. TRUSTEESHIP
U.S.A. Administration

GUAM
YAP
PALAU
C A R O L I N E   I.

Population Density
Persons per Square Mile
Under 5
5 to 100
101 to 250
Over 250

began the enormous task of industrializing and communizing the world's most populous nation.

This formidable undertaking was interrupted shortly after it had begun by China's involvement in the Korean War, 1950–1953 (see the following section). The Chinese Communists were greatly angered by the intervention of the United States, whose navy prevented them from driving Chiang Kai-shek's Nationalist forces from their last stronghold on Taiwan (Formosa) and ending the Chinese civil war. When the United Nations forces, which were mostly American, defeated the North Korean Communists and approached the Manchurian border, the Chinese Communist armies crossed the Yalu River into Korea, drove the Americans back, and stalemated the war. This was a remarkable accomplishment for such an industrially backward country fighting against the world's greatest military power, and it cost the Chinese Communists nearly a million casualties. This feat following the sweeping victories it had just won in China itself filled the young Red regime with pride and confidence.

In 1953 Mao Tse-tung launched his first five-year plan, which was very similar to Stalin's first five-year plan twenty-five years earlier. The Chinese Communists, however, were starting from a much more primitive base than the Russians. Industry and agriculture were both collectivized. The emphasis was on building heavy industry. These were years of bleak austerity, but the Chinese masses had never known anything else. In 1957 the government announced that the first five-year plan had been a great success. Most production quotas had been met or surpassed. The following year it launched its second five-year plan. The vast new goals in industry and agriculture were to be achieved by communizing Chinese society more completely than had ever been attempted in the Soviet Union. The entire population was organized into strictly regimented communes; the ancient and sacred Chinese family structure was drastically altered. China's huge and rapidly growing

population was set to building irrigation dams and ditches, steel mills, factories, railroads, schools, and hospitals, and in a frenzied hurry. Never in history had so vast a revolution been undertaken. It was called "the Great Leap Forward." But the plan was too ambitious. In 1959 a series of droughts and floods produced near-famine conditions in many areas. Overzealous local party officials provoked resentment and resistance among the harried populace. The realistic Red leaders slackened the pace and eased the regimentation.

The partial failure of the Great Leap Forward gave rise to ideological differences and set off a power struggle within the Communist Party hierarchy. A moderate group led by Liu Shao-chi, president of the republic and second in command to Party Chairman Mao Tse-tung, wished to slow down the pace of communization, produce more consumer goods, and encourage, at least temporarily, individual initiative, much on the order of the NEP in the early days of the Soviet Union. Mao took a different line. He believed many dangerous remnants of prerevolutionary capitalistic China had still to be destroyed. In 1966 he unleashed tens of thousands of Red Guards, fanatical Communist youths, upon the moderate element in what he called a "cultural revolution," and with the support of the regular army apparently succeeded in crushing the moderates.

The Chinese Communists' difficulties were intensified by their growing rift with the Soviet Union. An ideological dispute had begun when Khrushchev denounced Stalin in 1956 (see p. 896). Peking accused Moscow of becoming soft toward the capitalistic, imperialistic West. In 1960 the Soviet Union began to withhold promised economic and technological aid from China. By 1964 the two Red giants were vying with each other for allegiance and leadership in the Communist world, hurling epithets at each other and accusing each other of border violations.

But it was against the United States that Red China directed her greatest hostility.

The United States persistently refused to recognize her and blocked her admission to the United Nations. The American fleet continued to protect Chiang Kai-shek on Taiwan. American arms and armies prevented Communist regimes from winning complete victories in Korea, Vietnam, and Laos. American military bases in Japan and missile bases in Okinawa menaced China. In October 1964 Red China exploded her first nuclear device. It would appear that Communist China was destined to become some day a third world giant. She persecuted Christianity as a relic of Western imperialism, seized Buddhist properties, and adopted the religion of nationalism. Finally, she posed as the leader of the East against the West.

3. THE KOREAN WAR

The bitter left-right conflict among the Asiatic peoples and the global cold war struggle between the United States and the Soviet Union merged in Korea to produce a shooting war of major proportions. In August 1945, in accordance with the Yalta Agreements, the forces of the Soviet Union occupied Japanese-held Korea north of the thirty-eighth parallel. These moves were supposed to be for the purpose of setting up a free and united Korean nation. However, the Soviet Union immediately proceeded to set up a Communist dictatorship in North Korea. The land was distributed to the peasants, and industry was nationalized. In South Korea the United States authorities sponsored a right-wing government under the leadership of the aged and reactionary Korean patriot Syngman Rhee. Late in 1948 the Soviet forces withdrew from North Korea, leaving behind an energetic Communist regime well armed with the latest Soviet weapons. Six months later the American forces withdrew from South Korea, leaving behind the Syngman Rhee landlord regime armed mostly with the weapons that had been captured from the Japanese. Both the North and South Korean governments talked loudly of conquering each other.

On June 25 (June 24, American time), 1950, North Korea suddenly attacked South Korea. The high-spirited and well-armed North Korean Communists easily defeated the South Koreans. The armies of Syngman Rhee, made up largely of disgruntled landless tenant farmers, melted away. The Truman administration quickly decided that the Communist aggression in Korea was the Soviet Union's first move to conquer the world by military force and that there must not be another Munich. Secretary of State Dean Acheson persuaded the United Nations to take drastic action. Taking advantage of the absence of the Soviet Union's representative, the Security Council called upon all the members of the United Nations to furnish military forces to repel the North Korean aggression and asked President Truman to name the commander of the United Nations forces. Fifty-two of the fifty-nine members of the United Nations voted approval of this action, and a few of them contributed token forces. Truman named MacArthur to command them. Truman also announced that he had already ordered American forces into the Korean War, that the American navy would protect Chiang Kai-shek's Chinese Nationalists on Taiwan against the Chinese Communists, and that American aid to the French fighting the native Communists in Indo-China would be greatly increased.

The forces of the United Nations, mostly Americans, quickly defeated the North Koreans. By late October 1950, MacArthur's forces were approaching the Yalu River, which forms the Korean-Chinese border. At this point Red China entered the war and severely defeated MacArthur's forces, driving them in headlong retreat back down the peninsula. Eventually—January–March 1951—the battle line became stabilized along the thirty-eighth parallel, where the war had started.

MacArthur cried loudly for all available American military forces and for the blockade and bombing of Red China. However, the military authorities in Washington refused the request. They feared involvement in all-out war with the Soviet Union, which hitherto had limited its aid to the North Korean and Chinese Communists to the selling of weapons. The American military authorities were also opposed to stripping the home front and the critical Western European and Middle Eastern areas of defenses. Since the Communist aggression in Korea had been checked, Washington wished to see the Korean War simmer down with a minimum of further casualties. When MacArthur persisted in public criticism of his government's policies and disobeyed the orders of his superiors to cease making policy pronouncements, he was replaced in April 1951, both as commander of the United Nations forces in Korea and as supreme commander in Japan, by General Matthew Ridgway.

In June 1951, the Soviet Union proposed the beginning of peace negotiations in Korea. Both sides readily agreed. However, two years of haggling, accompanied by intermittent fighting at the front, ensued before an armistice was finally signed in July 1953. Total casualties—dead, wounded, and missing—are estimated to have been approximately a million and a half on each side, of which some 145,000 were Americans (including 54,000 dead) and 900,000 Chinese Communists. Most of the rest were Koreans. The war ended just about where it had started. However, the first Communist military aggression had been checked with severe punishment. The United Nations had functioned effectively and increased its prestige. Probably of equal significance is the fact that a revolutionary new Asiatic power, Red China, had fought the greatest Western power, the United States, to a standstill. American troops still stand guard along the truce line protecting a conservative regime in South Korea.

4. THE REVOLT OF SOUTHERN ASIA

The end of World War II found the huge British, Dutch, and French empires in Southern Asia aflame with the spirit of nationalism and revolt. The United States alone of the Western imperial powers escaped direct embroilment in this revolt by granting independence to the Philippines in 1946.

In India, by far the most populous country in this area, and Great Britain's richest colonial prize, the leader of the independence movement was Mohandas K. Gandhi (1869–1948), one of the most dynamic personalities of the twentieth century. This middle-class Hindu, educated in Great Britain, was a master of the psychology of the Indian masses. His chief tactics were passive resistance and civil disobedience. The British were unable to cope with him. The gentle little Mahatma (Great Spirit), whether sitting at his spinning wheel, subsisting on goat's milk, or fasting in a British prison, was a beloved symbol of national independence not only to India's millions, but also to millions of other Asiatic and African colonials.

Indian nationalism reached its peak during World War II, but Churchill would not hear of Indian independence. "I did not become the king's first minister," said the doughty warrior, "in order to preside over the liquidation of the British Empire." The British Labour party, however, upon coming to power in 1945 immediately announced its determination to grant Indian independence. In 1947 the Hindu portion of India, containing some 350 million (by 1970 over 500 million) people, became the Dominion of India. In the same year the Muslim portions, with a population of more than 70 million (by 1970 more than 100 million) became the Dominion of Paki-

Two great charismatic leaders of Asian independence, India's Jawaharlal Nehru and Mahatma Gandhi, are shown here during a meeting of the All India Congress in Bombay in 1946. Nehru, who became India's leader after Gandhi was assassinated in 1948, was the first prime minister of the independent Union of India. *Photo: United Press International* stan. Dominion status meant complete independence with voluntary membership in the British Commonwealth of Nations.

Religious and national strife soon broke out between Hindu India and Muslim Pakistan. Gandhi tried to quell the strife, but he was assassinated in 1948 by a fanatical Hindu nationalist. Thus the "Great Spirit" himself became another victim of malignant nationalism. Open war between the two states finally began in 1948 over possession of the disputed state of Kashmir. The United Nations was able to end the shooting, but not the dispute.

One of Gandhi's most devoted followers, Jawaharlal Nehru, a charming, wealthy British-educated Hindu of the highest (Brahmin) caste, became the first prime minister of the independent Union of India. The problems confronting him were staggering. Most of India's millions were poverty-stricken and illiterate. They spoke more than 800 languages and dialects (fewer than 50 percent spoke the official Hindi). Furthermore, their prevailing Hindu religion had long conditioned them to a placid acceptance of the status quo. Nehru inaugurated a liberal and mildly socialistic program somewhat similar to that of the British Labour government. Not the least of his problems was avoiding embroilment in the Soviet-American cold war. However, border clashes with Pakistan and with Red China frightened India into accepting military aid from both the United States and the Soviet Union.

Nehru's great charm and prestige kept India's restive millions fairly quiet. But when he died in 1964, his successors were confronted by rising discontent. In 1966 Nehru's daughter, Mrs. Indira Gandhi, became prime minister. Many Indians felt that the economic and social reform program of the Nehrus was not drastic enough. In spite of sizable loans and much technical assistance from the United States, Great Britain, and the Soviet Union, India's standard of living by 1970 had not kept abreast of her ever-mounting population. Her annual per capita income was still less than $60.

In 1948 the British Labour government granted complete independence to Burma and Dominion status to Ceylon. Burma immediately launched a liberal reform program more vigorous than that of India. The liberal regime encountered many difficulties including severe inflation and a growing Communist opposition. In 1962 the civilian leaders were overthrown by the army. Although claiming neutrality in the cold war, Burma's military dictatorship has appeared to be more friendly to Red China than to the United States. Malaya was granted independence in 1957, leaving only Hong Kong as a reminder of an era of British imperialism in Asia.

The rich and populous Dutch East Indies declared their independence at the end of World War II. Their leader was Achmed Sukarno. The Dutch resisted fiercely for four years, but finally yielded to pressure from the United Nations. Sukarno, the first president of the Republic of Indonesia, turned out to be a fiery nationalist, threatening and attacking his neighbors. In 1965, when Indonesia's large Communist Party attempted to seize control of the country, the coup was bloodily suppressed by the army. Sukarno, who appeared to be too friendly with the Communists and with Red China, was overthrown by a military junta which then aligned Indonesia with the United States.

Of all the European colonial regimes in Asia, that of the French in Indo-China was probably the most predatory and the most hated. Immediately after the surrender of Japan in August 1945, the Indo-Chinese nationalists, under the leadership of Ho Chi Minh, a Russian-trained Communist, proclaimed the independent "democratic" Republic of Vietnam. The returning French imperialists were fiercely resisted by the native Communist nationalists. Heavy fighting ensued, in which the French were aided by American Marshall Plan money. When the North Korean Communists began their aggression against South Korea in June 1950, the United States greatly

Rifle cradled in his arms, an American soldier moves warily through high grass near Khe Sanh, South Vietnam, in 1967. The war in Vietnam, begun at the end of World War II by Indochinese nationalists to prevent the French from reestablishing control, continues still, except that now it is America which pours a steady stream of men and materièl into an effort whose dubious and infinitestimal gains have cost the United States her domestic consensus and the respect of the world community. *Photo: Bill Hall–United Press International*

increased her aid to the French in Indo-China. Meanwhile, Ho Chi Minh began to receive aid from the Chinese Communists after they had overrun China in 1949. Thus a costly and dangerous war raged in Vietnam. The majority of the Vietnamese people apparently preferred the Communists to the French, and the forces of Ho Chi Minh won victory after victory in spite of American aid to the French.

In 1954 the French government of Premier Mendès-France agreed to a humiliating armistice with Ho Chi Minh and ceded the northern half of Vietnam to the Communists. Although South Vietnam technically remained a part of the French Union, French influence there quickly vanished. The United States, in accordance with its policy of military containment of communism—both Russian and Chinese—undertook to establish its power not only in South Vietnam, but in Laos and Cambodia as well, which France had also freed. Vigorous military and financial aid was given to the conservative Ngo Dinh Diem regime in South Vietnam. To many Asians, this policy smacked of the hated Western imperialism. Diem became increasingly unpopular. Almost immediately, he was faced with a rebellion of his own people supported and soon led by the Communists in both South and North Vietnam. No amount of American aid seemed to be able to hold back the tide against the unpopular and faltering Diem regime. In 1963 Diem was overthrown and assassinated by a group of his own officers. This left the American military position in South Vietnam dubious indeed. Early in 1965 the Vietnamese Communists with massive material aid from both the Soviet Union and Red China greatly stepped up their war against the American-supported but faltering South Vietnamese forces. The United States retaliated by bombing North Vietnam and increasing its armed forces in South Vietnam to 550,000 men. Vietnam was rapidly being devastated.

Meanwhile, public opinion all over the world, including in the United States itself, was becoming incensed at the wanton destruction. In 1968 representatives of North Vietnam and the United States began long and dreary peace talks in Paris, and the United States ceased bombing North but not South Vietnam. In 1969 Ho Chi Minh died, and the United States began slowly to reduce the size of its forces in Vietnam. This apparent simmering down of the war was marred by the violation by both sides of the territorial integrity of Laos and Cambodia. Much appeared to depend upon the ability and willingness of Washington, Moscow, and Peking to reach a living and working accommodation with one another.

5. THE EMBATTLED MIDDLE EAST

One of the most explosive areas in the mid-twentieth-century world was the Middle East—that area between and including Egypt and Iran, where East meets West. (The tendency in mid-twentieth-century usage is to include in the term "Middle East" much of the area that was formerly designated as "Near East.") In global terms it is probably the most strategic area in the world. It forms the bridge between the world's two greatest land masses, Eurasia and Africa; and through it pass the chief communication lines between the East and the West. The Middle East is the heart of the Muslim world, which stretches from Morocco to Indonesia and contains more than 300 million followers of the Prophet. It is also the heart of the tumultuous Arab world. Moreover, the area contains more than half the world's known oil reserves. At mid-twentieth century, the Middle East, the most fought-over area in history, was one of the most sensitive spots in the Soviet-American cold war.

During the early part of the century, while the great European powers competed for control of the Middle East, Arab nationalism was rising. This nationalism was vented first against the British, who were the dominant power in that area. Before World War I Great Britain controlled Egypt, including the Suez Canal, Cyprus, and a sphere of influence in Persia (in 1935 Persia changed its name to

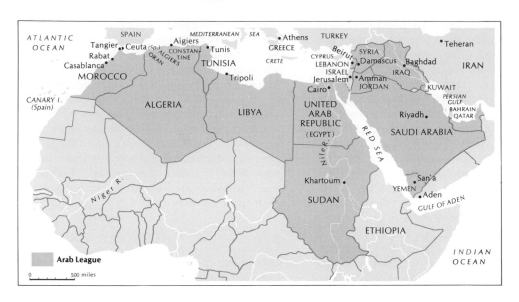

The Arab World 1970

Iran). After the war she took Palestine and Iraq as mandates under the League of Nations. (Trans-Jordan, created from part of the Palestine Mandate in 1921, became independent in 1927; it became Jordan in 1950.) As anti-British hostility mounted in the years between the wars, Great Britain began to relax her control. By the end of World War II only Cyprus, Palestine, and the Suez Canal remained in Britain's possession, and the British were bidding strongly for Arab friendship. But continued British possession of the Suez Canal and the admission of tens of thousands of Jews to Palestine under the Balfour Declaration of 1917 proved to be effective barriers to Anglo-Arab accord.

Palestine was the ancient home of the Jews. However, in A.D. 70 they were dispersed by the government of the Roman Empire. In the seventh century the Muslim Arabs conquered Palestine and lived there until the twentieth century—thirteen hundred years. In the late nineteenth century, the Zionist movement began. This was a movement to restore Palestine as a national home for the Jews. During the anti-Semitic persecutions of the Hitler era, thousands of European Jewish refugees, many of them wealthy, poured into Palestine, buy-

ing up the land and dispossessing the Arabs. The whole Arab and Muslim world became incensed. Great Britain favored the Arabs over the Jews, probably because of the Arabs' oil and their strategic location. With Great Britain's blessing, Egypt, Syria, Lebanon, Trans-Jordan, Iraq, Saudi Arabia, and Yemen formed the Arab League, embracing some 45 million people.

In 1948 the British Labour government turned Palestine over to the United Nations. The Jews immediately proclaimed the State of Israel and accepted the boundary lines that the United Nations had drawn to divide Palestine between the Jews and the Arabs. The Arab League refused to accept this arrangement, and began hostilities with a view to exterminating the Jewish state. Tiny Israel, however, well armed and well financed, was more than a match for the Arabs. After a year of fighting, the United Nations succeeded in bringing about a truce. But there were now nearly a million Arab refugees from Israel, Arab nationalism was thoroughly aroused, and border raids recurred as the Arabs armed for a revival of the struggle. Israel, in the meantime, receiving financial aid from Jews abroad, prospered, built modern cities, introduced irrigation and scientific agriculture, and became a vigorous, democratic, cooperative Western society in the midst of a feudalistic and largely primitive Muslim Arab world.

Great Britain continued to be a prime target of rampaging Arab nationalism. In 1951 the Iranian government nationalized the properties of the Anglo-Iranian Oil Company, including the largest refinery in the world. But Suez proved to be an even more critical issue. In 1952 a military coup led by extreme Egyptian nationalists overthrew the corrupt government of Egypt's King Farouk and brought to power the fiery agitator, Gamal Abdel Nasser, as dictator. Nasser set out to make himself the leader of the whole Arab world and to inflame it against the West.

His first targets were Israel and the Suez Canal Zone. Egyptian raids against Israel were stepped up, and preparations for a war of extermination were openly made. Threatening demands and gestures against the Canal Zone resulted in the British withdrawal in 1956. In 1956 Nasser nationalized the Suez Canal, thereby threatening the free access to the canal by all nations. The Soviet Union, seeing an opportunity to advance her interests in the Middle East by befriending the Arabs, sold arms to Nasser and helped him with a giant irrigation dam when the United States cut off its aid for the project.

In late October 1956, Israel suddenly attacked Egypt. In November she was joined by Britain and France. France was incensed at Nasser's encouragement and support of her rebellious Arab subjects in Algeria, Morocco, and Tunisia. The Israelis made rapid headway against the Egyptians, while the British and the French bombed Egyptian airfields and made landings in the Canal Zone. Nasser hastened to block the canal with sunken ships. Within a few days the Soviet Union threatened to enter the war on the side of Egypt. At this critical juncture the United States brought heavy pressure to bear on the British, French, and Israelis to cease hostilities. They had no alternative but to comply, and the United Nations supervised their withdrawal.

But nothing had been settled. Nasser continued to inflame Arab nationalism which had been stung to fanaticism by successive defeats at the hands of the Israelis. Almost every year witnessed some new crisis in the Middle East. The Arab states devoted much of their energy and resources to preparations for a

In a lookout post on the Israel-Lebanon border, Israeli soldiers stand constant duty as sporadic warfare between Israel and her Arab neighbors continues and the tension that has gripped the Middle East since the founding of the modern state of Israel in 1948 involves the superpowers—the U.S.S.R. and the United States.
Photo: United Press International

war of extermination against Israel. They received a constantly swelling stream of armaments, including tanks and planes, from the Soviet Union. They did relatively little to improve the social and economic conditions of their own people, and spurned all offers by the United Nations to help them resettle the destitute Arab refugees from Israel.

Nasser took the lead in bringing matters to a showdown in 1967. The armies of Egypt, Jordan, and Syria massed along the borders of Israel, and Egypt blockaded Israel's only port on the Red Sea (Israeli shipping had been barred from the Suez Canal since the 1956 war). In June 1967 the Israelis suddenly attacked these threatening Arab armies and crushed them in six days' time. Once again direct Soviet intervention in behalf of the Arabs was prevented only by the threat of counter action by the United States. The Soviet Union did proceed to rearm the defeated Arab states. Meanwhile, Israel occupied all Egyptian territory east of the Suez Canal (which Nasser kept closed to all shipping), Jordanian territory west of the Jordan River including the old section of Jerusalem with its sacred shrines, and a small strip of Syria overlooking the Sea of Galilee. These areas, of such great importance to the world—religiously, commercially, strategically—were the scenes of almost daily shooting and bombing.

6. THE AWAKENING OF AFRICA

By the mid-twentieth century large areas of Africa, the last of the continents to rise against Western imperialism, were also astir. Great Britain's troubles in Africa were by no means limited to Egypt. In one African colony after another, native populations caught the spirit of nationalism and turned in resentment against their white masters. Native terror bands, notably the Mau Mau in Kenya, made British life and property increasingly unsafe. In 1957 Great Britain granted independence to her Gold Coast colony, which became the Republic of Ghana in 1960. This proved to be the first step in the eventual freeing of her remaining African colonies. During the next few years one after another of Britain's African territories were freed, until by 1970 only the southern part of Rhodesia remained and that was in a state of rebellion against Great Britain.

The Dominion of South Africa had, of course, since 1931 (the Statute of Westminster) been completely free. There the prosperous white minority, constituting approximately one-fourth of the total population, clung desperately to its superiority. In 1948 and thereafter the white minority took severe measures to suppress the increasingly restless

The Nigerian civil war brought unimaginable misery and deprivation to the people of the secessionist province of Biafra. The trickle of emergency relief that international organizations managed to get into the country helped but a few of the hundreds of thousands of the starving, most of whom died for lack of food and medical care.
Photo: United Press International

Africa 1970

Colonies

Independent States

0 ___ 500 miles

Negro majority and to enforce *apartheid* (racial segregation). When in 1961 several of her fellow members of the British Commonwealth censored South Africa because of her racial policies, she withdrew from the Commonwealth, taking her large mandate, South-West Africa, with her.

The end of World War II found France's huge North African empire seething with unrest. Its population, largely Muslim, was agitated by the rampaging Arab nationalism in the Middle East. France, in 1956, granted independence to Morocco and Tunisia. The problem of independence or autonomy for Algeria was much more complex because of the presence there of more than a million French settlers who feared reprisals from the 8 million Muslim Algerians.

In 1954 the smoldering Algerian discontent with French rule burst into open revolt—a revolt that the regular French army was unable to quell. In May 1958 the harassed French army in Algeria, fearful that the government of the Fourth Republic was preparing to grant Algerian independence, mutinied and threatened to set up a military dictatorship in France. This emergency brought about the fall of the Fourth French Republic and the recall of Charles de Gaulle. De Gaulle undertook to restore the authority of the government over the army and to placate both the French and the Algerians in Algeria by means of a long-range program of economic and social improvements.

When it soon became evident that the inflamed Algerian Muslims would accept nothing short of complete independence, De Gaulle decided to take this difficult step. Algerian independence was granted in 1962. Meanwhile, he had granted independence to all the other French colonies, most of which were in Africa, and invited them to form a voluntary union with France. All but one, French Guinea, did so.

In 1960 Italy freed Somalia in East Africa and Belgium granted independence to the Congo. In the early 1960s even dictator Franco began to speak of freeing Spain's colonies in northwest Africa. Thus, by 1970 only Portugal, herself a Fascist dictatorship, was clinging stubbornly to her African colonies.

The granting of independence, of course, did not bring peace and prosperity to the African people, many of whom were illiterate tribesmen. The boundaries of the African states were drawn in many cases quite arbitrarily by nineteenth-century European imperialists sitting around plush green-topped tables in London or Brussels dividing up the spoils. In the Congo, for instance, tribal warfare flamed up immediately after independence. Russian and Chinese Communist agents moved in to exploit the chaos. UN Secretary-General Dag Hammarskjold lost his life there in a plane accident while trying to mediate the differences. In Nigeria, the Ibos in the Eastern Region attempted to secede and set up the independent Republic of Biafra. Thousands died in the ensuing struggle, and tens of thousands by starvation. Nevertheless, the Africans clearly preferred freedom with its problems to being a part of the "white man's burden."

The expansion of the European world, which began in the fifteenth century, had after five hundred years been very definitely reversed. The East now challenged the West. And human pride and fecundity threatened both.

7. LATIN AMERICA

Finally, there remains to be examined a large and populous area of the world which is, in a sense, neither East nor West—Latin America.

Just as Japan is a highly industrialized Western nation located in the East, Latin America is *in*, but, in many respects, not *of* the West. Her religion and her languages are, of course, Western. But the poverty and the illiteracy of her masses, her underdeveloped economy, and her unstable political institutions more closely resemble Southern Asia and Africa than Western Europe and the United States.

At the end of World War II the governments of the twenty independent Latin American states were all republics in name. In reality, however, most of them were Rightist dictatorships, representing the interests of the well-to-do bourgeoisie, the professional military, and the Roman Catholic hierarchy. Mexico was a noteworthy exception. There, a stable democratic regime in 1946 began a liberal program of economic, social, and educational reforms.

Throughout most of Latin America the poor, illiterate, and ever more numerous masses became increasingly restive after World War II. Many of them turned to communism, and were encouraged and supported by the Soviet Union. The United States, on the other hand, supported the rightist governments. In 1954 a military force armed by the United States invaded and overthrew the Leftist government of Guatemala. Ten years later a Rightist military takeover in Brazil was encouraged and applauded by the United States. In 1948 the twenty Latin American "republics" were persuaded to join the United States in an Organization of American States (OAS) for the purpose of resisting outside (Communist) interference. With the exception of the United States and Mexico, however, these governments represented only a tiny minority of the people of their respective states.

In Cuba the policy of the United States backfired. In 1959 the Rightist dictator, Fulgencio Batista, long supported by the United States, was overthrown by the Leftist revolutionary, Fidel Castro. Castro began a sweeping program of social and economic reforms including the seizure of property owned by individuals and corporations of the United

States. Fumbling efforts of the United States to overthrow the Castro regime drove it into the arms of the Soviet Union. Cuba became a Communist beachhead in the Western Hemisphere.

As the decade of the 1970s opened, Latin America was an area of sharp and dangerous contrasts. Rich natural resources were not being developed and used for the benefit of the rapidly increasing population which, for the most part, was poor and illiterate. Great modern cities such as Mexico City and Sao Paulo, which rivaled New York and Chicago in size and modernity, stood surrounded by wretched hovels and a depressed countryside. The government of the United States was ready, even eager, to offer financial and technical assistance, but as in Southern Asia and other parts of the world, it continued to support Rightist military regimes that were more interested in retaining their power than in aiding their people.

Suggested Reading

Japan Since 1945. One of the best studies of Japan since World War II, by an American ambassador to Japan during the period, is **E. O. Reischauer, *The United States and Japan* (Compass). Two excellent studies of Japan's remarkable economic recovery since 1945 are G. Allen, *Japan's Economic Recovery* (1958); and **R. Hall, Jr., *Japan: Industrial Power of Asia* (Searchlight). A scholarly examination of Japan and her place in the world since World War II is H. Borton, *Japan Between East and West* (1957).

Rise of Red China. An excellent history of China since 1911 is **O. Clubb, *Twentieth-century China* (Columbia University Press). E. Snow, *The Other Side of the River: Red China Today* (1962) is a scholarly and lucid account by an American who spent many years in China before and after the Communist takeover. This book was written before the internal upheaval—the so-called cultural revolution—and is perhaps overly optimistic about the success of the Red regime. The best biography of Mao to date is **S. Schram, *Mao Tse-tung* (Penguin) written in 1967. The best study of Chinese-American relations since World War II, by a leading American authority on China, is **J. Fairbank, *The United States and China* (Compass) written in 1958. Two good studies of the Sino-Soviet rift are K. Mehnert, *Peking and Moscow* (1964); and **D.

Zagoria, *The Sino-Soviet Conflict, 1956–1961* (Atheneum).

Korean War. A useful study of the situation in Korea before the outbreak of the war is G. McKune and A. Grey, *Korea Today* (1950). The Korean War itself is examined by J. Caldwell, *The Korean Story* (1953); and **R. Leckie, *Conflict: The History of the Korean War, 1950–1953* (Avon) published in 1962.

Revolt of Southern Asia. **B. Lamb, *India: A World in Transition* (Praeger) is a useful study. The student will find C. Bowles, *Ambassador's Report* (1954) enlightening and entertaining. Bowles was United States Ambassador to India, 1951–1953. The minds of the two greatest liberators and founders of the Dominion of India are revealed in **M. Gandhi, *Autobiography: The Story of My Experiments With Truth* (Beacon); and **J. Nehru, *Toward Freedom* (Beacon). Three valuable studies of Vietnam and the Vietnamese War are B. Fall, *The Two Viet-Nams* (1963); J. McAlister, *Vietnam: The Origins of Revolution* (1969); and J. Buttinger, *Vietnam: A Dragon Embattled* (2 vols., 1967). The last is a particularly detailed and scholarly work.

Embattled Middle East. Two useful studies of the situation in the Middle East since World

War II are **M. Harari, *Government and Politics in the Middle East* (Spectrum); and **P. Rondot, *Changing Patterns of the Middle East* (Praeger). American policy in the Middle East since World War II is carefully examined by **J. Campbell, *Defense of the Middle East* (Praeger). H. Sachar, *The Course of Modern Jewish History* (1958) furnishes excellent background material for an understanding of the State of Israel. J. Hurewitz, *The Struggle for Palestine* (1951) is a valuable study that covers the period of the first conflicts between Israel and her Arab neighbors. W. Douglas, *Strange Lands and Friendly People* (1951) gives an excellent description of Israel during the early years of its existence.

Awakening of Africa. R. Oliver and J. Fage, *A Short History of Africa* (1962) is a useful study of the background of the independence movement. **P. Bohannan, *Africa and Africans* (American Museum Science Books) is a perceptive and lucid survey. H. Kitchen, ed., *A Handbook of African Affairs* (1964) is the story of the struggles of the various African peoples for independence. An excellent study of the racial problem in South Africa is G. Carter, *The Politics of Inequality: South Africa Since 1948* (1958). See also **R. Emerson, *Africa and United States Policy* (1967); and D. Morison, *The U.S.S.R. and Africa* (1964) for background on Africa in a world context.

Latin America. **T. Draper, *Castro's Revolution: Myths and Realities* (Praeger) and T. Szulc, *The Winds of Revolution: Latin America Today and Tomorrow* (1963) are sound analyses of post-World War II Latin America written in a journalistic style. **F. Tannenbaum, *Ten Keys to Latin America* (Vintage) is a penetrating study of contemporary Latin America by a leading authority, written for the layman.

Conclusion. **A. Toynbee, *A Study of History* (12 vols., Galaxy), abridged by **D. Somervell (2 vols., Laurel) is the most prodigious effort ever made to synthesize and make a meaningful pattern of all human history. The student who reads Somervell's excellent abridgment of Toynbee's monumental work will be challenged and stimulated. W. McNeill, *The Rise of the West* (1963) is a provocative synthesis of world history and civilization. This is a very different interpretation from that of Toynbee. **A. N. Whitehead, *Science and the Modern World* (Free Press) is a brilliant analysis of the place of science in the twentieth century. A study of one of the most popular schools of philosophy since 1871 is R. Harper, *Existentialism: A Theory of Man* (1949). Various schools of philosophy in the twentieth century are examined in a series of thoughtful essays, D. D. Runes, ed., *Twentieth-century Philosophy* (1942).

RETROSPECT

The Europe of 1914 was shattered politically and socially by the two world wars and much of its science and technology were perverted to destructive purposes. Both wars were essentially the manifestation and the fruits of malignant nationalism. Both were centered around Germany, and it appears that Germany would have won both wars but for the intervention of the United States.

World War I began as a national power showdown between the German Empire on the one hand and France, Russia, and Great Britain on the other. It resulted in the destruction of the German, Russian, and Ottoman empires and the disintegration of the multilingual Austro-Hungarian national state. The British and French empires were both seriously weakened, as indeed were Britain and France themselves. Efforts to make a durable peace and to set up an international organization to keep the peace shattered on the rocks of national self-interests.

During World War I and largely as a result of it, the pioneer Marxist regime was set up in Russia. Quite a different, but equally antiliberal type of dictatorship—fascism—came to power in Germany, Italy, and Japan. These three militant Fascist powers armed themselves and banded together for world conquest. The only powers capable of stopping them—the three great liberal democracies, the United States, Great Britain, and France—were bogged down in depression and disillusionment and unwilling to cooperate with each other. The League of Nations, without their support, could do nothing. Attempts on the part of the democratic powers to appease the Fascist aggressors resulted in World War II.

During the first two years of World War II, Germany overran all of continental Europe west of Moscow except Sweden, Switzerland, Portugal, and Spain (a Fascist ally). Great Britain narrowly escaped defeat. The most productive part of the Soviet Union was conquered and devastated. By the end of 1941 Japan, thinking the hour of Fascist triumph was at hand, attacked the United States. As in 1917, the entry into the war of the United States, with her enormous industrial resources, turned the tide. The stubborn resistance of the British and the Russian people, of course, made the turning possible. Italy surrendered in 1943, and Germany and Japan two years later. The surrender of Japan was hastened by perhaps a few weeks by the dropping of two American atomic bombs, which destroyed two of her major cities. Much of Europe and Japan lay devastated.

As World War II was ending, the victors set up the United Nations. It was obvious to nearly everyone that now that nuclear weapons had arrived,

927

the curbing of irresponsible nationalism was a necessity. The greatest obstacle to the establishment of peace was the intense rivalry of the two remaining world powers, the United States and the Soviet Union, who competed fiercely and dangerously for world hegemony. Meanwhile, the peoples of Asia and Africa freed themselves from all but the last vestiges of Western imperialism.

Science and technology, which had long captivated the West, now became a world obsession. Philosophy, religion, and the arts in the Western world after 1914 continued much along the same lines they had followed during the period 1871–1914—disenchantment with traditional values and searching for new values which were secular, humanistic, and materialistic.

Conclusion 🌿 Western Civilization in the Twentieth Century

As we come closer to the present, it becomes more difficult to see and understand and write history. Current events—yesterday's headlines—are not history. Time must elapse before we can gain the perspective necessary to grasp their significance. In mountainous terrain—and history is mountainous terrain—the adjacent hill towers above us and looks big. But as we move away from it, higher hills loom up, and finally lofty mountain ranges emerge, turning our hill into a mole hill. Yet, bearing these pitfalls in mind, let us attempt to identify and explore the highlights of Western civilization in the twentieth century.

1. WAR

Much as we wish it were not so, the history of the twentieth century, perhaps more than any other century, has been dominated by war. World Wars I and II and the lesser wars of the century not only killed and maimed their tens of millions, but also destroyed nations, empires, and economic systems. Furthermore, they brutalized manners and morals and left in their wake a spirit of disillusionment that strongly influenced philosophy,

religion, literature, and the arts. With the advent of nuclear and biological weapons near the end of World War II, war became intolerable. By 1970 the United States and the Soviet Union possessed nuclear bombs that were more than a thousand times as powerful as the two that destroyed Hiroshima and Nagasaki. Each of the two superpowers had stockpiled enough nuclear weapons to kill all the citizens of the other many times over (the explosive power of the two stockpiles was believed to be equivalent to some fifteen tons of TNT for each person on the earth), and yet they continued to pour a major part of their wealth and resources into this race of death. And if nuclear weapons should for any reason prove to be insufficient, wonderful new biological and chemical weapons were reported to be stored and ready for use. War, therefore, was everybody's business.

War in the twentieth century was closely tied to nationalism. During the course of the century empires crumbled, and economic and social systems weakened and changed, but nationalism continued on unabated. Even communism, which was internationalist in theory, became increasingly nationalistic.

The controversy over racial discrimination and civil rights in the United States received world attention at the 1968 Olympics, when two black American athletes signaled their protest against their country's policies by receiving their medals with fists raised in the black power salute. *Photo: Ken Regan–Camera 5*

During the decade of the nineteen-sixties the United Nations became less effective in dealing with international problems as nation after nation turned inward for the solution of its own problems, and disarmament talks foundered repeatedly on the rock of national self-interest.

2. TECHNOLOGY

Apart from war, there can be little doubt that Western man's greatest obsession since 1914 has been with technology and science. Industrialization has continued at an ever-increasing pace. Consumer goods have become so plentiful in the Western world and the desire for them has been fanned to such an extent by the advertising industry that by the nineteen-sixties, people were rioting over conditions that would be thought luxurious in many parts of the world and that would have been considered normal in the West a few generations earlier. Industrialization was always accompanied by urbanization. At the opening of the century, the great majority of the people in the Western world still lived in rural areas or in small towns. By 1970 only 5 percent of the people in the United States were farmers, and much of their work was mechanized. But people were not just moving from the farms to the cities; the total population was rapidly increasing. At the opening of the modern era (1500) the population of the world is estimated to have been about one-half billion. Three centuries later (1800) it had doubled. One century later (1900) it had doubled again. By 1970 it had more than doubled again and was close to 4 billion. If the present acceleration continues, it will double again by the end of this century. To some observers, the threat of this uncontrolled population increase seemed to be greater than the threat of nuclear destruction.

One of the most serious byproducts of the increasing industrialization of the Western world and the increase in population of the whole world was the destruction and pollution of the earth's natural resources. Industrial wastes were poured with abandon into the lakes, the streams, the oceans, and the atmosphere. The decades following World War II were in a real sense the Age of the Bulldozer in the Western world. These monsters chewed up and gouged out hills and mountains, beauty spots and historic sites, forests and farmlands. Millions of productive acres were covered with highways and sub-

In July of 1969, man walked on the moon. The United States' Apollo 11 moon mission was launched from Cape Kennedy July 16, 1969; the moon landing was successfully made July 20, and four days later the three astronauts splashed down in the Pacific Ocean. This photograph was taken on the moon. *Photo: NASA* urbs. The automobiles, the television sets, and the creature comforts of the Western world, therefore, did not come without a price.

3. SCIENCE

While the consuming masses in the technologically advanced Western world were threatening to consume their own habitat, the intelligentsia of the West were consumed by their fascination with science. During the course of the twentieth century, interest in science has overshadowed all other intellectual interests and has drawn the best brains in the West away from the other disciplines. The main thrust in physics was to continue the probing of the atom, which was begun in the nineteenth century, to discover the last truths concerning the nature of matter. The results tended to be disillusioning. Albert Einstein had undermined the Newtonian world of physical stability with his relativity theory (see p. 755). A more shattering blow was delivered by Max Planck (1858–1947). Although he published his quantum theory in 1900, its full impact was not realized until the decades following World War I. According to this theory, energy is not transmitted in a steady measurable stream, as had long been supposed, but in little unpredictable leaps or packets (quanta), and the behavior of subatomic particles is so irregular and complex that man can never fathom the ultimate secrets of nature by objective observation. This left the materialists and positivists feeling alienated and alone in an uncertain, inscrutable universe. Physicists did, however, find out enough about the physical universe to produce the atom bomb (1945), orbit the earth (1957), and land on the moon (1969).

The most exciting discoveries in the biological sciences were in the field of genetics. In 1953 the nature of the complicated D N A molecule, which controls the pattern of all living things, was discovered. It is assumed that by tampering with this molecule new forms of life may be created, and that given characteristics in man can be controlled. The most beneficial discoveries in the field of biological science during the twentieth century have been those that prevent and cure human ailments. Shortly after World War I viruses were discovered. These organisms are so small that it is not certain whether they are animate or inanimate, but they were proved to be the cause of many diseases, including infantile paralysis, influenza, and the common cold. Vaccines were developed to combat successfully the infantile paralysis virus and a number of others—but the common cold still plagues most of humanity. During the decade of the 1930s the antibiotics, penicillin and the sulfa drugs, were discovered. These "miracle drugs" kill or control the bacteria causing many human infections. Since World War II, drugs have been found useful in treating mental illness, and artificial and transplanted kidneys and hearts have saved or lengthened many lives. The chief drawback in the application of these wonderful discoveries has been their high and continually soaring cost and the shortage of trained personnel to administer them. Some nations, notably Great Britain and Sweden, have recognized the enormous importance of public health by developing comprehensive programs of national health insurance. Communist regimes, of course, have always made the practice of medicine a public rather than a private matter.

In the social sciences, psychology strove to be an experimental laboratory science. Nevertheless, the influence of Freud (see p. 757) continued to be strong. The most important figure in economics between 1914 and 1970 was John Maynard Keynes (1883–1946). In 1936, in the midst of the Great Depression,

Keynes published *The General Theory of Employment, Interest and Money* advocating government regulation of the capitalistic system. In times of recession the government should increase the supply of money in circulation by lowering interest rates and by deficit spending on public works. In times of inflationary boom it should restrict the money supply by raising interest rates and by other means. Liberals, not only in Keynes' native Britain but throughout the capitalistic world, accepted his theories, as indeed did many conservatives. The general acceptance of so much of the Keynesian economics was the death knell of the classic laissez-faire economics of Adam Smith and Ricardo. Inflation, however, has continued to harass all capitalistic economies. Another important innovation in economic thought was made by John Kenneth Galbraith, whose *Affluent Society* was published in 1958. All previous economic theory had been based upon the concept of scarcity rather than the problem of superabundance. The social sciences, particularly sociology, tended to become increasingly quantitative.

During and after World War II technology and science combined to produce the computer—the mechanical brain. Faith in this device became such a rage, and so many billions were put into it, that some would call the period since 1945 the Age of the Computer. Since it is a hybrid—a cross between science and technology—perhaps we should call it the thinking mule.

4. PHILOSOPHY

Speculative thought in the Western world during the twentieth century was in large measure a continuation and further development of the philosophy of disenchantment of the late nineteenth century. The factors that had given rise to that philosophy—the depersonalizing effects of natural science in general and Darwinism in particular, the uprooting of the masses by industrialization and urbanization, materialism spawned by technology, and the decline in influence of the Christian religion—continued with increased tempo throughout the first three quarters of the twentieth century. To these factors were added the disillusionment resulting from the two world wars, the Great Depression, and the tensions of the cold war. The influence of all these forces is reflected in the most popular school of philosophy in the twentieth century—existentialism. Existentialism drew heavily from Friedrich Nietzsche (see p. 811), who was violently anti-Christian and antidemocratic. When Nietzsche said "God is dead," he meant that there are no absolutes. Existential philosophy was also influenced by the mid-nineteenth-century Danish theologian, Sören Kierkegaard, who rejected systematized and institutionalized Christianity in favor of personal inspiration and individual commitment. The most influential spokesman for existentialism has been Jean-Paul Sartre (1905——). Sartre defines his doctrine as an attempt to draw out all the logical implications of a consistent atheism. He rejects all absolute moral laws and values. Man is a finite but free creature responsible only to himself in a universe devoid of purpose. This sophisticated and often vague cult represents a revolt not only against Christianity, but also against such twentieth-century absolutes as Marxism and fascism.

Somewhat more optimistic and humanistic than Sartre and his fellow existentialists were Alfred North Whitehead (1861–1947) and Bertrand Russell (1872–1970) of Great Britain. On the eve of World War I they proclaimed a system of analytic philosophy that spurned any concept which could not be rationally and mathematically expressed. Unlike Sartre, who denied the existence of any meaning, they sought for a rational meaning behind existence. Both were tolerant men. Whitehead became a professor at Harvard University and eventually returned to Christianity, believing that philosophy begins and ends with wonder. Russell, however, became the twentieth century's chief proclaimer of atheism.

5. LITERATURE

The literature of the twentieth century, like the philosophy, was essentially an outgrowth and continuation of the literature of the late nineteenth century. A number of the great realistic writers of the period 1871–1914, such as Shaw and Dreiser, lived and wrote until the middle of the twentieth century. The realism that had shocked many Victorians was succeeded by the more starkly naked naturalism. In the United States Sinclair Lewis (1885–1951), much like Theodore Dreiser, ridiculed both the hypocritical and "Puritanical" bourgeoisie and the stupid, vulgar masses. Babbitt, Elmer Gantry, and Arrowsmith, deflated heroes in Sinclair Lewis' novels by those titles, became stereotypes of typical Americans in the minds of thousands of untypical American readers of books. Eugene O'Neill (1888–1953) wrote plays in which the dramatic tension was maintained by psychological conflict (like those of Anton Chekhov —see p. 813) rather than development of plot and action. Ernest Hemingway (1898–1961) was an existentialist, entertaining his readers with his crisp and sophisticated prose. William Faulkner (1897–1962) with greater depth and artistry tore away the veil woven by civilization to conceal the perverted and animal-like nature of ordinary people. He developed a complex stream-of-consciousness technique.

In Europe, James Joyce (1882–1941), an Irish expatriate in Paris, and T. S. Eliot (1888–1965), an American expatriate in London, developed still further the stream-of-consciousness technique, placing both words and thoughts out of sequence, with dramatic effect. Eliot was one of the few great writers of the twentieth century who revered mystic religion and tradition. He became a member of the Anglican Church and took seventeenth-century classicism as his literary model. Albert Camus (1913–1960) was in word and deed an apostle of existentialism. A Frenchman born in Algeria, he played a daring role in the French underground in World War II. Like Hemingway's characters and his own characters, he sought identity as a visceral creative individual in an amoral and purposeless universe.

Earlier in the century, Franz Kafka (1883–1924), a German Jew in Prague, depicted the alienation and frustrations of an intellectual in the World War I era. The haunting, ambiguous quality of his novels symbolizes the uncertainties and fears of his age. Most of his work was published after his death, and it is significant that he enjoyed wide popularity only after World War II, particularly in Germany. We have already taken note of Boris Pasternak (1890–1960), the Soviet Union's greatest man of letters in the twentieth century. His *Doctor Zhivago*, written in the grand manner of Tolstoy and Dostoevski, portraying the depressive effects of a totalitarian regime on the sensitive individual, was denounced and censored by his government. Of all the great literary figures of the twentieth century, probably the least revolutionary in style and content was Thomas Mann (1875–1955). In his magnificent prose he always revealed his reverence for man. Yet even he was clearly influenced by the philosophers of disenchantment, Schopenhauer and Nietzsche. He was a Jewish refugee from Nazi Germany to the United States and eventually to Switzerland. In his last major novel, *Doctor Faustus*, Mann describes the corruption of European humanism in his lifetime. With few exceptions, Western literature in the twentieth century was a literature of protest.

6. THE FINE ARTS

The fine arts in the Western world in the twentieth century, like the philosophy and the literature, have proceeded generally along the guidelines laid down by the artists and writers of the late nineteenth century—disenchantment, rejection of tradition, search for new values. These characteristics have become intensified by the materialism and the uncertainties of the twentieth century.

Without a doubt, the most gifted and influential painter of the twentieth century has been Pablo Picasso (1881——). A Spaniard, he emigrated to Paris as a young man. There he was influenced by the French post-Impressionists (see pp. 815–816). In order to penetrate the surface and reveal the inner reality of things, Picasso would take his subjects apart—arms, heads, violin parts—and rearrange and distort them for maximum effect. Early in the century, at about the same time that young Whitehead and Russell were proclaiming their analytic philosophy based upon mathematics, Picasso introduced cubism into the world of painting. This was an effort, suggested by Cézanne, to demonstrate the solidity of the material universe by portraying the geometric composition of objects—cubes, cones, and cylinders.

Most twentieth-century painters have attempted to follow or surpass Picasso. Generally they have turned inward, rejecting all tradition, sometimes even disregarding esthetics, and drawing and painting lines, shapes, and combinations of color to suit their whim or fancy. This type of painting is often called abstract expressionism. Picasso is obviously a genius. Whether his would-be imitators, so busy smashing all tradition and form

and values with their depersonalized, disjointed, abstract painting were doing more than reflecting the materialistic times in which they live remains for future critics to determine.

Twentieth-century architecture has been almost entirely in the functional style which was developed near the end of the nineteenth century by Louis Henry Sullivan (see p. 817). Sullivan's most illustrious student was Frank Lloyd Wright (1869–1959). Like his teacher, Wright believed that function is the sole purpose of architecture. He further insisted that form should conform to the materials used and to the setting. He made brilliant use of the cantilever (a projecting member supported at only one end) to achieve striking horizontal lines and an unobstructed spaciousness. These effects were made possible by the tensile strength of steel. Wright combined artistic skill with a Shavian scorn for traditional values and institutions. The most spectacular monuments of functional architecture are, of course, the great bridges and skyscrapers, most of them in the United States.

Twentieth-century music, too, was for the most part a continuation and development of styles formulated during the period 1871–1914. Richard Strauss (1864–1949) and Igor Stravinsky (1882——), two of the originators of modern music, have lived far into the twentieth century. During the course of the century, music in the Western world became increasingly dissonant, atonal, noisy, and experimental. These qualities probably found their ultimate composer in the Viennese Arnold Schoenberg (1874–1951), who abolished melody and key and replaced the seven-tone scale with one of twelve tones. Probably America's most original contribution to modern music was jazz, a development in which George Gershwin (1898–1937) played an important part. Some other great twentieth-century composers are Béla Bartók (1881–1945) in

Hungary, Paul Hindemith (1895–1963) in Germany, and Serge Prokofiev (1891–1953) and Dimitri Shostakovich (1906——) in the Soviet Union.

The prosperous masses, however, with their theater tickets and television sets demanded something more tuneful. After World War II, lyrics from "My Fair Lady" and "The Sound of Music" could be heard on pocket-size transistors throughout the Western World. Meanwhile, the younger masses gyrated to the sound of rock and roll by the Beatles and their successors. Granting membership to the Beatles in the Most Excellent Order of the British Empire in 1965 by Queen Elizabeth II must surely be of historical significance, whatever that significance may be.

7. RELIGION

Theology in the Western world during the twentieth century for the most part reflected the materialism of the age and the influence of existentialist philosophy. Strong efforts were made to update Christian theology by making it a secular philosophy. Paul Tillich (1886–1965), a German Protestant who spent his latter years in the United States, conceived of God as "ultimate truth" and "inner reality." Such traditional terms as "original sin," "salvation," "forgiveness," "immortality," and "atonement" were useful symbols actually referring to personal and social ethics. Harvey Cox (1929——) of Harvard University, in his widely read *The Secular City* (1965), defined Christianity as an endless social revolution. During the decade of the 1960s the phrase "God is dead" enjoyed popularity among quite a number of divinity school teachers and students. The phrase apparently meant a wide variety of things to its various users, including the belief that God is dead. On the other hand, a few powerful voices called for a return to an enlightened orthodoxy, notably

Changing ideas in art and in architecture, new blends and startling combinations of styles, materials, and functions—these trends are hallmarks of the twentieth century since World War II. This photograph shows the interior of the Guggenheim Museum in New York, designed by Frank Lloyd Wright. The use of a circular sloping ramp around the walls of the building, with the interior space open, is a controversial new concept of the use and function of a museum. *Photo: René Burri-Magnum*

Karl Barth (1886–1968) in Switzerland and Reinhold Niebuhr (1892——) in the United States, who were neo-Calvinists. God, they said, created the universe and runs it for his holy purpose, but man's selfish pride separates him from God. Only the Christian religion can remove that pride and bring man into God's purpose. Jacques Maritain

937

In the summer of 1968, the Russian invasion of Czechoslovakia to stop the movement for the liberalization of life and greater autonomy which had taken real hold among the Czech people brought vividly to world attention the continued strength of the Iron Curtain and of Soviet domination of Eastern Europe. Here crowds surround Russian tanks in Wenceslaus Square in Prague. *Photo: Sonja Bullaty and Angelo Lomeo from Nancy Palmer Photo Agency*

(1882————) in France called for a return to the teachings of St. Thomas Aquinas. These learned men contributed dignity to the continuing claims of traditional Christianity.

But the Christian churches continued to suffer a decline in influence. Many congregations adopted all sorts of devices, including rock sessions, to try to appeal to the young. Strenuous efforts were made to restore the lost unity of Christendom in order that the Christian church might face its enemies with a united front. In 1948 leaders of hundreds of Protestant and Orthodox denominations met

in Geneva and set up the World Council of Churches. The most spectacular step in this direction was taken by Pope John XXIII (1958–1963), head of the largest body of Christians, who called the Second Vatican Council (1962–1965) in the spirit of Christian tolerance and unity. Although John XXIII died during the first year of the council and was succeeded by Paul VI (1963————), who appears to be a less vigorous innovator, the Second Vatican Council introduced an ecumenical spirit into the Roman Catholic Church and a willingness to modernize the ritual and discipline that had been formalized by the Council of Trent in the sixteenth century. Whether such means can check the decline in influence of the Christian religion in the Western world, we cannot know. The dominant concerns of Western man as of 1970 were undoubtedly secular—war, science, technology.

8. MANNERS AND MORALS

The obsession of Western man with material values has taken its toll on his traditional manners and morals. The relentless march of technology with its accompanying urbanization, while bringing to the masses many creature comforts, has robbed millions of their manual skills and social contacts, and lost them in the lonely crowd. At the higher levels of industry, corporate man has tended to lose his independence and individual identity. The intricacy and specialization of twentieth-century science has tended to depersonalize the scientist. Furthermore, as the scientist has probed ever more deeply into the nature of the material universe, his findings have led to increased uncertainty rather than to the certainty that was sought and expected. War, of course, has always brutalized those who are engaged in it, but the wars of the twentieth century have vastly exceeded those of the past in size and destructiveness. Most of mankind apparently will discipline their bodies only under duress, and when forced to do so by war or great crisis, will "let themselves go," as it were,

afterwards. For instance, the Reign of Terror during the French Revolution was followed by the excesses of the Thermidorian Reaction. World War I was followed by the Jazz Age and the so-called "lost generation." The expected letdown after World War II was postponed by the Cold War tensions and full-scale wars in China, Korea, and Vietnam. However, in the late 1960s a wave of anarchy swept across the world. The sensitive philosophers, writers, and artists had foreseen and foretold it. Government at all levels staggered. Even national sovereignty was challenged as states and provinces, Flemings, Welsh, Ulsterites,

All over the world, young people in revolt against their elders' politics and value systems have experimented with life styles, modes of expression, and protest—both peaceful and violent. In the summer of 1969, hundreds of thousands of young Americans gathered at Woodstock, New York, to listen to music, to be with each other, and to demonstrate the utter chasm that divides them from the life style and the policies of their country. *Photo: Ken Regan—Camera 5*

French Canadians, and Biafrans asserted themselves. The crime rate mounted. Political parties and labor unions found themselves unable to control their members. The young, in particular, lacking physical outlets for their excess vitamins, and finding few if any spiritual and moral standards to guide them, revolted not only against their parents and teachers and all officials, but also against traditional standards of social and moral behavior. By 1970, Western civilization and its institutions, which had been so long developing—the family, the universities, the courts of law, the church, the state, traditions of social and moral behavior—were being severely tested.

Index

O

About the Authors

John B. Harrison was born in Lawrenceville, Virginia, and
grew up in Rich Square, North Carolina. He received his B.A.
and M.A. at the University of North Carolina, and his Ph.D. at
the University of Wisconsin. He taught history at Lees Junior
College, Jackson, Kentucky, the University of Wisconsin
extension, Ohio Northern University, and since 1942 has been
teaching at Michigan State University where he is Professor of
History. He was Visiting Professor at the University of North
Carolina, 1963-1964. Professor Harrison is a member of the
American Historical Association and the American Association
of University Professors. During four trips to Europe in 1951,
1955, 1960, and 1963, he visited nineteen European countries.
He is the author of *This Age of Global Strife* (1952), and of a
number of articles and book reviews.

Richard E. Sullivan was born and raised near Doniphan,
Nebraska. He received a B.A. degree from the University of
Nebraska in 1942, and an M.A. degree and a Ph.D. degree from
the University of Illinois in 1947 and 1949 respectively. His
doctorate was earned in the field of medieval history. He has
taught history at Northeast Missouri State Teachers' College
(1949-1954) and at Michigan State University (1954-1970) where
he is currently Dean of the College of Arts and Letters.
Professor Sullivan held a Fulbright Research Fellowship and
a John Simon Guggenheim Fellowship to Belgium in 1961-
1962. He is the author of *Coronation of Charlemagne* (1959),
Heirs of the Roman Empire (1960), and *Aix-la-Chapelle in the
Age of Charlemagne* (1963). His articles have appeared in
many scholarly journals.

A Note on the Type

The text of this book was set on the Linotype in Aster, a type-face designed by Francesco Simoncini for Ludwig and Mayer, the German type foundry. Starting out with the basic old-face letterforms that can be traced back to Francesco Griffo in 1495, Simoncini emphasized the diagonal stress by the simple device of extending diagonals to the full height of the letter-forms and squaring off. By modifying the weights of the individual letters to combat this stress, he has produced a type of rare balance and vigor.

The display type was set in Melior, a typeface designed by Hermann Zapf and issued in 1952. Melior, like Times Roman, was created specifically for use in a newspaper. With this functional end in mind, Zapf nonetheless chose to base the proportions of its letterforms on those of the Golden Section. The result is a typeface of unusual strength and surpassing sublety.

This book was composed, printed, and bound by
Kingsport Press Inc., Kingsport, Tennessee.
The maps were executed by Jean Paul Tremblay and
Francis & Shaw, Inc.
Cover design by Karin Batten

Typography by Hermann Strohbach